Americans Traveling Abroad
What You Should Know Before You Go

By Gladson I. Nwanna, Ph.D.

Third edition, completely revised

Frontline Publishers
Baltimore, Maryland

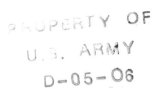
Library of Congress

LC Control Number: 96645138:
 Americans traveling abroad : what you should know before you go.
Baltimore, Md. : Frontline Publishers,
 c1994-
v. ; 28 cm.
[1994]- ISSN: 1070-3365

ISBN: 1-890605 -10 -7

Cover Design by David E. Ricardo

Printed in the United States of America

Visit Frontline Publishers Website at **http://www.frontlinepublishers.com**

Acknowledgement

A lot of people helped me with the first and second editions of this book and have continued to do so with this revised edition, giving me everything from encouragement to help with typesetting and other editorial advice. I would like to thank all of them, especially Mrs. Phyllis Desbordes for the relentless assistance in editing parts of the chapters and for other valuable suggestions.

A special thanks goes to the various agencies of the government whose research and publications have been reproduced in this book. There is no doubt that this book, like the previous editions, would not have materialized within the time it took to put it together without the assistance of the United States Departments of State, Commerce (Customs), Transportation, Treasury, Agriculture and Health and Human Resources, whose publications make up a substantial portion of the book

My gratitude and indebtedness also goes to the numerous organizations and firms that gave me permission to reproduce some of their proprietary works. These include:

Agora, Inc.: The material was excerpted from "The World Catalog" and from "International Living," both publications published by Agora Inc., 824 E. Baltimore St., Baltimore, MD 21202; Reprinted by permission. [Reference Code Used in the text **IL**]

Official Airline Guides: Reprinted by permission, Official Airline Guides. [Reference Code used in the text **OG**]

The Putnam Berkley Group, Inc.: Reprinted from Overcoming Jetlag by Charles Ehret and Lynne Scanlon, 1983. Reprinted by permission, The Berkley Publishing Group, Inc. [Reference Code used in text **PB**]

Runzheimer International: Reprinted by permission. All rights reserved by Runzheimer International. [Reference Code used in the text **RI**]

Airport Association Council International (AACI): Reprinted by permission. All rights reserved by AACI. [Reference Code used in the text **AI**]

Thomas Cook: Reprinted by permission. All rights reserved by Thomas Cook. [Reference Code used in the text **TC**]

Society for the Advancement of Travel for the Handicapped (SATH): Reprinted by permission. All rights reserved by SATH. [Reference Code used in the text **SH**]

Air Transport Association of America (ATAA): Reprinted by permission. [Reference Code used in the text **AT**]

Finally, I thank the thousands of travelers whose lives and trips have been enriched by information they found in the previous editions of this book, particularly those of you who either called or wrote us with praises for the content and coverage. Your encouragement and inspiration remains a driving force towards the completion of this new edition.

Preface

The events of September 11, 2001, and its aftermath provide the background for this revised third edition. At the time this edition went to press, Americans and the world continue to be limited and challenged by the fears and concerns the sad events unleashed. While almost every facet of American life and economy was affected, the impact on the travel industry especially international travel, will continue to be felt in the foreseeable future. Fear of terrorism, including the use of weapons of mass destruction, remains high in the minds of Americans at home, and those traveling overseas.

While the full impact of the September 11, events is yet to be realized, Americans traveling abroad, now more than ever ought to be more concerned about personal safety and hence must invest in pre-travel education and planning.

With careful and adequate preparation and safety planning, International travel can still be quite safe, enriching and exciting. On the other hand, it can become wasteful, expensive, boring, embarrassing and a nightmare if the traveler is not adequately informed.

The key to a successful trip overseas, however, will depend, to a large part, on how well you invest in preparing for such trips, particularly familiarizing yourself with a variety of conditions, laws, rules, regulations and requirements, that will affect your trip. Learning as much as you can about the host country, the general global political climate, as well as the political and social relationship between the U.S. and your host country is very important and should be considered a vital aspect of your trip overseas. Such a learning exercise is invaluable and will cut down on the potential for costly and avoidable mistakes. Above all, it will add more fun to your trip, rather than hurt your trip.

The key to having a successful trip abroad is to start preparing for the trip weeks or months before departure. Plans should include pre-flight considerations, as well as on-flight and post-flight considerations.

Admittedly, investment in pre-vacation planning aimed at ensuring a successful and enjoyable trip overseas can be time-consuming, expensive and frustrating to both seasoned and non-seasoned overseas travelers.

For most overseas travelers a major difficulty is having access to relevant and reliable information and resources in a timely manner . These goals have been met in this book.

The driving motive of the author is to compile a book that is informative and comprehensive in form, and reliable and authoritative as a source. It provides answers and sources of reference for the frequently asked questions, issues and concerns of Americans traveling abroad.

This book is, indeed, comprehensive and has several unique features that separate it from the numerous tour and travel books and guides available on the market. This book:

⬜ covers **over 170** countries and every continent or region of the world that Americans travel to.

It also includes tips and information:

- for Americans residing abroad;

- for first time as well as seasoned travelers;

- for business travelers;

- for disabled travelers, older travelers, student travelers, and for minors traveling unaccompanied;

- for Travelers to Canada;

- on passports and current visa, vaccination and other entry/exit requirements for most countries of the world;

- on safety, money, shopping, security, and health;

- on getting financial and other forms of assistance overseas;

- on the new democracies of Eastern Europe and the former Soviet Republics.

Importantly, in this (third) edition of the book readers will find additional unique features including:

- information that incorporates and reflects the post September 11 fears and concerns regarding overseas traveling;

- completely updated and revised information;

- world-wide web addresses and contact e-mails.

The Appendix section is filled with valuable addresses and telephone numbers of numerous organizations, institutions and agencies often sought after, but very often not readily accessible to Americans traveling abroad. It also includes country by country information, ranging from tipping, telephone codes, electricity requirements, commercial holidays and currencies to local weights and measures.

The book includes tips and advice on a variety of issues, questions and concerns of travelers to almost any part of the globe. The information will benefit the first time traveler, seasoned travelers, travel agencies, tour operators, tourists and those going on business trips;. It contains security information for both American citizens and American businesses operating overseas. It also includes tips and guidelines on cultural **Do's and Don'ts** for several countries and provides a unique perspective, considering that a large portion of the information is directly from the United States Government through its various agencies and directed particularly to Americans traveling abroad.

An additional and unique feature of this book is its wide appeal. Most of the information should be useful and beneficial to every international traveler, irrespective of the country of origin or country to be visited. Several of the topics discussed and tips provided have no boundaries, and are applicable to anyone traveling to a foreign country.

There are a number of helpful travel books readily found in bookstores, including those published by the major publishers referenced in Chapter 36 of this book. Although these guides are useful, most of them tell you what you need to know while you are already abroad, leaving out the more important things that you should know **BEFORE YOU GO**. This book provides you precisely with those important pieces of information you need to know **BEFORE YOU GO** and more. It covers more countries and provides detailed information that you will need **While Abroad**.

It is my expectation that the information contained in this revised edition will continue to make a big difference, particularly in ensuring a safe, enjoyable, rewarding and hitch-free trip for millions of Americans and overseas-bound travelers. I hope that your expectations will be met and when they are, I will appreciate hearing from you. Should this book fall short in meeting your expectations or in addressing adequately your overseas travel concerns, I would like to hear from you, so that an effort can be made to improve future editions. Suggestions and letters should be mailed to Public Relations Department, Frontline Publishers, P.O. Box 32674, Baltimore, Maryland 21208.

Editor's Note:

[1]   Perhaps little is known about the numerous publications and services for Americans traveling abroad made available by the United States Government through its various agencies. A good number is also available from several non-governmental agencies and organizations. Unfortunately, many overseas travelers are not aware of these resources. In this book, an effort has been made to fill in that gap by reproducing most of those publications with adequate references to other useful services and resources available to overseas travelers. Similarly, valuable expert advice and answers to questions of interest to travelers is available in the media, but are often limited to a few who subscribe to travel newsletters and magazines. This book provides these sources by incorporating the advice of experts in the field. To all these sources, I must say THANKS for facilitating the process of preparing this book.

[2]   The author, editor and publisher has made a determined effort to reproduce all the borrowed materials verbatim and in their entirety. For the most part, this objective was accomplished. Only in a few instances in the book, was it necessary to make minor alterations in order to facilitate reading and to ensure consistency and uniformity. This is the case with pagination, cross referencing and with the use of chapter, section and text in the place of brochure, publication, bulletin, pamphlet and leaflet as used in the original documents. I must also point out an important and deliberate feature of the book that could easily become obvious to a meticulous reader; that is, a seeming repetition of titles, topics, ideas, paragraphs and sections. This is a deliberate action due to our determination to represent, as much as possible, borrowed materials in their original forms and structure. It is also due to my desire and resolve to ensure that important tips and advice are not missed by those travelers or readers who, under the pressures of daily life, may not have the time to read the entire book and might only concentrate on a few select chapters. Furthermore, where repetition appears to be the case, it underscores my own belief in the importance of the information being conveyed. While it is realistic to assume that some readers and travelers may be pressed for time and thus may not be able to go through the entire book, I do encourage them (without prejudice) to include in their reading, Chapters 1, 4, 5 and 35. These chapters contain information that is more general than most of the other chapters.

[3]   I believe you will agree that we live in changing times, which include changing political, social, cultural and economic climates at home and abroad that may impact on international travels.

Whereas most of the information contained in this book will remain valid perhaps through the ages, some are bound to change. I have anticipated that to be the case; Therefore, I have provided you with relevant references, including postal and web addresses, phone numbers, and e-mail addresses of government and non-government agencies and organizations that will keep you up-to-date. (See Chapter 36)

I caution readers that some information contained in this book, including those related to prices of publications quoted/cited and addresses and phone numbers of various organizations cited throughout the book are subject to change by their respective sources by the time you consult this book. Lastly, for a book of this size, even with all the carefulness and diligence on the part of the publisher, errors and omissions both typographical and in content are bound to occur and I have acknowledged that. I urge you to inform us whenever you find such errors and omissions so that I may correct them in the next edition. At the time this book went to press, every effort was made to ensure that all of the prices and references were accurate. However, we make this explicit disclaimer:

DISCLAIMER:

The author and Frontline Publishers shall have neither liability nor responsibility to any person or entity with respect to any loss or damage caused, or alleged to have been caused, directly or indirectly, by information contained in this book. Nor will they be held responsible for the experiences of readers while they are traveling. The information contained in this book is meant to serve only as a general guide and to assist you in your travel plans and not as the only source or the ultimate source of information for travelers. This information is neither all inclusive, exhaustive nor cast in bronze. Similarly, we warn that neither the author nor the publisher recommends or attests to the legal status, reliability and quality of services and products provided by any of the agencies, organizations, and business firms mentioned in this book. Independent verification and assessment are strongly recommended, including checking with your local government's Consumer Affairs Office and the Better Business Bureau. If you do not wish to be bound by the above, you are advised not to purchase this book.

TABLE OF CONTENTS

**CHAPTER 8: HEALTH
INFORMATION FOR
INTERNATIONAL TRAVELS** *111*

**CHAPTER 9: TIPS FOR OLDER
AMERICANS** *143*

CHAPTER 15: TIPS FOR TRAVELERS TO CENTRAL AND SOUTH AMERICA *187*

CHAPTER 20: TIPS FOR TRAVELERS TO RUSSIA 273

CHAPTER 21: TIPS FOR TRAVELERS TO THE INDEPENDENT STATES (OF FORMER SOVIET UNION) 285

xix

APPENDIXES

INDEX

Chapter 1

Your Trip Abroad (Before, During and After)

[The information in this chapter is reprinted verbatim from a bulletin issued by the
U.S. State Department, Bureau of Consular Affairs. It is intended to serve as advice
to Americans traveling abroad.]

FOREWORD

Whether you are traveling overseas for business, pleasure or study, the best way to ensure a carefree and relaxing trip is to prevent problems before they happen. The more you learn about passports, visas, customs, immunizations, and other travel basics, the less likely you are to have difficulties during your travels.

The information in this chapter has been written to help you organize and take a pleasant, trouble-free trip. In the back of the book, we refer you to other sources of travel information covering such matters as customs regulations, agricultural restrictions, visa requirements, U.S. embassy addresses, foreign country information, and more. For your convenience, the addresses of the U.S. passport agencies are listed at the end of the pamphlet.

The Department of State in Washington, D.C., and its more than 250 U.S. embassies and consulates worldwide, as well as other U.S. Government agencies, are ready and pleased to offer assistance whenever possible. This is your trip. Make it an enjoyable one.

YOUR TRIP ABROAD

BEFORE YOU GO

There is much that you can do to prepare for your trip abroad, depending on where you are going, how long you are staying, and your reasons for traveling.

LEARN ABOUT THE COUNTRIES THAT YOU PLAN TO VISIT

The following suggestions and sources may be useful:

- Read as much as possible about the countries in which you plan to travel. Informing yourself about a nation's

- history, culture, customs and politics will make your stay more meaningful. Such information can be found in most libraries, bookstores and tourist bureaus. Although English is spoken in many countries, it is a good idea to learn what you can of the language of the country in which you will be traveling.

- Travel agents can provide brochures and tourist information about the countries that you wish to visit.

- Most international airlines can supply you with travel brochures about the countries that they serve. Many countries have tourist information offices in main cities in the United States where you can obtain travel brochures and maps.

- Foreign embassies or consulates in the United States can provide up-to-date information on their countries. Addresses and telephone numbers of the embassies of foreign governments are listed in the Congressional Directory, available at most public libraries. In addition to their embassies, some countries also have consulates in major U.S. cities. Look for their addresses in your local telephone directory, or find them in the publication, *Foreign Consular Offices in the United States*, available in many public libraries, or on

1

the Internet http://www.state.gov/
The Department of State publishes *Background Notes* on countries worldwide. These are brief, factual pamphlets with information on each country's culture, history, geography, economy, government, and current political situation. The *Background Notes* are available for approximately 170 countries. They often include a reading list, travel notes and maps. To purchase copies, you can contact the **Superintendent of Documents, U.S. Government Printing Office, Washington, D.C. 20402, or call (202) 512-1800**. Select issues are also available from the Department of State's Bureau of Public Affairs, fax-on-demand, **by calling (202) 736-7720 from your fax machine or on the Department of State's home page on the Internet at** http://www.state.gov/.

The **Consular Information Program** provides pertinent information for travelers. The U.S. Department of State issues fact sheets, known as *Consular Information Sheets*, on every country in the world. You should obtain the Department of State's *Consular Information Sheet* for any country that you will visit. The sheets contain information about crime and security conditions, areas of instability, and other details pertaining to travel in a particular country.

The Department of State also issues *Travel Warnings* and *Public Announcements*. *Travel Warnings* are issued when the Department of State recommends deferral of travel by Americans to a country because of civil unrest, dangerous conditions, terrorist activity and/or because the United States has no diplomatic relations with the country and cannot assist an American citizen in distress. *Public Announcements* are issued as a means to disseminate information quickly about terrorist threats and other relatively short-term and/or transnational conditions, which would pose significant risks to American travelers.

If the Department of State has issued a Travel Warning or Public Announcement for any country that you plan to visit, you should obtain this information. Instructions on how to access the Consular Information Program follow.

How to Access Consular Information Sheets, Travel Warnings and Public Announcements
Consular Information Sheets, Travel Warnings and Public Announcements may be heard at any time

by dialing the Office of Overseas Citizens Services, American Citizens Services and Crisis Management, Bureau of Consular Affairs, at **(202) 647-5225** from a touchtone phone. The recording is updated as new information becomes available. Consular Information Sheets, Travel Warnings and Public Announcements may also be obtained from any regional passport agency, from most airline computer reservation systems, from U.S. embassies or consulates abroad, or by sending your request, (indicating the desired country in the lower left corner of the envelope), in a self-addressed, stamped envelope to the **Office of Overseas Citizens Services, Bureau of Consular Affairs, Room 4811, U.S. Department of State, Washington, D.C. 20520-4818**.

By Fax
From your fax machine, dial **(202) 647-3000**, using the handset as you would a regular telephone. The system will prompt you on how to proceed.

By Internet
Information about travel and consular services is available on this site. Visitors to the site will find Travel Warnings, Public Announcements, Consular Information Sheets, passport and visa information, travel publications, background on international adoption and international child abduction services, and international legal assistance.

Consular Affairs Bulletin Board - CABB
If you have a personal computer, modem and communications software, you can access the Consular Affairs Bulletin Board (CABB). This service is free of charge. To view or download the documents, dial the CABB on **(301) 946-4400**, setting your software to N-8-1. The login is **travel** and the password is **info** (lower case required).

Tips for Travelers Series
The Department of State publishes a series of brochures on travel to specific regions of the world. The brochures cover a variety of topics such as import and export controls, customs and currency regulations, dual nationality, crime information, health precautions, and photography restrictions. The publications are available from **the Superintendent of Documents, U.S. Government Printing Office (GPO), Washington, D.C. 20402**. (Availability and prices

are subject to change without notice. Please check with the GPO before ordering at telephone 202-512-1800.)

REQUIRED DOCUMENTS

Travel document requirements vary from country to country, but you will need the following: a U.S. passport or other proof of citizenship, plus a visa or a tourist card, if required by the country or countries that you will visit. You may also need evidence that you have enough money for your trip and/or have ongoing or return transportation tickets.

A Valid Passport

[The Information on Passports slotted for this section is reproduced in the chapter entitled "Passports". Check the Table of Contents for location.]

How to Obtain Visas

A visa is an endorsement or stamp placed in your passport by a foreign government that permits you to visit that country for a specified purpose and a limited time - for example, a 3-month tourist visa. It is advisable to obtain visas before you leave the United States because you may not be able to obtain visas for some countries once you have departed. You should apply directly to the embassy or nearest consulate of each country that you plan to visit, or consult a travel agent. **Passport agencies *cannot* help you obtain visas.**
Foreign Entry Requirements

The Department of State publication M-264, *Foreign Entry Requirements*, gives entry requirements for every country and tells where and how to apply for visas and tourist cards. It can be ordered for 50 cents from the **Consumer Information Center, Pueblo, Colorado 81009; telephone: 719-948-4000; Internet** http://www.pueblo.gsa.gov/ **Please Note:** The publication is updated annually, but it may not reflect the most current requirements. It is advisable to verify the latest visa requirements directly with the embassy or consulate of each country that you plan to visit.

Because a visa is stamped directly onto a blank page in your passport, you will need to give your passport to an official of each foreign embassy or consulate. You may also need to fill out a form and submit one or more photographs with the form. Many visas require a fee. The process may take several weeks for each visa, so it is wise to apply well in advance of your trip, if possible.

Tourist Card

If the country that you plan to visit only requires a tourist card, you can usually obtain one from the country's embassy or consulate, from an airline serving the country, or at the port of entry. There is a fee for some tourist cards.

Proof of Citizenship

Check with the embassy or consulate of each country that you plan to visit to learn what proof of citizenship is required of visitors. Even if a country does not require a visitor to have a passport, it will require some proof of citizenship and identity. Remember that no matter what proof of citizenship a foreign country requires, U.S. Immigration has strict requirements for reentry into the United States.

Immunizations

Under international health regulations adopted by the World Health Organization, a country may require international certificates of vaccination against yellow fever and cholera. Typhoid vaccinations are not required for international travel, but are recommended for areas where there is risk of exposure. Smallpox vaccinations are no longer given. Check your health care records to ensure that your measles, mumps, rubella, polio, diphtheria, tetanus, and pertussis immunizations are up-to-date. Medication to deter malaria and other preventative measures are advisable for certain areas. No immunizations are needed to return to the United States.

Information on immunization requirements, U.S. Public Health Service recommendations, and other health guidance, including risks in particular countries, are included in the book, *Health Information for International Travel*. It may be purchased by sending a check or money order for $20.00 to the **Superintendent of Documents, U.S. Government Printing Office, P.O. Box 371954, Pittsburgh, PA 15250-7954.** Orders by telephone and a credit card (Visa, MasterCard, Discover) can be made by calling **202-512-1800; fax 202-512-2250.** In addition, you may obtain information on health from local and state health departments

3

or physicians. The information is also available from **the Centers for Disease Control and Prevention's 24-hour hotline at 1-888-232-3228,** from their automated faxback service at **1-888-232-3299,** or from their home page on the Internet at http://www.cdc.gov/.

It is not necessary to be vaccinated against a disease to which you will not be exposed, and few countries refuse to admit you if you arrive without the necessary vaccinations. Officials will either vaccinate you, give you a medical follow-up card, or, in rare circumstances, put you in isolation for the incubation period of the disease that you were not vaccinated against. It is a good idea to check immunization requirements before you depart.

If vaccinations are required, they must be recorded on approved forms, such as those in the booklet PHS-731, *International Certificates of Vaccination as Approved by the World Health Organization.* If your doctor or public health office does not have this booklet, it can be purchased for $1.00 from the **Superintendent of Documents, P.O. Box 371954, Pittsburgh, PA 15250-7954; telephone 202-512-1800,** or Government Printing Office bookstores. You should keep the booklet with your passport.

An increasing number of countries require that foreigners be tested for Human Immunodeficiency Virus (HIV) prior to entry. Testing is usually required as part of a medical exam for long term visitors (i.e., students and workers). Before traveling abroad, you can check with the embassy or consulate of the country that you intend to visit to learn about the latest information concerning entry requirements and, particularly, whether or not an AIDS/HIV test is a requirement.

Health Insurance

Obtaining medical treatment and hospital care can be costly for travelers who are injured or who become seriously ill overseas. **The Social Security Medicare/Medicaid program does *not* provide coverage for hospital or medical services outside the United States.** Before you leave the United States, you should be informed about which medical services your health insurance will cover abroad.

Senior citizens may wish to contact the American Association of Retired Persons for information about foreign medical care coverage with Medicare supplement plans.

If your health insurance policy does not provide coverage for hospital or medical costs abroad, you are urged to purchase a temporary health policy that does provide this type of coverage. There are short-term health and emergency assistance policies designed for travelers. You can find the names of companies that provide such policies from your travel agent, your health insurance company, or from advertisements in travel publications. Useful information on medical emergencies abroad is provided in the Department of State, Bureau of Consular Affairs' flyer, *Medical Information for Americans Traveling Abroad,* available by autofax service at **202-647-3000.** In addition to health insurance, many policies include trip cancellation, baggage loss, and travel accident insurance in the same package. Some traveler's check companies have protection policies available with the purchase of traveler's checks.

Medical Evacuation

Although some health insurance companies may pay "customary and reasonable" hospital costs abroad, very few will pay for medical evacuation back to the United States. Medical evacuation can easily cost $10,000 or more, depending on your location and medical condition. One of the main advantages of health and emergency assistance policies is that they often include coverage for medical evacuation to the United States. Even if your regular health insurance covers you for emergencies abroad, you should consider purchasing supplemental insurance to cover medical evacuation.

Whichever health insurance coverage you choose for travel overseas, remember to carry with you both your health insurance policy identity card and claim forms.

Do You Need Travel Insurance?

You may not need travel insurance, if you are already adequately covered by other insurance policies. Depending on the travel insurance plan, travel insurance usually promises to cover you for cancellation or interruption of your trip, some form of emergency medical care while you are traveling, lost or stolen luggage, and various other troublesome occurrences.

Before you decide on a travel insurance plan, it is wise to investigate the plan carefully and read the fine print. You should closely check any agreements with your travel agent, tour operator, airline, or other companies involved with your travel plans. The agreements may include written guarantees.

If you have a fully refundable airline ticket, you may decide that you would not need trip cancellation/interruption insurance.

On the other hand, it may be worthwhile noting that certain insurance plans can protect you by covering the financial costs in case of the following situations:

- A sudden, serious injury or illness to you, a family member, or a traveling companion.
- Financial default of the airline, cruise line or tour operator.
- Natural disasters or strikes that impede travel services.
- A terrorist incident in a foreign city within 10 days of your scheduled arrival in that particular city.

The fact that you, a traveling member of your family, or a traveling companion were quarantined, served with a court order or required to serve on a jury.

A circumstance in which you were directly involved in an accident enroute to departure for your trip.

It is a good idea to check your other insurance policies. For instance, your homeowners or tenants insurance may cover the loss or theft of your luggage.

Certain credit cards may also provide additional travel insurance, if you have used them to purchase the ticket for your trip.

Your health insurance may provide certain coverage, regardless of where you travel. But it is very important to note that some policies only partially cover medical expenses abroad. Moreover, as previously explained in the section on Health Insurance, Medicare/Medicaid will not cover hospital and medical services outside the United States. (Please See section on **Health Insurance** for more details about health emergencies abroad.)

Your travel agent should be able to advise you about the right plan for you. Before purchasing travel insurance, review the plan carefully, and be wary of buying coverage that you may already have.

How to Bring Money

Traveler's Checks

It is wise **not** to carry large amounts of cash. You should take most of your money in traveler's checks and remember to record the serial number, denomination and the date and location of the issuing bank or agency. Keep this information in a safe and separate place so, if you lose your traveler's checks, you can quickly get replacements.

Credit Cards

Some credit cards can be used worldwide, even for cash advances. Keep track of your credit card purchases so that you do not exceed your limit. Travelers have been arrested overseas for mistakenly exceeding their credit limit! Leave all unnecessary credit cards at home. Record the numbers of the credit cards that you do bring, and keep the list separately from the cards.

You should immediately report the loss or theft of your credit cards or traveler's checks to the credit card companies and to the local police. If you plan to stay in one place for some time, you might consider opening an account for check cashing and other transactions at a U.S. bank that has an overseas affiliate. U.S. embassies and consulates **cannot** cash checks for you.

Before leaving on your trip, you may wish to check with your bank to see if the country or countries that you plan to visit have Automated Teller Machine (ATM) service. The bank should be able to tell you if you can use your ATM card during your trip abroad.

Prepare for Emergency Funds

It is a good idea to keep the telephone number for your bank in the United States with you, in case you run out of cash and need to transfer money. In some countries, major banks and certain travel

5

agencies can help arrange a transfer of funds from your account to a foreign bank. If you do not have a bank account from which you can obtain emergency funds, you should make arrangements in advance with a relative or friend to send you emergency funds should it become necessary. If you find yourself destitute, contact the nearest U.S. embassy or consulate for assistance in arranging a money wire transfer from a relative or friend in the United States.

Foreign Currency

Before departing, you may wish to purchase small amounts of foreign currency to use for buses, taxis, phones, or tips when you first arrive. Foreign exchange facilities at airports may be closed when your flight arrives. You can purchase foreign currency at some U.S. banks, at foreign exchange firms, at foreign exchange windows, or even at vending machines in many international airports in the United States.

Some countries regulate the amount of local currency that you can bring into or take out of the country; others require that you exchange a minimum amount of currency. For currency regulations, check with a bank, a foreign exchange firm, your travel agent, or the embassy or consulate of the countries that you plan to visit.

If you leave or enter the United States with more than $10,000 in monetary instruments of any kind, you must file a report, **Customs Form 4790**, with U.S. Customs at the time. Failure to comply can result in civil and criminal proceedings.

Valuables -- Do Not Bring Them!

Do **not** bring anything on your trip that you would hate to lose, such as expensive jewelry, family photographs, or objects of sentimental value. If you bring jewelry, wear it discreetly to help prevent snatch-and-run robbery.

Other Things To Arrange Before You Depart

Lodging

Try to Make Lodging Reservations in Advance

Many travelers wait until they reach their destination before making hotel reservations. Some train stations and airports have travel desks to assist you in finding lodging. However, when you arrive, you may be tired and unfamiliar with your surroundings, and could have difficulty locating a

hotel to suit your needs. Therefore, when possible, reserve your lodging in advance and confirm your reservations along the way. During peak tourist season, it is important to have a hotel reservation for at least the first night that you arrive in a foreign city.

An alternative to hotels and pensions is the youth hostel system, which offers travelers of all ages clean, inexpensive, overnight accommodations in more than 6,000 locations in over 70 countries worldwide. Hostels provide dormitory-style accommodations with separate facilities for males and females. Some hostels have family rooms that can be reserved in advance. Curfews are often imposed and membership is frequently required. For more information, you may contact: **American Youth Hostels, P.O. Box 37613, Washington, D.C. 20013-7613; telephone (202) 783-6161.**

Organized Programs

The majority of private programs for vacation, study, or work abroad are reputable and financially sound. However, some charge exorbitant fees, use deliberately false "educational" claims, and provide working conditions far different from those advertised. Even programs of legitimate organizations can be poorly administered. Be cautious. **Before committing yourself or your finances, find out about the organization and what it offers.**

Travel Benefits for Students and Teachers

Students and teachers can save money on transportation and accommodations, and obtain other discounts if they have one of the following:

An **International Student Identity Card** - for students age 12 and older. You must be a junior high school, high school, college, university or vocational school student at least 12 years of age. Also, you must be enrolled in a study program leading to a diploma or degree at an accredited institution.

An **International Teacher Identity Card** - for full-time teachers and faculty at an accredited institution.

A **GO 25 International Youth Travel Card** - for youths ages 12 - 25. You must be at least 12 years of age, but not over 25 at the time that you apply.

These cards are available with proof of your status and a small fee from: **Council on International Educational Exchange; 205 East 42nd Street; New York, New York 10017; telephone 1-888-COUNCIL;** Internet http://www.counciltravel.com/idcards/default.asp

The international identity cards offer the following benefits:

- Reduced airfares on major international airlines
- Discounts in the United States and abroad, including transportation, accommodations, international phone calls, car rentals and museum admissions
- Toll-free, 24-hour, emergency **Help Line**
- **Basic insurance** to cover sickness, accident and emergency evacuation while traveling outside the United States (*only* **for cards purchased in the United States.**)
- International student/teacher/youth recognition.

For more details and information about applying for international identity cards, contact the Council on International Educational Exchange aas listed above.

Pre-Paid Telephone Card Service

You never know when you may wish or need to telephone home during your trip. For such purposes, you might consider purchasing a pre-paid telephone card. You can check with telephone companies about pre-paid telephone card service. They should be able to provide you with information about prices, sales locations in the United States and ordering the service by telephone. If you decide to purchase a pre-paid telephone card, be sure that the card you choose will work outside the United States.

Transportation

At the time of publication, U.S. citizens in the United States, who are traveling abroad, are required to pay a $12 airport departure tax and a $6 federal inspection fee that are included in the price of the air ticket.

Charter Flights and Airlines

There have been occasions when airlines or companies that sell charter flights or tour packages have gone out of business with little warning, stranding passengers overseas. If you know from the media or your travel agent that an airline is in financial difficulty, ask your travel agent or the airline what recourse you would have, if the airline ceased to operate. Some airlines may honor the tickets of a defunct airline, but they usually do so with restrictions.

It is a good idea to purchase tours only from operators that guarantee the safety of your money through a consumer protection plan.

Before you purchase a charter flight or tour package, read the contract carefully. Unless it guarantees to deliver services promised or give a full refund, you may consider purchasing travel insurance. If you are unsure of the reputation of a charter company or tour operator, consult your local **Better Business Bureau or the American Society of Travel Agents at 1101 King Street, Alexandria, VA 22314, Tel. (703) 739-2782.** They will help answer your questions and tell you whether or not a company has a complaint record.

Driver's License/Auto Insurance

If you intend to drive overseas, check with the embassy or consulate of the countries where you will visit to learn about requirements for driver's license, road permits, and auto insurance. If possible, obtain road maps of the countries that you plan to visit before you go.

Many countries do not recognize a U.S. driver's license. However, most countries accept an international driver's permit. Before departure, you can obtain one at a local office of an automobile association. The U.S. Department of State has authorized two organizations to issue international driving permits to those who hold valid U.S. driver's licenses: **AAA and the American Automobile Touring Alliance.** To apply for an international driving permit, you must be at least age 18, and you will need to present two passport-size photographs and your valid U.S. license. Certain countries require road permits, instead of tolls, to use on their divided highways, and they will fine those found driving without a permit.

7

Car rental agencies overseas usually provide auto insurance, but in some countries, the required coverage is minimal. When renting a car overseas, consider purchasing insurance coverage that is at least equivalent to that which you carry at home.

In general, your U.S. auto insurance does not cover you abroad. However, your policy may apply when you drive to countries neighboring the United States. Check with your insurer to see if your policy covers you in Canada, Mexico, or countries south of Mexico. Even if your policy is valid in one of these countries, it may not meet its minimum requirements. For instance, in most of Canada, you must carry at least $200,000 in liability insurance, and Mexico requires that, if vehicles do not carry theft, third party liability, and comprehensive insurance, the owner must post a bond that could be as high as 50% of the value of the vehicle. If you are under-insured for a country, auto insurance can usually be purchased on either side of the border.

U.S. Customs Pre-Registration

It is a good idea to be informed about U.S. Customs regulations. Foreign-made personal articles taken abroad are subject to U.S. Customs duty and tax upon your return, unless you have proof of prior possession such as a receipt, bill of sale, an insurance policy, or a jeweler's appraisal. If you do not have proof of prior possession, items such as foreign-made watches, cameras, or tape recorders that can be identified by serial number or permanent markings, may be taken to the Customs office nearest you, or to the port of departure for registration, before you depart the United States. The certificate of registration provided can expedite free entry of these items when you return to the United States.

The ATA Carnet

If you are interested in establishing business overseas, you may consider obtaining and ATA Carnet, which is an international Customs document for temporary, duty-free imports. The ATA Carnet offers many advantages for international business. For example, it reduces the cost of exporting by eliminating the value-added (VAT). It also simplifies the extensive Customs procedures by allowing temporary exporters to use a single document for all transactions and make arrangements for many countries and many trips in advance at a predetermined cost. For more information about obtaining an ATA Carnet, please contact the U.S. Council for International Business, 1212 Avenue of the Americas, New York, New York 10036; telephone 212-354-4480; fax 212-944-0012.

Documentation for Medications

If you go abroad with preexisting medical problems, you should carry a letter from you doctor describing your condition, including information on any prescription medicines that you must take. You should also have the generic names of the drugs. Please leave medicines in their original, labeled containers. These precautions make customs processing easier. A doctor's certificate, however, may not suffice as authorization to transport all prescription drugs to all foreign countries. Travelers have innocently been arrested for drug violations when carrying items not considered to be narcotics in the United States. To ensure that you do not violate the drug laws of the countries that you visit, you may consult the embassy or consulate of those countries for precise information before you leave the United States.

If you have allergies, reactions to certain medicines, or other unique medical problems, you may consider wearing a medical alert bracelet or carrying a similar warning.

Information About Physicians and Hospitals Abroad

Several private organizations provide listings of physicians abroad to international travelers. Membership in these organizations is generally free, although a donation may be requested. Membership entitles you to a number traveler's medical aids, including a directory of physicians with their overseas locations, telephone numbers and doctors' fee schedules. The physicians are generally English-speaking and provide medical assistance 24 hours a day. The addresses of these medical organizations are in travel magazines or may be available from your travel agent.

U.S. embassies and consulates abroad usually keep lists of physicians and hospitals in their area. Major credit card companies also can provide the names of local doctors and hospitals abroad.

8

For detailed information about physicians abroad, the authoritative reference is *the Directory of Medical Specialists*, published for the American Board of Medical Specialists and its 22 certifying member boards. The publication should be available in your local library.

More medical information may be found in the Department of State Bureau of Consular Affairs' brochure, *Medical Information for Americans Traveling Abroad*, available by autofax service at 202-647-3000.

Places to Receive Mail

If you are traveling for an extended period, you may want to arrange for the delivery of mail or messages to you abroad. Some banks and international credit card companies handle mail for customers at their overseas branches. General Delivery (Poste Restante) services at post offices in most countries will hold mail for you. U.S. embassies/consulates do not handle private mail.

Learn About Dual Nationality

Whether you are a U.S. citizen from birth or were naturalized as a U.S. citizen, a foreign country may claim you as its citizen if:

- You were born in that country.
- Your parent(s) is or was a citizen of that country.
- You are married to a citizen of that country.
- You are a naturalized U.S. citizen, but you are still considered to be a citizen under that country's laws.

If any of the possibilities for dual nationality applies to you, check on your status (including military obligations) with the embassy or consulate of the country that might claim you as a citizen. In particular, Americans may have problems with dual nationality in certain countries in the Middle East, in South America, and in Africa. Some foreign countries refuse to recognize a dual national's U.S. citizenship and do not allow U.S. officials access to arrested Americans.

Some Things to Leave Behind

Your Itinerary - Leave a Paper Trail

You should leave a detailed itinerary (with names, addresses, and phone numbers of persons and places to be visited) with relatives or friends in the United States so that you can be reached in an emergency. Also, include a photocopy of your passport information page.

Other Important Numbers

It is a good idea to make a list of all important numbers - your passport information as well as your credit card, traveler's checks, and airline ticket numbers. Leave a copy of the list at home, and carry a copy with you.

While You Are Overseas

How to Deal With the Unexpected

If you change your travel plans, miss your return flight, or extend your trip, be sure to notify relatives or friends at home. Should you find yourself in an area of civil unrest or natural disaster, please let your relatives or friends at home know **as soon as you can** that you are safe. Furthermore, upon arrival in a foreign country, you should contact the nearest U.S. embassy or consulate to register your presence and to keep the U.S. consul informed of your whereabouts.

Safety Tips

Protect Your Passport

Your passport is the most valuable document that you will carry abroad. It confirms your U.S. citizenship. Please guard it carefully. Do not use it as collateral for a loan or lend it to anyone. It is your best form of identification. You will need it when you pick up mail or check into hotels, embassies or consulates.

When entering some countries or registering at hotels, you may be asked to fill out a police card listing your name, passport number, destination, local address, and reason for travel. You may be required to leave your passport at the hotel reception desk overnight so that it may be checked by local police officials. These are normal procedures required by local laws. If your passport is not returned the following morning, immediately report the impoundment to local police authorities and to the nearest U.S. embassy or consulate.

Passport Fraud

Law enforcement records show that U.S. passports are sometimes used for illegal entry into the United States, or by criminals abroad seeking to establish another identity. This can cause embarrassment to innocent U.S. citizens whose names become associated with illegal activities. To protect the integrity of the U.S. passport and the security of the person bearing it, consular officers overseas have found it necessary to take precautions in processing lost passport cases. These precautions may involve some delay before a new passport is issued.

Safeguard Your Passport

Carelessness is the main cause for losing a passport or having it stolen. You may find that you have to carry your passport with you because you need to show it when you cash traveler's checks or the country that you are visiting requires you to carry it as an identity document. When you must carry your passport, hide it securely on your person. Do not leave it in a handbag nor in an exposed pocket. Whenever possible, leave your passport in the hotel safe, not in an empty hotel room, and not packed in your luggage. One family member should not carry all the passports for the entire family.

Guard Against Thieves

Coat pockets, handbags, and hip pockets are particularly susceptible to theft. Thieves will use all kinds of ploys to divert your attention just long enough to pick your pocket and grab your purse or wallet. These ploys include creating a disturbance, spilling something on your clothing, or even handing you a baby to hold! You can try to prevent theft by carrying your belongings in a secure manner. For example, consider not carrying a purse or wallet when going along crowded streets. Women who carry a shoulder bag should keep it tucked under the arm and held securely by the strap. Men should put their wallets in their front trouser pockets or use money belts instead of hip pockets. A wallet wrapped in rubber bands is more difficult to remove without notice. Be especially cautious in a large crowd _ in the subway, on buses, at the marketplace, at a festival, or if surrounded by groups of vagrant children. Do not make it easy for thieves!

Financial and Shopping Tips

Currency

Local banks usually offer better rates of exchange than hotels, restaurants, or stores. Rates are often posted in windows. Above all, avoid private currency transactions. In some countries, you risk more than being swindled or stuck with counterfeit currency _ you risk arrest. Avoid the black market --- learn and obey the local currency laws, wherever you go.

Shopping

Mail Small Items

When you purchase small items, it is a good idea to mail them personally to your home or to carry them in your luggage. This will help prevent misdirected packages, no receipt of merchandise, or receipt of wrong merchandise. When you mail purchases, be sure to ask about insurance. American embassies and consulates abroad cannot serve as post offices. **They cannot accept, hold, or forward mail for U.S. citizens abroad.**

Items mailed home are **not** eligible for your $400 personal exemption. If the item that you are mailing home is less than $200, duty will be waived. Be sure to write on the outside of the package that it contains goods for personal use.

Value Added Tax

Some European countries levy a value added tax (VAT) on the items that you buy. In some places, if you ship your purchases home, the VAT can be waived. Other places may require you to pay the VAT, but have a system to refund all of it or part of it to you by mail. You can ask the store clerk for an application to apply for the refund. The VAT refund is only for items that you can ship or carry with you. It does not apply to food, hotel bills, or other services. Because the rules for VAT refunds vary from country to country, you should check with the country's tourist office to learn the local requirements.

Beware When Making the Following Purchases:

Wildlife Souvenirs

Be careful when you buy articles made from animals and plants or when you purchase live, wild animals to bring back as pets. Some items, such as those made from elephant ivory, sea turtles, crocodile leather, or fur from endangered cats, and many species of live animals cannot be brought legally into the United States. Your wildlife souvenirs could be confiscated by government inspectors, and you could face other penalties for attempting to bring them into the United States. Do not buy wildlife or wildlife products unless you are certain that they are legal for import into the United States.

Glazed Ceramics

Beware of purchasing glazed ceramic ware abroad. It is possible to suffer lead poisoning, if you consume food or beverages that are stored or served in improperly glazed ceramics. Unless the ceramics are made by a firm with an international reputation, there is no immediate way to be certain that a particular item is safe. The U.S. Food and Drug Administration recommends that ceramic tableware purchased abroad be tested for lead release by a commercial laboratory on your return or be used for decorative purposes only.

Antiques

Certain countries consider antiques to be national treasures and the "inalienable property of the nation." In some countries, customs authorities seize illegally purchased antiques without compensation, and they may also levy fines on the purchaser. Americans have been arrested and prosecuted for purchasing antiques without a permit. Americans have even been arrested for purchasing reproductions of antiques from street vendors because a local authority believed the purchase was a national treasure.

Protect yourself. In countries where antiques are important, document your purchases as reproductions, if that is the case, or, if they are authentic, secure the necessary export permit. The documentation or export permit may be available through the country's national museum. A reputable dealer may provide the export permit or information on how to secure one. If you have questions about purchasing antiques, the country's tourist office can guide you. If you still have doubts, consult the Consular Section of the nearest U.S. embassy or consulate. In places where Americans have had problems because of purchasing antiques, the Consular Section is usually well aware of such situations. Consular officers can inform you about the local laws and the correct procedures to follow.

Customs

It is important that you keep all receipts for items you buy overseas. They will be helpful in making your U.S. Customs declaration when you return.

Legal Tips

Obey Foreign Laws

When you are in a foreign country, you are subject to its laws. It helps to learn about local laws and regulations and to obey them. Try to avoid areas of unrest and disturbance. Deal only with authorized outlets when exchanging money or buying airline tickets and traveler's checks. **Do *not* deliver a package for anyone, unless you know the person well and you are certain that the package does not contain drugs or other contraband.**

Before you think about selling personal effects, such as clothing, cameras, or jewelry, you should learn about the local regulations regarding such sales. You must adhere strictly to local laws because the penalties that you risk are severe.

Some countries are particularly sensitive about photographs. In general, refrain from photographing police and military installations and personnel; industrial structures, including harbor, rail, and airport facilities; border areas; and scenes of civil disorder or other public disturbance. Taking such photographs may result in your detention, in the confiscation of your camera and films, as well as the imposition of fines. For information on photography restrictions, check with the country's tourist office or its embassy or consulate in the United States. Once abroad, you can check with local authorities or with the Consular Section of the nearest U.S. embassy or consulate.

Drug Arrests

About 3,000 Americans are arrested abroad each year. Of these, approximately one-third are held on drug charges. Despite repeated warnings, drug arrests and convictions are still a common occurrence. Many countries have stiff penalties for drug violations and strictly enforce drug laws. If you are caught buying, selling, carrying or using any type of drug - from hashish to heroin, marijuana to mescaline, cocaine to quaaludes - you will be arrested. You are subject to foreign laws overseas, **not U.S. laws**, and, if arrested, you will find that:

- Few countries provide a jury trial.
- Trials are often long, with delays and postponements.
- Most countries do not accept bail.
- Pre-trial detention, often in solitary confinement, may last for months.

11

If you are convicted, you face a possible sentence of:

- 2 - 10 years in many countries
- A minimum of 6 years hard labor and a stiff fine in some countries
- The death penalty in a number of countries (e.g. Malaysia, Pakistan, Turkey, Thailand, Saudi Arabia)

During recent years, there has been an increase in the number of women arrested abroad. These are usually women who serve as drug couriers or "mules" and who believe that they can make fast money and have a vacation at the same time, without getting caught. Instead of a vacation, they receive a permanent residence in an overseas jail.

U.S. citizens have been arrested abroad on drug charges because they possessed just one ounce or less of marijuana. The risk of being jailed for just one marijuana cigarette is simply not worth it!

Once you are arrested, the U.S. consular officer **CANNOT** get you out of jail nor out of the country!

Likewise, the U.S. consular officer **CANNOT**

- Represent you at trial or give you legal counsel.
- Pay legal fees and/or fines with U.S. Government funds.

PLEASE REMEMBER!

- If someone offers you a free trip and some quick and easy money, just for bringing back a suitcase...SAY NO!
- Do not carry a package for anyone, no matter how small it may be.
- Do not let anyone pack your suitcases for you while you are abroad.
- If the drugs are in you suitcase, you will be caught.

Do not get involved with illegal drugs overseas! It can spoil more than your vacation. It can ruin your life!

For more details, you may wish to consult the Department of State, Bureau of Consular Affairs' publication, *Travel Warning on Drugs Abroad*, available by autofax service at 202-647-3000.

Legal Aid

Because you are subject to local laws abroad, there is little that a U.S. consular officer can do for you,

if you encounter legal difficulties. As stated previously, a consular officer cannot get you out of jail. What American officials can do is limited by both foreign and U.S. laws.

Although U.S. consular officers cannot serve as attorneys nor give legal advice, they can provide a list of local attorneys and help you find adequate legal representation. The lists of attorneys are carefully compiled from local bar association lists and responses to questionnaires, but neither the Department of State nor U.S. embassies or consulates abroad can assume responsibility for the caliber, competence, or professional integrity of the attorneys.

If you are arrested, you should ask the authorities to notify a consular officer at the nearest U.S. embassy or consulate. **Under international agreements and practice, you have the right to talk to the U.S. consul.** If you are denied this right, try to have someone get in touch with the U.S. consular officer for you.

When alerted, U.S. officials will visit you, advise you of your rights according to local laws, and contact your family and friends, if you wish. They will do whatever they can to protect your legitimate interests and to ensure that you are not discriminated against under local law. U.S. consuls can transfer money, food, and clothing to the prison authorities from your family or friends. They will try to get relief, if you are held under inhumane or unhealthy conditions or treated less favorably than others in the same situation.

Help From American Consuls Abroad

When to Register With the U.S. Embassy

You should register at the Consular Section of the nearest U.S. embassy or consulate:

- If you find yourself in a country or area that is experiencing civil unrest, has an unstable political climate, or is undergoing a natural disaster, such as an earthquake or a hurricane.
- If you plan to go to a country where there are no U.S. officials. In such cases, you should register at the U.S embassy or consulate in an adjacent country, leave an itinerary with the Consular Section, ask about conditions in the country that you will visit, and

ask about the third country that may represent U.S. interests there.

• If you plan to stay in a country longer than one month.

Registration at the U.S. Embassy or Consulate makes your presence and whereabouts known, in case it is necessary for a consular officer to contact you in an emergency. During a disaster overseas, American consular officers can assist in evacuation were that to become necessary. But they cannot assist you if they do not know where your are. Registration also makes it easier to apply for a replacement passport, if yours is lost or stolen.

If you are traveling with an escorted tour to areas experiencing political uncertainty or other problems, find out if registration at the U.S. embassy or consulate is being done for you by your tour operator. If it is not, or if you are traveling on your own, you should leave a copy of your itinerary at the nearest U.S. embassy or consulate soon after you arrive.

What U.S. Consuls Can Do To Help You

U.S. consular officers are located at U.S. embassies and consulates in most countries overseas. They are available to advise and help you, if you are in any serious trouble.

In the Case of Destitution

If you become destitute abroad, the U.S. consul can help you get in touch with your family, friends, bank, or employer and tell you how to arrange for them to send funds for you. These funds can sometimes be wired to you through the Department of State.

In the Case of Illness or Injury

If you become ill or injured while abroad, you can contact the nearest U.S. embassy or consulate for a list of local doctors, dentists, medical specialists, clinics and hospitals. If your illness or injury is serious, the U.S. consul can help you find medical assistance and, at your request, will inform your family or friends of your condition. If necessary, a consul can assist in the transfer of funds from the United States. Payment of hospital and other expenses is your responsibility. U.S. consular officers cannot supply you with medication. During an emergency, if you are unable to communicate, the consul will check your passport for the name and address of any relative, friend, or legal representative whom you wish to have notified. Because the U.S. Government cannot pay for medical evacuations, it is advisable to have private medical insurance to cover this.

Marriage Abroad

U.S. diplomatic and consular officials do not have the authority to perform marriages overseas. Marriage abroad must be performed in accordance with local law. There are always documentary requirements, and in some countries, there is a lengthy residence requirement before a marriage may take place. Before traveling, ask the embassy or consulate of the country in which you plan to marry about their regulations and how to prepare to marry abroad. Once abroad, the Consular Section of the nearest U.S. embassy or consulate may be able to answer some of your questions, but it is your responsibility to deal with local civil authorities.

Birth Abroad

A child born abroad to a U.S. citizen parent or parents generally acquires U.S. citizenship at birth. As soon as possible after the birth, the U.S. parent or parents should contact the nearest U.S. embassy or consulate to have a **Report of Birth Abroad of a Citizen of the United States of America** prepared. This document serves as proof of acquisition of U.S. citizenship and is acceptable evidence for obtaining a U.S. passport and for most other purposes where one must show a birth certificate or proof of citizenship.

Adoption Abroad

If you plan to adopt a child overseas, you should be aware that the U.S. government considers foreign adoptions to be a private, legal matter within the judicial sovereignty of the nation in which the child is residing. U.S. authorities have no right to intervene on behalf of American citizens in the courts of the country where the adoption takes place. But there are a number of ways in which U.S. embassies and consulates can assist prospective parents.

The U.S. embassy or consulate can provide you with information on the adoption process in that particular country. Consular officers can inquire on your behalf about the status of your case in the foreign court, and they can assist in clarifying documentary requirements, if necessary. Consular officers will also try to ensure that, as a U.S.

citizen, you will not be discriminated against by foreign courts, and they will provide you with information about the visa application process for your adopted child.

Because children in foreign adoptions are considered to be nationals of the country of origin, prospective parents must comply with local laws. One way to accomplish this is by dealing with a reputable international adoption agency, experienced in handling adoptions in the particular country in which you wish to adopt the child. In the case of a private adoption, you should hire a local attorney with expertise in adoptions.

Further information on adoption procedures can be obtained by requesting INS Form M-249, *The Immigration of Adopted and Prospective Adoptive Children*. You may also write for the free pamphlet, *International Adoption*. Please send a self-addressed, triple-stamped 9"x12" envelope to: Office of Children's Issues, Overseas Citizens Services, Bureau of Consular Affairs, Room 4817, Department of State, Washington, D.C. 20520-4818. If you are planning to adopt from a particular country, you should mention that in your request, because the Office of Children's Issues has specific information on the adoption procedures in countries around the world. Information is also available by autofax service on 202-647-3000.

International Child Custody Disputes

There are limits on the assistance that U.S. authorities can provide to parents involved in a child custody dispute. When an American child is abducted overseas by a parent, the U.S. Government's role is to help the remaining parent locate the child, monitor the child's welfare, and provide information about child custody laws and procedures in the country where the child has been taken. Consular officers overseas can issue a U.S. passport to a child involved in a custody dispute, if the child appears in person at a U.S. embassy or consulate, and if there is no court order from the foreign court of that country, which bars the child's departure from the country.

Parents who are involved in a custody dispute overseas should find out whether that country is a party to the Hague Convention on the Civil Aspects of International Child Abduction. Under the Hague Convention, a child who has been wrongfully removed from a parent may be returned to his or her place of habitual residence. For further information on international child abduction and the Hague Convention, please contact the **Office of Children's Issues, Overseas Citizens Services, Bureau of Consular Affairs, Room 4817, Washington, D.C., 20520; telephone 202-647-7000**. This office also has copies of the booklet, *International Parental Child Abduction*, which contains helpful information on what U.S. citizen parents can do to prevent their child from becoming a victim of parental child abduction. (The booklet is also available by autofax service at 202-674-3000. If you are overseas and would like information on this subject, please contact the nearest U.S. embassy or consulate for guidance.

Death Abroad

When a U.S. citizen dies abroad, the consular officer reports the death to the next of kin or legal representative and arranges to obtain from them the necessary private funds for local burial or return of the body to the United States. Before you begin your trip, please complete in **pencil** the address page in the front of your passport. Please provide the name, address and telephone number of someone to be contacted in an emergency. Do not give the names of your traveling companions, in case the entire party is involved in the same accident.

Because the U.S. Government cannot pay for local burial or shipment of remains to the United States, it is worthwhile to have insurance to cover this possibility. Following a death, a *Report of the Death of An American Citizen* (Optional Form 180) is prepared by the consular officer to provide the facts concerning the death and the custody of the personal estate of the deceased. Under certain circumstances, a consular officer becomes the provisional conservator of a deceased American's estate and arranges for the disposition of those effects.

A Variety of Non-Emergency Services

Consular officers provide non-emergency services as well. These include information about Selective Service registration, travel safety information, absentee voting, and the acquisition or loss of U.S. citizenship. They arrange for the transfer of Social Security and other Federal benefits to beneficiaries residing abroad, provide U.S. tax forms, and

14

notarize documents. Consuls can also provide information on how to obtain foreign public documents.

What U.S. Consuls Cannot Do

U.S. consular officers will do their best to assist U.S. citizens abroad. However, they must devote priority time and energies to those Americans who find themselves in the most serious legal, medical, or financial difficulties.

Because of limited resources, consuls **cannot** provide routine or commercial-type services. They cannot act as travel agents, information bureaus, banks, or law enforcement officers. U.S. Federal law forbids a consular officer from acting as your lawyer. Consular officers **cannot** find you employment; get you visas, residence permits or driving permits; act as interpreters; search for missing luggage; call your credit card company or bank; replace stolen traveler's checks; or settle disputes with hotel managers. However, they can tell you how to get assistance on these matters, as well as other issues.

When You Return

Return Transportation
You should confirm your return reservation at least twice, and at least 72 hours before your scheduled departure. Whenever possible, obtain a written confirmation. If you confirm your return reservation by phone, record the time, day, and the name of the agent who took your call. If your name does not appear on the reservations list, you have no recourse and may find yourself stranded.

Departure Tax
Some countries levy an airport departure tax on travelers, which can be as high as $50. Please ask the airline or a travel agent about this tax. **Make certain to have enough money at the end of your trip so that you will be able to get on the plane.**
Immigration and Customs

If a passport was required for your trip, have it ready when you go through Immigration and Customs. If you took other documents with you, such as an International Certificate of Vaccination, a medical letter, or a Customs certificate of registration for foreign-made personal articles, have them ready, also. Have your receipts handy, in case you need to support your customs declaration. When returning to the United States

by car from Mexico or Canada, have your certificate of vehicle registration available. It is a good idea to pack your baggage in a way to make inspection easier. For example, pack the articles you acquired abroad separately, if possible.

Articles acquired abroad and brought back with you are subject to duty and Internal Revenue tax. U.S. Customs currently allows each U.S. citizen to bring back $400 worth of merchandise duty free, provided the traveler has been outside the United States for at least 48 hours, has not already used this exemption within the preceding 30 day period, and provided the traveler can present the purchases upon his or her arrival at the port of entry. The next $1,000 worth of items brought back for personal use or gifts are subject to duty at a flat 10% rate. (Your duty-free exemption may include 100 cigars, 200 cigarettes, and one liter of wine, beer or liquor.)

There are two groups of destinations from which the duty-free exemption is higher. These are a group of 24 countries and dependencies in the Caribbean and Central America from which the exemption is $600, and a group of U.S. insular possessions (the U.S. Virgin Islands, American Samoa, and Guam), from which the exemption is $1,200. For details, you can consult your travel agent or the U.S. Customs Service publication, *Know Before You Go*, listed below.

Additional Sources of Information

Customs
The publication, ***Know Before You Go, Customs Hints for Returning U.S. Residents***, contains information on key U.S. Customs regulations and procedures, including duty rates. Single copies of the publication are free from any local Customs office or you may request copies by writing to: **U.S. Customs Service, P.O. Box 7407, Washington, D.C. 20044.**

Restrictions on the Entry of Products from Overseas into the United States
Fresh fruit, meat, vegetables, plants in soil, and many other agricultural products from abroad are prohibited entry into the United States because they may carry foreign insects and diseases that could damage U.S. crops, forests, gardens, and livestock. Other items may also be restricted, so it is advisable to be informed about such details before you return to the United States. The

15

restrictions also apply to mailed products from overseas. Prohibited items confiscated and destroyed at U.S. international postal facilities have almost doubled in recent years. Further information can be found in the pamphlet, *Travelers' Tips on Prohibited Agricultural Products*, obtainable from the Agricultural Affairs Office at the nearest U.S. embassy or consulate, or you may contact the **Animal and Plant Health Inspection Service, U.S. Department of Agriculture, 4700 River Road, Unit 51, Riverdale, Maryland 20737**; Internet http://www.usda.gov/

Wildlife and Wildlife Products

If, while abroad, you purchased any articles made from endangered animals and plants or any live wild animals to bring back as pets, you must be aware that according to U.S. laws and international treaties, it is a crime to bring many wildlife souvenirs into the United States. Some prohibited items include those made from sea turtle shell, most reptile skins, crocodile leather, ivory, furs from endangered cat species, as well as items made from coral reefs. So you should not buy wildlife souvenirs, if you are unsure about being able to bring them legally into the United States. The penalties that you risk are severe, and your purchases could be confiscated. To learn more about endangered wildlife and guidelines governing restrictions on imports into the United States, consult the pamphlet, *Buyer Beware!* You can request a free copy from **TRAFFIC (U.S.A.), World Wildlife Fund -- U.S., 1250 24th Street, N.W., Washington, D.C. 20037; telephone 202-293-4800**; Internet http://www.worldwide.org

Glazed Ceramic Purchases

The article, *An Unwanted Souvenir, Lead in Ceramic Ware*, explains the danger of lead poisoning from some glazed ceramic ware sold abroad. For a free copy, contact: **Office of Consumer Affairs, U.S. Food and Drug Administration, 5600 Fishers Lane, Rockville, MD. 20857; telephone 1-800-532-4440**; Internet http://www.fda.gov

Addresses for U.S. Embassies and Consulates
(See the Appendix A)

Other Important Publications

Note: All of the important State Department publications slated for inclusion here has been listed in Chapter 36 and has been reproduced elsewhere in this book.

Passport Agencies

[For a listing of U.S. Passport Agencies, See Appendix J]

Planning Another Trip?

See Chapter 36 for a listing of resources available to the general traveler from the U.S. Departments of State, Customs, Transportation, Health and various government and non-government organizations. Almost all of the available International travel-related pamphlets, brochures and publications issued by the U.S. Department of State and by the U.S. Customs have been reproduced in full in this book. See Table of Contents for location.

Chapter 2

Passports

[The Information in this chapter is reprinted verbatim from a bulletin issued by the U.S. State Department, Bureau of Consular Affairs. It is intended to serve as advice to Americans applying for passport.]

[Applying For Them The Easy Way] The Department of State's Bureau of Consular Affairs has prepared this publication to assist you in applying for your U.S. passport. This guide provides information on how, when and where to apply for your passport.

Other Than at Passport Agencies, Where Can I Apply for a Passport?
You can apply for a passport at over 5,000 passport acceptance facilities nationwide that include many Federal, state and probate courts, many post offices, some libraries and a number of county and municipal offices. These designated acceptance facilities are usually more convenient because they are near your home or workplace. (Most of the 13 passport agencies are designated to serve only those departing urgently and appointments are required.

When Do I Have to Apply in Person?
You must always apply in person if you are 13 or older and if you do not meet all of the requirements for renewing a previous passport by mail. *(Should you Apply for a Passport by Mail?)*
Usually, for children age 12 and under, only a parent or legal guardian need appear to apply for a passport on behalf of a child.

What Do I Need to Do to Apply for a Passport in Person?
See How to Apply in Person for a Passport.

Where Can I Get Passport Forms?
Passport acceptance facilities stock passport forms. (See Other Than at Passport Agencies, *Where do I get a Passport Application*? Passport forms can also be downloaded from the Internet at http://travel.state.gov or obtained by calling the National Passport Information Center at 1-900-225-5674 or from the passport agencies.

May I Apply for a Passport by Mail?
See How to Apply for a Passport Renewal.

When Should I Apply for a Passport?
Apply several months in advance of your planned departure. If you will need visas from foreign embassies, allow more time.

What Happens to My Passport Application After I Submit It?
If you apply at a passport acceptance facility, the same day that you apply, your application will be sent to Passport Services for processing. Your will receive your passport within 6 weeks via first class mail. If you apply at a passport agency, you will receive your passport within 5 weeks (25 business days) via first class mail. Your passport will be mailed to the mailing address you provided on your application. If you need your passport sooner, *see What If I Need a Passport in a Hurry?*

What Should I Do if My Passport Is Lost or Stolen?

If your still valid passport is lost or stolen, you can report the loss when you apply for a new passport. In addition to Form DS-11, you will need to complete a Form DS-64, "Statement Regarding a Lost or Stolen Passport." You may also call 202-955-0430, which has voice mail for nonbusiness hours, Eastern Time.

If you are abroad, immediately report the loss to local police authorities and the Consular Section of the nearest U.S. Embassy or Consulate. For more information, *see How to Replace a Lost or Stolen Passport.*

Do I Need to Obtain a Separate Passport for My Baby?

Yes. All persons, including newborn infants, are required to obtain passports in their own names.

What Do I Do if My Name Changes?

If you need to get a valid passport amended due to a name change, use Form DS-19. *See May I Apply for a Passport by Mail?* for the documentation needed to accompany the form and your current passport for amendment.

What If I Need a Passport in a Hurry?

If you are leaving on an emergency trip, apply in person at the nearest passport agency, presenting your tickets or airline-generated itinerary, as well as other required items listed in this publication. to ensure that customers with imminent travel receive their passports in time for their trips, many passport agencies are now operating by appointments and are generally serving only those leaving in less than 14 days.

If you do not live near a passport agency, but your overnight delivery service is reliable, departures within 7 to 10 business days may often be accommodated by appointments at a nearby passport acceptance facility. You will need to pay the additional $60 fee for expedited service and include a self-addressed, prepaid, two-way, overnight delivery envelope. (We have found that for states not densely populated and/or far from our Pittsburgh, PA cashiering facility, overnight service is not always reliable.) For all those customers leaving within 6 or fewer business days, apply at a passport agency. Whichever way you apply, be sure to include your departure date and travel plans on your application.

What Else Should I Know About Passports?

Before traveling abroad, make a copy of the identification page so it is easier to get a new passport, should it be necessary. It is also a good idea to carry two extra passport-size photos with you. If you run out of pages before your passport expires, submit Form DS-19, along with your passport to one of the passport agencies. (Please allow time for processing of the request.) If you travel abroad frequently, you may request a 48-page passport at the time of application.

Some countries require that your passport be valid at least 6 months beyond the dates of your trip. Check with the nearest embassy or consulate of the countries that you plan to visit to find out their entry requirements. In addition to foreign entry requirements, U.S. law must be considered. With certain exceptions, it is against U.S. law for U.S. citizens to enter or leave the country without a valid U.S. passport. Generally for tourists, the exceptions refer to direct travel within U.S. territories or between North, South, or Central America (except Cuba).

Passport Fees

Effective February 1, 1998

Routine Services (Form DS-11)*

Non-Refundable

Age 16 and older: The passport fee is $55. The execution fee is $30. The total is $85.
Under Age 16: The passport fee is $40. The execution fee is $30. The total is $70.
Note: When applying at other than one of the 13 Regional Passport Agencies and paying by check or money order, these fees must be paid separately because the $30.00 Execution Fee is retained locally by our 4,500

designated passport application acceptance facilities across the U.S. (Regional Passport Agencies also accept V, MC, D, and AE. Acceptance facilities may or may not accept credit cards.)

Passport Renewal (Form DS-82)
Non-Refundable

You may use this form if your previous passport:
1. Was issued when you were 16 or older.
2. Was issued in the last 15 years.
3. Is not damaged.
4. Is submitted with your application.

The total fee is $55.

Expedited Service - Add $60 for each application
For any service - e.g., first-time application, renewal, additional pages, name change

Additionally, to receive your passport as soon as possible, we strongly suggest that you arrange overnight delivery service for:
1. Sending your passport application
AND
2. Returning your passport to you.

How Long Will it Take to Process a Passport Application?

If you apply 1. At a Passport Acceptance Facility* or 2. By Mail for renewal, additional pages, amendment) and choose Routine Service, you will receive your passport within about 6 Weeks

If you apply 1. At a Passport Acceptance Facility* or 2. By Mail for renewal, additional pages, amendment) and choose Expedited Service or Expedited Service Plus Overnight delivery service for 1) Sending your application and 2) Returning your passport to you , you will receive your passport within about 2 Weeks

NOTE: •   Passport Agencies assist customers with urgent travel needs - generally if you are traveling within 2 weeks.
•   Most Passport Agencies are open by appointment only and require proof of your travel date or need for foreign visas. See List of Regional Passport Agencies.

How Can You Check the STATUS of the Application You ALREADY SUBMITTED?
To check status Call The National Passport Information Center

CALL
The National Passport Information Center (NPIC)
1-900-225-5674
1-888-362-8668
(for credit card users with Visa, MasterCard, American Express)
The Department of State receives NO income from the NPIC.
•   1-900: Automated information is 55 cents per minute.
•   1-900: Operator assisted calls are $1.50 per minute.
(Operators are available 8:30 a.m. to 5:30 p.m., Eastern Time, Monday - Friday, except Federal holidays; you must speak with an operator to check the status of a pending passport application.)

- 1-888: Flat rate is $5.50 per call.
- TDD - 1-900-225-7778 (for the hearing impaired)
- TDD - 1-888-498-3648 (for the hearing impaired)

Child Support Payments and Getting a U.S. Passport

Section 51.70 (a) (8) of Title 22 of the Code of Federal Regulations states, in part, that if you are certified to Passport Services by the U.S. Department of Health and Human Services (HHS) to be in arrears of child support payments in excess of $5,000, you are ineligible to receive a U.S. passport. If this applies to you, Passport Services strongly recommends that you contact the appropriate State child support enforcement agency to make payment arrangements before applying for a passport. This is because:

- The State agency must certify to the U.S. Department of Health and Human Services (HHS) that acceptable payment arrangements have been made.
- Then, HHS must notify Passport Services by the removal of your name from the electronic list HHS gives to Passport Services. (Passport Services cannot issue a passport until your name has been deleted by HHS.)
-

Please note that it can take 2-3 weeks from the time you make payment arrangements with the State agency until your name is removed from HHS' electronic list. Passport Services has no information concerning individuals' child support obligations and has no authority to take action until HHS removes your name from its list.

Please direct any questions to the appropriate State child support enforcement agency. You may go to the Department of Health and Human Services - State Child Support Enforcement Web Site for a listing of HHS state and local agencies.

Frequently Asked Questions:
Passports and Citizenship Documents
Where do I get a passport application?

- You may download forms from the State Department web site.
- Forms are also available at public offices like Post Offices, courthouses or municipal offices where passport applications are accepted.

Where are the instructions for filling out the passport forms?

Instructions are on the back of the forms.

I am traveling very soon. How do I get a passport in a hurry?

See How to Get Your Passport in a Hurry.

How do I renew my passport?

See How to Apply for a Passport Renewal.

I have never had a U.S. passport/My passport was lost or stolen. How do I get one?

See How to Apply in Person for a Passport.

My child who is under 18 needs a passport. How do I get it?

If your child is: Under 14 • then....

Your child need not appear in person.
- Both parents or legal guardians, can apply for your child.
- New legislation requires both parents' or legal guardians' consent for applications for minors under age 14. Both parents or legal guardians must show current, valid ID.
- If you do not have acceptable ID, someone with current, valid ID must vouch for you.

20

If your child is: 14 to 17
* Your child must appear in person.
* Your parental consent may be requested.

Is it true that passport applications for minors under 14 require the consent of both parents or legal guardians?
Effective July 2, 2001, Public Law 106-113, Section 236 requires that U.S. passport applications for children under the age of 14 require both parents' or legal guardians' consent.

What is the Children's Passport Issuance Alert Program (CPIAP)?
Separate from the Two-Parent Consent requirement for U.S. passport issuance for minors under the age of 14, parents may also request that their children's names be entered in the U.S. passport name-check system. The Children's Passport Issuance Alert Program provides:
* Notification to parents of passport applications made on behalf of minor children, and
* Denial of passport issuance if appropriate court orders are on file with CPIAP.
For more information, contact the Office of Children's Issues at 202-736-7000, or, by fax at 202-312-9743

I was recently married/divorced. How do I change my name on my passport?
You will need to complete Form DS-19, Passport Amendment/Validation Application and submit it along with the following:
* Certified documentation of your name change (e.g., marriage certificate, divorce decree with your new name); and
* Your current, valid passport.

My passport was lost/stolen. How do I report it?
Please apply for a new passport immediately. You may report your lost or stolen passport when you apply for the new one. Along with your application, you must submit the Statement Regarding Lost or Stolen Passport, Form DS-64.

If you decide not to apply for a new passport immediately, you may report your lost or stolen passport by completing Form DS-64 and mailing it to:

US Department of State
Passport Services
Consular Lost/Stolen Passport Section
1111 19th Street, NW, Suite 500
Washington, DC 20036
Or call us 24 hours/day at: (202) 955-0430
Voice mail - For non-business hours, Eastern Time

I was born abroad. How do I get a birth certificate proving my U.S. citizenship?
If one or both of your parents was a U.S. citizen when you were born abroad, your parent(s) should have registered your birth at a U.S. embassy or consulate, and, received a Consular Report of Birth Abroad, Form FS-240. This form is acceptable legal proof of birth and U.S. citizenship.

What should I do if my baby is born abroad?
As U.S. citizen parent(s), you should report your child's birth abroad as soon as possible to the nearest U.S. embassy or consulate to establish an official record of the child's claim to U.S. citizenship at birth. The official record will be the Consular Report of Birth of a Citizen of the United States of America, Form FS-240. This document, know as the Consular Report of Birth Abroad, is a basic United States citizenship document. An original FS-240 document will be given to you at the time registration is approved. (We have more information on these documents.)

21

A Consular Report of Birth can only be prepared at a U.S. embassy or consulate. It cannot be prepared if the child has been brought back into the United States, or, if the person is 18 years of age or older at the time the application is made.

What do I do if there is no birth record on file for me?

If you were born in the U.S. and there is no birth record on file, you will need several different documents to substantiate your citizenship. You will need:

A letter from the Vital Statistics office of the state of your birth with your name and what years were searched for your birth record. An official of the Vital Statistics office needs to issue a letter of no record found.

In addition, you will need early public records to prove your birth in the U.S.

If you were born outside the U.S. and your U.S. parent(s) did not register your birth at the U.S. embassy or consulate, you may:
Apply for a U.S. passport.
You will need:
Your foreign birth certificate that includes your parents' names; and
Evidence of your parent(s) U.S. citizenship; and
Your parents' marriage certificate.

I'm renewing my passport. Do I get the old one back?

Yes, we return the old, cancelled passport to you. It is a good idea to keep it in a safe place as it is considered proof of your U.S. citizenship.

My child is too young to sign his/her own passport. How do I sign my child's passport?

In the space provided for the signature, the mother or father must print the child's name and sign their own name. Then, in parenthesis by the parent's name, write the word (mother) or (father) so we know who signed for the child.

How do I get a certified copy of my birth certificate?

Contact the Vital Statistics office in the state where you were born.

How long is a passport valid?

If you were 16 or Older when the passport was issued then your passport is valid for 10 Years

If you were 15 or Younger when the passport was issued then your passport is valid for 5 Years

Who should maintain a valid U.S. passport?

Passport Services recommends that the following U.S. citizens maintain valid U.S. passports.... Those
- with family living or traveling abroad
- thinking about a vacation abroad, or
- with a job that could require international travel.

In the event of an emergency involving a family member abroad, a short-notice airfare bargain, or an unexpected business trip, already having a valid U.S. passport will save time, money and stress.

What if there is an error in the passport I just received?

Passport Services apologizes for the error in your passport. (Our error rate is significantly below 1 percent, but, when it happens to you, that does not mean very much.) In order for us to correct the error as quickly as possible, please submit the following:

Your new passport;

Completed Form DS-19, Amendment/Validation Application; and

Evidence to document the correct information, such as a certified birth certificate, previous U.S. passport, certified marriage certificate, or naturalization/citizenship certificate.

Please include your departure date on Form DS-19. **Mail the above to the Rewrite Desk of the Passport Agency that issued your passport.**

How to Apply in Person for a U.S. Passport

IF . . .	Should You Apply In Person?
You are applying for a U.S. passport for the first time.	Yes
Your previous U.S. passport was lost, stolen, or damaged.	Yes
Your previous U.S. passport has expired & was issued more than 15 years ago.	Yes
Your previous passport has expired and it was issued when you were under 16.	Yes
Your name is changed since your passport was issued and you do not have a legal document formally changing your name.	Yes
You are a minor child 14 or older	Yes

NOTE:

For All Minors Under Age 14:
- The child need not routinely appear in person.

However, we reserve the right to request that your child appear.
- All applications for children under 14 require both parents' or legal guardians' consent.

(See Special Requirements for Children Under Age 14.)
-

For All Minors Age 14 to 17
- The minor MUST appear in person.
- For security reasons, parental consent may be requested.
- If your child does not have identification of his/her own, you need to accompany your child, present identification and co-sign the application.

To Apply in Person for a U.S. Passport You MUST:

1. Provide Application for Passport, Form DS-11   •   Or, forms can be obtained from any passport agency or acceptance facility. (Call to check hours of availability.)
- Many travel agents stock application forms for their clients as well.

NOTE: *Please do NOT sign the DS-11 application form until the Passport Acceptance Agent instructs you to do so.*

2. **Present Proof of U.S. Citizenship**   **You may prove U.S. Citizenship with any one of the following:**
- Previous U.S. Passport
- Certified birth certificate issued by the city, county or state

NOTE: A certified birth certificate has a registrar's raised, embossed, impressed or multicolored seal, registrar's signature, and the date the certificate was filed with the registrar's office, which must be within 1 year of your birth
- Consular Report of Birth Abroad or Certification of Birth
- Naturalization Certificate
- Certificate of Citizenship

A Delayed Birth Certificate filed more than one year after your birth may be acceptable if it:
- Listed the documentation used to create it and
- Signed by the attending physician or midwife, or, lists an affidavit signed by the parents, or shows early public records.

If you do NOT have a previous U.S. passport or a certified birth certificate, you will need:

23

1. **Letter of No Record**

Issued by the State with your name, date of birth, which years were searched for a birth record and that there is no birth certificate on file for you.

2. **AND as many of the following as possible:**
- baptismal certificate
- hospital birth certificate
- census record
- early school record
- family bible record
- doctor's record of post-natal care

NOTES:
- *These documents must be early public records showing the date and place of birth, preferably created within the first five years of your life.*
- *You may also submit an Affidavit of Birth, form DS-10, from an older blood relative, i.e., a parent, aunt, uncle, sibling, who has personal knowledge of your birth. It must be notarized or have the seal and signature of the acceptance agent.*

NOTE: *The following are NOT proof of citizenship*
- Voter registration cards
- Army discharge papers

We have new information on foreign-born children adopted by U.S. citizens.

NOTE: If you travel extensively, you may request a larger, 48-page passport at no additional cost. To do so, please attach a signed request for a 48-page passport to your application.

FOR MINORS UNDER THE AGE OF 14:

The citizenship evidence submitted for minors under the age of 14 must list both parents' names. Read more information on the citizenship requirements for minors under the age of 14.

3. **Present Proof of Identity** You may prove your identity with any one of these, if you are **recognizable**:
- Previous U.S. passport
- Naturalization Certificate
- Certificate of Citizenship
- Current, valid
- Driver's license
- Government ID: city, state or federal
- Military ID: military and dependents

NOTE: *Your Social Security Card does NOT prove your identity.*

If none of these are available, you will need:

1. **Some signature documents, not acceptable alone as ID**

(ex: a combination of documents, such as your Social Security card, credit card, bank card, library card, etc.)

AND

2. **A person who can vouch for you. He/she must**
- Have known you for at least 2 years,
- Be a U.S. citizen or permanent resident,
- Have valid ID, and
- Fill out a Form DS-71 in the presence of a passport agent.

FOR MINORS UNDER THE AGE OF 14:

Normally, a child under the age of 14 does not need to appear in person. However, passport agents reserve the right to require the appearance of your child. Both parents or legal guardians must present evidence of identity when they apply for a minor under the age of 14. Read more information on the identity requirements for minors under the age of 14.

FOR MINORS 14 to 17:
- Your child MUST appear in person.
- For security reasons, parental consent may be requested.
- If your child does not have identification of his/her own, you need to accompany your child, present identification and co-sign the application.

4. Provide Two Passport Photos
Your photographs must be:
- 2x2 inches in size
- Identical
- Taken within the past 6 months, showing current appearance
- Color or black and white
- Full face, front view with a plain white or off-white background
- Between 1 inch and 1 3/8 inches from the bottom of the chin to the top of the head
- Taken in normal street attire
- Uniforms should not be worn in photographs except religious attire that is worn daily.
- Do not wear a hat or headgear that obscures the hair or hairline.
- If you normally wear prescription glasses, a hearing device, wig or similar articles, they should be worn for your picture.
- Dark glasses or nonprescription glasses with tinted lenses are not acceptable unless you need them for medical reasons. A medical certificate may be required.

NOTE: *Vending machine photos are not generally acceptable*

5. Pay the Applicable Fee   Passport Agencies Accept:
Credit Cards - VISA, MasterCard, American Express, Discover
Debit Cards (without pin numbers and not ATM cards)
Checks, money orders, bank drafts

Passport Acceptance Facilities:
All accept checks, money orders, bank drafts
Most accept exact cash
Some accept credit cards
Expedite Fee: (See How to Get Your Passport in a Hurry.)

Provide a Social Security Number   If you do not provide your Social Security Number, the Internal Revenue Service may impose a $500 penalty. If you have any questions please call your nearest IRS office.

Special Requirements for Children Under Age 14

As required by Public Law 106-113 Effective July 2, 2001,Minors Under Age 14 MUST:

1. Provide Application Form DS-11
- Or, forms can be obtained from any passport agency or acceptance facility. (Call to check hours of availability.)
- Many travel agents stock application forms for their clients as well.
NOTE: *Please do NOT sign the DS-11 application form until the Passport Acceptance Agent instructs you to do so.*

2. **Submit Proof of U.S. Citizenship (for minors under age 14)** Note: Previous U.S. passports are not acceptable as proof of relationship to the applying parent(s)/guardian(s). Please see box #3 for

documents that are acceptable as proof of relationship.
You will need to submit one of the following:
- Certified U.S. birth certificate; or
- Previous fully valid U.S. Passport; or
- Report of Birth Abroad (Form FS-240); or
- Certification of Birth Abroad (Form DS-1350); or
- Certificate of Citizenship or Naturalization from INS.

NOTE: *A certified birth certificate has a registrar's raised, embossed, Impressed or multicolored seal, registrar's signature, and the Date the certificate was filed with the registrar's office, which must be within 1 year of your birth*
A Delayed Birth Certificate filed more than one year after your birth may be acceptable if it:
- Listed the documentation used to create it and
- Signed by the attending physician or midwife, or, lists an affidavit signed by the parents, or shows early public records.

If you do NOT have a previous U.S. passport or a certified birth certificate, you will need:
1.   Letter of No Record
Issued by the state with your name, date of birth, which years were searched for a birth record and that there is no birth certificate on file for you.
2.   AND as many of the following as possible:
- Baptismal certificate
- Hospital birth certificate
- Census record
- Early school record
- Family bible record
- Doctor's record of post-natal care

NOTES:
- *These documents must be early public records showing the date and place of birth, preferably created within the first five years of your life.*
- *You may also submit an Affidavit of Birth, form DS-10A, from an older blood relative, i.e., a parent, aunt, uncle, sibling, who has personal knowledge of your birth. It must be notarized or have the seal and signature of the acceptance agent.*

NOTE: The following are NOT proof of citizenship
- Voter registration cards
- Army discharge papers

NOTE: If you travel extensively, you may request a larger, 48-page passport at no additional cost. To do so, please attach a signed request for a 48-page passport to your application.

3. Present Evidence of Child's Relationship to Parents/Guardians (for minors under age 14) Note: Previous U.S. passports are not acceptable as proof of relationship to the applying parent(s)/guardian(s).

You will need to submit one of the following:
- Certified U.S. birth certificate **(with parents' names)**; or
- Certified Foreign Birth Certificate **(with parents' names and translation, if necessary)**; or
- Report of Birth Abroad **(Form FS-240) (with parents' names)**; or
- Certification of Birth Abroad **(Form DS-1350) (with parents' names)**; or
- Adoption Decree **(with adopting parents' names)**; or
- Court Order Establishing Custody; or
- Court Order Establishing Guardianship.

NOTE: If the parent(s)'/guardian's name(s) is/are other than that on these documents, evidence of legal name change is required.

4. Provide Parental Identification (for minors under age 14) Each parent or guardian must submit one of the following:

- Valid Drivers License
- Valid Official U.S. Military ID
- Valid U.S. Gov't ID
- Valid U.S. or Foreign Passport with recognizable photo
- Naturalization/Citizenship Certificate from INS with recognizable photo
- Alien Resident Card from INS

NOTE: *Your Social Security Card does NOT prove your identity.*

If none of these are available, you will need:

1. **Some signature documents, not acceptable alone as ID**
(ex: a combination of documents, such as your Social Security card, credit card, bank card, library card, etc.)

AND

2. **A person who can vouch for you. He/she must**
- Have known you for at least 2 years,
- Be a U.S. citizen or permanent resident,
- Have valid ID, and
- Fill out a Form DS-71 in the presence of a passport agent.

5. Present Parental Application Permission Documentation
(for minors under age 14)

1. Both parents must appear together and sign **or**

2. One parent appears, signs, **and** submits second parent's Statement of Consent: Issuance of a Passport to a Minor Under Age 14, Form DS-3053 authorizing passport issuance for the child **or**

3. One parents appears, signs, and submits primary evidence of sole authority to apply (such as one of the following):
- Child's certified U.S. or foreign birth certificate (with translation, if necessary) listing only applying parent; or
- *Consular Report of Birth Abroad (Form FS-240) or Certification of Birth Abroad (Form DS-1350)* listing *only* applying parent; or
- Court order granting sole custody to the applying parent (unless child's travel is restricted by that order); or
- Adoption decree (if applying parents is *sole* adopting parent); or
- Court order specifically permitting applying parent's or guardian's travel with the child; or
- Judicial declaration of incompetence of non-applying parent; or
- Death certificate of non-applying parent.

If none of the above documentation is available, the applying parent/guardian should submit Form DS-3053: Statement of Consent: Issuance of a Passport to a Minor Under Age 14.

NOTE:

A third-party in loco parentis applying on behalf of a minor under the age of 14 must submit a notarized written statement or affidavit from both parents or guardians authorizing a third-party to apply for a passport. When the statement or affidavit is from only one parent/guardian, the third-party must present evidence of sole custody of the authorizing parent/guardian.

6. Provide Two Passport Photos
Your photographs must be:
- 2x2 inches in size
- Identical
- Taken within the past 6 months, showing current appearance
- Color *or* black and white
- Full face, front view with a plain white or off-white background

- Between 1 inch and 1 3/8 inches from the bottom of the chin to the top of the head
- Taken in normal street attire
- Uniforms should not be worn in photographs except religious attire that is worn daily.
- Do *not* wear a hat or headgear that obscures the hair or hairline.
- If you normally wear prescription glasses, a hearing device, wig or similar articles, they should be worn for your picture.

Dark glasses or nonprescription glasses with tinted lenses are not acceptable unless you need them for medical reasons. A medical certificate may be required.

NOTE: *Vending machine photos are not generally acceptable*

7. Pay the Applicable Fee

Passport Agencies Accept: Credit Cards – VISA, MasterCard, American Express, Discover Debit Cards (without pin numbers and not ATM cards) Checks, Money orders, Bank drafts

Passport Acceptance Facilities:

All accept Checks, Money orders, Bank drafts

Most accept Exact Cash

Some accept credit cards

Expedite Fee: (*See How to Get Your Passport in a Hurry* .)

8. Provide a Social Security Number   If you do not provide your Social Security Number, the Internal Revenue Service may impose a $500 penalty. If you have any questions please call your nearest IRS office.

How to Apply for a Passport Renewal

Should You Apply for a Passport Renewal by Mail?

YES, If You...

1.   Already have a passport that is not damaged; **and**
2.   Received it within the past 15 years; **and**
3.   Were over age 16 when it was issued; **and**
4.   Still have the same name as in passport (or you can legally document your name change).

NOTES:

- Residents abroad should renew their passports at nearest U.S. Embassy or U.S. Consulate.
- Passports renewed by mail in the U.S. can only be forwarded to U.S. addresses.
- If you mutilate or alter your U.S. passport, you may invalidate it and risk possible prosecution under the law (Section 1543 of Title 22 of the U.S. Code).
- If your passport has **been mutilated, altered or damaged**, you cannot apply by mail. You must **apply in person**. (*See How to Apply in Person.*)

If you can, then How Do You Renew Your Passport By Mail?

1. Complete Application For Passport By Mail, form DS-82

- Be sure to sign and date your application.

2. Attach to it:

- Your most recent passport
- Two identical passport photographs
- And, a $55 fee.
- If you need your passport urgently, you may request Expedited Service.

NOTE: Your previous passport will be returned to you with your new passport.

NOTE: If you travel extensively, you may request a larger, 48-page passport at no additional cost. To do so, please attach a signed request for a 48-page passport to your application.

3. If your name has changed since your passport was issued:

28

- Enclose a certified copy of the legal document specifying your name change (e.g. marriage certificate, divorce decree, adoption decree, or court order).
- No photocopies accepted.

NOTE: If your name has changed by other means, you must apply in person. (See How to Apply in Person.)

4. Mail in a padded envelope to:
National Passport Center
P.O. Box 371971
Pittsburgh, PA 15250-9971
5. If you use an overnight delivery service that does not deliver to a post office box, then send it to:
Passport Services - Lockbox
Attn: Passport Supervisor 371971
500 Ross Street, Rm. 154-0670
Pittsburgh, PA 15262-0001
NOTE: Include a prepaid overnight return envelope. Please note that overnight service will not speed up processing time unless the $60 fee for expedited service is also included.

How Can You Get Your Passport in a Hurry?
After you apply - You will receive your passport
Expedited Service
- Cost, **in addition** to regular application fees, is **$60** per application plus overnight delivery costs.
- Two-way overnight delivery is strongly suggested.
- If you mail in - clearly mark **Expedited** on the envelope.
- Anyone may request expedited service for any type of application (e.g., first-time applications, renewals, amendments of existing passports, etc.) See:
- How do I change my name on my passport?
- How to add extra visa pages to my passport?
- How do I apply to renew my passport?
- Passport applications sent together or at the same time do not necessarily remain together.
- Passports will be mailed separately.
Ordinarily, if you paid additionally for expedited service and two-way overnight delivery
Within about 2 weeks

Routine Service • Include your departure date on your application. ordinarily, Within 6 weeks
Life or Death Emergencies **Call The National Passport Information Center**

Payment Method

Passport Agency
- Major Credit Card - Visa, MasterCard, American Express, Discover or debit card (Not ATM and without a pin)
- Personal Check
- Bank Draft, Postal or Commercial Money Order
Mail-in
- Personal Check or Money Order (Pay to "U.S. Department of State")
- NO CASH
Post Office, Clerk of Court, Other Location
- Check with the facility for type of payment accepted.

Protect Yourself From Identity Fraud!
How to Report Your Lost or Stolen Passport

29

Please, provide detailed answers to all questions, sign, and submit Form DS-64, Statement Regarding a Lost or Stolen Passport, to:
US Department of State
Passport Services
Consular Lost/Stolen Passport Section
1111 19th Street, NW, Suite 500
Washington, DC 20036
Or call us 24 hours/day at: (202) 955-0430
Voice mail - For non-business hours, Eastern Time

IMPORTANT NOTICE
The information you provide on the DS-64, Statement Regarding a Lost or Stolen Passport will be entered in our Consular Lost/Stolen Passport System.

Passports reported lost or stolen are invalidated and can no longer be used for travel.
If you recover the passport after you have reported it lost or stolen, please submit it to the address listed above. When you submit it, if requested - we will cancel it and return it to you. If not requested, it will be destroyed.
Once a passport is reported lost or stolen, it cannot be re-validated.

How to Replace a Lost or Stolen Passport
See How to Replace a Lost or Stolen Passport.

How to Replace a Lost or Stolen Passport
To Replace Your Lost or Stolen Passport You Should:
1. Complete, Application for Passport, Form DS-11
Complete Question #18 as follows:
- Write your name as it appeared in your passport
- Write the approximate date of issue.
- Include the passport number if known
- Under "DISPOSITION", mark the appropriate box.
- If your passport was expired, write "EXPIRED" next to the "OTHER" box.
Note: If you travel extensively, you may request a larger, 48-page passport at no additional cost. To do so, please attach a signed request for a 48-page passport to your application.

2. Complete, Statement Regarding Lost Or Stolen Passport, Form DS-64
- **ONLY IF** your lost/stolen passport is **still valid.**
- Fill in as much of the passport information as you can.
- Answer all the other questions in detail.
3. Submit your form(s)
- To a passport acceptance facility.
- You will also need photos, documentation and fees.
See How to Apply in Person.

How to Add Extra Pages to Your U.S. Passport
IF:
1. Your passport pages are full **Then:** Mail completed form DS-19, Passport Amendment/Validation Application, with
your passport to the following address:
Charleston Passport Center
Attention: Amendments
1269 Holland Street

Charleston, SC 29405
- Under "Other Action Requested" write Add extra pages

2. **IF** You travel extensively and need a new passport **Then:** You may request a larger, 48-page passport at no additional cost. To do so, please attach a
signed request for a 48-page passport to your application.
NOTE: There is no fee for this service unless you require expedited service.
(See How do I get my passport in a hurry?)

See Special Requirements for Children Under Age 14.

How to Change Your Name in Your Valid U.S. Passport
IF:
Then:
1.   Your name has been legally changed since your passport was issued
- Send a completed form DS-19, Passport Amendment/Validation Application, a certified copy of your marriage certificate or your name change court decree, and your current valid passport to the following address:
Charleston Passport Center
Attention: Amendments
1269 Holland Street
Charleston, SC 29405

Photocopies and notarized copies are not acceptable
for passport purposes.
- If your name has changed by other means, you must apply in person. See How to **Apply in Person**
NOTE: There is no fee for this service unless you require expedited service.
(See How do I get my passport in a hurry?)

U.S. Passports Will No Longer be Issued Abroad
All passports, except those required for urgent travel, will be issued in the United States
using the new more secure photo-digitized imaging system.
Effective April 8, 2002, American citizens residing or traveling abroad, who require issuance of a U.S. passport, will be issued the latest, state-of-the-art passport. It incorporates a digitized image with other enhanced security features. Because this technology is not available at U.S. embassies and consulates, overseas passport issuance is being transferred to the National Passport Processing Center in Portsmouth, New Hampshire.

Travel documents in the post-September 11 world have become even more important. The new passport has many features that make it one of the most secure travel documents produced anywhere in the world. Getting these more secure passports into circulation will help minimize the misuse of American passports by criminals, terrorists, and others.

This new procedure will increase processing time at U.S. embassies and consulates, but the Department is committed to ensuring that American citizens receive secure documents in a timely manner. American citizens overseas are encouraged to apply early for renewal of expiring passports.

U.S. embassies and consulates will continue to issue passports that are needed for urgent travel. However, such passports will be limited in validity, and cannot be extended. Bearers will be required to exchange, at no additional cost, their limited-validity passports for a full-validity digitized passports upon completion of their urgent travel. Information on applying for a U.S. passport, passport application forms and requirements, and other travel-related information can be accessed through the Department of State's web site at: http://travel.state.gov.

Chapter 3

Visa and Other Entry Requirements of Foreign Governments

*[The Information in this chapter is reprinted verbatim from a bulletin issued by the
U.S. State Department, Bureau of Consular Affairs. It is intended to serve as advice
to Americans traveling abroad.]*

This listing is for U.S. citizens traveling on tourism/business and does not apply to persons planning to emigrate to foreign countries. Persons traveling on official business for the U.S. Government should obtain visa information from the agency sponsoring their travel. For purposes of this publication, a visa is an endorsement or stamp placed by officials of a foreign country on a U.S. passport that allows the bearer to visit that foreign country. **Note:** Wherever you see the words "photo(s) required" in this publication, it generally means that you will need to submit **passport-size (2"x2") photographs.**

IMPORTANT: THIS LISTING IS PREPARED FROM INFORMATION OBTAINED FROM FOREIGN EMBASSIES PRIOR TO MAY 2002. THIS INFORMATION IS SUBJECT TO CHANGE. CHECK ENTRY REQUIREMENTS WITH THE CONSULAR OFFICIALS OF THE COUNTRIES TO BE VISITED WELL IN ADVANCE.

PASSPORTS: U.S. citizens who travel to a country where a valid passport is not required will need documentary evidence of their U.S. citizenship and identity. Proof of U.S. citizenship includes an expired U.S. passport, a certified (original) birth certificate, Certificate of Naturalization, Certificate of Citizenship, or Report of Birth Abroad of a Citizen of the United States. To prove identity, a valid driver's license or government identification card are acceptable provided they identify you by physical description or photograph. However, for travel overseas and to facilitate reentry into the U.S., a valid U.S. passport is the best documentation available and unquestionably proves your U.S. citizenship.

Before you send your passport through the mail to apply for a visa, sign it in ink, and write in pencil your current address and daytime telephone number in the space provided. This will help the U.S. Postal Service return it to you should it become separated from the envelope during processing.

Some countries require that your **U.S. passport be valid at least six months** or longer beyond the dates of your trip. If your passport expires before the required validity, you will have to apply for a new one. Please check with the embassy or nearest consulate of the country that you plan to visit for their requirements.

Some Middle Eastern or African countries will not issue visas or allow entry if your passport indicates travel to Israel. Consult the National Passport Information Center (1-900-225-5674 or TDD: 1-900-225-7778 (fee of $0.35 per minute), or 1-888-362-8668 or TDD: 1-888-498-3648 (flat fee of $4.95 for people using a major credit card)) for guidance if this applies to you.

VISAS: If a visa is required, obtain it from the appropriate foreign consular representative before proceeding abroad. Allow sufficient time for processing your visa application, especially if you are applying by mail. Most foreign consular representatives are located in principal cities, and in many instances, a traveler may be required to obtain visas from the consular office in the area of his/her residence. IT IS THE RESPONSIBILITY OF THE TRAVELER TO OBTAIN VISAS, WHERE REQUIRED, FROM THE APPROPRIATE EMBASSY OR NEAREST CONSULATE OF THE COUNTRY YOU ARE PLANNING TO VISIT. As soon as you receive your visa, **check it** to make sure no mistakes **were made. Processing and visa fees vary, and most fees may not be refundable,** consult the embassy or consulate of the country you plan to visit for specific details.

IMMUNIZATIONS: Under the International Health Regulations adopted by the World Health Organization, a country may require International Certificates of Vaccination against yellow fever, especially if you are traveling from an area of the world that is infected with yellow fever. Check with health care providers or your records to ensure other immunizations (e.g. tetanus and polio) are up-to-date. Prophylactic medication for malaria and certain other preventive measures are advisable for travel to some countries. No immunizations are required to return to the United States. Detailed health information is included in Health Information for International Travel, available from the U.S. Government Printing Office (address on page 20) for $20 or may be obtained from your local health department or physician or by contacting the Centers for Disease Control and Prevention, telephone 1-877-FYI-TRIP (1-877-394-8747), toll-free autofax: 1-888-CDC-FAXX (1-888-232-3299), or Internet: http://www.cdc.gov.

AIDS/HIV TESTING: An increasing number of countries have established regulations regarding AIDS testing, particularly for long-term visitors. Although many are listed here, check with the embassy or consulate of the country that you plan to visit to verify if this is a requirement for entry.

ADDITIONAL FEES: All international flights are subject to U.S. Immigration and U.S. Customs fees paid in advance as part of your ticket. In addition, many countries have **departure fees** that are sometimes collected at the time of ticket purchase or upon exiting the foreign country.

AFGHANISTAN - *Passport and visa required. At the time of publication, the Afghan government was only allowing the issuance of a single entry visas to persons entering on sanctioned international relief flights at Kabul International Airport. For more information, consult the Embassy of Afghanistan located at 2000 L Street, NW, Washington, DC 20036, telephone 202-416-1620.

ALBANIA - *Passport required. Visa issued on arrival for tourists stay up to 90 days. Proof of round-trip travel required. Entry fee $45. For further information, contact the Embassy of the Republic of Albania at 2100 S Street, N.W., Washington, D.C. 20008 (202/223-4942).

ALGERIA - *Passport and visa required. Obtain visa before arrival. Visa valid up to 90 days, requires 2 application forms, 2 photos, and $55 fee (money order or certified check). For tourist visas an itinerary from airline and a hotel reservation is also needed. Company letter required for business visa. Enclose prepaid self-addressed envelope for return of passport by registered, certified or express mail. Validity of visa: Applicants must enter Algeria within 45 days of issuance. For currency regulations and other information, contact the Consular Section of the Embassy of the Democratic and Popular Republic of Algeria, 2137 Wyoming Ave., N.W., Washington, D.C. 20008(202/265-2800).
Internet: http://www.algeria-us.org

ANDORRA - (See France.)

ANGOLA - *Passport and visa required. Tourist/business visas require an application form, 1 recent photo with name on back, letter stating purpose of travel, letter of invitation sent by the individual or institution to be contacted in Angola, photocopy of a round-trip ticket or travel itinerary, proof of sufficient funds and $55 fee. Visa is good for stay up to 90 days. The Consular Office of the Embassy of Angola has the right to request additional information, if necessary. For additional information, contact: Embassy of Angola, 2100 16th Street, N.W., Washington, D.C. 20009 (202/452-1042/3). Internet: http://www.angola.org

ANTIGUA AND BARBUDA - Passport or proof of U.S. citizenship or voter's registration card, along with picture ID, required, return/onward ticket, and proof of funds needed for tourist stay up to 6 months. Contact the Embassy of Antigua and Barbuda, 3216 New Mexico Ave. N.W., Washington, D.C. 20016 (202/362-5122/5166/5211) for further information.

ARGENTINA - *Passport required. Visa not required for tourist stay up to 90 days. For information concerning longer stays, employment, or other types of visas contact the Consular

Section of the Argentine Embassy, 1718 Connecticut Ave., N.W., Washington, D.C. 20009 (202/238-6460) or the nearest Consulate: CA (213/954-9155), FL (305/373-7794), GA (404/880-0805, IL (312/819-2620), NY (212/603-0400) or TX (713/871-8935). Internet: http://www.uic.edu/orgs/argentina

ARMENIA - *Passport and visa required. Visa for stay up to 21 days, requires 1 application form, 1 photo and $60 to $95 processing fee (fees vary according processing time). For stays longer than 21 days, but not exceeding 90 days, an official invitation from a qualifying entity in Armenia is required ($35 to $65 fee). No fee for children under 18 years of age. If applying by mail, enclose a SASE or prepaid airbill indicating type of mail service (i.e. Federal Express, etc.), and money order or certified check in the appropriate amount, payable to the Embassy of Armenia. For more information, contact the Consular Section of the Embassy of the Republic of Armenia, 2225 R Street, N.W., Washington, D.C. 20008 (202/319-2983), or the Consulate General in Beverly Hills, CA (310/657-6102). Internet: http://www.armeniaemb.org

ARUBA - Passport or proof of citizenship (original-official birth or naturalization certificate and photo ID) required. Visa not required for stay up to 3 months after arrival. Proof of onward/return ticket or sufficient funds for stay may be required. Departure tax $20. AIDS test required for intending immigrants. For further information, consult Embassy of the Netherlands (202/244-5300), or nearest Consulate General: CA (310/266-1598), IL (312/856-0110), NY (212/246-1429) or TX (713/622-8000).

AUSTRALIA - *Passport, Electronic Travel Authority (ETA) or non-electronic label visa, proof of onward or return ticket, and sufficient funds are required. An ETA or non-electronic label visa is required for tourist or business stays of up to 3 months. An ETA is an electronically stored authority to travel to Australia. Application forms are available from participating travel agencies, airlines and Australian visa offices in Washington and Los Angeles. Minors not accompanied by a parent or traveling with only one parent need notarized written parental consent from the absent parent(s). AIDS test required for permanent resident visa for applicants age 15 and

older; tests taken in the U.S. are acceptable. For more information on longer stays, check with the Embassy of Australia, 1601 Mass. Ave., N.W., Washington, D.C. 20036 (202/797-3145) or the Consulate General in Los Angeles, CA (310/229-4840). Internet: http://www.immi.gov.au or http://www.austemb.org

AUSTRIA - *Passport required. Visa not required for tourist stay up to 90 days. For information concerning longer stays, employment, or other types of visas check with the Embassy of Austria, 3524 International Court, N.W., Washington, D.C. 20008 (202/895-6767) or nearest Consulate General: Los Angeles (310/444-9310), Chicago (312/222-1515) or New York (212/737-6400).

AZERBAIJAN - *Passport and visa required. Visa (no charge for visas issued within 5 working days) requires 1 application form, 2 photos, conformation from hotel, and a letter of invitation. (Fees are charged for express service, i.e., in less than 10 days.) Please include SASE or prepaid airbill for return of documents. For additional information, contact the Embassy of the Republic of Azerbaijan, 2741 34th Street, N.W., Washington, D.C. 20008 (202/337-3500).

AZORES - (See Portugal.)

BAHAMAS - Proof of U.S. citizenship, i.e. a passport (if you are using an expired passport it cannot be expired more than 5 years) or original or certified copy of a birth certificate with a photo ID, and onward/return ticket required for stay up to 8 months. Passport and residence/work permit needed for residence and business. Permit required for firearms and to import pets. Departure tax of $15 must be paid at airport. For further information call Embassy of the Commonwealth of the Bahamas, 2220 Massachusetts Ave., N.W., Washington, D.C. 20008 (202/319-2660) or nearest Consulate: Miami (305/373-6295) or New York (212/421-6420).

BAHRAIN - *Passport and visa required. Visa requires letter from applicant (for tourist visa) or company letter (for business visa) on company letterhead guaranteeing full responsibility for all expenses, and stating reason for visit and duration, 1 application form and $50 fee. Transit visa available upon arrival for stay up to 72 hours, must have return/onward ticket. Send SASE for return of passport by mail. For departure tax and other information, contact the Consular Section of the Embassy of the State of Bahrain, 3502 International Drive, N.W., Washington, D.C. 20008 (202/342-0741); or the Permanent Mission to the U.N., 866 Second Ave., 14th Floor, New York, NY 10017 (212/223-6200). Internet: http://www.bahrain embassy.org

BANGLADESH - *Passport, visa, and onward/return ticket required. Tourist/business visa requires 2 application forms, 2 photos, and $45 fee. Business visa also requires company letter. For longer stays and more information, consult the Embassy of the People's Repblic of Bangladesh, 3510 International Drive., N.W., Washington, D.C. 20008 (202/244-0183) or the Bangladesh Mission in New York at (212/867-3434). Internet: http://members.aol.com/banglaemb/embassy

BARBADOS - *Passport required. Tourists traveling directly from the U.S. to Barbados may be allowed to enter for up to 3 months stay with proof of U.S. citizenship (original or certified copy of birth certificate), photo ID and onward/return ticket. A passport is required for longer visits and other types of travel. Business visas $25, single-entry and $30 multiple-entry (may require work permit) must be obtained prior to entry. Departure tax of $12.50 US ($25 BDS) is paid at airport. Check information with Embassy of Barbados, 2144 Wyoming Ave., N.W., Washington, D.C. 20008 (202/939-9200), or Consulate General in New York (212/867-8435).

BELARUS - *Passport and visa required. Visa requires 1 application form, 1 photo, original letter of invitation from a citizen of Belarus (for visitor's visa) or a Belarusian organization, company or agency (for business visa). Tourist visa (for stay up to 30 days) requires 1 application form, 1 photo, confirmation from receiving tourist organization in Belarus, and proof of emergency medical insurance that is valid in Belarus. The visa processing fee is $50 for 5 working days, and $100 for next day processing. Transit visa is required when traveling through Belarus ($50). All foreigners visiting Belarus for more than 2 days must register their passports with the local law enforcement authorities. AIDS test required for persons staying longer than 3 months; tests taken in the U.S. are acceptable. For information about student visas and other questions, contact the Embassy of the Republic of Belarus, 1619 New Hampshire Ave., N.W., Washington, D.C. 20009 (202/986-1606), Consulate General, 708 3rd Ave., 21st Floor, New York, NY 10017 (212/682-5392).

BELGIUM - *Passport required. Visa not required for business/tourist stay up to 90 days. Temporary residence permit required for longer stays, and for study or work. For residence authorization, consult Embassy of Belgium, 3330 Garfield St., N.W., Washington, D.C. 20008 (202/333-6900), or nearest Consulate General: Los Angeles (323/857-1244), Atlanta (404/659-2150), Chicago (312/263-6624), or New York (212/586-5110).

BELIZE - *Passport, return/onward ticket and sufficient funds (at least $60 per night) required. Visa not required for stay up to 30 days. If visit exceeds 1 month, a stay permit must be obtained from the Immigration Authorities in Belize. AIDS test required for those staying more than 3 months; U.S. test accepted if within 3 months of visit. For longer stays and other information, contact the Embassy of Belize, 2535 Massachusetts Ave., N.W., Washington, D.C. 20008 (202/332-9636) or the Belize Mission in New York at (212/599-0233).

BENIN - *Passport and visa required. Visa for stay up to 36 months, requires $40 fee (certified check or money orders only), 2 application forms, 2 photos, proof of yellow fever vaccination, proof of return/onward transportation (guarantee from employer, travel agency, or photocopy of round trip ticket) and letter of guarantee from bank. Send prepaid envelope for return of passport by certified or express mail. Apply at Embassy of the Republic of Benin, 2737 Cathedral Ave., N.W., Washington, D.C. 20008 (202/232-6656/7/8).

BERMUDA - Passport (or proof of U.S. citizenship with photo ID) and onward/return ticket required for tourist stay up to 3 months. Departure tax of $10 is paid at airport. For further information, consult British Embassy (202/588-7800).

BHUTAN - *Passport and visa required. Tourist visas arranged by travel agency (valid for 15 days) and issued at entry point of entry in Bhutan. Visa requires $20 fee, 1 application, 1 photo, prepaid land tour, and onward/return ticket (approval time takes about 2 months). For further information, contact the Bhutan Mission to the U.N., 2 United Nations Plaza, 27th Floor, New York, NY 10017 (212/826-1919) or the Bhutan Travel Service, 120 E 56th Street, Suite 1130, New York, NY 10022 (1-800/950-9908 or 212/838-6382).

BOLIVIA - *Passport required. Visa not required for tourist stay up to 30 days. Tourist cards issued upon arrival in Bolivia. A "Defined Purpose Visa" for adoptions, business, or other travel requires 1 application form, 1 photo, $85 fee and for business travelers, a letter from company explaining purpose of trip. Send SASE for return of passport by mail. For more information, contact the Embassy of Bolivia (Consular Section), 3014 Mass. Ave., N.W., Washington, D.C. 20008 (202/232-4827 or 4828), or nearest Consulate General: Miami (305/358-3450), New York (212/687-0530), or San Francisco (415/495-5173).

BOSNIA AND HERZEGOVINA - *Passport required. A visa is not required for tourist stays up to three months. Unless the traveler is staying at a hotel, all foreigners must register with the local police within 48 hours of arrival. Visa must be renewed every 3 months during stay. Travelers planning to remain in Bosnia and Herzegovina for more than three months must obtain a temporary residence permit from the local police having jurisdiction over their place of residence. For more information, contact the Consulate General, 866 U.N. Plaza, Suite 580, New York, NY 10017 (212/593-0264). Internet: http://www.bosnianembassy.org

BOTSWANA - *Passport, onward/return ticket, and proof of sufficient funds required. Visa not required for U.S. citizens staying no more than 90 days. For further information, contact the Embassy of the Republic of Botswana, 1531 New Hampshire Ave., N.W., Washington, D.C. 20036 (202/244-4990) or nearest Honorary Consulate: Los Angeles (213/626-8484) or Houston (713/680-1155).

BRAZIL - *Passport and visa required. Tourist visas are issued within 24 hours if submitted in person by the applicant. Visas valid for multiple entries within 5 years from date of first entry for a stay up to 90 days (renewable for the same length

of stay by the Federal Police in Brazil), requires 1 application form, 1 passport size photo, and proof of onward/return transportation. There is a processing fee of $45 for tourist visas (money order only). There is a $10 service fee for applications sent by mail, or by anyone other than applicant. Provide SASE for return of passport by mail. Minors (under 18) traveling alone, with one parent or with a third party, must present written authorization by the absent parent(s) or legal guardian, specifically granting permission to travel alone, with one parent or with a third party. This authorization must be notarized, authenticated by the Brazilian Embassy or Consulate, and translated into Portuguese. For information about business visas, contact the Brazilian Embassy (Consular Section), 3009 Whitehaven St., N.W., Washington, D.C. 20008 (202/238-2828) or nearest Consulate: CA (323/651-2664 or 415/981-8170), FL (305/285-6200), IL (312/464-0244), MA (617/542-4000), NY (917/777-7777) or TX (713/961-3063). Internet: http://www.brasilemb.org

BRUNEI DARUSSALAM - *Passport and onward/return ticket required. Visa not required for tourist/business stay up to 90 days. AIDS test required for work permits; tests taken in the U.S. are not acceptable. For more information, contact the Embassy of Brunei Darussalam, 3520 International Court, N.W., Washington, D.C. 20008 (202/342-0159) or Brunei Darussalam Permanent Mission to the U.N., 711 United Nations Plaza, New York, NY 10017 (212/697-3465).

BULGARIA - *Passport required. Visa not required for a stay of up to 30 days. Border tax $20 (U.S.) must be paid when entering Bulgaria. For persons staying over 30 days, a visa is required and must be obtained in advance. Business travelers must provide an invitation from a business partner in Bulgaria and a letter from their company in the US. AIDS test may be required for those staying more than 1 month. For more information, contact the Consular Section of the Embassy of the Republic of Bulgaria, 1621 22nd St., N.W., Washington, D.C. 20008 (202/387-7969 or 387-0174) or the Bulgarian Consulate in New York at (212/935-4646). Internet: http://www.bulgaria-embassy.org

BURKINA FASO - *Passport and visa required.

Single-entry or multiple-entry visa valid 3 months for visit up to 3 months, extendible once in Burkina Faso, requires $25 fee, 2 application forms, and 2 photos. Send passport by registered mail and include postage or prepaid envelope for return by mail. Payment accepted in certified check, company check, or money order only. For further information call the Embassy of Burkina Faso, 2340 Mass. Ave., N.W., Washington, D.C. 20008 (202/332-5577) or Honorary Consulate in Decatur, GA (404/378-7278), Los Angeles, CA (310/575-5555) or New Orleans, LA (504/945-3152). Internet: http://burkinaembassy-usa.org

BURMA (Myanmar) - *Passport and visa required. Single-entry tourist visas (valid for 3 months), for stay up to 28 days, requires $20 fee, 2 application forms, 3 photos and itinerary . Tourists visas are issued for package or group tours as well as Foreign Independent Travelers (FITs). FITs over the age of 12 years holding tourist visas must exchange a minimum of $200 (U.S.) upon arrival. Overland travel into and out of Myanmar is only permitted at certain points (check with Embassy). Enclose prepaid envelope for return of passport by express mail. Allow 2 to 4 working days for processing. For business visas and further information, contact the Burmese Embassy (Embassy of the Union of Myanmar), 2300 S St., N.W., Washington, D.C. 20008 (202/332-9044 or 9045) or the Myanmar Consulate General Office, 10 East 77th St., New York, NY 10021 (212/535-1310).

BURUNDI - *Passport and visa required. Obtain visa before arrival to avoid long airport delay. Multiple-entry visa valid for 2 months (must be used within 2 months of date of issue) requires $40 (single-entry) or $80 (multiple-entry) fee, 3 application forms, 3 photos, return/onward ticket, proof of yellow fever immunization, and detailed itinerary from airline or travel agent. Company letter needed for business travel. Send U.S. postal money order or cash and SASE for return of passport by mail. For further information, consult Embassy of the Republic of Burundi, Suite 212, 2233 Wisconsin Ave., N.W., Washington, D.C. 20007 (202/342-2574) or Permanent Mission of Burundi to the U.N. (212/499-0001 thru 0006).

CAMBODIA - *Passport and visa required. Visa valid for a 30 day stay. Visa requires 3 photos, 3 application forms, and $20 (tourist visa) or $25 (business visa) fee. For further information, consult the Royal Embassy of Cambodia, 4500 16th Street, N.W., Washington D.C. 20011 (202/726-7742). Internet: http://www.embassy.org/cambodia

CAMEROON - *Passport and visa required. Obtain visa before arrival. Multiple-entry tourist visa for stay up to 3 months, requires $65.22 fee (money orders only), 2 application forms, 2 photos, proof of onward/return transportation and bank statement. If invited by family or friends, visa available for up to 3 months, may be extended 1 month. Authorities in Cameroon must sign invitation. Multiple-entry business visa, valid 12 months, requires company letter to guarantee financial and legal responsibility; include exact dates of travel. Enclose prepaid envelope for return of passport by registered, certified or express mail. For additional information, contact the Embassy of the Republic of Cameroon, 2349 Mass. Ave., N.W., Washington, D.C. 20008 (202/265-8790 to 8794).

CANADA - Passport or proof of U.S. citizenship and photo ID required. Minors (under 16) traveling alone or in someone else's custody, must present written authorization, signed before a notary, from the parent(s) or guardian. Visas are not required for visitors staying up to 180 days. Anyone with a criminal record (including a DWI charge) should contact the Canadian Embassy or nearest Consulate General before travel. U.S. citizens entering Canada from a third country must have a valid passport. For student or business travel, check with the Canadian Embassy, 501 Pennsylvania Ave., N.W., Washington, D.C. 20001 (202/682-1740) or nearest Consulate General: CA (213/346-2701), MI (313/567-2085), NY (212/596-1700 or 716/858-9501), or WA (206/443-1375). Internet: http://www.cic.gc.ca

CAPE VERDE - *Passport and visa required. Single-entry tourist visa, requires $20 fee, multiple-entry $40 fee, 1 application form, and 1 photo. Include SASE for return of passport by mail. For further information, contact the Embassy of the Republic of Cape Verde, 3415 Mass. Ave., N.W., Washington, D.C. 20007 (202/965-6820) or Consulate General, 535 Boylston St., 2nd Floor, Boston, MA 02116 (617/353-0014). Internet: http://www.capeverdeusembassy.org

CAYMAN ISLANDS - (See West Indies, British.)

CENTRAL AFRICAN REPUBLIC - *Passport and visa required. Visa must be obtained before arrival. Single-entry visa requires 2 application forms, 2 photographs, proof of onward or return ticket, yellow fever immunization, and $150 fee (no personal checks). Medical report, including AIDS test, required for work permits; U.S. test sometimes accepted. Company letter needed for business visa. For further information, contact the Embassy of Central African Republic, 1618 22nd St., N.W., Washington, D.C. 20008 (202/483-7800).

CHAD - *Passport and visa required. Tourist/business for a stay up to 30 days (extendible), requires $75 fee (no personal checks), 3 application forms, and 3 photos. Visa must be used within 2 months of issuance. For business visa need company letter stating purpose of trip. Send prepaid (express or certified/register mail)envelope for return of passport. Apply Embassy of the Republic of Chard, 2002 R St., N.W., Washington, D.C. 20009 (202/462-4009), and check specific requirements. Internet: http://www.chadembassy.org

CHILE - *Passport required. Visa not required for stay up to 90 days. Entry fee of $45 (U.S.) charged at airport. Dependent children under age 18 (including the children of divorced parents) arriving traveling alone, with one parent, or in someone else's custody, are required to present a notarized document certifying that both parents agree to their travel. This document must be notarized before a Chilean consular officer in the United States. For further information, consultthe Embassy of Chile, 1732 Mass. Ave., N.W., Washington, D.C. 20036 (202/785-1746 exts. 104 or 110) or nearest Consulate General: CA (310/785-0113 and 415/982-7662), FL (305/373-8623), IL (312/654-8780), PA (215/829-9520), NY (212/355-0612), TX (713/621-5853) or PR (787/725-6365). Internet: http://www.chile-usa.org

CHINA, PEOPLE'S REPUBLIC OF - *Passport and visa required. Transit visa required for any stop (even if you do not exit the plane or train) in China. Business travelers are required to obtain formal invitation from Chinese business contact. Tourist visas are issued only after receipt of a confirmation letter from a Chinese tour agency or letter of invitation from a relative in China. Single-entry visa requires $30 processing fee (no personal checks), 1 tourist visa application form, and 1 photo. Allow at least 5 business days processing time. Medical examination required for those staying 1 year or longer. AIDS test required for those staying more than 6 months. For longer stays and more detailed information, contact the Visa Section of the Chinese Embassy, 2201 Wisconsin Avenue, N.W., Washington, D.C. 20007 (202/338-6688) or nearest Consulate General: Chicago (312/803-0098), Houston (713/524-4311), Los Angeles (213/807-8018), New York (212/330-7409) or San Francisco (415/563-4857). Internet: http://www.china-embassy.org

COLOMBIA - *Passport and proof of onward/return ticket required for tourist stay up to 30 days. Minors (under 18), who are traveling alone, with one parent or with a third party must present a copy of their birth certificate and written authorization from the absent parent(s) or legal guardian, specifically granting permission to travel alone, with one parent or with a third party. Anyone suspected of being HIV-positive will not be admitted without a waiver from a Colombian consulate in the U.S. For additional information and information about other types of travel, contact the Colombian Consulate, 1875 Conn. Ave., N.W., Suite 218, Washington, D.C. 20009 (202/332-7476) or nearest Consulate General: CA (323/653-4299 or 415/495-7195), FL (305/448-5558 or 441-0437), GA (404/255-3038 or 256-2518), IL (312/923-1196), LA (504/525-5580 or 5582), MA (617/536-6222), NY (212/949-9898), or TX (713/527-8919). Internet: http://www.colombiaemb.org

COMOROS ISLANDS - *Passport and onward/return ticket required. Visa for up to 3 weeks (extendible) issued at airport upon arrival. For further information, consult Embassy of the Federal and Islamic Republic of Comoros, 336 East 45th St., 2nd Floor, New York, NY 10017 (212/972-8010).

CONGO-KINSHASA (formerly Zaire) - *Passport and visa required. Visa must be obtained before arrival. Tourist/business visa, valid 1 to 3 months depending on fee, requires 2 photos, 2 application forms, and onward/return ticket.

Business visa also requires company letter accepting financial responsibility for traveler. Single-entry visa $75 - $264; multiple-entry $120 - $360. No personal checks, send money order and enclose SASE for return of passport by mail. Apply Embassy of the Democratic Republic of the Congo, 1800 New Hampshire Ave., N.W., Washington, D.C. 20009 (202/234-7690/1) or Permanent Mission to the U.N., 747 Third Ave., New York, NY 10017.

CONGO-BRAZZAVILLE - *Passport and visa required. Tourist/business visa for a stay up to 3 months, requires 2 application forms, 2 photos, onward/return ticket, and $70 fee. For business visa company letter stating reason for trip. If applying by mail, include prepaid FedEx or Express mail envelope for return of passport. Apply Embassy of the Republic of the Congo, 4891 Colorado Ave., N.W., Washington, D.C. 20011 (202/726-5500).

COOK ISLANDS - *Passport, proof of sufficient funds, and onward/return ticket required. Visa not needed for visit up to 31 days. For longer stays and further information, contact the Consulate for the Cook Islands, Kamehameha Schools, #16, Kapalama Heights, Honolulu, HI 96817 (808/847-6377).

COSTA RICA - Passport or original U.S. birth certificate and photo ID required. (Persons under the age of 16 must use a valid passport to enter Costa Rica.) Tourist card issued upon arrival at airport upon presentation of aforementioned documents for approximately $4. U.S. citizens must have onward/return ticket. For stays over 90 days, you must apply for an extension (within the first week of visit) with Costa Rican Immigration and, after 90 days, obtain exit visa and possess a valid U.S. passport. For travel with pets and other information, contact the Consular Section of the Embassy of Costa Rica ,2112 S St. N.W. , Washington, D.C. 20008 (202/234-2945) or nearest Consulate General: CA (415/392-8488), GA (404/951-7025), FL (305/371-7485), IL (312/263-2772), LA (504/887-8131), NY (212/425-2620) or TX (713/266-1527). Internet: http://costarica-embassy.org

COTE D'IVOIRE (AKA Ivory Coast) - *Passport required. Visa not required for stay up to 90 days. Visa $33, requires 2 application forms,

2 photos, onward/return ticket, and financial guarantee. Include postage for return of passport by registered mail. For further information, contact the Embassy of the Republic of Cote D'Ivoire, 2424 Mass. Ave., N.W., Washington, D.C. 20008 (202/797-0300) or Honorary Consulate: CA (415/391-0176).

CROATIA - *Passport required. Visa not required for tourist/business stay up to 90 days. For stays over 3 months, a visa is required and should be obtained in advance. For additional information, consult the Embassy of Croatia, 2343 Massachusetts Ave., N.W., Washington, D.C. 20008 (202/588-5899 or 5906), or the nearest Consulate General in Los Angeles, CA (310/477-1009), Cleveland, OH (440/951-4246), or New York, NY (212/599-3066). Internet: http://www.croatiaemb.org

CUBA - *Passport and visa required. Tourist visa $26, business visa $50 valid for at stay of up to 30 days, requires 1 application form and 1 photo. Send money order only and SASE for return of passport. Apply Embassy of Switzerland, Cuban Interests Section, 2630 16th Street, N.W., Washington, D.C. 20009 (202/797-8518 (Spanish speakers 202/797-8609)). AIDS test required for those staying longer than 90 days. **Attention:** U.S. citizens need a Treasury Dept. license in order to engage in any transactions related to travel to and within Cuba (this includes the use of U.S. currency). Before planning any travel to Cuba, U.S. citizens should contact the Licensing Division, Office of Foreign Assets Control, Department of the Treasury, 1500 Penn. Ave., N.W., Washington, D.C. 20220 (202/622-0077) or http://www.ustreas.gov/ofac/.

CURACAO - (See Netherlands Antilles.)

CYPRUS - *Passport and round-trip ticket required. Visa not required for tourist/business stay up to 3 months. For employment and other travel, work permit required and must be obtained in advance. AIDS test required for work or study permits. For additional information consult Embassy of the Republic of Cyprus, 2211 R St., N.W., Washington, D.C. 20008 (202/462-5772) or the Consulate General in New York (212/686-6016) or the nearest Honorary Consulate: AR (602/264-9701), CA (310/397-0771), FL (904/953-2802), GA (770/941-3764), IL (847/296-

0064), IN (219/481-6897), MA (617/497-0219), MI (313/582-1411), OR (503/248-0500), PA (215/728-6980), TX (713/928-2264), VA (757/481-3583), or WA (425/827-1700).

CZECH REPUBLIC - *Passport required. Visa not required for stay of up to 30 days. For longer stays, U.S. citizens have to apply for the visa. Each visitor may be requested to provide proof of sufficient funds (approx. $25 per day) or documents confirming all expenses are prepaid, or an invitation verified by Czech Immigration Police. For more information, contact the Embassy of the Czech Republic, 3900 Spring of Freedom Street, N.W., Washington, D.C. 20008 (202/274-9123) or the nearest Consulate General: Los Angeles, CA (310/473-0889) or New York, NY (212/717-5643). Internet: http://www.czech.cz/washington

DENMARK (including GREENLAND) - *Passport required. Visa not required for a stay up to 90 days. (90 day period begins when entering Nordic area: Denmark, Finland, Iceland, Norway, and Sweden.) Special rules apply for entry into the U.S.-operated defense area in Greenland. For further information, contact the royal Danish Embassy, 3200 Whitehaven St., N.W., Washington, D.C. 20008 (202/234-4300) or nearest Consulate General: CA (310/443-2090), Chicago (312/787-8780) or New York (212/223-4545). Internet: http://www.denmarkemb.org

DJIBOUTI - *Passport and visa required. Visas must be obtained before arrival. Multiple-entry visa valid for 30 days, requires $50 fee, 2 application forms, 2 photos, onward/return ticket, and sufficient funds. Letter from current employer needed for business visa. Send prepaid envelope for return of passport by registered, certified, or express mail. Apply Embassy of the Republic of Djibouti, 1156 15th St., N.W., Suite 515, Washington, D.C. 20005 (202/331-0270) or the Djibouti Mission to the U.N., 866 United Nations Plaza, Suite 4011, New York, NY 10017 (212/753-3163).

DOMINICA - Passport or proof of U.S. citizenship and photo ID, and return/onward ticket required for tourist stay of up to 21 days. For longer stays and other information, consult Consulate of the Commonwealth of Dominica, 3216 New Mexico Avenue, N.W., Washington,

DC 20016 (202/364-6791).

DOMINICAN REPUBLIC - Passport or birth certificate and photo ID, and tourist card required. Tourist card for stay up to 2 months, available from Consulate or from airline serving the Dominican Republic, $10 fee. All persons must pay $10 airport departure fee. Minors under 18 years of age traveling alone, with only one parent, or a third party must present written authorization by the absent parent(s) or legal guardian. This authorization must be notarized at a Dominican consulate. AIDS test required for residence permit. U.S. test not accepted. For business travel and other information call the embassy of the Dominican Republic, 1715 22nd St., N.W., Washington, D.C. 20008 (202/332-6280) or nearest Consulate General: AL (334/342-5648), CA (510/864-7777), FL (305/375-9537 or 904/346-0909), HI (808/396-5702), GA (404/572-4814), IL (847/441-1831), LA (504/522-1843), MD (410/560-2101), MA (617/482-8121), MI (248/559-0684), MN (612/339-7566), NY (212/768-2480), PA (215/923-3006), PR (787/833-4756 or 725-9550), or TX (713/266-0165 or 512/224-1345). Internet: http://www.domrep.org

ECUADOR (including the Galapagos Islands) - *Passport required. Visa not required for a stay of up to 90 days. For information concerning longer stays or other types of travel, contact the Embassy of Ecuador, 2535 15th St., N.W., Washington, D.C. 20009 (202/234-7166) or nearest Consulate General: CA (323/658-6020 or 415/957-5921/22), FL (305/539-8214/15), IL (312/329-0266), LA (504/523-3229), MA (617/738-9465/68), NJ (201/985-2959/60), NY (212/808-0211/12), or TX (713/572-8731).

EGYPT - *Passport and visa required. Tourist visa, valid up to 3 months, requires $15 fee (cash or money order), 1 application form, and 1 photo. Enclose prepaid envelope for return of passport by certified mail. AIDS test required for study and work permits. Travelers must register with local authorities or at hotel within 7 days of arrival. For longer stays and additional information consult, the Embassy of the Arab Republic of Egypt, 3521 International Court, N.W., Washington, D.C. 20008 (202/895-5400) or nearest Consulate General: CA (415/346-9700), IL (312/828-9162), NY (212/759-7120), or TX (713/961-4915).

41

Internet: http://www.touregypt.net

EL SALVADOR - *Passport and visa required. (Length of validity of visa will be determined by Consulate.) Visa requires 1 application form, 2 photo, and flight itinerary. Allow 1 working day for processing. Send SASE for return of passport by mail. (Tourist cards issued at airport for emergencies or last minute travel, $10 fee.) AIDS test required for multiple-entry visas and residency permits. U.S. test not accepted. Apply Consulate general of El Salvador, 1424 16th St., N.W., Suite 200, Washington, D.C. 20036 (202/331-4032) or nearest Consulate: CA (213/383-5776, 415/781-7924 or 714/542-3250), FL (305/371-8850), LA (504/522-4266), MA (617/577-9111), NY (212/889-3608) or TX (713/270-6239 or 214/637-1018). Internet: http://www.elsalvador.org

ENGLAND - (See United Kingdom.)

EQUATORIAL GUINEA - *Passport required for a stay of less than 90 days. For more details, and information about business visas and longer stays, contact the Embassy of the Republic of Equatorial Guinea, the Embassy of the Republic of Equatorial Guinea, 2020 16th Street, N.W., Washington D.C. 20009 (202/518-5700).

ERITREA - *Passport, proof of onward/return ticket, and visa required. Tourist visa requires 1 application, 1 photo, $25 fee (no personal checks), and proof of sufficient funds. Business visa requires company letter stating purpose of travel. Include SASE for return of passport by mail. Allow 3 working days for processing. For more information, contact the Embassy of Eritrea, 1708 New Hampshire Ave., N.W., Washington, D.C. 20009, (202/319-1991).

ESTONIA - *Passport required. Visas are not required for stays up to 90 days, but for longer stays, a residency permit is required. For further information, contact the Consulate General of Estonia, 600 Third Ave., 26th Floor, New York, NY 10016 (212/883-0636). Internet: http://www.estemb.org

ETHIOPIA - *Passport and visa required. Tourist/business visa valid for stay up to 2 years, fee $70 or transit visa for 72 hours, $40 (money order only), requires 1 application, and 1 photo. Business visa requires company letter. Allow 3-4

working days for processing. Exit visas are required of all visitors remaining in Ethiopia for more than 30 days. For longer stays and other information, contact the Embassy of Ethiopia, 3506 International Dr., N.W., Washington, D.C. 20008, (202) 364-1200. Internet: http://www.ethiopianembassy.org.

FEDERAL REPUBLIC OF YUGOSLAVIA - *Passport and visa required. Visas must be obtained before arrival. The Federal Republic of Yugoslavia currently has no diplomatic or consular office issuing visas in the U.S. at this time. The Embassy of the Federal Republic of Yugoslavia in Ottawa, Canada (613/233-6289) will visa accept applications from U.S. citizens. Internet: http://www.mfa.gov.yu

FIJI - *Passport, proof of sufficient funds and onward/return ticket required. Visa not required for stay up to 4 months. All visitors over age 12 are required to pay $20 departure tax (tax must be paid in Fijian currency). For further information, contact the Embassy of the Republic of the Fiji Islands, 2233 Wisconsin Ave., N.W., #240, Washington, D.C. 20007 (202/337-8320). Internet: http://www.bulafiji.com/

FINLAND - *Passport required. Tourist/business visa not required for stay up to 90 days. (90 day period begins when entering Nordic area: Denmark, Finland, Iceland, Norway, and Sweden.) (For longer stays (e.g. employment, studies) residence/work permits required. Contact the Embassy of Finland, 3301 Massachusetts Ave., N.W., Washington, D.C. 20008 (202/298-5800), or nearest Consulate General: Los Angeles (310/203-9903) or New York (212/750-4400). Internet: http://www.finland.org/index.html

FORMER YUGOSLAV REPUBLIC OF MACEDONIA - *Passport required. Visa not required for tourist/business stay of up to 90 days. For more information check with the Embassy of the Former Yugoslav Republic of Macedonia, 3050 K St., N.W., Suite 210, Washington, D.C. 20007 (202/337-3063) or the Consulate General, 866 United Nations Plaza, Suite 4018, New York, NY 10017 (212/317-1727).

FRANCE - *Passport required. Visa not required for tourist/business stay up to 90 days in France, Andorra, Monaco, and Corsica, and 1 month in

42

French Polynesia. For further information, contact the Consulate General of France, 4101 Reservoir Rd., N.W., Washington, D.C. 20007 (202/944-6200) or nearest Consulate: CA (310/235-3200) or 415/397-4330), FL (305/372-9799), GA (404/495-1660), IL (312/787-5359), LA (504/523-5772), MA (617/542-7374), NY (212/606-3644) or TX (713/572-2799). Internet: http://www.info.france-usa.org

FRENCH GUIANA - *Passport required. Visa not required for tourist/business stay up to 3 months. For further information, contact the Consulate General of France, 4101 Reservoir Rd., N.W., Washington, D.C. 20007 (202/944-6200). Internet: http://www.france-consulat.org.

FRENCH POLYNESIA - (Includes Society Islands, French Southern and Antarctic Lands, Tuamotu, Gambier, French Austral, Marquesas, Kerguelen, Crozet, New Caledonia, Tahiti, Wallis and Furtuna Islands.) *Passport required. Visa not required for visit of up to 1 month. For further information, contact the Consulate General of France (202/944-6200). Internet: http://www.france-consulat.org.

GABON - *Passport and visa required. Visa for a stay of up to 4 months, requires 2 application forms, 2 photos, vaccination certificate for yellow fever, letter from sponsor or hotel in Gabon, and $60 fee. Business visas also require company letter. For longer stays and other information call Embassy of the Gabonese Republic, 2034 20th St., Suite 200, N.W., Washington, D.C. 20009 (202/797-1000 or 1021) or the Permanent Mission of the Gabonese Republic to the UN, 18 East 41st St., 6th Floor, New York, NY 10017 (212/686-9720).

GALAPAGOS ISLANDS - (See Ecuador.)

GAMBIA, THE - *Passport and visa required. Tourist/business visa for a stay up to 1 year, requires 1 application, 1 photo, and $45 fee (money order only). For business visa, you also need company letter stating purpose of visit and itinerary. Allow at least 2 weeks for processing. Include prepaid envelope for return of passport by mail. Apply Embassy of the Gambia, 1155 15th St., N.W., Washington, D.C. 20005 (202/785-1399) or Permanent Mission of The Gambia to the U.N., 820 2nd Ave., 9th floor, New York, NY

10017 (212/949-6640). Internet: http://www.gambia.com

GEORGIA - *Passport, visa and letter of invitation required. Visa requires passport (not a photo copy), 1 application, 1 photo, and processing fee ($40 -$70). Please provide SASE or prepaid airbill for return of documents. AIDS test required for persons staying longer than 1 month. For additional information, contact the Embassy of the Republic of Georgia, 1615 New Hampshire Ave., N.W., Suite 300, Washington, D.C. 20009 (202/393-6060).

GERMANY - *Passport required. Tourist/business visa not required for stay up to 90 days. For longer stays (e.g. employment, students) obtain temporary residence permit upon arrival. Applicants for residence permits staying over 90 days may be asked to undergo a medical examination. Every foreign national entering Germany is required to provide proof of sufficient health insurance and funds. For further information, contact the Embassy of the Federal Republic of Germany, 4645 Reservoir Rd., N.W., Washington, D.C. 20007 (202/298-4393) or nearest Consulate General: CA (415/775-1061, 213/930-2703), FL (305/358-0290), GA (404/659-4760), IL (312/580-1199), MA (617/536-4414), MI (313/962-6526), NY (212/610-9700), TX (713/627-7770), or WA (206/682-4312). Internet: http://www.germany-info.org

GHANA - *Passport and visa required. Tourist visa required for stay up to 30 days (extendible). Visa requires 1 application form, 4 photos, photocopy of onward/return ticket, and yellow fever immunization. Single-entry visa requires $20 fee, multiple-entry $50 fee (payment by money order only - payable to Embassy of Ghana. Allow 3 working days for processing. Include prepaid envelope for return of passport by overnight mail. Departure tax $15 paid at airport. For additional information, contact the Embassy of Ghana, 3512 International Drive, N.W., Washington, D.C. 20008 (202/686-4520) or Consulate General, 19 East 47th St., New York, NY 10017 (212/832-1300). Internet: http://www.ghana-embassy.org

GIBRALTAR - *Passport required. Visa not required for tourist stay up to 90 days. For further information, consult British Embassy (202/588-7800). Internet: http://www.britainusa.com

43

GILBERT ISLANDS - (See Kiribati.)

GREAT BRITAIN AND NORTHERN IRELAND - (See United Kingdom.)
GREECE - *Passport required. Visa not required for tourist/business stay up to 90 days. For additional information consult Consular Section of the Embassy of Greece, 2221 Mass. Ave., N.W., Washington, D.C. 20008 (202/939-5818 or 5800) or nearest Consulate: CA (310/826-5555 or 415/775-2102/4), GA (404/261-3313), IL (312/335-3915 or 17), LA (504/523-1167), MA (617/543-0100), NY (212/988-5500) or TX (713/840-7522). Internet:
http://www.greekembassy.org

GREENLAND - (See Denmark.)

GRENADA - Passport is recommended, but tourists may enter with birth certificate and photo ID. Visa not required for tourist stay up to 3 months, may be extended to maximum of 6 months. For additional information consult Consulate General of Grenada, 1701 New Hampshire Ave., N.W., Washington, D.C. 20009 (202/265-2561) or Permanent Mission of Grenada to the U.N. (212/599-0301).

GUADELOUPE - (See West Indies, French.)

GUATEMALA - *Passport required for a stay of up to 90 days. For travel by minors and general information, contact the Embassy of Guatemala, 2220 R St., N.W., Washington, D.C. 20008-4081 (202/745-4952), or nearest Consulate: CA (213/365-9251 or 415/788-5651), FL (305/443-4828), IL (312/332-3170), NY (212/686-3837) or TX (713/953-9531). Internet:
http://www.guatemala-embassy.org

GUIANA, FRENCH - (See French Guiana.)

GUINEA - *Passport and visa required. Tourist/business visa for a stay of up to 6 months, requires 3 applications forms, 3 photos, onward/return ticket, letter of purpose, yellow fever immunization and $45 fee (cash or money order only). Provide SASE for return of passport by mail. For more information, contact the Embassy of the Republic of Guinea, 2112 Leroy Pl., N.W., Washington, D.C. 20008 (202/483-9420).

GUINEA-BISSAU - *Passport, onward/return ticket, and visa required. Visa must be obtained in advance. For more information, contact the Embassy of Guinea-Bissau, 1511 K Street, NW, Suite 519, Washington, D.C. 20005.

GUYANA - *Passport and onward/return ticket required. For more information consult Embassy of Guyana, 2490 Tracy Pl., N.W., Washington, D.C. 20008 (202/265-6900/03) or Consulate General, 866 U.N. Plaza, 3rd Floor, New York, NY 10017 (212/527-3215).

HAITI - *Passport required. Visa not required for tourist/business stay of up to 90 days. For further information, consult: Embassy of Haiti 2311 Mass. Ave., N.W., Washington, D.C. 20008 (202/332-4090) or nearest Consulate: FL (305/859-2003), MA (617/266-3660), NY (212/697-9767), PR (809/764-1392), or IL (312/922-4004). Internet:
http://www.haiti.org

HOLY SEE, VATICAN CITY STATE - *Passport required for entry into Italy. (See entry requirements under "ITALY.") For further information, consult: Apostolic Nunciature, 3339 Mass. Ave., N.W., Washington, D.C. 20008 (202/333-7121).

HONDURAS - *Passport and onward/return ticket required. Visa not required for a stay of up to 90 days; holders of U.S. passports are issued a 30-day permit which can be renewed every 30 days for up to a maximum 90 day stay. Departure tax $25 (U.S.). For additional information, contact the Consular Section of the Embassy of Honduras, 2nd Floor, 1528 K Street, N.W., Washington, D.C. 20006 (202/737-2972/78), or nearest Consulate General: CA (213/383-9244 and 415/392-0076), FL (305/447-8927), IL (773/342-8281), LA (504/522-3118), NY (212/269-3611) or TX (713/622-7911). Internet:
http://www.hondurasembassy. Org

HONG KONG, SPECIAL ADMINISTRATIVE REGION - *Passport and onward/return transportation by sea/air required. Visa not required for tourist/business stay up to 90 days. Confirmed hotel and flight reservations recommended during peak travel months. Departure tax 100 Hong Kong dollars (approx. $13 U.S.) paid at airport. Visa required for work or study. For other types of travel, consult the Visa Section of the Embassy of the People's Republic of China (202/338-6688). Internet: http://www.china-embassy.org

HUNGARY - *Passport, onward/return ticket and proof of sufficient funds required. Visa not required for stay up to 90 days. AIDS test required for persons staying longer than 1 year. For longer stays and employment, visas must be obtained before you travel. For more information check Embassy of the Republic of Hungary, 3910 Shoemaker Street, N.W., Washington, D.C. 20008 (202/362-6730), or the nearest Consulate General: New York (212/752-0661) or Los Angeles (310/473-9344). Internet: http://www.hungaryemb.org

ICELAND - *Passport required. Visa not required for stay up to 90 days. (90 day period begins when entering Nordic area: Denmark, Finland, Iceland, Norway, and Sweden.) For additional information call Embassy of Iceland, 1156 15th Street, N.W., Suite 1200, Washington, D.C. 20005 (202/265-6653-5), or Consulate General in New York (212/593-2700).

INDIA - *Passport and visa required. Tourist visas require 1 application form, 2 photos, onward/return ticket, $150 fee, and proof of sufficient funds. Visa must be obtained before arrival. Include prepaid envelope for return of passport by certified mail. AIDS test required for all students and anyone over 18 staying 1 year or more; U.S. test from well known lab accepted. For information about business visas and other requirements, consult the Embassy of India, 2536 Mass. Ave., N.W., Washington, D.C. 20008 (202/939-9806/9839) or nearest Consulate General: Chicago (312/595-0405), Houston (713-626-2355), New York (212/774-0600) or San Francisco (415/668-0683). Internet: http://www.indiagov.org

INDONESIA - *Passport and onward/return ticket required. Visa not required for tourist stay up to 2 months (non-extendible). Letter of intent from employer or sponsor required for business/social and temporary stay visa. For longer stays and additional information, consult the Embassy of the Republic of Indonesia, 2020 Massachusetts Ave., N.W., Washington, D.C. 20036 (202/775-5200) or nearest Consulate General: CA (213/383-5126

or 415/474-9571), IL (312/595-1777), NY (212/879-0600) or TX (713/785-1691).

IRAN, ISLAMIC REPUBLIC OF - *Passport and visa required. The United States does not maintain diplomatic or consular relations with Iran. Travel by U.S. citizens is not recommended. Attention: U.S. citizens need a Treasury Dept. license in order to engage in any transactions related to travel to and within Iran. Before planning any travel to Iran, U.S. citizens should contact the Licensing Division, Office of Foreign Assets Control, Department of the Treasury, 1331 G St., N.W., Washington, D.C. 20220 (202/622-2480) or http://www.ustreas.gov/ofac/. For visa information, contact the Embassy of Pakistan, Iranian Interests Section, 2209 Wisconsin Ave., N.W., Washington, D.C. 20007 (202/965-4990). Internet: http://www.daftar.org

IRAQ - *Passport and visa required. Proof of an AIDS test required. The United States suspended diplomatic and consular operations in Iraq in 1990. Since February 1991, U.S. passports are not valid for travel in, to, or through Iraq without authorization from the Department of State. Application for exemptions to this restriction should be submitted in writing to Passport Services, Attn: CA/PPT/PAS, U.S. Department of State, 1111 19th St., N.W., Washington, D.C. 20524. Attention: U.S. citizens need a Treasury Dept. license in order to engage in any transactions related to travel to and within Iraq. Before planning any travel to Iraq, U.S. citizens should contact the Licensing Division, Office of Foreign Assets Control, Department of the Treasury, 1331 G St., N.W., Washington, D.C. 20220 (202/622-2480) or http://www.ustreas.gov/ofac/. For more visa information, contact the Iraqi Interests Section, 1801 P Street, N.W., Washington, D.C. 20036 (202-483-7500).

IRELAND - *Passport required. Tourists are not required to obtain visas for stays less than 90 days, but may be asked to show onward/return ticket. For further information, consult Embassy of Ireland, 2234 Mass. Ave., N.W., Washington, D.C. 20008 (202/462-3939) or nearest Consulate General: CA (415/392-4214), IL (312/337-1868), MA (617/267-9330) or NY (212/319-2555). Internet: http://www.irelandemb.org

ISRAEL - *Passport, onward/return ticket and proof of sufficient funds required. Visa not required for tourist or business stay of up to 90 days. Notarized consent from parent(s) required for children traveling alone, with one parent, or in someone else's custody. Consult the Consular Section of the Embassy of Israel, 3514 International Dr., N.W., Washington, D.C. 20008 (202/364-5527) or nearest Consulate General: CA (323/852-5500 and 415/844-7500), FL (305/925-9400), GA (404/487-6500), IL (312/297-4800), MA (617/535-0200), NY (212/499-5400), PA (215/546-5556) or TX (713/627-3780). Internet: http://www.israelemb.org

ITALY - *Passport required. Visa not required for tourist or business stays up to 90 days. For longer stays, employment, or study obtain visa in advance. For additional information, consult the Embassy of Italy, Whitehaven Street, N.W., Washington, D.C. 20008 (202/612-4400) or nearest Consulate General: CA (310/820-0622 or 415/931-4924), FL (305/374-6322), TX (713/850-7520), IL (312/467-1550), MA (617/542-0483/4), MI (313/963-8560), NY (212/737-9100), PA (215/592-7329) or TX (713/850-7520). Internet: http://www.italyemb.org

IVORY COAST - (See Cote d'Ivoire.)

JAMAICA - Passport or original birth or naturalization certificate and valid driver's license or state-issued photo ID, onward or return ticket, and proof of sufficient funds required. For business or study, visa must be obtained in advance, $45 fee. Departure tax $22 (paid at airport). Check information with Embassy of Jamaica, 1520 New Hampshire Ave., N.W., Washington, D.C. 20036 (202/452-0660) or nearest Consulate: CA (310/559-3822 or 510/266-0072), FL (305/374-8431), IL (312/663-0023), NY (212/935-9000), MA (617/266-8604), or WA (206/872-8950).

JAPAN - *Passport and onward/return ticket required. Visa not required for tourist/business stay up to 90 days. Passenger service facilities charge $20-$26 (2,040-2,650 yen) paid at airport. For specific information, consult the Embassy of Japan, 2520 Mass. Ave., N.W., Washington, D.C. 20008 (202/238-6800) or nearest Consulate General: AK (907/279-8428), CA (213/617-6700 or 415/777-3533), FL (305/530-9090), GA (404/892-2700), Guam (671/646-1290), HI (808/543-3111), IL (312/280-0400), LA (504/529-2101), MA (617/973-9772), MI (313/567-0120), MO (816/471-0111), NY (212/371-8222), OR (503/221-1811), CNMI (670/234-7201), TX (713/652-2977) or WA (206/682-9107). Internet: http://www.embjapan.org

JORDAN - *Passport and visa required. Single-entry visa requires 1 application form and $16.50 fee, multiple-entry visa requires a $31.50 fee (money order only). For a business visa, you also need a company letter stating purpose of your trip. If applying by mail, enclose a self-addressed prepaid airway bill or check payable to Federal Express, UPS, or DHL for return of passport. AIDS test required for persons staying longer than 3 months. For details, consult the Embassy of the Hashemite Kingdom of Jordan, 3504 International Dr., N.W., Washington, D.C. 20008 (202/966-2664) or nearest Consulate General: CA (415/546-1155), MI (248-/557-4377), NY (212/832-0119), or TX (713/224-2911). Internet: http://www.jordanembassyus.org

KAZAKHSTAN - *Passport, onward/return ticket and visa required. Visas require 1 application and 1 photo. Tourist visa requires a letter of invitation from Kazahstan's tourist agency with confirmation from the Ministry of Foreign Affairs. Requirements for business travel include confirmation from inviting organization with confirmation from the Ministry of Foreign Affairs. Cost of visa depends on duration of stay. Fees must be paid by money order, cashier's check, or traveler's cheque. Visa processing depends on length of stay and processing time. HIV test certificate required for anyone staying more than 30 days. Foreigners must register with the local office of the Ministry of Internal Affairs or at the hotel within 72 hours of arrival to Kazakhstan. For additional information, contact the Embassy of the Republic of Kazakhstan, 1401 16th Street, N.W., Washington, D.C. 20036 (202/232-5488) or their Consulate, 866 UN Plaza, Suite 586 A, New York, NY 10017 (212/888-3024).

KENYA - *Passport, visa, and onward/return ticket required. Visas should be obtained in advance, although airport visas are available. Travelers who opt to obtain an airport visa should expect delays upon arrival. Evidence of yellow fever immunization may be requested. Tourist

46

visas require 1 application form, 2 photos, onward/return ticket and $50 fee (money order or cashier's check only). Multiple-entry visa, $100 fee (money order or cashier's check only). Airport departure tax is $20. For additional information, consult the Embassy of Kenya, 2249 R St., N.W., Washington, D.C. 20008 (202/387-6101) or Consulate General: Los Angeles (310/274-6635) or New York (212/486-1300). Internet: http://www.kenya embassy.com

KIRIBATI (formerly Gilbert Islands) - *Passport, onward/return ticket, proof of sufficient funds, and visa required. Visa requires 1 application form, 2 photos, and $57.75 fee (for single-entry visa). For additional information consult the Embassy of Fiji (202/337-8320).

KOREA, DEMOCRATIC PEOPLE'S REPUBLIC OF (North Korea) - *Passport and visa required. Attention: U.S. citizens need a Treasury Dept. license in order to engage in any transactions related to travel to and within North Korea. Before planning any travel to North Korea, U.S. citizens should contact the Licensing Division, Office of Foreign Assets Control, Department of the Treasury, 1331 G St., N.W., Washington, D.C. 20220 (202/622-2480) or http://www.ustreas.gov/ofac/. The United States currently does not maintain diplomatic or consular relations with North Korea. Visa information must be obtained from a consulate in a country that maintains diplomatic relations with North Korea.

KOREA, REPUBLIC OF (South Korea) - *Passport and onward/return ticket required. Visa not required for a tourist stay up to 30 days. For longer stays and other types of travel, visa must be obtained in advance, $45 fee. Tourist visa requires passport, 1 application form, and 1 photo. Business visa requires 1 application form, 1 photo and company letter. Fine imposed for overstaying visa and for long-term visa holders not registered within 60 days after entry. If applying by mail, enclose SASE or prepaid airbill. Vaccination certificate required if coming from infected area within 14 days of arrival in Korea. AIDS test required for persons working as entertainers and staying longer than 90 days; U.S. tests results accepted. For further information check Embassy of the Republic of Korea, (Consular Division), 2320 Massachusetts Ave., N.W., Washington, D.C. 20008 (202/939-5663 or 60) or nearest

Consulate General: CA (213/385-9300 and 415/921-2251/3), FL (305/372-1555), GA (404/522-1611/3), Guam (671/472-6488), HI (808/595-6109), IL (312/822-9485), MA (617/348-3660), NY (212/752-1700), TX (713/961-0186) or WA (206/441-1011/4).

KUWAIT - *Passport and visa required. Business visa requires 2 application forms, 2 photos, a business letter, and $24 fee. Transit visa, valid for up to 72 hours, requires copy of onward/return ticket, visa for next destination (if applicable), $8 fee. AIDS test required for residency and work permits; U.S. test accepted. For further information, contact the Embassy of the State of Kuwait, 2940 Tilden St., N.W., Washington, D.C. 20008 (202/966-0702) or Consulate, 321 East 44th St., New York, NY 10017 (212/973-4318). Internet: http://www.kuwait-info.org

KYRGYZ REPUBLIC (Kyrgyzstan) - *Passport and visa required. Visa requires 1 application form, 1 photo, detailed letter of invitation, and appropriate fee ($25-$200). Visa and processing fees vary depending upon duration of stay and processing time requested. Include SASE for return of passport by mail (or proper fee for express mail service). AIDS test required for persons staying longer than 1 month; U.S. test results accepted. For additional information and fees, contact the Embassy of the Kyrgyz Republic, 1732 Wisconsin Ave., N.W., Washington, D.C. 20007 (202/338-5143). Internet: http://www.kyrgyzstan.org

LAOS - *Passport and visa required. Visa requires $30 fee, 1 application form, 1 photo, onward/return ticket, sufficient funds, and SASE for return of passport by mail. Tourist visas can be obtained upon arrival at certain entry points or before departure from the Lao Embassy. Visa available for a stay of up to15 days, extended. For business visas and more information, check with the Consular Section of the Embassy of the Lao People's Democratic Republic, 2222 S St., N.W., Washington, D.C. 20008 (202/667-0076). Internet: http://www.visit-laos.com

LATVIA - *Passport required. Visa not required for a stay of up to 90 days. AIDS test required for persons seeking residency permits; U.S. tests results accepted. For specific requirements, contact the Embassy of Latvia 4325 17th St., N.W.,

Washington, D.C. 20011 (202/726-8213).
Internet: http://www.latvia-usa.org

LEBANON - *Passport and visa required. Visa requires 1 application form, 2 photos, and cover letter detailing length of stay. Single-entry visa, $35 (stay cannot exceed 3 months) multiple-entry visa, $70 (stay cannot exceed 6 months). Business visa requires company letter stating purpose of travel. AIDS test required for those seeking residence permits; U.S. test is accepted. Minors need authorization from both parents (a notarized parental consent form/letter) to enter Lebanon. For further visa information, contact the Embassy of Lebanon, 2560 28th St., N.W., Washington, D.C. 20008 (202/939-6300) or nearest Consulate General: Los Angeles (323/467-1253), Detroit (313/567-0233), or New York (212/744-7905). Internet: http://www.lebanonembassy.org

LEEWARD ISLANDS - (See Virgin Islands, British.)

LESOTHO - *Passport, onward/return ticket, and proof of sufficient funds required. For more information, check with the Embassy of the Kingdom of Lesotho, 2511 Mass. Ave., N.W., Washington, D.C. 20008 (202/797-5533).

LIBERIA - *Passport and visa required. Travelers must obtain visas before arrival. Tourist/business entry visa valid 3 months, $45 fee, requires 2 application forms, 2 photos, onward/return ticket, proof of sufficient funds, and Certificate of Immunization against yellow fever. Company letter needed for business visa. Include SASE for return of passport by mail. Obtain exit permit from immigration authorities upon arrival, 1 photo required. For other requirements call the Embassy of the Republic of Liberia, 5201 16th Street, N.W., Washington, D.C. 20011 (202/723-0437). Internet: http://www.liberiaemb.org

LIBYA - *Passport and visa required. AIDS test required for those seeking residence permits; U.S. test accepted. Since December 1981, U.S. passports are not valid for travel in, to, or through Libya without authorization from the Department of State. Application for exemptions to this restriction should be submitted in writing to Passport Services, U.S. Department of State, 1111 19th St., N.W., Washington, D.C. 20524, Attn.: CA/PPT/PAS. Attention: U.S. citizens need a Treasury Dept. license in order to engage in any transactions related to travel to and within Libya. Before planning any travel to Libya, U.S. citizens should contact the Licensing Division, Office of Foreign Assets Control, Department of the Treasury, 1331 G St., N.W., Washington, D.C. 20220 (202/622-2480) or http://www.ustreas.gov/ofac/. Application and inquiries for visas must be made through a country that maintains diplomatic relations with Libya.

LIECHTENSTEIN - *Passport required. Visa not required for tourist/business stay up to 90 days. For further information, contact the Embassy of Switzerland, 2900 Cathedral Ave., N.W., Washington, D.C. 20008 (202/745-7900) or the nearest Consulate General: CA (310/575-1145 or 415/788-2272), GA (404/870-2000), IL (312/915-0061), NY (212/599-5700), or TX (713/650-0000). Internet: http://www.swissemb.org.

LITHUANIA - *Passport required. Visa not required for a stay up to 90 days. AIDS test required for persons seeking residency permits; U.S. tests results accepted. For further information, contact the Embassy of Lithuania, 2622 16th St., N.W., Washington, D.C. 20009 (202/234-5860) or Consulate General in New York, 420 Fifth Avenue, New York, NY 10018 (212/354-7849) or Chicago, 211 East Ontario Street, Suite 1500, Chicago, IL (312/397-0382).

LUXEMBOURG - *Passport required. Visa not required for tourist/business stay of up to 90 days. For additional information, contact the Embassy of Luxembourg, 2200 Mass. Ave., N.W., Washington, D.C. 20008 (202/265-4171) or the nearest Consulate: San Francisco (415/788-0816) or New York (212/888-6664).

MACAU, SPECIAL ADMINISTRATIVE REGION - *Passport required. Visa not required for visits up to 60 days. For further information, consult the Visa Section of the Chinese Embassy, 2201 Wisconsin Avenue, N.W., Washington, D.C. 20007 (202/338-6688) or the nearest Chinese Consulate General: Chicago (312/803-0098), Houston (713/524-4311), Los Angeles (213/807-8018), New York (212/330-7409) or San Francisco (415/563-4857), or the Macau Tourist Information Bureau, Suite 2R, 77 Seventh Avenue, New York, N.Y. 10011. Internet: http://www.macau.gov.mo

48

MACEDONIA - (See Former Yugoslav Republic of Macedonia.)

MADAGASCAR, REPUBLIC OF - *Passport and visa required. Visa allows entry in Madagascar within 6 months from the date of issue. Short-term visas valid for single-entry up to 30 days, $33.45; or double-entries, $39.01 (no personal checks). Requires 1 application form, 1 photo, proof of onward/return transportation, and sufficient funds for stay. For business visa, the aforementioned is required including company letter. Include a prepaid envelope for return of passport by registered mail. For longer stays and additional information, contact the Embassy of the Democratic Republic of Madagascar, 2374 Mass. Ave., N.W., Washington, D.C. 20008 (202/265-5525/6) or the U.N. Mission in New York, NY (212/986-9491). Internet: http://www.embassy.org/madagascar

MALAWI - *Passport required. Visa not required for stay up to 6 months. Exit fee $20. For further information, contact the Embassy of Malawi, 2408 Mass. Ave., N.W., Washington, D.C. 20008 (202/797-1007) or Malawi Mission to the U.N., 600 3rd Ave., New York, NY 10016 (212/949-0180).

MALAYSIA - *Passport required. Visa not required for stay up to 3 months. Medical exam required for work permits. U.S. test sometimes accepted. For entry of pets or other types of visits, consult the Embassy of Malaysia, 2401 Mass. Ave., N.W., Washington, D.C. 20008 (202/328-2700) or nearest Consulate: Los Angeles (213/892-1238) or New York (212/490-2722). Internet: http://www.undp.org/missions/malaysia

MALDIVES - *Passport required. Tourist visa issued upon arrival for 30 days validity, no charge (for stays longer than 30 days, you must apply at the immigration office in Maldives). Visitors must have proof of hotel reservations, onward/return transportation, and sufficient funds (minimum of $25 per person per day). Check with the Maldives Mission to the U.N. in New York (212/599-6195) for further information.

MALI - *Passport and visa required. Visa must be obtained in advance. Tourist/business visa for stay up to 1 month, may be extended after arrival,

requires $20 fee (cash or money order), 2 application forms, 2 photos, and proof of onward/return transportation. For business travel, must have company letter stating purpose of trip. Send SASE for return of passport if applying by mail and/or appropriate express mail fees. Apply at the Embassy of the Republic of Mali, 2130 R St., N.W., Washington, D.C. 20008 (202/332-2249).

MALTA - *Passport required. Visa not required for stay up to 90 days (extension must be applied for prior to end of 90-day period or expiration of original visa while in Malta). Residents of Commonwealth of Northern Mariana Islands need a visa. Visa requires 1 application form, 2 photos, proof of onward/return ticket, and $40 fee (check or money order). Transit visa available for $30 fee (fees are non-refundable). For additional information consult the Embassy of Malta, 2017 Conn. Ave., N.W., Washington, D.C. 20008 (202/462-3611/2) or nearest Consulate: CA (415/468-4321), MI (313/525-9777), MO (816/833-0033), MN (612/228-0935), NY (212/725-2345), PA (610/664-7475), or TX (713/428-7800 or 214/777-4463).

MARSHALL ISLANDS, REPUBLIC OF THE - Passport, sufficient funds for stay and onward/return ticket required for stay up to 30 days (extendible up to 90 days from date of entry). Departure fee $20. Health certificate required if arriving from infected areas. AIDS test may be required for visits over 30 days; U.S. test accepted. Check information with Embassy of Marshall Islands, 2433 Massachusetts Avenue, N.W., Washington, D.C. 20008 (202/234-5414) or Permanent Mission to the U.N., 220 East 42nd St., New York, NY 10017 (212/983-3040) or the Consulate General in Hawaii (808/545-7767). Internet: http://www.rmiembassyus.org

MARTINIQUE - (See West Indies, French.)

MAURITANIA - *Passport and visa required. Obtain visa before arrival. Visa valid 1 to 3 days, requires $50 fee, 3 days to 3 months, requires $125 fee (fees payable by certified check or money order only), 2 application forms, 4 photos, proof of sufficient funds (bank statement), letter of invitation, bank statement and proof of onward/return transportation. Business travelers must have letter from sponsoring company. For

49

further information, contact the Embassy of the Republic of Mauritania, 2129 Leroy Pl., N.W., Washington, D.C. 20008 (202/232-5700).

MAURITIUS - *Passport, sufficient funds for stay, confirmation from hotel, and onward/return ticket required. Visa not required for tourist/business stay up to 6 months. AIDS test performed upon arrival, when applicants are applying for permanent residency and work permits. For further information, consult the Embassy of Mauritius, Suite 441, 4301 Conn. Ave., N.W., Washington, D.C. 20008 (202/244-1491/2) or the Honorary Consulate: Los Angeles (818/788-3720).

MAYOTTE ISLAND - (See France.)

MEXICO - *Passport and visa not required of U.S. citizens for tourist/transit stay up to 90 days. Tourist card is required. Tourist card valid 3 months for single entry up to 180 days, no charge, requires proof of U.S. citizenship, photo ID and proof of sufficient funds. Tourist cards may be obtained in advance from Consulate, Tourism Office, and most airlines serving Mexico upon arrival. Departure tax $10 is paid at airport when not included in the cost of the airline ticket. Notarized consent from parent(s) required for children under age 18 traveling alone, with one parent, or in someone else's custody. For details and information on other types of travel, check with the Embassy of Mexico's Consular Section, 2827 16th St., N.W., Washington, DC 20009-4260 (202/736-1000) or nearest Consulate General: AZ (602/242-7398), CA (213/351-6800, 415/392-5554 and 619/231-8414), CO (303/331-1110), FL (305/716-4977), GA (404/266-1913), IL (312/855-1380), LA (504/522-3596), NY (212/689-0460), PR (809/764-0258) or TX (210/227-1085, 214/252-9250, 713/271-6800, 512/478-9031 and 915/533-4082).

MICRONESIA, FEDERATED STATES OF (Chuuk, Kosrae, Pohnei, and Yap) - Proof of citizenship, sufficient funds, and onward/return ticket required for tourist visit up to 30 days, extendible (up to 1 year from date of entry) after arrival in Micronesia. Entry permit is needed for other types of travel; obtain forms from airline. Departure fee for Chuuk and Kosrae $10 and $5 for Pohnpei (U.S. currency). Health certificate may be required if traveling from infected area.

AIDS test required if staying over 90 days; U.S. test is accepted. For further information, contact the Embassy of the Federated States of Micronesia, 1725 N St., N.W., Washington, D.C. 20036 (202/223-4383) or nearest Consulate: Hawaii (808/836-4775) or Guam (671/646-9154). Internet: http://www.fsmgob.org

MIQUELON ISLAND - Passport or proof of U.S. citizenship and official photo ID are sufficient for tourist/business stays of up to 3 months. (Stays from 2 weeks to 3 months require a valid *passport.) A visa is required for stays over 3 month. For further information, consult the Embassy of France (202/944-6000). Internet: http://www.france-consulat.org.

MOLDOVA - *Passport and visa required. Visa requires 1 application form, 1 photo, and processing fee. Single-entry visa, $40, multiple-entry $50-$200 (depending on length of stay), transit visa, single entry $20, double entry $40. There is an additional $5 visa application fee that must be paid separately. All fees must be paid with company checks or money orders only. No fee for visa for children under age 16. AIDS test required for persons staying over 90 days; U.S. tests results sometimes accepted. For additional information consult, the Embassy of the Republic of Moldova, 1533 K Street, N.W., Suite 333, Washington, D.C. 20005, (202/667-1130). Internet: http://www.moldova.org

MONACO - *Passport required. Visa not required for visit up to 90 days. For further information, contact the Embassy of France, (202/944-6000) or nearest Honorary Consulate of the Principality of Monaco: CA (213/655-8970 or 415/362-5050), IL (312/642-1242), LA (504/522-5700), NY (212/759-5227) or PR (809/721-4215). Internet: http://www.france.consulate.org

MONGOLIA - *Passport and visa required. Transit visa for stay up to 48 hours requires copy of onward ticket, visa for next destination and $35 fee. Tourist visa for up to 30 days requires confirmation from Mongolian Travel Agency (Zhuulchin) and $45 fee. Business visa requires letter from company stating purpose of trip and invitation from Mongolian organization and fee. Submit 1 application form, 1 photo, itinerary and prepaid envelope for return of passport by certified or special delivery mail. AIDS test required for students and anyone staying longer than 3 months; U.S. test accepted. All foreigners are required to be registered with the Civil Registration Information Center Police Department in Mongolia upon arrival regardless of duration of stay and are warned to do so in order to avoid any inconveniences they may face upon departure. For additional information, contact the Embassy of Mongolia, 2833 M Street, N.W., Washington, D.C. 20007 (202/333-7117) or the UN Mission of Mongolia, 6 East 77th St., New York, NY 10021 (212/861-9460). Internet: http://www.undp.org/missions/mongolia

MONTSERRAT - (See West Indies, British)

MOROCCO - *Passport required. Visa not required for stays up to 3 months, extendible. For additional information consult the Embassy of Morocco, 1601 21st St., N.W., Washington, D.C. 20009 (202/462-7734) or Consulate General in New York (212/213-9644).

MOZAMBIQUE - *Passport and visa required. Visa must be obtained in advance. Entry visa valid 3 months from date of issuance, requires 1 application form, 2 photos, $20 (single-entry) or $40 (multiple-entry) processing fee, and letter (from company or individual) giving detailed itinerary and address of where visitor is staying. Visitors must exchange $50 at point of entry and declare all foreign currency. Apply at the Embassy of the Republic of Mozambique, Suite 570, 1990 M St., N.W., Washington, D.C. 20036 (202/293-7146).

MYANMAR (see Burma.)

NAMIBIA - *Passport, onward/return ticket and proof of sufficient funds required. Visa not required for tourist or business stay up to 90 days. Person planning to work (this includes unpaid volunteers) in Namibia must obtain work and residency permits and/or visas from the Embassy of Namibia before traveling. Consult the Embassy of Namibia, 1605 New Hampshire Ave., N.W., Washington, D.C. 20009 (202/986-0540) for further information.

NAURU - *Passport, visa, onward/return ticket and sponsorship from a resident in Nauru required. For more information, contact the Consulate of the Republic of Nauru in Guam: Ada Professional Bldg., Marine Dr. 1st Floor, Agana, Guam 96910 (671/649-7106 or 7107).

NEPAL - *Passport and visa required. Tourist visa extendible to a maximum period of 150 days in one visa year (January to December). Single-entry visa for 60 days, $30; double-entry visa for 60 days, $55; triple entry visa for 60 days, $70; and multiple-entry visa with a validity for 60 days, $90; requires 1 application form and 1 photo. Entry visas are valid for entry into Nepal within six months from the date of issue. Tourist visa can also be obtained from Immigration Office at Katmandu Airport and other specified ports of entry. Airport tax of Rs.900 must be paid for all international flights into Nepal. For additional information about "trekking permits" and entry requirements, contact the Royal Nepalese Embassy, 2131 Leroy Pl., N.W., Washington, D.C. 20008 (202/667-4550), or Consulate General in New York (212/370-3988). Internet: http://www.undp.org/missions/nepal

NETHERLANDS - *Passport required. Visa not required for tourist/business visit up to 90 days. Tourists may be asked to show onward/return ticket, proof of sufficient funds and health insurance coverage, and that there is adequate housing available for length of stay. Long term visitors must register with the local police within 8 days of arrival. (No residency permits granted.) For further information, contact the Embassy of the Netherlands, 4200 Linnean Ave., N.W., Washington, D.C. 20008 (202/244-5300) or nearest Consulate General: CA (310/268-1598), IL (312/856-0110), NY (212/246-1429), or TX (713/622-8000). Internet: http://www.netherlands-embassy.org

NETHERLANDS ANTILLES - Islands include Bonaire, Curacao, Saba, Statia, St. Maarten. Passport or proof of U.S. citizenship (i.e. certified birth certificate or voter registration card with photo ID) required. Visa not required for stay up to 14 days, extendible to 90 days after arrival. Tourists may be asked to show onward/return ticket or proof of sufficient funds for stay. Departure tax $10 when leaving Bonaire and Curacao, $4 in Statia, $10 in St. Maarten. For further information, consult Embassy of the Netherlands (202/244-5300), or nearest Consulate General: CA (310/2681598), IL (312/856-0110), NY (212/246-1429) or TX (713/622-8000).

Internet: http://www.netherlands-embassy.org

NEW CALEDONIA - (See French Polynesia.)

NEW ZEALAND - *Passport and arrival card (to be completed upon arrival) required. Visa not required for tourist or business meeting or consultations stay up to 3 months, must have onward/return ticket, visa for next destination and proof of sufficient funds. For business or additional information, contact the Embassy of New Zealand, 37 Observatory Circle, N.W., Washington, D.C. 20008 (202/328-4800) or the Consulate General in Los Angeles (310/207-1605. Internet: http://www.emb.com/nzemb

NICARAGUA - *Passport valid 6 months beyond duration of stay, onward/return ticket and $5 entry fee required for a stay up to 30 days. Airport departure tax $18. If you change status from visitor to permanent resident while in Nicaragua, you will need to deposit with their immigration officials the equivalent cost of a one-way ticket from Nicaragua to the U.S. Business visa also requires a letter of invitation from business contact in Nicaragua. For further information, travelers may contact the Consulate of Nicaragua, 1627 New Hampshire Ave., N.W., Washington, D.C. 20009 (202/939-6531 or 32) or the nearest Consulate in CA (213/252-1170 or 415/765-6821), FL (305/220-6900), LA (504/523-1507), NY (212/983-1981), or TX (713/272-9628).

NIGER - *Passport and visa required. Visa must be used within 3 months of issuance. All visa types require 3 application forms, 3 photos, proof of onward/return transportation, and $35.58 (1 month stay) or $88.94 (longer stay) fee. Transit visas required for travelers continuing through Niger. For tourist visa the general requirements apply as well as 2 copies of bank statement, certifying the traveler has at least $500 in his/her bank account. For business visas, general requirements apply, plus 1 copy of a letter from the company that is being represented stating the purpose, activities, duration, and source of financial responsibility for the trip. Provide SASE or prepaid airbill for return of documents. For further information and fees, contact the Embassy of the Republic of Niger, 2204 R St., N.W., Washington, D.C. 20008 (202/483-4224).

NIGERIA - *Passport, proof of sufficient funds, hotel confirmation, and visa required. Visa requires 1 application, 1 photo, proof of onward/return transportation, fees (contact the Embassy of Nigeria for appropriate fees), and letter of invitation from Nigeria. Business visa requires letter from counterpart in Nigeria and letter of introduction from U.S. company. For information about visa fees and for other requirements, contact the Embassy of the Republic of Nigeria, 2201 M Street, N.W., Washington, D.C. 20037 (202/822-1500 or 1522) or the Consulate General in New York (212/715-7200).

NIUE - Passport, onward/return ticket, and confirmed hotel accommodations required. Visa not required for stay up to 30 days. For additional information, consult the Embassy of New Zealand (202/328-4800).

NORFOLK ISLAND - *Passport and visa required. Visa issued upon arrival for visit up to 30 days, extendible, requires confirmed accommodations and onward/return ticket. Business visa must be obtained before arrival, $27 fee. Australian transit visa must also be obtained in advance for travel to Norfolk Island. For both visas, consult the Australian Embassy (202/797-3000). Internet addresses: http://www.austemb.org or www.pitcairners.org

NORWAY - *Passport required. Visa not required for stay up to 90 days. (90 day period begins when entering Nordic area: Denmark, Finland, Iceland, Norway, and Sweden.) No pets. For further information, contact the royal Norwegian Embassy, 2720 34th St., N.W., Washington, D.C. 20008 (202/333-6000) or nearest Consulate General: CA (415/986-0766 to 68), FL (305/358-4386), MN (612/332-3338), NY (212/421-7333), or TX (713/521-2900). Internet: http://www.norway.org

OMAN - Passport (must be valid for not less than 12 months) and visa required. Tourist/business visas for multiple-entry issued for stay up to 6 months and valid for 2 years requires $60 fee (cash, cashier's check or money order). Single-entry visa requires $36 fee (cash, cashier's check or money order). Both types of visas require 1 application form and a SASE for return of passport by mail. AIDS test required for work permits. U.S. test not accepted. Allow 1-3 days for processing. For transit and road travel, check with the Embassy of the Sultanate of Oman, 2535 Belmont Rd., N.W., Washington, D.C. 20008 (202/387-1980, 1981 or 1982).

PAKISTAN - *Passport and visa required. Visa must be obtained before arrival. Tourist visa requires 1 application form, 2 photos, and proof of onward/return transportation. Validity depends on length of visit, multiple entries, and $45 fee. Need company cover letter and invitation for business visa. Include prepaid envelope for return of passport by registered mail. For applications and inquiries in Washington area, contact the Consular Section of the Embassy of Pakistan, 2315 Mass. Ave., N.W., Washington, D.C. 20008 (202/939-6295/61), or CA (310/441-5114), or NY (212/879-5800). Internet: http://www.pakistan-embassy.com

PALAU, THE REPUBLIC OF - Passport or proof of U.S. citizenship, visa, and onward/return ticket required. Visa, issued at airport, requires $50 fee for stays of up to 30 days. Obtain visa forms for entry permit from airline or shipping agent serving Palau. For further information, consult with Representative Office, 1150 18th St., N.W., Suite 750, Washington, D.C. 20036 (202/452-6814).

PANAMA - *Passport or proof of U.S. citizenship and photo ID, tourist card or visa, proof of sufficient funds, and onward/return ticket required. Visa and tourist card valid 30 days. Visa issued at Embassy of Panama or one of the consulates. Tourist card available from airline serving Panama for $10 fee. Stay can be extended up to 60 days, apply at the main office of Immigration and Naturalization in Panama. Visa requires 1 application form and 1 photo. Allow one working day for processing. Departure tax $20 is paid at airport. AIDS test required for persons adjusting visa status while in Panama. For longer stays and additional information regarding travel other than via a commercial airline, contact the Embassy of Panama, 2862 McGill Terrace, N.W., Washington, D.C. 20008 (202/483-1407) or the nearest Consulate: CA (415/391-4268), FL (305/371-7031 or 813/831-6685), LA (504/525-3458), NY (212/840-2450), PA (215/574-2994), or TX (713/622-445l).

PAPUA NEW GUINEA - *Passport, visa, onward/return ticket and proof of sufficient funds required. Tourist and business visas for a stay up to 60 days (extendible). multiple-entry visa requires 1 application form, 1 photo, letter of invitation, and $256.25 fee. Business visas also requires letter of invitation from sponsoring company, bio-data, recent annual report of parent company. AIDS other medical test required for work and residency permits; U.S. test accepted. Please provide SASE or prepaid airbill for return of documents. For longer stays and further information, contact the Embassy of Papua New Guinea, #805, 1779 Massachusetts Ave., N.W., Washington, D.C. 20036 (202/745-3680) or the Papua New Guinea Honorary Consulate, P.O. Box 893133, Mililani, Hono-lulu, Hawaii 96789 (808/623-8144). Internet: http://www.pngemb assy.org

PARAGUAY - *Passport required. Visa not required for tourist/business stay up to 90 days (extendible). Exit tax $20 (paid at airport). AIDS test required for resident visas. U.S. test sometimes accepted. For additional information, consult the Embassy of Paraguay, 2400 Mass. Ave., N.W., Washington, D.C. 20008 (202/483-6960). Internet: http://www.mre.gov.py/embaparusa/USA.htm

PERU - *Passport required. Visa not required for tourist stay up to 90 days, extendible after arrival. Tourists need onward/return ticket. Business visa requires 1 application form, 1 photo, company letter stating purpose of trip, and $27 fee. For further information, contact the Consulate General of Peru, 1625 Mass. Ave., N.W., Suite 605, Washington, D.C. 20036 (202/462-1084) or nearest Consulate: CA (213/252-5910 and 415/362-5185), FL (305/374-1305), IL (312/853-6174), NY (212/481-7410), or TX (713/355-9438).

PHILIPPINES - *Passport and onward/return ticket required. For entry by Manila International Airport, visa not required for transit/tourist stay up to 21 days, extendible to a maximum of 59 days with approval of immigration authorities. Visas requires 1 application form, 1 photo, $30 fee for single-entry and $90 fee multiple-entry. Company letter needed for business visa. For longer stays or more information, contact the Embassy of the Philippines, 1600 Mass. Ave., N.W., Washington, D.C. 20036 (202/467-9300) or nearest Consulate General: CA (213/639-0980 to 85 and 415/433-

6666 or 69), HI (808/595-6316), NY (212/764-1330 or 34), or CNMI (670/234-1848). Internet: us.sequel.net/RpinUS

POLAND - *Passport and proof of sufficient funds required. Visa not required for tourist/business stay of up to 90 days. Visitors must register at hotel or with local authorities within 48 hours after arrival. For longer stays or more information, contact the Embassy of the Republic of Poland (Consular Division), 2224 Wyoming Ave., N.W., Washington, D.C. 20008 (202/232-4517) or nearest Consulate General: Chicago, IL, 1530 Lakeshore Dr., 60610 (312/337-8166), Los Angeles, CA, 12400 Wilshire Blvd., Suite 555, 90025 (310/442-8500) or New York, NY, 233 Madison Ave., 10016 (212/889-8360). Internet: http://www.polishworld.com/polemb

PORTUGAL - (Includes travel to the Azores and Madeira Islands.) *Passport required. Visa not required for visit up to 90 days. For travel with pets and other information consult the Embassy of Portugal, 2310 Tracy Place, N.W., Washington, D.C. 20008 (202/332-3007) or the nearest Consulate: CA (415/346-3400), MA (617/536-8740 and 508/997-6151), NJ (973/643-4200), NY (212/246-4580) or RI (401/272-2003). Internet: http://www.portugalemb.org

QATAR - *Passport and visa required. Business visitors, tourists, those attending scientific or cultural symposia, and medical visitors are granted a 10-year multiple-entry visa at the Embassy in Washington, D.C. One application form, 1 photo, letter of invitation and a non-refundable application fee of $45 is required. Please provide a SASE for return of passport by mail. AIDS test required for persons seeking residency permits and visitors staying longer than 1 month; U.S. tests results not accepted. For specific information, contact the Embassy of the State of Qatar, Suite 200, 4200 Wisconsin Ave., N.W., Washington, D.C. 20016 (202/274-1603).

REUNION - (See France.)

ROMANIA - *Passport required. Visa not required for a stay up to 30 days. For stays exceeding 30 days, visa should be obtained in advance. Visa requires letter stating purpose of travel, duration, departure and return dates, and a SASE for return of passport by mail. For additional information, consult the Embassy of Romania, 1607 23rd St., N.W., Washington, D.C. 20008 (202/332-4851) or the nearest Consulate General: New York (212/682-9120) and Los Angeles (310/444-0043). Internet: http://www.roemembus.org

RUSSIA - *Passport and visa required. Tourist visa requires 1 application form, 3 photos, confirmation and voucher from travel agency and/or hotel in Russia, cover letter from travel agency, and processing fee. Business visa requires 1 application, 3 photos, cover letter from your company, and letter of an official invitation from an authorized Russian counterpart and visa processing fee. Visa processing fee for business and tourist visas is $70 for 2 weeks, $80 for one week, and $110 for less than three working days. Multiple-entry business visa (needs confirmation through the Russian MFA) - $200 to $450 processing fee. Fees must be paid by money order or cashier's check only. Transit visas required when traveling through Russia, even if you remain on the plane. Provide SASE for return of passport by mail. HIV test certificate required for anyone staying over 3 months. For additional information, contact the Consular Section of the Embassy of Russia, 2641 Tunlaw Road, N.W., Washington, D.C. 20007 (202/939-8907 or 8918) or the nearest Consulate General: NY (212/348-0926, 0955, 0626), CA (415/928-6878) or WA (206/728-1910). Internet: http://www.russianembassy.org

RWANDA - *Passport required. Visa not required for a stay of up to 30 days. For more information, contact the Embassy of the Republic of Rwanda, 1714 New Hampshire Ave., N.W., Washington, D.C. 20009 (202/232-2882), or the Permanent Mission of Rwanda to the U.N., 124 East 39th Street, New York, NY 10016 (212/696-0644/45/46), or the nearest Consulate General in Chicago (708/205-1188), or Denver (303/321-2400).

SAINT KITTS AND NEVIS - Passport or proof of U.S. citizenship, photo ID and onward/return ticket required for stay up to 3 months. AIDS test required for persons seeking residency/study/work permits; U.S. tests results sometimes accepted. For further information, consult the Embassy of St. Kitts and Nevis, 3216 New Mexico Ave., N.W., Washington, DC 20016 (202/686-2636) or Permanent Mission to the U.N., 414 East 75th St.,

Fifth Floor, New York, NY 10021 (212/535-1234). Internet: http://www.stkittsnevis.org

SAINT LUCIA - Passport (or proof of U.S. citizenship and photo ID) and return/onward ticket required for stay up to 6 months. For additional information, contact the Embassy of Saint Lucia, 3216 New Mexico Ave., Washington, D.C. 20016 (202/364-6792) or Permanent Mission to the U.N., 820 Second Ave., Suite 900E, New York, NY 10017 (212/697-9360).

ST. MARTIN (ST. MAARTEN*) - (See West Indies, French or *Netherlands Antilles.)
ST. PIERRE - Passport or proof of U.S. citizenship and official photo ID sufficient for tourist/business stays of up to 2 weeks. (Stays from 2 weeks to 3 months require a valid *passport.) A visa is required for stays over 3 month. For further information, consult the Embassy of France (202/944-6000). Internet: http://www.france-consulat.org.

SAINT VINCENT AND THE GRENADINES - Proof of U.S. citizenship, photo ID, and onward/return ticket and/or proof of sufficient funds required for tourist stay up to 6 months. AIDS test required for persons seeking residency permits; U.S. tests results accepted. For more information consult the Embassy of Saint Vincent and the Grenadines, 3216 New Mexico Ave., Washington, D.C. 20016 (202/364-6730) or Consulate, 801 Second Ave., 21st Floor, New York, NY 10017 (212/687-4490).

SAMOA - *Passport and onward/return ticket required. Visa not required for stay up to 30 days. For longer stays and more information, contact the Independent State of Samoa Mission to the U.N., 820 2nd Avenue, Suite 800, New York, NY (212/599-6196) or the Honorary Consul in Hawaii (808/677-7197).

SAN MARINO - *Passport required. Visa not required for tourist stay up to 90 days. For additional information, contact the nearest Honorary Consulate of the Republic of San Marino: Washington, D.C. (1899 L St., N.W., Suite 500, Washington, D.C. 20036, 202/223-3517), Detroit (313/528-1190) or New York (516/242-2212).

SAO TOME AND PRINCIPE - *Passport and visa required. Tourist visas for single entry of up to 3 months ($30) or multiple entry of up to 6 months ($35) and business visas for single entry of up to 3 months ($35) or multiple entry of up to 6 months ($40) require 1 application form, 1 photo, and letter stating purpose of travel. Fees are to be paid by money order only. Company letter is required for a business visa. Enclose prepaid envelope or postage for return of passport by FedEx service. Apply at the Permanent Mission of Sao Tome and Principe to the U.N., 400 Park Avenue, 7th Floor, New York, NY 10022 (212/317-0533).

SAUDI ARABIA - *Passport and visa required. (Tourist visas are not available for travel to Saudi Arabia.) Transit visa valid 72 hours, requires onward/return ticket, 1 application form, no fee. Business visa, for a stay not to exceed 30 days, requires $54 fee (money order only), 1 application form, 1 photo, company letter stating purpose of visit, invitation from Foreign Ministry in Saudi Arabia and SASE for return of passport by mail. Medical report, including AIDS test, required for work permits; U.S. test sometimes accepted. For details and requirements for family visits and religious travel, contact the Royal Embassy of Saudi Arabia, 601 New Hampshire Ave., N.W., Washington, D.C. 20037 (202/342-3800) or nearest Consulate General: Los Angeles (213/479-6000), New York (212/752-2740) or Houston (713/785-5577). Internet: http://www.saudiembassy.net

SCOTLAND - (See United Kingdom.)

SENEGAL - *Passport and onward/return ticket required. Visa not needed for stay up to 90 days. For further information, contact the Embassy of the Republic of Senegal, 2112 Wyoming Ave., N.W., Washington, D.C. 20008 (202/234-0540).

SERBIA AND MONTENEGRO - (See Federal Republic of Yugoslavia.)

SEYCHELLES - *Passport, onward/return ticket and proof of sufficient funds required. Visa issued upon arrival for stay up to 1 month, no charge, extendible up to 1 year. Medical exam, including AIDS test, performed upon arrival for work permits; U.S. test not accepted. For more information, consult Permanent Mission of Seychelles to the U.N., 800 Second Ave., Suite

400, New York, NY 10017 (212/972-1785) for further information.

SIERRA LEONE - *Passport and visa required. Single-entry visa valid 3 months, requires 1 application form, 1 photo, return/onward ticket, proof of financial support from bank or employer and $45 fee (money order only). Multiple-entry visa, $90 fee. Business visa also require a letter of invitation from a company in Sierra Leone and a profile of the company in the USA that the traveler is representing. Provide SASE or prepaid airbill for return of documentation. For business and additional information consult the Embassy of Sierra Leone, 1701 19th St., N.W., Washington, D.C. 20009 (202/939-9261).

SINGAPORE - *Passport, proof of sufficient funds for stay, and onward/return ticket required. Visa not required for tourist/business stay up to 3 months. AIDS test required for some work visas; U.S. test is not accepted. For additional information, contact the Embassy of Singapore, 3501 Int'l Place, N.W., Washington, D.C. 20008 (202/537-3100).

SLOVAK REPUBLIC - *Passport required. Visa not required for a stay of up to 30 days. AIDS test required for long term visas; U.S. test is not accepted. For more information, contact the Embassy of the Slovak Republic, 2201 Wisconsin Ave., N.W., Suite 250, Washington, D.C. 20007 (202/965-5160 ext. 270). Internet: http://www.slovakemb.com

SLOVENIA - *Passport required. Visa not required for business/tourist stay up to 90 days. For longer stays (e.g. employment, students) a temporary residence permit must be obtained before traveling. Additional information can be obtained from the Embassy of the Republic of Slovenia, 1525 New Hampshire Ave., N.W., Washington, D.C. 20036 (202/667-5363) or the Consulate General of Slovenia in New York (212/370-3006).

SOLOMON ISLANDS - *Passport, onward/return ticket and proof of sufficient funds required. Visitors permit issued on arrival for stay up to 2 months in 1-year period. For further information, consult Solomon Islands Mission to the U.N., 820 2nd Ave., Suite 800A, New York, NY 10017 (212/599-6192/93).

SOMALIA - *Passport required. For further information, contact the Consulate of the Somali Democratic Republic in New York (212/688-9410).

SOUTH AFRICA - *Passport, onward/return ticket, and proof of sufficient funds required. Tourist or business visa not required for stay up to 90 days. AIDS test required for all mine workers (irrespective of position); U.S. test sometimes accepted. For more information, contact the Embassy of South Africa, Consular Office, 3051 Massachusetts Ave., N.W., Washington, D.C. 20008 (202/232-4400) or the nearest Consulate in CA (323/651-0902), IL (312/939-7929), or NY (212/213-4880). Internet: http://www.southafrica.net

SPAIN - *Passport required. Visa not required for tourist or business stays up to 90 days. Medical report, including AIDS test, required for residency/student/work permits; U.S. test sometimes accepted. For additional information check with the Embassy of Spain, 2375 Pennsylvania Ave., N.W., Washington, D.C. 20037 (202/452-0100 and 728-2330) or nearest Consulate General in CA (415/922-2995 and 213/938-0158), FL (305/446-5511), IL (312/782-4588), LA (504/525-4951), MA (617/536-2506), NY (212/355-4080), PR (809/758-6090) or TX (713/783-6200). Internet: http://www.spainemb.org

SRI LANKA - *Passport, onward/return ticket and proof of sufficient funds ($30 per day) required. Tourist visa not required for stay up to 30 days (extendible in Sri Lanka). For business travel, visa required and must be obtained in advance. Business visa valid 30 days, requires 1 application form, 2 photos, a company letter, a letter from sponsoring agency in Sri Lanka and employing company in U.S., a copy of an onward/return ticket, and $45 fee. Include $6 postage for return of passport by registered mail. For further information, contact the Embassy of Sri Lanka, 2148 Wyoming Ave., N.W., Washington, D.C. 20008 (202/483-7954) or the Consulate in Los Angeles (323-634-0479 and 323-634-1079) or the nearest Honorary Consul General: GA (404-881-7164), LA (504-455-7600), or NY (212/966-7040 to 7043).

SUDAN - *Passport and visa required. Visa must be obtained in advance and visas are only issued at the Consulate General in New York. Transit visa valid up to 7 days, requires $50 fee (cash or money order), onward/return ticket and visa for next destination, if appropriate. Tourist/business visa for single entry up to 1 month (extendible), requires $50 fee, 1 application form, 2 photo, proof of sufficient funds for stay and SASE for return passport. Business visa requires company letter stating purpose of visit and invitation from Sudanese officials. Visas not granted to passports showing Israeli visas. Allow 4 weeks for processing. Travelers must declare currency upon arrival and departure. Check additional currency regulations for stays longer than 2 months. Contact the Embassy of the republic of the Sudan, 2210 Mass. Ave., N.W., Washington, D.C. 20008 (202/338-8565 to 8570) or Consulate General, 655 Third Ave., 5th Floor, New York, NY 10017 (212/573-6033 or 35). Internet: http://www.sudanembassyus.org

SURINAME - *Passport, visa and onward/return ticket required. Multiple-entry visa requires 2 application forms, 2 photos and appropriate fee. Business visa requires company letter explaining purpose of trip, name of institution to be visited and its address and telephone number in Suriname, and expected duration of visit. Processing fee: $45 (money order only). For return of passport by mail, include $8 for registered mail, or $15 for Express Mail (money order only), or enclose SASE. Allow 10 working days for processing. For additional requirements, contact the Embassy of the Republic of Suriname, Suite 460, 4301 Connecticut Ave., N.W., Washington, D.C. 20008 (202/244-7488 and 7590), or the Consulate in Miami (305/593-2697).

SWAZILAND - *Passport required. Visa not required for stay up to 60 days. Temporary residence permit available in Mbabane for longer stay. Visitors must report to immigration authorities or police station within 48 hours unless lodging in a hotel. For further information, consult the Embassy of the Kingdom of Swaziland, 3400 International Dr., N.W., Suite 3M, Washington, D.C. (202/362-6683).

SWEDEN - *Passport required. Visa not required for a stay up to 90 days. (90 day period begins when entering Nordic area: Denmark, Finland, Iceland, Norway, and Sweden.) For further information, consult the Embassy of Sweden, 1501 M St., N.W., Washington, D.C. 20005-1702 (202/467-2600) or nearest Consulate General: CA (310/445-4008), FL (954/467-3507), IL (312/781-6262), New York (212/583-2550) or any other consulate of Sweden in the United States. Internet: http://www.swedenemb.org

SWITZERLAND - *Passport required. Visa not required for tourist/business stay up to 90 days. For further information, contact the embassy of Switzerland, 2900 Cathedral Ave., N.W., Washington, D.C. 20008 (202/745-7900) or the nearest Consulate General: CA (310/575-1145 or 415/788-2272), GA (404/870-2000), IL (312/915-0061), NY (212/599-5700), or TX (713/650-0000). Internet: http://www.swissemb.org

SYRIA - *Passport and visa required. Obtain visa in advance. Single-entry visas valid for 3 months, require 2 application forms, 2 photos (signed), and $61 fee (payment must be money order only). Enclose SASE with appropriate postage (not metered stamps for certified mail) for return of passport by mail. AIDS test required for anyone staying over 15 days; U.S. test sometimes accepted. For group visas and other information, contact the Embassy of the Syrian Arab Republic, 2215 Wyoming Ave., N.W., Washington, D.C. 20008 (202/232-6313).

TAHITI - (See French Polynesia.)

TAIWAN - *Passport onward/return ticket, and valid visa for next destination, if applicable, required. Visa not required for stay up to 14 days. Health certificate, including AIDS test, is mandatory for anyone staying over 3 months; U.S. test not accepted. For business travel, longer stays or other information, contact the Tapei Economic and Cultural Represenative Office, 4201 Wisconsin Avenue, N.W., Washington, D.C. 20016-2137 (202/895-1800) or Taipei Economic and Cultural Office in Atlanta (404/872-0123), Boston (617/737-2050), Chicago (312/616-0100), Guam (671/472-5865), Honolulu (808/595-6347), Houston (713/626-7445), Kansas City (816/531-1298), Los Angeles (213/389-1215), Miami (305/443-8917), New York (212/317-7300), San Francisco (415-362-7680), and Seattle (206/441-4586). Internet: http://www.taipei.org or www.boca.gov.tw

TAJIKISTAN - *Passport and visa required. Travelers must obtain visas before arrival in Tajikistan. Visas may be obtained from the Russian Embassy or nearest Consulate in the U.S., for travel to Tajikistan. Travelers who intend to visit Tajikistan should also obtain double-entry Russian, Kazakh or Uzbek visas prior to departure, depending on intended transit points. AIDS test required for anyone staying longer than 90 days. U.S. test sometimes accepted. For additional information, contact the Consular Section of the Embassy of Russia, 2641 Tunlaw Road, N.W., Washington, D.C. 20007 (202/939-8907, 8913 or 8918) or the nearest Consulate General: NY (212/348-0926, 0955, 0626), CA (415/928-6878) or WA (206/728-1910).

TANZANIA - *Passport and visa required. Obtain visa before departure. Visas for mainland Tanzania are valid for Zanzibar. Business/tourist visa (valid 6 months from date of issuance) for 1 entry up to 30 days, may be extended after arrival. Requires 1 application form, 1 photo and $50 fee (no personal checks). Enclose prepaid envelope for return of passport by certified or registered mail. Allow 1 month for processing. For business visa and other information, consult Embassy of the United Republic of Tanzania, 2139 R St., N.W., Washington, D.C. 20008 (202/939-6125) or Tanzanian Permanent Mission to the U.N. 205 East 42nd St., 13th Floor, New York, NY 10017 (212/972-9160).

THAILAND - *Passport required. Tourists staying no longer than 30 days do not need a visa. For longer stays, obtain a visa in advance. Transit visa, for stay up to 30 days, $10 entry fee; or tourist visa for stay up to 60 days, $15 entry fee. For business visa valid up to 90 days, need $20 entry fee or $40 fee for multiple entry, and company letter stating purpose of visit. Submit 1 application form, 2 photos, and postage for return of passport by mail. (Note: All visa fees are payable in cash or money order, if applying in person, or by money order only, if applying by mail. Apply at the Royal Thai Embassy, 1024 Wisconsin Ave., N.W., Washington, D.C. 20007 (202/323-3600 ext. 767), or the nearest Consulate General: CA (213/962-9574-77), IL (312/664-3129), or NY (212/754-1770). For other Consulates General throughout the U.S., call 202/944-3600. Internet: http://www.thaiembdc.org

TOGO - *Passport and visa required. All types of visas (except diplomatic) require 3 application forms, 3 photos, proof of sufficient funds, and $45 fee. For information on additional visa related requirements, contact the Embassy of the Republic of Togo, 2208 Mass. Ave., N.W., Washington, D.C. 20008 (202/234-4212/3).

TONGA - *Passport and onward/return ticket required. Visa not required for stay up to 30 days. For additional information, consult the Consulate General of Tonga, 360 Post St., Suite 604, San Francisco, CA 94108 (415/781-0365).

TRINIDAD AND TOBAGO - *Passport required. Visa not required for tourist/business stay up to 3 months. Business visa requires 1 application form, 1 photo, $9 fee (no personal checks), company letter, and SASE (make sure you include enough stamps to cover the cost of postage, e.g. $11.75 for Post Office Express Mail Service, etc.) for return of passport by mail. For further information, consult Embassy of Trinidad and Tobago, 1708 Mass. Ave., N.W., Washington, D.C. 20036 (202/467-6490) or the nearest Consulate General: New York (212/682-7272) or Miami (305/374-2199).

TUNISIA - *Passport and onward/return ticket required. Visas not required for tourist/business stay up to 4 months. For further information, consult Embassy of Tunisia, 1515 Mass. Ave., N.W., Washington, D.C. 20005 (202/862-1850), or nearest Consulate: San Francisco (415/922-9222) or New York (212/272-6962).

TURKEY - *Passport and visa required. Visas can be obtained at Turkish border crossing points for tourist/business visits up to 3 months or through a Turkish consular office in the U.S. Visa requires a letter stating purpose of trip and $45 fee (cash or money order only). Visa must be obtained in advance for visits lasting longer stays, and for study, research, or employment purposes. For further information, contact the Consular Office of the Embassy of the republic of Turkey, 2525 Massachusetts Ave., N.W., Washington, D.C. 20008 (202/612-6740/41) or nearest Consulate: CA (323/937-0118), IL (312/263-0644), NY (212/949-0160) or TX (713/622-5849). Internet: http://www.turkey.org

TURKMENISTAN - *Passport and visa required. Visa requires 1 application, 1 photo, and letter of invitation. Visas are available in a variety of time periods, and fees are paid according to the type of visa and processing time needed. AIDS test required for foreigners staying longer than 3 months. U.S. test not accepted. For further information about visa fees and types, consult the Embassy of Turkmenistan, 2207 Massachusetts Ave., N.W., Washington, D.C. 20008 (202/588-1500). Internet: www.turkmenistanembassy.org

TURKS AND CAICOS - (See West Indies, British.)

TUVALU - *Passport and onward/return ticket and proof of sufficient funds required. Visitors permit issued on arrival. For further information, consult British Embassy (202/588-7800).

UGANDA - *Passport and visa required. For other information, contact the Embassy of the Republic of Uganda, 5911 16th St., N.W., Washington, D.C. 20011 (202/726-7100-02) or Permanent Mission to the U.N. (212/949-0110).

UKRAINE - *Passport and visa required. Visa requires 1 form, 1 photo, a letter of invitation, and $75 - $165 fee, depending upon whether you apply for a single, double or multiple entry visa (company check or money order only). Transit visa requires onward/return ticket. Anyone applying for a visa for a stay of 3 months or longer is required to present a certificate showing that they are HIV negative. Test performed in the U.S. are sometimes accepted. For additional information, contact the Consular Office of the Embassy of Ukrain, 3350 M St., N.W., Washington, D.C. 20007 (202/333-7507/08/09), or the Consulate in Chicago (312/642-4388), or the Consulate General in New York (212/371-5690). Internet: http://www.ukremb.com/

UNITED ARAB EMIRATES - *Passport and visa required. Tourist visa requires a typed letter from the applicant's employer indicating type and length of position held or, for students/homemakers/retirees, bank statement proving sufficient funds for stay. Business visas issued only by UAE Embassy, and require company letter and sponsor in UAE to send a fax or telex to UAE Embassy confirming trip and accepting financial responsibility. Single-entry visa valid within 2 months from the date of issuance for stay up to 30 days, $51 processing fee. Multiple-entry visa (for business only), valid 1 to 10 years from date of issue for maximum stay of 6 months per entry, no fee. Transit visa must be obtained in advance (through travel agency, hotel, or company in UAE), valid for a stay up to 15 days. To receive a visa, submit 2 application forms, 2 photos and prepaid envelope for return of passport by certified/registered mail (typed not handwritten). AIDS test required for residency permits; test performed upon arrival in the UAE. For further information, contact the Embassy of the United Arab Emirates, 1255 22nd Street, Suite 700, N.W., Washington, D.C. 20037 (202/955-7999).

UNITED KINGDOM (England, Northern Ireland, Scotland, and Wales) - *Passport required. Visa not required for stay up to 6 months. Medical exam, including AIDS test, sometimes required. For additional information consult the Consular Section of the British Embassy, 19 Observatory Circle, N.W., Washington, D.C. 20008 (202/588-7800) or nearest Consulate General: CA (310/477-3322), IL (312/346-1810), or NY (212/745-0200). Internet: http://www.britainusa.com

URUGUAY - *Passport required. Visa not required for stay up to 90 days. For additional information, consult the Consulate of Uruguay, 2715 M St., N.W., 3rd Floor, Washington, D.C. 20007 (202/331-4219) or nearest Consulate General: CA (310/394-5777), FL (305/443-7453 or 9764), or NY (212/753-8191 or 92). Internet: http://www.embassy.org/uruguay

UZBEKISTAN - *Passport and visa required. Visa requires 1 application, 1 photo, letter explaining purpose of visit, and $45 fee. Processing time is 7 days after receipt of application. AIDS test required for anyone staying longer than 15 days; U.S. test sometimes accepted. Check requirements with the Consular Section of the Embassy of the Republic of Uzbekistan, 1746 Massachusetts Ave., NW, 20036 (202/530-7284 or 91) or the Uzbekistan Consulate, 866 United Nations Plaza, Suite 327A, New York, NY 10017 (212/754-6178 or 7403). Internet: http://www.uzbekistan.org

VANUATU - *Passport and onward/return ticket

59

required. Visa not required for stay up to 30 days. For further information, consult the Vanuatu Mission to the U.N. (212/593-0144 or 0215).

VATICAN - (See Holy See.)

VENEZUELA - *Passport, onward/return ticket and proof of sufficient funds required. Business and other travelers require a visa. All travelers must pay departure tax ($40) at airport. For additional information, contact the Consular of the Embassy of Venezuela, 1099 30th Street, N.W., Washington, DC 20007 (202/342-2214) or the nearest Consulate: CA (415/955-1982), FL (305/577-4214), IL (312/236-9655), LA (504/522-3284), MA (617/266-9368), NY (212/826-1660), PR (809/766-4250/1) or TX (713/961-5166). Internet: http://www.embavenez-us.gov

VIETNAM - *Passport and visa required. Tourist/business visa, valid 6 months, requires 2 application forms, 2 photos, letter stating purpose of visit (or letter of invitation from Vietnamese authorities required for business visa) and $25 fee for a single-entry visa. Visa authorization is arranged by sponsor in Vietnam and the Embassy cannot process visas until it receives authorization or approval from Vietnam. For more information, contact the Embassy of Vietnam, 1233 20th St., N.W., Suite 400, Washington, D.C. 20036 (202/861-2293 or 861-0694). Internet: http://www.vietnamembassy-usa.org

VIRGIN ISLANDS, British - Islands include Anegarda, Jost van Dyke, Tortola and Virgin Gorda. Proof of U.S. citizenship, photo ID, onward/return ticket and sufficient funds required for tourist stay up to 6 months. Consult the British Embassy for further information (202/588-7800).

WALES - (See United Kingdom.)

WEST INDIES, British - Islands include Anguilla, Montserrat, Cayman Islands, Turks and Caicos. Proof of U.S. citizenship, photo ID, onward/return ticket and sufficient funds required for tourist stay up to 6 months. Consult the British Embassy for further information (202/588-7800).

WEST INDIES, French - Islands include Guadeloupe, Isles des Saintes, La Desirade, Marie Galante, Saint Barthelemy, St. Martin and Martinique. *Passport required. Visa not required for tourist/business stay of up to 3 months. For further information, consult the Embassy of France (202/944-6200). Internet: http://www.france-consulat.org

WESTERN SAMOA - (See Samoa)

YEMEN, REPUBLIC OF - *Passport and visa required. Visa valid 30 days from date of issuance for single-entry, requires 1 application form and 2 photos. For tourist visa need proof of onward/return transportation, employment, letter of invitation and $50 fee ($30 visa fee plus $20 application fee). Business visa requires $50, company letter stating purpose of trip. (Payment by money order only and include SASE with proper postage for return of passport by registered mail.) AIDS test required for residency/study/work permits; U.S. test not accepted. For more information, contact the Embassy of the Republic of Yemen, Suite 705, 2600 Virginia Ave., N.W., Washington, D.C. 20037 (202/965-4760) or Yemen Mission to the U.N., 866 United Nations Plaza, Rm. 435, New York, NY 10017 (212/355-1730).

ZAIRE - (See Congo, Democratic Republic of)

ZAMBIA - *Passport and visa required. Visa may be obtained in advance or at port of entry. Tourist/business multiple-entry visa, valid up to 3 years, requires $30 processing fee (no personal checks), 2 application forms, and 2 photos. Note: If applicant adds spouse and/or children to visa form, traveler must pay an additional $10 fee for each. When a visa is obtained at port of entry, it is only valid for stay of up to 3 months and the fee is $40. Business visa also requires company letter. For more information, consult the Embassy of the Republic of Zambia, 2419 Mass. Ave., N.W., Washington, D.C. 20008 (202/265-9717 to 19).

ZANZIBAR - (See Tanzania.)

ZIMBABWE - *Passport, visa, onward/return ticket and proof of sufficient funds required for a stay up to 3 months. Visas issued upon arrival in Zimbabwe, $30 fee. Anti-malarial pills are recommended. $20 exit fee paid at airport. Visitors must declare currency upon arrival. For regulations check with the Embassy of Zimbabwe, 1608 New Hampshire Ave., N.W., Washington, D.C. 20009 (202/332-7100).

Notes

SASE is self-addressed, stamped envelope. If applying in person, remember to call about office hours. Many consulates are only open in the morning and closed for local holidays.

This booklet is updated yearly. This publication and Passports-Applying for them the EASY WAY, which gives detailed information on how and where to apply for your U.S. passport, are both available from the **Consumer Information Center, Pueblo, CO 81009 for 50 cents each.**

The State Department's Bureau of Consular Affairs provides assistance and information to U.S. citizens traveling abroad. Consular Affairs issues Consular Information Sheets, Travel Warnings, Public Announcements, and other travel publications. The following gives a brief description of some of the information currently available through the Consular Information Program:

Consular Information Sheets, Travel Warnings, and Public Announcements

Consular Information Sheets are issued for every country in the world. They include such information as the location of the U.S. embassy or consulate in the subject country, health conditions, political disturbances, unusual currency and entry regulations, crime and security information, and drug penalties.

The State Department also issues *Travel Warnings* and *Public Announcements*. Travel Warnings are issued when the State Department decides to recommend that Americans avoid travel to a certain country. Countries where avoidance of travel is recommended will have Travel Warnings as well as Consular Information Sheets. Public Announcements are issued as a means to disseminate information quickly about terrorist threats and other relatively short-term and/or transnational conditions posing significant risks to the security of American travelers.

Consular Information Sheets, Travel Warnings, and Public Announcements may be heard anytime by dialing (202) 647-5225 from a touch-tone phone. They are also available at U.S. embassies and consulates abroad, and through airline computer reservation systems, or, by writing and sending a self-addressed, stamped business-size envelope to the Office of Overseas Citizens Services, Bureau of Consular Affairs, Room 4811, U.S. Department of State, Washington, D.C. 20520-4818.

Top Ten Tips for Travelers

1. Make sure you have a signed, valid passport and visa, if required. Also, before you go, fill in the emergency information page of your passport!

2. Read the Consular Information Sheets (and Public Announcements or Travel Warnings, if applicable) for the countries you plan to visit. (See the section "Consular Information Program.")

3. Leave copies of your itinerary, passport data page and visas with family or friends at home, so that you can be contacted in case of an emergency.

4. Make sure you have insurance, which will cover your emergency medical needs, while you are overseas.

5. Familiarize yourself with local laws and customs of the countries to which you are traveling. Remember, while in a foreign country, you are subject to its laws!

6. Do not leave your luggage unattended in public areas and never accept packages from strangers.

7. While abroad, avoid using illicit drugs or drinking excessive amounts of alcoholic beverages, and associating with people who do.

8. Do not become a target for thieves by wearing conspicuous clothing and expensive jewelry and do not carry excessive amounts of cash or unnecessary credit cards.

9. Deal only with authorized agents when you exchange money or purchase art or antiques in order to avoid violating local laws.

10. When overseas, avoid demonstrations and other situations that may become unruly or where anti-American sentiments may be expressed. Q

61

Chapter 4

A Safe Trip Abroad

[The information in this chapter is reprinted verbatim from a bulletin issued
by the U.S. State Department, Bureau of Consular Affairs. It is intended to serve as advice
to Americans traveling abroad.]

Foreword

When you travel abroad, the odds are in your favor that you will have a safe and incident-free trip. However, crime and violence, as well as unexpected difficulties, do happen to U.S. citizens in all parts of the world. No one is better able to tell you this than the U.S. consular officers who work in more than 250 U.S. embassies and consulates around the globe. Every day of the year, U.S. embassies and consulates receive calls from American citizens in distress.

Happily, most problems can be solved over the telephone or by a visit of the U.S. citizen to the Consular Section of the nearest U.S. embassy or consulate. But, there are less fortunate occasions when U.S. diplomats are called on to meet U.S. citizens at foreign police stations, hospitals, prisons and even at morgues. In these cases, the assistance that diplomats can offer is specific but limited.

In the hope of helping you avoid serious difficulties during your abroad, we have prepared the following travel tips. Thank you for taking the time to become an informed traveler. We wish you a safe and wonderful journey!

BEFORE YOU GO

What to Bring

Safety begins when you pack. To avoid being a target, dress conservatively. Don't wear expensive looking jewelry. A flashy wardrobe or one that is too casual can mark you as a tourist. As much as possible, avoid the appearance of affluence.

Always try to travel light. You can move more quickly and will be more likely to have a free hand. You will also be less tired and less likely to set your luggage down, leaving it unattended.

Carry the minimum amount of valuables necessary for your trip and plan a place or places to conceal them. Your passport, cash and credit cards are most secure when locked in a hotel safe. When you have to carry them on your person, you may wish to conceal them in several places rather than putting them all in one wallet or pouch. Avoid handbags, fanny packs and outside pockets that are easy targets for thieves. Inside pockets and a sturdy shoulder bag with the strap worn across your chest are somewhat safer. One of the safest places to carry valuables is in a pouch or money belt worn under your clothing.

If you wear glasses, pack an extra pair. Bring them and any medicines you need in your carry-on luggage.

To avoid problems when passing through customs, keep medicines in their original, labeled containers. Bring copies of your prescriptions and the generic names for the drugs. If a medication is unusual or contains narcotics, carry a letter from your doctor attesting to your need to take the drug. If you have any doubt about the legality of carrying a certain drug into a country, consult the embassy or consulate of that country first.

Bring travelers checks and one or two major credit cards instead of cash.

Pack an extra set of passport photos along with a photocopy of your passport information page to make replacement of your passport easier in the event it is lost or stolen.

Put your name, address and telephone numbers inside and outside of each piece of luggage. Use covered luggage tags to avoid casual observation of your identity or nationality. If possible, lock your luggage.

Consider getting a telephone calling card. It is a convenient way of keeping in touch. If you have one, verify that you can use it from your overseas location(s). Access numbers to U.S. operators are published in many international newspapers. Find out your access number before you go.

What to Leave Behind

Don't bring anything you would hate to lose. Leave at home:

● valuable or expensive-looking jewelry,

● irreplaceable family objects,

● all unnecessary credit cards,

● Social Security card, library cards, and similar items you may routinely carry in your wallet.

Leave a copy of your itinerary with family or friends at home in case they need to contact you in an emergency.

A Few Things to Bring AND Leave Behind

Make two photocopies of your passport identification page, airline tickets, driver's license and the credit cards that you plan to bring with you. Leave one photocopy of this data with family or friends at home; pack the other in a place separate from where you carry your valuables.

Leave a copy of the serial numbers of your travelers' checks with a friend or relative at home. Carry your copy with you in a separate place and, as you cash the checks, cross them off the list.

What to Learn About Before You Go

Security. The Department of State's **Consular Information Sheets** are available for every country of the world. They describe entry requirements, currency regulations, unusual health conditions, the crime and security situation, political disturbances, areas of instability, and special information about driving and road conditions. They also provide addresses and emergency telephone numbers for U.S. embassies and consulates. In general, the Sheets do not give advice. Instead, they describe conditions so travelers can make informed decisions about their trips.

In some dangerous situations, however, the Department of State recommends that Americans defer travel to a country. In such a case, a **Travel Warning** is issued for the country in addition to its Consular Information Sheet. **Public Announcements** are a means to disseminate information about relatively short-term and/or trans-national conditions posing significant risks to the security of American travelers. They are issued when there is a perceived threat, even if it does not involve Americans as a particular target group. In the past, Public Announcements have been issued to deal with short-term coups, pre-election disturbances, violence by terrorists and anniversary dates of specific terrorist events.

You can access Consular Information Sheets, Travel Warnings and Public Announcements 24-hours a day in several ways.

Internet

The most convenient source of information about travel and consular services is the Consular Affairs home page. The web site address is http://travel.state.gov. If you do not have access to the Internet at home, work or school, your local library may provide access to the Internet.

Fax

From your fax machine, dial **(202) 647-3000**, using the handset as you would a regular telephone. The system will instruct you on how to proceed.

Telephone

Consular Information Sheets and Travel Warnings may be heard any time by dialing the office of American Citizens Services at **(202) 647-5225** from a touchtone phone.

In Person/By Mail

Consular Information Sheets, Travel Warnings and Public Announcements are available at any of the regional passport agencies and U.S. embassies and consulates abroad, or, by writing and sending a self-addressed, stamped envelope to the Office of American Citizens Services, Bureau of Consular Affairs, Room 4811, U.S. Department of State, Washington, D.C. 20520-4818.

Local Laws and Customs. When you leave the United States, you are subject to the laws of the country where you are. Therefore, before you go, learn as much as you can about the local laws and customs of the places you plan to visit. Good resources are your library, your travel agent, and the embassies, consulates or tourist bureaus of the countries you will visit. In addition, keep track of what is being reported in the media about recent developments in those countries.

THINGS TO ARRANGE BEFORE YOU GO

Your Itinerary. As much as possible, plan to stay in larger hotels that have more elaborate security. Safety experts recommend booking a room from the second to seventh floors above ground level to deter easy entrance from outside, but low enough for fire equipment to reach.

Because take-off and landing are the most dangerous times of a flight, book non-stop flights when possible. When there is a choice of airport or airline, ask your travel agent about comparative safety records.

Legal Documents. Have your affairs at home in order. If you leave a current will, insurance documents, and power of attorney with your family or a friend, you can feel secure about traveling and will be prepared for any emergency that may arise while you are away. If you have minor children, consider making guardianship arrangements for them.

Credit. Make a note of the credit limit on each credit card that you bring. Make certain not to charge over that amount on your trip. In some countries, Americans have been arrested for innocently exceeding their credit limit. Ask your credit card company how to report the loss of your card from abroad. 800 numbers do not work from abroad, but your company should have a number that you can call while you are overseas.

Insurance. Find out if your personal property insurance covers you for loss or theft abroad. More importantly, check on whether your health insurance covers you abroad. Medicare and Medicaid do not provide payment for medical care outside the U.S. Even if your health insurance will reimburse you for medical care that you pay for abroad, normal health insurance does not pay for medical evacuation from a remote area or from a country where medical facilities are inadequate. Consider purchasing one of the short-term health and emergency assistance policies designed for travelers. Also, make sure that the plan you purchase includes medical evacuation in the event of an accident or serious illness.

PRECAUTIONS TO TAKE WHILE TRAVELING

Safety on the Street

Use the same common sense traveling overseas that you would at home. Be especially cautious in or avoid areas where you are likely to be victimized. These include crowded subways, train stations, elevators, tourist sites, market places, festivals and marginal areas of cities.

Don't use short cuts, narrow alleys or poorly-lit streets. Try not to travel alone at night. Avoid public demonstrations and other civil disturbances.

Keep a low profile and avoid loud conversations or arguments. Do not discuss travel plans or other personal matters with strangers.

Avoid scam artists. Beware of strangers who approach you, offering bargains or to be your guide.
Beware of pickpockets. They often have an accomplice who will:

- jostle you,
- ask you for directions or the time,
- point to something spilled on your clothing,
- or distract you by creating a disturbance.

A child or even a woman carrying a baby can be a pickpocket. Beware of groups of vagrant children who create a distraction while picking your pocket. Wear the shoulder strap of your bag across your chest and walk with the bag away from the curb to avoid drive-by purse-snatchers.

Try to seem purposeful when you move about. Even if you are lost, act as if you know where you are going. When possible, ask directions only from individuals in authority.

Know how to use a pay telephone and have the proper change or token on hand.

Learn a few phrases in the local language so you can signal your need for help, the police, or a doctor. Make a note of emergency telephone numbers you may need: police, fire, your hotel, and the nearest U.S. embassy or consulate.

If you are confronted, don't fight back. Give up your valuables. Your money and passport can be replaced, but you cannot.

Safety in Your Hotel

Keep your hotel door locked at all times. Meet visitors in the lobby.

Do not leave money and other valuables in your hotel room while you are out. Use the hotel safe.

Let someone know when you expect to return if you are out late at night.

If you are alone, do not get on an elevator if there is a suspicious-looking person inside.

Read the fire safety instructions in your hotel room. Know how to report a fire. Be sure you know where the nearest fire exit and alternate exits are located. Count the doors between your room and the nearest exit. This could be a life saver if you have to crawl through a smoke-filled corridor.

Safety on Public Transportation

If a country has a pattern of tourists being targeted by criminals on public transport, that information is mentioned in the Consular Information Sheets under the "Crime Information" section.

Taxis. Only take taxis clearly identified with official markings. Beware of unmarked cabs.

Trains. Well organized, systematic robbery of passengers on trains along popular tourists routes is a serious problem. It is more common at night and especially on overnight trains.

If you see your way being blocked by a stranger and another person is very close to you from behind, move away. This can happen in the corridor of the train or on the platform or station.

Do not accept food or drink from strangers. Criminals have been known to drug food or drink offered to passengers. Criminals may also spray sleeping gas in train compartments.

Where possible, lock your compartment. If it cannot be locked securely, take turns sleeping in shifts with your traveling companions. If that is not possible, stay awake. If you must sleep unprotected, tie down your luggage, strap your valuables to you and sleep on top of them as much as possible.

Do not be afraid to alert authorities if you feel threatened in any way. Extra police are often assigned to ride trains on routes where crime is a serious problem.

Buses. The same type of criminal activity found on trains can be found on public buses on popular tourist routes. For example, tourists have been drugged and robbed while sleeping on buses or in bus stations. In some countries whole bus loads of passengers have been held up and robbed by gangs of bandits.

Safety When You Drive

When you rent a car, don't go for the exotic; choose a type commonly available locally. Where possible, ask that markings that identify it as a rental car be removed. Make certain it is in good repair. If available, choose a car with universal door locks and power windows, features that give the driver better control of access to the car. An air conditioner, when available, is also a safety feature, allowing you to drive with windows closed. Thieves can and do snatch purses through open windows of moving cars.

Keep car doors locked at all times. Wear seat belts.

As much as possible, avoid driving at night.

Don't leave valuables in the car. If you must carry things with you, keep them out of sight locked in the trunk.

Don't park your car on the street overnight. If the hotel or municipality does not have a parking garage or other secure area, select a well-lit area.

Never pick up hitchhikers.

Don't get out of the car if there are suspicious looking individuals nearby. Drive away.

Patterns of Crime Against Motorists

In many places frequented by tourists, including areas of southern Europe, victimization of motorists has been refined to an art. Where it is a problem , U.S. embassies are aware of it and consular officers try to work with local authorities

66

to warn the public about the dangers. In some locations, these efforts at public awareness have paid off, reducing the frequency of incidents. You may also wish to ask your rental car agency for advice on avoiding robbery while visiting tourist destinations.

Carjackers and thieves operate at gas stations, parking lots, in city traffic and along the highway. Be suspicious of anyone who hails you or tries to get your attention when you are in or near your car.

Criminals use ingenious ploys. They may pose as good Samaritans, offering help for tires that they claim are flat or that they have made flat. Or they may flag down a motorist, ask for assistance, and then steal the rescuer's luggage or car. Usually they work in groups, one person carrying on the pretense while the others rob you.

Other criminals get your attention with abuse, either trying to drive you off the road, or causing an "accident" by rear-ending you or creating a "fender bender."

In some urban areas, thieves don't waste time on ploys, they simply smash car windows at traffic lights, grab your valuables or your car and get away. In cities around the world, "defensive driving" has come to mean more than avoiding auto accidents; it means keeping an eye out for potentially criminal pedestrians, cyclists and scooter riders.

How to Handle Money Safely
To avoid carrying large amounts of cash, change your travelers' checks only as you need currency. Countersign travelers' checks only in front of the person who will cash them.

Do not flash large amounts of money when paying a bill. Make sure your credit card is returned to you after each transaction.

Deal only with authorized agents when you exchange money, buy airline tickets or purchase souvenirs. Do not change money on the black market.

If your possessions are lost or stolen, report the loss immediately to the local police. Keep a copy of the police report for insurance claims and as an explanation of your plight. After reporting missing items to the police, report the loss or theft of:

- travelers' checks to the nearest agent of the issuing company,
- credit cards to the issuing company,
- airline tickets to the airline or travel agent,
- passport to the nearest U.S. embassy or consulate.

How to Avoid Legal Difficulties
When you are in a foreign country, you are subject to its laws and are under its jurisdiction **NOT** the protection of the U.S. Constitution.

You can be arrested overseas for actions that may be either legal or considered minor infractions in the United States. Be aware of what is considered criminal in the country where you are. Consular Information Sheets include information on unusual patterns of arrests in various countries when appropriate.

Some of the offenses for which U.S. citizens have been arrested abroad are:

Drug Violations. More than 1/3 of U.S. citizens incarcerated abroad are held on drug charges. Some countries do not distinguish between possession and trafficking. Many countries have mandatory sentences - even for possession of a small amount of marijuana or cocaine. A number of Americans have been arrested for possessing prescription drugs, particularly tranquilizers and amphetamines, that they purchased legally in certain Asian countries and then brought to some countries in the Middle East where they are illegal. Other U.S. citizens have been arrested for purchasing prescription drugs abroad in quantities that local authorities suspected were for commercial use. If in doubt about foreign drug laws, ask local authorities or the nearest U.S. embassy or consulate.

Possession of Firearms. The places where U.S. citizens most often come into difficulties for illegal possession of firearms are nearby - Mexico, Canada and the Caribbean. Sentences for possession of firearms in Mexico can be up to 30 years. In general, firearms, even those legally registered in the U.S., cannot be brought into a country unless a permit is first obtained from the embassy or a consulate of that country and the

67

firearm is registered with foreign authorities on arrival. (Note: If you take firearms or ammunition to another country, you cannot bring them back into the U.S. unless you register them with U.S. Customs before you leave the U.S.)

Photography. In many countries you can be harassed or detained for photographing such things as police and military installations, government buildings, border areas and transportation facilities. If you are in doubt, ask permission before taking photographs.

Purchasing Antiques. Americans have been arrested for purchasing souvenirs that were, or looked like, antiques and which local customs authorities believed were national treasures. This is especially true in Turkey, Egypt and Mexico. In countries where antiques are important, document your purchases as reproductions if that is the case, or if they are authentic, secure the necessary export permit (usually from the national museum.)

Terrorism

Terrorist acts occur at random and unpredictably, making it impossible to protect yourself absolutely. The first and best protection is to avoid travel to unsafe areas where there has been a persistent record of terrorist attacks or kidnapping. The vast majority of foreign states have good records of maintaining public order and protecting residents and visitors within their borders from terrorism.

Most terrorist attacks are the result of long and careful planning. Just as a car thief will first be attracted to an unlocked car with the key in the ignition, terrorists are looking for defenseless, easily accessible targets who follow predictable patterns. The chances that a tourist, traveling with an unpublished program or itinerary, would be the victim of terrorism are slight. In addition, many terrorist groups, seeking publicity for political causes within their own country or region, may not be looking for American targets.

Nevertheless, the following pointers may help you avoid becoming a target of opportunity. They should be considered as adjuncts to the tips listed in the previous sections on how to protect yourself against the far greater likelihood of being a victim of crime. These precautions may provide some degree of protection, and can serve as practical and psychological deterrents to would-be terrorists.

- Schedule direct flights if possible and avoid stops in high-risk airports or areas. Consider other options for travel, such as trains.
- Be aware of what you discuss with strangers or what may be overheard by others.
- Try to minimize the time spent in the public area of an airport, which is a less protected area. Move quickly from the check-in counter to the secured areas. On arrival, leave the airport as soon as possible.
- As much as possible, avoid luggage tags, dress and behavior that may identify you as an American.
- Keep an eye out for suspicious abandoned packages or briefcases. Report them to airport security or other authorities and leave the area promptly.
- Avoid obvious terrorist targets such as places where Americans and Westerners are known to congregate.

Travel to High-Risk Areas

If you must travel in an area where there has been a history of terrorist attacks or kidnapping, make it a habit to:

- Discuss with your family what they would do in the event of an emergency. Make sure your affairs are in order before leaving home.
- Register with the U.S. embassy or consulate upon arrival.
- Remain friendly but be cautious about discussing personal matters, your itinerary or program.
- Leave no personal or business papers in your hotel room.
- Watch for people following you or "loiterers" observing your comings and goings.
- Keep a mental note of safehavens, such as police stations, hotels, hospitals.
- Let someone else know what your travel plans are. Keep them informed if you change your plans.
- Avoid predictable times and routes of travel and report any suspicious activity to local police, and the nearest U.S. embassy or consulate.
- Select your own taxi cabs at random. Don't take a vehicle that is not clearly identified as a taxi. Compare the face of the driver with the one posted on his or her license.
- If possible, travel with others.
- Be sure of the identity of visitors before opening the door of your hotel room. Don't meet strangers at unknown or remote locations.

68

- Refuse unexpected packages.
- Formulate a plan of action for what you will do if a bomb explodes or there is gunfire nearby.
- Check for loose wires or other suspicious activity around your car.
- Be sure your vehicle is in good operating condition in case you need to resort to high-speed or evasive driving.
- Drive with car windows closed in crowded streets. Bombs can be thrown through open windows.
- If you are ever in a situation where somebody starts shooting, drop to the floor or get down as low as possible. Don't move until you are sure the danger has passed. Do not attempt to help rescuers and do not pick up a weapon. If possible, shield yourself behind or under a solid object. If you must move, crawl on your stomach.

Hijacking/Hostage Situations

While every hostage situation is different, some considerations are important.

The U.S. government's policy is firm. We will negotiate, but not make concessions - to do so would only increase the risk of further hostage-taking. When Americans are abducted overseas, we look to the host government to exercise its responsibility under international law to protect all persons within its territories and to bring about the safe release of hostages. We work closely with these governments from the outset of a hostage-taking incident to ensure that our citizens and other innocent victims are released as quickly and safely as possible.

Normally, the most dangerous phases of a hijacking or hostage situation are the beginning and, if there is a rescue attempt, the end. At the outset, the terrorists typically are tense, high-strung and may behave irrationally. It is extremely important that you remain calm and alert and manage your own behavior.

Avoid resistance and sudden or threatening movements. Do not struggle or try to escape unless you are certain of being successful.

- Make a concerted effort to relax. Prepare yourself mentally, physically and emotionally for the possibility of a long ordeal.
- Try to remain inconspicuous, avoid direct eye contact and the appearance of observing your captors' actions.
- Avoid alcoholic beverages. Consume little food and drink.
- Consciously put yourself in a mode of passive cooperation. Talk normally. Do not complain, avoid belligerency, and comply with all orders and instructions.
- If questioned, keep your answers short. Don't volunteer information or make unnecessary overtures.
- Don't try to be a hero, endangering yourself and others.
- Maintain your sense of personal dignity and gradually increase your requests for personal comforts. Make these requests in a reasonable low-key manner.
- If you are involved in a lengthier, drawn-out situation, try to establish a rapport with your captors, avoiding political discussions or other confrontational subjects.
- Establish a daily program of mental and physical activity. Don't be afraid to ask for anything you need or want - medicines, books, pencils, papers.
- Eat what they give you, even if it does not look or taste appetizing. A loss of appetite and weight is normal.
- Think positively. Avoid a sense of despair. Rely on your inner resources. Remember that you are a valuable commodity to your captors. It is important to them to keep you alive and well.

ASSISTANCE ABROAD

If you plan to stay more than two weeks in one place, if you are in an area experiencing civil unrest or a natural disaster, or, if you are planning travel to a remote area, it is advisable to register at the Consular Section of the nearest U.S. embassy or consulate. This will make it easier if someone at home needs to locate you urgently or in the unlikely event that you need to be evacuated in an emergency. It will also facilitate the issuance of a new passport should yours be lost or stolen.

The Consular Section can provide updated information on the security situation in a country.

If you are ill or injured, contact the nearest U.S. embassy or consulate for a list of local physicians and medical facilities. If the illness is serious, consular officers can help you find medical assistance from this list and, at your request, will inform your family or friends. If necessary, a consul can assist in the transfer of funds from family or friends in the United States. Payment of hospital and other medical expenses is your responsibility.

If you run out of money overseas and have no other options, consular officers can help you get in touch with your family, friends, bank or employer and inform them how to wire funds to you.

Should you find yourself in legal difficulty, contact a consular officer immediately. Consular officers cannot serve as attorneys, give legal advice, or get you out of jail. What they can do is provide a list of local attorneys who speak English and who may have had experience in representing U.S. citizens. If you are arrested, consular officials will visit you, advise you of your rights under local laws and ensure that you are held under humane conditions and are treated fairly under local law. A consular officer will contact your family or friends if you desire. When necessary, consuls can transfer money from home for you and will try to get relief for you, including food and clothing in countries where this is a problem. If you are detained, remember that under international treaties and customary international law, you have the right to talk to the U.S. consul. If you are denied this right, be persistent. Try to have someone get in touch for you.

Planning Another Trip?

See Chapter 36 for a listing of resources available to the general traveler from the U.S. Departments of State, Customs, Transportation, Health and various government and non-government organizations. Almost all of the available International travel-related pamphlets, brochures and publications issued by the U.S. Department of State and by the U.S. Customs have been reproduced in full in this book. See Table of Contents for location.

Chapter 5

Know Before You Go: U.S. State Department Hints

*[The information in this chapter is an excerpt from a bulletin issued by the
U.S. State Department, Bureau of Consular Affairs. It is intended to serve as advice
to Americans traveling abroad.]*

Soon you'll be experiencing the joys of international travel--meeting new people, exploring foreign lands, and discovering different cultures.

And whether you're a seasoned traveler or making your first trip abroad, you want your foreign experience to be as relaxing and enjoyable as possible.

That's why you should take the time to learn about the country you'll be visiting before you go, and use this chapter to help plan and guide you through your journey.

Inside you'll find up-to-date information on passports, foreign laws and customs, personal safety, and helpful travel tips.

Remember, the more you know before you go, the less likely you are to encounter difficulties while you're away.

I GETTING READY

(a) PASSPORTS AND VISA

Imagine the freedom a passport can give you-- taking off to an exotic country on a moment's notice. Every American citizen who anticipates traveling abroad should have a valid U.S. passport. It's easy to get a passport or renew one. It is the best documentation you can have while traveling overseas, and it is usually required to depart or enter the United States and most foreign countries. For detailed information on Passports See Chapter 2.

TIP:

If you plan to travel during the peak vacation season
(March-June), you should apply as soon as possible.

Allow several weeks for delivery to avoid unnecessary delays.

WILL I NEED A VISA?

Many countries require a visa--an official authorization stamped within the passport that permits travel within a country for a specified purpose and a limited time.

To find out if you need a visa:
*Contact the country's embassy or consulate here in the United States for the most up-to-date information on visa requirements

*Ask your travel agent

For written information on visa requirements, write to:

> Foreign Entry Requirements[1]
> Consumer Information Center
> Pueblo, CO 81009

Be sure to enclose 50 cents with your request for Foreign Entry Requirements.

(b) CASH, TRAVELER'S CHECKS AND CREDIT CARDS

Don't take chances carrying large amounts of cash when you travel. Protect yourself from loss and theft by using traveler's checks and credit cards.

Traveler's checks are the preferred alternative to cash. Buy them at your bank and use them as you would cash. When using traveler's checks, always remember to record the serial number, denominations, date and location of where they were purchased. Keep this information in a separate place so replacement checks can be issued quickly if they are lost or stolen. For convenience, carry $10 and $20 denominations with you.

It's helpful to know that most major credit cards are accepted abroad. If you plan to use credit cards on your trip, verify your available credit limit **before you leave the United States.** Avoid the potential embarrassment of overdrawing, having your card confiscated, or possibly being arrested. Many travelers mistakenly exceed their limit by overcharging and making cash withdrawals. Be sure to keep track of **all** your transactions. Take only those credit cards that can be used overseas; leave the rest at home.

BEFORE YOU GO...

Photocopy your passport descriptive data page and the contents of your wallet (credit cards, licenses, and insurance numbers). Keep this record in a separate place so if documents are lost or stolen, you can speed the replacement process.

Purchase a small amount of foreign currency for taxis, telephone calls, tips, etc. Most international airports have 24-hour currency exchange windows.

If you are bringing more than $10,000 out of the United States in coins, currency, or traveler's checks, you **must** file a report with U.S. Customs Service.

TIP:

Bring along a pocket calculator to help convert currencies.

(c) MEDICAL CARE, MEDICINES, IMMUNIZATIONS

Some foreign countries may require international certificates of vaccination. Depending on the areas you'll be visiting, you may be advised to carry special medication or follow other preventive steps to ensure your well-being. Be sure to ask your doctor or the local public health department for vaccination requirements of specific countries. Or, call the Centers for Disease Control in Atlanta at (404) 639-2572.

GET A HEALTHY START ON YOUR TRIP WHILE YOU'RE STILL IN THE STATES.

Take precautions to prevent yourself from becoming ill while you are abroad. Get a medical and dental checkup before your trip and make sure you are up-to-date with the following immunizations:

[] Measles [] Mumps
[] Rubella [] Diphtheria
[] Polio [] Tetanus
[] Whooping Cough

BE PREPARED

If you have allergies or other medical conditions, be sure to take along an ample supply of medication, and keep it in a carry-on bag. Don't make the common mistake of packing all your medications in your suitcase, which can get lost or stolen. Before you go, you may obtain a list of English-speaking doctors for the areas you plan to visit. Contact the International Association for Medical Assistance to Travelers for such a list at (716) 754-4883. [A listing of other Medical Assistance Organizations is provided in 3C.

BE AWARE

If you are planning to take any prescription drugs on your trip, check with your doctor, or the embassies of the countries you are visiting to ensure you do not violate foreign laws. Many travelers have been innocently arrested for possessing drugs not considered to be narcotic in the United States, but that are illegal in other countries, You can ask your doctor for a certificate attesting to your need to make customs processing easier. Note, however, that this may not be enough authorization to transport drugs into some foreign countries.

IMPORTANT TIPS TO REMEMBER...

Always leave medicines in original labeled containers. Ask your pharmacists for the generic name of any prescribed drug in case you need to refill the prescription. Brand names differ in other countries.

If you are allergic to certain medication, insect or snake bites wear a medical alert bracelet and carry a similar warning in your wallet.

If you wear glasses or contact lenses, bring an extra pair along with your lens prescription and ample supplies of lens solution and cleaner.

If you become injured or seriously ill abroad, a U.S. consular officer can help you find a physician. He or she can arrange the transfer of funds from your family or friends in the United States to pay for your treatment.

Carry a summary of your medical records. Be sure to include past illnesses and blood type.

An increasing number of countries are establishing entry regulations for AIDS, particularly for students and other long-term residents. Check with the embassy or consulate of the individual country to see if this applies to you.

INSURANCE

Enjoying yourself abroad means having your worries at home. That's why you should check with your insurance company to make sure your policy provides adequate medical coverage for you and your family. Did you know that Medicare programs do not provide payment for hospitals or medical services outside the United States? Check with your state insurance association for information on available protection plans for international travelers. The State Department recommends that you purchase the full available automobile insurance policy if you plan to drive. If you plan to rent a car while abroad, consider hiring a driver. In many countries the driver is detained in an accident until settlement is made.

Here are some important questions you should ask your insurance agent, travel agent, and automobile insurance agent:

Am I protected against trip cancellation, interruption, and baggage loss?

Will my medical expenses be covered if I incur an injury or illness while traveling abroad?

Will I be reimbursed for my flight if I have to curtail my trip due to an emergency?

Do I need additional automobile coverage if I am . going to be driving abroad?

Will I need additional life insurance coverage while overseas?

Will I need a driver's license?

TIP:

> If you plan to drive an automobile while in a foreign country, check with the Automobile Association of America (AAA) to see if you'll need an international driver's license and to find out where you can purchase supplemental insurance coverage, as needed. [For information on how to obtain an International Drivers License as well as where to purchase travel insurance See **Appendices K & 2B** respectively.]

BEFORE YOU GO

Protecting Yourself

Sometimes peace of mind can be just a phone call away. If you have any concerns or questions about local conditions or your destination, call the Department of State's Citizens Emergency Center as (202) 647-5225 for 24-hour-a-day recordings of all current travel advisories. You can also obtain travel advisories from U.S. passport agencies, or U.S. Embassies and consulates abroad. The Citizens Emergency Center also provides information on emergency services to U.S. citizens overseas. [See **Chapter 29** for additional information.]

TIP:

> Once you've reached your destination, if you have problems or concerns, visit the American Embassy to register. Let them know where you are staying, the areas you plan to visit, and when you will be returning to the United States.

II   WHILE YOU'RE ABROAD

(a) BE SMART!

When you're having a wonderful time in a new environment it's easy to let your guard down. That's why you need to use your common sense and be extra conscious of you actions so you do not become and easy target for crime.

Here are some precautions to take while traveling in a foreign country:

73

Keep a low profile. This means leaving your valuables, expensive jewelry, and luggage at home. These items might mark you as a wealthy or important American.

Avoid dangerous areas. Don't use short-cuts or walk down narrow alleys or poorly lit streets.

Never travel alone after dark. Always let someone know where you are going, and what time you expect to return, especially at night.

Meet visitors in the lobby of your hotel. Don't give out your room number. Always keep your hotel and car doors locked.

Carry belongings in a secure manner. Women should wear handbags tucked under their arm and hold the strap. Men should put their wallets in their front trouser pocket or wear a money belt.

Don't carry valuables in coat pockets, handbags, or hip pockets which are particularly susceptible to theft.

Avoid using "gypsy" taxis that pick up more that one person per cab. Use a hotel or airport taxi. If there is no meter, always agree on the fare in advance.

Be wary of street vendors. While one has your attention selling you goods, someone else may be picking your pocket.

Book hotel rooms between the second and seventh floors to prevent easy entrance from the outside, but low enough for fire equipment to reach. Check out the fire safety instructions and the exits.

If you have a problem, the local police department is the best place to go for help.

Learn a few important phrases in the local language so you can signal for fire, the police, the doctor, or the nearest bathroom.

Avoid displaying company name or logos on luggage and tags.

BE ALERT!

(b) GETTING TO KNOW FOREIGN LAWS

Be a Considerate Guest

Visiting a foreign country exposes you to different customs and different laws. That's why you should familiarize yourself with the local regulations before you go. Don't assume that what is acceptable in the United States is acceptable abroad. For example, some countries are particularly sensitive about photographs. It's best to refrain from taking pictures of police, military installations and personnel, or industrial structures unless you know for certain that it will not offend anyone, or break any laws. Check around to see what is considered appropriate clothing. What's acceptable in the United States may offensive elsewhere. And before you decide to sell personal effects such as clothing, cameras, or jewelry, make sure that the local law permits you to do so.

(c) BE INFORMED!

On the average, 2700 Americans are arrested abroad each year. About one-third are held on drug charges. **Do Not Get Involved With Illegal Drugs.** The consequences are serious. If arrested, you will be subject to local, not U.S. laws.

KNOW THE LAWS ABOUT ARREST LAWS!

Many countries do not provide a jury trial or accept bail, which means you may endure lengthy pretrial detention.

Prison conditions overseas can be harsh. Some lack minimal comforts, such as beds, toilets, and wash basins.

Officials may not speak English.

Diets are often inadequate. Payment for food and amenities may be expected.

Inhumane treatment and extortion are possible.

Depending upon your offense, if convicted of a drug charge, you could face up to 10 years in prison with a minimum of 6 years of hard labor, and stiff fines in some countries. The death penalty is possible in others.

(D) GETTING LEGAL AID ABROAD

If you are arrested, the U.S. Embassy or consulate will do what it can to protect your legitimate interests and ensure you are not discriminated against, but cannot pay your legal fees or get you out of jail. A list of local attorneys can be provided by a U.S. consular officer. However, neither the state Department nor the U.S. consular officer can act as your attorney or assume responsibility for the professional competence of local attorneys.

(e) DO'S AND DON'TS AT THE AIRPORT

Traveling abroad means you'll be spending time in foreign airports--going through customs, exchanging money and waiting for flights. That's why you should take a moment to review these practical tactics.

...... DO

Proceed to boarding gate as soon as possible.

Secure belongings.

Keep your distance from unattended luggage.

Keep a low profile, behave quietly and inconspicuously.

Be alert. Survey your surroundings and check out emergency exits.

...... DON'T

Discuss travel plans indiscriminately.

Leave bags unattended, even for a minute.

Carry any bags or packages for strangers or friends unless you are certain of what is inside.

Carry all your money in one place.

(f) WHEN EXCHANGING YOUR CURRENCY

Deal only with authorized outlets when you exchange money, or buy airline tickets or traveler's checks. Shop around for the best exchange rate.

If your passport, credit cards, or traveler's checks are stolen or lost, notify the **local police** at once! Apply for replacement passport at the nearest U.S. Embassy or consulate as soon a possible. If credit cards or traveler's checks are lost, contact the issuing companies promptly.

(g) WHAT TO DO IF THERE IS AN INCIDENT:

Try to remain calm and inconspicuous. Do not move until the situation is under control. Be passive, yet remain alert.

Avoid confrontation. Do not engage in political discussions or volunteer information.

Comply with requests. If you must surrender personal belongings, do so without a struggle.

Make any requests you may have in short, simple sentences.

If there is a rescue attempt, stay as close to the ground as possible.

Do not try to be a hero.

(h) TRAVEL CHECKLIST

Let's review some important details to consider before you leave the country. Take a moment to go through this checklist.

1. Is your passport valid? Will it be valid throughout the duration of your trip abroad? Do you have the necessary visas?

2. Are all your travel plans set--from tickets to seating arrangements to hotels to itinerary?

3. Does your family or a close friend know your specific travel plans? Did you leave a copy of your passport, credit cards and traveler's checks numbers?

4. Is your attire appropriate for your destination, that is, comfortable and conservative without indicating your nationality or religion?

5. Do you know the local conditions of your destination? Are there travel advisories for

the areas you'll be visiting?

6. Are you aware of the cultural and political differences of the areas you are visiting to avoid any misunderstandings and potential difficulties? For instance, in some Middle East countries, high fashion magazines are considered pornography!

7. Have you reviewed with a family member or close friend what is to be done in case of an emergency?

TIP:

If you are planning to bring valuables on your trip (watch, jewelry, cameras) check with U.S. Customs regarding registration requirements and proper proof of ownership. **Always** obtain a receipt before buying any foreign item, especially antiques.

AMERICAN CHILDREN ABROAD

If you plan to bring your children overseas, it is important that they become familiar with the local laws and customs. Foreign languages, symbols, and signs can be very confusing to young children. Be sure to prepare them well in advance for the differences they will encounter. Here are some common sense issues to discuss with your children before leaving the United States and once you have reached your destinations.

1. Make sure young children know the name and the address of the place where they are staying. A sample child I.D. a Form/Card has been provided. It should be filled out on both sides by an adult and kept in a safe place on your child at all times.

2. Using a foreign telephone can be confusing to a child. Show your child how to use the telephone, and be sure he or she has enough money to make several calls if needed.

3. Go over with your child who to call or approach in an emergency situation. These numbers and addresses should be kept on his or her I.D. card and, if possible, memorized. Point out a local, uniformed police officer to your child so he ore she will be able to recognize one.

4. Discuss traffic rules with your child. Red lights don't always necessarily mean stop.

5. Make sure your child is aware of the dangers of electrical outlets, appliances, and TVs that operate on strong current overseas.

6. Do not let your child go anywhere alone. Enforce the "Buddy System" and explain the importance of always being aware of his or her surroundings.

7. In crowded places such as open market, busy streets, and airports, keep your child close by. Always have a designated spot to meet in case you get separated.

RESOURCES FOR OVERSEAS TRAVELERS
See Chapter 36

THE BUREAU OF CONSULAR AFFAIRS PUBLISHES A VARIETY OF INTERNATIONAL TRAVEL BROCHURES, MOST OF THEM FREE-OF-CHARGE. See Chapter 36 for a listing.

Chapter 6

Security Awareness Overseas

[The information in this chapter is reprinted verbatim from a bulletin issued by the
U.S. State Department, Bureau of Diplomatic Security. It is intended to serve as advice
to Americans traveling abroad.]

Introduction

Personal security abroad is a major concern of individuals and companies. Information in this chapter, and infact the entire book should make a strong contribution to the security and well-being of American citizens who live and work abroad.

This chapter is intended as a guideline for business persons in the private sector who travel or reside abroad.

A rapidly changing political world has not lessened the attention one should pay to personal security when overseas. Natural disasters will continue, as will acts of terrorism. Indeed, one might expect increased incidents of civil unrest, some directed against Americans, as political situations remain unresolved. The guidelines, which follow, are suggested to assist American companies and their personnel abroad in planning to meet their individual needs and circumstances. Individuals should ensure, however, that any approach chosen is best suited to their individual situation.

Take the time to think through your upcoming travel and to use this chapter to plan for emergencies and other special contingencies. Hopefully, you will never be required to act upon your plan, but if an emergency does develop, the time spent planning may ensure your safety and that of your family.

Introduction

We gain a great sense of security and self confidence knowing we are prepared for potential crises. This chapter provides assistance in preparing us to face those emergencies we may encounter while living or traveling overseas. Many potential overseas crises may be eased or averted by taking the time to read and study the information that follows.

Cultural misunderstandings and inadequate local support services often make crises abroad more intense than similar situations in the United States. Overseas, we must assume greater responsibility for our own safety.

Information and suggestions in this chapter have been collected from several government and private sources. Personal experiences of those who have been through particular crises abroad have added substantially to the store of ideas and advice. The experience of each-whether hostage, crime victim, evacuee, or other-is distinct. Yet there are common threads that provide guidelines on how to handle crises successfully. We hope, in this chapter, to pass those guidelines on to you.

Although we have attempted to organize tips and information according to whether your stay will be temporary or permanent, most apply to either situation.

Preparing To Travel

Have Your Affairs in Order
Many hostages have expressed regret that their affairs were not left in better order for their families. An evacuation, illness, or death can often place a family in a similar situation. Three actions, taken before you depart, will alleviate this potential problem:

> Discuss and plan with your family what should be done in the case of any emergency separation. All adult family members should be aware of these plans.

> Supply family and close friends with the emergency notification numbers found on

this page. They serve both to notify you while you are overseas in the event of an illness or death in your family in the United States and to provide your family in the U.S. with information about you in case of a crisis abroad.

See that all important papers are up-to-date. List papers and leave originals with a family member or attorney in the United States. Carry only copies to your overseas assignment. Safe deposit boxes and bank accounts are very useful but may be sealed on the death of an owner. Therefore, make sure your representative has joint right of access.

Important Papers

Your collection of important papers might include:
Will
Birth and marriage certificates
Guardianship or adoption papers for children
Power of attorney for spouse or relative
Naturalization papers
Deeds, mortgages, stocks and bonds, car titles
Insurance papers-car, home, life, personal effects, medical
Tax records
Proof of termination of previous marriage(s)
Child support/alimony agreements Proof of membership in any organization or union that entitles the estate to any benefits

Useful Information

An Information List might include:
Bank account numbers and addresses
Passport numbers
Duplicate passport pictures in case passport needs to be replaced due to loss
U.S. and local driver's license numbers
Insurance policy numbers and names of carriers
Social Security numbers
Credit card numbers
Travelers check numbers and issuing bank
Medical and dental information, distinguishing marks and scars, and medicine and eyeglass prescriptions
Assets and debts
Names and addresses of business and professional contacts

Updated inventory of household and personal possessions with pictures/videos
Employment records for each family member; resumes, references, commendations
Personal address list
Fingerprints, current photos/videos, voice recording, known handwriting samples of family members

Emergency Notification

While abroad, you may need to be notified of an emergency involving someone in the United States. And during a political, social, or natural crisis abroad, your family in the United States will be anxious to get news of you.

The appropriate telephone numbers below should be given to your family for such purposes.
U.S. Embassy/consulate
...... (Day)
...... (Night)
U.S. Corporate HQ
...... (Day)
...... (Night)
Corporate Security
Local Legal Counsel
Local Police
Airline(s)
Red Cross
Department of State
Host Country Embassy, Washington, D.C.
Local Company Office
Residence
International Operator
Relatives

Before initiating calls, the caller in the United States should have the following information available:
Your name, company, and current location
Name and relationship of family member
In case of death-Date of death
In case of illness-Name, address, and telephone number of attending physician or hospital

Miscellaneous Tips

The corporate traveler should also consider the following, which will assist and possibly protect him/her during the actual journey:
Obtain International Driving Permit.

Prepare a wallet card identifying your blood type, known allergies, required medications, insurance company, and name of person to contact in case of emergency.

Remove from wallet all credit cards and other items not necessary for trip.

Remove unessential papers, such as reserve, military, or humorous cards, e.g., "Honorary Sheriff."

Put a plain cover on your passport (covers available in stationery stores);

Use hard, lockable luggage.

Be sure luggage tags contain your name, phone number, and full street address; that information is concealed from casual observation; and that company logos are not displayed on luggage.

Inform family member or friend of specific travel plans. Give your office a complete itinerary. Be sure to notify the local company manager of your travel plans.

Obtain the name(s) and address(es) of your local ...... office(s).

Obtain small amount of local currency if possible.

Be aware of airline safety records when booking vacation trips while overseas; do not include company name in reservation.

When possible, mail personal papers to yourself at the local overseas office.

Stay informed! Check for any travel advisories pertinent to countries you plan to visit. Call the Department of State's Citizens Emergency Center (see Chapter 29), or your company's Corporate Security Department.

In Transit

Most of the following suggestions apply to any travel; several are specifically directed at surviving a terrorist situation. It is recognized that the level of risk varies from country to country and time to time, so that you may need to choose among the suggested options or modify the concepts to meet your needs.

If you plan to stay in one country any length of time while traveling, especially in a country that is in a period of civil unrest, register with the embassy or consulate and provide a copy of your itinerary. Registration makes it easier to contact you in case of an emergency and to evacuate you if necessary.

On the Plane

Carry-on luggage should contain a supply of any regularly taken prescription medicines (in original containers labeled with the pharmacy name and prescribing physician), an extra pair of eyeglasses, passport, and carefully chosen personal documents (copies only!).

Dress inconspicuously to blend into the international environment.

Consider wearing no jewelry.

On foreign carriers, avoid speaking English as much as possible. Do not discuss business or travel plans with fellow passengers, crew, or even traveling companions. Select a window seat in the coach section. This position is less accessible by hijackers inflicting indiscriminate violence.

Memorize your passport number so you do not have to reveal your passport when filling out landing cards.

At an Overseas Airport

Maintain a low profile, and avoid public areas as much as possible. Check in quickly and do not delay in the main terminal area. Do not discuss travel plans indiscriminately.

Stay away from unattended baggage. Verify baggage claim checks before and after flight. Always maintain custody of your carry-on bag.

Survey surroundings, noting exits and safe areas.

If an incident occurs, survival may depend on your ability to remain calm and alert. During a terrorist attack or rescue operation, you do not want to be confused with the terrorists and shot. Avoid sudden moves; hide behind something and drop to floor.

Car Rentals

Ideally, choose a conservative model car with locking trunk, hood, and gas cap; power brakes and steering; seat belts; quick accelerating engine; heavy duty bumpers; smooth interior locks. In a hot climate, choose air conditioning. Keep the gas tank at least half full.

Before getting into the car, examine it for strange

objects or wires inside, around, or underneath it. If found, do not touch; clear the area and call police.

When driving, lock the doors, keep windows rolled up, avoid being boxed in by other cars. Vary routes. Check for suspicious individuals before getting out of the car.

Lock the car when unattended. Never let anyone place a package inside or enter the car unless you are present.

Public Transportation

Stay on your guard against pickpockets and petty thieves while in a bus/train terminal or at a taxi stop. Avoid carrying a wallet in your hip or easily accessible coat pocket. Carry a purse/handbag that you may firmly grip or secure to your body. Beware of people jostling you at busy stations.

Take only licensed taxis. Generally those found in front of terminals and the better hotels are the safest. You may pay a bit more, but the companies are reputable and normally the drivers have been screened. Be sure the photo on displayed license is of the driver. Have the address of your destination written out in local language and carry it with you. Get a map and learn the route to your destination; note if taxi driver takes you a different or longer way.

Try not to travel alone in a taxi, and never get out in deserted areas. If the door doesn't lock, sit near the middle of the seat so you will thwart thieves who might open the door to grab a purse, briefcase, or wallet.

On subways, choose a middle car but never an empty car. On buses, sit in an aisle seat near the driver. Stand back from the curb while waiting for a bus.

Avoid arriving anywhere at night and using dim or vacant entrances to stations or terminals. Utilize only busy, well-lit stations.

Take as little luggage as possible; ideally, no more than you can comfortably carry.

In-Transit Accommodations

Accommodations in many countries differ considerably from those found in North America and Western Europe. Safety features required in

U.S. hotels, such as sprinkler systems, fire stairwells, and emergency lighting, often are either lacking or inoperable. The following measures will enable you to better plan for unforeseen contingencies in hotels.

Hotel Crime

Stay alert in your hotel. Put the "do not disturb" sign on your door to give the impression that the room is occupied. Call the maid when you are ready for the room to be cleaned. Consider leaving the light or TV on when you are out of the room. Carry the room key with you instead of leaving it at front desk. Do not use your name when answering the phone. Do not accept packages or open the door to workmen without verification from the front desk.

When walking, remain on wide, well-lit streets. Know where you are going when you leave the hotel-if on a tour, enlist a reputable guide. Generally, the hotel will recommend or procure one. Do not take shortcuts through alleys or off the beaten path. If alone, be back in the hotel by dark. Never resist armed robbery; it could lead to violence. Always carry some cash to appease muggers who may resort to violence at finding no reward for their efforts.

Civil Unrest

In some areas of the world, civil unrest or violence directed against Americans and other foreigners is common. Travelers should be alert to indicators of civil unrest and take the following precautions in the event of such situations:

If in your hotel, stay there. Contact the U.S. Embassy, consulate or other friendly embassy. Hire someone to take a note to them if phones are out of order.

Contact your local office representative.

Do not watch activity from your window, and try to sleep in an inside room which provides greater protection from gunfire, rocks, grenades, etc.

If you are caught outside in the middle of a riot or unrest, do not take sides or attempt to gather information. Play the tourist who just wants to get home to his/her family.

80

Hotel Fires

Many hotels abroad are not as fire-resistant as those in the United States. Interior materials are often extremely flammable. Escape routes may not be posted in hallways and exits may be few or sealed. Fire fighting equipment and water supplies may be limited. There may be no fast method for

alerting a fire department. Sprinkler systems and smoke detectors may be nonexistent.

You must aggressively take responsibility for the safety of yourself and your family. Think "contingency plan" and discuss it with your dependents. Begin planning your escape from a fire as soon as you check in to a hotel. When a fire occurs, you can then act without panic and without wasting time.

Stay in the most modern hotel; consider a U.S. chain. Request a lower floor, ideally the second or third. Selecting a room no higher than the second floor enables you to jump to safety. Although most fire departments can reach above the second floor, they may not get to you in time or position a fire truck on your side of the building.

Locate exits and stairways as soon as you check in; be sure the doors open. Count the number of doors between your room and exit or stairway. In a smoke-filled hallway, you could have to "feel" your way to an exit. Form a mental map of your escape route.

If the hotel has a fire alarm system, find the nearest alarm. Be sure you know how to use it. You may have to activate it in the dark or in dense smoke.

Ensure that your room windows open and that you know how the latches work. Look out the window and mentally rehearse your escape through it. Make note of any ledges or decks that will aid escape.

Check the smoke detector by pushing the test button. If it does not work, have it fixed or move to another room. Better yet, carry your own portable smoke detector (with the battery removed while traveling). Place it in your room by the hall door near the ceiling.

Keep the room key and a flashlight on the bedside table so that you may locate the key quickly if you have to leave your room.

If a Fire Starts

If you awake to find smoke in your room, grab your key and crawl to the door on your hands and knees. Don't stand-smoke and deadly gases rise while the fresher air will be near the floor.

Before you open the door, feel it with the palm of your hand. If the door or knob is hot, the fire may be right outside. Open the door slowly. Be ready to slam it shut if the fire is close by. If your exit path is clear, crawl into the hallway. Be sure to close the door behind you to keep smoke out in case you have to return to your room. Take your key, as most hotel doors lock automatically. Stay close to the wall to avoid being trampled.

Do not use elevators during a fire. They may malfunction, or if they have heat-activated call buttons, they may take you directly to the fire floor.

As you make your way to the fire exit, stay on the same side as the exit door. Count the doors to the exit.

When you reach the exit, walk down the stairs to the first floor. Hold onto the handrail for guidance and protection from being knocked down by other occupants.

If you encounter heavy smoke in the stairwell, don't try to run through it. You may not make it. Instead, turn around and walk up to the roof fire exit. Prop the door open to ventilate the stairwell and to keep from being locked out. Find the windward side of the roof, sit down, and wait for fire fighters to find you.

If all exits are blocked or if there is heavy smoke in the hallway, you'll be better off staying in your room. If there is smoke in your room, open a window and turn on the bathroom vent. Don't break the window unless it can't be opened. You might want to close the window later to keep smoke out, and broken glass could injure you or people below.

If your phone works, call the desk to tell someone where you are, or call the fire department to report

81

your location in the building. Hang a bed sheet out the window as a signal.

Fill the bathtub with water to use for fire fighting. Bail water onto your door or any hot walls with an ice bucket or waste basket. Stuff wet towels into cracks under and around doors where smoke can enter. Tie a wet towel over your mouth and nose to help filter out smoke. If there is fire outside your window, take down the drapes and move everything combustible away from the window.

If you are above the second floor, you probably will be better off fighting the fire in your room than jumping. A jump from above the third floor may result in severe injury or death.

Remember that panic and a fire's byproducts, such as super-heated gases and smoke, present a greater danger than the fire itself. If you know your plan of escape in advance, you will be less likely to panic and more likely to survive.

Terrorism

Although for most of us it is not a probability, terrorism is a fact. The likelihood of terrorist incidents varies according to country or area of the world, generally depending on the

stability of the local government and the degree of frustration felt by indigenous groups or individuals.

Although the number of incidents worldwide has increased at the rate of 10 percent per year, less than a quarter of these have been directed against American businesses or their employees. Most acts of terrorism are directed against citizens of the country where they occur.

When an act of terrorism does occur, it often has dire consequences: murder, hostage taking, property destruction. Much has been learned about the mentality of terrorists, their methods of operation, and the behavior patterns of both victims and perpetrators.

Alert individuals, prepared for possible terrorist acts, can minimize the likelihood that these acts will be successfully carried out against them. While there is no absolute protection against terrorism, there are a number of reasonable precautions that can provide some degree of individual protection.

U.S. Policy

U.S. policy is firmly committed to resisting terrorist blackmail.

The U.S. Government will not pay ransom for the release of hostages. It will not support the freeing of prisoners from incarceration in response to terrorist demands. The U.S. Government will not negotiate with terrorists on the substance of their demands, but it does not rule out contact and dialogue with hostage takers if this will promote the safe release of hostages.

In terrorist incidents abroad affecting Americans, our government looks to the host government to provide for the safety of U.S. citizens in accordance with international agreements.

The U.S. Government is prepared to offer terrorist experts, specialized assistance, military equipment, and personnel should the foreign government decide such assistance could be useful.

Terrorist Demands

U.S. Government policy is to make no concessions to terrorist demands. However, such a decision on the part of private individuals or companies is a personal one and in some special circumstances may be made by the family or company of the victim. Whatever the decision, it should conform to local law.

Terrorist Surveillance

Terrorists may shadow an intended victim at length and with infinite patience before an actual abduction or assassination is attempted. Initial surveillance efforts may be clumsy and could be spotted by an alert target. In most cases, more than one individual is a likely candidate for the terrorist act. Usually the choice is based on the probability of success. In one documented instance, both an American and another country's representative were under surveillance. Though the American was the first choice of the terrorists, their surveillance showed that it would be more difficult to kidnap him. Consequently, the other individual was abducted and spent a long period in captivity.

Precise risks of surveillance and popular local tactics can be explained by your company's security representative. However, you must also learn to cultivate a "sixth sense" about your surroundings.

Know what is normal in your neighborhood and along your commute routes, especially at choke points. If you know what is ordinary, you will notice anything extraordinary-people who are in the wrong place or dressed inappropriately, or cars parked in strange locations.

Be particularly observant whenever you leave your home or office. Look up and down the street for suspicious vehicles, motorcycles, mopeds, etc. Note people near your home who appear to be repair personnel, utility crew teams, even peddlers. Ask yourself if they appear genuine.

Become familiar with vehicle makes and models; learn to memorize license numbers. Determine if a pattern is developing with specific vehicles. See if cars suddenly pull out of parking places or side streets when you pass. Cars with extra mirrors or large mirrors are suspicious.

Be aware of the types of surveillance: stationary (at residence, along route, at work); following (on foot, by car); monitoring (of telephone, mail); searching (of luggage, personal effects, even trash); and eavesdropping (electronic and personal). An elaborate system involving several people and cars might be used.

Make their job tougher by not being predictable. Eat at different times and places. Stagger professional and social activities; don't play tennis "every Wednesday at three," for example.

Know the choke points on your routes and be aware of other vehicles, vans, or motorcycles as you enter those bottleneck areas. Search out safe havens that you can pull into along the route.

Drive with windows rolled up to within 2 inches of the top and lock all doors. Report any suspicious activity promptly to law enforcement.

Avoid using unlicensed cabs or cabs that appear out of nowhere. Do not permit taxi drivers to deviate from desired route.

Be circumspect with members of the press, as terrorists often pose as journalists. Do not submit to interviews or allow photographs to be made in or of your home.

Always speak guardedly and caution children to do the same. Never discuss travel or business plans within hearing of servants. Surveillants consider children and servants to be a prime source of information. Always assume that your telephone is tapped.

In elevators, watch for anyone who waits for you to select your floor, then pushes a button for the one just above or below yours.

If you become aware of surveillance, don't let those watching you know you are onto them. And certainly never confront them. Immediately notify your appropriate company representative. Memorize emergency numbers, and carry change for phone calls.

Hijackings

The experience of others will be helpful to you if you are the victim of a hijacking. Blend in with the other airline passengers. Avoid eye contact with your captors. Remember there may be other hijackers covertly mixed among the regular passengers.

Although captors may appear calm, they cannot be trusted to behave reasonably or rationally at all times. Stay alert, but do not challenge them physically or verbally. Comply with their instructions.

If interrogated, keep answers short and limited to nonpolitical topics. Carry a family photo; at some point you may be able to appeal to captors' family feelings.

Minimize the importance of your job. Give innocuous reasons for traveling. Never admit to any accusations.

Armed Assault on the Ground

Hostages taken by ground assault are in a situation similar to hijacking except that it occurs within buildings. Business offices, banks, embassies, and trains have been targets. The same advice for dealing with hijackers applies to ground assaults. Should shooting occur, seek cover or lie flat on the floor.

Kidnappings

Kidnapping is a terrifying experience, but you

possess more personal resources than you may be aware of to cope with the situation. Remember, you are only of value to them alive, and they want to keep you that way.

The common hostage responses of fear, denial, and withdrawal are all experienced in varying degrees. You may be blindfolded, drugged, handled roughly, or even stuffed in the trunk of a car. If drugs are administered, don't resist. Their purpose will be to sedate you and make you more manageable; these same drugs may actually help you to get control of your emotions, which should be your immediate goal. If conscious, follow your captors' instructions.

Captivity

A hostage-taking situation is at its worst at the onset. The terrorists are nervous and unsure, easily irritated, often irrational. It is a psychologically traumatic moment for the hostage. Violence may be used even if the hostage remains passive, but resistance could result in death.

If taken hostage, your best defense is passive cooperation. You may be terrified, but try to regain your composure as soon as possible and to organize your thoughts. Being able to behave rationally increases your chances for survival. The more time that passes, the better your chances of being released alive.

Behavior Suggestions

Each captivity is different, but some behavior suggestions apply to most:

Try to establish some kind of rapport with your captors. Family is a universal subject. Avoid political dialogues, but listen attentively to their point of view. If you know their language, listen and observe; and if addressed, use it.

Plan on a lengthy stay, and determine to keep track of the passage of time. Captors may attempt to confuse your sense of time by taking your watch, keeping you in a windowless cell, or serving meals at odd hours. However, you can approximate time by noting, for example, changes in temperatures between night and day; the frequency and intensity of outside noises-traffic, whistles, birds; and by observing the alertness of guards.

Maintain your dignity and self respect at all times.

Manage your time by setting up schedules for simple tasks, exercises, daydreaming, housekeeping.

Build relations with fellow captives and with the terrorists. If hostages are held apart, devise ways to communicate with one another. Where hostages are moved back and forth, to bathrooms for example, messages can be written and left. However, do not jeopardize your safety or the safety or treatment of others if attempting to communicate with fellow captives seems too risky.

Maintain your physical and mental health; it is critical to exercise body and mind. Eat food provided without complaint; keep up your strength. Request medical treatment or special medicines if required.

Establish exercise and relaxation programs. Exercise produces a healthy tiredness and gives you a sense of accomplishment. If space is confined, do isometrics. Relaxation reduces stress. Techniques include meditation, prayer, daydreaming.

Keep your mind active; read anything available. Write, even if you are not allowed to retain your writings. If materials are not available, mentally compose poetry or fiction, try to recall Scripture, design a house, even "play tennis" (as one hostage did).

Take note of the characteristics of your captors and surroundings: their habits, speech, contacts; exterior noises (typical of city or country); and other distinctive sounds. This information could prove very valuable later.

If selected for early release, consider it an opportunity to help remaining hostages. Details you have observed on the terrorists and the general situation can assist authorities with a rescue.

You can expect to be accused of working for the government's intelligence service, to be interrogated extensively, and to lose weight. You may be put in isolation; your captives may try to disorient you. It is important that you mentally maintain control.

Avoidance of Capture or Escape
Efforts to avoid capture or to attempt escape have in most cases been futile. The decision, however, is a personal one, although it could affect fellow hostages by placing them in jeopardy. Several other considerations should be weighed.

To have any chance of success, you should be in excellent physical condition and mentally prepared to react before the terrorists have consolidated their position. This, also, is the riskiest psychological time. You would need to have a plan in mind, and possibly have been trained in special driving tactics or other survival skills.

If you are held in a country in which you would stand out because of race or other physical characteristics, if you know nothing of the language or your location, or if you are held in a country where anti-American or anti-Western attitudes prevail, you should consider the consequences of your escape before attempting it.

If you conclude that an escape attempt is worthwhile, take terrorists by surprise and you may make it. If their organization has a poor track record of hostage safety, it may be worth the risk.

Rescue
The termination of any terrorist incident is extremely tense. If an assault force attempts a rescue, it is imperative that you remain calm and out of the way. Make no sudden moves or take any action by which you could be mistaken for a terrorist and risk being injured or killed.

Even in a voluntary release or surrender by the terrorists, tensions are charged and tempers volatile. Very precise instructions will be given to the hostages, either by the captors or the police. Follow instructions precisely. You may be asked to exit with hands in the air, and you may be searched by the rescue team. You may experience rough treatment until you are identified and the situation has stabilized.

Finally, it's worth keeping in mind three facts about terrorism:

The overwhelming majority of victims have been abducted from their vehicles on the way to or from work.

A large number of people taken hostage ignored the most basic security precautions.

Terrorist tactics are not static. As precautions prove effective, they change their methods. There is a brief "window of vulnerability" while we learn to counter their new styles.

Additional Precautions
Do not settle into a routine. Vary times and routes to and from work or social engagements.

Remember, there is safety in numbers. Avoid going out alone. When traveling long distances by automobile, go in a convoy. Avoid back country roads and dangerous areas of the city.

A privately owned car generally offers the best security. Avoid luxury or ostentatious cars. Keep your automobile in good repair and the gas tank at least half full. Driving in the center lane of a multiple lane highway makes it difficult for the car to be forced off the road.

Overseas Crisis Planning

Culture Shock
Culture shock is the physiological and psychological stress experienced when a traveler is suddenly deprived of old, familiar cues-language, customs, etc. Both the seasoned traveler and the first-timer, whether in transit or taking up residence, are susceptible. The sensation may be severe or mild, last months or only hours, strike in a remote village or in a modern European city, in one country, but not another-or not at all.

Culture shock is most prevalent in the second or third month after arrival when the novelty of the new country fades. Symptoms typically disappear by the fourth to sixth month, when the family has settled in and a sense of equilibrium is restored.

Traveler disorientation is a form of culture shock. You may encounter so many strange sounds,

85

sights, and smells upon arrival in a country new to you that you may be more vulnerable to accidents or crime. You may experience this disorientation on a fast-paced business trip to several different cultures.

You can combat traveler disorientation by gathering, in advance, information of a practical nature-knowing the routine at the airport, which taxis are recommended, knowing the exchange rate, etc. Pay particular attention to any host nation cultural behavior which may affect your security or safety.

As with any type of stress, culture shock may manifest itself both physically and emotionally. If you should experience it at a time when you need to be alert to security concerns, your awareness could be impaired. But if you understand it, you can successfully deal with it.

Symptoms
In children, you may notice a drop in school work and disruptive or regressive behavior. Teens may rebel with drugs or sex.

Symptoms to watch for in adults and children include:
Sleepiness, apathy, depression
Compulsive eating or drinking
Exaggerated homesickness
Decline in efficiency
Negative stereotyping of nationals
Recurrent minor illnesses

Successful Handling
The trauma of culture shock is most successfully dealt with if you:
Realize that operating in a new setting with strange sights, sounds, smells, and possibly a new language, is a different experience for each person in the family.

Communicate with each other; have patience and understanding; be sensitive to each others' feelings and difficulties.

Exercise! Lack of proper rest, diet, and exercise aggravate culture shock stress symptoms. Establish a daily exercise schedule quickly.

Use the support system of experienced

associates at first. Begin to participate in the life of the new country to whatever extent possible. There are many possibilities for family or individual activities within the American and international communities and in the new country. Sightsee, join a tennis club, enroll at the university, join a church, go to a concert, volunteer with the Red Cross, join Rotary.

We never build up an absolute immunity to culture shock. Yet that same sensitivity to change also means that we have the capacity to be enriched by the new experience travel brings us. Remember, each positive effort at stepping into the local culture usually opens yet another door of opportunity and diminishes the effects of culture shock.

If severe culture shock symptoms persist past six months, seek professional help.

Helping Children Adjust

Before the Move
Set the stage with children before the transfer process begins. Discuss the contents of this booklet with them and share what you have learned about the new country. Keep discussions informal. Bring up selected subjects during routine activities-dinner or a weekend hike. Be careful not to be apologetic about any restrictions that living overseas may place on them.

Talk to them about:
Cultural restrictions: Teens need to understand any dress or behavior restrictions ahead of time. Help children accept the local mores rather than resent them. Make your guidelines clear.

Health precautions: It may be the first time children have not been able to drink tap water or eat the local fruits, vegetables, and meats. They may require shots or pills to prevent the onset of local diseases.

Stress factors: Discuss with them the stress placed on a family by such a move and how they can relieve it. Many children instinctively reduce stress through play with others or a pet or by spending hours on the phone with friends. Still, they may express anger at relocation and anxiety about what the future holds. Flashbacks and nightmares are not uncommon in these situations.

Relocation Crisis

Children are creatures of habit. Settling them into a daily routine helps them adjust more successfully to any situation-whether it's a normal move, an evacuation, a separation, or a catastrophic disaster that has affected the whole community.

Give them information on the crisis appropriate to their age level. Listen to them. Talk to them. Let them express their anxieties. Acknowledge their feelings.

Encourage them to be physically active. Little ones can play games, teenagers can help with community needs related to the crisis, such as organizing activities for younger children or cleaning up earthquake damage. Vigorous exercise and sports are good for everyone during periods of high stress.

Make opportunities for them to be with peers. The older the child the more important this is, but most need to interact with children their own age. Insist they attend school, as this is the center of life with peers.

Let them feel that they have complete parental support. In times of crisis, children regress to earlier developmental stages. Young children can become almost infantile, forget toilet training, cling to parents. School-age children may refuse to go to school, be disruptive. Even teens, who have begun to break away from parents, may need reassurance that they are still securely within the family circle.

Stress During Crisis

A crisis is best handled collectively. Parents, teachers, family, and friends can play a part in helping any child handle a crisis. Adults should support each other in guiding children through the crisis; there is no need to feel you're in this alone. Play groups or support groups may be formed.

Parents and teachers are models. If they handle a crisis calmly, children will be less anxious.

Children "borrow" strengths from adults around them. Help them put labels on their reactions; encourage them to verbalize feelings. Play is a natural form of communication for children; it will discharge bottled-up feelings. If allowed to work through their fears, most children will emerge strengthened from a crisis.

Children need to see you express your feelings of fear and grief, too. By example, parents and other adults can show children how these feelings are handled. It's important that they see not only the expression of grief and sadness, but that they understand that the feeling will pass.

Some parents attempt to protect children by not allowing discussion about a crisis. The healthy route is to let them discuss it until they can get some psychological distance from it. Verbal repetition is a natural cathartic process.

Give them information-real details in language appropriate to their ages. Children are more painfully aware of what's going on than adults realize. And, if it's not discussed, what they do know, or think they know, can become unpleasantly distorted in their minds.

If a child requires medical attention, someone from the immediate family should stay with him or her. See that the procedures that are to be done are explained to the child.

Security for Children

Rules for Children

Children must be taught:
> To keep a parent in sight in public places and to go to a store clerk if lost and in need of help.
> Not to go anywhere with anyone without a parent's permission.
> ...... A password known only to family and close friends.
> Not to accept packages or letters from people you don't now.
> To know at least key phrases in the local language.
> To let someone know their location and plans.

Rules for Parents

Parents need to:
> Teach your child never to get into a car or go

into a house without your permission. Don't leave your child alone in a public place, even for a moment.

Teach your child your home address and telephone number. Children should know how to use public phones. Keep a list of emergency numbers by your phone and make children aware of them.

Train children not to give personal information over the phone, even though the caller purports to be a friend. "Personal information" includes whether family members are away, travel plans, where parents work, or recreation and school routines.

Explain the importance of never divulging any information in front of strangers.

Caution children to always keep doors locked, and never to unlock a door to a stranger without adult approval.

Listen when your child tells you he or she does not want to be with someone; there may be a reason. Have the child present when you interview a servant who will be caring for him or her; observe their reactions.

Child-Watch Checklist
Post an information list by each phone. Your sitter should be familiar with every item.

  Family name
  Address
  Phone number
  Fire
  Police
  Medical
  Poison
  Neighbor's name
  Neighbor's address
  Neighbor's phone
  Nearest fire call box
  Miscellaneous information of importance

Checklist for Babysitters
Ensure all doors and windows are locked and that doors are not opened to anyone.

Do not give out any information over the telephone. Simply state that Mr./Mrs. X cannot come to the phone right now. Take a message.

Never leave the children alone, even for a minute.

Know the dangers to children of matches, gasoline, stoves, deep water, poisons, falls.

Know the locations of all exits (stairs, doors, windows, fire escapes) and phones in case of emergency.

List the names and ages of children.

Evacuation
Many evacuations have taken place in past years for reasons of political instability, acts of terrorism, and natural disasters. In a number of cases, people have gone back to their new home after a short time; in others they have not returned at all. Notification times can range from a couple of hours to several weeks.

No two evacuations are the same. But there are common threads that run through all; knowing them can make an evacuation easier. What we have learned, both as a government and from individuals who have been evacuated, is distilled here for you.

Preparation
Be prepared. Assume an evacuation could occur at any point and have everything in place to execute it. It is better to be ready and not need it, than to need it and be unprepared.

Determine the "who and where" with your family. Who should be contacted and where your family would go in case of an extended evacuation. This is especially important for single parents; employees could be required to stay in the new country while children must leave. Parents should make arrangements for emergency child care before leaving the United States.

Establish a line of credit to cover emergencies. Obtain individual credit cards for you and your spouse. Open two checking accounts; use one as an active account, and keep the other in reserve. If possible, arrange for your paycheck to be deposited in a U.S. bank. Keep only a small account in a local bank for currency exchange or local purchases.

Know the emergency evacuation plan of the school. If there is none, be an active parent organizer and ensure that one is instituted. Join or start a safety network of parents.

Keep a small bag packed with essentials-clothing changes, snack food (dry, nonperishable), bottled water, medications. Small means small; anything over 10 pounds is not small.

In your residence, group important papers together along with checkbooks, U.S. credit cards, some traveler's checks, a small amount of cash, and U.S. driver's licenses. Maintain a basic emergency supply of food, water, gasoline, and first-aid supplies.

Meet your neighbors. Learn the location of the nearest hospital, police station, and friendly embassy or consulate.

Remember pets; have inoculations current and arrange for a suitable home in case they must be left behind.

If Evacuated
In the event an evacuation order is given, it is crucial for parents to discuss with children what is going to happen. Even if there is very little time before a departure, talk with them about the parent who will be staying. Reassure them; explain what will take place in the evacuation. They also need to know that the same rules and routines that structured their lives during normal times will continue.

Establish a daily routine with the children as soon as possible after evacuation and relocation. Be sure to incorporate family rituals-bedtime stories, family meals, church, pancakes on Saturday morning, whatever! Accentuate any advantages of the alternate location museums, amusement park, proximity to grandma and grandpa.

Minimize separation from the remaining parent as much as possible. Try not to use day care for a while. The child's fear of abandonment will be intense for a time.

Residential Fire Safety
Although fire does not sound as dramatic as

terrorism, in fact it kills far more people each year than does terrorist activity overseas. In many countries fire regulations do not exist, fire fighting equipment is antiquated, water sources are inadequate, and buildings are constructed with minimum standards.

Each year thousands of people die in home fires, half of them killed in their sleep by the toxic gases and smoke. Many who do survive spend months in hospitals and suffer lifelong physical and emotional scars. Children are often killed because they panic and try to hide from fire under beds and in closets.

Most of this devastation can be prevented. In only a few years, the use of smoke detectors in the United States has cut in half the number of annual fire fatalities. Fire prevention education is gradually making the odds even better.

Take these basic steps to protect your family from fire, whether you are in the United States or overseas:
Use smoke detectors in your home.
Prepare a fire escape plan with your family.
Conduct a fire drill at least once every six months.

Smoke Detectors
If fire occurs in your home, you may never awaken; smoke and toxic gases kill quietly and quickly. Yet you can be saved by the same smoke that can kill you-if it activates a smoke detector.

A smoke detector sounds a warning before you can even smell the smoke or see any flames. Smoke detectors should be installed, on each floor of the residence. If you have only one, place it on the ceiling outside the sleeping area.

Smoke detectors must be tested once a month and whenever you return from vacation. Never paint them. Once a year they should be vacuumed to remove any dust or cobwebs inside that would interfere with their functioning. Be sure everyone in the family recognizes the sound of the alert; test it with all members in the bedrooms with doors closed to be sure that they can hear it.

Fire Escape Plan
Since fire and smoke travel quickly, you have, at most, only minutes to escape. It is imperative that each member of the family knows what to do,

89

automatically.

A fire escape plan is your best bet. With your family, draw a floor plan of your house marking all possible exits. Since fire could block any exit, always have an alternative way to escape. Know in advance where to go. Double check exits to be sure they open and that children can handle doors or windows by themselves.

Show all windows, doors, and outdoor features. Note escape aids such as a tree or balcony; check to ensure that they would work. Locate the nearest fire alarm box or the neighbor's house. Teach your children how to report a fire.

Designate a meeting place outside the house. You must know immediately who may be trapped inside.

Tape a copy of the floor plan by the telephone. Advise household employees and babysitters (see page 67).

Fire Drills

Practice your plan! Regular fire drills assure that everyone knows what to do. Change the imaginary situation from drill to drill. Decide where the "fire" is and what exits are blocked. When small children learn what to do by rote, they will be less likely to panic in real life situations.

Pets cannot be considered. The dangers of a fire are overwhelming, and the primary consideration is saving human lives. Often pets will escape before you do, anyway.

Fire Extinguishers

Every home should have at least one fire extinguisher and one smoke detector. Be sure that the extinguisher works and that you know how to operate it.

Portable fire extinguishers can be effective on a small, confined fire, such as a cooking fire. But if a fire is large and spreading, using an extinguisher may be unsafe; you risk the dangers of inhaling toxic smoke and having your escape route cut off.

Use a fire extinguisher only after you:
Are sure everyone else is out of the building.
Have called the fire department.
Are certain you can approach the fire safely.

Use of Window Escapes

Before using a window escape, be sure that the door to the room is closed; otherwise, a draft from the open window could draw smoke and fire into the room.

Use an escape ladder or balcony if possible. If there is none, don't jump, wait for rescue as long as you can. Open a window a few inches at the top and bottom while you wait; gases will go out through the top and fresher air will enter through the bottom.

Children must know that it is all right to break a window. Discuss how to do it, using a baseball bat or a chair. Stand aside to avoid flying glass shards. Place a rug or blanket over the sill before crawling out.

Lower small children from the window. Don't leave first and expect them to follow. If they panic and refuse to jump, you will be unable to get them.

A Summary of Fire Safety Reminders

After a smoke detector warns you of a fire, you have only a few moments to escape.

Even concrete buildings are not fireproof. Virtually all the contents of your home or office will burn very quickly and produce toxic gases that can overpower you.

Sleep with bedroom doors closed. A closed door can hamper the spread of a fire, and the chances of a fire starting in a bedroom are remote.

To escape, keep low and crawl on hands and knees. A safety zone of cleaner air exists nearer the floor.

Once out, no one should be permitted to re-enter a burning house for any reason. Hold on to children who may impulsively run back inside. Children panic in fire and tend to attempt hiding as a means of escape. Train them to react correctly. As you escape, try to close every door behind you. It may slow the fire's progress.

Feel every door before you open it. If it is hot, don't open it. If it is cool, brace yourself against the door and open it slowly, checking for fire. A fire that has died down due to lack of oxygen could flare up once the door is open. If that happens, close the door immediately. Never waste time getting dressed or grabbing valuables.

If clothes catch fire, drop to the ground and roll to extinguish flames, or smother the fire with a blanket or rug. Never run. Teach children to stop, drop, and roll.

The Final Word
Fires are preventable. The major causes of home fires are:

Carelessness with cigarettes. Never smoke in bed; poisonous gases from a smoldering mattress can kill long before there are flames. After a party, look under cushions for smoldering cigarettes.

Faulty electrical wiring. Many homes in lesser developed countries are wired insufficiently to handle the simultaneous use of many electrical appliances. Don't overload circuits. Limit appliances plugged into the same extension cord. Major appliances should have their own heavy-duty circuit. Know where the fuse box is and instruct older children and household employees on how to shut off power in case of an electrical fire. Household current and plugs/sockets in many countries are different than in the United States. Transformers may be required to adapt U.S. appliances to the local current. Be sure your appliance, transformer, and the local current are compatible before using.

Faulty lighting equipment. Check electrical cords for cracks, broken plugs, poor connections. Use correct size bulbs in lamps, and be sure shades are not too close to bulbs.

Carelessness with cooking and heating appliances. Don't leave food cooking unattended. Have heating system and fireplaces inspected professionally once a year.

Children playing with matches. Teach children fire safety; keep matches and combustibles out of their reach.

Community Participation in Security

Safety in Numbers
As you consider the issues of safety and security, remember you are not alone. Overseas, you have the support and guidance of your company, the U.S. Embassy, colleagues, and their families. The best security results from information and support flowing between these entities.

Remember, you also have a responsibility to them. Do your part to contribute to the safety and security of the community.

What You Can Do
Keep abreast of current events, not only in the country, but internationally. Know what's going on in the country and in the world that could affect that country. Watch TV news programs, read newspapers, attend embassy security briefings periodically. It is your responsibility to keep current.

Locate yourself in relation to emergency services and places of refuge. Assist newcomers to do the same.

Other Useful Steps
Assemble a list of telephone numbers.
Maintain a set of local maps.
Meet neighbors and friendly people in your neighborhood.
Locate fire department and police stations.
Pinpoint nearest hospitals and clinics.
Know how to reach friendly diplomatic missions.
Know how to get accurate information.
Don't repeat rumors.
Establish an I.D. system for children.
Establish and participate in a neighborhood warden plan and a buddy system.
Prepare and keep current a telephone notification system.
Identify an alternative notification system in the event telephone service is lost.
Be a good listener. Be sensitive to special needs in your community. Single parents and employed couples may need help arranging security for their children. People who are ill, pregnant, or have new babies may have limited mobility. Elderly, dependent parents are a growing concern. Those who are isolated may need help in getting information. You can refer those with needs

91

to the appropriate person.

......

Resources

Government Resources in the U.S.

Bureau of Consular Affairs, Citizens Emergency Center
Focal point of liaison between concerned families, friends and U.S. Consular posts and citizens overseas; may render assistance in the areas of passports, visas, inoculations; maintains and issues travel advisories.
Phone: (202) 647-5225 (24 hours)

Department of State Operations Center
Primary point of contact between U.S. citizens residing in the United States and American embassies and consulates overseas. Phone: (202) 647-1512 (24 hours)

Department of State Task Forces
Ad hoc groups formed to deal with civil disturbances, coups, natural disasters, etc., which occur overseas.
Phone: Contact through Department of State Operations Center

Foreign Commercial Service
Primary U.S. Government liaison with U.S. firms operating overseas.
Phone: (202) 377-5351 (6:30 a.m.-6:30 p.m. EST)

OSAC/Private Sector Liaison Staff, Department of State
Departmental point of contact for interface between Diplomatic Security and the private sector.
Phone: (703) 204-6185 (8:00-5:00 EST)

Overseas Resources

U.S. Embassy/Consulate Personnel
The Chief of Mission (with the title of Ambassador, Minister, or Charge d'Affaires) and the Deputy Chief of Mission head each U.S. diplomatic mission overseas. These officers are responsible for all components of the U.S. Mission within a country, including consular posts.

Commercial Officers, at larger posts, represent U.S. commercial interests within their country of assignment. They specialize in U.S. export promotion and will provide assistance to American business in furtherance of that effort. Economic/Commercial Officers fulfill these functions at smaller posts. Consular Officers extend the protection of the U.S. Government to U.S. citizens and their property abroad. They maintain lists of local attorneys, act as liaison with police and other officials, and have the authority to notarize documents. Business representatives residing overseas should register with the Consular Officer. In troubled areas, even travelers are advised to register.

Regional Security Officers are responsible for providing physical, procedural, and personal security services to U.S. diplomatic facilities and personnel. Their responsibilities extend to providing incountry security briefings and threat assessments to business executives.

Publications (See Chapter 36)

Conclusion
Although this chapter contains many tips for successful travel and residence abroad, it is by no means all inclusive. Additional information is available from a variety of sources, ranging from travel brochures, magazines, and books, to conversations with persons who have lived or traveled to your assigned country.

You can never know too much about what you're getting into. Prior organization and preparation will significantly reduce your anxieties, lessen the shock of adjustment, and enable you to settle in with relative ease to a safe and enjoyable experience abroad.

Chapter 7

Know Before You Go: U.S. Customs Hints for Returning Residents

[The information in this chapter is reprinted verbatim from a bulletin issued by the Department of the Treasury, U.S. Customs Service. It is intended to serve as Advice to Americans traveling abroad.]

KNOW BEFORE YOU GO: US CUSTOMS HINTS (including customs duties)

Introduction: The U.S. Customs Service is America's frontline against the smuggling of drugs and other prohibited goods. Customs has discovered large amounts of drugs in baggage, vehicles, and on passengers themselves.

When you return to the United States, we will treat you in a courteous, professional manner. We realize that very few travelers actually violate the law, but we may still need to examine your baggage or your vehicle, which, by law, we are allowed to do. We may ask you about your citizenship, your trip, and about anything you are bringing back to the United States that you did not have with you when you left.

If you need help clearing Customs, please do not hesitate to ask the Customs inspector for assistance.

"Duty" and "dutiable" are words you will find frequently throughout this chapter: Duty is the amount of money you pay on items coming from another country. It is similar to a tax, except that duty is collected only on imported goods. Dutiable describes items on which duty may have to be paid. Most items have specific duty rates, which are determined by a number of factors, including where you got the item, where it was made, and what it is made of.

To "declare" means to tell the Customs officer about anything you're bringing back that you did not have when you left the United States. For example, you would declare alterations made in a foreign country to a suit you already owned, and you would declare any gifts you acquired overseas.

U.S. Customs Mission We are the guardians of our Nation's borders - America's frontline. We serve and protect the American public with integrity, innovation, and pride. We enforce the laws of the United States, safeguard the revenue, and foster lawful international trade and travel.

When You Return to the United States

When you come back, you'll need to declare everything you brought back that you did not take with you when you left the United States. If you are traveling by air or sea, you may be asked to fill out a Customs declaration form. This form is almost always provided by the airline or cruise ship. You will probably find it easier and faster to fill out your declaration form and clear Customs if you do the following:

Keep your sales slips! As you read this chapter, you'll understand why this is especially important for international travelers. Try to pack the things you'll need to declare separately. Read the signs in the Customs area. They contain helpful information about how to clear Customs.

Be aware that under U.S. law, Customs inspectors are authorized to examine luggage, cargo, and travelers. Under the search authority granted to Customs by the U.S. Congress, every passenger who crosses a U.S. border may be searched. To stop the flow of illegal drugs and other contraband into our country, we need your cooperation. If you are one of the very few travelers selected for a search, you will be treated in a courteous, professional, and dignified manner. If you are searched and you believe that you were not treated in such a manner, or if you have any concerns about the search for any reason whatsoever, we want to hear from you. Please contact the Executive Director, Passenger Programs.

What You Must Declare

You Must Declare

Items you purchased and are carrying with you upon return to the United States.

Items you received as gifts, such as wedding or birthday presents.

Items you inherited.

Items you bought in duty-free shops or on the ship or plane.

Repairs or alterations to any items you took abroad and then brought back, even if the repairs/alterations were performed free of charge.

Items you brought home for someone else.

Items you intend to sell or use in your business.

Items you acquired (whether purchased or received as gifts) in the U.S. Virgin Islands, American Samoa, Guam, or in a Caribbean Basin Economic Recovery Act country (please see section on $600 exemption for a list of these countries) that are not in your possession when you return. In other words, if you acquired things in any of these island nations and asked the merchant to send them to you, you must still declare them when you go through Customs. (This differs from the usual procedure for mailed items, which is discussed in the section on Sending Goods to the United States.

You must state on the Customs declaration, in United States currency, what you actually paid for each item. The price must include all taxes. If you did not buy the item yourself - for example, if it is a gift - get an estimate of its fair retail value in the country where you received it. If you bought something on your trip and wore or used it on the trip, it's still dutiable. You must declare the item at the price you paid or, if it was a gift, at its fair market value.

Joint Declaration Family members who live in the same home and return together to the United States may combine their personal exemptions. This is called a joint declaration. For example, if Mr. And Mrs. Smith travel overseas and Mrs. Smith brings home a $600 piece of glassware, and Mr. Smith buys $200 worth of clothing, they can combine their $400 exemptions on a joint declaration and not have to pay duty.

Children and infants are allowed the same exemption as adults, except for alcoholic beverages.

Register Items Before You Leave the United States

If your laptop computer was made in Japan - for instance - you might have to pay duty on it each time you bring it back into the United States, unless you could prove that you owned it before you left on your trip. Documents that fully describe the item - for example, sales receipts, insurance policies, or jeweler's appraisals - are acceptable forms of proof. To make things easier, you can register certain items with Customs before you depart - including watches, cameras, laptop computers, firearms, and tape recorders - as long as they have serial numbers or other unique, permanent markings. Take the items to the nearest Customs Office and request a Certificate of Registration (Customs Form 4457). It shows Customs that you had the items with you before leaving the U.S. and all items listed on it will be allowed duty-free entry. Customs inspectors must see the item you are registering in order to certify the certificate of registration. You can register items with Customs at the international airport from which you're departing. Keep the certificate for future trips.

Duty-free Exemption

The duty-free exemption, also called the personal exemption , is the total value of merchandise you may bring back to the United States without having to pay duty. You may bring back more than your exemption, but you will have to pay duty on it. In most cases, the personal exemption is $800, but there are some exceptions to this rule, which are explained below.

Exemptions Depending on the countries you have visited, your personal exemption will be $600, $800, or $1,200. (The differences are explained in the following section.) There are also limits on the amount of alcoholic beverages, cigarettes, cigars, and other tobacco products you may include in your duty-free personal exemption.

The duty-free exemptions ($600, $800, or $1,200) apply if:

● The items are for your personal or household use.

● They are in your possession (that is, they accompany you) when you return to the United States. Items to be sent later may not be included in your $800 duty-free exemption.

● They are declared to Customs. If you do not declare something that should have been declared, you risk forfeiting it. If in doubt, declare it.

● You are returning from an overseas stay of at least 48 hours. For example, if you leave the United States at 1:30 p.m. on June 1, you would complete the 48-hour period at 1:30 p.m. on June 3. This time limit does not apply if you are returning from Mexico or from the U.S. Virgin Islands. (See the section on the $200 exemption.)

● You have not used your exemption, or any part of it, in the past 30 days. If you use part of your exemption - for example, if you go to England and bring back $150 worth of items - you must wait another 30 days before you are allowed another $800 exemption. (However, see the section on the $200 exemption.) The items are not prohibited or restricted as discussed in the section on Prohibited and Restricted Items. Note the embargo prohibitions on products of Cuba.

$200 Exemption If you can't claim other exemptions because you've been out of the country more than once in a 30-day period or because you haven't been out of the country for at least 48 hours, you may still bring back $200 worth of items free of duty and tax. As with the exemptions discussed earlier, these items must be for your personal or household use.

Each traveler is allowed this $200 exemption, but, unlike the other exemptions, family members may not group their exemptions. Thus, if Mr. and Mrs. Smith spend a night in Canada, each may bring back up to $200 worth of goods, but they would not be allowed a collective family exemption of $400.

Also, if you bring back more than $200 worth of dutiable items, or if any item is subject to duty or tax, the entire amount will be dutiable. Let's say you were out of the country for 36 hours and came back with a $300 piece of pottery. You could not deduct $200 from its value and pay duty on $100.

The pottery would be dutiable for the full value of $300.

You may include with the $200 exemption your choice of the following: 50 cigarettes and 10 cigars and 150 milliliters (5 fl. oz.) of alcoholic beverages or 150 milliliters (5 fl. oz.) of perfume containing alcohol.

$800 Exemption If you are returning from anywhere other than a Caribbean Basin country or a U.S. insular possession (U.S. Virgin Islands, American Samoa, or Guam), you may bring back $800 worth of items duty-free, as long as you bring them with you (this is called accompanied baggage).

Duty on items you mail home to yourself will be waived if the value is $200 or less. (See sections on "Gifts" and "Sending Goods to the United States.") Antiques that are at least 100 years old and fine art may enter duty-free, but folk art and handicrafts are generally dutiable.

This means that, depending on what items you're bringing back from your trip, you could come home with more than $800 worth of gifts or purchases and still not be charged duty. For instance, say you received a $700 bracelet as a gift, and you bought a $40 hat and a $60 color print. Because these items total $800, you would not be charged duty, because you have not exceeded your duty-free exemption. If you had also bought a $500 painting on that trip, you could bring all $1300 worth of merchandise home without having to pay duty, because fine art is duty-free.

Tobacco Products: Passengers/travelers may import previously exported tobacco products only in quantities not exceeding the amounts specified in exemptions for which the traveler qualifies. Any quantities of previously exported tobacco products not permitted by an exemption will be seized and destroyed. These items are typically purchased in duty-free stores, on carriers operating internationally, or in foreign stores. These items are usually marked "Tax Exempt. For Use Outside the U.S.," or "U.S. Tax Exempt For Use Outside the U.S." For example, a returning resident is eligible for the $800 exemption, which includes not more than 200 cigarettes and 100 cigars. If the resident declares 400 previously exported

95

cigarettes, the resident would be permitted 200 cigarettes, tax-free under the exemption and the remaining 200 previously exported cigarettes would be confiscated. If the resident declares 400 cigarettes, of which 200 are previously exported and 200 not previously exported, the resident would be permitted to import the 200 previously exported cigarettes tax free under the exemption and the resident would be charged duty and tax on the remaining 200 not previously exported cigarettes.

The tobacco exemption is available to each person. Tobacco products of Cuban origin, however, are prohibited unless you actually acquired them in Cuba and are returning directly or indirectly from that country on licensed travel. You may not, for example, bring in Cuban cigars purchased in Canada. Persons returning from Cuba may bring into the U.S. no more than $100 worth of goods.

Alcoholic Beverages: One liter (33.8 fl. oz.) of alcoholic beverages may be included in your exemption
if:
You are 21 years old.
It is for your own use or as a gift.
It does not violate the laws of the state in which you arrive.

Federal regulations allow you to bring back more than one liter of alcoholic beverage for personal use, but, as with extra tobacco, you will have to pay duty and Internal Revenue Service tax.

While federal regulations do not specify a limit on the amount of alcohol you may bring back for personal use, unusual quantities are liable to raise suspicions that you are importing the alcohol for other purposes, such as for resale. Customs officers are authorized by Alcohol Tobacco and Firearms (ATF) make on-the-spot determinations

that an importation is for commercial purposes, and may require you to obtain a permit to import the alcohol before leasing to you. If you intend to bring back a substantial quantity of alcohol for your personal use you should contact the Customs port you will be re-entering the country through, and make prior arrangements for entering the alcohol into the U.S.

Having said that, you should be aware that State

laws may limit the amount of alcohol you can bring in without a license. If you arrive in a state that has limitations on the amount of alcohol you may bring in without a license, that state law will be enforced by Customs, even though it may be more restrictive then Federal regulations. We recommend that you check with the state government before you go abroad about their limitations on quantities allowed for personal importation and additional state taxes that might apply.

In brief, for both alcohol and tobacco, the quantities discussed in this booklet as being eligible for duty-free treatment may be included in your $800 (or $600 or $1,200) exemption, just as any other purchase would be. But unlike other kinds of merchandise, amounts beyond those discussed here as being duty-free are taxed, even if you have not exceeded, or even met, your personal exemption. For example, if your exemption is $800 and you bring back three liters of wine and nothing else, two of those liters will be dutiable. Federal law prohibits shipping alcoholic beverages by mail within the United States.

$600 Exemption If you are returning directly from any one of the following 24 Caribbean Basin countries, your customs exemption is $600:

Antigua and Barbuda, Aruba, Bahamas, Barbados, Belize, British Virgin, Islands, Costa Rica, Dominica, Dominican Republic, El Salvador, Grenada, Guatemala, Guyana, Honduras, Jamaica, Montserrat, Netherlands, Antilles, Nicaragua, Panama, Saint Kitts, and Nevis, Saint Lucia, Saint Vincent and the Grenadines, Trinidad
and Tobago

You may include two liters of alcoholic beverages with this $600 exemption, as long as one of the liters was produced in one of the countries listed above (see section on Unaccompanied Purchases from Insular Possessions and Caribbean Basin Countries).

Travel to More Than One Country If you travel to a U.S. possession and to one or more of the Caribbean countries listed above (for example, on a Caribbean cruise), you may bring back $1,200 worth of items without paying duty. But only $600 worth of these items may come from the

Caribbean country(ies); any amount beyond $600 will be dutiable unless you acquired it in one of the insular possessions. For example, if you were to travel to the U.S. Virgin Islands and Jamaica, you would be allowed to bring back $1,200 worth of merchandise duty-free, as long as only $600 worth was acquired in Jamaica. (Keeping track of where your purchases occurred and having the receipts ready to show the Customs inspectors will help speed your clearing Customs.)

If you travel to any of the Caribbean countries listed above and to countries where the standard personal exemption of $800 applies - for example, a South American or European country - up to $800 worth of merchandise may come from the non-Caribbean country. For instance, if you travel to Venezuela and Trinidad and Tobago, your exemption is $600, only $200 of which may have been acquired in Venezuela.

$1,200 Exemption If you return directly or indirectly from a U.S. Insular possession (U.S. Virgin Islands, American Samoa, or Guam), you are allowed a $1,200 duty-free exemption. You may include 1,000 cigarettes as part of this exemption, but at least 800 of them must have been acquired in an insular possession. Only 200 cigarettes may have been acquired elsewhere. For example, if you were touring the South Pacific and you stopped in Tahiti, American Samoa, and other ports of call, you could bring back five cartons of cigarettes, but four of them would have to have been bought in American Samoa.

Similarly, you may include five liters of alcoholic beverages in your duty-free exemption, but one of them must be a product of an insular possession. Four may be products of other countries (see section on Unaccompanied Purchases from Insular Possessions and Caribbean Basin Countries).

Gifts Gifts you bring back from a trip abroad are considered to be for your personal use. They must be declared, but you may include them in your personal exemption. This includes gifts people gave you while you were out of the country, such as wedding or birthday presents, and gifts you've brought back for others. Gifts intended for business, promotional, or other commercial purposes may not be included in your duty-free exemption.

Gifts worth up to $100 may be received, free of duty and tax, by friends and relatives in the United States, as long as the same person does not receive more than $100 worth of gifts in a single day. If the gifts are mailed or shipped from an insular possession, this amount is increased to $200. When you return to the United States, you don't have to declare gifts you sent while you were on your trip, since they won't be accompanying you.

By federal law, alcoholic beverages, tobacco products, and perfume containing alcohol and worth more than $5 retail may not be included in the gift exemption.

Gifts for more than one person may be shipped in the same package, called a consolidated gift package, if they are individually wrapped and labeled with each recipient's name. Here's how to wrap and label a consolidated gift package:

Be sure to mark the outermost wrapper with:

- the words "UNSOLICITED GIFT" and the words "CONSOLIDATED GIFT PACKAGE" ;
- the total value of the consolidated package;
- the recipients' names; and
- the nature and value of the gifts inside (for example, tennis shoes, $50; shirt, $45; toy car, $15).

Packages marked in this way will clear Customs much more easily. Here's an example of how to mark a
consolidated gift package:

Unsolicited gift-consolidated gift package- total value $135 To John Jones-one belt, $20; one box of candy, $5; one tie, $20 To Mary Smith-one skirt, $45; one belt, $15; one pair slacks, $30.

If any item in the consolidated gift parcel is subject to duty and tax or worth more than the $100 gift allowance, the entire package will be dutiable.

You, as a traveler, cannot send a "gift" package to yourself, and people traveling together cannot send "gifts" to each other. But there would be no reason to do that anyway, because the personal exemption for packages mailed from abroad is $200, which is twice as much as the gift exemption. If a package is subject to duty, the United States Postal Service will collect it from the addressee along with any

97

postage and handling charges. The sender cannot prepay duty; it must be paid by the recipient when the package is received in the United States. (Packages sent by courier services are not eligible for this duty waiver.)

Duty-free or Reduced Rates
Items from Certain Countries The United States gives duty preferences - that is, free or reduced rates - to certain developing countries under a trade program called the Generalized System of Preferences (GSP). Some products that would otherwise be dutiable are not when they come from a GSP country. For details on this program, as well as the complete list of GSP countries, please ask your nearest Customs office for a copy of our pamphlet *GSP & The Traveler*.

Similarly, many products of Caribbean and Andean countries are exempt from duty under the Caribbean Basin Initiative, Caribbean Basin Trade Partnership Act, and Andean Trade Preference Act. Most products of certain sub-Saharan African countries are exempt from duty under the African Growth and Opportunity Act. Most products of Israel may also enter the United States either free of duty or at a reduced rate. Check with Customs for details on these programs.

The North American Free Trade Agreement (NAFTA) went into effect in 1994. If you are returning from Canada or Mexico , your goods are eligible for free or reduced duty rates if they were grown, manufactured, or produced in Canada or Mexico, as defined by the Act. Again, check with Customs for details.

Personal Belongings and Household Effects

What Items are Duty-free?
Personal Belongings Your personal belongings can be sent back to the United States duty-free if they are of U.S. origin and if they have not been altered or repaired while abroad. Personal belongings like worn clothing can be mailed home and will receive duty-free entry if you write the words "American Goods Returned" on the outside of the package.

Household Effects Household effects include furniture, carpets, paintings, tableware, stereos, linens, and similar household furnishings. Tools of trade, professional books, implements, and

instruments that you've taken out of the United States will be duty-free when you return.

You may import household effects you acquired abroad duty-free if:

You used them for at least one year while you were abroad.
They are not intended for anyone else or for sale.

Clothing, jewelry, photography equipment, portable radios, and vehicles are considered personal effects and cannot be brought in duty-free as household effects. However, the amount of duty collected on them will be reduced according to the age of the item.

Paying Duty
If you're bringing it back with you, you didn't have it when you left, and its total value is more than your Customs exemption, it is subject to duty.

The Customs inspector will place the items that have the highest rate of duty under your exemption. Then, after subtracting your exemptions and the value of any duty-free items, a flat rate of duty will be charged on the next $1,000 worth of merchandise. Any dollar amount beyond this $1,000 will be dutiable at whatever duty rates apply. The flat rate of duty may only be used for items for your own use or for gifts. As with your exemption, you may use the flat-rate provision only once every 30 days. Special flat rates of duty apply to items made and acquired in Canada or Mexico. The flat rate of duty applies to purchases whether the items accompany you or are shipped.

The flat duty rate will be charged on items that are dutiable but that cannot be included in your personal exemption, even if you have not exceeded the exemption. The best example of this is liquor: Say you return from Europe with $200 worth of items, including two liters of liquor. One liter will be duty-free under your exemption; the other will be dutiable at 4 percent, plus any Internal Revenue Service tax.

Family members who live in the same household and return to the United States together can combine their items to take advantage of a combined flat duty rate, no matter which family member owns a given item. The combined flat duty rate for a family of four traveling together would be $4,000.

If you owe duty, you must pay it when you arrive in the United States. You can pay it in any of the following ways:

U.S. currency (foreign currency is not acceptable).

Personal check in the exact amount, drawn on a U.S. bank, made payable to the U.S. Customs Service. You must present identification, such as a passport or driver's license. (The Customs Service does not accept checks bearing second-party endorsements.)

Government check, money order, or traveler's check if it does not exceed the duty owed by more than $50.

In some locations, you may pay duty with credit cards, either MasterCard or VISA.

Sending Goods to the United States

Items mailed to the United States are subject to duty when they arrive. They cannot be included in your Customs exemption, and duty on them cannot be prepaid.

If you are mailing merchandise from the U.S. insular possessions or from Caribbean Basin countries, you should follow different procedures than if you were mailing packages from any other country. These special procedures are described, in the section on " Unaccompanied Purchases ".

In addition to duty and, at times, taxes, Customs collects a user fee on dutiable packages. Those three fees are the only fees Customs collects; any additional charges on shipments are for handling by freight forwarders, Customs brokers, and couriers or for other delivery services. Some carriers may add other clearance charges that have nothing to do with Customs duties.

Note: Customs brokers are not U.S. Customs employees. Brokers' fees are based on the amount of work they do, not on the value of the items you ship, so travelers sometimes find the fee high in relation to the value of the shipment. The most cost-effective thing to do is to take your purchases with you if at all possible.

Unaccompanied Luggage Unaccompanied baggage is anything you do not bring back with you, as opposed to goods in your possession - that accompany you - when you return. These may be items that were with you when you left the United States or items that you acquired (received by any means) while outside the United States. In general, unaccompanied baggage falls into the following three categories.

U.S. Mail Shipments Shipping through the U.S. mail, including parcel post, is a cost-efficient way to send things to the United States. The Postal Service sends all foreign mail shipments to Customs for examination. Customs then returns packages that don't require duty to the Postal Service, which sends them to a local post office for delivery. The local post office delivers them without charging any additional postage, handling costs, or other fees.

If the package does require payment of duty, Customs attaches a form called a mail entry (form CF-3419A), which shows how much duty is owed, and charges a $5 processing fee as well. When the post office delivers the package, it will also charge a handling fee.

Commercial goods - goods intended for resale - may have special entry requirements. Such goods may require a formal entry in order to be admitted into the United States. Formal entries are more complicated and require more paperwork than informal entries. (Informal entries are, generally speaking, personal packages worth less than $2,000.) Customs employees may not prepare formal entries for you; only you or a licensed customs broker may prepare one. For more information on this subject, please request the Customs pamphlet U.S. Import Requirements or contact your local Customs office.

If you believe you have been charged an incorrect amount of duty on a package mailed from abroad, you may file a protest with Customs. You can do this in one of two ways. You can accept the package, pay the duty, and write a letter explaining why you think the amount was incorrect. You should include with your letter the yellow copy of the mail entry (CF-3419A). Send the letter and the form to the Customs office that issued the mail entry, which you'll find on the lower left-hand corner of the form.

99

The other way to protest duty is to refuse delivery of the package and, within five days, send your protest letter to the post office where the package is being held. The post office will forward your letter to Customs and will hold your package until the protest is resolved.

For additional information on international mailing, please ask Customs for the pamphlet International Mail Imports .

Express Shipments Packages may be sent to the United States by private-sector courier or delivery service from anywhere in the world. The express company usually takes care of clearing your merchandise through Customs and charges a fee for its service. Some travelers have found this fee to be higher than they expected.

Freight Shipments Cargo, whether duty is owed on it or not, must clear Customs at the first port of arrival in the United States. If you choose, you may have your freight sent, while it is still in Customs custody, to another port for Customs clearance. This is called forwarding freight in bond. You (or someone you appoint to act for you) are responsible for arranging to clear your merchandise through Customs or for having it forwarded to another port.

Frequently, a freight forwarder in a foreign country will take care of these arrangements, including hiring a customs broker in the United States to clear the merchandise through Customs. Whenever a third party handles the clearing and forwarding of your merchandise, that party charges a fee for its services. This fee is not a Customs charge. When a foreign seller entrusts a shipment to a broker or agent in the United States, that seller usually pays only enough freight to have the shipment delivered to the first port of arrival in the United States. This means that you, the buyer, will have to pay additional inland transportation, or freight forwarding charges, plus brokers' fees, insurance, and possibly other charges.

If it is not possible for you to secure release of your goods yourself, another person may act on your behalf to clear them through Customs. You may do this as long as your merchandise consists of a single, noncommercial shipment (not intended for resale) that does not require a formal entry-in other words, if the merchandise is worth less than

$2,000. You must give the person a letter that authorizes him or her to act as your unpaid agent. Once you have done this, that person may fill out the Customs declaration and complete the entry process for you. Your letter authorizing the person to act in your behalf should be addressed to the "Officer in Charge of Customs" at the port of entry, and the person should bring it along when he or she comes to clear your package. Customs will not notify you when your shipment arrives, as this is the responsibility of your carrier, If your goods are not cleared within 15 days of arrival you could incur storage fees.

Unaccompanied Purchases from Insular Possessions and Caribbean Countries

Unaccompanied purchases are goods you bought on a trip that are being mailed or shipped to you in the United States. In other words, you're not carrying them with you when you return. If your unaccompanied purchases are from an insular possession or a Caribbean Basin country and are being sent directly from those locations to the United States, you may enter them as follows:

Up to $1,200 worth will be duty-free under your personal exemption if the merchandise is from an insular possession.

Up to $600 worth will be duty-free if it is from a Caribbean Basin country.

Of these amounts ($1,200 or $600), up to $400 worth will be duty-free if the merchandise was acquired elsewhere than the insular possessions or the Caribbean Basin. However, merchandise that qualifies for the $400 exemption must be in your possession when you return (must accompany you) in order for you to claim the duty-free exemption. The duty-free exemptions for unaccompanied baggage apply only to goods from the insular possessions and the Caribbean Basin countries listed earlier.

An additional $1,000 worth of goods will be dutiable at a flat rate if they are from an insular possession, or from a Caribbean Basin country.(See chart under Paying Duty.)

If you are sending back more than $2,200 from an insular possession or more than $1,600 from a Caribbean Basin country, the duty rates in the Harmonized Tariff Schedules of the United States will apply. The Harmonized Tariff Schedule describes different rates of duty for different commodities; linen tablecloths, for example, will not have the same duty rates as handicrafts or plastic toy trucks.

Here's how you can take advantage of the duty-free exemption for unaccompanied tourist purchases from an insular possession or a Caribbean country:

Step 1. At place and time of purchase, ask your merchant to hold your item until you send him or her a copy of Customs Form CF-255 (Declaration of Unaccompanied Articles), which must be affixed to the package when it is sent.

Step 2. (a) On your Customs declaration (form CF-6059B), list everything you acquired on your trip, except the things you already sent home as gifts. (b) Check off on the declaration those items you are not bringing with you--that is, the unaccompanied items. (c) Fill out a separate Declaration of Unaccompanied Articles (form CF-255) for each package or container that will be sent to you after you arrive in the United States . You can often get this form where you make your purchase, but if not, ask a Customs officer for one when you clear Customs.

Step 3. When you return to the United States, the Customs officer will: (a) collect duty and tax, if any is owed, on the goods you've brought with you; (b) check to see that your list of unaccompanied articles, which you indicated on the Customs declaration, agrees with your sales slips, invoices, and so on; and (c) validate the CF-255 as to whether your purchases are duty-free under your personal exemption ($1,200 or $600) or whether they are subject to a flat rate of duty. Two copies of this three-part form will be returned to you.

Step 4. Send the yellow copy of the CF-255 to the foreign shopkeeper or vendor holding your purchase, and keep the other copy for your records. (When you make your purchase, it is very important to tell the merchant not to send your package to the United States until he or she gets the copy of form CF-255.)

Step 5. When the merchant gets your CF-255, he or she will put it in an envelope and attach the envelope securely to the outside wrapping of the package or container. The merchant must also mark each package "Unaccompanied Purchase." Please remember that each package or container must have its own CF-255 attached. This is the most important step to follow in order to gain the benefits allowed under this procedure.

Step 6. If your package has been mailed, the Postal Service will deliver it after it has cleared Customs. If you owe duty, the Postal Service will collect the duty along with a postal handling fee. If your package is delivered by a commercial courier, the delivery service will notify you of its arrival so you can go to the Customs office holding the shipment and complete the entry procedure. If you owe duty or tax, you can pay it at that time. Alternatively, you may hire a customs broker to do this for you, but be aware that brokers are not U.S. Customs employees, and they charge fees for their services.

Storage Charges: If freight or express packages from your trip are delivered before you return and you have not made arrangements to pick them up, Customs will place them in storage after 15 days. This storage will be at your risk and expense. If they are not claimed within six months, the items will be sold
at auction.

Packages sent by mail and not claimed within 30 days will be returned to the sender unless the amount of duty is being protested.

Duty-Free Shops
Many travelers are confused by the term "duty-free" shops. Travelers often think that what they buy in duty-free shops won't be dutiable when they return home and clear Customs. But this is not true: Articles sold in a duty-free shop are free of duty and taxes only for the country in which that shop is located. So if your purchases exceed your personal exemption, items you bought in a duty-free shop, whether in the United States or abroad, will almost certainly be subject to duty.

Articles sold in foreign duty-free shops are subject to U.S. Customs duty and other restrictions (for example, only one liter of liquor is duty-free), but you may include these items in your personal exemption. Articles sold in duty-free shops are meant to be taken out of the country; they are not meant to be used, worn, eaten, drunk, etc., in the country where you purchased them. Articles purchased in American duty-free shops are also subject to U.S. Customs duty if you bring them into the United States. For example, if you buy liquor in a duty-free shop in New York before entering Canada and then bring it back into the United States, it may be subject to duty and Internal Revenue Service tax.

Prohibited and Restricted Items

The Customs Service has been entrusted with enforcing some 400 laws for 40 other government agencies, such as the Fish and Wildlife Service and the Department of Agriculture. These other agencies have great interest in what people bring into the country, but they are not always at ports of entry, guarding our borders. Customs is always at ports of entry - guarding the nation's borders is what we do.

The products we want to keep out of the United States are those that would injure community health, public safety, American workers, children, or domestic plant and animal life, or those that would defeat our national political interests. Sometimes the products that cause injury, or have the potential to do so, may seem fairly innocent. But, as you will see from the material that follows, appearances can be deceiving.

Before you leave for your trip abroad, you might want to talk to Customs about the items you plan to bring back t6 be sure they're not prohibited or restricted. Prohibited means the item is forbidden by law to enter the United States, period. Examples are dangerous toys, cars that don't protect their occupants in a crash, or illegal substances like absinthe and Rohypnol. Restricted means that special licenses or permits are required from a federal agency before the item is allowed to enter the United States. Examples are firearms and certain fruits, vegetables, pets, and textiles.

Cultural Artifacts and Cultural Property (Art/Artifacts) Most countries have laws that protect their cultural property (art/artifacts/antiquities; archaeological and ethnological material are also terms that are used).Such laws include export controls and/or national ownership of cultural property. Even if purchased from a business in the country of origin or in another country, legal ownership of such artifacts may be in question if brought into the U.S. Make certain you have documents such as export permits and receipts, although these do not necessarily confer ownership. While foreign laws may not be enforceable in the U.S., they can cause certain U.S. law to be invoked. For example, as a general rule, under the U.S. National Stolen Property Act, one cannot have legal title to art/artifacts/antiquities that were stolen, no matter how many times such items may have changed hands. Articles of stolen cultural property (from museums or from religious or secular public monuments) originating in any of the countries party to the 1970 UNESCO Convention specifically may not be imported into the U.S.

In addition, U.S. law may restrict importation into the U.S. of specific categories of art/artifacts/antiquities:

1. U.S. law restricts the import of any Pre-Colombian monumental and architectural sculpture and murals from Central and South American countries.

2. U.S. law specifically restricts the importation of Native American artifacts from Canada; Maya Pre-Colombian archaeological objects from Guatemala; Pre-Colombian archaeological objects from El Salvador and Peru; archaeological objects (such as terracotta statues) from Mali; Colonial period objects such as paintings and ritual objects from Peru; Byzantine period ritual and ecclesiastic objects (such as icons) from Cyprus; Khmer stone archaeological sculpture from Cambodia.

Importation of items such as those above is permitted only when the items are accompanied by an export permit issued by the country of origin (where such items were first found). Purveyors of such items have been known to offer phony export certificates. As additional U.S. import restrictions may be imposed in response to requests from other countries, it is wise for the prospective purchaser to visit the State department's cultural property Web site. This Web site also has images representative of the categories of cultural property for which there are specific U.S. import restrictions.

Absinthe The importation of Absinthe and any other liquors or liqueurs that contain an excess of

Artemisia absinthium is prohibited.

Automobiles Automobiles imported into the United States must meet the fuel-emission requirements of the Environmental Protection Agency (EPA) and the safety, bumper, and theft-prevention standards of the Department of Transportation (DOT). (Please see Customs pamphlets Importing a Car and Pleasure Boats.) Trying to import a car that doesn't meet all the requirements can be a vexing experience. Here's why:

Almost all cars, vans, sport utility vehicles, and so on that are bought in foreign countries must be modified to meet American standards. Passenger vehicles that are imported on the condition that they be modified must be exported or destroyed if they are not modified acceptably.

And even if the car does meet all federal standards, it might be subject to additional EPA requirements, depending on what countries you drove it in. Or it could require a bond upon entry until the conditions for admission have been met. So before you even think about importing a car, you should call EPA and DOT for more information.

Information on importing vehicles can be obtained from the Environmental Protection Agency, Attn.: 6405J, Washington, DC 20460, telephone (202) 564-9660 , and the Department of Transportation, Office of Vehicle Safety Compliance (NEF 32) NHTSA, Washington, DC 20590.

Copies of the Customs Service's pamphlet Importing or Exporting a Car, can be obtained by writing to the U.S. Customs Service, P.O. Box 7407, Washington, DC 20044. EPA's Automotive Imports Fact Manual can be obtained by writing to the Environmental Protection Agency, Washington, DC 20460. Cars being brought into the United States temporarily (for less than one year) are exempt from these restrictions.

Trademarked and Copyrighted Articles U.S. Customs enforces laws relating to the protection of trademarks and copyrights. Articles that infringe a federally registered trademark or copyright, i.e., that use the protected right without the authorization of the trademark or copyright owner, are subject to detention and seizure.

Articles bearing marks that are counterfeit of a federally registered trademark are subject to seizure and forfeiture. Additionally, the importation of articles bearing counterfeit marks may subject an individual to a civil monetary penalty if the registered trademark has also been recorded with Customs. Articles bearing marks that are confusingly similar to a registered trademark, and gray market articles (goods bearing genuine marks not intended for importation into the United States) may be subject to detention and seizure.

However, passengers arriving into the United States are permitted to import one article, which must accompany the person, bearing a counterfeit, confusingly similar or restricted gray market trademark, provided that the article is for personal use and is not for sale. This exemption may be granted not more than once every thirty days. The arriving passenger may retain one article of each type accompanying the person. For example, an arriving person who has three purses, whether each bears a different infringing trademark, or whether all three bear the same infringing trademark, is permitted one purse. If the article imported under the personal exemption provision is sold within one year after the date of importation, the article or its value is subject to forfeiture.

In regard to copyright infringement, articles that are determined to be clearly piratical of a federally registered copyright, i.e., unauthorized articles that are substantially similar to a material protected part of a copyright, are subject to seizure. Articles that are determined to be possibly piratical may be subject to detention and possible seizure. A personal use exemption similar to that described above also applies in respect of copyrighted articles.

You may bring back genuine trademarked and copyrighted articles (subject to duties). The copyrighted products most commonly imported include CD-ROMs, tape cassettes, toys, stuffed animals, clothing with cartoon characters, videotapes, videocassettes, music CDs, and books.

Ceramic Tableware Although ceramic tableware is not prohibited or restricted, you should know that such tableware made in foreign countries may contain dangerous levels of lead in the glaze; this lead can seep into foods and beverages. The Food and Drug Administration Recommends that if you buy ceramic tableware abroad - especially in Mexico, China, Hong Kong, or India - you have it tested for lead release when you return, or use it for decorative purposes only.

Dog and Cat Fur It is illegal in the United States to import, export, distribute, transport, manufacture, or sell products containing dog or cat fur in the United States. As of November 9, 2000, the Dog and Cat Protection Act of 2000 calls for the seizure and forfeiture of each item containing dog or cat fur.

The Act provides that any person who violates any provision may be assessed a civil penalty of not more that $10,000 for each separate knowing and intentional violation, $5,000 for each separate gross negligent violation, or $3,000 for each separate negligent violation.

Drug Paraphernalia It is illegal to bring drug paraphernalia into the United States unless they have been prescribed for authentic medical conditions - diabetes, for example. Customs will seize any illegal paraphernalia. The importation, exportation, manufacture, sale, or transportation of drug paraphernalia is prohibited by law. If you're convicted of any of these offenses, you will be subject to fines and imprisonment.

Firearms The Bureau of Alcohol, Tobacco and Firearms (ATF) regulates and restricts firearms and ammunition; it also approves all import transactions involving weapons and ammunition. If you want to import (or export) either of them, you must do so through a licensed importer, dealer, or manufacturer. Also, if the National Firearms Act prohibits certain weapons, ammunition, or similar devices from coming into the country, you won't be able to import them unless the ATF specifically authorizes you, in writing, to do so.

You don't need an ATF permit if you can demonstrate that you are returning with the same firearms or ammunition that you took out of the United States. The best way is to register your firearms and related equipment by taking them to any Customs office before you leave the United States. The Customs officer will register them on the same form CF-4457 used to register cameras or computers (see "Register Items Before You

Leave the United States").

For further information about importing weapons, contact the Bureau of Alcohol, Tobacco and Firearms, U.S. Department of the Treasury, Washington, DC 20226; or call (202) 927-8320 .

Many countries will not allow you to enter with a firearm even if you are only traveling through the country on the way to your final destination. If you plan to take your firearms or ammunition to another country, you should contact officials at that country's embassy to learn about its regulations. And please visit your nearest Customs office before your departure to learn the latest requirements for weapons and ammunition registration.

Fish and Wildlife Fish, wildlife, and products made from them are subject to import and export restrictions, prohibitions, permits or certificates, and quarantine requirements. We recommend that you contact the U.S. Fish and Wildlife Service before you depart if you plan to import or export any of the following:

Wild birds, land or marine mammals, reptiles, fish, shellfish, mollusks, or invertebrates. Any part or product of the above, such as skins, tusks, bone, feathers, or eggs. Products or articles manufactured from wildlife or fish.

Endangered species of wildlife, and products made from them, generally may not be imported or exported. You'll need a permit from the Fish and Wildlife Service to import virtually all types of ivory, unless it's from a warthog. The Fish and Wildlife Service has so many restrictions and prohibitions on various kinds of ivory - Asian elephant, African elephant, whale, rhinoceros, seal, pre-Endangered Species Act, post-CITES (Convention on International Trade in Endangered Species), and many others - that they urge you to contact them before you even think of acquiring ivory in a foreign country. They can be reached at (800) 358-2104 .

But you may import an object made of ivory if it's an antique; that is, if it's at least 100 years old. You will need documentation that authenticates the age of the ivory. You may import other antiques containing wildlife parts with the same condition: they must be accompanied by documentation proving they are at least 100 years old. (Certain other requirements for antiques may apply.)

For example: If you plan to buy such things as tortoiseshell jewelry, leather goods, or articles made from whalebone, ivory, skins, or fur, please, before you go, contact the U.S. Fish and Wildlife Service, Division of Law Enforcement, P.O. Box 3247, Arlington, VA 22203-3247, or call (800) 358-2104 . Hunters can get information on the limitations for importing and exporting migratory game birds from this office as well. Ask for the pamphlet Facts About Federal Wildlife Laws .

The Fish and Wildlife Service has designated specific ports of entry to handle fish and wildlife entries. If you plan to import anything discussed in this section, please also contact the Customs Service. We'll tell you about designated ports and send you the brochure Pets and Wildlife, which describes the regulations we enforce for all agencies that oversee the importation of animals.

Some states have fish and wildlife laws and regulations that are stricter than federal laws and regulations. If you're returning to such a state, be aware that the stricter state laws and regulations have priority. Similarly, the federal government does not allow you to import into the United States wild animals that were taken, killed, sold, possessed, or exported from another country if any of these acts violated foreign laws.

Game and Hunting Trophies If you plan to import game or a hunting trophy, please contact the Fish and Wildlife Service before you leave at (800) 358-2104 . Currently, 14 Customs ports of entry are designated to handle game and trophies; other Customs ports must get approval from the Fish and Wildlife Service to clear your entry.

Depending on the species you bring back, you might need a permit from the country where the animal was harvested. Regardless of the species, you'll have to fill out a Fish and Wildlife form 3-177, Declaration for Importation or Exportation.

Trophies may also be subject to inspection by the U.S. Department of Agriculture's Animal and Plant Health Inspection Service (APHIS) for sanitary purposes. General guidelines for importing trophies can be found in APHIS's publication Traveler's Tips. Contact USDA-

APHIS-PPQ, Permit Unit, 4700 River Road, Unit 133, Riverdale, MD 20737, or call (301) 734-8645

Also, federal regulations do not allow the importation of any species into a state with fish or wildlife laws that are more restrictive than federal laws. And if foreign laws were violated in the taking, sale, possession, or export to the United States of wild animals, those animals will not be allowed entry into the United States.

Warning: There are many regulations, enforced by various agencies, governing the importation of animals and animal parts. Failure to comply with them could result in time-consuming delays in clearing your trophy through Customs. You should always call for guidance before you depart.

Food Products You may bring bakery items and certain cheeses into the United States. APHIS publishes a booklet, Traveler's Tips, that offers extensive information about bringing food products into the country. For more information, or for a copy of Traveler's Tips, contact USDA-APHIS (see the section on "Game and Hunting Trophies" section).

Some imported foods are also subject to requirements of the Food and Drug Administration.

Meats, Livestock, and Poultry The regulations governing meat and meat products are very strict: you may not bring back fresh, dried, or canned meats or meat products from most foreign countries. Also, you may not bring in food products that have been prepared with meat.

The regulations on importing meat and meat products change frequently because they are based on disease outbreaks in different areas of the world. APHIS, which regulates meats and meat products as well as fruits and vegetables, invites you to call for more information on importing meats. Contact USDA-APHIS Veterinary Services, National Center for Import/Export (NCIE), 4700 River Road, Unit 40, Riverdale, MD 20737-1231; call (301) 734-7830 .

Fruits and Vegetables Bringing home fruits and vegetables can be quite troublesome. That apple you bought in the foreign airport just before boarding and then didn't eat? Whether Customs

105

will allow it into the United States depends on where you got it and where you're going after you arrive in the United States. The same is true for those magnificent Mediterranean tomatoes. Fresh fruits and vegetables can carry plant pests or diseases into the United States.

You may remember the Med fly hysteria of the late 1980s: Stories about crop damage caused by the Mediterranean fruit fly were in the papers for months. The state of California and the federal government together spent some $100 million to get rid of this pest. And the source of the outbreak? One traveler who brought home one contaminated piece of fruit.

It's best not to bring fresh fruits or vegetables into the United States. But if you plan to, call APHIS and get a copy of Traveler's Tips, which lists what you can and can't bring, and also items for which you'll need a permit. For more information, visit http://www.aphis.usda.gov/travel/ or www.aphis.usda.gov/ppq/permits.

Plants The plants, cuttings, seeds, unprocessed plant products, and certain endangered species that are allowed into the United States require import permits; some are prohibited entirely. Threatened or endangered species that are permitted must have export permits from the country of origin. Every single plant or plant product must be declared to the Customs officer and must be presented for USDA inspection, no matter how free of pests it appears to be. Address requests for information to USDA-APHIS-PPQ, 4700 River Road, Unit 139, Riverdale, MD 20737-1236; phone (301) 734-8295 ; or visit www.aphis.usda.gov/travel/.

Gold Gold coins, medals, and bullion, formerly prohibited, may be brought into the United States. However, under regulations administered by the Office of Foreign Assets Control, such items originating in or brought from Afghanistan, Cuba, Iran, Iraq, Libya, Serbia, and Sudan are prohibited entry. Copies of gold coins are prohibited if not properly marked by country of issuance.

Medication Rule of thumb: When you go abroad, take the medicines you'll need, no more, no less.

Narcotics and certain other drugs with a high potential for abuse - Rohypnol, GHB, and Fen-

Phen, to name a few - may not be brought into the United States, and there are severe penalties for trying to bring them in. If you need medicines that contain potentially addictive drugs or narcotics (e.g., some cough medicines, tranquilizers, sleeping pills, antidepressants, or stimulants), do the following:

• Declare all drugs, medicinals, and similar products to the appropriate Customs official.
• Carry all drugs, medicinals, and similar products in their original containers.
• Carry only the quantity of such substances that a person with that condition(e.g., chronic pain)
would normally carry for his/her use.
• Carry a prescription or written statement from your physician that the substances are being
used under a doctor's supervision and that they are necessary for your physical well-being
while traveling.

U.S. residents entering the United States at international land borders, who are carrying a validly obtained controlled substance (except narcotics such as marijuana, cocaine, heroin, or LSD), are subject to certain additional requirements. If a U.S. resident wants to bring in a controlled substance other than narcotics such as marijuana, cocaine, heroine, or LSD, but does not have a prescription for the substance issued by a U.S.-licensed practitioner (e.g., physician, dentist, etc.) registered with and authorized by the Drug Enforcement Administration (DEA) to prescribe the mediation, the individual may not import more than 50 dosage units of the medication. if the U.S. Resident has a prescription for the controlled substance issued by a DEA registrant, more than 50 dosage units may be imported by that person, provided all other legal requirements are met.

Please note that only medications that can be legally prescribed in the United States may be imported for personal use. Be aware that possession of certain substances may also violate state laws.

Warning: The Food and Drug Administration (FDA) prohibits the importation, by mail or in person, of fraudulent prescription and nonprescription drugs and medical devices. These include unorthodox "cures" for such medical conditions as cancer, AIDS, arthritis, or multiple sclerosis. Although such drugs or devices may be legal elsewhere, if the FDA has not approved them for use in the United States, they may not legally enter the country and will be confiscated if found, even if they were obtained under a foreign physician's prescription.

For specifics about importing controlled substances call (202) 307-2414 . For additional information about traveling with medication, contact your nearest FDA office or write Food and Drug Administration, Division of Import Operations and Policy, Room 12-8 (HFC-170), 5600 Fishers Lane, Rockville, MD 20857, or read the FDA's Subchapter on Coverage of Personal Importations.

Merchandise from Embargoed Countries Generally, you may not bring in any goods from the following countries: Afghanistan, Cuba, Iran*, Iraq, Libya, Serbia, and Sudan. The Office of Foreign Assets Control of the U.S. Treasury Department enforces this ban.

You may, however, bring in informational materials - pamphlets, books, tapes, films or recordings - from these countries, except for Iraq.

If you want to import merchandise from any of these countries, you will first need a specific license from the Office of Foreign Assets Control. Such licenses are rarely granted.

There are restrictions on travel to these countries. The restrictions are strictly enforced, so if you're thinking about going to any of the countries on this list, write to the Office of Foreign Assets Control, Department of the Treasury, Washington, DC 20220, before you make your plans.

*The embargo on Iranian goods is being revised to allow the importation of carpets and foods for human consumption such as caviar and pistachios. Please check with your local port to find out when the new regulations are scheduled to take effect. Until the new regulations are published, the complete embargo is still in force.

Pets

If you plan to take your pet abroad or import one on your return, please get a copy of Customs booklet, Pets & Wildlife. You should also check with state, county, and local authorities to learn if

their restrictions and prohibitions on pets are more strict than federal requirements.

Importing animals is closely regulated for public health reasons and also for the well-being of the animals. There are restrictions and prohibitions on bringing many species into the United States.

Cats must be free of evidence of diseases communicable to humans when they are examined at the port of entry. If the cat does not seem to be in good health, the owner may have to pay for an additional examination by a licensed veterinarian.

Dogs , too, must be free of evidence of diseases that could be communicable to humans. Puppies must be confined at a place of the owner's choosing until they are three months old; then they must be vaccinated against rabies. The puppy will then have to stay in confinement for another 30 days.

Dogs older than three months must get a rabies vaccination at least 30 days before they come to the United States and must be accompanied by a valid rabies vaccination certificate if coming from a country that is not rabies-free. This certificate should identify the dog, show the date of vaccination and the date it expires (there are one-year and three-year vaccinations), and be signed by a licensed veterinarian. If the certificate does not have an expiration date, Customs will accept it as long as the dog was vaccinated 12 months or less before coming to the United states. Dogs coming from rabies-free countries do not have to be vaccinated.

You may import birds as pets as long as you comply with APHIS and U.S. Fish and Wildlife requirements. These requirements may include quarantining the birds at one of APHIS' three Animal Import Centers at your expense. You must make advance reservations at the quarantine facility. If you intend to import a bird, call APHIS' National Center for Import and Export at (301) 734-8364 for more information. In any case, birds may only be imported through ports of entry where a USDA port veterinarian is on duty, any you must make arrangements in advance to have the bird examined by a USDA port veterinarian at the first U.S. port of entry. There is a user fee for this service of a minimum of $23.00 based on an hourly rate of $76/hour. For more information, you may contact the USDA, APHIS, Veterinary Services, National Center for Import and Export (NCIE), 4700 River Road, Unit 40, Riverdale, MD 20737-1231; phone number (301) 734-8364 .

Textiles and Clothing In general, there is no limit to how much fabric and clothing you can bring back as long as it is for your personal use, that is, for you or as gifts. (You may have to pay duty on it if you've exceeded your personal exemption, but the amount you may bring in is not limited.)

Unaccompanied shipments (packages that are mailed or shipped), however, may be subject to limitations on amount. The quantity limitations on clothing and textiles are called "quotas." In order to enter the United States, clothing and textiles may need to be accompanied by a document - you could think of it as a passport for fabrics - called a "visa." Sometimes, instead of a visa, an export license or certificate is required from the country that produced the clothing. A formal entry must be filed for all made-to-order suits from Hong Kong, no matter what their value, unless they accompany you and an export license issued by Hong Kong is presented with this entry. If you plan to get clothing or fabric on your trip and have it sent to you by mail or courier, check with Customs about quota and visa requirements before you travel.

Money and Other Monetary Instruments

You may bring into or take out of the country, including by mail, as much money as you wish. But if it's more than $10,000, you'll need to report it to Customs. Ask the Customs officer for the Currency Reporting Form (CF 4790). The penalties for not complying can be quite severe.

"Money" means monetary instruments and includes U.S. or foreign coin currently in circulation, currency, traveler's checks in any form, money orders, and negotiable instruments or investment securities in bearer form.

Traveling Back and Forth Across the Border

If you cross the U.S. border into a foreign country and reenter the United States more than once in a short time, you might not want to use your personal exemption ($800 in this example) until you've returned to the United States for the last time. Here's why:

When you leave the United States, come back, leave again, and then come back again, all on the same trip, you can lose your Customs exemption, since you've technically violated the "once every 30 days" rule. So if you know that your trip will involve these so-called "swing-backs," you can choose to save your personal exemption until the end of your trip.

For example, say you go to Canada, buy a liter of liquor, reenter the United States, then go back to Canada and buy $500 worth of merchandise and more liquor. You would probably want to save your $800 exemption for those final purchases and not use it for that first liter of liquor. In this case, on your first swing-back, simply tell the Customs inspector that you want to pay duty on the liquor, even though you could bring it in duty-free. (If you did, you would lose the $800 exemption, since it's only available to you once every 30 days.) In other words, all you have to do is tell the inspector that you want to pay duty the first (or second or third) time you come back to the United States if you know that you'll be leaving again soon, buying goods or getting them as gifts, and then reentering before the 30 days are up. In such a case, you're better off saving your exemption until the last time you reenter the United States.

Photographic Film

Customs will not examine film you bought abroad and are bringing back unless the Customs officer has reason to believe it contains prohibited material, such as child pornography.

You won't be charged duty on film bought in the United States and exposed abroad, whether it's developed or not. But film you bought and developed abroad counts as a dutiable item.

Customer Service Programs and Other Travel-related Information

Customer Service Programs The Customs Service is expanding its methods of improving customer service to international travelers at major U.S. travel hubs. One method is having supervisory Customs inspectors, called passenger service representatives, available to travelers on a full-time basis at more than 20 international airports and some seaports and land border ports of entry. The representatives' major purpose is to help travelers clear Customs.

Photos of the passenger service reps are posted

wherever the program is operating, so you can find them if you need assistance. If you have a concern or need help understanding Customs regulations and procedures, ask to speak with the passenger service rep on duty.

The second initiative involves kiosks, the sort of automated booths you see in malls, banks, department stores, and airports. Customs Service kiosks are located at international airports.

Think of them as automated passenger service reps: They're self-service computers with a touch-screen display. All you have to do is type in your country of destination and the computer will print the information for you. The screen displays a telephone number to call for more information. The kiosks also have pockets with Customs pamphlets on a variety of topics of interest to travelers: regulations on transporting currency, agriculture and food items, medicines, and pets, to name just a few.

Customs kiosks are located in the outbound passenger lounges at the following international airports: Atlanta; Boston; Charlotte, North Carolina; Chicago; Dallas/Ft. Worth; Detroit; Houston; JFK, New York; Los Angeles; Miami; Newark, New Jersey; Philadelphia; San Francisco; San Juan; and Washington/Dulles. More kiosks are planned.

If you have any questions about Customs procedures, requirements, or policies regarding travelers, or if you have any complaints about treatment you have received from Customs inspectors or about your Customs processing, please contact:

Executive Director, Passenger Programs U.S. Customs Service 1300 Pennsylvania Avenue, NW Room 5.4D Washington, DC 20229

Allegations of criminal or serious misconduct may be reported to the Office of Internal Affairs at 1-877-IA CALLS . You may also write them at P.O. Box 14475, Washington, D.C. 20044.

Other Travel-related Information Frequently, we are asked questions that are not customs matters. If you want to know about:

Immigration - The U.S. Immigration and Naturalization Service (INS) is responsible for the movement of people in and out of the United States. Please contact the Department of Justice, INS, for questions concerning resident alien and nonresident visa and passport information at 800-375-5283

Passports are issued by the U.S. Department of State's Passport Agency. Please contact the passport agency nearest you for more information. Postal clerks also accept passport application.

Baggage allowance - Ask the airline or steamship line you are traveling for more information.

Currency of other Nations - Your local bank can be of assistance.

Foreign countries - For information about the country you will visit or about what articles may be taken into that country, contact its embassy, consular office, or tourist information office.

Chapter 8

Health Information For International Travels

[The information in this chapter is an excerpt from a bulletin issued by the
U.S. Department of Health and Human Services, Centers for Disease Control.
It is intended to serve as advice to Americans traveling abroad.]

Health Hints for International Travelers

Introduction

This section includes practical information on how the traveler can avoid potential health problems. Some of these recommendations are common sense precautions; others have been scientifically documented.

Personal and specific preventive measures against certain diseases might require advance planning and advice from a physician or the local health department concerning immunization and prophylaxis.

Travelers who take prescription medications should be advised to carry an adequate supply, accompanied by a signed and dated statement from a physician; the statement should indicate the major health problems and dosages of such medications to provide information for medical authorities in case of emergency. As applicable, travelers should also be advised to take an extra pair of glasses or lens prescription and a card, tag, or bracelet that identifies any physical condition that might require emergency care.

Motion Sickness

Travelers with a history of motion sickness can attempt to avoid symptoms by taking anti-motion-sickness medications (for example, antihistamines) before departure.

Protection against Mosquitoes and Other Arthropods

Although vaccines or chemoprophylactic drugs are available against important vector-borne diseases such as yellow fever and malaria, travelers still should be advised to use repellents and other general protective measures against biting arthropods.

The effectiveness of malaria chemoprophylaxis is variable, depending on patterns of resistance and compliance with medication, and no similar preventive measures exist for other mosquito-borne diseases such as dengue. For many vector-borne diseases, no specific preventives are available.

General Preventive Measures

The principal approach to prevention of vector-borne diseases is avoidance. Tick- and mite-borne infections characteristically are diseases of "place;" whenever possible, known foci of disease transmission should be avoided. Although many vector-borne infections can be prevented by avoiding rural locations, certain mosquito- and midge-borne arboviral and parasitic infections are transmitted seasonally, and simple changes in itinerary can greatly reduce risk for acquiring them.

Travelers should be advised that exposure to arthropod bites can be minimized by modifying patterns of activity or behavior. Some vector mosquitoes are most active in twilight periods at dawn and dusk or in the evening. Avoidance of outdoor activity during these periods can reduce risk of exposure. Wearing long-sleeved shirts, long pants, and hats minimizes areas of exposed skin. Shirts should be tucked in. Repellents applied to clothing, shoes, tents, mosquito nets, and other gear will enhance protection.

When exposure to ticks or biting insects is a possibility, travelers should be advised to tuck

111

their pants into their socks and to wear boots, not sandals. Permethrin-based repellents applied as directed (see the following section, "Repellents") will enhance protection. Travelers should be advised to inspect themselves and their clothing for ticks, both during outdoor activity and at the end of the day. Ticks are detected more easily on light-colored or white clothing. Prompt removal of attached ticks can prevent some infections.

When accommodations are not adequately screened or air conditioned, bed nets are essential to provide protection and comfort. Bed nets should be tucked under mattresses and can be sprayed with a repellent, such as permethrin. The permethrin will be effective for several months if the bed net is not washed. Aerosol insecticides and mosquito coils can help to clear rooms of mosquitoes; however, some coils contain dichlorodiphenyl- trichloroethane (DDT) and should be used with caution

Repellents

Travelers should be advised that permethrin-containing repellents (e.g., Permanone) are recommended for use on clothing, shoes, bed nets, and camping gear. Permethrin is highly effective as an insecticide and as a repellent. Permethrin-treated clothing repels and kills ticks, mosquitoes, and other arthropods and retains this effect after repeated laundering. There appears to be little potential for toxicity from permethrin-treated clothing. The insecticide should be reapplied after every five washings.

Most authorities recommend repellents containing N,N-diethylmetatoluamide (DEET) as an active ingredient. DEET repels mosquitoes, ticks, and other arthropods when applied to the skin or clothing. In general, the more DEET a repellent contains, the longer time it can protect against mosquito bites. However, there appears to be no added benefit of concentrations greater than 50%. A microencapsulated, sustained-release formulation can have a longer period of activity than liquid formulations at the same concentrations. Length of protection also varies with ambient temperature, amount of perspiration, any water exposure, abrasive removal, and other factors.

No definitive studies have been published about what concentration of DEET is safe for children. No serious illness has arisen from use of DEET according the manufacturer's recommendations. DEET formulations as high as 50% are recommended for both adults and children >2 months of age. Lower concentrations are not as long lasting, offering short-term protection only and necessitating more frequent reapplication. Repellent products that do not contain DEET are not likely to offer the same degree of protection from mosquito bites as products containing DEET. Non-DEET repellents have not necessarily been as thoroughly studied as DEET and may not be safer for use on children. Parents should choose the type and concentration of repellent to be used by taking into account the amount of time that a child will be outdoors, exposure to mosquitoes, and the risk of mosquito-transmitted disease in the area. The recommendations for DEET use in pregnant women do not differ from those for nonpregnant adults.

DEET is toxic when ingested and may cause skin irritation in sensitive persons. High concentrations applied to skin can cause blistering. However, because DEET is so widely used, a great deal of testing has been done, and over the long history of DEET use, very few confirmed incidents of toxic reactions to DEET have occurred when the product is used properly.

Travelers should be advised that the possibility of adverse reactions to DEET will be minimized if they take the following precautions:

Use enough repellent to cover exposed skin or clothing. Do not apply repellent to skin that is under clothing. Heavy application is not necessary to achieve protection. If repellent is applied to clothing, wash treated clothing before wearing again.

Do not apply repellent to cuts, wounds, or irritated skin.
After returning indoors, wash treated skin with soap and water.
Do not spray aerosol or pump products in enclosed areas.
Do not apply aerosol or pump products directly to the face. Spray your hands and then rub them carefully over the face, avoiding eyes and mouth.
When using repellent on a child, apply it to your own hands and then rub them on your child.

Avoid the child's eyes and mouth and apply sparingly around the ears.

Do not apply repellent to children's hands. (Children tend to put their hands in their mouths.)

Do not allow young children to apply insect repellent to themselves; have an adult do it for them. Keep repellents out of reach of children.

Bed nets, repellents containing DEET, and permethrin should be purchased before traveling and can be found in hardware, camping, sporting goods, and military surplus stores.

Risks From Food and Drink

Contaminated food and drink are common sources for the introduction of infection into the body. Among the more common infections that travelers can acquire from contaminated food and drink are Escherichia coli infections, shigellosis or bacillary dysentery, giardiasis, cryptosporidiosis, and hepatitis A. Other less common infectious disease risks for travelers include typhoid fever and other salmonelloses, cholera, infections caused by rotavirus and Norwalk-like viruses, and a variety of protozoan and helminthic parasites (other than those that cause giardiasis and cryptosporidiosis). Many of the infectious diseases transmitted in food and water can also be acquired directly through the fecal-oral route.

Water

Water that has been adequately chlorinated, using minimum recommended water treatment standards employed in the United States, will afford significant protection against viral and bacterial waterborne diseases. However, chlorine treatment alone, as used in the routine disinfection of water, might not kill some enteric viruses and the parasitic organisms that cause giardiasis, amebiasis, and cryptosporidiosis. In areas where chlorinated tap water is not available or where hygiene and sanitation are poor, travelers should be advised that only the following might be safe to drink:

Beverages, such as tea and coffee, made with boiled water.

Canned or bottled carbonated beverages, including carbonated bottled water and soft drinks.

Beer and wine.

Where water might be contaminated, travelers should be advised that ice should also be considered contaminated and should not be used in beverages. If ice has been in contact with containers used for drinking, travelers should be advised to thoroughly clean the containers, preferably with soap and hot water, after the ice has been discarded.

It is safer to drink a beverage directly from the can or bottle than from a questionable container. However, water on the outside of beverage cans or bottles might be contaminated also. Therefore, travelers should be advised to dry wet cans or bottles before they are opened, and to wipe clean surfaces with which the mouth will have direct contact. Where water might be contaminated, travelers should be advised to avoid brushing their teeth with tap water.

Treatment of Water

Travelers should be advised of the following methods for treating water to make it safe for drinking and other purposes.

Boiling is by far the most reliable method to make water of uncertain purity safe for drinking. Water should be brought to a vigorous rolling boil for 1 minute and allowed to cool to room temperature; ice should not be added. This procedure will kill bacterial and parasitic causes of diarrhea at all altitudes and viruses at low altitudes. To kill viruses at altitudes above 2,000 meters (6,562 feet), water should be boiled for 3 minutes or chemical disinfection should be used after the water has boiled for 1 minute. Adding a pinch of salt to each quart or pouring the water several times from one clean container to another will improve the taste.

Chemical disinfection with iodine is an alternative method of water treatment when it is not feasible to boil water. However, this method cannot be relied upon to kill Cryptosporidium unless the water is allowed to sit for 15 hours before it is drunk. Two well-tested methods for disinfection with iodine are the use of tincture of iodine (Table 4-1) and the use of tetraglycine hydroperiodide tablets (for example, Globaline®, Potable-Aqua®, or Coghlan's®). These tablets are available from pharmacies and sporting goods stores. The manufacturers' instructions should be followed. If water is cloudy, the number of tablets used should be doubled; if water is extremely cold ($<5°$ Celsius [$<41°$ Fahrenheit]), an attempt should be made to warm the water, and the recommended contact time should be increased to achieve reliable disinfection. Cloudy water should be strained through a clean cloth into a container to remove any sediment or floating matter, and then the water should be boiled or treated with iodine. Chlorine, in various forms, can also be used for chemical disinfection. However, its germicidal activity varies greatly with the pH, temperature, and organic content of the water to be purified and, therefore, it can produce less consistent levels of disinfection in many types of water. Chemically treated water is intended for short-term use only. If iodine-disinfected water is the only water available, it should be used for only a few weeks.

Portable filters currently on the market will provide various degrees of protection against microbes. Reverse-osmosis filters provide protection against viruses, bacteria, and protozoa, but they are expensive, are larger than most filters used by backpackers, and the small pores on this type of filter are rapidly plugged by muddy or cloudy water. In addition, the membranes in some filters can be damaged by chlorine in water. Microstrainer filters with pore sizes in the 0.1- to 0.3-micrometer range can remove bacteria and protozoa from drinking water, but they do not remove viruses. To kill viruses, travelers using microstrainer filters should be advised to disinfect the water with iodine or chlorine after filtration, as described previously. Filters with iodine-impregnated resins are most effective against bacteria, and the iodine will kill some viruses; however, the contact time with the iodine in the filter is too short to kill the protozoa Cryptosporidium and, in cold water, Giardia.

Proper selection, operation, care, and maintenance of water filters is essential to producing safe water. The manufacturers' instructions should be followed. NSF International, an independent testing company, tests and certifies water filters for their ability to remove protozoa, but not for their ability to remove bacteria or viruses. Few published reports in the scientific literature have evaluated the efficacy of specific brands or models of filters against bacteria and viruses in water. Until such information becomes available, the Centers for Disease Control and Prevention (CDC) cannot identify which specific brands or models of filters are most likely to remove bacteria and viruses. A list of filters that have passed NSF tests for parasite removal can be obtained by calling 1-

800-673-8010; by writing to NSF at 789 North Dixboro Road, P.O. Box 130140, Ann Arbor, Michigan 48113-0140; or online at http://www.NSF.org.

As a last resort, if no source of safe drinking water is available or can be obtained, tap water that is uncomfortably hot to touch might be safer than cold tap water; however, proper disinfection, filtering, or boiling is still advised.

Food

To avoid illness, travelers should be advised to select food with care. All raw food is subject to contamination. Particularly in areas where hygiene and sanitation are inadequate, the traveler should be advised to avoid salads, uncooked vegetables, and unpasteurized milk and milk products such as cheese, and to eat only food that has been cooked and is still hot, or fruit that has been peeled by the traveler personally. Undercooked and raw meat, fish, and shellfish can carry various intestinal pathogens. Cooked food that has been allowed to stand for several hours at ambient temperature can provide a fertile medium for bacterial growth and should be thoroughly reheated before serving. Consumption of food and beverages obtained from street food vendors has been associated with an increased risk of illness. The easiest way to guarantee a safe food source for an infant younger than 6 months of age is to have the infant breast feed. If the infant has already been weaned from the breast, formula prepared from commercial powder and boiled water is the safest and most practical food.

Some species of fish and shellfish can contain poisonous biotoxins, even when well cooked. The most common type of biotoxin in fish is ciguatoxin. The flesh of the barracuda is the most toxic laden and should always be avoided. Red snapper, grouper, amberjack, sea bass, and a wide range of tropical reef fish contain the toxin at unpredictable times. The potential for ciguatera poisoning exists in all subtropical and tropical insular areas of the West Indies and the Pacific and Indian Oceans where the implicated fish species are eaten. Symptoms of ciguatera poisoning include gastroenteritis followed by neurologic problems such as dysesthesias; temperature reversal; weakness; and, rarely, hypotension. Scombroid is another common fish poisoning that

114

occurs worldwide in tropical, as well as temperate, regions. Fish of the Scombridae family (for example, bluefin, yellowfin tuna, mackerel, and bonito), as well as some nonscombroid fish (for example, mahimahi, herring, amberjack, and bluefish) may contain high levels of histidine in their flesh. With improper refrigeration or preservation, histidine is converted to histamine, which can cause flushing, headache, nausea, vomiting, diarrhea, and urticaria.

Cholera cases have occurred among people who ate crab brought back from Latin America by travelers. Travelers should be advised not to bring perishable seafood with them when they return to the United States from high-risk areas.

Table 1.--Treatment of Water With Tincture of Iodine.

Tincture of Iodine	Drops* to be Added per Quart or Liter	
	Clear Water	Cold or Cloudy Water†
2%	5	10

Note: tincture of iodine can come from a medicine chest or first-aid kit.

1 drop = 0.05 milliliter. Water must stand for a minimum of 30 minutes before it is safe to use.

Very turbid or very cold water can require prolonged contact time; if possible, such water should be allowed to stand several hours prior to use. To ensure that *Cryptosporidium* is killed, water must stand for 15 hours before drinking.

Travelers' Diarrhea

Epidemiology

Travelers' diarrhea (TD) is a syndrome characterized by a twofold or greater increase in the frequency of unformed bowel movements. Commonly associated symptoms include abdominal cramps, nausea, bloating, urgency, fever, and malaise. Episodes of TD usually begin abruptly, occur during travel or soon after returning home, and are generally self-limited. The most important determinant of risk is the destination of the traveler. Attack rates of 20% to 50% are commonly reported. High-risk destinations include most of the developing countries of Latin America, Africa, the Middle East, and Asia. Intermediate-risk destinations include most of the southern European countries and a few Caribbean islands. Low-risk destinations include Canada, northern Europe, Australia, New Zealand, the United States, and some of the Caribbean islands.

TD is slightly more common in young adults than in older people. The reasons for this difference are unclear, but could include a lack of acquired immunity, more adventurous travel styles, and different eating habits. Attack rates are similar in men and women. The onset of TD is usually within the first week of travel, but can occur at any time during the visit and even after returning home.

TD is acquired through ingestion of fecally contaminated food or water, or both. Both cooked

115

and uncooked foods might be implicated if they have been improperly handled. Especially risky foods include raw or undercooked meat and seafood and raw fruits and vegetables. Tap water, ice, and unpasteurized milk and dairy products can be associated with increased risk of TD; safe beverages include bottled carbonated beverages (especially flavored beverages), beer, wine, hot coffee or tea, or water boiled and appropriately treated with iodine or chlorine.

The place food is prepared appears to be an important variable, with private homes, restaurants, and street vendors listed in order of increasing risk.

TD typically results in four to five loose or watery stools per day. The median duration of diarrhea is 3 to 4 days. Approximately 10% of the cases persist longer than 1 week, approximately 2% longer than 1 month, and <1% longer than 3 months. Persistent diarrhea is, thus, quite uncommon and can differ considerably from acute TD with respect to etiology and risk factors. Approximately 15% of ill people experience vomiting, and 2% to 10% have diarrhea accompanied by fever or bloody stools, or both. Travelers can experience more than one episode of TD during a single trip. Rarely is TD life threatening.

Etiology

Infectious agents are the primary cause of TD. Travelers from developed countries to developing countries frequently experience a rapid, dramatic change in the type of organisms in their gastrointestinal tract. These new organisms often include potential enteric pathogens. Those who develop diarrhea have ingested an inoculum of virulent organisms sufficiently large to overcome individual defense mechanisms, resulting in symptoms.

Enteric Bacterial Pathogens

Enterotoxigenic Escherichia coli (ETEC) are among the most common causative agents of TD in all countries where surveys have been conducted. ETEC produce a watery diarrhea associated with cramps and a low-grade or no fever.

Salmonella gastroenteritis is a well-known disease that occurs throughout the world. In developed nations, this large group of organisms is the most common cause of outbreaks of food-associated diarrhea. In developing countries, the proportion of cases of TD caused by nontyphoidal salmonellae varies, but is not high. Salmonellae also can cause dysentery characterized by small-volume stools containing bloody mucus.

Shigellae are well known as the cause of bacillary dysentery. The shigellae are the cause of TD in up to 20% of travelers to developing countries.

Campylobacter jejuni is a common cause of diarrhea throughout the world; it is responsible for a small percentage of the reported cases of TD, some with bloody diarrhea. Additional studies are needed to determine how frequently it causes TD.

Vibrio parahaemolyticus is associated with ingestion of raw or poorly cooked seafood and has caused TD in passengers on Caribbean cruise ships and in people traveling in Asia. How frequently it causes disease in other areas of the world is unknown.

Less common bacterial pathogens include other diarrheagenic E. coli, Yersinia enterocolitica, Vibrio cholerae O1 and O139, non-O1 V. cholerae, Vibrio fluvialis, and possibly Aeromonas hydrophila and Plesiomonas shigelloides.

Viral Enteric Pathogens--Rotaviruses and Norwalk-like Virus

Along with the newly acquired bacteria, the traveler can also acquire many viruses. In six studies, for example, as much as 36% of diarrheal illnesses in travelers (median 22%) was associated with rotaviruses in the stools. However, a comparable number of asymptomatic travelers also had rotaviruses, and up to 50% of symptomatic people with rotavirus infections also had nonviral pathogens. Approximately 10% to 15% of travelers develop serologic evidence of infection with Norwalk-like viruses. The roles of adenoviruses, astroviruses, coronaviruses, enteroviruses, or other viral agents in causing TD are even less clear. Although viruses are commonly acquired by travelers, they do not

116

appear to be frequent causes of TD in adults.

Parasitic Enteric Pathogens

While less commonly implicated as the cause of TD than bacteria, enteric protozoa are recognized etiologic agents of TD. In the small number of studies that have included appropriate testing for these parasites in travelers or expatriates in developing countries, a variable proportion of TD has been attributed to Giardia intestinalis (0% to 12%), Entamoeba histolytica (0% to 5%), Cryptosporidium parvum (2% to 5%), and Cyclospora cayetanensis (1% to 11%). The likelihood of a parasitic etiology is higher when diarrheal illness is prolonged. E. histolytica should be considered when the patient has dysentery or invasive diarrhea (bloody stools). Specific diagnostic testing is required to identify E. histolytica, C. parvum, and C. cayetanensis. Dientamoeba fragilis, Isospora belli, Balantidium coli, and Strongyloides stercoralis can cause occasional cases of TD. While not common causes of TD, these parasites should be considered in persistent, unexplained cases.

Unknown Causes

No data have been presented to support noninfectious causes of TD, such as changes in diet, jet lag, altitude, and fatigue. Existing evidence indicates that in all but a few instances, such as drug-induced or preexisting gastrointestinal disorders, an infectious agent or agents can cause diarrhea in travelers. However, even with the application of the best existing methods for detecting bacteria, viruses, and parasites, 20% to 50% of cases of TD remain without recognized etiologies.

Prevention

There are four possible approaches to prevention of TD: (1) instruction regarding food and beverage consumption, (2) immunization, (3) use of nonantimicrobial medications, and (4) use of prophylactic antimicrobial drugs. Data indicate that meticulous attention to food and beverage consumption, as mentioned previously, can decrease the likelihood of developing TD. Most travelers, however, encounter difficulty in observing the requisite dietary restrictions.

No available vaccines and none that are expected to be available in the next 3 years are effective against TD. Several nonantimicrobial agents have been advocated for prevention of TD. Available controlled studies indicate that prophylactic use of difenoxine, the active metabolite of diphenoxylate (Lomotil®), actually increases the incidence of TD, in addition to producing other undesirable side effects. Antiperistaltic agents (for example, Lomotil® and Imodium®) are not effective in preventing TD. No data support the prophylactic use of activated charcoal.

Bismuth subsalicylate, taken as the active ingredient of Pepto-Bismol® (2 ounces four times a day, or two tablets four times a day), has decreased the incidence of diarrhea by about 60% in several placebo-controlled studies. Side effects include temporary blackening of the tongue and stools; occasional nausea and constipation; and, rarely, tinnitus. Available data are not sufficient to exclude a risk to the traveler from the use of such large doses of bismuth subsalicylate for a period of more than 3 weeks. Bismuth subsalicylate should be avoided by travelers with aspirin allergy, renal insufficiency, and gout, and by those who are taking anticoagulants, probenecid, or methotrexate. In travelers already taking aspirin or related salicylates for arthritis, large concurrent doses of bismuth subsalicylate can produce toxic serum concentrations of salicylate. Caution should be used in giving bismuth subsalicylate to children and adolescents with chickenpox or influenza because of a potential risk of Reye's syndrome. Bismuth subsalicylate has not been approved for infants and children younger than 3 years of age. Bismuth subsalicylate appears to be an effective prophylactic agent for TD, but is not recommended for prophylaxis of TD for periods of more than 3 weeks. Further studies of the efficacy and side effects of lower dose regimens are needed.

Controlled data are available on the prophylactic value of several other nonantimicrobial drugs. Enterovioform® and related halogenated hydroxyquinoline derivatives (for example, clioquinol, iodoquinol, Mexaform®, and Intestopan®) are not helpful in preventing TD, can have serious neurologic side effects, and should never be used for prophylaxis of TD.

Controlled studies have indicated that a variety of antibiotics, including doxycycline, trimethoprim/sulfamethoxazole (TMP/SMX), trimethoprim alone, and the fluoroquinolone agents ciprofloxacin and norfloxacin, when taken prophylactically have been 52% to 95% effective in preventing TD in several areas of the developing world. The effectiveness of these agents, however, depends on the antibiotic resistance patterns of the pathogenic bacteria in each area of travel, and such information is seldom available. Resistance to fluoroquinolones is the least common, but this is changing as use of these agents increases worldwide.

Although effective in preventing some bacterial causes of diarrhea, antibiotics have no effect on the acquisition of various viral and parasitic diseases. Prophylactic antibiotics can give travelers a false sense of security about the risk associated with consuming certain local foods and beverages.

The benefits of widespread prophylactic use of doxycyline, fluroquinolones, TMP/SMX, or TMP alone in several million travelers must be weighed against the potential drawbacks. The known risks include allergic and other side effects (such as common skin rashes, photosensitivity of the skin, blood disorders, Stevens-Johnson syndrome, and staining of the teeth in children), as well as other infections that might be induced by antimicrobial therapy (such as antibiotic-associated colitis, Candida vaginitis, and Salmonella enteritis). Because of the uncertain risk involved in the widespread administration of these antimicrobial agents, their prophylactic use is not recommended. Although it seems reasonable to use prophylactic antibiotics in certain high-risk groups, such as travelers with immunosuppression or immunodeficiency, no data directly support this practice. There is little evidence that other disease entities are worsened sufficiently by an episode of TD to risk the rare undesirable side effects of prophylactic antimicrobial drugs. Therefore, prophylactic antimicrobial agents are not recommended for travelers. Instead, available data support the recommendation that travelers be instructed in sensible dietary practices as a prophylactic measure. This recommendation is justified by the excellent results of early treatment of TD as outlined in the following section. Some travelers might wish to consult with their physicians and might elect to use prophylactic antimicrobial agents for travel under special circumstances, once the risks and benefits are clearly understood.

Treatment

Travelers with TD have two major complaints for which they desire relief--abdominal cramps and diarrhea. Many agents have been proposed to control these symptoms, but few have been demonstrated to be effective in rigorous clinical trials.

Nonspecific Agents

A variety of "adsorbents" have been used in treating diarrhea. For example, activated charcoal has been found to be ineffective in the treatment of diarrhea. Kaolin and pectin have been widely used for diarrhea. While the combination appears to give the stools more consistency, it has not been shown to decrease cramps and frequency of stools or to shorten the course of infectious diarrhea. Lactobacillus preparations and yogurt have also been advocated, but no evidence supports use of these treatments for TD.

Bismuth subsalicylate preparation (1 ounce of liquid or two 262.5-milligram [mg] tablets every 30 minutes for eight doses) decreased the frequency of stools and shortened the duration of illness in several placebo-controlled studies. Treatment was limited to 48 hours at most, with no more than eight doses in a 24-hour period. There is concern about taking large amounts of bismuth and salicylate without supervision, especially for people who might be intolerant of salicylates, who have renal insufficiency, or who take salicylates for other reasons.

Antimotility Agents

Antimotility agents are widely used in treating diarrhea of all types. Natural opiates (paregoric, tincture of opium, and codeine) have long been used to control diarrhea and cramps. Synthetic agents, such as diphenoxylate and loperamide, come in convenient dosage forms and provide prompt symptomatic but temporary relief of uncomplicated TD. However, they should not be used by people with high fever or with blood in the stools. Use of these drugs should be discontinued if symptoms persist beyond 48 hours. Diphenoxylate and loperamide should not be used in infants younger than 2 years of age.

Antimicrobial Treatment

Travelers who develop diarrhea with three or more loose stools in an 8-hour period, especially if associated with nausea, vomiting, abdominal cramps, fever, or blood in the stools, might benefit from antimicrobial treatment. A typical 3- to 5-day illness can often be shortened to 1 to 1 1/2 days by effective antimicrobial agents. The effectiveness of antibiotic therapy will depend on the etiologic agent and its antibiotic sensitivity. The antibiotic regimen most likely to be effective is ciprofloxacin (500 mg) taken twice a day. Other fluroquinolones, such as norfloxacin, ofloxacin, or levofloxacin might be equally as effective. Fewer side effects and less widespread antibiotic resistance has been reported with the fluoroquinolones than with TMP/SMX. Three days of treatment is recommended, although 2 or fewer days might be sufficient. Nausea and vomiting without diarrhea should not be treated with antimicrobial drugs.

Travelers should be advised to consult a physician rather than attempt self-medication if the diarrhea is severe or does not resolve within several days; if there is blood or mucus, or both, in the stools; if fever occurs with shaking chills; or if there is dehydration with persistent diarrhea.

Oral Fluids

Most cases of diarrhea are self-limited and require only simple replacement of fluids and salts lost in diarrheal stools. This is best achieved by use of an oral rehydration solution such as World Health Organization oral rehydration salts (ORS) solution (Table 2). This solution is appropriate for treating as well as preventing dehydration. Travelers should be advised that ORS packets are available at stores or pharmacies in almost all developing countries. ORS is prepared by adding one packet to boiled or treated water. Packet instructions should be checked carefully to ensure that the salts are added to the correct volume of water. ORS solution should be consumed or discarded within 12 hours if held at room temperature or 24 hours if kept refrigerated.

Travelers should be advised to avoid iced drinks and noncarbonated bottled fluids made from water of uncertain quality. Dairy products aggravate diarrhea in some people and travelers with diarrhea should be advised to avoid them.

Infants With Diarrhea

Infants 2 years of age or younger are at high risk of acquiring TD. The greatest risk to the infant with diarrhea is dehydration (Table 3). Travelers should be advised that dehydration is best prevented by use of the WHO ORS solution in addition to the infant's usual food. ORS packets are available at stores or pharmacies in almost all developing countries. ORS is prepared by adding one packet to boiled or treated water. Travelers should be advised to check packet instructions carefully to ensure that the salts are added to the correct volume of water. ORS solution should be consumed or discarded within 12 hours if held at room temperature, or 24 hours if kept refrigerated. A dehydrated child will drink ORS avidly; travelers should be advised to give it to the child as long as the dehydration persists. An infant who vomits the ORS will usually keep it down if it is offered by spoon in frequent small sips. Breast-fed infants should continue nursing on demand. For bottle-fed infants, full-strength, lactose-free or lactose-reduced formulas should be administered. Older infants and children receiving semi-solid or solid foods should continue to receive their usual diet during the illness. Recommended foods include starches, cereals, yogurt, fruits, and vegetables. Immediate medical attention is required for the infant with diarrhea who develops signs of moderate to severe dehydration (Table 3), bloody diarrhea, >39° Celsius (>102° Fahrenheit) fever, or persistent vomiting. While medical attention is being obtained, the infant should be offered ORS.

More information is available from the CDC in a publication entitled, "The Management of Acute Diarrhea in Children: Oral Rehydration, Maintenance, and Nutritional Therapy" (MMWR No. RR-16, October 16, 1992). ORS packets are available in the United States from Jianas Brothers Packaging Company, 2533 Southwest Boulevard, Kansas City, Missouri 64108 (1-816-421-2880). Also, Cera Products, 8265 I Patuxent Range Road, Jessup, Maryland 20794 (1-410-997-2334 or 1-888-Ceralyte), markets a cereal- rather than a glucose-based product, Ceralyte, in several different flavors.

Table 2.--Composition of World Health Organization (WHO) Oral Rehydration Solution (ORS) for Diarrheal Illness.

Ingredient	Amount
Sodium chloride	3.5 grams per liter
Potassium chloride	1.5 grams per liter

119

Glucose   20.0 grams per liter

Trisodium citrate*   2.9 grams per liter

  * An earlier formulation that used sodium bicarbonate 2.5 grams per liter had a shorter shelf-life, but was physiologically equivalent and may still be produced in some countries.

Precautions for Children and Pregnant Women

Although infants and children do not make up a large proportion of travelers to high-risk areas, some children do accompany their families. Teenagers should follow the advice given to adults, with possible adjustments of doses of medication. Physicians should be aware of the risks of tetracyclines for infants and children younger than 8 years of age. Few data are available about the usage of antidiarrheal drugs in infants and children. Drugs should be prescribed with caution for pregnant women and nursing mothers.

Table 3.--Assessment of Dehydration Levels in Infants.

Signs	Severity		
	Mild	Moderate	Severe
General condition	Thirsty, restless, irritable	Thirsty, restless, agitated	Withdrawn, somnolent, or comatose
Pulse	Normal	Rapid, weak	Rapid, weak
Anterior fontanelle	Normal	Sunken	Very sunken
Eyes	Normal	Sunken	Very sunken
Tears	Present	Absent	Absent
Urine	Normal	Reduced, concentrated	None for several hours
Weight loss	4% to 5%	6% to 9%	10% or more

Cruise Ship Travel

Preventive Measures

International cruise ship travelers often are uncertain about the vaccines and prevention behaviors applicable to their particular cruise itineraries. Cruise ships often visit international ports and passengers disembark to sightsee and to experience the local culture; however, among cruise ship passengers, risk of exposure to geographic-specific infectious diseases is difficult to quantify because

of limited data. Because of this difficulty, the Centers for Disease Control and Prevention (CDC) recommends following those prevention and vaccine recommendations that apply to each country visited (as detailed in this text and at CDC's Travelers' Health website at http://www.cdc.gov/travel). The traveler should be advised to consult with a travel health advisor or a primary health care provider who may choose to modify the recommendations depending on the length of the traveler's visit ashore.

Sanitation

In 1975, because of several major disease outbreaks on cruise vessels, the Centers for Disease Control and Prevention (CDC) established the Vessel Sanitation Program (VSP) as a cooperative activity with the cruise ship industry. This joint program strives to achieve and maintain a level of sanitation on passenger vessels that will lower the risk of gastrointestinal disease outbreaks and provide a healthful environment for passengers and crews. CDC addresses the program goals by encouraging the industry to establish and maintain a comprehensive sanitation program and overseeing of its success through an inspection process. Every vessel having a foreign itinerary and carrying 13 or more passengers is subject to twice yearly unannounced inspections and, when necessary, reinspections. Inspections, conducted only at ports under U.S. control, cover such environmental aspects as:

Water supply, storage, distribution, backflow protection, and disinfection.

Food handling during storage, preparation, and service, and product temperature control.

Potential contamination of food, water, and ice.

Employee practices and personal hygiene.

General cleanliness, facility repair, and vector control.

Training programs in general environmental and public health practices.

A score of 86 or higher at the time of the inspection indicates that the ship is providing an acceptable standard of sanitation. In general, the lower the score, the lower the level of sanitation; however, a low score does not necessarily imply an imminent risk of an outbreak of gastrointestinal disease or other illness related to environmental sanitation. Each ship is required to document a plan for corrective action following each inspection. Inspectors will recommend a ship not sail if they detect an imminent health hazard aboard ship (for example, inadequate facilities for maintaining safe food temperatures or a contaminated drinking water system). Full information on inspection criteria can be obtained by writing to the VSP office at the address listed at the end of this section. At any time, the Director of CDC may determine that failure to implement corrective actions presents a threat of communicable disease being introduced into the United States and may take additional action, including detaining the ship in port.

The scores and inspection reports for each ship are available via the Internet at http://www.cdc.gov/nceh/vsp. Scores are also published biweekly in the Summary of Sanitation Inspections of International Cruise Ships, commonly known as the "Green Sheet." This sheet is distributed to travel-related services worldwide and is a way to communicate a ship's compliance with VSP recommendations both to the cruise ship industry and to the consumer. The Green Sheet is also available via the Internet site, as well as the CDC fax information service (1-888-232-6789; request information on "Cruise Ship Sanitation Inspection Updates"). Information can also be requested by sending an e-mail to vsp@cdc.gov or by writing to the Vessel Sanitation Program, National Center for Environmental Health, CDC, 4770 Buford Highway, NE, Mailstop F-16, Atlanta, Georgia 30341-3724.

Spraying Aircraft for Insects--Disinsection

International travelers should be advised that some countries require the spraying of the aircraft passenger compartment with insecticide while passengers are present. This practice is called disinsection, and is used to prevent the importation of insects such as mosquitoes. While these recommended disinsection procedures have been determined to be safe by the World Health Organization, they can aggravate certain health conditions (for example, allergies). Countries that might spray the passenger cabin for insects are located in Latin America, the Caribbean, Australia, and the South Pacific region.

Travelers who are interested in determining what disinsection procedures might be performed on a particular flight should be advised to see the U.S. Department of Transportation web site at http://www.ostpxweb.dot.gov/policy/safety/disin.htm.

Environmental Effects

International travelers can be subject to certain stresses that can lower resistance to disease, such as crowding; disruption of usual eating and drinking habits; and time changes, with "jet lag" contributing to a disturbed pattern of the sleep and wakefulness cycle. These conditions of stress can lead to nausea, indigestion, fatigue, or insomnia. Complete adaptation depends on the number of time zones crossed and can take a week or more.

Heat and cold can be directly or indirectly responsible for some diseases and can give rise to serious skin conditions. Dermatophytoses such as athlete's foot are often made worse by warm, humid conditions.

Excessive heat and humidity alone, or strenuous activity under those conditions, can lead to heat exhaustion from salt and water deficiency and to the more serious heat stroke or hyperthermia. Travelers who anticipate being exposed to excessive heat should be advised to increase consumption of nonalcoholic liquids and to be aware of signs of heat illness, such as headache; dizziness; and red, hot, and dry skin. The ultraviolet rays of the sun can cause severe and very debilitating sunburn in lighter skinned people. Wearing a wide-brimmed hat and using a sunscreen with a sun protection factor (SPF) of 15 or higher on exposed skin will reduce the likelihood of severe sunburn.

Excessive cold affects people who might be inadequately dressed or who remain outside for extended periods of time. Cold particularly affects the elderly and the young. Exposure to cold can lead to hypothermia and to frostbite of exposed parts of the body. Alcohol consumption can amplify the adverse effects of cold temperatures.

Breathing and swallowing dust when traveling on unpaved roads or in arid areas can be followed by nausea and malaise and can cause increased susceptibility to infections of the upper respiratory tract. The harmful effects of air pollution are

121

difficult to avoid when visiting some cities; limiting strenuous activity and not smoking can help.

Altitude Illness

Travelers whose itineraries will take them above an altitude of 1,829 to 2,438 meters (6,000 to 8,000 feet) should be aware of the risk of altitude illness. Travelers are exposed to higher altitudes in a number of ways: by mountain climbing or trekking in or to high-altitude destinations such as Cuzco, Peru (3,000 meters [11,000 feet]); La Paz, Bolivia (3,444 meters [11,300 feet]); or Lhasa, Tibet (3,749 meters [12,500 feet]). Travelers with underlying medical conditions, such as congestive heart failure or pulmonary insufficiency, should be advised to consult a doctor familiar with high-altitude illness before undertaking such travel. The risk of ischemic heart disease does not appear to be increased at high altitudes, but having a heart attack in a remote area increases the problems of obtaining appropriate treatment.

Travelers vary considerably in their susceptibility to altitude illness, and there are currently no screening tests that predict whether someone is at greater risk of getting altitude illness. Past experience is the most reliable guide; susceptibility to altitude illness appears to be genetic, and is not affected by training or physical fitness.

Altitude illness is divided into three syndromes: acute mountain sickness (AMS), high-altitude cerebral edema (HACE), and high-altitude pulmonary edema (HAPE). AMS is the most common presentation of altitude illness and, while it can occur at altitudes as low as 1,219 to 1,829 meters (4,000 to 6,000 feet), most often occurs in abrupt ascents to over 2,743 meters (9,000 feet). The symptoms resemble an alcohol hangover: headache; profound fatigue; loss of appetite; nausea; and, occasionally, vomiting. The onset of AMS is delayed, usually beginning at least 6 to 12 hours after arrival at a higher altitude.

HACE is considered a severe progression of AMS. In addition to the AMS symptoms, lethargy becomes profound, confusion can manifest, and ataxia will be demonstrated during the tandem gait test. The tandem gait test--having the traveler walk a straight line while placing the heel of the front foot against the toe of the rear foot--is the best test for determining whether HACE is present. A traveler who falls off the line while trying to do the tandem gait test has HACE by definition, and immediate descent is mandatory.

HAPE can occur by itself or in conjunction with HACE. The initial symptoms are increased breathlessness with exertion, and eventually increased breathlessness at rest. The diagnosis can usually be made when breathlessness fails to resolve after several minutes of rest. At this point, it is critical to descend to a lower altitude.

The main point of instructing travelers about altitude illness is not to prevent any possibility of getting altitude illness, but to prevent deaths from altitude illness. The onset of symptoms and clinical course are slow enough and predictable enough that there is no reason for someone to die from altitude illness unless trapped by weather or geography in a situation in which descent is impossible. The three rules that travelers should be made aware of to prevent death from altitude illness are:

Learn the early symptoms of altitude illness and recognize when personally suffering from them.
Never ascend to sleep at a higher altitude when experiencing any of the symptoms of altitude illness.
Descend if the symptoms become worse while resting at the same altitude.

Studies have shown that travelers who are on organized group treks to high-altitude locations are more likely to die of altitude illness than travelers who are by themselves. This is most likely the result of group pressure (whether perceived or real) and a fixed itinerary. The most important aspect of preventing severe altitude illness is to refrain from further ascent until all symptoms of altitude illness have disappeared.

Children are as susceptible to altitude illness as adults, and young children who cannot talk can show very nonspecific symptoms, such as loss of appetite and irritability. There are no studies or case reports of harm occurring to a fetus if the mother travels briefly to a high altitude during pregnancy. However, most authorities recommend that pregnant women stay below 3,658 meters (12,000 feet) if possible.

Three medications have been shown to be useful in

the prevention and treatment of altitude illness. Acetazolamide (Diamox®) can prevent AMS when taken prior to ascent, and can speed recovery if taken after symptoms have developed. The drug appears to work by acidifying the blood, which causes an increase in respiration and thus aids in acclimatization. The standard dose is 250 milligrams (mg) BID (bis in die, that is, "twice daily"), usually starting the day prior to ascent. Anecdotal observations support the use of 125 mg BID as being equally effective with fewer side effects. Allergic reactions to acetazolamide are extremely rare, but the drug is related to sulfonamides, and should not be used by sulfa-allergic travelers.

Dexamethasone has been shown to be effective in the prevention and treatment of AMS and HACE. The drug prevents symptoms, but there is no evidence that it aids acclimatization. Thus, there is a risk of a sudden onset of symptoms if the traveler goes off the drug while ascending. It is preferable for the traveler to use acetazolamide to prevent AMS while ascending, and to reserve the use of dexamethasone to treat severe symptoms. The dosage is 4 mg every 6 hours.

Nifedipine has been shown to prevent and ameliorate HAPE in people who are particularly susceptible to HAPE. The dosage is 10 mg every 8 hours.

For the majority of travelers, the best way to avoid altitude illness is to plan a gradual ascent. If this is not possible, acetazolamide may be used prophylactically, and dexamethasone and nifedipine may be carried for emergencies.

Natural Disasters and Environmental Hazards
Natural disasters can contribute to the transmission of some diseases; however, unless the causative agent is in the environment, transmission cannot take place. Natural disasters often disrupt water supplies and sewage systems. Epidemic typhoid has been conspicuously absent following natural disasters in developing countries where typhoid is endemic. It takes several weeks for typhoid antibodies to develop, and even then immunization provides only moderate protection. Floods pose no additional risk of typhoid. In flood areas where the organism has been present, recent studies have identified outbreaks of leptospirosis.

Of greatest important in preventing enteric disease transmission when water and sewage systems have been disrupted is ensuring that water and food supplies are safe to consume. If contamination is suspected, water should be boiled and appropriately disinfected. (See "Risks From Food and Drink" and "Water".)

Contamination of rivers and lakes with chemical or organic or inorganic compounds (such as heavy metals or other toxins) can be harmful both to fish and to the humans who eat the fish or who swim or bathe in the water. Sufficient warning that such a hazard exists in a body of water is often difficult to provide.

Air pollution is widespread in large cities. Uncontrolled forest fires have been known to cause widespread pollution over vast expanses of the world. Health risks associated with these environmental occurrences have not been fully studied, and travelers with chronic pulmonary disease might be more susceptible to respiratory infection. Any risk to short-term healthy travelers to such areas is probably small.

Chernobyl

Effects of the Radiological Release at Chernobyl

The Chernobyl nuclear power station, located in Ukraine about 100 kilometers (62 miles) northwest of Kiev, Ukraine, and 310 kilometers (km) (193 miles) southeast of Minsk, Belarus, had an uncontrolled release of radioactive material in April 1986. This event resulted in the largest short-term release of radioactive materials into the atmosphere ever recorded. The radiologic contamination primarily affected three republics: Ukraine, Belarus, and Russia. The highest radioactive ground contamination occurred within 30 km (19 miles) of Chernobyl. The level of contamination in any given area is decreasing with the passage of time, but it will be many years before levels of radioactivity in some parts of these countries return to the levels that existed prior to the Chernobyl event.

Area Considerations

Short-term international travelers (those who plan to stay in the region less than a few months) to

Ukraine, Belarus, and Russia should not be concerned about residing in areas that are not controlled (marked with signs or fenced). However, long-term travelers should be advised that, in some uncontrolled areas, they could receive a radiation dose from the radioactive ground contamination in excess of the international radiological health standards recommended for the public. Long-term travelers should investigate local conditions prior to choosing a long-term residence. (For example, ground contamination that exceeds 5 curies per square kilometer [5 Ci/km2] of cesium-137 could result in a radiation dose greater than the recommended standards.) Staff of the appropriate U.S. embassy should be able to assist in this investigation.

Food and Water Considerations

Officials of the three republics attempt to monitor all foodstuffs sold in the public markets for levels of radioactivity. Radioactive concentration limits have been established for various classes of food (for example, milk, meat, and vegetables). These limits are comparable with standards used by many western nations, including the European Union. Foods with contamination levels in excess of these limits are not allowed to be sold in the markets. Private farmers regularly make foods available for sale outside the official market system. These foods are not monitored for radioactivity, and travelers should not consume them. Likewise, travelers should be advised not eat any wild berries, wild mushrooms, or wild game from these regions and should drink only bottled water.

Age and Health Considerations

Young children, unborn babies, and nursing infants are potentially at greater risk from exposure to radiation than adults. Pregnant or nursing mothers should be advised to pay extra attention to acquiring food from reliable, well-monitored sources.

Injuries
Injuries, especially those from motor vehicle crashes, pose a great risk of serious disability or loss of life to international travelers. The risk of motor vehicle-related death is generally many times higher in developing countries than in the United States. Motor vehicle crashes result from a variety of factors, including inadequate roadway design, hazardous conditions, lack of appropriate vehicles and vehicle maintenance, unskilled or inexperienced drivers, inattention to pedestrians and cyclists, or impairment due to alcohol or drug use; all these factors are preventable or can be abated. Defensive driving is an important preventive measure. When driving or riding, travelers should be advised to request a vehicle equipped with safety belts and, where available, to use them. Travelers should carefully inspect vehicles to ensure that tires, windshield wipers, and brakes are in good condition and that all lights are in good working order. Travelers should also request a vehicle equipped with air bags, where available. Because a high proportion of crashes occur at night when drivers are returning from social events, travelers should avoid nonessential night driving, alcohol, and riding with people who are under the influence of alcohol or drugs. Night driving outside urban areas in developing countries is particularly risky. The risk of death in a motor vehicle crash is greater for people sitting in the front seat than for those in the rear seat. Travelers should ride in the rear seats of motor vehicles, where possible. In addition, travelers should be strongly urged to be familiar with local recommendations about what to do if their vehicle is involved in a crash, especially one involving injuries. Such situations can quickly become dangerous for drivers and passengers.

Pedestrian, bicycle, and motorcycle travel are often dangerous as well, and helmet use is imperative for bicycle and motorcycle travel. In developing countries where helmets will likely not be available, travelers should be advised to bring their own with them if they plan to ride bicycles or motorcycles. Travelers with young children should be advised to bring their own child safety seats.

Fire injuries are also a significant cause of injuries and death. Travelers should be reminded not to smoke in bed, and to inquire about whether hotels have smoke detectors and sprinkler systems. Travelers might wish to bring their own smoke detectors with them. Travelers should always locate primary and alternate escape routes from rooms in which they are meeting or staying. Travelers should also be advised to look for improperly vented heating devices that might cause carbon monoxide poisoning. Travelers should be reminded to escape a fire by crawling low under smoke.

Other major causes of injury trauma include drowning (see "Swimming Precautions," and injuries to water skiers and divers from boat propellers. Travelers should use boats equipped with propeller guards whenever possible, and wear a personal flotation device (life jacket) whenever riding in a boat.

Travelers should also be aware of the potential for violence-related injuries. Risk for assault or terrorist attack varies from country to country; travelers should heed advice from residents and tour guides about areas to be avoided, going out at night, and going out alone. Travelers should be advised not to fight attackers and, if confronted, to give up their valuables. For more information, travelers may be advised to contact the U.S. Department of State, Overseas Citizens Emergency Center at 1-202-647-5225 or the website, http://www.travel.state.gov, for specific country travel warnings and information.

Animal-Associated Hazards
Animals in general tend to avoid human beings, but they can attack, particularly if they are protecting their young or territory. Travelers should be reminded that, in areas of endemic rabies, domestic dogs, cats, or other animals should not be petted, handled, or fed. Wild animals should be avoided; most injuries from wild animals are the direct result of attempting to pet, handle, or feed the animals.

The bites and stings of and contact with some insects cause unpleasant reactions. Travelers should be advised to seek medical attention if an insect bite or sting causes redness, swelling, bruising, or persistent pain. Many insects also transmit communicable diseases. Some insects can bite and transmit disease without the traveler's being aware of the bite, particularly when the traveler is camping or staying in rustic or primitive accommodations. Travelers should be advised to use insect repellents, protective clothing, and mosquito netting when visiting many parts of the world. (See "Protection Against Mosquitoes and Other Arthropod Vectors".)
Poisonous snakes are hazards in many locations, although deaths from snake bites are relatively

rare. The Australian brown snake, Russell's viper and cobras in southern Asia, carpet vipers in the Middle East, and coral snakes and rattlesnakes in the Americas are particularly dangerous. Most snake bites are the direct result of handling or harassing snakes, which bite as a defensive reaction. Attempts to kill snakes are dangerous, often leading to bites on the fingers. The venom of a small or immature snake can be even more concentrated than that of larger ones; therefore, all snakes should be left alone.

Fewer than half of all snake bite wounds actually contain venom, but travelers should be advised to seek medical attention any time a bite wound breaks the skin. A pressure bandage, ice (if available), and immobilization of the affected limb are recommended first-aid measures while the victim is moved as quickly as possible to a medical facility. Specific therapy for snake bite is controversial, and should be left to the judgment of local emergency medical personnel. Snakes tend to be active at night and in warm weather. As a precaution, boots and long pants should be worn when walking outdoors at night in snake-infested regions. Bites from scorpions can be painful, but seldom are dangerous, except possibly in infants. In general, exposure to bites can be avoided by sleeping under mosquito nets and by shaking clothing and shoes before putting them on, particularly in the morning. Snakes and scorpions tend to rest in shoes and clothing.

Swimming Precautions
Swimming in contaminated water can result in skin, eye, ear, and certain intestinal infections, particularly if the swimmer's head is submerged. Generally, for infectious disease prevention, only pools that contain chlorinated water can be considered safe places to swim. In certain areas, fatal primary amebic meningoencephalitis has occurred following swimming in warm, dirty water. Travelers who swim should be advised to avoid beaches that might be contaminated with human sewage or with dog feces. Travelers should also be advised to avoid wading or swimming in freshwater streams, canals, and lakes that are likely to be infested with the snail hosts of schistosomiasis (bilharziasis) or contaminated with urine from animals infected with Leptospira. Biting and stinging fish, corals, and jellyfish can also be hazardous.

Travelers should be advised never to swim alone or when under the influence of alcohol or drugs. Likewise, they should never dive or jump into an unfamiliar body of water without first determining the depth (at least 9 feet for jumping and diving) and the terrain, and whether there are any hidden obstacles. Travelers should be advised to learn cardiopulmonary resuscitation (CPR) and basic first-aid. They should be aware of the weather conditions and forecasts. Thunderstorms or even strong winds are dangerous for swimmers and boaters. They should use a personal flotation device (life jacket) when boating, skiing, or using personal water craft regardless of the distance to be traveled, the size of the boat, or their swimming ability. Travelers should be cautioned to remember that open water usually has limited visibility, and conditions can sometimes change from hour to hour. Currents are often unpredictable, moving rapidly and quickly changing direction. A strong water current can carry even expert swimmers far from shore.

Recreational Water

A variety of infections (such as skin, ear, respiratory, and diarrheal infections) have been linked to wading or swimming in the ocean, freshwater lakes and rivers, and swimming pools. The water can be contaminated by other people, and from sewage, animal wastes, and waste water runoff.

Diarrhea can be spread when disease-causing germs from human or animal feces are introduced into the water. Accidentally swallowing small amounts of fecally contaminated water can then cause disease. Travelers should be warned to avoid swallowing water while engaging in aquatic activities. Some organisms (Cryptosporidium, Giardia, hepatitis A, and Norwalk virus) have moderate to very high resistance to chlorine levels commonly found in chlorinated swimming pools, so travelers also should avoid swallowing chlorinated swimming pool water.

Travelers should be advised to avoid swimming or wading with open cuts or abrasions that might serve as entry points for germs and to protect nasal membranes from germs by wearing nose plugs when entering untreated water venues. They should also avoid freshwater in schistosomiasis-endemic areas of the Caribbean, South America, Africa, and Asia, "Specific Recommendations for Vaccinations and Disease Prevention: Schistosomiasis" for further precautions).

Emerging Infectious Diseases

Emerging infectious diseases are diseases of infectious origin whose incidence in humans has increased within the past two decades or threatens to increase in the near future. Many factors, or combinations of factors, can contribute to disease emergence. New infectious diseases can emerge from genetic changes in existing organisms; known diseases can spread to new geographic areas and populations; and previously unknown diseases can appear in humans living or working in changing ecologic conditions that increase their exposure to insect vectors, animal reservoirs, or environmental sources of novel pathogens. Reemergence can occur because of the development of antimicrobial resistance in existing infections (for example, gonorrhea, malaria, and pneumococcal disease) or breakdowns in public health measures for previously controlled infections (for instance, cholera, tuberculosis, and pertussis). For current outbreak bulletins on diseases of international concern, travelers should be advised to call the Centers for Disease Control and Prevention Travelers' Health hotline at 1-877-FYI-TRIP (1-877-394-8747).

Illness Abroad

If Medical Care Is Needed Abroad

If an American citizen becomes seriously ill or is injured abroad, a U.S. consular officer can assist in locating appropriate medical services and informing family or friends. If necessary, a consular

officer can also assist in the transfer of funds from the United States. However, the traveler should be advised that payment of hospital and other expenses is his or her personal responsibility. See the U.S. Department of State website at http://www.travel.state.gov/acs.html#medical.

Protection against potentially hazardous drugs is nonexistent in some countries, increasing the risk of adverse reactions. Travelers should be advised not to buy medications "over the counter" unless they are familiar with the products.

Before going abroad, travelers should be advised to learn what medical services their health insurance will cover overseas. If the health insurance policy provides coverage outside the United States, travelers should be advised to carry both the insurance policy identity card (as proof of insurance) and a claim form. Although some health insurance companies will pay "customary and reasonable" hospital costs abroad, very few will pay for medical evacuation to the United States. Medical evacuation can easily cost $10,000 or more, depending on the location and medical condition.

World Health Organization (WHO) Blood Transfusion Guidelines for International Travelers

There is a growing public awareness of the acquired immunodeficiency syndrome (AIDS) epidemic and a resulting concern about acquiring human immunodeficiency virus (HIV) through blood transfusion. Accurate and systematic screening of all blood donations is not yet feasible in all developing countries. Travelers planning international itineraries have requested to have their own blood or blood from their home country available to them in case of urgent need. These requests raise logistical, technical, and ethical issues that are not easy to resolve. Ultimately, the safety of blood for such travelers will depend on the quality of blood transfusion services in the host country. The strengthening of these services is of the highest priority. While efforts are being made to achieve this end, other approaches are also needed.

Basic Principles

Unexpected, emergency blood transfusion is rarely required. It is needed only in situations of massive hemorrhage, such as severe trauma, gynecologic and obstetric emergency, or gastrointestinal bleeding.

In many cases, resuscitation can be achieved by use of colloid or crystalloid plasma expanders instead of blood.

Blood transfusion is not free of risk, even in the best of conditions. In most developing countries, the risk is increased by limited technical resources for screening blood donors for HIV infection and other diseases transmissible by blood.

The international shipment of blood for transfusion is practical only when handled by agreement between two responsible organizations, such as national blood transfusion services. This mechanism is not useful for the emergency needs of individual travelers and should not be attempted by private travelers or organizations not operating recognized blood programs.

Therefore, travelers should be made aware that:

There are no medical indications for travelers to take blood with them from their home countries.

The limited storage period of blood and the need for special equipment negate the feasibility of independent blood banking for individual travelers or small groups.

Blood should be transfused only when absolutely indicated. This applies even more forcefully in those countries where screening of blood for transmissible diseases is not yet widely performed.

Therefore, the following options should be recommended in emergency situations:

When urgent resuscitation is necessary, the use of plasma expanders rather than blood should always be considered.

In case of emergency need for blood, use of plasma expanders and urgent evacuation home might be the actions of choice.

When blood transfusion cannot be avoided, the attending physician should make every effort to ensure that the blood has been screened for transmissible diseases, including HIV.

International travelers should be advised to:

Take active steps to minimize the risk of injury, such as avoiding night driving, employing safe driving practices, and wearing safety belts whenever possible.

Establish a plan for dealing with medical emergencies.

Support the development within countries of safe and adequate blood supplies.

Death Overseas

Importation or Exportation of Human Remains

There are no federal restrictions on the importation of human remains, unless the cause of death was one of the following communicable diseases: cholera or suspected cholera, diphtheria, infectious tuberculosis, plague, suspected smallpox, yellow fever, or suspected viral hemorrhagic fevers (Lassa, Marburg, Ebola, Congo-Crimean, or others not yet isolated or named). If the death was the result of one of these diseases, the remains must be cremated or properly embalmed; placed in a hermetically sealed casket; and be accompanied by a death certificate, translated into English, that states the cause of death. The local mortician handling the remains following their importation will be subject to the regulations of the state and local health authorities for interstate and intrastate shipment.

The United States has no requirements for the exportation of human remains; however, travelers should be advised that the requirements of the country of destination must be met. Travelers should also be advised that information regarding these requirements may be obtained from the appropriate embassy or local consulate general.

The Post-Travel Period
Some diseases might not manifest themselves immediately. If travelers become ill after they return home, they should be advised to tell their physician where they have traveled.

Most travelers who acquire viral, bacterial, or parasitic infections abroad become ill within 6 weeks after returning from international travel. However, some diseases might not manifest themselves immediately; for example, malaria might not cause symptoms for as long as 6 months to a year after a traveler returns to the United States. The traveler should be advised to inform his or her physician of the countries visited within the 12 months preceding onset of illness. Knowledge of such travel and the possibility the traveler might be ill with a disease the physician rarely encounters will help the physician arrive at a correct diagnosis.

Animal Importation and Reentry
Travelers should be advised that pets that are transported internationally should be free of communicable diseases that can be transmissible to humans. U.S. Public Health Service (PHS) regulations place the following restrictions on the importation of dogs, cats, nonhuman primates, and turtles.

Dogs

Dogs older than 3 months of age presented for importation from countries where rabies is known to occur must be accompanied by a valid rabies vaccination certificate that includes the following information.

The breed, sex, age, color, markings, and other identifying information.

A vaccination date at least 30 pays prior to importation (see following).

The vaccination expiration date. If not shown, the date of vaccination must be within 12 months prior to importation.

The signature of a licensed veterinarian.

A dog not accompanied by the previously described certificate may be admitted, providing the importer completes a confinement agreement. Such a dog must be kept in confinement during transit to, and be vaccinated within 4 days of arrival at, the U.S. destination. Such a dog must remain in confinement for at least 30 days after the date of vaccination.

A dog younger than 3 months of age may be admitted, provided the importer completes a confinement agreement. Such a dog must be kept in confinement during transit and at the U.S. destination until it is vaccinated at 3 months of age and for at least 30 days after vaccination. Routine rabies vaccination of dogs is recommended in the United States and required by most state and local health authorities.

Cats

Although proof of rabies vaccination is not

required for cats, routine rabies vaccination of cats is recommended in the United States and required by most state and local health authorities.

Monkeys and Other Nonhuman Primates

Nonhuman primates can transmit a variety of serious diseases to humans. Live monkeys and other nonhuman primates may be imported into the United States only by importers registered with the Centers for Disease Control and Prevention (CDC) and only for scientific, educational, or exhibition purposes. Monkeys and other nonhuman primates may not be imported for use as pets.

Turtles

Turtles can transmit salmonellosis to humans, and because small turtles are often kept as pets, restrictions apply to their importation. Live turtles with a carapace (shell) length of less than 4 inches and viable turtle eggs may be imported into the United States if the importation is not for commercial purposes. The PHS has no restrictions on the importation of live turtles with a carapace length of more than 4 inches.

Measures at Ports of Entry

PHS regulations provide for the examination of admissible dogs, cats, nonhuman primates, and turtles presented for importation into the United States. Animals with evidence of disease that might be transmissible to humans may be subject to additional disease control measures.

General

For additional information regarding importation of these animals, travelers should be advised to contact the Centers for Disease Control and Prevention, Attention: National Center for Infectious Diseases, Division of Global Migration and Quarantine, Mailstop E03, Atlanta, Georgia 30333 (1-404-639-8107).

Travelers planning to import horses, ruminants, swine, poultry, birds, and dogs used handling livestock should be advised to contact the U.S. Department of Agriculture (1-301-734-8364) regarding additional requirements.

Travelers planning to import fish, reptiles, spiders, wild birds, rabbits, bears, wild members of the cat family, or other wild or endangered animals should be advised to contact the U.S. Department of the Interior, Fish and Wildlife Service (1-703-358-1949).

Travelers planning to take a pet to a foreign country should be advised to meet the entry requirements of the country of destination. To obtain this information, travelers should write or call the country's embassy in Washington, D.C., or the nearest consulate.

Medical Information for Americans Traveling Abroad

If an American citizen becomes seriously ill or injured abroad, a U. S. consular officer can assist in locating appropriate medical services and informing family or friends. If necessary, a consular officer can also assist in the transfer of funds from the United States. However, payment of hospital and other expenses is the responsibility of the traveler.

Before going abroad, learn what medical services your health insurance will cover overseas. If your health insurance policy provides coverage outside the United States, **REMEMBER** to carry both your insurance policy identity card as proof of such insurance and a claim form. Although many health insurance companies will pay "customary and reasonable" hospital costs abroad, very few will pay for your medical evacuation back to the United States. Medical evacuation can easily cost $10,000 and up, depending on your location and medical condition.

THE SOCIAL SECURITY MEDICARE PROGRAM DOES NOT PROVIDE COVERAGE FOR HOSPITAL OR MEDICAL COSTS OUTSIDE THE U.S.A.

Senior citizens may wish to contact the American Association of Retired Persons for information about foreign medical care coverage with Medicare supplement plans. To facilitate identification in case of an accident, complete the information page on the inside of your passport providing the name, address and telephone number of someone to be contacted in an emergency.

A traveler going abroad with any preexisting

medical problems should carry a letter from the attending physician, describing the medical condition and any prescription medications, including the generic name of prescribed drugs. Any medications being carried overseas should be left in their original containers and be clearly labeled. Travelers should check with the foreign embassy of the country they are visiting to make sure any required medications are not considered to be illegal narcotics.

A listing of addresses and telephone numbers of U.S. embassies and consulates abroad is contained in *Key Officers of Foreign Service Posts*. This publication may be obtained through the Superintendent of Documents, U.S. Government Printing Office, Washington, DC 20402. Also available from the Government Printing Office is *Health Information for International Travel* by the Centers for Disease Control and Prevention (CDC). This contains a global rundown of disease and immunization advice and other health guidance, including risks in particular countries. The CDC maintains the international travelers hotline at 1-877-FYI-TRIP (1-877-394-8747), an automated faxback service at 1-888-CDC-FAXX (1-888-232-3299) and a home page on the Internet at http://www.cdc.gov/.

For information about outbreaks of infectious diseases abroad, consult the World Health Organization's (WHO) website at http://www.who.int/en. The WHO also provides travel travel health information at http://www.who.int/iht. For detailed information on physicians abroad, the authoritative reference is *The Official ABMS Directory of Board Certified Medical Specialists* published for the American Board of Medical Specialists and its certifying member boards. This publication should be available in your local library. U.S. embassies and consulates abroad maintain lists of hospitals and physicians. Major credit card companies also can provide the names of local doctors and hospitals abroad.

Some countries require foreign visitors to have inoculations or medical tests before entering. Before traveling, check the latest entry requirements with the foreign embassy of the country to be visited.

Several private organizations will provide medical information and insurance for overseas travelers. Most charge a fee for this service. See the Table of Contents for the relevant Appendix covering Travel Insurance and Medical Assistance Organization.

VACCINATION INFORMATION
How To Use This Resource To Determine Vaccinations Required or Recommended

The following steps are suggested to determine vaccination requirements.

The traveler should be advised to list his or her itinerary in the sequence in which countries will be visited. The length of stay in each country also should be considered. For the purpose of the International Health Regulations, the incubation periods of the quarantinable diseases are:
Cholera--5 days
Plague--6 days
Yellow fever--6 days

Health care providers should use Yellow Fever Vaccine Requirements and Information on Malaria Risk and Prophylaxis, by Country to determine the yellow fever vaccination requirements for each country. Because some countries require vaccination only if a traveler arrives from an infected area, health care providers should check the current biweekly Summary of Health Information for International Travel (also known as the Blue Sheet) to determine if any country on the itinerary is currently infected with yellow fever. The Blue Sheet is available both from the Centers for Disease Control and Prevention (CDC) website at http://www.cdc.gov/travel/blusheet.htm and from the CDC Fax Information Service by telephoning 1-888-CDC-FAXX (232-3299) and requesting document number 220022.

Most immunizations are not required under the International Health Regulations, but are recommended to protect the health of the traveler. Health care providers should consider inoculating the traveler for the following diseases: tetanus, diphtheria, pertussis, poliomyelitis, measles, hepatitis A, hepatitis B, varicella, Japanese encephalitis, meningococcal meningitis, rabies, typhoid fever, and yellow fever. For those diseases for which no vaccines are available, specific preventive behaviors or medications are a necessity. Specific Recommendations for

130

Vaccinations and Disease Prevention provides detailed immunization and prophylaxis information for a variety of diseases. Subsequent chapters address the special needs of potentially at-risk or high-risk travelers, including infants, children, pregnant women, and those with compromised immune systems. Because the recommendations in this publication can change because of outbreaks or other events (such as natural disasters), travelers should be advised either to contact the CDC Fax Information Service (request document number 000005) or to consult the CDC Travelers' Health website at http://www.cdc.gov/travel for the most up-to-date information.

Vaccination Certificate Requirements
Under the International Health Regulations adopted by the World Health Organization, a country may, under certain conditions, require an International Certificate of Vaccination against yellow fever from international travelers.

The World Health Assembly amended the International Health Regulations in 1973 so that cholera vaccination is no longer required of any traveler. As a result, no country requires a certificate of cholera immunization and, indeed, cholera vaccine is no longer available in the United States.

Model of a Correctly Completed Certificate
An International Certificate of Vaccination must be complete in every detail; if incomplete or inaccurate, it is not valid. Revisions of this certificate dated 9-66, 9-69, 9-71, 1-74, 9-77, 1-82, or 11-91 are acceptable.

A copy of the International Certificate of Vaccination, PHS-731, may be purchased for $1.00 ($15.00 per 100) from the Superintendent of Documents, U.S. Government Printing Office, Washington, D.C. 20402, telephone 1-202-512-1800. The stock number is 017-001-00483-9.

Vaccination Certificate Requirements for Direct Travel From the United States To Other Countries
For direct travel from the United States, only the following countries require an International Certificate of Vaccination against yellow fever.

Benin
Burkina Faso
Cameroon
Central African Republic
Congo
Côte d'Ivoire
Democratic Republic of the Congo
French Guiana
Ghana
Liberia
Mali
Mauritania (for a stay of more than 2 weeks)
Niger
Rwanda
São Tomé and Príncipe
Togo
Gabon

For travel to and between other countries, individual country requirements should be checked.

Currently, no vaccinations are required to return to the United States.

Exemption From Vaccination

Age: Some countries do not require an International Certificate of Vaccination for infants younger than 6 months of age or 1 year of age. Travelers should be advised to check the individual country requirements in Yellow Fever Vaccine Requirements and Information on Malaria Risk and Prophylaxis, by Country.

Medical Grounds: If a physician concludes that a particular vaccination should not be administered for medical reasons, the traveler should be given a signed and dated statement of the reasons on the physician's letterhead stationary.

There are no other acceptable reasons for exemption from vaccination.

Unvaccinated Travelers
Travelers who do not have the required vaccinations upon entering a country might be subject to vaccination, medical follow up, or isolation, or a combination of these. In a few countries, unvaccinated travelers are denied entry.

Travel on Military Orders
Because military requirements may exceed the requirements indicated in this publication, any person who plans to travel on military orders

131

(civilians and military personnel) should be advised to contact the nearest military medical facility to determine the requirements for the trip.

Authorization To Provide Vaccinations and To Validate the International Certificate of Vaccination
A yellow fever vaccination must be given at an official yellow fever vaccination center as designated by respective state health departments or the Division of Global Migration and Quarantine, Centers for Disease Control and Prevention, and the accompanying certificate must be validated by the center that administers the vaccine. (Other vaccinations may be given under the supervision of any licensed physician.) Validation of the certificate can be obtained at most city, county, and state health departments, or from vaccinating physicians who possess a "Uniform Stamp." State health departments are responsible for designated nonfederal yellow fever vaccination centers and issuing Uniform Stamps to be used to validate the International Certificate of Vaccination. Information about the location and hours of yellow fever vaccination centers may be obtained by contacting local or state health departments. Physicians administering vaccine to travelers should emphasize that an International Certificate of Vaccination must be validated to be acceptable to quarantine authorities. Failure to secure validations can cause a traveler to be revaccinated, quarantined, or denied entry.

People Authorized To Sign the Certificate
The International Certificate of Vaccination must be signed by a licensed physician or by a person designated by the physician. A signature stamp is not acceptable.

Human Immunodeficiency Virus (HIV) Testing Requirements for Entry into Foreign Countries

An increasing number of countries require that foreigners be tested for Human Immunodeficiency Virus (HIV) prior to entry. It is usually required as part of a medical exam for long-term visitors (i.e., students and workers). The following list of country requirements is based on information available as of February 2002 and is subject to change. Before traveling abroad, check with the embassy of the country to be visited to learn about entry requirements and specifically whether AIDS testing is a requirement. If the list indicates U.S. test results are acceptable and the word "Yes" appears with an asterisk beside it (Yes*) in a particular country, prospective travelers should inquire at the embassy of that country for details (i.e., which laboratories in the United States may perform tests and where to have results certified and authenticated) before departing the United States.

132

HIV Testing Requirements

COUNTRY	TEST REQUIRED FOR	U.S. TEST ACCEPTED?
Aruba	Intending immigrants	
	No*	
Australia	All applicants for permanent residence over age 15 (All other applicants who require medical examinations are tested if it is indicated on clinical grounds.)	
		Yes*
Bahrain	Individuals employed in jobs involving food handling, and patient or child care	No
Belarus	All persons staying longer than 3 months	Yes
Belize	All persons applying for residency permits	No
Brunei	All persons applying for work permits	No
Bulgaria	All intending immigrants (and may be required for foreigners staying longer than 1 month for purposes of study or work)	Yes*
Canada	Any foreigner suspected of being HIV positive (HIV testing is not mandatory for entry)	Yes*
Central African Republic	Anyone seeking residence, work and student permits must submit to a medical exam (which includes an HIV test)	Yes
China, People's Republic of	Foreigners planning to stay for more than 6 months (Testing is not required for entry or residency in Hong Kong or Macau.)	Yes*
Colombia	Anyone suspected of being HIV positive (HIV positive persons are not admitted without a waiver from a Colombian consulate in the U.S.) No*	
Cuba	Anyone staying over 90 days, excluding diplomats	Yes*
Cyprus	All foreigners working or studying are tested after entry	N/A
Dominican Republic	Foreigners planning to reside, study or work	No
Egypt	Foreigners applying for study, training or work permits (spouses of applicants are exempt)	Yes*
El Salvador	Anyone age 15 and older applying for temporary and permanent residency	No
Georgia	All foreigners staying longer than 1 month	Yes, if issued 30 days before arrival*
Greece	Prostitutes (as defined by Greek law)	Yes*
Hungary	Anyone staying over 1 year, and all intending immigrants (some employers may require workers to be tested)	Yes*
India	All students over 18, anyone between the ages of 18 and 70 with a visa valid for 1 year or more, and anyone extending a stay to a year or more, excluding accredited journalists and those working in foreign missions Test must be taken within 30 days of arrival*	
Iraq	All foreigners (except diplomats, Muslim pilgrims transiting through Iraq, children under 14 who do not suffer from hemophilia, men over 60 and women over 50 years of age) will be tested upon entry and are required to pay a $50 (US) fee for the test (Persons possessing a current medical certificate confirming that they do not suffer from AIDS may also be exempt from being tested.)	Yes*
Jordan	Anyone staying longer than 3 months	No
Kazakstan	All visitors staying more then 1 month must present a certificate of an HIV test within 10 days of their arrival Yes, if issued 30 days before arrival*	
Korea, Republic of	Foreigners working as entertainers staying over 90 days	Yes
Kuwait	Those seeking to obtain a residence permit	No
Kyrgyzstan	All foreigners, excluding diplomats, staying more than one month	Yes
Latvia	Anyone seeking a residency permit	Yes
Lebanon	Those planning to reside or work (Universities may require testing of foreign students)	

133

		No*
Libya	Those seeking residency permits, excluding official visitors	Yes
Lithuania	Applicants for permanent residence permits	Yes*
Malaysia	Foreigners seeking work permits as unskilled laborers	Yes*
Marshall Islands, Republic of the	Temporary visitors staying more than 30 days, and applicants for residence and work permits	Yes*
Mauritius	Foreigners planning to work or seek permanent residence (testing performed upon arrival in Mauritius)	No
Micronesia, (Federated States of)	Anyone applying for a permit needs to obtain a medical clearance, which may include an HIV test	Yes
Moldova	Anyone staying more than 3 months	Yes*
Montserrat	University students and applicants for work and residency	Yes*
Oman	Those newly-employed by private sector companies and upon renewal of work permit	No
Panama	Women intending to work in prostitution and anyone who adjusts visa status once in Panama	No*
Papua New Guinea	Applicants seeking work or residency visas and their dependents	Yes
Paraguay	Applicants seeking temporary or permanent residency status	Yes*
Qatar	Applicants seeking work or residency visas and visitors staying more than 1 month	No
Russia	All foreign visitors staying longer than 3 months	Yes*
Saudi Arabia	Applicants for residency/work permits	Yes*
St. Vincent	Applicants seeking temporary and permanent residency visas	Yes
St. Kitts and Nevis	Students, intending immigrants and anyone seeking employment	Yes*
Seychelles	Foreigners planning to work must under go a medical exam, which includes an HIV test, upon arrival	No
Singapore	Workers who earn less than $1,250 per month and applicants for permanent resident status (except spouses and children of Singapore citizens)	No
Slovakia	Applicants for long term or permanent residency visas	No*
South Africa	All mine workers (irrespective of their positions)	Yes*
Spain	Anyone seeking residence, work and student permits must submit to a medical exam (which may include an AIDS test)	Yes*
Syria	All foreigners (ages 15 to 60 years) staying more than 15 days	Yes*
Taiwan	Applicants for residency and work permits (Testing is also required for anyone staying over 90 days.)	No*
Tajikistan	Anyone staying more than 90 days (pending legislation)	Yes*
Turkmenistan	All foreigners staying longer than 3 months	No*
Turks and Caicos	Foreign workers (HIV testing is part of the medical exam that is required for work permits.)	No
United Arab Emirates	Applicants for work or residence permits except those under age 18	No, testing performed upon arrival
Ukraine	Anyone staying longer than 3 months	Yes, if issued 30 days before arrival*
United Kingdom	Anyone who does not appear to be in good health may be required to undergo a medical exam (including an HIV test) prior to being granted or denied entry	No*
Uzbekistan	Anyone staying more than 15 days (Long-term visitors must renew HIV certificate after the first 3 months in Uzbekistan and annually thereafter.)	Yes*
Yemen	Applicants seeking permanent residence including work or study (students over age 16), all foreigners staying longer than 1 month, and foreign spouses of Yemeni nationals (excludes experts, teachers, and foreign missions who are required to work in Yemen)	No

Summary of Health Information for International Travel

Countries with areas infected with quarantinable diseases according to the World Health Organization (WHO)

NOTE: No country requires cholera vaccination for direct travel from the United States, and no vaccinations are required to reenter the United States. This listing supplements information in Health Information for International Travel, 2001-2002 and should be used in conjunction with that document to determine required and recommended vaccinations.

- Countries added during the 14 days prior to the date above.
* Countries considered a threat in the introduction of plague.

CHOLERA-INFECTED COUNTRIES

This list represents those countries reporting cholera cases to WHO 14 days prior to the date above.

Africa

Angola
Benin
Burkina Faso
Burundi
Cameroon
Cape Verde
Central African
Republic
Chad
Comoros
 Congo
Côte d'Ivoire
Democratic
Republic of Congo
Djibouti
Ghana
Guinea
Guinea-Bissau
Kenya
Liberia
Madagascar
Malawi
Mali
Mauritania
Mozambique
Niger
Nigeria
Rwanda
SãoTomé &
Príncipe
Senegal
Sierra Leone
Somalia
South Africa
Swaziland
Tanzania

Togo
Uganda
Zambia
Zimbabwe

Central America
El Salvador
Guatemala
Nicaragua

South East Asia
East Timor

East Asia
China
Republic of Korea

Indian Subcontinent
Afghanistan Bhutan India Nepal

Middle East
Iran
Iraq

South America
Brazil
Ecuador
Peru
Venezuela

Southeast Asia
 Cambodia
Laos
Myanmar
Philippines
Vietnam

135

Countries removed during the 14 days prior to date above

YELLOW FEVER-INFECTED COUNTRIES

Africa

COUNTRY/ REGION WITHIN COUNTRY

Angola: Provinces: Bengo and Luanda
Benin: Department: Atakora, du Borgou
Burkina Faso: Gaoua Region
Cameroon: Northern Province
Côte d'Ivoire Department de l'Ouest
Democratic Republic of Congo: North of 10°
South
Gabon: Ogooue'-Ivindo Province
Gambia: Upper River Division
Ghana: Upper West Region, Upper East Region
Guinea: Siguiri Region, Macenta Region
Liberia: Counties: Bassa County, Boma County,
Bong County, Lofa County, Rivercess County,
Sinoe County
Nigeria: States: Anambra, Bauchi, Bendel,
Benue, Cross River, Imo, Kaduna, Kano, Kwara,
Lagos, Niger, Ogun, Ondo, Oyo, and Plateau
Sierra Leone: Kenema District
Senegal   Kolda, Diourbel, Fatick,
Tambacounda, Ziguinchor, Louga, Thies, and
Dakar
Sudan: South of 12° North

South America

COUNTRY/ REGION WITHIN COUNTRY

Bolivia: Departments: Beni, Cochabamba, La
Paz, and Santa Cruz
Brazil: States: Acre, Amapá, Amazonas,
Goiás, Maranhão, Mato Grosso, Motto Grosso do
Sul, Pará, Rondonia, Roraima, and Tocantins, and
certain areas of Bahia, Minas Gerais, Parana,
Piaui, Rio Grande do Sul, São Paulo, Santa
Catarina
Colombia: Departments: Antioquia, Boyaca,
Caqueta, Casanare, Cesar, Choco, Cundinamarca,
Meta, Norte de Santander, Santander, and
Vichada. Intendencias: Arauca, Cucuta, Guaviare,
and Putumayo
Ecuador: Provinces: Morona-Santiago, Napo,
Pastaza, Sucumbios, and Zamora Chinchipe
French Guiana: Saint Laurent-du-Moroni

region
Peru: Departments: Amazonas, Ancash,
Ayacucho, Cusco, Huanuco, Junin, Loreto, Madre
de Dios, Puno, Pasco, San Martin, and Ucayali
Venezuela: Amazonas State, Bolivar
State

PLAGUE-INFECTED COUNTRIES

OUTBREAK NOTICES

Notice: Notice: Brazil yellow fever outbreak
waning
Updated March 6, 2003
Notice: Ebola hemorrhagic fever, Congo
Updated March 5, 2003
Notice: Meningococcal disease, Burkina Faso
Updated March 5, 2003
Notice: Human Cases of Avian Influenza A
(H5N1) Infection Hong Kong (SAR), China, 2003
Released February 26, 2003
Notice: Acute respiratory syndrome in China
Released February 25, 2003
Notice: Gastrointestinal illness aboard cruise ships
Updated February 13, 2003
Notice: Yellow Fever Cases, Guinea
Updated February 7, 2003
Notice: Yellow fever, Senegal

Updated December 3, 2002

Please also check the Outbreaks section and the Diseases section of this site.

Food and Water Precautions and Travelers' Diarrhea Prevention

Please see the **Destinations** section for recommendations for specific countries. Travelers with special needs should see the **Special Needs** section for additional information about food and water safety.

Contaminated food and drink are the major sources of stomach or intestinal illness while traveling. Intestinal problems due to poor sanitation are found in far greater numbers outside the United States and other industrialized nations.

Water

In areas with poor sanitation, only the following beverages may be safe to drink: boiled water, hot beverages (such as coffee or tea) made with boiled water, canned or bottled carbonated beverages, beer, and wine. Ice may be made from unsafe water and should be avoided. It is safer to drink from a can or bottle of beverage than to drink from a container that was not known to be clean and dry. However, water on the surface of a beverage can or bottle may also be contaminated. Therefore, the area of a can or bottle that will touch the mouth should be wiped clean and dry. In areas where water is contaminated, travelers should not brush their teeth with tap water.

Treatment of Water

Boiling is the most reliable method to make water safe to drink. Bring water to a vigorous boil, and then allow it to cool; do not add ice. At high altitudes, allow water to boil vigorously for a few minutes or use chemical disinfectants. Adding a pinch of salt or pouring water from one container to another will improve the taste.

Chemical disinfection can be achieved with either iodine or chlorine, with iodine providing greater disinfection in a wider set of circumstances. For disinfection with iodine, use either tincture of iodine or tetraglycine hydroperiodide tablets, such as Globaline®* and Potable-Aqua®*. These disinfectants can be found in sporting goods stores and pharmacies. Read and follow the manufacturer's instructions. If the water is cloudy, then strain it through a clean cloth and double the number of disinfectant tablets added. If the water is very cold, either warm it or allow increased time for disinfectant to work.

CDC makes no recommendation as to the use of any of the portable filters on the market due to lack of independently verified results of their efficacy. As a last resort, water that is uncomfortably hot to touch may be safe for drinking and brushing teeth after it is allowed to cool. However, many disease-causing organisms can survive the usual temperature reached by the hot water in overseas hotels.

Food

Food should be selected with care. Any raw food could be contaminated, particularly in areas of poor sanitation. Foods of particular concern include salads, uncooked vegetables and fruit, unpasteurized milk and milk products, raw meat, and shellfish. If you peel fruit yourself, it is generally safe. Food that has been cooked and is still hot is generally safe.

Infants younger than 6 months should either be breast-fed or be given powdered commercial formula prepared with boiled water.

Some fish are not guaranteed to be safe even when cooked because of the presence of toxins in their flesh. Tropical reef fish, red snapper, amber jack, grouper, and sea bass can occasionally be toxic at unpredictable times if they are caught on tropical reefs rather than in open ocean. The barracuda and puffer fish are often toxic, and should generally not be eaten. Highest risk areas include the islands of the West Indies, and the tropical Pacific and Indian Oceans.

Travelers'Diarrhea

The typical symptoms of travelers' diarrhea (TD) are diarrhea, nausea, bloating, urgency, and malaise. TD usually lasts from 3 to 7 days. It is rarely life threatening. Areas of high risk include the developing countries of Africa (Central, East, North, Southern, and West), the Middle East, and Central America. The risk of infection varies by type of eating establishment the traveler visits—from low risk in private homes to high risk for food from street vendors.

TD is slightly more common in young adults than in older people, with no difference between males and females. TD is usually acquired through ingestion of fecal contaminated food and water.

The best way to prevent TD is by paying meticulous attention to choice of food and beverage. CDC does not recommend use of antibiotics to prevent TD because they can cause additional problems.

For treatment, oral fluids should be administered to sufferers of diarrhea. Fruit juices, soft drinks (preferably without caffeine), and salted crackers are advised. For severe dehydration, the use of an oral rehydration solution (ORS) is advised (see below). Avoid dairy products and all beverages that contain water of questionable quality.

Antimicrobial drugs such as doxycycline, and trimethoprim/sulfamethoxazole (Bactrim®, Septra®), and fluoroquinolones (Cipro®, Noroxin®) may shorten the length of illness and may especially benefit persons with severe abdominal cramping, fever, and/or bloody diarrhea. Notably, high levels of resistance in many parts of the developing world to doxycycline and trimethoprim-sulfamethoxazole now limit the utility of these drugs for persons traveling to such areas. Consult your physician for prescription and dose schedules. Antidiarrheals, such as Lomotil®* or Immodium®*, can decrease the number of diarrheal stools, but can cause complication for persons with serious infections.

It is important for the traveler to consult a physician about treatment of diarrhea in children and infants because some of the drugs mentioned are not recommended for them. The greatest risk for children, and especially for infants, is dehydration. Prevention of dehydration through administration of soups, thin porridges, and other safe beverages is advised. Infants with diarrhea who exhibit signs of mild dehydration, such as thirst and restlessness, should be given an oral rehydration solution (ORS) to drink. This is a packet of salt and carbohydrates that should be prepared following the package instructions and using boiled or treated water. It is widely available abroad. If bloody diarrhea, dehydration, fever in excess of 102° F, or persistent vomiting occurs, seek immediate medical help.

Most episodes of TD resolve in a few days. As with all diseases it is best to consult a physician rather than attempt self-medication, especially for pregnant women and children. Travelers should seek medical help if diarrhea is severe, bloody, or does not resolve within a few days or if it is accompanied by fever and chills or if the traveler is unable to keep fluids intake up and becomes dehydrated.

For more extensive information on food and water precautions and on travelers' diarrhea, please read Risks from Food and Drink and Travelers' Diarrhea.
*The use of trademarks is for identification only and does not imply an endorsement by the Public Health Service or the U.S. Department of Health and Human Services.

Risks From Food and Drink

Contaminated food and drink are common sources for the introduction of infection into the body. Among the more common infections that travelers can acquire from contaminated food and drink are *Escherichia coli* infections, shigellosis or bacillary dysentery, giardiasis, cryptosporidiosis, and hepatitis A. Other less common infectious disease risks for travelers include typhoid fever and other salmonelloses, cholera, infections caused by rotavirus and Norwalk-like viruses, and a variety of protozoan and helminthic parasites (other than those that cause giardiasis and cryptosporidiosis). Many of the infectious diseases transmitted in food and water can also be acquired directly through the fecal-oral route.

Water

Water that has been adequately chlorinated, using minimum recommended water treatment standards employed in the United States, will afford significant protection against viral and bacterial waterborne diseases. However, chlorine treatment alone, as used in the routine disinfection of water, might not kill some enteric viruses and the parasitic organisms that cause giardiasis, amebiasis, and cryptosporidiosis. In areas where chlorinated tap water is not available or where hygiene and sanitation are poor, travelers should be advised that only the following might be safe to drink:

- Beverages, such as tea and coffee, made with boiled water.
- Canned or bottled carbonated beverages, including carbonated bottled water and soft drinks.
- Beer and wine.

Where water might be contaminated, travelers should be advised that ice should also be considered contaminated and should not be used in beverages. If ice has been in contact with containers used for drinking, travelers should be advised to thoroughly clean the containers, preferably with soap and hot water, after the ice has been discarded.

It is safer to drink a beverage directly from the can or bottle than from a questionable container. However, water on the outside of beverage cans or bottles might be contaminated also. Therefore, travelers should be advised to dry wet cans or bottles before they are opened, and to wipe clean surfaces with which the mouth will have direct contact. Where water might be contaminated, travelers should be advised to avoid brushing their teeth with tap water.

Treatment of Water

Travelers should be advised of the following methods for treating water to make it safe for drinking and other purposes.

Boiling is by far the most reliable method to make water of uncertain purity safe for drinking. Water should be brought to a vigorous rolling boil for 1 minute and allowed to cool to room temperature; ice should not be added. This procedure will kill bacterial and parasitic causes of diarrhea at all altitudes and viruses at low altitudes. To kill viruses at altitudes above 2,000 meters (6,562 feet), water should be boiled for 3 minutes or chemical disinfection should be used after the water has boiled for 1 minute. Adding a pinch of salt to each quart or pouring the water several times from one clean container to another will improve the taste.

Chemical disinfection with iodine is an alternative method of water treatment when it is not feasible to boil water. However, this method cannot be relied upon to kill *Cryptosporidium* unless the water is allowed to sit for 15 hours before it is drunk. Two well-tested methods for disinfection with iodine are the use of tincture of iodine (Table 1) and the use of tetraglycine hydroperiodide tablets (for example, Globaline", Potable-Aqua", or Coghlan's"). These tablets are available from pharmacies and sporting goods stores. The manufacturers' instructions should be followed. If water is cloudy, the number of tablets used should be doubled; if water is extremely cold ($<5°$ Celsius [$<41°$ Fahrenheit]), an attempt should be made to warm the water, and the recommended contact time should be increased to achieve reliable disinfection. Cloudy water should be strained through a clean cloth into a container to remove any sediment or floating matter, and then the water should be boiled or treated with iodine. Chlorine, in various forms, can also be used for chemical disinfection. However, its germicidal activity varies greatly with the pH, temperature, and organic content of the water to be purified and, therefore, it can produce less consistent levels of disinfection in many types of water. Chemically treated water is intended for short-term use only. If iodine-disinfected water is the only water available, it should be used for only a few weeks.

Portable filters currently on the market will provide various degrees of protection against microbes. Reverse-osmosis filters provide protection against viruses, bacteria, and protozoa, but they are expensive, are larger than most filters used by backpackers, and the small pores on this type of filter are rapidly plugged by muddy or cloudy water. In addition, the membranes in some filters can be damaged by chlorine in water. Microstrainer filters with pore sizes in the 0.1- to 0.3-micrometer range can remove bacteria and protozoa from drinking water, but they do not remove viruses. To kill viruses, travelers using microstrainer filters should be advised to disinfect the water with iodine or chlorine after filtration, as described previously. Filters with iodine-impregnated resins are most effective against bacteria, and the iodine will kill some viruses; however, the contact time with the iodine in the filter is too short to kill the protozoa *Cryptosporidium* and, in cold water, *Giardia*. Proper selection, operation, care, and maintenance of water filters is essential to producing safe water. The manufacturers' instructions should be followed. NSF International, an independent testing company, tests and certifies water filters for their ability to remove protozoa, but not for their ability to remove bacteria or viruses. Few published reports in the scientific literature have evaluated the efficacy of specific brands or models of filters against bacteria and viruses in water. Until such information becomes available, the Centers for Disease Control and Prevention (CDC) cannot identify which specific brands or models of filters are most likely to remove bacteria and viruses. A list of filters that have passed NSF tests for parasite removal can be obtained by calling 1-800-673-8010; by writing to NSF at 789 North Dixboro Road, P.O. Box 130140, Ann Arbor, Michigan 48113-0140; or online at http://www.nsf.org/.

As a last resort, if no source of safe drinking water is available or can be obtained, tap water that is uncomfortably hot to touch might be safer than cold tap water; however, proper disinfection, filtering, or boiling is still advised.

Table 1.--Treatment of Water With Tincture of Iodine.

Tincture of Iodine	Drops* to be Added per Quart or Liter	
	Clear Water	Cold or Cloudy Water†
2%	5	10

Note: tincture of iodine can come from a medicine chest or first-aid kit.

1 drop = 0.05 milliliter. Water must stand for a minimum of 30 minutes before it is safe to use.

Very turbid or very cold water can require prolonged contact time; if possible, such water should be allowed to stand several hours prior to use. To ensure that *Cryptosporidium* is killed, water must stand for 15 hours before drinking.

Protection against Mosquitoes and Other Arthropods

Although vaccines or chemoprophylactic drugs are available against important vector-borne diseases such as yellow fever and malaria, travelers still should be advised to use repellents and other general protective measures against biting arthropods.

The effectiveness of malaria chemoprophylaxis is variable, depending on patterns of resistance and compliance with medication, and no similar preventive measures exist for other mosquito-borne diseases such as dengue. For many vector-borne diseases, no specific preventives are available.

General Preventive Measures

The principal approach to prevention of vector-borne diseases is avoidance. Tick- and mite-borne infections characteristically are diseases of "place;" whenever possible, known foci of disease transmission should be avoided. Although many vector-borne infections can be prevented by avoiding rural locations, certain mosquito- and midge-borne arboviral and parasitic infections are transmitted seasonally, and simple changes in itinerary can greatly reduce risk for acquiring them.

Travelers should be advised that exposure to arthropod bites can be minimized by modifying patterns of activity or behavior. Some vector mosquitoes are most active in twilight periods at dawn and dusk or in the evening. Avoidance of outdoor activity during these periods can reduce risk of exposure. Wearing long-sleeved shirts, long pants, and hats minimizes areas of exposed skin. Shirts should be tucked in. Repellents applied to clothing, shoes, tents, mosquito nets, and other gear will enhance protection.

When exposure to ticks or biting insects is a possibility, travelers should be advised to tuck their pants into their socks and to wear boots, not sandals. Permethrin-based repellents applied as directed (see the following section, "Repellents") will enhance protection. Travelers should be advised to inspect themselves and their clothing for ticks, both during outdoor activity and at the end of the day. Ticks are detected more easily on light-colored or white clothing. Prompt removal of attached ticks can prevent some infections.

When accommodations are not adequately screened or air conditioned, bed nets are essential to provide protection and comfort. Bed nets should be tucked under mattresses and can be sprayed with a repellent, such as permethrin. The permethrin will be effective for several months if the bed net is not washed. Aerosol insecticides and mosquito coils can help to clear rooms of mosquitoes; however, some coils contain dichlorodiphenyl- trichloroethane (DDT) and should be used with caution

Repellents

Travelers should be advised that permethrin-containing repellents (e.g., Permanone) are recommended for use on clothing, shoes, bed nets, and camping gear. Permethrin is highly effective as an insecticide and as a repellent. Permethrin-treated clothing repels and kills ticks, mosquitoes, and other arthropods and retains this effect after repeated laundering. There appears to be little potential for toxicity from permethrin-treated clothing. The insecticide should be reapplied after every five washings.

Most authorities recommend repellents containing N,N-diethylmetatoluamide (DEET) as an active ingredient. DEET repels mosquitoes, ticks, and other arthropods when applied to the skin or clothing. In general, the more DEET a repellent contains, the longer time it can protect against mosquito bites. However, there appears to be no added benefit of concentrations greater than 50%. A microencapsulated, sustained-release formulation can have a longer period of activity than liquid formulations at the same concentrations. Length of protection also varies with ambient temperature, amount of perspiration, any water exposure, abrasive removal, and other factors.

No definitive studies have been published about what concentration of DEET is safe for children. No serious illness has arisen from use of DEET according the manufacturer's recommendations. DEET formulations as high as 50% are recommended for both adults and children >2 months of age. Lower concentrations are not as long lasting, offering short-term protection only and necessitating more frequent reapplication. Repellent products that do not contain DEET are not likely to offer the same degree of protection from mosquito bites as products containing DEET. Non-DEET repellents have not necessarily been as thoroughly studied as DEET and may not be safer for use on children. Parents should choose the type and concentration of repellent to be used by taking into account the amount of time that a child will be outdoors, exposure to mosquitoes, and the risk of mosquito-transmitted disease in the area. The recommendations for DEET use in pregnant women do not differ from those for nonpregnant adults.

DEET is toxic when ingested and may cause skin irritation in sensitive persons. High concentrations applied to skin can cause blistering. However, because DEET is so widely used, a great deal of testing has been done, and over the long history of DEET use, very few confirmed incidents of toxic reactions to DEET have occurred when the product is used properly.

Travelers should be advised that the possibility of adverse reactions to DEET will be minimized if they take the following precautions:

- Use enough repellent to cover exposed skin or clothing. Do not apply repellent to skin that is under clothing. Heavy application is not necessary to achieve protection. If repellent is applied to clothing, wash treated clothing before wearing again.
- Do not apply repellent to cuts, wounds, or irritated skin.
- After returning indoors, wash treated skin with soap and water.
- Do not spray aerosol or pump products in enclosed areas.
- Do not apply aerosol or pump products directly to the face. Spray your hands and then rub them carefully over the face, avoiding eyes and mouth.
- When using repellent on a child, apply it to your own hands and then rub them on your child. Avoid the child's eyes and mouth and apply sparingly around the ears.
- Do not apply repellent to children's hands. (Children tend to put their hands in their mouths.)
- Do not allow young children to apply insect repellent to themselves; have an adult do it for them. Keep repellents out of reach of children.

Bed nets, repellents containing DEET, and permethrin should be purchased before traveling and can be found in hardware, camping, sporting goods, and military surplus stores.

142

Chapter 9

Tips for Older Americans

[The information in this chapter is reprinted verbatim from a bulletin issued by the U.S. State Department, Bureau of Consular Affairs. It is intended to serve as advice to Americans traveling abroad.]

Forward
International travel can be a rich and rewarding adventure. Whether you have waited a lifetime to take the perfect trip or are an experienced world traveler, we would like to offer some advice to help you plan a safe and healthy trip.

American consuls at U.S. embassies and consulates abroad are there to help if you encounter serious difficulties in your travels. They are happy to meet you if you come in to register your passport at the Consular Section of the U.S. embassy or consulate. But it is also their duty to assist American citizens abroad in times of emergency--at hospitals or police stations, for instance. Information in this chapter is written in the hopes that it will help you to prevent such emergencies from arising.

PREPARATION FOR YOUR TRIP
Start Early. Apply for your passport as soon as possible. Three months before your departure date should give you plenty of time. See the section, Passports and Visas, for details on how to apply.

Learn About the Countries You Plan to Visit. Before you go, read up on the culture, people, and history for the places you will travel. Bookstores and libraries are good resources. Travel magazines and the travel sections of major newspapers tell about places to visit and also give advice on everything from discount airfares to international health insurance. Many travel agents and foreign tourist bureaus provide free information on travel abroad.

For up-to-date travel information on any country in the world that you plan to visit, obtain the Department of State's Consular Information Sheet. They cover such matters as health conditions, unusual currency and entry regulations, crime and security conditions, drug penalties, and areas of instability. In addition, the State Department issues Travel Warnings when it recommends Americans defer travel to a country because of unsafe conditions. Travel Warnings are under continuous review by the Department of State and are removed when conditions warrant. The Department of State also issues Public Announcements as a means to disseminate information quickly about relatively short-term and/or trans-national conditions which would pose significant risks to the security of American travelers.

How to Access Consular Information Sheets, Travel Warnings and Public Announcements Consular Information Sheets, Travel Warnings and Public Announcements may be heard any time by dialing the Office of Overseas Citizens Services at (202) 647-5225 from a touchtone phone. The recording is updated as new information becomes available. They are also available at any of the 13 regional passport agencies, field offices of the Department of Commerce, and U.S. embassies and consulates abroad, or, by sending a self-addressed, stamped envelope and indicating the desired country to the Office of Overseas Citizens Services, Bureau of Consular Affairs, Room 4811, U.S. Department of State, Washington, D.C. 20520-4818.

By Fax
From your fax machine, dial (202) 647-3000, using the handset as you would a regular telephone. The

143

system prompts you on how to proceed.

By Internet
Information about travel and consular services is now available on the Internet's World Wide Web. The address is http://travel.state.gov. Visitors to the web site will find Travel Warnings, Public Announcements and Consular Information Sheets, passport and visa information, travel publications, background on international adoption and international child abduction services, international legal assistance, and the Consular Affairs mission statement. There is also a link to the State Department's main site on the Internet's World Wide Web that provides users with current foreign affairs information. The address is http://www.state.gov.

Consular Affairs Bulletin Board - CABB
If you have a personal computer, modem and communication software, you can access the Consular Affairs Bulletin Board (CABB). This service is free of charge. To view or download the documents from a computer and modem, dial the CABB on (301) 946-4400. The login is **travel**; the password is **info**.

Passport. Pack an "emergency kit" to help you get a replacement passport in case yours is lost or stolen. To make a kit: photocopy the data page at the front of your passport; write down the addresses and telephone numbers of the U.S. embassies and consulates in the countries you plan to visit; and put this information along with two recent passport-size photographs in a place separate from your passport.

Leave a Detailed Itinerary. Give a friend or relative your travel schedule. Include names, addresses, and telephone numbers of persons and places to be visited; your passport number and the date and place it was issued; and credit card, travelers check, and airline ticket numbers. Keep a copy of this information for yourself in a separate place from your purse or wallet. If you change your travel plans--for example, if you miss your return flight to the United States or extend your trip--be sure to notify relatives or friends at home.

Don't Overprogram. Allow time to relax and really enjoy yourself. Even if this is your once-in-a-lifetime trip, don't feel you have to fill every available minute.

If you are visiting a country such as China, where physical activity can be quite strenuous and sudden changes in diet and climate can have serious health consequences for the unprepared traveler, consult your physician before you depart.

What to Pack. Carefully consider the clothing you take. Don't pack more than you need and end up lugging around heavy suitcases. Wash-and-wear clothing and sturdy walking shoes are good ideas. Consider the climate and season in the countries you will visit and bring an extra outfit for unexpectedly warm or cool weather. A sweater or shawl is always useful for cooler evenings and air-conditioned planes and hotels. Dress conservatively--a wardrobe that is flashy or too causal may attract the attention of thieves or con artists.

Include a change of clothing in your carry-on luggage. Otherwise, if your bags are lost, you could be wearing the same clothes you were traveling in during the entire time it takes to locate your luggage--an average of 72 hours. Do not pack anything that you would hate to lose such as valuable jewelry, family photographs, or objects of sentimental value.

PASSPORTS AND VISAS

Passports. It is a good idea to apply 3 months before you plan to travel. If you also need visas, allow more time as you must have a valid passport before applying for a visa. If this is your first passport, you must apply in person, bringing with you proof of U.S. citizenship (usually a certified copy of your birth certificate, previous U.S. passport, a naturalization certificate, or a Consular Report of Birth Abroad); 2 identical recent front-view photos (2" x 2"); a completed passport application (Form DS-11); proof of

144

identity, such as a valid drivers license or other photo or physical-description I.D.; and the appropriate fee for a passport valid for 10 years. Click here to see a chart of passport fees.

You may apply at any passport agency (see list at the end of this chapter) or at one of the many clerks of court or post offices designated to accept passport applications. Your birth certificate or other documents will be returned to you by mail, along with your new passport.

You may be eligible to apply for a passport by mail. If you have had a passport issued within the past 12 years and you are able to mail that passport with your application, you can use Form DS-82, "Application for Passport by Mail," to apply. Obtain this form from any office that accepts passport applications or from your travel agent. Follow the instructions on the back of the form. Click here to see a chart of passport fees.

If you are leaving on an emergency trip within two weeks, apply in person at the nearest passport agency and present your tickets and itinerary from an airline, as well as the other required items. Or, apply at a court or post office and arrange to have the application sent to the passport agency through an overnight delivery service of your choice. (You should also include a self-addressed, pre-paid envelope for the return of the passport by express mail.) Be sure to include your dates of departure, travel plans on your application and all appropriate fees (including the $35 expedite fee).

When you receive your passport, be sure to sign it on page 1 and to pencil in on page 4 the requested information. This will help us notify your family or friends in case of an accident or other emergency. Do not designate your traveling companion as the person to be notified in case of an emergency. (**See Chapter 2** for more information on passports)

Visas. Many countries require a visa--an endorsement or stamp placed in your passport by a foreign government that permits you to visit that country for a specified purpose and a limited time. A number of countries require you to obtain a visa from the embassy or consular office nearest to your residence. The addresses of foreign consular offices can be found in telephone directories of large cities or in the Congressional Directory, available in most libraries; or you may write to the appropriate embassy in Washington, D.C. and request the address of their consulate that is nearest to you. You can also obtain the Department of State booklet, *Foreign Entry Requirements*, which lists visa and other entry requirements and locations of all foreign embassies and consulates in the U.S.. Apply for your visa directly to the embassy or consulate of each country you plan to visit or ask your travel agent to assist you with visas. U.S. passport agencies cannot obtain visas for you.

An increasing number of countries are establishing entry requirements regarding AIDS testing, particularly for long-term residents and students. Check with the embassy or consulate of the countries you plan to visit for the latest information.

HEALTH

Health problems sometimes affect visitors abroad. Information on health precautions can be obtained from local health departments or private doctors. General guidance can also be found in the Centers for Disease Control and Prevention's (CDC) book, Health Information for International Travel, available for $14.00 from the Superintendent of Documents, U.S. Government Printing Office, Washington, D.C. 20402, or the CDC's international travelers hotline at (404) 332-4559.

Health Insurance. It is wise to review your health insurance policy before you travel. In some places, particularly at resorts, medical costs can be as high or higher than in the United States. If your insurance policy does not cover you abroad, it is strongly recommended that you purchase a policy that does. There are short-term health insurance policies designed specifically to cover travel. If your travel agent cannot direct you to a medical assistance company, look for information in travel magazines. The U.S. government cannot pay to have you medically evacuated to the United States.

The Social Security Medicare program does not provide for payment of hospital or medical services obtained outside the United States. However, some Medicare supplement plans offer foreign medical care coverage at no extra cost for treatments considered eligible under Medicare. These are reimbursement plans. You must pay the bills first and obtain receipts for submission them later for compensation. Many of these plans have a dollar ceiling per trip.

Review your health insurance policy. Obtaining medical treatment and hospital care abroad can be expensive. If your Medicare supplement or other medical insurance does not provide protection while traveling outside the United States, we strongly urge you to buy coverage that does. The names of some of the companies offering short-term health and emergency assistance policies are listed in the Bureau of Consular Affairs flyer, *Medical Information for Americans Traveling Abroad.* The flyer is available by sending a stamped, self-addressed envelope to Bureau of Consular Affairs, Room 6831, U.S. Department of State, Washington, D.C. 20520-4818 (or via the automated systems mentioned under How to Access Consular Information Sheets).

Trip Insurance. One sure way to ruin a vacation is to lose money because an emergency forces you to postpone or cancel your trip. Except for tickets on regularly scheduled airlines, almost any travel package you purchase will have a penalty for cancellation and some companies will give no refund at all. Regularly scheduled airlines usually give a refund if an illness or death in the family forces you to cancel. Airlines require a note from the doctor or a death certificate. Take careful note of the cancellation penalty for any other large travel purchase you make, such as a tour package, charter flight, or cruise. Unless you can afford to lose the purchase amount, protect yourself by buying trip insurance. If you invest in trip insurance, make sure your policy covers all reasonable possibilities for having to cancel. For instance, if an emergency with a family member would force you to cancel, insure against that as well.

Some trip insurance policies will give a refund if the company goes out of business or otherwise does not make good on its offering. The best insurance against company default is to choose a reputable company that guarantees a refund if they do not provide the services procured. If, however, you are tempted to purchase a tour at a great bargain price and you can't find a guarantee of delivery in the fine print, protect yourself by purchasing trip insurance that covers company default.

Shop around for the trip insurance policy that offers the most benefits. Some credit card and traveler's check companies offer travel protection packages for an additional fee. Benefits may even include accident and illness coverage while traveling.

Immunizations. Information on immunizations and health precautions for travelers can be obtained from local health departments, the Centers for Disease Control and Prevention's international travelers hotline at (404) 332-4559, private doctors, or travel clinics. General guidance can also be found in the U.S. Public Health Service book, *Health Information for International Travel.* Immunizations are normally recommended against diptheria, tetanus, polio, typhoid, and hepatitis A for travelers. Generally, these immunizations are administered during childhood.

Medical Assistance Programs. One strong advantage of medical assistance programs is that they also cover the exorbitant cost of medical evacuation in the event of an accident or serious illness. As part of the coverage, these companies usually offer emergency consultation by telephone. They may refer you to the nearest hospital or call directly for help for you. If you need an interpreter, they may translate your instructions to a health care worker on the scene. Another benefit that is normally part of such coverage is payment for the return of remains to the United States in case of death.

If your regular health insurance already covers you for medical expenses abroad, you can buy a medical assistance program that offers all the consultative and evacuation services listed above except for the health insurance itself. Cost of medical assistance coverage is usually inexpensive without health insurance coverage or a little more for the complete medical assistance program including health insurance. On the other hand, escorted medical evacuation can cost thousands of dollars.

If your travel agent cannot direct you to a medical assistance company, look for information on such services in travel magazines. Once you have adequate coverage, carry your insurance policy identity cards and claim forms with you when you travel.

Medication. If you require medication, bring an ample supply in its original containers. Do not use pill cases. Because of strict laws concerning narcotics throughout the world, bring along copies of your prescriptions and, if possible, carry a letter from your physician explaining your need for the drug. As an extra precaution, carry the generic names of your medications with you because pharmaceutical companies overseas may use different names from those used in the United States.

If you wear eyeglasses, take an extra pair with you. Pack medicines and extra eyeglasses in your hand luggage so they will be available in case your checked luggage is lost. To be extra secure, pack a backup supply of medicines and an additional pair of eyeglasses in your checked luggage. If you have allergies, reactions to certain medications, foods, or insect bites, or other unique medical problems, consider wearing a "medical alert" bracelet. You may also wish to carry a letter from your physician explaining desired treatment should you become ill.

Medical Assistance Abroad. If you get sick, you can contact a consular officer at the nearest U.S. embassy or consulate for a list of local doctors, dentists, and medical specialists, along with other medical information. If you are injured or become seriously ill, a consul will help you find medical assistance and, at your request, inform your family or friends. The list of English speaking doctors is also available before you travel by writing to the Office of Overseas Citizens Services, Room 4811, 2201 C Street, N.W., Washington, D.C. 20520. Please specify to which country you will be traveling.

Health Precautions. Air pollution abroad may sometimes be severe. Air pollution and high altitudes are a particular health risk for the elderly and persons with high blood pressure, anemia, or respiratory or cardiac problems. If this applies to you, consult your doctor before traveling.

In high altitude areas most people need a short adjustment period. If traveling to such an area, spend the first few days in a leisurely manner with a light diet and reduced intake of alcohol. Avoid strenuous activity, this includes everything from sports to rushing up the stairs. Reaction signs to high altitude are lack of energy, a tendency to tire easily, shortness of breath, occasional dizziness, and insomnia.

If possible, drink only bottled water or water that has been boiled for 20 minutes. Be aware of ice cubes that may not have been made with purified water. Vegetables and fruits should be peeled or washed in a purifying solution. A good rule to follow is if you can't peel it or cook it, do not eat it. Diarrhea may be treated with antimicrobial treatment which may be prescribed or purchased over the counter. Travelers should consult a physician, rather than attempt self-medication, if the diarrhea is severe or persists several days.

Charter Flights. Before you pay for a charter flight or travel package, read your contract carefully and see what guarantee it gives that the company will deliver the services that it is trying to sell you. Tour operators sometimes go out of business in the middle of a season, leaving passengers stranded, holding unusable return tickets and unable to obtain a refund for the unused portion of their trip. Unless you are certain a company is reputable, check its credentials with your local Better Business Bureau (BBB). The BBB maintains complaint files for a year. You can also check with the consumer affairs office of the American Society of Travel Agents, 1101 King Street, Alexandria, VA 22314, tel. (703) 739-2782 to learn if a travel company has a complaint record.

147

MONEY AND VALUABLES

Don't Take Your Money in Cash. Bring most of your money in traveler's checks. Have a reasonable amount of cash with you, but not more than you will need for a day or two. Convert your traveler's checks to local currency as you use them rather than all at once.

You may also wish to bring at least one internationally-recognized credit card. Before you leave, find out what your credit card limit is and do not exceed it. In some countries, travelers who have innocently exceeded their limit have been arrested for fraud. Leave unneeded credit cards at home.

ATMs (Automated Teller Machines) are becoming increasingly popular in some of the more modern countries abroad. Often these ATMs can be accessed by your local bank card depending on which service is available. The exchange rates are comparable to the going rate of exchange. Check with your local bank to find out which ATM service is available in the country you plan to visit. Because ATMs may not always be available, this should be used as only a backup method and not depended on solely for all your financial transactions abroad.

If you must take jewelry or other valuables, use hotel security vaults to store them. It is wise to register such items with U.S. Customs before leaving the United States to make customs processing easier when you return.
It is a violation of law in some countries to enter or exit with that countrys currency. Check with a travel agent or the embassy or consulate of the countries you plan to visit to learn their currency restrictions. Before departing from the U.S., you may wish, if allowed, to purchase small amounts of foreign currency and coins to use for buses, taxis, telephone calls, and other incidentals when you first arrive in a country. You may purchase foreign currency from some banks or from foreign exchange dealers. Most international airports also have money exchange facilities.

Once you are abroad, local banks generally give more favorable rates of exchange than hotels, restaurants, or stores for converting your U.S. dollars and traveler's checks into foreign currency.

YOUR TRIP

Driving. U.S. auto insurance is usually not valid outside of the United States and Canada. When you drive in any other country, be sure to buy adequate auto insurance in that country. When renting a car abroad, make certain that adequate insurance is part of your contract; otherwise, purchase additional coverage in an amount similar to that which you carry at home. Also, prior to driving in a foreign country, familiarize yourself with the metric system since countries abroad display speed limits in kilometers per hour. **REMEMBER:** If you plan to rent a car, keep in mind which side of the road traffic moves. Unlike the U.S., many countries drive on the left hand side of the road.

Flying. On overseas flights, break up long periods of sitting. Leave your seat from time to time and also do in-place exercises. This will help prevent you from arriving tired and stiff-jointed. Also, get some exercise after a long flight. For example, take a walk or use your hotel's exercise room.

Reconfirm. Upon arrival at each stopover, reconfirm your onward reservations. When possible, obtain a written confirmation. International flights generally require confirmation 72 hours in advance. If your name does not appear on the reservation list, you could find yourself stranded.

Register. If you plan to be in a location for 2 weeks or more or in an area where there is civil unrest or any other emergency situation, register with the nearest U.S. embassy or consulate. This will help in locating you, should someone in the United States wish to confirm your safety and welfare or need to contact you urgently.

PRACTICAL SAFETY PRECAUTIONS

Respect the Local Laws and Customs. While abroad, you are subject to the laws and regulations of your host country and are not protected by the U.S. Constitution. If you should be detained by local authorities, ask them to notify a U.S. consular officer. Under international agreements and practice, you have a right to contact an American consul. Although U.S. consuls cannot act as your attorney or get you out of jail, they can provide you with a list of local attorneys and inform you of your rights under local laws. They will also monitor the status of detained Americans and make sure they are treated fairly under local laws.

Guard Your Passport. Your passport is the most valuable document you carry abroad. It confirms that you are an American citizen. Do not carry your passport in the same place as your money or pack it in your luggage. Remember to keep your passport number in a separate location in case it is lost or stolen. In some countries, you may be required to leave your passport overnight or for several days with the hotel management. This may be local practice--do not be concerned unless the passport is not returned as promised. If your passport is lost or stolen abroad, immediately report it to the local police, obtain a copy of the report, and contact the nearest U.S. embassy or consulate to apply for a new passport.

Be Alert. Move purposefully and confidently. If you should find yourself in a crowded area, such as in an elevator, subway, marketplace, or in busy tourist areas, exercise special caution to avoid theft.

Robbery. Help prevent theft by carrying your belongings securely. Carry purses tucked under an arm and not dangling by a strap. Carry valuables hidden in an inside front pocket or in a money belt, not in a hip pocket. You may wish to wrap your wallet with rubber bands to make it more difficult for someone to slip it from your pocket unnoticed. Money belts or pouches that fit around your shoulder, waist or under clothing are available through some luggage shops and department stores.

ASSISTANCE FROM U.S. EMBASSIES AND CONSULATES

Emergencies. If you encounter serious legal, medical, or financial difficulties or other problems abroad, contact the nearest U.S. embassy or consulate for assistance. Although consular officers cannot serve as attorneys, they can help you find legal assistance. Consular officers cannot cash checks, lend money, or act as travel agents. However, in an emergency, consular officers can help you get in touch with your family back home to inform them on how to wire funds to you and to let them know of your situation. Consular officers can also provide you with the latest information about adverse conditions abroad.

Nonemergencies. Consular officers also provide nonemergency services such as information on absentee voting and acquisition or loss of U.S. citizenship. They can arrange for the transfer of Social Security and other benefits to Americans residing abroad, provide U.S. tax forms, notarize documents, and advise U.S. citizens on property claims.

Safeguarding Your Health. If you are injured or become seriously ill abroad, a U.S. consular officer will assist you in finding a physician or other medical services, and, with your permission, will inform your family members or friends of your condition. If needed, consular officers can assist your family in transferring money to the foreign country to pay for your treatment.

Death Abroad. Each year, about 6,000 Americans die abroad. Two thirds of them are Americans who live overseas, but approximately 2,000 Americans per year die while visiting abroad. Consular officers will contact the next of kin in the United States and will explain the local requirements. It is a worthwhile precaution to have insurance that covers the cost of local burial or shipment of remains home to the United States (see information on medical assistance programs). Otherwise, this cost must be borne by your next of kin and can be extremely expensive. The U.S. government cannot pay for shipment of remains to the United States.

149

SHOPPING--SOME THINGS TO AVOID

Beware of purchasing souvenirs made from endangered wildlife. Many wildlife and wildlife products are prohibited either by U.S. or foreign laws from import into the United States. You risk confiscation and a possible fine if you attempt to import such things. Watch out for and avoid purchasing the following prohibited items:

All products made from sea turtles.

All ivory, both Asian and African.

Furs from spotted cats.

Furs from marine mammals.

Feathers and feather products from wild birds.

All live or stuffed birds from Australia, Brazil, Colombia, Costa Rica, Ecuador, Guatemala, Mexico, Paraguay, Venezuela, and some Caribbean countries.

Most crocodile and caiman leather.

Most coral, whether in chunks or in jewelry.

WHEN YOU RETURN

Be Prepared. On arrival in the United States, have your passport ready when you go through immigration and customs controls.

Keep receipts for any items you purchased abroad. U.S. citizens may bring back and orally declare $400 worth of merchandise duty free. The next $1000 is taxed at a flat rate of 10%. Check with U.S. Customs for further information.

Currency. There is no limit on the amount of money or negotiable instruments which can be brought into or taken out of the United States. However, any amount over $10,000 must be reported to U.S. Customs on Customs Form 4790 when you depart from or enter into the United States.

Foreign Produce. Don't bring home any fresh fruits or vegetables. Such items will be confiscated.

OTHER USEFUL TRAVEL PUBLICATIONS
(See Chapter 36)

PASSPORT AGENCIES

(See the Appendix C for a listing of US Government Passport Agencies)

Planning Another Trip?

See Chapter 36 for a listing of resources available to the general traveler from the U.S. Departments of State, Customs, Transportation, Health and various government and non-government organizations. Almost all of the available International travel-related pamphlets, brochures and publications issued by the U.S. Department of State and by the U.S. Customs have been reproduced in full in this book. See Table of Contents for location.

Chapter 10

Travel Tips for the Disabled

*[The information in this chapter is intended to serve as
advice to disabled travelers.]*

Suggestions for Convenient Travel

Over 43 million people in the U.S. with some kind of a disability need to use air transportation for business or pleasure. With the passage of the Air Carrier Access Act of 1986 and the Americans with Disabilities Act of 1990, air transportation providers have made great strides to increase accessible services for people with disabilities.

The following suggestions offer tips to help travelers with disabilities and older people to experience a trouble-free trip:

Advance Reservations

It will be helpful to give the airline ample time to supply any special equipment or services you may need. This procedure will allow the reservation agent to program your request into the airline computer system and distribute it to other airline representatives who you may encounter on your trip.

Request information about the airline's special services for people who are disabled and/or older, as well as any other customer service requests such as: special meals, braille briefing procedures, open-captions on videos, visual displays at gate areas, procedures for packaging battery-powered wheelchairs, and special senior fares.

Request written confirmation after you make your reservation. Ask the reservation or travel agent to repeat your request to make sure they have recorded it correctly.

Deadlines for purchasing reservations will vary according to the airline and type of fares you are investigating.

Make sure you confirm the deadline for purchasing your ticket(s) with the reservation agent.

If you are hearing impaired, inform the reservation or travel agent of a relay telephone number, as well as your TDD number, in case they need to reach you.

Inform the airline as to whether you wish to transport your own wheelchair and if so, whether it is battery-powered and the type of battery it has so the airline can provide appropriate packaging. Be sure you understand the airline's procedure for transporting battery-powered wheelchairs.

Make sure a baggage destination tag and a personal I.D. tag are attached to your wheelchair before you check it in.

Inform the airline/travel agent if you will be traveling with a service animal or will need special equipment during the flight such as portable oxygen, on board wheelchair, or a stretcher, among other items.

Upon request, airlines, by law, will provide assistance for boarding, exiting the aircraft, flight connections, and for transportation between gates.

Advance Check-In

It is helpful to check in early, at least (1) hour before departure to provide enough time for the airline to accommodate your wishes.

If paying by check, make sure you have the proper identification-a drivers license, major credit card, etc.

When checking in be sure to give the

151

final destination and not the city where you might connect to go to another flight.

Make sure your tickets have the correct originating city, connecting city, and final destination.
Make sure your claim ticket and luggage tag matches your final destination.

Carry on luggage is limited to two pieces of luggage that will fit underneath the passengers seat, in the overhead bin or closet of the aircraft. Assistive devices such as canes, TDDs, wheelchairs, crutches, prosthetic devices etc., are not counted as carry on baggage according to the Air Carrier Access Act of 1986.

Many airports provide printed access guides which outline accessible services available in the airport. These brochures may be found at travelers aid stations, information counters, and airport administration offices. Airport authorities will be happy to send you a copy of their brochure if requested in advance.

Procedures for Boarding, In-Flight and Deplaning

Airlines must offer the opportunity for you to pre-board upon request. Be prepared to provide instructions on how to best help you. If you are hearing impaired, ask the agent to let you know when it is time to board. Confirm the flight number and destination before boarding, and sit facing the boarding station if possible.

If you are unable to hear announcements in-flight, request that they be communicated to you, in person, by the flight attendant.

Federal Aviation Regulations require in-flight crews to brief passengers on evacuation procedures. It may be necessary to provide you with an independent briefing. Ask the attendant for print or braille instructions to facilitate the briefing.

If you need assistance leaving the plane upon arrival, advise the in-flight crew during the flight to make arrangements with ground crew personnel.

Medical Traveling Tips

According to the American Academy of Otolaryngology Head and Neck Surgery, ear problems are the most common medical complaint of airplane travelers. Many people experience a sensation of fullness in the ears or popping when in-flight. During an airplane descent babies often cry due to this discomfort.

A fullness or blocked sensation can be experienced when the middle ear pressure cannot be equalized. The Eustachian tube must open frequently and widely enough to equalize the changes in pressure. Since air travelers can experience rapid changes in air pressure, the following tips can help to equalize the pressure in the middle ear.

Swallow frequently when you are in-flight, especially before descent. Chewing gum or allowing mints to melt in your mouth will create a need for you to swallow more often.
Avoid sleeping during descent, because you may not be swallowing often enough to keep up with pressure changes.

If yawning or swallowing is not effective, use the 'valsalva' maneuver:

- Pinch your nostrils shut.

- Breathe in a mouthful of air.

- Using only your cheek and throat muscles, create pressure and force the air into the back of your nose as if you were trying to blow your thumb and fingers off your nostrils.

- Be very gentle and blow in short successive attempts. When you hear or feel a pop in your ears, you have succeeded.

- Never use force from your chest (lungs) or abdomen (diaphragm) which can create pressures that are too intense.

- If travelling with a baby, allow the baby to suck on a pacifier or bottle, and do not allow the baby to sleep during descent.

- If you have a cold, a sinus infection or allergy attack, postpone the airplane trip if at all possible.

- Decongestant tablets and nasal sprays can be used an hour or so before descent. Travelers with allergy problems should take their medication at the beginning of the flight.
Decongestant tablets and sprays should be avoided by persons with heart disease, high blood pressure, irregular heart rhythms, thyroid diseases or excessive nervousness. Pregnant women should consult their physicians first before using these over the counter medications.

- After landing you may continue the pressure equalizing techniques, but if your ears fail to open or pain persists, seek the help of a physician who has experience in the care of ear disorders.

- Do not put medication or glasses in checked bags; always bring them with you in carry-on bags. Bring a copy of your prescriptions for medication, glasses, and a statement from your physician explaining any special medical problems

ADVICE TO TRAVEL AGENTS AND HANDICAPPED TRAVELLERS ON ALERTING AIR CARRIERS TO SPECIAL NEEDS[SH]

It concerns the use of SSR (Special Services Request) and OSI (Other Service Information) codes which are used to alert the airlines to the individual client's special needs. Entered in the PNR (Passenger Name Record) the SSR "sends an action message to the airline and station that will provide the service and product. "while the OSI merely alerts boarding agents or inflight personnel of some special condition. Following is a list of special services, some provided as a matter of course others requiring action on the agent's part.

Advance boarding: This is standard procedure and requires no advance notification. The passenger should, however, be advised to check in early if they desire it.

Blind passengers - There is no restriction on the number of guide dogs per flight, but they must be properly harnessed.

Canes and Cruches - FAA regulations allow these in the cabin but require them to be secured at least during take-off and landing.

Deaf passengers: Hearing dogs are also not restricted, but must be properly harnessed.

Special Meal Requirement: An SSR must specify the type of meal, e.g. diabetic. low cholesterol, low sodium, vegetarian and must be entered at least 24 hours before the flight. Escort Service: An SSR to "meet and assist" can be sent for the disabled or elderly.

Inability to sit upright: If a reclining seat is needed even during take-off and landing, special arrangements must be made. Some carriers will not allow this, while others will do so only for seats in front of the bulkhead or if the row behind can be closed off.

Mentally handicapped: Those who are self-sufficient can travel alone. An SSR to "meet and assist" will help ensure that all goes smoothly. Those who require an attendant must also have a physician's statement that they can travel without causing inconvenience or injury to themselves or others. The carrier must be notified in advance and sent the doctor's release. Early check-in is necessary to allow for pre-boarding.

Obesity: Those who require it can travel as a "passenger occupying two seats". Usually this allows them to reserve two adjacent seats for one and a half fares. and entitles them to twice the normal free baggage allowance.

Oxygen: Therapeutic inflight oxygen is provided

by many carriers but requires advance notification. The traveller must have a doctor's certificate which gives the maximum oxygen usage per hour and the flow rate per minute. For reasons of safety, the patient's own equipment normally must be checked as cargo, packed and labeled as required for hazardous materials. The charge for inflight oxygen varies by carrier.

Pregnancy: In order to be checked in, expectant mothers in their ninth month must have a doctor's release no more than three days old and which gives the estimated delivery date. To avoid inconvenience, those with visibly advanced pregnancies but not yet in their ninth month may want to have a certificate as well.

Prosthetic devices and walkers: Carried at no charge, but may have to be transported as checked baggage. Consult the carrier and request special assistance if needed.

Seating restrictions: The standard policy is that handicapped persons not be seated in emergency exit rows. SATH feels that the physically handicapped should, if anything, be seated so that they can get to exits without undue hinderance. In general, the handicapped should be allowed to sit where they choose: they do not constitute a safety problem.

Wheelchairs: airline owned: Send an SSR to all stations on the passenger itinerary so that a wheelchair is available for each departure and arrival. The three types of wheelchair requests are as follows: WCHC - completely immobile, WCHR - Can ascend/descend stairs, WCHS - Cannot ascend/descend stairs, can walk in cabin.

Wheelchairs: passenger owned: Carried at no charge as checked baggage on a last on first off basis, (this ensures that it is immediately available on landings, On electric chairs, batteries are frequently disconnected in flight for safety reasons. Reconnecting them after arrival and making sure the chair is working should be the airline's responsibility. Advise the passenger to label all detachable parts of the wheelchair (surgical tape works well) with his/her name, destination address, and how long he/she will be there so that the part can be forwarded if it gets lost. However if possible he/she should remove them and keep them with him/her if possible. Also

advise the passenger to get wheelchair insurance: airline insurance policies are restricted to $600.00 maximum at time of writing.

OTHER HELPFUL RESOURCES AND REFERENCES

A Guide to Recreation, Leisure and Travel for the Handicapped, vol., 2: **Travel and Transportation.** This reference manual is available (for a price), from Resource Directories, Toledo, Ohio, (419)-536-5353

A Travel Guide for the Disabled: Western Europe by Mary Meister. This book is available (for a price), from Van Nostrand Reinhold Co. Inc. 135, W. 50th Street, New York, N.Y. 10020.

A World of Options for the 1990's A Guide to International Educational Exchange, Community Service and Travel for Persons With Disabilities published by Mobility International, Eugene Oregon. (503) 343-1284

Access to the World: A travel guide for the Handicapped, by Louise Weiss. Available from Facts on File, Inc. 460 Park Avenues South, New York, NY 10016 (212) 683-2244.

Access Travel: *A Guide to Accessibility of Airport Terminals* Available free of charge from Consumer Information Center, Pueblo Colorado, 81009. and from Airport Operators Councils International Inc., 1220 19th Street, N.W. Suite 200, Washington D.C. 20036, Fax: (202) 331-1362

Airline Seating Guide, Available from Carlson Publishing Company, 3535 Farguhar Ave., P.O. Box 888 Los Alamitos CA 90720.

Dialysis World-Wide, published by N.A.P.H.T. 7628 Densmore Ave., Van Nuys, CA 91406, Tel. (818) 782-7328.

Directory of Travel Agencies for the Disabled; Travel for the Disabled and *Wheelchair Vagabond* published by Twin Peaks Press, P.O. Box 129, Vancouver, WA 98666 (800) 637-2256 or (206) 694-2462. Twin Peaks also publish travel information on accommodations, as well as provide travel hints and advice directed to travelers who are disabled.

Frommer's A Guide For The Disabled Traveler by Frances Barish Published by Frommer/Pasmantler Publishers, A Division of Simon & Schuster 1230 Avenue of The Americas, New York, NY 10020

Handi-Travel A Resource Book for Disabled & Elderly Travellers by Cinnie Noble Published by the Canadian

Rehabilitation Council for the Disabled One Yonge Street, Ste. 2110, Toronto, Ontario M5E lE3

Incapacitated Passengers Handling Guide, T.A.T.A. Travel Services, Director, International Air Transport association, 1000 Sherbrooke Street, West Montreal, Quebec, Canada, H3A 2R4

International Directory of Access Guides, Travel Survey Rehabilitation International U.S.A. 20 West 40th St. New York, NY 10018

Moss Rehabilitation Hospital (Travel Information Service), 1200 W. Tabor Road. Philadelphia PA 19141 (215) 456-9602

Ten Questions and Answers About Air Travel for Wheel Chair Users. This booklet is available free from Eastern Paralyzed Veterans Association, Jackson heights, N.Y. (718) 803-3782.

The Guide to Recreation, Leisure & Travel for The Handicapped, Vol.2 Travel & Transportation by Rod W. Durgin, PH.D. Resource Directories 3103 Executive Parkway Toledo, OH 43606

The Handicapped Traveller: A Guide for Travel Counsellors by Cinnie Noble Published by the Canadian Institutes of Travel Counsellors/Instituts Canadiens des Conseillers de Voyages 2333 Dundas St. W Ste 302 Toronto, Ontario M6R 3A6

The Real Guide, Able To Travel. True Stories by and for People with Disabilities edited by Allison Walsh with Jodi Abbott and Peg L.Smith.Published by Prentice Hall Travel, New York .

The Physically Disabled Traveler's Guide is also available from Resource Directories, Toledo, Ohio, (419) 536-5353.

The *Handicapped Driver's Mobility Guide* published by the American Automobile

Association. This guide is free to AAA members. or write to the Traffic Safety Department, 8111 Gatehouse Road, Falls Church VA 22047.

The Itinerary (a bimonthly magazine) For subscription write to Box 2012, Bayonne NJ 07002; (201) 858-3400

The Braille Institute Press, Braille Institute, 741 N. Vermont Ave., Los Angeles CA 90020; (213) 663-1111. The Braille Institute publishes a number of travel books in Braille.

Travel Tips for People with Arthritis, published by the Arthrities Foundation. For a free copy call the foundation. Washington, D.C. Chapter at (202) 276-7555, or (800) 242-9945.

Travel Ability by Lois Reamy, Macmillan Publishing Co, Inc 866 Third Avenue New York, NY 10022. Collier Macmillan Canada Ltd

Travel For The Disabled: A Handbook of Travel Resources & 500 Worldwide Access Guide by Helen Hecker R.N. Published by Twin Peaks Press, P.O. Box 8097, Portland, OR 97207

Additional information could be obtained from:

- The airport, rail, and other transportation authorities.

- The airline(s) you plan to use in your travels.

- The tourist offices or tourist boards of foreign governments located here in the U.S.

Once you have decide on the countries to visit, check Appendix L for addresses and phone numbers of that country's tourist office.

When making inquiries find out what services and considerations if any, are given to disabled persons. Request for brochures, addresses and telephone number if available.

SERVICES

Write or call these organizations and request for their catalogue as well on any other services they offer to disabled persons or disabled international

155

travelers.

TOUR COMPANIES FOR THE DISABLED

Accessible Journeys, 412 S. 45th St, Philadelphia, PA 19104, Tel. (215) 747-0171.

Dialysis & Sea Cruises/Unique Reservations Inc., 611 Barry Place, Indian Rocks Beach, FL 34635, Tel. (800) 544-7604 or (813) 596-7604.

Dialysis Travel Services, 9301 East Shea Blvd., Scottsdale, AZ, Tel. (800) 832-5445.

Dialysis in Wonderland, 1130 West Center St., North Salt Lake city, UT 84054, Tel. (800) 777-5727.

Evergreen Travel Services (Wings on Wheels), 4114 198th Ave. Lynnwood WA 98036. (800) 435-2288 or (206) 776-1184.

Flying Wheels Travel, 143 West Bridge St, P.O. Box 382, Owatonna, MN 55060. (800) 535-6790) or (507) 451-5005.

Interpret Tours, 1730 Citronia Street, North Ridge CA 91325 Telephone:TTY (818) 885-6921; In California dial (800) 342-5833

Med Escort International, Inc., ABE International Airport, P.O. Box 8766, Allentown, PA 18105, Tel. (800) 255-7182 or (215) 791-3111.

The Guided Tour Inc. 613 Cheltenham Ave, St. 200 Melrose Park, PA 19126. (215) 782-1370.

Travel Care Health Services, 630-21 10405 Jasper Avenue, Edmonton, Alberta, T5J 3S2, Canada, Tel. (403) 429-2323.

U.S. Travel, 11 East 44th Street, New York, NY 10017, Tel. (800) 487 8787 or (212) 883-5687.

Whole Person Tours, P.O. Box 1084 Bayonne New Jersey 07002. (201) 858-3400

HELPING HANDS (Also See Appendix 14N)

American Foundation for the Blind, 15 West 16th St., New York (800)232-5463 or (212) 620-2159.

Directions Unlimited, 720 N. Bedford Rd., Bedford Hills, NY 10507 (800) 533-5343

Medic Alert Foundation International, P.O. Box 1009, Turlock California 95831. (800)432-5378. Medic Alert manufactures and distributes the Medic Alert Identification Tag, a useful device for those overseas travelers with special medical conditions.

Opening Door, Rte. 2, Box 1805, Woodford, VA 22580, Tel. (804) 633-6752

Mobility International P.O. Box 3551, Eugene, OR 97403 (503) 343-1284 (voice and TDD).

Society for the Advancement of Travel for the Handicapped, 347 Fifth Ave., Suite 610, New York, NY 10016 (212) 447-7284 fax (212) 725-8253. Membership required.

The American Diabetes Association 1660 Duke St. Alexandria, VA 2324 (800) 232-3472.

The Information Center for Individuals with Disabilities, Fort Point Pl., Worm wood St., Boston MA 02210 (617) 727-5540

The Access Foundation for the Disabled, Malverne, New York (516)887-5798

Travel Industry and Disabled Exchange, 5435 Donna Ave., Tarzana CA 91356. (818) 368-5648

Traveling Nurses Network, P.O. Box 129, Vancouver, Washington, (202) 694-2462

Chapter 11

Tips for Women Traveling Alone

*[The information in this chapter is intended to serve as advice
To disabled travelers.]*

Information contained in this chapter has been prepared by the U.S. State Department Bureau of Consular Affairs to provide general information for women who plan to travel abroad alone. There has been an increase in the number of Americans traveling abroad - especially women traveling alone either for business or pleasure.

Each country and culture has their own views of what is appropriate behavior for women. Although you may not agree with these views, it is wise to abide by the local laws and customs to avoid problems. Please become familiar with the laws and customs of the places where you wish to go. Here are two examples of situations you may encounter:

It is illegal in Laos to invite Lao nationals of the opposite sex to one's hotel room.
Foreigners in Saudi Arabia have been arrested in the past for "improper dress."
Women traveling alone can be more vulnerable to problems in certain cultures. Keeping in mind the following information can help make your trip as safe and rewarding as possible.

PREPARING FOR YOUR TRIP
Passports & Visas: Make sure your passport is still valid or apply for a new one long before you plan to travel. Make sure you have the right travel documents and visas for your destinations. For information on individual countries' entry and exit requirements, refer to our publication Foreign Entry Requirements.

Your Destinations: Make an effort to learn about the locations you plan to visit, their culture, and any problems that might be occurring there.

The Bureau of Consular Affairs constantly updates its published and on-line information to reflect developing situations in each country.

http://travel.state.gov

Many exciting and exotic destinations may have very conservative views about women. Being a foreigner makes you stand out; a woman traveling alone can be even more of an oddity in some places.

What to Leave Behind: Leave a detailed itinerary and a copy of your passport's identification page with a friend or relative at home. Include names, addresses and telephone numbers where you will be staying. Leave a copy of your flight and ticket information with them as well.

You may wish to establish certain check in dates when you will either call, e-mail, fax, etc. to let someone know that you are all right. But remember that if you happen to miss a check-in, your loved ones may assume that you are having a problem or are in trouble.

Leave any valuables, extra credit cards and jewelry - even fake jewelry - at home. Thieves often won't know the real from the fake until after they take it, so why risk your personal safety?

Health: Make sure you have adequate health insurance coverage while abroad and that your coverage includes medical evacuations. Your policy might not cover you overseas and you may need to purchase traveler's insurance. See our publication Medical Information for Americans Traveling Abroad.

If you have any condition that might develop complications- especially if you are pregnant, check with your doctor before you go abroad. If you experience complications, a medical evacuation might still take several precious hours to arrange.

157

If you take prescription medication, make sure you have enough to last the duration of the trip, including extra medication in case you are delayed. Always carry your prescriptions in their labeled containers as many countries have strict narco-trafficking laws and might be suspicious of pills in unlabeled bottles. Bring your prescription information and the names of their generic equivalents with you just in case.

OFF YOU GO

Safety and Security: Use common sense and be alert and aware of your surroundings. If you are unsure in general about the local situation, feel free to check with the American Citizens Services section of the local U.S. Embassy or Consulate for the latest security information.

Don't announce that you are traveling alone! Some guides for women even advise wearing a wedding ring if you're single. If you feel like you're being followed, step into a store or other safe place and wait to see if the person you think is following has passed. Do not be afraid or embarrassed to ask for someone to double check for you to see if all is safe. Display confidence. By looking and acting as if you know where you're going, you may be able to ward off some potential danger.

Ask for directions before you set out. No matter how modest your lodgings are, your hotel concierge or other hotel staff should be able to help. If you find yourself lost, do not be afraid to ask for directions. Generally, the safest people to ask are families or women with children. Getting the right information may save you from ending up in a potentially unsafe area.

Hotels: Choose a hotel where security is good and transportation is readily available and nearby. Check that all the doors and windows in your room have locks and that they work. If you feel uncomfortable, ask hotel security to escort you to and from parking lots or your room at night. Always use your peephole and common sense about letting strangers into your room.

Clothing: There is no doubt that fashion makes a statement. Unfortunately, not everyone will interpret how you dress the same way you would. What you consider casual clothing might be seen as provocative or inappropriate in other cultures.

Thieves might choose you over another potential target based on your style of dress or the amount of makeup or jewelry you are wearing. Other might single you out for harassment or even physical violence because they find your clothing offensive, based on their cultural norms. By taking your cues from local women, or at least by dressing conservatively, you could save yourself a great deal of trouble.

- - - - - - - - - - - - - - - - - - -

There is a wealth of literature available both on the Internet and in books and journals with information and advice for women traveling alone. Take the time to search the web and your local library and/or bookstore.

Consular Affairs regularly updates its Consular Information Sheets, Public Announcements, Travel Warnings and other information materials. Please check these out on the Internet at http://travel.state.gov. This information is also available by phone at 202-647-5225. See Chapter 36 for a list of important U.S. Government publications reprinted elsewhere in this book.

‾ REMINDERS ‾

1. Make sure you have a signed, valid passport and visas, if required. Also, before you go, fill in the emergency information page of your passport!
2. Read the Consular Information Sheets (and Public Announcements or Travel Warnings, if applicable) for countries you plan to visit.
3. Leave copies of your itinerary, passport data page and visas with family and friends at home, so you can be contacted in case of an emergency
4. Make sure you have insurance that will cover your medical needs while you are overseas.
5. Familiarize yourself with local laws and customs, especially when it comes to dressing and socializing.
6. Do not leave your luggage unattended in public areas and never accept packages from strangers.
7. Do not announce that you are traveling alone!
8. Do not wear conspicuous clothing and expensive jewelry and do not carry excessive amounts of cash or unnecessary credit cards.
9. Before leaving your hotel ask for directions.
10. Ensure that the hotel you plan on staying at has good security and easy access to transportation.

Chapter 12

Tips For Students Traveling or Studying Abroad

Introduction

So you are a student and you are preparing to travel abroad. You are not alone. Every year tens of thousands of American students travel overseas either unaccompanied by or in the company of their parents, friends or guardians. The purpose of these travels vary. Whereas some of the students go abroad to continue their education, in which case they take up semi-permanent residence; others go in search of summer jobs or as volunteers.

Whatever the reasons or motives for your trip, you will inevitably be exposed to the same type of problems often experienced by the majority of non-student Americans who travel abroad. This means that you should engage yourself in the same type of preparation and take the same general precautions suggested throughout this book, particularly in Chapters 1, 4, 5 and 35. Like the rest of the population of Americans traveling abroad, you are concerned with security issues, health issues, time, as well as money saving opportunities. Ultimately, you want to have an exciting, safe and incident-free trip.

This book addresses precisely those issues aimed at enabling you to make a successful trip and, enabling to learn in particular, the things you need to know before you go. This theme has been echoed in several chapters throughout this book. I suggest, therefore, that you refer to the relevant chapters for those aspects of international travel that you may be interested in, that have not been addressed in this chapter.

In the course of my research and travels, I have come to appreciate the importance of a number of subjects of real interest to international student travelers. Few, if any, have matched the wishes of these students to learn about cost-saving opportunities to finance their trip. Of course, students are not alone in this category; except to say that a number of such opportunities, specifically limited to students, do exist, and

student travelers should know about them and take advantage of them.

First and foremost, you should avail yourself of the services of the Council on International Education Exchange (CIEE).

Founded in 1947, CIEE is a world-renowned organization known for its active promotion and sponsorship of International Education Exchange.

Today, CIEE services the interest of students, youths and teachers, assisting them in a variety of ways with study, hospitality and travel programs. In cooperation with member institutions world-wide, CIEE administers several study programs, including language programs, voluntary service opportunities for American students in Europe, and a variety of work camps for American and non-American youths, as well as exchange programs between secondary schools in the U.S. and in several countries of the world.

The budget-conscious student traveler may want to explore CIEE's international travel programs. CIEE distinguishes itself as a clearing house for information and services relating to all aspects of student travel. They arrange low cost transportation for individuals and groups, including students flights to Europe, Asia and various destinations in Latin America. Furthermore, CIEE provides information on low-cost hotel accommodations available to students overseas.

International Identification Cards

Further, CIEE issues a number of identification cards, including the International Student Identity Cards (ISIC), the International Teachers Identification (ITIC), and the Federation of International Youth Organization Cards (FIYTO). These cards are available from CIEE and other centers listed in the section of this chapter entitled "Helping Hands". They usually have a one year expiration date, the cost is less than $20.00 each and they often require a passport photo 1 1/2 x 2 inches and some form of identification, such as a letter from your school, your grade report or transcript.

ADVANTAGES OF THE ISIC:

Although you may be able to receive just about the same services with your standard university or college I.D. card as those available to ISIC holders, the ISIC has the unique feature of being the most widely recognized proof of student status all over the world. As a holder of the ISIC, you will have access to a variety of money-saving discount opportunities and services, from airfare, bus, ferry and train rides to accommodations to museums and theaters. These money saving opportunities may not be advertised and may not be available in every country. Therefore, always initiate the request. Ask your travel or ticket agent if there are discounts available to students. If one exists, request to receive such discounts or considerations. Remember, "If You Don't Ask, You Don't Receive!" Do not forget to be polite and courteous; it could make the difference.

The other advantage of the ISIC is that, if bought in the United States, it also provides you with some amount of accident and health insurance, an important asset for every traveler going abroad.

Not the least of the ISIC advantages is its unique 'classy look'. Besides, the card serves as an important piece of identification, one that could become very useful in the event of an incident. That is the primary reason you should carry it with you at all times.

LODGING:

Finding suitable lodging overseas has not always been a problem, particularly if you have lots of money to spend. However for those on a limited budget this may not be so. Some avenues, nevertheless, exist for the budget-conscious student traveler. Some of these avenues may require some flexibility and tolerance on your part, while others may require long-term planning.

An alternative to hotels and pensions are the youth hostels. These hostels offer travelers of all ages clean, inexpensive, overnight accommodations in more than 6000 locations in over 70 countries world wide. Hostels provide dormitory-style accommodations with separate facilities for males and females. Some hostels have family rooms that can be reserved in advance. Curfews are often imposed, and membership is often required. For more information contact the American Youth Hostels, P.O. Box 37613, Washington, D.C. 20013-7613 or call (202) 783-4943. Some of the other agencies listed below in the section "Helping Hands" would be willing to assist you in finding inexpensive lodging. Should you, on the other hand, wish to use instead, a hotel or pension for lodging, present your ISIC or school I.D. card and request a discount. Who knows, they might be able to give you one.

The other alternative available to student budget travelers is to identify in the countries they plan to visit, a university or college with boarding facilities for its students, preferably, one located closest to your intended destination. Write to the "President of the Student Union/Organization/Council" of that institution requesting accommodations on campus, if possible. Your letter should explain briefly who you are, your school affiliation, your intended travel plans to that country (not your detailed day-to-day itinerary), the length of time for which you seek accommodation, and more important, that you are writing because you are traveling on a budget and do not have enough funds to cover your lodgings. Of course, you must have some funds, sufficient to subsist on for a few days in a hotel, but you do not want to include that in your request. If you succeed, that might provide you with a token gift to leave with your host or hostess. When carefully done, success with this plan has quite a number of advantages. Besides saving you money on lodging, you may be lucky enough to get free or discounted meals. As a special guest, you may have the opportunity to visit and explore many more exciting places than you probably would see in the absence of this type of accommodation.

The camaraderie created between you and your host/hostess, and their friends and relatives may provide just another opportunity for future trips at even cheaper costs.

Alternatively, you may consider renting a room in a nearby college or university (University Hostels). Several institutions abroad do have room and board facilities that are rented out to students and non-student travelers, during vacation time. The rates charged to students are usually lower than rates charged non-students. Inquiries should be directed to the Director of Housing at the respective institutions

There are, of course, several, other less conventional and cheap lodging facilities available to the international traveler. They include, farms, camps, road-side shelters and parks

Not withstanding which plans you chose, or which countries you visit, remember you are in a foreign country and that all of the precautions emphasized elsewhere in this book should be followed to safeguard your valuables, health and safety.

It is important, as with every American traveling abroad, to register immediately your presence with the Consular Section of the American Embassy immediately upon arrival. The usefulness of such registration has been stated and emphasized in Chapters 1 and 35 of this book.

For a country-by-country listing of foreign universities and other institutions of higher learning, including their addresses, consult your college or local public library.

USEFUL PUBLICATIONS
You will find the following publications helpful *Work, Study, Travel Abroad: The Whole World Handbook; The Teenager's Guide to Study, Travel and Adventure Abroad; The Student Travel Catalog* and *Volunteer*. These publications are produced by CIEE. The first two publications are available from CIEE and at many bookstores. The student travel catalog which is updated annually is offered free of charge. CIEE also distributes directories and brochures on foreign travel and study programs.

-LET'S GO SERIES of travel books published by Harvard Student Agencies, Inc. Cambridge, MA. (671) 495-9695. These travel books are widely available in bookstores across the country. Also check your local libraries.

Study Abroad, Published by UNESCO and *The World of Learning*, published by Europe Publications Ltd: These and other sources should be available in your local public or school library.

You may, also, contact the respective education departments of the Embassies for a complete listing and location of institutions of higher learning with boarding facilities in their country.

HELPING HANDS (National and International Student Organizations)
The following organizations have a reputation for catering to the needs of students, youths and teachers traveling abroad.

They provide a wide range of services and products including bargain fares, discount travel guides, insurance, accommodation, international rail passes, and identification cards (ISIC, ITIC & FIYTO Cards). Write and request for information on their services.

Council on International Education Exchange (CIEE) 205 E. 42nd St., New York NY. 10017 (212) 661-1414. OTHER CIEE OFFICES are located in the following cities: Boston: 729 Boylston St., Boston, MA 02116. (617) 266-1926; Los Angeles: 1093 Broxton Ave., Los Angeles, CA 90024, (213) 208-3551; Chigago: 1153 N. Dearborn St., Chicago, IL 60610 (312) 951-0585; San Francisco: 919 Irvin St., San Francisco, CA 94122, (415) 566-9222, Austin : 2000 Guadelupe St. Austin TX 78705, (512) 472-4931.:The ISIC, ITIC and the YIYTO cards are administered by CIEE and are available from any of their offices.

Education Travel Center (ETC) 438 North Frances St. Madison, Wisconsin (608) 256-5551.

International Student Exchange Flights (ISE), 5010 East Shea Blvd. Suite A 104, Scottsdale, Arizona 85254. (602) 951-1177.

Let's Go Travel Services, Harvard Student Agencies Inc. Thayer Hall, B. Harvard University, Cambridge MA. 02138 (617) 495-9649.

Council Travel (is a subsidiary of CIEE. See CIEE

STA Travel, 17 East 45th St. New York, NY 10017 (800) 777-0112 or (212) 986-9470.

American Youth Hostels, P.O.Box 37613 Washington, D.C. 20013 (202) 783-4943.

Institute For Foreign Study (AIFS), 102

Greenwich Ave., Greenwich, CT 06830. (800) 727 AIFS or (203) 869-9090 or (203) 863-6087

Experiment in International Living, Kipling Rd., Brattleboro, VT. 05302, (800) 345-2929, or (802) 257-7751.

Institute of International Education, 809 United Nations Plaza, New York NY 10017, (800) 883-8200

* Your Student Office: Check with the student office of your institution. They may have valuable information, references and contacts that may save you both time and money. Some student offices do issue the ISIC card.

More Travel Tips For Students Traveling or Studying Abroad [*from the U.S. Department of State*]

This section was to provide students, who are planning to travel or study abroad, with a few reminders about safety.

Although most trips abroad are trouble free, being prepared will go a long way to avoiding the possibility of serious trouble.

Become familiar with the basic laws and customs of the country you plan to visit before you travel.

Remember: Reckless behavior while in another country can do more than ruin your vacation; it can land you in a foreign jail or worse! To have a safe trip, avoid risky behavior and plan ahead.

Preparing for Your Trip Abroad

Apply early for your passport and, if necessary, any visas: Passports are required to enter and/or depart most countries around the world. Apply for a passport as soon as possible. Some countries also require U.S. citizens to obtain visas before entering. Most countries require visitors who are planning to study or work abroad to obtain visas before entering. Check with the embassy of the foreign country that you are planning to visit for up-to-date visa and other entry requirements. (Passport and visa information is available on the Internet at http://travel.state.gov.)

Learn about the countries that you plan to visit. Before departing, take the time to do some research about the people and their culture, and any problems that the country is experiencing that may affect your travel plans. The Department of State publishes Background Notes on about 170 countries. These brief, factual pamphlets contain information on each country's culture, history, geography, economy, government, and current political situation. Background Notes are available at www.state.gov.

Read the Consular Information Sheet. Consular Information Sheets provide up-to-date travel information on any country in the world that you plan to visit. They cover topics such as entry regulations, the crime and security situation, drug penalties, road conditions, and the location of the U.S. embassy, consulates, and consular agencies.
Check for Travel Warnings and Public Announcements. Travel Warnings recommend U.S. citizens defer travel to a country because of dangerous conditions. Public Announcements provide fast-breaking information about relatively short-term conditions that may pose risks to the security of travelers.

Find out the location of the nearest U.S. embassy or consulate. If you are traveling to a remote area or one that is experiencing civil unrest, find out the location of the nearest U.S. embassy or consulate and register with the Consular Section when you arrive. (U.S. embassy and consulate locations can be found in the country's Consular Information Sheet.) If your family needs to reach you because of an emergency, they can pass a message to you through the Office of Overseas Citizens Services at 202-647-5225. This office will contact the embassy or consulate in the country where you are traveling and pass a message from your family to you. Remember consular officers cannot cash checks, lend money or serve as your attorney. They can, however, if the need arises, assist you in obtaining emergency funds from your family, help you find an attorney, help you find medical assistance, and replace your lost or stolen passport.

Find out what information your school offers. Find out whether your school offers additional information for students who are planning to study, travel, or work abroad. Many student advisors can provide you with information about studying or working abroad. They may also be able to provide you with information on any travel benefits for students (e.g. how to save money on transportation and accommodations, and other resources.)

Before committing yourself or your finances, find out about the organization and what it offers. The majority of private programs for vacation, study or work abroad are reputable and financially sound. However, some charge exorbitant fees, use deliberately false "educational" claims, and provide working conditions far different from those advertised. Even programs of legitimate organizations can be poorly administered.

How to Access Consular Information Sheets, Travel Warnings, and Public Announcements

There are four ways to obtain *Consular Information Sheets*, *Travel Warnings*, and *Public Announcements*:

- *Internet:* http://travel.state.gov
- *Telephone:* Dial the Office of Overseas Citizens Services at 202-647-5225.
- *Mail:* Send a self-addressed, stamped business-size envelope to: Overseas Citizens Services, Room 4811, Department of State, Washington, DC 20520-4818. On the outside envelope, write the name of the country or countries needed in the lower left corner.
- Also available at http://travel.state.gov: passport applications and procedures, foreign and U.S. visa information, travel publications (including the pamphlet *Travel Warning on Drugs Abroad*), links to several U.S. embassy and consulate web sites worldwide, and other sources of information for students.

Top Ten Travel Tips for Students

1. Make sure you have a signed, valid passport and visas, if required. Also, before you go, fill in the emergency information page of your passport!
2. Read the Consular Information Sheets

(and Public Announcements or Travel Warnings, if applicable) for the countries you plan to visit.
3. Leave copies of your itinerary, passport data page and visas with family or friends at home, so that you can be contacted in case of an emergency. Keep your host program informed of your whereabouts.
4. Make sure you have insurance that will cover your emergency medical needs (including medical evacuation) while you are overseas.
5. Familiarize yourself with local laws and customs of the countries to which you are traveling. Remember, while in a foreign country, you are subject to its laws!
6. Do not leave your luggage unattended in public areas and never accept packages from strangers.
7. While abroad, avoid using illicit drugs or drinking excessive amounts of alcoholic beverages, and associating with people who do.
8. Do not become a target for thieves by wearing conspicuous clothing and expensive jewelry and do not carry excessive amounts of cash or unnecessary credit cards.
9. Deal only with authorized agents when you exchange money to avoid violating local laws.
10. When overseas, avoid demonstrations and other situations that may become unruly or where anti-American sentiments may be expressed.

STUDENTS SHOULD LEARN AS MUCH AS POSSIBLE ABOUT THE COUNTRIES IN WHICH THEY PLAN TO TRAVEL OR STUDY

- Students should read the State Department's Consular Information Sheet for the country in which they plan to study or visit, and check any Public Announcements or Travel Warnings that may pertain to that particular country. A Consular Information Sheet is available for every country in the world and provides an overview of conditions pertaining to travel in each

163

country.

- Students to learn about the history, culture, politics and customs of the country/countries in which they travel and study, and to respect the country's customs, manners, rules and laws. For instance, various countries and cultures respect certain manners and dress codes. American students should also abide by these manners and dress codes as much as possible.

- It is a good idea for students to learn as much as they can of the language of the country in which they plan to travel or study. Learning basic phrases of the language can be helpful, and it indicates a willingness on the part of students to make an effort to communicate in the language of the country.

- The Department of State publishes *Background Notes* on countries worldwide. These are brief, factual pamphlets with information on each country's culture, history, geography, economy, government and current political situation. *Background Notes* are available for approximately 170 countries. They often include a reading list, travel notes and maps.

- It is important that students learn about the local laws abroad and obey them. **Remember, while in a foreign country, you are subject to its laws!** This year, the State Department has issued a spring break fact sheet for the Bahamas and two press releases: a press release for college newspapers on travel safety abroad for students and a press release on spring break in Cancun, reminding students about drug laws and drunk and disorderly conduct during spring and summer breaks.

WHAT STUDENTS NEED TO KNOW ABOUT OBTAINING PASSPORTS AND VISAS TO TRAVEL, STUDY AND OR WORK ABROAD

- Students must have a signed, valid passport and visas, if required. Students studying abroad must be sure that they have the proper visa to study there. A visitors visa or entry without a visa may not allow one to study. Refer to our

Foreign Entry Requirements brochure for information on foreign visas and to *Your Trip Abroad* for U.S. passport information.

- Students should remember to fill in the emergency information page of their passport.

- It is a good idea for relatives of students abroad to obtain and maintain a valid passport as well, in case of an emergency requiring them to travel.

- Students who wish to work part-time in conjunction with their studies or when their studies are finished, should make sure that they understand the laws that apply and comply with them.

- The United States requires student visas for study in the United States.

- Students should make copies of their passport's data page and any visas. They should keep a copy separately from the originals while traveling and leave one at home with their family and with their student advisor. This will help to obtain a replacement passport in the event that a passport is lost or stolen. Refer to our brochure *Your Trip Abroad* for more information on U.S. passports.

- Students are encouraged to travel with extra photos, in case they need to get a new passport quickly. Refer to our brochures *Passports-Applying for Them the Easy Way* and *Your Trip Abroad* for more information.

STUDENTS SHOULD LEARN ABOUT MEDICAL INSURANCE AND EVACUATION INSURANCE IN CASE OF A MEDICAL EMERGENCY ABROAD

Every year, hundreds of students become ill or suffer injuries overseas. It is essential that students have medical insurance and medical evacuation insurance that would cover a medical emergency abroad. For further information, see our flyer on *Medical Information for Americans Traveling Abroad, Your Trip Abroad* and visit the Centers for Disease Control and Prevention's web site at http://www.cdc.gov.

STUDENTS ARE ENCOURAGED TO KNOW THE LOCATION OF THE NEAREST U.S.

EMBASSY OR CONSULATE AND TO REGISTER

If students are going to be in a country for more than a couple of weeks, they should to register at the American Embassy or Consulate. This is helpful to students and their families, if there is need to locate family members in the event of an emergency. See our links to U.S. embassies and consulates worldwide.

WHAT U.S. CONSULAR OFFICERS *CAN* AND *CAN NOT* DO TO HELP U.S. CITIZENS ABROAD

If students find themselves in trouble overseas, the Consular Officer at the nearest U.S. embassy or consulate can provide certain assistance and advice. Consular Officers can also help in the event of illness, injury, natural catastrophe, evacuations, destitution, or death. See our brochures *Crisis Abroad*, *U.S. Consuls Help Americans Abroad* and *Overseas Citizens Services* for more information.

In the United States, the Office of Overseas Citizens Services can also assist American students abroad and their families in the USA in emergency cases. There is a 24 hour number to call (202) 647-5225.

There are certain things that consular officers at American embassies **CAN NOT** for American citizens abroad. For example, they can not cash checks, lend money or serve as your attorney. See our brochure *U.S. Consuls Help Americans Abroad*

GENERAL PRECAUTIONS THAT STUDENTS SHOULD TAKE WHILE TRAVELING OR STUDYING ABROAD

Remember not to leave luggage unattended and not to carry packages for anyone. The packages could contain drugs or other illegal items. Refer to our brochure *Travel Warning on Drugs Abroad.*

Do not become a target for thieves by wearing conspicuous clothing and expensive looking jewelry.—

There are restrictions on photography in certain countries. Students should check the Consular Information Sheet for the countries where they plan to visit or travel. -- Students should avoid demonstrations or civil disturbances, which could turn violent. Demonstrations could also turn anti-American.

The Department of State is engaged in outreach efforts to education-related organizations to publicize road safety risks in other countries. Students, who may chose less expensive, often less reliable methods of local travel while in foreign countries, should be aware of the potential danger.

OTHER SOURCES OF INFORMATION FOR STUDENTS. [For links on the web, Go to http://travel.state.gov/studentinfo.html]

U.S. Department of State
 Centers for Disease Control and Prevention
Center for Global Education
Council on International Educational Exchange for
Peace Corps
The University of Southern California (USC) has information on Personal Safety and Adjustment Abroad, Crisis and Risk Management and Crime and Violence Abroad.

Foreign Embassies in the United States

[For a complete listing of foreign embassies in the United States see **Appendix B**].

United States Embassies and Consulates Abroad

[For a complete listing of United States embassies and consulates abroad, including their addresses, telephone, fax, and telex numbers see **Appendix A**].

Planning Another Trip?

See Chapter 36 for a listing of resources available to the general traveler from the U.S. Departments of State, Customs, Transportation, Health and various government and non-government organizations. Almost all of the available International travel-related pamphlets, brochures and publications issued by the U.S. Department of State and by the U.S. Customs have been reproduced in full in this book. See Table of Contents for location.

165

Chapter 13

Tips for Travelers to Canada

[The information in this chapter is reprinted verbatim from a bulletin issued by the U.S. State Department, Bureau of Consular Affairs. It is intended to serve as advice to Americans traveling abroad.]

INTRODUCTION

Millions of U.S. citizens visit Canada each year. We hope this chapter will help you avoid problems, but if you should need assistance as a result of an accident, illness, or even the loss of your passport, our Embassy in Ottawa and Consulates General in Halifax, Quebec City, Montreal, Toronto, Calgary, and Vancouver are there to assist you.

PART ONE: BEFORE YOU GO

For up-to-date travel information on Canada or any country in the world that you plan to visit, obtain the Department of State's Consular Information Sheet. Consular Information Sheets cover such matters as health conditions, unusual currency and entry regulations, crime and security conditions, drug penalties, and areas of instability. In addition, the State Department issues Travel Warnings when we recommend Americans defer travel to a country because of unsafe conditions. Travel Warnings are under continuous review by the Department of State. Before you depart for a country that has a Travel Warning, make certain that you have the most recent revision of the Warning. The Department of State also issues Public Announcements as a means to disseminate information quickly about relatively short-term and/or trans-national conditions which would pose significant risks to the security of American travelers.

Travel Information

How to Access Consular Information Sheets, Travel Warnings and Public Announcements
Consular Information Sheets, Travel Warnings and Public Announcements may be heard any time by dialing the Office of Overseas Citizens Services at (202) 647-5225 from a touchtone phone. The recording is updated as new information becomes available. They are also available at the 13 regional U.S. passport agencies, field offices of the Department of Commerce, and U.S. embassies and consulates abroad, or, by sending a self-addressed, stamped envelope and indicating the desired country to the Office of Overseas Citizens Services, Bureau of Consular Affairs, Room 4811, U.S. Department of State, Washington, D.C. 20520-4818.

By Internet

Information about travel and consular services is also available on the Internet's World Wide Web. The address is http://travel.state.gov. Visitors to the web site will find Travel Warnings, Public Announcements and Consular Information Sheets, passport and visa information, travel publications, background on international adoption and international child abduction services and international legal assistance. There is also a link to the State Department's main site on the Internet's World Wide Web with current foreign affairs information. The address is: http://www.state.gov.

By Fax

From your fax machine, dial (202) 647-3000, using the handset as you would a regular telephone. The system prompts you on how to proceed.

Consular Affairs Bulletin Board - CABB

If you have a personal computer, modem and communication software, you can access the Consular Affairs Bulletin Board (CABB). This service is free of charge. To view or download the documents using a computer and modem, dial CABB on (301) 946-4400. The login is **travel**; the password is **info**.

Visas and travel documents

General

Visas are not required for U.S. tourists entering Canada from the U.S. for stays up to 180 days. You will, however, need (1) proof of your U.S. citizenship such as (a) your U.S. passport or (b) original or certified copy of your birth certificate and photo identification. (For information on obtaining a U.S. passport, check with the nearest passport agency located at 13 locations throughout the U.S.) If you are a naturalized citizen and do not have a passport, you should travel with your naturalization certificate. A driver's license or Social Security card is not valid proof of citizenship. All U.S. citizens entering Canada from a third country must have a valid passport. Alien permanent residents of the U.S. must present their Alien Registration Card, commonly called the "Green Card." If you are a dual U.S./Canadian citizen you should always present yourself as a Canadian citizen when entering Canada.

However, U.S. citizens should use their U.S. passports when entering or leaving the United States.

Due to international concern over child abduction, single parents, grandparents, or guardians traveling with children often need proof of custody or notarized letters from the other parent authorizing travel. (This is in addition to proof of citizenship as explained above.) Any person under the age of 18 and traveling alone should carry a letter from his/her parent or guardian authorizing the trip. Travelers without such documentation may experience delays at the port of entry.

For further information, including information on student or business travel, visitors can contact the Embassy of Canada at 501 Pennsylvania Ave, NW, Washington, DC 20001, (202) 682-1740 or the nearest Canadian consulate.

NAFTA and Information For Business Travelers

The North American Free Trade Agreement (NAFTA) facilitates the cross border movement of business persons who are citizens of member countries to the NAFTA. The provisions of NAFTA do not replace Canada's provisions for temporary entry or for immigration. A U.S. citizen can enter Canada under NAFTA provisions as a business visitor, intra-company transferee,

professional, or trader. Prior to seeking entry into Canada under the NAFTA, it is advisable to call Canada's Trade Info Line at 1-613-944-4000. Their fax number is (613) 944-9500. The Canadian government publication, Cross Border Movement of Business Persons and the North American Free Trade Agreement, is available from the Info Centre, Department of Foreign Affairs and International Trade.

U.S. business people who are crossing into Canada for a meeting, trade show, convention or exhibition may be eligible for special treatment concerning the importation of advertising materials, office materials and souvenirs. Revenue Canada and Canada Customs have established criteria for duty-free and tax-free importing of certain convention materials. Additional information is available through the National Convention Services, Department of Revenue Canada at (613) 946-0237.

NAFTA allows business persons to engage in certain business activities without an employment authorization - provided they otherwise comply with existing immigration requirements applicable to temporary entry. Examples are conducting market research, marketing products, negotiating contracts, or taking orders.

General Qualifying Criteria for Business Visitors

You may qualify as a business visitor if you are a citizen of a member country; you are seeking entry for business purposes; the proposed business activity is international in scope; you have no intention of entering the labor market; and your primary source of remuneration is outside of the country in which you are seeking entry. In addition, the principal place of business and the accrual of profits must remain outside of the country you are seeking to enter.

U.S. Business Visitors Entering Canada

Business visitors seeking temporary entry into Canada must meet the General Qualifying criteria listed above. A business visitor may temporarily import certain goods duty-free. Goods that qualify are professional equipment (tools of the trade), equipment for the press or for radio or television broadcasters, cinematographic equipment, goods for sports purposes, and goods for display.

Professionals

General Qualifying Criteria

Professionals are exempt from the job-validation process normally required of individuals looking to enter a foreign country's labor market. To qualify as a professional under the NAFTA you must be a citizen of a member country. The occupation you are to be engaged in must be listed in Appendix 1603.D.1 of the NAFTA; you must be qualified to work in the occupation; and you must have pre-arranged employment or a contracted agreement.

You will need to provide documentation indicating the professional level activity to be carried out, your job title, a summary of your job duties, the expected length of stay, and the arrangement for remuneration.

U.S. professionals entering Canada may apply for an Employment Authorization at any Canadian embassy, consulate, or port of entry. When applying at the port of entry, no written application is required and determination can be made at the time of application. The processing fee for issuing employment authorization is C$125. After admittance into Canada, a Social Insurance Number can be obtained from a local Canada Employment Centre.

Intra Company Transferees

Intra-company transferees are business persons employed by an enterprise who are seeking to render services to a branch, parent, subsidiary, or affiliate of that enterprise, in a managerial or executive capacity or in a manner that involves specialized knowledge. The total period of stay for a person employed in an executive or managerial capacity cannot exceed seven years. The total period of stay for a person employed in a capacity that requires specialized knowledge cannot exceed five years.

Traders and Investors

An Application for an Employment Authorization Form (Form IMM1295) must be completed at a Canadian embassy or consulate prior to seeking entry. You will also be required to provide information on your business by completing an Application for Trader/Investor Status. There is a $125 processing fee (payable in Canadian currency) for issuing employment authorizations. Upon arrival, traders and investors should obtain a Social Insurance Number from a local Canada Employment Centre.

In the event that you take up permanent residence in Canada, you should be advised that U.S. citizens residing abroad are required to file taxes with the Internal Revenue Service. If you have any questions on tax liability or the submission of tax forms, etc. you should contact the IRS located at 60 Queen Street, Suite 201, Ottawa, Canada, K1P 5Y7, telephone (613) 563-1834 or fax (613) 230-1376.

Medical Advice

Insurance

Double check that your insurance policy covers you during your time in Canada. Consider purchasing supplemental or other insurance if your own policy is not enough. You may wish to check with your health insurance company to ensure that your policy includes coverage for medical evacuations to the United States as well as escort to the United States, hospitalization abroad, premature birth abroad, and other coverage for a beneficiary who is involved in an accident or illness outside the United States. Carry details of your insurance plan with you (and leave a copy with a relative or friend at home).

Please note: The Social Security Medicare Program does not provide for payment of hospital or medical services outside the United States.

AIDS

U.S. citizen visitors are not required to have an AIDS test prior to entering Canada.

Medication

If you are entering Canada with prescription drugs and syringes used for medical reasons, be sure to keep the medication in its original and labeled container to avoid problems. Syringes should be accompanied by a medical certificate that shows they are for medical use and should be declared to Canadian Customs officials. It may also be wise to carry with you an extra prescription from your doctor in the event your medication is lost or stolen and to attest to your need to take such prescriptions.

Traveling by Car

U.S. citizens do not need to obtain an international driver's license to drive in Canada. Your valid

U.S. license is good for trips in Canada as long as you are a visitor and are actually resident in the U.S. Should you wish information on provincial traffic laws, please contact the Department of Transport, Motor Vehicle Division of the particular province you wish to visit. You may also contact the American Automobile Association (AAA) or Canadian Automobile Association (CAA) if you are a member. AAA members are covered by the CAA while traveling in Canada. Be sure to carry proof of your car insurance.

PART TWO: ASSISTANCE IS AVAILABLE

Register at the U.S. Embassy or Consulate General

If you will be in Canada for three months or more, you may wish to formally register at the U.S. Embassy or nearest U.S. Consulate General.

Consular Assistance

Please dial 1-800 529-4410 for information on how to reach each U.S. consular section in Canada to report the death, injury, or arrest of an American citizen. Recordings specific to each Consulate General provide guidance on how to reach a duty officer after hours as well. The 800 line service also provides valuable information regarding U.S. passport issuance in Canada, registration of births for U.S. citizens born in Canada, claims to U.S. citizenship, notarial services, tax information, voting procedures, Social Security, U.S. Customs, and travel safety information. This service requires a touchtone phone.

Wiring Money

In the event you encounter a financial emergency, your relatives or friends can wire you money in Canada. Western Union Wire services allow money to be picked up through local money mart centers, mail boxes, Miracle Mart and some grocery stores. Funds are paid in Canadian dollars. In addition, many U.S. automated teller machine (ATM) cards, such as those on the PLUS or CIRRUS system, can be used throughout Canada to obtain Canadian funds on your U.S. bank account.

PART THREE: WHILE TRAVELING

Laws

It is important to respect the laws of Canada while you are a guest in their country.

Weapons

Firearms are strictly controlled and generally are not permitted in Canada. While handguns are prohibited, hunting rifles are allowed into Canada with advance permission. Anyone wishing to take a hunting rifle into Canada can contact the nearest Canadian consulate in advance for detailed information. In all cases, travelers must declare any firearms in their possession to Canadian authorities when entering Canada. If a traveler is denied permission to take the firearm into Canada, in some cases there are facilities near the border where firearms may be stored pending the traveler's return to the United States. For example, in Alberta, the Wy Moberlie Company operates such a facility at duty free shops on the U.S. side of the border. They accept items for storage (including weapons) and either forward these items to the traveler's home address in the United States or store them until the traveler picks the items up upon returning to the United States. Canadian law requires that officials confiscate weapons from individuals crossing the border who deny having such weapons in their possession. Confiscated firearms are virtually never returned and are destroyed. A new firearms act slated to take effect in 1998/1999 will include a license and registration requirement through Canada Customs for all guns, including hunting guns, before entering the country.

Please check with your nearest Canada Customs office for further information.

Pepper spray, mace and similar defensive weapons are prohibited under the Criminal Code of Canada. Travelers who declare prohibited weapons are allowed to abandon them or export them without penalty.

Drugs

Penalties for possession, use, and dealing in illegal drugs are strict in Canada. Convicted offenders can expect jail sentences and fines.

Drunk Driving

Driving under the influence of alcohol is a serious offense. Penalties are heavy, and any prior conviction (no matter how long ago or how minor the infraction) is cause for exclusion from Canada. A waiver of exclusion may be obtained from a

Canadian consulate in the United States, but several weeks are required. There is a processing fee for the waiver.

Automobile Radar Detectors

It is illegal to take automobile radar detectors into the provinces of Quebec, Ontario, and Manitoba or into the Yukon and Northwest territories. The police will confiscate radar detectors, whether in use or not, and may impose fines up to $1000.

Previous Convictions

Section 19 of Canada's Immigration Act prohibits the admission of people who pose a threat to public health, safety, order, and national security. Prior to attempting a border crossing, American citizens who have had a criminal conviction in the past must contact the nearest Canadian embassy or consulate well in advance to determine their admissibility as visitors into Canada. If found inadmissible, an immigration officer will advise whether a waiver (Minister's Permit) is possible.

Arrest

There are currently over 100 American citizens incarcerated in Canadian prisons. An American citizen who is arrested in Canada will be informed by the police of his/her right to contact the American Embassy or one of the Consulates General. When notified, a consular officer will contact the citizen by phone, and subsequently make a personal visit. Collect calls will be accepted by the U.S. Embassy or Consulates General if coming from a U.S. citizen for the initial notification of arrest.

U.S. consular officers can provide lists of lawyers from each local area, but cannot recommend a particular lawyer and can not act as a legal representative on behalf of the arrestee. Arrestees are responsible for their own legal fees. Legal Aid programs are administered by the provinces, and may not cover individuals who are visitors to Canada. There are no public defenders as we know them in the United States. As a foreigner, under Bill C44, work release programs, day parole or bail may be difficult to obtain or refused in view of the flight risk involved. Under the Treaty on the Execution of Penal Sentences signed by the U.S. and Canada 1977, prisoners may request to be transferred to an American prison.

Customs Restrictions for U.S. Visitors to

Canada

Alcoholic Beverages and Tobacco Products

For short-term visitors to Canada, the following restrictions apply per person:

-- 1.14 liters (40 oz.) of liquor or wine or 24 x 355ml (12 oz.) bottles or cans of beer or ale (8.5 liters)

You must be 18 years of age or older to import alcoholic beverages into the provinces of Alberta, Manitoba, and Quebec. To import alcoholic beverages into all other provinces and territories, you must be 19 years of age or older .

-- 200 cigarettes, 50 cigars or cigarillos, 400 grams of manufactured tobacco, and 400 tobacco sticks . You must be 18 years of age or older to import tobacco products into the provinces of Quebec, Manitoba, Saskatchewan, Alberta, the Yukon Territory, and the Northwest Territories. To import tobacco products into all other provinces, you must be 19 years or older .

Other Goods

Certain goods are restricted from entering Canada. If you are considering importing meat or dairy products, weapons, plants, vehicles, or exotic animals or products made from their skins or feathers, please contact Canada Customs beforehand for guidance. (See phone number listed below.)

Obscene materials, hate propaganda, most weapons and firearms, and goods harmful to the environment are prohibited from entering Canada.

If you have any questions about what you can and cannot bring into Canada, call Canada Customs. Customs officers are available from 8:00 a.m. to 4:30 p.m. Monday through Friday to answer your questions. If you're calling in Canada, dial 1-800-461-9999 for the Automated Customs Information System. Outside Canada, call (613) 993-0534.

Pets

To bring your dog or cat into Canada, you will have to present Canada Customs with a valid Rabies Certificate, showing that your dog or cat has been vaccinated between 30 days and three years ago. For information on importation of other pets, contact Canada Customs at (613) 993-0534.

Where to find consular assistance while in Canada

The State Department maintains a number of diplomatic offices in Canada. The U.S. Embassy is located in Ottawa, and there are U.S. Consulates General in Calgary, Halifax, Montreal, Quebec, Vancouver, and Toronto. At each of these offices, there are U.S. consular officers available to help you with problems.

These offices, in cooperation with the Office of Overseas Citizens Services at the State Department in Washington, D.C., provide a range of services to resolve problems during your visit to Canada. The services include:

Support and assistance in the event you are a victim of crime, become ill, are arrested, die abroad, or are involved in a disaster
-- Communications with friends and relatives in the event of an emergency, and help with arrangements for emergency fund transfers.
-- Notarizing documents. (There is a fee for this service.)
-- Issuance of U.S. passports and Reports of Birth of U.S. citizens born abroad. (There are fees for these services.)

OTTAWA
Embassy of the United States
Consular Section
85 Albert Street
Ottawa, Ontario

The mailing address is:

Embassy of the United States
Consular Section
100 Wellington Street
Ottawa, Ontario K1P 5T1
Telephone: 613-238-4470

Consular district includes Baffin Island, the following counties
in eastern Ontario: Lanark, Leeds, Prescott, Renfrew, Russell and
Stormont, and the following counties in western Qubec: Gatineau,
Hull, Labelle, Papineau, Pontiac and Tamiscamingue.

CALGARY
U.S. Consulate General
615 Macleod Trail, SE
Calgary, Alberta, T2G 4T8

Telephone: (403) 266-8 962

Consular district includes Alberta, Manitoba, Saskatchewan and the
Districts of MacKenzie and Keewatin in the Northwestern
Territories.

HALIFAX
U.S. Consulate General
Suite 910
Cogswell Tower
Scotia Square
Halifax, N.S., B3J 3K1
Telephone: (902) 429-2480

Consular district includes New Brunswick, Newfoundland, Nova
Scotia, and Prince Edward Island.

MONTREAL
U.S. Consulate General
1155 St. Alexander Street
Montreal, Quebec, H2Z 1Z2
Telephone: (514) 398-9695

Consular district includes southwestern Quebec with the exception
of the six counties served by the U.S. Embassy at Ottawa.

QUEBEC CITY
U.S. Consulate
2 Place Terrasse Dufferin,
Quebec, Que., G1R 4T9
Telephone: (418) 692-2095

Consular district includes the counties of Abitibi-West, Abitibi-East, St. Maurice, Trois-Rivieres, Nicolet, Wolfe, Frontenac and all other counties to the north or east within the province.

TORONTO
U.S. Consulate General
360 University Avenue
Toronto, Ont., M5G 1S4
Telephone: (416)-595-1700

Consular district includes the entire Province of Ontario except those areas east of Kingston, which are included in the Ottawa consular district.

VANCOUVER

U.S. Consulate General
1095 West Pender Street,
Vancouver, BC., V6E 4E9
Telephone: (604) 685-4311

Consular district includes British Columbia and the Yukon.

PART FOUR: RETURNING TO THE U.S.

Immigration

To re-enter the United States, returning U.S. citizens need to show the Immigration and Naturalization Service officer proof of identity and citizenship, such as a passport, birth certificate, or certificate of naturalization (for citizenship) and photo identification (such as a driver's license) for identity. A U.S. passport is proof of both citizenship and identity. Persons who are dual nationals should enter using U.S. documents only, as they could be fined under U.S. law for entering the U.S. on a foreign passport.

U.S. Customs

Articles acquired abroad and brought back with you into the United States are subject to duty and internal revenue tax. As a returning U.S. resident, you are allowed to bring back $400 worth of merchandise duty free. However, you must have been outside the U.S. for at least 48 hours, and you must not have used this exemption within the preceding 30-day period. The next $1,000 worth of items you bring back with you for personal use or gifts are dutiable at a flat 10 percent rate. Any dollar amount of an article or articles over $1000 is subject to variable duties.

There is no limit on the total amount of money that may be brought into or taken out of the United States, nor is it illegal to do so. However, if you transport or cause to be transported (including by mail or other means) more than $10,000 in monetary instruments on any occasion into or out of the United States, or if you receive more than that amount, you must file a report (Customs form 4790) with U.S. Customs. Failure to comply can result in civil and criminal penalties, including seizure of the currency or monetary instruments. Monetary instruments include U.S. or foreign coin, currency, traveler's checks, money orders, and negotiable instruments or investment securities in bearer form.

Restrictions of Food, Plant, and Animal Products

Citrus products of any origin are prohibited. Most other products produced or grown in Canada are allowed. This includes vegetables, fruits other than black currants; and meat and dressed poultry, if accompanied by proof of origin or labeled as a product of Canada.

CANADIAN EMBASSY AND CONSULATES IN THE UNITED STATES

Canadian Embassy
501 Pennsylvania Avenue, N.W.
Washington, DC 20001
Telephone: (202) 682-1740

California
Canadian Consulate General
300 S. Grand Avenue, 10th Floor
Los Angeles, CA 90071
Telephone: (213) 346-2700

Florida
Canadian Consulate
First Union Financial Centre
200 Biscayne Boulevard, Suite 1600
Miami, FL 33131
Telephone: (305) 579-1600

Georgia
Canadian Consulate General
South Tower
1 CNN Center, Suite 400
Atlanta, GA 30303-2705
Telephone: (404) 577-6810

Illinois
Canadian Consulate General
2 Prudential Plaza
180 N. Stetson Avenue, Suite 2400
Chicago, IL 60601
Telephone: (312) 616-1860

Massachusetts
Canadian Consulate General
3 Copley Place, Suite 400
Boston, MA 02116
Telephone: (617) 262-3760

Michigan
Canadian Consulate General
600 Renaissance Center, Suite 1100
Detroit, MI 48243-1798

Telephone: (313) 567-2340

Minnesota
Canadian Consulate General
701 4th Avenue, S., 9th Floor
Minneapolis, MN 55415-1899
Telephone: (612) 333-4641

New York
Canadian Consulate General
3000 Marine Midland Center, 30th Floor
Buffalo, NY 14203-2884
Telephone: (716) 858-9500

Canadian Consulate General
1251 Avenue of the Americas
New York, NY 10020
Telephone: (212) 596-1600

Puerto Rico
Consulate of Canada
107 Cereipo Street
Alturas de Santa Maria
Guaynabo, PR
Telephone: (809) 790-2210

Texas
Canadian Consulate General
750 N. Saint Paul Street, Suite 1700
Dallas, TX 75201
Telephone: (214) 922-9806

Washington
Canadian Consulate General
412 Plaza 600
6th & Stewart Streets
Seattle, WA 98101
Telephone: (206) 443-1777

Planning Another Trip?
See Chapter 36 for a listing of resources available
to the general traveler from the U.S. Departments
of State, Customs, Transportation, Health and
various government and non-government
organizations. Almost all of the available
International travel-related pamphlets, brochures
and publications issued by the U.S. Department of
State and by the U.S. Customs have been
reproduced in full in this book. See Table of
Contents for location.

Chapter 14

Tips for Travelers to the Caribbean

[The information in this chapter is reprinted verbatim from a bulletin issued by the U.S. State Department, Bureau of Consular Affairs. It is intended to serve as advice to Americans traveling abroad.]

Anguilla, Antigua, Aruba, Bahamas, Barbados, Barbuda, Bermuda, Bimini, Bonaire, British Virgin.Is., Caicos, Cayman Islands, Cuba, Curacao, Dominica, Dominican Republic, Grenada, Grenadines, Guadeloupe, Haiti, Jamaica, Martinique, Montserrat, Netherlands Antilles,St. Kitts, St. Lucia, St Vincent, Trinidad and Tobago, U.S. Virgin Is.

Foreword

Since colonial times, the Caribbean has been a favorite place for American visitors. In the past 50 years, tourism to the area has increased greatly, and today millions of U.S. citizens visit the islands every year. The majority of these visitors have a safe trip. To help you have a similar experience, the Department of State's Bureau of Consular Affairs has prepared these tips for you.

Consular Affairs provides services to Americans who travel or reside abroad. If, in spite of your best precautions, you find yourself in difficulties abroad, please contact the U.S. consul at the nearest U.S. embassy or consulate. There is a list of U.S. embassies and consulates in the Caribbean at the end of this publication.

We hope you have a safe and enjoyable experience during your visit to the Caribbean!

Originally named the West Indies by explorers seeking a sea route to India, the Caribbean is the region of tropical islands in the Caribbean Sea situated between North and South America and east of Central America. The islands extend for nearly 1,700 miles from Cuba in the west to Barbados in the east.

Note: There are special conditions relating to travel to Cuba, including U.S. Treasury restrictions

Travel to Mexico and to Central and South America is covered in separate chapter.

If you plan to visit the most popular islands during high tourist season (from mid-December to mid-April), confirm your hotel reservations two to three months in advance. There are, however, lesser-known islands where you may be able to book first class accommodations on short notice. In addition, you can usually book reservations with ease during the off-season, but be aware of hurricane season, which runs from June to November. During this period, travelers are wise to check weather reports before departure from the U.S., as well as periodically, during their stay.

Most of the islands in the Caribbean belong to one of 13 independent countries. In addition, several islands and groups of islands in the Caribbean are part of or dependent upon France, the Netherlands, the United Kingdom, or the United States. A directory of the major islands is located at the end of this document.

Preparation for Your Trip

Start Early. If a passport is required for you to enter the country where you are planning to travel, apply for it as soon as possible. (See the section, *Visa and Other Entry Requirements*.)

Learn about the countries you plan to visit. Before departing, read up on the culture and people for the places you will travel.

As you travel, keep abreast of local news coverage. If you are in an area experiencing civil unrest or a natural disaster, if you will be staying more than two weeks in an area, or if you are going to a place where communications are poor, you are encouraged to register with the nearest U.S. embassy or consulate. (See addresses at the end of this document.) Registration takes only a

175

few moments, and it may be invaluable in case of an emergency. Remember to leave a detailed itinerary and the numbers of your passport or other citizenship documents with a friend or relative in the United States.

For up-to-date travel information on any country in the world that you plan to visit, obtain the Department of State's Consular Information Sheet. This covers topics such as entry regulations, the crime and security situation, drug penalties, and location of the nearest U.S. embassy, consulate or consular agency.

The Department also issues Travel Warnings and Public Announcements. A Travel Warning advises travelers not to go to a country because of dangerous conditions and/or U.S. government's ability to assist a U.S. citizen in distress there is severely limited. A Public Announcement is issued as a means to disseminate information quickly about relatively short-term and/or trans-national conditions which would pose significant risks to the security of American travelers.

How to Access Consular Information Sheets, Travel Warnings and Public Announcements

Consular Information Sheets, Travel Warnings and Public Announcements are available at the regional U.S. passport agencies; from U.S. embassies and consulates abroad; or by sending a self-addressed, stamped business-size envelope to: Overseas Citizens Services, Room 4811, Department of State, Washington, DC 20520-4818. On the outside envelope, write the name of the country or countries needed in the lower left corner.

There are three electronic methods to access Consular Information Sheets, Travel Warnings and Public Announcements 24-hours a day:

By Telephone : Consular Information Sheets, Travel Warnings and Public Announcements may be heard any time by dialing the Office of Overseas Citizens Services at 202-647-5225 from a touchtone phone. The recording is updated as soon as new information becomes available.

By Internet : Information about travel and consular services is also available on the Internet. The address is http://travel.state.gov.

By Fax : From your fax machine, dial 202-647-3000 and follow the voice prompts.

Entry and Exit Requirements

Entering: Every island in the Caribbean has its own entry requirements. Most countries allow you to visit for up to two or three months if you show proof of U.S. citizenship and a return or onward ticket. Some countries, however, require that you have a valid passport. If you are arriving from an area infected with yellow fever, many Caribbean countries require you to have a certificate of vaccination against yellow fever. Some countries have an airport departure tax of up to $25. For authoritative information on a country's entry and exit requirements and on its customs and currency regulations, contact its embassy, consulate, or tourist office in the United States.

Returning - Caution! Make certain that you can return to the United States with the proof of citizenship that you take with you. Although some Caribbean countries may allow you to enter with only a birth certificate, U.S. Immigration requires that you document both your U.S. citizenship and identity when you reenter the United States.

The best document to prove your U.S. citizenship is a valid U.S. passport. Other documents of U.S. citizenship include an expired U.S. passport, a certified copy of your birth certificate, a Certificate of Naturalization , a Certificate of Citizenship , or a Report of Birth Abroad of a U.S. Citizen.

To prove your identity, either a valid driver's license or a government identification card that includes a photo or a physical description is acceptable.

If you lose or have your U.S. passport stolen while overseas, report it immediately to the local police and the nearest U.S. embassy or consulate. A lost or stolen birth certificate or driver's license cannot be replaced outside the United States. There are several countries, most notably Barbados, the Dominican Republic, Grenada, Haiti, and Jamaica, where airlines have consistently refused to board American citizens with insufficient proof of U.S. citizenship. The resulting delays can be inconvenient as well as expensive.

Bringing Your Own Boat or Plane
If you plan to arrive in the Caribbean in your own

boat or plane, contact the embassy, consulate, or tourist office of each country you plan to visit to learn what is required for entry and exit. Besides title of ownership, most ports of entry will require proof of insurance coverage for the country you are entering. Some countries require a temporary import permit for your boat or plane.

Authorities in the Caribbean are familiar with U.S. regulations for documentation of air and sea craft. They will detain improperly documented craft that enter their territory. In some countries, authorities will confiscate firearms found on a boat or plane unless the owner or master can show proof that U.S. licensing and export procedures have been followed. In addition, some countries impose stiff prison terms for the importation of illegal firearms.

Customs, Firearms, and Currency Regulations

Customs formalities are generally simple in the Caribbean. As a rule, one carton of cigarettes and one quart of liquor are permitted duty free into the islands. Most countries tax additional quantities at a high rate. In general, tourists are permitted to enter with other commodities required for personal use. If you wish to bring firearms into any country, inquire at the country's embassy or consulate about the permit required. As noted above, some countries in the Caribbean impose a stiff prison term for importing illegal firearms.

Currency regulations vary. Inquire about them when you check on entry requirements. In some countries, you must declare all currency and are not allowed to take out more money than you brought in. Other countries limit the amount of their own currency that can be brought in or taken out.

Check with your travel agent about extra fees and taxes that may be overlooked in the tourist literature. Examples are hotel taxes, obligatory restaurant gratuities, and airport departure taxes.

When you convert your money to local currency, retain receipts. You will need to show them if you wish to reconvert money upon departure. It is usually advantageous to reconvert local currency before departure. Although U.S. currency is used along with local currency, in some places there may be an advantage to using local currency.

Health

Information on health precautions for travelers can be obtained from local health departments, private doctors, or travel clinics. You may also call the Centers for Disease Control and Prevention's 24-hour hotline on (404) 332-4559 or check the Internet at http://www.cdc.gov for information on immunizations and health risks worldwide.

Review your health insurance policy. U.S. medical insurance is often not valid outside the United States. Medicare/Medicaid does not provide payment for medical services obtained outside the U.S. In addition to medical insurance, consider obtaining insurance to cover evacuation in the event of an accident or serious illness. Considering air evacuation to the United States can easily cost $15,000 if you are not insured, insurance to cover a medical evacuation is relatively inexpensive. There are short-term health and emergency assistance policies designed for travelers. Ask your travel agent about them or look for ads in travel publications.

If you need medical attention during your trip, your hotel may be able to recommend the nearest clinic, hospital or doctor, or you can obtain a list of local medical services from the nearest U.S. embassy or consulate. In a medical emergency, a U.S. consul can help you locate medical treatment.

The most prevalent health hazard in the Caribbean is one you can avoid -- overexposure to the sun. Use sunscreen and bring a shirt to wear over your bathing suit, especially if you plan to snorkel.

Where the quality of drinking water is questionable, bottled water is recommended. Travelers to remote areas should boil or chemically treat drinking water.

Safety Tips

Crime Information. Most visitors to the Caribbean have a relatively safe trip. However, thievery, purse snatching, and pick pocketing do happen, particularly in cities and at beaches. There has also been an increase in violent crimes, such as rape and assault against tourists. In some places, U.S. passports and identity documents are especially attractive to thieves. Robbery of yachts is a problem in some marinas.

Here are some precautions to keep in mind:

-- Safety begins when you pack. Leave expensive jewelry, unnecessary credit cards, and anything you would hate to lose at home.

-- Use a concealed money pouch or belt for passports, cash, and other valuables.

-- To facilitate replacing a lost or stolen passport, carry two extra passport photos and a photocopy of your passport information page and other identity documents with you in a separate place from those items.

-- Do not take valuables to the beach. When possible, use the hotel safe when you go to the beach or into town.

-- When you enter a marina, register with the local government authorities.

Water Safety. Make certain that sports equipment, including scuba equipment, that you rent or buy meets international safety standards.

If you use a beach without a lifeguard, exercise extreme caution. Drowning is one of the leading causes of death for Americans in the Caribbean.

Do not dive into unknown bodies of water because hidden rocks or shallow depths can cause serious injury or death. In some places, you may need to wear sneakers in the water for protection against sea urchins.

Civil Aviation Oversight. This information applies only to foreign flag carriers, not U.S. flag carriers who travel to the following countries: At the time of publication, an assessment conducted by The U.S. Federal Aviation Administration (FAA) concluded that the Dominican Republic's, Haiti's, Jamaica's, and Trinidad & Tobago's civil aviation authorities were not in compliance with international aviation safety standards for oversight of air carrier operations. The same applies to the civil aviation authorities of the Organization of Eastern Caribbean States (Anguilla, Antigua & Barbuda, Dominica, Grenada, Montserrat, St. Lucia, St. Vincent & the Grenadines, and St. Kitts & Nevis). For further information, travelers may contact the Department of Transportation's travel advisory line at (1-800) 322-7873.

Drug Offenses
Most countries in the Caribbean have strict laws against the use, possession, or sale of narcotics. Foreigners arrested for possession of even small amounts of marijuana, cocaine or other illegal drugs are often charged and tried as international traffickers. The penalty for carrying narcotics into or out of the country can be 20 years imprisonment. There are usually expensive fines as well. In some places, there is no bail and there are long judicial delays where you can spend more than two years awaiting trial. Conditions in most Caribbean prisons do not meet even minimum U.S. standards.

If you carry prescription drugs, keep them in their original container, clearly labeled with the doctor's name, pharmacy, and contents.

Judicial Systems
When you travel abroad, you are subject to the laws of the country you are in. If you find yourself in serious difficulty while abroad, contact a consular officer at the nearest U.S. embassy or consulate. U.S. consuls cannot serve as attorneys or give legal assistance, and they cannot get you out of jail. They can, however, provide lists of local attorneys and advise you of your rights under local law. If you are detained, a consul can monitor your case to assure your treatment is in accordance with local law.

Driving in the Caribbean
If you plan to rent a car, be aware that most jurisdictions of the Caribbean drive on the left. The only places where you drive on the right are Aruba, Cuba, Dominican Republic, Guadeloupe, Haiti, Martinique, and the Netherlands Antilles. In other places, if you are not used to driving on the left, proceed slowly and with utmost caution. You may wish to ride as a passenger for a while before trying to drive yourself.

Driving conditions and local driving patterns are different from the U.S. Many roads are narrow or winding, signs may not be in English, and in some places, domestic animals roam freely. Defensive driving is a must.

Shopping: Avoid Wildlife Products
Beware of purchasing a live animal or plant or an item made from one. Many such items are prohibited from international traffic. You risk confiscation and a possible fine by U.S. Customs if you attempt to import certain wildlife or wildlife products. In particular, watch out for and avoid:

-- All products made from sea turtles, including turtle leather boots, tortoiseshell jewelry, and sea turtle oil cosmetics.
-- Fur from spotted cats.
-- Feathers and feather products from wild birds.
-- Birds, stuffed or alive, such as parrots or parakeets.
-- Crocodile and caiman leather.
-- Black coral and most other coral, whether in chunks or in jewelry.

Residence or Investments in the Caribbean

You will need a passport and visas to reside in or to conduct or start a business in the Caribbean. Although some Caribbean countries welcome retirees or others of independent means as long-term residents, requests for work permits are rarely granted. Before you travel, apply to the country's embassy or consulate in the United States to obtain a visa if you wish to reside, go into business, or work in the country.

U.S. citizens who wish to invest in the Caribbean, such as in real estate or a business, should first thoroughly investigate the company making the offer and, in addition, learn about the investment climate in the country. A good resource is the Trade Information Center of the U.S. Department of Commerce, telephone 1-800-USA-TRADE. The Center can tell you how to access the National Trade Data Bank. Among the things you can learn are how to find out if the company is registered with local authorities and how to get in touch with local trade associations. Before signing a contract for a timeshare or other real estate, you may wish to consult with a lawyer. You will need to check whether the contract contains the same safeguards as do similar contracts in the U.S., such as the retention of timeshare rights if the property is sold. You should also determine whether the builder or seller has a clear title.

Country Information

Antigua and Barbuda

Medical Care. Medical care is limited.
Crime Information . Violent crimes have increased and armed assaults have been perpetrated against tourists. Petty street crime also occurs and valuables left unattended on beaches are subject to theft.

Bahamas

Medical Care. Medical care is generally good, but may be limited in outlying areas.
Drug Penalties. Criminal penalties for possession of or trafficking in drugs in the Bahamas are severe. The Bahamian court system has a heavy volume of pending cases, and U.S. citizens arrested for drugs or other offenses are often held in prison for months while awaiting trial.

Crime Information. Visitors should exercise normal caution in safeguarding valuables left on the beach. Woman may wish to avoid deserted areas, especially at night. Crime is more prevalent in major population centers, particularly the "over-the-hill" area of Nassau.

General Information. In the Bahamas, be sure to budget for hotel room tax, an energy surtax, a 15% obligatory gratuity in restaurants, and a departure tax of $15, which must be paid in cash.

Barbados

Medical Care. Medical care is generally good, but may be limited in outlying areas.
Crime Information . Street crime sometimes occurs. Valuables left unattended on beaches are subject to theft.

Bermuda

Medical Care. Medical care is generally good.
General Information. Although it is often thought of as part of the Caribbean, Bermuda is not actually in the Caribbean Sea, it is located in the Atlantic about 650 miles east of North Carolina.
Crime Information . Bermuda has a low crime rate. However, during the tourist season, pickpocketing and theft of unattended baggage can occur.

British Virgin Islands

General Information. The islands of Anegada, Jost Van Dyke, Tortola and Virgin Gorda make up the British Virgin Islands.

British West Indies

General Information. The British West Indies include Anguilla, Montserrat, Cayman Islands and Turks & Caicos.
Special Information for Montserrat. There is potentially dangerous volcanic activity on the island. For more information, refer to the Consular Information Sheet for Barbados.

Cuba

Financial Restrictions . The Cuban Assets Control Regulations of the U.S. Department of the Treasury require that transactions incident to the travel to and within Cuba of U.S. citizens or residents be licensed. A **general license** needs no application. Transactions under a general license are authorized only for the following categories of travelers:

-- U.S. and foreign government officials, including representatives of international organizations of which the U.S. is a member, traveling on official business;

-- journalists regularly employed in such capacity by a news reporting organization;
-- persons visiting close relatives who reside in Cuba due to extreme humanitarian needs once within any twelve month period;
Transactions relating to the following categories of travel must be authorized by a **specific license** based upon a written application to Treasury's Office of Foreign Assets Control:

-- humanitarian travel by persons traveling to visit close relatives more than once within 12 months;
-- persons traveling to accompany licensed humanitarian donations (other than gift parcels);
-- persons traveling in connection with activities of recognized human rights organizations;
-- persons traveling for professional research or similar activities;
-- persons traveling in connection with clearly defined educational or religious activities;
-- persons traveling in connection with the exportation, importation, or transmission of information and informational materials, including provision of telecommunications services.
U.S. citizens whose transactions are not authorized by general or specific licenses may not buy goods (a meal at a hotel or restaurant, for example) or services (an airline ticket or hotel room) related to Cuban travel.

Important Information: Transactions relating to travel to Cuba for tourism or business purposes are not authorized by a general license, nor would they be authorized in response to an application for a specific license. This restriction includes transactions related to tourist and business travel from or through a third country such as Canada or Mexico. Any payments to the Marina Hemingway International Yacht Club by unlicensed travelers are prohibited and a violation of the Cuban Assets Control Regulations.

Under U.S. Treasury regulations, authorized travelers may spend no more than $100 per day for living expenses in Cuba, and, except for informational materials which are not limited, may bring back to the U.S. no more than $100 total worth of Cuban goods. Failure to comply with U.S. Treasury regulations could result in prosecution upon return to the United States.

For more information, contact the Licensing Division, Office of Foreign Assets Control, Department of Treasury, Washington, D.C. 20220, (202) 622-2480.

Cuban Entry Regulations. Cuba requires a passport and a visa for entry. Attempts to enter or exit Cuba illegally or to aid the illegal exit of Cuban nationals are punishable by jail terms. Entering Cuban territory, territorial waters or airspace without prior authorization from the Cuban government many result in arrest. Violators may also be putting their lives at risk. On February 24, 1996, the Cuban military shot down two U.S. registered civil aircraft in international airspace.

Dual Nationals. For all practical purposes, the government of Cuba considers Cuban-born U.S. citizens to be solely Cuban citizens. The Cuban government does not recognize the right or obligation of the U.S. government to protect dual U.S.-Cuban citizens. Cuban authorities have consistently denied U.S. consular officers the right to visit incarcerated dual nationals and to ascertain their welfare and proper treatment under Cuban law. Dual U.S.-Cuban nationals may be subject to a range of restrictions and obligations, including military service.

Crime Information . As severe economic problems continue in Cuba, street crime against tourists has increased noticeably. Foreigners are prime targets for purse snatchings, pickpocketing and thefts from hotel rooms, beaches, historic sites and other attractions.

Credit Card Transactions. Credit cards issued by U.S. financial institutions are not valid in Cuba. Personal checks drawn on U.S. banks are not accepted in Cuba. However, some non-U.S.

180

travelers checks are sometimes acceptable.

Restriction on Photography. Photographing military or police installations or personnel, harbor, rail or airport facilities is forbidden.

U.S. Interests Section. U.S. travelers in Cuba should register in person, in writing, or by telephone during business hours at the U.S. Interests Section which is part of the Embassy of Switzerland. Further information is available in the Consular Information Sheet for Cuba.

Dominica
Medical Care. Medical care is limited.

General Information. Dominica is a developing island nation. The tourist industry is not highly developed.

Crime Information . Street crime occurs. Valuables left unattended on beaches are subject to theft.

Dominican Republic
Medical Care. Medical care is limited.

Entry Requirements. A valid U.S. passport or proof of U.S. citizenship along with photo ID, and tourist card or visa are required. A Naturalization Certificate or Certificate of Citizenship, along with proper photo identification, may be accepted. Minors traveling without their parents require additional documentation.

Currency Regulations. Currency can only be exchanged at commercial banks, authorized exchange booths in hotels and exchange houses. No more than $10,000.00 (U.S.) (or its equivalent) may be taken out of the Dominican Republic at the time of departure.

Crime Information . Valuables left unattended in parked cars, on beaches, and in other public places are subject to theft. Burglaries of private residences have increased. Some resort areas have experienced an increase in violent crime. The larger resort complexes, which rely on private security services, have generally not been affected.

French West Indies
Medical Care. Medical care is limited.

General Information. The French West Indies

include the islands of Guadeloupe, Isles des Saintes, La Desirade, Marie Galante, St. Barthelemy, St. Martin and Martinique.

Crime Information . Street crime, sometimes involving armed assault, appears to be on the rise in St. Martin. In the other territories, petty street crime occurs. Valuables left unattended on beaches are subject to theft.

Grenada
Medical Care. Medical care is limited.

General Information. Grenada is a developing island nation. Tourism facilities vary according to price and area.

Crime Information . Tourists have been victims of armed robbery in isolated areas, particularly after dark. Valuables left unattended on beaches are subject to theft.

Special Exit Requirements. There is an airport departure charge of $14 (Eastern Caribbean $35) per person.

Haiti
Medical Care. Medical care in Port-au-Prince is limited and the level of community sanitation is low. Medical facilities outside the capital are almost always below U.S. standards. Life-threatening emergencies may require evacuation by air ambulance at the patient's expense. You might want to consider supplemental medical insurance with specific overseas coverage, including medical evacuation. In mid-1996, the government ordered Haitian-manufactured pharmaceuticals taken off shelves. Be alert to the presence of Haitian brands in people's homes or in remote pharmacies, and obtain the Consular Information Sheet for Haiti (page 4) for up-to-date information.

Special Entry/Exit Requirements. Haitian law requires a passport to enter. In practice, officials frequently waive this requirement if travelers have other documentation, such as a U.S. birth certificate. Due to fraud concerns, however, airlines will not board passengers for return to the U.S. unless they are in possession of a valid U.S. passport. Haiti's airport departure tax, currently $25 plus 10 Haitian gourdes (U.S. $.65), must be paid in cash in U.S. currency. It cannot be paid as

181

part of the airline ticket.

General Information. Haiti continues to experience occasional civil unrest, including unofficial roadblocks. There have been attacks on some government buildings by unidentified perpetrators. Travelers are urged to use common sense in avoiding large crowds, which have turned violent.

Crime Information . Reports of crime, including armed and sometimes violent robbery, are increasing. Crimes involving occupied and unoccupied vehicles along Route Nationale No. 1 in the port area, in Cite Soleil, and along the airport road continue to be a problem.

Jamaica

Medical Care. Medical care is limited in comparison to care available in the U.S.

Drug Penalties. Criminal penalties for possession, use and dealing in illegal drugs, including marijuana, are strict. Substantial fines and mandatory sentences of six to nine months are common and longer prison sentences can be levied under Jamaican law. Departing visitors are thoroughly screened for drug possession.

Crime Information . Crime is a serious problem in and around Kingston, Jamaica's capital. Criminal acts can rapidly turn violent. Visitors should exercise common sense, not walk around at night, and use only licensed taxis or hotel-recommended transportation. In tourist areas, be careful at isolated villas and small establishments.

Netherlands Antilles

Medical Care. Medical care is generally good, but may be limited in more remote areas.

General Information. The Netherlands Antilles are autonomous parts of the Kingdom of the Netherlands. The Netherlands Antilles include the islands of Bonaire, Curacao, Saba, St. Eustatius (also known as Statia), and St. Maarten.

Insurance for Rented Aquatic/Land Vehicles. Caution should be exercised when renting motorized aquatic and land vehicles. Renters should note the insurance underwriter and the amount of deductible that they would be responsible for in case of an accident. (When accidents occur, the renter is often charged exorbitant charges against his/her credit card for repairs or replacement of the vehicle.)

Crime Information . Petty street crime and armed robbery, including shooting of the victims, are increasing.

St. Kitts and Nevis

Medical Care. Medical care is limited.

Crime Information. Petty street crime occurs. Valuables left unattended on beaches are subject to theft.

St. Lucia

Medical Care. Medical care is limited.

Crime Information . Petty street crime occurs. Valuables left unattended on beaches are subject to theft.

St. Vincent and the Grenadines

Medical Care. Medical care is limited.

Crime Information . Petty street crime occurs. Valuables left unattended on beaches are subject to theft.

Trinidad and Tobago

Medical Care. Medical care is limited.

Drug Penalties. Drug laws are severe and strictly enforced in Trinidad and Tobago. Possession of even small amounts of narcotics can result in lengthy jail sentences and expensive fines. The penalty for carrying narcotics into or out of the country is five to 15 years imprisonment with no possibility of parole.

Crime Information . Violent crime, including murder, is on the rise. While crime is significantly lower in Tobago, travelers may wish to avoid traveling alone.

Foreign Embassies in the United States

In addition to the embassies listed below, some Caribbean countries have consulates or tourist offices in large cities in the United States. Look for them in your telephone book.

Embassy of **Antigua and Barbuda**
3216 New Mexico Ave., N.W.
Washington, DC 20016

(202) 362-5122 or 5166

Embassy of the **Bahamas**
2220 Massachusetts Ave., N.W.
Washington, DC 20008
(202) 319-2660

Embassy of **Barbados**
2144 Wyoming Ave., NW
Washington, DC 20008
(202) 939-9200

Embassy of Switzerland
Cuban Interests Section
2639 16th Street, NW
Washington, DC 20009
(202) 362-5122 or 5166

Consulate of the Commonwealth of **Dominica**
820 2nd Ave., Suite 900
New York, NY 10017
(212) 599-8478

Embassy of the **Dominican Republic**
1715 22nd Street., NW
Washington, DC 20008
(202) 332-6280

Embassy of **France**
4101 Reservoir Road, NW
Washington, DC 20007-2172
(202) 944-6200 or 6187

Embassy of **Grenada**
1701 New Hampshire Ave., NW
Washington, DC 20009
(202) 265-2561

Embassy of **Haiti**
2144 Wyoming Ave., NW
Washington, DC 20008
(202) 939-9200

Embassy of **Jamaica**
1520 New Hampshire Ave., NW
Washington, DC 20036
(202) 452-0660

Embassy of the **Netherlands**
4200 Linnean Ave., NW
Washington, DC 20008
(202) 244-5300
Embassy of **St. Kitts and Nevis**

3216 New Mexico Ave., NW
Washington, DC 20016
(202) 686-2636

Embassy of **St. Lucia**
3216 New Mexico Ave., NW
Washington, DC 20016
(202) 364-6792

Embassy of **St. Vincent and the Grenadines**
1717 Massachusetts Ave., NW
Washington, DC 20036
(202) 462-7803

Embassy of **Trinidad and Tobago**
1708 Massachusetts Ave., NW
Washington, DC 20036
(202) 467-6490

United Kingdom
British Embassy
3100 Massachusetts Ave., NW
Washington, DC 20008
(202) 462-1340

U.S. Embassies and Consulates Abroad

Note that the Bahamas , Cuba , Haiti , and Jamaica are on Eastern Time. All others are one hour ahead. Note: Some (809) area codes are expected to change. If you are unable to get through on (809), consult your telephone directory or the operator.

BAHAMAS
American Embassy
Queen Street
Nassau, BAHAMAS
(1-242) 322-1181 or 328-2206

BARBADOS
American Embassy
Canadian Imperial Bank of Commerce Bldg.
Broadstreet
Bridgetown, BARBADOS
(1-246) 436-4950

American Consulate
ALICO Building
Cheapside
Bridgetown, BARBADOS
(1-246) 431-0225

183

BERMUDA
American Consulate General
Crown Hill, 16 Middle Rd.
Devonshire
Hamilton, BERMUDA
(1-441) 295-1342

CUBA
Swiss Embassy (USINT)
Calzada between Land M
Vedado
Havana, CUBA
(537) 33-4401

DOMINICAN REPUBLIC
American Embassy
Calle Cesar Nicolas Penson and Calle Leopoldo
Navarro
Santo Domingo,
DOMINICAN REPUBLIC
(1-809) 221-2171

GRENADA
American Embassy
Point Salines
St. George's, GRENADA
(1-809) 444-1173 thru 5

HAITI
American Embassy
Harry Truman Blvd.
Port-au-Prince, HAITI
(1-509) 22-0200 or 0612
American Consulate General
Rue Oswald Durand #104
Port-au-Prince, HAITI
(1-509) 23-7011

JAMAICA
American Embassy
Jamaica Mutual Life Center
2 Oxford Road
Kingston, JAMAICA
(1-809) 929-4850 to 4859

NETHERLANDS ANTILLES
American Consulate General
J.B. Gorsiraweg No. 1
Willemstad, CURACAO
(599-9) 461-3066

TRINIDAD and TOBAGO

American Embassy
15 Queen's Park West
Port of Spain, TRINIDAD and TOBAGO
(1-809) 622-6371

U.S. Consular Agents

To supplement the consular services available to American citizens at U.S. embassies and consulates, resident consular agents have been designated in the Caribbean. You may contact the consular agent directly or through the U.S. embassy in the country where he or she is located.

American Consular Agent
George Town, Grand Cayman*
Tel: (246) 949-7955
*Assists Americans in the Cayman Islands.

American Consular Agent
Bluff House, Nelson's Dockyard P.O.
English Harbour, Antigua*
Tel: (268) 463-6531
Fax: (268) 460-1569
*Assists Americans in Antigua & Barbuda, St. Kitts & Nevis, the British West Indies, Montserrat and Anguilla.

American Consular Agent
Calle Beller 51, Second Floor, Office 6
Puerto Plata, Dominican Republic*
Tel: (809) 586-4204
*Assists Americans in the Dominican Republic.

American Consular Agent
9 Rue Des Alpinias, Didier
Fort de France, Martinique*
Tel: (596) 71-96-90
(596) 71-96-74 (after hours)
*Assists Americans in Martinique, Guadeloupe, Isles Des Saintes, La Desirade, Marie-Galant, St. Barthelemy and St. Martin (French side).

American Consular Agent
St. James Place, 2nd Floor, Gloucester Ave.
Montego Bay, Jamaica*
Tel: (809) 949-7955
*Assists Americans in Jamaica.

184

Directory of Islands	Political Status	Location of U.S. Embassy or Consulate With Consular Jurisdiction

(Islands in *italics* are parts (see codes below) (addresses listed above)
of larger political units.)

Anguilla	UK	Bridgetown, Barbados
Antigua and Barbuda	I	Bridgetown, Barbados
Aruba	N	Curacao, Netherlands Antilles*
Bahamas	I	Nassau, Bahamas
Barbados	I	Bridgetown, Barbados
Barbuda	part of Antigua and Barbuda	
Bermuda (in the Atlantic)	UK	Hamilton, Bermuda*
Bimini	part of Bahamas	
Bonaire	part of Netherlands Antilles	
British Virgin Islands	UK	St. John's, Antigua
Caicos	part of Turks and Caicos	
Cayman Islands	UK	Kingston, Jamaica
Cuba	I	U.S. Interests Section, Swiss Embassy, Havana, Cuba
Curacao	part of Netherlands Antilles	
Dominica	I	Bridgetown, Barbados
Dominican Republic	I	Santo Domingo, Dominican Republic
Eleuthera; Exuma	parts of Bahamas	
Grenada	I	St. George's, Grenada
Grenadines	part of St. Vincent/Grenadines	
Guadeloupe	F	Bridgetown, Barbados
Haiti	I	Port-au-Prince, Haiti
Jamaica	I	Kingston, Jamaica
Marie-Galante	part of Guadeloupe	
Martinique	F	Bridgetown, Barbados
Montserrat	UK	Bridgetown, Barbados
Netherlands Antilles	N	Curacao, Netherlands Antilles*
Nevis	part of St. Kitts and Nevis	
Puerto Rico	US	(not applicable, U.S. commonwealth)
Saba	part of Netherlands Antilles	
St. Barthelemy (St. Barts)	part of Guadeloupe	
St. Croix	part of U.S. Virgin Is.	
St. Eustatius (Statia)	part of Netherlands Antilles	
St. John	part of U.S. Virgin Is.	
St. Kitts and Nevis	I	Bridgetown, Barbados
St. Lucia	I	Bridgetown, Barbados
St. Maarten (Dutch)	part of Netherlands Antilles	
St. Martin (French)	part of Guadeloupe	
St. Thomas	part of U.S. Virgin Is.	
St. Vincent and the Grenadines	I	Bridgetown, Barbados
San Salvador	part of Bahamas	
Tortola	part of British Virgin Is.	
Trinidad and Tobago	I	Port of Spain, Trinidad

Turks and Caicos	UK	Nassau, Bahamas
U.S. Virgin Islands	US	
		(not applicable, U.S. territory)
Virgin Gorda	part of British Virgin Is.	

Code:

F = overseas department of France;
I = independent country;
N = commonwealth of the Netherlands;
UK = dependency of the United Kingdom;
US = commonwealth or territory of the United States
* = U.S. Consulate General

Planning Another Trip?

See Chapter 36 for a listing of resources available to the general traveler from the U.S. Departments of State, Customs, Transportation, Health and various government and non-government organizations. Almost all of the available International travel-related pamphlets, brochures and publications issued by the U.S. Department of State and by the U.S. Customs have been reproduced in full in this book. See Table of Contents for location.

Chapter 15

Tips for Travelers to Central and South America

[The information in this chapter is reprinted verbatim from a bulletin issued by the U.S. State Department, Bureau of Consular Affairs. It is intended to serve as advice to Americans traveling abroad.]

Argentina, Belize, Bolivia, Brazil, Chile, Colombia, Costa Rica, Ecuador, El Salvador, French Guiana, Guatemala, Guyana, Honduras, Nicaragua, Panama, Paraguay, Peru, Suriname, Uruguay, Venezuela

FOREWORD

Travelers to Central and South America are usually welcomed with courtesy and warmth. There is great diversity in the region. You can visit major cosmopolitan cities, ruins of great ancient civilizations, primeval tropical rainforests and breathtaking locales. However, there are important things that you should know before you travel. That is why we have prepared this publication. We wish you an enjoyable and memorable journey.

Please note that travel to Mexico and the Caribbean are covered in their own chapters. Please refer to the Table of Contents for further details.

The information in this publication is in the public domain and may be reproduced without permission. When this material is reproduced, the Department of State would appreciate receiving a copy at: CA/P/PA, Room 6831, Department of State, Washington, D.C. 20520.

CURRENT TRAVEL INFORMATION

The Department of State's Consular Information Sheets are available for every country of the world. They describe topics such as unusual entry regulations, the crime and security situation, political disturbances, areas of instability and drug penalties. They also provide addresses and emergency telephone numbers for U.S. embassies and consulates in the subject country. In general, the sheets do not give advice. Instead, they describe conditions so travelers can make informed decisions about their trips.

In some dangerous situations, however, the Department of State recommends that Americans defer travel to a country. In such a case, a Travel Warning is issued for the country in addition to its Consular Information Sheet.

Public Announcements are a means to disseminate information about terrorist threats and other relatively short-term and/or trans-national conditions posing significant risks to the security of American travelers. They are issued when there is a perceived threat, usually involving Americans as a particular target group. In the past, Public Announcements have been issued to deal with short-term coups, pre-election disturbances, violence by terrorists and anniversary dates of specific terrorist events.

Consular Information Sheets, Travel Warnings and **Public Announcements** are available at U.S. regional passport agencies; at U.S. embassies and consulates abroad; or by sending a self-addressed, stamped envelope to: Overseas Citizens Services, Room 4811, Department of State, Washington, DC 20520-4818. They are also available through airline computer reservation systems when you or your travel agent make your international air reservations.

Before you travel, check to see if a Travel Warning is in effect for the country or countries that you plan to visit.

You can access Consular Information Sheets, Travel Warnings and Public Announcements 24 hours-a-day in several ways.

Telephone
To listen to them, call (202) 647-5225 from a touchtone phone.

Fax

From your fax machine, dial (202) 647-3000, using the handset as you would a regular telephone. The system prompts you on how to proceed.

Internet

Information about travel and consular services is available on the Bureau of Consular Affairs' World Wide Web home page. The address is http://travel.state.gov. It includes Consular Information Sheets, Travel Warnings and Public Announcements, passport and visa information, travel publications, background on international adoption and international child abduction services and international legal assistance. The site also links to the State Department's main home page at http://www.state.gov, which contains current foreign affairs information.

Consular Affairs Bulletin Board

If you have a personal computer, modem and communication software, you can access the Consular Affairs Bulletin Board (CABB). To view or download the documents from a computer and modem, dial the CABB on (301) 946-4400. The login is **travel**; the password is **info**.

There is no charge to use the telephone, fax and bulletin board systems other than normal long distance charges.

As you travel, keep abreast of local news coverage. If you plan more than a short stay in one place, if you intend travel to an area where communications are poor, or if you are in an area experiencing civil unrest or some natural disaster, you are encouraged to register with the nearest U.S. embassy or consulate. Registration takes only a few moments, and it may be invaluable in case of an emergency. Remember to leave a detailed itinerary and your passport number with a friend or relative in the United States. If your itinerary is not fixed, try to get in touch with family and friends frequently so they will know how to reach you if necessary.

ENTERING AND LEAVING - PASSPORTS AND VISAS

U.S. citizens must have a valid U.S. passport to travel to all Central and South American countries with the exception of Panama and short stays in French Guiana. (Panama and French Guiana require proof of U.S. citizenship such as a birth certificate or passport. However, the U.S. Embassy in Panama encourages U.S. citizens to travel to Panama using their U.S. passports.) Visa requirements for U.S. citizens vary from country to country. Certain countries do not require a visa for a short tourist stay. For some, you need to obtain a tourist card from the airline office or at the destination airport. Other countries require you to obtain a visa in advance from that country's embassy or consulate. Some places have additional entry requirements such as proof of sufficient funds and/or onward or return tickets. If you do NOT meet the entry requirements upon arrival in a country, you will not be admitted and will have to leave on the next plane.

In addition, most Central and South American countries require a departure tax. If you are departing to a neighboring country, the tax may be small, but if you are returning to the U.S., the tax could be fairly substantial per person, regardless of age. Be sure to have enough money at the end of your trip to be able to pay the departure tax so you can get on the plane!

For authoritative information on a country's entry and exit requirements, contact its embassy or consulate (see the list of foreign embassies at the end of this chapter). When you make your inquiries, ask about:

-- where to obtain a tourist card or visa;
-- visa price, length of validity, and number of entries;
-- financial requirements: proof of sufficient funds, proof of onward or return ticket;
-- special requirements for children traveling alone or with only one parent (see below);
-- health requirements;
-- currency regulations: how much local or dollar currency can be brought in or out;
-- export/import restrictions; and
-- departure tax: how much and who must pay.

RESTRICTIONS ON MINORS

Many countries impose restrictions on minor children who travel alone, with only one parent, with someone who is not their parent or who are nationals of the country, including dual nationals. A child must present written authorization for travel from the absent parent, parents, or legal guardian. If the parent or guardian traveling with the child is the sole custodian, the court order granting custody may, in some cases, serve as the authorization document. For certain countries, the documentation must be translated into Spanish or Portuguese and/or authenticated at the embassy of the country in question before departure from the U.S.

If any of this applies to you, inquire about the following at the embassy or consulate of the country your child plans to visit:

-- the age of majority at which the restriction no longer applies (i.e., age 15 in Argentina, age 18 in Brazil);
-- the type of document that can overcome the restriction (i.e., court order, statement of absent parent or parents);
-- whether notarizing the document is sufficient or if it must also be authenticated by the country's embassy or consulate;
-- whether the document must be translated.
-- whether the permission of the mother, father or both parents is required.

BRINGING YOUR OWN CAR, PLANE OR BOAT

If you plan to drive to Central or South America or arrive in a private plane or boat, contact the embassy or consulate of each country you plan to visit to learn what is required for entry and exit. You may not be able to enter certain countries unless you have had your vehicle documented by that country's embassy or consulate before you leave the United States. Besides title and ownership, at most borders you will need to show insurance coverage effective for the country you are entering. If your U.S. insurance does not cover you abroad, you can usually purchase insurance when you enter a country. In some countries, if you are involved in an accident that causes injury, you will automatically be taken into police custody until it can be determined who is liable and whether you have the insurance or financial ability to pay any judgment. There may also be criminal liability assigned if the injuries or damages are serious.

If you are a visitor, you will not ordinarily have to pay import duty on your car, but you may have to post a bond or otherwise satisfy customs officials that you will not sell or dispose of the vehicle in the country. Before you get behind the wheel, be sure you are in compliance with the automobile import regulations of your destination country or countries.

If driving, check the Consular Information Sheet for information regarding security threats that might be encountered on the highway. You should also keep in mind that in many countries road conditions and local drivers' concern for safety fall far short of what is customary in the U.S.

HEALTH

Information for travelers on health precautions, immunizations and areas with specific health issues can be obtained from local health departments, private doctors, travel clinics or the Centers for Disease Control and Prevention in Atlanta, Georgia (CDC). The CDC can be reached by telephone at 404-332-4559, or, you can visit their home page on the Internet at http://www.cdc.gov. General guidance can be found in the U.S. Public Health Service book, Health Information for International Travel, available for $14.00 from the U.S. Government Printing Office, Washington, D.C. 20402.

Insurance. Review your health insurance policy. If it does not cover you abroad, consider purchasing insurance that does. Also consider obtaining insurance to cover the very high cost of medical evacuation in the event of accident or serious illness.

Insects. Mosquito avoidance measures, if used day and night, may help prevent malaria and other less prevalent insect-borne diseases found in parts of Central and South America.

Food. Throughout most of Central and South America, fruits and vegetables should be washed with care and meats and fish thoroughly cooked. Water is generally not potable and should be boiled or chemically treated. Diarrhea caused by contaminated food or water is potentially serious. If it persists, seek medical attention.

Beaches. Certain beaches in the region are dangerously polluted. Avoid swimming at beaches that might be contaminated with human sewage or dog feces. Swimming in fresh water in the areas where schistosomiasis is found should also be avoided.

189

Mountains. Visitors in the Andes may experience symptoms of altitude sickness such as insomnia, headache, and nausea. If you become sick, descend to a lower altitude if possible. Mountaineers should learn about the symptoms of high altitude pulmonary edema, a condition that is fatal unless remedied by immediate descent.

Another hazard of high altitudes is sunburn. Exposure to ultraviolet radiation increases not only as you approach the equator, but also as you ascend in altitude. Sunscreens may help prevent this.

SAFETY TIPS - CRIME

As in a number of places around the world, crime in many parts of Central and South America seems to be increasing. Visitors should take common sense precautions:

-- Safety begins when you pack. Leave expensive jewelry behind. Dress conservatively; a flashy wardrobe or one that is too casual can mark you as a tourist. Use travelers checks, not cash. Leave photocopies of your passport personal information page and your airline tickets with someone at home and carry an extra set with you.

-- Use a money belt or a concealed money pouch for passports, cash and other valuables.

-- In a car, keep doors locked, windows rolled up and valuables out of sight. A common trick is for a thief to reach through a car window and grab a watch from a persons wrist or a purse or package from the seat while you are driving slowly or stopped in traffic.

-- When you leave your car, try to find a guarded parking lot. Lock the car and keep valuables out of sight.

-- When walking, avoid marginal areas of cities, dark alleys and crowds. Do not stop if you are approached on the street by strangers, including street vendors and beggars. Be aware that women and small children, as well as men, can be pickpockets or purse snatchers. Keep your billfold in an inner front pocket, carry your purse tucked securely under your arm, and wear the shoulderstrap of your camera or bag across your chest. To guard against thieves on motorcycles, walk away from the curb, carrying your purse away from the street.

-- Use official taxi stands rather than cruising taxis. Illegal taxis can be decoys for robbers.

-- Whenever possible, do not travel alone. If you travel in isolated areas, go with a group or a reputable guide.

-- Avoid travel at night.

-- Do not take valuables to the beach.

Any U.S. citizen who is criminally assaulted should report the incident to the local police and to the nearest U.S. embassy or consulate.

SAFETY TIPS - CIVIL UNREST

Some countries in Latin America experience periodic political violence aimed at national government targets or even at foreigners. In a number of countries, kidnapping for political and/or profit motives is widespread and U.S. citizens sometimes fall victim. In addition to checking the latest Consular Information Sheets, Travel Warnings and Public Announcements, you may also want to contact the U.S. embassy in the country or countries you plan to visit for the most up-to-date information on the security situation.

Always carry your papers with you and do not overstay the validity of your visa or tourist card.

Avoid public demonstrations. Travelers can accidentally become injured if caught up in them. Also, American citizens have been arrested when local authorities have thought they were participating in civil demonstrations. If you are detained or arrested for any reason, ask to speak with a U.S. consular officer.

DRUG AND FIREARMS OFFENSES

Most Central and South American countries strictly enforce laws against the use, possession and sale of narcotics. Foreigners arrested for possession of even small amounts of narcotics are generally charged and tried as international traffickers. There is no bail, judicial delays are lengthy, and you can spend 2 to 4 years in prison awaiting trial and sentencing. If you carry prescription drugs, keep them in their original container, clearly labeled with the doctors name, pharmacy and contents. Check with the embassy of the country you plan to visit for specific customs requirements for prescription drugs.

Laws concerning importation and possession of firearms can also be strict, with stiff penalties for violations. U.S. citizens who legally keep weapons in their boat or car in the U.S. sometimes forget to remove them before arrival in a foreign country, resulting in imprisonment.

PHOTOGRAPHY

Be cautious when taking pictures. Local authorities in many Central and South American countries consider all airports, police stations, military locations, oil installations, harbors, mines and bridges to be security-related. Photography of demonstrations or civil disturbances is also usually prohibited. Tourists have had their film confiscated and have been detained for trying to take these types of pictures. When in doubt about whether you can take a picture, ask first.

U.S. WILDLIFE REGULATIONS

Endangered species and products made from them may not be brought into the United States. The penalty is confiscation and a possible fine. These items are prohibited from import: virtually all birds originating in Brazil, Ecuador, Paraguay, and Venezuela; furs from spotted cats; most lizard-skin products from Brazil and Paraguay; many snakeskin products from Brazil, Ecuador, and Paraguay; skins from the Orinoco crocodile; and all sea turtle products.

SHOPPING FOR ANTIQUES

Most countries in Central and South America control the export of objects from their pre-Columbian and colonial heritage. This may also include relics and/or reproductions of antiques. Some countries claim ownership of all such material and consider the export of antiques, without the permission of the government, to be an act of theft. In addition, under U.S. law, importers of all pre-Columbian monumental and architectural sculpture, murals and certain archaeological and ethnological materials are required to provide proof to the U.S. Customs Service that these artifacts are legally exported from the country of origin. Beware of purchasing artifacts unless they are accompanied by an export permit issued by the government of origin.

DUAL NATIONALITY

Some countries in Central and South America do not recognize acquisition of U.S. citizenship unless the naturalized U.S. citizen renounces his or her original nationality at an embassy or consulate of the country of origin. A person born in the United States of a parent or parents who were citizens of another country may also be considered by that country to be their national. If arrested, a dual national may be denied the right to communicate with the U.S. embassy or consulate. Dual nationals may also be forced to serve in the military of their former country, or they may not be allowed to depart the country when their visit is over.

If you are a naturalized U.S. citizen, a dual national or have any reason to believe another country may consider you its national, check with the embassy of that country as to your citizenship status and any obligations you may have while visiting. When you research your citizenship status, bear in mind the purpose of your planned trip can affect your status. Your acquired U.S. citizenship may be recognized by your former country if you only visit there. If, however, you take up residence, the country may consider you as having resumed your former nationality. This can happen even if the embassy of the country has stamped a visa in your U.S. passport.

Dual nationals should also be aware that they may be required to use a passport from their country of origin to enter or leave that country. The U.S. Government does not object to the use of a foreign passport in such situations. U.S. citizens may not, however, use a foreign passport to enter or leave the United States and must travel on their U.S. passports.

If you have any questions about dual nationality, contact the Office of Overseas Citizens Services, Room 4811, Department of State, Washington, D.C. 20520, telephone (202) 647-5225.

ADOPTING A CHILD ABROAD

While most foreign adoptions are processed without significant difficulty, in some instances and in some countries U.S. citizens have experienced problems when attempting to adopt children from some Central or South American countries. Several countries in the region have either outlawed adoptions by foreigners or passed a law requiring formal court adoption of the child in the country before the child is permitted to emigrate to the U.S. These changes have lessened the potential for legal challenges to the adoption, but have not necessarily streamlined the procedures for U.S. citizens.

Any citizen interested in adopting a child from a country in Central or South America is encouraged to contact either the U.S. embassy in the country, or, in the United States, the Department of State's Office of Children's Issues (telephone 202-736-7000) to obtain information on the adoption process in that country.

INFORMATION ON SPECIFIC COUNTRIES

Argentina
Argentina is a medium income nation with a developing economy. The quality of facilities for tourism varies according to price and area. U.S. citizens who are also citizens of Argentina (dual nationals) should call the Argentine Embassy or nearest consulate to clarify their status and to obtain the latest information and requirements for travel.

Belize
Belize is a developing country. Facilities for tourism vary in quality.

Bolivia
Bolivia is a developing nation with a slowly growing economy. Facilities for tourism are adequate but vary greatly in quality. Roads outside the major cities are frequently unpaved. Rail transportation is below standard. In addition to the American Embassy in La Paz, you may also seek assistance at two consular agencies, one located in Santa Cruz and the other in Cochabamba.

Brazil
Brazil has a developing economy. Facilities for tourism are good in the major cities, but vary in quality in remote areas. Those arriving in Brazil without a visa are usually required to depart on the next available flight. Minors (under 18) traveling alone, with one parent or with a third party must present written authorization by the absent parent(s) or legal guardian, specifically granting permission to travel alone, with one parent or with a third party. This authorization must be notarized, authenticated by the Brazilian Embassy or nearest consulate, and translated into Portuguese.

Street crime is a problem in Brazil, especially in areas surrounding hotels, bars, nightclubs, discotheques and other establishments where visitors tend to gather, including locations adjacent to the main beach areas in Rio. In addition to the American Embassy in Brasilia, you may seek assistance at the Consulates General located in Rio de Janeiro and Sao Paulo, the Consulate in Recife and the Consular Agencies in Belem, Manaus and Salvador de Bahia.

Chile
Chile has a stable government and a strong economy. Civil disorder is rare. Tourist facilities vary according to price and area. American citizens are required to pay a "processing fee" of $20 in U.S. currency (exact change) at the international airport check in point. Those considering scientific, technical or mountaineering activities in areas classified as frontier areas are required to obtain authorization from the Chilean government. Requests for authorization must be presented to Chilean authorities at least 90 days prior to the beginning of the expedition. The portions of Antarctica claimed by Chile are exempt from these pre-approval requirements.

Colombia
There is a Travel Warning in effect for Colombia. Colombia is one of the most dangerous countries in the world. Violence affects a significant portion of the country. As a result, all in-country travel, both official and private, to all destinations by U.S. government employees is restricted. Kidnapping for ransom and political purposes is increasing in Colombia. In recent years, several U.S. citizens have been kidnapped, and two U.S. citizen kidnap victims were killed.

If you must travel to Colombia, a valid U.S. passport and a return or onward ticket are required. U.S. citizens do not require entry visas for stays of less than 30 days. Stiff fines are imposed if passports are not stamped on arrival and if stays exceeding 30 days are not authorized by the Colombian Immigration Agency (DAS Extranjeria). Minors under 18 traveling alone, with one parent or with a third party must present written authorization from the absent parent or legal guardian. The authorization must be notarized, authenticated and translated into Spanish. Minors must also present a notarized copy of their birth certificate. If the child was born in the United States, the birth certificate must be notarized by a Colombian consulate within the U.S. If the child was born in Colombia, the birth certificate must have been issued by a Colombian notary.

Costa Rica

Costa Rica is a developing country. Tourist facilities, particularly in the capital, are generally adequate. It is strongly recommended that U.S. citizens use a valid U.S. passport to enter Costa Rica. U.S. citizens must have an onward or return ticket. Kidnapping of foreigners is on the increase. Money exchangers on the street pass off counterfeit U.S. dollars and local currency. Credit card fraud is growing.

Ecuador

Ecuador has a developing economy. Tourist facilities are adequate but vary in quality. Avoid the areas within approximately 30 miles of the Colombian border because of criminal and Colombian guerrilla violence. Refer to the Consular Information Sheet for further details. There are numerous traffic accidents involving buses. Bus travel throughout Ecuador can be particularly dangerous because of the frequency of crimes perpetrated against bus travelers. Kidnappings of foreigners, including Americans, is on the rise. Maritime safety standards on some tour vessels to the Galapagos Islands are deficient. It may be useful to verify the credentials of tour vessels in advance. Under provision of Ecuadorian law, a business dispute that would normally be handled by civil litigation in the U.S. may be converted into a criminal proceeding. This provision of law has been used to impose travel prohibitions against resident Americans and has resulted in U.S. businesspersons being arrested.

El Salvador

El Salvador has a developing economy. Tourist facilities are not fully developed. Credit cards are widely accepted. The Salvadoran constitution prohibits foreigners from participating in domestic political activities, including public demonstrations. The government of El Salvador considers such involvement to be a violation of the participant's tourist visa status. Mine removal efforts have ended, but land mines and unexploded ammunition in back country regions still pose a threat to off-the-road tourists, backpackers and campers. Currently, it is extremely difficult for prospective adoptive parents to begin adoption proceedings in El Salvador.

French Guiana

French Guiana, which is an overseas department of France, is a sparsely populated wilderness. Tourist facilities are available, but in some instances are not highly developed.

Guatemala

Guatemala has a developing economy. Except for luxury hotels in major cities and tourist destinations, tourist facilities are not fully developed. U.S. citizens whose passports are lost or stolen in Guatemala must obtain a new passport and present it along with a police report of the loss or theft to the main immigration office in Guatemala City to obtain permission to depart. Identification must be carried at all times.

In the past, unfounded rumors that foreigners are involved in the theft of children for the purpose of using their organs in transplants have led to threats and incidents of mob violence in parts of Guatemala. If you visit areas outside of the major tourist and business destinations, there is a greater likelihood, albeit small, of such an incident. The risk is also increased for tourists who have contact with Guatemalan children. Adoptive parents, in particular, are encouraged to travel within Guatemala without their adoptive children or to limit such travel when possible.

There have been sporadic terrorist incidents during periods surrounding key political events. Violent crime is a very serious and growing problem throughout the country, including murder, rape and kidnapping. U.S. citizens have been among the victims. Night travel between cities anywhere in Guatemala is extremely dangerous.

Guyana

Guyana is a developing nation. Except for hotels in the capital city of Georgetown, tourist facilities are not fully developed. Road conditions throughout the country are poor. Bring prescription medicine sufficient for your length of stay and be aware that Guyana's humid climate may affect some medicines. Many birds are protected species. Visitors wishing to take a tropical bird back to the U.S. need to obtain quarantine space in advance from the U.S. Department of Agriculture's Animal and Plant Inspection Service. Proof that space has been reserved for the bird in the U.S. must be presented to the Guyana Ministry of Agriculture before permission for export will be given.

Honduras

Honduras has a developing economy. Tourist facilities are generally adequate, but vary in quality. Judicial delays are common. Suspected criminals, including U.S. citizens, have been detained for years without trial or sentencing. Although safe bottled water is widely available, tap water is not potable in Honduras and should be boiled or chemically treated to help prevent cholera and gastrointestinal disorders. Medical care is limited, particularly outside of Tegucigalpa and San Pedro Sula. It is usually impossible for visitors to cash personal checks in Honduras. It is also extremely difficult to arrange for the transfer of funds from abroad to Honduras, especially to the Bay Islands, where banking facilities are limited. If you travel to rural areas and to the border regions near Guatemala, El Salvador and Nicaragua, exercise caution because armed bands have operated in these areas.

Nicaragua

Nicaragua has a developing economy and lacks an extensive tourist infrastructure. Travelers checks are accepted at a few major hotels and may be exchanged for local currency at authorized exchange facilities. Although many restaurants and hotels now accept credit cards, acceptance is not as widespread as in the U.S. Travel in remote areas in the northern and central departments is strongly discouraged because of violent crime.

Panama

Panama has a developing economy. Outside the Panama City area, tourist facilities vary in quality. The Pan American Highway ends at Yaviza in the Darien Province, and the final portion from Chepo to Yaviza is reasonably passable only during the dry season (January-April). If you plan to travel to South America by car, you may wish to take the automobile ferry "Crucero-Express" to Cartagena, Colombia, or ship your car on a freighter. Travel beyond Yaviza may be dangerous, and there is no

Panamanian police presence in much of Darien Province, which is known to be frequented by guerrillas, smugglers, and undocumented aliens.

Paraguay

Paraguay is a medium income nation with a developing economy. Tourist facilities are good in Asuncion, poor in other major cities and almost nonexistent in remote areas. Minors under 20 traveling alone, with one parent or with a third party must present written authorization from the absent parent(s) or legal guardian, which grants permission to travel alone, with one parent or a third party. The authorization will need to be notarized and translated into Spanish. Due to serious problems in the international adoption process in Paraguay, including chronic unpredictability in the issuance of final decrees, uncertainty over case processing and prospects for proposed new adoption regulations, prospective adoptive parents are strongly urged to postpone any commitment to adopt a Paraguayan child until such time as the adoption situation is clarified.

Peru

Peru is a developing country with significant tourist and commercial activity. The quality of tourist facilities varies, depending on cost and location. The U.S. Embassy has placed restrictions on official travel of U.S. government employees to several areas because terrorist groups and narcotics traffickers continue to use violence. (For information on the restricted areas, please consult the Consular Information Sheet on Peru.) If you visit places high in the Andes, such as Cuzco and Puno, you should be aware of the effects of high altitude and the sickness it can cause. In addition to the American Embassy in Lima, you may seek assistance at the Consular Agency located in Cuzco.

Suriname

Suriname is a developing nation. Transportation, communications and other infrastructure elements do not meet U.S. standards. Roads in the interior are poorly maintained and often impassable. Tourist facilities vary, depending on price and area. The government of Suriname and private tourism companies have expanded tourism in the interior by establishing several guest houses and tour packages. Visitors to Suriname who are injured or become ill during their visit will not be admitted to the only hospital with emergency and intensive care facilities unless they pay an advance deposit equal to ten days stay (payable only in U.S. dollars) or provide proof of adequate insurance coverage in a form the hospital will accept. You may experience disruptions in travel plans due to the varying scheduled airline service to and from Suriname.

Uruguay

Uruguay is a medium income nation with a developing economy. The quality of tourist facilities varies according to price and area.

Venezuela

Venezuela is a middle income country with a well developed transportation infrastructure. Scheduled air service and good all-weather roads, some poorly marked and congested around urban centers, connect major cities and all regions of the country. Its tourism infrastructure varies in quality according to location and price. If you do not have a Venezuelan identity card, you will need to carry your U.S. passport with you at all times. Certain areas along the border with Colombia have travel restrictions. If you visit those areas, you may be subject to search and seizure. Foreign exchange transactions must take place through commercial banks and exchange houses at the official rate. Credit cards are accepted at most tourist establishments. Outside of major cities, Venezuelan currency is required for most transactions. Visitors departing Venezuela can exchange local currency up to $5,000.

FOREIGN EMBASSIES IN THE UNITED STATES

Embassy of **ARGENTINA**
1718 Connecticut Ave., N.W.
Washington, DC 20009
(202) 797-8826

Embassy of **BELIZE**
2535 Massachusetts Ave., N.W.
Washington, DC 20008
(202) 332-9636

Embassy of **BOLIVIA**
Consular Section
3014 Massachusetts Ave., N.W.
Washington, DC 20008
(202) 232-4828 or 483-4410

Embassy of **BRAZIL**
Consular Section
3009 Whitehaven St., N.W.
Washington, DC 20008
(202) 745-2820 or 745-2831

Embassy of **CHILE**
1732 Massachusetts Ave., N.W.
Washington, DC 20036
(202) 785-1746

Embassy of **COLOMBIA**
2118 Leroy Place, N.W.
Washington, DC 20008
(202) 387-8338

Embassy of **COSTA RICA**
2112 S St., N.W.
Washington, DC 20008
(202) 234-2945

Embassy of **ECUADOR**
2535 15th St., N.W.
Washington, DC 20009
(202) 234-7200

Embassy of **EL SALVADOR**
2308 California St., N.W.
Washington, DC 20008
(202) 265-9671

FRENCH GUIANA
Embassy of France
4101 Reservoir Road, N.W.
Washington, DC 20007
(202) 944-6187

Embassy of **GUATEMALA**
2220 R St., N.W.
Washington, DC 20008-4081
(202) 745-4952

Embassy of **GUYANA**
2490 Tracy Place, N.W.
Washington, DC 20008
(202) 265-6900 or 265-6903

Embassy of **HONDURAS**
Consular Section
Suite 310
1612 K St., N.W.
Washington, DC 20006
(202) 223-0185

Embassy of **NICARAGUA**
1627 New Hampshire Ave., N.W.
Washington, DC 20009
(202) 939-6531 or 939-6532

Embassy of **PANAMA**
2862 McGill Terrace, N.W.
Washington, DC 20008
(202) 483-1407

Embassy of **PARAGUAY**
2400 Massachusetts Ave., N.W.
Washington, DC 20008
(202) 483-6960

Embassy of **PERU**
1700 Massachusetts Ave., N.W.
Washington, DC 20036
(202) 833-9860 through 9869

Embassy of **SURINAME**
4301 Connecticut Ave., N.W.
Suite 108
Washington, DC 20008
(202) 244-7488

Embassy of **URUGUAY**
1918 F Street, N.W.
Washington, DC 20008
(202) 331-1313 through 1316
or (202) 331-4219
Embassy of **VENEZUELA**
1099 30th Street, N.W.
Washington, DC 20007
(202) 342-2214

U.S. EMBASSIES AND CONSULATES ABROAD

ARGENTINA
American Embassy
4300 Colombia
1425 Buenos Aires
Tel: (54)(1) 777-4533 and 777-4534
Fax: (54)(1) 777-0197
Mailing address:
American Embassy
APO AA 34034

BELIZE
American Embassy
Gabourel Lane and Hutson St.
Belize City
Tel: (501)(2) 77161 through 77163
Fax: (501)(2) 30802
Mailing address:
American Embassy
APO AA 34025

BOLIVIA
American Embassy La Paz
Avenue Arce No. 2780
La Paz
Tel: (591)(2) 430251
Fax: (591)(2) 433854
Mailing address:
American Embassy
APO AA 34032

BRAZIL
American Embassy
Avenida das Nacoes, Lote 3
Brasilia
Tel: (55)(61) 321-7272
Fax: (55)(61) 225-9136
Mailing address:

American Embassy
Unit 3500
APO AA 34030

American Consulate General
Rio de Janeiro
Avenida Presidente Wilson
147 Castelo
Rio de Janeiro
Tel: (55)(21) 292-7117
Fax: (55)(21) 220-0439
Mailing address:
American Consulate General
Rio de Janeiro
Unit 3501
APO AA 34030

American Consulate General
Sao Paulo
Rua Padre Joao Manoel, 933
Sao Paulo
Tel: (55)(11) 881-6511
Fax: (55)(11) 852-5154
Mailing address:
American Consulate General
Sao Paulo
P.O. Box 8063
APO AA 34030

American Consulate Recife
Rua Goncalves Maia, 163
Recife
Tel: (55)(81) 421-2441
Fax: (55)(81) 231-1906
Mailing address:
American Consulate Recife
APO AA 34030

CHILE
American Embassy
Av. Andres Bello 2800
Santiago
Tel: (56)(2) 232-2600
Fax: (56)(2) 330-3710
Mailing address:
American Embassy
U.S. Department of State
Washington, DC 20521-3460

COLOMBIA
American Embassy
Calle 22D-BIS, No. 47-51
Ave. El Dorado & Carrera 50

Bogota
Tel: (57)(1) 315-0811
Fax: (57)(1) 315-2197
Mailing address:
American Embassy
APO AA 34038

COSTA RICA
American Embassy
Pavas
San Jose
Tel: (506) 220-3939
Fax: (506) 220-2305
Mailing address:
American Embassy
APO AA 34020

ECUADOR
American Embassy
Avenida 12 de Octubre y
Avenida Patria
Quito
Tel: (593)(2) 562-890
Fax: (593)(2) 502-052
Mailing address:
American Embassy
APO AA 34039-3420
American Consulate General
9 de Octubre y Garcia Moreno
Guayaquil
Tel: (593)(4) 323-570
Fax: (593)(4) 325-286
Mailing address:
American Consulate General
APO AA 34039

EL SALVADOR
American Embassy
Final Blvd. Santa Elena
Antiguo Cuscatlan
San Salvador
Tel: (503) 278-4444
Fax: (503) 278-6011
Mailing Address:
American Embassy
APO AA 34023

FRENCH GUIANA
American Embassy
Dr. Sophie Redmondstraat 129
Paramaribo, Suriname
Tel: (597) 472-900
Fax: (597) 410-972

196

GUATEMALA

American Embassy
7-01 Avenida de la Reforma
Zone 10
Guatemala
Tel: (502) 331-1541
Fax: (502) 331-0564
Mailing Address:
American Embassy
Unit 3303
APO AA 34024

GUYANA

American Embassy
99-100 Young and Duke
Streets
Kingstown, Georgetown
Tel: (592)(2) 54900-9
Fax: (592)(2) 58497
Mailing Address:
American Embassy
U.S. Department of State
Washington, DC 20521-3170

HONDURAS

American Embassy
Avenido La Paz
Tegucigalpa
Tel: (504) 36-9320 or 38-5114
Fax: (504) 37-1792 (Consular fax))
Mailing Address:
American Embassy
Unit 2909
APO AA 34022

NICARAGUA

American Embassy
Km. 4-1/2 Carretera Sur
Managua
Tel: (505)(2) 66010 through 666013
Fax: (505)(2) 669074
Mailing Address:
American Embassy
APO AA 34021

PANAMA

American Embassy
Apartado 6959 Panama 5
Panama City

Tel: (507) 227-1777
Fax: (507) 227-1964
Mailing Address:
American Embassy
APO AA 34002

PARAGUAY

American Embassy
1776 Mariscal Loipez Avenida
Asuncion
Tel: (595)(21) 213-715
Fax: (595)(21) 213-728
Mailing Address:
American Embassy
Unit 4711
APO AA 34036-0001

PERU

American Embassy
Consular Section
Av. La Encalada s/n
Block 17
Monterrico
Lima33, Lima
Tel: (51)(1) 434-3000
Fax: (51)(1) 434-3037
Mailing Address:
Consular Section
Unit 3740
APO AA 34031

SURINAME

American Embassy
Dr. Sophie Redmondstraat 129
Paramaribo
Tel: (597) 472900
Fax: (597) 410972
Mailing Address:
AmEmb Paramaribo
Department of State
Washington, DC 20521-3390

URUGUAY

American Embassy
Lauro Muller 1776
Montevideo
Tel: (598)(2) 23-60-61
Fax: (598)(2) 48-86-11
Mailing Address:
American Embassy
APO AA 34035

VENEZUELA

American Embassy
Calle F con Calle Suapure
Colinas de Valle Arriba
Caracas
Tel: (58)(2) 977-2011
Fax: (58)(2) 977-0843
Mailing Address:
American Embassy
APO AA 34037

Planning Another Trip?

See Chapter 36 for a listing of resources available to the general traveler from the U.S. Departments of State, Customs, Transportation, Health and various government and non-government organizations. Almost all of the available International travel-related pamphlets, brochures and publications issued by the U.S. Department of State and by the U.S. Customs have been reproduced in full in this book. See Table of Contents for location.

Chapter 16

Tips for Travelers to the People's Republic of China

*[The information in this chapter is reprinted verbatim from a bulletin issued by the
U.S. State Department, Bureau of Consular Affairs. It is intended to serve as advice
to Americans traveling abroad.]*

Foreword
The information in this chapter has been gathered for you by consular officers - both in the Department of State and in the People's Republic of China - to assist you with your trip. We hope this chapter will be of help to you in making your trip both safe and enjoyable.

The People's Republic of China (P.R.C.) has a communist government. It is one of the world's largest and fastest growing economies. Modern tourist facilities are not widely available, except in major cities.

About China
China is the oldest continuous major world civilization, with records dating back over 3,500 years. Successive dynasties developed a system of bureaucratic control which gave the agrarian-based Chinese an advantage over neighboring nomadic and hill cultures. Chinese civilization was further strengthened by the development of a common written language that bridged the gaps among the country's many local languages and dialects.

There are several major Chinese dialects and many subdialects. The Beijing dialect, often called Mandarin (or Putonghua), is taught in all schools and is the medium of government. Almost two-thirds of Han Chinese are native speakers of Mandarin; the rest, concentrated in southwest and southeast China, speak one of the other major Chinese dialects.

China's population in mid-1995 was over 1.2 billion, with an estimated growth rate of 1.2%. The largest ethnic group is the Han Chinese, who constitute about 93% of the total population. The remaining 7% are Zhuang (16 million), Manchu (9 million), Hui (8 million), Miao (8 million), Uygur (7 million), Yi (7 million), Tibetan (5 million),

Mongol (5 million), and Korean (1 million).

China is full of natural and man-made wonders. Its great rivers include the Yellow and the Yangtze. There are also many mountain ranges including the Himalayas along the southern border of Tibet and the Kunlun Mountains stretching east and west along Tibet's northern edge. Part of the Gobi desert is located in China's Inner Mongolia.

China's most popular man-made wonder is the Great Wall. The Great Wall was built in the 3rd century B.C. (completed in 204 B.C.). It extends for about 1500 miles from Gansu province to the Bohai Gulf. The wall averages 20 to 50 feet high and 15 to 25 feet thick. The actual length, including branches and windings, is more than 2000 miles.

Consular Information Program
For up-to-date travel information on the P.R.C., see the Department of State's Consular Information Sheet for China. Consular Information Sheets cover such matters as health conditions, unusual currency and entry regulations, crime and security conditions, drug penalties, and areas of instability. In addition, the State Department issues Travel Warnings when we recommend Americans defer travel to a country because of unsafe conditions. Travel Warnings are under continuous review by the Department of State. Before you depart for a country that has a Travel Warning, make certain that you have the most recent revision of the Warning. The Department of State also issues Public Announcements. Public Announcements are issued as a means to disseminate information quickly about relatively short-term and/or trans-national conditions which would pose significant risks to the security of American travelers. At the time of publication, there were no Travel Warnings nor were there any

199

Public Announcements issued for travel to China.

There are several ways to access Consular Information Sheets, Travel Warnings and Public Announcements. You can listen to them 24-hours a day by calling 202-647-5225 from a touchtone phone. You can receive copies of them by sending a self-addressed, stamped envelope to Overseas Citizens Services, Room 4800, Department of State, Washington, DC 20520-4818. (Write the name of the requested country or countries on the outside of the envelope.) You can also find Consular Information Sheets and Travel Warnings at the 13 regional passport agencies and at U.S. embassies and consulates abroad. The information can also be accessed through an airline or travel agent's computer reservation system, the Bureau of Consular Affairs' 24- hour automated fax system at 202/647-3000, or through many computer bulletin boards, including the Consular Affairs Bulletin Board (CABB). You may call the CABB on modem number 301-946-4400. The login is **travel**; the password is **info**.

Entry and Other Visa Requirements
To enter the People's Republic of China, a U.S. citizen must have a valid U.S. passport and P.R.C. visa Most tourist visas are valid for only one entry. Travelers required a new visa for additional entries into China. Chinese authorities fine those who arrive without a visa up to 5,000 renminbi (about $600 U.S.) at the port of entry and may not allow them to enter China.

An application for a business visa should include an invitation from the applicant's host or counterpart in China. Visas for tour group members are often obtained by the travel agent as part of the tour package. You may book China tours through a number of travel agencies and airlines in the United States and abroad. You can find advertisements for these tours in newspapers or magazines, or you may contact the China National Tourist Office at: 60 E. 42nd Street, Suite 3126, New York, NY 10165; (212) 867-0271.

Tourist visas for individuals are routinely issued at Chinese embassies or consulates abroad. Expedited processing is often available for an increased fee or by working through a Chinese tour operator.

Apply for a visa at the Chinese Embassy in Washington, D.C., or at a Chinese consulate in Chicago, Houston, Los Angeles, New York, or San Francisco. (Addresses are listed at the end of this chapter.) At this time, the cost of a visa for China is $30 (not including fees for expedited handling). To apply, each person must send an application form, valid passport, two photographs and the fee. U.S. citizens applying for visas outside the United States may be requested to fill out visa application forms both in English and in Chinese.

Whether you visit on your own or with a tour, allow several weeks for visa processing. The Chinese Embassy and consulates in the United States often require 10 working days to process visas.

In addition to the requirements above, long-term visitors to China may be required to provide evidence of an AIDS test. Negative HIV exam results are required for students, teachers, and visiting scholars who plan to stay 9 months or more and for business persons who plan to stay over a year. If this applies to you, you may have the medical exam done in the United States using blank forms issued by the Chinese Embassy or a consulate. However, the test results must indicate the test was done by a government facility such as your states health department or, if done at a private health facility, the results must be notarized by a notary public. Attach your photograph to the test form. The notary seal should be applied to the photograph and it should run off on to the page.

For individuals visiting Hong Kong en route, tours to China depart regularly from that city and may be booked through China Travel Service, LTD., 77 Queens Road, Central, Hong Kong (tel: 2525-2284, fax: 2541-9777) or 27-33 Nathan Road, Kowloon, Hong Kong (tel: 2315-7149, fax: 2721-7757). (Cable address: TRAVEL BANK.) For a handling fee, individual visas for travel originating in Hong Kong may be obtained through these agencies in two working days. If you have made travel arrangements and wish to obtain your visa on your own, apply to the Visa Office of the Ministry of Foreign Affairs of the People's Republic of China, 5th Floor, Low Block, 26 Harbour Road, Wanchai, Hong Kong.

Note: Hong Kong became a special administrative region of China on July 1, 1997.

While You Are in China

All American citizens visiting China for a month or more are encouraged to register with the U.S. Embassy in Beijing or the nearest U.S. consulate. Registration will assist our posts in China in locating you in the event of an emergency back home or in replacing a lost or stolen passport. You should also photocopy the data page of your passport and keep it in a separate place from your passport. In the event that your passport is lost, stolen, or in the possession of government officials, travel agents or tourism representatives, you will have the requisite information available, as well as proof of your identity and citizenship.

Customs Regulations

Foreign visitors to the People's Republic of China are allowed to import 4 bottles of wine or spirits and 600 cigarettes along with their personal belongings. Items such as watches, radios, cameras, and calculators imported duty free for personal use may not be transferred or sold to others. Gifts and articles carried on behalf of others must be declared to the customs inspector and are subject to duty.

Chinese customs regulations prohibit the import or export of the following items:

(a) arms, ammunition, and explosives;
(b) radio transmitter-receivers and principal parts;
(c) Chinese currency (renminbi);
(d) books, films, records, tapes, etc. which are "detrimental to China's politics, economy, culture, and ethics" (e.g. pornographic or religious content)
(e) poisonous drugs and narcotics;
(f) infected animal or plant products; and
(g) infected foodstuffs.

Note: Videotapes may be confiscated by Chinese customs to determine that they do not violate prohibitions noted in item (d), above. Tapes are sometimes held for several months before being returned. (There is no guarantee that they will ever be returned.)

Export of the following items is also prohibited:
(a) valuable cultural relics and rare books relating to Chinese history, culture, and art;
(b) rare animals, rare plants and their seeds; and
(c) precious metals and diamonds and articles made from them.

Antiques and imitations which are approved for export are marked with a red wax seal.

According to the U.S. Food and Drug Administration, improper glazing of some dinnerware for sale in China can cause lead contamination in food. Therefore, unless you have proof of its safety, dinnerware purchased in China should be used for decorative purposes only. Chinese commercial shipments of dinnerware to the United States are tested to conform to U.S. safety standards.

Movie cameras and videotaping equipment should be declared upon entry into China.

Crime

China has a low crime rate; however crime has increased in the past few years, principally in the major cities. U.S. citizens and other foreigners have seldom been victims of violent crime.

Currency Regulations

Chinese currency is called yuan or, more commonly, renminbi (RMB). Foreign currency (cash or traveler's checks) may be exchanged for Chinese currency at licensed exchange facilities of the Bank of China and other authorized banks.

Money exchange facilities are available at major airports, hotels, and department stores. Major brands of traveler's checks are accepted at such exchange facilities and cash advances against a credit card can be arranged, a service charge is usually added. Consult with your bank before departing the United States to be sure that your brand of check or credit card will be accepted. Major credit cards (American Express, Mastercard and Visa) are accepted by most major hotels and in many well-known restaurants.

Legal Matters

While in China, a U.S. citizen is subject to Chinese laws and regulations. Laws in China sometimes differ significantly from those in the United States and do not afford the protections available to the individual under U.S. law. Exercise caution and carefully obey local laws. Penalties for breaking the law can be more severe than in the United States for similar offenses. Persons violating the law, even unknowingly, may be expelled, arrested or imprisoned. Chinese laws prohibit public demonstrations without a valid permit obtained from the Chinese Public Security Bureau in the city where the demonstration is planned.

Chinese authorities have seized documents, literature, and letters which they deem to be pornographic or political in nature or those which are intended for religious proselytizing. If you seek to enter China with religious materials in a quantity greater than what is considered needed for personal use, you could be detained and fined. Religious proselytizing or passing out of religious materials is strictly forbidden. Americans suspected of engaging in such activities have been fined, arrested or deported. Magazines with photographs considered commonplace in Western countries, including some advertisements, may be regarded as sexually explicit pornography. Books, films, records, tapes, etc., which are "detrimental to China's politics, economy, culture, and ethics" will be seized by Chinese Customs to determine that they do not violate these prohibitions.

American citizens should be aware that foreign visitors and residents in China have sometimes been detained and heavily fined for having improper sexual relations with Chinese citizens. In most of these cases, the foreigners involved had invited Chinese citizens to their hotel rooms. Any U.S. citizen who is detained by Chinese authorities for questioning regarding this or any other violation of Chinese law or regulations should notify the U.S. Embassy or nearest U.S. consulate as soon as possible.

Under the U.S. -P.R.C. Consular Convention of 1980, U.S. consular officers shall be notified if a U.S. citizen is arrested or detained no later than four days after the arrest or detention. Under the Convention, U.S. consular officers must be informed upon request of the reasons for the arrest or detention and have a right to visit the citizen after a formal request is made by the consular officer. U.S. consular officers cannot serve as attorneys or give legal advice. They can, however, provide a list of local English speaking attorneys you may retain and help you find legal representation.

U.S. citizens are encouraged to carry photocopies of their passport data and photo pages with them at all times so that, if questioned by P.R.C. officials, proof of U.S. citizenship is readily available. (Do not carry your original passport with you. Your passport and other valuables should be placed in a hotel safety deposit box.) U.S. citizens have rights to consular access under the U.S. - P.R.C. Consular Convention and should insist upon contact with the U.S. Embassy or one of the U.S. consulates general. If you are denied this right, continue to protest.

Criminal penalties for possession, use, or trafficking of illegal drugs in China are strict. Convicted offenders may receive severe jail sentences and fines.

Dual Nationality
China does not recognize dual nationality. U.S. citizens who are also Chinese nationals have experienced difficulty entering and departing China on U.S. passports, and some U.S. passports have been seized by Chinese authorities. Dual nationals may be subject to Chinese laws which impose special obligations. Such persons are often required to use Chinese documentation to enter China. The United States requires that all U.S. citizens enter and depart the United States on U.S. passports. Dual nationals who enter and depart China using a U.S. passport and a valid P.R.C. visa retain the right of U.S. consular access and protection under the U.S.-P.R.C. Consular Convention. The ability of the U.S. Embassy or consulates general to provide normal consular services would be extremely limited should a dual national enter China on a Chinese or other passport. China does not recognize the U.S. citizenship of children born in China, when one of the parents is a P.R.C. national. Such children are required to depart China on P.R.C. travel documents. Children born in the United States to P.R.C. national parents, who are neither lawful permanent residents nor U.S. citizens, are not recognized as U.S. citizens under Chinese nationality law. Although Chinese consulates have frequently issued visas to such individuals in error, they are treated solely as P.R.C. nationals by Chinese authorities when in China. Before traveling to China, dual nationals should contact the Office of Overseas Citizens Services at (202) 647-6769 or the U.S. Embassy in Beijing (see address at end of this booklet) for additional information.

Passport Confiscation and Business Disputes
U.S. citizens conducting business in China are

advised to be vigilant in investigating the companies they plan to work with to ensure they are reputable or to learn whether a prior history of disputes exists.

The confiscation of foreign passports of persons involved in business disputes has increased in China in recent years frequently resulting in individuals being placed under house arrest or unable to leave China until the dispute is satisfactorily resolved. As a valid Chinese visa is required in order to depart China, obtaining a replacement for a confiscated U.S. passport will not facilitate exiting the P.R.C. and the Chinese government will block your departure.

Adoptions

After completing lengthy pre-adoption procedures in the United States, Americans wishing to adopt a child in China can expect to spend at least two weeks there to complete the adoption. Current adoption information can be obtained by calling the U.S. Department of State's Office of Children's Issues at (202) 736-7000, or writing to that office in Room 4800, U.S. Department of State, Washington, D.C. 20520. Once in China, and after the adoption has been completed the U.S. Consulate General in Guangzhou will process the immigrant visa to enable you to bring your newly adopted child back to the United States. Consult the Consulate for further details to arrange an interview appointment.

Health

Information on health precautions for travelers can be obtained in the United States from local health departments, private doctors, travel clinics, and the Centers for Disease Control & Prevention's international travelers hotline at (404) 332-4559. For China, immunizations are recommended for hepatitis B and Japanese B encephalitis. (Immunization for Japanese B encephalitis is only recommended during the epidemic summer months for visitors planning to stay longer than two or three weeks in rural areas.) An immune globulin shot may offer protection against hepatitis A. Malaria occurs in China, particularly in rural areas and in southern China. Depending on the season and your destination, you may need to take antimalarial drugs, use insect repellant, and take other measures to reduce contact with mosquitoes.

There are no Western-style pharmacies stocked with drugs common in the United States. Therefore, carry medications in hand luggage packed in their original and labelled containers to avoid emergencies should checked luggage go astray.

Foreign visitors who become ill in China are usually provided with the best medical care available in the country. Generally speaking, the doctors and nurses are qualified and competent, although hospital accommodations are spartan, medical technology is not up-to-date, and sanitary conditions problematic.

Hospital costs for non-Chinese visitors are similar to those charged for similar services in the United States. Prospective travelers should review their health insurance policies. If your policy does not provide coverage overseas, consider buying coverage that does. In addition, insurance covering medical evacuation is highly recommended. There are two internationally-recognized emergency medical assistance firms with representatives in Beijing:

Asia Emergency Assistance Ltd. (AEA)
14 Liangmahe South Road, 1/F
Beijing 100600
Tel: 462-9112
Fax: 462-9100

International SOS Assistance (SOS)
Kunlun Hotel, Office Suite 433
2 Xin Yuan Nan Lu, Beijing
Tel: 500-3419
Fax: 501-6048.

Such insurance is inexpensive (less than $100 for a 30 day visit). Without insurance, the cost of evacuation can be extremely high. For example, the estimated cost of evacuation, using a stretcher and a medical escort, from Beijing to San Francisco is over $20,000.

Tourist travel in China can be extremely strenuous and may be especially debilitating to someone in poor health. Tours often involve walking long distances and up steep hills. All visitors, especially those with a history of coronary/pulmonary problems, should have a complete medical checkup before making final travel plans. Plans should include rest time. Travelers should avoid overly full schedules which could lead to exhaustion or illness. China discourages travel by persons who are ill, pregnant, or of advanced age. Visa applicants over 60 are sometimes required to complete a health questionnaire. If medical problems exist, a letter from your physician in the United States explaining treatment and, if relevant, copies of your most recent electrocardiograms, would be helpful in case a medical emergency occurs in China.

Air pollution in the large cities is severe, particularly in winter. Respiratory ailments are common.

Visitors are advised not to drink tapwater in China. Hotels almost always supply boiled water that is safe to drink. Bottled water and carbonated drinks are readily available. Travelers should carry water purification tablets to use when neither boiled water nor bottled drinks are available.

Travel Arrangements Within China

Packaged tours, while often more expensive than self arranged travel, will insulate you from the difficulties of booking travel by air, rail, bus or car in China. Transportation systems have not expanded as fast as the number of Chinese and international travelers has increased. Planes and trains are often overbooked.

Tickets or reservations for onward travel should be reconfirmed at each stop. Hotels, for a fee, will assist in making reservations and purchasing tickets.

Train travel can be difficult to reserve, even for the experienced traveler. Round trip rail tickets are not generally available without the services of a travel agency. Beware of counterfeit train tickets. Unethical entrepreneurs manufacture and sell such tickets at railway stations.

Restricted Areas

Visitors to China should be aware that Chinese regulations strictly prohibit travel in "closed" areas without special permission. However, over 1,200 cities and areas in China are open to visitors without special travel permits, including most major scenic and historical sites. If you need to know if an area is open to travel without a permit, seek advice from the nearest Chinese embassy or consulate, or, if you are already in China, from the U.S. Embassy in Beijing, the nearest U.S.

consulate, or the local Chinese public security bureau. (See addresses at the end of the document.)

Travel to Tibet

Americans visiting Tibet, whether individually or in tour groups, must obtain permission in advance from the Tibet Travel Bureau. U.S. should be aware that all areas of the region are closed to foreign traveler except for Lhasa, Shigatze (Xigaze), Naqu, Zedong, Zhang Muxkhasa, and the main roads between these points. Special permission to visit any of the closed areas must be obtained from the regions public security bureau. Travel arrangements booked through Chinese travel agencies will include necessary advance approvals. Occasionally, visitors have been refused admission or had difficulty entering Tibet from Nepal. In addition, the Kathmandu/Lhasa Highway that connects Nepal and Tibet can be washed out in the monsoon season, from June through September. Avoid this road during the monsoon. You should also be aware that foreign travelers have been the victims of robberies on this road.

Virtually all of the Tibetan autonomous region, much of Qinghai and Xinjiang, and parts of Sichuan, Yunnan, and Gansu are above 13,000 feet (4,000 meters) in altitude. Some main roads in Tibet, Qinghai, and Xinjiang go above 17,000 feet (5,200 meters), where available oxygen is only half of that at sea level. Conditions in Tibet are primitive, and travel there can be particularly arduous. Medical facilities are practically nonexistent. Many otherwise healthy visitors to the high altitude areas may suffer severe headaches, nausea, dizziness, shortness of breath, or a dry cough. These symptoms usually disappear after a few days of acclimatization. However, if symptoms persist, sufferers should descend to a lower altitude, or seek medical assistance as soon as possible. Visitors with respiratory or cardiac problems should avoid such high altitudes. Consult a physician before making the trip.

Travel on the Trans-Siberian Express

If you wish to take the Trans-Siberian railway from Beijing to Europe, you must obtain visas for Mongolia, Russia and other countries en route. Plan ahead. The Mongolian Consulate in Beijing is only open a few hours per week.

Chinese Embassy and Consulates in the United States
www.china-embassy.org

Embassy of the People's Republic of China
2300 Connecticut Avenue, NW
Washington, D.C. 20008
(202) 328-2517

Visa Section of the Embassy of the People's Republic of China
2201 Wisconsin Avenue, NW
Washington, D.C. 20007
(202) 338-6688)

Chinese Consulate General
100 West Erie Street
Chicago, Illinois 60610
(312) 803-0095

Chinese Consulate General
3400 Montrose Boulevard
Houston, Texas 77006
(713) 524-4311

Chinese Consulate General
443 Shatto Place, Suite 300
Los Angeles, California 90020
(213) 807-8006

Chinese Consulate General
520 12th Avenue
New York, New York 10036
(212) 868-2078

Chinese Consulate General
1450 Laguna Street
San Francisco, California 94115
(415) 674-2940

U.S. Embassy and Consulates in China
www.usembassy-china.org.cn

U.S. Embassy in China
2 Xiu Shui Dong Jie
Beijing 100600
Tel: (86-10) 6532-3431, 6532-3831
After-hours: (86-10) 6532-1910
Fax (86-10) 6532-4153, 6532-3178
The Embassy consular district includes the following provinces/regions of China: Beijing, Tianjin, Shandong, Shanxi, Inner Mongolia, Ningxia, Shaanxi, Qinghai, Xinjiang,

Hebei, Henan, Hubei, Hunan, and Jiangxi.

U.S. Consulate General
Number 4 Lingshiguan Road
Section 4, Renmin Nanlu,
Chengdu 610041
Tel: (86-28) 558-3992, 555-3119
After-hours (86-0) 13708001422.
Fax (86-28) 558-3520
This consular district includes the following provinces/regions of China: Guizhou, Sichuan, Xizang (Tibet), and Yunnan, as well as the municipality of Chongqing.

U.S. Consulate General
Number 1 South Shamian Street
Shamian Island 200S1
Guangzhou 510133
Tel: (86-20) 8121-8000 or (86-20) 8121-8418
After-hours: (86-0) 13902203169
Fax: (86-20) 8121-8428
This consular district includes the following provinces/regions of China: Guangdong, Guangxi, Hainan, and Fujian.

U.S. Consulate General
1469 Huaihai Zhonglu
Shanghai 200031
telephone: (86-21) 6433-6880
after-hours: (86-21) 6433-3936
fax: (86-21) 6433-4122, 6471-1148
This consular district includes the following provinces/regions of China: Shanghai, Anhui, Jiangsu, and Zhejiang.

U.S. Consulate General
No. 52, 14th Wei Road
Heping District
Shenyang 110003
telephone: (86-24) 2322-1198, 2322-0368
after-hours: (86-0) 13704019790
fax (86-24) 2322-2374
This consular district includes the following provinces/regions of China: Liaoning, Heilongjiang, and Jilin.

U.S. Consulate in Hong Kong
http://hongkong.usconsulate.gov

U.S. Consulate General Hong Kong
26 Garden Road
Central
Hong Kong

telephone: (852) 2523-9011
after-hours: (852) 2523-9011: follow prompts
fax: (852) 2845-4845
Email: acshnk@netvigator.com
This consular district includes Hong Kong and
Macau.

Planning Another Trip?

See Chapter 36 for a listing of resources available
to the general traveler from the U.S. Departments
of State, Customs, Transportation, Health and
various government and non-government
organizations. Almost all of the available
International travel-related pamphlets, brochures
and publications issued by the U.S. Department of
State and by the U.S. Customs have been
reproduced in full in this book. See Table of
Contents for location.

Chapter 17

Tips for Travelers to Eastern Europe

[The information in this chapter is excepted from a bulletin issued by the U.S. State Department, Bureau of Consular Affairs. It is intended to serve as advice to Americans traveling abroad.]

Albania, Bulgaria, Croatia, Czech Republic, Hungary, Poland, Serbia and Montenegro, Slovak Republic, Slovenia, Romania. Eastern Europe also includes the western part of the former Soviet Union. For travel information on the former Soviet Union, see Tips for Travelers to RUSSIA[1].

Conditions in Eastern European countries are unlike those in Western European countries. Americans traveling to any of the countries of former Eastern Block need to take the utmost precaution, particularly, during this period. Most of the countries, although moderately developed, are undergoing profound economic and political changes. Tourist facilities are not highly developed and many of the goods and services taken for granted in Western European countries are not yet available.

With the easing of entry and exit requirements, the opportunity to travel to Eastern Europe has gained popularity with U.S. citizens. In visiting the countries in Eastern Europe, you will see many of the changes that have taken place since the crumbling of the Berlin Wall.

This is a truly exciting time in history to visit Eastern Europe. Nevertheless, there are a few cautionary measures you can take to ensure a pleasant and rewarding stay. The Department of State's Bureau of Consular Affairs has prepared the informationcontained in this chapter to acquaint you with the services we provide to Americans traveling or residing in Eastern Europe.

Any additional guidance not covered here may be obtained from the Bureau of Consular Affairs in the Department of State or from the nearest U.S. embassy or consulate in Eastern Europe at one of the addresses listed in **Appendix A**.

The countries of Eastern Europe are rich in history with civilizations and traditions dating back to the beginning of recorded European history. These countries are in a period of transition, and their rules for visitors are changing. Before you go, contact the embassy of each country you plan to visit for the latest information on visa requirements, customs and currency regulations.

Although tourist facilities are expanding to meet the rapid increase in tourism to Eastern Europe, in most of the region they are quite limited. In many places, you will have to be patient with scarce or inadequate hotels, rental cars, and other facilities. To be certain of accommodations, make reservations for hotels and transportation, and make them well in advance. If you cannot get a hotel reservation, check with the country's tourist office, because many cities have a bureau that arranges accommodations in small hotels or private homes.

The Department of State issues travel advisories concerning serious health or security conditions that may affect U.S. citizens. Travel advisories are available in the 13 regional passport agencies, or by calling or writing the Citizens Emergency Center,

Entry Requirements

U.S. citizens should travel to Eastern Europe with a valid U.S. passport and with appropriate visas when necessary. Visa regulations change, so check with each embassy's consular section for current information.

Remember to leave a detailed itinerary and your passport information with a friend or relative in the United States in case of an emergency. If you are a national of both the United States and an Eastern European country, also see the section on dual

207

nationality in the Table of Contents before you travel to Eastern Europe.

Albania

COUNTRY DESCRIPTION: Since the 1991-1992 period of political upheaval and the serious civil disturbances in 1997, Albania has been in a period of economic transition and steady recovery. Albania ranks among the countries with the lowest per capital income in Europe. The security situation throughout Albania remains somewhat unstable. Tourist facilities are not highly developed, and though EU market integration is slowly underway, many of the goods and services taken for granted in other European countries are not yet available. Hotel accommodations are limited outside of major cities. The capital is Tirana.

ENTRY REQUIREMENTS: A passport is required. An entry card will be issued at the point of entry for $10.00 (U.S.) that is valid for a stay up to 30 days. An extension up to 180 days may be obtained by applying at the local police station. For stays exceeding 180 days, The Ministry of Interior accepts extension requests. There is also a departure fee of $10.00 (U.S.), payable in U.S. dollars or local currency (lek).

For additional information, please contact the Embassy of the Republic of Albania at 2100 S Street, N.W., Washington, D.C. 20008, tel. (202) 223-4942; Fax (202 628-7324. Albania also maintains Honorary Consuls in Louisiana at 701 Poydras St. Suite 4200, New Orleans, LA 70139 (504)596-4229; in Massachusetts at 140 Northern Ave., Boston, MA 02210 (617)482-6262; and Texas at 20682 Sweetglen Dr., Houston, TX 77365-6385 (281)345-9599.

In an effort to prevent international child abduction, many governments have initiated procedures at entry/exit points. These often include requiring documentary evidence of relationship and permission for the child's travel from the parent(s) or legal guardian not present. Having such documentation on hand, even if not required, may facilitate entry/departure.

DUAL NATIONALITY: In addition to being subject to all Albanian laws affecting U.S. citizens, dual nationals may be subject to Albanian laws that impose special obligations. The Albanian government considers any person born in Albania of Albanian parents to be an Albanian citizen. Male Albanian citizens are subject to the compulsory military draft regulations. If such persons are found guilty of draft evasion in Albania, they are subject to prosecution by the Albanian court. Those who might be affected should inquire at an Albanian embassy or consulate outside Albania regarding their status before traveling. In some instances, dual nationality may hamper U.S. Government efforts to provide protection abroad. For additional information on dual citizenship, please see the Consular Affairs home page on the Internet at http://travel.state.gov for our Dual Nationality flyer. A useful Albanian government website in English is at http://www.mfa.al.

SAFETY AND SECURITY: Organized criminal gangs are endemic to all regions, and corruption is pervasive. The U.S. Government maintains security procedures regarding the travel of U.S. Government employees to areas north (north and east of Shkoder) of Mamuras (with the exception of cities along the national road) and to the southern town of Lazarat, with such travel restricted to secure vehicles with escort. In most cases, traditional police assistance and protection is minimal. A high level of security awareness should be maintained at all times. Taking photographs of anything that could be perceived as being of military or security interest may result in problems with authorities. All gatherings of large crowds should be avoided, particularly those involving political causes or striking workers.

CRIME: Albania has a high crime rate outside Tirana with instances of armed robberies, assaults, and bombings. Carjackings are a matter of considerable concern, especially for drivers of four-wheel drive and sport-utility vehicles. Anyone who is carjacked should surrender the vehicle without resistance. Armed crime is common in Shkoder and frequent in other towns further up north and throughout northwestern Albania. Throughout the country, street crime is fairly common, and it occurs particularly at night. Criminals do not deliberately target U.S. citizens, but criminals seek targets of opportunity selecting those who appear to have anything of value. Pick-pocketing is widespread; U.S. citizens have reported the theft of their passports by pickpockets.

The loss or theft abroad of a U.S. passport should be reported immediately to the local police and the nearest U.S. embassy or consulate. If you are the victim of a crime while overseas, in addition to reporting to local police, please contact the nearest U.S. embassy or consulate for assistance. The embassy/consulate staff can, for example, assist you to find appropriate medical care, to contact family members or friends, and explain how funds could be transferred. Although the investigation and prosecution of the crime is solely the responsibility of local authorities, consular officers can help you to understand the local criminal justice process and to find an attorney if needed.

U.S. citizens may refer to the Department of State's pamphlet, *A Safe Trip Abroad,* for ways to promote a more trouble-free journey. The pamphlet is available by mail from the Superintendent of Documents, U.S. Government Printing Office, Washington, D.C. 20402, via the Internet at http://www.access.gpo.gov/su_docs, or via the Bureau of Consular Affairs home page at http://www. travel.state.gov.

If you are the victim of a crime while overseas, in addition to reporting to local police, please contact the nearest U.S. embassy or consulate for assistance. The embassy/consulate staff can, for example, assist you to find appropriate medical care, to contact family members or friends, and explain how funds could be transferred. Although the investigation and prosecution of the crime is solely the responsibility of local authorities, consular officers can help you to understand the local criminal justice process and to find an attorney if needed.

MEDICAL FACILITIES: Medical facilities and capabilities are limited beyond rudimentary first aid treatment. Emergency and major medical care requiring surgery and hospital care is inadequate due to lack of specialists, diagnostic aids, medical supplies, and prescription drugs. Travelers with previously diagnosed medical conditions may wish to consult their physician before travel. As prescription drugs may be unavailable locally, travelers may also wish to bring extra supplies of required medications.

MEDICAL INSURANCE: The Department of State strongly urges Americans to consult with their medical insurance company prior to traveling abroad to confirm whether their policy applies overseas and if it will cover emergency expenses such as a medical evacuation. U.S. medical insurance plans seldom cover health costs incurred outside the United States unless supplemental coverage is purchased. Further, U.S. Medicare and Medicaid programs do not provide payment for medical services outside the United States. However, many travel agents and private companies offer insurance plans that will cover health care expenses incurred overseas, including emergency services such as medical evacuations.

When making a decision regarding health insurance, Americans should consider that U.S medical insurance is not always valid outside the United States. Moreover, many foreign doctors and hospitals require payment in cash prior to providing service and that a medical evacuation to the United States may cost well in excess of $50,000. Uninsured travelers who require medical care overseas often face extreme difficulties. When consulting with your insurer prior to your trip, please ascertain whether payment will be made to the overseas healthcare provider or if you will be reimbursed later for expenses that you incur. Some insurance policies also include coverage for psychiatric treatment and for disposition of remains in the event of death.

Useful information on medical emergencies abroad, including overseas insurance programs, is provided in the Department of State's Bureau of Consular Affairs brochure, *Medical Information for Americans Traveling Abroad,* available via the Bureau of Consular Affairs home page or autofax: (202) 647-3000.

OTHER HEALTH INFORMATION: Information on vaccinations and other health precautions may be obtained from the Centers for Disease Control and Prevention's hotline for international traveler's at 1-877-FYI-TRIP (1-877-394-8747); fax 1-888-CDC-FAXX (1-888-232-3299), or via the CDC's Internet site at http://www.cdc.gov.

TRAFFIC SAFETY AND ROAD CONDITIONS: While in a foreign country, U.S. citizens may encounter road conditions that differ significantly from those in the United States. The information below concerning Albania is provided for general reference only, and it may not be totally accurate in a particular location or circumstance.

Safety of Public Transportation: Poor
Urban Road Condition/Maintenance: Poor
Rural Road Condition/Maintenance: Poor
Availability of Roadside Assistance: None

Major roads in Albania are often in very poor repair. Travel at night outside the main urban areas is particularly dangerous and should be avoided due to deplorable road conditions. During the winter months, travelers may encounter dangerous snow and ice conditions on the roads through the mountains in Northern Albania. Buses travel between most major cities almost exclusively during the day, but they may be unreliable and uncomfortable. Many travelers looking for public transport prefer to use privately owned vans, which function as an alternate system of bus routes and operate almost wholly without schedules or set fares. Please note that many of these privately owned vans may not have official permission to operate a bus service and may not adhere to accepted safety and maintenance standards. Persons wishing to use privately owned vans should exercise caution. There are no commercial domestic flights and few rail connections.

For additional general information about road safety, including links to foreign government sites, please see the Department of State, Bureau of Consular Affairs home page at http://travel.state.gov/road_safety.html. For specific information concerning Albania driving permits, vehicle inspection, road tax and mandatory insurance, please contact the Albanian National Tourist Organization offices in New York via the Internet at: albaniatourism@e-mail.com. Please see also road safety information from other sources in Albania.

AVIATION SAFETY OVERSIGHT: As there is no direct commercial air service by local carriers at present, nor economic authority to operate such service between the United States and Albania, the U.S. Federal Aviation Administration (FAA) has not assessed Albania's Civil Aviation Authority for compliance with international aviation safety standards. For further information, travelers may

contact the Department of Transportation within the United States at tel. 1-800-322-7873, or visit the FAA's Internet website at http://www.faa.gov/avr/iasa.

The U.S. Department of Defense (DOD) separately assesses some foreign air carriers for suitability as official providers of air services. For information regarding the DOD policy on specific carriers, travelers may contact the DOD at tel. (618) 229-4801.

CUSTOMS REGULATIONS: Albania's customs authorities may enforce strict regulations concerning temporary importation into or export from Albania of some items. It is advisable to contact the Embassy of Albania in Washington, D.C. or one of Albania's consulates in the United States for specific information regarding customs requirements.

CRIMINAL PENALTIES: While in a foreign country, a U.S. citizen is subject to that country's laws and regulations, which sometimes differ significantly from those in the United States and may not afford the protections available to the individual under U.S. law. Penalties for breaking the law can be more severe than in the United States for similar offenses. Persons violating Albania's laws, even unknowingly, may be expelled, arrested or imprisoned. Penalties for possession, use or trafficking of illegal drugs in Albania are strict, and convicted offenders can expect jail sentences and heavy fines.

U.S. citizens are encouraged to carry a copy of their U.S. passports with them at all times, so that, if questioned by local officials, proof of identity and U.S. citizenship are readily available.

SPECIAL CIRCUMSTANCES: Albania is a cash economy. Credit cards and travelers checks are not generally accepted, except at the major new hotels in Tirana and some international airline offices. Travelers' checks can be changed at banks in larger towns.

CHILDREN'S ISSUES: For information on international adoption of children and international parental child abduction, please refer to our Internet site at http://travel.state.gov/children's_issues.html, or telephone (202) 736-7000.

REGISTRATION/EMBASSY LOCATION: Americans living in or visiting Albania are urged to register at the Consular Section of the U.S. Embassy and obtain updated information on travel and security within Albania. The U.S. Embassy in Tirana is located at Rruga E Elbasanit 103, tel. (355)(42) 32875, fax (355)(42) 74957. The U.S. Embassy website is: http://www.usemb-tirana.usia.co.at.

Bulgaria

COUNTRY DESCRIPTION: Bulgaria is a moderately developed European nation undergoing significant economic changes. Tourist facilities are widely available although conditions vary, and some facilities may not be up to Western standards. Goods and services taken for granted in other European countries are still not available in many areas of Bulgaria.

ENTRY REQUIREMENTS: A passport is required. U.S. citizen visitors who enter the country on regular passports without a Bulgarian visa are authorized to stay for a total of 30 days within a six-month period. Travelers who intend to stay more than 30 days, or travelers using official or diplomatic passports, must secure a Bulgarian visa from a Bulgarian embassy/consulate prior to arrival. American citizens who intend to stay and live or work in Bulgaria must obtain a special 30-day visa prior to arrival. Once in Bulgaria, this visa facilitates application for a residence permit. Travelers who have a one-year multiple-entry visa for Bulgaria may stay for a total of 90 days within a six- month period. If a traveler comes to Bulgaria on a one-year multiple-entry visa, stays in the country 90 days and then leaves, he/she will not be able to enter the country within the next 90 days.

All travelers are required to register with the regional passport office for foreigners or the police within 48 hours after their arrival in the country and to inform the office about any change in their address. For those staying at a hotel, a private boarding house or an apartment rented through an accommodation company, registration is taken care of by the proprietor. The Bulgarian authorities do not consider presentation of a copy of the passport sufficient for identification purposes. Visitors should carry their passport with them at all times. For further information concerning entry requirements, travelers should contact the Embassy of the Republic of Bulgaria at 1621 22nd St. N.W., Washington, D.C. 20008; Internet http://www.bulgaria-embassy.org, tel. (202) 483-5885 (main switchboard (202) 387-7969) or the Bulgarian Consulate in New York City.

In an effort to prevent international child abduction, many governments have initiated procedures at entry/exit points. These often include requiring documentary evidence of parental relationship and permission for the child's travel from the parent(s) or legal guardian not present. Having such documentation on hand, even if not required, may facilitate entry/exit.

CRIME INFORMATION: Petty street crime, much of which is directed against foreigners or others who appear to have money, continues to be a problem. Pick-pocketing and purse snatching are frequent occurrences, especially in crowded markets and on shopping streets. Con artists operate on public transportation and in bus and train stations. Travelers should be suspicious of "instant friends" and should also require persons claiming to be government officials to show identification. There have been numerous incidents in which tourists have accepted offers of coffee or alcoholic beverages from "friendly people" met by chance at the airport, bus stations, hotels or train stations and have been drugged or assaulted and robbed. Travelers should be wary of unfamiliar individuals who encourage them to drink or eat products that may be tainted with strong tranquilizers (such as valium) that can lead rapidly to unconsciousness.

Taxi drivers at Sofia Airport often overcharge unwary travelers. Travelers who pre-negotiate a fare may avoid excessive payment. Taximeters are frequently rigged to accrue charges faster than normal. Because incidents of pilferage of checked baggage at Sofia Airport are common, travelers should not include items of value in checked luggage. Automobile theft is also a frequent problem, with four-wheel drive vehicles and late model European sedans the most popular targets. Very few vehicles are recovered. Thieves also sometimes smash vehicle windows to steal valuables left in sight. Break-ins at residential apartments occur frequently. Persons who plan to reside in Bulgaria on a long-term basis should take

211

measures to protect their dwellings. Long term residents should consider installation of window grills, steel doors with well-functioning locks, and an alarm system that alerts an armed response team. Potential travelers should also be cautious about making credit card charges over the Internet as recent experience has shown that some offers come from scam artists posing as legitimate businesses. Travelers should also be careful about making credit card payments to Bulgarian tour operators over the Internet before coming to Bulgaria, because some entities listed there do not actually exist.

The loss or theft abroad of a U.S. passport should be reported immediately to the local police and the nearest U.S. embassy or consulate. If you are the victim of a crime while overseas, in addition to reporting to local police, please contact the nearest U.S. embassy or consulate for assistance. The Embassy/Consulate staff can, for example, assist you to find appropriate medical care, to contact family members or friends and explain how funds could be transferred. Although the investigation and prosecution of the crime is solely the responsibility of local authorities, consular officers can help you to understand the local criminal justice process and to find an attorney if needed.

MEDICAL FACILITIES: Although Bulgarian physicians are trained to a very high standard, most hospitals and clinics are generally not equipped and maintained at U.S. or Western European levels. Basic medical supplies are widely available, but specialized treatment may not be obtainable. Serious medical problems requiring hospitalization and/or medical evacuation to the United States can cost thousands of dollars or more. Doctors and hospitals often expect immediate cash payment for health services.

MEDICAL INSURANCE: As of December 1, 2001, all foreign citizens traveling to Bulgaria must present valid evidence of health insurance to the Bulgarian border authorities in order to be admitted into the country. The insurance should be valid for the duration of the traveler's stay in Bulgaria. The Department of State strongly urges Americans to consult with their medical insurance company prior to traveling abroad to confirm whether their policy applies overseas and if it will cover emergency expenses such as a medical evacuation. U.S. medical insurance plans seldom cover health costs incurred outside the United States unless supplemental coverage is purchased. Further, U.S. Medicare and Medicaid programs do not provide payment for medical services outside the United States. However, many travel agents and private companies offer insurance plans that will cover health care expenses incurred overseas, including emergency services such as medical evacuations.

When making a decision regarding health insurance, Americans should consider that many foreign doctors and hospitals require payment in cash prior to providing service and that a medical evacuation to the United States may cost more than $50,000. Uninsured travelers who require medical care overseas often face extreme difficulties, whereas travelers who have purchased overseas medical insurance have found it to be life-saving when a medical emergency has occurred. When consulting with your insurer prior to your trip, please ascertain whether payment will be made to the overseas healthcare provider or if you will be reimbursed later for expenses that you incur. Some insurance policies also include coverage for psychiatric treatment and for disposition of remains in the event of death. Useful information on medical emergencies abroad, including overseas insurance programs, is provided in the Department of State's Bureau of Consular Affairs brochure, *Medical Information for Americans Traveling Abroad*, available via the Bureau of Consular Affairs home page or autofax: (202) 647-3000.

OTHER HEALTH INFORMATION: Information on vaccinations and other health precautions may be obtained from the Centers for Disease Control and Prevention's hotline for international travelers at 1-877-FYI-TRIP (1-877-394-8747); fax 1-888-CDC-FAXX (1-888-232-3299), or via their Internet site at http://www.cdc.gov.

TRAFFIC SAFETY AND ROAD CONDITIONS: While in a foreign country, U.S. citizens may encounter road conditions which differ significantly from those in the United States. The information below concerning Bulgaria is provided for general reference only, and it may not be totally accurate in a particular location or circumstance.

Safety of Public
Transportation: Good
Urban Road
Conditions/Maintenance:
Fair
Rural Road
Conditions/Maintenance:
Poor
Availability of Roadside
Assistance: Fair

The Bulgarian road system is underdeveloped. There are few sections of limited-access divided highway. Some roads are in poor repair and full of potholes. Rockslides and landslides may be encountered on roads in mountainous areas. Livestock and animal-drawn carts present road hazards throughout the country, especially during the agricultural season. Travel conditions deteriorate during the winter as roads become icy and potholes proliferate. The U.S. Embassy in Sofia advises against night driving because road conditions are more dangerous in the dark. Some roads lack pavement markings and lights, and motorists often drive with dim or missing headlights.

The number of serious accidents and the death toll from them over the last few years has remained high. In 1999, there were 7,586 serious accidents which resulted in 1,047 deaths. In 2000, there were 6,886 accidents, in which 1,012 people were killed. In 2001, there were 6,709 serious road accidents with 1,011 fatalities.

Heavy truck traffic along the two-lane routes from the Greek border at Kulata to Sofia and from the Turkish border at Kapitan Andreevo to Plovdiv creates numerous hazards. Motorists should expect long delays at border crossings. A U.S. state driver's license is valid in Bulgaria only when used in conjunction with an International Driving Permit. For information on how to obtain a permit, please see

http://travel.state.gov/road_safety.html#permits.
Persons operating vehicles with foreign license plates frequently complain of being stopped by police and being fined on the spot for offenses that they have not committed.
Buses, trams, and trolleys are inexpensive, but they are often crowded and of widely varying quality. Passengers on the busiest lines have

reported pick-pocketing, purse-slashing, and pinching.

The use of seat belts is mandatory in Bulgaria. Child car seats are required by law, but only on the back seats. Speed limits are 50 KM/H in the cities/towns, 90 KM/H out of town and 120 KM/H on the highways. The same speed limits apply for motorcycles; motorcyclists must drive with helmets and with lights on at all times. At crossings that are not regulated, the driver who is on the right has the right-of-way, but this rule is frequently ignored. Drivers may be charged with driving under the influence of alcohol with a blood level as low as 0.05%. Right turns on red lights are not permitted unless specifically authorized. The penalties for drivers involved in an accident resulting in injury or death range from a $25 (US) fine up to imprisonment for life.

The most generally encountered local traffic custom is a driver flashing high beams, which usually means that a traffic police post is ahead. Motorists should avoid confrontations with aggressive drivers in Bulgaria. Drivers of late-model sedans (BMW, Mercedes, Audi) are known to speed and drive dangerously. Motorists should exercise caution and not engage in altercations with the drivers of such vehicles because some are armed organized crime figures.

In case of emergency, drivers should contact the police at telephone number 166 and/or the Roadside Assistance at telephone number 146. For an ambulance, please call 150.

For additional general information about road safety, including links to foreign government sites, please see the Department of State, Bureau of Consular Affairs home page at http://travel.state.gov/road_safety.html. For specific information concerning Bulgarian driving permits, vehicle inspection, road tax and mandatory insurance, please contact the Bulgarian Embassy via the Internet at http://www.bulgaria-embassy.org.

AVIATION SAFETY OVERSIGHT: The U.S. Federal Aviation Administration (FAA) has assessed the Government of Bulgaria's Civil Aviation Authority as Category One -- in compliance with the international aviation safety standards for the oversight of Bulgarian air carrier operations.

For further information, travelers may contact the Department of Transportation at tel. 1 (800) 322-7873, or visit the FAA Internet home page at http://www.faa.gov/avr/iasa/. The U.S. Department of Defense (DOD) separately assesses some foreign air carriers for suitability as official providers of air services. For information regarding the DOD policy on specific carriers, travelers may contact the DOD at tel. (618) 229-4801.

CUSTOMS REGULATIONS: Travelers should declare jewelry, cameras, computers, and other valuables upon arrival in order to avoid difficulties when departing. Travelers entering Bulgaria with more than 5,000 Bulgarian Leva or the equivalent (around USD 2,500) in either foreign currency or travelers checks must declare the money and/or checks to Customs officials upon arrival. Travelers entering Bulgaria with any amount of cut or uncut gems, unworked gold or unworked silver must also declare these valuables. Americans intending to declare money or valuables who enter Bulgaria through Sofia Airport are strongly encouraged to use the red "Something to Declare" line and not the green "Nothing to Declare" line at Customs, even if specifically invited into the green line by a Customs official. The Bulgarian government considers entry through the green line to be a formal, irrevocable declaration that the traveler is carrying less than 5,000 Leva, and Customs authorities have sometimes confiscated travelers' entire funds if they are carrying undeclared cash in excess of that amount.

Travelers who have with them the equivalent of 20,000 Bulgarian Leva or more upon departure must have a permit to export the money issued by the Bulgarian National Bank's Headquarters, if they had less than the equivalent of 20,000 Bulgarian Leva upon entry in the country. Please contact the Embassy of Bulgaria in Washington, D.C. or one of Bulgaria's consulates in the United States for specific information regarding customs regulations.

Bulgaria's customs authorities encourage the use of an ATA (Admission Temporaire/Temporary Admission) Carnet for the temporary admission of professional equipment, commercial samples, and/or goods for exhibitions and fair purposes. ATA Carnet Headquarters, located at the U.S. Council for International Business, 1212 Avenue of the Americas, New York, NY 10036, issues and guarantees the ATA Carnet in the United States. For additional information, please call (212) 354-4480, or send an e-mail to atacarnet@uscib.org, or visit http://www.uscib.org for details.

CRIMINAL PENALTIES: While in a foreign country, a U.S. citizen is subject to that country's laws and regulations, which sometimes differ significantly from those in the United States and may not afford the protections available to the individual under U.S. law. Penalties for breaking the law can be more severe than in the United States for similar offenses. Persons violating Bulgarian law, even unknowingly, may be expelled, arrested or imprisoned. Penalties for possession, use, or trafficking in illegal drugs in Bulgaria are strict, and convicted offenders can expect jail sentences and heavy fines. Foreigners charged with a crime may be denied permission to depart Bulgaria. Criminal cases have been known to take years to resolve, regardless of outcome.

SPECIAL CIRCUMSTANCES: Bulgaria is still largely a cash economy. Visitors should exchange cash at banks or Change Bureaus, but they should know that Change Bureaus sometimes post misleading rate quotations that confuse travelers. People on the street who offer high rates of exchange are usually con artists intent on swindling the unwary traveler. Damaged or very worn U.S dollar bank notes are often not accepted at banks or Change Bureaus. Major branches of the following Bulgarian banks will cash travelers' checks on the spot for Leva, the Bulgarian currency, or another desired currency: Bulbank, Bulgarian Postbank, Biochim, First Investment Bank, and United Bulgarian Bank (UBB). UBB also serves as a Western Union agent and provides direct transfer of money to travelers in need. ATM cash machines are increasing in numbers in Sofia and other major cities. Most shops, hotels and restaurants, with the exception of the major hotels, still do not accept travelers' checks or credit cards. Due to the potential of fraud and other criminal activity, credit cards and ATM's should be used with caution.

CHILDREN'S ISSUES: For information on international adoption of children and international parental child abduction, please refer to our Internet site at http://travel.state.gov/children's_issues.html or telephone (202) 736-7000.

For information on international adoptions in Bulgaria, please contact the Department of State's Office of Children's Issues, the Consular Section of the Embassy, or the U.S. Embassy web site at http://www.usembassy.bg.

REGISTRATION/EMBASSY AND CONSULATE LOCATION: Americans living in or visiting Bulgaria are encouraged to register at the Consular Section of the U.S. Embassy in Bulgaria and obtain updated information on travel and security within Bulgaria. The U.S. Embassy is located in Sofia at 1 Suborna (formerly 1 A. Stamboliyski Boulevard); tel. (359) (2) 937-5100; fax: (359) (2) 981-8977. The Consular Section of the Embassy is located at 1 Kapitan Andreev Street in Sofia; tel. (359) (2) 963-2022; fax (359) (2) 963-2859. The Embassy's web site address is http://www.usembassy.bg. Questions regarding consular services may be directed via e-mail to: niv@usconsulate.bg, iv@usconsulate.bg and acs@usconsulate.bg.

Croatia

Country Description: Croatia is a moderately developed nation in transition to a market economy. Facilities for tourism are available throughout the country, and the Adriatic coast is an increasingly popular tourist destination.

Entry Requirements: A passport is required for travel to Croatia. A visa is not required for U.S. passport holders for tourist or business trips of less than 90 days. Visas are required for all other types of stays and must be obtained prior to arrival in the country. Unless the traveler is staying at a hotel, all foreign citizens must register with the local police within 48 hours of arrival. Failure to register is a misdemeanor offense; some Americans have been fined and/or expelled as a result of their failure to register. Additional information on entry requirements may be obtained from the Embassy of Croatia at 2343 Massachusetts Ave., N.W., Washington, D.C.

20008, tel. (202) 588-5899 or from the Croatian Consulates in New York City, Cleveland, Chicago and Los Angeles. Overseas, inquiries may be made at the nearest Croatian embassy or consulate. The Internet home page of the Croatian embassy in Washington is http://www.croatiaemb.org.

Dual Nationality: In addition to being subject to all laws affecting U.S. citizens, dual nationals may be subject to other laws that impose special obligations on Croatian citizens. The government of Croatia does not recognize the U.S. citizenship of persons who are citizens of both Croatia and the United States. This may hinder the ability of a U.S. Consular officer to assist U.S. citizens who do not enter Croatia on a U.S. passport. Dual nationals may also be subject to national obligations, such as taxes and military service. Travelers should contact a Croatian embassy or consulate for further information. For additional information, see the Bureau of Consular Affairs home page on the Internet at http://travel.state.gov for our *dual nationality flyer*.

Safety and Security: Although fighting in all parts of the country ended in 1995, the conflict over Croatia's independence led to the laying of land mines on Croatian territory, mostly along the former confrontation lines. De-mining is not complete; marking of mined areas is similarly incomplete. Travelers in former conflict areas, including the Danube region (eastern Slavonia) and the former Krajina, should exercise caution and not stray from known safe roads and areas. Mine clearance work often leads to the closure of major roads, including roads to the coast.

There are occasional attacks targeted at specific persons or property as a result of organized criminal activity or actions prompted by ethnic tensions residual from Croatia's war for independence.

Crime Information: Croatia has a relatively low crime rate, and violent crime is rare. Foreigners do not appear to be singled out; however, as in many countries, displays of wealth increase chances of becoming the victim of a pickpocket or mugger. Such crimes are more likely to occur in bus or railroad stations.

The loss or theft of a U.S. passport should be reported immediately to the local police and the nearest U.S. Embassy or Consulate. U.S. citizens may refer to the Department of State's pamphlet, *A Safe Trip Abroad*, for ways to promote a more trouble-free journey. It is available from the Superintendent of Documents, U.S. Government Printing Office, Washington, D.C. 20402, via the Internet at http://www.access.gpo.gov/su_docs, or via the Bureau of Consular Affairs home page at http://travel.state.gov.

Medical Facilities: Health facilities in Croatia, although generally of Western caliber, are under severe budgetary strains. Some medicines are in short supply in public hospitals and clinics. The number of private medical and dental practitioners is substantial, and private pharmacies stock a variety of medicines not readily available through public health facilities. Croatian health care facilities, doctors and hospitals may expect immediate cash payment for health services.

Medical Insurance: The Department of State strongly urges Americans to consult with their medical insurance company prior to traveling abroad to confirm whether their policy applies overseas and whether it will cover emergency expenses such as a medical evacuation. U.S. medical insurance plans seldom cover health costs incurred outside the United States unless supplemental coverage is purchased. Further, U.S. Medicare and Medicaid programs do not provide payment for medical services outside the United States. However, many travel agents and private companies offer insurance plans that will cover health care expenses incurred overseas including emergency services such as medical evacuations.

When making a decision regarding health insurance, Americans should consider that many foreign doctors and hospitals require payment in cash prior to providing service and that a medical evacuation to the U.S. may cost well in excess of $50,000. Uninsured travelers who require medical care overseas often face extreme difficulties. When consulting with your insurer prior to your trip, ascertain whether payment will be made to the overseas healthcare provider or whether you will be reimbursed later for expenses you incur. Some insurance policies also include coverage for psychiatric treatment and for disposition of remains in the event of death.
Useful information on medical emergencies abroad, including overseas insurance programs, is provided in the Department of State's Bureau of Consular Affairs brochure, *Medical Information for Americans Traveling Abroad*, available via the Bureau of Consular Affairs home page or autofax: (202) 647-3000.

Other Health Information: Information on vaccinations and other health precautions may be obtained from the Centers for Disease Control and Prevention's hotline for international travelers at 1-877-fyi-trip (1-877-394-8747), fax 1-888-cdc-faxx (1-888-232-3299), or via CDC's Internet site at http://www.cdc.gov.

Traffic Safety and Road Conditions: While in a foreign country, U.S. citizens may encounter road conditions that differ significantly from those in the United States. The information below concerning Croatia is provided for general reference only, and it may not be totally accurate in a particular location or circumstance.

Safety of Public Transportation: good
Urban Road Conditions/Maintenance: good
Rural Road Conditions/Maintenance: fair
Availability of Roadside Assistance: fair

Since gaining independence in 1991, Croatia has seen an increase in the number of cars, leading to heavy congestion on major routes on weekends (towards the coast, for example) and in major cities during rush hour. Parking can be difficult and expensive in city centers, and drivers can be aggressive. In Zagreb, motorists and pedestrians alike must also pay special attention to trams (streetcars), which in downtown areas may travel at a high rate of speed through the narrow, congested streets. Primary roads are generally adequate, but most have only one lane in each direction, including roads going to and from the coast. Coastal roads are narrow and congested, and tend to be very slippery when wet. Right turns on red lights are strictly forbidden in Croatia, unless an additional green light (in the shape of an arrow) allows it. At unmarked intersections, right of way is always to the vehicle entering from the right. Front seat belts are obligatory and passengers in vehicles equipped with rear seat belts are required to use them.

The legal limit for blood alcohol content in Croatia is .05 percent. Police routinely spot-check motorists for drinking and driving and will administer breathalyzer tests at even the most minor accident. Drivers who refuse to submit to a breathalyzer are automatically presumed to have admitted to driving while intoxicated. In case of accidents resulting in death or serious injury, Croatian law obligates police to take blood samples to test blood alcohol levels. Drivers traveling through former conflict areas should stay on paved roads to reduce the risk of encountering mines and unexploded ordnance left over from the war.

Within Croatia, emergency road help and information may be reached by dialing 987, a service of the Croatian Automobile Association (HAK), staffed by English speaking operators. The police can be reached by dialing 92 and ambulance by dialing 94. Additional road condition and safety information may be obtained from HAK at tel. (385)(1) 455-4433, or via their web page, http://www.www.hak.hr.

For additional information about road safety, including links to foreign government sites, please see the Department of State, Bureau of Consular affairs home page at http://travel.state.gov/road_safety.html. For additional information on road conditions specific to Croatia, see the U.S. Embassy home page at http://www.usembassy.hr/consular/traffic.htm.
For specific information concerning Croatian driver's permits, vehicle inspection, road tax and mandatory insurance, please contact the Croatian National Tourist Office, 350 Fifth Avenue, Suite 4003, New York, NY 10118; phone 1-800-829-4416 or 212-278-8672; fax 212-279-8683.

Aviation Safety Oversight: As there is no direct commercial air service by local carriers between the United States and Croatia at present, nor economic authority to operate such service, the U.S. Federal Aviation Administration (FAA) has not assessed Croatia's Civil Aviation Authority for compliance with international aviation safety standards. For further information, travelers may contact the Department of Transportation within the U.S. at 1-800-322-7873, or visit the FAA Internet web site at http://www.faa.gov/avr/iasa.

The U.S. Department of Defense (DOD) separately assesses some foreign air carriers for suitability as official providers of air services. For information regarding the DOD policy on specific carriers, travelers may contact the DOD at tel. (618) 229-4801.

Customs Regulations: Croatian customs authorities encourage the use of an ATA (Admission Temporaire/Temporary Admission) carnet for the temporary admission of professional equipment, commercial samples, and/or goods for exhibitions and fair purposes. ATA Carnet Headquarters, located at the U.S. Council for International Business, 1212 Avenue of the Americas, New York. N.Y. 10036, issues and guarantees the ATA Carnet in the United States. For additional information, please call (212) 354-4480, or send e-mail to atacarnet@uscib.org, or visit http://www.uscib.org for details. It is advisable to contact the Embassy of Croatia in Washington or one of Croatia's consulates in the United States for specific information regarding customs requirements.

Criminal Penalties: While in a foreign country, U.S. citizens are subject to the laws and regulations of the country in which they travel. Such laws sometimes differ significantly from those in the United States and may not afford the protections available to the individual under U.S. law. Penalties for breaking the law can be more severe than in the United States for similar offenses. Persons violating Croatian laws, even unknowingly, may be expelled, arrested or imprisoned. Penalties for possession, use, or trafficking in illegal drugs in Croatia are strict, and convicted offenders can expect jail sentences and fines.

Special Circumstances: With the proliferation of automated teller machines and ever-wider acceptance of credit cards in Croatia, traveler's checks are accepted less and less frequently or exchanged at an unfavorable rate.

Children's Issues: For information on international adoption of children and international parental child abduction please refer to our Internet web site at http://travel.state.gov/children's_issues.html or telephone (202) 736-7000.

Registration and Embassy Location: U.S. citizens are encouraged to register at the U.S.

Embassy and obtain updated information on travel and security within Croatia. The U.S. Embassy in Zagreb is located at Andrije Hebranga 2, tel. (385)(1) 661-2300, Internet home page: http://www.usembassy.hr. On weekends, holidays, and after hours, an Embassy duty officer can be reached at tel. (385)(1) 661-2400 or (385)(91) 455-2247.

Czech Republic

COUNTRY DESCRIPTION: The Czech Republic is a rapidly developing European nation undergoing profound economic and social change. Tourist facilities, particularly those found in the capital, Prague, are quickly approaching the level of those found in most Western European countries. Outside Prague, these facilities are not as developed, and some goods and services taken for granted in other European countries may not yet be available.

ENTRY REQUIREMENTS: A valid passport is required, but a visa is not necessary for U.S. citizens for tourism, short study or business visits up to 90 days. Visas are required for longer stays and for any gainful activity; application can be made at any Czech embassy or consulate (outside the Czech Republic). For further information concerning entry requirements for the Czech Republic, travelers can contact the Embassy of the Czech Republic at 3900 Spring of Freedom Street, N.W., Washington, D.C. 20008, telephone (202)274-9103 or visit the Embassy's web site at http://www.mzv.cz/washington/.

CRIME INFORMATION: The Czech Republic has a low rate of violent crime. However, there has been a dramatic increase in street crime, particularly pick-pocketing, especially in major tourist areas in Prague and on public transportation. Visitors should be alert to the potential for substantial overcharging by taxis, particularly in areas frequented by tourists. The loss or theft abroad of a U.S. passport should be reported immediately to the local police and to the nearest U.S. embassy or consulate. The Department of State's pamphlet, *A Safe Trip Abroad*, is available from the Superintendent of Documents, U.S. Government Printing Office, Washington, D.C. 20402. It provides useful information on safeguarding valuables and protecting personal security while traveling abroad.

MEDICAL FACILITIES: Medical facilities are available but may be limited, particularly in remote areas. Doctors and hospitals often expect cash payment for health services. Serious medical problems requiring hospitalization and/or medical evacuation to the United States can cost thousands of dollars or more.

MEDICAL BCISURANCE: U.S. medical insurance is not always valid outside the United States. U.S. Medicare and Medicaid programs do not provide payment for medical services outside the United States. Uninsured travelers who require medical care overseas may face extreme difficulties. Please check with your own insurance company to confirm whether your policy applies overseas, including provision for medical evacuation. Please ascertain whether payment will be made to the overseas hospital or doctor or if you will be reimbursed later for expenses that you incur. Some insurance policies also include coverage for psychiatric treatment and for disposition of remains in the event of death. Useful information on medical emergencies abroad, including overseas insurance programs, is provided in the Department of State's Bureau of Consular Affairs brochure, *Medical Information for Americans Traveling Abroad*, available via the Bureau of Consular Affairs home page.

OTHER HEALTH INFORMATION: Information on vaccinations and other health precautions may be obtained from the Centers for Disease Control and Prevention's hotline for international travelers at 1-877-FYI-TRIP (1-877-394-8747); fax 1-888-CDC-FAXX (1-888-232-3299), or via their Internet site at http://www.cdc.gov.

TRAFFIC SAFETY AND ROAD CONDITIONS: While in a foreign country, U.S. citizens may encounter road conditions that differ significantly from those in the United States. The information below concerning the Czech Republic is provided for general reference only, and it may not be totally accurate in a particular location or circumstance.

Safety of Public Transportation: Good
Urban Road Conditions/Maintenance: Good

Rural Road Conditions/Maintenance: Poor
Availability of Roadside Assistance: Good

First-class roads in the Czech Republic generally meet Western European standards. However, on side roads drivers should be prepared to encounter uneven surfaces, irregular lane markings, and sign placements that are not clear. Roads are often under construction. Streets in towns are not always in good condition. U.S. drivers should pay special attention to driving on cobblestone and among streetcars in historic city centers. Speed limits are 50 km/h in towns and 120 km/h on highways. A U.S. drivers license must be accompanied by an International Driving Permit (IDP), available from AAA (in the United States only); failure to have the IDP with a valid license may result in denial of an insurance claim after an accident.

Persons driving into the Czech Republic should be aware that a road usage tax sticker is required to drive legally on major highways, including the E-50 motorway. Signs stating this requirement are posted near the border, but they are easy to miss. The stickers are available at gasoline stations on the highways. The fine for failing to display a motorways toll sticker is assessed on the spot.

Taxi fares in Prague are often the subject of tourist complaints. Taxis operating from stands or cruising for customers often do not use a meter. Passengers should determine the fare to be charged and agree on it before beginning a taxi ride. Information on normal charges for common routes is available at Prague Airport and at many tourist information offices. Airport taxis are allowed to charge a higher than normal tariff. Radio-dispatched taxis are generally reliable and cheaper than taxis flagged on the street. For specific information concerning the Czech Republic on drivers permits, vehicle inspection, road tax and mandatory insurance, please contact the Czech Tourist Authority offices in New York at tel. (212) 288-0830 or nycenter@pop.net.

AVIATION SAFETY OVERSIGHT: The U.S. Federal Aviation Administration (FAA) has assessed the Government of the Czech Republic Civil Aviation Authority as Category 1 -- in compliance with international aviation safety standards for oversight of the Czech Republic air carrier operations.

For further information, travelers may contact the Department of Transportation within the United States at tel. 1-800-322-7873, or visit the FAA's Internet web site at http://www.faa.gov/avr/iasa/. The U.S. Department of Defense (DOD) separately assesses some foreign air carriers for suitability as official providers of air services. For information regarding the DOD policy on specific carriers, travelers may contact the DOD at tel. (618) 256-4801.

CUSTOMS REGULATIONS: Czech customs authorities encourage the use of an ATA (Admission Temporaire/Temporary Admission) Carnet for the temporary admission of professional equipment, commercial samples, and/or goods for exhibitions and fair purposes. ATA Carnet Headquarters, located at the U.S. Council for International Business, 1212 Avenue of the Americas, New York, NY 10036, issues and guarantees the ATA Carnet in the United States. For additional information, please call (212) 354-4480, or send an e-mail to atacarnet@uscib.org, or visit http://www.uscib.org for details.

CRIMINAL PENALTIES: While in a foreign country, a U.S. citizen is subject to that country's laws and regulations, which sometimes differ significantly from those in the United States and may not afford the protections available to the individual under U.S. law. Penalties for breaking the law can be more severe than in the United States for similar offenses. Persons violating Czech laws, even unknowingly, may be expelled, arrested or imprisoned. Penalties for possession, use, or trafficking in illegal drugs in the Czech Republic are strict, and convicted offenders can expect jail sentences and heavy fines.

CHILDREN'S ISSUES: For information on international adoption of children and international parental child abduction, please refer to our Internet site at http://travel.state.gov/children's_issues.html or telephone (202) 736-7000.

REGISTRATION/EMBASSY AND CONSULATE LOCATIONS: Americans living in or visiting the Czech Republic are encouraged to register at the Consular Section of the U.S. Embassy in the Czech Republic and obtain updated information on travel and security within the Czech Republic. Information is also available on the Embassy's web site at http://www.usembassy.cz. The U.S. Embassy in Prague is located at Trziste 15, 118 01 Prague, Czech Republic; tel. (420) (2) 5753-0663; for after hours emergencies only - tel. (420) (2) 5753-2716.

Hungary

COUNTRY DESCRIPTION: Hungary is a stable democracy with a market economy. Tourist facilities outside Budapest are widely available, if not as developed as those found in Western Europe. Visitors considering a trip are encouraged to read the Embassy's consular web site: http://www.usembassy.hu/consular.htm.

ENTRY REQUIREMENTS: A passport is required. A visa is not required for tourist stays of up to three months. If you plan to reside or study in Hungary, a visa must be obtained from the Embassy of the Republic of Hungary at 3910 Shoemaker Street N.W., Washington, D.C. 20008, telephone (202) 362-6730, internet address http://www.hungaryemb.org, or the nearest Hungarian Consulate in Los Angeles or New York.

In an effort to prevent international child abduction, many governments have initiated procedures at entry/exit points. These often include requiring documentary evidence of relationship and permission for the child's travel from the parent(s) or legal guardian not present. Having such documentation on hand, even if not required, may facilitate entry or departure.

SAFETY AND SECURITY: Prior police approval is required for public demonstrations in Hungary and police oversight is routinely provided to ensure adequate security for participants and passers-by. Nonetheless, situations may develop which could pose a threat to public safety. U.S. citizens are advised to avoid areas in which public demonstrations are taking place. For the latest security information, Americans traveling abroad should regularly monitor the Department's Internet web site at http://travel.state.gov, where the current Worldwide Caution, Travel Warnings, and Public Announcements can be found.

CRIME: Hungary has a low rate of violent crime. However, street crime, which occasionally involves violence, has increased, especially at night near major hotels and restaurants and on public transportation. Theft of passports, currency, and credit cards is a frequent problem, especially in youth hostels, train stations, and on public transportation.

The U.S. Embassy's Consular Section offers an informational brochure for tourists in Hungary, including a section on crimes and scams that have been encountered by other tourists. To consult this advisory, please visit the Embassy's consular website at http://usembassy.hu/tourist.htm.

The number of highway robberies has increased over the past few years. Drivers should be cautious when stopping at gas stations and highway parking lots, or fixing flat tires or other mechanical problems, especially at night. There have been reports of scams perpetrated on unwitting victims while travelling the highways. One reported scam involves someone who attracts the driver's attention by saying that there is something wrong with his/her car (e.g. a smoking hood, or a flat tire) in order to encourage the driver to pull over to the side of the road. Once pulled over, the people participating in the scam will remove purses, passports, etc. from the car and drive away. Luggage and valuables should not be left unattended inside any vehicle.

Tourists who become victims of a crime in Hungary are strongly encouraged to call a 24-hour multilingual crime reporting telephone number. The number from 8 a.m. to 8 p.m. is 01-438-8080; from 8 p.m. to 8 a.m., the number is 06-8066-0044. There is also a 24-hour police Tourinfo office that provides service in English and German and is located in one of downtown Budapest's busiest tourist areas: Vigado Utca 6, 1051 Budapest.

The loss or theft abroad of a U.S. passport should be reported immediately to the local police and the nearest U.S. Embassy or Consulate. If you are the victim of a crime while overseas, in addition to reporting to local police, please contact the nearest U.S. Embassy or Consulate for assistance. The Embassy/Consulate staff can, for example, assist you to find appropriate medical care, to contact family members or friends and explain how funds could be transferred. Although the investigation and prosecution of the crime is solely the responsibility of local authorities, consular officers can help you to understand the local criminal justice process and to find an attorney if needed.

U.S. citizens may refer to the Department of State's pamphlet, "*A Safe Trip Abroad*," for ways to promote a trouble-free journey. The pamphlet is available by mail from the Superintendent of Documents, U.S. Government Printing Office, Washington, D.C. 20402, via the Internet at http://www.access.gpo.gov/su_docs, or via the Bureau of Consular Affairs home page at http://travel.state.gov.

MEDICAL FACILITIES: Medical treatment available in Hungary is adequate at best, but hospital facilities and nursing support are not comparable to those in the United States. Physicians are generally well trained, but there is a lack of adequate emergency services. A language barrier can exist as well, if one does not speak Hungarian. Doctors and hospitals usually expect immediate cash payment for health services.

MEDICAL INSURANCE: The Department of State strongly urges Americans to consult with their medical insurance company prior to traveling abroad to confirm whether their policy applies overseas and whether it will cover emergency expenses such as a medical evacuation. U.S. medical insurance plans seldom cover health costs incurred outside the United States unless supplemental coverage is purchased. Further, U.S. Medicare and Medicaid programs do not provide payment for medical services outside the United States. However, many travel agents and private companies offer insurance plans that will cover health care expenses incurred overseas including emergency services such as medical evacuations.

When making a decision regarding health insurance, Americans should consider that many foreign doctors and hospitals require payment in cash prior to providing service and that a medical evacuation to the U.S. may cost well in excess of $50,000. Uninsured travelers who require medical care overseas often face extreme difficulties. When consulting with your insurer prior to your trip, ascertain whether payment will be made to the overseas healthcare provider or whether you will be reimbursed later for expenses you incur. Some insurance policies also include coverage for psychiatric treatment and for disposition of remains in the event of death.

Useful information on medical emergencies abroad, including overseas insurance programs, is provided in the Department of State's Bureau of Consular Affairs brochure, "*Medical Information for Americans Traveling Abroad*," available via the Bureau of Consular Affairs home page or autofax:(202) 647-3000.

OTHER HEALTH INFORMATION: Information on vaccinations and other health precautions may be obtained from the Centers for Disease Control and Prevention's international travelers hotline at 1-877-FYI-TRIP (1-877-394-8747); fax: 1-888-CDC-FAXX (1-888-232-3299, or by visiting CDC's Internet home page at http://www.cdc.gov. For information about outbreaks of infectious diseases aboad consult the World Health Organization's web site at http://www.who.int/en. Further health information for travelers is available at http://www.who.int/iht.

TRAFFIC SAFETY AND ROAD CONDITIONS: While in a foreign country, U.S. citizens may encounter road conditions that differ significantly from those in the United States. The information below concerning Hungary is provided for general reference only and may not be accurate in a particular location or circumstance.

Safety of Public Transportation:	Good
Urban Road Condition/Maintenance:	Good
Rural Road Condition/Maintenance:	Fair
Availability of Roadside Assistance:	Good

In Hungary, the number of fatal traffic accidents is approximately 1,200 per year, with approximately 7,000 traffic accidents per year resulting in serious injuries. Road travel is more dangerous during the Christmas season, summer months, and at night. Roadside assistance, including medical and other services, is generally available. Ambulance service can be reached by dialing 104, and the police can be reached by dialing 107. Bus, train, and taxi services are readily available for inter-city travel.

Hungarian motorways and highways are generally in good condition. In urban areas, roads and road maintenance are also good. However, in rural areas, roads are often narrow, badly lit, and can be in a state of poor repair in some areas. Pedestrians, agricultural machinery, and farm animals often use these small rural roads. This requires increased caution on the part of drivers. Additional information on road conditions is available from "Utinform" at phone number (36)(1)322-7052.

Hungary has a policy of zero tolerance for driving under the influence of alcohol. Police often conduct routine roadside checks where breath-analyzer tests are administered. Persons found to be driving while intoxicated face jail and/or fines. Possible penalties for a car accident involving injury or death are one to five years in prison. Police have instituted a widespread practice of stopping vehicles to check driver identity documents in the search for illegal aliens and residents in Hungary, and to check vehicle registration and fitness documentation, particularly in Budapest.

Hungary recognizes international driver's permits (IDP) issued by the American Automobile Association (AAA) and the American Automobile Touring Alliance when presented in conjunction with a state driver's license. American driver's licenses will be accepted in Hungary for one year after arrival, provided that a certified Hungarian translation has been attached to the license. Those with IDPs do not need to have the license translated, but must present both IDP and state driver's license together. After one year in Hungary, U.S. citizens must obtain a Hungarian driver's license. For further information on this procedure, please contact the American Citizen Services office at the U.S. Embassy in Budapest, e-mail address: acs.budapest@state.gov.

The speed limit for cars and motorcycles on the motorway is 130 km per hour (approximately 81 mph); on highways, the limit is 110 km per hour (approximately 69 mph); and in town and village areas, the speed limit is 50 km per hour (approximately 30 mph). Special seats are required for children under age 12. Seat belts are mandatory for everyone in the car. Unless another instruction sign is displayed, yielding right of way is prevalent. Making right turns during a red light is prohibited. If another car flashes its high beams at you, it means the driver is giving you precedence at an intersection or calling your attention to the presence of something that may affect your driving.

In the past, it was common for fines to be collected on the spot by the police for any alleged traffic violation. Now, tickets are written up by the police, thus documenting the infraction and fine(s). The police will give the offender a postal check (money order), on which the amount of the fine to be paid is written, and this postal check may be presented and paid for at any Hungarian post office. Sometimes, in disputes about fines or the offense, the police will confiscate the person's passport and issue a receipt for the passport plus an "invitation letter" to appear at the police station the next day or day after to resolve the dispute. The passport is given back after resolution and/or the payment of the fine.

For additional general information about road safety, including links to foreign government sites, see the Department of State, Bureau of Consular Affairs, home page at http://travel.state.gov/road_safety.html. For specific information about Hungarian driver's permits, vehicle inspection, road taxes and mandatory insurance, please contact the Hungarian National Tourist Organization Office in New York via the Internet at http://www.gotohungary.com.

AVIATION SAFETY OVERSIGHT: The U.S. Federal Aviation Administration (FAA) has assessed the Government of Hungary's civil aviation authority as Category 1 -- in compliance with international aviation safety standards for the oversight of Hungary's air carrier operations. For further information, travelers may contact the U.S. Department of Transportation at 1-800-322-7873, or visit the FAA's Internet website at http://www.faa.gov/avr/iasa.

The U.S. Department of Defense (DOD) separately assesses some foreign carriers for suitability as official providers of air services. For information regarding the DOD policy on specific carriers, travelers may contact DOD at (618) 229-4801.

CUSTOMS REGULATIONS: Hungary's customs authorities may enforce strict regulations concerning temporary importation into or export from Hungary of items such as firearms, antiquities, and prescription medications. It is advisable to contact the Embassy of Hungary in

Washington or one of Hungary's consulates in the United States for specific information regarding customs requirements. Hungary's customs authorities encourage the use of an ATA (Admission Temporaire/Temporary Admission) Carnet for the temporary admission of professional equipment, commercial samples, and/or goods for exhibitions and fair purposes. ATA Carnet Headquarters, located at the U.S. Council for International Business, 1212 Avenue of the Americas, New York, NY 10036, issues and guarantees the ATA Carnet in the United States. For additional information call 212-354-4480, send an e-mail to atacarnet@uscib.org, or visit http://www.uscib.org for details.

CRIMINAL PENALTIES: While in a foreign country, a U.S. citizen is subject to that country's laws and regulations, which sometimes differ significantly from those in the United States and may not afford the protections available to the individual under U.S. law. Penalties for breaking the law can be more severe than in the United States for similar offenses. Persons violating Hungary's laws, even unknowingly, may be expelled, arrested or imprisoned. Penalties for possession, use, or trafficking in illegal drugs in Hungary are strict, and convicted offenders can expect jail sentences and heavy fines.

SPECIAL CIRCUMSTANCES: The acceptance of traveler's checks and credit cards is not universal in Hungary. The presence of ATMs is increasing in Budapest and other major cities.

CHILDREN'S ISSUES: For information on international adoption of children and international parental child abduction, please refer to our Internet site at http://travel.state.gov/children's issues.html, or telephone (202) 736-7000.

REGISTRATION/EMBASSY AND CONSULATE LOCATION: Americans living in or visiting Hungary are encouraged to register at the Consular Section of the U.S. Embassy in Budapest, and to obtain updated information on travel and security in Hungary. The U.S. Embassy is located at 1054 Budapest, Szabadsag Ter 12; telephone (36)(1)475-4400 between the hours of 8 a.m. - 5p.m., or if calling after hours, on weekends or holidays, (36)(1)475-4703 or (36)(1)475-4929. The Consular Section's fax is (36)(1)475-4188 or (36)(1)475-4113, and the Consular Section's website is located at: http://www.usembassy.hu/consular.htm.

Poland

COUNTRY DESCRIPTION: Poland is a moderately developed European nation and a democracy rapidly implementing a free market transformation. While improving rapidly, tourist facilities are not highly developed in all areas, and some of the services taken for granted in other European countries can be difficult to find in some parts of the country.

ENTRY REQUIREMENTS: A valid passport is required. U.S. citizens do not need visas for stays up to 90 days for tourist, business, or transit purposes. Americans should ensure that their passports are date-stamped upon entry. Persons planning to stay in Poland for longer than 90 days or who will be employed in Poland must obtain a visa in advance. Polish law requires every traveler to be able to show means of support, if asked. For persons above 16 years of age, this has been defined as 100 Polish zloty per day or the equivalent in foreign currency or other negotiable instruments. For further information on entry requirements, please contact the Embassy of the Republic of Poland, Consular Section, at 2224 Wyoming Ave N.W., Washington, D.C. 20008, tel. (202) 232-4517 or 232-4528, or the Polish consulates in Chicago, Los Angeles, and New York. The Polish Embassy can also be contacted via its web site at http://www.polishworld.com/polemb.

DUAL NATIONALITY: Poland is now enforcing a law that requires Polish citizens to enter and depart Poland using a Polish passport (including Polish citizens who are also American citizens). Americans who are also Polish citizens or who are unsure if they hold Polish citizenship are advised to contact the nearest Polish consular office for information about citizenship requirements and travel documentation. Poland has compulsory military service for all males between the ages of eighteen and twenty-eight. A dual national would not be subject to conscription if he can prove that he does not live in Poland. While recognizing that some Americans are also citizens of other countries, the U.S. Government does not encourage its citizens to become or remain dual nationals due to an array of complications that may ensue from the obligations owed to the country of second nationality. Additional information about the U.S. Government's policy with respect to dual nationality may be found at the Bureau of Consular Affairs web site at http://travel.state.gov/dualnationality.html.

CRIME INFORMATION: Crime rates in Poland vary. Warsaw, Krakow, and other major cities have higher rates of crime against residents and foreign visitors. The tri-cities area of Gdynia, Sopot, and Gdansk has a high incidence of muggings, sometimes in broad daylight. Organized groups of thieves and pickpockets operate at major tourist destinations, in train stations, and on trains, trams, and buses in major cities. Thefts have occurred on overnight trains, including thefts from passengers in second-class closed compartments. Most pickpocketing on trains occurs when boarding. A common practice is for groups of well-dressed young men to surround a passenger in the narrow aisle of the train and jostle/pickpocket him or her as they supposedly attempt to get around the passenger. (This often occurs in first-class cars).

Racially motivated verbal and, on occasion, physical harassment of Americans and others of non-Caucasian ethnicity can occur. Most of the incidents that have occurred were perpetrated by groups of young males generally identified as skinheads.

Car thefts, carjackings, and theft from cars are commonplace. Drivers should be wary of persons indicating they should pull over or that something is wrong with their car. Often, a second car or person is following, and when the driver of the targeted car gets out to see if there is a problem, the person who has been following will get in and drive off with the car. Drivers should never get out of the car to check for damage without first turning off the ignition and taking the keys. There has been an increasing incidence of thieves opening or breaking passenger-side doors and windows in slow or stopped traffic to take purses or briefcases left on the seat beside the driver.

The loss or theft abroad of a U.S. passport should be reported immediately to the local police and the nearest U.S. embassy or consulate. U.S. citizens may refer to the Department of State's pamphlet, *A*

Safe Trip Abroad, for ways to promote a more trouble-free journey. The pamphlet is available by mail from the Superintendent of Documents, U.S. Government Printing Office, Washington, D.C. 20402, via the Internet at http://www.access.gpo.gov/su_docs, or via the Bureau of Consular Affairs home page at http://travel.state.gov.

MEDICAL FACILITIES AND INSURANCE: Adequate medical care is available in Poland, but it generally does not meet Western standards. U.S. medical insurance is not always valid outside the United States. U.S. Medicare and Medicaid programs do not provide payment for medical services outside the United States. Doctors and hospitals often expect immediate cash payment for health services. Uninsured travelers who require medical care overseas may face extreme difficulties.

Please check with your own insurance company to confirm whether your policy applies overseas, including provision for medical evacuation, and for adequacy of coverage. Serious medical problems requiring hospitalization and/or medical evacuation to the United States can cost tens of thousands of dollars. Please ascertain whether payment will be made to the overseas hospital or doctor or whether you will be reimbursed later for expenses that you incur. Some insurance policies also include coverage for psychiatric treatment and for disposition of remains in the event of death.

Useful information on medical emergencies abroad, including overseas insurance programs, is provided in the Department of State's Bureau of Consular Affairs brochure *Medical Information for Americans Traveling Abroad*, available via the Bureau of Consular Affairs home page or autofax: (202) 647-3000.

OTHER HEALTH INFORMATION:
Information on vaccinations and other health precautions may be obtained from the Centers for Disease Control and Prevention's hotline for international travelers at 1-877-FYI-TRIP (1-877-394-8747); fax 1-888-CDC-FAXX (1-888-232-3299), or via CDC's Internet site at http://www.cdc.gov.

TRAFFIC SAFETY AND ROAD

CONDITIONS: While in a foreign country, U.S. citizens may encounter road conditions that differ significantly from those in the United States. Roadside services, while not at Western levels, are rapidly improving. Polski Zwiazek Motorowy Auto-Tour has multi-lingual operators and provides assistance country-wide. Their phone numbers are 981 or 9637. The police emergency number is 997, fire service is 998, and ambulance service is 999. Mobile phone users can dial 112 for roadside assistance. Seat belts are compulsory in both the front and back seats, and children under the age of 10 are prohibited from riding in the front seat. Headlights must be used at all times from October through March. The information below concerning Poland is provided for general reference only, and it may not be totally accurate in a particular location or circumstance.

Safety of Public Transportation: Fair
Urban Road Conditions/Maintenance: Fair
Rural Road Conditions/Maintenance: Poor
Availability of Roadside Assistance: Fair

The number of cars in Poland has increased substantially. Driving, especially after dark, is very hazardous. Roads are generally narrow, badly lit, frequently under repair, especially in the summer months, and are often also used by pedestrians and animals. The Ministry of Transportation has a program called black spots (czarny punkt), which puts signs in places where the number of accidents and casualties are particularly high. These signs have a black spot on a yellow background, and the road area around the "black spot" is marked with diagonal red lines. A map of Poland with marked black spots is available at the Ministry of Transportation web site: http://www.mtigm.gov.pl/czarne3.html.

Alcohol consumption is frequently a contributing factor in accidents. Polish laws provide virtually zero tolerance for driving under the influence of alcohol, and penalties for drunk driving (defined as a blood alcohol level of 0.05) include a fine and probation or imprisonment for up to 2 years. Penalties for drivers involved in accidents can be severe. If an accident results in injury or death, the penalty can be imprisonment from 6 months up to 8 years.

Within cities, taxis are available at major hotels and designated stands, or they may be ordered in advance. Some drivers take credit cards and/or speak English. Travelers should be wary of hailing taxis on the street, especially those that do not have a telephone number displayed because these may not have meters, and many of them charge more.

For additional general information about road safety, including links to foreign government sites, please see the Departments of State, Bureau of Consular Affairs home page at: http://state.gov.road_safety.html. For information about Polish driving permits, vehicle inspection, road tax and mandatory insurance, please contact the Polish National Tourist Organization Office in New York or the U.S Embassy Warsaw's Consular Section web page at http://www.usinfo.pl.

AVIATION SAFETY OVERSIGHT: The U.S. Federal Aviation Administration (FAA) has assessed the Government of Poland's civil aviation authority as Category One -- in compliance with the international aviation safety standards for the oversight of Polish air carrier operations.

For further information, travelers may contact the Department of Transportation at 1-800-322-7873, or visit the FAA's Internet web site at http://www.faa.gov/avr/iasa/. The U.S. Department of Defense (DOD) separately assesses some foreign air carriers for suitability as official providers of air services. For information regarding the DOD policy on specific carriers, travelers may contact the DOD at tel. (618) 256-4801.

CUSTOMS REGULATIONS: Polish customs authorities may enforce strict regulations concerning temporary import and export of items such as works of art, particularly those created before 1945. Works of art produced by living artists after 1945 may be exported with the permission from the Provincial Conservator of Relics. Some works of art produced after 1945 may still be subject to a ban on exportation if the artist is no longer living and the work is considered of high cultural value. It is advisable to contact the Embassy of Poland in Washington, D.C. or one of Poland's consulates in the United States for specific information regarding customs requirements.

Poland's customs authorities encourage the use of an ATA (Admission Temporaire/Temporary Admission) Carnet for the temporary admission of professional equipment, commercial samples, and/or goods for exhibitions and fair purposes. ATA Carnet Headquarters, located at the U.S. Council for International Business, 1212 Avenue of the Americas, New York, N.Y. 10036, issues and guarantees the ATA Carnet in the United States. For additional information, please call (212) 354-4480, or send e-mail to atacarnet@uscib.org, or visit http://www.uscib.org for details.

CRIMINAL PENALTIES: While in a foreign country, a U.S. citizen is subject to that country's laws and regulations, which sometimes differ significantly from those in the United States and may not afford the protections available to the individual under U.S. law. Penalties for breaking the law can be more severe than in the United States for similar offenses. Persons violating Poland's laws, even unknowingly, may be expelled, arrested or imprisoned. Penalties for possession, use, or trafficking in illegal drugs in Poland are strict, and convicted offenders can expect jail sentences and heavy fines.

Special Circumstances: Upon entry into Poland, visitors must request a form to declare currency, travelers checks, and other cash instruments in amounts in excess of 5,000 euros (please check exchange rate for approximate dollar amount). The declaration form must be stamped by Polish customs and retained by the traveler for presentation on departure. Undeclared cash may be confiscated upon departure, and visitors carrying undeclared cash may be subject to criminal penalties. Most major banks now cash traveler's checks. ATM machines are readily available in all major cities and credit cards are becoming increasingly accepted.

Children's Issues: For information on international adoption of children and international parental child abduction, please refer to our Internet site at http://travel.state.gov/children's_issues.html or tel. (202) 736-7000.

Registration/Embassy and Consulate Locations: U.S. citizens are encouraged to register with the U.S. Embassy or the U.S. Consulate, where they can obtain updated information on travel and security within Poland. The U.S. Embassy in Warsaw is located at Aleje Ujazdowskie 29/31. The Consular Section entrance is located around the corner at Ulica Piekna 12, tel (48)(22) 628-3041, fax (48)(22) 625-0289, after-hours tel (48)(22) 625-0055. The U.S. Consulate in Krakow is located at Ulica Stolarska 9, tel (48)(12) 429-6655, fax (48)(12) 421-8292, after-hours cellular phone, 0601-483-348. A Consular Agency providing limited consular services in Poznan is located at Ulica Paderewskiego 7, tel (48)(61) 851-8516, fax (48)(61) 851-8966.

Slovak Republic

COUNTRY DESCRIPTION: The Slovak Republic is a moderately developed European nation undergoing profound economic and political changes. Tourist facilities are not as developed as those found in Western Europe and many of the goods and services taken for granted in other European countries are not yet available.

ENTRY REQUIREMENTS: A passport is required. A visa is not required for stays up to thirty days. For stays longer than thirty days a visa must be obtained prior to entry at Slovak embassies or consulates abroad. Visas cannot be obtained at border points upon arrival. Travelers to the Slovak Republic can obtain entry information at the Embassy of the Slovak Republic at 3523 International Court N.W., Suite 250, Washington, DC 20007, telephone (202) 965-5160/1, Internet http://www.slovakemb.com.

The new Slovak law on foreigners stipulates that as of April 1, 2002, all foreigners seeking entry into Slovakia will have to carry proof of a medical insurance policy contracted for payment of all costs for hospitalization and medical treatment in Slovakia. Also, the border police will have right to request evidence of finances available to pay for the stay in Slovakia in the amount of $50 per person per day.

In an effort to prevent international child abduction, many governments have initiated procedures at entry/exit points. These often include requiring documentary evidence of relationship and permission for the child's travel from the parent(s) or legal guardian not present. Having such documentation on hand, even if not required, may facilitate entry/departure.

DUAL NATIONALITY: In addition to being subject to all Slovak Republic laws affecting U.S. citizens, dual nationals may be subject to Slovak laws, which impose special obligations. For additional information, see the Consular Affairs home page on the Internet at http://travel.state.gov for our Dual Nationality flyer.

SAFETY/SECURITY: Taking photographs of anything that could be perceived as being of military or security interest may result in problems with authorities.

CRIME: Slovakia has a medium rate of crime. Police forces suffer from lack of manpower, resources and equipment. Local police are not likely to speak English. Western visitors, especially short-term visitors such as tourists and students, are the primary foreign targets. The majority of street crime is non-violent. Street crimes range from pick-pocketing (particularly in the summer) and purse and cellular telephone snatchings to muggings, armed robbery, shooting, drugging and robbing unsuspecting victims at nightspots and bars. Most reported thefts occur at crowded tourist sites or on public buses or trains. Thieves in Slovakia often work in groups or pairs. In most cases, one thief distracts a victim while an accomplice performs the robbery. Groups of street children are known to divert tourists' attention so that a member of their group can pick-pocket them while they are distracted.

Reports of racially motivated incidents against foreigners and persons of color, perpetrated by groups with a history of targeting persons of African or Asian descent, have occurred in Slovakia. In addition to incidents of assault, persons of African or Asian heritage may be subject to various types of harassment, such as verbal abuse.

The loss or theft abroad of a U.S. passport should be reported immediately to the local police and the nearest U.S. embassy or consulate. U.S. citizens can refer to the Department of State's pamphlet, *A Safe Trip Abroad*, for ways to promote a trouble-free journey. The pamphlet is available by mail from the Superintendent of Documents, U.S.

Government Printing Office, Washington, D.C. 20402, via the Internet at http://www.access.gpo.gov/su_docs, or via the Bureau of Consular Affairs home page at http://travel.state.gov.

If you are the victim of a crime while overseas, in addition to reporting to local police, please contact the nearest U.S. embassy or consulate for assistance. The embassy/consulate staff can, for example, assist you to find appropriate medical care, to contact family members or friends, and explain how funds could be transferred. Although the investigation and prosecution of the crime is solely the responsibility of local authorities, consular officers can help you to understand the local criminal justice process and to find an attorney if needed.

MEDICAL FACILITIES: Medical facilities are available. However, only a limited number of doctors speak English speakers. Doctors and hospitals expect cash payment for health services unless the patient can present an insurance number from the Slovak National Insurance Company. Serious medical problems requiring hospitalization and/or medical evacuation to the United States can cost thousands of dollars or more.

MEDICAL INSURANCE: The Department of State strongly urges Americans to consult with their medical insurance company prior to traveling abroad to confirm whether their policy applies overseas and whether it will cover emergency expenses such as a medical evacuation. U.S. medical insurance plans seldom cover health costs incurred outside the United States unless supplemental coverage is purchased. Further, U.S. Medicare and Medicaid programs do not provide payment for medical services outside the United States. However, many travel agents and private companies offer insurance plans that will cover health care expenses incurred overseas including emergency services such as medical evacuations.

When making a decision regarding health insurance, Americans should consider that many foreign doctors and hospitals require payment in cash prior to providing service and that a medical evacuation to the U.S. may cost well in excess of $50,000. Uninsured travelers who require medical care overseas often face extreme difficulties, whereas travelers who have purchased overseas medical insurance have, when a medical emergency occurs, found it life-saving. When consulting with your insurer prior to your trip, ascertain whether payment will be made to the overseas healthcare provider or whether you will be reimbursed later for expenses you incur. Some insurance policies also include coverage for psychiatric treatment and for disposition of remains in the event of death.

Useful information on medical emergencies abroad, including overseas insurance programs, is provided in the Department of State's Bureau of Consular Affairs brochure, *Medical Information for Americans Traveling Abroad*, available via the Bureau of Consular Affairs home page or autofax: (202) 647-3000.

OTHER HEALTH INFORMATION: Information on vaccinations and other health precautions may be obtained from the Centers for Disease Control and Prevention's hotline for international travelers at 1-877-FYI-TRIP (1-877-394-8747); fax 1-888-CDC-FAXX (1-888-232-3299), or CDC's Internet site at http://www.cdc.gov.

TRAFFIC SAFETY AND ROAD CONDITIONS: While in a foreign country, U.S. citizens may encounter road conditions that differ significantly from those in the United States. The information below concerning Slovakia is provided for general reference only, and may not be totally accurate in a particular location or circumstance.

Safety of Public Transportation: Fair
Urban Road Conditions/Maintenance: Good
Rural Road Conditions/Maintenance: Fair
Availability of Roadside Assistance: Poor

The roads in Slovakia are typically safe and well maintained. Four-lane highways exist in and around Bratislava. However, Most roads outside of built-up areas are two lanes only, and aggressive drivers attempting to pass at unsafe speeds pose a serious hazard. Due to poor lighting and narrow, winding roads, nighttime driving outside of built-up areas is not recommended.

From November through March there is often heavy snowfall, which is not adequately cleared from many rural roads. Roads in the mountainous northern part of the country are particularly prone to hazardous conditions during winter months. Winter tires and chains are recommended for travel to mountain and ski resorts.

In Slovakia, drivers drive on the right side of the road. The maximum legal speed on highways is 130 kilometers per hour (78 mph). On smaller roads the maximum speed is 90 kph (54mph). The limit in towns is 60 kph (36 mph). Use of cellular phones while driving is strictly prohibited.

Drivers must yield the right of way to all vehicles with flashing blue lights (police, ambulances, fire trucks, motorcades). Vehicles with yellow or orange lights usually mean that traffic must slow down. Drivers must always be cautious, however, as many slowly moving vehicles, such as agricultural vehicles, are not well marked.

Driving under the influence of alcohol is strictly prohibited. The blood alcohol tolerance level is zero percent.

Penalties for drivers involved in car accidents involving injury or death are decided by a court of law. Penalties for minor offences are bot generally large, but foreigners are sometimes targeted for additional sums. Anyone suspecting that this has occurred should ask for a written receipt and note the number of the traffic officer imposing the fine.

Gasoline is readily available, although many gas stations are closed on Sunday. Gas stations typically do not offer repair service; private mechanics must be found. Few gas stations and mechanics accept credit cards, so travelers should expect to pay for these services in cash.

A highway user decal must be purchased for travel on most major roads outside of Bratislava. The decal is valid for the calendar year in which it is purchased, and is available at gas stations, post offices and some newspaper kiosks. The cost is either Sk 400 or Sk 800, depending on the size of the engine.

Emergency numbers:
Police: 158
Ambulance: 155
Fire: 150
Public Transportation: Taxi companies provide generally reliable, safe, and economical services. Avoid, however, independent cabs, which do not

prominently display a company name. Buses, trolleys, and trams are mechanically safe, but there have been reports of thefts on city transportation, and of harassment by the transport police. Inter-city travel is widely available by bus, train, or taxi and is generally safe (inquire about taxi fares in advance). There are regular international trains and buses, which are mechanically safe. However, there is a danger of theft, even from locked compartments, on international night trains serving Warsaw, Prague, and Budapest. Taxi drivers with special permits may provide international taxi service.

Motorcycles: A motorcycle driver's license and helmet are required. Small motorcycles are not allowed on highways. All traffic regulations apply.

General Recommendations: Tourists coming to Slovakia are required to have an International Drivers' Permit. Otherwise, they may have problems entering neighboring countries.

For additional general information about road safety, including links to foreign government sites, see the Department of State, Bureau of Consular Affairs home page at http://travel.state.gov/road_safety.html. For specific information concerning Slovak driver's permits, vehicle inspection, road tax and mandatory insurance, contact the Slovak Information Center office in New York via the Internet at http://www.inx.net/~matica. See also road safety from other sources in Slovakia (http://www.zjazdnost.ssc.sk).

AVIATION SAFETY OVERSIGHT: The U.S. Federal Aviation Administration (FAA) has assessed the Government of Slovakia' civil aviation authority as Category 1 -- in compliance with international aviation safety standards for oversight of Slovak air carrier operations. For further information, travelers may contact the Department of Transportation within the U.S. at 1-800-322-7873, or visit the FAA's Internet website at http://www.faa.gov/avr/iasa.

The U.S. Department of Defense (DOD) separately assesses some foreign air carriers for suitability as official providers of air services. For information regarding the DOD policy on specific carriers, travelers may contact DOD at (618) 229-4801.

CUSTOMS REGULATIONS: Slovak customs authorities may enforce strict regulations concerning temporary importation into or export from Slovakia of items such as firearms, antiquities, medications, etc. It is advisable to contact the Embassy of the Slovak Republic in Washington or one of the Slovak consulates in the United States for specific information regarding customs requirements.

Slovak customs authorities encourage the use of an ATA (Air Transport Association) carnet for the temporary admission of professional equipment, commercial samples, and/or goods for exhibitions and fair purposes. ATA Carnet Headquarters, located at the U.S. Council for International Business, 1212 Avenue of the Americas, New York, NY 10036, issues and guarantees the ATA Carnet in the United States. For additional information call (212) 354-4480, send e-mail to atacarnet@uscib.org, or visit http://www.uscib.org for details.

CRIMINAL PENALTIES: While in a foreign country, a U.S. citizen is subject to that country's laws and regulations, which sometimes differ significantly from those in the United States and may not afford the protections available to the individual under U.S. law. Penalties for breaking the law can be more severe than in the United States for similar offenses. Persons violating Slovak laws, even unknowingly, may be expelled, arrested or imprisoned. Penalties for possession, use, or trafficking in illegal drugs in Slovakia are strict and convicted offenders can expect jail sentences and heavy fines.

CHILDREN'S ISSUES: For information on international adoption of children, international parental child abduction, and international child support enforcement issues, please refer to our Internet site at http://travel.state.gov/children's_issues.html or telephone (202) 736-7000.

REGISTRATION/EMBASSY AND CONSULATE LOCATIONS: Americans living in or visiting Slovakia are encouraged to register at the Consular Section of the U.S. Embassy in Slovakia and obtain updated information on travel and security within Slovakia. The U.S. Embassy is located at Hviezdoslavovo nam. 4, telephone

(421)(7) 5443 0861, (421)(7) 5443 3338, fax (421)(7) 5441 8861, web site: http://www.usis.sk.

Slovenia

COUNTRY DESCRIPTION: Slovenia operates under a parliamentary democracy. A mountainous country, half of Slovenia is covered by forests, with 29 miles of coastline along the Adriatic Sea. Tourist facilities are widely available throughout the country.

ENTRY REQUIREMENTS: A valid passport is required for entry into Slovenia. A visa is not required for a tourist/business stay of up to 90 days. Visitors not staying at hotels or other tourist facilities should register with the nearest local police station within three days after their arrival in Slovenia. For further information on entry requirements for Slovenia, travelers may contact the Embassy of Slovenia at 1525 New Hampshire Avenue N.W., Washington, D.C. 20036, tel. (202) 667-5363; the Consulate General of Slovenia in New York City, tel. (212) 370-3006; or the Consulate General of Slovenia in Cleveland, Ohio, tel. (216) 589-9220. The web site of the Slovenian Embassy in the United States is http://www.embassy.org/slovenia/.

In an effort to prevent international child abduction, many governments have initiated procedures at entry/exit points. These often include requiring documentary evidence of relationship and permission for the child's travel from the parent(s) or legal guardian not present. Having such documentation on hand, even if not required, may facilitate entry/departure.

DUAL NATIONALITY: In addition to being subject to all Slovene laws affecting U.S. citizens, dual nationals may also be subject to other laws that impose special obligations on Slovene citizens, such as obligatory military service. For additional information, please see the Consular Affairs home page on the Internet at http://travel.state.gov for our *Dual Nationality flyer*.

CRIME: Slovenia has a low crime rate. But travelers should take normal precautions, as they are sometimes the targets of pick-pockets and purse-snatchers, especially on the trains. The loss

or theft abroad of a U.S. passport should be reported immediately to the local police and the nearest U.S. embassy or consulate.

If you are the victim of a crime while overseas, in addition to reporting to local police, please contact the nearest U.S. embassy or consulate for assistance. The embassy/ consulate staff can, for example, assist you to find appropriate medical care, to contact family members or friends, and explain how funds could be transferred. Although the investigation and prosecution of the crime is solely the responsibility of local authorities, consular officers can help you to understand the local criminal justice process and to find an attorney if needed.

U.S. citizens can refer to the Department of State's pamphlet, *A Safe Trip Abroad*, for ways to promote a more trouble-free journey. The pamphlet is available by mail from the Superintendent of Documents, U.S. Government Printing Office, Washington, D.C. 20402, or via the Internet at http://www.access.gpo.gov/su_docs, or via the Bureau of Consular Affairs home page at http://travel.state.gov.

MEDICAL FACILITIES: Adequate medical care is readily available.

MEDICAL INSURANCE: The Department of State strongly urges Americans to consult with their medical insurance company prior to traveling abroad to confirm whether their policy applies overseas and whether it will cover emergency expenses such as a medical evacuation. U.S. medical insurance plans seldom cover health costs incurred outside the United States unless supplemental coverage is purchased. Further, U.S. Medicare and Medicaid programs do not provide payment for medical services outside the United States. However, many travel agents and private companies offer insurance plans that will cover health care expenses incurred overseas including emergency services such as medical evacuations.

When making a decision regarding health insurance, Americans should consider that many foreign doctors and hospitals require payment in cash prior to providing service and that a medical evacuation to the U.S. may cost well in excess of $50,000. Uninsured travelers who require medical care overseas often face extreme difficulties. When consulting with your insurer prior to your trip, ascertain whether payment will be made to the overseas healthcare provider or whether you will be reimbursed later for expenses you incur. Some insurance policies also include coverage for psychiatric treatment and for disposition of remains in the event of death.

Useful information on medical emergencies abroad, including overseas insurance programs, is provided in the Department of State's Bureau for Consular Affairs brochure, *Medical Information for Americans Traveling Abroad*, available via the Bureau of Consular Affairs home page or autofax: (202) 647-3000.

OTHER HEALTH INFORMATION: Travelers to Slovenia may obtain a list of English-speaking physicians at the U.S. Embassy. Antibiotics, allergy medication and all other prescription medication are available at local pharmacies. Some over-the-counter medications are available locally. For those persons who engage in outdoor activities, a vaccine to prevent tick-borne encephalitis is recommended.

Information on vaccinations and other health precautions may be obtained from the Centers for Disease Control and Prevention's hotline for International travelers at 1-877-FYI-TRIP (1-877-394-8747); fax: 1-888-CDC-FAXX (1-888-232-3299), or via the CDC's Internet site at http://www.cdc.gov.

TRAFFIC SAFETY AND ROAD CONDITIONS: While in a foreign country, U.S. citizens may encounter road conditions that differ significantly from those in the United States. The information below concerning Slovenia is provided for general reference only and may not be totally accurate in a particular location or circumstance.

Safety of public transportation: Good
Urban road conditions/maintenance: Good
Rural road conditions/maintenance: Good
Availability of roadside assistance: Good

Slovenia has a well-developed road network, safe for travel. Highways connect to neighboring cities and countries and are clearly sign-posted. As the number of cars in Slovenia continues to rise, roads are becoming more heavily congested during the weekends on major routes and during rush hours. Parking is difficult and can be expensive in the city center. Traffic moves on the right; road signs and traffic rules are similar to those used throughout Europe. Third party liability insurance is required for all vehicles; coverage is purchased locally. Travelers should be alert to aggressive drivers both in cities and on highways. Many of the serious accidents in Slovenia occur as a result of high speed driving. Emergency roadside help and information may be reached by dialing 987 for vehicle assistance and towing services, 112 for an ambulance or fire brigade, and 113 for police. U.S. visitors or U.S. residents in Slovenia must be in possession of both a valid U.S. driver's license and an International driver's license if they wish to drive here. This will allow them to drive for a maximum of one year after which residents of Slovenia are required to obtain a Slovenian driver's license.

The speed limit is 50-kph/30 mph in residential areas and 130-kph/78 mph on highways. Motorists are required to have their headlights on during the daytime and drivers and passengers must wear seat belts. For additional information, visit the website of the U.S. Embassy in Slovenia at http://www.usembassy.si.

For specific information on Slovenian driver's permits, vehicle inspection, road tax and mandatory insurance contact the Slovenian National Tourist Office at (212) 358-9686, or via the Internet at http://www.Slovenia-tourism.si. For information about international driving permits, contact AAA or the American Automobile Touring Alliance at http://www.aaa.com.

AVIATION SAFETY OVERSIGHT: As there is no direct commercial air service by local carriers at present, or economic authority to operate such service, between the U.S. and Slovenia, the U.S. Federal Aviation Administration (FAA) has not assessed Slovenia's Civil Aviation Authority for compliance with international aviation safety standards. For further information, travelers may contact the Department of Transportation within the U.S. at 1-800-322-7873, or visit the FAA's Internet website at http://www.faa.gov/avr/iasa.

The U.S. Department of Defense (DOD) separately assesses some foreign air carriers for suitability as official providers of air services. For information regarding the DOD policy on specific carriers, travelers may Contact DOD at (618) 229-4801.

CUSTOMS REGULATIONS: Slovenia customs authorities may enforce strict regulations concerning temporary importation or export from Slovenia of items such as firearms, antiquities, medications, business equipment, and other items. It is advisable to contact the Embassy of Slovenia in Washington, D.C. or the Consulate General of Slovenia in New York for specific information regarding customs requirements.

As of March 15, 2001, Slovenian Customs authorities accept ATA (Air Transport Association) Carnets for the temporary importation of commercial samples, exhibitions and fairs and professional equipment into Slovenia. The U.S. Council for International Business, 1212 avenue of the Americas, New York, NY 10036, issues and guarantees the ATA Carnet in the United States. For additional information call (212) 354-4480, send an email to atacarnet@uscib.org, or visit http://www.uscib.org for details.

CRIMINAL PENALTIES: While in a foreign country, U.S. citizens are subject to that country's laws and regulations, which sometimes differ significantly from those in the United States and may not afford the protections available to the individual under U.S. law. Penalties for breaking the law can be more severe than in the United States for similar offenses. Persons violating the laws of Slovenia, even unknowingly, may be expelled, arrested or imprisoned. Penalties for possession, use, or trafficking in illegal drugs in Slovenia are strict and convicted offenders can expect jail sentences and heavy fines.

DISASTER PREPAREDNESS: Slovenia is rated high for earthquake probability by the U.S. Federal Management Agency. In 1895 Ljubljana, the capital of Slovenia, was leveled by an earthquake. On April 12, 1998, 3,000 buildings in the Soca Valley were damaged from a 5.5 scale earthquake which was centered in the valley. Although 700 homes were damaged irrevocably, there were no injuries or fatalities. Earthquake probability ratings and other information about earthquake preparedness is available via the Internet from the U.S. Federal Management Agency (FEMA) at http://www.fema.gov.

CHILDREN'S ISSUES: For information on international adoption of children, international parental child abduction, and international child support enforcement issues, please refer to our Internet site at http://travel.state.gov/children's_issues.html or telephone (202) 736-7000.

REGISTRATION/EMBASSY LOCATION: Americans living in or visiting Slovenia are encouraged to register at the Consular Section of the U.S. Embassy in Ljubljana to obtain updated information on travel and security within Slovenia. The U.S. Embassy is located at Presernova 31, Ljubljana 1000, Tel: (386)(1) 200-5500 or Fax: (386)(1) 200-5535. The Embassy website address is http://www.usembassy.si.

Romania

COUNTRY DESCRIPTION: Romania has undergone profound political and economic changes since the 1989 revolution, and it is in a period of economic transition. Most tourist facilities, while being upgraded, have not yet reached Western European standards. The capital is Bucharest.

ENTRY REQUIREMENTS: A passport is required. Tourist visas for stays up to ninety days are not required. An exit visa must be obtained only in cases when the original passport used to enter the country was lost or stolen and a replacement passport has been issued by the Embassy. For stays longer than ninety days, visas should be obtained from a Romanian embassy or consulate abroad. These should be extended at passport offices in Romania in the area of residence. Travelers should be advised that the Romanian Government has begun enforcing visa regulations more vigorously, and a record of visa overstay can result in the denial of future visas or entry without visa for a specified time. Visitors can obtain visas and other information regarding entry requirements from the Romanian Embassy at 1607 23rd St. N.W., Washington, D.C. 20008, telephone number (202) 232-4747, or the Romanian consulates in Los Angeles, Chicago, or New York City. The Romanian Embassy maintains a web site at http://www.roembus.org.

In an effort to prevent international child abduction, many governments have initiated procedures at entry/exit points. These often include requiring documentary evidence of relationship and permission for the child's travel from the parent(s) or legal guardian not present. Having such documentation on hand, even if not required, may facilitate entry/departure.

DUAL NATIONALITY: In addition to being subject to all Romanian laws affecting U.S. citizens, dual nationals may also be subject to other laws that impose special obligations on Romanian citizens. For additional information, please see the Consular Affairs home page on the Internet at http://travel.state.gov for our Dual Nationality flyer.

CRIME: While most crimes in Romania are non-violent and non-confrontational, crimes do occur in which the victim suffers personal harm. Crimes against tourists (robbery, mugging, pick-pocketing and confidence scams) remain a problem in Romania. Organized groups of thieves and pickpockets operate in the train stations and on trains, subways, and buses in major cities. A number of thefts and assaults have occurred on overnight trains, including thefts from passengers in closed compartments. Money exchange schemes targeting travelers are common in Romania. Some of these scams have become rather sophisticated, involving individuals posing as plainclothes policemen, who approach the potential victim, flash a badge and ask for his/her passport and wallet. In many of these cases, the thieves succeed in obtaining passports, credit cards, and other personal documents. Credit card and Internet fraud remain among the most common crimes affecting foreigners in Romania (please see the section below on "Special Circumstances").

The loss or theft abroad of a U.S. passport should be reported immediately to the local police and the nearest U.S. embassy or consulate. If you are the victim of a crime while overseas, in addition to reporting to local police, please contact the nearest U.S. embassy or consulate for assistance. The Embassy/Consulate staff can, for example, assist you to find appropriate medical care, to contact family members or friends and explain how funds could be transferred. Although the investigation and prosecution of the crime is solely the responsibility of local authorities, consular officers can help you to understand the local criminal justice process and to find an attorney if needed.

U.S. citizens may refer to the Department of State's pamphlet, *A Safe Trip Abroad*, for ways to promote a trouble-free journey. The pamphlet is available by mail from the Superintendent of Documents, U.S. Government Printing Office, Washington, D.C. 20402, via the Internet at http://www.access.gpo.gov/su_docs, or via the Bureau of Consular Affairs home page at http://travel.state.gov.

MEDICAL FACILITIES: Medical care in Romania generally is not up to Western standards, and basic medical supplies are limited, especially outside major cities. Some medical providers that are up to Western quality standards are available in Bucharest and other cities, but they can be difficult to identify and locate. Therefore, travelers seeking medical treatment should choose their provider carefully.

MEDICAL INSURANCE: The Department of State strongly urges Americans to consult with their medical insurance company prior to traveling abroad to confirm whether their policy applies overseas and if it will cover emergency expenses such as a medical evacuation. U.S. medical insurance plans seldom cover health costs incurred outside the United States unless supplemental coverage is purchased. Further, U.S. Medicare and Medicaid programs do not provide payment for medical services outside the United States. However, many travel agents and private companies offer insurance plans that will cover health care expenses incurred overseas, including emergency services such as medical evacuations.

When making a decision regarding health insurance, Americans should consider that many foreign doctors and hospitals require payment in cash prior to providing service and that a medical evacuation to the United States may cost well in excess of $50,000. Uninsured travelers who require medical care overseas often face extreme difficulties. When consulting with your insurer prior to your trip, please ascertain whether payment will be made to the overseas healthcare provider or if you will be reimbursed later for expenses that you incur. Some insurance policies also include coverage for psychiatric treatment and for disposition of remains in the event of death.

Useful information on medical emergencies abroad, including overseas insurance programs, is provided in the Department of State's Bureau of Consular Affairs brochure, *Medical Information for Americans Traveling Abroad*, available via the Bureau of Consular Affairs home page or autofax: (202) 647-3000.

OTHER HEALTH INFORMATION: Information on vaccinations and other health precautions, such as safe food and water precautions and insect bite protection, may be obtained from the Centers for Disease Control and Prevention's hotline for international travelers at 1-877-FYI-TRIP (1-877-394-8747), fax 1-888-CDC-FAXX (1-888-232-3299), or via the CDC's Internet site at http://www.cdc.gov/travel. For information about outbreaks of infectious diseases abroad, please consult the World Health Organization's website at http://www.who.int/en. Further health information for travelers is available at http://www.who.int/ith.

TRAFFIC SAFETY AND ROAD CONDITIONS: While in a foreign country, U.S. citizens may encounter road conditions that differ significantly from those in the United States. The information below concerning Romania is provided for general reference only, and it may not be totally accurate in a particular location or circumstance.

Safety of Public Transportation: Good
Urban Road Conditions/Maintenance: Fair
Rural Road Conditions/Maintenance: Poor
Availability of Roadside Assistance: Fair

Road conditions vary widely throughout Romania. While major streets in larger cities and major inter-city roads are in fair to good condition, most other roads are in poor repair, badly lit, narrow, and often do not have marked lanes. Many roads, particularly in rural areas, are also used by pedestrians, animals, people on bicycles, and horse-drawn carts that are difficult to see, especially at night. Road travel can be particularly dangerous when roads are wet or covered with snow or ice. This is especially the case concerning mountain roads.

Romanian traffic laws are very strict. Any form of driver's license or permit can be confiscated by the traffic police for one to three months, and payment of fines may be requested at the time of many infractions. Some examples are: failure to yield the right of way, failure to yield to pedestrians at crossroads, or not stopping at a red light or stop sign. Romanian traffic law provides for retention of licenses and possible imprisonment from one to five years for driving under the influence (alcohol level over 0.1% limit) or for causing an accident resulting in injury or death. In spite of these strict rules, however, many drivers in Romania often do not follow traffic laws or yield the right of way. Therefore, it is strongly recommended that defensive driving be practiced while driving in Romania.

U.S. driver's licenses are only valid in Romania for up to 30 days. Before the 30-day period has expired, U.S. citizens must either obtain an international driving permit in addition to their U.S. driver's license or obtain a Romanian driver's license. Wearing a seat belt is mandatory only in the front seats of a car. Children under 12 years of age cannot be transported on the front seat. Drivers must yield to pedestrians at all marked pedestrian crosswalks, but many of these are poorly marked and difficult to see. Unless otherwise marked with road signs, speed limits are as follows: inter-city traffic on highways, 120 km/hr for cars, 100 km/hr for motorcycles, 90 km/hr for vans. On all other roads: 90 km/hr for cars, 80 km/hr for motorcycles, and 70 km/hr for vans. Inner-city traffic: 50 km/hr. Speed limits for motor vehicles with trailers and for drivers with less than one year of driving experience are 10 km/hr slower than those listed above.

Inter-city travel is generally done via trains and buses, which are relatively safe, inexpensive, and reliable. However, travelers should beware of pickpockets while on night trains or in train stations. Inter-city travel by taxi is much more expensive, and safety depends on the quality of the driver. Many older taxis are not equipped with seat belts. To avoid being overcharged, those using inner-city taxis should request the taxi by phone, make sure the taxi has an operational meter, or agree upon a price before entering the taxi.

The host country authority responsible for road safety is the Traffic Police of the Romanian Ministry of Interior. The Traffic Police maintain a web site at http://www.politiarutiera.ro.

Emergency roadside help and information may be reached by dialing 9271 for vehicle assistance and towing services, 961 for ambulance services, 981 for fire brigade, and 955 for police.

For additional information about road travel in Romania, please see the U.S. Embassy home page at http://www.usembassy.ro. For additional general information about road safety, including links to foreign government web sites, please see the Department of State, Bureau of Consular Affairs home page at http://travel.state.gov/road_safety.html. For specific information concerning Romanian driving permits, vehicle inspection, road tax and mandatory insurance, please contact the Romania National Tourist Organization offices in New York via the Internet at http://www.towd.com.

AVIATION SAFETY OVERSIGHT: The U.S. Federal Aviation Administration (FAA) has assessed the Government of Romania's civil aviation authority as Category 1 -- in compliance with international aviation safety standards for oversight of Romania's air carrier operations. For further information, travelers may contact the Department of Transportation within the United States at tel. 1-800-322-7873, or visit the FAA's Internet website at http://www.faa.gov/avr/iasa.

The U.S. Department of Defense (DOD) separately assesses some foreign air carriers for suitability as official providers of air services. For information regarding the DOD policy on specific carriers, travelers may contact the DOD at tel. (618) 229-4801.

CUSTOMS REGULATIONS: Romania's customs authorities may enforce strict regulations concerning temporary importation into or export from Romania of items such as firearms, antiquities, and medications. Romanian law allows foreigners to bring up to $10,000 in cash into Romania, and no amount in excess of that declared upon entry may be taken out of Romania upon departure. Sums larger than $10,000 must be transferred through banks. No more than 1,000,000 Romanian lei (rol) may be brought into or taken out of the country. It is advisable to contact the Embassy of Romania in Washington, D.C. or one of Romania's consulates in the United States for specific information regarding customs requirements.

Romania customs authorities encourage the use of an ATA (Admission Temporaire/Temporary Admission) carnet for the temporary admission of professional equipment, commercial samples, and/or goods for exhibitions and fair purposes. ATA Carnet headquarters, located at the U.S. Council for International Business, 1212 Avenue of the Americas, New York, N.Y. 10036, issues and guarantees the ATA Carnet in the United States. For additional information, please telephone (212) 354-4480, or send an e-mail to atacarnet@uscib.org, or visit http://www.uscib.org for details.

CRIMINAL PENALTIES: While in a foreign country, a U.S. citizen is subject to that country's laws and regulations, which sometimes differ significantly from those in the United States and may not afford the protections available to the individual under U.S. Law. Penalties for breaking the law can be more severe than in the United States for similar offenses. Persons violating Romanian laws, even unknowingly, may be expelled, arrested or imprisoned. Penalties for possession, use, or trafficking in illegal drugs in Romania are strict, and convicted offenders can expect jail sentences and heavy fines.

SPECIAL CIRCUMSTANCES: Romania is largely a "cash only" economy. While an increasing number of businesses do accept credit cards, travelers are advised to use cash for goods and services rendered due to an increase in credit card fraud. Venders have been known to misuse credit card information by making illegal purchases on individuals' accounts. There are an increasing number of ATM machines located throughout major cities. Travelers' checks are of limited use, but they may be used to exchange local currency at some exchange houses.

There is a significant population of stray dogs in and around Bucharest, and attacks on pedestrians and joggers are not uncommon. While there have not been any reported problems with rabies, travelers are advised to avoid all stray dogs.

DISASTER PREPAREDNESS: Romania is an earthquake-prone country. General information about natural disaster preparedness is available via the Internet from the U.S. Federal Emergency

Management Agency (FEMA) at
http://www.fema.gov/.

CHILDREN'S ISSUES: There is currently a
moratorium on adoptions in Romania. For
information on international adoption of children
and international parental child abduction, please
refer to our Internet site at
http://travel.state.gov/children's_issues.html or
telephone (202) 736-7000

International Adoptions: Before traveling to
Romania, prospective parents may wish to obtain
information about both United States visa
requirements and Romanian adoption laws from
the U.S. Embassy in Bucharest or from the
Embassy's web site at http://www.usembassy.ro.
Romanian adoption law mandates criminal
penalties for offering money or goods to obtain the
release of children for adoption. A guidebook
detailing the adoption process can be found on the
Embassy's web site or by requesting a copy from
the U.S. Embassy, Consular Section, Immigrant
Visas Unit, Tudor Arghezi 7-9, Bucharest,
Romania or adoptions@usembassy.ro.

**REGISTRATION/EMBASSY AND
CONSULATE LOCATION:** Americans living in
or visiting Romania are encouraged to register
with the Consular Section of the U.S. Embassy in
Romania and obtain updated information on travel
and security within Romania. The U.S. Embassy is
located at Strada Tudor Arghezi 7-9, telephone
(40) 21-210-4042. In life or death emergencies, an
after hours duty officer may be reached by
telephoning (40) 21-210-0149. Consular services
for U.S. citizens are performed in the Consular
Section located at Strada Filipescu No. 26
(formerly Strada Snagov), one block from the U.S.
Embassy at the corner of Strada Batistei. The
telephone number of the Consular Section is (40)
21-210-4042, and faxes can be sent to (40) 21
211-3360. The Embassy Information Office in
Cluj-Napoca is located at Universitatii 7-9, Etaj 1,
telephone (40) 264-193-815. This office is able to
provide limited consular information.

Chapter 18

Tips for Travelers to Mexico

[The information in this chapter is reprinted verbatim from a bulletin issued by the U.S. State Department, Bureau of Consular Affairs. It is intended to serve as advice to Americans traveling abroad.]

General Information

Between 15 and 16 million U.S. citizens visit Mexico each year, while more than 460,000 Americans reside there year round. Although the majority of visitors thoroughly enjoy their stay, a small number experience difficulties and serious inconveniences.

Travel conditions in Mexico can contrast sharply with those in the United States. This chapter offers advice to help you avoid inconveniences and difficulties as you go. The Department of State and its Embassy and consulates in Mexico offer a wide range of services to assist U.S. citizens in distress. U.S. consular officials meet regularly with Mexican authorities to promote the safety of U.S. citizens in Mexico.

Before you go, learn as much as you can about your destination. Your travel agent, local bookstore, public library, the Internet and the embassy of the country or countries you plan to visit are all useful sources of information. Another source is the Department of State s *Background Notes* series, which features a pamphlet regarding each specific country to which you wish to travel. To obtain specific pamphlet prices and information, contact the Superintendent of Documents, U.S. Government Printing Office, Washington, D.C. 20402; tel: (202) 512-1800. You may also obtain selected copies by fax by calling the State Department s Bureau of Public Affairs (202) 736-7720 from your fax machine or from the State Department home page at http://www.state.gov/.

Important: This chapter contains information obtained prior to August 1998 and is subject to change. Please consult the latest Consular Information Sheet for current information.

How To Have a Safe and Healthy Trip

Know Before You Go

As you travel, keep abreast of local news coverage. If you plan a stay in one place for longer than a few weeks, or, if you are in an area where communications are poor, experiencing civil unrest or some natural disaster, you are encouraged to register with the nearest U.S. embassy or consulate. Registration takes only a few moments, and it may be invaluable in case of an emergency.

Other useful precautions are:

- Leave a detailed itinerary and the numbers of your passport or other citizenship documents with a friend or relative in the United States.
- Bring either a U.S. passport or a certified copy of a birth certificate and photo identification.
- Carry your photo identification and the name of a person to contact with you in the event of serious illness or other emergency.
- Keep photocopies of your airline or other tickets and your list of travelers checks with you in a separate location from the originals and leave copies with someone at home.
- Leave things like unnecessary credit cards and expensive jewelry at home.
- Bring travelers checks, not cash.
- Use a money belt or concealed pouch for passport, cash and other valuables.
- Do not bring firearms or ammunition into Mexico without written permission from the Mexican government.

Consular Information Program

Before traveling, obtain the Consular Information Sheet for Mexico and any other countries you plan to visit. You should also check to see if the Department of State has issued a Travel Warning or Public Announcement for the country or countries you will be visiting. *Travel Warnings* are issued when the Department of State decides, based on all relevant information, to recommend that all Americans avoid travel to a certain country. *Public Announcements* are issued as a means to disseminate information quickly about relatively short-term and/or trans-national conditions which would pose significant risks to the security of American travelers. *Consular Information Sheets* are available for every country in the world. They include such information as the location of the U.S. embassy or consulate in the country, unusual immigration practices, health conditions, unusual currency and entry regulations, crime and security information, and drug penalties. A description of political disturbances may be included in the Consular Information Sheet under an optional section entitled "Areas of Instability." On limited occasions, the Department also restates in this section U.S. Embassy advice given to official employees. Consular Information Sheets present information so that travelers can make knowledgeable decisions concerning travel to a particular country. Countries where we suggest that you not travel will have Travel Warnings as well as Consular Information Sheets.

How to Access Consular Information Sheets, Travel Warnings and Public Announcements

By Internet

The most convenient source of information about travel and consular services is available from the Consular Affairs home page on the Internet s World Wide Web. The address is http://travel.state.gov. If you do not have access to the Internet at home, work or school, check with you local library to see if it has access to the Internet.

In Person/By Mail

Consular Information Sheets, Travel Warnings and Public Announcements are available at any of the regional passport agencies, field offices of the Department of Commerce, and U.S. embassies and consulates abroad, or, by writing and sending a self-addressed, stamped envelope to the Office of American Citizens Services, Bureau of Consular Affairs, Room 4811, U.S. Department of State, Washington, D.C. 20520-4818.

By Telephone

Consular Information Sheets and Travel Warnings may be heard any time by dialing the office of American Citizens Services at **(202) 647-5225** from a touchtone phone. The recording is updated as new information becomes available.

By Fax

From your fax machine, dial **(202) 647-3000**, using the handset as you would a regular telephone. The system will instruct you on how to proceed.

Entry Requirements

Proof of citizenship and photo identification are required for entry by all U.S. citizens. A passport and visa are not required for a tourist/transit stay of up to 180 days. A tourist card, issued by Mexican consulates and most airlines serving Mexico, is required. Minors require notarized consent from parent(s) if traveling alone, with one parent, or in someone else's custody. Mexican regulations limit the value of goods brought into Mexico by U.S. citizens arriving by air or sea to $300 per person and by land to $50 per person. Amounts exceeding the duty-free limit are subject to a 32.8 percent tax. Upon arrival in Mexico, business travelers must complete a form (FM-N 30 days) authorizing the conduct of business, but not employment, for a 30-day period. If the business traveler departs and re-enters, the 30-day period begins again. For further information concerning entry requirements, travelers may contact the Embassy of Mexico at 1911 Pennsylvania Avenue N.W., Washington, D.C. 20006, telephone (202) 736-1000, or any of the Mexican consulates in major U.S. cities. In response to the increased interest in immigration matters in the U.S., Mexican authorities may scrutinize more closely the visa situation of U.S. citizens residing or working in Mexico. U.S. citizens planning on working or living in Mexico should apply for the appropriate Mexican visa (FM-2 or 3).

Visitors intending to participate in humanitarian aid missions, human rights advocacy groups or international observer delegations should contact the nearest Mexican Consulate or Embassy for guidance on how to obtain the appropriate visa before traveling to Mexico. This is particularly relevant in light of the tension and polarization in Chiapas and the international interest the situation there has attracted.

Returning to the United States – Caution! Make certain that you can return to the United States with the proof of citizenship that you take with you. Although some countries may allow you to enter with only a birth certificate, U.S. law requires that you document both your U.S. citizenship and identity when you reenter the United States.

The best document to prove your U.S. **citizenship** is a valid U.S. passport. Other documents that establish U.S. citizenship include an expired U.S. passport, a certified copy of your birth certificate, a Certificate of Naturalization, a Certificate of Citizenship, or a Report of Birth Abroad of a U.S. citizen. To prove your **identity**, either a valid driver's license or a government identification card that includes a photo or physical description is acceptable.

Health

Health problems sometimes affect visitors to Mexico. Information on health precautions can be obtained from local health departments or private doctors. General guidance can also be found in the U.S. Public Health Service book, *Health Information for International Travel*, available from the Superintendent of Documents, U.S. Government Printing Office, Washington, D.C. 20402.

For the most current information on immunizations and heath risks, the Centers for Disease Control and Prevention (CDC) maintains an international travelers hotline at 1-888-232-3228, an automated faxback service at 1-888-232-3299 and a home page on the Internet at http://www.cdc.gov/.

It is wise to review your health insurance policy before you travel. In some places, particularly at resorts, medical costs can be as high or higher than in the United States. Medicare/Medicaid does not cover you when you are outside the United States. If your insurance policy does not cover you in Mexico, it is strongly recommended that you purchase a policy that does. There are short-term health insurance policies designed specifically to cover travel.

Medical facilities in Mexico differ from those in the United States. Adequate medical care can be found in all major cities. There are some excellent health facilities in Mexico City. Some remote areas or coastal islands may have few or no medical facilities. For these reasons, in addition to medical insurance that you can use in Mexico, consider obtaining insurance or joining a medical assistance program to cover the very high cost of medical evacuation in the event of an accident or serious illness. As part of the coverage, these programs usually offer emergency consultation by telephone. They may refer you to the nearest hospital or call for help on your behalf; they may translate your instructions to a health care worker on the scene. The cost of medical evacuation coverage can be as low as $50.00 for a trip of 30 days. Without this insurance, medical evacuation can cost thousands of dollars.

If your travel agent cannot direct you to a medical assistance company, look for information in travel magazines. The names of some companies that provide medical evacuation coverage or services are listed in our publication, *Medical Information for Americans Traveling Abroad*, accessible at our Internet site (http://travel.state.gov). The U.S. government cannot pay to have you medically evacuated to the United States.

Immunizations are normally recommended against diphtheria, tetanus, polio, typhoid, and hepatitis A for travelers. Generally, these immunizations are administered during childhood. For visitors coming directly from the United States, no immunization certification is required to enter Mexico. If you are traveling from an area known to be infected with yellow fever, a vaccination certificate is required.

Malaria is found in some rural areas of Mexico, particularly those near the southwest coast. Travelers to malarial areas should consult their physician or the U.S. Public Health Service and take the recommended dosage of chloroquine or other anti-malarial medication. Although chloroquine is not considered necessary for travelers to the major resort areas on the Pacific and Gulf coasts, travelers to those areas should use insect repellent and take other personal protection measures to reduce contact with mosquitoes, particularly from dusk to dawn when malaria transmission is most likely.

Air pollution in Mexico City is severe. It is most dangerous during thermal inversions which occur most often from December to May. Air pollution plus Mexico City s high altitude are a particular health risk for the elderly and persons with high blood pressure, anemia, or respiratory or cardiac problems. If this applies to you, consult your doctor before traveling to Mexico City.

In high altitude areas, such as Mexico City, most people need a short adjustment period. Spend the first few days in a leisurely manner, with a light diet and reduced intake of alcohol. Avoid strenuous activity, including everything from sports to rushing up the stairs. Reaction signs to high altitude are lack of energy, a tendency to tire easily, shortness of breath, occasional dizziness, and insomnia.

Drink only bottled water or water that has been boiled for 20 minutes. Beware of ice cubes that may not have been made with purified water. Vegetables and fruits should be peeled or washed in a purifying solution. A good rule to follow is if you can t peel it or cook it, do not eat it. Diarrhea may benefit from antimicrobial treatment which may be prescribed or purchased over the counter. Travelers should consult a physician, rather thanattempt self-medication, if the diarrhea is severe or persists several days.

Safety Tips

In an emergency, call [91] (5) 250-0123, the 24-hour hotline of the Mexican Ministry of Tourism. They also have two toll free numbers: if calling within Mexico [91] 800-90-392 and from the U.S. 1-800-482-9832. The hotline is for immediate assistance but it can give you general, nonemergency guidance as well. It is an important number to keep with you. If necessary, in an emergency, you may also call the U.S. Embassy or the nearest U.S. consulate or consular agency. (See telephone numbers at the end of this chapter.)

As a visitor to Mexico, be alert to your new surroundings. Problem situations in Mexico may be different from those you are used to, and safety regulations and their enforcement are generally not equivalent to U.S. standards.

In large cities, take the same precautions against assault, robbery, or pickpockets that you would take in any large U.S. city. Be aware that women and small children, as well as men, can be pickpockets or purse snatchers. Keep your billfold in an inner front pocket; carry your purse tucked securely under your arm; and wear the shoulder strap of your camera or bag across your chest. To guard against thieves on motorcycles, walk away from the curb and carry your purse away from the street.

At the Hotel. Travelers to Mexico should leave valuables and irreplaceable items in a safe place. All visitors are encouraged to make use of hotel safes when available.

On Public Transport. Be vigilant in bus and train stations and on public transport. Watch for pickpockets in these areas.

On Streets and Highways. Be wary of persons representing themselves as Mexican police or other local officials. It is not uncommon for Americans to become victims of harassment, mistreatment and extortion by Mexican law enforcement and other officials. Mexican authorities are concerned about these incidents and have cooperated in investigating such cases. *You must, however, have the officer s name, badge number, and patrol car number to pursue a complaint.* Make a note of this information if you are ever involved with police or other officials.

Do not be surprised if you encounter several types of police in Mexico. The Preventive Police, the Transit Police and the Federal Highway Police all wear uniforms. The Judicial Police who work for the public prosecutor are not uniformed.

At the Pool or Beach. Do not leave your belongings on the beach while you are swimming. Keep your passport and other valuables in the hotel safe.

Visitors to Mexican resorts should carefully assess the risk potential of recreational activities. Sports and aquatic equipment that you rent may not meet U.S. safety standards nor be covered by any accident insurance. For example, unless you are certain that scuba diving equipment is up to standard, do not use it. Inexperienced scuba divers should beware of dive shops that promise to "certify" you after a few hours instruction. Safe diving requires lengthy training.

Parasailing is offered at many Mexican beach resorts. Be aware that by putting your name on the passenger list, you may be relieving the boat operator and owner of responsibility for your safety. There have been cases in which tourists have been dragged through palm trees or slammed into hotel walls while participating in this activity.

Be extremely careful when renting jet-skis. Several tourists have been killed or injured in jet-ski accidents, particularly when participating in group tours. Often inexperienced tour guides allow their clients to follow too closely or operate the jet-skis in other unsafe manners. In one case the jet-ski rental company carried liability insurance limited to $2,500 U.S. dollars. Make sure that the rental company has adequate medical/accident insurance, is staffed with personnel on-site with water rescue training, and properly demonstrates safe operation of the vehicle to you before you rent or operate such equipment.

Do not use pools or beaches without lifeguards, or, if you do, exercise extreme caution. Do not dive into unknown bodies of water because hidden rocks or shallow depths can cause serious injury or death. Some Mexican beaches, such as those in Cancun, have warning signs about undertow; take them seriously. Newer resorts may lack comprehensive medical facilities.

Travel by Car
People are often surprised when inconveniences occur because they were unaware of the laws regarding crossing the border. The government of Mexico strictly regulates the entry of vehicles into Mexico.

It is important for visitors to remember the following steps when crossing the border between the United States and Mexico by automobile. There are no procedures to comply with if you are traveling within the Border Zone or Free Trade Zone (including the Baja California Peninsula and the Sonora Free Trade Zone). If you wish to travel past these zones, you will need to adhere to certain procedures.

The first step to take is to obtain the original and

photocopies of the appropriate immigration form, the vehicle state registration certificate or document certifying legal ownership, and leasing contract. If the vehicle is leased or rented then it must be in the name of the person who is driving the car. If the vehicle belongs to a company, proper documentation is necessary to show you work for the company. A valid driver s license and an international credit card (American Express, Diner s Club, Mastercard or Visa) are needed in the name of the owner of the vehicle. If you do not possess an international credit card, you will be asked to post a bond, payable to the Federal Treasury, issued by an authorized bonding company in Mexico. An alternative is to make a cash deposit at Banco del Ejercito in an amount equal to the value of the vehicle according to the tables of vehicle values for bonding companies. This is often a substantial percentage of the vehicle s value.

The second step is to present the documents you have received to the Vehicular Control Module located in Mexican Customs to process the importation permit. Carry this document with you at all times! The permit is valid for periods up to six months. The vehicle may be driven across the border multiple times during the authorized period of the permit. Other persons may drive the car as long as the owner is in the vehicle. Other foreigners with the same "tourist" status as the vehicle owner may drive the vehicle without the owner present in the car. If you wish to authorize another person to drive your car, record the authorization with Mexican officials when you enter Mexico - even if you expect to be a passenger when the other person drives.

Do not, under any circumstances, allow an unauthorized person to drive the vehicle when the owner is not in it. Such a person would have to pay a fine amounting to a substantial percentage of the vehicle s value, and your vehicle would be confiscated. All documents and the credit card must be in the name of the owner, who must be present upon crossing the border. We caution American citizens not to loan their vehicles to Mexican citizens resident in Mexico as those vehicles are subject to seizure by Mexican authorities. If confiscated, they are not returned.

In the third step, your credit card will be charged an amount in national currency equivalent to U.S.

$10 at the Banco del Ejercito. If you do not have a credit card, the bank will accept cash in an amount equal to the value of your vehicle shown in the table of vehicle values for bonding companies. Your deposit plus any interest it may earn will be returned upon departure from Mexico. You may also, instead, obtain a bond through an authorized Mexican bonding company located at all border crossings. The bonding companies require a refundable deposit equal to a substantial percentage of the vehicle s value. The bonding company will also assess taxes and processing costs for this service.

Finally, upon your departure from Mexico, and if the vehicle will not be driven back into Mexico, the permit for temporary importation must be canceled at Customs. If these steps are carefully followed, there should be no problem taking your car to Mexico. Remembr, if your car is found in Mexico beyond the authorized time or without the proper documents, it will be immediately confiscated. Also, the sale, abandonment, or use of the vehicle for financial gain will result in its confiscation. Travelers are advised to consult with the nearest Mexican Consulate in the U.S. for additional detailed information prior to departing the U.S.

If you bring spare auto parts to Mexico, declare them when you enter the country. When you leave, be prepared to show that you are taking the unused parts with you or that you have had them installed in Mexico. Save your repair receipts for this purpose.

All vehicular traffic is restricted in the capital city of Mexico City in order to reduce air pollution. The restriction is based on the last digit of the vehicle license plate. (This applies equally to permanent and temporary plates. There is no specific provision regarding plates with letters only.)

Monday: no driving if license plate ends with 5 or 6.

Tuesday: no driving if license plate ends with 7 or 8.

Wednesday: no driving if license plate ends with 3 or 4.

Thursday: no driving if license plate ends with 1 or 2.

Friday: no driving if license plate ends with 9 or 0.

Saturday and Sunday: all vehicles may be driven.

Avoid excessive speed and, if at all possible, do not drive at night. Loose livestock can appear at any time. Construction sites or stranded vehicles are often unmarked by flares or other warning signals. Sometimes cars have only one headlight. Many cars lack brake lights. Bicycles seldom have lights or reflectors. This makes for very dangerous driving conditions at night. Be prepared for a sudden stop at any time. *Mexican driving conditions are such that, for your safety, you must drive more slowly than you do at home.*

Learn local driving signals. In Mexico, a blinking left turn signal on the vehicle in front of you could mean that it is clear ahead and you may pass, or it could mean the driver is making a left turn. An outstretched left arm may mean an invitation for you to pass. When in doubt, do not pass.

An oncoming vehicle flashing its headlights is a warning for you to slow down or pull over because you are both approaching a narrow bridge or place in the road. The custom is that the first vehicle to flash has the right of way and the other must yield.

When it begins to rain, immediately slow to a crawl. Freshly wet roads are dangerous because oil and road dust mix with water and form a lubricant. Until this mixture washes away, driving is extremely hazardous. Beware of sudden rains. Stop, or go extremely slowly, until conditions improve.

To avoid highway crime, try not to drive at night and never drive alone during this time. Never sleep in vehicles along the road. Do not, under any circumstances, pick up hitchhikers who not only pose a threat to your physical safety, but also put you in danger of being arrested for unwittingly transporting narcotics or narcotics traffickers in your vehicle. Your vehicle can be confiscated if you are transporting marijuana or other narcotics. There are checkpoints and temporary roadblocks where vehicles are checked.

If you plan to drive, learn about your route from

an auto club, guide book or a Mexican government tourist office. Some routes have heavy truck and bus traffic, others have poor or nonexistent shoulders and many have animals on the loose. Also, some of the newer roads have very few restaurants, motels, gas stations or auto repair shops. You may not be able to avoid all problems, but at least you will know what to expect if you have done some research. For your safety, have your vehicle serviced and in optimum condition before you leave for Mexico. It is wise to bring an extra fan belt, fuses and other spare parts. Pack a basic first-aid kit and carry an emergency water supply in your vehicle. Unleaded gasoline (magna sin) is generally available throughout Mexico. Bring a flexible funnel to fill your gas tank because some gas stations have nozzles too large to fit unleaded tanks.

If you have an emergency while driving, call the Ministry of Tourism s hotline or (91)(5) 250-8221/8555 et. 130/297 to obtain help from the "Green Angels," a fleet of radio dispatched trucks with bilingual crews that operate daily. Services include protection, medical first aid, mechanical aid for your car, and basic supplies. You will not be charged for services, only for parts, gas, and oil. The Green Angels patrol daily, from dawn until sunset. If you are unable to call them, pull off the road and lift the hood of your car; chances are good they will find you.

Insurance. Mexican auto insurance is sold in most cities and towns on both sides of the border. U.S. automobile liability insurance is not valid in Mexico nor is most collision and comprehensive coverage issued by U.S. companies. Therefore, when you cross the border, purchase auto insurance adequate for your needs in Mexico. A good rule of thumb is to buy coverage equivalent to that which you carry in the United States.

Motor vehicle insurance is invalid in Mexico if the driver is found to be under the influence of alcohol or drugs. Regardless of whether you have insurance, if you are involved in an accident, you will be taken into police custody until it can be determined who is liable and whether you have the ability to pay any judgment. If you do not have Mexican liability insurance, you are almost certain to spend some time in jail until all parties are satisfied that responsibility has been assigned and adequate financial satisfaction received. There may

also be criminal liability assigned if the injuries or damages are serious.

Rental Cars

Renting in the United States. Many car rental companies in the United States have clauses in their contracts prohibiting drivers from traveling out of the country. The Mexican police are aware of these regulations and will sometimes impound rental vehicles driven from the United States. When renting a vehicle in the United States, check with the company to see if your contract allows you to drive it into Mexico.

Renting a Car in Mexico. The standard insurance included with many car rental contracts in Mexico provides only nominal liability coverage, often as little as the equivalent of $200. Because Mexican law permits the jailing of drivers after an accident until they have met their obligations to third parties and to the rental company, renters should read their contracts carefully and purchase additional liability and comprehensive insurance if necessary.

Yucantan-Campeche and Quintana Roo Borders
The State of Yucatan has agricultural inspection stations on its border to eradicate swine fever and inspectors may confiscate pork products that arrive at these inspection stations. Yucatan health inspectors may hold travelers for possible arrest by Federal authorities if travelers appear in violation of any Mexican laws, such as immigration, firearms, narcotics, etc.

Military Checkpoints
Military and law enforcement checkpoints aimed at detecting narcotics, alien smuggling, and firearms traffic are located at various places throughout Mexico. Areas known to possess these checkpoints include the Yucatan peninsula, Chiapas, Oaxaca and Guerrero. Many checkpoints will have a red flag marker and are operated by uniformed officials; however, others will not be marked and are manned by police/military officers not in uniform. These checkpoints have "spiked devices" and are sometimes used to deflate tires of vehicles attempting to evade these checkpoints.

Travel through Mexico to Central American Countries
Mexican authorities require that all international transit of persons (transmigrantes) and

merchandise through Mexico, destined for Central America, from the area from Ciudad Acuna to Matamoros, be handled by the Lucio Transmigrantes. Persons and merchandise entering Mexico from areas other than the Ciudad Acuna-Matamoros zone continue to use their regular ports of entry. Mexican authorities require that a customs broker handle the temporary entry into Mexico of all non-personal property of travelers destined for Central American countries. Fees will be processed through the customs broker. For more detailed information, travelers can contact the nearest Mexican consulate or tourism office, or the U.S. Consulate in Matamoros prior to departing the U.S.

Bringing Your Own Plane or Boat to Mexico
Private aircraft and boats are subject to the same Mexican customs regulations as are motor vehicles. When you arrive at a Mexican port in your private boat, you can obtain a temporary import permit similar to the one given for motor vehicles.

Flying your own plane to Mexico, however, is more complicated. Well before your trip, inquire about private aircraft regulations and procedures from a Mexican consulate or Mexican Government Tourist Office.

Crime
In Mexico City, crime has reached critical levels. Low apprehension and conviction rates of criminals contribute to the high rate of crime. Metropolitan areas other than the capital are considered to have lower but still serious levels of crime activity. Travelers to Mexico should leave valuables and irreplaceable items at home in the U.S. All visitors to Mexico are encouraged to make use of hotel safes when available, avoid wearing obviously expensive jewelry or designer clothing and carry only the cash or credit cards that will be needed on each outing. Travelers are discouraged from bringing very large amounts of cash into Mexico, as officials may suspect money laundering or other criminal activity. During 1998, criminal activity in Mexico City continued at a high rate, with a marked increase in violent crime, including sexual assaults committed against women.

The most frequently reported crimes involve taxi robberies, armed robbery, pickpocketing and purse snatching. In several cases, tourists report that uniformed police are the crime perpetrators, stopping vehicles and seeking money or assaulting and robbing tourists walking late at night. The area behind the U.S. Embassy and the Zona Rosa, a restaurant/shopping area near the Embassy, are frequent sites of street crime against foreigners. Caution should be exercised when walking in these areas, especially at night. Any U.S. citizen victims of crime in Mexico are encouraged to report the incident to local police authorities and to the nearest U.S. consular office.

U.S. citizens should be very cautious in using ATM cards nd machines in Mexico. If an ATM machine must be used, it should be only during the business day at large protected facilities (preferably inside commercial establishments, rather than at a glass-enclosed, highly visible ATM machine on streets where criminals can observe financial transactions.)

U.S. citizens are advised to be careful when ordering beverages in local nightclubs and bars, especially at night. Some establishments may contaminate or drug the drinks to gain control over the patron. Victims, who are almost always unaccompanied, have been robbed of personal property and abducted and held while their credit cards were used at various businesses and ATM locations around the city.

U.S. citizens should not hitchhike or accept rides from strangers anywhere in Mexico.
Metro (subway) robberies are also becoming more frequent in Mexico City. If riding the Metro, U.S. citizens should hold valuables and belongings tightly. Avoid using Metro during busy commuting hours in the morning or afternoon. Incidents of people boarding long distance buses as passengers and robbing and assaulting all real passengers while underway have also been reported. If someone attempts to rob you, it is generally considered safest to immediately comply by handing over the requested items.

U.S. citizens should avoid providing personal identifying information to individuals not known to them. Information obtained from unaware travelers has been used by individuals in Mexico to extort money from families in the U.S. by contacting them and fraudulently informing them that a family member has been arrested in Mexico or requires urgent medical care. The caller gains their confidence by providing this personal information and requests that funds be sent to assist their family member.

Kidnapping, including the kidnapping of non-Mexicans, is increasing. U.S. businesses with offices in Mexico or concerned U.S. citizens may contact the Embassy to discuss precautions to take. Travelers to Mexico should exercise caution when traveling on all highways in Mexico. Of specific concern are Highway 190 (Tuxtla to Tapachula,) Highway 195 (Tuxtla to Villahermosa,) Highway 186 (Chetumal to Villahermosa,) Highway 15 (Sinaloa) and Express Highway 1 (Sinaloa). These highways have recently seen particularly high levels of criminal assaults and robberies. In addition, the Embassy recommends avoiding the highway from Altamirano to Ixtapa/Zihuatanejo, where a number of serious assaults have recently occurred. The U.S. Embassy advises its personnel to exercise extreme caution and not to travel on Mexican highways after dark for safety reasons.

All bus travel should be done during daylight and on first-class conveyances. These buses travel on toll roads that have a markedly lower rate of incidents than buses (second and third class) that travel the less secure free highways. While many of the assaults have occurred in daylight, the Embassy nevertheless encourages daytime travel to lower the chance of auto accidents.

Tourists should exercise caution by not walking on lightly frequented beaches, off-the-path ruins or trails. Additionally, visitors should not carry excessive cash or valuables, and, should place travel documents in a safe place. In the past two years, several U.S. citizens have been murdered in the vicinity of Puerto Escondido, Oaxaca, including a U.S. citizen woman who was raped and murdered in March 1998.

Taxicab Crime: U.S. citizens visiting Mexico City should absolutely avoid taking any taxi not summoned by telephone or on their behalf by a responsible individual or contracted in advance at the airport. Robbery assaults on passengers in taxis have become more frequent and violent, with passengers subjected to beatings, sexual assault and in December 1997, the murder of a U.S. citizen. When in need of a taxi, telephone a radio taxi or "sitio" (pronounced "C-T-O"). Ask the dispatcher for the driver s name and the cab s license plate number. If you walk to a "sitio" taxi stnd, use only a driver known to you. Ask the hotel concierge or other responsible individual calling on your behalf to write down the license plate number. Passengers arriving at Mexico City s Benito Juarez International Airport should take only airport taxis (yellow with an airport symbol on the door) after pre-paying the fare at one of the special booths inside the airport. Radio taxis may be called at telephone numbers: 271-9146, 271-9058 and 272-6125. U.S. citizens should avoid taking taxis parked outside the Bellas Artes theater, in front of nightclubs, restaurants or cruising throughout the city.

In Case of Emergency. Call the Mexican Ministry of Tourism s emergency hotline, [91] (5) 250-0123, for immediate assistance. Or, in Mexico City, dial 06 for police assistance.

If You Have Been the Victim of a Crime. Immediately contact the U.S. Embassy or the nearest U.S. consulate or consular agency. For addresses and telephone numbers, see the end of this chapter. You should also report the crime to the local police immediately.

Avoiding Legal Problems

While traveling in Mexico, you are subject to Mexican laws and not U.S. laws. Tourists who commit illegal acts have no special privileges and are subject to full prosecution under the Mexican judicial system.

Avoid drug offenses. Mexico rigorously prosecutes drug cases. Under Mexican law, possession of and trafficking in illegal drugs are federal offenses. For drug trafficking, bail does not exist. Convicted offenders can expect lengthy jail sentences and fines. Sentences for possession of drugs in Mexico can be as long as 25 years plus fines. Just as in the U.S., the purchase of controlled medication requires a doctor s prescription. The Mexican list of controlled medication differs from the U.S. list and Mexican public health laws concerning controlled medication are unclear. Possession of excessive amounts of a psychotropic drug such as valium can result in your arrest if the authorities suspect abuse. Mexican law does not differentiate between types of narcotics. Heroin, marijuana, and amphetamines, for example, are treated the same. *Offenders found guilty of possessing more than a token amount of any narcotic substance are subject to a minimum sentence of 10 years, and it is not uncommon for persons charged with drug offenses to be detained for up to 1 year before a verdict is reached.*

Remember, if narcotics are found in your vehicle, you are subject to arrest and your vehicle can be confiscated.

Avoid public drunkenness. It is against the law to be drunk in public in Mexico. Certain border towns have become impatient with teenage (and older) Americans who cross the border to drink and carouse. This behavior can lead to fights, arrests, traffic accidents and even fatalities.

WARNING ON FIREARMS

The Department of State warns U.S. citizens against taking any type of firearm or ammunition into Mexico without prior written authorization. Entering Mexico with a firearm or a single round of ammunition carries a penalty of up to five years in jail, even if the firearm or ammunition is taken into Mexico unintentionally.

The Mexican Government strictly enforces laws restricting the entry of firearms and ammunition along borders and at air and seaports. This has resulted in arrests, convictions and long prison sentences for U.S. citizens who have unintentionally crossed the border with firearms or ammunition in their possession. Those who are approaching Mexico along the land border who realize they are in possession of unauthorized firearms or ammunition should immediately return to the U.S. and not go through Mexican Customs.

The **only** way to **legally** import firearms and/or ammunition into Mexico is to **secure a permit in advace** from the Mexican Embassy in Washington, D.C. or from a Mexican Consulate.

Remember that, even when you enter Mexican waters on your private boat or airplane, you are subject to the ban on importing firearms and ammunition.

Some cities, such as Nuevo Laredo, have ordinances prohibiting the possession of knives, similar weapons or anything that might be construed as a weapon. Tourists have even been arrested for possessing souvenir knives. Most arrests for knife possession occur in connection with some other infraction, such as drunk and disorderly behavior.

Failure to pay hotel bills or for other services rendered is considered fraud under Mexican law. Those accused of these offenses are subject to arrest and conviction with stiff fines and jail sentences.

Be cautious when purchasing real estate. U.S. citizens who become involved in time-share or other real property purchases should be aware that Mexican laws and practices regarding real estate are markedly different from those in the United States. Foreigners purchasing real estate or time-shares in Mexico have no protection under Mexican law and should be aware of the high risks involved. Foreigners may be granted the right to own real property only under very specific conditions and the purchase of real property in Mexico is far more complicated than in the United States. For example no title insurance is available in Mexico for the purchaser and the builders frequently go bankrupt leaving the investors with little recourse to recoup their funds. The U.S. Embassy strongly recommends the use of competent local legal assistance for any significant real property or business purchase. A list of local attorneys can be obtained from the U.S. Embassy or the nearest consulate in Mexico.

To Avoid Disputes With Merchants, Be a Careful Shopper. Make sure the goods you buy are in good condition and always get a receipt. There is a federal consumer protection office, the Procuraduria Federal del Consumidor, to assist you if you have a major problem with a faulty product or service. However, if the problem is with a service of the tourist industry, you should bring the matter to the Mexican Government Tourist Office (Secretaria de Turismo).

U.S. Assistance in Mexico

Where To Turn If You Have Serious Legal, Medical, or Financial Difficulties
Legal Problems. If you find yourself in serious difficulty while in Mexico, contact a consular officer at the U.S. Embassy or the nearest U.S. consulate for assistance. U.S. consuls cannot serve

as attorneys or give legal assistance. They can, however, provide lists of local attorneys and advise you of your rights under Mexican laws.

Worldwide, Mexico has the highest number of arrests of Americans abroad - over 1,000 per year - and the highest prison population of U.S. citizens outside of the United States - about 450 at any one time. If you are arrested, ask permission to notify the U.S. Embassy or nearest U.S. consulate. Under international agreements and practice, you have the right to talk with an American consul. Although U.S. consuls are limited in what they can do to assist you in legal difficulties, they can monitor the status of detained U.S. citizens and make sure they are treated fairly under local laws. They will also notify your relatives or friends upon your request.

An individual is guaranteed certain rights under the Mexican constitution, but those rights differ significantly from U.S. constitutional guarantees. The Mexican judicial system is based on Roman and Napoleonic law and presumes a person accused of a crime to be guilty until proven innocent. There is no trial by jury nor writ of habeas corpus in the Anglo-American sense. Trial under the Mexican system is a prolonged process based largely on documents examined on a fixed date in court by prosecution and defense counsel. Sentencing usually takes 6 to 10 months. Bail can be granted after sentencing if the sentence is less than 5 years. Pre-trial bail exists but is ever granted when the possible sentence upon conviction is greater than 5 years.

Medical or Financial Problems. If you become seriously ill, U.S. consular officers can assist in finding a doctor and in notifying your family and friends about your condition. Consular officers can also help arrange the transfer of emergency funds to you if you become destitute as a result of robbery, accident or other emergency.

Advice on Dual Nationality
U.S. law recognizes that Americans may also be citizens of other countries. As of March 20, 1998, Mexican law recognizes dual nationality for Mexicans by birth, those born in Mexico or born abroad to Mexican parents. U.S. citizens who are also Mexican nationals should be aware that they will be considered Mexican by local authorities and that their dual nationality status could

therefore hamper U.S. government efforts to provide consular protection. Dual nationals will not, however, be subject to compulsory military service. It is important to note that travelers possessing both U.S. and Mexican nationalities must carry with them proof of their citizenship of both counties. Under Mexican law, dual nationals entering or departing Mexico must identify themselves as Mexican citizens or face a stiff fine. Under U.S. law, U.S. citizens must enter U.S. territory with documents proving U.S. citizenship.

A Guide to Entry and Exit Regulations

Getting Into Mexico
U.S. citizens visiting Mexico for no more than 72 hours and remaining within 25 kilometers of the border do not need a permit to enter. Those wishing to travel past the 25 kilometer border area of Mexico must be properly documented. Those transiting Mexico to another country need a transit visa which costs a nominal fee and is valid for up to 30 days.

Tourist Cards. All U.S. citizens visiting Mexico for tourism or study for up to 180 days need a document, called a tourist card (in English) or FMT (in Spanish), to enter and leave Mexico. The tourist card is free and may be obtained from Mexican consulates, Mexican tourism offices, Mexican border crossing points and from most airlines serving Mexico. If you fly to Mexico, you must obtain your tourist card before boarding your flight; it cannot be obtained upon arrival at an airport in Mexico.

The tourist card is issued upon presentation of proof of citizenship, such as a U.S. passport or a U.S. birth certificate, plus a photo I.D., such as a driver s license. Tourist cards are issued for up to 90 days with a single entry, or if you present proof of sufficient funds, for 180 days with multiple entries.

Upon entering Mexico, retain and safeguard the pink copy of your tourist card so you may surrender it to Mexican immigration when you depart. You must leave Mexico before your tourist card expires or you are subject to a fine. A tourist card for less than 180 days may be revalidated in Mexico by the Mexican immigration service (Direccion General de Servicios Migratorios.)

Visas. If you wish to stay longer than 180 days, or if you wish to do business or conduct religious work in Mexico, contact the Mexican Embassy or the nearest Mexican consulate to obtain a visa or permit. Persons conducting religious work on a tourist card are subject to arrest and deportation.

Residing or Retiring in Mexico. If you plan to live or retire in Mexico, consult a Mexican consulate on the type of long-term visa you willneed. As soon as possible after you arrive in the place you will live, it is a good idea to register with the U.S. Embassy or the nearest U.S. consulate or consular agent. Bring your passport or other identification with you. Registration makes it easier to contact you in an emergency. (Registration information is confidential and will not be released to inquirers without your express authorization.)

Traveling Minors. A child under the age of 18 traveling with only one parent must have written, notarized consent from the other parent to travel, or must carry, if applicable, a decree of sole custody for the accompanying parent or a death certificate for the other parent. Children traveling alone or in someone else s custody must have notarized consent from both parents to travel, or, if applicable, notarized consent from a single parent plus documentation that the parent is the only custodial parent.

Operating Citizens Band (CB) Equipment
American tourists are permitted to operate CB radios in Mexico. You must, however, obtain a 180 day permit for a nominal fee by presenting your U.S. citizen s band radio authorization at a Mexican consulate or Mexican Government Tourist Office. This permit cannot be obtained at the border.

Transmissions on CB equipment are allowed only on channels 9, 10 and 11 and only for personal communication and emergency road assistance. Any device which increases transmission power to over 5 watts is prohibited. CB equipment may not be used near radio installations of the aeronautical and marine services.

What You May Bring Into Mexico

Customs Regulations. Tourists should enter Mexico with only the items needed for their trip.

Entering with large quantities of an item a tourist might not normally be expected to have, particularly expensive appliances, such as televisions, stereos or other items, may lead to suspicion of smuggling and possible confiscation of the items and arrest of the individual.

Mexican regulations limit the value of goods brought into Mexico by U.S. citizens arriving by air or sea to $300 U.S. per person and by land to $50 U.S. per person. Other travel-related items may also be brought in duty-free. Amounts exceeding the duty-free limit are subject to a 32.8 percent tax.

Unless you prepare ahead, you may have difficulty bringing computers or other expensive electronic equipment into Mexico for your personal use. To prevent being charged an import tax, write a statement about your intention to use the equipment for personal use and to remove it from Mexico when you leave. Have this statement signed and certified at a Mexican consulate in the United States and present it to Mexican customs as you enter Mexico.

Land travelers should verify from Mexican customs at the border that all items in their possession may be legally brought into Mexico. You will be subject to a second immigration and customs inspection south of the Mexican border where unlawful items may be seized and you could be prosecuted regardless of whether or not the items passed through the initial customs inspection. Guns and ammunition cannot be brought into Mexico without a permit from a Mexican Consulate in the United States.

Currency. The Mexican government permits tourists to exchange dollars for pesos at the fluctuating free market rate. There are no restrictions on the import or export of bank notes and none on the export of reasonable quantities of ordinary Mexican coins. However, gold or silver Mexican coins may not be exported.

Take travelers checks with you because personal U.S. checks are rarely accepted by Mexican hotels or banks. Major credit cards are accepted in many hotels, shops and restaurants. An exchange office (casa de cambios) usually gives a better rate of exchange than do stores, hotels or restaurants.

248

Pets. U.S. visitors to Mexico may bring a dog, cat or up to four canaries by presenting the following certificates at the border:

(1) a pet health certificate signed by a registered veterinarin in the United States and issued not more than 72 hours before the animal enters Mexico; and

(2) a pet vaccination certificate showing that the animal has been treated for rabies, hepatitis, pip and leptospirosis.

Certification by Mexican consular authorities is not required for the health or vaccination certificate. A permit fee is charged at the time of entry into Mexico.

Shopping - Some Things To Beware of Buying

Wildlife and Wildlife Products. Beware of purchasing souvenirs made from endangered wildlife. Mexican markets and stores abound with wildlife, most of it prohibited from international traffic. You risk confiscation and a possible fine by U.S. Customs if you attempt to import virtually any wildlife from Mexico. In particular, watch out for and avoid:

- All products made from sea turtles, including such items as turtle leather boots, tortoise-shell jewelry, and sea turtle oil cosmetics
- Fur from spotted cats
- Mexican birds, stuffed or alive, such as parrots, parakeets, or birds of prey
- Crocodile and caiman leather
- Black coral jewelry
- Wildlife curios, such as stuffed iguanas

When driving across state lines within Mexico, you can expect to be stopped at agricultural livestock inspection stations.

Antiques. Mexico considers all pre-Colombian objects to be the "inalienable property of the Nation" and that the unauthorized export of such objects is theft and is punishable by arrest, detention and judicial prosecution. Under U.S. law, to import pre-Colombian monumental and architectural sculpture and murals, you must present proof that they were legally exported from the country of origin. U.S. law does not prohibit the import of nonmonumental or nonarchitectural artifacts from Mexico.

Glazed Ceramics. According to the U.S. Food and Drug Administration, it is possible to suffer lead poisoning if you consume food or beverages that have been stored or served in improperly glazed ceramic ware. Analysis of many ceramic pieces from Mexico has shown them to contain dangerous levels of lead. Unless you have proof of their safety, use glazed ceramics purchased in Mexico for decorative purposes only.

Returning to the United States

You must present the pink copy of your tourist card at your point of departure from Mexico. If you are returning by motor vehicle, you will need to show your vehicle import permit when you cross the border. At the time of publication, the airport departure tax is $10 or the equivalent in Mexican currency for those returning by commercial airline.

The U.S. Customs Service currently permits U.S. citizens returning from international travel to bring back $400 worth of merchandise, including 1 liter of alcohol, duty free. The next $1,000 worth of items brought back is subject to a duty of 10%.

In addition to U.S. Customs regulations, be aware that some U.S. border states (most notably, Texas) have imposed state restrictions on liquor, wine and beer imports from Mexico. If you are planning to bring back alcoholic beverages, inquire about these restrictions from the liquor control office of the state through which you plan to return.

Useful Addresses & Telephone Numbers

American Embassy
Paseo de la Reforma 305
Colonia Cuauhtemoc
Mexico 06500, D.F.
Tel [52] (5) 209-9100
U.S. Export Development Office/U.S. Trade Center
31 Liverpool
Mexico 06600, D.F.
Tel [52] (5) 591-0155
U.S. Consulates General

American Consulate General
Avenue Lopez Mateos 924-N
Ciudad Juarez, Chihuahua

Tel: [52] (16) 11-3000

American Consulate General
Progreso 175
Guadalajara, Jalisco
Tel [52] (3) 825-2998/2700

American Consulte General
Avenida Constitucion 411 Poniente
Monterrey, Nuevo Leon, 64000
Tel [52] (8) 345-2120

American Consulate General
Tapachula 96
Tijuana, Baja California
Tel [52] (66) 81-7400
U.S. Consulates

American Consulate
Ave. Monterrey 141 Pte.
Hermosillo, Sonora
Tel [52] (62) 17-2375

American Consulate
Ave. Primera 2002
Matamoros, Tamaulipas
Tel [52] (88) 12-44-02

American Consulate
Paseo Montejo 453
Merida, Yucatan
Tel [52] (99) 25-5011
American Consulate
Calle Allende 3330, Col. Jardin
Nuevo Laredo, Tamaulipas
Tel [52] (87) 14-0512

U.S. Consular Agents
Resident consular agents have been designated in other locations in Mexico to assist U.S. citizens in serious emergencies. Each consular agent is supervised by one of the above-listed offices and may be contacted through it or by calling the consular agent s direct number.

Acapulco, Hotel Acapulco Continental Costera M. Alema 121-Local 14
[52] (748)40-300 or 52-74-690-556

Cabo San Lucas, Blvd. Marina y Perdregal #1, Local 3 Zona Cento, [52] (114) 3-35-66

Cancun, Plaza Caracol two, third level, no. 320-

323, Boulevard Kukulcan, km. 8.5, Zona Hotelera, [52] (988) 3-02-72

Mazatlan, Hotel Playa Mazatlan, Rodolfo T. Loaiza 202 Zona Dorada, 82110,
[52] (69) 134-444 Ext. 285

Oaxaca, Alcala 201 Deps. 206, [52] (951) 4-3054

Puerto Vallarta, Edif. Vallarta, Plaza Zaragoza 160-Piso 2 Int-18, [52](322) 2-0069

San Luis Potosi, Francisco de P. Moriel 103-10, [52] (481) 2-1528

San Miguel de Allende, Dr. Hernandez Marcias 72, [52] (465) 2-2357

Foreign Embassies in the United States

[For a complete listing of foreign embassies in the United States see **Appendix B**].

United States Embassies and Consulates Abroad

[For a complete listing of United States embassies and consulates abroad, including their addresses, telephone, fax, and telex numbers see **Appendix A**].

Planning Another Trip?

See Chapter 36 for a listing of resources available to the general traveler from the U.S. Departments of State, Customs, Transportation, Health and various government and non-government organizations. Almost all of the available International travel-related pamphlets, brochures and publications issued by the U.S. Department of State and by the U.S. Customs have been reproduced in full in this book. See Table of Contents for location.

Chapter 19

Tips for Travelers to the Middle East and North Africa

[The information in this chapter is reprinted verbatim from a bulletin issued by the U.S. State Department, Bureau of Consular Affairs. It is intended to serve as advice to Americans traveling abroad.]

Algeria, Bahrain, Egypt, Iran, Iraq, Israel, Jordan, Kuwait, Lebanon, Libya, Morocco, Oman, Quatar, Saudi Arabia, Syria, Tunisia, United Arab Emirates, Yemen

Foreword

Travel to the Middle East and North Africa can be a rich and rewarding adventure. Whether you are a novice or an experienced world traveler, we think that this chapter will be of assistance to you as you plan a safe and enjoyable trip.

Remember: If you encounter serious difficulties in your travels, American consuls at U.S. embassies and consulates abroad are there to help you. If you are planning to stay for a long period of time, or are visiting an area that is experiencing political unrest or other problems, please register at the Consular Section of the nearest U.S. embassy or consulate.

How to Prepare for a Safe Trip

The policies of the countries in the Middle East and North Africa toward foreign visitors vary greatly from country to country. Some countries encourage tourism and put very few restrictions on visitors.

Other countries do not allow tourism and carefully regulate business travel. Some areas in the region have experienced military conflict over an extended period.

A little planning and knowledge will go a long way toward making your trip to the Middle East and North Africa go smoothly. If you learn about the countries you will visit and obey the laws and respect the customs of those places, you can make your stay as pleasant and incident-free as possible.

Consular Information Sheets, Public Announcements & Travel Warnings

The State Department's Bureau of Consular Affairs is responsible for providing assistance and information to U.S. citizens traveling abroad. Consular Affairs issues *Consular Information Sheets, Travel Warnings,* and *Public Announcements. Consular Information Sheets* are issued for every country in the world. They include such information as the location of the U.S. embassy or consulate in the subject country, health conditions, political disturbances, unusual currency and entry regulations, crime and security information, and drug penalties.

The State Department also issues *Travel Warnings* and *Public Announcements. Travel Warnings* are issued when the State Department decides to recommend that Americans avoid travel to a certain country. Countries where avoidance of travel is recommended will have *Travel Warnings* as well as *Consular Information Sheets. Public Announcements* are issued as a means to disseminate information quickly about terrorist threats and other conditions overseas that pose significant risks to the security of American travelers.

How to Access Consular Information Sheets, Public Announcements & Travel Warnings

By Internet: The most convenient source of information about travel and consular services is the Consular Affairs home page on the Internet's World Wide Web. The web site address is **http://travel.state.gov**. If you do not have access to the Internet at home, work or school, your local library may provide access to the Internet.

By Telephone: Consular Information Sheets and Travel Warnings may be heard any time by dialing the office of American Citizens Services at **(202)**

251

647-5225 from a touch-tone phone.

By Fax: From your fax machine, dial **(202) 647-3000**, using the handset as you would a regular telephone. The system will instruct you on how to proceed.

By Mail: Consular Information Sheets, Travel Warnings and Public Announcements can be obtained by sending a self-addressed, stamped business-size envelope to: **Office of American Citizens Services, Room 4811, Department of State, Washington, DC 20520-4818**. On the outside envelope, write the name of the country or countries needed in the lower left corner.

Registration

As you travel, keep abreast of local news coverage. If you plan more than a short stay in one place, or if you are in an area experiencing civil unrest or a natural disaster, you are encouraged to register with the nearest U.S. embassy or consulate. Remember to leave a detailed itinerary with a friend or relative in the United States in case of an emergency.

U.S. Passport Information

Make a record or photocopy of the data from your passport's identification page and from your visas. Also, make a copy of the addresses and telephone numbers of the U.S. embassy and consulates in the countries you will visit. Put this information along with two passport photos in a place separate from your passport to be available in case of loss or theft of your passport.

To obtain a U.S. passport for a minor under age 14, both parents' signatures are now required on the passport application form, or, if only one parent is applying, a signed statement from the non-applying parent, or evidence proving sole custody of the minor. For more information, please refer to the Bureau of Consular Affairs' Internet site at http://travel.state.gov/passport_services.html or contact the Passport Information Center; telephone 1-900-225-5674 (there is a fee of $0.35 per minute for this service) or 1-888-362-8668 (credit card users can pay a flat fee of $4.95).

Visa and Other Entry Requirements

A U.S. passport is required for travel to all countries in the region. U.S. citizens are not required to have visas for short-term tourist or business travel to Israel, Morocco, or Tunisia, but may need to supply proof of sufficient funds for the trip and proof of onward or round trip travel arrangements. All other countries in the Middle East and North Africa require U.S. citizens to have visas.

If you plan to travel extensively in the region, entry and exit stamps could quickly fill the pages of your passport. Before you go, you may wish to ask the nearest passport agency to add extra pages to your passport, or, if applying for a new passport, you can request one with 48 pages instead of the usual 24.

Each country has its own set of entry requirements. For authoritative visa information, contact the embassy or consulate of the country you plan to visit. (See address and telephone list under *Foreign Embassies in the United States* at the end of this publication.)

When you make inquiries, ask about the following:

- Visa price, length of validity, number of entries allowed.
- Financial requirements - proof of sufficient funds and proof of onward/return ticket.
- Immunization requirements - yellow fever immunization is often required if arriving from a yellow-fever-infected area.
- Import and export restrictions and limitations. (Several countries prohibit the import and consumption of alcoholic beverages and pork products. Some countries prohibit the import of non-Islamic religious materials and items deemed pornographic.)
- Departure tax. (Be sure to keep enough local currency to be able to depart as planned.)

Some Arab countries will not allow travelers to enter if their passports show any evidence of previous or expected travel to Israel. Other Arab countries apply the ban inconsistently, sometimes refusing and at other times allowing entry when a passport shows evidence of travel to Israel. If passport restrictions imposed by other countries may be a problem for you, contact the nearest

U.S. passport agency, embassy, or consulate for guidance.

Several Arab countries ask visa applicants to state their religious affiliation. The U.S. government is opposed to the use of this information to discriminate against visa applicants, and has made its views known to the governments concerned. In turn, the United States has received assurances that visa applications are not denied based on religious affiliation.

Exit Permits

Countries that require visitors to be sponsored usually also require them to obtain exit permits from their sponsors. U.S. citizens can have difficulty obtaining exit permits if they are involved in business disputes. A U.S. citizen who is the wife or child of the local sponsor needs the sponsor's permission to leave the country. Do not accept sponsorship to visit a country unless you are certain you will also be able to obtain an exit permit.

Family Issues

In many Islamic countries, even those that give tourist visas and do not require sponsorship, a woman needs the permission of her husband, and children need the permission of their father, to leave the country. If you travel or allow your children to travel, be aware of the laws of the country you plan to visit. Once overseas, you are subject to the laws of the country where you are; U.S. law cannot protect you.

In an effort to prevent international child abduction, many governments have initiated procedures at entry/exit points. These often include requiring documentary evidence of relationship and permission for the child's travel from the parent(s) or legal guardian not present. Having such documentation on hand, even if not required, may facilitate entry/departure.

For information on international adoption of children and international parental child abduction, please refer to the Consular Affairs Internet site at http://travel.state.gov/children's_issues.html or telephone (202) 736-7000.

Dual Nationality

Some countries in the Middle East and North Africa do not recognize acquisition of U.S. citizenship by their nationals. Unless the naturalized U.S. citizen renounces his or her original nationality at an embassy or consulate of the country of origin, he or she may still be considered a citizen of that country. A person born in the United States with a parent who was a citizen of another country may also be considered a citizen of that country. The laws of some countries provide for automatic acquisition of citizenship when a person marries a national of that country.

If arrested, a dual national may be denied the right to communicate with the U.S. embassy or consulate. Another consequence could be having to serve in the military of one's former country. If you are a naturalized U.S. citizen, a dual national, or have any reason to believe another country may claim you as their national, check with the embassy of that country as to your citizenship status and any obligations you may have while visiting. Dual nationals who have not researched their citizenship status before traveling have sometimes, to their surprise, encountered difficulties, such as not being allowed to depart.

Even countries that recognize acquired U.S. citizenship may consider their former citizens as having resumed original citizenship if they take up residence in their country of origin. This can happen even if the embassy of the country of origin stamps a visa in the U.S. passport of its former citizen.

Currency and Customs Regulations

Some countries in the region have no restrictions on currency imports or exports. Some prohibit Israeli currency. Most countries in the Middle East and North Africa, however, have detailed currency regulations, including a requirement to declare all currency, including travelers' checks, upon entry. In those countries, the export of foreign currency is limited to the amount that was imported and declared. Be sure to make the required currency declaration, have it validated, and retain it for use at departure. Buy local currency only at banks or other authorized exchange places and retain your receipts for use at departure. Currency not accounted for may be confiscated.

Several countries prohibit the import and consumption of alcoholic beverages. Most countries restrict the entry of products containing pork, as well as any literature, videotapes, and cassette tapes deemed pornographic. Also, some countries will not permit the import of books or other goods from Israel.

Shopping - Be Wary of Antiques

Americans have been arrested in some countries in the region for the unauthorized purchase of antiques or other important cultural artifacts. If you purchase such items, always insist that the seller provide a receipt and the official museum export certificate required by law. Travelers have also been detained at customs for possessing reproductions of antiques. The safest policy is to purchase copies of antiques from reputable stores and have them documented as such. Obtain receipts for all such purchases.

Health

Immunizations

Under the International Health Regulations adopted by the World Health Organization, a country may require International Certificates of Vaccination against yellow fever. A cholera immunization may be required if you are traveling from an infected area. Check with health care providers or your records to ensure other immunizations (e.g. tetanus and polio) are up-to-date. Prophylactic medication for malaria and certain other preventive measures are advisable for travel to some countries. No immunizations are required to return to the United States. Detailed health information may be obtained from your local health department or physician or by contacting the Centers for Disease Control and Prevention, telephone 1-877-FYI-TRIP (1-877-394-8747), toll-free autofax: 1-888-CDC-FAXX (1-888-232-3299), or Internet: www.cdc.gov.

An increasing number of countries have established regulations regarding AIDS testing, particularly for long-term residents and students. Check with the embassy or consulate of the country that you plan to visit for the latest information. (See address and telephone list under *Foreign Embassies in the United* States at the end of this publication.)

Health Insurance Policy

If your health insurance does not provide coverage overseas, you should buy temporary insurance that does. In addition, obtain insurance to cover the exorbitant cost of medical evacuation in the event of an illness or for the return of remains in case of death. Insurance companies and some credit card and travelers check companies offer short-term health and emergency assistance policies designed for travelers. The Department of State's Bureau of Consular Affairs provides information on medical emergencies abroad, including overseas insurance programs in its brochure *Medical Information for Americans Traveling Abroad*, available via the Bureau of Consular Affairs home page http://travel.state.gov or autofax: (202) 647-3000.

Medical facilities vary in the region; in some countries they are similar to U.S. standards. U.S. embassies or consulates can furnish you with a list of local hospitals and English-speaking physicians. (See address list under *U.S. Embassies and Consulates Abroad* at the end of this publication.)

Health Precautions

In the hot and dry climates that prevail in the Middle East and North Africa, it is important to avoid water depletion and heat stroke. Safe tap water is available in many areas. In some places, however, it is highly saline and should be avoided by persons on sodium-restricted diets. In many rural and some urban areas, tap water is not potable, and travelers should drink only boiled or chemically treated water or bottled carbonated drinks. In these areas, avoid fresh vegetables and fruits unless they are washed in a purifying solution and peeled. Diarrhea is potentially serious. If it persists, seek medical attention.

Schistosomiasis (or bilharzia) is present in the area of the Nile and in several other areas in North Africa and the Middle East. These parasites are best avoided by not swimming in fresh water in endemic areas. For more information, contact the Centers for Disease Control and Prevention, telephone 1-877-FYI-TRIP (1-877-394-8747), toll-free autofax: 1-888-CDC-FAXX (1-888-232-3299), or Internet: www.cdc.gov.

Drug Offenses

Drug enforcement policies in the region are strict. Possession of even small amounts of narcotics, including substances such as heroin, LSD, marijuana, ecstasy or amphetamines, can lead to arrest. If found guilty, drug offenders are subject to lengthy prison sentences. Because what is considered "narcotics" varies from country to country, learn and obey the laws in the places that you will visit. Keep all prescription drugs in their original containers clearly labeled with the doctor's name, pharmacy and contents. In addition, if you take an unusual prescription drug, carry a letter from your doctor explaining your need for the drug and a copy of the prescription.

Dress and Local Customs

Dress

Conservative Western street clothing (except for shorts) is appropriate in most areas. In more traditional societies, however, attire for women should be more conservative, garments should have sleeves, and dress length should be below the knee. On the other hand, in some areas of the region visited by many tourists - for example, the beaches of Israel and Morocco - attire similar to that worn in the United States is acceptable.

Islam

Islam is the preeminent influence on local laws and customs in much of the Middle East and North Africa. The extent of this influence varies. Some Arab countries have secular governments, but in certain other countries, particularly those in the Arabian Peninsula, Islam dictates a total way of life. It prescribes the behavior for individuals and society, codifying law, family relations, business etiquette, dress, food, personal hygiene, and much more. Among the important values is a family-centered way of life, including a protected role for women and clear limits on their participation in public life. In traditional societies, Muslims believe open social relations between the sexes result in the breakdown of family life. Contact between men and women, therefore, is rigidly controlled in traditional societies.

Travel during Ramadan, the holiest time in the Islamic year, can prove to be very difficult. Business is rarely conducted during this time and not observing the Ramadan tradition of fasting during daylight hours can carry penalties in some countries.

Etiquette

In the traditional societies of the region, it is considered rude to face the soles of one's feet toward other people. At traditional meals, the left hand is not used for eating.

The Workweek

In many countries in the Middle East and North Africa, the weekend is either Thursday/Friday or Friday/Saturday. Workweek information is included in the list of U.S. embassies at the end of this document.

Country Information

(Note: Before you travel, please check the Consular Affairs Internet site at http://travel.state.gov to see if any Travel Warnings or Public Announcements have been issued for the country(ies) you plan to visit.)

ALGERIA

Algeria is a republic with a developing economy. Facilities for travelers are widely available, but sometimes limited in quality. English is not widely spoken in Algeria.

Entering Algeria

A valid passport and visa are required. Obtain visa before arrival. For tourist visas, an itinerary from an airline and a hotel reservation are also needed. A letter from your company is quired for a business visa. Applicants must enter Algeria within 45 days of issuance.

Terrorism/Security

Travelers to Algeria should evaluate carefully the implications for their security and safety before deciding to travel to Algeria. Although terrorist attacks have fallen considerably recently, unpredictable attacks still occur in rural villages, on roadsides and public transport, and at night. Most recent terrorist activity has occurred in rural areas in northern Algeria.

The crime rate in Algeria is moderately high, and is increasing. Serious crimes have been reported in which armed men posing as police officers have entered homes of occupants, held them at gun point, and robbed them. Armed carjacking is also a serious problem.

Customs Regulations

Algerian currency and customs regulations are strictly enforced. All currency must be declared upon entering the country, and completely accounted for when departing. Nonresidents are required to change the equivalent of approximately $200 into Algerian dinars at the official exchange rate while in Algeria. You will need to present evidence of this currency exchange before you are allowed to depart the country. All hotel bills must be paid in hard currency such as U.S. dollars. Paid hotel receipts may be used as evidence of currency exchange.

Family Issues

Algerian fathers of minor children (under 18 years of age for boys, 19 years for girls) may legally prevent their children from leaving Algeria.

BAHRAIN

Entering/Exiting Bahrain

A valid passport and visa are required. Two-week visas may be obtained for a fee upon arrival at the airport. Prior to travel, visitors may obtain from Bahraini embassies overseas five-year multiple entry visas valid for stays as long as one month. Visitors who fail to depart the country at the end of their authorized stay are fined. An AIDS test is required for individuals employed in jobs involving food handling, and patient or child care. U.S. test results are not accepted.

An exit tax is charged all travelers upon departure. Residents of Bahrain who intend to return must obtain a re-entry permit before departing.

Dual Nationality

The Bahrain government does not recognize dual nationality. Bahrain authorities have confiscated the U.S. passports of dual Bahrain/U.S. nationals when they applied for a Bahrain passport. This does not constitute loss of U.S. citizenship, but should be reported to the U.S. Embassy in Manama.

Special Circumstances

Water is drinkable though often highly saline. Conservative dress is recommended. Bahrain prohibits the import of pornography, firearms, ammunition, or of items such as knives, swords, or daggers that are capable of being used as weapons. Videotapes may be screened by customs in Bahrain and either confiscated or held until the traveler departs the country.

Consumption of alcohol is allowed in most bars and restaurants, except during the month of Ramadan. If there is any indication that a driver has consumed alcohol, authorities will regard that as evidence of driving under the influence of alcohol. The penalty for drunken driving may be

incarceration or a fine of 500 Bahraini dinars, the equivalent of $1,300. This fine can be increased to up to double that amount, depending on the circumstances of the case and the judge's decision. Under Bahraini law, convicted drug traffickers may receive the death penalty.

EGYPT

Entering Egypt

A valid passport and visa are required. Travelers can obtain a renewable 30-day tourist visa at any port of entry, except at Taba and Rafah, for a $15 fee, payable in U.S. dollars. Visitors arriving overland from Israel and/or those previously experiencing difficulty with their visa status in Egypt, must obtain a visa prior to arrival. Military personnel arriving on commercial flights are not exempt from passport and visa requirements. Proof of cholera, yellow fever and meningitis immunization is required if arriving from an infected area. Proof of an AIDS test is required for anyone planning to apply for a study or work permit.

Foreigners are required to register with the police within 7 days of arrival. Hotels usually take care of this.

All travelers to Egypt should be aware that Egyptian authorities strictly enforce drug laws. The death penalty may be imposed on anyone convicted of smuggling or selling marijuana, hashish, opium, or other narcotics.

Customs Regulations

The maximum amount of Egyptian currency that can be brought in or taken out of Egypt is 1,000 Egyptian pounds. Personal use items such as jewelry, laptop computers and electronic equipment are exempt from customs fees. However, Egyptian customs authorities may enforce strict regulations concerning temporary importation into or export from Egypt of items such as computer peripherals, including printers and modems, which are subject to customs fees. For tourists, electronic equipment is annotated in their passport, and the person is required to show the same items upon exiting Egypt. For residents, a deposit, refunded upon departure, may be made in lieu of customs fees. Commercial merchandise and samples require an import/export license issued by the Egyptian Ministry of Trade and Supply in Egypt prior to travel and should be declared upon arrival. It is advisable to contact the Embassy of Egypt in Washington or one of Egypt's consulates in the United States for specific information regarding customs requirements.

Dual Nationality

If a dual national resides in Egypt for extended periods, proof of Egyptian citizenship, such as a family ID. card, is required. Male dual nationals of military age, who have not completed military service, are not generally required to enlist in the armed forces. However, before they can leave Egypt, they must obtain an exemption certificate through the Ministry of Defense Draft Office. Individuals who may be affected can inquire at an Egyptian consular office in the U.S. (see address and telephone list under *Foreign Embassies in the United States* at the end of this publication) before traveling to Egypt. Dual Egyptian-American nationals may enter and leave Egypt on their U.S. passports. Persons with dual nationality who travel to Egypt on their Egyptian passports are normally treated as Egyptian citizens by the local government. The ability to provide U.S. consular assistance to such persons, therefore, is extremely limited.

Family Issues

The Government of Egypt considers all children born to Egyptian fathers to be Egyptian citizens. Even if the children bear American passports, immigration officials may require proof that the father approves their departure before the children will be allowed to leave Egypt. Americans married to Egyptians do not need their spouse's permission to depart Egypt as long as they have a valid Egyptian visa. To renew a visa, or to leave the country after a visa has expired, an American woman married to an Egyptian must present proof of the husband's consent.

IRAN

In 1999, President Khatami called for a "dialogue of civilizations" and an increase of private exchanges between Iranians and Americans; some limited exchanges have taken place. There is, however, evidence that hostility to the United States remains in some segments of the Iranian population and some elements of the Iranian government. In July 1999, violent anti-government demonstrations took place in Tehran and other cities around the country. There were accusations that the U.S. was behind these demonstrations.

Prior to and since that time, some groups of American travelers have encountered harassment by vigilante groups.

The U.S. government does not currently have diplomatic or consular relations with the Islamic Republic of Iran and therefore cannot provide protection or routine consular services to American citizens in Iran. The Swiss government, acting through its embassy in Tehran, serves as protecting power for U.S. interests in Iran.

Entering/Exiting Iran

A valid passport and visa are required. U.S. passports are valid for travel to Iran. However, the authorities have often confiscated the U.S. passports of U.S.-Iranian dual nationals upon arrival. U.S.-Iranian dual nationals have been denied permission to depart Iran documented as U.S. citizens. Despite the fact that these individuals possess U.S. citizenship, they must enter and exit Iran bearing an Iranian passport. To prevent the confiscation of U.S. passports, the Department of State suggests that dual nationals leave their U.S. passports at the nearest U.S. embassy or consulate overseas for safekeeping before entering Iran, and to use their Iranian passports to enter the country. To facilitate their travel if their U.S. passports are confiscated, dual nationals may, prior to entering Iran, obtain in their Iranian passports the necessary visas for the country which they will transit on their return to the U.S., and where they may apply for a new U.S. passport. Exit visas are required for dual nationals to depart Iran.

Dual Nationality

U.S. citizens who were born in Iran, who have become naturalized citizens of Iran, or who were at one time citizens of Iran, and the children of such persons, are considered Iranian nationals by Iranian authorities. U.S.-Iranian dual nationals are subject to Iranian laws that impose special obligations upon Iranian nationals, such as military service or taxes. Exit permits for departure from Iran may be denied until such obligations are met.

U.S. citizens of Iranian origin who are considered by Iran to be Iranian citizens have been detained and harassed by Iranian authorities. Former Muslims who have converted to other religions, as well as persons who encourage Muslims to convert, are subject to arrest and possible execution. The Iranian government reportedly has the names of all individuals who filed claims against Iran, and who received awards, at the Iran-U.S. claims tribunal at The Hague pursuant to the 1981 Algerian Accords. There are restrictions on both the import and the export of goods between Iran and the United States. Neither U.S. passports nor visas to the United States are issued in Tehran.

Economic Sanctions

On May 6, 1995, President Clinton signed Executive Order 12959, 60 Federal Register 24757 (May 9, 1995), which prohibits exporting goods or services to Iran, re-exporting certain goods to Iran, making new investments in Iran and dealing in property owned or controlled by the government of Iran. The importation of Iranian-origin goods or services into the United States has been prohibited since October 19, 1987. The Office of Foreign Assets Control, Department of Treasury, provides guidance to the public on the interpretation of the order. For additional information, consult the Licensing Division, Office of Foreign Assets Control (OFAC), U.S. Department of Treasury at the OFAC home page on the Internet at http://www.treas.gov/ofac/.

Customs Regulations

All luggage is searched upon traveling into and departing from Iran. Tourists can bring in and take out the following non-commercial goods, if they are recorded on the tourist's goods slip upon arrival at customs: personal jewelry, one camera, an amateur video camera, one pair of binoculars, a portable tape recorder, a personal portable computer, first aid box, and a camping tent with its equipment. Iranian authorities allow the departing passenger to take an unlimited amount of Iranian goods and foreign goods up to $160 (US), and their personal non-commercial equipment. Air passengers may also take one carpet up to six square meters. However, the U.S. government only allows the importation of up to $100 worth of Iranian-origin goods. Iranian authorities prohibit the export of antique carpets and carpets portraying women not wearing the proper Islamic covering, antiques, original works of art, calligraphic pieces, miniature paintings, different kinds of coins, and precious stones. They likewise prohibit the export and import of alcoholic beverages, weapons, ammunitions, swords and sheaths, military devices, drugs and illegal goods.

Special Circumstances

In addition to the U.S. government economic sanctions on trade and investment restrictions, travelers should be aware that most hotels and restaurants do not accept credit cards. Cash-dollars (not traveler checks) are accepted as payment. In general, hotel rooms have to be paid with cash-dollars. ATM machines are not available. Foreign currency has to be declared at Customs upon entry into the country, and the amount is entered in the passport. This amount can then be changed at the bank.

Family Issues

Children of Iranian citizens, under the age of 18, must have the father's permission to depart Iran, even if the mother has been granted full custody by an Iranian court. Even the non-Iranian wife of an Iranian citizen (who obtains Iranian nationality through marriage and must convert to Islam) requires the consent of her husband to leave Iran. In case of marital problems, women in Iran are often subject to strict family controls. Because of Islamic law, compounded by the lack of diplomatic relationships between the United States and Iran, the U.S. Interests Section in Tehran can provide very limited assistance if an American woman encounters difficulty in leaving Iran.

IRAQ - See Page 269

ISRAEL, THE WEST BANK AND GAZA

The State of Israel is a parliamentary democracy with a modern economy. Tourist facilities are widely available. Israel occupied the West Bank, Gaza Strip, Golan Heights, and East Jerusalem as a result of the 1967 War. Pursuant to negotiations between Israel and the Palestinians, an elected Palestinian Authority now exercises jurisdiction in parts of Gaza and the West Bank. Palestinian Authority police are responsible for keeping order in those areas and the Palestinian Authority exercises a range of civil functions. The division of responsibilities and jurisdiction in the West Bank and Gaza between Israel and the Palestinian Authority is complex. Definitive information on entry, customs requirements, arrests, and other matters in the West Bank and Gaza is subject to change without prior notice or may not be available.

Western dress is appropriate in Israel. At religious sites and in certain religious neighborhoods, attire should be modest. Religious holidays in Israel and Jerusalem are determined according to the Hebrew calendar and fall on different dates each year. It is likely that religious holidays in the Gaza Strip and the West Bank will be determined by the Moslem calendar, and also will fall on different dates each year. Because hotels are usually heavily booked before and during religious holidays, tourists should check holiday schedules with their travel agent or with the Embassy of Israel in Washington, DC. (See address and telephone list under "U.S. Embassies and Consulates" at the end of this publication.) Travelers should make reservations for holiday periods well in advance.

Entering/Exiting Israel
A valid passport is required. U.S. visitors to Israel, the West Bank, the Golan Heights, and the Gaza Strip can obtain a tourist visa that is renewable and valid for 3 months at no cost upon arrival in Israel. However, anyone who has been refused entry to Israel or experienced difficulties with their visa status during a previous visit, or who has overstayed a visa, should contact the nearest Israeli embassy or consulate before attempting to return to Israel. Permission must be obtained from Israel for anyone attempting to claim the status of a returning resident. At ports of entry, Israeli officials determine a U.S. citizen's eligibility to enter Israel. Applicants may be questioned in detail and/or required to post a departure bond. American citizens have, on occasion, had their U.S. passports taken as a guarantee of their departure. If this should happen to you, contact a U.S. consular officer and report the seizure of your passport.

The Allenby Bridge crossing from the West Bank into Jordan, and the Rafah crossing from Gaza into Egypt are under the jurisdiction of the Israeli Government, which also controls entry and exit via the Gaza International Airport. This may have special ramifications for Palestinian Americans and other Arab Americans.

Palestinian Americans: American citizens of Palestinian origin who were born on the West Bank or Gaza or resided there for more than three months, may be considered by Israeli authorities to be residents, especially if they or their parents were issued a Palestinian ID number. Any American citizen whom Israel considers to be a resident is required by Israel to hold a valid Palestinian passport to enter or leave the West Bank or Gaza via Israel, the Gaza International Airport, or the Rafah or Allenby Bridge border crossing. American citizens in this category who arrive without a Palestinian passport will generally be granted permission to travel to the West Bank or Gaza to obtain one, but may only be allowed to depart via Israel on a Palestinian passport rather than on their U.S. passport. The Government of Israel does not require travel on a Palestinian passport for visits of less than 90 days, but may instead require a transit permit for travel to the West Bank or Gaza.

During periods of heightened security restrictions, Palestinian Americans with residency status in the West Bank or Gaza may not be allowed to enter or exit Gaza or the West Bank, even if using their American passports. Specific questions may be addressed to the nearest Israeli Embassy or Consulate.

Israel-Jordan Crossings: International crossing points between Israel and Jordan are the Arava crossing (Wadi al-'Arabah) in the south, near Eilat, and the Jordan River crossing (Sheikh Hussein Bridge) in the north, near Beit Shean. American citizens using these two crossing points to enter either Israel or Jordan need not obtain prior visas, but will have to pay a fee at the bridge. Visas should be obtained in advance for those wanting to cross the Allenby Bridge between Jordan and the occupied West Bank. (Note: The Government of Israel requires that Palestinian Americans with residency status in the West Bank or Gaza only enter Jordan by land by means of the Allenby Bridge.) Procedures for all crossings into Jordan are subject to frequent changes.

Persons leaving Israel by air are subjected to lengthy and detailed security questioning. Travelers should arrive at the airport several hours before flight time. There is no departure tax when leaving Israel.

Customs Requirements
Video cameras, among other items, must be declared upon entry to Israel and travelers carrying these items must go through the red zone at customs. Definitive information on customs requirements for the Palestinian Authority is not available.

Security Measures

Israel has strict security measures that may affect visitors. Prolonged questioning and detailed searches may take place at the time of entry and/or departure at all points of entry to Israel, including entry from any of the areas under Palestinian jurisdiction. During searches and questioning, American citizens may be denied access to U.S. consular officers, lawyers, or family members.

Terrorism/Security

In light of several terrorist bombings in Israel and continuing violence in Gaza and the West Bank, American citizens should exercise extreme caution and avoid shopping areas, malls, public buses and bus stops as well as crowded areas and demonstrations. U.S. Embassy and Consulate employees and their families have been prohibited from using public buses. American citizens should maintain a low profile and take appropriate steps to reduce their vulnerability.

Because of violent clashes and confrontations that have taken place throughout the West Bank and Gaza, U.S. Embassy and Consulate employees have been prohibited from traveling to the West Bank, Gaza, commercial districts of East Jerusalem, and the Old City of Jerusalem, except for mission essential business. Private American citizens should avoid travel to these areas.

From time to time, the Embassy or Consulate General will temporarily suspend public services as necessary to review its security posture.

Areas of Instability

Jerusalem: In Jerusalem, travelers should exercise caution at religious sites on holy days, Fridays, Saturdays, and Sundays. Dress appropriately when visiting the Old City and ultra-orthodox Jewish neighborhoods. Most roads into ultra-orthodox Jewish neighborhoods are blocked off on Friday nights and Saturdays. Assaults on secular visitors, either for being in cars or for being "immodestly dressed," have occurred in these neighborhoods. Isolated street protests and demonstrations can occur in the commercial districts of East Jerusalem (Salah Eddin Street and Damascus Gate areas) during periods of unrest. U.S. Government employees have been prohibited from traveling to the commercial areas of East Jerusalem, including the Old City, except for mission essential business.

Private American citizens should avoid travel to these areas at this time.

West Bank and Gaza: The U.S. Government currently prohibits U.S. Government employees, officials, and dependents from traveling to the West Bank and Gaza, except for mission essential business. Private American citizens should avoid travel to these areas at this time. Embassy staff have also been prohibited from using Rt. 443 (the Modi'in Road) in Israel to travel to Jerusalem.

During periods of unrest, access to the West Bank and Gaza are sometimes closed off by the Israeli government. Travel restrictions may be imposed with little or no warning. Strict measures have frequently been imposed following terrorist actions and the movement of Palestinian Americans with residency status in the West Bank or Gaza and foreign passport holders have been severely impaired

Golan Heights: In the Golan Heights, there are live land mines in many areas and visitors should walk only on established roads or trails. Near the northern border of Israel, rocket attacks from Lebanese territory can occur without warning.

Dual Nationality

Israeli citizens naturalized in the United States retain their Israeli citizenship, and their children usually become Israeli citizens. In addition, children born in the United States to Israeli parents usually acquire both U.S. and Israeli nationality at birth. Israeli citizens, including dual nationals, are subject to Israeli laws requiring service in Israel's armed forces. U.S.-Israeli dual nationals of military age who do not wish to serve in the Israeli armed forces should contact the Israeli Embassy in Washington, DC to learn more about an exemption or deferment from Israeli military service before going to Israel. Without this document, they may not be able to leave Israel without completing military service or may be subject to criminal penalties for failure to serve. Israeli citizens, including dual nationals, must enter and depart Israel on their Israeli passports.

Palestinian Americans whom the Government of Israel considers residents of the West Bank or Gaza may face certain travel restrictions (see *Entering/Exiting Israel* page 18). These individuals are subject to restrictions on movement between

Israel, the West Bank and Gaza and within the West Bank and Gaza imposed by the Israeli Government on all Palestinians for security reasons. During periods of heightened security concerns these restrictions can be burdensome. Palestinian-American residents of Jerusalem are normally required to use laissez-passers (documents issued by the Israeli Government) which contain re-entry permits approved by the Israeli Ministry of Interior.

All U.S. citizens with dual nationality must enter and depart the U.S. on their U.S. passports

JORDAN
While Jordan is modern and Western-oriented, Islamic ideals and beliefs provide the conservative foundation of the country's customs, laws and practices.

Entering/Exiting Jordan
A passport and a visa are required. Visitors may obtain a visa for Jordan at international ports of entry, not including the King Hussein (Allenby) Bridge, upon arrival, for a fee. Foreigners who wish to stay fourteen days or more in Jordan must register at a Jordanian police station by their fourteenth day in the country. Failure to do so subjects the traveler to a fine of one Jordanian dinar per day overstay. This fine is usually assessed at departure. An AIDS test is required for persons planning to stay longer than 3 months. U.S. test results are not accepted.

Travel Between Jordan and Israel
International crossing points between Israel and Jordan are the Arava crossing (Wadi al-'Arabah) in the south, near Eilat, and the Jordan River crossing (Sheikh Hussein Bridge) in the north, near Beit Shean. American citizens using these two crossing points to enter either Israel or Jordan need not obtain prior visas, but will have to pay a fee at the bridge. Visas should be obtained in advance for those wanting to cross the Allenby Bridge between Jordan and the occupied West Bank. (Note: The Government of Israel requires that Palestinian Americans with residency status in the West Bank or Gaza only enter Jordan by land by means of the Allenby Bridge.) Procedures for all crossings into Jordan are subject to frequent changes. Check Jordan's web site for current entry regulations. (See address and telephone list under "Foreign Embassies in the United States" at the end of this publication)

Special Circumstances
Caution and sensitivity should be exercised at religious sites on holy days and Friday Sabbath. Modest attire should be worn at all holy sites.

There have been isolated incidents of sexual harassment, assault and unwelcome advances of a sexual nature against Western women, both visiting and residing in Jordan. These incidents, while troubling, are not pervasive. However, women are advised to use common sense and to take reasonable precautions; they should dress conservatively and not travel alone.

Proselytizing
Islam is the state religion of Jordan. The Jordanian Government does not interfere with public worship by the country's Christian minority. However, while Christians are allowed to practice freely, some activities, such as proselytizing or encouraging conversion to the Christian faith— both considered legally incompatible with Islam— are prohibited. It is illegal for a Muslim to convert to Christianity.

Terrorism/Security
U.S. citizens traveling or residing in Jordan are urged to continue to review their security practices, to remain alert to changing situations, and to exercise prudence. U.S. citizens should generally avoid crowds and gatherings, keep a low profile, and vary routes and times of travel.

Crime is generally not a serious problem for travelers in Jordan, but petty crime is prevalent in the downtown Amman Hashimiyah Square area and near the Roman Theater. In the narrow streets of the Old City, crowded conditions invite pickpockets and other petty criminals. It is safer to travel in groups when visiting the center of Amman.

Family Issues

Husbands/fathers may deny permission to travel to their wives and children, regardless of the wives' religion or nationality.

KUWAIT
Day-to-day life has returned to normal after the 1991 Gulf War, and facilities for travelers are

widely available. However, travel to and near the Iraq-Kuwait border is very hazardous and unexploded bombs, mines, booby traps, and other items remain in open areas and beaches throughout Kuwait.

Entering Kuwait

A valid passport and visa are required for U.S. citizens traveling to Kuwait. An AIDS test is required for anyone seeking a residency permit. U.S. test results are not accepted.

Special Circumstances

Visitors to Kuwait should be aware of the danger of unexploded land mines, bombs, and shells throughout the country. Stay on main roads, do not travel on unpaved roads, and avoid open areas and beaches.

The crime rate in Kuwait has increased from prewar levels and women have been objects of increased harassment. Women should take precautions as they would in any large city, remaining alert to the possibility of being followed, whether they are walking or driving. They should not respond to any approach from strangers and should avoid travel alone in unfamiliar or isolated parts of the city, especially at night. Conservative dress is recommended for both men and women. Garments should fit loosely and cover elbows and knees.

No alcohol, pork products, or pornographic materials may be imported into or used in Kuwait. If customs officials discover prohibited items in a traveler's effects, he or she may be arrested and prosecuted.

U.S. citizens should not go near the border with Iraq, and should be very careful when traveling north or west of Kuwait City. In recent years, a number of foreigners traveling near the border have been taken into custody by Iraqi officials and some have received lengthy prison sentences. Anyone who must travel or work near the demilitarized zone is strongly advised to contact the U.S. Embassy for further advice before his or her travel begins.

LEBANON

The Republic of Lebanon is a parliamentary republic. The country is emerging from a long period of civil war, which has damaged the economy and the social fabric. The population is composed of both Christians and Muslims from a variety of sects. Although the government of Lebanon has made efforts to extend its control, limited areas of the country remain outside of effective government control.

Entering Lebanon

A valid passport and visa are required. Travelers holding passports which contain visas or entry/exit stamps for Israel may be refused entry into Lebanon. Travelers whose passports contain Israeli stamps or visas and who also hold an "Arab Nationality" according to Lebanese law may be subject to arrest and imprisonment.

Travelers who enter Lebanon on work visas under the sponsorship of a Lebanese company or individual may face problems and be unable to leave the country before the completion of their contract without the agreement of their employer. In cases of a business dispute, if jurisdiction falls under local law, the Lebanese party to a contract may obtain an injunction to prevent the departure of a foreign party from the country until the dispute is settled.

Lebanese males 18 to 30 years old are subject to mandatory military service of one year. Dual nationals who visit Lebanon are not exempt, except as allowed by Lebanese law. Even Americans who have never visited or resided in Lebanon may be considered Lebanese and required to complete military service if their fathers were Lebanese. Dual nationals should contact the Military Office of the Embassy of Lebanon for details prior to traveling to Lebanon.

Because of the prevalence of Syrian troops in Lebanon, Syrian-American males of draft age who are planning to visit Lebanon are strongly urged to check with the Syrian Embassy prior to travel. Even Americans who have never visited or resided in Syria may be considered Syrian and required to complete military service if their fathers were Syrian. Possession of a U.S. passport does not absolve the bearer of this obligation.

An AIDS test is required for anyone planning to obtain a work or residency permit. U.S. test results are not accepted.

Terrorism/Security

The Department of State warns U.S. citizens of the risks of travel to Lebanon and recommends that Americans exercise caution while traveling there. During Lebanon's civil conflict from 1975 to 1990, Americans were the targets of numerous terrorist attacks in Lebanon. While there have been very few such incidents in recent years, the perpetrators of these attacks are still present in Lebanon and retain the ability to act.

The U.S. government considers the potential threat to U.S. personnel sufficiently serious to require that U.S. citizen employees of the American Embassy live and work under a strict security regime. Hizballah, an anti-West and anti-Israel terrorist organization that was formed in Lebanon, has not been disarmed, and it maintains a presence in several areas of the country, including training camps in the Biqaa' Valley. There are thousands of Syrian troops in the country. Palestinian groups hostile to both the Lebanese government and the U.S. operate largely autonomously inside refugee camps in different areas of the country.

Visitors should also be aware that the U.S. Embassy in Beirut operates under tight security conditions, which limit the Embassy's ability to assist Americans.

Customs Regulations
Lebanese customs authorities prohibit the import or export of firearms and antiquities, except with special permission.

Special Circumstances
Local telephone service is unreliable, and it is extremely difficult to contact the U.S. Embassy or place a local call from most of the country.

Family Issues
Lebanese fathers of minor children (under 18 years of age) may legally prevent their children from leaving or being taken from Lebanon. Likewise, a Lebanese husband may take legal action to prevent his wife from leaving the country, regardless of her nationality. Once such legal orders are in place, the U.S. Embassy cannot assist American citizens to leave Lebanon.

LIBYA

Entering Libya
Passports and visas are required. On December 11, 1981, U.S. passports ceased to be valid for travel to, in, or through Libya and may not be used for that purpose without a special validation. The request must be accompanied by supporting documentation according to the category under which validation is sought. (See information under *"Entering Iraq"* for details). Visa application and inquiries must be made through a Libyan Embassy in a third country. The land border with Egypt is subject to periodic closures even to travelers having valid Libyan visas. Short-term closures of other land borders occur with little notice.

All financial and commercial transactions with Libya are prohibited, unless licensed by the Office of Foreign Assets Control, U.S. Treasury Department. For the addresses to which applications can be made to overcome both the U.S. passport and the U.S. Treasury restrictions, see the section on Iraq under *"Entering Iraq"* for details.

Those persons granted exceptions to travel to Libya should be aware that there is no U.S. mission in Libya and U.S. interests are represented by the government of Belgium which can provide only limited protection for U.S. citizens.

An AIDS test is required for persons seeking residency permits. U.S. test results are accepted.

Family Issues
Children under 18 whose fathers are Libyan must have the father's permission to depart Libya, even if the mother has been granted full custody by a Libyan court. Women in Libya are often subjected to strict family controls; on occasion families of Libyan-American women visiting Libya have attempted to prevent them from leaving the country. Young single women are most likely to be vulnerable in these circumstances. Finally, a Libyan husband is permitted to take legal action to prevent his wife from leaving the country, regardless of her nationality.

MOROCCO
Morocco has a mixed economy based largely on agriculture, fishing, light industry, phosphate mining, tourism, and remittances from citizens working abroad. Modern tourist facilities and means of transportation are widely available, but they may vary in quality depending on price and location. The workweek in Morocco is Monday

263

through Friday.

Entering Morocco

A valid passport is required. Visas are not required for American tourists traveling in Morocco for less than 90 days. For visits of more than 90 days, Americans are required to obtain a residence permit and return visa should they wish to return to Morocco for extended periods. A residence permit and return visa may be requested and obtained from immigration (*Service d'Etranger*) at the central police station of the district of residence.

Crime Information

Morocco has a high crime rate in urban areas. Criminals have targeted tourists for robberies, assaults, muggings, thefts, pickpocketing, and scams of all types. Commonly reported crimes include falsifying credit-card vouchers, and shipping inferior rugs as a substitute for the rugs purchased by the traveler, and thefts occurring in the vicinity of ATM machines. Some travelers have been befriended by persons of various nationalities who have offered them food, drink, or cigarettes that are drugged. Harassment of tourists by unemployed Moroccans posing as "guides" is a common problem. Travelers should hire only official tour guides through hotels and travel agencies. Aggressive panhandling is common. Traveling alone in the Rif Mountain area is risky, as tourists have fallen victim to schemes involving the purchase and/or trafficking of hashish. Unescorted women in any area of Morocco may experience verbal abuse.

Family Issues

The government of Morocco considers all children born to Moroccan fathers to be Moroccan citizens. Even if the children bear American passports, immigration officials may require proof that the father approves their departure before the children will be allowed to leave Morocco. Although women are normally granted custody of their children in divorces, regardless of nationality, the children's departure from Morocco must be approved by their father. Women must obtain permission to move the children more than 100 kilometers (about 62 miles) from their last residence before the divorce.

OMAN

Entering Oman

A valid passport and visa are required. Omani embassies and consulates issue two-year, multiple-entry tourist and/or business visas to qualified American citizens. "No-objection certificates" for entry into Oman may also be arranged through an Omani sponsor. Evidence of yellow fever immunization is required if the traveler enters from an infected area. An AIDS test is required for persons newly-employed by private sector companies and anyone applying for renewal of a work permit. U.S. test results are not accepted.

Customs Regulations

Travelers entering Oman may not carry with them or in accompanied baggage any firearms, ammunition, or pornography; all are subject to seizure if found. No more than one bottle of liquor is permitted per non-Muslim adult. Books, videotapes, and audiotapes may be reviewed prior to being released to the owner.

Special Circumstances

Omani employers often ask that expatriate employees deposit their passports with the company as a condition of employment. Although customary, this practice is not required by Omani law. The U.S. Embassy advises Americans to exercise caution in agreeing to employer confiscation of passports, since this operates as a restraint on travel and could give undue leverage to the employer in any dispute.

Family Issues

Children of Omani fathers automatically acquire Omani citizenship at birth and must enter and leave the country on Omani passports, whether or not they are dual nationals. Child custody decisions in Oman are based on Islamic law. It is difficult for an American woman, even a Muslim, to obtain custody of her children through the Omani courts. Minor children of Omani fathers must have their father's permission to depart the country, even if they are U.S. citizens.

QATAR

Qatar is a traditional Muslim country. Conservative dress and behavior are strongly recommended for all visitors. Travelers to Qatar may not bring in narcotics, weapons, items deemed pornographic, or pork products. Luggage is subject to careful inspection by customs officials.

Although Arabic is the official language, English is widely spoken.

Entering Qatar
A valid passport and visa are required. To receive a visa, an applicant must be sponsored by a resident of Qatar, a local business, or by the hotel at which he or she will be staying. After obtaining a sponsor, travelers may apply for visas at a Qatari embassy or consulate. An AIDS test is required for persons seeking residency or work permits and anyone staying longer than one month. U.S. test results are not accepted.

Dual Nationality
Qatari law does not recognize dual nationality. Persons who possess Qatari citizenship in addition to U.S. citizenship are considered Qatari citizens by the State of Qatar and are subject to Qatar's laws.

Family Issues
Qatari citizenship imposes special obligations, particularly with regard to child custody and exiting or entering the country. Qatar is not a party to any international or bilateral treaty regarding international child abduction, adoption or child support enforcement issues

SAUDI ARABIA
Islam dominates all aspects of life in Saudi Arabia — government policy, cultural norms, and social behavior. Islam is the only official religion of the country, and public observance of any other religion is forbidden. The Saudi government considers it a sacred duty to safeguard two of the greatest shrines of Islam, the holy mosques located in the cities of Mecca and Medina. Travel to Mecca and Medina is forbidden to non-Muslims. Muslims throughout the world turn to Mecca five times a day for prayer. Restaurants, stores, and other public places close for approximately a half-hour upon hearing the call to prayer, and Muslims stop their activities to pray during that time. Government and business activities are noticeably curtailed during the month of Ramadan, during the celebrations at the end of Ramadan, and during the time of the annual pilgrimage to Mecca, the Hajj. Travel facilities into, out of, and within Saudi Arabia are crowded during these periods.

Although Westerners have some leeway in dress and social contacts within company residential compounds, both men and women should dress conservatively in public. Women's clothing should be loose fitting and concealing, with high necks, skirts worn well below the knee, and sleeves below the elbow. It is recommended that women not wear pants.

Females are prohibited from driving vehicles or riding bicycles on public roads, or in places where they might be observed. Males and females beyond childhood are not free to congregate together in most public places, and a man may be arrested for being seen with, walking with, traveling with, or driving a woman other than his wife or immediate relative. In Saudi Arabia, playing of music or dancing in public, mixed bathing, public showing of movies, and consumption of alcoholic beverages are forbidden.

Saudi religious police, known as *mutawwa* , have been empowered to enforce the conservative interpretation of Islamic codes of dress and behavior for women, and may rebuke or harass women who do not cover their heads or whose clothing is insufficiently concealing. In addition, in more conservative areas, there have been incidents of private Saudi citizens stoning, accosting, or pursuing foreigners, including U.S. citizens, for perceived dress code or other infractions. While most such incidents have resulted in little more than inconvenience or embarrassment for the individual targeted, there have been incidents where Westerners were physically harmed.

U.S. citizens in Saudi Arabia should be aware of Saudi social practices, and that any infractions may be dealt with aggressively. If you are accosted by Saudi authorities, cooperate fully in accordance with local customs and regulations. U.S. citizens who are harassed by private Saudi citizens or Saudi authorities should report the incidents immediately to the U.S. Embassy in Riyadh or the U.S. Consulate General either in Dhahran or in Jeddah. (See address and telephone list under *Foreign Embassies in the United States* at the end of this publication.)

Entering/Exiting Saudi Arabia
A valid passport and visa are required. Visas are issued for business and work, to visit close relatives, and for transit and religious visits. Visas for tourism are issued only for approved tour

groups following organized itineraries. Airport and seaport visas are not available. All visas require a sponsor, can take several months to process, and must be obtained prior to arrival. Women visitors and residents are required to be met by their sponsor upon arrival. Women traveling alone, who are not met by sponsors, have experienced delays before being allowed to enter the country or to continue on to other flights.

Visitors to Saudi Arabia generally obtain a meningitis vaccination prior to arrival. A medical report or physical examination is required to obtain work and residence permits. An AIDS test is required for persons planning to seek a residency or work permit. U.S. test results are sometimes accepted.

Health
Malaria is endemic to the low-lying coastal plains of southwest Saudi Arabia, primarily in the Jizan region extending up the coast to the rural area surrounding Jeddah. Visitors to the region are advised to take precautions to avoid being bitten by mosquitoes. As a further precaution, all persons intending to travel to this region should seek medical advice regarding recommendations for prophylactic anti-malarial medications. Cases of meningicoccal disease or meningitis in Americans traveling to Saudi Arabia are rare. However, during the Hajj season when there is an increased incidence of this disease among those traveling in the vicinity of Mecca and Medina, the Saudi Ministry of Health may require proof of immunization against meningitis. Visitors should check with the Centers for Disease Control, their travel agent, and a Saudi consulate or embassy regarding recommended or required shots.

Employment/Commercial and Business Disputes
Residents working in Saudi Arabia generally must surrender their passports while in the Kingdom. The sponsor (normally the employer) obtains work and residence permits for the employee and for any family members. Family members of those working are not required by law to surrender their passports, though they often do. Residents carry a Saudi residence permit (Iqama) for identification in place of their passports.

The written, Arabic text of a contract governs employment and business arrangements under Saudi law. Before signing a contract, American companies should obtain an independent translation to ensure a full understanding of the contract's terms, limits, and agreements. Verbal assurances or side letters are not binding under Saudi law. In the event of any contract dispute, the Saudi authorities refer to the contract.

Since the Saudi sponsor holds the employee's passport and controls the issuance of exit permits, Americans cannot simply leave Saudi Arabia in the event of a labor or business dispute. An American who wishes to break an employment or business contract may have to pay substantial penalties before being allowed to leave Saudi Arabia. To change employers in Saudi Arabia requires the permission of the previous employer, which is discretionary. Saudi courts take seriously their responsibility to adjudicate disputes. This process, which is performed in accordance with Saudi law and customs, may require the hiring of legal counsel, should not be entered into without an Arabic translator, and can take several months. The U.S. Embassy and U.S. Consulates General cannot adjudicate labor or business disputes.

The Hajj
All travel plans should be made through a travel agent in order to book accommodations in advance. Hajj visas are required and are valid only for travel to the two holy cities. Onward travel to Riyadh or other cities in Saudi Arabia is not permitted.

Foreign Muslim residents of the Kingdom may perform the Hajj once every five years. Advance approval must be obtained from an immigration office with the approval of the Saudi sponsor.

During the Hajj, about two million pilgrims from all over the world are concentrated in a relatively small space for a short period of time. The scale of this event, and the very basic living conditions it entails may be overwhelming to some. Housing, food, and sanitation are very basic.

Family Issues
A married woman residing with her Saudi husband should be aware that she must have her husband's permission to depart or have their children depart from Saudi Arabia. This is true even if the woman or children are U.S. citizens. The husband is the sponsor of his foreign wife and of his children, and is, as such, the only individual who can

request an exit visa for the wife or children.

In Saudi Arabia, child custody decisions are based on Islamic law. Saudi Arabia is not party with the U.S. to any extradition, judicial assistance or child abduction treaties. Saudi law does not recognize U.S. court orders, including child custody and divorce decrees, which are consequently unenforceable in Saudi Arabia. It is quite difficult for an American parent to resolve to his/her satisfaction a child custody dispute involving Saudi-American children. The role of U.S. officials in a child custody dispute is to determine the welfare and whereabouts of the disputed child, try to open lines of communication between the parties and assist the left-behind parent to find local counsel. Even when visitation is granted by a Saudi court, American mothers have, in some cases, experienced difficulties obtaining a Saudi visitor's visa enabling them to visit their Saudi-American children. Females and children need the permission of the eldest/closest male relative in their family to depart Saudi Arabia. A child born anywhere to a Saudi father is generally held to be a Saudi citizen, Muslim, and eligible for a Saudi passport.

Customs Regulations
Saudi customs authorities enforce strict regulations concerning importation into Saudi Arabia of such banned items as alcohol products, weapons and any item that is held to be contrary to the tenets of Islam. This includes non-Islamic religious materials, pork products, and pornography. Saudi customs and postal officials broadly define what is contrary to Islam, and therefore prohibited. Christmas decorations, fashion magazines, and "suggestive" videos may be confiscated and the owner subjected to penalties and fines. It is advisable to contact the Embassy of Saudi Arabia or one of Saudi Arabia's consulates in the United States for specific information regarding customs requirements. The private ownership of weapons is prohibited. Imported and domestic audiovisual media and reading matter are censored.

Items considered pornographic by Saudi standards, including magazines and videocassettes, are strictly forbidden. It is also illegal to import firearms of any type, ammunition, related items such as gun sights and gun magazines, food items, and banned books.

Personal religious items such as a Bible or a rosary are usually permitted, but travelers should be aware that on occasion, these items have been seized at entry and not returned to the traveler.

Special Circumstances and Criminal Penalties
Visitors should not photograph mosques, people who are praying, military or government installations, and key industrial, communications, or transportation facilities. If you have any doubts about what you may photograph, request permission first.

Homosexual activity is considered to be a criminal offense and those convicted may be sentenced to lashing and/or a prison sentence, or death.
Penalties for the import, manufacture, possession, and consumption of alcohol or illegal drugs are severe. Convicted offenders can expect jail sentences, fines, public flogging, and/or deportation. The penalty for drug trafficking in Saudi Arabia is death.

SYRIA
Conservative dress is recommended for Syria. Travelers should exercise caution when photographing historic sites. Photographs may be taken of regular tourist attractions, such as ancient ruins and temples, but warnings are issued against photographing government buildings, government property, and anything other than tourist sites.

Entering Syria
A passport and a visa are required. Visas must be obtained prior to arrival in Syria. Entry to Syria is not granted to persons with passports bearing an Israeli visa or entry/exit stamps, or to persons born in the Gaza region or of Gazan descent. Entry into Syria via the land border with Israel is not possible. Foreigners who wish to stay 15 days or more in Syria must register with Syrian Immigration by their 15th day in Syria. Americans between the ages of 18 and 45 who are of Syrian birth or recent descent are subject to the Syrian compulsory military service requirement, unless they receive an exemption from the Syrian Embassy in the United States prior to their entry into Syria. An AIDS test is required for persons between the ages of 15 and 60 years who are planning to stay longer than 15 days. U.S. test results are sometimes accepted.

Customs Regulations

267

Syrian pounds cannot be taken out of Syria. Travelers cannot convert Syrian pounds back into convertible currency, and should therefore not purchase more of the currency than they expect to spend in Syria. There are no foreign banks and no ATMs in Syria, and it is impossible to wire or otherwise transfer money from the United States to Syria.

Syrian customs authorities may enforce strict regulations concerning temporary importation into or export from Syria of items such as weapons, narcotics, alcohol, tobacco, cheese, fruits, pharmaceuticals, modems, cosmetics, and some electrical appliances. It is advisable to contact the Embassy of Syria in Washington, DC. for specific information regarding customs requirements

Dual Nationality/ Family Issues
U.S.-Syrian dual nationals may be subject to laws that impose special obligations on Syrian citizens. Under Syrian law, children of Syrian fathers, even those who have never been to Syria and do not speak Arabic, are Syrian. American men over the age of 18 who have never resided in or visited Syria, but whose fathers are/were Syrian, are required to complete military service or pay to be exempted. Possession of a U.S. passport does not absolve the bearer of this obligation.

Syrian-American and Palestinian-American men who have never served in the Syrian military and who are planning to visit Syria are strongly urged to check with the Syrian Embassy in Washington, DC prior to traveling, concerning their requirement for compulsory military service.

TUNISIA

Entering Tunisia
A valid passport is required. A visa is not required for a stay of up to four months. For longer visits, Americans are required to obtain a residence permit. A residence permit may be requested and obtained from the central police station of the district of residence. Americans born in the Middle East or with Arabic names have experienced delays in clearing immigration at airports upon arrival. American citizens of Tunisian origin are expected to enter Tunisia, on their Tunisian passports. If a Tunisian-American succeeds in entering on an American passport, there is a high probability that a Tunisian passport will be required before exiting the country.

Customs Regulations
Travelers' checks and credit cards are accepted at some establishments in Tunisia, mainly in urban or tourist areas. The Tunisian dinar is not yet a fully convertible currency. Tunisian law prohibits the export or import of Tunisian bank notes or coins. Tunisian law permits the export of foreign currency declared when entering Tunisia. Tourists are expected to make foreign exchange transactions at authorized banks or dealers and to retain receipts for dinars obtained. Under foreign currency regulations, a tourist can reconvert to foreign currency 30 percent of what has been exchanged into dinars, up to a maximum of 100 dollars. Declaring foreign currency on entering Tunisia and obtaining a receipt for dinars purchased thereafter will facilitate reconverting dinars to U.S. dollars. Keep all receipts of monetary transactions for presentation when leaving the country.

UNITED ARAB EMIRATES
The United Arab Emirates (UAE) is a federation of seven independent emirates, each with its own ruler. The federal government exists as a constitutional republic, headed by a president and council of ministers. Islamic ideals and beliefs provide the conservative foundation of the country's customs, laws and practices.

Entering the UAE
A valid passport and visa are required. In addition, an AIDS test is required of persons seeking a residency or work permit; testing must be performed upon arrival in the UAE. A U.S. AIDS test is not accepted.

Dual Nationality
The UAE government does not recognize dual nationality. Children of UAE fathers automatically acquire UAE citizenship at birth and must enter the UAE on UAE passports. UAE authorities have in the past confiscated U.S. passports of dual (UAE/U.S.) nationals. This does not constitute loss of U.S. citizenship, but should be reported to the U.S. Embassy in Abu Dhabi or the U.S. Consulate General in Dubai. Dual nationals may be subject to UAE laws that impose special obligations.

Customs Regulations

UAE customs authorities enforce strict regulations concerning temporary importation into or export from the UAE of items such as firearms (including fireworks), pornographic materials, medications, religious materials and communication equipment. It is advisable to contact the Embassy of the UAE in Washington for specific information regarding customs requirements.

UAE customs authorities also impose additional requirements for the importation of pets into the country. Prior permission in the form of a permit from the UAE Ministry of Agriculture and Fisheries must be secured before the pet's travel. To obtain the permit, please contact the UAE Ministry of Agriculture and Fisheries at the following address: P.O. Box 213, Abu Dhabi, UAE, telephone 971-2-662-781 or 971-2-485-438.

Special Circumstances
Visitors may apply for a temporary UAE driver's license upon presentation of a valid U.S. license. There are strict penalties for persons involved in traffic accidents while under the influence of alcohol, including lashings for Muslims.

Family Issues
Women residing in the UAE do not require their husband's permission to travel abroad, but a husband may block his wife's departure by submitting her name to immigration authorities. The UAE does not recognize dual nationality, and UAE citizenship is transmitted through the father regardless of the child's place of birth. Dual national children generally must enter and depart the UAE using their UAE passports.

YEMEN
Conditions in Yemen remain unsettled due to the recent end of Yemen's civil war. Ordnance such as mines, left over from the war, may pose a hazard to travelers. U.S. citizens should exercise caution in Yemen and avoid travel in remote areas. Local tribal disputes have occasionally led to violence. Westerners, including U.S. citizens, have been kidnapped as a result of such local disputes, and vehicles have been hijacked. Sixteen Western tourists, including two Americans, were abducted in Southern Yemen on December 28, 1998, by an anti-Western terrorist group. Four of the tourists died in a subsequent clash between the terrorists and Yemeni government forces. Anti-Western terrorists are still at large in Yemen. Urban violence and crime is a growing problem in Yemen, including within the capital, Sanaa.

Photography of military installations, including airports, equipment, or troops, is forbidden. In the past, such photography has led to the arrest of U.S. citizens. Military sites are not always obvious. If in doubt, it is wise to ask specific permission from Yemeni authorities.

Entering Yemen
A valid passport and visa are required. A yellow fever vaccination is recommended. Americans who consider studying in Yemen should make this fact clear to a Yemeni consular official in the U.S. and apply for the appropriate visa. Some Americans studying in Yemen without official permission have been deported. An AIDS test is required for persons seeking residency, study or work permits and anyone staying longer than 1 month, and foreign spouses of Yemeni nationals. U.S. test results are not accepted.

Dual Nationality
The Government of Yemen may not recognize the U.S. citizenship of persons who are citizens of both Yemen and the United States. This may hinder the ability of U.S. consular officials to assist persons who do not enter Yemen on a U.S. passport. Dual nationals may also be subject to national obligations, such as taxes or military service. Travelers can contact an embassy or consulate of Yemen for further information on Yemeni policy.

Iraq

Note: As of the time this publication went to press, the situation in Iraq remains uncertain and unstable. The following information is current as of December, 2003

COUNTRY DESCRIPTION: Iraq is currently administered by the Coalition Provisional Authority (CPA). Three decades of war and government mismanagement have stunted Iraq's economy, leading to increased crime and poverty. Infrastructure is antiquated. Conditions in Iraq are extremely dangerous. The workweek in Iraq is Saturday through Thursday. Information about the

269

CPA can be found at http://www.cpa-iraq.org.

SPECIAL CIRCUMSTANCES: There is a U.S. consular officer who provides limited emergency services to U.S. citizens only. Because police and civil structures are in the process of being rebuilt, U.S. citizens may have little recourse to these entities in emergency situations, and may have to seek assistance from coalition military police. At the present time, there is an 11:00 pm to 4:30 am curfew in Baghdad.

The banking and financial infrastructure has been disrupted and is in the process of rebuilding. Hotels usually require payment in foreign currency. No ATM machines exist. Restrictions on the use of the U.S. passport have been lifted.

ENTRY REQUIREMENTS: A person seeking entry to Iraq must appear before an authorized officer of the CPA at a port of entry, border control station, or at any place designated by the Senior Advisor of the Iraqi Ministry of Interior, in coordination with the Interim Minister of the Interior, for examination to determine whether the person may be granted entry to Iraq. Officers issue permits valid for up to 90 days, which may be renewed at CPA offices in Iraq. Permits will eventually be issued by Iraqi missions abroad.

In an effort to prevent international child abduction, many governments have initiated procedures at entry/exit points. These often include requiring documentary evidence of relationship and permission for the child's travel from the parent(s) or legal guardian not present. Having such documentation on hand, even if not required, may facilitate entry/departure.

DUAL NATIONALITY: In addition to being subject to all Iraqi laws affecting U.S. citizens, dual nationals may also be subject to other laws that impose special obligations on Iraqi citizens. For additional information, see the Consular Affairs home page on the Internet at http://travel.state.gov for our Dual Nationality flyer.

TERRORISM: The risk of terrorism directed against U.S. citizens and interests in Iraq remains high.

AREAS OF INSTABILITY/SAFETY AND SECURITY: Remnants of the former Baath regime, transnational terrorists, and criminal elements remain active throughout Iraq. Coalition-led military operations continue, and there continue to be attacks against Coalition forces throughout the country. While a number of attacks have been concentrated in Baghdad, Fallujah, Ramadi, Tikrit, Bayji, Baqubah, Mosul and Kirkuk, the security environment across Iraq remains volatile and unpredictable. Attacks on Coalition forces as well as civilian targets can occur at any time, especially during nighttime hours. There has been an increase in the use of Improvised Explosive Devices and/or mines on roads, particularly in plastic bags, soda cans, and animal carcasses. Grenades and explosives have been thrown into vehicles from overpasses, particularly in crowded areas.

Large demonstrations have occurred in Baghdad and other areas of the country, some of which have turned violent. Security conditions are improving, but demonstrations and civil strife are likely to continue into the near future. Detailed security information is available at http://www.centcom.mil http://www.centcom.mil.

U.S. citizens traveling abroad should regularly monitor the State Department's Internet website at http://travel.state.gov where the current Worldwide Caution Public Announcement, Travel Warnings, including the Travel Warning for Iraq, and Public Announcements can be found.

CRIME INFORMATION: The CPA is working with Iraqi police to establish law enforcement and civil structures throughout the country. U.S. and British military personnel are providing police protection as well as the security situation permits. Petty theft is common in Iraq, including thefts of money, jewelry, or valuable items left in hotel rooms and pickpocketing in busy places such as markets. Carjackings by armed thieves are increasing, even during daylight hours.

The loss or theft abroad of a U.S. passport should

be reported immediately to the local police or coalition military personnel and to the U.S. consular officer in Baghdad. Where needed, the U.S. consular officer may be able to assist you to find appropriate medical care, to contact family members or friends, and explain how funds could be transferred.

MEDICAL FACILITIES: Basic modern medical care and medicines are not widely available in Iraq. The recent conflict in Iraq has left some medical facilities non-operational and medical stocks and supplies severely depleted. The facilities in operation do not meet U.S. standards, and the majority lack medicines, equipment and supplies.

MEDICAL INSURANCE: The Department of State strongly urges U.S. citizens to consult with their medical insurance company prior to traveling abroad to confirm whether their policy applies overseas and whether it will cover emergency expenses such as a medical evacuation. U.S. medical insurance plans seldom cover health costs incurred outside the United States unless supplemental coverage is purchased. Further, U.S. medicare and medicaid programs do not provide payment for medical services outside the United States.

Traffic Safety and Road Conditions: While in a foreign country, U.S. citizens may encounter road conditions that differ significantly from those in the United States. The information below concerning Iraq is provided for general reference only and may not be totally accurate in a particular location or circumstance:

Safety of public transportation: Poor

Urban road conditions/maintenance: Good

Rural road conditions/maintenance: Poor

Availability of roadside assistance: Poor

Travel at night is extremely dangerous and should be avoided. There have been attacks on civilian as well as military convoys on Highways 1, 5, 10 and 15, even during daylight. Travelers are strongly urged to travel in convoys with at least 4 vehicles

in daylight hours only.

Buses run irregularly and frequently change routes. Poorly maintained city transit vehicles are often involved in accidents. Long distance buses are available, but are often in poor condition and drive at unsafe speeds. Jaywalking is common. Drivers usually do not yield to pedestrians at crosswalks and ignore traffic lights (if available), traffic rules and regulations. Roads are congested. Driving at night is extremely dangerous. Some cars do not use lights at night and urban street lights may not be functioning. Some motorists drive at excessive speeds, tailgate and force other drivers to yield the right of way. For additional general information about road safety, see the Department of State, Bureau of Consular Affairs home page at http://travel.state.gov/road_safety.html. See also road safety information on Iraq at http://www.arab.net/iraq/iraq_contents.htm.

AVIATION SAFETY OVERSIGHT: There are no commercial flights to and from Iraq. For further information, travelers may contact the U.S. Department of Transportation within the U.S. at 1-800-322-7873, or visit the FAA Internet website at http://www.intl.faa.gov.

CUSTOMS REGULATIONS: Customs and CPA officers have the broad authority to search persons or vehicles at Iraq ports of entry. Officers may confiscate any goods that may pose a threat to the peace, security, health, environment, or good order of Iraq or any antiquities or cultural items suspected of being illegally exported. Goods that are not declared may be confiscated by an officer. Persons may also be ordered to return such goods, at their expense, to the jurisdiction from which they came.

CRIMINAL PENALTIES: While in a foreign country, a U.S. citizen is subject to that country's laws and regulations, which sometimes differ significantly from those in the U.S. and may not afford the protections available to the individual under U.S. law. Penalties for breaking the law can be more severe than in the U.S. for similar offenses. Persons violating Iraqi laws, even unknowingly, may be expelled, arrested or imprisoned.

TELECOMMUNICATIONS:

Telecommunications are very poor. There is very limited international phone service in Iraq at this time. Local calls are often limited to a neighborhood network. There are no public telephones in the cities; however, calls may be made from hotels, restaurants or shops. Limited cellular telephone service is available in Baghdad. Public Internet service is not available.

U.S. CONSULAR OFFICER : U.S. citizens residing in or visiting Iraq are encouraged to make their presence in Iraq known to the U.S. consular officer, whose office is located in the Iraq Forum (formerly known as the Iraq Conference Hall) across from the al-Rashid Hotel in Baghdad. The e-mail address is payneba@orha.centcom.mil . Tel: 1-914-360-1025. (this is a New York number that rings in Baghdad).

*** *Please consult the State Department Travel Warnings Website at http://travel.state.gov. for up-to-date information on Iraq. American citizens may obtain the latest security information or other information about Iraq by phone: 1-914-360-1025, or by e-mail: payneba@orha.centcom.mil. Detailed security information is also available at http://www.centcom.mil and security.advisor@us.army.mi . Also consult Services for American Citizens In Iraq at (http://travel.state.gov/iraq_amcitservices.html)*

See Appendix B for a list and addresses of Foreign Embassies in the United States

See Appendix A for a list and addresses of U.S. Embassies and Consulates Abroad

Planning Another Trip?

See Chapter 36 for a listing of resources available to the general traveler from the U.S. Departments of State, Customs, Transportation, Health and various government and non-government organizations. Almost all of the available International travel-related pamphlets, brochures and publications issued by the U.S. Department of State and by the U.S. Customs have been reproduced in full in this book. See Table of Contents for location.

Chapter 20

Tips for Travelers to Russia

[The information in this chapter is reprinted verbatim from a bulletin issued by the U.S. State Department, Bureau of Consular Affairs. It is intended to serve as advice to Americans traveling abroad.]

General Information

Travel and living conditions in Russia can contrast sharply with those in the United States. This chapter offers advice to help you avoid inconveniences and difficulties. The Department of State and the U.S. Embassy and consulates in Russia offer a wide range of services to U.S. citizens. U.S. consular officials meet regularly with local authorities to promote the safety of U.S. citizens in the country.

In advance of your trip, learn as much as you can about your destination. Your travel agent, local bookstore, public library, the Internet and the embassy of the country or countries you plan to visit are all useful sources of information. Another source is the Department of State's *Background Notes* series, which features a pamphlet on each country. You may obtain B*ackground Notes* from the State Department home page at http://www.state.gov.

IMPORTANT: This information in this booklet is subject to change. Please consult the latest Consular Information Sheet for the most recent information on each country that you plan to visit.

Know Before You Go

Before and during your travels, keep abreast of local news coverage. If you plan to stay in one place for longer than a few weeks, or, if you are in an area where communications are poor, there is civil unrest or a natural disaster has occurred, you should register with the nearest U.S. embassy or consulate. Registration takes only a few moments and may be invaluable in case of an emergency.

Here are some other useful precautions:

Leave a detailed itinerary and the number of your passport or other citizenship documents with a friend or relative in the United States.

Carry your photo identification and the name of a person to contact with you in the event of serious illness or other emergency.

Keep photocopies of your passport, visa, airline or other tickets and a list of your traveler's checks with you in a separate location from the originals and leave copies with someone at home.

Leave things like unnecessary credit cards and expensive jewelry at home.

Use a money belt or concealed pouch for your passport, cash and other valuables.

Consular Information Program

Before traveling, obtain the Consular Information Sheets for all the countries you plan to visit. You should also check to see if the Department of State has issued a Travel Warning or Public Announcement for the country or countries you will be visiting.

Travel Warnings are issued when the Department of State decides, based on all relevant information, to recommend that Americans avoid travel to a certain country.

Public Announcements are issued as a means to disseminate information quickly about relatively short-term and/or regional conditions that could pose significant risks to the security of American travelers.

Consular Information Sheets are available for every country in the world. They include such information as the location of the U.S. embassy or consulate in the country, unusual immigration practices, health conditions, unusual currency and entry regulations, crime and security information, and drug penalties. A description of political disturbances may be included in the Consular

273

Information Sheet under an optional section entitled "Areas of Instability." On limited occasions, the Department also restates in this section U.S. embassy advice given to official employees. Consular Information Sheets present information so travelers can make knowledgeable decisions concerning travel to a particular country. Countries where we suggest that you not travel will have Travel Warnings in addition to Consular Information Sheets.

How to Access Consular Information Sheets, Travel Warnings and Public Announcements

By Internet

The most convenient source of information about travel and consular services is the Consular Affairs home page on the Internet's World Wide Web. The web site is http://travel.state.gov. If you do not have access to the Internet at home, work or school, your local library may provide access to the Internet.

By Telephone

Consular Information Sheets and Travel Warnings may be heard any time by dialing the office of American Citizens Services at **(202) 647-5225** from a touchtone phone.

By Fax

From your fax machine, dial **(202) 647-3000**, using the handset as you would a regular telephone. The system will instruct you on how to proceed.

In Person/By Mail

Consular Information Sheets, Travel Warnings and Public Announcements are available at any of the regional passport agencies, field offices of the Department of Commerce, U.S. embassies and consulates abroad, or, by writing and sending a self-addressed, stamped envelope to the Office of American Citizens Services, Bureau of Consular Affairs, Room 4811, U.S. Department of State, Washington, D.C. 20520-4818.

Visas and Other Entry Requirements

U.S. citizens must possess a valid U.S. passport and appropriate visas for travel to, or transit through, Russia and many of its neighboring countries, whether by train, car, ship or airplane. Travelers who arrive without an entry visa will be unable to enter Russia and face immediate ordered

departure by route of entry, at the traveler's expense. Visas should be obtained in advance of your trip at the embassy or consulate of the country you wish to visit. If possible, obtain your visa(s) in the United States, because this can be difficult and time-consuming to do in a third country. It is impossible to obtain a Russian entry visa upon arrival into the country. Errors in dates or other information on the visa can occur and it is helpful to have someone who reads the local language check the visa before departing the U.S.

Visas are valid for specific dates. An entry/exit visa reflects two dates written in the European style (date, month, year). The first date indicates the day you may enter Russia; the second date indicates the day you must leave the country. Sometimes, the length of a visa may not correspond to the length of your planed stay. Before starting your trip, be sure your visa is valid for the dates of your planned entry and departure. In Russia, travelers who spend more than three days in the country must register their visa through their hotel or sponsor. It is helpful to make a photocopy of your visa in the event of loss. A copy of your visa will not be sufficient for leaving the country. Russian border officials always ask for the original.

Amendment of a visa necessitated by illness or changes in travel plans must be approved in advance by the office that issued your visa. If travelers experience entry and exit visa problems they and/or their sponsor must contact the nearest Russian visa and passport office for assistance. Visitors who overstay their visa's validity, even for one day, or, who neglect to register their visa will be prevented from leaving. Due to the possibility of random document checks by police, U.S. citizens should carry their original or photocopies of their passports and registered visas with them at all times. Failure to provide proper documentation can result in detention and/or heavy fines.

Business and Transit Visas

A business visa requires a letter of invitation from a business contact in the country to which you are traveling. A transit visa requires a copy of your confirmed ticket and visa, if required, to your onward destination.

Sponsorship for Visas

Russia and many of its neighboring countries issue visas (with the exception of transit visas) on the basis of support from a sponsor, usually an individual or local organization. It is important to know who your sponsor is and how to contact them because, in many of these countries, the law requires that your sponsor apply on your behalf for replacement, extension or changes to your visa. Even if your visa was obtained through a travel agency in the U.S., there is always a Russian legal entity whose name is indicated on the visa and who is considered to be your legal sponsor. The U.S. Embassy cannot act as your sponsor. U.S. citizens should contact their tour company or hotel in advance for information on visa sponsorship.

Exit Visas

An exit visa is usually required to depart Russia. For short stays, the exit visa is issued along with the entry visa and is only valid until the date listed on the visa. In Russia and many neighboring countries, travelers who spend more than three days in the country must register their visa through their hotel or sponsor. Visitors who overstay their visa's validity, even for one day, or who neglect to register their visa will be prevented from leaving.

How to Obtain More Visa Information

Authoritative and current information on visas can only be obtained from the embassies or consulates of the countries you plan to visit. When you inquire about visas, ask about price, length of validity, the number of entries that are permitted and whether or not you will need an exit visa.

Your U.S. Passport

Thefts of U.S. passports are increasing rapidly. The theft or loss of a passport, especially when the nearest U.S. consular office is hundreds or thousands of miles away, is a major source of inconvenience and expense to travelers. Before your trip, make photocopies of the data page of your passport. A copy of the addresses and telephone numbers of the U.S. embassies and consulates in the countries you will visit may also be helpful. Put one set of the photocopies along with two passport photos in a place separate from your passport. If your passport is lost or stolen abroad, this will make issuance of a new passport faster and easier. Leave the second set of copies and your itinerary with a relative or friend in the U.S.

While in Russia and in many countries, you may be asked to turn over your passport to hotel personnel or a tour leader for short periods of time for registration with police or for other purposes. Your passport should be returned within two or three days. However, for U.S. citizens on long-term business or studies, the registration process can often take longer. It is not unusual for sponsors and local authorities to hold on to American passports for as much as several weeks while visas are registered or while exit visas are processed. Be sure to safeguard your passport at all other times, as its loss can cause you delays and problems.

If your passport is lost or stolen, you must apply for a replacement passport at a U.S. embassy or consulate. If possible, bring with you:

> identification, especially photo ID
> proof of U.S. citizenship (a birth certificate, naturalization certificate, Report of Birth Abroad or a copy of your passport)
> two 2" by 2" passport size photos, in color or black and white, and
> the police report that you filed when you notified the local authorities that your passport was lost or stolen.

In most cases, a new passport can be issued quickly. If U.S. passport records must be checked, the process may delay the issuance of a new passport.

In Russia you must also obtain a new or duplicate visa from OVIR (Office of Visas and Registration) if your visa is lost or stolen. (This office is also known as the "Passport-Visa Service" in some areas.) The passport number on your visa must match that of any new passport. Obtaining a replacement visa takes approximately 10 working days. A police certificate verifying the theft of your visa and passport may be necessary to obtain a new visa.

U.S. Visas for Foreigners

Questions regarding U.S. visas for foreigners should be directed to the nearest U.S. embassy or consulate.

275

Adoptions

Russia has well-established procedures governing international adoption; however, adoption laws vary greatly and are subject to change with little prior notice. Prospective adoptive parents should be prepared to go through a lengthy and complicated process before being allowed to adopt a child. For country specific information about current laws and procedures for international adoption, U.S. citizens may contact the Department of State's Office of Children's Issues at (202) 736-7000. They can also consult the Bureau of Consular Affairs' web site at http://travel.state.gov. Prospective adoptive parents are encouraged to contact their state's social services department for assistance in locating an adoption agency specializing in international adoption.

Travel in Russia

Areas of Instability. Due to continued civil and political unrest throughout most of the Caucasus region of Russia, the Department of State warns U.S. citizens against travel to the areas of Chechnya, all areas bordering Chechnya, North Ossetia, Ingushetia, Dagestan, Stavropol, Karachayevo-Cherkessiya and Kabardino-Balkariya. United States Government personnel are prohibited from traveling to these areas and American citizens residing in these areas should depart immediately as the safety of Americans and other foreigners cannot be effectively guaranteed. Throughout the region, local criminal gangs routinely kidnap foreigners, including Americans, for ransom. U.S. citizens have disappeared in Chechnya and remain unaccounted for. In December 1998, four foreign hostages were decapitated by their captors. Close contacts with the local population do not guarantee safety. The U.S. Government's ability to assist Americans who travel to the Northern Caucasus is extremely limited.

Air Travel Within Russia. After extensive joint reviews with the State Civil Aviation Authority (SCAA), the U.S. Federal Aviation Administration (FAA) has concluded under its International Aviation (IASA) Program that the SCAA oversees and licenses Russia's air carriers in accordance with international safety oversight provisions. For further information, travelers may contact the Department of Transportation within the U.S. at 1-800-322-7873, or visit the FAA web site at http://www.faa.gov/avr/iasa/. Travelers should note that air travel within Russia, particularly in remote regions, can be unreliable at times. Small local airlines do not have advance reservation systems but sell tickets for cash at the airport. Flights often get cancelled if more than 30% of the seats remain unsold.

Overland Travel. When traveling by train or automobile in Russia, it is advisable to bring food and water with you. You cannot rely on the availability or quality of these goods throughout the region. When traveling overland between Central European countries and Russia, be sure that you have visas for all countries through which you will pass. For example, you will need a Belarusian transit visa if you take the train from Warsaw, Poland to Vilnius, Lithuania because the train passes through Grodno, Belarus. Most transit problems can be avoided if you research your routes well.

Travel By Car. Driving conditions in Russia and the region are drastically different from those in Western Europe. In some areas, roads are practically non-existent. Throughout the region, service stations are few and far between and the lines are often quite long for the scarce amount of available fuel. Avoid excessive speed and, if at all possible, do not drive at night. Loose livestock can appear at any time. Construction sites or stranded vehicles are often unmarked by flares or other warning signals. Sometimes cars have only one headlight. Many cars lack brake lights. Bicycles seldom have lights or reflectors. This makes for very dangerous driving conditions at night. Be prepared for sudden stops at any time.

If you plan to drive, travelers should adhere to all local driving regulations. These are strictly enforced and violators are subject to severe legal penalties. Learn about your route from an auto club, guide book or a government tourist office. Some routes have heavy truck and bus traffic, others have poor or nonexistent shoulders and many have animals on the loose. Also, some of the newer roads have very few restaurants, motels, gas stations or auto repair shops. You may not be able to avoid all problems, but at least you will know what to expect if you have done some research. For your safety, have your vehicle serviced and in optimum condition before you travel. It is wise to bring an extra fan belt, fuses and other spare parts.

To avoid highway crime, try not to drive at night and never drive alone during this time. Never sleep in vehicles along the road. Do not, under any circumstances, pick up hitchhikers, who not only pose a threat to your physical safety, but also put you in danger of being arrested for unwittingly transporting narcotics or narcotics traffickers in your vehicle. Your vehicle can be confiscated if you are transporting marijuana or other narcotics.

A valid U.S. driver's license, a valid international driver's license or a valid license from the country in which you are traveling are necessary to drive a vehicle in Russia. International driver's licenses, good for one year, are available through the American Automobile Association. Foreigners who plan to drive in the region for more than six months must have a Russian driver's license. If you will be there for less than six months, you can use your American driver's license but need to carry an official translation, into Russian. Moreover, legal residents of Russia are required to obtain a Russian driver's license. In order to do that one has to take an appropriate exam. An American drivers' license cannot be exchanged for a Russian license. Travelers without a valid license are often subject to prolonged stops by highway police.

Insurance. Your automobile should be fully insured under a policy valid for the country in which you are traveling. U.S. automobile liability insurance is not valid nor are most collision and comprehensive coverage policies issued by U.S. companies. A good rule of thumb is to buy coverage equivalent to that which you carry in the United States.

Checkpoints. Law enforcement checkpoints aimed at detecting narcotics, alien smuggling and firearms traffic are located at various places throughout the region. Many checkpoints are operated by uniformed officials; however, others will not be marked and are manned by police or military officers not in uniform.

Crime and Safety
As a visitor to Russia, be alert to your surroundings. Problem situations in these countries may be different from those you are used to and safety regulations and their enforcement are generally not equivalent to U.S. standards.

Crime against foreigners is a problem. In large cities, take the same precautions against assault, robbery, or pickpockets that you would take in any large U.S. city. Be aware that women and small children, as well as men, can be pickpockets or purse snatchers. Keep your billfold in an inner front pocket, carry your purse tucked securely under your arm and wear the shoulder strap of your camera or bag across your chest. Walk away from the curb and carry your purse away from the street. The most vulnerable areas include underground walkways and the subway, overnight trains, train stations, airports, markets, tourist attractions, restaurants, hotel rooms and residences, even when locked or occupied. Groups of children are known to assault and rob foreigners on city streets or underground walkways. Members of religious and missionary groups have been robbed by people pretending to be interested in their beliefs. Foreigners who have been drinking alcohol are especially vulnerable to assault and robbery in or around nightclubs or bars, or on their way home. U.S. citizens are advised to be careful when ordering beverages in local nightclubs and bars, especially at night. Some establishments may contaminate or drug the drinks to gain control over the patron. Victims, who are almost always unaccompanied, have been robbed of personal property and abducted and held while their credit cards were used at various businesses and ATM locations around the city. Robberies may occur in taxis shared with strangers. Travelers have found it safer to travel in groups organized by reputable tour agencies.

NOTE: U.S. citizens should avoid providing personal identifying information to individuals not known to them. Information obtained from unsuspecting travelers has been used by individuals to extort money from families in the U.S. by contacting them and fraudulently informing them that a family member has been arrested or requires urgent medical care. The caller gains their confidence by providing this personal information and requests that funds be sent to assist their family member.

Public Transport. Be vigilant in bus and train stations and on public transport. Crime aboard trains has also increased. For example, travelers have been victimized without their knowledge and robbed on the train from Moscow to St. Petersburg. Crimes such as armed robbery have also been reported on trains between Moscow and Warsaw and between Moscow and Ulaanbaatar, Mongolia. On some trains, thieves have been able to open locked compartment doors. Always watch for pickpockets in these areas.

Streets and Highways. U.S. citizens should never hitchhike or accept rides from strangers. Be wary of persons representing themselves as police or other local officials. It is not uncommon for Americans to become victims of harassment, mistreatment and extortion by law enforcement and other officials. Authorities are concerned about these incidents and have cooperated in investigating such cases. *You must, however, have the officer's name, badge number, and patrol car number to pursue a complaint.* Make a note of this information if you are ever involved with police or other officials.

Skinheads. There have been sporadic attacks on foreigners by "skinhead" groups in some Russian urban centers. Many of these attacks appear to target university students, particularly those of Asian and African origin. Travelers are urged to exercise caution in areas frequented by "skinhead" groups and wherever large groups have gathered.

Crime Against Foreign Businesses and Businesspersons. Extortion and corruption are common in the business environment. Organized criminal groups target foreign businesses in many cities and have been known to demand protection money under threat of serious violence. Many Western firms hire security services that have improved their overall security, although this is no guarantee. Small businesses are particularly vulnerable. Since the mid-1990's, several American business people have been attacked, kidnapped and even killed. U.S. citizens are encouraged to report all extortion attempts to the Russian authorities and to inform consular officials at the U.S. Embassy or nearest consulate.

Travelers should be aware that in Russia certain activities, which would be normal business activities in the United States and other countries, are still either illegal under the Russian legal code or are considered suspect by the FSB (Federal Security Service.) Americans should be particularly aware of potential risks involved in any commercial activity with the Russian military-industrial complex, including research institutes, design bureaus, and production facilities or other high technology, government-related institutions. Any misunderstanding or dispute in such transactions can attract the involvement of the security services and lead to investigation or prosecution for espionage. Rules governing the treatment of information remain poorly defined. During the last several years, there have been a number of such incidents involving the arrest and/or detention of U.S. citizens. While the U.S. Embassy has had consular access to these individuals, arrested Americans faced lengthy sentences - sometimes in deplorable conditions - if convicted.

Safety Tips
Although officials in Russia have in many cases expressed willingness to cooperate with U.S. officials in emergencies involving U.S. citizens, communications and transportation can be slow and difficult, and the U.S. Embassy or nearest consulate may be more than a day's travel away. To reduce the risk of becoming a victim of crime, exercise the same precautions that you would in any large city and follow these tips:

Safety begins when you pack. Leave expensive jewelry, unnecessary credit cards and anything you would hate to lose at home.

Never display large sums of money when paying a bill. Conceal your passport, cash and other valuables on your person. Do not trust waist packs or fanny packs. Pickpockets have learned that is where the valuables are stored.

Be vigilant on public transport and at tourist sites, food markets, flea markets, art exhibitions and all places where crowds gather.

Even slight intoxication is noted by professional thieves. Therefore, if you drink in a public place, do so only with a trusted friend who has agreed to remain sober.

Avoid hailing unmarked cars as taxis. Although this is a common practice in Russia, foreigners have been robbed and assaulted by the drivers of such unmarked cabs. Never accept a ride from a driver who already has other passengers.

Demonstrations are frequently held in front of U.S. embassies and consulates. While these demonstrations are usually peaceful and controlled, it is best to avoid such gatherings.

If you have been the victim of a crime, immediately contact the U.S. Embassy or the nearest U.S. consulate or consular agency. For addresses and telephone numbers, see the end of this chapter. You should also report the crime to the local police immediately.

Useful information on safeguarding valuables, protecting personal security, and other matters while traveling abroad is provided in the Department of State pamphlet, *A Safe Trip Abroad*, which is available on the Consular Affairs web site at http://travel.state.gov and for sale from the U.S. Government Printing Office. (See the end of the booklet for ordering information.)

Medical Care and Health Insurance

Medical Care. Medical care is usually far below Western standards, with severe shortages of basic medical supplies. Access to the few quality facilities that exist in major cities usually requires cash payment at Western rates upon admission. The U.S. Embassy and consulates maintain lists of such facilities and English-speaking doctors. Many resident Americans travel to the West for virtually all of their medical needs. Such travel can be very expensive if undertaken under emergency conditions. Travelers may therefore wish to check their insurance coverage and consider supplemental coverage for medical evacuation. Elderly travelers and those with existing health problems may be at particular risk.

Health Insurance. Medicare/Medicaid does **not** cover you when you are outside the United States. If your insurance policy does not cover you outside the United States, it is strongly recommended that you purchase a policy that does. There are short-term health insurance policies designed specifically to cover travel, which can be as low as $50.00 for a trip of 30 days. As part of the coverage, these programs usually offer emergency consultation by telephone. They may refer you to the nearest hospital or call for help on your behalf. They may translate your instructions to a health care worker on the scene. Because conditions in many hospitals are not adequate to ensure recovery, medical evacuation is frequently necessary for illnesses or injuries that could be treated locally in other countries. This is an expensive option. For example, minimum cost from Moscow to New York on a stretcher is more than $15,000. Medical evacuation by hospital aircraft on the same route approaches $130,000. Such services require a substantial down payment before they commit themselves to arranging a flight out of Russia. In addition, medical evacuation from remote areas can be especially long and difficult. Evacuation from the interior of the country, such as Siberia, can take a day to organize and set into motion.

If your travel agent cannot direct you to a medical assistance company, look for information in travel magazines. The names of some companies that provide medical evacuation coverage or services are listed in the publication, *Medical Information for Americans Traveling Abroad*, on our Internet site http://travel.state.gov under Travel Publications. The U.S. government cannot pay to have you medically evacuated to the United States.

Potential Health Problems

Health problems sometimes affect visitors to Russia. Information on health precautions can be obtained from local health departments or private doctors. General guidance can also be found in the U.S. Public Health Service book, *Health Information for International Travel*, available from the Superintendent of Documents, U.S. Government Printing Office, Washington, D.C. 20402.

Travel in Russia and its neighboring states can be strenuous, particularly for the elderly and individuals with special health problems. When you plan your trip, be careful not to overschedule. Leave time for rest and relaxation. Tourists in frail health are strongly advised not to visit because of the harsh conditions and lack of adequate medical facilities.

Outbreaks of diphtheria have been reported throughout the region, even in large cities such as Moscow and St. Petersburg. The U.S. Centers for Disease Control and Prevention recommend up-to-date diphtheria immunizations before traveling to Russia and its neighboring countries. Typhoid can be a concern for those who plan to travel extensively in the region. Cases of cholera have also been reported throughout the area; the risk of exposure to cholera can be reduced by refraining from drinking local water supplies.

Immunizations. No immunizations are required for travelers to Russia. However, diphtheria, tetanus, polio and gamma globulin vaccinations are recommended for the region. The following vaccines should be considered, depending on the locations to be visited, planned activities and the health of the traveler: hepatitis A, hepatitis B, rabies, encephalitis and typhoid.

Information on vaccinations and other health precautions may be obtained from the Centers for Disease Control and Prevention's international travelers hotline at 1-877-FYI-TRIP (1-877-394-8747); the automated fax information system at 1-888-CDC-FAXX (1-888-232-3299) or by visiting the CDC Internet home page at http://www.cdc.gov/.

AIDS Testing. Russia requires submission of an appropriate HIV-negative certificate at the time of applying for a visa in case of an intended stay of 3 months or longer. Positive test results for HIV could be grounds for expulsion from the country. All travelers intending to reside in Russia are strongly advised to have the requisite tests performed in the United States, as the testing conditions in the region tend to be very unsanitary and could pose a hazard to your health. Requirements for HIV testing are likely to change as new legislation is adopted. Please refer to the current Consular Information Sheet or contact the U.S. Embassy or nearest consulate for the latest requirements.

Drinking Water. Drink only bottled water or water that has been boiled for 20 minutes. The U.S. Public Health Service warns that many visitors to the region have returned to the United States infected with the intestinal parasite giardia lamblia. This infection is usually contracted by drinking local tap water. In addition, you should avoid ice cubes, salads and uncooked vegetables and fruits that cannot be peeled. Use only bottled water for brushing teeth. A good rule to follow is if you can't peel it or cook it, don't eat it! Local water supplies can be avoided in several ways. Some travelers to the region bring drinking water with them in their luggage. If you cannot import your drinking water, drink only bottled carbonated drinks. Some portable water filters are specially constructed to remove the giardia parasite.

However, if you are relying on a water filter, it is still highly advisable to boil the water after filtering. In many large cities, bottled water of imported or Russian origin can be purchased in stores. However, travelers should not rely on the availability of bottled water from these sources. In addition, carry iodine tablets to disinfect drinking water (though it should be noted that some iodine tablets take several hours to work.) Travelers returning from the region who develop a diarrheal illness lasting more than five days should consult a physician.

Bring Your Own Medicines. Bring any necessary medications with you and keep them in the original, labeled containers in your hand luggage. Because of strict laws on narcotics, carry a letter from your physician explaining your need for any prescription drugs in your possession. Also bring along any toiletries and personal hygiene items that you will need. These items can be difficult to obtain in major cities and virtually nonexistent elsewhere.

Legal Matters

How to Avoid Legal Problems. While in a foreign country, U.S. citizens are subject to that country's laws and regulations. In some instances, laws in Russia differ significantly from those in the United States and do not afford the protections available to the individual under U.S. law. Exercise caution and carefully obey local laws. Penalties for breaking the law can be more severe than in the United States for similar offenses. Persons violating the law, even unknowingly, may have difficulties with the authorities and may be expelled and forced to forfeit the unused part of a pre-purchased tour. Serious transgressions of the law can lead to arrest and imprisonment.

Under Article 12 of the U.S.-USSR Consular Convention of 1964 (which the U.S. considers to remain in force), government authorities in Russia are required to inform the U.S. Embassy or consulate of the arrest or detention of a U.S. citizen and to permit communication with the detained citizen within two to four days of arrest. If you are detained by authorities, ask that a U.S. consular officer be informed and that you be allowed to meet with a consular officer without delay.

Dual Nationality

Russian law may require naturalized U.S. citizens of Russian origin to enter and depart Russia using a Russian passport. In addition, a Russian visa may not be issued to U.S. citizens who are still considered Russian citizens under Russian law. Dual nationals who enter Russia on a Russian passport will be considered Russian citizens. Dual nationals who enter Russia on a U.S. passport and Russian visa will be considered U.S. citizens during their stay. While recognizing that some Americans are also citizens of other countries, the U.S. Government does not encourage its citizens to become or remain dual nationals due to an array of complications that may ensue from the obligations (payment of taxes, military service, etc.) owed to the country of second nationality. It may be necessary for such persons to "withdraw" or renounce their former Russian or Soviet nationality before a Russian consular official in the United States. Those who are unsure whether they hold Russian citizenship are advised to contact the nearest Russian consular office for information about citizenship requirements and travel documentation.

The United States recognizes as an established principle of international law that every sovereign state has the right to decide under the provisions of its own laws who is and who is not its citizen.

The U.S. Department of State maintains the following:

U.S. citizens, whether by birth or naturalization, possess full American citizenship and its accompanying benefits and responsibilities despite any additional entitlement to other citizenship(s).

U.S. citizens cannot lose their U.S. citizenship because of automatic acquisition of foreign citizenship. However, if a U.S. citizen contemplates voluntarily accepting dual nationality in connection with assuming duties as a government official in any country, he or she should first consult with the Department of State's Office of Overseas Citizens Services at **202-647-5225** or with the nearest U.S. embassy or consulate.

Additional information about the U.S. Governments policy with respect to dual nationality may be found at the Bureau of Consular Affairs web site at http://travel.state.gov/dualnationality.html.

Legal Permanent U.S. Residents

The ability of U.S. authorities to assist legal permanent U.S. residents is limited. These individuals should travel with appropriate documentation of their legal status in the U.S. Those who are citizens of Russia or any country should ensure that they have the correct entry/exit permission from the appropriate embassy in the United States before they travel.

Marriage Abroad

Americans contemplating marriage to a citizen of Russia or other country should contact the Consular Section of the nearest American embassy or consulate before the marriage takes place. Consular officers cannot perform marriages, but can provide information about local regulations concerning marriage.

Photography Restrictions

The majority of areas formerly closed to foreigners have been opened. Use good judgment when photographing in museums, churches and sensitive areas. Many museums do not permit photography near the exhibits. At the time you are purchasing your tickets, inquire as to whether or not photography is allowed in the museum, if a permit is required, how much the permit will cost, and, if photos taken with high-speed film and without a flash are allowed. When in doubt, ask your tour guide or someone else in authority if it is acceptable to take a photograph.

The following are general guidelines for photography in Russia:

Photographs are permitted of architectural monuments, cultural, educational and medical buildings, theaters, museums, parks, stadiums, streets and squares, and living quarters and landscape scenes.

If prior permission is obtained from officials of the institution concerned, photographs may be taken of industrial enterprises that manufacture non-military products, farms, railroad stations, airports, riverports, riverlocks, dams, construction sites, and governmental, educational and social organizations.

Telephone Service

Long distance telephone calls can usually be made

from a hotel. AT&T, MCI and other telecommunications companies can provide calling card service with local access numbers. Check with your phone card provider for specific information. Calls can also be made from phone kiosks, located near Metro and train stations, tourist attractions and in downtown areas, with pre-paid, locally purchased phone cards.

It is also possible to make calls from the local Telephone and Telegraph office. This is the cheapest way to call, but it also necessitates standing in line and putting in a request to make an international call. A rudimentary knowledge of the local language is extremely helpful for those placing a call through the Telephone and Telegraph office.

U.S. Priority Mail Services
Federal Express, DHL, TNT and United Parcel Service all offer priority mail services between the U.S. and Russia. However, even packets sent by priority mail may be held up in customs for up to a week. Local regulations forbid the mailing of Russian passports to or from a foreign country.

Currency
The ruble is the only legal tender. It is illegal to pay for goods and services in U.S. dollars except at authorized retail establishments. Old or very worn dollar bills are often not accepted at banks and exchange offices, even though this constitutes a violation of currency laws. Russia operates on the basis of a cash-only economy. This means that traveler's checks and credit cards are not widely, if ever, accepted as currency. Travelers' checks and credit cards are not generally accepted outside of Moscow and St. Petersburg. Even in these cities, the acceptance of credit cards is subject to change. Before you leave home, check with your credit card and travelers check companies to learn if and where these can be used in Russia. Travelers should expect some difficulty in obtaining dollars in Russia, although dollars can be easily exchanged into rubles. Travelers should not rely on automated teller machines (ATM) for cash. Major hotels or the American Express offices in Moscow or St. Petersburg may be able to suggest locations for cashing travelers checks or obtaining cash advances on credit cards. Western Union agents in Moscow, St. Petersburg and some other large cities disburse money wired from the U.S. Russia sometimes experiences periodic cash shortages. The difficulties of a currency shortage can be avoided by taking a prepaid tour that includes all meals and hotels. Most travelers go to Russia with a sufficient supply of hard currency to cover their obligations during travel. Some hotel restaurants and shops will accept payment only in dollars or other hard currency.

Generally, U.S. dollars can be exchanged for local currency only at official exchange offices or in banks. Anyone caught dealing on the black market can expect to be detained by the local militia.

Shopping
Artwork, souvenirs and handicrafts purchased at special stores for tourists may be taken out of Russia. Be wary of antiques! The authorities define antiques as anything of historical or cultural value and they apply this definition to a wide range of articles. Antiques and artifacts (such as samovars) often may not be taken out of Russia without inspection by local cultural authorities and payment of a substantial export duty. This can be an inconvenient and time-consuming process. Items such as samovars, which are not purchased at tourist stores and not cleared by cultural authorities, are normally confiscated at pre-departure customs inspections. You should obtain a receipt for all items of value that you have purchased. The receipt must indicate that the items were bought in a store clearly licensed to sell to foreigners. Furthermore, icons, art, rugs, antiques and other culturally significant objects must have a certificate indicating that they have no historical value. This certificate can be obtained either from the store at the time the item is purchased or from the Ministry of Culture.

Customs Regulations
Russian customs laws and regulations are in a state of flux and are not consistently enforced. Travelers to Russia should declare all items of value, including cash, on a customs form upon arrival and keep this form until their departure from Russia. Make an accurate and complete customs declaration of all money, travelers' checks and valuables in your possession. Include all personal jewelry, such as wedding rings and watches, and other high-value items, such as personal computers. Have your customs declaration stamped by the authorities and keep it with you until you leave the country. Keep your exchange receipts to account for your expenditures. Without

these records, customs officials could confiscate your cash and valuables upon departure. Currently, travelers **leaving** Russia with more than $1,500 dollars must declare the amount of cash they are carrying on their customs declaration. Lost or stolen customs forms should be reported to the Russian police, and a police report (spravka) should be obtained to present to customs officials upon departure.

Travelers should obtain receipts for all high-value items (including caviar) purchased in Russia. Any article that could appear old to the customs service, including icons, samovars, rugs and other antiques must have a certificate indicating that it has no historical value. It is illegal to remove such items from Russia without this certificate. These certificates may be obtained either from the vendor of the item or from the Russian Ministry of Culture. For further information, Russian speakers may call the customs service of the Russian Federation at Sheremetyevo-2 Airport in Moscow at (7) (095) 578-2120/2125.

Attempts to bring any of the following articles into Russia has caused difficulties for U.S. citizens in the past:

- *Narcotics* - Drug laws are strict. U.S. citizens have received long sentences for trying to enter or transit with illegal narcotics. Under Russian law, any amount of marijuana or other narcotic is considered to be a large amount of drugs.
- *Pornography* - Magazines with sexually explicit photographs, that may be considered commonplace in Western countries, may be regarded as pornography and are often confiscated.
- *Gifts for Persons in Russia* - A high rate of customs duty may be assessed on gifts that you bring into Russia. U.S. citizens have had to abandon gifts at the airport because they lacked funds to pay the customs duty.
- *Video Cassettes* - Customs regulations allow for the import and re-export of a limited number of blank or commercially recorded video cassettes for personal use. Some travelers with a large number of cassettes have had them confiscated. Travelers are advised to leave blank video cassettes sealed in their wrappers when entering a country.

Electronic Devices

The importation and use of Global Positioning Systems (GPS) and other radio electronic devices are subject to special rules and regulations in Russia. In general, mapping and natural resource data collection activities associated with normal, commercial and scientific collaboration may result in seizure of the equipment and/or arrest of the user. The penalty for using a GPS device in a manner which is determined to have compromised Russia's national security can carry a prison term of ten to twenty years. In December 1997, a U.S. citizen was imprisoned in Rostov-na-Donu for ten days on charges of espionage for using a GPS device to check the efficacy of new-installed telecommunications equipment. He and his company believed the GPS had been legally imported and were not aware that Russian authorities considered nearby government installations secret.

No traveler should seek to import or use GPS equipment in any manner unless it has been properly and fully documented by the traveler in accordance with the instructions of the Glavgossvyaznadzor (Main Inspectorate in Communications) and is declared in full on a customs declaration at the point of entry to the Russian Federation.

All radio electronic devices brought into Russia must have a certificate from Glavgossvyaznadzor of the Russian Federation. This includes all emitting, transmitting, and receiving equipment such as GPS devices, cellular telephones, satellite telephones, and other kinds of radio electronic equipment. Excluded from the list are consumer electronic devices such as AM/FM radios.

Cellular Telephones. To obtain permission to bring in a cellular telephone, an agreement for service from a local cellular provider in Russia is required. That agreement and a letter of guarantee to pay for the cellular service must be sent to Glavgossvyaznadzor along with a request for permission to import the telephone. Based on these documents, a certificate is issued. This procedure is reported to take two weeks. Without a certificate, no cellular telephone can be brought into the country, regardless of whether or not it is meant for use in Russia. Permission for the above devices may also be required from the State Customs Committee of the Russian Federation.

Cellular phone rentals are available and recommended.

U.S. Embassy and Consulate Locations in Russia

U.S. Embassy in Moscow
Novinskiy Bulvar 19/23
tel. (7-095) 728-5000
After hours duty officer: (7-095) 728-5109 h
http://usembassy.state.gov/moscow/
E-mail address: Consulmo@state.gov

U.S. Consulates General
St. Petersburg
Ulitsa Furshtadskaya 15 t
el. (7-812) 275-1701
After hours duty officer: (7-812) 274-8692
E-mail: Acs_stpete@state.gov

Vladivostok
Ulitsa Pushkinskaya 32
tel. (7-4232) 30-00-70 (also for after hour emergencies)
http://usembassy.state.gov/vladivostok/

Yekaterinburg
Ulitsa Gogolya 15 ;tel. (7-3432) 62-98-88
After hours duty officer: (8-29) 05-15-06
Elsewhere within Russia for Yekaterinburg tel. (8-3439) 05-15-06 ; http://www.uscgyekat.ur.ru
E-mail: uscgyekat@gin.ru

Russian Embassy and Consulate Locations in the U.S.

Embassy of the Russian Federation
2641 Tunlaw Road, N.W.
Washington, D.C. 20007
Telephone: 202-939-8907, 202-939-8913, 202-939-8918 ; http://www.russianembassy.org

Consulates General of the Russian Federation
New York City
9 East 91st Street
New York, NY 10128
Telephone: 212-348-0926

San Francisco
2790 Green Street
San Francisco, CA 94123
Telephone: 415-928-6878

Seattle
2323 Westin Building
2001 6th Avenue
Seattle, WA 98121
Telephone: 206-728-1910

Foreign Embassies in the United States
[For a complete listing of foreign embassies in the United States see **Appendix B**].

United States Embassies and Consulates Abroad

[For a complete listing of United States embassies and consulates abroad, including their addresses, telephone, fax, and telex numbers see **Appendix A**].

Planning Another Trip?
See Chapter 36 for a listing of resources available to the general traveler from the U.S. Departments of State, Customs, Transportation, Health and various government and non-government organizations. Almost all of the available International travel-related pamphlets, brochures and publications issued by the U.S. Department of State and by the U.S. Customs have been reproduced in full in this book. See Table of Contents for location.

Chapter 21

Tips for Travelers to The Independent States (of former Soviet Union)

[The information in this chapter is reprinted verbatim from a bulletin issued by the U.S. State Department, Bureau of Consular Affairs. It is intended to serve as advice to Americans traveling abroad.]

Armenia, Azerbaijan, Belarus, Estonia, Georgia, Latvia, Lithuania, Moldova, Kazakhstan, Kyrgyz Rep. Tajikistan, Turkmenistan, Ukraine, Uzberkistan

ARMENIA

COUNTRY DESCRIPTION: Armenia, located in the southern Caucasus Mountains, is the smallest of the former Soviet republics. Armenia's borders with Turkey and Azerbaijan are closed due to the dispute over the status of the Nagorno-Karabakh region of Azerbaijan. Long transportation routes and economic difficulties limit the availability of imported goods, though the extreme shortages of the early- and mid-1990s have eased significantly. Tourist facilities, especially outside Yerevan, the capital, are not highly developed, and many of the goods and services taken for granted in other countries may be difficult to obtain. Travelers frequently experience problems with local officials seeking bribes to perform basic duties.

ENTRY REQUIREMENTS: A passport and visa are required. For further information on entry requirements, please contact the Armenian Embassy at 2225 R St. NW, Washington, D.C. 20008, tel. (202) 319-1976; the Armenian Consulate General in Los Angeles at 50 N. La Cienega Blvd., Suite 210, Beverly Hills, CA 90211, tel. (310) 657-6102 or visit the Armenian Embassy's website at http://www.armeniaemb.org.

In an effort to prevent international child abduction, many governments have initiated procedures at entry/exit points. These often include requiring documentary evidence of relationship and permission for the child's travel from the parent(s) or legal guardian not present. Having such documentation on hand, even if not required, may facilitate entry/departure.

DUAL NATIONALITY: In addition to being subject to all Armenian laws affecting U.S. citizens, dual nationals may also be subject to other laws that impose special obligations on Armenian citizens. For additional information, please see the Consular Affairs home page on the Internet at http://travel.state.gov for our *Dual Nationality flyer.*

SAFETY AND SECURITY: Since 1988, armed conflict has taken place in and around the self-proclaimed "Republic of Nagorno-Karabakh," a breakaway autonomous republic of Azerbaijan. A cease-fire has been in effect since May 1994, although there have been some reports of minor violations. Because of the existing state of hostilities, consular services are not available to Americans in Nagarno-Karabakh. Travelers should exercise caution near the Armenia-Azerbaijan border and consult the Consular Information Sheet for Azerbaijan if considering travel to Nagorno-Karabakh from Armenian territory. Armenia's land borders with Turkey, Azerbaijan and the Nakhichevan Autonomous Republic of Azerbaijan remain closed and continue to be patrolled by armed troops who stop all persons attempting to cross. There are still land mines in numerous areas in and near the conflict zones.

Visitors are advised to place valuables in the hotel safe for safekeeping during their stay.

CRIME: Armenia has a low rate of violent crime, but common street crime has increased, especially at night. Generally, incidents are limited to pick-pocketing and other petty thefts. However, expatriates have been victims of several attacks involving knives in the last few years.

The loss or theft abroad of a U.S. passport should be reported immediately to the local police and the nearest U.S. embassy or consulate. If you are the victim of a crime while overseas, in addition to reporting to local police, please contact the nearest U.S. embassy or consulate for assistance. The Embassy/Consulate staff can, for example, assist you to find appropriate medical care, to contact family members or friends and explain how funds could be transferred. Although the investigation and prosecution of the crime is solely the responsibility of local authorities, consular officers can help you to understand the local criminal justice process and to find an attorney if needed.

U.S. citizens may refer to the Department of State's pamphlet, *A Safe Trip Abroad*, for ways to promote a trouble-free journey. The pamphlet is available by mail from the Superintendent of Documents, U.S. Government Printing Office, Washington, D.C. 20402, via the Internet at http://www.access.gpo.gov/su_docs, or via the Bureau of Consular Affairs home page at http://travel.state.gov.

MEDICAL FACILITIES: Though there are many competent physicians, medical care facilities in Armenia are limited, especially outside the major cities. The U.S. Embassy maintains a list of English speaking physicians in the area. Most prescription medications are available, but the quality varies. Elderly travelers and those with existing health problems may be at risk due to inadequate medical facilities.

MEDICAL INSURANCE: The Department of State strongly urges Americans to consult with their medical insurance company prior to traveling abroad to confirm whether their policy applies overseas and if it will cover emergency expenses such as a medical evacuation. U.S. medical insurance plans seldom cover health costs incurred outside the United States unless supplemental coverage is purchased. Further, U.S. Medicare and Medicaid programs do not provide payment for medical services outside the United States. However, many travel agents and private companies offer insurance plans that will cover health care expenses incurred overseas, including emergency services such as medical evacuations.

When making a decision regarding health insurance, Americans should consider that many foreign doctors and hospitals require payment in cash prior to providing service and that a medical evacuation to the United States may cost well in excess of $50,000. Uninsured travelers who require medical care overseas often face extreme difficulties. When consulting with your insurer prior to your trip, please ascertain whether payment will be made to the overseas healthcare provider or if you will be reimbursed later for expenses that you incur. Some insurance policies also include coverage for psychiatric treatment and for disposition of remains in the event of death.

Useful information on medical emergencies abroad, including overseas insurance programs, is provided in the Department of State's Bureau of Consular Affairs brochure, *Medical Information for Americans Traveling Abroad*, available via the Bureau of Consular Affairs home page or autofax: (202) 647-3000.

OTHER HEALTH INFORMATION:
Information on vaccinations and other health precautions, such as safe food and water precautions and insect bite protection, may be obtained from the Centers for Disease Control and Prevention's hotline for international travelers at 1-877-FYI-TRIP (1-877-394-8747); fax 1-888-CDC-FAXX (1-888-232-3299), or via the CDC's Internet site at http://www.cdc.gov/travel.

TRAFFIC SAFETY AND ROAD CONDITIONS: While in a foreign country, U.S. citizens may encounter road conditions, which differ significantly from those in the United States. The information below concerning Armenia is provided for general reference only, and it may not be totally accurate in a particular location or circumstance.

Safety of public transportation: Fair
Urban road condition/ maintenance: Fair
Rural road condition/maintenance: Poor
Availability of roadside assistance: Fair
Travel in Armenia requires caution. Public transportation, while very inexpensive, may be unreliable and uncomfortable. Travel at night is not recommended, and winter travel can be extremely hazardous in mountain areas and higher elevations.

With the exception of a few major arteries, primary roads are frequently in poor repair, with sporadic stretches of missing pavement and large potholes. Some roads shown as primary roads on maps are unpaved and can narrow to one lane in width, while some newer road connections have not yet been marked even on recently produced maps.

Secondary roads are normally in poor condition and are often unpaved and washed out in places. Street and road signs are poor to nonexistent. Truck traffic is not heavy except on the main road linking Yerevan to the Iranian border.

Though crime on the roads is rare, the police themselves often seek bribes at periodic checkpoints on main routes. Drivers in Armenia often take great risks, and traffic laws are frequently ignored. This problem is only slightly offset by the fact that congestion on city streets is light.

Pedestrians are as prone to risky behavior as are drivers. Travelers driving in towns at night should be especially cautious. In the cities, a pedestrian dressed all in black crossing an unlit street in the middle of the block is a common occurrence.

The quality of gasoline in Armenia ranges from good at some of the more reliable stations in cities to very poor. The gasoline and other fuels sold out of jars, barrels and trucks by independent roadside merchants should be considered very unreliable.

For additional general information about road safety, including links to foreign government sites, please see the Department of State, Bureau of Consular Affairs home page at http://travel.state.gov/road_safety.html. Please see also road safety information from other sources in Armenia at http://www.international.fhwa.dot.gov/links/intl.cfm

AVIATION SAFETY OVERSIGHT: As there is no direct commercial air service by local carriers at present, nor economic authority to operate such service between the United States and Armenia, the U.S. Federal Aviation Administration (FAA) has not assessed Armenia's Civil Aviation Authority for compliance with international aviation safety standards. For further information, travelers may contact the Department of Transportation within the United States at tel. 1-800-322-7873, or visit the FAA's Internet website at http://www.faa.gov/avr/iasa.

The U.S. Department of Defense (DOD) separately assesses some foreign air carriers for suitability as official providers of air services. For information regarding the DOD policy on specific carriers, travelers may contact the DOD at tel. (618) 229-4801.

CUSTOMS REGULATIONS: Armenian customs authorities may enforce strict regulations concerning temporary importation into or export from Armenia of items such as firearms, pornographic materials, medication and communications equipment. For export of antiquities and other items that could have historical value, such as paintings, carpets or other artisan goods, a special authorization is required in advance from the Armenian Ministry of Culture. It is advisable to contact the Embassy of Armenia in Washington, D.C. or consulate in Los Angeles for specific information regarding customs requirements.

CRIMINAL PENATIES: While in a foreign country, a U.S. citizen is subject to that country's laws and regulations, which sometimes differ significantly from those in the United States and may not afford the protections available to the individual under U.S. law. Penalties for breaking the law can be more severe than in the United States for similar offenses. Person's violating Armenian laws, even unknowingly, may be expelled, arrested or imprisoned. Penalties for possession, use, or trafficking in illegal drugs in Armenia are strict, and convicted offenders can expect jail sentences and heavy fines.

SPECIAL CIRCUMSTANCES: Armenia remains largely a cash-only economy, and credit cards are accepted at some businesses, but not at hotels. Limited facilities exist for cashing traveler's checks and wiring money into the country. Dollars are readily exchanged at market rates.

DISASTER PREPAREDNESS: Armenia is an earthquake-prone and landslide-prone country. In addition to these natural disasters, the possibility of chlorine gas spills and radiation poisoning due to industrial accidents exists. General information about natural disaster preparedness is available via the Internet from the U.S. Federal Emergency Management Agency (FEMA) at http://www.fema.gov. All U.S. citizens visiting Armenia are advised to register at the Consular Section of the U.S. Embassy upon arrival.

CHILDREN'S ISSUES: For information on international adoption of children and international parental child abduction, please refer to our Internet site at http://travel.state.gov/children's_issues.html or telephone (202) 736-7000.

REGISTRATION/EMBASSY AND CONSULATE LOCATION: Americans living in or visiting Armenia are encouraged to register at the Consular Section of the U.S. Embassy in Armenia and obtain updated information on travel and security within Armenia. The U.S. Embassy in Yerevan is located at 18 General Bagramian Street, telephone 011 (3741) 151-551 and fax 011 (3741) 151-550. The Consular Section is open from 9:00 a.m. until 5:30 p.m., with time reserved for American citizen services from 2:00 p.m. until 5:30 p.m. Monday through Friday. For more information, please see the Embassy of Armenia's Internet home page at http://www.armeniaemb.org.

AZERBAIJAN

COUNTRY DESCRIPTION: The Republic of Azerbaijan, located in the southeastern Caucasus mountains on the southwestern shore of the Caspian, became an independent nation in 1991 following the break-up of the former Soviet Union. Western-style amenities are increasingly found in the capital, Baku, but they are generally not available outside that city.

ENTRY REQUIREMENTS: A passport and visa are required. Travelers may obtain single-entry visas for USD 40 by mail or in person from either the Azerbaijani Embassy in Washington, D.C. or any other Azerbaijani embassy offering consular services. Travelers may also obtain single-entry visas at the airport upon arrival. Two-entry visas (cost $80 U.S.) and one-year multiple-entry visas (cost $250 U.S.) are only available through an Azerbajini embassy or through the Ministry of Foreign Affairs. A letter of invitation from a contact in Azerbaijan is required, and travelers who expect to travel in the region should request a one-year, multiple-entry visa.

U.S. citizens who obtain a one-entry visa at the port of entry are permitted to remain in Azerbaijan for up to one month, after which an extension of stay must be requested. For persons in Azerbaijan, visa applications, extensions or renewals are made at the Ministry of Foreign Affairs, Shikhali Kurbanov Str., 4, Baku; tel. (9-9412) 93 59 40. For additional information, please contact the Embassy of Azerbaijan, 2741 34th Street, N.W., Washington, D.C. 20008 (tel. 202-337-3500); e-mail azerbaijan@tidalwave.net; Internet: http://www.azembassy.com.

SAFETY AND SECURITY: As a result of conflict in the Nagorno-Karabakh area of Azerbaijan, insurgent forces occupy 16 percent of Azerbaijani territory (in the southwest along the borders with Iran and Armenia). A cease-fire has been in effect since 1994, although reports of armed clashes along the cease-fire line and along the border with Armenia continue. Anti-personnel mines are a danger in areas close to the front lines. It is not possible to enter the self-proclaimed "Republic of Nagorno-Karabakh" from Azerbaijan. Travelers are cautioned to avoid travel to Nagorno-Karabakh and the surrounding occupied areas. Because of the existing state of hostilities, consular services are not available to Americans in Nagorno-Karabakh.

Several unsanctioned political rallies have occurred in recent months. In the past, some of these rallies have become confrontational and have escalated into violence. Americans are advised to avoid all demonstrations.

CRIME: Although the Republic of Azerbaijan has a low rate of violent crime, incidents of street crime and assaults on foreigners are common. Visitors should follow the same precautions they would in any major city. Visitors should not walk alone at night, if possible. All crime incidents should be reported to the local police and U.S. Embassy.

The loss or theft abroad of a U.S. passport should be reported immediately to the local police and the nearest U.S. embassy or consulate. If you are the victim of a crime while overseas, in addition to reporting to local police, please contact the nearest

U.S. embassy or consulate for assistance. The Embassy/Consulate staff can, for example, assist you to find appropriate medical care, to contact family members or friends and explain how funds could be transferred. Although the investigation and prosecution of the crime is solely the responsibility of local authorities, consular officers can help you to understand the local criminal justice process and to find an attorney if needed.

U.S. citizens may refer to the Department of State's pamphlet, *A Safe Trip Abroad*, for ways to promote a trouble-free journey. The pamphlet is available by mail from the Superintendent of Documents, U.S. Government Printing Office, Washington, D.C. 20402, via the Internet at http://www.access.gpo.gov/su_docs, or via the Bureau of Consular Affairs home page at http://travel.state.gov.

MEDICAL FACILITIES: A few Western-type medical clinics, the quality of which is comparable to those in Western countries, have recently opened in Baku. The quality of these clinics is good. However, medical facilities outside the capital remain inadequate, unsanitary, and unsafe. There is often a shortage of basic medical supplies, including disposable needles and vaccines.

MEDICAL INSURANCE: U.S. medical insurance is not always valid outside the United States. U.S. Medicare and Medicaid programs do not provide payment for medical services outside the United States. Uninsured travelers who require medical care overseas may face extreme difficulties.

Please check with your own insurance company to confirm whether your policy applies overseas, including provision for medical evacuation, and adequacy of coverage. Serious medical problems requiring hospitalization and/or medical evacuation to the United States can cost tens of thousands of dollars. Please ascertain whether payment will be made to the overseas hospital or doctor or if you will be reimbursed later for expenses that you may incur. Some insurance policies also include coverage for psychiatric treatment and for disposition of remains in the event of death.

Useful information on medical emergencies abroad, including overseas insurance programs, is provided in the Department of State's Bureau of Consular Affairs brochure, *Medical Information for Americans Traveling Abroad,* available via the Bureau of Consular Affairs home page or autofax: (202) 647-3000.

OTHER HEALTH INFORMATION: Information on vaccinations and other health precautions may be obtained from the Centers for Disease Control and Prevention's hotline for international travelers at 1-877-FYI-TRIP (1-877-394-8747); fax 1-888-CDC-FAXX (1-888-232-3299), or via the CDC's Internet site at http://www.cdc.gov.

TRAFFIC SAFETY AND ROAD CONDITIONS: While in a foreign country, U.S. citizens may encounter road conditions that differ significantly from those in the United States. The information below concerning Azerbaijan is provided for general reference only, and it may not be totally accurate in a particular location or circumstance.

Safety of Public Transportation: Very Poor
Urban Road Conditions/Maintenance: Very Poor
Rural Road Conditions/Maintenance: Very Poor
Availability of Roadside Assistance: Very Poor

Driving hazards such as open manholes, debris, and potholes are common. Drivers pay little heed to traffic regulations, signals, lanes, or other drivers. Drivers often travel at extremely high rates of speed, and accidents are frequent. Driving in Baku should be considered extremely hazardous. Outside the city, even where roads are present, conditions are similar. Roads are often in poor repair, unlit, and lack lane markings, traffic signs, and warnings. Many rural roads are unpaved and rarely traveled.

Public transportation throughout the country is overcrowded and poorly maintained. The U.S. Embassy strongly discourages use of the Baku Metro. Train travel in the Caucasus region is not secure. For additional information about road safety, including links to foreign government sites, please see the Department of State, Bureau of Consular Affairs home page at http://travel.state.gov/road_safety.html.

AVIATION SAFETY OVERSIGHT: As there is no direct commercial service at present between the United States and the Republic of Azerbaijan, nor economic authority to operate such service, the U.S. Federal Aviation Administration (FAA) has not assessed Azerbaijan's Civil Aviation Authority for compliance with international aviation safety standards for oversight of Azerbaijan air carrier operations.

For further information, travelers may contact the Department of Transportation within the U.S. at tel. 1-800-322-7873, or visit the FAA Internet web site at http://www.faa.gov/avr/iasa/. The U.S. Department of Defense (DOD) separately assesses some foreign air carriers for suitability as official providers of air services. For information regarding the DOD policy on specific carriers, travelers may contact the DOD at tel. (618) 229-4801.

Travelers on airlines among the countries of the Caucasus may experience prolonged delays and sudden cancellations of flights. In addition to frequent delays, flights are often overcrowded with passengers without seats standing in the aisle along with excess unsecured cabin luggage. Even basic safety features such as seat belts are sometimes missing. Air travel to Azerbaijan on international carriers via the United Kingdom, Germany, and Turkey is more reliable.

CRIMINAL PENALTIES: While in a foreign country, a U.S. citizen is subject to that country's laws and regulations, which sometimes differ significantly from those in the United States and may not afford the protections available to the individual under U.S. law. Penalties for breaking the law can be more severe than in the United States for similar offenses. Persons violating Azerbaijani laws, even unknowingly, may be expelled, arrested, or imprisoned. Penalties for possession, use, or trafficking in illegal drugs in Azerbaijan are strict, and convicted offenders can expect jail sentences and heavy fines.

SPECIAL CIRCUMSTANCES: The Republic of Azerbaijan is mostly a cash economy country. Traveler's checks and credit cards are accepted only in some hotels and a few restaurants and supermarkets. The national currency is the manat. In recent months, an increasing number of commercial establishments have begun to enforce the requirement that purchases be made with manats.

CHILDREN'S ISSUES: For information on international adoption of children and international child support enforcement issues, please refer to our Internet site at http://travel.state.gov/children's_issues.html or telephone (202) 736-7000.

REGISTRATION AND EMBASSY LOCATION: Americans living in or visiting the Republic of Azerbaijan are encouraged to register at the Consular Section of the U.S. Embassy in Baku and obtain updated information on travel and security within Azerbaijan. The U.S. Embassy is located at Prospect Azadlig 83; tel. (9-9412) 98-03-35, 36, or 37; (9-9412) 90-66-71. More information can be obtained from Embassy Baku's Internet site at http://www.usembassybaku.org/.

BELARUS

COUNTRY DESCRIPTION: Economic and political reform in Belarus has stalled or reversed under the current authoritarian government. Human rights are regularly abused by the Belarusian authorities. Tourist facilities are not highly developed, and many of the goods and services taken for granted in other countries are not readily available. Localized street disturbances relating to political events may occur without warning, most frequently in Minsk, the capital. Bystanders, including foreign nationals, face the possibility of arrest, beating, and detention. Since April 1999, three prominent members of the opposition and a journalist have disappeared without a trace, and are believed to be dead.

ENTRY REQUIREMENTS: A passport and visa are required. A visa must be obtained before entering Belarus. Travelers who do not have a visa cannot register at hotels. U.S. citizens residing in Belarus are required to register with the local Office of Visas and Registration (OVIR). Failure to do so can result in fines and visits from local law enforcement authorities. U.S. citizens staying in hotels are automatically registered at check-in. Visa validity dates are strictly enforced; travelers should request sufficient time to allow for delays in arrival and departure.

Foreign missionaries may not engage in religious activities outside the institutions that invited them. One-year validity, multiple-entry, "spiritual activities" visas, which are required officially of foreign missionaries, can be difficult to get, even for faiths that registered with the government and have a long history in the country. Foreign clergy or religious workers who do not register with the authorities or who have tried to preach without government approval or without an invitation from, and the permission of, a registered religious organization, have been expelled from the country. Approval often involves a difficult bureaucratic process.

Belarus requires all foreign nationals (other than accredited diplomats) entering the country to purchase medical insurance at the port-of-entry regardless of any other insurance one might have. Costs for this insurance vary according to the length of stay. (Subject to change, current information puts costs at $1.00 for a one-day stay; $15.00 for a stay of 60 days, up to a maximum of $85.00 for a stay of a year.)

U.S. citizens traveling through Belarus to other countries are strongly reminded that there is a transit visa requirement for entering and leaving Belarus. Transit visas should be obtained prior to any journey that requires travel through Belarus. Commonwealth of Independent States (CIS) and Russian visas are no substitute for this transit visa. U.S. citizens attempting to transit Belarus without a valid Belarusian transit visa have been denied entry into the country and forcibly removed from trains. Most travel agencies, including those in Russia and CIS countries as well as train ticket sales personnel, are often not aware of this visa requirement and may not seek a transit visa for a traveler unless instructed by the traveler to do so.

For more information concerning entry requirements, travelers should contact the Belarus Embassy located at 1619 New Hampshire Ave, N.W. Washington, D.C. 20009, tel. (202) 986-1606; Internet: http://www.belarusembassy.org or the Belarus Consulate in New York at 708 Third Avenue, 21st floor, New York, NY, 10017, tel. (212) 682-5392.

In an effort to prevent international child abduction, many governments have initiated procedures at entry/exit points. These often include requiring documentary evidence of relationship and permission for the child's travel from the parent(s) or legal guardian not present.

Having such documentation on hand, even if not required, may facilitate entry/departure.

SAFETY AND SECURITY: Security personnel may at times place foreign visitors under surveillance. Hotel rooms, telephones and fax machines may be monitored, and personal possessions in hotel rooms may be searched. Taking photographs of anything that could be perceived as being of military or security interest may result in problems with authorities. These sites are not always clearly marked, and application of these restrictions is subject to interpretation.

There have been numerous situations involving American citizens traveling through Belarus by train in which Americans have been required to disembark while in transit. In some instances, local border and train authorities have threatened passengers with jail or extorted "fines" when it was learned that they did not possess a valid transit visa. In some cases, American citizens have been subjected to rude and threatening treatment, including body and baggage searches. American citizens are advised not to pay any border or train officials for transit visas. These officials are not authorized to issue such visas. Nor should Americans pay "transit visa fines." Americans finding themselves in Belarus without transit visas should, if confronted by border or train personnel, demand to be put in contact with consular officials at the American Embassy in Minsk.

CRIME INFORMATION: Belarus has a moderate rate of crime, and common street crime continues to increase, especially at night and in or near hotels frequented by foreigners. Foreigners, and particularly foreign cars, tend to be targets of crime. Travelers should keep a copy of their passport in a separate location from their original passport.

The loss or theft abroad of a U.S. passport should be reported immediately to the local police and the nearest U.S. embassy or consulate. U.S. citizens can refer to the Department of State's pamphlet, *A Safe Trip Abroad*, for ways to promote a more trouble-free journey. The pamphlet is available by mail from the Superintendent of Documents, U.S. Government Printing Office, Washington, D.C. 20402, via the Internet at http://www.access.gpo.gov/su_docs, or via the

Bureau of Consular Affairs home page at http://travel.state.gov.

MEDICAL FACILITIES: Medical care in Belarus is limited. There is a severe shortage of basic medical supplies, including anesthetics, vaccines and antibiotics. Elderly travelers and those with existing health problems may be at risk due to inadequate medical facilities.

MEDICAL INSURANCE: the Department of State strongly urges Americans to consult with their medical insurance company prior to traveling abroad to confirm whether their policy applies overseas and if it will cover emergency expenses such as a medical evacuation. U.S. medical insurance plans seldom cover health costs incurred outside the United States unless supplemental coverage is purchased. Further, U.S. Medicare and Medicaid programs do not provide payment for medical services outside the United States. However, many travel agents and private companies offer insurance plans that will cover health care expenses incurred overseas, including emergency services such as medical evacuations. Please note that Belarus requires all foreign nationals (other than accredited diplomats) entering the country to purchase medical insurance at the port-of-entry (Please see "Entry Requirements" section.)

When making a decision regarding health insurance, Americans should consider that many foreign doctors and hospitals require payment in cash prior to providing service and that a medical evacuation to the U.S. may cost well in excess of $50,000. Uninsured travelers who require medical care overseas often face extreme difficulties. When consulting with your insurer prior to your trip, please ascertain whether payment will be made to the overseas healthcare provider or if you will be reimbursed later for expenses that you incur. Some insurance policies also include coverage for psychiatric treatment and for disposition of remains in the event of death.

Useful information on medical emergencies abroad, including overseas insurance programs, is provided in the Department of State's Bureau of Consular Affairs brochure, *Medical Information for Americans Traveling Abroad*, available via the Bureau of Consular affairs home page or autofax: (202) 647-3000.

OTHER HEALTH INFORMATION: The U.S. Embassy recommends against drinking the local water even in larger cities. It is recommended that visitors instead drink only bottled or filtered water. While the effects of radiation from the Chernobyl disaster have diminished, it is inadvisable to eat any food grown in the contaminated areas near Chernobyl, and the Embassy cautions against eating any mushrooms or berries. Consumption of Belarusian milk is best avoided as well.

Information on vaccinations and other health precautions may be obtained from the Centers for Disease Control and Prevention's hotline for international travelers at 1-877-FYI-TRIP (1-877-394-8747); fax 1-888-CDC-FAXX (1-888-232-3299), or via CDC'S Internet site at http://www.cdc.gov.

TRAFFIC SAFETY AND ROAD CONDITIONS: While in a foreign country, U.S. citizens may encounter road conditions that differ significantly from those in the United States. The information below concerning Belarus is provided for general reference only, and it may not be totally accurate in a particular location or circumstance.

Safety of Public Transportation: Fair
Urban Road Conditions/Maintenance: Fair
Rural Road Conditions/Maintenance: Fair
Availability of Roadside Assistance: Poor

U.S. citizens may drive in Belarus with their home country driver's license for up to six months from arrival. Foreign drivers should, therefore, always carry their passports to prove date of entry into the country in the event they are stopped by the police. After residing in Belarus for six months, one may apply for a local driver's license. A medical exam at the driver's clinic, which will include a chest x-ray, is the only exam required to receive a local driver's license.

Radar traps, often unlit at night, are widespread. Except for a stretch of the main east-west superhighway, where the speed limit is 100 km/h (60 mph), the maximum speed limit on divided highways or main roads outside village, town or city limits is 90 km/h (55 mph). Speed limits inside city limits vary widely from 40 km/h to 70 km/h, with frequent radar traps. Visible and hidden dangers exist, including potholes, the absence of road signs, and lack of service areas. Other hazards include unlit or poorly lit streets, inattentive and dark-clothed pedestrians walking on unlit roads, drivers under the influence of alcohol, and a common disregard for traffic rules. Driving in winter is especially dangerous because many roads are not properly cleared of ice and snow. Driving with caution is urged at all times.

Taxi service is prompt, although fares vary greatly and the automobiles themselves are often in poor condition. Buses and trolleys are poorly maintained, lack heating or cooling capabilities, and are usually crowded. For additional information about road safety, please see the Department of State, Bureau of Consular Affairs home page's road safety overseas feature at http://travel.state.gov/road_safety.html.

AVIATION SAFETY OVERSIGHT: As there is no direct commercial air service at present, nor economic authority to operate such service between the United States and Belarus, the U.S. Federal Aviation Administration (FAA) has not assessed Belarus' Civil Aviation Authority for compliance with international aviation safety standards. For further information, travelers may contact the Department of Transportation within the United States at tel. 1-800-322-7873, or visit the FAA's Internet web site at http://www.faa.gov/avr/iasa/.

The U.S. Department of Defense (DOD) separately assesses some foreign air carriers for suitability as official providers of air services. For information regarding the DOD policy on specific carriers, travelers may contact the DOD at tel. (618) 229-4801.

CUSTOMS REGULATIONS: Belarus's customs authorities may enforce strict regulations concerning temporary importation into or export from Belarus of items such as icons, art, rugs, antiquities, etc. It is advisable to contact the Embassy of Belarus in Washington, D.C. or one of Belarus' consulates in the United States for specific information regarding customs requirements.

CRIMINAL PENALTIES: While in a foreign country, a U.S. citizen is subject to that country's laws and regulations, which sometimes differ significantly from those in the United States and may not afford the protections available to the individual under U.S. law. Penalties for breaking the law can be more severe than in the United States for similar offenses. Persons violating Belarus' laws, even unknowingly, may be expelled, arrested or imprisoned. Penalties for possession, use, or trafficking in illegal drugs in Belarus are strict, and convicted offenders can expect jail sentences and heavy fines.

SPECIAL CIRCUMSTANCES: Traveler's checks are not widely accepted in Belarus. Most Intourist hotels accept either American Express or Visa credit cards. In addition, one hotel in Minsk, The Planeta, provides cash from VISA credit cards during business hours. Travelers face arrest if they attempt to buy items with currency other than Belarusian rubles.

CHILDREN'S ISSUES: For information on international adoption of children and international parental child abduction, please refer to our Internet site at http://travel.state.gov/children's_issues.html or telephone (202) 736-7000.

REGISTRATION/EMBASSY AND CONSULATE LOCATION: Americans living in or visiting Belarus are encouraged to register at the Consular Section of the U.S. Embassy in Belarus and to obtain updated information on travel and security within Belarus. The U.S. Embassy is located in Minsk at 46 Starovilenskaya Ulitsa; telephone (375) 172-10-12-83 or 234-77-61, fax (375) 172-76-88-62.

ESTONIA

COUNTRY DESCRIPTION: Estonia is a rapidly developing nation that has experienced significant success in reforming its political and economic institutions since regaining independence in 1991. Tourist facilities are generally good though some amenities may be lacking in rural areas. Some goods and services may not be available outside of major cities. The capital is Tallinn.

ENTRY REQUIREMENTS: A valid passport is required. Tourists and business travelers may stay in Estonia for up to 90 days within a six month period without a visa. U.S. citizens who wish to

293

work in Estonia or remain longer than 90 days must obtain a visa or residence permit. For further information concerning entry requirements and residency permits, please contact the Estonian Embassy, temporarily located at 1730 M. Street, N.W. Suite 503, Washington, D.C. 20036, tel. (202) 588-0101, or the Consulate General of Estonia in New York City (212) 883-0636. Also, please see the Embassy's Internet home page at http://www.estemb.org.

In an effort to prevent international child abduction, many governments have initiated procedures at entry/exit points. These often include requiring documentary evidence of relationship and permission for the child's travel from the parent(s) or legal guardian if not present. Having such documentation on hand, even if not required, may facilitate entry/departure.

CRIME: Travelers in Estonia should exercise the same precautions with regard to their personal safety and belongings that they would take in major U.S. cities. The most common crimes encountered by foreign tourists are purse snatching, pick-pocketing and mugging. Violent crime, though rarely directed against foreigners, does occur. Intoxicated people leaving bars alone or in small groups late at night are a favorite target for muggings, which can turn violent. Car thefts are common, and they can occur in daylight. Police capabilities in Estonia are improving, but they still suffer from lack of equipment, training, personnel and resources. Few police officers speak English. Credit card fraud is on the rise. Travelers should take prudent precautions to safeguard their credit cards and report any suspected unauthorized transactions to the credit card company immediately. Racially motivated verbal and, on occasion, physical harassment of Americans of non-Caucasian ethnicity can occur. If an incident occurs, it should be reported to the U.S. Embassy.

The loss or theft abroad of a U.S. passport should be reported immediately to the local police and the nearest U.S. embassy or consulate. If you are the victim of a crime while overseas, in addition to reporting to local police, please contact the nearest U.S. embassy or consulate for assistance. The Embassy/Consulate staff can, for example, assist you to find appropriate medical care, to contact family members or friends and explain how funds could be transferred. Although the investigation and prosecution of the crime is solely the responsibility of local authorities, consular officers can help you to understand the local criminal justice process and to find an attorney if needed.

U.S. citizens can refer to the Department of State's pamphlet, *A Safe Trip Abroad*, for ways to promote a trouble-free journey. The pamphlet is available by mail from the Superintendent of Documents, U.S. Government Printing Office, Washington, D.C. 20402, via the Internet at http://www.access.gpo.gov/su_docs, or via the Bureau of Consular Affairs home page at http://travel.state.gov.

MEDICAL FACILITIES: The quality of medical care in Estonia is improving, but it still falls short of Western standards. Estonia has many highly trained medical professionals, but hospitals and clinics still lack equipment and resources. Elderly travelers and those with health problems may be at increased risk.

MEDICAL INSURANCE: U.S. medical insurance is not always valid outside the United States. U.S. Medicare and Medicaid programs do not provide payment for medical services outside the United States. Doctors and hospitals often expect immediate cash payment for health services. Uninsured travelers who require medical care overseas may face extreme difficulties.

Check with your own insurance company to confirm whether your policy applies overseas, including provision for medical evacuation, and for adequacy of coverage. Serious medical problems requiring hospitalization and/or medical evacuation to the United States can cost tens of thousands of dollars. Please ascertain whether payment will be made to the overseas hospital or doctor or if you will be reimbursed later for expenses that you incur. Some insurance policies also include coverage for psychiatric treatment and for disposition of remains in the event of death.

Useful information on medical emergencies abroad, including overseas insurance programs, is provided in the Department of State's Bureau of Consular Affairs brochure, *Medical Information for Americans Traveling Abroad*, available via the Bureau of Consular Affairs home page or autofax: (202) 647-3000.

294

OTHER HEALTH INFORMATION: Cases of resistant strains of tuberculosis have been reported in Estonia. Visitors to forest areas in warm weather should also guard against tick-borne encephalitis. Information on vaccinations and other health precautions may be obtained from the Centers for Disease Control and Prevention's hotline for international travelers at 1-877-FYI-TRIP (1-877-394-8747); fax 1-888-CDC-FAXX (1-888-232-3299), or via the CDC's Internet site at http://www.cdc.gov.

TRAFFIC SAFETY AND ROAD CONDITIONS: While in a foreign country, U.S. citizens may encounter road conditions that differ significantly from those in the United States. The information below concerning Estonia is provided for general reference only, and it may not be totally accurate in a particular location or circumstance.

Safety of Public Transportation: Fair
Urban Road Conditions/Maintenance: Fair
Rural Road Conditions/Maintenance: Fair
Availability of Roadside Assistance: Poor

Driving in Estonia can be more dangerous than in much of the United States. Many roads, especially in rural areas, are poorly lit and not up to Western standards. Some drivers can be aggressive and drive above the speed limit. Pedestrians should be careful when crossing the streets, as drivers do not always stop at marked crosswalks. Icy road conditions and wild animals, such as moose, can create unexpected hazards. Driving at night, especially in the countryside, can be particularly risky. Dark-clothed pedestrians walking along unlit roads or darting across dimly lit streets or highways pose a risk to unsuspecting drivers.

Local law requires that headlights be turned on while driving during the day as well as at night. Use of seatbelts by all passengers is required, and children too small to be secure in seatbelts must use child car seats. The speed limit is 50 km/h in town and 90 km/h out of town unless otherwise indicated. A right turn on a red light is prohibited unless otherwise indicated by a green arrow. Laws against driving under the influence of alcohol are strict, and they follow a policy of zero tolerance. It is not uncommon for the police to set up checkpoints on major streets, and drivers should pull over when asked. Americans planning to drive in Estonia must obtain an international driver's license prior to arrival.

For information about international driving permits, please contact AAA or the American Automobile Touring Alliance. The Eesti Autoklubi (Estonian Auto Club) which is affiliated with AAA provides emergency roadside assistance. Drivers do not need to be a member to receive assistance, however, the fees charged are higher for non-members. The number to call for roadside vehicle assistance and towing service is 118. For ambulance, fire or police assistance, the number is 112. Please note that for both numbers, the operator may speak little English.

For additional information about road safety, please see the Department of State, Bureau of Consular Affairs home page road safety overseas feature at http://travel.state.gov/road_safety.html.

AVIATION SAFETY AND OVERSIGHT: As there is no direct air commercial service at present between the United States and Estonia, nor economic authority to operate such service, the U.S. Federal Aviation Administration (FAA) has not assessed Estonia's Civil Aviation Authority for compliance with international aviation safety standards for oversight of Estonia's air carrier operations.

For further information, travelers may contact the Department of Transportation within the United States at tel. 1-800-322-7873, or visit the FAA Internet web site at http://www.faa.gov/avr/iasa/. The U.S. Department of Defense (DOD) separately assesses some foreign air carriers for suitability as official providers of air services. For information regarding the DOD policy on specific carriers, travelers may contact the DOD at tel. (618) 229-4801.

CRIMINAL PENALTIES: While in a foreign country, a U.S. citizen is subject to that country's laws and regulations, which sometimes differ significantly from those in the United States and may not afford the protections available to the individual under U.S. law. Penalties for breaking the law can be more severe than in the United States for similar offenses. Persons violating Estonia's laws, even unknowingly, may be expelled, arrested or imprisoned. Penalties for possession, use, or trafficking in illegal drugs in

Estonia are strict, and convicted offenders can expect jail sentences and heavy fines.

CUSTOMS REGULATIONS: Estonia's customs authorities encourage the use of an ATA (Admission Temporaire/Temporary Admission) Carnet for the temporary admission of professional equipment, commercial samples, and/or goods for exhibitions and fair purposes. ATA Carnet Headquarters, located at the U.S. Council for International Business, 1212 Avenue of the Americas, New York, NY 10036, issues and guarantees the ATA Carnet in the United States. For additional information, please call (202) 354-4480, or send an e-mail to atacarnet@uscib.org, or visit http://www.uscib.org for details.

CHILDREN'S ISSUES: For information on international adoption of children and international parental child abduction, please refer to our Internet site at http://travel.state.gov/children's_issues.html or telephone (202) 736-7000.

REGISTRATION/EMBASSY LOCATION: U.S. citizens living in or visiting Estonia are encouraged to register at the Consular Section of the U.S. Embassy and obtain updated information on travel and security within Estonia. The U.S. Embassy in Tallinn is located at Kentmanni 20, tel. (372) 668-8100; fax (372) 668-8267; emergency cell phone: (011)(372) 509-2129, if dialed from the United States, and 0-509-2129, if dialed from within Estonia. The Embassy's home page on the Internet is at http://www.usemb.ee.

This replaces the Consular Information Sheet dated October 17, 2000, to update information on Entry Requirements, Crime, Traffic Safety and Road Conditions and Children's Issues.

GEORGIA

COUNTRY DESCRIPTION: A mountainous republic situated in the heart of the Caucasus range, Georgia has borders with Turkey, Armenia, Azerbaijan, and Russia. Living conditions do not meet Western standards. Tourist facilities outside of Tbilisi, the capital, are not highly developed, and many of the goods and services taken for granted in other countries are not yet available.

Georgia is facing a chronic energy crisis. During the winter months, frequent and prolonged power outages are common, especially outside of Tbilisi. The lack of lighting in public places, even when electricity is available, heightens vulnerability to crime. (Please see the Crime section below for details.)

ENTRY REQUIREMENTS: A passport and visa are required. U.S. citizens may obtain a visa upon arrival at Tbilisi Airport, the Port of Poti, and the Red Bridge ("Tsiteli Khidi") crossing on Georgia's border with Azerbaijan. Americans intending to enter Georgia at other points-of-entry must obtain a visa beforehand at a Georgian embassy or consulate abroad. Armenian and Azerbaijani visas are no longer valid for transit through Georgia. Travelers to Georgia must fill out a customs declaration upon arrival that is to be presented to customs officials when departing the country. (Please see also the section on Georgian Customs Regulations.) For further information, please contact the Embassy of Georgia at 1615 New Hampshire Avenue, N.W., Suite 300, Washington, D.C. 20009, tel. (202) 387-2390, fax: (202) 393-4537; Internet: http://www.georgiaemb.org.

In an effort to prevent international child abduction, many governments have initiated procedures at entry/exit points. These often include requiring documentary evidence of relationship and permission for the child's travel from the parent(s) or legal guardian not present. Having such documentation on hand, even if not required, may facilitate entry/departure.

SAFETY AND SECURITY: The U.S. Embassy advises American citizens to avoid travel to the separatist-controlled region of Abkhazia where a tense truce exists between previously warring Georgian and Abkhaz military forces. In addition, there have been bombings, attacks and kidnappings in Abkhazia. The mining of roads poses a serious threat to vehicular traffic. While Abkhaz "border officials" may demand that travelers entering the region purchase "visas" from the so-called "Ministry of Foreign Affairs of Abkhazia," the U.S. Government does not recognize the separatists' declaration of Abkhazia's independence from Georgia. As a result of the restricted access of U.S. officials to Abkhazia, the ability of the U.S. Government to assist American citizens there is extremely limited, even in emergencies. American citizens in areas of Western Georgia near the Abkhaz border are advised to be aware of their surroundings at all times and to avoid straying off main roads or travelling after dark.

American citizens should be aware that they cannot legally cross overland between Russia and Georgia, even if in possession of valid Russian or Georgian visas.

In recent months, Georgia's armed forces have conducted operations against suspected international terrorists, Chechen fighters and criminals who have taken refuge in the Pankisi Gorge. American citizens should avoid all travel to the Pankisi Gorge north of Akhmeta. American citizens are also advised to avoid travel to other areas of continuing security concern: specifically, the northern mountainous areas of Georgia bordering the Russian Federation, especially the Chechnya and Dagestan sectors. It is not advisable for Americans to travel to certain areas such as Svaneti without a Georgian citizen familiar with the area accompanying them. There have been instances of kidnappings for ransom in these regions.

Americans should be advised that kidnappings and the threat of kidnapping are not limited to the above- mentioned outlying regions. In the past year, several foreign businessmen have been kidnapped for ransom and kidnapping threats to Americans have been received in the Tbilisi region. The possibility of a similar risk to Americans elsewhere in the country cannot be discounted.

As a result of a threat posed by banditry and other criminal activities, American citizens should also carefully evaluate the implications for their security before considering travel to the separatist Georgian region of South Ossetia.

Travelers are advised that the Autonomous Republic of Ajara, which is a part of Georgia, requires the presentation of photo identification at land crossings with the rest of Georgia. Also, travelers in the Autonomous Republic of Ajara may be subject to document verification at police checkpoints at which authorities may attempt to charge travelers additional fees.

In a separate and unrelated matter, within the past year there have been numerous violent attacks directed against religious minorities in Georgia. The victims are primarily Jehovah's Witnesses, but also include Pentecostals, Baptists, and members of the "Assembly of God." Incidents include the burning of literature, the destruction of private property and the beating (sometimes severe) of believers, including American citizens.

CRIME: Crime is a critical problem in Georgia. All Americans visiting Tbilisi are advised to be cautious while traveling during the day and not/not to walk alone after dark in the city. Incidents of pickpocketing, purse snatching, and cell-phone theft remain common. After dark, persons are advised to use personal cars or established taxi company taxis that will take passengers door-to-door. People should travel in pairs or in groups and exercise common-sense security measures. Foreigners in Georgia, especially Westerners and including Americans, continue to be victimized by violent muggings, home break-ins and other crimes. Most muggings have occurred on side streets near Tbilisi's city center, including areas off the main avenues in the Vake and Vera districts, and Chavchavadze and Rustaveli avenues. In many instances, the mugging victims have first been knocked unconscious by blows to the head.

Petty theft is particularly a problem on the Tbilisi metro system and in mini-vans used for public transit. While the security of overland travel in Georgia has improved, vehicular and rail traffic remains vulnerable to robbery. Americans visiting or residing in Tbilisi should take the same precautions they would take in any major city where crime is a problem. American citizens in Tbilisi are advised to remain aware of their surroundings at all times, day or night; and to stay off dark or unlit streets even when traveling in a group; to avoid carrying large sums of cash; and to be particularly cautious of being singled out for victimization at establishments frequented by foreigners. Americans ought to be aware of the great disparity of affluence between themselves and most Georgians.

Westerners are often perceived as being rich and are therefore lucrative targets for crime.

The loss or theft abroad of a U.S. passport should be reported immediately to the local police and the nearest U.S. Embassy or Consulate. If you are the victim of a crime while overseas, in addition to reporting to local police, please contact the nearest U.S. Embassy or Consulate for assistance. The Embassy/Consulate staff can, for example, assist you to find appropriate medical care, to contact family members or friends and explain how funds could be transferred. Although the investigation and prosecution of the crime is solely the responsibility of local authorities, consular officers can help you to understand the local criminal justice process and to find an attorney, if needed. U.S. citizens may refer to the Department of State's pamphlet, "*A Safe Trip Abroad*," for ways to promote a trouble-free journey. The pamphlet is available by mail from the Superintendent of Documents, U.S. Government Printing Office, Washington, D.C. 20402, via the Internet at http://www.access.gpo.gov/su_docs, or via the Bureau of Consular Affairs home page at http://travel.state.gov.

MEDICAL FACILITIES: Medical care in Georgia is limited. There is a severe shortage of basic medical supplies, including disposable needles, anesthetics, and antibiotics. Elderly travelers and those with pre-existing health problems may be at risk due to inadequate medical facilities. Georgian doctors and hospitals often expect immediate cash payment before rendering medical services.

MEDICAL INSURANCE: The Department of State strongly urges Americans to consult with their medical insurance company before traveling abroad to confirm whether their policy applies overseas and if it will cover emergency expenses such as a medical evacuation. U.S. medical insurance plans seldom cover health costs incurred outside the United States unless supplemental coverage is purchased. Further, U.S. Medicare and Medicaid programs do not provide payment for medical services outside the United States. However, many travel agents and private companies offer insurance plans that will cover health care expenses incurred overseas, including emergency services such as medical evacuations.

When making a decision regarding health insurance, Americans should consider that many foreign doctors and hospitals require payment in cash before providing service and that a medical evacuation to the U.S. may cost well in excess of $50,000. Uninsured travelers who require medical care overseas often face extreme difficulties. When consulting with your insurer before your trip, please ascertain whether payment will be made to the overseas hospital or doctor or if you will be reimbursed later for expenses that you incur. Some insurance policies also include coverage for psychiatric treatment and for disposition of remains in the event of death.

Useful information on medical emergencies abroad, including overseas insurance programs, is provided in the Department of State's Bureau of Consular Affairs brochure, "*Medical Information for Americans Traveling Abroad*," available via the bureau of Consular Affairs' home page http://travel.state.gov or autofax: (202) 647-3000.

OTHER HEALTH INFORMATION: Information on vaccinations and other health precautions, such as safe food and water precautions and insect bite protection, may be obtained from the Centers for Disease Control and Prevention's hotline for international travelers at 1-877-FYI-TRIP (1-877-394-8747); fax 1-888-CDC-FAXX (1-888-232-3299), or via the CDC's Internet site at http://www.cdc.gov/travel. For information about outbreaks of infectious diseases abroad consult the World Health Organization's website at http://www.who.int/en. Further health information for travelers is available at http://www.who.int/iht.

TRAFFIC SAFETY AND ROAD CONDITIONS: While in a foreign country, U.S. citizens may encounter road conditions that differ significantly from those in the United States. The information below concerning Georgia is provided for general reference only, and may not be totally accurate in a particular location or circumstance.

Safety of Public Transportation: Fair
Urban Road Conditions/Maintenance: Poor
Rural Road Conditions/Maintenance: Poor
Availability of Roadside Assistance: Poor

As in the United States, vehicular traffic in Georgia moves along the right side of roadways. Speed limits range from 80 to 100 km/hr. on highways, and from 30 to 60 km/hr. on urban thoroughfares. Motorists are not permitted to make

298

right turns on red at traffic lights. While legislation mandating seat belt use has yet to be enacted, drivers and passengers are nevertheless strongly advised to buckle up on Georgian roads. Children under seven (7) years of age are required to be restrained in child-safety seats. Under Georgian law, a driver may be considered to be driving under the influence of alcohol with any blood alcohol concentration exceeding zero.

The Georgian Traffic Police, who come under the authority of the Ministry of Internal Affairs, are responsible for maintaining traffic safety in Georgia. As many local drivers do not operate their vehicles in accordance with established traffic laws, motorists should exercise extreme caution when driving. Vehicular traffic can be very dangerous in Georgia. Pedestrians should be extremely careful when crossing streets.

Roads in Georgia are generally in poor condition and often lack shoulder markings and centerlines. In addition, traffic signals may not work as a result of power outages or poor maintenance. Traffic signals and rules of the road are often completely ignored. Motorists drive erratically, often recklessly and at excessive speeds. Pedestrians enjoy no right of way and need to be cautious when crossing streets.

Undivided two-lane roads connect most major cities. Motorists may frequently encounter oncoming high-speed traffic attempting to pass other vehicles at blind turns or over hilltops. Driving at night can be especially dangerous. Travel on mountain roads is treacherous in both rain and snow, and during winter heavy snowfalls may make some roads impassable. During the first ten months of the year 2001, 457 traffic-related fatalities and 1,976 traffic-related injuries were reported to the police. These figures reflect a continuing increase in fatality and injury rates on Georgian roads over previous years.

For additional information about road safety, including links to foreign government sites, please see the Department of State, Bureau of Consular Affairs home page at http://travel.state.gov/road_safety.html.

AVIATION SAFETY OVERSIGHT: As there is no direct commercial air service by local carriers at present, nor economic authority to operate such service between the U.S. and Georgia, the U.S. Federal Aviation Administration (FAA) has not assessed Georgia's Civil Aviation Authority for compliance with international aviation safety standards.

For further information, travelers may contact the Department of Transportation within the United States at 1-800-322-7873, or visit the FAA Internet website at http://www.faa.gov/avr/iasa.

The U.S. Department of Defense (DOD) separately assesses some foreign air carriers for suitability as official providers of air services. For information regarding the DOD policy on specific carriers, travelers may contact the DOD at tel. 618-229-4801.

CUSTOMS REGULATIONS: Travelers to Georgia must fill out a customs declaration upon arrival that is to be presented to customs officials when departing the country. Travelers are advised to declare all items of value on the customs form. Failure to declare currency and items of value can result in fines or other penalties. If your customs form is lost or stolen, please report the loss to the police to obtain a certificate to show to customs officials when you depart the country.

Traveler's should be aware that Georgia's customs authorities may enforce strict regulations concerning the temporary importation into or export from Georgia of items such as alcohol, tobacco, jewelry, religious materials, art or artifacts, antiquities, and business equipment. Only personal medicines with a doctor's statement can be imported without the permission of the Georgian Department of Healthcare.

U.S. citizens may not import firearms into Georgia; however, hunting weapons may be brought into the country for a two-week period based on valid Georgian hunting licenses. While there is no limit to the amount of currency that can be imported, if more money is exported than was declared at the time of entry, the traveler is obligated to prove it was legally obtained. There are limits on the amount of Georgian currency that may be exported.

The Ministry of Culture, Department of Expertise and Evaluation must license any valuables such as artwork, antiques, jewelry, paintings, etc. This

299

license describes the object, assesses its value and provides permission to export it from Georgia.

The U.S. Embassy in Tbilisi, Georgia, can provide more specific information on quantities of items that can be imported duty-free, as well as duties excised for specific items. It is also advisable to contact the Embassy of Georgia in Washington, D.C. for specific information regarding customs requirements.

Note that the U.S. Customs Service may impose corresponding import restrictions in accordance with the Convention on Cultural Property Implementation Act. (Please contact the U.S. Customs Service at tel. 202 927-2336 or on the Internet at http://exhanges.state.gov/education/culprop for further information).

CRIMINAL PENALTIES: While in a foreign country, a U.S. citizen is subject to that country's laws and regulations, which sometimes differ significantly from those in the United States and may not afford the protections available to the individual under U.S. law. Penalties for breaking the law can be more severe than in the United States for similar offenses. Persons violating the laws of Georgia, even unknowingly, may be expelled, arrested, or imprisoned. Penalties for possession, use, or trafficking in illegal drugs are strict, and convicted offenders can expect jail sentences and fines.

DISASTER PREPAREDNESS: Georgia is an earthquake- and landslide-prone country. General information about natural disaster preparedness is available via the Internet from the U.S. Federal Emergency Management Agency (FEMA) at http://www.fema.gov.

CURRENCY INFORMATION: While the Georgian lari is the only legal tender, dollars can be freely exchanged for laris at market rates. Credit cards are rarely accepted outside of upscale hotels and restaurants, and travelers' checks are difficult to cash. Incidents of credit card fraud and identity theft have been reported by American citizens in Georgia.

CHILDREN'S ISSUES: For information on international adoption of children and international parental child abduction, please refer to our Internet site at http://travel.state.gov/children's_issues.html or telephone the Overseas Citizens Services (OCS) call center at 1-888-407-4747. The OCS call center can answer general inquiries regarding international adoptions and will forward calls to the appropriate Country Officer. This number is available from 8:00 a.m. to 8:00 p.m. Eastern Standard Time, Monday through Friday (except U.S. federal holidays). Callers who are unable to use toll-free numbers, such as those calling from overseas, may obtain information and assistance during these hours by calling 1-317-472-2328.

REGISTRATION AND EMBASSY LOCATION: U.S. citizens living in or visiting Georgia are strongly encouraged to register at the Consular Section of the U.S. Embassy in Tbilisi, where they may obtain updated information on travel and security within Georgia. The U.S. Embassy in Tbilisi is located at 25 Atoneli Street, tel. (995)(32)98-99-67 or (995)(32)98-99-68, fax: (995)(32)93-37-59. The Embassy web site address is located at: http://web.sanet.ge/usembassy/

LATVIA

COUNTRY DESCRIPTION: Latvia is a nation undergoing economic transition. Most tourist facilities found in a western European city are available in Riga, the capital. However, many of the services taken for granted in other countries are not yet available outside Riga.

ENTRY REQUIREMENTS: A passport valid for at least six months is required. No visa is required for travelers remaining up to 90 days in a half-calendar year (from January to June and from July to December). Travelers remaining in Latvia for more than 90 days, including 180 day periods that cross over two half-calendar years, must apply for temporary residence. Travelers who plan to remain in Latvia for more than 90 days must apply in-country for temporary residence. For more information, travelers may contact the Latvian Embassy, at 4325 17th Street, N.W., Washington, D.C. 20011, tel. (202) 726-8213, web site http://www.latvia-usa.org. Within Latvia, please contact the Citizenship and Immigration Department at Raina bulv. 5, Riga, LV 1508, tel. (371) 721-9424 or (371) 721-9427, fax (371) 782-0306, http://www.pid.gov.lv. Any traveler to

Russia, even in transit, is advised to obtain a Russian visa prior to entry into Latvia. The process of obtaining a visa at the Russian Embassy in Riga can be lengthy and involve surrender of the passport for an undetermined period of time.

DUAL NATIONALITY: Dual nationals may be subject to Latvian laws which impose special obligations. Whether or not a person with United States citizenship would also be considered a Latvian citizen is a legal question dependent upon an individual's date and place of birth and the nationality of both parents. For more information on this issue, please consult the Latvian Citizenship and Immigration Department, Raina bulv 5, Riga, LV 1050, tel. 371-721-9424, http://www.pid.gov.lv. For additional information, please see the Consular Affairs home page on the Internet at http://travel.state.gov for the Department of State's *Dual Nationality flyer*.

SAFETY AND SECURITY: Civil unrest is not a problem in Riga, and there have been no incidents of terrorism directed toward American interests. Incidents of anti-Americanism are rare.

CRIME: Crime in Riga is generally non-violent, although there have been cases of serious assaults. Street crime is a serious problem, particularly for tourists. In addition to falling prey to pickpockets in all public areas, there have been cases of tourists and residents being drugged in bars and restaurants and then taken outside or to their residences and robbed. In any public area, one should always be alert to being surrounded by two or more people at once. It is not uncommon for groups of juvenile pickpockets to attempt to overwhelm their victim. In addition, Riga has one of the highest rates of car theft in the world.

The loss or theft abroad of a U.S. passport should be reported immediately to the local police and the U.S. Embassy. If you are the victim of a crime while overseas, in addition to reporting to local police, please contact the nearest U.S. embassy. The Embassy staff can, for example, assist you to find appropriate medical care, to contact family members or friends and explain how funds could be transferred. Although the investigation and prosecution of the crime is solely the responsibility of local authorities, consular officers can help you to understand the local criminal justice process and to find an attorney if needed.

U.S. citizens may refer to the Department of State's pamphlet, *A Safe Trip Abroad*, for ways to promote a more trouble-free journey. The pamphlet is available by mail from the Superintendent of Documents, U.S. Government Printing Office, Washington, D.C. 20402, via the Internet at http://www.access.gpo.gov/su_docs, or via the Bureau of Consular Affairs home page at http://travel.state.gov.

MEDICAL FACILITIES: Medical care in Latvia is steadily improving, but it remains limited in several important respects. There are a few private clinics with medical supplies and services, including disposable needles and basic modern diagnostics, which are nearly equal to Western Europe or U.S. standards. However, any major invasive procedures or surgeries in Latvia are not recommended because of lack of equipment and resources. Hospital services are not equal to Western standards. Most, but not all, antibiotics and prescription medications are available, but as they are generally European or Russian produced, they often have different names, and labels are usually not printed in English. Elderly travelers and those with existing health problems may be at risk due to inadequate medical facilities. Diptheria, hepatitis and tick-borne encephalitis are widespread. According to the World Health Organization, tuberculosis is a significant problem in Latvia, with 9% of all cases being multi-drug resistant. State ambulance service for emergencies is available by dialing 03 anywhere in Latvia. However, response is poor in rural areas. Air ambulance service is available for medical evacuations. In general, private air ambulance services are very expensive.

MEDICAL INSURANCE: U.S. medical insurance is not always valid outside the United States. U.S. Medicare and Medicaid programs do not provide payment for medical services outside the United States. Doctors and hospitals often expect immediate cash payment for health services. Uninsured travelers who require medical care overseas may face extreme difficulties.

Please check with your own insurance company to confirm whether your policy applies overseas, including provision for medical evacuation, and for adequacy of coverage. Serious medical problems requiring hospitalization and/or medical evacuation to the United States can cost tens of thousands of dollars. Please ascertain whether payment will be made to the overseas hospital or doctor or if you will be reimbursed later for expenses that you incur. Some insurance policies also include coverage for psychiatric treatment and for disposition of remains in the event of death.

Useful information on medical emergencies abroad, including overseas insurance programs, is provided in the Department of State's Bureau of Consular Affairs brochure, *Medical Information for Americans Traveling Abroad,* available via the Bureau of Consular Affairs home page or autofax: (202) 647-3000.

OTHER HEALTH INFORMATION: Information on vaccinations and other health precautions may be obtained from the Centers for Disease Control and Prevention's hotline for international travelers at 1-877-FYI-TRIP (1-877-394-8747); fax 1-800-CDC-FAXX (1-888-232-3299), or via the CDC's Internet site at http://www.cdc.gov.

TRAFFIC SAFETY/ROAD CONDITIONS: While in a foreign country, U.S. citizens may encounter road conditions that differ significantly from those in the United States. The information below concerning Latvia is provided for general reference only, and it may not be totally accurate in a particular location or circumstance.

Safety of Public Transportation: Good
Urban Road Conditions/Maintenance: Good
Rural Road Condition/Maintenance: Fair
Availability of Roadside Assistance: Fair

Latvia has one of the highest per capita rates of automobile accidents and fatalities in Europe. Drivers should be alert to pedestrians and slow moving vehicles in traffic. Widespread private ownership of automobiles is quite new, and drivers can be both inexperienced and highly aggressive. Violation of traffic rules is common. It is not unusual to be overtaken by other automobiles, traveling at high speed, even in crowded urban areas. Drivers do not always yield to pedestrians, even at marked intersections. During winter, most major roads are cleared of snow. However, drivers should be alert for fog, snow, and ice while driving. Winter tires are mandatory from December 1 until March 30. Studded tires are not permitted from May 1 through September 30.

Driving while intoxicated is a very serious offense and carries heavy penalties. Local authorities use roadblocks and breathalyzer tests as enforcement tools. Because alcohol is a serious societal problem, drivers and pedestrians should be alert to the possibility of drunk drivers. Drivers should also be alert to the possibility of drunk pedestrians wandering onto the road. Drivers must use their headlights at all times day and night. Speed limits are usually 50 km/hr in the city and 90 km/hr on the highways. Latvia has a mandatory seat belt law, and children must use approved child car seats. Latvia uses standard European road signs. However, traffic lights and signs may not be clearly visible. U.S. driving licenses are not valid in Latvia, and American tourists must possess a valid international driving permit. In the United States, international driving permits are issued by the American Automobile Association (AAA) and the American Automobile Touring Alliance. After six months in Latvia, American citizens must apply for a Latvian Driving License.

Latvian highways are slowly being upgraded after years of little or no maintenance. Information about road safety and accidents statistics is available on the website of the Latvian Road Safety Administration http://www.csdd.lv.

Public transportation is generally safe. There have been no major bus or train accidents resulting in death.

Rescue service is available by dialing 01 or 112 and ambulance service by dialing 03. The response may be slow in rural areas.

For additional general information about road safety, including links to foreign government sites, please see the Department of State, Bureau of Consular Affairs home page at http://travel.state.gov/road_safety.html. For specific information about Latvian driving permits, vehicle inspection, road tax and mandatory insurance, please contact the Latvia Tourist Board at 4 Pils Square, Riga, Latvia, LV 1050, tel and fax: 371-722-9945, or via the Internet at http://222.latviatravel.com.

AVIATION SAFETY OVERSIGHT: As there is no direct commercial air service by local carriers at present, nor economic authority to operate such service, between the United States and Latvia, the U.S. Federal Aviation Administration (FAA) has not assessed Latvia's Civil Aviation Authority for compliance with international aviation safety standards.

For further information, travelers may contact the Department of Transportation within the United States at tel. 1-800-322-7873, or visit the FAA Internet website at http://www.faa.gov/avr/iasa/. The U.S. Department of Defense (DOD) separately assesses some foreign air carriers for suitability as official providers of air services. For information regarding the DOD policy on specific carriers, travelers may contact the DOD at tel. (618) 256-4801.

CUSTOMS REGULATIONS: Latvia customs authorities may enforce strict regulations concerning temporary importation into or export from Latvia of items such as firearms, religious materials, antiquities, medications, business equipment, drugs etc. It is advisable to contact the Embassy of Latvia in Washington, D.C. or one of Latvia's consulates in the United States for specific information regarding customs requirements.

CRIMINAL PENALTIES: While in a foreign country, a U.S. citizen is subject to that country's laws and regulations, which sometimes differ significantly from those in the United States and may not afford the protections available to the individual under U.S. law. Penalties for breaking the law can be more severe than in the United States for similar offenses. Persons violating Latvia' laws, even unknowingly, may be expelled, arrested or imprisoned. Penalties for possession, use, or trafficking in illegal drugs in Latvia are strict and convicted offenders can expect jail sentences and heavy fines.

SPECIAL CIRCUMSTANCES: Telephone connections with the United States are reliable. However, 1-800 numbers cannot be accessed from Latvia. Please check with your long-distance carrier before departure to see if they offer service in Latvia. Local Internet cafes offer computer access, and fax machines are widely available. ATMs are available in Riga and in other major towns.

CHILDREN'S ISSUES: For information on international adoption of children and international parental child abduction please refer to our Internet site at http://travel.state.gov/children's_issues.html or telephone at (202) 736-7000.

REGISTRATION/EMBASSY AND CONSULATE LOCATION: Americans living in or residing in Latvia are encouraged to register at the Consular Section of the U.S. Embassy in Riga and obtain updated information on travel and security within Latvia. The U.S. Embassy is located at Raina Boulevard 7; tel. (371) 703-6200; fax (371) 781-4088. Consular information and current travel information can also be found on the Embassy Riga home page at http://www.usembassy.lv.

LITHUANIA

COUNTRY DESCRIPTION: Lithuania is a country undergoing rapid economic transition. Tourist facilities in Vilnius, the capital, and to a lesser extent in Kaunas and Klaipeda, are similar to those available in a Western European city. In other parts of the country, however, some of the goods and services taken for granted in other countries may not be available.

ENTRY REQUIREMENTS: A valid passport is required to enter Lithuania. The passport must be valid for at least 6 months from the date of entry. U.S. citizens do not need Lithuanian visas for most stays of 90 days or less. Travelers remaining in Lithuania for more than 90 days within any six-month period must apply for temporary residency. U.S. citizens should contact the Lithuanian Embassy at 2622 16th Street N.W., Washington, D.C. 20009, tel. (202) 234-5860, www.ltembassyus.org for current information on visa requirements.

Travelers to Lithuania who also plan to enter Russia, even in transit, need a Russian visa. The Russian Embassy in Lithuania is able to provide same-day processing of tourist visas with payment of an additional fee. Proof of medical insurance valid through the period of travel is required.

In an effort to prevent international child abduction, many governments have initiated procedures at entry and exit points. These often include requiring documentary evidence of family relationship and permission from the non-accompanying parent(s) or legal guardian for the child's travel. Having such documentation on hand, even if not required, may facilitate entry and departure.

DUAL NATIONALITY: In addition to being subject to all Lithuanian laws affecting U.S. citizens, those travelers also holding Lithuanian citizenship may be subject to other laws imposing special obligations on Lithuanian citizens. Lithuanian law views dual nationals in the same way as those who have only Lithuanian citizenship, which could hamper U.S. efforts to provide consular protection. More information regarding Lithuanian citizenship can be obtained from the Ministry of Foreign Affairs of the Republic of Lithuania, J. Tumo Vaizganto Street 2, 2600 Vilnius, telephone: (370) 2-362-539, e-mail: urm@urm.lt, website: www.urm.lt and from the Migration Department of the Ministry of Internal Affairs of the Republic of Lithuania, Sventaragio 2, 2600 Vilnius, telephone: (370) 2-717-236, fax: (370) 2-718-210, website: www.vrm.lt. For additional information regarding dual nationality, please see the Consular Affairs home page on the Internet at http://travel.state.gov/ for our Dual Nationality flyer.

SAFETY AND SECURITY: Civil unrest is not a problem in Lithuania and there have been no incidents of terrorism directed toward American interests. Incidents of anti-Americanism are rare.

CRIME: Crimes against foreigners, while usually non-violent, are becoming more common. Pickpocketing and theft are problems, so personal belongings should be well protected at all times. Car thefts, carjackings, and theft from cars are increasingly commonplace. Drivers should be wary of persons indicating they should pull over or that something is wrong with their car. Often, a second car or person is following, and when the driver of the targeted car gets out to see if there is a problem, the person who has been following will either steal the driver's belongings from the vehicle or get in and drive off with the car. Drivers should never get out of the car to check for damage without first turning off the ignition and taking the keys. Valuables also should not be left in plain sight in parked vehicles, as there have

been increasing reports of car windows smashed and items stolen. Burglary of foreigners' homes is also prevalent; home alarm systems should be used whenever possible. American citizens should avoid walking alone or in small groups after dark. There have been cases of American citizens being drugged in bars and then taken elsewhere to be robbed. In any public area, one should always be alert to being surrounded by two or more people at once. Racially motivated verbal, and sometimes physical, harassment of American citizens of non-Caucasian ethnicity has been reported in major cities. Incidents of racially motivated attacks against foreigners have been reported in Klaipeda in particular.

If you are the victim of a crime while in Lithuania, in addition to reporting the crime to the local police, please contact the Consular Section of the U.S. Embassy. Although the investigation and prosecution of the crime is solely the responsibility of local Lithuanian authorities, the Consular Section can provide information on the local criminal justice process. In Vilnius, an English-speaking Lithuanian police officer should always be available at 716-222.

The loss or theft abroad of a U.S. passport should be reported immediately to the local police and the nearest U.S. Embassy or Consulate. U.S. citizens may refer to the Department of State's pamphlet, "*A Safe Trip Abroad*," for ways to promote a trouble-free journey. The pamphlet is available by mail from the Superintendent of Documents, U.S. Government Printing Office, Washington, D.C. 20402, via the Internet at http://www.access.gpo.gov/su_docs, or via the Bureau of Consular Affairs home page at http://travel.state.gov.

MEDICAL FACILITIES: Medical care in Lithuania is improving but medical facilities do not always meet Western standards. There are a few private clinics with medical supplies and services that are nearly equal to Western European or U.S. standards. Most medical supplies are now widely available, including disposable needles, anesthetics, antibiotics and other pharmaceuticals. Lithuania has many highly trained medical professionals, but hospitals and clinics still suffer from a lack of equipment and resources. Western-quality dental care can be obtained in major cities. Elderly travelers who require medical care may face extreme difficulties. Most pharmaceuticals sold here are from Europe; travelers will not necessarily find the same brands that they use in the U.S. Serious medical problems requiring hospitalization and/or medical evacuation to the United States can cost thousands of dollars or more. Doctors and hospitals often expect immediate cash payment for health services.

Tick-borne encephalitis and Lyme disease are widespread. Those intending to visit parks or forested areas in Lithuania are urged to speak with their health care practitioners about immunization. The Lithuanian Government does not require HIV testing for U.S. citizens. However, sexually transmitted diseases are a growing concern.

MEDICAL INSURANCE: The Department of State strongly urges Americans to consult with their medical insurance company prior to traveling abroad to confirm whether their policy applies overseas and if it will cover emergency expenses such as a medical evacuation. U.S. medical insurance plans seldom cover health costs incurred outside the United States unless supplemental coverage is purchased. Further, U.S. Medicare and Medicaid programs do not provide payment for medical services outside the United States. However, many travel agents and private companies offer insurance plans that will cover health care expenses incurred overseas including emergency services such as medical evacuations.

When making a decision regarding health insurance, Americans should consider that many foreign doctors and hospitals require payment in cash prior to providing service and that a medical evacuation to the U.S. may cost well in excess of $50,000. Uninsured travelers who require medical care overseas often face extreme difficulties. When consulting with your insurer prior to your trip, ascertain whether payment will be made to the overseas healthcare provider or if you will be reimbursed later for expenses you incur. Some insurance policies also include coverage for psychiatric treatment and for disposition of remains in the event of death.

Useful information on medical emergencies abroad, including overseas insurance programs, is provided in the Department of State's Bureau of Consular Affairs brochure, "*Medical Information for Americans Traveling Abroad*," available via the Bureau of Consular Affairs home page or autofax: (202) 647-3000.

OTHER HEALTH INFORMATION: Information on vaccinations and other health precautions, such as safe food and water precautions and insect bite protection, may be obtained from the Centers for Disease Control and Prevention's hotline for international travelers at 1-877-FYI-TRIP (1-877-394-8747); fax 1-888-CDC-FAXX (1-888-232-3299), or via the CDC's Internet site at http://www.cdc.gov/travel. For information about outbreaks of infectious diseases abroad consult the World Health Organization's website at http://www.who.int/en. Further health information for travelers is available at http://www.who.int/ith.

TRAFFIC SAFETY AND ROAD CONDITIONS: While in a foreign country, U.S. citizens may encounter road conditions that differ significantly from those in the United States. The information below concerning Lithuania is provided for general reference only, and may not be totally accurate in a particular location or circumstance.

Safety of Public Transportation: Good
Urban Road Conditions/Maintenance: Good
Rural Road Conditions/Maintenance: Fair
Availability of Roadside Assistance: Good (on major highways)

Roads in Lithuania range from well maintained two to four-lane highways connecting major cities, to small dirt roads traversing the countryside. Violation of traffic rules is common. It is not unusual to be overtaken by other automobiles traveling at high speeds, even in crowded urban areas. Driving at night, especially in the countryside, can be particularly hazardous. In the summer, older "seasonal" vehicles and inexperienced drivers are extra hazards. During the winter, most major roads are cleared of snow. Driving with caution is urged at all times. The speed limit is 60 km/hr in town and 90 km/hr out of town unless otherwise indicated. The phone number for roadside assistance is 8-800-0000 from a regular phone and 188 from a GSM mobile phone.

Seatbelts are mandatory for the driver and all passengers except children under the age of 12.

Studded tires are not allowed from April 1st through November 1st. Headlights must be turned on at all times from September 1st through 7th (the first week of school) and November 1st through March 1st. The police allow Americans to drive in Lithuania with an American driver's license for up to 3 months. Public transportation may be slow, but is generally safe.

For additional general information about road safety, including links to foreign government sites, see the Department of State, Bureau of Consular Affairs home page at http://travel.state.gov/road_safety.html. For specific information concerning Lithuanian driving permits, vehicle inspection, road tax and mandatory insurance, contact the Lithuanian State Department of Tourism at Vilniaus gatve 4/35, 2600 Vilnius, telephone: (370) 2-622-610, e-mail: info@tourism.lt, website: www.tourism.lt. See also road safety information from the Lithuanian Road Administration at www.lra.lt/index_en.html. (Note: "index_en").

AVIATION SAFETY OVERSIGHT: As there is no direct commercial air service by local carriers at present, or economic authority to operate such service, between the U.S. and Lithuania, the U.S. Federal Aviation Administration (FAA) has not assessed Lithuania's Civil Aviation Authority for compliance with international aviation safety standards. For further information, travelers may contact the Department of Transportation within the U.S. at 1-800-322-7873, or visit the FAA's Internet website at http://www.faa.gov/avr/iasa.

The U.S. Department of Defense (DOD) separately assesses some foreign air carriers for suitability as official providers of air services. For information regarding the DOD policy on specific carriers, travelers may contact DOD at (618) 229-4801.

CUSTOMS REGULATIONS: Lithuanian customs authorities may enforce strict regulations concerning temporary importation into or export from Lithuania of items such as firearms and antiquities. It is advisable to contact the Embassy of Lithuania in Washington or one of Lithuania's consulates in the United States for specific information regarding customs requirements. Special permission from the Ministry of Culture is required before one can remove antiques from Lithuania. Travelers are advised to contact the Foreign Export Valuation Control Section of the Ministry of Culture, Snipiskiu 3, Vilnius, tel: 2-724-113 or 2-724-005 before removing any object more than 50 years old from Lithuania; the definition of antiquity depends on the type of object. To export firearms, one needs special permission from the Ministry of the Interior. Cash in excess of 10,000 Lithuanian litai (or its equivalent in other currencies) must be declared in written form upon entry and exit.

Lithuanian customs authorities encourage the use of an ATA (Admission Temporaire/Temporary Admission) Carnet for the temporary admission of professional equipment, commercial samples, and/or goods for exhibitions and fair purposes. ATA Carnet Headquarters, located at the U.S. Council for International Business, 1212 Avenue of the Americas, New York, NY 10036, issues and guarantees the ATA Carnet in the United States. For additional information call (212) 354-4480, send an e-mail to atacarnet@uscib.org, or visit www.uscib.org for details.

CRIMINAL PENALTIES: While in a foreign country, a U.S. citizen is subject to that country's laws and regulations, which sometimes differ significantly from those in the United States and may not afford the protections available to the individual under U.S. law. Penalties for breaking the law in Lithuania can be more severe than in the United States for similar offenses. Persons violating Lithuanian laws, even unknowingly, may be expelled, arrested, or imprisoned. Penalties for possession, use, or trafficking in illegal drugs in Lithuania are strict and convicted offenders can expect jail sentences and heavy fines.

SPECIAL CIRCUMSTANCES: Telephone connections are generally good, though phone numbers are in the process of being changed, especially in Vilnius. American 1-800 numbers can be accessed from Lithuania but not on a toll-free basis; the international long distance rate per minute will be charged. Local Internet cafes offer computer access. ATMs are widely available. Most hotels, restaurants and other businesses now accept major credit cards.

CHILDREN'S ISSUES: For information on international adoption of children, international parental child abduction, and international child support enforcement issues, please refer to our Internet site at http://travel.state.gov/children's_issues.html or telephone (202) 736-7000.

REGISTRATION/EMBASSY LOCATION: Americans living in or visiting Lithuania are encouraged to register at the Consular Section of the U.S. Embassy in Vilnius and obtain updated information on travel and security within Lithuania. The U.S. Embassy is located at Akmenu gatve 6; telephone (370)(5) 266-5500 or 266-5600, fax (370)(5) 266-5590. Consular information can also be found on the Embassy Vilnius home page at www.usembassy.lt

MOLDOVA

COUNTRY DESCRIPTION: Moldova has been an independent nation since 1991. The capital, Chisinau, offers adequate hotels and restaurants, but tourist facilities in other parts of the country are not highly developed, and many of the goods and services taken for granted in other countries are not yet available. Moldova is a democracy with a freely elected government.

ENTRY REQUIREMENTS: Visas are required of American citizens traveling to (or transiting) Moldova. All visas must be obtained in advance of arrival from a Moldovan embassy or consulate. Only those U.S. citizens who can provide evidence that they reside in a country in which Moldova has no embassy or consulate are permitted to obtain a tourist/business visa at the Chisinau airport. No invitation is necessary. Any person applying for a visa for a stay of more than three months must present a certificate showing that the individual is HIV negative. Only tests performed at designated clinics in Moldova are accepted. For more information on entry requirements, please contact the Moldovan Embassy, 2101 S. Street N.W., Washington, D.C. 20008, telephone: (202) 667-1130, (202) 667-1131, or (202) 667-1137, fax: (202) 667-1204, e-mail: moldova@dgs.dgsys.com.

IMPORTANT NOTES: All foreign citizens staying in Moldova for three days or longer are required to register with local authorities at the Office of Visas and Registration. The place of registration (usually, a district police station) depends on where a visitor is staying in Moldova. Most hotels will register guests automatically. The U.S. Embassy encourages U.S. citizens to ask about registration when checking into a hotel. U.S. citizens not staying in a hotel are responsible for registering with authorities. To find out exactly where to register, a U.S. citizen may call the central Office for Visas and Registration at (373) (2) 21-30-78, and should be prepared to give the address of the residence in Moldova. Under Moldovan law, those who fail to register with authorities may be required to appear in court and pay a fine. For more information on registering with Moldovan authorities, U.S. citizens are encouraged to call the Consular Section at the U.S. Embassy in Chisinau at telephone (373) (2) 40-83-00.

In an effort to prevent international child abduction, many governments have initiated procedures at entry/exit points. These often include requiring documentary evidence of relationship and permission for the child's travel from the parent(s) or legal guardian not present. Having such documentation on hand, even if not required, may facilitate entry/departure.

SAFETY/SECURITY: A separatist regime controls a narrow strip of land in the Transnistria region of eastern Moldova. The United States and other countries do not recognize this regime. Since no formal diplomatic relations exist between the United States and local authorities there, the provision of consular assistance to American citizens cannot be ensured. Travelers should exercise caution in visiting or transiting the area. Travelers should be aware that there are numerous road checkpoints in the Transnistria region.

CRIME INFORMATION: Moldova's economic difficulties in recent years, as well as increased organized criminal activity and more frequent travel by foreigners to Moldova, contribute to the risk to visitors of street crime and other crime, potentially involving violence. While this risk is no greater than in most cities in the United States, many Americans have reported theft of money and small valuables from hotel rooms and local apartments. Cases of breaking and entering into homes and offices are not uncommon. It is wise for travelers to exercise the same precautions with regard to personal safety and protection of valuables in Chisinau that they would in any major U.S. city.

Train and bus service are below Western standards, and some U.S. citizens have been victims of crime such as thefts, while traveling on international trains to and from Moldova.

The loss or theft abroad of a U.S. passport should be reported immediately to the local police and the nearest U.S. embassy or consulate. If you are the victim of a crime while overseas, in addition to reporting to local police, please contact the nearest U.S. embassy or consulate for assistance. The Embassy/Consulate staff can, for example, assist you to find appropriate medical care, to contact family members or friends and explain how funds can be transferred. Although the investigation and prosecution of the crime is solely the responsibility of local authorities, consular officers can help you understand the local criminal justice process and find an attorney if needed.

U.S. citizens may refer to the Department of State's pamphlet, *A Safe Trip Abroad*, for ways to promote a trouble-free journey. The pamphlet is available by mail from the Superintendent of Documents, U.S. Government Printing Office, Washington, D.C. 20402, via the Internet at http://www.access.gpo.gov/su_docs, or via the Bureau of Consular Affairs home page at http://travel.state.gov.

MEDICAL FACILITIES: Medical care in Moldova is limited, and there are severe shortages of basic medical supplies. Elderly travelers and those with existing health problems may be at risk due to inadequate medical facilities. The U.S. Embassy maintains lists of such facilities and English-speaking doctors. Rabies vaccinations may be useful because casual exposure to stray dogs is common throughout Chisinau. The Centers for Disease Control (CDC) recommends the Hepatitis A or IG, and B series for certain travelers. The CDC also recommends typhoid vaccinations for travelers to Moldova. Please consult your physician about immunizations.

MEDICAL INSURANCE: The Department of State strongly urges Americans to consult with their medical insurance company prior to traveling abroad to confirm whether their policy applies overseas and if it will cover emergency expenses such as a medical evacuation. U.S. medical insurance plans seldom cover health costs incurred outside the United States unless supplemental coverage is purchased. Further, U.S. Medicare and Medicaid programs do not provide payment for medical services outside the United States. However, many travel agents and private companies offer insurance plans that will cover health care expenses incurred overseas, including emergency services such as medical evacuations.

When making a decision regarding health insurance, Americans should consider that many foreign doctors and hospitals require payment in cash prior to providing service and that a medical evacuation to the United States may cost well in excess of $50,000. Uninsured travelers who require medical care overseas often face extreme difficulties. When consulting with your insurer prior to your trip, please ascertain whether payment will be made to the overseas healthcare provider or if you will be reimbursed later for expenses that you incur. Some insurance policies also include coverage for psychiatric treatment and for disposition of remains in the event of death.

Useful information on medical emergencies abroad, including overseas insurance programs, is provided in the Department of State's Bureau of Consular Affairs brochure, *Medical Information for Americans Traveling Abroad*, available via the Bureau of Consular Affairs home page or autofax: (202) 647-3000.

OTHER HEALTH INFORMATION: Information on vaccinations and other health precautions may be obtained from the Centers for Disease Control and Prevention's hotline for international travelers at 1-877-FYI-TRIP (1-877-394-8747); fax 1-888-CDC-FAXX (1-888-232-3299), or via their Internet site at http://www.cdc.gov.

TRAFFIC SAFETY AND ROAD CONDITIONS: While in a foreign country, U.S. citizens may encounter road conditions that differ significantly from those in the United States. The information below concerning Moldova is provided for general reference only, and it may not be totally accurate in a particular location or circumstance.

Safety of Public Transportation: Poor
Urban Road Conditions/Maintenance: Poor
Rural Road Conditions/Maintenance: Poor
Availability of Roadside Assistance: Poor

Moldova's highway infrastructure consists mainly of two-lane roads, which are unevenly maintained and unlighted. Caution should be taken to prevent collisions with agricultural vehicles. Travel before dawn and after dusk should be avoided if possible. Drivers and pedestrians should exercise extreme caution to avoid accidents, which are commonplace. Many accidents involve drunk drivers.

For additional general information about road safety, including links to foreign government sites, please see the Department of State, bureau of Consular Affairs home page at http://travel.state.gov/road_safety.html.

AVIATION SAFETY OVERSIGHT: As there is no direct commercial service by local carriers at present, nor economic authority to operate such service between the United States and Moldova, the U.S. Federal Aviation Administration (FAA) has not assessed Moldova's Civil Aviation Authority for compliance with international aviation safety standards. For further information, travelers may contact the Department of Transportation within the United States. at tel. 1-800-322-7873, or visit the FAA's Internet website at http://www.faa.gov/avr/iasa.

The U.S. Department of Defense (DOD) separately assesses some foreign air carriers for suitability as official providers of air services. For information regarding the DOD policy on specific carriers, travelers may contact the DOD at tel. (618) 229-4801.

CUSTOMS REGULATIONS: Moldovan customs authorities may enforce strict regulations concerning temporary importation into or export from Moldova of items such as firearms, religious materials, antiquities, medications, business equipment, and foreign currency. Travelers are advised to register any foreign currency brought into Moldova with customs authorities upon entering the country. It is advisable to contact the Embassy of Moldova in Washington, D.C. for specific information regarding customs requirements.

Moldovan customs authorities encourage the use of an ATA (Admission Temporaire/Temporary Admission) Carnet for the temporary admission of professional equipment, commercial samples, and/or goods for exhibitions and fair purposes. ATA Carnet Headquarters, located at the U.S. Council for International Business, 1212 Avenue of the Americas, New York, NY 10036, issues and guarantees the ATA Carnet in the United States. For additional information, please call (212) 354-4480, or send an e-mail to atacarnet@uscib.org, or visit http://www.uscib.org for details.

CRIMINAL PENALTIES: While in a foreign country, a U.S. citizen is subject to that country's laws and regulations, which sometimes differ significantly from those in the United States and may not afford the protections available to the individual under U.S. law. Penalties for breaking the law can be more severe than in the United States for similar offenses. Persons violating Moldova's laws, even unknowingly, may be expelled, arrested or imprisoned. Penalties for possession, use, or trafficking in illegal drugs in Moldova are strict, and convicted offenders can expect jail sentences and heavy fines.

SPECIAL CIRCUMSTANCES: Outside of Chisinau, travelers may have difficulty finding public telephones and receiving and making international and local calls. Losses have been reported from international letter and package mail, both of which are subject to a customs inspection before delivery. "Express" mailing services such as DHL and Federal Express are available in Chisinau, although prices are expensive in most cases, and shipments arrive from (or reach) the United States in no less than five business days.

Moldova is generally a cash-only economy. Traveler's checks and credit cards are accepted only at a few select locations in Chisinau, and some travelers have reported incidents of unauthorized expenditures made via their credit cards during or following their use of the cards in Moldova.

CHILDREN'S ISSUES: For information on international adoption of children, international parental child abduction, and international child support enforcement issues, please refer to our Internet site at http://travel.state.gov/children's_issues.html or telephone (202) 736-7000.

309

NOTE: Due to changes in Moldovan law, it is not currently possible for U.S. citizens to adopt in Moldova, nor is it possible to predict when this situation might change. Please check the Web site noted above for updated information.

REGISTRATION/EMBASSY

AND CONSULATE LOCATION: Americans living in or visiting Moldova are encouraged to register at the Consular Section of the U.S. Embassy in Chisinau and obtain updated information on travel and security within Moldova. The U.S. Embassy is located in Chisinau, Moldova, Strada Alexei Mateevici 103; telephone (373)(2) 23-37-72, after-hours telephone (373)(2) 23-73-45.

KAZAKHASTAN

COUNTRY DESCRIPTION: The Republic of Kazakhstan celebrated the eleventh anniversary of its independence in 2002. Kazakhstan is the ninth largest country in area in the world, but it has a relatively small population of 15 million. In 2000, the Government of Kazakhstan completed its move to the new capital, Astana. The U.S. Embassy is still located in Almaty, which remains the country's largest city, business center and transportation hub. Many Americans also travel to Atyrau and Aktau, cities in the heart of Kazakhstan's oil producing region on the Caspian Sea. Kazakhstan's tourist facilities are not highly developed; the availability of goods and services is better than most neighboring countries, but not up to standards in North America and Western Europe. Internal travel and travel to neighboring countries, both by air and land, can be subject to delays due to infrastructure shortcomings and winter weather.

ENTRY REQUIREMENTS: A valid passport and visa are required. The Kazakhstani Embassy in Washington, D.C. and the Kazakhstani Consulate in New York issue visas based on an invitation from an individual or organizational sponsor in Kazakhstan. The U.S. Embassy in Almaty does not issue letters of invitation to citizens interested in private travel to Kazakhstan. All travelers, even those simply transiting Kazakhstan for less than 72 hours, must obtain a Kazakhstani visa before entering the country. Travelers may also be asked to provide proof at the border of their onward travel arrangements. Travelers transiting through Kazakhstan are reminded to check that their visas allow for sufficient number of entries to cover each transit trip and to check the length of validity of the visa. Crossing the land border to and from the neighboring Kyrgyz Republic can result in delays or demands from border officials to pay fines. For complete information concerning entry requirements, U.S. citizens should contact the Kazakhstani Embassy at 1401 16th Street N.W., Washington, D.C. 20036, telephone (202) 232-5488, fax (202) 232-5845, e-mail kazakhembusa@earthlink.net or kazakh.consul@verizon.net, or home page http://www.kazakhembus.com or the Kazakhstani Consulate at 866 United Nations Plaza, Suite 586, New York, N.Y. 10017, telephone (212) 888-3024, fax (212) 888-3025, e-mail kzconsulny@un.int, or home page http://www.kazconsulny.org.

In an effort to prevent international child abduction, many governments have initiated procedures at entry/exit points. These often include requiring documentary evidence of relationship and permission for the child's travel from the parent(s) or legal guardian not present. Having such documentation on hand, even if not required, may facilitate entry/departure.

DUAL NATIONALITY: In addition to being subject to all Kazakhstani laws affecting U.S. citizens, dual nationals may also be subject to other laws that impose special obligations on Kazakhstani citizens. For instance, Kazakhstan requires that all Kazakhstani citizens who have emigrated from Kazakhstan complete the permanent exit visa process or face penalties upon return to Kazakhstan. For additional information specific to Kazakhstan, please consult the Kazakhstani Embassy. For additional general information, please see the Consular Affairs home page on the Internet at http://travel.state.gov for our Dual Nationality flyer.

SAFETY AND SECURITY: Travel to several border areas with China and cities in close proximity to military installations require prior permission from the government. In 2001, the government declared the following areas closed to foreigners: Gvardeyskiy village, Rossavel village, and Kulzhabashy railway station in Zhambyl

Oblast; Bokeyorda and Zhangaly districts in Western Kazakhstan Oblast; the town of Priozersk and Gulshad village in Karaganda Oblast; and Baykonur, Karmakshy, and Kazakly districts in Kyzylorda Oblast. Americans traveling within Kazakhstan have on occasion reported local officials who demand documentation authorizing travel within their area of jurisdiction, despite appropriate registration in Almaty or Astana. Americans should report any trouble with local authorities to the U.S. Embassy in Almaty.

There are local Kazakhstani registration requirements. All travelers staying for more than five calendar days must register with the Office of Visas and Registration (OVIR) within that time period. OVIR offices are located in Almaty, Astana, and all other major cities. Visitors who do not register may have to pay fines upon departure. All visitors who plan to stay more than 30 days must also present to the OVIR office within 30 days of arrival a certificate indicating a negative HIV test conducted no more than one month before registration. Evidence of an HIV test performed abroad is acceptable. Testing may also be done at the Center for the Prevention and Control of AIDS (7 Talgarskaya Street, Almaty).

Note: For additional regional security information concerning Central Asia, U.S. citizens should check on a regular basis the Consular Information Sheets and current Travel Warnings or Public Announcements for nearby countries, including the Kyrgyz Republic, Tajikistan, Turkmenistan, and Uzbekistan. The U.S. Embassy in each of those countries can provide up-to-date information about local crime and safety issues. Information about how to contact each embassy directly is available on the Consular Affairs homepage, http://www.travel.state.gov.

CRIME: Travelers in Kazakhstan should exercise the same precautions concerning personal safety and protection of valuables as they would in any major U.S. city. Using good judgment and avoiding high-risk areas can reduce the crime threat. The most common crimes foreign tourists encounter are purse snatching, pick-pocketing and mugging. Pick-pocketings or robberies occur most frequently in the vicinity of Western hotels and at open-air markets, including the central open-air market in Almaty (known locally as the "green market"). Americans are advised to exercise caution in the vicinity of hotels and when shopping. The U.S. Embassy strongly recommends that Americans do not carry large sums of money on the street. There have also been multiple reports of robberies in Almaty residences occupied by American citizens.

Be wary of persons representing themselves as police or other local officials. It is not uncommon for Americans to become victims of harassment and extortion by law enforcement and other officials. A genuine police official should always present his own credentials when approaching someone on the street. If the officer cannot produce identification, he is most likely not a real police officer. Never voluntarily hand over your wallet to a police officer. Tell the officer that you will report his behavior to the U.S. Embassy and his supervisors. Authorities are concerned about these incidents and have cooperated in investigating such cases. Try to obtain the officer's name, badge number, and license plate number, and note where the incident happened because this information assists local officials in identifying the perpetrators. Report crimes committed against you by persons presenting themselves as police or other governmental authorities to a police station and the U.S. Embassy.

The "lost wallet" scam continues to be common in Kazakhstan. One version of this swindle involves the discovery of a lost wallet in your presence. A first person will discover the wallet and offer to divide its contents with you. A second person will then appear, claim to be the owner of the wallet, and demand compensation for the missing money. A second version involves a person looking for a lost wallet who will ask you if you have seen it. The person asks you to reveal the contents of your pockets, wallet, or bag to prove that you do not have the missing wallet. The wallet seeker will then surreptitiously remove your valuables. When initially approached by the finder or seeker of the lost wallet, simply walk away. Never hand over your wallet or belongings to someone who approaches you on the street. The perpetrators will eventually go looking for another target.

Another swindle has occurred at the Almaty International Airport. Men posing as "meet and greet" airport facilitators lure foreigners into cars purportedly to take them to their hotels. However, the driver takes the passengers to a secluded destination and then demands approximately $100 for gas to take the foreigner back to the city. All travelers should make prior arrangements with their contacts in Almaty for concrete identification upon arrival at the airport. Americans should not leave with anyone who does not show pre-arranged identification, even if the person is holding a sign with the traveler's name.

Corruption at the airport in Almaty has been reported. Some foreigners have been told by customs or border guard officials that they must pay a $50-$500 fine for violating an undisclosed local regulation, despite the fact that the foreign citizen has fully complied with local laws. Some Americans reportedly were asked to pay a large fine upon exiting Kazakhstan. When encountering such irregularities, U.S. citizens are advised to seek clarification from supervisory airport officials or contact the U.S. Embassy before paying.

Given the crime situation, the U.S. Embassy has made arrangements with the Kazakhstani Government to allow Americans in the Almaty Oblast to carry a certified copy of their passport and visa rather than the original. These copies can be obtained from the U.S. Embassy Consular Section during business hours Monday to Friday, 9:00 a.m. to 5:00 p.m.

The loss or theft abroad of a U.S. passport should be reported immediately to the local police and the nearest U.S. embassy or consulate. If you are the victim of a crime while overseas, in addition to reporting to local police, please contact the nearest U.S. embassy or consulate for assistance. The Embassy/Consulate staff can, for example, assist you to find appropriate medical care, to contact family members or friends and explain how funds could be transferred. Although the investigation and prosecution of the crime is solely the responsibility of local authorities, consular officers can help you to understand the local criminal justice process and to find an attorney if needed.

U.S. citizens may refer to the Department of State's pamphlet, "A Safe Trip Abroad," for ways to promote a trouble-free journey. The pamphlet is available by mail from the Superintendent of Documents, U.S. Government Printing Office, Washington, D.C. 20402, via the Internet at http://www.access.gpo.gov/su_docs, or via the Bureau of Consular Affairs home page at http://travel.state.gov.

MEDICAL FACILITIES: Medical care in Kazakhstan is limited and well below North American and Western European standards. The U.S. Embassy maintains a list of English-speaking physicians. Basic medical supplies, including disposable needles, anesthetics, and antibiotics can be in short supply. Elderly travelers and those with pre-existing health problems may be at risk due to inadequate medical facilities. Most resident Americans travel to Western Europe for serious medical treatment. Such travel can be extremely expensive if undertaken under emergency conditions. Travelers requiring prescription medications or specific brand-name medicines should bring sufficient supplies of medications and not rely on local availability.

MEDICAL INSURANCE: The Department of State strongly urges Americans to consult with their medical insurance company prior to traveling abroad to confirm whether their policy applies overseas and if it will cover emergency expenses such as a medical evacuation. U.S. medical insurance plans seldom cover health costs incurred outside the United States unless supplemental coverage is purchased. Further, U.S. Medicare and Medicaid programs do not provide payment for medical services outside the United States. However, many travel agents and private companies offer insurance plans that will cover health care expenses incurred overseas, including emergency services such as medical evacuations.

When making a decision regarding health insurance, Americans should consider that many foreign doctors and hospitals require payment in cash prior to providing service and that a medical evacuation to the United States may cost well in excess of $50,000. Uninsured travelers who require medical care overseas often face extreme difficulties. When consulting with your insurer before your trip, please ascertain whether payment will be made to the overseas healthcare provider or if you will be reimbursed later for expenses that you incur. Some insurance policies also include coverage for psychiatric treatment and for disposition of remains in the event of death.
Useful information on medical emergencies abroad, including overseas insurance programs, is provided in the Department of State's Bureau of

Consular Affairs brochure, "Medical Information for Americans Traveling Abroad," available via the Bureau of Consular Affairs home page or autofax: (202) 647-3000.

OTHER HEALTH INFORMATION: Information on vaccinations and other health precautions, such as safe food and water precautions and insect bite protection, may be obtained from the Centers for Disease Control and Prevention's hotline for international travelers at 1-877-FYI-TRIP (1-877-394-8747); fax 1-888-CDC-FAXX (1-888-232-3299), or via the CDC's Internet site at http://www.cdc.gov/travel. For information about outbreaks of infectious diseases abroad, please consult the World Health Organization's website at http://www.who.int/en. Further health information for travelers is available at http://www.who.int/ith.

TRAFFIC SAFETY AND ROAD CONDITIONS: While in a foreign country, U.S. citizens may encounter road conditions that differ significantly from those in the United States. The information below concerning Kazakhstan is provided for general reference only, and it may not be totally accurate in a particular location or circumstance.

Safety of Public Transportation: Fair
Urban Road Conditions/Maintenance: Poor
Rural Road Conditions/Maintenance: Poor
Availability of Roadside Assistance: Poor

Roads are in poor repair, especially in rural areas. The road between Almaty and Bishkek, Kyrgyzstan is especially treacherous at night or during poor weather. Americans and other travelers have been killed in traffic accidents on that road, and travel at night is not recommended. Street lighting, especially on side streets, may be turned off at night. Drivers often ignore lane markings. Potholes are common, and they are often dangerously deep. Pedestrians frequently dart out in front of cars. Visitors should use special caution if driving at night. Defensive driving is a must because many local drivers do not follow traffic laws. Accidents involving severe injury and/or death are common. Traffic police have reportedly stopped cars to seek bribes on main city streets and at periodic checkpoints on major highways.

Travelers should be particularly careful when using public transportation and taxis. Buses tend to be very crowded and can be unsafe and unreliable. Due to the danger of theft or assault, travelers should be selective regarding which taxi they contract and always avoid entering a cab that already contains persons other than the driver.

Americans wishing to drive in Kazakhstan should possess a valid American driver's license and an international driver's license. For specific information, travelers may contact the Embassy of the Republic of Kazakhstan at 1401 16th Street N.W., Washington, D.C. 20036, telephone (202) 232-5488.

For additional general information about road safety, including links to foreign government sites, please see the Department of State, Bureau of Consular Affairs home page at http://travel.state.gov/road_safety.html.

AVIATION SAFETY OVERSIGHT: As there is no direct commercial air service by local carriers at present nor economic authority to operate such service between the United States and Kazakhstan, the U.S. Federal Aviation Administration (FAA) has not assessed Kazakhstan's Civil Aviation Authority for compliance with international aviation safety standards. For further information, travelers may contact the Department of Transportation within the United States at tel. 1-800-322-7873, or visit the FAA's Internet home page at http://www.faa.gov/avr/iasa.

The U.S. Department of Defense (DOD) separately assesses some foreign air carriers for suitability as official providers of air services. For information regarding the DOD policy on specific carriers, travelers may contact the DOD at tel. (618) 229-4801.

CUSTOMS REGULATIONS: Kazakhstani customs authorities may enforce strict regulations concerning export from Kazakhstan of items such as antiquities. Foreigners must complete a customs declaration upon entering Kazakhstan and may face fines upon departure if unable to produce certificates verifying legal conversion of foreign currency. Tenge, Kazakhstan's currency, can be exported in amounts up to $10,000 without written certification on the origin of funds. For legal requirements on the export of Tenge, travelers

313

should consult with local Customs officials. In practice, travelers have been erroneously charged duty on Tenge exports or asked to surrender Tenge before departing the country. It is advisable to contact the Embassy of the Republic of Kazakhstan in Washington, D.C. for specific information at 1401 16th Street NW, Washington, D.C. 20036, telephone (202) 232-5488.

CRIMINAL PENALTIES: While in a foreign country, a U.S. citizen is subject to that country's laws and regulations, which sometimes differ significantly from those in the United States and may not afford the protections available to the individual under U.S. law. Penalties for breaking the law can be more severe than in the United States for similar offenses. Persons violating Kazakhstani laws, even unknowingly, may be expelled, arrested, or imprisoned. Penalties for possession, use, or trafficking in illegal drugs in Kazakhstan are strict, and convicted offenders can expect jail sentences and heavy fines.

SPECIAL CIRCUMSTANCES: Kazakhstan remains largely a cash economy. Traveler's checks and credit cards are not widely accepted, except at large hotels and restaurants catering to international visitors. U.S. dollars can easily be exchanged for the local currency (Tenge) at local and authorized currency exchanges, but all denominations of U.S. currency except $1 bills must be new series (large portraits) and all must have been issued after 1995 and be in good condition (not worn or torn and without any writing or marks).

DISASTER PREPAREDNESS: Kazakhstan, especially the mountainous southeast region, is an earthquake-prone country. The U.S. Department of State has ranked the earthquake threat level within Almaty as a Level 4 (the highest level assigned). Building practices within Kazakhstan do not generally meet U.S. seismic standards. In addition, local authorities do not have sufficient resources to respond to a large-scale disaster. American citizens traveling to Kazakhstan are encouraged to register with the U.S. Embassy Consular Section to assist in contacting them in the event of an emergency. General information about natural disaster preparedness is available via the Internet from the U.S. Federal Emergency Management Agency (FEMA) at http://www.fema.gov.

CHILDREN'S ISSUES: For information on international adoption of children and international parental child abduction, please refer to the Bureau of Consular Affairs' Internet site at http://travel.state.gov/children's_issues.html or telephone (202) 736-7000.

While Kazakhstani law affirms the right of foreigners to adopt Kazakhstani children, implementation of the law is not uniform. Adoption procedures vary widely from region to region, and Americans should expect bureaucratic delays during the adoption process.

Before traveling to Kazakhstan, prospective adoptive parents should carefully clarify with their agency that everything is in order to complete their adoption.

For current information on adoptions in Kazakhstan, please contact the U.S. Embassy in Almaty.

REGISTRATION/EMBASSY LOCATION: Americans living in or visiting Kazakhstan are encouraged to register at the U.S. Embassy Consular Section in Almaty and obtain updated information on travel and security within Kazakhstan. Registration with the Embassy is different from Kazakhstani OVIR registration. It can help the U.S. Embassy contact you in case of an emergency, and it can streamline replacement of a lost or stolen passport. The U.S. Embassy in Almaty is 11 hours ahead of U.S. Eastern Standard Time, and it is located at 99/97A Furmanova Street, tel. 7-3272-63-39-21, after-hour emergencies 7-3272-50-76-27, fax 7-3272-50-62-69, e-mail ConsularAlmaty@state.gov, or web site http://www.usembassy-kazakhstan.freenet.kz.

KYRGYZ REPUBLIC

COUNTRY DESCRIPTION: The Kyrgyz Republic (informally known as Kyrgyzstan) is a newly independent nation in Central Asia undergoing profound political and economic change. Tourist facilities are not highly developed, and many of the goods and services taken for granted in other countries are not yet available.

ENTRY REQUIREMENTS: A passport and visa as well as an invitation are required. For further information regarding entry requirements, contact the Embassy of the Kyrgyz Republic at 1732 Wisconsin Ave., N.W., Washington, DC 20007, telephone (202) 338-5141, fax: (202) 338-5139, or on the Internet at http://www.kyrgyzstan.org. Effective March 2002, a one-month single-entry tourist visas can be obtained upon arrival at the airport "Manas" for $60 fee without invitation. Please be aware, you cannot obtain a tourist visa at land borders. Americans are required to register their passports with the Office of Visas and Registration, of the Kyrgyz Internal Affairs Ministry, within five business days of arrival in the Kyrgyz Republic. There are fines for failure to register and fines for late registration. This requirement does not apply to official delegation members and bearers of diplomatic passports. The Embassy also recommends Americans traveling in the Kyrgyz Republic obtain Kazakhstani visas, as commercial air travel out of the Kyrgyz Republic is limited and Americans might need to travel through Kazakhstan to return to the United States.

DUAL NATIONALITY: The Kyrgyz Republic does not recognize dual citizenship. In addition to being subject to all laws of the Kyrgyz Republic affecting U.S. citizens, dual nationals may also be subject to other laws that impose special obligations on Kyrgyz citizens. For additional general information on dual nationality, see the Consular Affairs home page on the Internet at http://travel.state.gov for our dual nationality flyer.

SAFETY AND SECURITY: The Department of State urges U.S. citizens to avoid all travel to rural areas along the Kyrgyz-Uzbek and Kyrgyz-Tajik borders, and all areas to the south and west of the provincial capital of Osh. Security conditions in these parts of the southern Kyrgyz Republic differ from security conditions in the north, and a threat of terrorist violence in the southern Kyrgyz Republic continues.

Military and insurgent activity created volatile and dangerous situations in the southern Kyrgyz Republic in the summers of 1999 and 2000. There are land mines in Batken Oblast and near the Kyrgyz-Tajik border. Hostage-taking incidents involving foreigners have occurred during each of the last two summers, including one in the summer of 2000 involving American citizens. All U.S. Government personnel are prohibited from traveling to areas of the Kyrgyz Republic south and west of Osh and in rural areas along the Kyrgyz-Uzbek border because of the volatile security situation in these areas.

Note: U.S. citizens should check the Consular Information Sheets and current Travel Warnings or Public Announcements for nearby countries, including Kazakhstan, Tajikistan, Turkmenistan, and Uzbekistan on a regular basis. The U.S. Embassy in each of those countries can provide up-to-date information about local crime and safety issues. Information about how to contact each Embassy directly is available on the Internet at the Consular Affairs home page, http://travel.state.gov, or by calling the U.S. Embassy, Bishkek.

CRIME: the U.S. Embassy cautions U.S. citizens to exercise caution in urban areas of the Kyrgyz Republic due to the high rate of violent crimes against foreigners. Travelers should not take public transportation or walk after dark, and should be extremely cautious in or near hotels, bars, parks and all places that attract an expatriate clientele. The Kyrgyz Republic has a high rate of violent crime due to unemployment and an increase in the number of organized gangs. Economically motivated street crime against U.S. citizens is rising. Common crimes include auto theft, muggings, and pickpocketing in crowded places such as markets and public transportation.

Harassment and extortion by people who purport to be Kyrgyz police officers are common. According to Kyrgyz law, any person claiming to be a police officer must show identifying documents on demand. U.S. citizens should not accept requests by people, whether in civilian dress or in police uniform, if they have no official identification.

Further, Americans should exercise caution in traveling to Bishkek from the Kazakh border crossing at Georgievka on the Bishkek-Almaty road. The Embassy has received several reports of robbery of foreigners entering Kyrgyzstan by this route. Persons in plainclothes claiming to be police officers have stopped vehicles and robbed the occupants under the pretense of a search for contraband.

The loss or theft of a U.S. passport should be reported immediately to the local police and the nearest U.S. embassy or consulate. U.S. citizens can refer to the Department of State's pamphlet, *A Safe Trip Abroad*, which provides useful information on guarding valuables and ways to promote a more trouble-free journey. The pamphlet is available by mail from the Superintendent of Documents, U.S. Government Printing Office, Washington DC 20402, via the Internet at http://www.access.gpo.gov/su_docs, or visit the Consular Affairs Internet home page at http://travel.state.gov.

MEDICAL FACILITIES: The Consular Section of the U.S. Embassy in Bishkek maintains a list of foreign and local physicians who have agreed to give medical assistance to Americans. Basic medical supplies, including disposable needles, anesthetics, and antibiotics, are in short supply in the Kyrzgyz Republic. Elderly travelers and those with existing health problems may be at risk due to inadequate medical facilities. Travelers to the Kyrgyz Republic may find it prudent to consult with medical evacuation companies regarding costs and insurance rates prior to their arrival. Please see the Consular Affairs Internet home page for contact information for air ambulance or medical evacuation companies.

MEDICAL INSURANCE: U.S. medical insurance is not always valid outside the United States. U.S. Medicare and Medicaid programs do not provide payment for medical services outside the United States. Doctors and hospitals often expect immediate cash payment for health services. Uninsured travelers who require medical care overseas may face extreme difficulties.

Check with your own insurance company to confirm whether your policy applies overseas, including provision for medical evacuation, and for adequacy of coverage. Serious medical problems requiring hospitalization and/or medical evacuation to the United States can cost tens of thousands of dollars. Ascertain whether payment will be made to the overseas hospital or doctor or whether you will be reimbursed later for expenses you incur. Some insurance policies also include coverage for psychiatric treatment and for disposition of remains in the event of death.

Useful information on medical emergencies abroad, including overseas insurance programs, is provided in the Department of State's Bureau of Consular Affairs brochure *Medical Information for Americans Traveling Abroad*, available via the Consular Affairs Internet home page at http://travel.state.gov or by autofax: (202) 647-3000.

OTHER HEALTH INFORMATION: Information on vaccinations and other health precautions may be obtained from the Center for Disease Control and Prevention's international travelers' hotline, at 1-877-FYI-TRIP (1-877-394-8747); fax: 1-888-CDC-FAXX (1-888-232-3299), or via the CDC's internet site at http://www.cdc.gov.

TRAFFIC SAFETY AND ROAD CONDITIONS: While in a foreign country, U.S. citizens may encounter road conditions that differ significantly from those in the United States. The information below concerning the Kyrgyz Republic is provided for general reference only, and may not be totally accurate in a particular location or circumstance.

Safety of public transportation: Poor
Urban road conditions/maintenance: Poor
Rural road conditions/maintenance: Poor
Availability of roadside assistance: Poor

Most of the Kyrgyz Republic's road infrastructure consists of two-lane roads, all of which are in various states of disrepair. Many local drivers tend to disobey fundamental traffic laws – such as stopping at a red light. As a result, driving can be very dangerous. Accidents involving severe injury and/or death are not uncommon.

Drivers must exercise particular caution to avoid uneven pavement, potholes and open drains and manholes. Night driving should be avoided, as roads are inadequately lit. In winter, roads are seldom plowed and ice and snow make the poor driving conditions even more hazardous. Pedestrians routinely walk in the road necessitating even greater caution for drivers.

Mountain roads in the Kyrgyz Republic are often narrow and tortuous, and may close without notice. Guardrails and barriers preventing falling rocks are often missing. The Bishkek-Osh road is

316

currently undergoing extensive renovation along much of its length and construction-related activity can create additional hazards and delays.

The Kyrgyz Republic does not have a roadside assistance infrastructure. Towing companies do not exist. Although mechanics are available in cities there is little organized oversight or certification of their practices or abilities. Rest areas are infrequent and very primitive. Service stations are generally available in and near cities, but the fuel they provide may be adulterated or of poor quality. Generally, speed limits are 60 km per hour in the cities and 90 km per hour in rural areas. Kyrgyz law mandates that all automobile passengers wear seat belts and that motorcycle riders wear helmets. International driving permits are recognized in the Kyrgyz Republic.

Drivers may face harassment by traffic police, who have been known to demand arbitrary "fines" for purported infractions. The Kyrgyz Republic has a "zero tolerance" policy for driving under the influence of alcohol.

Public transportation in the Kyrgyz Republic is limited to buses and taxis. Travelers should be particularly careful when using public transportation. Buses tend to be very crowded and can be unsafe and unreliable. Taxis too can be unsafe and dangerous. Due to the danger of theft or assault, travelers should avoid entering a cab that already contains passengers. Taxis are seldom metered, and travelers should negotiate a fare prior to entering a cab and be aware that cab drivers often try to charge foreigners a high fare. Drivers of vehicles that are not taxis are often willing to drive people for fares, however, U.S. Citizens should avoid using all of these "private taxis" and unmarked taxis.

For additional general information about road safety, including links to foreign government sites, see the Department of State, Bureau of Consular Affairs home page at http://travel.state.gov/road_safety.html. For specific information concerning Kyrgyz Republic driver's permits, vehicle inspection, road tax and mandatory insurance, contact the Kyrgyz Ministry of Transportation through the Kyrgyz Embassy in Washington, DC at 1732 Wisconsin Ave., N.W., Washington, DC 20007, telephone (202)338-5141, fax: (202) 338-5139, or on the Internet at http://www.kyrgyzstan.org.

AVIATION SAFETY OVERSIGHT: As there is no direct commercial air service by local carriers at present, or economic authority to operate such service, between the U.S. And the Kyrgyz Republic, the U.S. Federal Aviation Administration (FAA) has not assessed the Kyrgyz Republic's civil aviation authority for compliance with international aviation safety standards.

For further information, travelers may contact the Department of Transportation within the U.S. At 1-800-322-7873, or visit the FAA's internet web site at http://www.faa.gov/avr/iasa/. The U.S. Department of Defense (DOD) separately assesses some foreign air carriers for suitability as official providers of air services. For information regarding the DOD policy on specific carriers, travelers may contact DOD at (618) 229-4801.

CUSTOMS REGULATIONS: Kyrgyz customs authorities may enforce strict regulations concerning temporary importation into or export from the Kyrgyz Republic of items such as antiquities or hunting trophies. It is advisable to contact the Embassy of the Kyrgyz Republic in Washington for specific information at 1732 Wisconsin Ave., N.W., Washington, DC 20007, telephone (202)338-5141, fax: (202) 338-5139, or on the Internet at http://www.kyrgyzstan.org.

CRIMINAL PENALTIES: While in a foreign country, a U.S. citizen is subject to the country's laws and regulations, which sometimes differ significantly from those in the united states and may not afford the protections available to the individual under U.S. law. Penalties for breaking the law can be more severe than in the united states for similar offenses. Persons violating the Kyrgyz Republic's laws, even unknowingly, may be expelled, arrested or imprisoned. Penalties for possession, use, or trafficking in illegal drugs in the Kyrgyz Republic are strict and convicted offenders can expect jail sentences and heavy fines.

Hunting in the Kyrgyz Republic without proper licenses is illegal. Foreign hunters who do not have official permission to hunt or take trophies out of the country may face criminal and civil charges.

CONSULAR ACCESS: U.S. citizens are encouraged to carry a copy of their U.S. passport with them at all times, so that, if questioned by local officials, proof of identity and citizenship are readily available. To this end, the American Citizen Services Unit of the Consular Section at U.S. Embassy Bishkek provides free-of-charge certified photocopies of the passports of U.S. citizens who register with the Consular Section. For information on how to take advantage of this service, please refer to the paragraph on Registration below.

In accordance with the Vienna Convention on Consular Relations and certain bilateral treaties, a consular officer from the U.S. Embassy must be given access to any U.S. citizen arrested in the Kyrgyz Republic. U.S. citizens who are arrested or detained should ask for the U.S. Embassy to be contacted immediately.

SPECIAL CIRCUMSTANCES: The Kyrgyz Republic is a cash-only economy. The banking system is not well developed and there are no automated teller machines. One or two hotels or banks may, on occasion, accept travelers checks or credit cards but fees can be quite high for travelers checks, as much as 20 percent.

DISASTER PREPAREDNESS: The Kyrgyz Republic is an earthquake-prone country. General information about natural disaster preparedness is available via the internet from the U.S. Federal Emergency Management Agency (FEMA) at http://www.fema.gov.

CHILDREN'S ISSUES: For information on international adoption of children and international parental child abduction please refer to our Internet site at http://travel.state.gov/children's_issues.html or telephone (202) 736-7000.

REGISTRATION/EMBASSY
LOCATION: Americans living or visiting the Kyrgyz Republic are encouraged to register at the U.S. Embassy and obtain updated information on travel and security in the Kyrgyz Republic. The U.S. Embassy in Bishkek is located at 171 Prospect Mira, 720016 Bishkek, Kyrgyz Republic. The phone number is 996-312-551-241, fax 996-312-551-264.

TAJIKISTAN

COUNTRY DESCRIPTION: Tajikistan, an independent country in Central Asia, has been undergoing profound political and economic changes since the break-up of the Soviet Union. Tourist facilities are undeveloped, and many goods and services taken for granted in other countries are unavailable. The capital is Dushanbe. After the civil war in 1992, sporadic fighting continued, largely in remote areas. Comprehensive peace accords were signed in June 1997, though some armed clashes involving renegade forces took place subsequently.

ENTRY REQUIREMENTS: A passport and visa are required to enter Tajikistan. Travelers must produce the visa to register at hotels. Failure to produce a valid visa may cause a traveler to leave the country immediately. Visas issued by the Russian embassies and consulates are no longer valid for travel to Tajikistan. Tajik visas can be obtained at Tajik embassies or consulates abroad. Tajik visas can be obtained at the Dushanbe airport upon arrival only through prior arrangement with the Ministry of Foreign Affairs of Tajikistan. Visitors to Tajikistan require an official invitation to Tajikistan from a sponsoring organization or individual. Entry into Tajikistan at points along the Gorno-Badakhshan border requires special authorization in advance in addition to a valid Tajik visa.

Tajik authorities advise that requests for visas need to be submitted by sponsoring organizations or individuals to the Ministry of Foreign Affairs or OVIR (Department of Visas and Registration) at least three weeks in advance of the planned travel. Travelers who would like their visas to be extended need to apply for extension in advance through the Ministry of Foreign Affairs (official travelers) or OVIR (tourist or commercial travlers). Travelers staying in Tajikistan three days or longer must obtain registration stamps at the Ministry of Foreign Affairs or OVIR. The registering agency also depends on whether the purpose of the visit to Tajikistan is for official or personal travel.

For further information on entry requirements, please contact the Mission of the Republic of Tajikistan to the United Nations, 136 East 67th

318

St., New York, NY 10021; telephone (212) 472-76-45.

Note: To ensure admission to another country when leaving Tajikistan, travelers should obtain the appropriate double entry Russian, Kazakh or Uzbek visas before departure from Tajikistan.

In an effort to prevent international child abduction, many governments have initiated procedures at entry/exit points. These often include requiring documentary evidence of relationship and permission for the child's travel from the parent(s) or legal guardian not present. Having such documentation on hand, even if not required, may facilitate entry/departure.

SAFETY AND SECURITY: Tajikistan has suffered from severe security problems since gaining independence. Instability in Afghanistan has adversely affected the security situation in the Central Asian countries sharing a border, including Tajikistan. It is currently unclear how anti-terrorist operations in Afghanistan have affected the risk of future terrorist actions in Tajikistan. In addition, organized crime continues to be a serious problem in the capital city of Dushanbe and its environs, and security forces have a strong presence in Dushanbe and areas to the south.

The Islamic Movement of Uzbekistan (IMU) a foreign terrorist organization which has targeted Americans in the past, has been affected by the U.S. military actions in Afghanistan due to their ties to Al-Qaida and the Taliban. Their current operational capabilities remain unclear. In 1999 and 2000, IMU fighters used Tajik territory to stage cross-border attacks into the Kyrgyz Republic and Uzbekistan, taking American, Japanese, and Kyrgyz citizens hostage in the process.

Sporadic violence does occur in Tajikistan. The violence is largely the result of fighting between rival clan-based heavily armed factions competing for control of markets and narcotics trafficking. Past incidents have included several spontaneous shootouts between factions in public marketplaces (particularly the Green Market), a marketplace bombing in April 2001, and a suicide bombing in September 2001. Though such incidents have not specifically targeted Americans, innocent bystanders have been injured or killed during these attacks. Criminal and terrorist groups in Tajikistan do not distinguish between civilian and official targets, and for this reason, U.S. travelers should avoid demonstrations, places where military personnel congregate, and crowds. Americans should be aware that the danger increases greatly after dark.

In addition, there have been clashes between government troops and criminal groups outside of Dushanbe. In summer 2001, the Tajik government conducted security operations in order to eliminate one such criminal group, which was responsible for the June 2001 hostage-taking of foreign aid workers (including an American citizen) in the Karategin Valley. This operation resulted in the deaths or arrests of many of the group's members. Other Tajik security initiatives include a campaign to disarm factional militias operating in Dushanbe.

Outside of Dushanbe, the situation has generally remained calm in the northern province of Sughd (formerly Leninabad) and in Gorno-Badakhshan in the east. However, the security situation in former opposition-held areas such as the Karategin Valley remains fluid. In the past, renegade groups in these areas have targeted foreigners for violence. U.S. citizens should check with the U.S. Embassy in Dushanbe for current information before traveling outside Dushanbe.

Security personnel may at times place foreign visitors under surveillance. Hotel rooms, telephones and fax machines may be monitored, and personal possessions in hotel rooms may be searched. Taking photographs of anything that could be perceived as being of military or security interest may result in problems with the authorities.

From time to time, the U.S. Embassy may suspend or otherwise restrict the travel of U.S. Embassy personnel to Tajikistan and within Tajikistan. The Department of State relocated U.S. Embassy operations from Dushanbe, Tajikistan to Almaty, Kazakhstan in 1998 due to instability in Tajikistan, threats against Americans and American interests worldwide, and the limited ability to secure the safety of U.S. Embassy personnel in Dushanbe. American diplomatic personnel currently reside in Almaty, Kazakhstan, and travel frequently to Tajikistan.

319

Note: U.S. citizens should check the Consular Information Sheets and current Travel Warnings or Public Announcements for nearby countries, including Afghanistan, Kazakhstan, the Kyrgyz Republic, Turkmenistan and Uzbekistan on a regular basis. The U.S. Embassy in each of those countries can provide up-to-date information about local crime and safety issues. Information about how to contact each Embassy directly is available on the Internet at the Consular Affairs home page, http://travel.state.gov, or by calling the U.S. Embassy in Dushanbe.

CRIME: Tajikistan is a country with a struggling economy and widespread unemployment. This has resulted in considerable street crime, in addition to the organized crime described in the above section on "Safety and Security." There have been a number of pickpocketings, muggings and armed robberies in the homes of persons perceived to have money, including foreigners. Travelers should not travel alone or on foot after dark.

The loss or theft abroad of a U.S. passport should be reported immediately to the nearest U.S. embassy or consulate. U.S. citizens may refer to the Department of State's pamphlet, *A Safe Trip Abroad*, for ways to promote a trouble-free journey. The pamphlet is available by mail from the Superintendent of Documents, U.S. Government Printing Office, Washington, D.C. 20402, via the Internet at http://www.access.gpo.gov/su_docs/, or via the Bureau of Consular Affairs home page at http://travel.state.gov.

MEDICAL FACILITIES: The medical infrastructure of Tajikistan is significantly below Western standards, with severe shortages of basic medical supplies, including disposable needles, anesthetics, and antibiotics. Many trained medical personnel left the country. Elderly travelers and those with pre-existing health problems may be at particular risk due to inadequate medical facilities.

MEDICAL INSURANCE: The Department of State strongly urges Americans to consult with their medical insurance company prior to traveling abroad to confirm whether their policy applies overseas and if it will cover emergency expenses such as a medical evacuation. U.S. medical insurance plans seldom cover health costs incurred outside the United States unless supplemental coverage is purchased. Further, U.S. Medicare and Medicaid programs do not provide payment for medical services outside the United States. However, many travel agents and private companies offer insurance plans that will cover health care expenses incurred overseas, including emergency services such as medical evacuations.

When making a decision regarding health insurance, Americans should consider that doctors and hospitals in Tajikistan require payment in cash before providing service and that a medical evacuation to the United States may cost well more than $50,000. Due to long distances and poor infrastructure, medical evacuations from Tajikistan may take as long as 24 hours. Uninsured travelers who require medical care overseas often face extreme difficulties. When consulting with your insurer prior to your trip, please ascertain whether payment will be made to the overseas healthcare provider or if you will be reimbursed later for expenses that you incur. Some insurance policies also include coverage for psychiatric treatment and for disposition of remains in the event of death.

Useful information on medical emergencies abroad, including overseas insurance programs, is provided in the Department of State's Bureau of Consular Affairs brochure, *Medical Information for Americans Traveling Abroad*, available via the Bureau of Consular Affairs home page, http://travel.state.gov, or autofax: (202) 647-3000.

OTHER HEALTH INFORMATION: Significant disease outbreaks are possible due to population shifts and the breakdown in immunization activity. There have been outbreaks of typhoid in the Dushanbe area and in the south, and the risk of cholera and water-borne illnesses is high. Throughout Central Asia, rates of infection of various forms of hepatitis and tuberculosis (including drug-resistant strains) are on the rise. Information on vaccinations and other health precautions may be obtained from the Centers for Disease Control and Prevention's hotline for international travelers at 1-877-FYI-TRIP (1-877-394-8747); fax 1-888-CDC-FAXX (1-888-232-3299), or via the CDC's Internet site at http://www.cdc.gov.

The government of Tajikistan requires visitors who remain in country for more than 90 days to present a medical certificate showing that they are HIV-free, or to submit to an HIV test in Tajikistan. This testing requirement is not currently being implemented, but enforcement could begin at any time. Because of the lack of medical supplies, submitting to an HIV test in Tajikistan could pose a health risk. HIV is a growing health threat in Tajikistan.

TRAFFIC SAFETY AND ROAD CONDITIONS: While in a foreign country, U.S. citizens may encounter road conditions that differ significantly from those in the United States. The information below concerning Tajikistan is provided for general reference only, and it may not be totally accurate in a particular location or circumstance.

Safety of Public Transportation: Poor
Urban Road Conditions/Maintenance: Fair
Rural Road Conditions/Maintenance: Poor
Availability of Roadside Assistance: Poor

Road travel outside of Dushanbe can be made difficult by checkpoints, where police or soldiers staffing the checkpoints are armed. They have been known to shoot if vehicles do not stop upon request. There are also checkpoints on the road east of Dushanbe, operated by independent armed groups. These independent groups have targeted foreigners in the past. For this reason, road travel to the east is strongly discouraged. Vehicles with Tajik license plates have frequently been refused permission to enter Uzbekistan. A change of vehicles at the Uzbek border may be required. Road travel should be undertaken only in daylight hours and on routes known to the traveler or a reliable escort.

For additional general information about road safety, including links to foreign government sites, please see the Department of State, Bureau of Consular Affairs home page at http://travel.state.gov/road_safety.html.
For specific information concerning Tajikistan driving permits, vehicle inspection, road tax and mandatory insurance, please contact the Permanent Mission of Tajikistan, 136 East 67th Street, New York, NY 10021, telephone (212) 472-7645.

AVIATION SAFETY OVERSIGHT: As there is no direct commercial air service by local carriers at present, nor economic authority to operate such service between the United States and Tajikistan,

the U.S. Federal Aviation Administration (FAA) has not assessed Tajikistan's Civil Aviation Authority for compliance with international aviation safety standards.

For further information, travelers may contact the Department of Transportation within the United States at telephone 1-800-322-7873, or visit the FAA's Internet web site at http://www.faa.gov/avr/iasa/. The U.S. Department of Defense (DOD) separately assesses some foreign air carriers for suitability as official providers of air services. For information regarding the DOD policy on specific carriers, travelers may contact the DOD at telephone (618) 229-4801.

CUSTOMS REGULATIONS: Tajik customs authorities may subject all items that are imported into or exported from Tajikistan to a high level of scrutiny. The Government of Tajikistan may enforce strict customs regulations against those who import and export goods. There are currency restrictions. Travelers must fill out a Customs Declaration Form upon arrival. Travelers retain the form until departure to demonstrate that they are not taking more money out of Tajikistan than was brought into the country. Please contact the U.S.- Tajikistan Chamber of Commerce, 1250 24th St., N.W., Suite 350, Washington, D.C. 20037, telephone (202) 776-7770 or the U.S.- Tajikistan Chamber of Commerce, 1250 24th St., N.W. Suite 350, Washington D.C. 20037, telephone (202) 776-7770, for specific information about customs requirements.

CRIMINAL PENALITIES: While in a foreign country, a U.S. citizen is subject to that country's laws and regulations, which sometimes differ significantly from those in the United States and may not afford the protections available to the individual under U.S. law. Penalties for breaking the law can be more severe than in the United States for similar offenses. Persons who violate Tajikistan's laws, even unknowingly, may be expelled, arrested or imprisoned. Penalties for possession, use or trafficking in illegal drugs in Tajikistan are strict, and convicted offenders can expect jail sentences and heavy fines.

CONSULAR ACCESS: Travelers to Tajikistan are subject to frequent document inspections. U.S. citizens are strongly encouraged to carry a copy of their U.S. passports and Tajik visas at all times. In accordance with the Vienna Convention on Consular Relations and certain bilateral agreements, local authorities must grant a United States Consular officer access to any U.S. citizen who is arrested. U.S. citizens who are arrested or detained should ask to contact the U.S. Embassy immediately.

SPECIAL CIRCUMSTANCES: Travel to, from, and within Tajikistan is difficult and unreliable. Flights may be canceled or substantially delayed. Neighboring countries may unilaterally close borders. Commercial charter flights are frequently overloaded with merchandise. International train connections are dangerous because of criminals reportedly operating onboard.

Tajikistan is a cash-only economy. International banking services are not available. Credit cards and traveler's checks are not accepted. Travel with large amounts of cash can be dangerous. Tajikistan's national currency is the Somoni, which is convertible. Please contact the U.S.-Tajikistan Chamber of Commerce, 1250 24th St., N.W. Suite 350, Washington D.C. 20037, telephone (202) 776-7770, for information on currency restrictions.

DISASTER PREPAREDNESS: Tajikistan is an earthquake-prone country. General information about natural disaster preparedness is available via the Internet from the U.S. Federal Emergency Management Agency (FEMA) at http://www.fema.gov/.

CHILDREN'S ISSUES: For information on international adoption of children and international parental child abduction, please refer to our Internet site at http://travel.state.gov/children's_issues.html or telephone (202) 736-7000.

REGISTRATION/EMBASSY LOCATIONS: U.S. citizens are encouraged to register with the Consular Section of the U.S. Embassy in Dushanbe. The American Embassy can provide updated information on travel and security within Tajikistan. The U.S. Embassy is located at 10 Pavola Street, Dushanbe, telephone (24-hour operator) 011 (992)(372) 21-03-48/52 or 24-15-60 fax 011 (992)(372) 21-03-62. Embassy personnel are resident in Almaty, Kazakhstan, and their presence in Dushanbe is not continuous. Consular services for Tajikistan are handled in coordination with the U.S. Embassy in Almaty, Kazakhstan. The telephone number for the American Embassy in Almaty is 7-3272-63-39-21; 50-76-27. U.S. citizens are reminded that resources limit the availability of most non-emergency and emergency consular services.

TAJIKISTAN

This Travel Warning is being revised to update security information. The overall security situation in Tajikistan has improved. Nevertheless, the presence of terrorist groups allied with Al-Qaida and limitations on the Embassy's ability to provide consular services still pose risks to travelers. This Travel Warning supersedes the Travel Warning for Tajikistan dated September 25, 2001.

The Department of State warns U.S. citizens of the potential danger of travel to Tajikistan. The security situation has improved since the conclusion of the civil war in 1997. However, incidents of hostage-taking and assassination occurred in recent years and threats against Americans, including the threat of kidnapping, continue. The Islamic Movement of Uzbekistan (IMU), a foreign terrorist organization, fought alongside Al-Qaida and the Taliban in Afghanistan against U.S. military forces. Following U.S. military actions, the IMU's operational capabilities were diminished, but the threat of terrorist actions by the IMU and its sympathizers still exists. Americans should particularly avoid the vicinity of Kofarhihon and areas along the borders with Afghanistan and the Kyrgyz Republic, the Karategin Valley, and Tavildara District. From time to time, the U.S. Embassy restricts the travel of U.S. Embassy personnel to certain parts of Tajikistan. U.S. citizens should check with the U.S. Embassy in Dushanbe before traveling outside Dushanbe.

The Department of State relocated Embassy operations from Dushanbe, Tajikistan, to Almaty, Kazakhstan, in 1998 due to threats to Americans and American interests worldwide, instability in Tajikistan at the time, and the limited ability to secure the safety of U.S. Embassy personnel in the Embassy facility in Dushanbe. Although still officially resident in Almaty, Embassy staff work primarily out of Dushanbe at an interim Embassy facility. U.S. citizens are reminded that resources and security considerations limit the availablity of most consular services, including those of an emergency nature.

Departure options from Tajikistan may be limited in an emergency. U.S. citizens, their family members and their dependents can maximize departure options by obtaining extended visas for travel to countries with direct flight or reliable land connections to Tajikistan. These include Kazakhstan, Uzbekistan, Kyrgyz Republic, Russia, and India, for which visas in advance are required. Other destinations, via weekly flight only are Turkey and Germany, which do not require visas in advance. Please note, however, that in certain emergency situations, flights may be suspended.

U.S. citizens are strongly advised to register and obtain updated security information at the American Embassy in Dushanbe, Tajikistan. Contact information in Dushanbe (switchboard staffed 24 hours per day): 992-372-21-03-48; 24-15-60; 51-00-28. Consular services for Tajikistan are handled in coordination with the U.S. Embassy in Almaty, Kazakhstan. The telephone number for the American Embassy in Almaty is 7-3272-63-39-21; 50-76-27.
For further information on Tajikistan, please consult the Department of State's Consular Information Sheet on Tajikistan and the Worldwide Caution Public Announcement which are located on the Department's Internet web site at http://travel.state.gov.

TURKMENISTAN

COUNTRY DESCRIPTION: Turkmenistan is a Central Asian nation roughly the size of California. It shares borders with Kazakhstan, Uzbekistan, Afghanistan and Iran. Turkmenistan gained its independence in 1991 during the dissolution of the Soviet Union. Primarily a desert country, it has a small population of around 5 million people. Tourist facilities, especially outside of the capital city of Ashgabat, are not highly developed. Many of the goods and services taken for granted in North American and Western European countries are not yet available. Travel within the country can be difficult due to limited infrastructure and government imposed internal travel restrictions.

ENTRY/EXIT REQUIREMENTS: American citizens must have a valid passport and visa to enter and exit Turkmenistan. To apply for a visa, all U.S. citizens must complete an application and have a letter of invitation approved by the Ministry of Foreign Affairs (MFA) in Ashgabat. The letter of invitation on behalf of an American citizen must be submitted to the MFA by an individual or organization in Turkmenistan. The MFA requires at least ten working days for approval. The U.S. Embassy in Ashgabat does not issue letters of invitation to citizens interested in private travel to Turkmenistan. Applications for a Turkmen visa can be submitted to the Turkmen Embassy in Washington, D.C. or directly to the MFA in Ashgabat. Recent travelers to Turkmenistan have found it difficult to secure visa issuance from the Embassy of Turkmenistan in Washington, D.C. A traveler with a stamped and approved invitation letter from the MFA may also obtain a visa at the Ashgabat Airport upon arrival in Turkmenistan.

The price for the visa will vary according to the intended length of stay. For an additional charge the visa can be extended at the MFA in Ashgabat from its initial validity for any period of time up to one year. Any traveler arriving without a visa or without the needed documents to obtain a visa will be denied entry and may be held at the airport or border until the traveler has secured transportation out of Turkmenistan. Travelers departing Turkmenistan must have a valid visa or they will be denied exit until they extend the validity of the visa. In addition, U.S. citizens traveling in Turkmenistan should be aware that they may require special permission from the MFA to travel to some areas of the country that have been restricted by the Government of Turkmenistan.

There are local Turkmen registration requirements. Americans who plan to stay more than three working days in Turkmenistan must register with the Office of Visas and Registration (OVIR). OVIR offices are located in all of Turkmenistan's five major cities: Ashgabat, Dashoguz, Mary, Turkmenabat and Turkmenbashi. Visitors who do not register may have to pay fines upon departure. Additionally, according to a decree issued December 10, 2002, by Ashgabat city authorities, foreign guests in Ashgabat for temporary stays are required to stay in hotels. Unless they are legally resident in Turkmenistan, foreigners may not rent or buy private residences and may not stay at the private residences of Turkmen citizens in Ashgabat. Similar decrees have not been issued for other areas in Turkmenistan.

According to the MFA, all foreigners staying in Turkmenistan more than 3 months must be tested for HIV. Testing should be performed upon arrival in Turkmenistan. Before extending a visa, the MFA requires a certificate from the Blood Transfusion Center located on 53 Gerogly Street, Ashgabat. U.S. test results are not accepted. Previous travelers have reported sporadic enforcement of this regulation.

For complete information concerning entry and exit requirements, as well as internal travel restrictions, U.S. citizens should contact the Embassy of Turkmenistan at 2207 Massachusetts Ave. NW, Washington, D.C. 20008, telephone (202) 588-1500. The Embassy may also be reached at its homepage on the Internet: http://www.turkmenistanembassy.org.

In an effort to prevent international child abduction, many governments have initiated procedures at entry/exit points. These often include requiring documentary evidence of relationship and permission for the child's travel from the parent(s) or legal guardian not present. Having such documentation on hand, even if not required, may facilitate entry/departure.

SAFETY AND SECURITY: Turkmenistan's proximity to regions of past and current instability should be weighed carefully by travelers to the country. The Government of Turkmenistan has designated many areas throughout the country as "restricted zones," particularly the border areas next to Iran, Uzbekistan and Afghanistan. Other areas have also been designated as "restricted zones," including the city of Dashoguz and areas of the Caspian coast. Travel to these areas is forbidden without special permission from the Government of Turkmenistan. Turkmen Air, the national airline, will not sell a ticket to any traveler who intends to travel to a "restricted zone" without proof of permission from the Government. Travelers who wish to visit a "restricted zone" must have a valid passport and visa and must

apply to the Ministry of Foreign Affairs. There is a minimum processing time of 10 working days.

The November 25, 2002, attack on the motorcade of the President of Turkmenistan has led to a heightened state of security in which police have conducted widespread questioning, home searches, and car searches. Security personnel have set up checkpoints on major roads. Foreigners have sometimes been singled out for harassment.

For additional regional security information concerning Central Asia, U.S. citizens should check the Consular Information Sheets and current Travel Warnings or Public Announcements for nearby countries, including Kazakhstan, the Kyrgyz Republic, Tajikistan, and Uzbekistan on a regular basis. The U.S. Embassy in each of these countries can provide up-to-date information about local crime and safety issues. Information about how to contact each Embassy directly is available on the Internet at the Consular Affairs home page, http://www.travel.state.gov, or by calling the U.S. Embassy in Ashgabat. For the latest security information, Americans traveling abroad should regularly monitor the Department's Internet web site at http://travel.state.gov where the current Worldwide Caution Public Announcement, Travel Warnings and Public Announcements can be found.

CRIME: Turkmenistan has a low rate of violent crime, but ordinary street crime is common. Foreign visitors, including American citizens, present an attractive target for criminals. Travelers should exercise the same common sense, good judgment and caution in their activities as they would in any major U.S. city. There is a high incidence of petty theft and pickpockets in crowded public places, especially in the local bazaars. Visitors should take appropriate measures to safeguard their passports and valuables in such areas.

The U.S. Embassy strongly recommends that Americans avoid carrying large sums of money on the street. Travelers, especially women, should not take public transportation or walk alone, after dark. Taxi service should be used with caution. Unregistered taxis should be avoided. Visitors in bars and restaurants, particularly men, should be aware of women who may attempt to steal money and valuables. It is not advisable to go alone to unpopulated locations with an unknown person. The U.S. Embassy has received reports of police asking to view passports, and refusing to return the passports until the owner has paid a "fine."

The loss or theft abroad of a U.S. passport should be reported immediately to the local police and the nearest U.S. Embassy or Consulate. If you are the victim of a crime while overseas, in addition to reporting to local police, please contact the nearest U.S. Embassy or Consulate for assistance. The Embassy/Consulate staff can, for example, assist you to find appropriate medical care, to contact family members or friends and explain how funds could be transferred. Although the investigation and prosecution of the crime is solely the responsibility of local authorities, consular officers can help you to understand the local criminal justice process and to find an attorney if needed.

Additional information on the region can be found in the brochure, "*Tips for Travelers to Russia and the New Independent States.*"

U.S. citizens may refer to the Department of State's pamphlet, "*A Safe Trip Abroad,*" for ways to promote a trouble-free journey. The pamphlet is available by mail from the Superintendent of Documents, U.S. Government Printing Office, Washington, D.C. 20402, via the Internet at http://www.access.gpo.gov/su_docs, or via the Bureau of Consular Affairs home page at http://travel.state.gov.

MEDICAL FACILITIES: Medical care in Turkmenistan is limited and well below North American and Western European standards. The U.S. Embassy maintains a list of public hospitals and English-speaking physicians in the country. Basic medical supplies, including disposable needles, anesthetics, and antibiotics are often in short supply. Two clinics can conduct consultations and/or operations performed by foreign (German and Turkish) specialists. Elderly travelers and those with pre-existing health problems may be at risk due to inadequate medical facilities. Most resident American citizens travel to Western Europe for treatment of any serious medical condition. Such travel can be extremely expensive if undertaken under emergency conditions. Travelers requiring prescription medications should bring sufficient supplies of all necessary medications.

MEDICAL INSURANCE: The Department of State strongly urges Americans to consult with their medical insurance company prior to traveling abroad to confirm whether their policy applies overseas and whether it will cover emergency expenses such as a medical evacuation. U.S. medical insurance plans seldom cover health costs incurred outside the United States unless supplemental coverage is purchased. Further, U.S. Medicare and Medicaid programs do not provide payment for medical services outside the United States. However, many travel agents and private companies offer insurance plans that will cover health care expenses incurred overseas including emergency services such as medical evacuations.

When making a decision regarding health insurance, Americans should consider that many foreign doctors and hospitals require payment in cash before providing service and that a medical evacuation to the U.S. may cost more than $50,000. Uninsured travelers who require medical care overseas often face extreme difficulties. When consulting with your insurer before your trip, ascertain whether payment will be made to the overseas healthcare provider or whether you will be reimbursed later for expenses you incur. Some insurance policies also include coverage for psychiatric treatment and for disposition of remains in the event of death. Useful information on medical emergencies abroad, including overseas insurance programs, is provided in the Department of State's Bureau of Consular Affairs brochure, "*Medical Information for Americans Traveling Abroad,*" available via the Bureau of Consular Affairs home page at http://www.travel.state.gov or Autofax: (202) 647-3000.

OTHER HEALTH INFORMATION: The Embassy recommends that travelers ensure that their hepatitis, diphtheria, and typhoid fever vaccinations are current. Information on vaccinations and other health precautions, such as safe food and water precautions and insect bite protection, may be obtained from the Centers for Disease Control and Prevention's hotline for international travelers at 1-877-FYI-TRIP (1-877-394-8747); fax 1-888-CDC-FAXX (1-888-232-3299), or via the CDC's Internet site at http://www.cdc.gov/travel. For information about outbreaks of infectious diseases abroad consult the

World Health Organization's website at http://www.who.int/en. Further health information for travelers is available at http://www.who.int/ith.

TRAFFIC SAFETY AND ROAD CONDITIONS: While in a foreign country, U.S. citizens may encounter road conditions that differ significantly from those in the United States. The information below concerning Turkmenistan is provided for general reference only, and may not be totally accurate in a particular location or circumstance:

Safety of public transportation: Fair
Urban road conditions/maintenance: Fair
Rural road conditions/maintenance: Poor
Availability of roadside/ambulance assistance: Poor

Road conditions in Turkmenistan can make driving difficult and sometimes dangerous. Most roads outside of major cities are narrow, riddled with potholes, unlit at night, and without proper road signs. Driving at night on these roads should be avoided. City roads are better in comparison to rural routes but may be hazardous due to potholes, uncovered manholes and poor lighting. Many city streets lack designated crosswalks, forcing pedestrians to cross against traffic and creating dangerous conditions. Traffic accidents involving serious injury to drivers, passengers, and pedestrians are not uncommon.

In general, visitors should use caution when driving in Turkmenistan and be prepared for surprises and behavior not normally exhibited in the United States. Drivers may pay little attention to lanes and other road markings, with weaving and sudden lane changes a common occurrence (usually without use of the turn signal). Drivers will often encounter cars going the wrong way on one-way streets or divided highways. Cars also frequently make left-turns from the right lane and vice-versa.

Roadside assistance does not exist in Turkmenistan, where vast stretches of highway are often unmarked. Police checkpoints (where cars are required to stop and register) are a common feature on major routes between cities. The Embassy in Ashgabat has received reports that police stationed at checkpoints may arbitrarily fine motorists. Turkmen law requires that traffic fines

be paid within twelve hours. If a fine is not paid within that period, the amount may double every 12 hours up to 72 hours, after which the vehicle may be seized.

Travelers who wish to drive in Turkmenistan must have a valid international driving permit. Foreigners who plan to reside in Turkmenistan must apply for a Turkmen Driver's License with the Road Police Department of the Ministry of Internal Affairs of Turkmenistan. American citizens, who want more specific information about driving in Turkmenistan should contact the Embassy of Turkmenistan at 2207 Massachusetts Ave. NW, Washington, D.C. 20008, telephone (202) 588-1500. Local traffic customs will appear unfamiliar to American drivers.

For additional general information about road safety, including links to foreign government sites, see the Department of State, Bureau of Consular Affairs home page at http://travel.state.gov/road_safety.html. For specific information concerning Turkmenistan driving permits, vehicle inspection, road tax and mandatory insurance, contact the Turkmenistan national tourist organization offices at its Permanent Mission in New York. The address is: 136 East 67th Street, NY, NY 10021. The phone number is 1-212-472-5921.

AVIATION SAFETY OVERSIGHT: As there is no direct commercial service at present between the United States and Turkmenistan, nor economic authority to operate such service, the U.S. Federal Aviation Administration (FAA) has not assessed the Turkmenistan Civil Aviation Authority for compliance with international aviation standards for oversight of Turkmenistan's air carrier operations. Travelers may experience significant delays, unexpected re-routing and sudden cancellations of flights, including those of Turkmen Air (Turkmenhowayollary), the Turkmen national airline.

For further information, travelers may contact the Department of Transportation within the U.S. at 1-800-322-7873, or visit the FAA's Internet website at http://www.intl.faa.gov. The U.S. Department of Defense (DOD) separately assesses some foreign air carriers for suitability as official providers of air services. For information regarding DOD policy on specific air carriers, travelers may contact the DOD at tel. (618) 229-4801

CUSTOMS REGULATIONS: Turkmenistan customs authorities may enforce strict regulations concerning temporary importation into or export from Turkmenistan of items such as carpets, jewelry, musical instruments, pieces of art, archaeological artifacts, antiques, etc. It is advisable to contact the Embassy of Turkmenistan in Washington for specific information regarding customs requirements. Travelers who want to take carpets out of Turkmenistan must obtain a certificate from the Carpet Museum in central Ashgabat indicating that the carpet is not of historical value. In addition, buyers may have to pay a tax calculated on the size of the carpet.

CRIMINAL PENALTIES: While in a foreign country, a U.S. citizen is subject to that country's laws and regulations, which sometimes differ significantly from those in the United States and may not afford the protections available to the individual under U.S. law. Penalties for breaking the law can be more severe than in the United States for similar offenses. Persons violating Turkmenistan laws, even unknowingly, may be expelled, arrested or imprisoned. Penalties for possession, use or trafficking in illegal drugs in Turkmenistan are strict and convicted offenders can expect jail sentences and heavy fines.

CONSULAR ACCESS: U.S. citizens are encouraged to carry a copy of their U.S. passports and Turkmeni visas with them at all times, so that, if questioned by local officials, proof of identity and U.S. citizenship are readily available. In the aftermath of the November 25, 2002, attack against the president's motorcade, the government did not notify U.S. government officials when American citizens were detained or arrested, and U.S. government access to these Americans was problematic.

SPECIAL CIRCUMSTANCES: Turkmenistan is a cash-only economy. However, several new hotels accept credit cards. Vnesheconombank and the National Bank of Pakistan cash traveler's checks and personal checks for a fee, although cashing a personal check is a lengthy process that could require up to two months. Vnesheconombank also accepts Visa for cash advances, for a fee. The Turkmen-Russian Karz Bank, right next to the U.S. Embassy, has a Western Union office.

Although the Manat is the official currency, U.S. dollars are widely accepted and are required in payment for certain goods and services. Travelers may wish to bring sufficient U.S. currency to exchange into Manat to cover expenses not payable in U.S. Dollars. Old U.S. dollar bills (issued before 1990) and/or those in poor condition (with tears, writing or stamps) are not acceptable forms of currency in Turkmenistan. Banks frequently do not have small bills for change. More detailed information is available at the U.S. Embassy in Ashgabat.

DISASTER PREPAREDNESS: Turkmenistan is an earthquake-prone country. Building practices within Turkmenistan do not generally meet U.S. seismic standards. In addition, local authorities do not have sufficient resources to respond to a large-scale disaster. American citizens traveling to Turkmenistan are encouraged to register with the U.S. Embassy Consular Section. Registration can assist the Embassy in quickly contacting American citizens during an emergency. General information about natural disaster preparedness is available via the Internet from the U.S. Federal Emergency Management Agency (FEMA) at http://www.fema.gov.

CHILDREN'S ISSUES: For information on international adoption of children and international parental child abduction issues, please refer to our Internet site at http://www.travel.state.gov/children's issues.html or telephone: (202) 736-7000. There is no specific legislation in Turkmenistan that governs the adoption of a Turkmen citizen by a foreigner. Accordingly, adoption procedures vary widely. American citizens should expect long bureaucratic delays during the adoption process.

REGISTRATION/EMBASSY AND CONSULATE LOCATIONS: Americans living in or visiting Turkmenistan are encouraged to register at the Consular Section of the U.S. Embassy in Ashgabat to obtain updated information on travel and security within Turkmenistan. Registration with the Embassy can assure quick communication during an emergency and help replacement of a lost and/or stolen passport. The U.S. Embassy is located at 9

Pushkin Street, off Magtymguly Street, tel. (993-12) 35-00-45; fax (993-12) 39-26-14. The Consular Section can also be contacted by e-mail at: consularashgab@state.gov. The Embassy's Internet address is http://www.usemb-ashgabat.rpo.at/

UKRAINE

COUNTRY DESCRIPTION: Ukraine is a nation undergoing profound political and economic change as it moves towards a market economy and integrates into Western institutions. In recent years, availability of goods and services has increased, and facilities for travelers have improved. Nevertheless, the availability of travel and tourist services remains uneven throughout the country, and Ukraine still lacks the abundance of many of the goods and services taken for granted in other countries. Travel within Ukraine is unrestricted; however, travelers should be prepared to show their documents to police upon demand.

ENTRY REQUIREMENTS: A passport valid for sixth months beyond the date of travel is required. In addition, all travelers to Ukraine must have a valid single - or multiple entry visa before arriving in the country. A visa may be obtained from the Consular Office of the Embassy of Ukraine, in Washington, D.C. or from Consulates General in New York or Chicago. No invitation letter is necessary for EU, Canadian and U.S. citizens for business, official, cultural, sporting, and private visas. However, to receive a tourist visa, you have to submit one of the following: a letter of invitation from a Ukrainian or American tourist agency, confirmation from a hotel, an itinerary, or copies of tickets with valid dates.

IF YOU LIVE IN ONE OF THESE STATES: Alabama, Ohio, Alaska, Oklahoma, Arizona, Oregon, Arkansas, South Carolina, California, Tennessee, Colorado, Texas, Delaware, Utah, District of Columbia, Virginia, Florida, Washington, Georgia, West Virginia, Hawaii, Wyoming, Idaho, Kentucky, Louisiana, Maryland, Mississippi, Missouri, Montana, Nevada, New Mexico, North Carolina

APPLY FOR YOUR VISA AT THE: Embassy of Ukraine,
3350 M Street, NW, Washington, D.C. 20007
Tel. (202) 333-0606
Fax (202) 333-0817
web site: http://www.ukremb.com
Connecticut, Maine, Massachusetts, New Hampshire, New Jersey, New York, Pennsylvania, Rhode Island, Vermont

Consulate General of Ukraine
240 East 49th Street
New York, NY 10017
Tel. 212-371-5690
Fax: 212-371-5547
web site: http://www.brama.com/ua-consulate
Illinois, Indiana, Iowa, Kansas, Michigan, Minnesota, Nebraska, North Dakota, South Dakota, Wisconsin

Consulate General of Ukraine
10 East Huron St.,
Chicago, IL, 60611
Tel. 312-642 4388
fax: 312-642 4385
web site: http://www.ukrchicago.com

U.S. citizens who stay in Ukraine for less than six months on a private, tourist, or business visa, do not need to register with local authorities. Once inside Ukraine, it is possible to get an extension of stay, over and beyond the validity of the visa, for up to six months, from the Ministry of Interior's Office of Visas and Registration (OVIR). However, the extension is only valid for continued presence in the country. It is not possible to depart Ukraine and return on the extension.

The Government of Ukraine does not issue visas at the point of entry into Ukraine. All visitors without a valid entry visa will be turned back to the United States or will have to travel to another European country to obtain a visa. Please check your visa carefully upon receipt. Each traveler is responsible for understanding the type of visa issued and the provisions of the visa. American citizens have been refused entry to Ukraine because they thought they possessed a multiple entry visa when actually their visa was valid for only a single entry. Or, Americans have tried to reenter Ukraine after using their single entry visa thinking they had unlimited travel for six months. In rare cases,

Americans attempted to enter Ukraine before their visa became valid. This is due to the fact that in Ukraine the date is spelled day-month-year, not month-day-year like in the United States. Thus, a visa issued on May 1, 2002 is valid from January 5, 2002 and NOT from May 1, 2002.

These travelers were turned away as well. The U.S. Embassy in Kiev is not able to assist travelers in these situations.

Travelers who intend to visit Russia from Ukraine must also have a Russian visa. The Russian Embassy in Ukraine is located at Prospekt Kutuzova 8, Kiev, tel. (380-44) 294-7797 or 294-6816.

Effective July 1, 2002 the Ukrainian Government introduced visa free travel for stays of up to eight days for American citizens arriving at the international airports of Simferopol and Odessa and at the international port of Odessa. Travel must originate abroad and end at these ports of entry without any other initial stop in Ukraine. Travelers must also depart Ukraine from the same port used at the time of arrival.

In an effort to prevent international child abduction, many governments have initiated procedures at entry/exit points. These often include requiring documentary evidence of a child's relationship to accompanying travelers and permission for the child's travel from the parent(s) or legal guardian not present. Having such documentation on hand, even if not required, may facilitate entry/departure.

DUAL NATIONALITY: Ukraine does not recognize dual nationality. American citizens entering Ukraine with a Ukrainian passport will be treated as Ukrainian citizens by the local authorities. This may include being required to perform mandatory national service. Also, Ukrainians who have immigrated to the United States without obtaining the proper exit visa from Ukrainian authorities may be subject to civil or criminal penalties and will be required to obtain an exit visa before returning to the United States. For additional information, please see the Consular Affairs home page on the Internet at http://travel.state.gov for our *Dual Nationality flyer* or the Embassy's web site at

http://usinfo,usemb.kiev/ua.amcitmiscdualnateng.html.

SAFETY AND SECURITY: Although most travelers encounter no problems with crime while in Ukraine, Western foreigners, perceived to be wealthier than most local residents, still remain a favorite target for criminals. Occasionally, Americans of African or Asian heritage also report incidents of racially motivated assaults or harassment. In cases involving the latter, complaints center on being frequently stopped on the street by both civilians and local law enforcement officials.

Over the past several years, we have also received a number of reports of harassment and intimidation directed against foreign businesspersons and interests. While these reports have become considerably less frequent in recent years, they have not ended. Reported incidents range from physical threats (possibly motivated by rival commercial interests tied to organized crime), to local government entities engaging in such practices as arbitrary termination or amendment of business licenses, dilution of corporate stock to diminish U.S. investor interest, delays of payment or delivery of goods, and arbitrary "inspections" by tax, safety or other officials. These activities appear designed to harm the business rather than be a genuine attempt at good governance.

As in all countries undergoing political and economic change, organized or spontaneous demonstrations can and do occur in Ukraine. When such protests occur, they most often occur in the capital or larger cities. We wish to remind American citizens though the intent for these events may be peaceful, even demonstrations intended to be peaceful can sometimes become confrontational and escalate into violence. Therefore, we urge American citizens to avoid demonstrations and protest gatherings and to exercise caution when near such gatherings.

CRIME: As stated earlier, most travelers do not encounter problems with crime while in Ukraine. Nonetheless, the country is undergoing a severe economic, political and social transformation, and income disparities have grown sharply. As a result, visitors perceived to be wealthier are targets for criminals. Americans stand out in Ukraine, and they are more likely to be targeted than in Western

European countries where incomes are higher and Americans may blend in better. Most street crime is relatively low level, but crimes involving small caliber firearms have been reported. Street crime ranges from wallet scams, simple pick-pocketing and purse snatching, to muggings, armed robbery, or drugging unsuspecting victims at nightspots and bars (where they are then robbed). Cases of assaults in apartment building corridors and stairwells, and armed break-ins have also been reported.

Credit card and ATM fraud is widespread. Ukraine operates as a cash economy, and money scams are widespread. We strongly recommend that visitors and permanent residents of Ukraine refrain from using credit cards or ATM cards

Burglaries of apartments and vehicles represent the most significant threat to long-term residents. Although few cars are actually stolen, primarily because of increased use of alarm systems and security wheel locks, vehicular break-ins and vehicular vandalism are becoming more common. Computer fraud is also becoming more common in Ukraine. Internet scams appear to be on the increase. We suggest refraining from wiring money unless the recipient is well known and the purpose of business is clear.

Americans citizens have reported transferring money to Ukraine to pay for goods purchased from residents of Ukraine via on-line auction sites, but never having received the goods in return. The U.S. Embassy regularly receives complaints from Americans regarding scams involving marriage and dating services. Numerous Americans have lost money to agencies that claimed they could have unmarried Ukrainians sponsored for student or fiancée visas to the United States. Additional information is available on our web site in a document titled "Marriage Brokers" at http://usinfo.usemb.kiev.ua/amcit_marriage_broke rs_eng.html.

Please note that the loss or theft abroad of a U.S. passport should be reported immediately to the local police and the nearest U.S. embassy or consulate. If you are the victim of a crime while overseas, in addition to reporting the incident to the local police, please contact the nearest U.S. embassy or consulate for assistance. The Embassy/Consulate staff can, for example, assist you to find appropriate medical care, to contact family members or friends, and to explain how funds can be transferred from the U.S. Although the investigation and prosecution of the crime is solely the responsibility of local authorities, consular officers can help you to understand the local criminal justice process and to find an attorney if needed.

U.S. citizens may refer to the Department of State's pamphlet, A Safe Trip Abroad, for ways to promote a more trouble-free journey. The pamphlet is available by mail from the Superintendent of Documents, U.S. Government Printing Office, Washington, D.C. 20402, via the Internet - http://www.access.gpo.gov/su_docs, or via the Bureau of Consular Affairs home page at http://travel.state.gov.

Additional information and recommendations on how to avoid becoming a victim of criminal activity are available on the Embassy web site in a separate document, "Security Information for Ukraine," at http://usinfo.usemb.kiev.ua/amcit_security_eng.ht ml.

MEDICAL FACILITIES: Medical care in Ukraine is limited. The U.S. Embassy maintains a list of hospitals and physician with some English-speaking staff. Many facilities have only limited English-speakers. Ukrainian standards do not meet American and Western-European professional standards of care. Some facilities are adequate for basic services. Basic medical supplies are available, but travelers requiring prescription medicine should bring their own medications with them. Elderly travelers and those with existing health problems may be at risk due to inadequate medical facilities. When hospitalized, patients or their relatives or acquaintances are often expected to provide for their own medication, bandages, etc.

The Consular Section of the U.S. Embassy has information on various air ambulance companies that perform medical evacuations to Europe and the United States. Serious medical problems requiring hospitalization and/or medical evacuation to Europe can cost from $25,000 to $50,000, and to the United States it can cost over $70,000.

More information can be found on the Embassy's web site in a separate document on Medical Services in Kiev at http://usinfo.usemb.kiev.ua/amcitmedicalserveng.html.

Please note that while the U.S. Embassy can help an individual or his or her family make contact with a medevac service, the U.S. Government cannot pay for the medical evacuation.

MEDICAL INSURANCE: The Department of State strongly urges Americans to consult with their medical insurance company prior to traveling abroad to confirm whether their policy applies overseas and if it will cover emergency expenses such as a medical evacuation. U.S. medical insurance plans seldom cover health costs incurred outside the United States unless supplemental coverage is purchased. Further, U.S. Medicare and Medicaid programs do not provide payment for medical services outside the United States. However, many travel agents and private companies offer insurance plans that will cover health care expenses incurred overseas, including emergency services such as medical evacuations.

When making a decision regarding health insurance, Americans should consider that many foreign doctors and hospitals require payment in cash prior to providing service and that a medical evacuation to the United States may cost well in excess of $50,000. Uninsured travelers who require medical care overseas often face extreme difficulties. When consulting with your insurer prior to your trip, please ascertain whether payment will be made to the overseas healthcare provider or if you will be reimbursed later for expenses that you incur. Some insurance policies also include coverage for psychiatric treatment and for disposition of remains in the event of death.

Useful information on medical emergencies abroad, including overseas insurance programs, is provided in the Department of State's Bureau of Consular Affairs brochure, *Medical Information for Americans Traveling Abroad*, available via the Bureau of Consular Affairs home page or autofax: (202) 647-3000.

OTHER HEALTH INFORMATION: Information on vaccinations and other health precautions, such as safe food and water precautions and insect bite protection, may be obtained from the Centers for Disease Control and Prevention's hotline for international travelers at 1-877-FYI-TRIP (1-877-394-8747); fax 1-888-CDC-FAXX (1-888-232-3299), or via CDC's Internet site at http://www.cdc.gov/travel. For information about outbreaks of infectious diseases abroad, please consult the World Health Organization's website at http://www.who.int/en. Further health information for travelers is available at http://www.who.int/ith.

TRAFFIC SAFETY AND ROAD CONDITIONS: While in a foreign country, U.S. citizens may encounter road conditions that differ significantly from those in the United States. The information below concerning Ukraine is provided for general reference only, and it may not be totally accurate in a particular location or circumstance.

Safety of Public Transportation: Fair
Urban Road Conditions/Maintenance: Fair
Rural Road Conditions/Maintenance: Poor
Availability of Roadside Assistance: Poor

Generally, roads in Ukraine outside major urban areas are in poor condition and poorly lit. Defensive driving is an absolute necessity since drivers often disregard traffic rules. Drivers are often poorly trained or drive without a valid driver's license. Drivers can also be very aggressive, and they normally do not respect the rights of pedestrians, even at clearly marked pedestrian crossings. Pedestrians should also be aware of cars driving or attempting to park on sidewalks. Many cars do not meet the safety standards common in America.

Overland travel at night and in winter can be particularly dangerous. We strongly recommend that visitors and permanent residents of Ukraine refrain from driving their private vehicles after dark outside of Kiev. However, major roads are driveable during daylight hours. Roadside services such as gas stations and repair facilities are becoming more common, particularly on the main national and regional overland highways and in large and mid-size cities. Nonetheless, such services are far from American standards, and travelers should plan accordingly. There have been isolated reports of carjackings of western-made or foreign-registered cars. There has been an increase in the number of documented reports of criminal acts occurring on trains.

AVIATION SAFETY OVERSIGHT: The U.S. Federal Aviation Administration (FAA) has assessed Ukraine's civil aviation authority as Category 1 - in compliance with international aviation safety standards for oversight of Ukraine's air carrier operations. For further information, travelers may contact the Department of Transportation within the United States at tel. 1-800-322-7873, or visit the FAA's Internet website at http://www.faa.gov/avr/iasa.

The U.S. Department of Defense (DOD) separately assesses some foreign air carriers for suitability as official providers of air services. For information regarding the DOD policy on specific carriers, travelers may contact the DOD at tel. (618) 256-4801.

CUSTOMS REGULATIONS: Ukrainian law requires that travelers declare all cash and jewelry, regardless of value, upon entering Ukraine. Travelers should fill out a customs declarations and ask customs officials to stamp it. According to Ukrainian law, foreign citizens may bring up to $10,000 cash or up to $50,000 in traveler's checks into Ukraine without a special license. Travelers must declare the cash or checks. If customs officials determine that a traveler entering or leaving the country has undeclared cash on their person, they can and often do confiscate the undeclared funds. When leaving the country, travelers are only allowed to take out a maximum of $1,000 in cash or as much cash as they declared upon entry into Ukraine. A traveler wishing to depart the country with more than $1,000 must be able to present a customs declaration proving he or she brought the corresponding sum of money into the country.

If you wish to bring more than $10,000 you must obtain a special license AFTER entering the Ukraine. Details for obtaining this license are available on the Embassy web site in a document entitled, "Ukrainian Customs Procedures for Transporting Currencies, Monetary Instruments, or Precious Metals" at:

http://usinfo.usemb.kiev.ua/amcittravelukrcustoms eng.htm.

Ukraine also has strict limitations for the export of antiques and other goods and artifacts deemed to be of particularly important historical or cultural value.

According to Ukrainian customs laws, travelers are allowed to take up to 10,000 hryvnya out of Ukraine as long as the entire amount is declared. Additionally, travelers are only allowed to bring back the same amount of hryvnya as they originally took out of Ukraine, as substantiated by their customs declaration.

It is advisable to contact the Embassy of Ukraine in Washington, D.C. or one of Ukraine's consulates in the United States for specific information regarding customs requirements.

CRIMINAL PENALTIES: While in a foreign country, a U.S. citizen is subject to that country's laws and regulations, which sometimes differ significantly from those in the United States and may not afford the protections available to the individual under U.S. law. Penalties for breaking the law can be more severe than in the United States for similar offenses. Persons violating Ukrainian laws, even unknowingly, may be expelled, arrested or imprisoned. Penalties for possession, use, or trafficking in illegal drugs in Ukraine are strict, and convicted offenders can expect jail sentences and heavy fines.

CONSULAR ACCESS: U.S. citizens are encouraged to carry a copy of their U.S. passports with them at all times, so that, if questioned by local officials, proof of identity and U.S. citizenship are readily available. If stopped or detained, Americans should comply with instructions from law enforcement officers but also make it known that they are American citizens. In accordance with a bi-lateral agreement between the USSR and the United States, which remains in force for the successor states of the Soviet Union, including Ukraine, U.S. Consular Officers are to be notified of an arrest or detention of a U.S. citizen within one to three days, and access to the arrestee/detainee is to be granted in two to four days. If arrested, American citizens should insist on calling a Consular Officer at tel. (044) 490-4422 or (044) 490-4000 after-hours. Please be advised that consular access and assistance does not allow the U.S. Embassy to act as your legal counsel, or otherwise intervene on your behalf if you are detained or arrested. Only a lawyer can represent you. The U.S. Embassy, however, can assist you in obtaining legal counsel from a list of lawyers and law firms that it maintains.

SPECIAL CIRCUMSTANCES: Ukraine is a cash economy. While Travelers' Checks and credit cards are gaining wider acceptance in larger cities, acceptance of credit cards is not nearly as widespread as in the United States or in Western European countries. Expect credit card use to be limited to better hotels, upscale restaurants, international airlines and the rapidly growing, but still select number of up-market stores. When bringing U.S. dollars into Ukraine, ensure that bills are in good condition because those that are worn, torn or written on may not be accepted.

Travelers should also note that customs regulations prohibit sending cash, travelers' checks, personal checks, credit cards, or passports through the international mail system. Customs authorities regularly confiscate these items as contraband. Exchanging U.S. dollars into the national Ukrainian currency hryvnya is simple and unproblematic, as licensed exchange booths are widespread, and exchange rates are normally clearly advertised. Exchanging U.S. dollars into Ukrainian currency or other currencies is legal only at banks, currency exchange desks at hotels, and licensed exchange booths; anyone caught dealing on the black market can expect to be detained by the local militia.

ATMs (a.k.a. Bankomats) are becoming available throughout Ukraine, particularly in Kiev and in other larger cities. In smaller cities and towns, ATMs are still virtually non-existent. Most ATMs disperse cash only in the local currency, hryvnya. However, because the incidence of credit card and ATM bankcard fraud is high, it is strongly recommend that visitors and permanent residents of Ukraine refrain from using credit cards or ATM cards. The difficulties of a currency shortage can be avoided by coming to Ukraine with a sufficient supply of hard currency to cover necessary obligations during travel. Funds may be transferred by wire; advances may be drawn on credit cards at secure locations and travelers checks may be cashed at many locations.

CHILDREN'S ISSUES: For information on international adoption of children, international parental child abduction, and international child support enforcement issues, please refer to our Internet site at http://travel.state.gov/children's_issues.html or telephone (202) 736-7000.

REGISTRATION/EMBASSY LOCATION: All U.S. citizens residing in Ukraine for more that a few days are encouraged to register at the Consular Section of the U.S. Embassy in Kiev and obtain updated information on travel and security within Ukraine.

The completely voluntary registration system allows the Embassy to:
-- help you more quickly if your passport is lost;
-- contact you in case of an emergency;
-- provide information on your whereabouts to family and friends (you must sign a Privacy Act Waiver - which is included in the registration form - in order for us to provide this service);
-- inform you, via our email-based warden system, of changes in the assessed security situation in Ukraine or elsewhere, and otherwise keep you informed about issues of interest to Americans present in Ukraine.

To register, you simply need to present your U.S. passport at the Consular Section during American Citizen Services' public hours and complete a simple form. There is no charge for this service. The form may also be downloaded at http://www.usinfo.usemb.kiev.ua and mailed or faxed, along with a copy of the citizen's passport to the Consular Section.

The Consular Section of the U.S. Embassy is located at #6, Pimonenko St., 01901 Kiev, Ukraine, tel. (380-44) 490-4422, fax 236-4892. The U.S. Embassy is located at 10 Vulitsa Yuria Kotsubinskoho, 01901 Kiev, Ukraine, tel. (380-44) 490-4000; after-hours 240-0856. Mail using U.S. domestic postage should be addressed to U.S. Embassy Kiev, U.S. Department of State, Washington, D.C. 20521-5850. Please visit the Embassy's Internet home page at http://www.usemb.kiev.ua.

UZBEKISTAN

COUNTRY DESCRIPTION: Uzbekistan is a newly independent nation in the midst of profound political and economic change. Tourist facilities are not highly developed, and many of the goods and services taken for granted in other countries are not yet available. Internal travel and travel to other New Independent States (NIS), including both air and land routes, can be erratic and disrupted by fuel shortages, overcrowding and other problems. The capital is Tashkent.

ENTRY REQUIREMENTS: A passport and visa are required; official invitations from a sponsoring organization or individual are no longer required for American citizens. Visas are issued by Uzbek embassies and consulates abroad. Visitors coming from countries where Uzbekistan does not have diplomatic or consular representation should obtain visas in a third country. Visas are not available upon arrival at any Uzbek airport.

Importantly, Uzbek visas indicate not only the validity of the visa, but also the period of time a person is allowed to stay in Uzbekistan on a given trip. Although Uzbek visas given to private American citizens are generally valid for four years with multiple entries, a visitor will have to leave the country after the number of days indicated as the duration of stay on the visa. Therefore, it is important to indicate your intended period of stay when applying for your Uzbek visa. Further visa information is available at the Embassy of the Republic of Uzbekistan, located a 1746 Massachusetts Ave., N.W., Washington, D.C. 20036; telephone (202) 887-5300; http://www.uzbekistan.org; or the Uzbek Consulate in New York, located at 866 United Nations Plaza, Suite 327A, New York, N.Y. 10017; telephone (212) 754-6178 or (212) 754-7403; http://www.uzbekconsul.org.

Note 1: All travelers, even those simply transiting Uzbekistan for less than 72 hours, must obtain an Uzbek visa before traveling to Uzbekistan. Uzbekistan has suspended the 72-hour transit rule that allowed travelers with visas from other members of the Commonwealth of Independent States to transit Uzbekistan without an Uzbek visa.

Note 2: On December 1, 2001, the Uzbek Government imposed travel restrictions on large parts of the Surkhandarya Oblast region bordering Afghanistan, including the border city of Termez. Foreign citizens intending to travel to this region must obtain a special permission card from the Ministry of Foreign Affairs, the Ministry of

Internal Affairs or Uzbek embassies and consulates abroad.

Registration after Entry: All travelers present in Uzbekistan for more than three days must register with the Office of Entry, Exit, and Citizenship. Hotel guests are registered automatically, but all other travelers are responsible for registering themselves. Visitors without proper registration are subject to fines and possible harassment by local authorities. Uzbek law mandates that visitors carry a medical certificate attesting that they are not infected with HIV. However, this requirement is only sporadically enforced.

In an effort to prevent international child abduction, many governments have initiated procedures at entry/exit points. These often include requiring documentary evidence of relationship and permission for the child's travel from the parent(s) or legal guardian not present. Having such documentation on hand, even if not required, may facilitate entry/departure.

SAFETY AND SECURITY: On December 1, 2001, the Uzbek Government imposed travel restrictions on large parts of the Surkhandarya Oblast region bordering Afghanistan, including the border city of Termez. Please keep in mind that the border between Afghanistan and Uzbekistan remains closed to all but official traffic.

In August 2000, fighting broke out on the Tajikistan-Kyrgyz and Tajikistan-Uzbekistan borders in response to insurgency activity by the Islamic Movement of Uzbekistan (IMU). As a result of operations by government security forces, portions of the Uzbek borders with Tajikistan, the Kyrgyz Republic and Kazakhstan were subsequently closed to civilians and tourists; such closures can be expected if IMU activity recurs in the summer. Restricted personal movement, including the closing of roads to traffic, and frequent document, vehicle and personal identification checks should be anticipated. The IMU has been responsible for several hostage-taking incidents in the Kyrgyz Republic directly targeting foreign citizens, including Americans. U.S. citizens should remain vigilant about their personal safety.

Americans traveling to or residing in Uzbekistan are urged to contact the Consular Section of the

U.S. Embassy in Tashkent for up-to-date information on security developments.

Note: U.S. citizens should check the Consular Information Sheets and current Travel Warnings or Public Announcements for nearby countries, including Afghanistan, Kazakhstan, the Kyrgyz Republic, Tajikistan, and Turkmenistan on a regular basis. The U.S. Embassy in each of those countries can provide up-to-date information about local crime and safety issues. Information about how to contact each Embassy directly is available on the Internet at the Consular Affairs home page, http://travel.state.gov, or by calling the U.S. Embassy, Tashkent.

CRIME: Uzbekistan has a relatively low rate of violent crime, but recent attacks against foreigners, including American citizens, indicate that it is increasing. Also, common street crime has increased, especially at night. In urban areas, travelers are urged to take the same precautions against crime that they would take in a large American city.

Although using private cars as taxicabs is a common practice in Uzbekistan, Americans should not consider this a safe practice, especially women and those traveling alone. Americans are encouraged to use clearly marked taxicabs, such as those at hotels.

The loss or theft abroad of a U.S. passport should be reported immediately to the local police and the nearest U.S. embassy or consulate. U.S. citizens can refer to the Department of State's pamphlet, *A Safe Trip Abroad*, for ways to promote a trouble-free journey. The pamphlet is available by mail from the Superintendent of Documents, U.S. Government Printing Office, Washington, D.C. 20402, via the Internet at http://www.access.gpo.gov/su_docs, or via the Bureau of Consular Affairs home page at http://travel.state.gov.

MEDICAL FACILITIES: Medical care in Uzbekistan is below Western standards, with severe shortages of basic medical supplies, including disposable needles, anesthetics, and antibiotics. Elderly travelers and those with pre-existing health problems may be at particular risk due to inadequate medical facilities. Most resident Americans travel to North America or Western Europe for their medical needs.

MEDICAL INSURANCE: U.S. medical insurance is not always valid outside the United States. U.S. Medicare and Medicaid programs do not provide payment for medical services outside the United States. Doctors and hospitals often expect immediate cash payment for health services. Uninsured travelers who require medical care overseas may face extreme difficulties.

The Department of State strongly urges Americans to consult with their medical insurance company prior to traveling abroad to confirm whether their policy applies overseas and whether it will cover emergency expenses such as a medical evacuation. U.S. medical insurance plans seldom cover health costs incurred outside the United States unless supplemental coverage is purchased. Further, U.S. Medicare and Medicaid programs do not provide payment for medical services outside the United States. However, many travel agents and private companies offer insurance plans that will cover health care expenses incurred overseas, including emergency services such as medical evacuations.

When making a decision regarding health insurance, Americans should consider that many foreign doctors and hospitals require payment in cash prior to providing service and that a medical evacuation to the United States may cost well in excess of $50,000. Uninsured travelers who require medical care overseas often face extreme difficulties. When consulting with your insurer prior to your trip, please ascertain whether payment will be made to the overseas healthcare provider or if you will be reimbursed later for expenses that you incur. Some insurance policies also include coverage for psychiatric treatment and for disposition of remains in the event of death.

Useful information on medical emergencies abroad, including overseas insurance programs, is provided in the Department of State's Bureau of Consular Affairs brochure, *Medical Information for Americans Traveling Abroad*, available via the Bureau of Consular Affairs home page or autofax: (202) 647-3000.

OTHER HEALTH INFORMATION: Travelers are advised to drink only boiled water, peel all fruits and vegetables, and avoid undercooked meat. Due to inadequate sanitation conditions, travelers should avoid eating dairy products and most food sold in the streets. Information on vaccinations and other health precautions may be obtained from the Center for Disease Control and Prevention's hotline for international travelers at 1-877-FYI-TRIP (1-877-394-8747); fax 1-888-CDC-FAXX (1-888-232-3299), or via the CDC's Internet site at http://www.cdc.gov.

TRAFFIC SAFETY AND ROAD CONDITIONS: While in a foreign country, U.S. citizens may encounter road conditions that differ significantly from those in the United States. The information below concerning Uzbekistan is provided for general reference only, and it may not be totally accurate in a particular location or circumstance.

Safety of Public Transportation: Good
Urban Road Conditions/Maintenance: Poor
Rural Road Conditions/Maintenance: Poor
Availability of Roadside Assistance: Poor

Uzbekistan has a developed but deteriorating traffic infrastructure. Although roads in Tashkent are relatively well-maintained, many roads outside Tashkent, and particularly those in the Tien Shan and Fan Mountains, are in poor condition and may be passable only by four-wheel-drive vehicles. Driving at night can be quite dangerous because only the main roads in Tashkent have streetlights; rural roads and highways generally are not lit. Visitors are strongly urged to avoid driving at night outside Tashkent.

Livestock, farm equipment and carts drawn by animals are found on both urban and rural roads at any hour. Local drivers are not familiar with safe driving techniques. Pedestrians in cities and rural areas cross streets unexpectedly and often without looking for oncoming traffic. Uzbekistan has a large road police force, which frequently stops drivers for minor infractions or simple document checks. There have been reports of harassment of foreign drivers by the road police, with reported minor police corruption in the form of solicitation of bribes.

For additional general information about road safety, including links to foreign government sites, please see the Department of State, Bureau of Consular Affairs home page at http://travel.state.gov/road_safety.html. For specific information concerning Uzbekistan driver's permits, vehicle inspection, road tax and mandatory insurance, please fax your question to the Uzbek Embassy in Washington, D.C. at (202) 293-9633 or the Consulate General in New York at (212) 838-9812.

AVIATION SAFETY OVERSIGHT: The U.S. Federal Aviation Administration (FAA) has assessed the Government of Uzbekistan's Civil Aviation Authority as Category One -- in compliance with international aviation safety standards for oversight of Uzbekistan's air carrier operations. For further information, travelers may contact the Department of Transportation within the United States at telephone (800) 322-7873, or visit the FAA's Internet web site at http://www.faa.gov/avr/iasa/.

The U.S. Department of Defense (DOD) separately assesses some foreign air carriers for suitability as official providers of air services. For information regarding the DOD policy on specific carriers, travelers may contact the DOD at telephone (618) 229-4801.

CUSTOMS REGULATIONS: Uzbek customs authorities may enforce strict regulations concerning temporary import or export from Uzbekistan of items such as armaments and ammunition, space technology, encryption devices, X-ray and isotope equipment, nuclear materials, poisons, drugs, precious and semi-precious metals, nullified securities, pieces of art and antiques of historical value. It is advisable to contact the Embassy of Uzbekistan in Washington, D.C. or the Consulate of Uzbekistan in New York for specific information regarding customs requirements.

CRIMINAL PENALTIES: While in a foreign country, a U.S. citizen is subject to that country's laws and regulations, which sometimes differ significantly from those in the United States and may not afford the protections available to the individual under U.S. law. Penalties for breaking the law can be more severe than in the United States for similar offenses. Persons violating Uzbek laws, even unknowingly, may be expelled. Penalties for possession, use or trafficking of illegal drugs in Uzbekistan are strict, and offenders can expect jail sentences and heavy fines.

CONSULAR ACCESS: Travelers to Uzbekistan are subject to frequent document inspections. Therefore, U.S. citizens are strongly encouraged to carry a copy of their U.S. passport and their Uzbek visa with them at all times so that they may more readily prove that they are U.S. citizens. In accordance with the Vienna Convention on Consular Relations and certain bilateral agreements, local authorities must grant a United States consular officer access to any U.S. citizen who is arrested. U.S. citizens who are arrested or detained should ask to contact the U.S. Embassy immediately.

SPECIAL CIRCUMSTANCES: Most transactions are conducted on a cash-only, local currency (som) basis. Credit cards are accepted only at the main hotels and a few shops and restaurants; traveler's checks can be cashed into dollars at the National Bank of Uzbekistan. The commission fee is two percent. Importation of currency exceeding $10,000 (US) is subject to a one percent duty.

Foreigners must complete a customs declaration upon entering Uzbekistan and may face fines upon departure if unable to produce certificates verifying legal conversion of foreign currency. Old U.S. dollar bills (prior to 1990) and/or those in poor condition (with tears, writing or stamps) are not acceptable forms of currency in Uzbekistan. Although payment in U.S. dollars is required for certain hotel charges, plane tickets, and visa fees, other dollar transactions, as well as black market currency exchanges, are prohibited.

DISASTER ASSISTANCE: Uzbekistan is an earthquake-prone country. General information about natural disaster preparedness is available via the Internet from the U.S. Federal Emergency Management Agency (FEMA) at http://www.fema.gov/.

CHILDREN'S ISSUES: For information on international adoption of children and international parental child abduction, please refer to our Internet site at http://travel.state.gov/children's_issues.html or telephone (202) 736-7000.

REGISTRATION/EMBASSY LOCATION: Americans are encouraged to register at the Consular Section of the U.S. Embassy and obtain updated information on travel and security in Uzbekistan. The U.S. Embassy in Tashkent, is located at Ulitsa Chilanzarskaya, 82. The main Embassy telephone number is (998 71) 120-5450, fax (998 71) 120-6335; the Consular Section's direct line is (998 71) 120-5444, e-mail address: consular@usembassy.us. Current information may also be obtained from the Embassy web site at http://www.usembassy.uz.

Chapter 22

Tips for Travelers to South Asia

[The information in this chapter is reprinted verbatim from a bulletin issued by the
U.S. State Department, Bureau of Consular Affairs. It is intended to serve as advice
to Americans traveling abroad.]

Afghanistan, Bangladesh, Bhutan, India, Maldives, Nepal, Pakistan, and Sri Lanka

AFGHANISTAN

COUNTRY DESCRIPTION: Afghanistan faces daunting challenges - recovering from over two decades of civil strife, dealing with years of severe drought, and rebuilding a shattered infrastructure. Meanwhile, Operation Enduring Freedom continues. The Emergency Loya Jeirga, a national assembly held in June 2002, established the Transitional Islamic State of Afghanistan.

ENTRY REQUIREMENTS: A passport is required. The Transitional Islamic State of Afghanistan requires American citizens to obtain a visa for entry into the country Information on entry requirements can be obtained from the Embassy of Afghanistan located at 2341 Wyoming Avenue, NW, Washington, DC 20008, phone no. 202-483-6410, fax no. 202-483-6488, website: www.afghanistanembassy.org.

In an effort to prevent international child abduction, many governments have initiated procedures at entry/exit points. These often include requiring documentary evidence of relationship and permission for the child's travel from the parent(s) or legal guardian not present. Having such documentation on hand, even if not required, may facilitate entry/departure.

DUAL NATIONALITY: In addition to being subject to all Afghan laws affecting U.S. citizens, dual nationals may also be subject to other laws that impose special obligations on Afghan citizens, including military service. For additional information, see the Consular Affairs home page on the Internet at http://travel.state.gov for the Dual Nationality flyer reprinted elsewhere in this book. See the chapter on Dual Nationality.

SECURITY AND SAFETY: The latest Travel Warning for Afghanistan states clearly that the security situation remains critical for American citizens. There are remnants of the former Taliban regime and the terrorist al-Qaida network in various parts of Afghanistan. There is a continuing threat of terrorist actions, including attacks using vehicular or other bombs. The country faces a difficult period in the near term, and American citizens could be targeted or placed at risk by unpredictable local events. There is also a real danger from the presence of millions of unexploded land mines and other ordnance. The Afghan government has lifted their curfew in Kabul; however, U.S. Embassy in Kabul continues to observe a curfew.

Afghan-Americans returning to Afghanistan to recover property have become involved in complicated disputes and, even given favorable court proceedings, often face retaliatory actions including threats of kidnapping for ransom.

CRIME: A large portion of the Afghan population is unemployed and displaced from their traditional places of residence, and the food situation is of critical concern throughout Afghanistan. Basic services are rudimentary or not existent. These factors may directly contribute to crime and lawlessness. Diplomats and international relief workers have reported incidents of highway robbery and household burglaries. Any American citizen who enters Afghanistan should remain vigilant for possible banditry, including attacks with violence.

The loss or theft abroad of a U.S. passport should be reported immediately to the local police and the nearest U.S. Embassy or Consulate. If you are the victim of a crime while overseas, in addition to reporting to local police, please contact the nearest U.S. Embassy or Consulate for assistance. (Currently, the U.S. Embassy in Kabul is not issuing passports and cannot replace a lost passport.) The Embassy/Consulate staff can, for example, assist you to find appropriate medical care, to contact family members or friends and explain how funds could be transferred. Although the investigation and prosecution of the crime is solely the responsibility of local authorities, consular officers can help you to understand the local criminal justice process and to find an attorney if needed.

U.S. citizens may refer to the Department of State's pamphlet, *A Safe Trip Abroad*, for ways to promote a trouble-free journey. The pamphlet is available by mail from the Superintendent of Documents, U.S. Government Printing Office, Washington, D.C. 20402, via the Internet at http://www.access.gpo.gov/su_docs, or via the Bureau of Consular Affairs home page at http://travel.state.gov.

MEDICAL FACILITIES: Well-equipped medical facilities are few and far between throughout Afghanistan. European and American medicines are generally unavailable, and there is a shortage of basic medical supplies. Basic medicines manufactured in Iran, Pakistan and India are available. Travelers will not be able to find Western-trained medical personnel in most parts of the country. Hospitals throughout the country can provide only the most-limited services. There are also some international aid groups temporarily providing basic medical assistance in various cities and villages. For any medical treatment, payment is required in advance. Commercial medical evacuation capability from within Afghanistan is limited.

MEDICAL INSURANCE: The Department of State strongly urges Americans to consult with their medical insurance company prior to traveling abroad to confirm whether their policy applies overseas and whether it will cover emergency expenses such as a medical evacuation. U.S. medical insurance plans seldom cover health costs incurred outside the United States unless supplemental coverage is purchased. Further, U.S. Medicare and Medicaid programs do not provide payment for medical services outside the United States. However, many travel agents and private companies offer insurance plans that will cover health care expenses incurred overseas including emergency services such as medical evacuations.

When making a decision regarding health insurance, Americans should consider that many foreign doctors and hospitals require payment in cash prior to providing service and that a medical evacuation to the U.S. may cost in excess of $50,000. Uninsured travelers who require medical care overseas often face extreme difficulties. When consulting with your insurer prior to your trip, ascertain whether payment will be made to the overseas healthcare provider or whether you will be reimbursed later for expenses you incur. Some insurance policies also include coverage for psychiatric treatment and for disposition of remains in the event of death.

Useful information on medical emergencies abroad, including overseas insurance programs, is provided in the Department of State's Bureau of Consular Affairs brochure, *Medical Information for Americans Traveling Abroad*, available via the Bureau of Consular Affairs home page or autofax: (202) 647-3000.

OTHER HEALTH INFORMATION: Information on vaccinations and other health precautions, such as safe food and water precautions and insect bite protection, may be obtained from the Centers for Disease Control and Prevention's hotline for international travelers at 1-877-FYI-TRIP (1-877-394-8747); fax 1-888-CDC-FAXX (1-888-232-3299), or via the CDC's Internet site at http://www.cdc.gov/travel. For information about outbreaks of infectious diseases abroad consult the World Health Organization's website at http://www.who.int/en. Further health information for travelers is available at http://www.who.int/ith.

TRAFFIC SAFETY AND ROAD CONDITIONS: While in a foreign country, U.S. citizens may encounter road conditions that differ significantly from those in the United States. The information below concerning Afghanistan is provided for general reference only, and may not be totally accurate in a particular location or circumstance.

Safety of Public Transportation: Poor
Urban Road Conditions/Maintenance: Poor

340

Rural Road Conditions/Maintenance: Poor
Availability of Roadside Assistance: Poor

All traffic is in danger of land mines that have been randomly planted on and near roadways. An estimated 5-7 million landmines and large quantities of unexploded ordnance are scattered throughout the countryside and alongside roads, posing a danger to travelers. Robbery and crime are also prevalent on highways outside of Kabul. The transportation system in Afghanistan is marginal. Vehicles are poorly maintained and often overloaded; traffic laws are not enforced; drivers are erratic. Vehicular traffic is chaotic and must contend with numerous pedestrians and animals. Many urban streets have large potholes and are not well lit. Rural roads often are not paved.

For additional general information about road safety, including links to foreign government sites, see the Department of State, Bureau of Consular Affairs home page at http://travel.state.gov/road_safety.hmtl.

AVIATION SAFETY OVERSIGHT: A few commercial airlines offer service to Afghanistan.

As there is no direct commercial air service by local carriers at present, or economic authority to operate such service, between the U.S. and Afghanistan, the U.S. Federal Aviation Administration (FAA) has not assessed Afghanistan's Civil Aviation Authority for compliance with international aviation safety standards. For further information, travelers may contact the Department of Transportation within the U.S. at 1-800-322-7873, or visit the FAA's Internet website at http://www.intl.faa.gov.

The U.S. Department of Defense (DOD) separately assesses some foreign air carriers for suitability as official providers of air services. For information regarding the DOD policy on specific carriers, travelers may contact DOD at (618) 229-4801.

CUSTOM REGULATIONS: Afghan customs authorities may enforce strict regulations concerning temporary importation into or export from Afghanistan of items such as firearms, alcoholic beverages, religious materials, antiquities, medications, and printed materials. It is advisable to contact the Embassy of Afghanistan in Washington or one of Afghanistan's other diplomatic missions for specific information regarding customs requirements.

CRIMINAL PENALTIES: While in a foreign country, a U.S. citizen is subject to that country's laws and regulations, which sometimes differ significantly from those in the United States and may not afford the protections available to the individual under U.S. law. Penalties for breaking the law can be more severe than in the United States for similar offenses. Persons violating Afghanistan's laws, even unknowingly, may be expelled, arrested or imprisoned. Penalties for possession, use, or trafficking in illegal drugs in Afghanistan are strict and convicted offenders can expect jail sentences and heavy fines. Proselytizing remains illegal and violators will be punished.

CONSULAR ACCESS: U.S. citizens are encouraged to carry a copy of their U.S. passports with them at all times, so that, if questioned by local officials, proof of identity and U.S. citizenship are readily available. As stated in the Travel Warning for Afghanistan, consular assistance for American citizens in Afghanistan is limited.

SPECIAL CIRCUMSTANCES: Because of the poor infrastructure in Afghanistan, access to banking facilities is extremely limited and unreliable. Afghanistan's economy operates on a "cash-only" basis for most transactions. Credit card transactions are not operable. International bank transfers are not available. No ATM machines exist.

TELECOMMUNICATIONS: International communications are difficult. Local telephone networks do not operate reliably. Many rely on satellite telephone communications even to make local calls. There is cellular phone service available locally. Injured or distressed foreigners could face long delays before being able to communicate their needs to colleagues or family outside Afghanistan. Internet access through local service providers is limited.

CHILDREN'S ISSUES: For information on international adoption of children and international parental child abduction, please refer to our Internet site at

341

http://travel.state.gov/children's_issues.html or telephone (202) 736-7000.

REGISTRATION/EMBASSY LOCATION: The Embassy is located at Great Masood Road between Radio Afghanistan and the Ministry of Public Health, Kabul. It can provide no passport or visa services, but does perform emergency and routine citizens services. U.S. citizens who travel to or reside in Afghanistan are encouraged to register at the consular section of the U.S. Embassy in Kabul, phone numbers: (93-2) 290002, 290005, 290154; INMARSAT line, tel 00 [872](761)837-927; fax: 00[873](76) 183-7374, and obtain updated information on travel and security within Afghanistan. The U.S. Embassy in Kabul web site can be accessed at http://usembassy.state.gov/afghanistan/

BANGLADESH

COUNTRY DESCRIPTION: Bangladesh has a developing economy. Tourist facilities outside major cities and tourist areas are minimal. The capital city is Dhaka.

ENTRY/EXIT REQUIREMENTS: A passport, visa and onward/return ticket are required. All travelers to Bangladesh, including American citizens, must have a valid visa in their passport prior to arrival. Note that airport visas (landing permits) are no longer available upon arrival by air. Some Americans seeking visas from the Bangladesh Embassy in Washington, D.C. or from Bangladesh embassies or consulates in other countries have reported that they are erroneously advised to enter Bangladesh on a landing permit. New exit requirements are in effect for persons working and residing long term in Bangladesh. As of April 15, 2002, departing foreign nationals are required to comply with the Income Tax Ordinance of 1984 and submit an income tax clearance

certificate/income tax exemption certificate to local airline offices upon departure from Bangladesh. For further information on entry requirements and possible exceptions to the exit requirements, please contact the Embassy of the People's Republic of Bangladesh, 3510 International Drive, N.W., Washington, D.C. 20008, telephone 202-244-0183, fax 202-244-5366, website http://www.bangladeshembassy.com, or the Bangladesh Consulates in New York, 211 E. 43rd Street, Suite 502, New York, NY 10017, telephone 212-599-6767, or Los Angeles, 10850 Wilshire Boulevard, Suite 1250, Los Angeles, CA 90024, telephone 310-441-9399.

SAFETY AND SECURITY: American citizens residing in or visiting Bangladesh are urged to consider carefully the security risks in deciding whether to attend large public gatherings. Bombings in public places have occurred from time to time. In December 2002, bombs exploded at four packed movie theaters in the town of Mymensingh, located approximately 70 mi/112 km north of Dhaka, killing 20 people and injuring 100 others. Police officers in the town of Gaibandha later located another device in a movie theater and safely defused it. A similar coordinated attack occurred in September 2002, when bombs exploded in a movie theater and at a circus in the town of Satkhira, located approximately 112 mi/180 km southwest of Dhaka. More than 100 people were injured in this attack. There have been no American citizens among the victims of these bombings. The Mymensingh bombings reinforce continued embassy warnings about the possibility of violence in public places where large crowds gather.

While the coordinated nature of these bombings raises further security concerns in Bangladesh, the State Department has no information to indicate that these bombings are related to terrorist attacks against Americans elsewhere in the world. However, we wish to remind Americans in Bangladesh that worldwide terrorist attacks against private American citizens and civilians of all nationalities demonstrate that, as security is increased at official U.S. facilities, terrorists and their sympathizers will seek softer targets. Such targets may include facilities at which Americans or possibly other foreigners are generally known to congregate or visit, such as residential areas, clubs, restaurants, places of worship, schools, hotels, cinemas, outdoor recreation events or resorts and beaches. Americans should increase their security awareness when they are at such locations, avoid them, or switch to other locations at which Americans in large numbers generally do not congregate.

Bangladesh continues to experience some anti-American sentiment as a result of U.S. Military and other actions in the war against terrorism and events in the Middle East. Anti-American demonstrations throughout Bangladesh frequently occur on Friday afternoons but have the potential to take place at any time and to be unruly.

Domestic, politically inspired violence has not abated since the 2001 election campaign. Such violence is a particular problem on university campuses. While Americans in Bangladesh have not been the targets of the violence, they should consider it when planning their movements. Public demonstrations, marches and labor strikes are widely used as means of political expression in Bangladesh. The political opposition over the past several years has called a number of general strikes, or "hartals," resulting in the virtual shutdown of transportation and commerce, and sometimes attacks on individuals who do not observe the hartals. Clashes between rival political groups during hartals have resulted in deaths and injuries. American citizens are therefore urged to avoid all political protests, demonstrations, and marches. During hartals, American citizens should exercise caution in all areas and remain inside their hotels, residences, schools, or workplaces, whenever possible.

Due to several kidnappings, including those of foreign nationals, U.S. citizens are advised against traveling to the Khagrachari, Rangamati and Bandarban Hill Tracts districts (collectively known as the Chittagong Hill Tracts) unless the travel is absolutely essential. Individuals who choose to visit these districts are urged to exercise extreme caution. Visitors to Bangladesh should check with the Consular Section at the U.S. Embassy in Dhaka for updated information on planned political activities.

For the latest security information, Americans traveling abroad should regularly monitor the Department's Internet web site at http://travel.state.gov where the current Worldwide Caution Public Announcement, Travel Warnings and Public Announcements can be found.

CRIME: Crime is a growing problem in Bangladesh, particularly in the major cities of Dhaka and Chittagong. Armed criminal incidents are on the rise. Pick-pocketing, purse-snatching, and other forms of street crime occur often, especially in areas frequented by foreigners. Visitors should avoid walking alone after dark, carrying large sums of money, and wearing expensive jewelry. Valuables should be stored in the hotel safety deposit box and should not be left unattended in hotel rooms.

The loss or theft abroad of a U.S. Passport should be reported immediately to local police and to the U.S. Embassy in Dhaka. If you are the victim of a crime while overseas, please report it to the local authorities and contact the nearest U.S. Embassy or Consulate for assistance. The Embassy/Consulate staff can, for example, assist you in finding appropriate medical care, contacting family members or friends, and explaining how funds may be transferred. Although the investigation and prosecution of a crime is solely the responsibility of local authorities, consular officers may help you understand the local criminal justice process and find an attorney, if needed.

U.S. Citizens may refer to the Department of State's pamphlets, *A Safe Trip Abroad* and *Tips for Travelers to South Asia*, for ways to promote a more trouble-free journey. The pamphlets are available by mail from the Superintendent of Documents, U.S. Government Printing Office, Washington, D.C. 20402, via the internet at http://www.access.gpo.gov/su_docs, or via the Bureau of Consular Affairs home page at http://travel.state.gov.

MEDICAL FACILITIES: Medical facilities in Bangladesh do not approach U.S. standards, even in tourist areas. Medical evacuations to Bangkok or Singapore are often needed for serious conditions.

MEDICAL INSURANCE: the Department of State strongly urges Americans to consult with their medical insurance company prior to traveling abroad to confirm whether their policy applies overseas and if it will cover emergency expenses such as a medical evacuation. U.S. medical insurance plans seldom cover health costs incurred outside the United States unless supplemental coverage is purchased. Further, U.S.

Medicare and Medicaid programs do not provide

payment for medical services outside the United States. However, many travel agents and private companies offer insurance plans that will cover health care expenses incurred overseas, including emergency services such as medical evacuations. When making a decision regarding health insurance, Americans should consider that many foreign doctors and hospitals require payment in cash prior to providing service and that a medical evacuation to the United States may cost in excess of $50,000. Uninsured travelers who require medical care overseas often face extreme difficulties. When consulting with your insurer prior to your trip, please ascertain whether payment will be made to the overseas healthcare provider or if you will be reimbursed later for expenses that you incur. Some insurance policies also include coverage for psychiatric treatment and for disposition of remains in the event of death.

Useful information on medical emergencies abroad, including overseas insurance programs, is provided in the Department of State's Bureau of Consular Affairs brochure, Medical Information for Americans Traveling Abroad, available via the Bureau of Consular Affairs home page or autofax: 202-647-3000.

OTHER HEALTH INFORMATION: Information on vaccinations and other health precautions may be obtained from the Centers for Disease Control and Prevention's hotline for international travelers at telephone 1-877-fyi-trip (1-877-394-8747); fax: 1-888-cdc-faxx (1-888-232-3299), or via the CDC's internet site at http://www.cdc.gov/travel. For information about outbreaks of infectious diseases abroad consult the World Health Organization's website at http://www.who.int/en. Further health information for travelers is available at http://www.who.int/ith.

TRAFFIC SAFETY AND ROAD CONDITIONS: While in a foreign country, U.S. Citizens may encounter road conditions that differ significantly from those in the United States. The information below concerning Bangladesh is provided for general reference only, and it may not be totally accurate in a particular location or circumstance.

Safety of public transportation: Poor
Urban road conditions/maintenance: Poor
Rural road conditions/maintenance: Poor

Availability of roadside assistance: Poor

The Bangladesh road network is in poor condition. The streets of Dhaka are extremely congested. Hundreds of thousands of bicycle rickshaws compete for limited road space with baby taxis, auto tempos, cars, overloaded buses, and trucks. Inter-city roads are narrow and also in poor condition. Driving at night is especially dangerous. Streetlights are rare, even in cities.

Road accidents are common in Bangladesh. Numerous American residents of Bangladesh report having had at least one traffic accident. Fatal head-on collisions on inter-city roads are common. When vehicle accidents occur, a crowd quickly gathers and judges the more affluent party to be at fault. Travelers are strongly urged not to use rickshaws or three-wheeled baby taxis due to their high accident rate, as well as the increased possibility of purse snatchings or muggings. Rental cars with drivers and normal taxis are the preferred means of transportation.

For additional general information about road safety, including links to foreign government sites, please see the Department of State, Bureau of Consular Affairs home page at http://travel.state.gov/road_safety.html or contact the Bangladesh Parjan Corporation, National Tourism Organization, 233 Airport Road, Tejgaon, Dhaka-1214, telephone (880-2) 811-9192 or 811-8559, fax (880-2) 811-7235, internet web site http://www.parjatan.org, e-mail address: bpcho@bangla.net.

WATER TRANSPORTATION: Bangladesh is a riverine country with a wide network of waterways used for public transportation. Ferries and other boats compete with the railroads as a major means of public transport. Typically overloaded and top heavy, ferries are subject to capsizing, particularly during the monsoon season from May to October when encountering thunderstorms and wind gusts that arise unpredictably. In May 2002, over 500 fatalities occurred from three capsized ferry incidents.

AVIATION SAFETY OVERSIGHT: The U.S. Federal Aviation Administration (FAA) has assessed the Government of Bangladesh's Civil Aviation Authority as Category 2 -- not in compliance with international aviation safety standards for oversight of Bangladesh's air carrier operations. While consultations to correct the deficiencies are ongoing, the Bangladesh air carriers currently flying to the United States will be subject to heightened FAA surveillance. No additional flights or new service to the United States by Bangladesh's air carriers will be permitted unless they arrange to have the flights conducted by an air carrier from a country meeting international safety standards. Because of safety concerns about the operation of Biman Airlines, the Department of State authorizes its personnel to use alternative carriers or means of transportation whenever practical for trips to/from Bangladesh. Americans who are required to travel by air within Bangladesh may wish to consider using an alternative airline, if available, or consider alternate means of transportation. For further information, travelers may contact the Department of Transportation within the United States at telephone 1-800-322-7873, or visit the FAA's internet web site at http://www.faa.gov/avr/iasa.

The U.S. Department of Defense (DOD) separately assesses some foreign carriers for suitability as official providers of air services. In addition, the DOD does not permit its personnel to use air carriers from Category 2 countries for official business except for flights originating from or terminating in the United States local exceptions may apply. For information regarding the DOD policy on specific carriers, travelers may contact the DOD at telephone 618-229-4801.

CUSTOMS REGULATIONS: Bangladesh customs authorities may enforce strict regulations concerning temporary importation into or export from Bangladesh of items such as currency, household appliances, alcohol, cigarettes and weapons. It is advisable to contact the Embassy of Bangladesh in Washington, D.C. for specific information regarding customs requirements.

CRIMINAL PENALTIES: While in a foreign country, a U.S. Citizen is subject to that country's laws and regulations, which sometimes differ significantly from those in the United States and may not afford the protections available to the individual under U.S. law. Penalties for breaking the law can be more severe than in the United States for similar offenses. Persons violating Bangladesh's laws, even unknowingly, may be expelled, arrested or imprisoned. Penalties for

possession, use, or trafficking in illegal drugs in Bangladesh are strict. The death penalty or life imprisonment can be imposed for some drug-related crimes, and convicted offenders can expect jail sentences and heavy fines. The judicial system is slow, trial proceedings are subject to frequent delays, and the U.S. Embassy in Dhaka hears complaints of corruption. Jail conditions are far below U.S. standards.

CONSULAR ACCESS: U.S. citizens are encouraged to carry a copy of their U.S. passports with them at all times, so that, if questioned by local officials, proof of identity and U.S. citizenship are readily available. In accordance with the Vienna Convention on Consular Relations to which Bangladesh is a signatory, a U.S. citizen under detention in Bangladesh has a right to request that the U.S. Embassy in Dhaka be notified regarding his or her situation and gain access. Bangladeshi authorities have repeatedly failed to notify U.S. Consular officials of the arrest of American citizens.

CHILDREN'S ISSUES: Bangladesh is not a party to the Hague Convention on Civil Aspects of International Child Abduction, nor do any U.S. States have reciprocal child support enforcement agreements with Bangladesh. For information on international adoption of children and international parental child abduction, please refer to our Internet site http://travel.state.gov/children's_issues.html or telephone (202) 736-7000.

REGISTRATION/EMBASSY LOCATION: Americans living in or visiting Bangladesh are encouraged to register at the Consular Section of the U.S. Embassy in Dhaka and obtain updated information on travel and security within Bangladesh. The U.S. Embassy is located some four miles south of Zia International Airport, and five miles north of downtown in the Diplomatic Enclave, Madani Avenue, Baridhara, Dhaka, telephone (880-2) 882-4700, fax number (880-2) 882-3744. The workweek is Sunday - Thursday. The Consular Section is open for American citizen services Sunday through Thursday from 8:30 to 10:30 a.m. and 1:30 to 3:30 p.m. For emergency services during business hours, please call (880-2) 882-3805. For emergency services after hours, please call (880-2) 882-4700 and ask for the duty officer. The Embassy's Internet home page is http://www.usembassy-dhaka.org/state/embassy.htm.

BHUTAN

COUNTRY DESCRIPTION: Bhutan is a small land-locked Himalayan monarchy. By treaty it accepts the guidance of India in foreign affairs. Facilities for tourism are limited.

ENTRY/EXIT REQUIREMENTS: Independent travel is not permitted. Tourists are admitted only in groups by pre-arrangement with the Tourism Authority of Bhutan, P.O. Box 126, Thimpu, Bhutan, telephone (975-2) 23251, 23252; fax(975-2)23695. Entry is available only via India, Bangladesh, Nepal, and Thailand. The border with China is closed.

Visitors to Bhutan are required to book travel through a registered tour operator in Bhutan. This can be done directly or through a travel agent abroad. The minimum daily tariff is regulated and fixed by the Royal Government. The rate includes all accommodations, all meals, transportation, services of licensed guides and porters, and cultural programs where and when available.

A passport and visa are required for entry into and exit from Bhutan. Most visitors, including those on official U.S. government business, should obtain visas prior to entering the country. Those travelers with prepaid, pre-approved, guided package tours may be issued visas on arrival. Such travelers must forward their passport details to the travel group organizing their trip at least 15 days before the travelers arrive in Bhutan. The tour operator in Bhutan applies for the visas, which take a minimum of five working days to process. The only carrier servicing Bhutan is Druk Air, the Bhutanese government airline. Druk Air will board only travelers with visa clearance from the Tourism Authority of Bhutan.

For additional entry/exit information, please contact the Bhutan Mission to the United Nations (Consulate General), 2 UN Plaza, 27th floor, New York, NY 10017, telephone(212)826-1919, fax (212)826-2998, or via the Internet at http://www.embassy.org/embassies/bt.html.

CRIME INFORMATION: There is relatively little crime in Bhutan. Petty crime, such as pickpocketing and purse snatching, is occasionally reported. The loss or theft of a U.S. passport abroad should be reported immediately to local police and the nearest U.S. embassy or consulate. U.S. citizens may refer to the Department of State's pamphlets, *A Safe Trip Abroad* and *Tips for Travelers to South Asia*, for ways to promote a more trouble-free journey. The pamphlets are available by mail from the Superintendent of Documents, U.S. Government Printing Office, Washington, D.C. 20402, via the Internet at http://www.access.gpo.gov/su_docs, or via the Bureau of Consular Affairs home page at http://travel.state.gov.

MEDICAL FACILITIES: Medical facilities in Bhutan are limited. Some medicine is in short supply. Doctors and hospitals often expect immediate cash payment for health services.

MEDICAL INSURANCE: The Department of State strongly urges Americans to consult with their medical insurance company prior to traveling abroad to confirm whether their policy applies overseas and if it will cover emergency expenses such as a medical evacuation. U.S. medical insurance plans seldom cover health costs incurred outside the United States unless supplemental coverage is purchased. Further, U.S. Medicare and Medicaid programs do not provide payment for medical services outside the United States. However, many travel agents and private companies offer insurance plans that will cover health care expenses incurred overseas, including emergency services such as medical evacuations.

When making a decision regarding health insurance, Americans should consider that many foreign doctors and hospitals require payment in cash prior to providing service and that a medical evacuation to the United States may cost in excess of $50,000. Uninsured travelers who require medical care overseas often face extreme difficulties. When consulting your insurer prior to your trip, please ascertain whether payment will be made to the overseas healthcare provider or if you will be reimbursed later for expenses that you incur. Some insurance policies also include coverage for psychiatric treatment and for disposition of remains in the event of death.

Useful information on medical emergencies

abroad, including overseas insurance programs, is provided in the Department of State's Bureau of Consular Affairs brochure, *Medical Information for Americans Traveling Abroad,* available via the Bureau of Consular Affairs home page or autofax: (202) 647-3000.

OTHER HEALTH INFORMATION: Information on vaccinations and other health precautions may be obtained from the Centers for Disease Control and Prevention's hotline for international travelers at 1-877-FYI-TRIP (1-877-394-8747); fax 1-888-CDC-FAXX (1-888-232-3299), or via their Internet site at http://www.cdc.gov.

TRAFFIC SAFETY AND ROAD CONDITIONS: While in a foreign country, U.S. citizens may encounter road conditions that differ significantly from those in the United States. The information below concerning Bhutan is provided for general reference only, and it may not be totally accurate in a particular location or circumstance.

Safety of Public Transportation: Not Applicable (Tourists pay a set fee per day, which includes supplied transportation)
Road Conditions/Maintenance in Urban Areas: Good
Road Conditions/Maintenance in Rural Areas: Poor
Availability of Roadside Assistance: Poor

Although Bhutan's road network is not extensive, principal sites likely to be visited by travelers are connected by reasonably well-maintained, paved, two-lane roads. Traffic is rarely heavy, but sharp curves, narrow lanes, and limited visibility in mountainous terrain make traveling slow and potentially hazardous. Reduced speeds and special caution are advisable.

For additional general information about road safety, including links to foreign government sites, please see the Department of State, Bureau of Consular Affairs home page at http://travel.state.gov/road_safety.html.

AVIATION SAFETY OVERSIGHT: As there is no direct commercial air service by local carriers at present, nor economic authority to operate such service between the United States and Bhutan, the U.S. Federal Aviation Administration (FAA) has not assessed Bhutan's Civil Aviation Authority for compliance with international aviation safety standards.

For further information, travelers may contact the Department of Transportation within the United States at telephone 1-800-322-7873, or visit the FAA's Internet web site at http://www.faa.gov/avr/iasa. The U.S. Department of Defense (DOD) separately assesses some foreign air carriers for suitability as official providers of air services. For information regarding the DOD policy on specific carriers, travelers may contact the DOD at telephone (618) 229-4801.

CUSTOMS REGULATIONS: Bhutan customs authorities enforce strict regulations concerning temporary importation into or export from Bhutan of items such as firearms, ammunition, explosives and military stores; narcotics and drugs (except medically prescribed drugs); wildlife products, especially those of endangered species; and antiques. Please contact the Tourism Authority of Bhutan for specific information on customs requirements. (Please see also the above section on Entry/Exit Requirements)

CRIMINAL PENALTIES: While in a foreign country, a U.S. citizen is subject to that country's laws and regulations, which sometimes differ significantly from those in the United States and may not afford the protections available to the individual under U.S. law. Penalties for breaking the law can be more severe than penalties for similar offenses in the United States. Persons violating Bhutan laws, even unknowingly, may be expelled, arrested or imprisoned. Penalties for possession of, use of, or trafficking in illegal drugs are strictly enforced. Convicted offenders can expect jail sentences and heavy fines.

SPECIAL CIRCUMSTANCES: Visitors are advised to carry cash or travelers checks, since credit cards are not widely accepted in Bhutan. Druk Air, the only carrier servicing Bhutan, has rigid restrictions on the amount and size of luggage passengers may carry into the country. Passengers are advised to book bulky items ahead as unaccompanied baggage, since the aircraft servicing Bhutan have limited space available for large bags, and airline employees may not load

347

large pieces of luggage. Flights into Paro Airport are restricted to daylight hours and are dependent on weather. Flights are sometimes delayed or cancelled. Passengers are advised to allow at least 24 hours transit time for connecting flights from Paro Airport and to travel on non-restricted air tickets so that they can be rebooked on the first available air carrier if a connecting flight is missed.

DISASTER PREPAREDNESS: Bhutan is an earthquake-prone country. General information about natural disaster preparedness is available via the Internet from the U.S. Federal Emergency Management Agency (FEMA) at http://www.fema.gov/.

CHILDREN'S ISSUES: For information on international adoption of children and international parental child abduction, please refer to our Internet site at http://travel.state.gov/children's_issues.html or telephone (202) 736-7000.

EMBASSY LOCATION AND REGISTRATION: There is no U.S. Embassy or Consulate in Bhutan. Although no formal diplomatic relations exist between the United States and Bhutan, informal contact is maintained through the U.S. Embassy in New Delhi. Updated information on travel and security in Bhutan may be obtained at any U.S. Consulate or Embassy in India or Bangladesh. Americans living in or visiting Bhutan are encouraged to register at the U.S. Embassy in New Delhi. They may also obtain assistance from the U.S. Consulates in India or, to a more limited degree, from the U.S. Embassies in Dhaka, Bangladesh or Kathmandu, Nepal.

--The U.S. Embassy in New Delhi is located at Shanti Path, Chanakyapuri 110021, telephone (91)(11)419-8000, fax:(91)(11)419-0017. The Embassy's Internet home page address is http://usembassy.state.gov/posts/in1/wwwhmain.ht ml

--The U.S. Consulate General in Mumbai (Bombay) is located at Lincoln House, 78 Bhulabhai Desai Road, 400026, telephone (91)(22) 363-3611/ Internet home page address is http://usembassy.state.gov/mumbai.
--The U.S. Consulate General in Calcutta is at 5/1

Ho Chi Minh Sarani, 700071, telephone (91)(033)282-3611 through 282-3615. The Internet home page address is http://usembassy.state.gov/posts/in4/wwwhmain.ht ml
--The U.S. Consulate General in Chennai (Madras) is at Mount Road, 600006, telephone (91)(44)827-3040. Internet home page address is http://usembassy.state.gov/chennai/.
--The U.S. Embassy in Dhaka is located at Diplomatic Enclave, Madani Ave, Baridhara, Dhaka 1212, telephone (880) (2) 882-4700-22, fax (880)(2) 882-3744.
--The U.S. Embassy in Kathmandu is located at Pani Pokhari, Kathmandu, telephone (977)(1)411179, 410531, fax(977)(1)419963. The Internet home page address is http://www.south-asia.com/usa/.

This replaces the Consular Information Sheet dated October 24, 2000, to expand information in the Entry/Exit Requirements, Customs Regulations, and Medical Insurance, and to include a section on Special Circumstances.

INDIA

COUNTRY DESCRIPTION: India is an economically developing democratic republic. Tourist facilities varying in degree of comfort and amenities are widely available in the major population centers and main tourist areas.

ENTRY REQUIREMENTS: All American citizens require a passport and visa for entry into and exit from India for any purpose. All visitors, including those on official U.S. government business, must obtain visas at an Indian embassy or consulate abroad prior to entering the country. There are no provisions for visas upon arrival. Those arriving in India without a visa bearing the correct validity dates and number of entries are subject to immediate deportation on the return flight. The U.S. Embassy and consulates in India are unable to assist when U.S. citizens arrive without visas. For further information on entry requirements, please contact the Embassy of India at 2536 Massachusetts Avenue N.W., Washington, D.C. 20008, telephone (202) 939-9849 or 939-9806 or the Indian consulates in Chicago, New York, San Francisco, or Houston. The Internet address of the Embassy of India is http://www.indianembassy.org/. Outside the

United States, inquiries should be made at the nearest Indian embassy or consulate.

In an effort to prevent international child abduction, many governments have initiated procedures at entry/exit points. These often include requiring documentary evidence of relationship and permission for the child's travel from the parent(s) or legal guardian not present. Having such documentation on hand, even if not required, may facilitate entry/departure.

SAFETY/SECURITY: Since 1996, New Delhi has been the site of occasional terrorist bombing incidents. These bomb blasts have occurred in public places, as well as on public transportation such as trains and buses. In December 1999, an Indian Airlines plane carrying one American citizen was hijacked en route from Kathmandu to New Delhi. The American was not injured. In December 2000, a terrorist attack on Delhi's Red Fort, a major tourist attraction, left three Indians dead. While no U.S. citizens were among the victims, other foreign visitors were injured. No reliable pattern has emerged in these attacks; nor is there any indication that they are directed against Americans or other foreigners. Nevertheless, U.S. citizens should be alert to suspicious packages in public places and avoid crowds, political demonstrations, and other manifestations of civil unrest.

AREAS OF INSTABILITY AND TERRORISM: JAMMU and KASHMIR The Department of State strongly urges private U.S. citizens to avoid all travel to the Kashmir Valley, Doda district, and Srinagar in the state of Jammu and Kashmir. These are areas of ongoing terrorist activities and violent civil disturbances. In October 2001, a bomb exploded at the Jammu and Kashmir State Assembly complex, killing 38 people and injuring over 100 others. Also, in the past year, several Western foreigners have been attacked in an effort to ensure tourism does not get a new start in these areas. The few tourists who do go to these areas are quite visible and vulnerable and definitely at risk. Even Ladakh has occasionally been affected by terrorist violence. In 2000, a German tourist was killed by Kashmiri militants in Ladakh's Zanskar region. U.S. Government employees are prohibited from traveling to the Kashmir portion of the state of Jammu and Kashmir without permission from the U.S. Embassy in New Delhi.

In 1999, the terrorist organization Harakat Ul Mujahideen issued a ban on Americans, including tourists, visiting Kashmir. In 1995, the terrorist organization Al Faran kidnapped seven Western tourists who were trekking, including two Americans, in the Kashmir Valley. One of the hostages was brutally murdered, another escaped, and the other five - including one American - have never been found. Srinagar has also been the site of a great deal of violence. Within the past year, it has been the site of a number of car bombings, market bombings, and land mine deaths. In May 2000, a Czech tourist was shot and wounded in Srinagar. During that same month, a minister for the state of Jammu and Kashmir was killed in a land mine explosion south of Srinagar. Also in May 2000, rocket-propelled grenades fired at a government building in Srinagar, killed a government employee and wounded others. In October 1999, a French tourist was shot and wounded. An American tourist was fatally shot in Srinagar in 1994.

AREAS OF INSTABILITY: NORTHEAST STATES - Sporadic incidents of violence by ethnic insurgent groups, including the bombing of buses and trains, are reported from parts of Assam, Manipur, Nagaland, Tripura, and Meghalaya. While U.S. citizens have not been specifically targeted, visitors are cautioned not to travel outside major cities at night. Security laws are in force, and the central government has deployed security personnel to several Northeast states. Travelers may check with the U.S. Consulate in Calcutta for information on current conditions. (Please see the section on Registration/Embassy and Consulate Locations below.)

AREAS OF INSTABILITY: INDIA-PAKISTAN BORDER - Tensions run high between India and Pakistan, particularly over Kashmir. The only official India-Pakistan border crossing point is between Atari, India, and Wagah, Pakistan. A Pakistani visa is required for entry into Pakistan. Since January 1, the border crossing has been closed due to tensions between India and Pakistan, and all commercial travel links, including air, train and bus, between India and Pakistan have been suspended. Travelers are advised to confirm the current status of the border crossing prior to commencing travel.

349

Both India and Pakistan claim an area of the Karakoram mountain range that includes the Siachen Glacier. The two countries have military outposts in the region, and armed clashes have occurred. Because of this situation, U.S. citizens traveling to or climbing peaks anywhere in the disputed areas face significant risk of injury and death. The disputed area includes the following peaks: Rimo Peak; Apsarasas I, II, and III; Tegam Kangri I, II and III; Suingri Kangri; Ghiant I and II; Indira Col.; and Sia Kangri.

RESTRICTED AREAS: Permission from the Indian Government (from Indian diplomatic missions abroad or in some cases from the Ministry of Home Affairs) is required to visit the states of Mizoram, Manipur, Nagaland, Arunachal Pradesh, Sikkim, parts of Kulu district and Spiti district of Himachal Pradesh, border areas of Jammu and Kashmir, some areas of Uttar Pradesh, the area west of National Highway No. 15 running from Ganganagar to Sanchar in Rajasthan, the Andaman and Nicobar Islands, and the Union Territory of the Laccadive Islands.

CIVIL DISTURBANCES: Urban demonstrations pose risks to travelers' personal safety and can disrupt transportation systems and city services. In response to such events, Indian authorities occasionally impose curfews and/or restrict travel. Political rallies and demonstrations in India have the potential for violence, especially immediately preceding and following elections. Americans are urged to avoid demonstrations and rallies. In addition, religious and inter-caste violence occasionally occurs unpredictably. While such violence rarely targets foreigners, mobs have attacked Indian Christian workers. Missionary activity has aroused strong reactions in some areas -- usually rural areas -- and in January 1999, a mob murdered an Australian missionary and his two sons in the eastern state of Orissa. Nevertheless, the principal risk for foreigners is that of becoming inadvertent victims. U.S. citizens should read local newspapers and contact the U.S. Embassy or the nearest U.S. consulate for further information about the current situation in areas where they wish to travel.

CRIME INFORMATION: Petty crime, especially theft of personal property, is common. Although violent crime is uncommon, some Westerners, including Americans, have been the victims of robberies and violent attacks that resulted in serious injuries and, in two recent cases, death. The common thread for most attacks on travelers has been that the travelers were traveling on their own. Travelers are cautioned not to travel alone in India. Because Americans' purchasing power is comparatively large, relative to that of the general population, travelers should always exercise modesty and caution in their financial dealings in India to reduce the chance of being a target for robbery.

The Embassy also urges Americans arriving at major tourist points such as airports and train stations to use pre-paid taxis as much as possible. There have been a number of cases where drivers and others have solicited travelers with "come-on" offers of cheap transportation and/or hotels. Such travelers often then find themselves the victims of various scams, including disproportionately expensive hotel rooms, unwanted "tours," unwelcome "purchases," and even threats when the tourists try to decline to pay. There have also been unconfirmed reports of individual tourists being given drugged drinks or tainted food to make them more vulnerable to theft. Travelers should exercise significant care when hiring transportation and/or guides.

Travelers should be aware of a number of other scams that have been perpetrated against foreign travelers, particularly in the Jaipur area. The scams generally target younger travelers and involve suggestions that money can be made by privately transporting gems or gold (both of which can result in arrest) or by taking delivery abroad of expensive carpets, supposedly while avoiding customs duties. The scam artists describe the theoretical profits that can be made upon delivery of the goods. Most such schemes require that the traveler first put up a "deposit" to either show "sincerity" or as a "down payment" or as the "wholesale cost." All travelers are strongly cautioned that the schemes invariably result in the traveler being fleeced. The "gems" or "gold" are nearly always fake. And if they were real, the traveler could be subject to arrest. Such schemes often pull the unsuspecting traveler in over the course of several days and begin with a new "friend" who offers to show the traveler the sights so that the "friend" or another new acquaintance can "practice his English." Offers of cheap lodgings and meals also can place the traveler in the physical custody of the scam artist and can leave the traveler at the mercy of threats or even physical coercion.

CRIME IN UTTARANCHAL AND HIMACHAL PRADESH - In the last two years, two Americans were murdered in the Haridwar/Rishikesh region of Uttaranchal state. Both Americans had become heavily involved with the Hindu religious community there. The police have confirmed that both crimes were financially motivated. Several other foreigners have also been attacked in Uttaranchal, including two Spaniards and one Japanese tourist who were murdered in 2000. Several U.S. citizens have reported their passports and other belongings stolen in the last year. Crime and violence have also increased in the popular hiking and rafting destination of Kulu/Manali, Uttaranchal, where the number of foreign backpackers and tourists has been growing and where drugs are readily available. In the last year, an Italian was murdered and a missing Russian hiker is presumed to be dead. Foreigners are the targets of criminal activities primarily because of the disproportionately large sums of money they are thought to carry. Visitors to the area are strongly cautioned not to travel alone and to be aware of their environment and their belongings. Travelers may check with the U.S. Embassy in New Delhi on current conditions. (Please see the section on Registration/Embassy and Consulate Locations below.)

CRIME IN ANDHRA PRADESH - Americans traveling to or residing in Andhra Pradesh should also be aware that there have been media and other reports of inappropriate sexual behavior by a prominent local religious leader. Most of the reports indicate that the subjects of these approaches have been young male devotees, including a number of Americans. Although these reports are unconfirmed, American citizens should be aware of this information.

The loss or theft of a U.S. passport abroad should be reported immediately to local police and the nearest U.S. embassy or consulate. U.S. citizens may refer to the Department of State's pamphlets, *A Safe Trip Abroad* and *Tips for Travelers to South Asia*, for ways to promote a more trouble-free journey. The pamphlets are available by mail from the Superintendent of Documents, U.S.

Government Printing Office, Washington, D.C. 20420; via the Internet at http:/www.acess.gpo.gov/su_docs, or from the Bureau of Consular Affairs home page at http://travel.state.gov.

MEDICAL FACILITIES AND INSURANCE: Adequate to excellent medical care is available in the major population centers, but it is usually very limited or unavailable in rural areas. The Department of State strongly urges Americans to consult with their medical insurance company prior to traveling abroad to confirm whether their policy applies overseas and if it will cover emergency expenses such as a medical evacuation. U.S. medical insurance plans seldom cover health costs incurred outside the United States unless supplemental coverage is purchased. Further, U.S. Medicare and Medicaid programs do not provide payment for medical services outside the United States. However, many travel agents and private companies offer insurance plans that will cover health care expenses incurred overseas, including emergency services such as medical evacuations.

When making a decision regarding health insurance, Americans should consider that many foreign doctors and hospitals require payment in cash prior to providing service and that a medical evacuation to the United States may cost well in excess of $50,000. Uninsured travelers who require medical care overseas often face extreme difficulties. When consulting with your insurer prior to your trip, please ascertain whether payment will be made to the overseas healthcare provider or if you will be reimbursed later for expenses that you incur. Some insurance policies also include coverage for psychiatric treatment and for disposition of remains in the event of death.

Useful information on medical emergencies abroad, including overseas insurance programs, is provided in the Department of State's Bureau of Consular Affairs brochure, *Medical Information for Americans Traveling Abroad*, available via the Bureau of Consular Affairs home page or autofax: (202) 647-3000.

OTHER HEALTH INFORMATION: Information on vaccinations and other health precautions may be obtained from the Centers for Disease Control and Prevention's international traveler's hotline at telephone 1-877-FYI-TRIP (1-

877-394-8747); fax 1-888-CDC-FAXX (1-888-232-3299), or via CDC'S Internet home page at http://www.cdc.gov. It is important to note that Indian health regulations require all travelers arriving from Sub-Sahara Africa or other yellow fever areas to have evidence of vaccination against yellow fever. Travelers who do not have such proof are subject to immediate deportation or a six-day detention in the yellow fever quarantine center. Americans who transit through any part of sub-Sahara Africa, even for one day, are advised to carry proof of yellow fever immunization.

TRAFFIC SAFETY AND ROAD CONDITIONS: While in a foreign country, U.S. citizens may encounter road conditions that differ significantly from those in the United States. The information below concerning traffic safety and road conditions in India is provided for general reference only, and it may not be totally accurate in a particular location or circumstance.

Safety of Public Transportation: Poor
Urban Road Condition/Maintenance: Poor
Rural Road Condition/Maintenance: Poor
Availability of Roadside Assistance: Poor to nonexistent

Travel by road is dangerous. In recent years, Delhi alone has experienced over 2,000 road deaths annually. A number of Americans have suffered fatal traffic accidents in recent times. Travel at night is particularly hazardous. In March 1996, five Americans were killed when a tour bus crashed at night near the city of Agra. Buses, patronized by hundreds of millions of Indians, are convenient in that they serve almost every city of any size. However, they are usually driven fast, recklessly, and without consideration for official rules of the road. Accidents are quite common. Trains are somewhat safer than buses, but train accidents still occur more frequently than in developed countries.

On Indian roads, the safest driving policy is to assume that other drivers will not respond to a traffic situation in the same way you would in the United States. For instance, buses will often run straight through red lights and will merge directly into traffic at yield points and traffic circles. Cars, auto-rickshaws, bicycles and pedestrians behave only slightly more cautiously. It has been said that the Indian driver looks only ahead; all drivers

consider themselves responsible only for traffic in front of them, not behind or to the side. Frequent use of one's horn to announce presence is both customary and wise. It is always preferable to have a licensed experienced driver who has a "feel" for road and driving conditions.

Outside major cities, main roads and other roads are poorly maintained and always congested. Even main roads often have only two lanes, with poor visibility and inadequate warning markers. Heavy traffic is the norm, and it includes (but is not limited to) overloaded trucks and buses, scooters, pedestrians, bullock and camel carts, horse or elephant riders en route to weddings, and free-roaming livestock.

It is very important to keep in mind that if a driver hits a pedestrian or a cow, the vehicle and its occupants are at risk of being attacked by passersby. Such attacks put the vehicle's occupants at significant risk of injury or death, or at least incineration of the vehicle. It can thus be unsafe to remain at the scene of an accident of this nature, and drivers may wish to consider seeking out the nearest police station instead.

Emergency Numbers: The following emergency numbers work in New Delhi:
Police 100
Fire Brigade 101
Ambulance 102

Traffic in India moves on the left. For specific information concerning Indian driver's permits, vehicle inspection, road tax and mandatory insurance, please contact the Indian National Tourist Organization offices via the Internet at http://www.tourisminindia.com/

PILOTING CIVIL AIRCRAFT: There have been a number of incidents in which civil aircraft have been detained for deviating from approved flight plans. U.S. citizens piloting civil aircraft in India must file any changes to previous flight plans with the appropriate Indian authorities and may not over-fly restricted airspace.

AVIATION SAFETY OVERSIGHT: The U.S. Federal Aviation Administration (FAA) has assessed the government of India's civil aviation authority as category 1 - in compliance with international aviation safety standards for oversight of India's air carrier operations.

For further information, travelers may contact the Department of Transportation within the United States at telephone 1-800-322-7873 or visit the FAA's Internet web site at http://www.faa.gov/avr/iasa.pdf. The U.S. Department of Defense (DOD) separately assesses some foreign air carriers for suitability as official providers of air services. For information regarding the DOD policy on specific carriers, travelers may contact the DOD at telephone 1-618-256-4801.

CUSTOMS CONSIDERATIONS: Indian customs authorities enforce strict regulations concerning temporary importation into or export from India of items such as firearms, antiquities, electronic equipment, currency, ivory, gold objects, and other prohibited materials. It is advisable to contact the Embassy of India in Washington, D.C. or one of India's consulates in the United States for specific information regarding customs requirements.

DRUG AND CRIMINAL PENALTIES: While in a foreign country, a U.S. citizen is subject to that country's laws and regulations, which sometimes differ significantly from those in the United States and may not afford the protections available to the individual under U.S. law. Penalties for breaking the law can be more severe than in the United States for similar offenses. Persons violating Indian laws, even unknowingly, may be expelled, arrested or imprisoned. Penalties for possession of, use of, or trafficking in illegal drugs are strictly enforced; convicted offenders in India can expect a minimum jail sentence of ten (10) years, plus fines. In addition, they can face lengthy detention without bail pending trial. Conditions in Indian jails range from austere to severe.

CONSULAR ACCESS: U.S. citizens are encouraged to carry a photocopy of their U.S. passports with them at all times, so that proof of identity and U.S. citizenship are readily available if they are questioned by local officials. In accordance with the Vienna Convention, Indian authorities must allow U.S. citizens to contact a U.S. Consular Officer if arrested or detained in India.

CHILDREN'S ISSUES: For information on international adoption of children and international parental child abduction, please refer to the Internet site at http://travel.state.gov/children's_issues.html or telephone (202) 736-7000.

REGISTRATION/EMBASSY AND CONSULATE LOCATIONS: Americans living in or visiting India are encouraged to register at the U.S. Embassy in New Delhi or at one of the U.S. consulates in India. They may also obtain updated information on travel and security in India and request a copy of the booklet, "Guidelines for American travelers in India."

-- The U.S. Embassy in New Delhi is located at Shantipath, Chanakyapuri 110021; telephone (91) (11) 2419-8000; fax (91) (11) 2419-0017. The Embassy's Internet home page address is http://usembassy.state.gov/delhi/html.
-- The U.S. Consulate General in Mumbai (Bombay) is located at Lincoln House, 78 Bhulabhai Desai Road, 400026, telephone (91) (22) 2363-3611; fax (91)(22) 2363-0350. Internet home page address is http://usembassy.state.gov/posts/in3/wwwhmain.html.
-- The U.S. Consulate General in Calcutta (now oftencalled Kolkata) is at 5/1 Ho Chi Minh Sarani, 700071;telephone (91) (033) 2282-3611 through 2282-3615; fax(91) (33) 2282-2335. The Internet home page address is http://usembassy.state.gov/posts/in4/wwwhmain.html.
-- The U.S. Consulate General in Chennai (Madras) is at Mount Road, 600006, telephone (91) (044) 811-2000; fax (91)(044) 811-2020. The Internet home page address is http://usembassy.state.gov/chennai/.

This replaces the Consular Information Sheet for India dated November 23, 2001, to update information on Safety and Security (Areas of Instability: India-Pakistan Border) and Crime.

MALDIVES

COUNTRY DESCRIPTION: The Republic of Maldives consists of 1,190 islands (fewer than 200 are inhabited) located southwest of Sri Lanka, off the southern tip of India. The Maldives has a population of 270,000, of which about 70,000 reside in Male, the capital city. The only international airport is on the nearby island of Hulhule. Beautiful atolls inhabited by over 1,100 species of fish and other sea life attract thousands of visitors each year. Tourism facilities are well developed on the resort islands.

ENTRY/EXIT REQUIREMENTS: A valid passport, along with an onward or return ticket and sufficient funds, is required for entry. A no-cost visit visa valid for 30 days is issued upon arrival. If a traveler stays in a resort or hotel, the Department of Immigration and Emigration routinely approves requests for extensions of stays up to 90 days with evidence of sufficient funds. Anyone staying over 60 days without proper authorization faces heavy fines and deportation. All travelers (except diplomats and certain exempted travelers) departing the Republic of the Maldives must pay an airport departure tax.

Arrival by Private Boat: Travelers arriving by private yacht or boat are granted no-cost visas, usually valid until the expected date of departure. Vessels anchoring in atolls other than Male must have prior clearance from the Ministry of Defense and National Security. The clearances can be obtained through local shipping agents in Male. Maldivian customs, police and/or representatives of Maldivian Immigration will meet all vessels, regardless of where they anchor. Vessels arriving with a dog on board will be permitted anchorage, but the dog will not be allowed off the vessel. Any firearms or ammunition on board will be held for bond until the vessel's departure.

Specific inquiries should be addressed to the Maldives High Commission in Sri Lanka at No. 23, Kaviratne Place, Colombo 6, telephone (94) (1) 586-762/500-943, or the Maldives Mission to the U.N. in New York, telephone (212) 599-6195.

In an effort to prevent international child abduction, many governments have initiated procedures at entry/exit points. These often include requiring documentary evidence of relationship and permission for the child's travel from the parent(s) or legal guardian not present. Having such documentation on hand, even if not required, may facilitate entry/departure.

DUAL NATIONALITY: The Republic of the Maldives recognizes dual nationality. Dual nationals are not required to use their Maldivian

passports when entering the country, but they must use them when departing.

CRIME INFORMATION: The Maldives has a low crime rate, but thefts of valuables left unattended on beaches or in hotels do occur. The loss or theft abroad of a U.S. passport should be reported immediately to the local police and the nearest U.S. embassy or consulate. U.S. citizens may refer to the Department of State's pamphlet, *A Safe Trip Abroad*, for ways to promote a more trouble-free journey. The pamphlet is available by mail from the Superintendent of Documents, U.S. Government Printing Office, Washington, D.C. 20402, via the Internet at http://www.access.gpo.gov/su_docs, or via the Bureau of Consular Affairs home page at http://travel.state.gov.

MEDICAL FACILITIES: There are two main hospitals in Male: the government-owned Indira Ghandi Memorial Hospital (IGM) and the privately owned Abdurahman Don Kaleyfan Hospital (ADK). Both hospitals provide a relatively high standard of medical care, including general and orthopedic surgery and neurosurgery. ADK accepts most major credit cards and some foreign medical insurance packages. IGM accepts neither credit cards nor medical insurance. Both hospitals accept U.S. dollars.

There are two recompression chambers in the Maldives; one is located near Male on Bandos Island and the other is in Kuramathi, North Ari Atoll. There are no trauma units in the country, and spinal surgery is not available. There is an air medical service to Singapore; however, medical evacuations are very costly.

MEDICAL INSURANCE: The Department of State strongly urges Americans to consult with their medical insurance company prior to traveling abroad to confirm whether their policy applies overseas and if it will cover emergency expenses such as medical evacuation. U.S. medical insurance plans seldom cover health costs incurred outside the United States unless supplemental coverage is purchased. Further, U.S. Medicare and Medicaid programs do not provide payment for medical services outside the United States. However, many travel agents and private companies offer insurance plans that will cover health care expenses incurred overseas, including emergency services such as medical evacuations.

When making a decision regarding health insurance, Americans should consider that many foreign doctors and hospitals require payment in cash prior to providing service and that a medical evacuation to the United States may cost in excess of $50,000. Uninsured travelers who require medical care overseas often face extreme difficulties. When consulting your insurer prior to your trip, please ascertain whether payment will be made to the overseas healthcare provider or if you will be reimbursed later for expenses that you incur. Some insurance policies also include coverage for psychiatric treatment and for disposition or remains in the event of death.

Useful information on medical emergencies abroad, including overseas insurance programs, is provided in the Department of State's Bureau of Consular Affairs brochure, *Medical Information for Americans Traveling Abroad*, available via the Bureau of Consular Affairs home page or autofax: (202) 647-3000.

OTHER HEALTH INFORMATION: Information on vaccinations and other health precautions may be obtained from the Centers for Disease Control and Prevention's hotline for international travelers at 1-877-FYI-TRIP (1-877-394-8747); fax: 1-888-CDC-FAXX (1-888-232-3299), or by visiting the CDC's Internet home page at http://www.cdc.gov.

TRAFFIC SAFETY AND ROAD CONDITIONS: While in a foreign country, U.S. citizens may encounter road conditions that differ significantly from those in the United States. The information below concerning the Republic of Maldives is provided for general reference only and may not be totally accurate in a particular location or circumstance.

Safety of Public Transportation: Good to Excellent
Urban Road Conditions/Maintenance: Excellent
Rural road conditions/Maintenance: Fair
Availability of Roadside Assistance: Poor

Only a few of the islands are large enough to support automobiles. Most transportation in the Maldives is by boat or seaplane. The Maldives has good safety standards for land, sea, and air travel. Roads in Male and on the airport island are brick

and generally well maintained. Sand roads on resort islands are well kept by the resorts.

Transportation on the small island on which the capital, Male, is situated is either by foot or by readily available taxi. Transportation between the airport and Male, as well as to nearby resort islands, is by motorized water taxis (known as dhoni) and by speedboat. Several local companies provide seaplane (air taxi) and helicopter service to outlying islands. Air taxis stop flying one hour before sunset, and some resorts do not transport passengers by boat between the airport and the resort island later than one hour before sunset. Visitors to distant resorts arriving in the country at night can expect to stay overnight at a hotel in Male or at the Hulhule Airport hotel. All travelers should confirm their transfer arrangements in advance.

For additional general information about road safety, including links to foreign government sites, please see the Department of State, Bureau of Consular Affairs home page at http://travel.state.gov/road_safety.html. For specific information concerning Maldivian driving permits, vehicle inspection, road tax and mandatory insurance, please contact the Maldivian National Tourist Organization Office in Male via the Internet at http://www.visitmaldives.com.

AVIATION SAFETY OVERSIGHT: As there is no direct commercial air service at present, nor economic authority to operate such service between the United States and the Republic of Maldives, the U.S. Federal Aviation Administration (FAA) has not assessed Maldives' civil aviation authority for compliance with international aviation safety standards.

For further information, travelers may contact the Department of Transportation within the United States at telephone 1-800-322-7873 or visit the FAA Internet home page at http://www.faa.gov/avr/iasa/. The U.S. Department of Defense (DOD) separately assesses some foreign air carriers for suitability as official providers of air services. For information regarding the DOD policy on specific carriers, travelers may contact the DOD at telephone 1-618-229-4801.

CUSTOMS REGULATIONS: Maldivian customs

authorities prohibit the importation of non-Islamic religious materials, including religious statues. Personal Bibles are permitted. The importation of pork and pork by-products is restricted. Dogs are not permitted, but visitors may bring their cats. (Many hotels and resorts do not allow pets; travelers should confirm a particular hotel's policy prior to arrival.) Please see the "Arrival by Private Boat" section above regarding dogs on anchored vessels. Items such as alcohol and religious items will be kept and held for bond until the traveler departs. Pornographic materials are banned, and they will be destroyed upon arrival in the country. A complete summary of custom regulations is available at http://www.customs.gov.mv/.

CRIMINAL PENALTIES: While in a foreign country, a U.S. citizen is subject to that country's laws and regulations, which sometimes differ significantly from those in the United States and may not afford the protections available to the individual under U.S. law. Penalties for breaking the law can be more severe than those in the United States for similar offenses. Persons violating Maldivian laws, even unknowingly, may be expelled, arrested or imprisoned. Penalties for possession of, use of, or trafficking in illegal drugs are strictly enforced in the Maldives. Convicted offenders can expect jail sentences, deportation, and/or heavy fines. It is illegal to bring alcohol into the Maldives. Alcoholic beverages are legally available for retail sale to tourists on resort islands, but not on the island city of Male.

SPECIAL CIRCUMSTANCES:
Religious Laws: Public observance of any religion other than Islam is prohibited. All Maldivian citizens living in the Republic of Maldives are Moslem, and places of worship for adherents of other religions do not exist. Religious gatherings such as Bible study groups are prohibited; however, a family unit of foreigners may practice its religion, including Bible readings, privately within its residence. It is against the law to invite or encourage Maldivian citizens to attend these gatherings. Offenders may face jail sentences, expulsion and/or fines.

In 1998, several foreign families, including some Americans, were expelled for allegedly engaging in religious proselytizing. Although Maldivian law prohibits importing "idols for religious worship," tourists going to the resort islands are generally

allowed to bring in items and texts used for personal religious observances. Please refer to the "Customs Regulations" section above for information about other restrictions.

Currency: Credit cards are not widely accepted outside large hotels and resorts; however, more shops are slowly moving toward accepting them. Cash payment in dollars is accepted at most retail shops and restaurants and by taxi drivers.

CHILDREN'S ISSUES: For information on international adoption of children and international parental child abduction, please refer to our Internet site at http://travel.state.gov/children's_issues.html or telephone (202) 736-7000.

REGISTRATION/EMBASSY LOCATION: There is no U.S. Embassy in Republic of Maldives, but the U.S. Ambassador to Sri Lanka is also accredited to the Maldives. The former U.S. Consular Agency in Male closed on August 9, 1995. Americans living in or visiting the Maldives are encouraged to register at the Consular Section of the U.S. Embassy in Sri Lanka and to obtain updated information on travel and security within the Republic of Maldives. The U.S. Embassy is located at 210 Galle Road, Colombo 3, Sri Lanka. The Embassy's telephone number during normal business hours Monday through Friday is (94) (1) 448-007. The Embassy's after-hours and emergency telephone number is (94)(1) 448-601. The Consular Section fax number is (94)(1) 436-943. The Internet address is http://usembassy.state.gov/srilanka. The e-mail address for the Consular Section is consularcolombo@state.gov.

NEPAL

COUNTRY DESCRIPTION: Nepal is a developing country with extensive tourist facilities, which vary widely in quality and price. The capital is Kathmandu. The country is currently suffering increasing incidents of violence related to a brutal Maoist insurgency.

ENTRY/EXIT REQUIREMENTS: A passport and visa are required. Tourist visas can be purchased upon arrival at Tribhuvan International Airport in Kathmandu and at all other ports of entry. All foreigners also must pay an airport exit tax, regardless of the length of their stay. Travelers may obtain further information on entry/exit requirements by contacting the Royal Nepalese Embassy at 2131 Leroy Place, N.W., Washington, D.C. 20008, telephone (202) 667-4550 or the Consulate General in New York at (212) 370-3988. The Internet address of the Embassy of Nepal is http://www.nepalembassyusa.org/.

Travelers occasionally report immigration difficulties with Chinese authorities when crossing the Nepal-China border overland in either direction. U.S. citizens planning to travel to Tibet from Nepal should contact the U.S. Embassy in Kathmandu for current information on the status of the border-crossing points. Travelers may also wish to check with the People's Republic of China Embassy in Nepal for current regulations for entry into Tibet.

In an effort to prevent international child abduction, many governments have initiated procedures at entry/exit points. These often include requiring documentary evidence of relationship and permission for the child's travel from the parent(s) or legal guardian not present. Having such documentation on hand, even if not required, may facilitate entry/departure.

SAFETY/SECURITY: Since November 2001, violence from the Maoist insurgency in Nepal that began in 1996 has increased. The insurgents have escalated armed attacks throughout Nepal. Maoist cadres have engaged in a variety of guerrilla and terrorist tactics that have victimized, and in many cases brutalized, civilians. The insurgents have detonated explosive devices both within and outside the Kathmandu Valley, causing numerous injuries and some fatalities. The frequency of bombings has been increasing, and public areas, including a few frequented by tourists, have been targeted. The random, indiscriminate, and unpredictable nature of these attacks increases the likelihood that Americans in Nepal could be caught in the wrong place at the wrong time.

In a November 2002 press release, the Maoists claimed responsibility for targeting and murdering two locally hired U.S. Embassy security guard employees in separate incidents. Included in the press release are threats of further violence against any party or "diplomatic communities...working against the Maoists," specifically mentioning the "American Diplomatic Mission." While the Maoist press release states that Maoist actions are not targeted at foreign tourists, its repeated threatening references to the "American Mission" may imply a heightened risk for both official and private Americans in Nepal. Moreover, increasing Maoist robberies of trekkers, attacks on the property of several businesses perceived to have an American affiliation, and continuing anti-American rhetoric by the Maoist leadership could portend a threat to Americans in Nepal, particularly outside the Kathmandu Valley. The Embassy cannot rule out the potential for violence anywhere, even in traditional tourist areas.

In most areas outside the Kathmandu Valley, the situation is tense and uncertain. Of Nepal's 75 Districts, all but one have suffered violence and/or armed conflicts relating to the Maoist insurgency. Maoist landmine explosions, armed attacks, and vehicle burnings occur sporadically on main highways, including the roads linking Kathmandu with the Tibetan and Indian borders and with the tourist destinations of Pokhara and Chitwan National Park. Visitors throughout Nepal, including in Kathmandu, should avoid public buses and use metered taxis. The U.S. Embassy in Kathmandu requires pre-clearance of all travel outside the Kathmandu Valley by U.S. Government employees and forbids official American travel to many districts outside Kathmandu. Private Americans who decide to travel outside the Valley are strongly urged to contact the U.S. Embassy in Kathmandu to discuss and register their planned itinerary and to receive the most recent security information before traveling. Nighttime road travel should be strictly avoided outside the Kathmandu Valley and minimized within Kathmandu.

Maoists have attacked the offices of non-governmental organizations (NGO's), their local partners, and multinational businesses working in Nepal. Since the fall of 2000, NGO workers have reported a substantial increase in Maoist intimidation and extortion. Many workers have left their projects in rural areas because of concerns about possible Maoist violence and in response to Maoist threats.

BANDHS (GENERAL STRIKES) - A "bandh"

(general strike) is a longstanding form of political expression in Nepal used increasingly by the Maoist insurgency and enforced through intimidation and violence. Past bandhs have resulted in the shutdown of businesses, schools, offices and vehicular traffic. Both within and outside the Kathmandu Valley the Maoists have established a pattern of bombings, targeted assassinations (usually of security personnel), and other acts of intimidation prior to scheduled bandhs. In the lead-up to past bandhs, Maoists have attacked public buses, Nepalese Government vehicles, schools and private businesses with firebombs and explosive devices in an effort to terrorize the population into observing the strike. They have attacked civilian vehicles as well. In anticipation of a bandh planned for October 2002, for example, Maoists detonated three small bombs in the heart of Kathmandu, injuring four Nepalese.

Inside the Kathmandu Valley, American citizens are urged to pay attention to the volume of traffic on the roads, waiting until a pattern of traffic is well established before undertaking travel, and to maintain a low profile throughout bandh periods. Buses, taxis, and other forms of public transportation may not operate during a bandh. Observance of bandhs, particularly in the transportation sector, may be higher outside the Valley, where a number of private buses and trucks have been stopped and torched and their drivers beaten. Americans are strongly urged to avoid road travel outside the Kathmandu Valley during scheduled bandhs, and to exercise additional caution both during the lead-up to bandhs and during the bandhs. Americans planning air travel to or from Nepal during scheduled bandhs should be aware that transportation to and from airports throughout Nepal could be affected.

Americans are advised to consult the U.S. Embassy in Nepal's website at http://nepal.usembassy.gov for up-to-date information on upcoming bandhs as well as the latest security information. A link to the Embassy's website is provided in the Registration/Embassy Location section below.

CRIME INFORMATION: Although the rate of violent crime is low in Kathmandu relative to that in comparably sized American cities, minor street crime does occur in Kathmandu as well as in other areas frequented by foreigners. To avoid being victimized, visitors should avoid walking alone after dark and carrying large sums of cash or expensive jewelry. In addition, visitors should consider exchanging money only at banks and hotels and limiting shopping to daylight hours. Valuables should be stored in the hotel safety deposit box and should never be left unattended in hotel rooms.

Travelers should be especially alert at or near major tourist sites, where most pick-pocketing occurs. Passports and cash should be carried in a protected neck pouch or money belt--not in a backpack. The loss or theft abroad of a U.S. passport should be reported immediately to local police and to the nearest U.S. Embassy or Consulate. If you are the victim of a crime while overseas, in addition to reporting to local police, please contact the nearest U.S. Embassy or Consulate for assistance. The Embassy/Consulate staff can, for example, assist you to find appropriate medical care, to contact family members or friends and explain how funds could be transferred. Although the investigation and prosecution of a crime is solely the responsibility of local authorities, consular officers can help you to understand the local criminal justice process and to find an attorney if needed.

U.S. citizens may refer to the Department of State's pamphlets "*A Safe Trip Abroad*" and "Tips for Travelers to South Asia" for ways to promote a trouble-free journey. The pamphlets are available by mail from the Superintendent of Documents, U.S. Government Printing Office, Washington, D.C. 20402, via the Internet at http://www.access.gpo.gov/su_docs, or via the Bureau of Consular Affairs home page at http://travel.state.gov/.

MEDICAL FACILITIES: Medical care is limited and is generally not up to Western standards. Serious illnesses often require evacuation to the nearest adequate medical facility (in Singapore, Bangkok or New Delhi). Illnesses and injuries suffered while on trek in remote areas often require evacuation by helicopter to Kathmandu. Travelers should be aware that emergency services like evacuations and rescues from remote areas have been compromised by Maoist attacks on helicopters and airfields and the destruction of regular phone service in most trekking areas.

MEDICAL INSURANCE: The Department of State strongly urges Americans to consult with their medical insurance company prior to traveling abroad to confirm whether their policies apply overseas and whether they will cover emergency expenses such as helicopter rescues and other medical evacuations. U.S. medical insurance plans seldom cover health costs incurred outside the United States unless supplemental coverage is purchased. Further, U.S. Medicare and Medicaid programs do not provide payment for medical services outside the United States. However, many travel agents and private companies offer insurance plans that will cover health care expenses incurred overseas, including emergency rescue services such as medical evacuations.

When making a decision regarding health insurance, Americans should consider that many foreign doctors and hospitals require payment in cash prior to providing service and that a medical evacuation on commercial airlines to the U.S. may cost in excess of $50,000. An air ambulance medevac to Singapore costs in excess of $55,000. Helicopter evacuation from within Nepal to Kathmandu typically costs between $3,500 and $10,000. Uninsured travelers who require medical care overseas often face extreme difficulties. When consulting with your insurer prior to your trip, ascertain whether payment will be made to the overseas healthcare provider or whether you will be reimbursed later for expenses you incur. Some insurance policies also include coverage for psychiatric treatment and for disposition of remains in the event of death.

Useful information on medical emergencies abroad, including overseas insurance programs, is provided in the Department of State's Bureau of Consular Affairs brochure *"Medical Information for Americans Traveling Abroad,"* available via the Bureau of Consular Affairs home page or autofax: (202) 647-3000.

OTHER HEALTH INFORMATION: Information on vaccinations and other health precautions may be obtained from the Centers for Disease Control and Prevention's hotline for international travelers at 1-877-FYI-TRIP (1-877-394-8747); fax 1-888-CDC-FAXX (1-888-232-3299), or via CDC's Internet site at http://www.cdc.gov/travel. For information about outbreaks of infectious diseases abroad, consult the World Health Organization's website at http://www.who.int/en. Further health information for travelers is available at http://www.who.int/ith.

TRAFFIC SAFETY AND ROAD CONDITIONS: While in a foreign country, U.S. citizens may encounter road conditions that differ significantly from those in the United States. The information below concerning Nepal is provided for general reference only, and may not be totally accurate in a particular location or circumstance.
Safety of Public Transportation: Poor
Urban Road Conditions/Maintenance: Poor
Rural Road Conditions/Maintenance: Poor
Availability of Roadside Assistance: Poor

American citizens are strongly warned against undertaking any road travel outside the Kathmandu Valley at night or during or immediately preceding bandhs (general strikes). Additionally, American citizens should be extremely cautious when traveling overland in Nepal, especially by bus. A number of public buses have been held up and/or burned by Maoists over recent months. In general, roads are in poor condition and lack basic safety features. Many mountain and hill roads are impassable during monsoon season (June-September) due to landslides, and are hazardous even in the best weather. Avoid travel on night buses; fatal accidents are frequent. In the Kathmandu Valley, motor vehicles, bicycles, pedestrians and animals, all traveling at different speeds, congest narrow roads. Traffic is poorly regulated, and the volume of vehicles on the roads has been increasing by 15 percent a year. Many drivers are neither properly licensed nor trained. Many vehicles are poorly maintained. Sidewalks and pedestrian crossings are non-existent in most areas, and drivers do not yield the right-of-way to pedestrians. Pedestrians account for over 40% of all traffic fatalities in Nepal.

INFORMATION FOR TREKKERS: The past year has seen an increase in the number of foreign trekkers and climbers, including a number of American citizens, who have been robbed, extorted from and even assaulted by armed Maoists on the trails. Many formerly popular trekking routes traverse areas seriously affected by the Maoist insurgency and are no longer safe for travel. With the exceptions of the Everest region above Lukla, Upper Mustang and the Annapurna

359

Circuit region (see further information below regarding incidents in the Annapurna area), trekking routes in Nepal pose security risks and should be avoided.

Reports indicate that nearly all trekkers traveling on formerly popular trails from Jiri (in Dolakha District), the trails to Makalu Base Camp (in Sankuwasabha District), and trekking routes in the Kanchenjunga area (in the eastern Taplejung District) encounter Maoists and enforced demands for payments. The Dhaulagiri, Manaslu and Langtang trails also traverse Maoist-affected areas.

The safest trekking area in Nepal has been Mustang District, where no incidents of robbery or Maoist encounters have been reported. (Note that trekking in Upper Mustang requires a special permit from the Nepal Government at a minimum cost of $700/person.) In terms of reported incidents of Maoist encounters, the second safest trekking area has been the Everest region above Lukla. There have been, however, a few incidents of Maoist violence in and above Lukla, including the bombing of Lukla Airport's control tower in March 2002 and the burning down of a Village Development Committee office in Cheplung (north of Lukla) in October 2002. Areas to the immediate east, west and south of Lukla have been affected by increasing Maoist violence and should be avoided.

Although thousands of Westerners trekked this year without incident in the Annapurna region, a growing number of Maoist robberies have been reported there. In addition, on at least two occasions, groups of Maoists attacked and destroyed offices and buildings in Ghandruk (also transliterated as Ghandrung), a gateway village for both the Annapurna Circuit and the route to the Annapurna Base Camp.

When confronted by Maoists' demands for "donations," some trekkers have reported success in negotiating downwards the amount of money and equipment they are forced to turn over to the Maoists. However, Americans are urged to refrain from arguing with or "talking back" to Maoists; any Maoist encounter involves a risk of violence. American citizens are advised never to hike alone or to become separated from larger traveling parties while on a trail.

Maoist destruction of telephone service to most trekking areas complicates efforts to locate Americans and make arrangements for medical evacuations. U.S. citizens are strongly encouraged to contact the Embassy in Kathmandu for the latest security information and to register their itinerary before undertaking treks outside the Kathmandu Valley (see Registration/Embassy Location below). Trekkers are also advised to leave their itinerary with family or friends in the U.S. and to check in at police checkpoints where trekking permits are logged.

Trekking in Nepal involves walking over rugged, steep terrain, where one is exposed to the elements, often at high altitudes. Many popular trekking routes in Nepal cross passes as high as 18,000 feet. The U.S. Embassy in Kathmandu strongly advises all U.S. citizens to exercise extreme caution when trekking at higher altitudes. Only experienced mountain travelers should tackle the Himalayas. Trekkers of all ages, experience, and fitness levels can experience Acute Mountain Sickness (AMS), which can be deadly.

Trekkers should also be alert to the possibility of avalanches and landslides, even when trails are clear. Avalanches at the narrow gorge above Deurali on the route to the Annapurna Base Camp regularly result in the deaths of trekkers and climbers. Avalanches and landslides caused by severe storms have killed many foreign trekkers and their Nepalese guides, and have stranded hundreds of others.

More than any other factor, solo trekking contributes to injuries and deaths. The safest option for all trekkers is to join an organized group and/or use a reputable firm that provides an experienced guide and porters who communicate in both Nepali and English. Before leaving Kathmandu, trekkers can check with the U.S. Embassy or the Himalayan Rescue Association (phone 977-1-440292/440293) for good information about trail conditions and possible hazards in the high country.

AVIATION SAFETY OVERSIGHT: As there is no direct commercial air service by local carriers at present, or economic authority to operate such service, between the U.S. and Nepal, the U.S. Federal Aviation Administration (FAA) has not assessed Nepal's Civil Aviation Authority for compliance with international aviation safety standards. For further information, travelers may contact the Department of Transportation within the U.S. at 1-800-322-7873, or visit the FAA Internet home page at http://www.intl.faa.gov/.

The U.S. Department of Defense (DOD) separately assesses some foreign air carriers for suitability as official providers of air services. For information regarding the DOD policy on specific carriers, travelers may contact the DOD at (703)-697-7288.

CUSTOMS REGULATIONS: Nepalese customs authorities may enforce strict regulations concerning importation (even temporary) into or export from Nepal of items such as valuable metals, articles of archeological and religious importance, wildlife and related articles, drugs, arms and ammunition, and communications equipment. It is advisable to contact the Embassy of Nepal in Washington or Nepal's Consulate General in New York for specific information regarding customs requirements.

CRIMINAL PENALTIES: While in a foreign country, a U.S. citizen is subject to that country's laws and regulations, which sometimes differ significantly from those in the United States and may not afford the protections available to the individual under U.S. law. Penalties for breaking the law can be more severe than those in the United States for similar offenses. Persons violating Nepalese laws, even unknowingly, may be expelled, arrested or imprisoned. Penalties for possession of, use of, or trafficking in illegal drugs in Nepal are strict, and convicted offenders can expect jail sentences and heavy fines.

DISASTER PREPAREDNESS: Nepal is an earthquake-prone country. General information about natural disaster preparedness is available via the Internet from the U.S. Federal Emergency Management Agency (FEMA) at http://www.fema.gov/.

CHILDREN'S ISSUES: For information on international adoption of children and international parental child abduction, please refer to our Internet site at http://travel.state.gov/children's_issues.html or telephone (202) 736-7000.

REGISTRATION/EMBASSY LOCATION:

Americans living in or visiting Nepal are strongly encouraged to register at the Consular Section of the U.S. Embassy in Nepal and to obtain updated information on travel and security within Nepal. The U.S. Embassy is located at Pani Pokhari in Kathmandu, telephone (977) (1) 411179; fax (977) (1) 419963. Citizens may also register by accessing the U.S. Embassy's home page at http://nepal.usembassy.gov/ or by e-mail at amemb@cons.col.com.np. Please include the following information: full name; date of birth; U.S. passport number, date and place of issuance; home address and phone number; emergency contact person's name, phone number, fax or e-mail address; travel/medevac insurance information; address and phone number in Nepal; travel or trekking agency contact in Nepal; planned itinerary in Nepal; and traveling companions' names and nationalities. Finally, please indicate to whom, if anyone, the Embassy may divulge information regarding your welfare and whereabouts in Nepal.

This replaces the Consular Information Sheet for Nepal dated November 4, 2002, to expand the sections on Safety/Security, Bandhs (general strikes), Medical Facilities, Medical Insurance, Road Conditions, and Information for Trekkers.

PAKISTAN

WARNING (Issued March 22, 2002): This Travel Warning is being issued to alert Americans that the Department has ordered the departure of all non-emergency personnel and family members of the U.S. Embassy and Consulates in Pakistan. The possibility of threats to Americans continues, as demonstrated by the March 17 attack on worshippers at a church service in Islamabad underscoring the possibility that terrorists may seek civilian targets. This Travel Warning supersedes the Travel Warning for Pakistan dated March 18, 2002.

The Department of State warns U.S. citizens to defer travel to Pakistan. Terrorist groups have demonstrated a willingness to hit civilian as well as official targets. An American journalist was kidnapped and brutally murdered in Karachi in early 2002. The Department has reports that American citizens generally have been targeted for kidnapping or other terrorist actions. The March 17 attack on worshippers at the Protestant International Church in Islamabad, where two Americans were killed and several more were injured, underscores the growing possibility that as security is increased at official U.S. facilities, terrorists and their sympathizers will seek less well-protected targets. These may include facilities where Americans are generally known to congregate or visit, such as clubs, restaurants, places of worship, schools or outdoor recreation events.

As a result of these concerns, the Department has ordered the departure of non-emergency personnel and family members of the Embassy and Consulates in Pakistan. Americans in Pakistan are urged to consider departing the country. The Embassy and Consulates in Pakistan will remain available for American citizen services. However, from time to time, the missions in Pakistan may temporarily close or suspend public services as necessary to review their security posture. Americans seeking assistance should telephone the Embassy or Consulates before visiting there in person to ensure the offices are open.

The Government of Pakistan continues to give full support to the international campaign against terrorism. As Operation Enduring Freedom defeats Al-Qaida strongholds in Afghanistan, some Al-Qaida members have fled to Pakistan and other countries. This, coupled with the presence of indigenous sectarian and militant groups in Pakistan, requires that all Americans in or traveling through Pakistan take appropriate security measures. Events in the Middle East also increase the possibility of violence.

American citizens should also be aware that there are many areas of Pakistan which are restricted by the Government of Pakistan and require non-Pakistanis to obtain official permission before they may travel to them. This includes the tribal areas of Pakistan's Northwest Frontier Province, areas along the Line of Control, the Pakistan-India border and near other sensitive areas and facilities. Travelers need to determine beforehand whether the areas they intend to visit have any Pakistan government restrictions on them. If so, then the appropriate authorities must be contacted and approval obtained before travel is undertaken.

Americans who reside in or visit Pakistan should exercise maximum caution and take prudent measures. They should avoid crowds, demonstrations, and areas where Americans generally congregate.

U.S. citizens who remain in Pakistan are strongly urged to register and obtain updated security information at the U.S. Embassy or Consulates listed in the Registration/Embassy Location section near the end of this document.

COUNTRY DESCRIPTION: Pakistan is a developing country. Its elected government was overthrown by the military in October 1999, and it is now ruled by President Pervez Musharraf and an appointed civilian cabinet.

ENTRY/EXIT REQUIREMENTS: A passport is required. All U.S. citizens traveling to Pakistan are required to have valid visas issued at a Pakistani Embassy or Consulate. Other information on entry requirements can be obtained from the Embassy of Pakistan, 2315 Massachusetts Avenue, N.W., Washington, DC, 20008, telephone (202)939-6295 or 6261, Internet home page: http://www.pakistan-embassy.com. Travelers may also contact one of the Consulates General of Pakistan located at 12 East 65th St., New York, NY 10021, telephone (212)879-5800, fax (212)517-6987, or 10850 Wilshire Blvd., Suite 1100, Los Angeles, CA 90024, telephone (310)441-5114, fax (310)441-9256. If a traveler plans to stay longer than the time listed on the visa, he or she must extend the stay with the local passport office of Ministry of Interior. Airlines may require travelers departing the United States to present multiple photographs and complete copies of passports and other travel documents. Tourist facilities are available in the principal population centers of the country.

In an effort to prevent international child abduction, many governments have initiated procedures at entry/exit points. These often include requiring documentary evidence of relationship and permission for the child's travel from the parent(s) or legal guardian not present. Having such documentation on hand, even if not required, may facilitate entry/departure.

SAFETY/SECURITY/AREAS OF INSTABILITY: Bombings continue to occur throughout Pakistan with frequency. Bombs have exploded in public markets, on a train, at a bus station and in other public venues during the past year causing numerous casualties. Two Americans were killed and several more were injured in a church bombing on March 17, 2002. Rallies, demonstrations and processions occur from time to time throughout Pakistan on very short notice and have occasionally taken on an anti-American or anti-Western character. Karachi and the southern parts of Punjab province have experienced protracted political or sectarian violence that, although not explicitly anti-American, poses a potential danger to American travelers. During the Islamic religious observance of Moharram, sectarian rivalry and violence often increase. Family feuds are frequently fatal and may be followed by retaliation. Women do not walk out alone and it is not wise to travel in the streets late at night. Travelers may wish to maintain a low profile, blend in, and seek security in the traveler's family or sponsoring organization. An American citizen reporter was kidnapped and killed in Karachi in January 2002 after being lured from a public place to a private one.

Northern Areas - Visitors wishing to trek in Gilgit, Hunza, Chitral and the upper Swat valley should use only licensed guides and tourist agencies. There have been occasional assaults, and in 1998, a U.S. tourist who was not accompanied by a guide was murdered in Gilgit.

Northwest Frontier Province - The Government of Pakistan requires all citizens of countries other than Pakistan and Afghanistan to obtain permission from the Home and Tribal Affairs Department prior to visiting these tribal areas, which lie outside the normal jurisdiction of the Government of Pakistan. Substantial areas within the Northwest Frontier Province are designated tribal areas and are outside the normal jurisdiction of government law enforcement authorities. If visitors must enter the tribal areas, a permit from the Home and Tribal Affairs Department is required. The permit may stipulate that an armed escort must accompany the visitor. Even in the settled areas of the Northwest Frontier Province, there is occasional ethnic, sectarian, and political violence as well as anti-foreign rhetoric; foreigners should steer clear of such demonstrations or known areas of conflict. However, the periodic steam train excursion for tourists from Peshawar through the Khyber Pass is well protected by local authorities.

Kashmir: Military operations continue along the Line of Control in Kashmir, and military exchanges between Pakistani and Indian forces often result in deaths and injuries on both sides. Militant groups, some of whom have made anti-American statements, are active in the area. Many areas are restricted. Americans planning travel in Pakistan-controlled Kashmir should contact the U.S. Embassy in Islamabad prior to travel in the area and assure that they have taken appropriate security precautions. Americans should defer travel to Kashmir and the Pakistan - India border areas at this time. The Wagah border crossing into India near Lahore remains open (from 9:30 a.m. to 3:30 p.m.) for travel to and from India if the passport holder has a valid visa for either country. Travelers are advised to confirm the current status of the border crossing prior to commencing travel. An American and other Westerners were kidnapped in Indian-controlled Kashmir in 1995 and have never been found.

Punjab Province - Sectarian violence decreased considerably in recent years, although there continue to be isolated attacks on places of worship of all faiths. While Americans are not targets of this violence, the foreign community is not immune, as evidenced by the 1997 assassination of five Iranians in an attack widely believed to have had sectarian overtones. As a precaution against possible dangers resulting from sectarian violence, U.S. citizens are cautioned to avoid public transportation and crowded areas.

Sindh Province - In the areas of Karachi and Hyderabad there have been recurring outbreaks of ethnic and sectarian violence characterized by random bombings, shootings and demonstrations. These have resulted in deaths and the imposition of curfews. There have also been numerous incidents of kidnappings for ransom. In rural Sindh Province, the security situation is hazardous, especially in regard to overland travel. Foreigners have occasionally been kidnapped or killed, most notably an American citizen reporter who was kidnapped and murdered in Karachi in early 2002. In 1997, four U.S. businessmen and their driver were also murdered in Karachi. In 1995, employees from the U.S. Consulate General in Karachi were murdered on their way to work. The Government of Pakistan has recommended that

363

travelers limit their movements in Sindh Province to the city of Karachi. If visitors must go into the interior of Sindh Province, the Government of Pakistan requests that travelers inform police authorities well in advance of the trip so that necessary police security arrangements can be made.

Baluchistan Province - The province of Baluchistan, which borders both Iran and Afghanistan, is notorious for cross-border smuggling. Armed battles between clans are frequent. Because provincial police presence is limited, travelers wishing to visit the interior of Baluchistan should consult with the province's Home Secretary. Advance permission from provincial authorities is required for travel into some areas. Local authorities have detained travelers who lack permission. Quetta, the provincial capital, has experienced serious ethnic violence that has led to gun battles in the streets and the imposition of curfews.

Returning Americans of Afghan origin are sometimes targets for harassment for extortion by the local populace and even by police, local immigration and customs officials--especially if they do not have a well-established family structure in Pakistan.

CRIME: Crime is a serious concern for foreigners throughout Pakistan, with violent crime increasing faster than any other category. Carjackings, armed robberies, house invasions and other violence against civilians have increased steadily in the major urban areas. Lahore and Karachi, in particular, experience high levels of crime. They are large cities beset by poverty, high unemployment, and underpaid, under-manned police forces. Travelers in Karachi are encouraged to use hotel shuttles from the airport rather than taxis, which are subject to police harassment, especially after dark. Petty crime, especially theft of personal property, is common throughout Pakistan.

The loss or theft of a U.S. passport abroad should be reported immediately to local police and to the nearest U.S. embassy or consulate. U.S. citizens may refer to the Department of State pamphlets, *A Safe Trip Abroad* and *Tips for Travelers to South Asia*, for ways to promote a more trouble-free journey. The pamphlets are available by mail from the Superintendent of Documents, U.S. Government Printing Office, Washington, D.C. 20402, via the Internet at http://www.access.gpo.gov/su_docs, or via the Bureau of Consular Affairs home page at http://travel.state.gov.

MEDICAL FACILITIES: Adequate medical care is available in major cities in Pakistan, but it is limited in rural areas. With the exception of the Agha Khan Hospital in Karachi and Doctors' Hospital in Lahore, Americans may find hospital care and cleanliness below U.S. standards. Medical facilities often require prepayment and do not accept credit cards.

MEDICAL INSURANCE: The Department of State strongly urges Americans to consult with their medical insurance company prior to traveling abroad to confirm whether their policy applies overseas and if it will cover emergency expenses such as a medical evacuation. U.S. medical insurance plans seldom cover health costs incurred outside the United States unless supplemental coverage is purchased. Further, U.S. Medicare and Medicaid programs do not provide payment for medical services outside the United States. However, many travel agents and private companies offer insurance plans that will cover health care expenses incurred overseas, including emergency services such as medical evacuations.

When making a decision regarding health insurance, Americans should consider that many foreign doctors and hospitals require payment in cash prior to providing service and that a medical evacuation to the United States may cost more than $50,000. Uninsured travelers who require medical care overseas often face extreme difficulties, whereas travelers who have purchased overseas medical insurance have found it to be life-saving when a medical emergency has occurred. When consulting with your insurer prior to your trip, please ascertain whether payment will be made to the overseas healthcare provider or if you will be reimbursed later for expenses that you incur. Some insurance policies also include coverage for psychiatric treatment and for disposition of remains in the event of death.

Useful information on medical emergencies abroad, including overseas insurance programs, is provided in the Department of State's Bureau of

364

Consular Affairs brochure, *Medical Information for Americans Traveling Abroad,* available via the Bureau of Consular Affairs home page or autofax: (202) 647-3000.

OTHER HEALTH INFORMATION: The water is not potable anywhere in Pakistan, and sanitation in many restaurants is inadequate. Stomach illnesses are frequent and dangerous. Information on vaccinations and other health precautions may be obtained from the Centers for Disease Control and Prevention's hotline for international travelers from the United States at 1-877-FYI-TRIP (1-877-394-8747); fax: 1-888-CDC-FAXX (1-888-232-3299), or via the CDC's Internet site at http://www.cdc.gov.

TRAFFIC SAFETY AND ROAD CONDITIONS: While in a foreign country, U.S. citizens may encounter road conditions that differ significantly from those in the United States. The information below concerning traffic safety and road conditions in Pakistan is provided for general reference only, and it may not be totally accurate in a particular location or circumstance

Safety of Public Transportation: Poor
Urban Road Condition/Maintenance: Good to Poor
Rural Road condition/Maintenance: Poor
Availability of Roadside Assistance: Poor

Road travel in Pakistan is risky. Roads are crowded, drivers are aggressive and poorly trained, and many vehicles, particularly large trucks and buses, are badly maintained. Roads, including most major highways, also suffer from poor maintenance and often have numerous potholes, sharp drop-offs and barriers that are not sign-posted. Extreme caution should be exercised when traveling at night by road since many vehicles do not have proper illumination or dimmers nor are most roads properly illuminated or sign posted. Driving without experienced local drivers or guides is not recommended.

For additional information about road safety, please see the Department of State, Bureau of Consular Affairs home page at http://travel.state.gov/road_safety.html

AVIATION SAFETY OVERSIGHT: The U.S. Federal Aviation Administration (FAA) has assessed the Government of Pakistan's civil aviation authority as Category 1 -- in compliance with international aviation safety standards for oversight of Pakistan's air carrier operations.

For further information, travelers may contact the Department of Transportation within the United States at tel. 1-800-322-7873, or visit the FAA's Internet web site at http://www.faa.gov/avr/iasa. The U.S. Department of Defense (DOD) separately assesses some foreign carriers for suitability as official providers of air services. For information regarding the DOD policy on specific carriers, travelers may contact the DOD at tel. 618-229-4801.

CUSTOMS REGULATIONS: Import of firearms, pornographic material and alcohol is restricted. An import permit and health certificate are required for animals. There are also restrictions on leaving Pakistan with antiquities or animals. It is advisable to contact the Pakistani Embassy in Washington, D.C. or the nearest Pakistani consulate for specific information regarding customs requirements.

CRIMINAL PENALTIES: While in a foreign country, a U.S. citizen is subject to that country's laws and regulations, which sometimes differ significantly from those in the United States and may not afford the protections available to the individual under U.S. law. Penalties for breaking the law can be more severe than in the United States for similar offenses. Persons violating Pakistani laws, even unknowingly, may be expelled, arrested or imprisoned. Penalties for possession, use, or trafficking in illegal drugs are strictly enforced. Long jail sentences are frequently imposed, and large fines are assessed in some cases. Legislation passed in 1994 makes trafficking offenses punishable by death.

SPECIAL CIRCUMSTANCES: Pakistan is largely a cash economy. Personal checks are not commonly accepted. Most Pakistanis do not use checking accounts for routine transactions. Only a few establishments in the larger cities accept credit cards and traveler's checks, and there have been numerous reports of credit card fraud. There are bank branches as well as registered moneychangers in all international airports. ATMs are usually not found in airports. English is widely spoken by professional level airport staff. It is best to agree on taxi fares before hiring a driver. Currently, U.S. Embassy employees are restricted from using taxis for security reasons.

CHILDREN'S ISSUES: For information on international adoption of children and international parental child abduction, please refer to our Internet site at http://travel.state.gov/children's_issues.html or telephone 202-736-7000.

REGISTRATION/EMBASSY AND CONSULATE LOCATIONS: American citizens living in or visiting Pakistan are encouraged to register at the Consular Section of the U.S. Embassy or Consulate in Pakistan and obtain updated information on travel and security within Pakistan. They are located at the following addresses:

-- The U.S. Embassy in Islamabad is located at Diplomatic Enclave, Ramna 5, telephone (92-51) 2080-0000; Consular Section telephone (92-51) 2080-2700, fax (92-51) 282-2632, web site http://www.usembassy.state.gov/pakistan.
-- The U.S. Consulate General in Karachi is located at 8 Abdullah Haroon Road, telephone (92-21) 568-5170 (after hours: 92-21-568-1606), fax (92-21) 568-0496, web site http://www.usembassy.state.gov/pakistan
-- The U.S. Consulate in Lahore is located on 50-Empress Road near Shimla Road or Sharah-E-Abdul Hamid Bin Badees, (Old Empress Road), telephone (92-42) 636-5530, fax (92-42) 636-5177, website http://usembassy.state.gov/pakistan. Email address: amconsul@brain.net.pk
-- The U.S. Consulate in Peshawar is located at 11 Hospital Road, Cantonment, Peshawar, telephone (92-91) 279-801 through 803, fax (92-91) 276-712, web site http://usembassy.state.gov/pakistan
The normal workweek in Pakistan is Monday through Saturday, with a half-day worked on Friday. However, the U.S. Embassy and consulates are open Monday through Friday.

SRI LANKA

COUNTRY DESCRIPTION: Sri Lanka is a presidential parliamentary democracy with a developing economy. The country has been seriously disrupted since 1983 by a civil war and

related urban terrorism. Despite the armed insurgency, Sri Lanka's beaches and archeological sites attract tens of thousands of visitors from around the world. The capital city of Colombo, the Cultural Triangle (Kandy, Anuradhapura, and Polonnaruwa), and the west and southwest coasts all have good tourist facilities.

ENTRY/EXIT AND REGISTRATION REQUIREMENTS: A passport and an onward/return ticket and proof of sufficient funds are required. A no-cost visit visa, valid for 30 days, will be granted to tourists at the time of time of entry into Sri Lanka. Business travelers are required to have a visa prior to arrival. Visitors staying more than 30 days for any purpose must pay residency visa fees. Yellow fever and cholera immunizations are needed if arriving from an infected area. All travelers departing Sri Lanka (except diplomats and certain exempted travelers) must pay an airport tax, in cash. Sri Lankan law requires all persons, including foreigners, who are guests in private households to register in person at the nearest local police station. Individuals who stay in private households without registering may be temporarily detained for questioning. This requirement does not apply to individuals staying in hotels or guesthouses.

Specific inquiries should be addressed to the Embassy of the Democratic Socialist Republic of Sri Lanka, 2148 Wyoming Avenue, N.W., Washington, D.C. 20008, telephone (202) 483-4025 through 28, fax numbers (202) 232-7181 or 483-8017, e-mail address: slembassy@clark.net, home page: http://www.slembassy.org. There is a Consulate General in Los Angeles at 5371 Wilshire Blvd., Suite 201, Los Angeles, CA 90036, telephone (323) 634-0479 or (323) 634-1079 and a Consulate in New York City telephone (212) 986-7040. There are two honorary Sri Lankan consuls in the United States: New Orleans, LA telephone (504) 455-7880 and Atlanta, GA (404) 881-7164. Sri Lanka maintains a Permanent Mission to the United Nations at 630 3rd Avenue, 20th floor, New York, NY 10017.

In an effort to prevent international child abduction, many governments have initiated procedures at entry/exit points. These often include requiring documentary evidence of relationship and permission for the child's travel from the parent(s) or legal guardian not present.

Having such documentation on hand, even if not required, may facilitate entry/departure.

DUAL NATIONALITY: Sri Lanka recognizes dual nationality in some cases. For further information, please contact either the Sri Lankan Embassy or one of the consulates.

SAFETY/SECURITY:

TERRORISM:
Since 1997, the Liberation Tigers of Tamil Eelam (LTTE) have been on the State Department list of foreign terrorist organizations. Terrorist activities in the capital city of Colombo and other areas of the country remain a serious threat. On July 24, The Liberation Tigers of Tamil Eelam (LTTE) attacked the Colombo International Airport and destroyed both commercial and military aircraft. Several military personnel were killed in the attack, military and airport employees were injured, and civilians were caught in the crossfire. In the past several years, the LTTE has also attacked several commercial ships flying foreign flags in the waters off the north and east of the country. In 1998, threats were directed at domestic air carriers flying between Colombo and Jaffna, and in September of that year, a domestic civilian aircraft flying from Colombo to Jaffna crashed, killing everyone on board. The cause of the accident is still unknown.

Bomb attacks remain the greatest terrorist hazard. The LTTE has attempted or carried out numerous political assassinations or attempts. In 1999, suicide bombings resulted in the death of 30 persons and injury to 143 others in Colombo, Trincomalee, Batticaloa, Jaffna and Medawachchi. In January 2000, a suicide bomber killed more than a dozen and wounded several passers-by when she detonated her bomb outside the Prime Minister's Office after being detected by security personnel. In March 2000, as many as eight LTTE terrorists attacked a government motorcade traveling on a major Colombo thoroughfare, killing 25 people and wounding many others. In June 2000, a suicide bomber assassinated the Minister for Industrial Development in a Colombo suburb. Twenty-one others were killed and 60 people were injured in the attack. In October 2000, two American and one British women and their Sri Lankan driver were seriously injured in their vehicle in Central Colombo when an LTTE suicide bomber confronted by police exploded his device rather than surrender. Three policemen were killed. In October 2001, an LTTE suicide bomber stopped by police in the vicinity of an election rally in Colombo detonated his device rather than surrender, killing five people and injuring 16 others.

In addition to individual suicide bombers, vehicle-mounted bombs have been used by the LTTE. Major hotels have been directly affected by terrorist activities and could be again because of their proximity to likely economic, government and military targets. In October 1997, a number of American citizens suffered minor injuries when a vehicle bomb was detonated near five-star hotels in Colombo. In January 1998, the Temple of the Tooth, an important religious and tourist site in Kandy, was subjected to a truck bomb; eight people were killed, and the temple, nearby businesses and an historic hotel were damaged.

Small bombs have frequently been placed against infrastructure targets such as telephone switchgear or electrical power transformers. Public buses have also been the targets of terrorist attacks. In September 1999, bombs were detonated in buses in separate incidents in Negombo and Badula. In one week in February 2000, seven separate explosions of bombs left on public buses in Colombo and other cities killed three and wounded over 140 people. Bombs have also been found on trains and on train roadbeds, resulting in one death and injuries to over 50 people.

Although U.S. citizens have not been specifically targeted, LTTE operations have been planned and executed with the knowledge that Americans and other foreigners might be killed or injured. Tourists or business representatives traveling in Sri Lanka may be inadvertently caught up in random acts of violence. Security is very tight in major cities, particularly Colombo and Kandy, and along roads linking Colombo with the north and east. U.S. citizens and other visitors, particularly those of Sri Lankan ancestry, may be subject to unwelcome scrutiny by irregular neighborhood security units known as the Home Guards. . Travel in restricted areas is dangerous. In April 2001, an American citizen was seriously injured by grenade fragments when caught in a skirmish between government and insurgent forces in the eastern part of the country.

367

Americans are urged to exercise extreme caution in Colombo because of possible terrorist activities there. In addition, Americans are advised to avoid political rallies and other mass gatherings, limit exposure to government and military installations and avoid public transportation if possible. Street and highway checkpoints staffed by security personnel are common; travelers should closely follow any instructions given. Non-Sri Lankan citizens of Tamil heritage have occasionally been detained during security operations. U.S. citizens of any ethnic heritage are encouraged to keep their passports with them at all times. In the event of a terrorist attack, Americans should monitor local radio and television, seek cover away from windows and return to their homes or hotels when it is safe to do so. The Government of Sri Lanka has periodically imposed curfews in Colombo; Americans should strictly observe curfew regulations and monitor local radio and television. In May 2000, the Sri Lankan Government activated provisions of the Public Security Ordinance, giving certain government authorities sweeping powers to deal with threats to national security.

TRAVEL RESTRICTIONS:

American citizens are advised not to travel north of a line drawn from Puttalam on the west coast through Anuradhapura in the central north and Nivaveli (just north of Trincomalee) in the east. Areas north of this line contain many land mines, making travel off paved roads very dangerous. In addition, the LTTE rather than the Government of Sri Lanka is effectively the civil administration in many sections of the north. Official travel by U.S. Government personnel to this area is restricted, and their unofficial travel is prohibited. Travel in the east in the area south of the Anuradhapura-Nivaveli line (including Trincomalee, Batticaloa and points south) poses significant safety risks. Roads are often substandard, and police, medical and other emergency help is severely limited or not available. Communications within the eastern areas are also limited, with no cell phone accessibility and very limited landline telephone access. Because of these considerations, the U.S. Embassy may not be able to provide consular services in a timely manner to American citizens who travel to the north and east. You can see a map of the areas affected by the travel restrictions.

CRIME INFORMATION: Sri Lanka has a rising crime rate, and criminals, including outlaw gangs of military deserters, increasingly use automatic weapons when committing crimes. There have been reports of police inaction in certain cases. In January 2001, bandits raided a resort in the southern coastal town of Tangalla with the intention of robbing Europeans guests; the owner, a German national, resisted and was killed; his daughter was reportedly raped. In recent years, the U.S. Embassy has received reports of criminal incidents involving violence in the towns of Negombo and Hikkaduwa. Please exercise caution in these towns, especially at night. Children should not be left unattended, even on hotel/resort premises. There have been reports of attempted child molestation by hotel staff. Petty street crime such as purse snatching and pick-pocketing is common, especially on crowded local public transportation. In addition, visitors should be alert to outbreaks of communal violence, such as a May 2001 disturbance between Buddhist and Muslim communities near Kandy that reportedly resulted in one death during a police shootout and extensive property damage.

The loss or theft of a U.S. passport should be reported immediately to local police and the U.S. Embassy. U.S. citizens may refer to the Department of State's pamphlets, *A Safe Trip Abroad* and *Tips for Travelers to South Asia*, for ways to promote a more trouble-free journey. The pamphlets are available from the Superintendent of Documents, U.S. Government Printing Office, Washington, D.C. 20402, via the Internet at http://www.access.gpo.gov/su_docs, or via the Bureau of Consular Affairs home page at http://travel.state.gov.

MEDICAL FACILITIES: Medical facilities outside Colombo are limited. The U.S. Embassy maintains a list of private physicians who may be consulted in emergency cases. Medical supplies are uneven; travelers should carry any special drugs with them. There are five large hospitals in the Colombo area, including two with emergency trauma service, which are Asiri Hospital and the government General Hospital. Serious medical problems may require evacuation to the United States or to the nearest country where adequate medical facilities or treatment are available, usually Thailand or Singapore. Neither Thailand nor Singapore requires American citizens to have an entry visa.

MEDICAL INSURANCE: The Department of State strongly urges Americans to consult with their medical insurance company prior to traveling abroad to confirm whether their policy applies overseas and if it will cover emergency expenses such as a medical evacuation. U.S. medical insurance plans seldom cover health costs incurred outside the United States unless supplemental coverage is purchased. Further, U.S. Medicare and Medicaid programs do not provide payment for medical services outside the United States. However, many travel agents and private companies offer insurance plans that will cover health care expenses incurred overseas, including emergency services such as medical evacuations.

When making a decision regarding health insurance, Americans should consider that many foreign doctors and hospitals require payment in cash prior to providing service and that a medical evacuation to the United States may cost in excess of $50,000. Uninsured travelers who require medical care overseas often face extreme difficulties. When consulting your insurer prior to your trip, please ascertain whether payment will be made to the overseas healthcare provider or if you will be reimbursed later for expenses that you incur. Some insurance policies also include coverage for psychiatric treatment and for disposition of remains in the event of death.

Useful information on medical emergencies abroad, including overseas insurance programs, is provided in the Department of State's Bureau of Consular Affairs brochure, *Medical Information for Americans Traveling Abroad*, available via the Bureau of Consular Affairs home page or autofax: (202) 647-3000.

OTHER HEALTH INFORMATION: Information on vaccinations and other health precautions may be obtained from the Centers for Disease Control and Prevention's hotline for international travelers at 1-877-FYI-TRIP (1-877-394-8747), autofax 1-888-CDC-FAXX (1-888-232-3299), or via the CDC's Internet site at http://www.cdc.gov.

TRAFFIC SAFETY AND ROAD CONDITIONS: While in a foreign country, U.S. citizens may encounter road conditions that differ significantly from those in the United States. The information below concerning Sri Lanka is provided for general reference only and may not be totally accurate in a particular location or circumstance:
Safety of Public Transportation: Poor
Urban Road Conditions/Maintenance: Fair
Rural Road Conditions/Maintenance: Poor
Availability of Roadside Assistance: Poor

Vehicular traffic moves on the left (British style). Traffic in Colombo is very congested. Narrow, two-lane highways, dangerously driven buses, overloaded trucks and the variety of vehicles on the road, ranging from ox carts, elephants and bicycles to new four-wheel drive jeeps, make driving a challenge and dangerous. Many visitors hire cars and drivers or use radio taxicabs.

For additional general information about road safety, including links to foreign government sites, please see the Department of State, Bureau of Consular Affairs home page at http://travel.state.gov/road_safety.html. For specific information concerning Sri Lankan driving permits, vehicle inspection, road tax and mandatory insurance, please contact the Sri Lankan National Tourist Organization offices in New York via the Internet at http://www.lanka.net.

AVIATION SAFETY OVERSIGHT: As there is no direct commercial air service at present, nor economic authority to operate such a service between the United States and Sri Lanka, the U.S. Federal Aviation Administration (FAA) has not assessed Sri Lanka's Civil Aviation Authority for compliance with international aviation safety standards.

For further information travelers may contact the Department of Transportation within the United States at tel. 1-800-322-7873, or visit the FAA's Internet web site at http://www.faa.gov/avr/iasa/. The U.S. Department of Defense (DOD) separately assesses some foreign air carriers for suitability as official providers of air services. For information regarding the DOD policy on specific carriers, travelers may contact the DOD at telephone (618) 256-4801.

CUSTOMS REGULATIONS: Sri Lankan customs authorities may enforce strict regulations concerning temporary importation into or export from Sri Lanka of items such as firearms, antiquities, business equipment, obscene materials, currency, gems and precious metals. It is advisable to contact the Embassy of Sri Lanka in Washington, D.C., or one of Sri Lanka's consulates in the United States for specific information regarding customs requirements.

CRIMINAL PENALTIES: While in a foreign country, a U.S. citizen is subject to that country's laws and regulations, which sometimes differ significantly from those in the United States and may not afford the protections available to the individual under U.S. law. Penalties for breaking the law can be more severe than those in the United States for similar offenses. Persons violating Sri Lankan laws, even unknowingly, may be expelled, arrested or imprisoned. Penalties for possession of, use of, or trafficking in illegal drugs in Sri Lanka are strict, and convicted offenders can expect jail sentences and heavy fines. Persons charged with crimes may be remanded without possibility of bail for months prior to a trial date. Prison conditions in Sri Lanka do not meet international standards and suffer from overcrowding, inadequate food and medical resources, poor sanitation and risk of violence and extortion.

CHILDREN'S ISSUES: For information on international adoption of children and international parental child abduction, please refer to our Internet site at http://travel.state.gov/children's_issues.html or telephone (202) 736-7000.

REGISTRATION AND EMBASSY LOCATION: Americans living in or visiting Sri Lanka are encouraged to register at the Consular Section of the U.S. Embassy in Colombo and obtain updated information on travel and security within Sri Lanka. The U.S. Embassy is located at 210 Galle Road, Colombo 3, Sri Lanka. The Embassy's telephone number during normal business hours Monday through Friday is (94)(1) 448-007. The after-hours and emergency telephone number is (94)(1) 447-601. The Consular Section fax number is (94)-(1)-436-943. The Embassy's Internet address is http://usembassy.state.gov/srilanka. The e-mail address for the consular section is consularcolombo@state.gov. The Embassy in

Colombo also covers the Republic of the Maldives. U.S. citizens are strongly encouraged to register at the Embassy upon arrival in Sri Lanka or by e-mail.

Planning Another Trip?

See Chapter 36 for a listing of resources available to the general traveler from the U.S. Departments of State, Customs, Transportation, Health and various government and non-government organizations. Almost all of the available International travel-related pamphlets, brochures and publications issued by the U.S. Department of State and by the U.S. Customs have been reproduced in full in this book. See Table of Contents for location.

Chapter 23

Tips for Travelers to Sub-Saharan Africa

[The information in this chapter is reprinted verbatim from a bulletin issued by the U.S. State Department, Bureau of Consular Affairs. It is intended to serve as advice to Americans traveling abroad.]

Angola, Benin, Botswana, Burkina Faso, Burundi, Cameroon, Cape Verde, Central African Republic, Chad, Comoros, Cote D'Ivoire, Djibouti, Equatorial Guinea, Ethiopia, Gabon, Gambia, Ghana, Guinea, Guinea-Bissau, Kenya, Lesotho, Liberia, Madagascar, Malawi, MAli, Mauritania, Mauritius, Mozambique, Namibia, Niger, Nigeria, Rwanda, Sao Tome and Principe, Senegal, Seychelles, Sierra Leone, Somalia, South Africa, Sudan, Swaziland, Tanzania, Togo, Uganda, Zaire, Zambia, Zimbabwe.

Foreword

Your trip to Africa will be an adventure off the beaten path. Conditions and customs in sub-Saharan Africa can contrast sharply with those in the United States. These pages contain advice to help you avoid inconvenience and difficulties. Take our advice seriously but don't let it keep you at home. Most Americans have unforgettable experiences in Africa. We are often welcomed and helped by Africans who are happy to share not just their scenery, but their culture and traditions as well.

This chapter covers all of Africa except the five nations bordering the Mediterranean. Sub-Saharan Africa includes 48 nations. Forty-two of these nations are on the mainland. In addition, four island nations in the southwest Indian Ocean (Madagascar, The Comoros, Mauritius, and Seychelles) and two island nations in the Atlantic Ocean (Cape Verde and Sao Tome and Principe) are considered part of Africa. For convenience, we will often use the word "Africa" to refer to the sub-Saharan region. For information on the five northern African nations of Tunisia, Algeria, Morocco, Libya, and Egypt, see the chapter enttled *Tips for Travelers to the Middle East and North Africa*.

Before you go, learn as much as you can about your destination. Your travel agent, local bookstore, public library and the embassies of the countries you plan to visit are all useful sources of information. The Department of State's *Background Notes* series includes a pamphlet for every country worldwide, including those in Africa. You may obtain Background Notes via the Internet by visiting the Department of State home page at http://www.state.gov.

Consular Information Program

Before traveling, obtain the Consular Information Sheet for any countries you plan to visit. You should also check to see if the Department of State has issued a Travel Warning or Public Announcement for the country or countries you will be visiting. *Travel Warnings* are issued when the Department of State decides based on all relevant information, to recommend that all Americans avoid travel to a certain country. *Public Announcements* are issued as a means to disseminate information quickly about relatively short-term and/or trans-national conditions that would pose significant risks to the security of American travelers. *Consular Information Sheets* are available for every country in the world. They include such information as the location of the U.S. embassy or consulate in the country, unusual immigration practices, health conditions, crime and security information, road safety, unusual currency and entry regulations, and drug penalties. A description of political disturbances may be included in the Consular Information Sheet under an optional section entitled "Safety/Security." On limited occasions, the Department also restates in this section U.S. Embassy advice given to official employees. Consular Information Sheets present information so travelers can make knowledgeable decisions concerning travel to a particular country. Countries to which we suggest that you not travel will have Travel Warnings as well as Consular

Information Sheets.

How to Access Consular Information Sheets, Travel Warnings and Public Announcements

By Internet
The most convenient source of information about travel and consular services is the Consular Affairs home page on the Internet's World Wide Web. The web site address is http://travel.state.gov. If you do not have access to the Internet at home, work or school, your local library may provide access to the Internet.

By Telephone
Consular Information Sheets and Travel Warnings may be heard any time by dialing the office of American Citizens Services at **(202) 647-5225** from a touchtone phone.

In Person/By Mail
Consular Information Sheets, Travel Warnings and Public Announcements are available at any of the regional passport agencies, field offices of the Department of Commerce, and U.S. embassies and consulates abroad, or by writing and sending a self-addressed, stamped envelope to the Office of American Citizens Services, Bureau of Consular Affairs, Room 4811, U.S. Department of State, Washington, D.C. 20520-4818.

By Fax
From your fax machine, dial **(202) 647-3000**, using the handset as you would a regular telephone. The system will instruct you on how to proceed.

Visa and Other Entry Requirements
A valid, unexpired U.S. passport is required for travel to all countries in Africa. In addition, most countries in sub-Saharan Africa require U.S. citizens to have a visa. If visas are required, obtain them before you leave home. Be particularly attentive to visa requirements for countries you may transit en route to your country of destination. If you decide to visit additional countries en route, it may be difficult or impossible to obtain visas. In most African countries, if you arrive without a visa, you will not be admitted into the country and will have to depart on the next plane. This can be extremely inconvenient if the next plane does not arrive for several days, the airport hotel is full, and the airport has no other sleeping accommodations.

The best authority on a country's visa and other entry requirements is its embassy or consulate. The Department of State publication, *Foreign Entry Requirements*, gives basic information on entry requirements and tells where and how to apply for visas. You can order a copy for 50 cents from the Consumer Information Center, Pueblo, Colorado 81009.

Foreign Entry Requirements is also available on the Internet at http://travel.state.gov/foreignentryreqs.html.
Allow plenty of time to apply for visas. An average of two weeks for each visa is recommended. When you inquire, check the following:

- Visa price, length of validity, and number of entries
- Financial data required
- Proof of sufficient funds, proof of onward/return ticket
- Immunizations required
- Currency regulations
- Import/export restrictions
- Departure tax - if required. Be sure to keep sufficient hard currency so that you may leave the country on schedule.
- HIV clearance certification; some countries require travelers to submit certification or be tested upon arrival for HIV.

Restricted Areas
A visa is good only for those parts of a country that are open to foreigners. Several countries in Africa have areas of civil unrest or war zones that are off-limits to visitors without special permits. Others have similar areas that are open but surrounded by security checkpoints where travelers must show their passport, complete with valid visa. When traveling in such a country, keep your passport with you at all times. It is recommended that you leave photocopies of your passport, including copies of those pages containing visas, at your hotel or in some other safe location. No matter where you travel in Africa, do not overstay the validity of your visa. Renew it if necessary.

If stopped at a roadblock, be courteous and responsive to questions asked by persons in authority. Outside major cities, try to avoid travel at night. For information on restricted or risky areas, consult Department of State Consular Information Sheets or, if you are already in Africa, the nearest U.S. embassy or consulate. If you plan on spending an extended period of time in a country, register with the nearest U.S. embassy or consulate.

In some areas, when U.S. citizens are arrested or detained, police or prison officials fail to inform the U.S. embassy or consulate. If you are detained for any reason, it is your right to speak with a U.S. consular officer immediately.

Health

Health problems affect visitors to Africa more than any other difficulty. For travel health information on the Internet, visit the Centers for Disease Control and Prevention's (CDC) home page at http://www.cdc.gov. The CDC also provides recorded information on their international travelers hotline at 1-877-FYI-TRIP (1-877-394-8747) and by fax at 1-888-CDC-FAXX (1-888-232-3299). Additional general information can be found in the U.S. Public Health Service book, Health Information for International Travel, available from the Superintendent of Documents, U.S. Government Printing Office, Washington, DC 20402, via the Internet at http://www.access.gpo.gov/su_docs or by calling (202) 512-1800.

Human immunodeficiency virus (HIV), which causes acquired immunodeficiency syndrome or AIDS, is epidemic in sub-Saharan Africa. In its December 2000 *AIDS Epidemic Update*, the United Nations AIDS/World Health Organization Working Group on Global HIV/AIDS/STI Surveillance reported that 25.3 million adults and children are living with HIV/AIDS in sub-Saharan Africa. 3.8 million people were newly infected, mainly through heterosexual contact. HIV is found primarily in the bodily fluids of an infected person. It is spread through intimate sexual contact, needle sharing among intravenous drug users and transfusions of infected blood and blood clotting factors.

Hepatitis B is a viral infection of the liver transmitted through activities resulting in the exchange of blood or blood derived fluids and/or through sexual activity. Meningococcal disease (bacterial meningitis) is an infection in the lining of the brain or spinal cord. This is spread when an infected person sneezes or coughs near you, as is tuberculosis, both of which are significant risks in crowded, confined spaces.

Many diseases are transmitted through the bite of infected insects such as mosquitoes, flies, fleas, ticks and lice. Travelers must protect themselves from insect bites by wearing proper clothing, using bed nets, and applying the proper insect repellent. Mosquitoes are most active between dusk and dawn. Malaria is a very serious, sometimes fatal, parasitic infection transmitted to humans by mosquitoes, and is endemic in most parts of sub-Saharan Africa. Travelers at risk for malaria should consult with a doctor for advice on whether or not it is necessary to take Mefloquine or an alternative drug as a preventative measure. Yellow fever and Dengue fever are prevalent viral infections also transmitted by mosquito bites.

Food and waterborne diseases also cause illnesses in travelers, most frequently diarrhea. Drink only bottled, chemically treated or boiled water. Avoid ice cubes. Unless you are sure that they are pasteurized, avoid dairy products. Eat only thoroughly cooked food. Vegetables and fruits should be peeled or washed in a purifying solution. A good rule of thumb is, "If you can't peel it or cook it, don't eat it." Severely ill individuals should receive immediate medical attention.

Schistosomiasis is an infection that develops after the larvae of a flatworm penetrate the skin. Water treated with chlorine or iodine is virtually safe and salt water poses no risk. The risk is a function of the frequency and degree of contact with contaminated fresh water for bathing, wading or swimming. It is often difficult to distinguish between infested and non-infested water. Swimming in fresh water in rural areas should be avoided.

Rabies is a viral infection that affects the central nervous system. The virus is introduced by an animal bite. Any animal bite should receive prompt attention.

Some countries have shortages of medicines. Bring an adequate supply of any prescription and over-the-counter medicines that you need to take. Keep all prescriptions in their original, labeled containers.

Some medical devices, such as insulin pumps, may not be available in some countries. Those travelers requiring these devices should take spares. In addition, certain formulations of drugs, such as insulin, may not be available. Be aware of alternative substitute formulations. There are instances where "type A" of insulin is available locally, but, not "type B" or "type C," which may include the kind that the traveler may currently be taking.

Medical facilities may be limited, particularly in rural areas. Should you become seriously ill or injured abroad, contact the nearest U.S. embassy or consulate. A U.S. consular officer can furnish you with a list of local hospitals and English-speaking doctors. Consular officers can inform your family or friends in the United States of your condition. Because medical coverage overseas can be quite expensive, prospective travelers should review their health insurance policies. Doctors and hospitals expect immediate cash payment in full for health services in many sub-Saharan countries. If your policy does not provide medical coverage overseas, consider buying supplemental insurance. It is also advisable to obtain insurance to cover the cost of medical evacuation in the event of an emergency, as this can be extremely expensive.

Crime
Crime is a worldwide problem, particularly in urban populated areas. Travelers should be alert to the increasing crime problem throughout sub-Saharan Africa. In places where crime is especially acute, we have noted this problem under the county-specific section later in this chapter.

Weather
Sub-Saharan Africa is tropical, except for the high inland plateaus and the southern part of South Africa. Within 10 degrees of the Equator, the climate seldom varies and is generally hot and rainy. Further from the Equator, the seasons become more apparent. If possible, you should plan your trip in the cooler months. If traveling to rural areas, avoid the rainy months that generally run from May through October north of the equator and November through April south of the equator. Roads may be washed out during these times.

U.S. Citizens Married to Foreign Nationals
Women who travel to Africa should be aware that in some countries, either by law or by custom, a woman and her children need the permission of her husband to leave the country. If you or your children travel, be aware of the laws and customs of the places you visit. Do not visit or allow your children to visit unless you are confident that you will be permitted to leave. Overseas, you are subject to the laws of the country you visit. U.S. law cannot protect you.

Currency Regulations
The amount of money, including traveler's checks, which may be taken into or out of African countries, varies. In general, visitors must declare all currency and travelers checks upon arrival. Do not exchange money on the black market. Use only banks and other authorized foreign exchange offices and keep your receipts. You may need to present the receipts as well as your original currency declaration when you depart. Currency not accounted for may be confiscated and you may be fined or detained. Many countries require that hotel bills be paid in hard currency. Some require that a minimum amount of hard currency be changed into the local currency upon arrival. Some countries prohibit the import or export of local currency. Also, some countries prohibit the destruction of local currency, no matter how small the denomination.

U.S. Wildlife Regulations
The United States prohibits the importation of products from endangered species, including the fur of any spotted cats. Most African countries have enacted laws protecting wildlife, but poaching and illegal trafficking in wildlife are still commonplace. Importing products made from endangered species may result in the seizure of the product and a possible fine. Generally, African ivory cannot be legally imported into the United States.

The import of most types of parrots and other wild birds from Africa is restricted and subject to licensing and other controls. Birds are required to be placed in quarantine upon arrival to ensure they are free from disease. For further information on the import of wildlife and related products, visit the U.S. Fish and Wildlife Service web site at http://international.fws.gov or the TRAFFIC USA web site at http://www.traffic.org.

Air Travel

If you are flying to places in Africa other than the major tourist destinations, you may have difficulty securing and retaining reservations and experience long waits at airports for customs and immigration processing. If stranded, you may need proof of a confirmed reservation in order to obtain food and lodging vouchers from some airlines. Flights are often overbooked, delayed or canceled and, when competing for space on a plane, you may be dealing with a surging crowd rather than a line. Traveling with a packaged tour may insulate you from some of these difficulties. Not all problems can be avoided, but you can:

- Learn the reputation of the airline and the airports you will use to prevent problems and avoid any unpleasant surprises.
- Reserve your return passage before you go and reconfirm immediately upon arrival.
- Ask for confirmation in writing, complete with file number or locator code, when you make or confirm a reservation.
- Arrive at the airport earlier than required in order to put yourself at the front of the line - or the crowd, as the case may be.
- Travel with funds sufficient for an extra week's subsistence in case you are stranded.

Photography

Africa is filled with breathtaking scenery and photography is generally encouraged. However, most governments prohibit photography of military installations or locations having military significance, including airports, bridges, tunnels, port facilities and public buildings. Visitors can seek guidance on restrictions from local tourist offices or from the nearest U.S. embassy or consulate. Taking such photographs without prior permission can result in arrest or the confiscation of film and/or equipment.

Shortages, High Prices, and Other Problems

Consumer goods, gas and food are in short supply in some African countries and prices for these commodities may be high by U.S. standards.

Shortages of hotel accommodations also exist so confirm reservations well in advance. Some countries experience disruptions in electricity and water supply or in services such as mail and telecommunications.

Local Transportation

Rental cars, where available, may be expensive. Hiring a taxi which is in good condition is often the easiest way to go sightseeing. Taxi fares should be negotiated in advance. Travel on rural roads can be slow and difficult in the dry season and disrupted by floods in the rainy season.

Country Information

Angola

The Department of State warns U.S. citizens against travel to Angola because of renewed military conflict and continuing violent crime. Angola is a developing country that has experienced war and civil strife since its independence from Portugal in 1975. In 1993, the U.S. recognized the Angolan government and a U.S. Embassy was established in Luanda. Facilities for tourism are virtually nonexistent. Visas are required. Persons arriving without visas are subject to possible arrest or deportation. Violent crime exists throughout the country. Travel in many parts of Luanda is considered unsafe at night because of the increased incidence of armed robberies and carjackings. Adequate medical facilities are scarce in Angola and most medicine is not available. Travelers are advised to purchase medical evacuation insurance. Embassy of Angola Web Site: http://www.angola.org

Benin

Benin is a developing West African country. Its capital is Porto Novo; however, the adjoining city of Cotonou is the main port and site of most government and tourist activity. Tourist facilities in Cotonou are available but not fully developed elsewhere in Benin. U.S. citizens are required to have a visa and vaccination certificates for yellow fever and cholera. Medical facilities in Benin are limited. Crime rates are rising, particularly in Cotonou.

Botswana

Botswana is a developing Southern African nation with a democratically elected system of government. Facilities for tourism are available. No visa is necessary for stays of less than 90 days. Medical facilities in Botswana are limited. Some petty crime, such as pickpocketing and purse snatching is common in the capital city of Gaborone. It is dangerous for visitors to walk alone at night in unfamiliar areas. Travel by automobile outside of large towns may be dangerous. Although major roads are generally in good condition, the combination of long stretches of two-lane highway, high speed limits, and the occasional presence of large animals on the roads makes accidents a frequent occurrence. Driving at night, particularly on rural highways, is strongly discouraged. When on safari or other game viewing activities, visitors should remember that wild animals are unpredictable and can be extremely dangerous. Visitors should use reputable tour operators and carefully follow all safety instructions when engaged in such activities. U.S. Embassy Web Site: http://usembassy.state.gov/posts/bc1/wwwhmain.html

Burkina Faso

Burkina Faso, previously known as Upper Volta, is a developing West African country of dry savannah that borders the Sahara Desert. The official language is French. Facilities for tourism are not widely available. A visa is required but may be purchased at the airport in Ouagadougou and at some border stations (bring along extra passport sized photos). Malaria is prevalent. Cholera and yellow fever immunizations are recommended. Medical facilities in Burkina Faso are very limited and medicine is in short supply. Petty crime is on the increase. Street crime poses a risk within Ouagadougou City and some armed banditry has been reported on border region routes. Public transportation is unreliable and generally unsafe. Traveling at night is extremely hazardous and should be avoided if possible. Travel on roads is difficult due to lack of maintenance and banditry. There are restrictions on photography. A valid photo permit may be obtained from the Ministry of Tourism. The U.S. Embassy in Ouagadougou can provide information on specific photography regulations. Credit cards are rarely accepted. Traveler's checks can sometimes be cashed at local banks that charge a fee for services. Telephone service is available at telecenters but it is expensive. Embassy of Burkina Faso Web Site: http://www.burkinaembassy-usa.org

Burundi

The Department of State warns U.S. citizens to avoid travel to Burundi due to continuing unstable conditions throughout the country. Burundi is a small, inland African nation passing through a period of instability following a coup attempt in October 1993. Facilities for tourism, particularly in the interior, are limited. A visa and immunizations for yellow fever and cholera are required. Medical facilities are limited. Street crime poses a high risk for visitors. Burundi has a good network of roads between major towns and border posts. Travel on other roads is difficult, particularly in the rainy season. Public transportation to border points is often difficult and frequently unavailable.

Cameroon

Cameroon is a developing African country. The official language is French. Facilities for tourism are limited. A visa and proof of inoculation against yellow fever and cholera are required. Obtain your visa before arrival to avoid difficulty at the airport. Airport security is stringent and visitors may be subjected to baggage searches. Medical facilities are limited. Armed banditry is a problem in the extreme north and in major cities. Petty crime is common throughout the country. Persons traveling at night on rural highways are at extreme risk. While photography is not officially forbidden, security officials are extremely sensitive about the photographing of government buildings and military installations, many of which are unmarked. Photography of these subjects may result in seizure of photographic equipment by Cameroonian authorities.

Cape Verde

The Republic of Cape Verde consists of several rugged volcanic islands off the West Coast of Africa. The climate is warm and dry. Tourist facilities are limited. A visa is required. If arriving from an infected area, evidence of immunization against yellow fever is required. Medical facilities in Cape Verde are extremely limited. Some petty theft is common. Embassy of Cape Verde Web Site: http://www.capeverdeusembassy.org

Central African Republic

The Central African Republic is a developing

African country. The U.S. Embassy maintains a limited staff and only emergency consular services are available. Facilities for tourism are limited. A visa is required. Medical facilities in the Central African Republic are limited. Petty crime such as pickpocketing can occur throughout the country, and armed highway robbery in rural areas is common. Photography of police or military installations, as well as government buildings, is prohibited.

Chad

Chad is a developing country in north central Africa that has experienced sporadic armed disturbances over the past several years. Facilities for tourism are limited. Visitors to Chad must have a visa before arrival and present evidence of a yellow fever vaccination. Medical facilities are extremely limited and medicines are in short supply. Pickpocketing and purse snatching are endemic in market and commercial areas. A permit is required for all photography. Even with a permit, there are prohibitions against taking pictures of military establishments and official buildings. U.S. citizens traveling across the southwestern border into Cameroon should consult with the U.S. Embassy N'djamena for updates on the incidence of highway banditry in the region. Embassy of Chad Web Site: http://www.chadembassy.org

The Comoros

The Comoros is a developing island nation located in the Indian Ocean, off the east coast of Africa. Facilities for tourism are limited. A visa is required. Visas for stays of three weeks or less can be issued at the airport upon arrival, provided an onward/return ticket is presented. Medical facilities in the Comoros are limited. Petty thievery is common.

Republic of the Congo (Brazzaville)

Although the 1998-99 civil conflict has ended and security in the country in general is improving, the Department of State warns U.S. citizens to defer travel to Republic of the Congo because of the uncertain security situation in some regions. The U.S. Embassy is closed. The Republic of the Congo is a developing nation in central Africa. Facilities for tourism are limited. A visa is required. Medical facilities are limited and some medical supplies are in short supply. Petty street crime, including mugging and purse snatching, occasionally occur in Brazzaville and Pointe Noire, as well as in parts of the countryside. Driving may be hazardous, particularly at night, and travelers should be alert to possible roadblocks. Travelers may wish to contact the U.S. Embassy in Kinshasa in the Democratic Republic of Congo for the latest information on conditions in the Republic of Congo.

Cote d'Ivoire

Cote d'Ivoire, previously known as the Ivory Coast, is a developing West African nation. Tourism facilities in the capital city of Abidjan include some luxury hotels. Other accommodations, especially outside the capital, may be limited in quality and availability. A visa is not required for a stay of up to 90 days. All travelers arriving in Cote d'Ivoire must be in possession of a World Health Organization (WHO) vaccination card reflecting a current yellow fever inoculation. The WHO card is inspected by Ivorian health officials at the airport before admittance into the country. Medical facilities are adequate in Abidjan but may be limited elsewhere. Not all medicines are available. Street crime of the "grab and run" variety, as well as pickpocketing in crowded areas, has increased. Automobile accidents are one of the greatest threats to Americans in Cote d'Ivoire. Night driving is particularly hazardous due to poorly lit roads and vehicles. Airline travel in Cote d'Ivoire and many other parts of West Africa is routinely overbooked, schedules are limited and airline assistance is of varying quality.

Democratic Republic of the Congo

The Department of State warns U.S. citizens against travel to the Democratic Republic of the Congo (DRC) because of security and political uncertainties. DRC is the largest sub-Saharan African country. Although DRC has substantial human and natural resources, in recent years, the country has suffered a profound political and economic crisis. This has resulted in the dramatic deterioration of the physical infrastructure of the country, insecurity and an increase in crime in urban areas (including occasional episodes of looting and murder in Kinshasa's streets.) There has also been occasional official hostility to U.S. citizens, U.S. interests and nationals of European countries; periodic shortages of basic needs such as gasoline; chronic shortages of medicine and supplies for some basic medical care; hyperinflation and corruption. In some urban areas, malnutrition and starvation are acute. Tourism facilities are minimal. A visa and vaccination certificate, showing valid yellow fever immunization, are required for entry. Medical facilities are extremely limited. Medicine is in short supply. Most intercity roads are difficult or impassable in the rainy season. Government permission is required for travel outside Kinshasa. Credit cards are generally not accepted, except by a few major hotels and restaurants. Photography of public buildings and/or military installations is forbidden, including photography of the banks of the Congo River. Offenders may be arrested, held for a minimum of several hours, fined and the film and camera may also be confiscated. Armed groups operate in parts of the DRC outside government control. These groups have been responsible for pillaging, vehicle thefts, carjackings, extrajudicial settling of differences, ethnic tensions and continued military/paramilitary operations. Travelers in these areas run the risk of attack or detention.

Djibouti

Djibouti is a developing East African country. Facilities for tourism are limited. Visitors to Djibouti must obtain a visa before arrival. Evidence of yellow fever immunization must be presented. Medical facilities are limited. Medicine is often unavailable. Petty crime occurs in Djibouti City and elsewhere in the country.

Equatorial Guinea

Equatorial Guinea is a developing country in West Africa. Tourism facilities are minimal. A visa is not required. Proof of smallpox, yellow fever and cholera immunizations required for a stay of less than 90 days. Medical facilities are extremely limited. Many medicines are unavailable. Petty crime is common. The government of Equatorial Guinea has established stringent currency restrictions, applied both on arrival and departure from the country. Special permits may be needed for some types of photography. There is no U.S. Embassy in Equatorial Guinea. Contact the U.S. Embassy in neighboring Yaounde, Cameroon for the latest information.

Eritrea

Eritrea is a poor but developing East African country. Formerly a province of Ethiopia, Eritrea became an independent country in 1993, following a 30-year long struggle for independence. Tourism facilities in Eritrea are very limited. A visa is required. Airport visas are unavailable. Medical facilities in Eritrea are extremely limited. Travelers must bring their own supplies of prescription drugs and preventative medicines. Street crime is not a frequent occurrence but is on the increase. Visitors should exercise normal safety precautions with regard to what valuables are carried and what environs are visited. Credit cards are generally not accepted in Eritrea. Foreigners must pay bills in U.S. dollars or U.S. dollar denomination travelers checks.

Ethiopia

Ethiopia and Eritrea signed a final, comprehensive peace agreement on December 12, 2000, ending their two-year border conflict. Travel near or across the Ethiopia/Eritrea border should be avoided. Ethiopia is a developing East African country. Tourism facilities, although available in larger cities, are limited. A visa is required, as well as evidence of yellow fever immunization. Travelers must enter Ethiopia by air, either at Addis Ababa or Dire Dawa. Individuals entering overland risk being detained by immigration authorities and/or fined. Airport visas may be obtained if 48 hours advance notice has been provided by the traveler's sponsoring organization to proper authorities within Ethiopia. Visitors must declare hard currency upon arrival and may be required to present this declaration when applying for an exit visa. Upon departure, travelers should remember that antiquities and religious artifacts require export permission. There is a black market for hard currency, although the official and unofficial exchange rates continue to converge. Black market exchanges remain illegal and visitors are encouraged to exchange funds at banks or hotels.

Domestic and international air services generally operate on schedule. Internal travel is usually safe along major arteries. However, in rural areas and at night, bandit attacks are common, especially along the border with Somalia. Additionally, not all land mines have been disabled and cleared, especially in rural and isolated areas. Pickpocketing is rampant, and there have been numerous reports of thieves snatching jewelry.

Although physicians are well trained, medical facilities are minimal. Hospitals in Addis Ababa suffer from inadequate facilities, antiquated equipment and shortages of supplies, particularly medicine. Certain buildings and public places may not be photographed. U.S. Embassy Web Site: http://www.telecom.net.et/~usemb-et/ Embassy of Ethiopia Web Site: http://www.ethiopianembassy.org

Gabon

Gabon is a developing West African nation. French is the official language. Facilities for tourism are limited, especially outside the capital city. A visa is required, and must be obtained in advance of arrival in Gabon. Medical facilities in Gabon are limited. Some medicines are not available. Petty crime, such as robbery and mugging, is common, especially in urban areas.

The Gambia

The Gambia is a developing West African nation. Facilities for tourists such as hotels and restaurants are common near the coast. In inland areas, there are few tourist facilities, mostly consisting of campgrounds and small wildlife parks. A visa is required. Evidence of yellow fever immunization must be submitted with the visa application. Malaria is common and is predominately the most dangerous variety, *Plasmodium Falciparum.* Malaria prophylaxis is highly recommended, and visitors should be aware that any fever or flu-like illness while in The Gambia or within three months of travel to The Gambia requires urgent medical attention. Health facilities and services do not meet U.S. standards and there is a limited selection of medicines available. Petty street crime such as pickpocketing and purse snatching is a problem in some urban areas. Embassy of Gambia Web Site: http://www.gambia.com/index.html

Ghana

Ghana is a developing country on the west coast of Africa. A visa and evidence of immunization for yellow fever is required. Medical facilities in Ghana are limited, particularly outside the capital city of Accra. Malaria is common, as are other tropical diseases. Petty crime, such as pickpocketing, is a problem. Robberies often occur in public places and at the beach. In order to comply with Ghanaian law, currency transactions must be conducted with banks or foreign exchange bureaus. Visitors arriving in Ghana with electronic equipment, particularly video cameras and laptop computers may be required to pay a refundable deposit of 17.5% of the item's value prior to entry into the country. In some areas, possession of a camera is considered to be suspicious. Individuals have been arrested for taking pictures near sensitive installations. The government of Ghana does not recognize dual nationality except for minors under 21 years of age. The wearing of any military apparel, such as camouflage jackets or pants, or any clothing or items that may appear military in nature is strictly prohibited. U.S. Embassy Web Site: http://usembassy.state.gov/ghana/ Embassy of Ghana Web Site: http://www.ghana-embassy.org

Guinea

Guinea is a developing coastal West African country. The Department of State advises against travel in or near southern border regions. Due to armed incursions across Guinea's borders with Sierra Leone and Liberia, the Department of State has recalled all U.S. government employees formerly residing within 63 miles (100 kilometers) of the southern borders back to Conakry. Travelers should consult the latest State Department Consular Information Sheet before making travel plans to Guinea, and should register with the U.S. Embassy in Conakry upon arrival. Facilities for tourism are minimal. A visa is required. Diseases such as malaria, including cerebral malaria, hepatitis and intestinal hepatitis disorders are endemic. Evidence of yellow fever immunization is required and the Guinean government recommends taking of malarial suppressants. Medical facilities are limited. Street crime is very common. Criminals particularly target visitors at the airport in Conakry. Pickpockets or persons posing as officials sometimes offer assistance and then steal bags, purses or wallets. Travelers may wish to be met at the airport by travel agents, business contacts, family members or friends to avoid this possibility. Permission from the Guinean government's security personnel is required for photographing government buildings, airports, bridges or official looking buildings. Credit cards are rarely accepted in Guinea. Fund transfers between banks are frequently difficult, if not impossible, to accomplish. Western Union and Moneygram have offices in Conakry. The communications system is poor. It is recommended that travelers keep their

379

passport in a safe place and carry copies of the passport and visa(s) with them. U.S. Embassy Web Site: http://www.eti-bull.net/usembassy/

Guinea-Bissau

The Department of State warns American citizens against travel to Guinea-Bissau. The U.S. Embassy has suspended operations and all official Americans have departed the country. Guinea-Bissau is a developing nation on the west coast of Africa. Portuguese is the official language; French is also widely spoken. Facilities for tourism are minimal, particularly outside the capital city of Bissau. A visa must be obtained in advance; recent visitors arriving without visas via land or air have been turned back. Two photos and evidence of yellow fever immunization must accompany visa applications. Medical facilities in Guinea-Bissau are extremely limited. Medicines often are not available. Malaria and other tropical diseases are common. Petty thievery and pickpocketing are increasingly common, particularly at the airport, in markets and at public gatherings. Thieves have occasionally posed as officials and stolen bags and other personal items. Visitors should request permission from security personnel before photographing military or police installations. Small U.S. currency denominations are most useful for exchange into Guinea-Bissau pesos. Credit cards and travelers checks are rarely accepted in Guinea-Bissau. Fund transfers between banks are frequently difficult and time-consuming to accomplish. Taking pesos out of the country is prohibited. Travelers may have difficulty finding public phones and receiving international calls. Telephone services are expensive.

Kenya

Kenya is a developing East African country known for the wildlife in its national park system. Tourist facilities are widely available in Nairobi, on the coast and in the game parks and reserves. No visa is required for a tourist stay of up to one month. Proof of yellow fever immunization is required if traveling from infected areas. Adequate medical services are available in Nairobi. There is a high rate of street crime against tourists in downtown Nairobi, Mombasa, and at the coastal beach resorts. Pickpockets and thieves are also involved in "snatch and run" crimes near crowds. While traveling in wildlife areas, visitors should use reputable travel firms and knowledgeable guides

and avoid camping alone. Water in Nairobi is potable. In other parts of the country, water must be boiled or bottled. Travel by passenger train in Kenya may be unsafe, particularly during the rainy season, because of the lack of routine maintenance and safety checks.

Embassy of Kenya Web Site: http://www.kenyaembassy.com

Lesotho

Lesotho is a developing country surrounded on all sides by the Republic of South Africa. Facilities for tourists are limited. Visas are required and should be obtained at a Lesotho diplomatic mission abroad. However, some Americans have obtained visas without difficulties at the immigration office in Maseru after entering the country from South Africa. Although basic medical facilities and medicines are available in Lesotho, medical attention should be sought in South Africa if possible. The political situation has been stable for the last two years and is expected to remain so in the near term. Travel at night and travel in local mini-vans/taxis is dangerous. Travelers up-country in winter (May-Sept) should be prepared for cold weather and snow. Street crime, car jacking and break-ins are common in Maseru and can occur elsewhere as well. Credit cards are only accepted at a few establishments in Maseru. The local currency, the maloti, is pegged to the South African rand, which is accepted everywhere in Lesotho. Tap water is not reliably potable.

Liberia

U.S. citizens are warned to avoid travel due to unsettled security conditions. Liberia is a West African country that has suffered internal strife for the past several years. Tourism facilities are poor, and in some cases, non-existent. Travelers are required to have a visa prior to arrival. Evidence of yellow fever vaccination is also required. An exit permit must be obtained from Liberian immigration authorities upon arrival. Medical facilities have been disrupted and medicines are scarce. Monrovia's crime rate is high. Foreigners have been targets of street crime. Lodging, water, electricity, fuel, transportation, telephone and postal services continue to be uneven in Monrovia.

Embassy of Liberia Web Site: http://www.liberiaemb.org

Madagascar

Madagascar, the "Great Red Island," is a developing island nation off the east coast of Africa. It is a living museum offering endless fascination to the zoologist and botanist. Antananarivo, the capital, enjoys a temperate climate but the island has a wide range of microclimates ranging from rain forests in the northeast to desert in the southwest. Facilities for tourism are available, but vary in quality. Visas are required; a 3-month non-renewable tourist visa is available at the airport. Evidence of yellow fever immunizations is also required for all travelers who have been in an infected zone 6 months prior to their arrival here. If you will be traveling outside of Antananarivo, malaria prophylactics are highly recommended. Check with your insurance company to confirm whether your policy applies overseas, including provisions for medical evacuations, as medical facilities are minimal and many medicines are unavailable. Most crime in Madagascar is non-confrontational (pickpockets, snatch and grab, burglary) and travelers are reminded to be aware of their surroundings and not to carry valuables openly. There is little political unrest in Madagascar but travelers are reminded not to photograph political gatherings or demonstrations, especially in towns outside Antananarivo as this may put one at risk of arrest. Roads outside of the capital are generally not kept in good repair and tend to be narrow and winding with many one-lane bridges. Travel at night on these roads is not recommended due to the possibility of serious accidents. Embassy of Madagascar Web Site: http://www.embassy.org/madagascar/

Malawi

Malawi is a developing African nation. The country had multiparty democratic elections in 1994 and 1999. Facilities for tourism exist in major cities, resort areas and games parks, but, are limited and vary in quality. Medical facilities are limited and not up to U.S. standards. Medicines and medical equipment are in short supply. Lake Malawi is not bilharzia-free. Dress code restrictions, which applied to all visitors in Malawi, are no longer in effect. Travelers may wear comfortable clothes, but may wish to dress modestly, especially when visiting remote areas. Petty crime including pickpocketing and purse snatching occurs in urban areas. Residential crime and vehicle thefts are on the increase. Road travel at night, particularly outside the three major cities is not recommended due to the high number of serious road accidents. Major credit cards are generally accepted for payment of hotel bills. It is forbidden to take more than 200 kwacha (Malawi currency) out of the country.

Mali

Mali is a West African nation with a democratically elected system of government. Facilities for tourism are limited but developing. A visa is required. Evidence of a yellow fever vaccination is also required. Medical facilities are limited and many medicines are unavailable. Petty crime, including pickpocketing and purse snatching, is common. Incidents of banditry and vehicle theft have been reported along major travel routes, near the principal cities and in smaller towns, especially in the far north. Victims have included foreigners. The roads from Bamako to Mopti, Douentza, Koutiala, Sikasso, and Bougouni, and a few other roads are paved. Otherwise, road conditions are poor, particularly in the rainy season from mid-June to mid-September. Driving is hazardous after dark, and nighttime travel may be dangerous. Photography of military subjects is restricted; however, interpretation of what may be considered off limits varies. Other subjects may be considered sensitive from a cultural or religious viewpoint and it is helpful to obtain permission before taking pictures. The Malian currency is the CFA franc which is exchangeable for French francs at a fixed rate. Exchange of dollars in cash or travelers checks is slow and often involves out-of-date rates. Use of credit cards is limited to payments for services at only two hotels in Bamako. Cash advances on credit cards are performed by one bank in Mali, the BMCD Bank in Bamako, and only with a VISA credit card. International calls are expensive and difficult to make outside of Bamako. Collect calls cannot be made from Mali. Embassy of Mali Web Site: http://www.maliembassy-usa.org

Mauritania

Mauritania is a moderate Muslim republic located in northwestern Africa. A visa is required, as is evidence of yellow fever immunization and proof of sufficient funds. Facilities for tourism and internal travel are limited. Medical facilities in Mauritania are limited, and medicines are difficult to obtain. While Mauritania is safer than most African countries, petty crime exists, and the regions bordering Morocco and Mali may be hazardous due to land mines and banditry. Local currency may not be imported or exported. Dollars, especially $100 bills, may be easily exchanged in exchange offices or banks. Credit cards are only accepted in a few hotels in Nouakchott and Nouadhibou. Cash advances on credit cards and collect calls are not available from Mauritania.

Mauritius

The Republic of Mauritius has a democratic stable government and a growing economy. Facilities for tourism are highly developed. Although the spoken languages are French and Creole, English is the official language. An onward/return ticket and evidence of sufficient funds are required for entrance to Mauritius. U.S. citizens do not need visas for a stay of three months or less for business or tourism. Petty crime is common in Mauritius. U.S. Embassy Web Site: http://usembassymauritius.mu/ Embassy of Mauritius Web Site: http://www.idsonline.com/usa/embasydc.html

Mozambique

Mozambique, a less developed country in southern Africa, ended a 17-year civil war in October 1992 with the signing of a peace agreement between the government and the rival rebel group. Facilities for tourism are severely limited outside of Maputo. Travel by road outside of the major urban areas is possible; however, road conditions vary greatly. A visa is required and must be obtained in advance. Evidence of a yellow fever and cholera vaccination is also required. Medical facilities are minimal and many medicines are unavailable. Maputo's special clinic, which requires payment in hard currency, can provide general non-emergency services. Economic conditions in the country, spotty police protection and years of war have caused an increase in violent and armed robberies, break-ins and auto thefts. Victims, including members of the foreign community, have been killed. Traveling alone or at night is particularly risky. Currency can be converted at locations authorized by the Mozambican government. Currency conversions on the black market are illegal and very risky. Credit cards are not widely accepted in Mozambique. Some merchants prefer to be paid in U.S. dollars. Embassy of Mozambique Web Site: http://www.embamoc-usa.org

Namibia

Namibia is a Southern African country with a moderately developed economy. Facilities for tourism are available. An onward/return ticket and proof of sufficient funds are required for entrance into Namibia. A visa is not required for tourist or business visits under 90 days. Medical facilities are relatively modern, especially in the city of Windhoek. Some petty crime occurs. U.S. Embassy Web Site: http://www.usembassy.namib.com

Niger

Niger is an inland African nation whose northern area includes a part of the Sahara Desert. Tourism facilities are minimal, particularly outside of Niamey. A visa is required to enter Niger. Visas are valid for a period of one week to three months from the date of issuance, depending on the type of visa and category of traveler. Yellow fever vaccinations are required for entry into Niger. Medical facilities are minimal in Niger, particularly outside the capital of Niamey. Some medicines are in short supply. Armed bandits operate in northern Niger, and a number of people have been killed. Thieves and pickpockets are especially active in tourist areas. Care must be taken in walking city streets anywhere, at any time, but especially at night. There have been incidents of groups of men assaulting women who are, or appear to be, African, and who are wearing garments other than the traditional ankle-length wrap known as "pagnes." Tourists are free to take pictures anywhere in Niger, except near military installations, radio and television stations, the Presidency Building, and the airport. There are no laws restricting currency transactions in Niger. International telephones service to and from Niger is expensive and callers experience delays getting a line. Faxes are often garbled due to poor quality.

Nigeria

The Department of State warns U.S. citizens of the dangers of travel to Nigeria. A visa is required for admission the country and no visas are issued at the airport. Evidence of yellow fever vaccination is also required. Tourist facilities are limited. Violent crime is a serious problem, especially in Lagos, and the southern half of the country. Foreigners in particular are vulnerable to armed robbery, assault, burglary, carjackings and extortion.

382

Disease is widespread and the public is not always informed in a timely manner about outbreaks of typhoid, cholera and yellow fever. Malaria, including potentially fatal cerebral malaria, and hepatitis are endemic. Medical facilities are limited. Not all medicines are available. Permission is required to take photographs of government buildings, airports, bridges or official looking buildings.

Permission may be obtained from Nigerian security personnel. Persons seeking to trade at lower rates on the "black market" could be arrested or shaken down. To avoid problems, dollars should be exchanged for naira (Nigerian currency) only at the official rate and at approved exchange facilities, including many major hotels. (This is no longer true. Foreign exchange is now liberalized.) Credit cards are rarely accepted, and their use is generally ill advised because of the prevalence of credit card fraud in Nigeria and perpetrated by Nigerians in the United States. Travelers' checks can be exchanged at the airport, but due to insecurity at and near the airport, travelers are advised not to cash large amounts at the airport. There are very few, if any, facilities in Nigeria for cashing travelers checks other than as a courtesy for guests at major hotels. Check with your hotel before arrival to see if they offer this service. It is often necessary to bring currency in sufficient amounts to cover the trip. Transfers between banks are practically impossible to accomplish. Prospective visitors should consult the Consular Information Sheet for Nigeria. Because of the incidence of business scams and swindles, persons interested in doing business in Nigeria are advised to consult Tips for Business Travelers to Nigeria before providing any information or funds in response to an unverified business offer. This publication is available free of charge by sending a self-addressed, stamped envelope to the Office of Overseas Citizens Services, Department of State, Washington, DC 20520-4818, or, visit the Bureau of Consular Affairs web site at http://travel.state.gov/tips_nigeria.html.

Rwanda

Rwanda is a central East African country recovering from civil war and a genocide in 1994. Visas are not required for stays of less than 90 days. A yellow fever immunization is required. Medical facilities are severely limited and extremely overburdened. Looting and street crime are common. Civilian law enforcement authorities may be limited. Sporadic attacks by insurgents still occur in the northwest and unexploded ordnance remains a danger off well-traveled roads in the northwest as well.

Embassy of Rwanda Web Site: http://www.rwandemb.org

Sao Tome and Principe

Sao Tome and Principe is a developing island nation off the west coast of Africa. Facilities for tourism are not widely available. A visa is required and must be obtained prior to arrival in country. Medical facilities in Sao Tome and Principe are limited. Some crime occurs. There is no U.S. Embassy in Sao Tome and Principe. Inquiries may be made at the U.S. Embassy in neighboring Gabon.

Senegal

Senegal is a French speaking West African country. Facilities for tourists are widely available although of varying quality. Visas are not required for stays of less than 90 days. Medical facilities are limited, particularly in areas outside the capital city, Dakar. Street crime in Senegal poses moderate risks for visitors. Most reported incidents involve pickpockets, purse snatchers and street scam artists.

U.S. Embassy Web Site: http://usembassy.state.gov/posts/sg1/wwwhemb.html

Seychelles

Seychelles is a tropical island nation in the Indian Ocean off the east coast of Africa. The principle island of Mahe has a population of about 50,000. The two other islands with significant permanent populations are Praslin and La Digue. Facilities for tourism are generally well developed. A visa is required and may be issued on arrival for a stay of up to one month. There is no charge. The visa may be extended for a period of up to one year. Medical facilities in Seychelles are limited, especially in the isolated outer islands, where doctors are often unavailable. Petty crime occurs, although violent crime against tourists is considered to be rare. Keep valuables in hotel safes. Close and lock hotel windows at night, even while the room is occupied to minimize the risk of crime.

Sierra Leone

Sierra Leone is a developing country that has few facilities for tourism and poses considerable risks for travelers. Outside the capital city of Freetown, approximately 60% of the country remains under rebel control, and travel to these areas should not be attempted. A visa is required. Airport visas are not available upon arrival in Sierra Leone. Cholera and yellow fever immunizations are required if arriving from an infected area. Malaria suppressants are recommended. Medical facilities are limited and medicines are in short supply. Sterility of equipment is questionable and treatment is often unreliable. Travelers must declare foreign currency being brought into Sierra Leone. Declaration is made on an exchange control form that must be certified and stamped at the port of entry. Petty crime and theft of wallets and passports are common. Main roads and highways throughout the country have many roadblocks manned by the military, rebels or civil defense forces, who demand payment in exchange for passage. Permission is required to photograph government buildings, airports, bridges or official-looking buildings. Areas forbidding photography are not marked or defined. Telephone service is unreliable.

Somalia

U.S. citizens are warned not to travel to Somalia. The Liaison Office in Mogadishu ceased operations in September 1994. No visas are required because there is no functioning government. Anyone entering Somalia must receive immunization against cholera, typhoid and yellow fever, and obtain a doctor's advice regarding any other immunizations that might be necessary. There are virtually no health facilities or medicines available in Somalia. Looting, banditry and all forms of violent crime are common in Somalia, particularly in the capital city of Mogadishu. Electricity, water, food and lodging are unobtainable on a regular basis. Parts of the north, including much of the self-declared "Republic of Somaliland," are relatively peaceful and calm.

South Africa

Although South Africa is in many respects a developed country, much of its population, particularly in rural areas, lives in poverty. There are adequate facilities in all urban centers, game parks and areas most commonly visited by tourists. A passport valid for at least six months is required but a visa is not required for visits for holiday, business or transit purposes. However, visas are required for extended stays, employment, study and for diplomatic and official passport holders. Evidence of a yellow fever vaccination is necessary if arriving from an infected area. Medical facilities are good in urban areas and in the vicinity of game parks and beaches, but may be limited elsewhere. Food and water are generally safe and a wide variety of consumer goods and pharmaceuticals are readily available. There is continuing and significant street crime such as muggings, pickpocketing, and random street violence, which affects foreigners as well as local residents, especially in the center of major cities such as Johannesburg. Road conditions are generally good but there is a very high incidence of highway casualties, especially over holiday weekends. U.S. Embassy Web Site: http://usembassy.state.gov/posts/sf1/wwwhmain.html Embassy of South Africa Web Site: http://usaembassy.southafrica.net

Sudan

The Department of State warns U.S. citizens against all travel to Sudan. The Government of Sudan has been fighting a civil war against a southern secessionist movement for more than 17 years. The war is active in southern and eastern parts of the country. The United States has no permanent diplomatic presence in Sudan, and updated information is not available because of the decreased of diplomatic presence there. Sudan is a large under-developed country in northeastern Africa. Tourism facilities are minimal. A visa is required to enter Sudan. Visas are not granted in passports showing Israeli visas. Travelers are required to register with police headquarters within three days of arrival. Travelers must obtain police permission before moving to another location in Sudan and must register with police within 24 hours of arrival at the new location. The Sudanese government recommends that malarial suppressants be taken, and that yellow fever, cholera and meningitis vaccinations are in order. The exchange of money at other than an authorized banking institution may result in arrest and loss of funds though unscrupulous black marketeers. A permit must be obtained before taking photographs anywhere in Khartoum, as well as in the interior of the country. Photographing military areas, bridges, drainage stations, broadcast stations, public utilities and slum areas or beggars is prohibited. Disruption of water and electricity is frequent. Telecommunications are slow and often not possible. Unforeseen circumstances such as sandstorms and electrical outages may cause flight delays. Embassy of Sudan Web Site: http://www.sudanembassyus.org

Swaziland

Swaziland is a small developing nation in southern Africa. Facilities for tourism are available. Visas are not required of tourists planning to stay less than 60 days. Temporary residence permits are issued in Mbabane, the capital. For longer stays, visitors must report to immigration authorities or to a police station within 48 hours of arrival, if they are not lodged in a hotel. Yellow fever and cholera immunizations are required for visitors arriving from an infected area. Anti-malarial treatment is recommended. Medical facilities are limited. Petty street crime, primarily theft of money and personal property occurs with some frequency.

Tanzania

Tanzania is an East African nation. Tourist facilities are adequate in major cities but limited in remote areas. A visa is required for entrance into the country. Visas for mainland Tanzania are also valid for Zanzibar. Airport visas may be obtained only in Zanzibar; they are not available at mainland airports. Yellow fever and cholera immunizations are required if arriving from an affected area. Airport officials often require current immunization records from travelers arriving from non-infected areas as well. Medical facilities are limited. Some medicines are in short supply or unavailable. Malaria is endemic in Tanzania and anti-malarial prophylaxis is advisable. Numerous cases of meningococcal meningitis and cholera have been reported throughout the country. Crime is a concern in both urban and rural areas of Tanzania. Incidents include muggings, vehicle thefts and residential break-ins. Valuables such as passports, travelers' checks, cameras and jewelry are particular targets for thieves, and are easily stolen if left in luggage at airline check-ins or hotel lobbies. Photography of military installations is forbidden. Individuals have been detained and/or had their cameras and film confiscated for taking pictures of hospitals, schools, bridges, industrial sites and airports.

Togo

Togo is a small West African nation with a developing economy. Tourism facilities are limited, especially outside the capital city. A visa is required. Yellow fever immunizations are also required. Medical facilities in Togo are limited under normal conditions and have degraded because of a long general strike, the departure of medical personnel and the closure or reduction of service in clinics and hospitals. Some medicines are available through local pharmacies. Petty crime, including pickpocketing, has increased.

Uganda

Uganda is an East African nation. Tourism facilities are adequate in Kampala; they are limited, but are improving in other areas. U.S. travelers may obtain a visa at a Ugandan embassy, consulate or at Entebbe Airport, near Kampala. Travelers are urged to procure a visa from the nearest Ugandan embassy or consulate at their earliest convenience. Evidence of immunization for yellow fever is required. Immunization for cholera and typhoid is recommended. Medical facilities in Uganda are limited. Medical supplies, equipment and medication are often in short supply or not available. Incidents of armed vehicle hijacking and armed highway robbery occur throughout the country with varying frequency. Many roads in Uganda are poor and bandit activity in some areas is both frequent and unpredictable. Insurgent activities have made travel to the northern area of the country risky. Highway travel at night is particularly dangerous. Photographing security forces or government installations is prohibited. Embassy of Uganda Web Site: http://www.ugandaweb.com/ugaembassy/

Zambia

Zambia is a developing African country. Tourist facilities outside of well-known game parks are not fully developed. A visa is required prior to entering the country. Medical facilities are limited. Cholera and yellow fever are endemic. Crime is prevalent in Zambia. Muggings and petty theft are commonplace, especially in Lusaka in the vicinity of Cairo Road and in other commercial areas. Road travel at night is not recommended, especially outside of urban areas.

Zimbabwe

Zimbabwe is a landlocked Southern African nation

385

with extensive tourist facilities. To enter the country, a passport, return ticket, and adequate funds are required. U.S. citizens travelling to Zimbabwe for tourism, business and transit can obtain a visa at the airports and border points of entry or in advance from the Embassy of Zimbabwe in Washington, D.C. U.S. travelers are required to pay a visa entry fee at the point of entry into Zimbabwe, and there is an airport departure tax of $20 payable by all U.S. citizens. Medical facilities in Zimbabwe are limited, and many medicines are in short supply. Carjacking, street crime, rape and credit card fraud are on the increase, particularly in Harare and tourist resort areas. Bus travel can be dangerous due to overloaded buses, inadequate maintenance, and unskilled drivers, and fuel shortages can complicate any travel plans within the country whether by bus or automobile. Zimbabwean authorities are extremely sensitive about photographing certain locations and buildings, including government offices, airports, military installations, official residences and embassies. Deteriorating economic conditions have sparked sporadic and sometimes violent riots and U.S. citizens should avoid all demonstrations and political rallies. Squatters have occupied many commercial farms, and those occupations have led to significant violence. Numerous game reserves and lodges around the country have been affected by these occupations and many have closed. U.S. citizens are urged to avoid occupied farms and to

reconfirm lodging reservations immediately prior to departure for Zimbabwe. Embassy of Zimbabwe Web Site: http://www.zimweb.com/Embassy/Zimbabwe/

U.S. Embassies and Consulates Abroad

Note: The workweek is Monday-Friday except where noted. Mail to APO and FPO addresses must originate in the United States; the street address must not appear in an APO or FPO address.

ANGOLA
American Embassy
Rua Houari Boumedienne
P.O. Box 6468
Luanda
Tel: (244-2) 34-54-81

BENIN
American Embassy
Rue Caporal Anani Bernard
B.P. 2012
Cotonou
Tel: (229) 30-06-50

BOTSWANA
American Embassy
P.O. Box 90
Gaborone
Tel: (267) 353-982

BURKINA FASO
American Embassy
B.P. 35
Ouagadougou 01
Tel: (226) 30-67-23

BURUNDI
American Embassy
B.P. 34 1720
Bujumbura
Tel: (257)(2) 23454

CAMEROON
American Embassy

Rue Nachtigal, B.P. 817
Yaounde
Tel: (237) 23-40-14

CAPE VERDE
American Embassy
Rua Abilio Macedo 81
C.P. 201
Praia
Tel: (238) 61-56-16

CENTRAL AFRICAN REPUBLIC
American Embassy
Avenue David Dacko
B.P. 924
Bangui
Tel: (236) 61-02-00

CHAD
American Embassy
Avenue Felix Eboue
B.P. 413
N'djamena
Tel: (235) 516-218

THE COMOROS
Services provided by the American Embassy in Port Louis, Mauritius.

CONGO
American Embassy
Avenue Amilcar Cabral
B.P. 1015, Box C
Brazzaville
Tel: (242) 83-20-70

COTE d'IVOIRE
American Embassy
5 Rue Jesse Owens 01
B.P. 1712
Abidjan
Tel: (225) 21-09-79

DEMOCRATIC REPUBLIC OF CONGO
American Embassy
310 Avenue des Aviateurs
Unit 31550
Kinshasa
Tel: (243)(12) 21523

DJIBOUTI
American Embassy
Plateau du Serpent
Blvd. Marechal Joffre
B.P. 185
Djibouti
Tel: (253) 353-995

EQUATORIAL GUINEA
American Embassy
Calle de Los Ministros
P.O. Box 597
Malabo
Tel: (240-9) 2406

ERITREA
American Embassy
34 Zera Yacob St.
P.O. Box 211
Asmara
Tel: (291-1) 12-00-04

ETHIOPIA
American Embassy
Entoto St., P.O. Box 1014
Addis Ababa
Tel: (251-1) 550-666, ext.
316/336

GABON
American Embassy
Blvd. de la Mer
B.P. 4000
Libreville
Tel: (241) 762-003, 743-492

THE GAMBIA
American Embassy
Kairaba Ave.
P.M.B. No. 19
Banjul
Tel: (220) 392856, 392858,
391970/1

GHANA
American Embassy
Ring Road East
P.O. Box 194
Accra
Tel: (223-21) 775-347

GUINEA
American Embassy

2nd Blvd. and 9th Ave.
B.P. 603
Conakry
Tel: (224) 41-15-20/1/3

GUINEA-BISSAU
American Embassy
C.P. 297
1067 Codex
Bissau
Tel: (245) 25-2273

KENYA
American Embassy
Mombassa Rd.
P.O. Box 30137
Nairobi
Tel. 254-2-537-800

LESOTHO
American Embassy
254 Kingsway
P.O. Box 333, Maseru 100
Maseru
Tel: (266) 312-666

LIBERIA
American Embassy
111 United Nations Dr.
P.O. Box 10-0098
Mamba Point
Monrovia
Tel: (231) 222-991

MADAGASCAR
American Embassy
14 and 16 Rue Rainitovo,
Antsahavola
B.P. 620
Antananarivo
Tel: (261)(2) 21257, 20089

MALAWI
American Embassy
Area 40, Plot #24
Kenyatta Road
P.O. Box 30016
Lilongwe 3, Malawi
Tel: (265) 783-166

MALI
American Embassy
Rue de Rochester N.Y.

B.P. 34
Bamako
Tel: (223) 223-678,225-470

MAURITANIA
American Embassy
B.P. 222
Nouakchott
Tel: (222)(2) 52660
Workweek: Sunday-Thursday

MAURITIUS
American Embassy
John F. Kennedy Street
Port Louis
Tel: (230) 208-9764

MOZAMBIQUE
American Embassy
Avenida Kaunda 193
Maputo
Tel: (258)(1) 49-27-97

NAMIBIA
American Embassy
Private Bag 12029
Ausspannplatz
Windhoek, Namibia
Tel: (264-61) 22-1601

NIGER
American Embassy
B.P. 11201
Niamey
Tel: (227) 722-661

NIGERIA
American Embassy
2 Eleke Crescent
Victoria Island, Lagos
Tel: (234)(1) 261-0050

RWANDA
American Embassy
Blvd. de la Revolution
B.P. 28
Kigali
Tel: (250) 75601

SAO TOME AND PRINCIPE
Falls under the jurisdiction of
the American Embassy in
Libreville, Gabon

387

SENEGAL
American Embassy
Avenue Jean XXIII
B.P. 49
Dakar
Tel: (221) 23-42-96

SEYCHELLES
American Embassy
Box 148, Unit 62501
Victoria
Tel: (248) 225-256

SIERRA LEONE
American Embassy
Corner Walpole and Siaka
Stevens St.
Freetown
Tel: (232-22) 226-481

SOMALIA
U.S. Liaison Office ceased
operation September 1994;
services provided through the
U.S. Embassy in Nairobi,
Kenya

SOUTH AFRICA
American Embassy
887 Pretorius St.
Pretoria
Tel: (27)(12) 342-1048

American Consulate General
Broadway Industries Center
Heerengracht
Foreshore
Cape Town
Tel: (27)(21) 214-280

American Consulate General
Durban House, 29th Fl.
333 Smith St.
Durban 4001
Tel: (27)(31) 304-4737

American Consulate General
1 River Street, Killarney
Johannesburg
Tel: (27)(11) 644-8000

SUDAN

American Embassy
Sharia Ali Abdul Latif
P.O. Box 699
Khartoum
Tel: 74700, 74611
Workweek: Sunday-Thursday

SWAZILAND
American Embassy
Central Bank Bldg.
Warner Street
P.O. Box 199
Mbabane
Tel: (268) 464-41/5

TANZANIA
American Embassy
30 Laibon Rd. (off Ali Hassan
Mwinyi Rd.)
P.O. Box 9123
Dar Es Salaam
Tel: (255)(51) 66010/4

TOGO
American Embassy
Rue Pelletier Caventou & Rue
Vauban
B.P. 852
Lome
Tel: (228)(21) 29-91

UGANDA
American Embassy
Parliament Ave.
P.O. Box 7007
Kampala
Tel: (256)(41) 259-792, 259-
795

ZAMBIA
American Embassy
Independence and United
Nations Aves.
P.O. Box 31617
Lusaka
Tel: (260)(1) 250-955

ZIMBABWE
American Embassy
P.O. Box 3340
Harare
Tel: (263)(4) 794-521

Foreign Embassies in the U.S.

Embassy of **Angola**
1819 L Street, NW
Suite 400
Washington, DC 20036
(202) 452-1042/43

Embassy of the Republic of
Benin
2737 Cathedral Ave., NW
Washington, DC 20008
(202) 232-6656

Embassy of the Republic of
Botswana
1531 New Hampshire Ave.,
NW
Washington, DC 20036
(202) 244-4990

Embassy of **Burkina Faso**
2340 Mass. Ave., NW
Washington, DC 20008
(202) 332-5577

Embassy of the Republic of
Burundi
2233 Wisconsin Ave., NW
Suite 212
Washington, DC 20007
(202) 342-2574

Embassy of the Republic of
Cameroon
2349 Mass. Ave., NW
Washington, DC 20008
(202) 265-8790 to 8794

Embassy of the Republic of
Cape Verde
3415 Mass. Ave., NW
Washington, DC 20007
(202) 965-6820

Embassy of **Central African
Republic**
1618 22nd Street, NW
Washington, DC 20008
(202) 483-7800

Embassy of the Republic of

Chad
2002 R Street, NW
Washington, DC 20009
(202) 462-4009

Embassy of the Federal and
Islamic Republic of **Comoros**
336 East 45th Street
2nd Floor
New York, NY 10017
(212) 972-8010

Embassy of the **Republic of
Congo**
4891 Colorado Ave., NW
Washington, DC 20011
(202) 726-5500

Embassy of the Republic of
Cote d'Ivoire
2424 Mass. Ave., NW
Washington, DC 20008
(202) 797-0300

Embassy of the **Democratic
Republic of Congo**
1800 New Hampshire Ave.,
NW
Washington, DC 20009
(202) 234-7690/1

Embassy of the Republic of
Djibouti
1156 15th Street, NW
Suite 515
Washington, DC 20005
(202) 331-0270

Embassy of the Republic of
Equatorial Guinea
1511 K Street, NW
Suite 405
Washington, DC 20005
(202) 393-0348

Embassy of **Eritrea**
910 17th Street, NW
Suite 400
Washington, DC 20009
(202) 429-1991

Embassy of **Ethiopia**
2134 Kalorama Road, NW

Washington, DC 20008
(202) 234-2281/2

Embassy of the **Gabon**ese
Republic
2034 20th Street, NW
Washington, DC 20009
(202) 797-1000

Embassy of the **Gambia**
1155 15th Street, NW
Washington, DC 20005
(202) 785-1399

Embassy of **Ghana**
3512 International Drive, NW
Washington, DC 20008
(202) 686-4520

Embassy of the Republic of
Guinea
2112 Leroy Place, NW
Washington, DC 20008
(202) 483-9420

Embassy of **Guinea-Bissau**
1511 K Street, NW
Suite 519
Washington, DC 20005
(202) 347-3950

Embassy of **Kenya**
2249 R Street, NW
Washington, DC 20008
(202) 387-6106

Embassy of the Kingdom of
Lesotho
2511 Mass. Ave., NW
Washington, DC 20008
(202) 797-5533

Embassy of the Republic of
Liberia
5303 Colorado Ave., NW
Washington, DC 20011
(202) 723-0437

Embassy of the Democratic
Republic of **Madagascar**
2374 Mass. Ave., NW
Washington, DC 20008
(202) 265-5525/6

Embassy of **Malawi**
2408 Mass. Ave., NW
Washington, DC 20008
(202) 797-1007

Embassy of the Republic of
Mali
2130 R Street, NW
Washington, DC 20008
(202) 332-2249

Embassy of the Republic of
Mauritania
2129 Leroy Place, NW
Washington, DC 20008
(202) 232-5700/01

Embassy of **Mauritius**
4301 Connecticut Ave., NW
Suite 441
Washington, DC 20008
(202) 244-1491/2

Embassy of the Republic of
Mozambique
1990 M Street, NW
Suite 570
Washington, DC 20036
(202) 293-7146

Embassy of **Namibia**
1605 New Hampshire Ave.
NW
Washington, DC 20009
(202) 986-0540

Embassy of the Republic of
Niger
2204 R Street, NW
Washington, DC 20008
(202) 483-4224

Embassy of the Republic of
Nigeria
2201 M Street, NW
Washington, DC 20037
(202) 822-1500 or 1522

Embassy of the Republic of
Rwanda
1714 New Hampshire Ave.,
NW

Washington, DC 20009
(202) 232-2882

Permanent Mission of **Sao Tome & Principe**
to the U.N.
400 Park Avenue
7th Floor
New York, NY 10022
(212) 317-0533

Embassy of the Republic of
Senegal
2112 Wyoming Ave., NW
Washington, DC 20008
(202) 234-0540

Permanent Mission of the
Seychelles to the U.N.
800 Second Avenue
Suite 400
New York, NY 10017
(212) 972-1785

Embassy of **Sierra Leone**
1701 19th Street, NW
Washington, DC 20009
(202) 939-9261

Consulate of the **Somali**
Democratic Republic
New York, NY
(212) 688-9410

Embassy of **South Africa**
Consular Office
3051 Mass. Ave., NW
Washington, DC 20016
(202) 966-1650

Embassy of the Republic of
Sudan
2210 Mass. Ave., NW
Washington, DC 20008
(202) 338-8565 to 8570

Embassy of the Kingdom of
Swaziland
3400 International Drive, NW
Suite 3M
Washington, DC
(202) 362-6683

Embassy of the United
Republic of **Tanzania**
2139 R Street, NW
Washington, DC 20008
(202) 939-6125

Embassy of the Republic of
Togo
2208 Mass. Ave., NW
Washington, DC 20008
(202) 234-4212/3

Embassy of the Republic of
Uganda
5911 16th Street, NW
Washington, DC 20011
(202) 726-7100 to 02

Embassy of the Republic of
Zambia
2419 Mass. Ave., NW
Washington, DC 20008
(202) 265-9717 to 19

Embassy of **Zimbabwe**
1608 New Hampshire Ave.,
NW
Washington, DC 20009
(202) 332-7100

Planning Another Trip?

See Chapter 36 for a listing of
resources available to the
general traveler from the U.S.
Departments of State, Customs,
Transportation, Health and
various government and non-
government organizations.
Almost all of the available
International travel-related
pamphlets, brochures and
publications issued by the U.S.
Department of State and by the
U.S. Customs have been
reproduced in full in this book.
See Table of Contents for
location.

Chapter 24

Tips for Travelers to Western Europe and Australia

Australia, Austria, Belgium, Cyprus, Denmark, Finland, France, Germany, Greece, Greenland, Iceland, Ireland, Italy, Luxembourg, Liechtenstein, Monaco, Netherlands, New Zealand, Norway, Portugal, Spain, Sweden, Switzerland, Turkey, United Kingdom.

Australia

COUNTRY DESCRIPTION: Australia is a highly developed, stable democracy with a federal-state system. Tourist facilities are widely available. The Australian Tourist Commission, which has a wide range of information of interest to travelers, can be contacted via the Internet at http://www.australia.com.

ENTRY REQUIREMENTS: U.S. citizens may travel to Australia on a valid U.S. passport with an Australian visa or, if eligible, on a valid U.S. passport and an Electronic Travel Authority (ETA), which replaces a visa and allows a stay of up to three months. The ETA is free of charge and is available from airlines and many travel agents. American citizens who overstay their ETA or visa, even for short periods, may be subject to detention and removal. More information about the ETA and entry requirements may be obtained from the Embassy of Australia at 1601 Massachusetts Avenue, N.W., Washington, D.C. 20036, telephone (202) 797-3000, via the Australian Embassy home page on the Internet at http://www.austemb.org/, or from the Australian Consulate General in Los Angeles, tel (310) 229-4840.

In an effort to prevent international child abduction, many governments have initiated procedures at entry/exit points. These often include requiring documentary evidence of relationship and permission for the child's travel from the parent(s) or legal guardian not present. Having such documentation on hand, even if not required, may facilitate entry/departure.

DUAL NATIONALITY: In addition to being subject to all Australian laws affecting U.S. citizens, dual nationals may also be subject to other laws that impose special obligations on Australian citizens. For additional information, please see the Consular Affairs home page on the Internet at http://travel.state.gov for our *Dual Nationality flyer*. For recent information concerning the Government of Australia's approach to dual nationality, please see http://www.citizenship.gov.au.

CRIME: Australia's crime rate is low. However, foreign visitors from the United States or elsewhere are sometimes targets for pick-pockets, purse snatchers and petty thieves. Automobile burglaries and theft of personal belongings also occur. The loss or theft abroad of a U.S. passport should be reported immediately to the local police and the nearest U.S. embassy or consulate. U.S. citizens may refer to the Department of State's pamphlet, *A Safe Trip Abroad*, for ways to promote a trouble-free journey. The pamphlet is available by mail from the Superintendent of Documents, U.S. Government Printing Office, Washington, D.C. 20402, via the Internet at http://www.access.gpo.gov/su_docs, or via the Bureau of Consular Affairs home page at http://travel.state.gov.

MEDICAL FACILITIES: Excellent medical care is available. Serious medical problems requiring hospitalization and/or medical evacuation to the United States can cost thousands of dollars. Doctors and hospitals often expect immediate cash payment for health services.

MEDICAL INSURANCE: The Department of State strongly urges Americans to consult with their medical insurance company prior to traveling abroad to confirm whether their policy applies overseas and if it will cover emergency expenses

391

such as a medical evacuation. U.S. medical insurance plans seldom cover health costs incurred outside the United States unless supplemental coverage is purchased. Further, U.S. Medicare and Medicaid programs do not provide payment for medical services outside the United States. However, many travel agents and private companies offer insurance plans that will cover healthcare expenses incurred overseas including emergency services such as medical evacuations.

When making a decision regarding health insurance, Americans should consider that many foreign doctors and hospitals require payment in cash prior to providing service and that a medical evacuation to the United States may cost well in excess of $50,000. Uninsured travelers who require medical care overseas often face extreme difficulties. When consulting with your insurer prior to your trip, please ascertain whether payment will be made to the overseas healthcare provider or if you will be reimbursed later for expenses that you incur. Some insurance policies also include coverage for psychiatric treatment and for disposition of remains in the event of death.

Useful information on medical emergencies abroad, including overseas insurance programs, is provided in the Department of State's Bureau of Consular Affairs brochure, *Medical Information for Americans Traveling Abroad*, available via the Bureau of Consular Affairs home page or autofax: (202) 647-3000.

OTHER HEALTH INFORMATION: Information on vaccinations and other health precautions may be obtained from the Centers for Disease Control and Prevention's hotline for international travelers at 1-877-FYI-TRIP (1-877-394-8747); fax 1-888-CDC-FAXX (1-888-232-3299), or via CDC's Internet site at http://www.cdc.gov.

TRAFFIC SAFETY AND ROAD CONDITIONS: While in a foreign country, U.S. citizens may encounter road conditions that differ significantly from those in the United States. The information below concerning Australia is provided for general reference only, and may it not be totally accurate in a particular location or circumstance.

Safety of Public Transportation: Good

Urban Road Conditions/Maintenance: Good
Rural Road Conditions/Maintenance: Good
Availability of Roadside Assistance: Good

Visitors are reminded that all traffic operates on the left side of the road, and that all vehicles use right-hand drive. Visitors should use caution when crossing streets and when driving. When crossing roads, pedestrians are reminded to look carefully in all directions. Seat belts are mandatory. Speed limits and laws regarding driving while intoxicated are rigorously enforced. Roads and streets are frequently narrower and less graded than U.S. highways. Outside the major metropolitan areas, most highways are two-lane roads with significant distances between destinations.

Drivers are urged to exercise caution while passing or merging with adjacent traffic. When driving in rural areas, particularly in the Northern Territory where there are no speed limits, drivers should be cautious of free-roaming animals and "road-trains" (several semi-truck trailers hooked together). It is dangerous to pass road-trains, and it is advisable to pull over and allow on-coming road-trains to pass to avoid being sideswiped. A number of fatalities have occurred in the Northern Territory when vehicles, driven at high rates of speed, have skidded and overturned after hitting the loose gravel shoulder of the road. U.S. drivers, especially those inexperienced with 4-wheel drive vehicles, should exercise common-sense judgment when driving in outback Australia.

For additional general information about road safety, including links to foreign government sites, please see the Department of State, Bureau of Consular Affairs, home page at http://travel.state.gov/road_safety.html. For specific information concerning Australian driving permits, vehicle inspection, road tax, mandatory insurance and the rental and operation of motor vehicles in Australia, please contact the Australian Tourist Commission via the Internet at http://www.australia.com.

AVIATION SAFETY OVERSIGHT: The U.S. Federal Aviation Administration (FAA) has assessed the Government of Australia's civil aviation authority as Category 1 -- in compliance with international aviation safety standards for oversight of Australia's air carrier operations. For further information, travelers may contact the

Department of Transportation within the United States at telephone 1-800-322-7873, or visit the FAA's Internet web site at http://www.faa.gov/avr/iasa.

The U.S. Department of Defense (DOD) separately assesses some foreign air carriers for suitability as official providers of air services. For information regarding the DOD policy on specific carriers, travelers may contact the DOD at telephone (618) 229-4801.

CUSTOMS REGULATIONS: Australian customs authorities enforce very strict regulations concerning the temporary importation from all countries of items such as agricultural and wood products, as well as very strict quarantine standards for other products, animals and pets. It is advisable to contact the Embassy of Australia in Washington or one of Australia's consulates in the United States for specific information regarding customs requirements, or see http://www.aqis.gov.au.

Australian customs authorities encourage the use of an ATA (Admission Temporaire/Temporary Admission) Carnet for the temporary admission of professional equipment, commercial samples, and/or goods for exhibitions and fair purposes. ATA Carnet Headquarters, located at the U.S. Council for International Business, 1212 Avenue of the Americas, New York, NY 10036, issues and guarantees the ATA Carnet in the United States. For additional information, please call (212) 354-4480, or send an e-mail to atacarnet@uscib.org, or visit http://www.uscib.org for details.

CRIMINAL PENALTIES: While in a foreign country, a U.S. citizen is subject to that country's laws and regulations, which sometimes differ significantly from those in the United States and may not afford the protections available to the individual under U.S. law. Penalties for breaking the law can be more severe than in the United States for similar offenses. Persons violating Australia's laws, even unknowingly, may be arrested, imprisoned and/or deported. Penalties for possession, use, or trafficking in illegal drugs in Australia are strict, and convicted offenders can expect jail sentences and fines.

DISASTER PREPAREDNESS: Australia is located in an area of low seismic activity. Although the probability of a major earthquake occurring during an individual trip is remote, earthquakes can and do occur. General information about natural disaster preparedness is available via the Internet at http://travel.state.gov/crisismg.html, and from the U.S. Federal Emergency Management Agency (FEMA) at http://www.fema.gov/.

CHILDREN'S ISSUES: For information on international adoption of children and international parental child abduction, please refer to our Internet site at http://travel.state.gov/children's_issues.html or telephone (202) 736-7000.

REGISTRATION/EMBASSY AND CONSULATE LOCATIONS: Americans living in or visiting Australia are encouraged to register at the nearest U.S. consulate and obtain updated information on travel and security within Australia.

The U.S. Embassy in Canberra is located at Moonah Place, Yarralumla, A.C.T. 2600, telephone (61)(2) 6214-5600, fax (61)(2) 6273-3191, home page http://usembassy-australia.state.gov.

NOTE: Registration, passports, and other routine citizen services for Canberra and the rest of the Australian Capital Territory (A.C.T.) are provided by the U.S. Consulate in Sydney (please see contact information below). The Embassy may be contacted for emergency services (i.e. the arrest, death or serious injury of American citizens) within the ACT or Queanbeyan.

The U.S. Consulate General in Sydney serves New South Wales, Queensland, and the Australian Capital Territory and is located on Level 59, MLC Centre, 19-29 Martin Place, Sydney NSW 2000, telephone (61)(2) 9373-9200, fax (61)(2) 9373-9184, home page http://usembassy-australia.state.gov/sydney/.

The U.S. Consulate General in Melbourne serves Victoria, Tasmania, South Australia, and the Northern Territory and is located at 553 St. Kilda Road, P.O. Box 6722, Melbourne Vic 3004, telephone (61)(3) 9526-5900, fax (61)(3) 9525-

0769, home page http://usembassy-australia.state.gov/melbourne/.

The U.S. Consulate General in Perth serves Western Australia and is located on Level 13, 16 St. Georges Terrace, Perth WA 6000, telephone (61)(8) 9202-1224, fax (61)(8) 9231-9444, home page http://usembassy-australia.state.gov/perth/.

Austria

COUNTRY DESCRIPTION: Austria is a highly developed stable democracy with a modern economy.

ENTRY REQUIREMENTS: A passport is required. A visa is not required for business or tourist stays up to three months. For further information concerning entry requirements for Austria, travelers should contact the Embassy of Austria at 3524 International Court, N.W.., Washington, D.C. 20008, tel. (202) 895-6767, or the nearest Austrian Consulate General in Chicago, Los Angeles, or New York. The Austrian Embassy to the United States maintains a web page in English that answers questions concerning the laws and regulations of Austria, including residency, driver's license requirements, and permission to work: http://www.austria.org/index.html.

In an effort to prevent international child abduction, many governments have initiated procedures at entry/exit points. These often include requiring documentary evidence of relationship and permission for the child's travel from the parent(s) or legal guardian not present. Having such documentation on hand, even if not required, may facilitate entry/departure.

CRIME: Austria has a low crime rate, and violent crime is rare. However, crimes involving theft of personal property have increased in recent years. Travelers can become targets of pickpockets and purse-snatchers who operate where tourists tend to gather; favorite spots include Vienna's two largest train stations and the pedestrian shopping area in the first district. The loss or theft of a U.S. passport overseas should be reported immediately to the local police and the nearest U.S. embassy or consulate. U.S. citizens can refer to the Department of State's pamphlet, *A Safe Trip Abroad*, for ways to promote a more trouble-free

trip. The pamphlet is available from the Superintendent of Documents, U.S. Government Printing Office, Washington, D.C. 20402.

If you are the victim of a crime while overseas, in addition to reporting to local police, please contact the nearest U.S. embassy or consulate for assistance. The Embassy/Consulate staff can, for example, assist you to find appropriate medical care, to contact family members of friends, and explain how funds could be transferred. Although the investigation and prosecution for the crime is solely the responsibility of local authorities, consular officers can help you to understand the local criminal justice process and to find an attorney if needed.

MEDICAL FACILITIES AND BCISURANCE: Good medical care is widely available. The Department of State strongly urges Americans to consult with their medical insurance company prior to traveling abroad to confirm whether their policy applies overseas and if it will cover emergency expenses such as a medical evacuation. U.S. medical insurance plans seldom cover health costs incurred outside the United States unless supplemental coverage is purchased. Further, U.S. Medicare and Medicaid programs do not provide payment for medical services outside the United States. However, many travel agents and private companies offer insurance plans that will cover health care expenses incurred overseas, including emergency services such as medical evacuations.

When making a decision regarding health insurance, Americans should consider that many foreign doctors and hospitals require payment in cash prior to providing medical service and that a medical evacuation to the United States may cost in excess of $50,000. Uninsured travelers who require medical care overseas often face extreme difficulties. When consulting with your insurer prior to your departure, please ascertain whether payment will be made to the overseas healthcare provider or if you will be reimbursed later for expenses that you incur. Some insurance policies also include coverage for psychiatric treatment and for the disposition of remains in the event of death.

Useful information on medical emergencies abroad, including overseas insurance programs, is provided in the Department of State's Bureau of Consular Affairs brochure, *Medical Information for Americans Traveling Abroad*, available via the Bureau of Consular Affairs home page or autofax: (202) 647-3000.

OTHER HEALTH INFORMATION: Information on vaccinations and other health precautions may be obtained from the Centers for Disease Control and Prevention's hotline for international travelers at 1-877-FYI-TRIP (1-877-394-8747); fax 1-888-CDC-FAXX (1-888-232-3299), or via their Internet site at http://www.cdc.gov.

TRAFFIC SAFETY AND ROAD CONDITONS: While in a foreign country, U.S. citizens may encounter road conditions that differ significantly from those in the United States. The information below concerning Austria is provided for general reference only, and it may not be totally accurate in a particular location or circumstance.

Safety of Public Transportation: Excellent
Urban Road Conditions/Maintenance: Excellent
Rural Road Conditions/Maintenance: Excellent
Availability of Roadside Assistance: Excellent

Road conditions in Austria are generally excellent. During the winter, however, roads in alpine areas may become dangerous due to snowfall, ice, or avalanches. Some mountain roads may be closed for extended periods, and tire chains are often required. Drivers should exercise caution during the heavily traveled vacation periods (December-February, Easter, and July-August). Extra caution is recommended when driving through autobahn construction zones, particularly on the A-1 East/West Autobahn. Reduced lanes and two-way traffic in these zones have resulted in several deadly accidents in recent years. Traffic information and road conditions are broadcast on the English language channel fm4, located between 91 and 105 FM depending on the locale.

A U.S. driver's license alone is not sufficient to drive in Austria. The U.S. driver's license must be accompanied by an international driver's permit (obtainable in the U.S. from American Automobile Association and the American Automobile Touring Alliance) or by an official translation of the U.S. driver's license, which can be obtained at one of the Austrian automobile clubs (OAMTC or ARBO). This arrangement is only acceptable for

the first six months of driving in Austria, after which all drivers must obtain an Austrian license.

Austria requires all vehicles using the autobahn to display a highway tax sticker "Autobahn Vignette" on the inside windshield of the vehicle. The sticker may be purchased at border crossings, gas stations in Austria, as well as small "Tabak" shops located in Austrian towns. Fines for failing to display a valid autobahn vignette on the windshield of the car are usually around $120.00.

Austrian autobahns have a maximum speed limit of 130 km/hr, although drivers often drive much faster and pass aggressively. The use of hand-held cell phones while driving is prohibited. Turning right on red is also prohibited throughout Austria. The legal limit for blood alcohol content in Austria is .05 percent, and penalties for driving under the influence tend to be stricter than in many U.S. states.

Tourists driving rented vehicles should pay close attention to the provisions of their rental contract. Many contracts prohibit drivers from taking rented vehicles into eastern European countries. Drivers attempting to enter countries listed as "prohibited" on the car rental contract may be arrested, fined, and/or charged with attempted auto theft. The vehicle can be held by Austrian police for the car rental company.

Emergency roadside help and information may be reached by dialing 123 or 120 for vehicle assistance and towing services (Austrian Automobile Clubs), 122 for the fire department, 133 for police, and 144 for ambulance.

For additional general information about road safety, including links to foreign government sites, please see the Department of State, Bureau of Consular Affairs home page at http://travel.state.gov/road_safety.html. For specific information concerning Austrian driving permits, vehicle inspection, road tax and mandatory insurance, please contact the Austrian government website at http://www.austria.org/visa.html. Additional official tourist information can be obtained from the Austrian National Tourist Office in New York at tel. 212-944-6880 or in Los Angeles at tel. 818-999-4030.

395

AVIATION SAFETY OVERSIGHT: The U.S. Federal Aviation Administration (FAA) has assessed the Government of Austria's Civil Aviation Authority as Category 1 -- in compliance with international aviation safety standards for oversight of Austria's air carrier operations. For further information, travelers may contact the Department of Transportation within the United States at telepone 1-800-322-7873, or visit the FAA's Internet website at http://www.faa.gov/avr/iasa.htm. The U.S. Department of Defense (DOD) separately assesses some foreign air carriers for suitability as official providers of air services. For information regarding the DOD policy on specific carriers, travelers may contact the DOD at tel. (618) 256-4801.

CUSTOMS REGULATIONS: Austrian customs authorities encourage the use of an ATA (Admission Temporaire/Temporary Admission) Carnet for the temporary admission of professional equipment, commercial samples, and/or goods for exhibitions and fair purposes. ATA Carnet Headquarters, located at the U.S. Council for International Business, 1212 Avenue of the Americas, New York, NY 10036, issues and guarantees the ATA Carnet in the United States. For additional information, please call (212) 354-4480, or send an e-mail to atacarnet@uscib.org, or visit http://www.uscib.org for details.

DRUG PENALTIES: U.S. citizens are subject to the laws of the country in which they are traveling. Penalties for possession, use, or trafficking in illegal drugs in Austria are strict, and convicted offenders can expect jail sentences and fines.

CHILDREN'S ISSUES: For information on international adoption of children and international parental child abduction, please refer to our Internet site at http://travel.state.gov/children's_issues.html or telephone (202) 736-7000.

REGISTRATION AND EMBASSY/CONSULATE LOCATION: U.S. citizens are encouraged to register at the Consular Section of the U.S. Embassy in Vienna or at the Consular Agency in Salzburg and obtain updated information on travel and security within Austria. The U.S. Embassy in Vienna is located at Boltzmanngasse 16 in the Ninth District. The Consular Section of the U.S. Embassy is located in the Marriott Building, on the fourth floor of Gartenbaupromenade 2, in the First District. The telephone number for both the Embassy and the Consular Section is (43)(1) 31-339. There is also a Consular Agency in Salzburg at Alter Markt 1, tel. (43) (662) 84-87-76, open Monday, Wednesday, and Thursday from 9:00 a.m. to 12:00 noon. U.S. citizens in Salzburg who require assistance outside of these hours may contact the U.S. Embassy in Vienna. The Embassy also maintains a website, at http://www.usembassy-vienna.at with security updates and other information helpful to American citizens.

CYPRUS

COUNTRY DESCRIPTION: Cyprus is a developed Mediterranean island nation divided "de facto" into two areas. The government of the Republic of Cyprus is the internationally recognized authority on the island but, in practice, its control extends only to the Greek Cypriot southern part of the island. The northern area operates under an autonomous Turkish-Cypriot administration. In 1983, this administration declared itself the "Turkish Republic of Northern Cyprus," which is only recognized by Turkey. Facilities for tourism in the Republic of Cyprus are highly developed. Most facilities in north Cyprus, while adequate, tend to be smaller and less modern.

ENTRY REQUIREMENTS: A passport is required for travel to Cyprus. Tourist and business visas are issued at the port of entry for a stay of up to three months. For further information on entry requirements for Cyprus, travelers can contact the Embassy of the Republic of Cyprus at 2211 R Street NW, Washington, D.C. 20008, tel. (202) 462-5772, or the Consulate in New York, 13 E. 40th St., New York, New York, 10016, tel. (212) 686-6016. The Embassy's Internet address is http://www.cyprusembassy.org, or e-mail info@us.cyprusembassy.org.

Since 1974, the Cypriot government has designated Larnaca and Paphos international airports, and the seaports of Limassol, Larnaca, and Paphos, as the only legal points of entry into and exit from Cyprus. These ports are all in the government-controlled southern part of the island. Entry or exit via any other air or seaport is not authorized by the Cypriot government. It is possible for visitors to arrive at non-designated airports and seaports in the north, but they should not expect to cross the United Nations-patrolled "green line" to the government-controlled areas in the south. Such travel is not permitted by the government of Cyprus, even for transit purposes.

Visitors arriving through designated ports of entry in the south are normally able to cross into the north for day trips. Policy and procedures regarding such travel are subject to change. Information on this may be obtained at the U.N. "Buffer Zone" Checkpoint.

In an effort to prevent international child abduction, many governments have initiated procedures at entry/exit points. These often include requiring documentary evidence of relationship and permission for the child's travel from the parent(s) or legal guardian not present. Having such documentation on hand, even if not required, may facilitate entry/departure.

DUAL NATIONALITY: In addition to being subject to all Cypriot laws affecting U.S. citizens, dual nationals may also be subject to other laws that impose special obligations on Cyprus citizens. U.S. citizens whom the Government of Cyprus considers to be Cypriot citizens may be subject to compulsory military service and other aspects of Cypriot law while in Cyprus. Those who may be affected should inquire at the Cypriot Embassy regarding their status. U.S. citizens whom the Turkish-Cypriot authorities consider to be "citizens" may be subject to compulsory military service in north Cyprus. For additional information, please see the Consular Affairs home page on the Internet at http://travel.state.gov for our *Dual Nationality flyer.*

SAFETY AND SECURITY: While civil disorder is uncommon in Cyprus, demonstrations sometimes occur, and there have been occasional violent incidents along the "green line" dividing the two sides of the island. In previous years, terrorist groups from the Middle East have used Cyprus as a base for carrying out acts of terrorism against third country targets.

CRIME: Cyprus has a low rate of crime. The loss or theft abroad of a U.S. passport should be reported immediately to the local police and the nearest U.S. embassy or consulate. If you are the victim of a crime while overseas, in addition to reporting to local police, please contact the nearest U.S. embassy or consulate for assistance. The Embassy/Consulate staff can, for example, assist you to find appropriate medical care, to contact family members or friends and explain how funds could be transferred. Although the investigation and prosecution of the crime is solely the responsibility of local authorities, consular officers can help you to understand the local criminal justice process and to find an attorney if needed.

U.S. citizens may refer to the Department of State's pamphlet, *A Safe Trip Abroad,* for ways to promote a trouble-free journey. The pamphlet is available by mail from the Superintendent of Documents, U.S. Government Printing Office, Washington, D.C. 20402, via the Internet at http://www.access.gpo.gov/su docs, or via the Bureau of Consular Affairs home page at http://travel.state.gov.

MEDICAL FACILITIES: Medical care is available at a combination of government hospitals and private clinics. Many of the private-sector doctors have been trained in the United Kingdom or the United States. While fees are generally lower than those in the United States, medical supplies are often more expensive. Additionally, most ambulances are unable to provide medical care en route to the hospital.

MEDICAL INSURANCE: The Department of State strongly urges Americans to consult with their medical insurance company prior to traveling abroad to confirm whether their policy applies overseas and if it will cover emergency expenses such as a medical evacuation. U.S. medical insurance plans seldom cover health costs incurred outside the United States unless supplemental coverage is purchased. Furthermore, U.S. Medicare and Medicaid programs do not provide payment for medical services outside the United States. However, many travel agents and private companies offer insurance plans that will cover health care expenses incurred overseas, including emergency services such as medical evacuations.

When making a decision regarding health insurance, Americans should consider that many foreign doctors and hospitals require payment in cash prior to providing service and that a medical evacuation to the United States may cost well in excess of $50,000. Uninsured travelers who require medical care overseas often face extreme difficulties. When consulting with your insurer prior to your trip, please find out whether payment will be made to the overseas healthcare provider or if you will be reimbursed later for expenses that you incur. Some insurance policies also include coverage for psychiatric treatment and for disposition of remains in the event of death.

Useful information on medical emergencies abroad, including overseas insurance programs, is provided in the Department of State's Bureau of Consular Affairs brochure, *Medical Information for Americans Traveling Abroad*, available via the Bureau of Consular Affairs home page or autofax: (202) 647-3000.

OTHER HEALTH INFORMATION: The World Health Organization considers Cyprus to be one of the healthiest areas of the Mediterranean. Water supplies are potable, and the refuse collection/sewage disposal system is adequate. Communicable diseases such as typhoid are rare. Respiratory ailments and allergies are sometimes exacerbated by the dry and dusty climate. Information on vaccinations and other health precautions may be obtained from the Centers for Disease Control and Prevention's hotline for international travelers at 1-877-FYI-TRIP (1-877-394-8747); fax 1-888-CDC-FAXX (1-888-232-3299), or via the CDC's Internet site at http://www.cdc.gov.

TRAFFIC SAFETY AND ROAD CONDITIONS: While in a foreign country, U.S. citizens may encounter road conditions that differ significantly from those in the United States. The information below concerning Cyprus is provided for general reference only, and it may not be totally accurate in a particular location or circumstance.

Safety Of Public Transportation: Good
Urban Road Condition/Maintenance: Good
Rural Road Condition/Maintenance: Fair
Availability of Roadside Assistance: Fair

There are few public buses and no rail lines. Taxis are widely available, but they often do not have operating seat belts.

The Cypriot transportation system is comparable to that of Western Europe. Traffic moves on the left side of the road, British style, and modern motorways link the major cities. Secondary roads, especially in mountainous areas, tend to be narrow and winding, and they are not as well-maintained as major highways. Traffic laws, signs and speed limits are consistent with the standards used throughout Europe. Traffic circles (roundabouts) are often utilized at major intersections. The use of seat belts (in front seats) and child car seats is compulsory. Motorcyclists are required to wear helmets, and the use of cellular phones while driving is prohibited. Motorway speed limits are set at 100 kph (62 mph). Liability insurance is mandatory.

Enforcement of traffic laws and regulations is inconsistent, and the government is looking at ways to improve road safety. In recent years Cyprus has ranked among the top three countries in Europe, on a per capita basis, in regard to traffic fatalities. Speeding, tailgating, overtaking and the running of caution lights are commonplace, and major causes of accidents. Emergency assistance is available by calling 199.

The information above applies only to those areas under the control of the Republic of Cyprus. Road safety conditions in north Cyprus (the Turkish-Cypriot administered areas) are similar to conditions in the south, except that the road network is less developed. Insurance purchased in the Republic of Cyprus is not valid in the Turkish-Cypriot administered areas, but it may be purchased near the U.N. "Buffer Zone" Checkpoint. Emergency assistance is available by calling 155.

For additional general information about road safety, including links to foreign government sites, please see the Department of State, Bureau of Consular Affairs home page at http:/travel.state.gov/road_safety.html. For specific information concerning Cyprus driving permits, vehicle inspection, road tax and mandatory insurance, please contact the Cyprus Tourism Organization in New York via the Internet at http://www.cyprustourism.org.

AVIATION SAFETY OVERSIGHT: As there is no direct commercial air service by local carriers at present, nor economic authority to operate such service, between the United States and Cyprus, the U.S. Federal Aviation Administration (FAA) has not assessed Cyprus's Civil Aviation Authority for compliance with international aviation safety standards. For further information, travelers may contact the Department of Transportation within the United States at tel. 1-800-322-7873, or visit the FAA's Internet website at http://www.faa.gov/avr/iasa/.

The U.S. Department of Defense (DOD) separately assesses some foreign air carriers for suitability as official providers of air services. For information regarding the DOD policy on specific carriers, travelers may contact the DOD at tel. (618) 229-4801.

CUSTOMS REGULATIONS: Cyprus customs authorities may enforce strict regulations concerning temporary importation into or export from Cyprus of items such as firearms. There are no restrictions on religious materials and medication for personal use. It is advisable to contact the Embassy of Cyprus in Washington, D.C. for specific information regarding customs requirements. Cyprus restricts the export of Byzantine period ecclesiastical material and all archeological material. The U.S. Customs Service has imposed corresponding import restrictions in accordance with the Convention on Cultural Property Implementation Act on certain categories of Byzantine, Pre-Classical and Classical antiquities that are restricted from leaving Cyprus without an export permit. For further information, please contact the Customs Service at tel. (202) 927-2336 or on the Internet at http://exchanges.state.gov/culprop/.

Cyprus customs authorities encourage the use of an ATA (Admission Temporaire/Temporary Admission) Carnet for the temporary admission of professional equipment, commercial samples, and/or goods for exhibitions and fair purposes. ATA Carnet Headquarters, located at the U.S. Council for International Business, 1212 Avenue of the Americas, New York, NY 10036, issues and guarantees the ATA Carnet in the United States. For additional information, please call (212) 354-4480, or send an e-mail to atacarnet@uscib.org, or visit http://www.uscib.org for details.

CRIMINAL PENALTIES: While in a foreign country, a U.S. citizen is subject to that country's laws and regulations, which sometimes differ significantly from those in the United States and may not afford the protections available to the individual under U.S. law. Penalties for breaking the law can be more severe than in the United States for similar offenses. Persons violating Cyprus's laws, even unknowingly, may be expelled, arrested or imprisoned. Penalties for possession, use, and dealing in illegal drugs in Cyprus are strict, and convicted offenders can expect jail sentences and heavy fines. The legal system in Cyprus is based on English common law and is similar to that of the United States in many respects.

SPECIAL CIRCUMSTANCES: There are restrictions on the photographing of military installations in both south and north Cyprus. English-language signs are generally posted in sensitive areas advising of the restrictions. However, visitors should refrain from photographing military installations and/or personnel regardless of whether warning signs are posted, and if confronted by local authorities, they should comply with all reasonable requests regarding the use of photographic equipment.

CHILDREN'S ISSUES: For information on international adoption of children and international parental child abduction, please refer to our Internet site at http://travel.state.gov/children's_issues.html or telephone (202) 736-7000.

REGISTRATION/EMBASSY AND CONSULATE LOCATIONS: Americans living in or visiting Cyprus are encouraged to register with the Consular Section of the U.S. Embassy in Cyprus and obtain updated information on travel and security within Cyprus. The U.S. Embassy in Nicosia is located at Metochiou and Ploutarchou Streets, Engomi, telephone (357)(22) 776-400; Internet address: http://www.americanembassy.org.cy. The U.S. Government also maintains an office in North Cyprus at 6 Serif Arzik Street, Koskluestlik, Nicosia, telephone (392) 669-965.

Denmark, Greenland, and the Faroe Islands

COUNTRY DESCRIPTION: Denmark is a highly developed stable democracy with a modern economy. Tourist facilities are extensive. English, which is a compulsory subject in the public school system, is widely spoken. Denmark is the only Nordic/Baltic member of both the European Union (EU) and NATO.

Greenland, a self-governing dependency of Denmark, is not a member of the EU. Greenland is located in the Arctic region and is thus characterized by an extreme climate. Its economy is based primarily on fishing, although presently Greenland is experiencing an upswing in ecotourism.

The Faeroes are an island group in the North Atlantic Ocean. They are a self-governing overseas administrative division of Denmark and are not members of the European Union. Precipitous terrain limits habitation to small coastal lowlands and tourism is minimal. However, there are tourist facilities available, ranging from cabins to four-star hotels, and guided tours available from May through September.

ENTRY REQUIREMENTS: Passport and visa regulations are similar for Denmark, Greenland and the Faeroe Islands. A valid passport is required. Tourist and business travelers do not need visas for visits of up to three months (the 90-day period begins when entering any of the following countries which are parties to the Schengen Agreement: Austria, Belgium, Denmark, Finland, France, Germany, Greece, Iceland, Italy, Luxembourg, The Netherlands, Norway, Portugal, Spain, and Sweden). For further information on entry requirements for Denmark/Greenland/Faeroe Islands, travelers may contact the Royal Danish Embassy at 3200 Whitehaven Street, N.W., Washington, D.C. 20008, phone (202) 234-4300, on-line at http://www.denmarkemb.org/, or the Danish Consulates General in Chicago, Los Angeles, or New York.

In an effort to prevent international child abduction, many governments have initiated procedures at entry/exit points. These often include requiring documentary evidence of relationship and permission for the child's travel from the parent(s) or legal guardian not present.

Having such documentation on hand, even if not required, may facilitate entry/departure.

SAFETY AND SECURITY: Prior police approval is required for public demonstrations in Denmark, and police oversight is routinely provided to ensure adequate security for participants and passers-by. Nonetheless, situations may develop which could pose a threat to public safety. U.S. citizens are advised to avoid areas in which public demonstrations are taking place.

For the latest security information, Americans traveling abroad should regularly monitor the Department's Internet web site at http://travel.state.gov, where the current Worldwide Caution Public Announcement, Travel Warnings and Public Announcements can be found.

CRIME: Denmark, Greenland, and the Faeroe Islands all have relatively low crime rates. However, travelers to Copenhagen and other major Danish cities can become targets for pickpockets and sophisticated purse snatchers. Purses and luggage are particular targets for thieves in hotel lobbies and breakfast rooms, fast food outlets, and Copenhagen's main train station. Car and home break-ins are also on the rise.

The loss or theft abroad of a U.S. passport should be reported immediately to local police and the nearest U.S. Embassy or Consulate. If you are the victim of a crime while overseas, in addition to reporting to local police, please contact the nearest U.S. Embassy or Consulate for assistance. The Embassy/Consulate staff can, for example, assist you to find appropriate medical care, to contact family members or friends and explain how funds could be transferred. Although the investigation and prosecution of the crime is solely the responsibility of local authorities, consular officers can help you to understand the local criminal justice process and to find an attorney if needed.

If your U.S. passport is lost or stolen while you are in Denmark, please contact the U.S. Embassy in Copenhagen for information about passport replacement. U.S. citizens may refer to the Department of State's pamphlet *A Safe Trip Abroad* for ways to promote a trouble-free journey. The pamphlet is available by mail from the Superintendent of Documents, U.S.

Government Printing Office, Washington, D.C. 20402, via the Internet at http://www.access.gpo.gov/su_docs, or via the Bureau of Consular Affairs home page at http://travel.state.gov/.

MEDICAL FACILITIES AND INSURANCE: Excellent medical facilities are widely available in Denmark. In Greenland and the Faeroe Islands, medical facilities are limited and evacuation is required for serious illness or injury. Although emergency medical treatment is free of charge, the patient is charged for follow-up care.

The Department of State strongly urges Americans to consult with their medical insurance company prior to traveling abroad to confirm whether their policy applies overseas and whether it will cover emergency expenses such as a medical evacuation. U.S. medical insurance plans seldom cover health costs incurred outside the United States unless supplemental coverage is purchased. Further, U.S. Medicare and Medicaid programs do not provide payment for medical services outside the United States. However, many travel agents and private companies offer insurance plans that will cover health care expenses incurred overseas including emergency services such as medical evacuations.

When making a decision regarding health insurance, Americans should consider that many foreign doctors and hospitals require payment in cash prior to providing service and that a medical evacuation to the U.S. may cost well in excess of $50,000. Uninsured travelers who require medical care overseas often face extreme difficulties, whereas travelers who have purchased overseas medical insurance have, when a medical emergency occurs, found it life-saving. When consulting with your insurer prior to your trip, ascertain whether payment will be made to the overseas healthcare provider or whether you will be reimbursed later for expenses you incur. Some insurance policies also include coverage for psychiatric treatment and for disposition of remains in the event of death.

Useful information on medical emergencies abroad, including overseas insurance programs, is provided in the Department of State's Bureau of Consular Affairs brochure *Medical Information for Americans Traveling Abroad*, available via the

Bureau of Consular Affairs home page or autofax: (202) 647-3000.

OTHER HEALTH INFORMATION: Travelers should be aware that increasing numbers of illegal drug users, particularly young people, experience unanticipated serious health emergencies, including permanent brain damage and even death, stemming from use of Methylenedioxinmethylamphetamine (MDA), commonly known as Ecstasy or XTC, and other illegal narcotics.

Information on vaccinations and other health precautions, such as safe food and water precautions and insect bite protection, may be obtained from the Centers for Disease Control and Prevention's hotline for international travelers at 1-877-FYI-TRIP (1-877-394-8747); fax 1-888-CDC-FAXX (1-888-232-3299), or via the CDC's Internet site at http://www.cdc.gov/travel/. For information about outbreaks of infectious diseases abroad consult the World Health Organization's website at http://www.who.int.en/. Further health information for travelers is available at http://www.who.int/ith.

TRAFFIC SAFETY AND ROAD CONDITIONS: While in a foreign country, U.S. citizens may encounter road conditions that differ significantly from those in the United States. The information below concerning Denmark is provided for general reference only, and may not be totally accurate in a particular location or circumstance.

Safety of Public Transportation: Good
Urban Road Conditions/Maintenance: Excellent
Rural Road Conditions/Maintenance: Excellent
Availability of Roadside Assistance: Excellent

Danish expressways, highways, and secondary roads are of high quality and connect all areas of the country. It is possible to drive from the northern tip of Denmark to the German border in the south in just four hours. Greenland has no established road system, and domestic travel is performed on foot, by boat or by air. The majority of the Faeroe Islands are connected by bridges or serviced by boat. Although the largest islands have roads, most domestic travel is done on foot, on horseback, by boat or by air.

For additional general information about road safety, including links to foreign government sites, see the Department of State, Bureau of Consular Affairs home page at http://travel.state.gov/road_safety.html. For specific information concerning Danish driver's permits, vehicle inspection, road tax and mandatory insurance, contact the Danish Tourist Board in New York via the Internet at http://www.denmark.org/.

EMERGENCY NUMBERS: The emergency telephone number for police/fire/ambulance in Denmark and the Faeroe Islands is 112. In Greenland local police should be contacted.

AVIATION SAFETY OVERSIGHT: The U.S. Federal Aviation Administration (FAA) has assessed the Government of Denmark's Civil Aviation Authority as Category One -- in compliance with international aviation safety standards for the oversight of Denmark's air carrier operations. This rating applies to Greenland and the Faeroe Islands as well.

For further information, travelers may contact the Department of Transportation at 1 (800) 322-7873, or visit the FAA's Internet web site at http://www.faa.gov/avr/iasa/. The U.S. Department of Defense (DOD) separately assesses some foreign air carriers for suitability as official providers of air services. For information regarding the DOD policy on specific carriers, travelers may contact DOD at (618) 229-4801.

CUSTOMS REGULATIONS: Customs authorities may enforce strict regulations concerning temporary importation into and export from Denmark of items such as firearms and medications. It is advisable to contact the Embassy of Denmark in Washington or one of Denmark's Consulates in the United States for specific information regarding customs requirements.

Danish customs authorities encourage the use of an ATA (Admission Temporaire/Temporary Admission) Carnet for the temporary admission of professional equipment, commercial samples, and/or goods for exhibitions and fair purposes. ATA Carnet headquarters, located at the U.S. Council for International Business, 1212 Avenue of the Americas, New York, NY 10036, issues and guarantees the ATA Carnet in the United States. For additional information call (212) 354-4480, send an e-mail to atacarnet@uscib.org, or visit http://www.uscib.org/ for details.

CRIMINAL PENALTIES: While in a foreign country, a U.S. citizen is subject to that country's laws and regulations, which sometimes differ significantly from those in the United States and may not afford the protections available to the individual under U.S. law. Penalties for breaking the law can be more severe than in the United States for similar offenses. Persons violating Denmark's laws, even unknowingly, may be expelled, arrested or imprisoned. Penalties for possession, use, or trafficking in illegal drugs in Denmark are strict and convicted offenders can expect jail sentences and heavy fines.

CHILDREN'S ISSUES: For information on international adoption of children and international parental child abduction, please refer to our Internet site at http://travel.state.gov/children's_issues.html or telephone (202) 736-7000.

REGISTRATION/EMBASSY LOCATION: Americans living in or visiting Denmark are encouraged to register at the Consular Section of the U.S. Embassy in Copenhagen and obtain updated information on travel and security within Denmark. The U.S. Embassy is located at Dag Hammarskjolds Alle 24; 2100 Copenhagen, Tel: (45) 35-55-31-44. Fax: (45) 35-43-02-23. After hours emergencies: Tel: (45) 35-55-92-70. Information is also available via the U.S. Embassy home page at http://www.usembassy.dk/. The U.S. has no consular presence in Greenland or the Faeroe Islands.

Finland

COUNTRY DESCRIPTION: Finland is a highly developed democracy with a modern economy. It is a member of the European Union. Tourist facilities are widely available.

ENTRY REQUIREMENTS: A passport is required. A visa is not required for tourist or business stays of up to 90 days. For additional information concerning entry requirements, travelers can contact the Embassy of Finland at 3301 Massachusetts Avenue, N.W., Washington, DC 20008, tel: (202) 298-5800, or the Finnish Consulate General in Los Angeles or New York. Additional information is available via the Internet at http://www.finland.org.

In an effort to prevent international child abduction, many governments have initiated procedures at entry/exit points. These often include requiring documentary evidence of relationship and permission for the child's travel from the parent(s) or legal guardian not present. Having such documentation on hand, even if not required, may facilitate entry/departure.

DUAL NATIONALITY: In addition to being subject to all Finnish laws affecting U.S. citizens, dual nationals may also be subject to other laws that impose special obligations on Finnish citizens. For additional information, see the Consular Affairs home page on the Internet at http://travel.state.gov for our Dual Nationality flyer.

CRIME: Although the crime rate in Finland is low compared to the U.S. and most European countries, it has increased in recent years. However, Finland remains a relatively safe environment. Americans visiting Finland are seldom victims of crime, but visitors should not be complacent regarding personal safety or the protection of valuables. The same precautions employed in the U.S. should be followed in Finland. Finnish police services are excellent; however, some police officers speak little English. The telephone number for police and other emergency services throughout Finland is 112. All forms of public transportation are considered safe. Street crimes, such as muggings and pickpocketing, remain relatively uncommon, but do occur.

The loss or theft abroad of a U.S. passport should be reported immediately to the local police and the nearest U.S. Embassy or Consulate. If you are the victim of a crime while overseas, in addition to reporting to local police, please contact the nearest U.S. Embassy or Consulate for assistance. The Embassy/Consulate staff can, for example, assist you to find appropriate medical care, to contact family members or friends and explain how funds could be transferred. Although the investigation and prosecution of the crime is solely the responsibility of local authorities, consular officers can help you to understand the local criminal justice process and to find an attorney if needed.

U.S. citizens may refer to the Department of State's pamphlet, *A Safe Trip Abroad*, for ways to promote a trouble-free journey. The pamphlet is available by mail from the Superintendent of Documents, U.S. Government Printing Office, Washington, D.C. 20402, via the Internet at http://www.access.gpo.gov/su_docs, or via the Bureau of Consular Affairs home page at http://travel.state.gov.

MEDICAL FACILITIES AND INSURANCE: Medical facilities are widely available for emergency services. The public hospital system and many private hospitals honor foreign credit cards. The department of state strongly urges Americans to consult with their medical insurance company prior to traveling abroad to confirm whether their policy applies overseas and whether it will cover emergency expenses such as a medical evacuation. U.S. medical insurance plans seldom cover health costs incurred outside the United States unless supplemental coverage is purchased. Further, U.S. Medicare and Medicaid programs do not provide payment for medical services outside the United States. However, many travel agents and private companies offer insurance plans that will cover health care expenses incurred overseas including emergency services such as medical evacuations.

When making a decision regarding health insurance, Americans should consider that many foreign doctors and hospitals require payment in cash prior to providing service and that a medical evacuation to the U.S. may cost well in excess of $50,000. Uninsured travelers who require medical care overseas often face extreme difficulties. When consulting with your insurer prior to your trip, ascertain whether payment will be made to the overseas healthcare provider or whether you will be reimbursed later for expenses you incur. Some insurance policies also include coverage for psychiatric treatment and for disposition of remains in the event of death.

Useful information on medical emergencies abroad, including overseas insurance programs, is provided in the Department of State's Bureau of Consular Affairs brochure, *Medical Information for Americans Traveling Abroad*, available via the Bureau of Consular Affairs home page or autofax: (202) 647-3000.

OTHER HEALTH INFORMATION: Information on vaccinations and other health precautions, such as safe food and water precautions and insect bite protection, may be obtained from the Centers for Disease Control and Prevention's hotline for international travelers at 1-877-FYI-TRIP (1-877-394-8747); fax 1-888-CDC-FAXX (1-888-232-3299), or via the CDC's Internet site at http://www.cdc.gov/travel. For information about outbreaks of infectious diseases abroad consult the World Health Organization's website at http://www.who.int/en. Further health information for travelers is available at http://www.who.int/ith.

TRAFFIC SAFETY AND ROAD CONDITIONS: While in a foreign country, U.S. citizens may encounter road conditions that differ significantly from those in the United States. The information below concerning Finland is provided for general reference only, and may not be totally accurate in a particular location or circumstance.

Safety of Public Transportation:
Excellent
Urban Road Condition/Maintenance:
Excellent
Rural Road Condition/Maintenance:
Excellent
Availability of Roadside Assistance:
Excellent

Finland has an extensive network of highways throughout the country, as well as excellent public transportation services. Travelers should be aware that drunk-driving laws are strict, and acceptable blood alcohol levels are much lower in Finland than in the U.S. Police strictly enforce all traffic laws and institute random roadside Breathalyzer tests. Those drivers who register a .05 or above alcohol content are subject to immediate arrest. Drivers should be aware that regulations and traffic signs differ significantly from those in the U.S. Visitors should be familiar with both prior to operating a vehicle in Finland. Driving in Finland

during the winter months can be hazardous. Icy road conditions are common. If driving in Finland, the vehicle must be winterized with studded snow tires, and engine heaters are strongly recommended. When driving at night, drivers must be alert to moose wandering onto major roadways. There have been incidents of moose being struck by vehicles, causing severe damage to the vehicle and injury, sometimes fatal, to the occupants.

For specific information concerning Finnish driver's permits, vehicle inspection, road tax and mandatory insurance, contact the Finland National Tourist Organization offices in New York via the Internet at http://www.mek.fi. The e-mail address is med@mek.fi. For specific real-time updates on road conditions in Finland, see the Finnish Road Administration's travel and traffic information web page at http://finnra.fi/alk/english/.

AVIATION SAFETY OVERSIGHT: The U.S. Federal Aviation Administration (FAA) has assessed the Government of Finland's Civil Aviation Authority as Category 1 -- in compliance with international aviation safety standards for oversight of Finland's air carrier operations. For further information, travelers may contact the Department of Transportation within the U.S. at 1-800-322-7873, or visit the FAA's Internet website http://www.faa.gov/avr/iasa/.

The U.S. Department of Defense (DOD) separately assesses some foreign air carriers for suitability as official providers of air services. For information regarding the DOD policy on specific carriers, travelers may contact the DOD at (618) 229-4801.

CUSTOMS REGULATIONS: Finland's customs authorities encourage the use of an ATA (Admission Temporaire/Temporary Admission) Carnet for the temporary admission of professional equipment, commercial samples, and/or goods for exhibitions and fair purposes. ATA Carnet Headquarters, located at the U.S. Council for International Business, 1212 Avenue of the Americas, New York, NY 10036, issues and guarantees the ATA Carnet in the United States. For additional information call 212-354-4480, send an e-mail to atacarnet@uscib.org, or visit www.uscib.org for details.

404

CRIMINAL PENALTIES: While in a foreign country, a U.S. citizen is subject to that country's laws and regulations, which sometimes differ significantly from those in the United States and may not afford the protections available to the individual under U.S. law. Penalties for breaking the law can be more severe than in the United States for similar offenses. Persons violating Finland's laws, even unknowingly, may be expelled, arrested or imprisoned. Penalties for possession, use, or trafficking in illegal drugs in Finland are strict and convicted offenders can expect jail sentences and heavy fines.

CHILDREN'S ISSUES: For information on international adoption of children and international parental child abduction, please refer to our Internet site at http://travel.state.gov/children's_issues.html or telephone (202) 736-7000.

REGISTRATION AND EMBASSY LOCATION: Americans living in or visiting Finland are encouraged to register at the Consular Section of the U.S. Embassy in Helsinki and obtain updated information on travel and security within Finland. The U.S. Embassy is located at Itainen Puistotie 14B; tel: 358-9-171931 or after hours tel 358-9-605414; fax 358-9-652057; e-mail consular@usembassy.fi; or visit the Embassy's Internet home page at http://www.usembassy.fi/.

France and Monaco

COUNTRY DESCRIPTION: France is a developed and stable democracy. Monaco is a developed constitutional monarchy.

ENTRY REQUIREMENTS: A passport is required for entry to France and Monaco. A visa is not required for tourist/business stays up to 90 days in France and Monaco. For further information concerning entry requirements for France, travelers may contact the Embassy of France at 4101 Reservoir Road, N.W. Washington, D.C. 20007, tel. (202) 944-6000, or the French Consulate General in Atlanta, Boston, Chicago, Houston, Los Angeles, Miami, New Orleans, New York, or San Francisco. The web site for the Consular Section of the French Embassy in the United States is: http://www.france-consulat.org. For further information on entry requirements to Monaco,

travelers may contact the Consulate General of Monaco at 565 5th Avenue, New York, N.Y. 10017, tel. (212) 759-5227. The Consulate General's web site is http://www.monaco-consulate.com.

In an effort to prevent international child abduction, many governments have initiated procedures at entry/exit points. These often include requiring documentary evidence of relationship and permission for the child's travel from the parent(s) or legal guardian not present. Having such documentation on hand, even if not required, may facilitate entry/departure.

DUAL NATIONALITY: Dual nationals, who are French or Monegasque citizens as well as U.S. citizens, are subject to all French and Monegasque laws that affect U.S. citizens. Moreover, dual nationals also may be subject to other laws that impose special obligations on French and Monegasque citizens. In some instances, dual nationality may hamper U.S. Government efforts to provide protection abroad. For additional information, please see the Bureau of Consular Affairs home page on the Internet at http://travel.state.gov for our Dual Nationality flyer.

SAFETY AND SECURITY: The Government of France maintains a national anti-terrorism plan, "Vigipirate Renforce." Under this plan, in times of heightened security concerns, the government mobilizes police and armed forces and installs them at airports, train and metro stations, as well as other high profile locations such as schools, embassies, and government installations.

In recent years, France has experienced political assassinations and random bombings. One U.S. citizen was injured in these attacks, but none have been killed. All passengers on subways and trains are urged to be aware of their surroundings and to report any unattended baggage to the nearest authority.

The Basque Separatist Party (ETA) and the National Front for the Liberation of Corsica (FLNC) continue to operate in the south of France and occasionally bomb local government institutions, banks, travel agencies, etc. During the summer of 2001, there were seven politically motivated bombings on the island of Corsica. No deaths were caused by any of these acts of terrorism. However, Americans should remain vigilant when traveling to Corsica.

Violent civil disorder is rare in France. In the past, however, student demonstrations, labor protests or other routine demonstrations have turned into violent confrontations between demonstrators and police. Americans are advised to avoid street demonstrations. Americans can obtain current travel information at the State Department's Consular Affairs web site at http://travel.state.gov.

CRIME: France and Monaco both have relatively low rates of violent crime. But the overall crime rate has been rising over the past two years. Crimes involving vehicles with non-local license plates are common. Criminals frequent tourist attractions such as museums, monuments, restaurants, hotels, beaches, trains, train stations, airports and subways. Americans in France and Monaco should be particularly alert to pickpockets in train stations and subways. Although thieves may operate anywhere, the U.S. Embassy in Paris receives frequent reports of theft from several particular areas:

Paris: --
- Gangs of thieves operate on the rail link from Charles de Gaulle Airport to downtown Paris by preying on jet-lagged, luggage-burdened tourists. Often, one thief distracts the tourist with a question about directions while an accomplice takes a momentarily unguarded backpack, briefcase or purse. Thieves also time their thefts to coincide with train stops so that they may quickly exit the car. Travelers may wish to consider traveling from the airport to the city by bus or taxi.

- There have been a number of violent armed robberies, including knife attacks, in the vicinity of the Eiffel Tower late at night.

- There have been reports of robberies involving thieves on motorcycles who reach into a moving car by opening the car door or reach through an open window to steal purses and other bags visible inside. Those traveling by car in Paris should remember to keep windows closed and doors locked.

- The Number One Subway Line, which runs by many major tourist attractions (including the Grand Arch at La Defense, Arc de Triomphe, Champs Elysees, Concorde, Louvre, and Bastille), is the site of many thefts. Pickpockets are especially active on this metro line during the summer months.

- Gare du Nord train station, where the express trains from the airport arrive in Paris, is also a high-risk area for pickpocketing and theft.

- Many thefts occur at the major department stores (Galeries Lafayette, Printemps, and Samarataine) where tourists often leave wallets, passports, and credit cards on cashier counters during transactions.

- In hotels, thieves frequent lobbies and breakfast rooms, and take advantage of a minute of inattention to snatch jackets, purses and backpacks. Also, while many hotels do have safety latches that allow guests to secure their rooms while they are inside, this feature is not as universal as it is in the United States. If no chain or latch is present, a chair placed up against the door is usually an effective obstacle to surreptitious entry during the night.

- In restaurants, many Americans have reported that women's purses placed on the floor under the table at the feet of the diner are stolen during the meal.

- ATMs (Automatic Teller Machines) are very common in France and provide ready access to cash, allowing travelers to carry as much money as they need for each day. The rates are competitive with local exchange bureaus and an ATM transaction is easier than the cashing of travelers' checks. However, crimes committed around ATMs have been reported. Travelers should not use an ATM in isolated, unlit areas or when loiterers are in the vicinity. Travelers should be especially aware of persons standing close enough to see the PIN (Personal Identification Number) being entered into the machine. Thieves often conduct successful scams by simply observing the PIN as it is entered. If the card becomes stuck, travelers should be wary of persons offering to help and even asking for the PIN to "fix" the machine. Legitimate bank employees never have a reason to ask for the PIN.

- Pigalle is the red-light district of Paris. Many entertainment establishments in this area engage in aggressive marketing and charge well beyond the normal rate for their drinks. There have been reports of threats of violence to coerce patrons into paying exorbitant beverage tabs.

Southern France: --
- Thefts from cars stopped at red lights are common, particularly in the Nice-Antibes-Cannes area, and in Marseille. Car doors should be kept locked at all times while traveling to prevent incidents of "snatch and grab" thefts. In this type of scenario, the thief is usually a passenger on a motorcycle. Similar incidents have also occurred at tollbooths and rest areas. Special caution is advised when entering and exiting the car, because that offers opportunity for purse-snatchings.

- Break-ins of parked cars are also frequent. Locking valuables in the trunk is not a safeguard. Valuables should not be left unattended in a car.

- Purse snatching and pickpocketing occur throughout the south of France. Passports should be carried on the body when necessary and over-the-shoulder bags should not be used.

The loss or theft abroad of a U.S. passport should be reported immediately to local police and the nearest U.S. embassy or consulate, where you may obtain information about passport replacement. U.S. citizens may refer to the Department of State's pamphlet, *A Safe Trip Abroad*, for ways to promote a more trouble-free journey. The pamphlet is available by mail from the Superintendent of Documents, U.S. Government Printing Office, Washington, D.C. 20402, or via the Internet at http://www.access.gpo.gov/su_docs, or via the Bureau of Consular Affairs home page at http://travel.state.gov.

MEDICAL FACILITIES: Medical care comparable to that found in the United States is widely available.

MEDICAL INSURANCE: The Department of State strongly urges Americans to consult with their medical insurance company prior to traveling abroad to confirm whether their policy applies overseas and if it will cover emergency expenses such as medical evacuation. U.S. medical insurance plans seldom cover health costs incurred outside the United States unless supplemental coverage is purchased. Further, U.S. Medicare and Medicaid programs do not provide payment for medical services outside the United States. However, many travel agents and private companies offer insurance plans that will cover health care expenses incurred overseas, including emergency services such as medical evacuations.

When making a decision regarding health insurance, Americans should consider that many foreign doctors and hospitals require payment in cash prior to providing service and that a medical evacuation to the United States may cost well in excess of $50,000. Uninsured travelers who require medical care overseas often face extreme difficulties, whereas travelers who have purchased overseas medical insurance have found it to be life-saving when a medical emergency has occurred. When consulting with your insurer prior to your trip, please ascertain whether payment will be made to the overseas healthcare provider or if you will be reimbursed later for expenses that you incur. Some insurance policies also include coverage for psychiatric treatment and for disposition of remains in the event of death.

Useful information on medical emergencies abroad, including overseas insurance programs, is provided in the Department of State's Bureau of Consular Affairs brochure, *Medical Information for Americans Traveling Abroad,* available via the Bureau of Consular Affairs home page or autofax: (202) 647-3000.

OTHER HEALTH INFORMATION: Information on vaccinations and other health precautions may be obtained from the Centers for Disease Control and Prevention's hotline for international travelers at 1-877-FYI-TRIP (1-877-394-8747); fax 1-888-CDC-FAXX (1-888-232-3299), or via CDC's Internet site at http://www.cdc.gov.

TRAFFIC SAFETY AND ROAD CONDITIONS: While in a foreign country, U.S. citizens may encounter road conditions that differ significantly from those in the United States. The information below concerning France and Monaco is provided for general reference only, and it may not be totally accurate in a particular location or circumstance.

Safety of Public Transportation: Good
Urban Road Conditions/Maintenance: Good
Rural Road Conditions/Maintenance: Good
Availability of Roadside Assistance: Good

Roads in France are generally comparable to those in the United States, but traffic engineering and driving habits pose special dangers. Usually, lane markings and sign placements are not as clear as in the United States. Drivers should be prepared to make last-minute maneuvers, as most French drivers do. French drivers usually drive more aggressively and faster than Americans and tend to exceed posted speed limits. Right-of-way rules in France may differ from those in the United States. Drivers entering intersections from the right have priority over those on the left (unless specifically indicated otherwise) even when entering relatively large boulevards from small side streets. Many intersections in France are being replaced by circles, where the right-of-way belongs to drivers in the circle.

On the major highways, service stations are situated every 25 miles or less. Service stations are as plentiful on secondary roads as in the United States.

Paris, the capital and largest city in France, has an extensive and efficient public transportation system. The interconnecting system of buses, subways, and commuter rails serves more than 4 million people a day with a safety record comparable to or better than the systems of major American cities. Similar transportation systems are found in all major French cities. Between cities, France is served by an equally extensive rail service, which is safe and reliable. High-speed rail links connect the major cities in France. Many cities are also served by frequent air service.

For additional general information about road safety, including links to foreign government sites, please see the Department of State, Bureau of Consular Affairs home page at http://travel.state.gov/road_safety.html. For specific information concerning French and Monegasque driver's permits, vehicle inspection, road tax and mandatory insurance, please contact the French and Monegasque National Tourist Office hotline at New York at (202) 659-7779 or via the Internet at: http://www.franceguide.com.

AVIATION SAFETY OVERSIGHT: The U.S. Federal Aviation Administration (FAA) has assessed the Government of France's Civil Aviation Authority as Category 1 -- in compliance with international aviation safety standards for oversight of France's air carrier operations.

For further information, travelers may contact the Department of Transportation within the United States at tel. 1-800-322-7873, or visit the FAA's Internet web site at http://www.faa.gov/avr/iasa/. The U.S. Department of Defense (DOD) separately assesses some foreign air carriers for suitability as official providers of air services. For information regarding the DOD policy on specific carriers, travelers may contact the DOD at tel. (618) 256-4801.

CUSTOMS REGULATIONS: French customs authorities enforce strict regulations concerning temporary importation into or export from France of items such as firearms, antiquities, medications, business equipment, sales samples, and other items. It is advisable to contact the Embassy of France in Washington, D.C. or one of France's consulates in the United States for specific information regarding customs requirements.

French customs authorities encourage the use of an ATA (Admission Temporaire/Temporary Admission) Carnet for the temporary admission of professional equipment, commercial samples, and/or goods for exhibitions and fair purposes. ATA Carnet Headquarters, located at the U.S. Council for International Business, 1212 Avenue of the Americas, New York, NY 10036, issues and guarantees the ATA Carnet in the United States. For additional information, please call (212) 354-4480, or send an e-mail to atacarnet@uscib.org, or visit http://www.uscib.org for details.

CRIMINAL PENALTIES: While in a foreign country, a U.S. citizen is subject to that country's laws and regulations, which sometimes differ significantly from those in the United States and may not afford the protections available to the individual under U.S. law. Penalties for breaking the law can be more severe than in the United States for similar offenses. Persons violating French or Monegasque laws, even unknowingly, may be expelled, arrested or imprisoned. Penalties for possession, use, or trafficking in illegal drugs in France or Monaco are strict, and convicted offenders can expect jail sentences and heavy fines.

SPECIAL CIRCUMSTANCES: In January 2002, the Eurozone Countries, including France, converted from their national currencies to the Euro for all monetary transactions. Monaco also converted from the French franc to the Euro.

The emergency numbers in France for the police, fire and medical assistance are as follows: 17 (police emergency), 18 (fire department) and 15 (emergency medical/paramedic team/ambulance). In Monaco, the numbers are 17 (police emergency), 18 (fire department) and 9375-2525 (medical/paramedic team/ambulance).

CHILDREN'S ISSUES: For information on international adoption of children and international parental child abduction please refer to our Internet site at http://travel.state.gov/children's_issues.html or telephone (202) 736-7000.

REGISTRATION/EMBASSY AND CONSULATE LOCATIONS: Americans living in or visiting France or Monaco are encouraged to register at the Consular Section of the U.S. Embassy in Paris or the nearest consulate and obtain updated information on travel and security within France and Monaco. The Consular Section of the U.S. Embassy in Paris is located at 2 Rue St. Florentin, 75001 Paris (Place de La Concorde, Metro Stop Concorde). Tel. 011-33-1-43 12 22 22 or (in France)01-43 12 22 22; fax 01-42 61 61 40. Further information can be obtained at the U.S. Embassy's web site at http://www.amb-usa.fr.

The Consulate General in Marseille is located at Place Varian Fry, 13086 Marseilles; tel. 011-33-4-91 54 92 00 (Consular Section extension: 304), fax 011-33-4-91 55 09 47.

The Consulate General in Strasbourg is located at 15 Avenue d'Alsace, 67082 Strasbourg tel. 011-33-3-88 35 31 04, fax 011-33-3-88 24 06 95. The Consulate General in Strasbourg does not produce passports on the premises. American citizens in this area whose passports are lost or stolen and who have urgent travel needs should contact the U.S. Embassy in Paris.

The Consular Agency in Nice is located at 7, Avenue Gustave V, 3rd floor, 06000 Nice; tel. 011-33-4-93 88 89 55, fax 011-33-4-93 87 07 38.

The U.S. Government also has consular representation in Bordeaux, Lille, Lyon, Rennes, and Toulouse that provide some emergency services to Americans. However, their primary focus is economic and commercial.

Germany

COUNTRY DESCRIPTION: Germany is a modern and stable democracy. Tourist facilities are highly developed. In larger towns, many people can communicate in English.

ENTRY REQUIREMENTS: A passport is required. A visa is not required for tourist/business stays up to 90 days within the Schengen Group of countries, which includes Germany. Further information on entry, visa and passport requirements may be obtained from the German Embassy at 4645 Reservoir Road N.W., Washington, D.C. 20007, telephone (202) 298-4000, or the German Consulates General in Atlanta, Boston, Chicago, Houston, Los Angeles, Miami, New York, or San Francisco, and on the Internet at www.germany-nfo.org/newcontent/index_consular.html. Inquiries from outside the United States may be made to the nearest German embassy or consulate.

In an effort to prevent international child abduction, many governments have initiated procedures at entry/exit points. These often include requiring documentary evidence of relationship and permission for the child's travel from the parent(s) or legal guardian, if not present. Having such documentation on hand, even if not required, may facilitate entry/departure.

SAFETY AND SECURITY: Overall, the security risk to travelers in Germany is low. Germany experiences, however, a number of demonstrations every year on a variety of political and economic themes. These demonstrations have a tendency to spread and turn violent, and anyone in the general area can become the victim of a random attack. Prior police approval is required for public demonstrations in Germany, and police oversight is routinely provided to ensure adequate security for participants and passers-by. Nonetheless, situations may develop which could pose a threat to public safety. All Americans are cautioned to avoid the area around protests and demonstrations and to check local media for updates on the situation.

In addition, hooligans, most often young intoxicated "skinheads," have been known to harass or even attack people whom they believe to be foreigners or members of rival youth groups. While U.S. citizens have not been specific targets, several Americans have reported that they were assaulted for racial reasons or because they appeared "foreign." For the latest security information, Americans traveling abroad should regularly monitor the Department's Internet web site at http://travel.state.gov, where the current Worldwide Caution Public Announcement, Travel Warnings and Public Announcements can be found.

CRIME: Violent crime is rare in Germany, but can occur, especially in larger cities or high-risk areas such as train stations. Most incidents of street crime consist of theft of unattended items and pickpocketing. There have been a few reports of aggravated assault against U.S. citizens in higher-risk areas. American travelers are advised to take the same precautions against becoming crime victims as they would in any American city.

The loss or theft abroad of a U.S. passport should be reported immediately to the local police and the nearest U.S. Embassy or Consulate. If you are the victim of a crime while overseas, in addition to reporting to local police, please contact the nearest U.S. Embassy or Consulate for assistance. The Embassy/Consulate staff can, for example, assist you to find appropriate medical care, to contact family members or friends and explain how funds could be transferred. Although the investigation and prosecution of the crime is solely the responsibility of local authorities, consular officers can help you to understand the local criminal justice process and to find an attorney if needed.

U.S. citizens may refer to the Department of State's pamphlet, "*A Safe Trip Abroad*," for ways to promote a trouble-free journey. The pamphlet is available by mail from the Superintendent of Documents, U.S. Government Printing Office, Washington, D.C. 20402, via the Internet at http://www.access.gpo.gov/su_docs, or via the Bureau of Consular Affairs home page at http://travel.state.gov.

MEDICAL FACILITIES: Good medical care is widely available. Doctors and hospitals may expect immediate payment in cash for health services from tourists and persons with no permanent address in Germany. Most doctors, hospitals and pharmacies do not accept credit cards.

MEDICAL INSURANCE: The Department of State strongly urges Americans to consult with their medical insurance company prior to traveling abroad to confirm whether their policy applies overseas and if it will cover emergency expenses such as a medical evacuation. U.S. medical insurance plans seldom cover health costs incurred outside the United States unless supplemental coverage is purchased. Further, U.S. Medicare and Medicaid programs do not provide payment for medical services outside the United States. However, many travel agents and private companies offer insurance plans that will cover health care expenses incurred overseas including emergency services such as medical evacuations.

When making a decision regarding health insurance, Americans should consider that many foreign doctors and hospitals require payment in cash prior to providing service and that a medical evacuation to the U.S. may cost well in excess of $50,000. Uninsured travelers who require medical care overseas often face extreme difficulties. When consulting with your insurer prior to your trip, ascertain whether payment will be made to the overseas healthcare provider or if you will be reimbursed later for expenses you incur. Some insurance policies also include coverage for psychiatric treatment and for disposition of remains in the event of death.

Useful information on medical emergencies abroad, including overseas insurance programs, is provided in the Department of State's Bureau of Consular Affairs brochure, "*Medical Information for Americans Traveling Abroad*," available via the Bureau of Consular Affairs home page or autofax: (202) 647-3000.

OTHER HEALTH INFORMATION: Information on vaccinations and other health precautions, such as safe food and water precautions and insect bite protection, may be obtained from the Centers for Disease Control and Prevention's hotline for international travelers at 1-877-FYI-TRIP (1-877-394-8747); fax 1-888-CDC-FAXX (1-888-232-3299), or via the CDC's Internet site at http://www.cdc.gov/travel. For information about outbreaks of infectious diseases abroad, consult the World Health Organization's website at http://www.who.int/en. Further health information for travelers is available at http://www.who.int/ith.

TRAFFIC SAFETY AND ROAD CONDITIONS:
While in a foreign country, U.S. citizens may encounter road conditions that differ significantly from those in the United States. The information below concerning Germany is provided for general reference only, and may not be totally accurate in a particular location or circumstance:

Safety of Public Transportation: Excellent
Urban Road Conditions/Maintenance: Excellent
Rural Road Conditions/Maintenance: Excellent
Availability of Roadside Assistance: Excellent

Road conditions in general are excellent, although caution should be exercised while traveling on older roads in eastern Germany. The high speed permitted on the German autobahn, weather, and unfamiliar road markings can pose significant hazards, and driver error is a leading cause of accidents involving American motorists in Germany. Rules on right-of-way differ significantly from the U.S. Notice should be taken that it is generally illegal in Germany to pass vehicles from the right and that the threshold for determining whether a person has been driving under the influence of alcohol is lower than in some U.S. states. For specific information on travel within Germany contact the German National Tourist Board Office in New York at (212) 661-7200, fax (212) 661-7174 or via the Internet at http://www.us.germany-tourism.de/e.

Travelers should also note that railroad crossings are differently marked in Germany than in the U.S. There have been several accidents involving Americans in recent years at railroad crossings. In addition to the standard crossbuck (X-shaped) sign, railroad crossings are often marked by signal lights. Signal lights flash only when a train is approaching. Regardless of the color of the light, a flashing light at a railroad crossing means that a train is approaching and that all vehicles should stop.

Individuals holding U.S. drivers' licenses may drive in Germany for up to six months without acquiring a German driver's license. For additional information about road safety, see the Department of State, Bureau of Consular Affairs home page's road safety overseas feature at http://travel.state.gov/road safety.html.

AVIATION SAFETY OVERSIGHT:
The U.S. Federal Aviation Administration (FAA) has assessed the Government of Germany's civil aviation authority as Category 1 -- in compliance with international aviation safety standards for oversight of Germany's air carrier operations. For further information, travelers may contact the Department of Transportation within the U.S. at 1-800-322-7873, or visit the FAA's Internet website at http://www.faa.gov/avr/iasa.

The U.S. Department of Defense (DOD) separately assesses some foreign air carriers for suitability as official providers of air services. For information regarding the DOD policy on specific carriers, travelers may contact DOD at (618) 229-4801.

CUSTOMS REGULATIONS/CURRENCY AND BANKING:
Germany's customs authorities may enforce strict regulations concerning temporary importation into or export from Germany of certain items such as firearms, military artifacts (particularly those pertaining to the Second World War), antiques, medications/pharmaceuticals and business equipment. Under German law it is also illegal to bring into or take out of Germany literature, music CDs, or other paraphernalia that glorifies fascism, the Nazi past or the former "Third Reich." It is advisable to contact the German Embassy in Washington or one of the German consulates in the United States for specific information regarding customs requirements.

Germany's customs authorities encourage the use of an ATA (Admission Temporaire/Temporary Admission) Carnet for the temporary admission of professional equipment, commercial samples, and/or goods for exhibitions and fair purposes. ATA Carnet headquarters, located at the U.S. Council for International Business, 1212 Avenue

411

of the Americas, New York, NY 10036, issues and guarantees the ATA Carnet in the United States. For additional information, please call 212-354-4480, send an e-mail to atacarnet@uscib.org, or visit http://www.uscib.org for details.

CURRENCY/BANKING: Germany adopted the Euro as its official currency on January 1, 2002. Automatic Teller Machines (ATMs) are widely available throughout Germany. They utilize many of the same account networks that are found in the U.S., so it is possible in most cases to get German currency directly from your U.S. bank while you are in Germany.

CRIMINAL PENALTIES: While in a foreign country, a U.S. citizen is subject to that country's laws and regulations, which sometimes differ significantly from those in the United States and may not afford the protections available to the individual under U.S. law. Penalties for breaking the law can be more severe than in the United States for similar offenses. Persons violating Germany's laws, even unknowingly, may be expelled, arrested or imprisoned. Penalties for possession, use, or trafficking in illegal drugs in Germany are strict and convicted offenders can expect jail sentences and heavy fines.

CHILDREN'S ISSUES: Custody and access issues for children in dual American-German families have been a recent, high-profile concern in Germany. For information on children's issues, including international adoption of children and international parental child abduction, please refer to our Internet site at http://travel.state.gov/children's_issues.html or telephone (202) 736-7000.

REGISTRATION/EMBASSY AND CONSULATE LOCATIONS: Americans living in Germany are encouraged to register at the consular section of the U.S. Embassy or any of the U.S. consulates and obtain updated information on travel and security within Germany. Individuals planning extended stays in Germany are encouraged to register in person at their local consular section.

A new initiative of the American Embassy in Berlin allows all Americans in Germany to obtain automatic security updates and Public Announcements by e-mail. To subscribe to this service, simply send a blank e-mail to GermanyACS@state.gov and put the word "SUBSCRIBE" on the subject line.

U.S. EMBASSY BERLIN IS LOCATED AT: Neustaedtische Kirchstrasse 4-5; Tel: (49)(30) 238-5174 or 8305-0; the consular section is located at Clayallee 170; Tel: (49)(30) 832-9233; Fax: (49)(30) 8305-1215

U.S. Consulates General are located at: Duesseldorf: Willi-Becker-Allee 10, Tel: (49)(211) 788-8927; Fax: (49)(211) 788-8938; Frankfurt: Siesmayerstrasse 21, Tel: (49)(69) 75350; Fax: (49)(69) 7535-2304;

Hamburg: Alsterufer 27/28, Tel: (49)(40) 4117-1351; Fax: (49)(40) 44-30-04; Leipzig: Wilhelm-Seyfferth-Strasse 4, Tel: (49)(341) 213-8418; Fax: (49)(341) 21384-17 (emergency services only);

Munich: Koeniginstrasse 5, Tel: (49)(89) 2888-0; Fax: (49)(89) 280-9998. There is also a U.S. consular agency in Bremen located at Bremen World Trade Center, Birkenstockstrasse 15, Tel: (49)(421) 301-5860; Fax: (49)(421) 301-5861.
When calling another city from within Germany, dial a zero before the city code (for example, when calling Berlin from Munich, the city code for Berlin is 030).

Greece

COUNTRY DESCRIPTION: Greece is a developed and stable democracy with a modern economy.

ENTRY REQUIREMENTS: A passport is required, but no visa is needed for tourist or business stays of up to three months. For other entry requirements, travelers should contact the Embassy of Greece at 2221 Massachusetts Avenue, NW, Washington, DC 20008, telephone (202) 939-5800, or Greek consulates in Atlanta, Boston, Chicago, Houston, Los Angeles, New Orleans, New York, and San Francisco, and

Greek embassies and consulates around the world. Additional information is available at http://www.greekembassy.org.

In an effort to prevent international child abduction, many governments have initiated procedures at entry/exit points. These often include requiring documentary evidence of relationship and permission for the child's travel from the parent(s) or legal guardian not present. Having such documentation on hand, even if not required, may facilitate entry/departure.

DUAL NATIONALITY: In addition to being subject to all Greek laws affecting U.S. citizens, dual nationals may also be subject to other laws that impose special obligations on Greek citizens. For additional information, see the Citizenship and Nationality section of the Consular Affairs home page at http://travel.state.gov.

SAFETY AND SECURITY: Civil disorder is rare, although strikes and demonstrations are a regular occurrence. During 2002, Greek authorities made important progress toward alleviating domestic terrorism by arresting and charging 18 alleged members of "November 17." Other left-wing and anarchist groups continue to pose a threat to American commercial interests in Greece, however, through their use of small explosive devices. Travelers should always review their security practices and be alert to their surroundings. Americans are encouraged to check the Consular Affairs home page for updated travel and security information.

CRIME: Crime against tourists (purse-snatchings, pickpocketing) appears to be on the rise at popular tourist sites and on crowded public transportation, particularly in Athens. Reports of date or acquaintance rape have also increased, with most of the offenses occurring on the islands. The usual safety precautions practiced in any urban or tourist area ought to be practiced during a visit to Greece.

The loss or theft abroad of a U.S. passport should be reported immediately to the local police and the nearest U.S. Embassy or Consulate. If you are the victim of a crime while overseas, in addition to reporting to local police, please contact the nearest U.S. Embassy or Consulate for assistance. The Embassy/Consulate staff can, for example, assist you to find appropriate medical care, to contact family members or friends and explain how funds could be transferred. Although the investigation and prosecution of the crime is solely the responsibility of local authorities, consular officers can help you to understand the local criminal justice process and to find an attorney if needed.

U.S. citizens may refer to the Department of State's pamphlet, *A Safe Trip Abroad*, for ways to promote a trouble-free journey. The pamphlet is available by mail from the Superintendent of Documents, U.S. Government Printing Office, Washington, D.C. 20402, via the Internet at http://www.access.gpo.gov/su_docs, or via the Bureau of Consular Affairs home page at http://travel.state.gov.

MEDICAL FACILITIES: Medical facilities are adequate, and some in Athens and Thessaloniki are quite good. Nursing care, however, particularly in public hospitals, may be less than adequate.

MEDICAL INSURANCE: The Department of State strongly urges Americans to consult with their medical insurance company prior to traveling abroad to confirm whether their policy applies overseas and whether it will cover emergency expenses such as a medical evacuation. U.S. medical insurance plans seldom cover health costs incurred outside the United States unless supplemental coverage is purchased. Further, U.S. Medicare and Medicaid programs do not provide payment for medical services outside the United States. However, many travel agents and private companies offer insurance plans that will cover health care expenses incurred overseas including emergency services such as medical evacuations.

When making a decision regarding health insurance, Americans should consider that many foreign doctors and hospitals require payment in cash prior to providing service and that a medical evacuation to the U.S. may cost well in excess of $50,000. Uninsured travelers who require medical care overseas often face extreme difficulties. When consulting with your insurer prior to your trip, ascertain whether payment will be made to the overseas healthcare provider or whether you will be reimbursed later for expenses you incur. Some insurance policies also include coverage for psychiatric treatment and for disposition of remains in the event of death.

Useful information on medical emergencies abroad, including overseas insurance programs, is provided in the Department of State's Bureau of Consular Affairs brochure, *Medical Information for Americans Traveling Abroad*, available via the Bureau of Consular Affairs home page or autofax: (202) 647-3000.

OTHER HEALTH INFORMATION: Information on vaccinations and other health precautions may be obtained from the Centers for Disease Control and Prevention's international travelers hotline at 1-877-FYI-TRIP (1-877-394-8747); fax: 1-888-CDC-FAXX (1-888-232-3299, or by visiting CDC's Internet home page at http://www.cdc.gov. For information about outbreaks of infectious diseases abroad consult the World Health Organization's web site at http://www.who.int/en. Further health information for travelers is available at http://www.who.int/ith.

TRAFFIC SAFETY AND ROAD CONDITIONS: While in a foreign country, U.S. citizens may encounter road conditions that differ significantly from those in the United States. The information below concerning Greece is provided for general reference only and may not be accurate in a particular location or circumstance.

Safety of Public Transportation: Good
Urban Road Condition/Maintenance: Good
Rural Road Condition/Maintenance: Fair
Availability of Roadside Assistance: Poor

Visitors to Greece must be prepared to drive defensively. Heavy traffic and poor highways pose hazards, especially at night. Extreme care is warranted in operating a motorbike. The majority of U.S. citizen traffic casualties in Greece have involved motorbikes. Drivers must carry a valid U.S. license as well as an international driver's permit. The U.S. Department of State has authorized two organizations to issue international driving permits to those who hold valid U.S. driver's licenses: AAA and the American Automobile Touring Alliance. Vehicles may be rented without the permit, but the driver will be penalized for failure to have one in the event of an accident. Fines are high. Small motorbike rental firms frequently do not insure their vehicles; the customer is responsible for damages. Review your coverage before renting.

For additional general information about road safety, including links to foreign government sites, see the Department of State, Bureau of Consular Affairs, home page at http://travel.state.gov/road_safety.html. For specific information concerning Greek driving permits, vehicle inspection, road tax and mandatory insurance, contact the Greek National Tourism Office via the Internet at http://www.gnto.gr.

AVIATION SAFETY OVERSIGHT: The U.S. Federal Aviation Administration (FAA) has assessed the Greek Government's civil aviation authority as Category 2 -- not in compliance with international aviation safety standards for the oversight of Greek air carrier operations. While consultations to correct the deficiencies are ongoing, the Greek air carriers currently flying to the U.S. will be subject to heightened FAA surveillance. No additional flights or new service to the U.S. by Greek air carriers will be permitted unless they arrange to have the flights conducted by an air carrier from a country meeting international safety standards. For further information, travelers may contact the U.S. Department of Transportation at 1-800-322-7873, or visit the FAA Internet web site at http://www.faa.gov/avr/iasa/.

The U.S. Department of Defense (DOD) separately assesses some foreign carriers for suitability as official providers of air services. In addition, DOD does not permit its personnel to use air carriers from Category 2 countries for official business except for flights originating from or terminating in the United States. Local exceptions may apply. For information regarding the DOD policy on specific carriers, travelers may contact DOD at (618) 229-4801.

CUSTOMS REGULATIONS: Greek customs authorities may enforce strict regulations concerning the export from Greece of antiquities, including rocks from archaeological sites. Penalties range from large fines to prison terms. It is advisable to contact the Embassy of Greece in Washington or one of Greece's consulates in the United States for specific information regarding customs requirements. Customs authorities encourage the use of an ATA (Admission Temporaire/Temporary Admission) Carnet for the temporary admission of professional equipment, commercial samples, and/or goods for exhibitions and fair purposes. ATA Carnet headquarters, located at the U.S. Council for International Business, 1212 Avenue of the Americas, New York, NY 10036, issues and guarantees the ATA Carnet in the United States. For additional information call 212-354-4480, send an e-mail to atacarnet@uscib.org, or visit http://www.uscib.org for details.

CRIMINAL PENALTIES: While in a foreign country, a U.S. citizen is subject to that country's laws and regulations, which sometimes differ significantly from those in the United States and may not afford the protections available to the individual under U.S. law. Penalties for breaking the law can be more severe than in the United States for similar offenses. Persons violating Greek laws, even unknowingly, may be expelled, arrested or imprisoned. Penalties for possession, use, or trafficking in illegal drugs in Greece are strict, and convicted offenders can expect jail sentences and heavy fines.

SPECIAL CIRCUMSTANCES: Labor strikes in the transportation sector (national airline, city bus lines, and taxis) occur frequently. Most are announced in advance and are of short duration. Reconfirmation of domestic and international flight reservations is highly recommended.

The Government of Greece does not permit the photographing of military installations. In 2001, several British and other nationals who photograph military aircraft as a hobby were arrested while taking photographs of aircraft taking off and landing at a military base. Although they were eventually acquitted, the Embassy strongly recommends against participating in such activities.

EMERGENCY ASSISTANCE: People traveling in Greece who do not speak Greek may call 112 if they require emergency services. This is a 24-hour toll-free number. Callers will be able to receive information in English and French (as well as Greek) to request ambulance services, the fire department, the police and the coast guard.

CHILDREN'S ISSUES: For information on international adoption of children and international parental child abduction, please refer to our Internet site at http://travel.state.gov/children's issues.html or telephone the Overseas Citizens

Services (OCS) call center at 1-888-407-4747. The OCS call center can answer general inquiries regarding international adoptions and will forward calls to the appropriate Country Officer. This number is available from 8:00 a.m. to 8:00 p.m. Eastern Standard Time, Monday through Friday (except U.S. federal holidays). Callers who are unable to use toll-free numbers, such as those calling from overseas, may obtain information and assistance during these hours by calling 1-317-472-2328.

REGISTRATION/EMBASSY AND CONSULATE LOCATION: Americans living in or visiting Greece are encouraged to register at the consular section of the U.S. Embassy/Consulate General and to obtain updated information on travel and security in Greece. The U.S. Embassy in Athens is located at 91 Vasilissis Sophias Boulevard, tel: (30)(210) 721-2851. The U.S. Consulate General in Thessaloniki is located at Plateia Commercial Center, 43 Tsimiski Street, 7th floor, tel: (30)(2310) 242-905. The Embassy's web site is http://www.usembassy.gr. The e-mail address for the Consular Section is athensconsul@state.gov. The U.S. Consulate's web site addresses are http://www.usconsulate.gr and http://thessaloniki.usconsulate.gov. The e-mail address for the U.S. Consulate General Thessaloniki is amcongen@compulink.gr.

Iceland

COUNTRY DESCRIPTION: Iceland is a highly developed stable democracy with a modern economy. The national language is Icelandic, but English is widely spoken, especially in the capital city of Reykjavik.

ENTRY REQUIREMENTS: A passport is required, but no visa is needed for tourist or business stays of up to three months within any six-month period. U.S. citizens should be aware, however, that because Iceland is now part of the EU's Schengen area, the three-month period begins as soon as they enter any Schengen country.

For stays longer than three months, or for visitors who will be studying or working in Iceland, a visa is required. Applications for Icelandic visas are processed by the Embassy of Denmark in

415

Washington D.C., and the Danish Consulates General in Los Angeles and New York. The Embassy of Iceland in Washington, D.C., and the Consulate General of Iceland in New York no longer process visas. For further information concerning entry requirements for Iceland, please contact the Royal Danish Embassy at 3200 Whitehaven Street, N.W., Washington, D.C. 20008, tel (202) 234-4300, on-line at http://denmarkemb.org, or the Danish Consulates General in Los Angeles or New York.

In an effort to prevent international child abduction, many governments have initiated procedures at entry/exit points. These often include requiring documentary evidence of relationship and permission for the child's travel from the parent(s) or legal guardian if not present. Having such documentation on hand, even if not required, may facilitate entry/departure.

DUAL NATIONALITY: In addition to being subject to all Icelandic laws affecting U.S. citizens, dual nationals may also be subject to other laws that impose special obligations on Icelandic citizens. For additional information, please see the Consular Affairs home page on the Internet at http://travel.state.gov for our *Dual Nationality flyer*.

CRIME: Iceland has a relatively low crime rate, but minor assaults and other street crimes have become more common, especially in the capital city of Reykjavik. Tourists should be aware that downtown Reykjavik can become especially disorderly on weekend evenings. Violent crime is rare, but it does occur, and it appears to be increasing.

The loss or theft abroad of a U.S. passport should be reported immediately to the local police and the nearest U.S. embassy or consulate. If you are the victim of a crime while overseas, in addition to reporting to local police, please contact the nearest U.S. embassy or consulate for assistance. The Embassy/Consulate staff can, for example, assist you to find appropriate medical care, to contact family members or friends and explain how funds could be transferred. Although the investigation and prosecution of the crime is solely the responsibility of local authorities, consular officers can help you to understand the local criminal justice process and to find an attorney if needed.

U.S. citizens may refer to the Department of State's pamphlet, *A Safe Trip Abroad*, for ways to promote a trouble-free journey. The pamphlet is available by mail from the Superintendent of Documents, U.S. Government Printing Office, Washington, D.C. 20402, via the Internet at http://www.access.gpo.gov/su_docs, or via the Bureau of Consular Affairs home page at http://travel.state.gov.

MEDICAL FACILITIES: Excellent medical facilities are available in Iceland. To obtain emergency medical assistance anywhere in the country, please dial 112. To obtain non-emergency medical assistance outside of normal business hours, please dial 1770. The nurse who answers will offer advice on how to handle the problem, suggest that the patient come to an after-hours clinic, or send a physician to make a house call. For information on after-hours dental care, please call 575-0505.

MEDICAL INSURANCE: The Department of State strongly urges Americans to consult with their medical insurance company prior to traveling abroad to confirm whether their policy applies overseas and if it will cover emergency expenses such as a medical evacuation. U.S. medical insurance plans seldom cover health costs incurred outside the United States unless supplemental coverage is purchased. Further, U.S. Medicare and Medicaid programs do not provide payment for medical services outside the United States. However, many travel agents and private companies offer insurance plans that will cover health care expenses incurred overseas, including emergency services such as medical evacuations.

When making a decision regarding health insurance, Americans should consider that many foreign doctors and hospitals require payment in cash prior to providing service and that a medical evacuation to the United States may cost well in excess of $50,000. Uninsured travelers who require medical care overseas often face extreme difficulties. When consulting with your insurer prior to your trip, please ascertain whether payment will be made to the overseas healthcare provider or if you will be reimbursed later for expenses that you incur. Some insurance policies also include coverage for psychiatric treatment and for disposition of remains in the event of death.

Useful information on medical emergencies abroad, including overseas insurance programs, is provided in the Department of State's Bureau of Consular Affairs brochure, *Medical Information for Americans Traveling Abroad*, available via the Bureau of Consular Affairs home page or autofax: (202) 647-3000.

OTHER HEALTH INFORMATION: Information on vaccinations and other health precautions, such as safe food and water precautions and insect bite protection, may be obtained from the Centers for Disease Control and Prevention's hotline for international travelers at 1-877-FYI-TRIP (1-877-394-8747); fax 1-888-CDC-FAXX (1-888-232-3299), or via the CDC's Internet site at http://www.cdc.gov/travel.

TRAFFIC SAFETY AND ROAD CONDITIONS: While in a foreign country, U.S. citizens may encounter road conditions that differ significantly from those in the United States. The information below concerning Iceland is provided for general reference only, and may not be totally accurate in a particular location or circumstance.

Safety of Public Transportation: Excellent
Urban Road Conditions/Maintenance: Excellent
Rural Road Conditions/Maintenance: Fair
Availability of Roadside Assistance: Good

Less than a third of the country's total road network is paved (2,262 miles of paved road versus 5,774 miles of gravel or dirt road). Most of the 900-mile ring road (Highway 1) that encircles the country is paved, but many other roads outside the capital, especially those that run through the center of the country, are dirt or gravel tracks. Even those roads that are paved tend to be narrow and lack a shoulder or margin. Most bridges are only one lane wide, requiring drivers to be cognizant of oncoming traffic.

Extreme care should be taken when driving in rural areas during the winter (October through March), when daylight hours are limited and the weather and road conditions can quickly change. Many routes in the interior of the country are impassable until July due to muddy conditions caused by snowmelt. When driving in the interior, travelers should consider traveling with a second vehicle and always inform someone of their travel plans. For information on current road conditions

throughout the country, please call the Public Roads Administration (Vegagerdin) at 1777 or consult its web site at http://www.vegag.is. For recorded weather information in English, please call the Icelandic Weather Office (Vedurstofa Islands) at 902-0600, ext. 44.

The law requires drivers to keep headlights on at all times. Unless otherwise posted, the speed limit in urban areas is 50 km per hour (31 mph). In rural areas, the speed limit is 80 km per hour (50 mph) on dirt and gravel roads, and 90 km per hour (56 mph) on paved highways. There is no provision for turning right on red in Iceland. An increasing number of intersections in the capital city area are now equipped with automatic cameras to catch drivers who run red lights. The use of seatbelts is mandatory in both the front and rear seats, and children under the age of six must be secured in a special car seat designed for their size and weight. Drivers are held responsible for any passenger under the age of fifteen who is not wearing a seatbelt. No one who is less than 140 cm (approximately 54 inches) tall or weighs less than 40 kilograms (88 lbs.) is allowed to ride in a front seat equipped with an airbag. Since November 2001, the use of cell phones while driving has been banned.

Driving under the influence of alcohol is considered a serious offense in Iceland. The threshold blood alcohol test (BAT) level is very low. Drivers can be charged with DWI with a BAT as low as .05%. Drivers stopped under suspicion for DWI are usually given a balloon or breathalizer test. If that shows positive, a blood test is routinely administered. Under Icelandic law, a blood test cannot be refused and will be administered by force if necessary. The minimum punishment for a first offense is a fine of ISK 50,000 (about $500) and the loss of driving privileges for two months.

For additional general information about road safety, please see the Department of State, Bureau of Consular Affairs home page road safety overseas feature at http://travel.state.gov/roads.html. U.S. citizens staying for less than 90 days can drive in Iceland using their U.S. licenses. For specific information concerning Icelandic driver's permits, vehicle inspection, road tax and mandatory insurance, please contact the Iceland National Tourist

Organization offices in New York via the Internet at http://www.iceland.org/oeku.htm.

AVIATION SAFETY OVERSIGHT: The U.S. Federal Aviation Administration (FAA) has assessed the Government of Iceland's civil aviation authority as Category 1 -- in compliance with international aviation safety standards for oversight of Iceland's air carrier operations. For further information, travelers may contact the Department of Transportation within the United States at tel. 1-800-322-7873, or visit the FAA's Internet web site at http://www.faa.gov/avr/iasa.

The U.S. Department of Defense (DOD) separately assesses some foreign air carriers for suitability as official providers of air services. For information regarding the DOD policy on specific carriers, travelers may contact the DOD at tel. (618) 229-4801.

CUSTOMS REGULATIONS: Icelandic customs authorities encourage the use of an ATA (Admission Temporaire/Temporary Admission) Carnet for the temporary admission of professional equipment, commercial samples, and/or goods for exhibitions and fair purposes. ATA Carnet Headquarters, located at the U.S. Council for International Business, 1212 Avenue of the Americas, New York, NY 10036, issues and guarantees the ATA Carnet in the United States. For additional information, please call (212) 354-4480, or send an e-mail to atacarnet@uscib.org, or visit http://www.uscib.org for details.

CRIMINAL PENALTIES: While in a foreign country, a U.S. citizen is subject to that country's laws and regulations, which sometimes differ significantly from those in the United States and may not afford the protections available to the individual under U.S. law. Penalties for breaking the law can be more severe than in the United States for similar offenses. Persons violating Icelandic laws, even unknowingly, may be expelled, arrested or imprisoned. Penalties for possession, use, or trafficking in illegal drugs in Iceland are strict, and convicted offenders can expect jail sentences and heavy fines.

SPECIAL CIRCUMSTANCES: Extreme care should be exercised when touring Iceland's numerous nature attractions, which include glaciers, volcanic craters, lava fields, ice caves, hot springs, boiling mud pots, geysers, waterfalls and glacial rivers. There are few warning signs or barriers to alert travelers to the potential hazards. Several tourists are scalded each year because they get too close to an erupting geyser, or because they fall or step into a hot spring or boiling mud pot. High winds and icy conditions can exacerbate the dangers of visiting these nature areas.

Hikers and backpackers are well advised to stay on marked trails, travel with someone, let someone else know their travel plans, and check weather reports.

DISASTER PREPAREDNESS: Iceland is subject to natural disasters in the form of earthquakes, volcanic eruptions, avalanches, and violent storms. Travelers should learn how to prepare for and react to such events by consulting the web site of Iceland's National Civil Defense Agency at http://www.avrik.is. General information about natural disaster preparedness is available via the Internet from the U.S. Federal Emergency Management Agency (FEMA) at http://www.fema.gov.

CHILDREN'S ISSUES: For information on international adoption of children and international parental child abduction, please refer to our Internet site at http://travel.state.gov/children's_issues.html or telephone (202) 736-7000.

REGISTRATION/EMBASSY AND CONSULATE LOCATIONS: Americans living in or visiting Iceland are encouraged to register at the Consular Section of the U.S. Embassy in Reykjavik and obtain updated information on travel and security within Iceland. The U.S. Embassy is located at Laufasvegur 21, tel. +354-562-9100; fax +354-562-9110. Information about consular services can be found in the Consular Section of the Embassy home page at http://www.usa.is.

Ireland

COUNTRY DESCRIPTION: Ireland is a highly developed democracy with a modern economy.

ENTRY REQUIREMENTS: A passport is necessary, but a visa is not required for tourist or business stays of up to three months. For information concerning entry requirements for Ireland, travelers can contact the Embassy of Ireland at 2234 Massachusetts Avenue N.W., Washington, D.C. 20008; telephone:(202) 462-3939, fax: 202-232-5993, or the nearest Irish consulate in Boston, Chicago, New York, or San Francisco. The Internet address of the Irish Embassy is: http://www.irelandemb.org.

SAFETY/SECURITY: A peace agreement for Northern Ireland was ratified by voters in Ireland and Northern Ireland in May 1998. Nonetheless, there have been periodic incidents of violence in Northern Ireland associated with paramilitary organizations, with at least the potential for some spill over into Ireland. Travelers to Northern Ireland should consult the Consular Information Sheet for the United Kingdom for more specific information.

CRIME INFORMATION: Although Ireland has a low rate of violent crime, there have been incidents in which non-nationals and tourists have been victims of assault, including instances that appear to have been racially motivated. There is a high incidence of petty crime, mostly theft, burglary, and purse snatching. Rental cars and tourists, particularly in the vicinity of tourist attractions, are targeted by thieves.

There has been an increase over the last year in the number of crimes involving credit cards and Automatic Teller Machines (ATMS). The use of "skimmers" to record credit card details has increased, and these recorded details are being sent elsewhere to program false and stolen credit cards. The primary target of these scams have been individuals, often tourists, at ATMs.

The loss or theft abroad of a U.S. passport should be reported immediately to local police and the nearest U.S. embassy or consulate. U.S. citizens can refer to the Department of State's pamphlet, *A Safe Trip Abroad*, for ways to promote a trouble-free trip. The pamphlet is available from the Superintendent of Documents, U.S. Government Printing Office, Washington, D.C. 20402, via the Internet at http://www.access.gpo.gov/su_docs, or via the Bureau of Consular Affairs home page at http://travel.state.gov.

MEDICAL FACILITIES: Modern medical facilities and highly skilled medical practitioners are available. Serious medical problems requiring hospitalization and/or medical evacuation to the United States can cost thousands of dollars or more. Doctors and hospitals often expect immediate cash payment for health services

MEDICAL INSURANCE: U.S. medical insurance is not always valid outside the United States. U.S. Medicare and Medicaid programs do not provide payment for medical services outside the United States. Uninsured travelers who require medical care overseas may face extreme difficulties. Please check with your own insurance company to confirm whether your policy applies overseas. Additional coverage for medical evacuation is recommended. Some insurance policies also include coverage for psychiatric treatment and for disposition of remains in the event of death. Useful information on medical emergencies abroad, including overseas insurance programs, is provided in the Department of State's Bureau of Consular Affairs brochure, *Medical Information for Americans Traveling Abroad*, available via the Bureau of Consular Affairs home page or autofax: (202) 647-3000.

OTHER HEALTH INFORMATION: Information on vaccinations and other health precautions may be obtained from the Centers for Disease Control and Prevention's hotline for international travelers at tel. 1-877-FYI-TRIP (1-877-394-8747); fax 1-800-CDC-FAXX (1-800-232-3299), or via their Internet site at http://www.cdc.gov.

TRAFFIC SAFETY AND ROAD CONDITIONS: While in a foreign country, U.S. citizens may encounter road conditions that differ significantly from those in the United States. The information below concerning Ireland is provided for general reference only, and it may not be totally accurate in a particular location or circumstance.

Safety of Public Transportation: Good
Urban Road Conditions/Maintenance: Good
Rural Road Conditions/Maintenance: Fair
Availability of Roadside Assistance: Good

Driving is on the left side of the road in Ireland, and motorists without experience in left-drive countries should be extra cautious. Tourists driving on the wrong side of the road are the cause of several serious accidents each year. The vast majority of the rental cars are stick shift; it can be difficult to find automatic transmission rental cars. Road conditions are generally very good, but once off main highways, country roads quickly become narrow, uneven and winding. Roads are more dangerous during the summer and on holiday weekends due to an increase in traffic.

Taxis are reasonably priced, but availability varies with time of day. Bus service in cities is generally adequate, though many buses are overcrowded and frequently late. Inter-city bus and train services are reasonably good.

For additional general information about road safety, including links to foreign government sites, please see the Department of State, Bureau of Consular Affairs home page at http://travel.state.gov/road_safety.html. For specific information concerning Irish driving permits, vehicle inspection, road tax and mandatory insurance, please contact the Irish National Tourist Organization (Bord Failte) web site at http://www.ireland.travel.ie.

AVIATION SAFETY OVERSIGHT: The U.S. Federal Aviation Administration (FAA) has assessed the Government of Ireland's Civil Aviation Authority as Category 1 -- in compliance with international aviation safety standards for oversight of Ireland's air carrier operations. For further information, travelers may contact the Department of Transportation within the United States at tel. 1-800-322-7873, or visit the FAA's web site at http://www.faa.gov/avr/iasa/. The U.S. Department of Defense (DOD) separately assesses some foreign air carriers for suitability as official providers of air services. For information regarding the DOD policy on specific carriers, travelers may contact the DOD at tel. (618) 229-4801.

CUSTOMS REGULATIONS: Irish customs authorities may enforce strict regulations concerning temporary importation into or export from Ireland of items such as firearms. It is advisable to contact the Embassy of Ireland in Washington, D.C. or one of Ireland's consulates in the United States for specific information regarding customs requirements. Customs authorities encourage the use of an ATA (Admission Temporaire/Temporary Admission) Carnet for the admission of professional equipment, commercial samples, and/or goods for exhibitions and fair purposes. ATA Carnet Headquarters, located at the U.S. Council for International Business, 1212 Avenue of the Americas, New York, NY 10036, issues and guarantees the ATA Carnet in the United States. For additional information, please call 212-354-4480, or send an e-mail to atacarnet@uscib.org, or visit http://www.uscib.org for details.

CRIMINAL PENALTIES: While in a foreign country, a U.S. citizen is subject to that country's laws and regulations, which sometimes differ significantly from those in the United States and may not afford the protection available to the individual under U.S. law. Penalties for breaking the law can be more severe than in the United States for similar offenses. Persons violating Irish laws, even unknowingly, may be expelled, arrested or imprisoned. Penalties for possession, use, or trafficking in illegal drugs in Ireland are strict, and convicted offenders can expect jail sentences and heavy fines.

CURRENCY/BANKING: Ireland will adopt the Euro as its official currency on January 1, 2002. Irish pounds will be accepted for cash transactions, along with Euros, until midnight February 9, 2002. After that, travelers to Ireland must pay in Euros, although banks will change Irish pounds to Euros for some months afterward.

Most Irish banks will not accept $100 (US) dollar bills. Automated Teller Machines are widely available, but some ATM's, particularly in rural areas, may not accept U.S. bank ATM cards. Credit cards are widely accepted throughout Ireland.

420

CHILDREN'S ISSUES: For information on international adoption of children, international child support enforcement issues, or international parental child abduction, please refer to our Internet site at: http://travel.state.gov/children's_issues.html, or telephone (202) 786-7000.

REGISTRATION/EMBASSY LOCATION: Americans living in or visiting Ireland are encouraged to register with the Consular Section of the U.S. Embassy and obtain updated information on travel and security in Ireland. The U.S. Embassy in Dublin is located at 42 Elgin Road, Ballsbridge, tel. (353)(1)668-7122; after hours tel. (353)(1)668-9612/9464; fax (353)(1) 668-9946. Travelers to Northern Ireland may consult the Consular Information Sheet for the United Kingdom. Further information and answers to many frequently asked questions are available on the Embassy's Internet home page (http://www.usembassy.ie).

Italy

COUNTRY DESCRIPTION: Italy is a developed democracy with a modern economy. Tourist facilities are widely available. Additional information may be obtained from the Italian Government Tourist Board by telephone at 212-245-5618 or via the Internet: http://www.enit.it.

ENTRY REQUIREMENTS: A valid passport is required. Italian authorities may deny entry to travelers who attempt to enter Italy without a valid passport. A visa is not required for tourist stays up to three months. For further information concerning entry requirements for Italy, travelers may contact the Embassy of Italy at 1601 Fuller St. N.W., Washington, D.C. 20009, tel. 202-328-5500 or via the Internet: http://www.italyemb.org, or the Italian Consulates General in Boston, Chicago, Detroit, Houston, Los Angeles, Miami, Newark, New Orleans, New York, Philadelphia, or San Francisco.

Tourists staying other than in hotels for more than one month should register with the local police station and obtain a "permesso di soggiorno"

(permit to stay) within eight days of arrival in Italy. Visitors to Italy may be required to demonstrate to the police upon arrival sufficient means of financial support. Credit cards, ATM cards, travelers' checks, prepaid hotel/vacation vouchers, etc. can be used to show sufficient means.

In an effort to prevent international child abduction, many governments have initiated procedures at entry/exit points. These often include requiring documentary evidence of relationship and permission for child's travel from the parent(s) or legal guardian not present. Having such documentation on hand, even if not required, may facilitate entry/departure.

DUAL NATIONALITY: U.S. citizens born in Italy and/or who are also Italian citizens may be subject to compulsory military service and other laws imposing special obligations upon them in Italy. Those who might be affected should inquire at an Italian embassy or consulate regarding their status before traveling to Italy. In some instances, dual nationality may hamper U.S. Government efforts to provide protection abroad. For additional information, please see the Consular Affairs home page on the Internet: http://www.travel.state.gov for our *Dual Nationality flyer*.

SAFETY/SECURITY: There have been occasional episodes of violence in Italy, most often connected to Italian internal developments or social issues. In 2001, there was violence associated with the demonstrations against the G-8 Meeting in Genoa. At various times, Italian authorities have found bombs outside public buildings; they have received bomb threats and were themselves the subjects of letter bombs. These incidents have all been ascribed to organized crime or anarchist movements. Americans were not targeted or injured in these instances. In March 2002, Americans were warned by the Department of State about possible actions by extremist groups in Italy.

CRIME: Italy has a low rate of violent crime, little of which is directed toward tourists. But petty crimes such as pick-pocketing, theft from parked cars, and purse snatching are serious problems, especially in large cities. Most reported thefts occur at crowded tourist sites, on public buses or trains, or at the major railway stations, Rome's

Termini, Milan's Centrale, Florence's Santa Maria Novella, and Naples' Centrale. Clients of Internet cafes in major cities have been targeted. Elderly tourists who have tried to resist petty thieves on motor scooters have suffered broken arms and collarbones.

Thieves in Italy often work in groups or pairs. Pairs of accomplices or groups of street urchins are known to divert tourists' attention so that another can pick-pocket them. In one particular routine, one thief throws trash or waste at the victim; a second thief assists the victim in cleaning up the mess; and the third discreetly takes the victim's belongings. Criminals on crowded public transportation slit the bottoms of purses or bags with a razor blade or sharp knife, then remove the contents. Theft of small items such as radios, luggage, cameras, briefcases, and even cigarettes from parked cars is a major problem. Robbers take items from cars at gas stations often by smashing car windows. Thefts have also been reported from occupied vehicles waiting in traffic or stopped at traffic lights.

In a scam practiced on the highways, one thief punctures the tire of a rental or out-of-town car. An accomplice signals the flat tire to the driver and encourages the driver to pull over. When the driver stops, one thief helps change the tire, while the other takes the driver's belongings. Please use particular caution driving at night on highways, when there may be a greater incidence of robbery attempts. There have been occasional reports of break-ins of rental cars driven by Americans when the precautions mentioned above were not followed during stops at highway service areas.

On trains, a commonly reported trick involves one or more persons who pretend to befriend a traveler and offer drugged food or drink. Also, thieves have been known to impersonate police officers to gain the confidence of tourists. The thief shows the prospective victim a circular plastic sign with the words "police" or "international police." If this happens, the tourist should insist on seeing the officer's identification card (documento), as impersonators tend not to carry forged documents. Tourists should immediately report thefts or other crimes to the local police.

The loss or theft abroad of a U.S. passport should be reported immediately to the local police and the nearest U.S. embassy or consulate. If you are the victim of a crime while overseas, in addition to reporting to local police, please contact the nearest U.S. embassy or consulate for assistance. The embassy/consulate staff can, for example, assist you to find appropriate medical care, to contact family members or friends and explain how funds could be transferred. Although the investigation and prosecution of the crime is solely the responsibility of local authorities, consular officers can help you to understand the local criminal justice process and to find an attorney if needed.

U.S. citizens can refer to the Department of State's pamphlet, *A Safe Trip Abroad*, for ways to promote a more trouble-free journey. The pamphlet is available by mail from the Superintendent of Documents, U.S. Government Printing Office, Washington, D.C. 20402, via the Internet at http://www.access.gpo.gov/su_docs, or via the Bureau of Consular Affairs home page at http://travel.state.gov.

MEDICAL FACILITIES AND INSURANCE: Medical facilities are available, but they may be limited outside urban areas. Public hospitals sometimes do not maintain the same standards as hospitals in the United States, so travelers are encouraged to obtain insurance that would cover a stay in a private Italian hospital or clinic. It is almost impossible to obtain an itemized hospital bill from public hospitals, as required by many U.S. insurance companies, because the Italian National Health Service charges one inclusive rate (care services, bed and board). The Department of State strongly urges Americans to consult their medical insurance company prior to traveling to confirm whether their policy applies overseas and if it will cover emergency expenses such as a medical evacuation. U.S. medical insurance plans seldom cover health costs incurred outside the United States unless supplemental coverage is purchased. U.S. Medicare and Medicaid programs do not provide payment for medical services outside the United States. Many travel agents and private companies offer insurance plans to cover overseas health care expenses, including emergency services such as medical evacuations.

When making a decision regarding health insurance, Americans should consider that many foreign doctors and hospitals require payment in cash prior to providing service and that a medical evacuation to the United States may cost well in excess of $50,000. Uninsured travelers who require medical care overseas often face extreme difficulties, whereas travelers who have purchased overseas medical insurance have found it to be life-saving when a medical emergency has occurred. When consulting with your insurer prior to your trip, please ask if payment will be made to the overseas healthcare provider or whether you will be reimbursed later for incurred expenses.

Some insurance companies include coverage for psychiatric treatment and for disposition of remains in the event of death. Information on medical emergencies abroad, including overseas insurance programs, is provided in the Department of State's Bureau of Consular Affairs brochure, *Medical Information for Americans Traveling Abroad*, available via the Bureau of Consular Affairs home page or autofax: (202) 647-3000.

OTHER HEALTH INFORMATION: Travelers should always carry a prescription for any prescription drugs they are taking and should know the generic name of the drug. Most prescription drugs available in the United States* can also be found in Italy. If you are taking an unusual medicine that is difficult to find even in the United States, we suggest that you bring an ample supply of the medicine with you when you travel. Mailing prescription drugs to Italy is time-consuming and complicated. Information on vaccinations and other health precautions may be obtained from the Centers for Disease Control and Prevention's international traveler's hotline at 1-877-FYI-TRIP (1-877-394-8747); fax 1-888-CDC-FAXX (1-888-232-3299), or by visiting the CDC Internet home page at http://www.cdc.gov.

TRAFFIC SAFETY AND ROAD CONDITIONS: While in a foreign country, U.S. citizens may encounter road conditions that differ significantly from those in the United States. The information below concerning Italy is provided for general reference only, and it may not be totally accurate in a particular location or circumstance.

Safety of Public Transportation: Good
Urban Road Condition/Maintenance: Fair
Rural Road Condition/Maintenance: Good
Availability of Roadside Assistance: Excellent

Streets in cities are often narrow, winding and congested; lane markings are often nonexistent; traffic lights are limited and often disobeyed; and a different convention of right-of-way is observed. Italy has over 5,600 kilometers (3,480 mi.) of "Autostrada", or superhighways. Commercial and individual drivers travel and pass on these well-maintained roads at very high speeds. Accidents in which excessive speed is a contributing factor do occur.

In rural areas, a wide range of speed on highways makes for hazardous driving. Roads are generally narrow and often do not have guardrails. Travelers in northern Italy, especially in winter, should be aware of ground fog and poor visibility, which cause multiple-car accidents each year. Most Italian-specification automobiles are equipped with special fog lights. Roadside assistance in Italy is excellent on the well-maintained toll roads, but limited on secondary roads.

For specific information concerning Italy's drivers' licenses, vehicle inspection, road tax and mandatory insurance, please contact the Italian Government Tourist Board (ENIT) offices via the Internet at: http://www.enit.it, tel. 212-245-4822 or the A.C.I. (Automobile Club Italiano) at Via Magenta 5, 00185 Rome, tel. 39-06-4477. For information on obtaining international drivers' licenses, please contact AAA or the American Automobile Touring Alliance.

AVIATION SAFETY OVERSIGHT: The U.S. Federal Aviation Administration (FAA) has assessed the Government of Italy's Civil Aviation Authority as Category 1 -- in compliance with international aviation safety standards for oversight of Italy's air carrier operations. For further information, travelers may contact the Department of Transportation within the United States at telephone 1-800-322-7873, or visit the FAA Internet website at http://www.faa.gov/avr/iasa/. The U.S. Department of Defense (DOD) separately assesses some foreign air carriers for suitability as official providers of air services. For information regarding the DOD policy on specific carriers, travelers may contact the DOD at telephone (618) 229-4801.

CUSTOMS REGULATIONS: Italian customs authorities may enforce strict regulations concerning temporary importation into or export

423

from Italy of items such as professional equipment, commercial samples, advertising materials and/or goods for exhibition and fair purposes. Tax-free shopping rules are strictly enforced. Please be sure you have read and understood all the procedures and conditions regarding refunds before purchasing any item. It is advisable to contact the Embassy of Italy in Washington, D.C. or one of Italy's consulates in the United States for specific information regarding customs requirements. The U.S. Customs Service may impose corresponding import restrictions in accordance with the Convention on Cultural Property Implementation Act. (Please contact the Customs Service at telephone 202-927-2336 or Internet http://exchanges.state.gov/education/culprop for further information.)

Italy's customs authorities encourage the use of an ATA (Admission Temporaire/Temporary Admission) Carnet. ATA Carnet Headquarters, located at the U.S. Council for International Business, 1212 Avenue of the Americas, New York, NY 10036, issues and guarantees the ATA Carnet in the United States. For additional information, please call (212) 354- 4480, or send an e-mail to atacarnet@uscib.org, or visit http://www.uscib.org for details.

CRIMINAL PENALTIES: While in a foreign country, a U.S. citizen is subject to that country's laws and regulations, which sometimes differ significantly from those of the United States and may not afford the protections available to the individual under U.S. law. Penalties for breaking the law can be more severe than in the United States for similar offenses. Persons violating Italian law, even unknowingly, may be expelled, arrested or imprisoned. Penalties for possession, use or trafficking in illegal drugs in Italy are strict, and convicted offenders can expect jail sentences and heavy fines.

SPECIAL CIRCUMSTANCES: Strikes and other work stoppages occur frequently in the transportation sector (national airlines, airports, trains, and bus lines). Most are announced in advance and are of short duration. Reconfirmation of domestic and international flight reservations is highly recommended

DISASTER PREPAREDNESS: Several major earthquake fault lines cross Italy. Large Italian

cities do not lie near fault lines, however, smaller tourist cities, such as Assisi do lie near fault lines and have experienced earthquakes. General information about disaster preparedness is available via the Internet from the U.S. Federal Management Agency (FEMA) at http://www.fema.gov. Detailed information on Italy's earthquake fault lines is available from the U.S. Geological Survey (USGS) at http://www.usgs.gov.

Italy also has several active volcanoes generating geothermal events. Mt. Etna, on the eastern tip of the Island of Sicily, has been erupting intermittently since 2000. The eruptions are relatively small in scale. Mt. Vesuvius, located next to Naples, is currently capped and not active. Activity at Mt. Vesuvius is monitored by an active seismic network and sensor system, and no recent seismic activity has been recorded. Two of Italy's smaller islands (Stromboli and Vulcano in the Aeolus Island chain north of Sicily) also have active volcanoes with lava flows. Detailed information on volcano activity in Italy is available from the U.S. Geological Survey (USGS) at http://www.usgs.gov.

CHILDREN'S ISSUES: For information on international adoption of children and international parental child abduction, please refer to our Internet site at http://travel.state.gov/children's_issues.html or telephone (202) 736-7000.

REGISTRATION/EMBASSY AND CONSULATE LOCATIONS: Americans living in or visiting Italy are encouraged to register at the Consular Section of the U.S. Embassy in Rome or at one of the three U.S. Consulates General and obtain updated information on travel and security within Italy.

The U.S. Embassy in Rome is located at Via V. Veneto 119/A. Tel: 39-06-46741 and fax: 39-06-4674-2217. Internet address: http://www.usembassy.it.
The U.S. Consulates are located in:
Florence, at Lungarno Amerigo Vespucci 38. Tel. 39-055-239-8276/7/8/9, or 39-055-217-605; fax: 39-055-284-088.
Milan, at Via Principe Amedeo 2/10. Tel. 39-02-290-351 and fax: 39-02-290-35-273.

Naples, at Piazza della Repubblica. Tel. 39-081-583-8111 and fax: 39-081-761-1804.
There are U.S. Consular Agents located in:
Genoa, at Via Dante 2. Tel. 39-010-584-492 and fax: 39-010- 553-3033.
Palermo, at Via Vaccarini 1. Tel. 39-091-305-857 and fax: 39- 091-625-6026.
Trieste, at Via Roma 15. Tel. 39-040-660-177 and fax: 39-040-631-240.

Luxembourg

COUNTRY DESCRIPTION: Luxembourg is a highly developed stable constitutional monarchy. Tourist facilities are widely available.

ENTRY REQUIREMENTS: A passport is required. A visa is not required for American citizens for business or tourist stays of up to 90 days. For further information concerning entry requirements for Luxembourg, travelers can contact the Embassy of Luxembourg at 2200 Massachusetts Avenue, NW, Washington, D.C. 20008, Tel. (202) 265-4171 or 4172, or the Luxembourg consulates general in New York Tel: (212) 888-6664 or San Francisco Tel: (415) 788-0816.

In an effort to prevent international child abduction, many governments have initiated procedures at entry/exit points. These often include requiring documentary evidence of relationship and permission for the child's travel from the parent(s) or legal guardian if not present. Having such documentation on hand, even if not required, may facilitate entry/departure.

CRIME: The crime rate in Luxembourg is generally low. However, travelers should take common-sense precautions while in Luxembourg. In particular, travelers should be especially cautious while in airports and train terminals, where pickpockets can be a problem.

The loss or theft abroad of a U.S. passport should be reported immediately to the local police and the nearest embassy or consulate. Embassy staff can, for example, assist you to find appropriate medical care, to contact family members or friends and explain how funds could be transferred. Although the investigation and prosecution of the crime is solely the responsibility of local authorities, consular officers can help you to understand the local criminal justice process and to find an attorney if needed.

U.S. citizens can refer to the Department of State's pamphlet, *A Safe Trip Abroad*, for ways to promote a trouble-free journey. The pamphlet is available from the Superintendent of Documents, U.S. Government Printing Office, Washington, D.C. 20402, via the Internet at http://www.access.gpo.gov/su docs, or via the Bureau of Consular Affairs home page at http://travel.state.gov/.

MEDICAL FACILITIES: Medical facilities are available, but may be limited outside urban areas.

MEDICAL INSURANCE: The Department of State strongly urges Americans to consult with their medical insurance company prior to traveling abroad to confirm whether their policy applies overseas and if it will cover emergency expenses such as a medical evacuation. U.S. medical insurance plans seldom cover health costs incurred outside the United States unless supplemental coverage is purchased. Further, U.S. Medicare and Medicaid programs do not provide payment for medical services outside the United States. However, many travel agents and private companies offer insurance plans that will cover health care expenses incurred overseas including emergency services such as medical evacuations.

When making a decision regarding health insurance, Americans should consider that many foreign doctors and hospitals require payment in cash prior to providing service and that a medical evacuation to the U.S. may cost well in excess of $50,000. Uninsured travelers who require medical care overseas often face extreme difficulties. When consulting with your insurer prior to your trip, ascertain whether payment will be made to the overseas healthcare provider or if you will be reimbursed later for expenses you incur. Some insurance policies also include coverage for psychiatric treatment and for disposition of remains in the event of death.

Useful information on medical emergencies abroad, including overseas insurance programs, is provided in the Department of State's Bureau of Consular Affairs brochure, *Medical Information*

425

for Americans Traveling Abroad, available via the Bureau of Consular Affairs home page or autofax: (202) 647-3000.

OTHER HEALTH INFORMATION: Information on vaccinations and other health precautions, such as safe food and water precautions and insect bite protection, may be obtained from the Centers for Disease Control and Prevention's hotline for international travelers at 1-877-FYI-TRIP (1-877-394-8747); fax 1-888-CDC-FAXX (1-888-232-3299), or via the CDC's Internet site at http://www.cdc.gov/travel. For information about outbreaks of infectious diseases abroad, consult the World Health Organization's Internet site at http://www.who.int/en. Further health information for travelers is available at http://www.who.int/ith.

TRAFFIC SAFETY AND ROAD CONDITIONS: While in a foreign country, U.S. citizens may encounter road conditions that differ significantly from those in the United States. The information below concerning Luxembourg is provided for general reference only, and may not be totally accurate in a particular location or circumstance.
Safety of Public Transportation: Good
Urban Road Conditions/Maintenance: Good
Rural Road Conditions/Maintenance: Good
Availability of Roadside Assistance: Good

Luxembourg has a modern, well-maintained system of highways and secondary roads. In mountainous areas, winding roads and cyclists sometimes slow traffic, and roads can be congested during rush hour in the Luxembourg City environs. Visitors should drive defensively in high-volume commuter and tourist traffic, or during winter fog and ice.

For additional general information about road safety, including links to foreign government sites, see the Department of State, Bureau of Consular Affairs home page at http://travel.state.gov/road_safety.html. For specific information concerning Luxembourg driver's permits, vehicle inspection, road tax and mandatory insurance contact the Luxembourg National Tourist Office in New York at 212-935-8888, or via the Internet at http://www.visitluxembourg.com/. For international driving permits (IDPs) contact the

American Automobile Association (AAA) at http://www.aaa.com/ or call the American Automobile Touring Alliance (AATA) at 1-800-622-7070.

AVIATION SAFETY OVERSIGHT: The U.S. Federal Aviation Administration (FAA) has assessed Luxembourg Civil Aviation Authority as category 1 --in compliance with international aviation safety standards for oversight of Luxembourg's air carrier operations. For further information, travelers may contact the Department of Transportation within the U.S. at 1-800-322-7873, or visit the FAA's Internet website at http://www.faa.gov/avr/iasa.

The U.S. Department of Defense (DOD) separately assesses some foreign air carriers for suitability as official providers of air services. For information regarding the DOD policy on specific carriers, travelers may contact DOD at (618) 229-4801.

CUSTOMS REGULATIONS: Luxembourg customs authorities encourage the use of an ATA (Admission Temporaire/Temporary Admission) Carnet for the temporary admission of professional equipment, commercial samples, and/or goods for exhibitions and fair purposes. ATA Carnet Headquarters, located at the U.S. Council for International Business, 1212 Avenue of the Americas, New York, NY 10036, issues and guarantees the ATA Carnet in the United States. For additional information call (212) 354-4480, send an e-mail to mailto:atacarnet@uscib.org, or visit http://www.uscib.org/ for details.

CRIMINAL PENALTIES: While in a foreign country, U.S. citizens are subject to that country's laws and regulations, which sometimes differ significantly from those in the United States and may not afford the protections available to the individual under U.S. law. Penalties for breaking the law can be more severe than in the United States for similar offenses. Persons violating Luxembourg law, even unknowingly, may be expelled, arrested or imprisoned. Penalties for possession, use, or trafficking in illegal drugs in Luxembourg are strict and convicted offenders can expect jail sentences and heavy fines.

CHILDREN'S ISSUES: For information on international adoption of children and international parental child abduction, please refer to our Internet site at http://travel.state.gov/children's_issues or call (202) 736-7000.

REGISTRATION AND EMBASSY LOCATION: Americans living in or visiting Luxembourg are encouraged to register with the Consular Section of the U.S. Embassy in Luxembourg to obtain updated information on travel and security within Luxembourg. The U.S. Embassy is located at 22 Boulevard Emmanuel Servais in Luxembourg City, tel: (352) 46-01-23 extension 213 (2:00 - 5:00pm), fax: (352) 46-19-39, email: mailto:usconsul@pt.lu. The Embassy's Internet address is http://www.amembassy.lu/.

Switzerland and Liechtenstein

COUNTRY DESCRIPTIONS: Switzerland is a highly developed democracy. Liechtenstein is a democratically run constitutional monarchy.

ENTRY REQUIREMENTS: A passport is required for travel to both Switzerland and Liechtenstein. A visa is not required for U.S. citizens for stays of up to 90 days in either country. For more information on entry requirements for both countries, travelers may contact the Embassy of Switzerland at 2900 Cathedral Avenue, N.W., Washington, D.C. 20008, telephone (202) 745-7900, or the nearest Swiss Consulate General in Atlanta, Chicago, Houston, Los Angeles, New York, or San Francisco. Additional information for both countries is available at http://www.swissemb.org.

In an effort to prevent international child abduction, many governments have initiated new procedures at entry/exit points. These procedures often include requiring documentary evidence of relationship and permission for a child to travel, if the parent(s) or legal guardian is not present. Having such documentation on hand, even if not required, may facilitate entry/departure.

DUAL NATIONALITY: U.S. citizens who are also considered by the Swiss Government to have Swiss citizenship may be subject to compulsory military service and other requirements while in Switzerland. Those who might be affected should inquire at a Swiss Embassy or Consulate regarding their status. In some instances, dual nationality may hamper U.S. government efforts to provide protection abroad. In addition to being subject to all Swiss laws affecting U.S. citizens, dual nationals may also be subject to other laws that impose special obligations on Swiss citizens. For additional information, see the Consular Affairs home page on the Internet at http://travel.state.gov for our *Dual Nationality flyer.*

CRIME: Switzerland has a low rate of violent crime. However, pick-pocketing and purse snatching do occur in the vicinity of train and bus stations, airports, and some public parks, especially during peak tourist periods (such as summer and Christmas) and when conferences, shows, or exhibits are scheduled in major cities. Liechtenstein has a low crime rate.

Travelers may wish to exercise caution on trains, especially on overnight trains to neighboring countries. Even locked sleeping compartments can be entered by thieves, who steal from passengers while they sleep. The loss or theft abroad of a U.S. passport should be reported immediately to the local police and the nearest U.S. Embassy or Consulate. U.S. citizens may refer to the Department of State's pamphlet, *A Safe Trip Abroad* to promote a more trouble-free journey. The pamphlet is available from the Superintendent of Documents, U.S. Government Printing Office, Washington, D.C. 20402, and via the Internet at http://www.access.gpo.gov/su docs, or via the Bureau of Consular Affairs home page at http://travel.state.gov.

MEDICAL FACILITIES: Good medical care is widely available. Serious medical problems requiring hospitalization and/or medical evacuation to the United States can cost many thousands of dollars. Doctors and hospitals often expect immediate cash payment for health services.

MEDICAL INSURANCE: The Department of State strongly urges Americans to consult with their medical insurance company prior to traveling abroad to confirm whether their policy applies overseas and whether it will cover emergency expenses such as a medical evacuation. U.S. medical insurance plans seldom cover health costs incurred outside the United States unless supplemental coverage is purchased. Further, U.S. Medicare and Medicaid programs do not provide payment for medical services outside the United States. However, many travel agents and private companies offer insurance plans that will cover health care expenses incurred overseas including emergency services such as medical evacuations.

When making a decision regarding health insurance, Americans should consider that many foreign doctors and hospitals require payment in cash prior to providing service and that a medical evacuation to the U.S. may cost well in excess of $50,000. Uninsured travelers who require medical care overseas often face extreme difficulties. When consulting with your insurer prior to your trip, ascertain whether payment will be made to the overseas healthcare provider or whether you will be reimbursed later for expenses you incur. Some insurance policies also include coverage for psychiatric treatment and for disposition of remains in the event of death.

Supplemental medical insurance with specific overseas coverage, including provision for mountain rescue and/or medical evacuation, is strongly advised, particularly for those who plan to participate in mountain activities (summer or winter). Rescue insurance is available inexpensively in Switzerland. Information can be obtained from the Swiss National Tourist Office or the U.S. Embassy in Bern. Such insurance has proved useful as uninsured rescues can easily cost $25,000 or more.

Useful information on medical emergencies abroad, including overseas insurance programs, is provided in the Department of State's Bureau of Consular Affairs brochure, *Medical Information for Americans Traveling Abroad*, available via the Bureau of Consular Affairs home page or autofax: (202) 647-3000.

OTHER HEALTH INFORMATION: Information on vaccinations and other health precautions may be obtained from the Centers for Disease Control and Prevention's hotline for International Travelers at 1-877-FYI-TRIP (1-877-394-8747); fax 1-888-CDC-FAXX (1-888-232-3299), or via their Internet site at http://www.cdc.gov.

TRAFFIC SAFETY AND ROAD CONDITIONS: While in a foreign country, U.S. citizens may encounter road conditions that differ significantly from those in the United States. The information below concerning Switzerland and Liechtenstein is provided for general reference only, and may not be totally accurate in a particular location or circumstance.

Safety of public transportation: Excellent
Urban road conditions/maintenance: Excellent
Rural road conditions/maintenance: Excellent
Availability of roadside assistance: Excellent

Although many roads are mountainous and winding, road safety standards are high. In some mountain areas, vehicle snow chains are required in winter. Road travel can be more dangerous during summer, winter holidays, and Whitsunday weekend (late spring) because of increased traffic. Travel on highways (indicated by green signs with a white highway symbol) requires purchase of a sticker ("vignette") which must be affixed to the car's windshield. Vignettes can be purchased at most border crossing points and at Swiss post offices. Drivers using the highway system without a vignette are subject to hefty fines levied on the spot. All forms of public transportation in Switzerland and Liechtenstein are generally excellent.

AVIATION SAFETY OVERSIGHT: The U.S. Federal Aviation Administration (FAA) has assessed the Swiss civil aviation authority's oversight of Switzerland's air carrier operations as category 1 -- in compliance with international aviation safety standards.. For further information, travelers may contact the Department of Transportation within the U.S. at 1-800-322-7873, or visit the FAA Internet website at http://www.faa.gov/ avr/iasa/index/htm. The U.S. Department of Defense (DOD) separately assesses some foreign air carriers for suitability as official providers of air services. For information regarding the DOD policy on specific carriers, travelers may contact the Pentagon at 703-697-7288.

CUSTOMS REGULATIONS: Switzerland's customs authorities encourage the use of an ATA (Admission Temporair/Temporary Admission) Carnet for the temporary admission of professional equipment, commercial samples, and/or goods for exhibitions and fair purposes. ATA Carnet

Headquarters, located at the U.S. Council for International Business, 1212 Avenue of the Americas, New York, N.Y. 10036, issues and guarantees the ATA Carnet in the United States. For additional information call 212-354-4480, send an e-mail to atacarnet@uscib.org, or visit http://www.uscib.org for details.

CRIMINAL PENALTIES: U.S. citizens are subject to the laws of the country in which they are traveling. Sometimes these laws can differ significantly from those in the United States and may not afford the protections available to individuals under U.S. law. Penalties for breaking the law can be more severe than in the United States for similar offenses. In Switzerland and Liechtenstein, penalties for possession, use, and dealing in illegal drugs are strict, and convicted offenders can expect jail sentences and heavy fines.

CHILDREN'S ISSUES: For information on the international adoption of children, international parental child abduction, and international child support enforcement issues, please refer to our Internet site at http://travel.state.gov/childrens_issues.html or tel. (202) 736-7000.

REGISTRATION AND EMBASSY AND CONSULATE LOCATIONS: U.S. citizens may register and obtain updated information on travel and security within Switzerland at the locations below:

The U.S. Embassy in Bern is located at Jubilaeumsstrasse 93,Telephone (41)(31) 357-7011, FAX (41)(31) 357-7280.

The 24 hours emergency telephone number is (41)(31) 357-7218. The U.S. Embassy website at http://www.us-embassy.ch answers many questions of interest to Americans visiting and residing in Switzerland.

The U.S. Consular Agency in Zurich is located at the American Center of Zurich, Dufourstrasse 101, 8008 Zurich, telephone (41)(1) 422-2566, FAX(41) (1) 383-9814.

The U.S. Consular Agency in Geneva is located at the American Center Geneva, 7 Rue Versonnex, 1207 Geneva, telephone (41)(22) 840-5160, fax (41)(22) 840-5162.

U.S. Consular Agencies offer limited consular services to U.S. citizens.

There is no U.S. Embassy or Consulate in Liechtenstein. For assistance and information on travel and security in Liechtenstein, U.S. citizens may contact or register at the U.S. Embassy in Bern at the address above.

The Netherlands

COUNTRY DESCRIPTION: The Netherlands is a highly-developed, stable democracy.

ENTRY REQUIREMENTS: A passport is required. A visa is not required for U.S. citizens for visits up to 90 days. For further information on entry requirements for the Netherlands, travelers may contact the Embassy of The Netherlands at 4200 Linnean Avenue, N.W., Washington, D.C. 20008, telephone (202) 244-5300, or the Dutch consulate in Chicago, Houston, Los Angeles, New York, or San Francisco. Additional information is available at http://www.netherlands-embassy.org and the National Bureau for Tourism in New York at http://www.goholland.com.

In an effort to prevent international child abduction, many governments have initiated procedures at entry/exit points. These often include requiring documentary evidence of relationship and permission for the child's travel from the parent(s) or legal guardian not present. Having such documentation on hand, even if not required, may facilitate entry/departure.

SAFETY AND SECURITY: Prior police approval is required for public demonstrations in the Netherlands, and police oversight is routinely provided to ensure adequate security for participants and passers-by. Nonetheless, situations may develop which could pose a threat to public safety. U.S. citizens are advised to avoid areas in which public demonstrations are taking place.

CRIME: While the rate of violent crime in the Netherlands is low, tourists are occasionally targeted, usually in conjunction with robbery attempts. Visitors to larger cities frequently fall prey to pickpockets, bag snatchers, and other petty thieves. Visitors should never leave baggage or other valuables unattended.

While thieves may operate anywhere, the U.S. Consulate General in Amsterdam receives frequent reports of thefts from several specific areas. The train from Schiphol Airport to Amsterdam Central Station is particularly plagued by thieves, who often work in pairs. In those instances, one thief distracts the victim, often by asking for directions, while an accomplice moves in on the victim's momentarily unguarded handbag, backpack, laptop or briefcase. The thieves typically time their thefts to coincide with train stops so they may quickly exit. Within Amsterdam, thieves are very active in and around train and tram stations, the city center and public transport.

Advance Fee Fraud: Confidence artists have victimized a number of Americans. Typically, this involves the U.S. citizen being contacted in the United States and advised of an inheritance or other offer - often originating in Africa - that requires their assistance and cooperation to conclude. The American is requested to forward advance payments for alleged "official expenses" and often asked to come to Amsterdam to conclude the operation. Several Americans have lost tens of thousands of dollars in such scams. For further information, please contact the nearest office of the United States Secret Service and/or the Fraud Unit, Amsterdam Police, Police Headquarters, PB 2287, 1000 CG Amsterdam, Netherlands, tel. 559-2380, fax 559-5755.

The loss or theft abroad of a U.S. passport should be reported immediately to local police and the nearest U.S. embassy or consulate. If you are the victim of a crime while overseas, in addition to reporting to local police, please contact the nearest U.S. embassy or consulate for assistance. The Embassy/Consulate staff can, for example, assist you to find appropriate medical care, to contact family members or friends and explain how funds could be transferred. Although the investigation and prosecution of the crime is solely the responsibility of local authorities, consular officers can help you to understand the local criminal justice process and to find an attorney if needed.

If your U.S. passport is lost or stolen while you are in the Netherlands, please contact the U.S. Consulate General in Amsterdam for information about passport replacement. U.S. citizens may refer to the Department of State's pamphlet, A Safe Trip Abroad, for ways to promote a more trouble-free journey. The pamphlet is available by mail from the Superintendent of Documents, U.S. Government Printing Office, Washington, D.C. 20402, via the Internet at http://www.access.gpo.gov/su_docs, or via the Bureau of Consular Affairs home page at http://travel.state.gov.

MEDICAL FACILITIES AND INSURANCE: Good medical facilities are widely available. The Department of State strongly urges Americans to consult with their medical insurance company prior to traveling abroad to confirm whether their policy applies overseas and if it will cover emergency expenses such as a medical evacuation. U.S. medical insurance plans seldom cover health costs incurred outside the United States unless supplemental coverage is purchased. Further, U.S. Medicare and Medicaid programs do not provide payment for medical services outside the United States. However, many travel agents and private companies offer insurance plans that will cover health care expenses incurred overseas, including emergency services such as medical evacuations.

When making a decision regarding health insurance, Americans should consider that many foreign doctors and hospitals require payment in cash prior to providing service and that a medical evacuation to the United States may cost well in excess of $50,000. Uninsured travelers who require medical care overseas often face extreme difficulties, whereas travelers who have purchased overseas medical insurance have found it to be life-saving when a medical emergency has occurred. When consulting with your insurer prior to your trip, please ascertain whether payment will be made to the overseas healthcare provider or if you will be reimbursed later for expenses that you incur. Some insurance policies also include coverage for psychiatric treatment and for disposition of remains in the event of death.

Useful information on medical emergencies abroad, including overseas insurance programs, is provided in the Department of State's Bureau of Consular Affairs brochure, *Medical Information for Americans Traveling Abroad*, available via the Bureau of Consular Affairs home page or autofax: (202) 647-3000.

OTHER HEALTH INFORMATION: Travelers should be aware that increasing numbers of illegal drug users, particularly young people, experience unanticipated serious health emergencies, including permanent brain damage and even death, stemming from use of Methylenedioxinmethylamphetamine (MDA), commonly known as Ecstasy or XTC, and other illegal narcotics. Information on vaccinations and other health precautions may be obtained from the Centers for Disease Control and Prevention's hotline for international travelers at 1-877-FYI-TRIP (1-877-394-8747, fax 1-888-CDC-FAXX (1-888-232-3299), or via the CDC's Internet site at http://www.cdc.gov.

TRAFFIC SAFETY AND ROAD CONDITIONS: While in a foreign country, U.S. citizens may encounter road conditions that differ significantly from those in the United States. The information below concerning the Netherlands is provided for general reference only, and it may not be totally accurate in a particular location or circumstance.

Safety of Public Transportation: Excellent
Urban Road Conditions/Maintenance: Excellent
Rural Road Conditions/Maintenance: Excellent
Availability of Roadside Assistance: Excellent

Travel in, around, and between cities is possible through a highly advanced national train, light rail, and tram network, by use of an extensive system of bike paths, and by automobile and motorcycle using the highway system. Rail is often a convenient alternative to driving, particularly in the areas around Amsterdam, The Hague, and Rotterdam, where road congestion is frequent. Rail network information is available at http://www.ns.nl.

Inter-city travel by road is relatively safe, in comparison with some other European countries. Nonetheless, over 1000 people die and another 10,000 are injured from traffic accidents in the Netherlands each year. More than two-thirds of the fatal accidents occur outside urban areas.

Seat belt and child seat use is compulsory. Driving is on the right side of the road. The maximum speed limit on highways is 120 km/h, with a highway speed limit of 100 km/h posted in most urban areas. Secondary roads have a speed limit of 80 km/h. The speed limit in towns and cities is 50 km/h, with 30 km/h posted in residential areas. Drivers must yield the right-of-way to drivers from the right at intersections or traffic circles, unless otherwise posted. The maximum allowable blood alcohol level in the Netherlands is 0.5. Use of cellular telephones while driving is discouraged.

Lanes at the center of many urban two-way streets are reserved for buses, trams, and taxis. In cities, pedestrians should be very mindful of trams, which often cross or share bicycle and pedestrian paths. Motorists must be especially mindful of the priority rights of bicyclists. Pedestrians should also pay particular attention not to walk along bicycle paths, which are often on the sidewalk and usually designated by red pavement.

Taxi service in the Netherlands is safe, but it is expensive. Trams and buses are both convenient and economical, but they are often frequented by pick-pockets.

For additional general information about road safety, including links to foreign government sites, please see the Department of State, Bureau of Consular Affairs home page at http://travel.state.gov/road_safety.html. For specific information concerning the Netherlands, please contact the Netherlands Bureau for Tourism in New York via the Internet at http://www.goholland.com. More information is available from the Netherlands Ministry of Transportation, Public Works, and Water Management (Ministerie van Verkeer en Waterstraat) at http://www.minvenw.nl.

AVIATION SAFETY OVERSIGHT: The U.S. Federal Aviation Administration (FAA) has assessed the Government of the Netherlands' Civil Aviation Authority as Category One -- in compliance with international aviation safety standards for the oversight of the Netherlands' air carrier operations.

For further information, travelers may contact the Department of Transportation at telephone 1 (800) 322-7873, or visit the FAA's Internet web site at http://www.faa.gov/avr/iasa/. The U.S. Department of Defense (DOD) separately assesses some foreign air carriers for suitability as official providers of air services. For information regarding the DOD policy on specific carriers, travelers may contact DOD at tel. (618) 229-4801.

CUSTOMS REGULATIONS: Customs authorities may enforce strict regulations concerning temporary import into the Netherlands of items such as firearms. It is advisable to contact the Embassy of The Netherlands in Washington, D.C. or one of the Dutch Consulates in Chicago, Houston, Los Angeles, or New York for specific information regarding customs requirements.

Dutch customs authorities encourage the use of an ATA (Admission Temporaire/Temporary Admission) Carnet for the temporary admission of professional equipment, commercial samples, and/or goods for exhibitions and fair purposes. ATA Carnet headquarters, located at the U.S. Council for International Business, 1212 Avenue of the Americas, New York, N.Y. 10036, issues and guarantees the ATA Carnet in the United States. For additional information, please call tel. (212) 354-4480, send an e-mail to atacarnet@uscib.org, or visit http://www.uscib.org for details.

CRIMINAL PENALTIES: While in a foreign country, a U.S. citizen is subject to that country's laws and regulations, which sometimes differ significantly from those in the United States and may not afford the protections available to the individual under U.S. law. Penalties for breaking the law can be more severe than in the United States for similar offenses. Persons violating Dutch laws, even unknowingly, may be expelled, arrested or imprisoned. Drug possession and trafficking are illegal in the Netherlands.

CHILDREN'S ISSUES: For information on international adoption of children and international parental child abduction, please refer to our Internet site at http://travel.state.gov/children's_issues.html or telephone (202) 736-7000.

REGISTRATION/EMBASSY AND CONSULATE LOCATION: Americans living in or visiting the Netherlands are encouraged to register at the Consulate General in Amsterdam and obtain updated information on travel and security within the Netherlands. The U.S. Embassy is located in The Hague, at Lange Voorhout 102; telephone (31)(20) 310-9209. However, all requests for consular assistance

should be directed to the Consulate General in Amsterdam at Museumplein 19, telephone

(31)(20) 664-5661, (31)(20) 679-0321, or (31)(20) 575-5309. The after-hours emergency telephone number is (31)(70) 310-9499. The U.S. Embassy and Consulate General website at http://www.usembassy.nl answers many questions of interest to Americans visiting or residing in the Netherlands.

New Zealand

COUNTRY DESCRIPTION: New Zealand is a highly developed, stable parliamentary democracy, which recognizes the British monarch as sovereign. It has a modern economy, and tourist facilities are widely available. The New Zealand Tourist Board, which has a wide range of information of interest to travelers, can be contacted via the Internet at http://www.newzealandtourism.com.

ENTRY REQUIREMENTS: U.S. citizens eligible for a visa waiver do not need a visa for tourist stays of three months or less. For more information about visa waivers and entry requirements, please contact the Embassy of New Zealand, 37 Observatory Circle, N.W., Washington, D.C. 20008, telephone (202) 328-4800, or the Embassy's home page at http://www.nzemb.org, or the Consulate General of New Zealand in Los Angeles, telephone (310) 207-1605.

CRIME INFORMATION: Crime in New Zealand is comparatively low, but it has increased in recent years. The most prevalent crime is theft or attempted theft from cars, camper vans and hostels. To help protect against theft, please do not leave passports or other valuable documents in unattended vehicles. Violent crime against tourists is unusual.

The loss or theft abroad of a U.S. passport should be reported immediately to the local police, and the nearest U.S. embassy or consulate. If you are the victim of a crime while overseas, in addition to reporting to local police, please contact the nearest U.S. embassy or consulate for assistance. The embassy/consulate staff can, for example, assist you to find appropriate medical care, to contact family members or friends and explain how funds could be transferred. Although the investigation and prosecution of the crime is solely the responsibility of local authorities, consular officers can help you to understand the local criminal justice process and to find an attorney if needed.

U.S. citizens may refer to the Department of State's pamphlet, *A Safe Trip Abroad*, for ways to promote a more trouble-free journey. The pamphlet is available by mail from the Superintendent of Documents, U.S. Government Printing Office, Washington, D.C. 20402, via the Internet at http://www.access.gpo.gov/su_docs or via the Bureau of Consular Affairs home page at http://travel.state.gov.

MEDICAL FACILITIES: Quality medical care is widely available, but waiting lists exist for certain types of treatment. Serious medical problems requiring hospitalization and/or medical evacuation to the United States can cost thousands of dollars. Doctors and hospitals often expect immediate cash payment for health services.

MEDICAL INSURANCE: U.S. medical insurance is not always valid outside the United States. U.S. Medicare and Medicaid programs do not provide payment for medical services outside theUnited States. Uninsured travelers who require medical care overseas may face extreme difficulties. Please check with your own insurance company to confirm whether your policy applies overseas, including provisions for medical evacuation. Please ascertain whether payment will be made to the overseas hospital or doctor or if you will be reimbursed later for expenses that you incur. Some insurance policies also include coverage for psychiatric treatment and for disposition of remains in the event of death. Useful information on medical emergencies abroad, including overseas insurance programs, is provided in the Department of State's Bureau of Consular Affairs brochure,*Medical Information for Americans Traveling Abroad*, available via the Bureau of Consular Affairs home page.

OTHER HEALTH INFORMATION: Information on vaccinations and other health precautions may be obtained from the Centers for Disease Control and Prevention's hotline for international travelers at 1-877-FYI-TRIP (1-877-394-8747); fax 1-888-CDC-FAXX (1-888-232-3299), or via the CDC's Internet site at http://www.cdc.gov.

TRAFFIC SAFETY AND ROAD CONDITIONS: While in a foreign country, U.S. citizens may encounter road conditions that differ significantly from those in the United States. The information below concerning New Zealand is provided for general reference only, and it may not be totally accurate in a particular location or circumstance:

Safety of Public Transportation: Good
Urban Road Conditions/Maintenance: Good
Rural Road Conditions/Maintenance: Good
Availability of Roadside Assistance: Good

All traffic travels on the left side of the road in New Zealand, and many roads have only two lanes. Drivers should exercise extra caution if accustomed to driving on the right side of the road. Cars turning left must yield to oncoming cars turning in the same direction. This is especially important to remember on two-lane roads. Travelers should proceed carefully through intersections and be wary of drivers who may run yellow and red lights. Drivers should use caution to avoid animals when driving in rural areas. Pedestrians are advised to look carefully in all directions before crossing a street or roadway, and to use crosswalks. Traffic always yields to the right, and pedestrians do not have the right of way except at crosswalks.

For specific information concerning the operation and rental of motor vehicles, please contact the New Zealand Tourist Board via the Internet at http://www.newzealandtourism.com or the Land Transport Safety Authority at http://www.ltsa.govt.nz.

AVIATION OVERSIGHT: The U.S. Federal Aviation Administration (FAA) has assessed the government of New Zealand's civil aviation authority as category 1 - in compliance with international aviation standards for oversight of New Zealand's air carrier operations. For further information, travelers may contact the Department of Transportation in the United States at telephone 1-800-322-7873, or visit the FAA's Internet web site at http://www.faa.gov/avr/iasa/. The U.S. Department of Defense (DOD) separately assesses some foreign air carriers for suitability as official providers of air services. For information regarding the DOD policy on specific carriers, travelers may contact the DOD at telephone (618) 229-4801.

CUSTOMS REGULATIONS: New Zealand's customs authorities may enforce strict regulations concerning temporary importation into or export from New Zealand of certain items, including firearms and agricultural products. Handguns may not be brought into the country, and a permit for other firearms must be obtained from the New Zealand police immediately after arrival. Tourists have also faced police inquiries as a result of importing or brandishing toy weapons. The Ministry of Agriculture of New Zealand has stringent requirements for the entry of food and agricultural products. Travelers are required to declare any items that come under agricultural quarantine restrictions as stated on the customs form at the port of entry. Heavy fines have been levied against those attempting to bring in undeclared prohibited items. For more information, please contact the New Zealand Customs Service at http://www.customs.govt.nz and the Ministry of Agriculture and Forestry at http://www.maf.govt.nz. It is also advisable to contact the Embassy of New Zealand in Washington, D.C. at telephone (202) 775-5200, or one of New Zealand's consulates in the United States, for specific information regarding customs requirements.

New Zealand Customs officials encourage the use of an ATA (Admission Temporaire/Temporary Admission) Carnet for the temporary admission of professional equipment, commercial samples, and/or goods for exhibitions and fair purposes. ATA Carnet Headquarters, located at the U.S. Council for International Business, 1212 Avenue of the Americas, New York, NY 10036, issues and guarantees the ATA Carnet in the United States. For additional information, please call (212) 354-4480 or send an e-mail to atacarnet@uscib.org or visit their web site at http://www.uscib.org.

CRIMINAL PENALTIES: While in a foreign country, a U.S. citizen is subject to that country's laws and regulations, which sometimes differ significantly from those in the United States and do not always afford the protections available to the individual under U.S. law. Penalties for breaking the law can be more severe than in the United States for similar offenses. Persons violating New Zealand's laws, even unknowingly, may be expelled, arrested or imprisoned. Penalties for possession, use, or trafficking of illegal drugs in New Zealand are strict, and convicted offenders can expect jail sentences and fines. Vessels used to import or convey prohibited drugs are liable to seizure.

If you are the victim of a crime while overseas, in addition to reporting to local police, please contact the nearest U.S. embassy or consulate for assistance. The Embassy/Consulate staff can, for example, assist you to find appropriate medical care and contact family members or friends, and explain how funds could be transferred. Although the investigation and prosecution of the crime is solely the responsibility of local authorities, consular officers can help you to understand the local criminal justice process and to find an attorney if needed.

SPECIAL CIRCUMSTANCES: In 1998, a New Zealand court ruled that Section 21 of the New Zealand Maritime and Transportation Act of 1994 does not require foreign-flagged pleasure craft to pass a safety inspection before setting sail from New Zealand. Nevertheless, New Zealand's Director of Maritime Safety urges the owners of such craft to ensure that they are adequately equipped and have sufficient crew for an ocean voyage. In particular, carrying an Electronic Position Indicating Radio Beacon (EPIRB) is recommended.

DISASTER PREPAREDNESS: Some heavily populated parts of New Zealand are located in an area of very high seismic activity. Although the probability of a major earthquake taking place during an individual trip is remote, earthquakes can and do occur. General information regarding disaster preparedness is available via the Internet at http://travel.state.gov/crisismg.html, and from the U.S. Federal Emergency Management Agency (FEMA) home page at http://www.fema.gov.

CHILDREN'S ISSUES: For information on international adoption of children or international parental child abduction, please refer to our Internet site at

http://travel.state.gov/children's_issues.html   or
telephone (202) 736-7000.

REGISTRATION/U.S. EMBASSY AND CONSULATE GENERAL LOCATIONS: Americans living in or visiting New Zealand are encouraged to register at the Consular Section of the U.S. Consulate General in Auckland by mail, phone, fax or in person, where they can obtain updated information on travel and security.

The U.S. Consulate General in Auckland is located on the third floor of the Citibank Centre, 23 Customs Street East, between Commerce and Queen Streets. The telephone number is (64)(9) 303-2724. The fax number is (64-9) 366-0870. Please see also the Consulate General home page via the Internet at http://www.usembassy.org.nz.

The U.S. Embassy is located at 29 Fitzherbert Terrace, Thorndon, Wellington; the telephone number is (64)(4) 462-6000. The fax number is (64)(4) 471-2380.

For after-hours emergencies anywhere in New Zealand, a duty officer can be contacted by telephone. Persons seeking such assistance after hours may call (64)(4) 462-6000; after listening to a brief recording, the caller may leave a message on the voice mail system, describing the nature of the emergency and giving a point of contact. The phone system will automatically call the duty officer in Wellington or in Auckland, who will listen to the message and take the appropriate action.

Norway

COUNTRY DESCRIPTION: Norway is a highly developed stable democracy with a modern economy. The cost of living in Norway is high, and tourist facilities are well developed and widely available. Tourism to Norway is increasing, and outdoor activities are popular. English is a popular second language in Norway. Additional information about Norway is available at http://www.usa.no.

ENTRY REQUIREMENTS: A valid passport is required. U.S. citizens may enter Norway for tourist or general business purposes without a visa

for up to 90 days. Since March 2001, Norwegian entry visas are governed by the rules of the Schengen Agreement. Under this agreement, a visa issued for admission to most European Union (EU) countries (including non EU members Norway and Iceland) is also valid for admission to other member countries. EU members Ireland and the United Kingdom have opted not to participate in the Schengen arrangement at this time. Under Schengen visa procedures, a tourist is only permitted to spend a total of three months in the "Schengen area" within any six month period.

Tourists who enter Norway without a visa cannot usually change status in Norway in order to reside or work there. Travelers planning a long-term stay, marriage or employment in Norway should therefore seek the appropriate visa before departing the United States. For information concerning entry requirements, travelers can contact the Royal Norwegian Embassy at 2720 34th Street, N.W., Washington, D.C. 20008-2714, tel. 1-202-333-6000, or the nearest Norwegian consulate; and on the Internet at http://www.norway.org. Norwegian consulates are located in Houston, Miami, Minneapolis, New York City, and San Francisco. Information can also be obtained from the Norwegian Directorate of Immigration at http://www.udi.no.

Travelers should also be aware that in an effort to prevent international child abduction, many governments have initiated procedures at entry/exit points which often include requiring documentary evidence of relationship and permission for the child's travel from the parent(s) or legal guardian not present. Having such documentation on hand, even if not required, may facilitate entry/departure.

DUAL NATIONALITY: In addition to being subject to all Norwegian laws affecting U.S. citizens, dual nationals may also be subject to other laws that impose special obligations on Norwegian citizens. For additional information, please see the Consular Affairs home page on the Internet at http://travel.state.gov for our *Dual Nationality* information leaflet.

SAFETY AND SECURITY: The threat Americans face from political violence and terrorism in Norway is low. Anti-American sentiments are most commonly expressed in small, planned, usually peaceful demonstrations against a particular U.S. policy. These protests are most often staged near the American Embassy or in central areas of Oslo, and they target specific official U.S. Government policies rather than U.S. citizens.

CRIME INFORMATION: Norway has a relatively low crime rate. Most crimes involve the theft of personal property. Residential burglaries, auto theft, and vandalism to parked cars can also occur. Most high-end value vehicles, especially in Oslo, have visible alarm system indicators to discourage joy-riders or thieves. Persons who appear affluent or disoriented may become targets of pickpockets and purse-snatchers, especially during the peak tourist seasons (May-September). Thieves frequently target tourists in hotels, particularly lobby/reception and restaurant areas. Often, such thieves work in pairs, and use distraction as a method to steal purses or briefcases. While passports are frequently stolen in the course of these thefts, money, credit cards and jewelry are the actual objects of interest. In some cases, stolen passports are recovered. Violent crime, although rare, occurs and appears to be increasing. Some thieves or burglars may have weapons.

The loss or theft abroad of a U.S. passport should be reported immediately to the local police and the nearest U.S. embassy or consulate. U.S. citizens may refer to the Department of State's pamphlet, *A Safe Trip Abroad*, for ways to promote a more trouble-free journey. The pamphlet is available by mail from the Superintendent of Documents, U.S. Government Printing Office, Washington, D.C. 20402, via the Internet at http://www.access.gpo.gov/su_docs, or via the Bureau of Consular Affairs home page at http://travel.state.gov.

MEDICAL FACILITIES: Medical facilities are widely available and of high quality, but they may be limited outside the larger urban areas. The remote and sparse populations in northern Norway, and the dependency on ferries to cross fjords of western Norway, may affect transportation and ready access to medical facilities. The U.S. Embassy in Oslo maintains a list of emergency clinics in major cities.

MEDICAL INSURANCE: The Department of State strongly urges Americans to consult with their medical insurance company prior to traveling abroad to confirm whether their policy applies overseas and if it will cover emergency expenses such as a medical evacuation. U.S. medical insurance plans seldom cover health costs incurred outside the United States unless supplemental coverage is purchased. Further, U.S. Medicare and Medicaid programs do not provide payment for medical services outside the United States. However, many travel agents and private companies offer insurance plans that will cover health care expenses incurred overseas, including emergency services such as medical evacuations.

When making a decision regarding health insurance, Americans should consider that many foreign doctors and hospitals require payment in cash prior to providing service and that a medical evacuation to the United States may cost well in excess of $50,000. Uninsured travelers who require medical care overseas often face extreme difficulties. When consulting with your insurer prior to your trip, please ascertain whether payment will be made to the overseas healthcare provider or if you will be reimbursed later for expenses that you incur. Some insurance policies also include coverage for psychiatric treatment and for disposition of remains in the event of death.

Useful information on medical emergencies abroad, including overseas insurance programs, is provided in the Department of State's Bureau of Consular Affairs brochure, *Medical Information for Americans Traveling Abroad*, available via the Bureau of Consular Affairs home page or autofax: (202) 647-3000.

OTHER HEALTH INFORMATION: Information on vaccinations and other health precautions may be obtained from the Centers for Disease Control and Prevention's hotline for international travelers at 1-877-FYI-TRIP (1-877-394-8747); fax 1-888-CDC-FAXX (1-888-232-3299), or via the CDC's Internet site at http://www.cdc.gov.

TRAFFIC SAFETY AND ROAD CONDITIONS: While in a foreign country, U.S. citizens may encounter road conditions that differ significantly from those in the United States. The information below concerning Norway is provided for general reference only, and it may not be totally accurate in a particular location or circumstance.

Safety of Public Transportation: Good
Urban Road Conditions/Maintenance: Good
Rural Road Conditions/Maintenance: Fair
Availability of roadside assistance: Fair

Public transportation in Norway is generally safe, and the maintenance and condition of urban roads are generally good. Rural road conditions are fair, and the availability of roadside assistance is limited. The roadway system beyond Oslo's limits and other major cities tends to be simple two-lane roads. In mountainous areas of Norway, the roads also tend to be narrow and winding, and there are many tunnels. The northerly latitude can also cause road conditions to vary greatly depending on weather and time of year. Many mountain roads are closed due to snow from late fall to late spring. The use of winter tires is mandatory on all motor vehicles from November to April.

Norwegian law requires that drivers always use their vehicle headlights when driving. Norwegian law also requires drivers to yield to vehicles coming from the right. In some, but not all, instances, major roads with "right of way" are marked. Seat belts are mandatory for drivers and passengers. The maximum legal blood alcohol content level for driving a car in Norway is 0.2 per   cent.

Automatic cameras placed by the police along roadways help to maintain speed limits, which are often lower than in other European countries. Frequent road checks with mandatory breathalyzer tests and the promise of stiff jail sentences encourage alcohol-free driving.

For additional general information about road safety, including links to foreign government sites, please see the Department of State, Bureau of Consular Affairs home page at http://travel.state.gov/road_safety.html. For specific information concerning Norwegian driver's permits, vehicle inspection, road tax and mandatory insurance, please contact the Norwegian Tourist Board office located at P.O. Box 4649, Grand Central Station, New York, New York 10163-4649 (tel. 212-885-9700; fax - 212/885-9710) or visit their web site on the Internet at http://www.norway.org/travel.

AVIATION SAFETY OVERSIGHT: The U.S. Federal Aviation Administration (FAA) has assessed the Government of Norway's Civil Aviation Authority as Category 1 -- in compliance with international aviation safety standards for oversight of Norway's air carrier operations. For further information, travelers may contact the Department of Transportation within the United States at tel. 1-800-322-7873, or visit the FAA's Internet web site at http://www.faa.gov/avr/iasa.

The U.S. Department of Defense (DOD) separately assesses some foreign air carriers for suitability as official providers of air services. For information regarding the DOD policy on specific carriers, travelers may contact the DOD at tel. (618) 229-4801.

CUSTOMS REGULATIONS: Norway's customs authorities may enforce strict regulations concerning temporary importation into or export from Norway such items as firearms, antiques, etc. It is advisable to contact the Embassy of Norway in Washington, D.C. or one of Norway's consulates in the United States for specific information regarding customs requirements.

Norway's customs authorities encourage the use of an ATA (Admission Temporaire/Temporary Admission) Carnet for the temporary admission of professional equipment, commercial samples, and/or goods for exhibitions and trade fair purposes. ATA Carnet Headquarters located at the U.S. Council for International Business, 1212 Avenue of the Americas, New York, NY 10036, issues and guarantees the ATA Carnet in the United States. For additional information, please call tel. (212) 354-4480, or send an e-mail to atacarnet@uscib.org, or visit http://www.uscib.org for details.

Travelers with pets should note that Norway is a rabies-free country, and they should seek advance information about the strict quarantine requirements for all incoming pets.

CRIMINAL PENALTIES: While in a foreign country, a U.S. citizen is subject to that country's laws and regulations, which sometimes differ significantly from those in the United States and may not afford the protections available to the individual under U.S. law. Penalties for breaking

437

the law can be more severe than in the United States for similar offenses. Persons violating Norway's laws, even unknowingly, may be expelled, arrested or imprisoned. Penalties for possession, use, or trafficking in illegal drugs in Norway are strict, and convicted offenders can expect jail sentences and heavy fines. All controlled substances are prohibited in Norway. The possession of even small amounts of drugs (e.g. marijuana, hashish) can result in arrest in Norway. If drugs or controlled substances are discovered upon one's arrival in Norway, the result can be a charge of importation, which is a more serious crime than simple possession. Penalties usually include detention, a hefty fine and deportation, usually back to the United States.

CHILDREN'S ISSUES: For information on international adoption of children and international parental child abduction, please refer to our Internet site at http://travel.state.gov/children's_issues.html or telephone (202) 736-7000.

REGISTRATION AND EMBASSY LOCATION: Americans living in or visiting Norway are encouraged to register at the Consular Section of the U.S. Embassy and to obtain updated information on travel and security within Norway. The U.S. Embassy is located in Oslo near the Royal Palace at Drammensveien 18; tel. (47) 22-44-85-50, Consular Section fax (47) 22-56-27-51. Information about consular services can be found in the Consular Section of the Embassy's home page at http://www.usa.no.

Portugal

COUNTRY DESCRIPTION: Portugal is a developed and stable democracy with a modern economy. Tourist facilities are widely available.

ENTRY REQUIREMENTS: A passport is required for entry into Portugal. A visa is not required for tourist or business stays of up to 90 days. Portuguese law requires some non-European Union foreign nationals to register with immigration officials within three days of entering Portugal. The law affects those who transit a Schengen country (Austria, Belgium, Denmark,

Finland, France, Germany, Greece, Italy, Luxembourg, Spain, Sweden and The Netherlands) by air en route to Portugal and stay at noncommercial accommodations. For further information concerning entry requirements for Portugal, travelers may contact the Embassy of Portugal at 2125 Kalorama Road N.W., Washington, D.C. 20008, tel. (202) 328-8610, or the Portuguese consulates in Boston, MA; New Bedford, MA; Providence, RI; New York, NY; Newark, NJ; San Francisco, CA; or Los Angeles, CA.

DUAL NATIONALITY: In addition to being subject to all Portuguese laws affecting U.S. citizens, dual nationals may also be subject to other laws that impose special obligations on Portuguese citizens. U.S. citizens who are considered to have acquired Portuguese citizenship may be subject to certain aspects of Portuguese law such as mandatory voting and military service. For additional information, please see the Consular Affairs home page on the Internet at http://travel.state.gov for our flyer on *Dual Nationality*.

CRIME INFORMATION: Though Portugal has a relatively low rate of violent crime, petty crime against tourists is on the rise in continental Portugal. Travelers may become targets of pickpockets and purse-snatchers, particularly at popular tourist sites, restaurants, and on public transportation. Rental cars and vehicles with non-local license plates are targets for break-ins, and travelers should remove all luggage from vehicles upon parking. Travelers should also avoid using automatic teller machines in isolated or poorly lit areas. Drivers in continental Portugal should keep car doors locked when stopped at intersections.

In general, visitors to Portugal should carry limited cash and credit cards, and leave extra cash, credit cards, and personal documents at home or in a hotel safe. While thieves may operate anywhere, the U.S. Embassy receives frequent reports of theft from the following areas:

Lisbon Area: Pick-pocketing and purse-snatching in the Lisbon area occur in buses, restaurants, the airport, trains, train stations, and trams, especially tram number twenty-eight to the Castle of Sao Jorge. Gangs of youths have robbed passengers on the Lisbon-Cascais train. At restaurants, thieves snatch items hung over the backs of chairs or placed on the floor. There have been reports of theft of unattended luggage from the Lisbon Airport. Special care should be taken at the Santa Apolonia and Rosso train stations, the Alfama and Bairro Alto districts, the Castle of Sao Jorge and Belem.

Other Areas: Thefts have been reported in Sintra, Cascais, Mafra and Fatima. Automobile break-ins occur in parking areas at tourist attractions and near restaurants. Special care should be taken in parking at the Moorish Castle and Pena Palace in Sintra; and at the beachfront areas of Quincho, Cabo da Roca, and Boca do Inferno.

Azores: In contrast to continental Portugal, pick-pocketing and purse-snatching are not common occurrences in the Azores. There are no reports of organized crime or gangs.

The loss or theft abroad of a U.S. passport should be reported immediately to the local police and the nearest U.S. embassy or consulate. The emergency number for medical and police assistance is 112. U.S. citizens can refer to the Department of State's pamphlet, *A Safe Trip Abroad*, for ways to promote a more trouble-free journey. The pamphlet is available by mail from the Superintendent of Documents, U.S. Government Printing Office, Washington, D.C. 20402, via the Internet at http://www.access.gpo.gov/su_docs, or via the Bureau of Consular Affairs home page at http://travel.state.gov.

MEDICAL FACILITIES AND INSURANCE: Medical facilities are available in Portugal, but in some cases they may not meet U.S. standards. U.S. medical insurance is not always valid outside the United States. U.S. Medicare and Medicaid programs do not provide payment for medical services outside the United States. Doctors and hospitals often expect immediate cash payment for health services. Uninsured travelers who require health care overseas may face extreme difficulties. Please check with your insurance company to confirm whether your policy applies overseas, including provision for medical evacuation and for adequacy of coverage. Serious medical problems requiring hospitalization and/or medical evacuation to the United States can cost tens of thousands of dollars. Please ascertain whether payment will be made to the overseas hospital or doctor or if you will be reimbursed later for expenses that you incur. Some insurance policies also include coverage for psychiatric treatment and for disposition of remains in the event of death.

Useful information on medical emergencies abroad, including overseas insurance programs, is provided in the Department of State, Bureau of Consular Affairs brochure, *Medical Information for Americans Traveling Abroad*, available via the Bureau of Consular Affairs home page at http://travel.state.gov or autofax service at (202) 647-3000.

OTHER HEALTH INFORMATION: Information on vaccinations and other health precautions may be obtained from the Centers for Disease Control and Prevention's international traveler's hotline at 1-877-fyi-trip (1-877-394-8747); fax: 1-888-cdc-faxx (1-888-232-3299), or by visiting the CDC Internet home page at http://www.cdc.gov.

TRAFFIC SAFETY AND ROAD CONDITIONS: While in a foreign country, U.S. citizens may encounter road conditions that differ significantly from those in the United States. The information below concerning Portugal is provided for general reference only, and it may not be totally accurate in a particular location or circumstance.

Safety of Public Transportation: Good
Urban Road Conditions/Maintenance: Good to Fair
Rural Road Conditions/Maintenance: Fair to Poor
Availability of Roadside Assistance: Good to Fair

Portugal has one of the highest rates of automobile accidents and fatalities in Europe. Portuguese driving habits, high speeds, and poorly marked roads pose special hazards. In continental Portugal, fines for traffic violations are substantial and usually must be paid on the spot. Taxis are a reliable means of transportation, though travelers should pay attention to discrepancies between the meter fare and the amount requested by the driver. Buses are reliable and inexpensive.

In the Azores, driving can be treacherous due to narrow cobblestone streets, blind curves, unprotected embankments, herds of cows in the

439

countryside roads, and the high speeds of other drivers. In contrast to the continent, traffic violations are registered by radar and later forwarded to the offender via the postal service - payments are not made on the spot. Taxis do not have meters. The fare consists of a base fee plus a posted rate per kilometer traveled. Public buses are inexpensive. Bus services begin at 7:00 a.m. and generally operate until 8:00 p.m. depending on the destination.

U.S. visitors to Portugal may drive with a valid U.S. driver's license for up to six months. For international driving permits, please contact AAA in the U.S. at tel. 1-800-222-4357. For specific information concerning Portuguese driver's permits, vehicle inspection and mandatory insurance, please contact the Portuguese National Tourist Office by telephone at 1-800-767-8842 or via the Internet at http://www.portugal.org.

AVIATION SAFETY OVERSIGHT: The U.S. Federal Aviation Administration (FAA) has assessed the government of Portugal's Civil Aviation Authority as category 1 - in compliance with international aviation safety standards for oversight of Portugal's air carrier operations. For further information, travelers may contact the Department of Transportation within the United States at tel. 1-800-322-7873, or visit the FAA's Internet web site at http://www.faa.gov/avr/iasa/. The U.S. Department of Defense (DOD) separately assesses some foreign air carriers for suitability as official providers of air services. For information regarding the DOD policy on specific carriers, travelers may contact the DOD at tel. (618) 229-4801.

CUSTOMS REGULATIONS: Portuguese customs authorities may enforce strict regulations concerning temporary importation into or export from Portugal of such items as firearms, antiquities, medications, business equipment, sales samples and other items. It is advisable to contact the Embassy of Portugal in Washington, D.C. or one of the Portuguese consulates in the United States for specific information regarding customs requirements. Portugal's customs authorities encourage the use of an ATA (Admission Temporaire/Temporary Admission) carnet for the temporary admission of professional equipment, commercial samples, and/or goods for exhibitions and fair purposes. ATA Carnet Headquarters,

located at theU.S Council for International Business, 1212 Avenue of The Americas, New York, NY 10036, issues and guarantees the ATA carnet in the United States. For additional information, please telephone (212) 354-4480, or send an e-mail to atacarnet@uscib.org, or visit http://www.uscib.org for details.

CRIMINAL PENALTIES: While in a foreign country, a U.S. citizen is subject to that country's laws and regulations, which sometimes differ significantly from those in the United States and may not afford the protections available to the individual under U.S. law. Penalties for breaking the law can be more severe than in the United States for similar offenses. Persons violating Portuguese laws, even unknowingly, may be expelled, arrested or imprisoned. In 2001, Portugal made consumption, acquisition and possession for personal use of small amounts of drugs, not to exceed 2.5 grams of hashish or 1 gram of cocaine or heroin, an administrative offense. Criminal penalties for trafficking in illegal drugs, however, are strict and can range up to 15 years in prison. If the defendant belongs to a criminal organization, jail sentences range from a minimum of 10 years to a maximum of 20 years.

DISASTER PREPAREDNESS: Portugal has a history of infrequent but severe seismic activity. Responsibility for caring for disaster victims, including foreigners, rests with the Portuguese authorities. General information regarding disaster preparedness is available via the Internet from the U.S Federal Emergency Management Agency (FEMA) home page at http://www.fema.gov.

CHILDREN'S ISSUES: For information on international adoption and international parental child abduction, please refer to our Internet site at http://travel.state.gov.children's_issues.html or telephone(202) 736-7000.

REGISTRATION/EMBASSY AND CONSULATE LOCATIONS: Americans living in or visiting Portugal may register at the Consular Section of the U.S Embassy in Lisbon and obtain updated information on travel and security within Portugal. Embassy is located on Avenida das Forças Armadas, Sete Rios, telephone (351)(21) 727-3300, fax (351)(21) 726-9109, Internet home page: http://www.american-embassy.pt. The U.S. Consulate is located in Ponta Delgada on the

Island of San Miguel in the Azores. The address is Avenida D. Henrique, telephone (351)(96) 282216/ 7/ 8/ 9. There is also a Consular Agency located in Funchal, Madeira, on Rua Tentente Coronel Sarmento, Ed. Infante, Bloco B-4 Andar, Apt. B, 9000 Funchal, telephone (351)(29) 174-3429 or fax (351)(29) 174-3808, open Monday through Friday from 10:00 a.m. to 12:00 noon.

Spain and Andorra

COUNTRY DESCRIPTION: Spain and Andorra are both highly developed and stable democracies with modern economies. Spain is a member of the European Community. Additional information on Spain may be obtained from the Tourist Office of Spain (http://www.okspain.org), telephone (212) 265-8822, or via the Internet at http://www.okspain.org. Additional information on Andorra may be obtained from the Andorran Mission to the U.N., 2 U.N. Plaza, 25th Floor, New York, New York 10018, telephone (212) 750-8064.

ENTRY REQUIREMENTS: A passport is required for both countries, but a visa is not required for tourist or business stays up to 90 days. Individuals who enter Spain without a visa are not authorized to work. For further information concerning entry requirements for Spain, travelers should contact the Embassy of Spain at 2375 Pennsylvania Avenue NW, Washington, D.C. 20037, telephone (202) 728-2330, or the nearest Spanish consulate in Boston, Chicago, Houston, Los Angeles, Miami, New Orleans, New York, San Francisco, or San Juan. The web site of the Spanish Embassy in the United States is http://www.spainemb.org. For further information on entry requirements in Andorra, travelers should contact the Andorran Mission to the U.N., 2 U.N. Plaza, 25th Floor, New York, NY 10018, telephone (212) 750-8064.

Students planning to study in Spain should be aware of a recent change in Spanish immigration laws, which require applications for student visas to be submitted a minimum of 60 days before anticipated travel to Spain.

In an effort to prevent international child abduction, many governments have initiated procedures at entry/exit points. These often include requiring documentary evidence of relationship and permission for the child's travel from the parent(s) or legal guardian not present. Having such documentation on hand, even if not required, may facilitate entry/departure.

DUAL NATIONALITY: In addition to being subject to all Spanish laws affecting U.S. citizens, dual nationals may also be subject to other laws that impose special obligations on Spanish citizens. For additional information, please see the Consular Affairs home page on the Internet at http://travel.state.gov for our *Dual Nationality flyer*.

SAFETY AND SECURITY: The ETA terrorist organization remains active in Spain. Although ETA efforts have historically been directed against police, military, and other Spanish government targets, in March 2001, ETA issued a communique announcing its intention to target Spanish tourist areas. Americans have not been the specific targets of ETA activities. The Spanish government is vigorously engaged in combating terrorism at home and abroad and has been able to avert many terrorist activities. Over the years, ETA has conducted many successful attacks, many of which have resulted in deaths and injuries. Last year, ETA attacks included a number of car bomb incidents, which occurred in areas frequented by tourists, including the Madrid and Malaga airports. While there were no tourist fatalities from any of these incidents, a number of innocent bystanders suffered injuries. A smaller Marxist group, GRAPO, has also mounted several attacks since 1999 and killed three people. U.S. tourists traveling to Spain should exercise caution and refer to the guidance offered in the Worldwide Caution Public Announcements issued in the wake of the September 11 attacks against New York and Washington.

CRIME: While most of Spain has a moderate rate of crime, and most of the estimated one million American tourists have trouble free visits to Spain each year, the principal tourist areas have been experiencing an increase in violent crime. Madrid and Barcelona, in particular, have reported growing incidents of muggings and violent attacks, and older tourists and Asian-Americans seem to be particularly at risk. Criminals frequent tourist areas and major attractions such as museums, monuments, restaurants, hotels, beach resorts, trains, train stations, airports, subways and ATM machines. In Barcelona, violent attacks have occurred near the Picasso Museum and in the Gothic Quarter, Parc Guell, Plaza Real and Mont Juic. In Madrid, reported incidents occur in key tourist areas, including the area near the Prado Museum and Atocha train station, and areas of old Madrid like Sol, El Rastro flea market and Plaza Mayor. Travelers should exercise caution, carry limited cash and credit cards, and leave extra cash, credit cards, passports and personal documents in a safe location. Crimes have occurred at all times of day and night.

Thieves often work in teams or pairs. In most cases, one person distracts a victim while the accomplice performs the robbery. For example, a stranger might wave a map in your face and ask for directions or "inadvertently" spill something on you. While your attention is diverted, an accomplice makes off with the valuables. Attacks can also be initiated from behind, with the victim being grabbed around the neck and choked by one assailant while others rifle through the belongings. A group of assailants may surround the victim, maybe in a crowded popular tourist area or on public transportation, and only after the group has departed does the person discover he/she has been robbed. Some attacks have been so violent that victims have needed to seek medical attention after the attack.

Theft from parked cars is also common. Small items like luggage, cameras or briefcases are often stolen from parked cars. Travelers are advised not to leave valuables in parked cars, and to keep doors locked, windows rolled up and valuables out of sight when driving. "Good Samaritans" scams are unfortunately common. A passing car will attempt to divert the driver's attention by indicating there is a mechanical problem. If the driver stops to check the vehicle, accomplices steal from the car while the driver is looking elsewhere. Drivers should be cautious about accepting help from anyone other than a uniformed Spanish police officer or Civil Guard. Andorra has a low rate of crime.

The loss or theft abroad of a U.S. passport should be reported immediately to the local police and the nearest U.S. embassy or consulate. U.S. citizens may refer to the Department of State's pamphlet, *A Safe Trip Abroad*, for ways to promote a more trouble-free journey. The pamphlet is available by mail from the Superintendent of Documents, U.S. Government Printing Office, Washington, D.C. 20402, via the Internet at http://www.access.gpo.gov/su_docs, or via the Bureau of Consular Affairs home page at http://travel.state.gov.

MEDICAL FACILITIES AND INSURANCE: Good medical care is available. The Department of State strongly urges Americans to consult with their medical insurance company prior to traveling abroad to confirm whether their policy applies overseas and if it will cover emergency expenses such as a medical evacuation. U.S. medical insurance plans seldom cover health costs incurred outside the United States unless supplemental coverage is purchased. Further, U.S. Medicare and Medicaid programs do not provide payment for medical services outside the United States. However, many travel agents and private companies offer insurance plans that will cover health care expenses incurred overseas, including emergency services such as medical evacuations.

When making a decision regarding health insurance, Americans should consider that many foreign doctors and hospitals require payment in cash prior to providing service and that a medical evacuation to the United States. may cost well in excess of $50,000. Uninsured travelers who require medical care overseas often face extreme difficulties, whereas travelers who have purchased overseas medical insurance have found it to be life-saving when a medical emergency has occurred. When consulting with your insurer prior to your trip, please ascertain whether payment will be made to the overseas healthcare provider or if you will be reimbursed later for expenses that you incur. Some insurance policies also include coverage for psychiatric treatment and for disposition of remains in the event of death.

Useful information on medical emergencies abroad, including overseas insurance programs, is provided in the Department of State's Bureau of Consular Affairs brochure, *Medical Information for Americans Traveling Abroad*, available via the Bureau of Consular Affairs home page or autofax: (202) 647-3000.

OTHER HEALTH INFORMATION:
Information on vaccinations and other health precautions may be obtained from the Centers for Disease Control and Prevention's hotline for international travelers at 1-877-FYI-TRIP (1-877-394-8747); fax: 1-888-CDC-FAXX (1-888-232-3299), or via the CDC's Internet site at http://www.cdc.gov.

TRAFFIC SAFETY AND ROAD CONDITIONS: While in a foreign country, U.S. citizens may encounter road conditions that differ significantly from those in the United States. The information below concerning Spain is provided for general reference only, and it may not be totally accurate in a particular location or circumstance.

Safety of Public Transportation: Good
Urban Road Conditions/Maintenance: Excellent
Rural Road Conditions/Maintenance: Good
Availability of Roadside Assistance: Good

Traffic in Madrid and Barcelona is faster-paced than in U.S. cities. Pedestrians should use designated crossing areas when crossing streets and obey traffic lights. Night driving on Fridays and Saturdays in urban areas may be dangerous due to drivers under the influence of alcohol. Night driving in isolated rural areas can be dangerous because of farm animals and poorly marked roads. Rural traffic is generally heavier in July and August as well as during the Christmas and Easter seasons.

Public transportation in large cities is generally excellent. Taxi services are relatively inexpensive, and the use of meters is common, although there have been reports of taxi drivers occasionally overcharging tourists coming from the airport. Travelers are advised to use registered cabs only.

For additional general information about road safety, including links to foreign government sites, please see the Department of State, Bureau of Consular Affairs home page at http://travel.state.gov/road_safety.html. For specific information concerning Spanish driving permits, vehicle inspection, road tax and mandatory insurance, please contact the Spanish National Tourist Organization offices in New York via the Internet at http://www.okspain.org.

AVIATION SAFETY OVERSIGHT: The U.S. Federal Aviation Administration (FAA) has assessed the Government of Spain's Civil Aviation Authority as Category 1 -- in compliance with international aviation safety standards for oversight of Spain's air carrier operations. For further information, travelers may contact the Department of Transportation within the United States at telephone 1-800-322-7873, or visit the FAA's Internet website at http://www.faa.gov/avr/iasa. The U.S. Department of Defense (DOD) separately assesses some foreign air carriers for suitability as official providers of air services. For information regarding the DOD policy on specific carriers, travelers may contact the DOD at telephone (618) 229-4801.

CUSTOMS REGULATIONS: It is advisable to contact the Embassy of Spain in Washington, D.C. or one of Spain's consulates in the United States for specific information regarding customs requirements. This is especially important if you are attempting to send any medications to Spain through postal channels. Spain's customs authorities encourage the use of an ATA (Admission Temporaire/Temporary Admission) Carnet for the temporary admission of professional equipment, commercial samples, and/or goods for exhibitions and fair purposes. ATA Carnet Headquarters, located at the U.S. Council for International Business, 1212 Avenue of the Americas, New York, NY 10036, issues and guarantees the ATA Carnet in the United States. For additional information, please call (212) 354-4480, or send an e-mail to atacarnet@uscib.org, or visit http://www.uscib.org for details.

CRIMINAL PENALTIES: While in a foreign country, a U.S. citizen is subject to that country's laws and regulations, which sometimes differ significantly from those in the United States and may not afford the protections available to the individual under U.S. law. Penalties for breaking the law can be more severe than in the United States for similar offenses. Persons violating Spanish law, even unknowingly, may be expelled, arrested or imprisoned. Penalties for possession of, use of, or trafficking in illegal drugs in Spain are strict, and convicted offenders can expect jail sentences and fines.

CHILDREN'S ISSUES: For information on international adoption of children and international parental child abduction, please refer to our Internet site at http://travel.state.gov/children's_issues.html or telephone (202) 736-7000.

REGISTRATION/EMBASSY AND CONSULATE LOCATIONS: Americans living in or visiting Spain or Andorra are encouraged to register at the Consular Section of the U.S. Embassy in Madrid or at the U.S. Consulate General in Barcelona where they may obtain updated information on travel and security within Spain or Andorra. The U.S. Embassy in Madrid, Spain is located at Serrano 75; telephone (34)(91) 587-2200, and fax (34)(91) 587-2303. U.S. citizens who register in the Consular Section at the U.S. Embassy or Consulate listed below can obtain updated information on travel and security within Spain or Andorra. Additional information is also available through the U.S. Embassy's Internet homepage at http://www.embusa.es/indexbis.html.

There is a U.S. Consulate in Barcelona, at Paseo Reina Elisenda 23-25; telephone (34)(93) 280-2227 and fax (34)(93) 205-5206.

There are also Consular Agencies in the following locations:

Malaga, at Avenida Juan Gomez Juanito #8, Edificio Lucia 1C, 29640, Fuengirola, telephone (34)(952)474-891 and fax (34)(952) 465-189, hours 10:00 a.m. to 1:00 p.m.;

La Coruna, at Canton Grande 16-17, telephone(34)(981) 213-233 and fax (34)(981) 222-808, hours 10:00 a.m. to 1:00 p.m.;

Las Palmas, at Edificio Arca, Calle Los Martinez de Escobar 3, Oficina 7, telephone (34)(928) 222-552 and fax (34)(928) 225-863, hours 10:00 a.m. to 1:00 p.m.;

Palma de Mallorca, Edificio Reina Constanza, c/ Porto Pi, 8 -9D, 07015 Palma de Mallorca, telephone (34) 971-403-707 or (34) 971-403-905 and fax (34) 971-403-971, hours 10:30 a.m. to 1:30 p.m.;

Seville, at Paseo de Las Delicias 7, telephone (34)(954) 231-885 and fax (34)(954) 232-040, hours 8:30 a.m. to 1:30 p.m.;

Valencia, at Doctor Romagosa #1, 2-J, 46002, Valencia telephone (34)(96)-351-6973 and fax (34)(96) 352-9565, hours 10:00 a.m. to 1:00 p.m. For Andorra, please contact the U.S. Consulate in Barcelona.

Sweden

COUNTRY DESCRIPTION: Sweden is a highly developed stable democracy with a modern economy. Detailed information about Sweden is available at the following Internet sites: http://www.gosweden.org and http://www.webcom.com/sis.

ENTRY REQUIREMENTS: A valid passport is required. Tourist and business travelers do not need visas for stays of less than 90 days. Since March 2001, Sweden entry visas are governed by the rules in the Schengen Agreement. Under the Agreement, all the European Union countries (except Ireland and the United Kingdom), as well as the European Economic Area countries of Norway and Iceland, have opened their borders to one another. A visa issued for a visit to one of these countries is normally valid in all of the other countries as well. For further information on entry requirements, please contact the Royal Swedish Embassy at 1501 M St., N.W., Washington, D.C. 20005, tel. (202) 467-2600, or the Swedish Consulate General in New York at (212) 583-2550 or check their homepage at http://www.webcom.com/sis. Sweden's immigration authorities (Migrationsverket) also maintain a homepage at htt://www.migrationsverket.se. In an effort to prevent international child abduction, many governments have initiated procedures at entry/exit points. These often include requiring documentary evidence of relationship and permission for the child's travel from the parent(s) or legal guardian not present. Having such documentation on hand, even if not required, may facilitate entry/departure.

DUAL NATIONALITY: In addition to being subject to all Swedish laws affecting U.S. citizens, dual nationals may also be subject to other laws that impose special obligations on Swedish citizens. For additional information, please see the Consular Affairs home page on the Internet at http://travel.state.gov for our *Dual Nationality flyer*.

CRIME: Sweden has a relatively low crime rate, and violent crimes are uncommon although increasing. Most crimes involve theft of personal property from cars or residences or in public areas. Pick-pockets and purse-snatchers often work in pairs or groups with one distracting the victim while another grabs valuables. Major tourist attractions like Stockholm's Old Town, restaurants, amusement parks, museums, bars, buses and subway trains are prime locations for pick-pockets to operate. Hotel breakfast rooms and lobbies attract professional, well-dressed thieves who blend in with guests and target purses and briefcases left unguarded by unsuspecting tourist and business travelers. Valuables should not be left unguarded in parked vehicles.

The loss or theft abroad of a U.S. passport should be reported immediately to the local police and the nearest U.S. embassy or consulate. If you are the victim of a crime while overseas, in addition to reporting to local police, please contact the nearest U.S. embassy or consulate for assistance. The embassy/consulate staff can, for example, assist you to find appropriate medical care, to contact family members or friends, and explain how funds could be transferred. Although the investigation and prosecution of the crime is solely the responsibility of local authorities, consular officers can help you to understand the local criminal justice process and to find an attorney if needed.

U.S. citizens may refer to the Department of State's pamphlet, *A Safe Trip Abroad,* for ways to promote a trouble-free journey. The pamphlet is available by mail from the Superintendent of Documents, U.S. Government Printing Office, Washington, D.C. 20402, via the Internet at http://www.access.gpo.gov/su_docs, or via the Bureau of Consular Affairs home page at http://travel.state.gov.

MEDICAL FACILITIES: Medical care comparable to that found in the United States is widely available. The Swedish medical system is a state run system, so instead of visiting a local private general practitioner, travelers can visit a local medical center or clinic, called an "Akutmottagning" or "Vardcentral." Patients should be prepared to present their passport. Non-European citizens should consult with their travel agents about the need for insurance before they travel. In case of a medical emergency, the emergency telephone number "112" (equivalent of U.S. "911") can be used to contact the appropriate emergency service.

Travelers with special medical needs should consult with their personal physician and take appropriate precautions, including bringing adequate supplies of necessary medication. Medicines may be brought into the country as long as they are intended for the traveler's personal use. Medications classified as narcotics may only be brought into the country to cover the traveler's personal use for a maximum of five days, and they must be accompanied by a medical certificate that states why the traveler needs them. Forwarding drugs to Sweden after a traveler has arrived is prohibited by stringent Swedish customs regulations. Travelers may also find local physicians reluctant to prescribe equivalent quantities or dosages. Prescriptions are dispensed at state-run pharmacies called "Apotek" in Swedish. Most pharmacies are open during normal shopping hours, but major cities have a 24-hour pharmacy.

MEDICAL INSURANCE: The Department of State strongly urges Americans to consult with their medical insurance company prior to traveling abroad to confirm whether their policy applies overseas and if it will cover emergency expenses such as a medical evacuation. U.S. medical insurance plans seldom cover health costs incurred outside the United States unless supplemental coverage is purchased. Further, U.S. Medicare and Medicaid programs do not provide payment for medical services outside the United States. However, many travel agents and private companies offer insurance plans that will cover health care expenses incurred overseas, including emergency services such as medical evacuations.

When making a decision regarding health insurance, Americans should consider that many foreign doctors and hospitals require payment in cash prior to providing service and that a medical evacuation to the United States may cost well in excess of $50,000. Uninsured travelers who require medical care overseas often face extreme difficulties. When consulting with your insurer prior to your trip, please ascertain whether payment will be made to the overseas healthcare provider or whether you will be reimbursed later for expenses that you incur. Some insurance policies also include coverage for psychiatric treatment and for disposition of remains in the event of death.

Useful information on medical emergencies abroad, including overseas insurance programs, is provided in the Department of State's Bureau of Consular Affairs brochure, *Medical Information for Americans Traveling Abroad*, available via the Bureau of Consular Affairs home page or autofax: (202) 647-3000.

OTHER HEALTH INFORMATION: Information on vaccinations and other health precautions, such as safe food and water precautions and insect bite protection, may be obtained from the Centers for Disease Control and Prevention's hotline for international travelers at 1-877-FYI-TRIP (1-877-394-8747); fax 1-888-CDC-FAXX (1-888-232-3299), or via the CDC's Internet site at http://www.cdc.gov/travel. For information about outbreaks of infectious diseases abroad, please consult the World Health Organization's website at http://www.who.int/en. Further health information for travelers is available at http://www.who.int/ith.

TRAFFIC SAFETY AND ROAD CONDITIONS: While in a foreign country, U.S. citizens may encounter road conditions that differ significantly from those in the United States. The information below concerning Sweden is provided for general reference only, and it may not be totally accurate in a particular location or circumstance.

Safety of Public Transportation: Good
Urban Road Conditions/Maintenance: Good
Rural Road Conditions/Maintenance: Good
Availability of Roadside Assistance: Good

A valid U.S. driver's license may be used while visiting Sweden, but the drivers must be at least 18 years of age. Driving in Sweden is on the right side of the road. Road signs use standard international symbols and Swedish text. Many urban streets have traffic lanes reserved for public transport only.

Swedish roads are comparable to roads in the United States, but due to Sweden's sparse population outside the major urban areas, secondary roads may be less heavily traveled. Outside urban areas, roads often narrow to two lanes with a wider shoulder. Slower vehicles are expected to move onto the shoulder to allow faster moving vehicles to pass. All vehicles must have headlights lit when on the road, no matter what time of day. The use of snow tires is mandatory between December 1 and March 31 and, due to the country's northerly climate, experience in driving on ice and snow is recommended before negotiating Sweden's winter roads.

Public transport in Sweden is of good quality, and it is the recommended method of travel. Passenger trains, intercity buses and air flights provide regular service over longer distances. Public transportation in urban centers includes buses, subways, trams, suburban trains and taxis. Taxis are relatively more expensive than in major U.S. cities. Most local residents use public transport in Stockholm because parking can be hard to find and expensive. The bus, train and subway systems are relatively safe.

Use of seat belts is mandatory for drivers and all passengers, and children under seven must be seated in approved child or booster seats. The maximum speed limit is 110 kilometers per hour. Driving under the influence of alcohol or drugs, including prescription drugs, is considered to be a very serious offense. The rules are stringently enforced, and fines can be severe. Violations can result in severe fines and possible jail sentences. Emergency services (equivalent to "911" in the United States) for traffic accidents and emergency roadside assistance can be reached by calling 112.

For additional general information about road safety, including links to foreign government sites, please see the Department of State, Bureau of Consular Affairs, home page at http://travel.state.gov/road_safety.html. Specific information on road safety is available at http://www.vv.se.

AVIATION SAFETY OVERSIGHT: The U.S. Federal Aviation Administration (FAA) has assessed the Government of Sweden's civil aviation authority as Category 1 -- in compliance with international aviation safety standards for oversight of Sweden's air carrier operations. For further information, travelers may contact the Department of Transportation within the United States at tel. 1-800-322-7873, or visit the FAA's Internet website at http://www.faa.gov/avr/iasa.

The U.S. Department of Defense (DOD) separately assesses some foreign air carriers for suitability as official providers of air services. For information regarding the DOD policy on specific carriers, travelers may contact the DOD at tel. (618) 229-4801.

CUSTOMS REGULATIONS: Sweden's customs authorities may enforce strict regulations concerning temporary importation into or export from Sweden of items such as firearms, knives and similar weapons, narcotics, medications and pharmaceuticals, specific animal food products and live animals, including dogs, cats, birds, fish and reptiles. An import permit is required for pets. It is advisable to contact the Embassy of Sweden in Washington, D.C. or one of Sweden's consulates in the United States for specific information regarding custom requirements and appropriate application forms.

Customs authorities encourage the use of an ATA (Admission Temporaire/Temporary Admission) carnet for the temporary admission of professional equipment, commercial samples, and/or goods for exhibitions and fair purposes. ATA Carnet Headquarters, located at the U.S. Council for International Business, 1212 Avenue of the Americas, New York, NY 10036, issues and guarantees the ATA carnet in the United States. For additional information, please call tel. 212-354-4480, or send an e-mail to atacarnet@uscib.org, or visit http://www.uscib.org for details.

CRIMINAL PENALTIES: While in a foreign country, a U.S. citizen is subject to that country's laws and regulations, which sometimes differ significantly from those in the United States and may not afford the protections available to the individual under U.S. law. Penalties for breaking the law can be more severe than in the United States for similar offenses. Persons violating Sweden's laws, even unknowingly, may be expelled, arrested or imprisoned. Penalties for possession, use, or trafficking in illegal drugs in Sweden are strict, and convicted offenders can expect jail sentences and heavy fines. There is no bail system in Sweden, and non-resident Americans who are arrested may be held in custody until the trial is complete.

CHILDREN'S ISSUES: For information on the international adoption of children and international parental child abduction, please refer to our Internet site at http://travel.state.gov/children's_issues.html or telephone (202) 736-7000.

REGISTRATION AND EMBASSY LOCATION: Americans living in or visiting Sweden are encouraged to register at the Consular Section of the U.S. Embassy in Stockholm and obtain updated information on travel and security within Sweden. The U.S. Embassy is located at Dag Hammarskjoldsvag 31, tel. (46)(8) 783-5300, fax (46)(8) 660-5879 and after-hours telephone (46)(8) 783-5310. The Embassy's Internet website is http://www.usemb.se and U.S. citizens can also use the website to register on-line. Normal hours for public visitors are Monday-Friday, 9:00 a.m.-11:00a.m., holidays excepted. Routine passport and U.S. citizen service inquiries are handled at telephone (46)(8)783-5375 Monday-Friday between 1:30 p.m. and 4:00 p.m.

Turkey

COUNTRY DESCRIPTION: Turkey is a moderately developed nation with a wide range of tourist facilities of all classes in the main tourist destinations.

ENTRY REQUIREMENTS: A passport and visa are required. Holders of all types of passports can purchase a 90-day sticker visa at the port of entry for $100, if they are traveling to Turkey as tourists. For further information, travelers in the U.S. may contact the Embassy of the Republic of Turkey at 2525 Massachusetts Avenue, NW, Washington, D.C. 20008, telephone: (202) 612-6700, or the Turkish consulates general in Chicago, Houston, Los Angeles, or New York. Information may also be found at Internet address http://www.turkey.org/. Overseas, travelers may contact a Turkish embassy or consulate. Holders of official and diplomatic passports on official business must obtain a visa from a Turkish embassy or consulate before arrival in Turkey. Holders of official and diplomatic passports on private travel may receive a visa free of charge from a Turkish embassy or consulate, or obtain one upon arrival at the port of entry for $100. All those who are planning to stay more than three months for any purpose are required to obtain a visa from a Turkish embassy or consulate. Such travelers must also apply for a residence/work permit or Turkish ID card within the first month of their arrival in Turkey. For example, this would include anyone who plans to spend more than three months doing research, studying, or working in Turkey.

All travelers are advised to obtain entry stamps on the passport page containing their visa at the first port of entry before transferring to domestic flights. Failure to obtain entry stamps at the port of entry has occasionally resulted in serious difficulties for travelers when they attempt to depart the country.

In an effort to prevent international child abduction, many governments have initiated procedures at entry/exit points. These often include requiring documentary evidence of relationship and permission for the child's travel from the parent(s) or legal guardian not present. Having such documentation on hand, even if not required, may facilitate entry/departure.

DUAL NATIONALITY: In addition to being subject to all Turkish laws affecting U.S. citizens, dual nationals may also be subject to other laws that impose special obligations on Turkish citizens. Male U.S. citizens over the age of 18 who are also considered to be Turkish citizens may be subject to conscription and compulsory military service upon arrival, and to other aspects of Turkish law while in Turkey. Those who may be affected are strongly advised to consult with Turkish officials and inquire at a Turkish embassy or consulate to determine their status before traveling. For additional information on dual nationality, see the Consular Affairs home page on the Internet at http://travel.state.gov/ for our Dual Nationality flier.

SAFETY AND SECURITY: The general security situation throughout Turkey is stable, but sporadic incidents involving terrorist groups have occurred. The Turkish government is committed to eliminating terrorist groups such as the Kurdistan Worker's Party (PKK) and various leftist and fundamentalist groups. Although these groups have not completely disbanded, their operational capabilities have greatly diminished. These groups have used terrorist activity to make political

statements, particularly in Istanbul and other urban areas of Turkey. No Americans appear to have been targeted in any recent terrorist incidents in Turkey, but Americans simply in the wrong place at the wrong time during a terrorist incident could be victims. In 2000 and 2001, terrorists targeting Turkish officials and various civilian facilities in Istanbul were responsible for deaths and injuries of several dozen people. The civilian targets included a number of fast food restaurants.

SOUTHEAST TURKEY: The PKK retains a residual presence in certain parts of southeastern Turkey. The following provinces are under a state of emergency: Sirnak, and Diyarbakir. The following additional areas are considered "sensitive areas" or one level below state-of-emergency status: Van, Siirt, Mus, Mardin, Batman, Bingol, Tunceli, Hakkari, and Bitlis. The southeast provinces of Adana, Adiyaman, Hatay, Elazig, Gaziantep, Kahraman Maras, Kilis, Malatya, Icel, Osmaniye and Sanliufra are not under a heightened state of alert. Mount Ararat is a special military zone and access permission must be obtained from the Turkish Government. Visitors to the emergency and sensitive areas of southeastern Turkey are advised to travel only during daylight hours and on major highways. The Turkish Jandarma and police forces monitor checkpoints on roads throughout the southeastern region. Drivers and all passengers in the vehicle should be prepared to provide identification if stopped at a checkpoint.

Travelers are cautioned not to accept letters, parcels, or other items from strangers for delivery either in or outside of Turkey. The PKK has attempted to use foreigners to deliver messages and packages in or outside of Turkey. If discovered, individuals could be arrested for aiding and abetting the PKK - a serious charge.

A "Southeastern Turkey Briefing" is available on the Embassy Ankara website under "Security Matters" at http://www.usemb-ankara.org.tr/.

CRIME: Street crime is relatively low in Turkey, although it is increasing in large urban centers such as Istanbul and Izmir. Women appear to have been targeted for muggings or robberies. Visitors should not be complacent regarding personal safety or the protection of valuables. The same precautions employed in the US should be followed in Turkey. As in other large metropolitan areas throughout the world, common street crimes include pickpocketing, purse-snatching, and mugging. English-or French-speaking foreigners, who identified themselves as Tunisian, Moroccan, Egyptian, Kuwaiti, or Romanian, have also targeted foreign tourists. These persons have befriended the tourists and then drugged them, using teas, juice, alcohol, or food. Two common drugs used are nembitol, known on the street as sari bomba (the yellow bomb) and benzodiazepine; when used incorrectly they can cause death. In similar cases, tourists are invited to visit clubs or bars, and then presented with inflated bills (often exceeding $1000), and coerced to pay them by credit card.

The loss or theft abroad of a U.S. passport should be reported immediately to the local police and the nearest U.S. Embassy or Consulate. Travelers are encouraged to carry a photocopy of their passport, to assist in getting a replacement passport if the original is stolen. U.S. citizens may refer to the Department of State's pamphlet, *A Safe Trip Abroad*, for ways to promote a trouble-free journey. The pamphlet is available by mail from the Superintendent of Documents, U.S. Government Printing Office, Washington, D.C. 20402, via the Internet at http://www.access.gpo.gov/su_docs, or via the Bureau of Consular Affairs home page at http://travel.state.gov./ An "Istanbul Street Crime Briefing" is available on the U.S. Embassy Ankara's web site at http://www.usemb-ankara.org.tr or from the Consular Affairs website at http://travel.state.gov/turkey.html

MEDICAL FACILITIES: Turkish hospitals vary greatly. The new, private hospitals in Ankara and Istanbul have the most modern facilities and equipment, but still may be unable to treat certain serious conditions. The State Department recommends medical evacuation for its personnel who will be giving birth. Those planning to remain in Turkey should consider bringing a 6-month supply of necessary chronic medications (e.g., heart medications, birth control pills). Not all diagnostic testing (including mammograms) is up to American standards.

MEDICAL INSURANCE: The Department of State strongly urges Americans to consult with their medical insurance company prior to traveling abroad to confirm whether their policy applies overseas and whether it will cover emergency expenses such as a medical evacuation. U.S. medical insurance plans seldom cover the health care costs incurred outside the United States unless supplemental coverage is purchased. Further, U.S. Medicare and Medicaid programs do not provide payment for medical services outside the United States. However, many travel agents and private companies offer insurance plans that will cover health care expenses incurred overseas including emergency services such as medical evacuations.

When making a decision regarding health insurance, Americans should consider that many foreign doctors and hospitals require payment in cash prior to providing service and that a medical evacuation to the U.S. may cost more than $50,000. Uninsured travelers who require medical care overseas often face extreme difficulties. When consulting with your insurer before your trip, ascertain whether payment will be made to the overseas healthcare provider or whether you will be reimbursed later for expenses you incur. Some insurance policies also include coverage for psychiatric treatment and for disposition of remains in the event of death.

Useful information on medical emergencies abroad, including overseas insurance programs, is provided in the Department of State's Bureau of Consular Affairs brochure, *Medical Information for Americans Traveling Abroad*, available via the Bureau of Consular Affairs home page or autofax: (202) 647-3000.

OTHER HEALTH INFORMATION: Travelers are advised to drink only bottled water or water that has been filtered and boiled. Bottled beverages are considered safe to drink. Most local dairy products, including milk, yogurt, and cheese, are safe to consume. However, care must be taken when purchasing all perishable products, as many vendors do not have adequate refrigeration. Travelers are advised to wash vegetables and fruits thoroughly and to cook meat thoroughly as well.

Information on vaccinations and other health precautions can be obtained from the Centers for Disease Control and Prevention's hotline for international travelers at 1-877-FYI-TRIP (1-877-394-8747), fax 1-800-CDC-FAXX (1-800-232-

3299), or via CDC's Internet site at http://www.cdc.gov/.

TRAFFIC SAFETY AND ROAD CONDITIONS: While in a foreign country, U.S. citizens may encounter road conditions that differ significantly from those in the United States. The information below concerning Turkey is provided for general reference only, and may not be totally accurate in a particular location or circumstance.

Safety of Public Transportation: Fair
Urban Road Conditions/Maintenance: Fair
Rural Road Conditions/Maintenance: Fair
Availability of Roadside Assistance: Poor

Roads in Turkey run the full spectrum from single lane country roads to modern, divided, Trans-European motorways built to European standards. Highways in the southwestern, coastal portion of the country, which is frequented by tourists, are generally in good condition and well maintained. Further information is available on the Embassy's website, under "driver safety." For additional information about road safety, see the Department of State, Bureau of Consular Affairs home page road safety overseas feature at http://travel.state.gov/road_safety.html or the Turkey Road Report on http://www.asirt.org/.

For specific information concerning Turkish driving permits, vehicle inspection, road tax and mandatory insurance, contact the Turkish Tourism and Information Office in New York via the Internet at http://www.turkey.org/Turkey, or by writing to 821 United Nations Plaza, New York, NY 10017, telephone (212) 687-2194, 687-2195, fax (212) 599-7568.

AVIATION SAFETY OVERSIGHT: The U.S. Federal Aviation Administration (FAA) has assessed the Government of Turkey's civil aviation authority as Category 1 -- in compliance with international aviation safety standards for oversight of Turkey's air carrier operations. For more information, contact the Department of Transportation within the U.S. at 1-800-322-7873, or visit the FAA's Internet website at http://www.faa.gov.avr/iasa/

The U.S. Department of Defense (DOD) separately assesses some foreign air carriers for suitability as official providers of air services. For information regarding the DOD policy on specific carriers, travelers may contact DOD at (618) 229-4801.

CUSTOMS REGULATIONS: Turkish customs authorities may enforce strict regulations concerning temporary importation into or export from Turkey of items such as antiquities (very broadly defined) or other important artwork and cultural artifacts. At the time of departure, travelers who purchase such items may be asked to present a receipt from the seller, as well as the official museum export certificate required by law. Smuggling of large quantities of other items, such as cigarettes, out of Turkey is also a punishable offense. Contact the Embassy of Turkey in Washington or one of Turkey's consulates in the United States for specific information regarding customs requirements.

Customs authorities encourage the use of an ATA (Admission Temporaire/Temporary Admission) carnet for the temporary admission of professional equipment, commercial samples, and/or goods for exhibitions and fair purposes. ATA Carnet Headquarters located at the U.S. Council for International Business, 1212 Avenue of the Americas, New York, NY 10036, issues and guarantees the ATA carnet in the United States. For additional information contact the Council at (212) 354-4480, e-mail at mailto:acarnet@uscib.org, or visit their web site at http://www.atacarnet.com/.

CRIMINAL PENALTIES: While in a foreign country, a U.S. citizen is subject to that country's laws and regulations, which sometimes differ significantly from those in the United States and may not afford the protections available to the individual under U.S. law. Penalties for breaking the law can be more severe than in the United States for similar offenses. Persons violating Turkey's laws, even unknowingly, may be expelled, arrested, or imprisoned. Penalties for possession, use, or trafficking in illegal drugs in Turkey are strict and convicted offenders can expect jail sentences and heavy fines. Sentences range from 4 to 24 years.

Below are some of the laws foreign travelers should be aware of:
--Insulting the State: It is illegal to show disrespect to the name or image of Mustafa Kemal Ataturk,

the founder of the modern Turkish Republic, or to insult the Turkish government, flag, or security forces.

--Proselytizing: Although there is no specific law against proselytizing, some activities can lead to arrest under laws that regulate expression, educational institutions, and religious meetings. The Department of State's Annual Report on International Religious Freedom contains additional information on religious freedom in Turkey. The report is available on the Department's website, http://www.state.gov/.

--Cultural Artifacts: Turkish law has a broad definition of "antiquities" and makes it a crime to remove any from the country. Offenders are prosecuted. Under Turkish law, all historic sites such as fortresses, castles and ruins, and everything in them or on the grounds or in the water, is the property of the Turkish government. While many sites do not have signs cautioning the unwary, official silence does not mean official consent. One may buy certain antiquities, but only from authorized dealers who have been issued a certificate by a museum for each item they are authorized to sell. If one has acquired a possible antiquity without having obtained the necessary certificate, competent museum personnel should evaluate it before its removal from Turkey.

DISASTER PREPAREDNESS: Several major earthquake fault lines cross Turkey. A number of Turkish cities including Istanbul, Izmir, and Erzincan lie on or near fault lines, making these areas particularly vulnerable to earthquakes. General information about natural disaster preparedness is available via the Internet from the U.S. Federal Management Agency (FEMA) at http://www.fema.gov/. Detailed information on Turkey's earthquake fault lines is available from the U.S. Geological Survey (USGS) at http://www.usgs.gov/.

CHILDREN'S ISSUES: For information on international adoption of children and international parental child abduction please refer to our Internet site at http://travel.state.gov/children's_issues.html or tel: (202) 736-7000. Since August 2000, the Republic of Turkey has been party to the Hague Convention on the Civil Aspects of International Child Abduction.

REGISTRATION/EMBASSY AND CONSULATE LOCATIONS: Americans living in or visiting Turkey are encouraged to register at the nearest Consular Office, at the U.S. Embassy in Ankara, the U.S. consulates in Istanbul or Adana, or the Consular Agency in Izmir. Updated information on travel and security within Turkey is available while registering, or on the Embassy website at http://www.usemb-ankara.org.tr/.

The U.S. Embassy in Ankara is at 110 Ataturk Boulevard, tel: (90)(312) 455-5555, fax (90)(312) 468-6131. Visa information is available at (90)(312) 468-6110. The Internet address is http://www.usemb-ankara.org.tr. Non-emergency e-mail messages about consular matters may be sent to mailto:ca-ankara@state.gov.

The U.S. Consulate in Istanbul is at 104-108 Mesrutiyet Caddesi, Tepebasi, tel: (90)(212) 251-3602, fax (90)(212) 252-7851. Istanbul-specific information can also be accessed via the Consulate's website http://www.usconsulate-istanbul.org.tr/. Non-emergency e-mail messages about consular matters may be sent to email: mailto:ca_istanbul@state.gov.

The U.S. Consulate in Adana is at the corner of Vali Yolu and Ataturk Caddesi, tel: (90)(322) 459-1551, fax (90)(322) 457-6591.

The U.S. Consular Agent in Izmir is at Kazim Dirik Caddesi 13/8, Atabay Is Merkezi, Daire 805, Pasaport, Izmir, 35210, tel: (90)(232) 441-0072/2203, fax (90)(232) 441-2373. A variety of information on visa procedures, American citizen services, road safety, etc. is also available on the mission's web site, http://www.usemb-ankara.org.tr/.

United Kingdom

COUNTRY DESCRIPTION: The United Kingdom is a highly developed constitutional monarchy comprising England, Scotland, Wales, and Northern Ireland; Gibraltar is a British Overseas Territory. Tourist facilities are widely available.

ENTRY REQUIREMENTS: A passport is required. Tourists are not obliged to obtain a visa for stays of up to six months in the United

Kingdom or to enter Gibraltar. Those wishing to remain longer than one month in Gibraltar should regularize their stay with Gibraltar immigration authorities.

In an effort to prevent international child abduction, many governments have initiated procedures at entry/exit points. These often include requiring documentary evidence of relationship and permission for the child's travel from the parent(s) or legal guardian if not present. Having such documentation on hand, even if not required, may facilitate entry/departure.

Further information on entry requirements may be obtained from the British Embassy at 3100 Massachusetts Avenue, NW, Washington, DC 20008; tel: (202) 588-7800. Inquiries may also be directed to British consulates in Atlanta, Boston, Chicago, Houston, Los Angeles, New York, and San Francisco. The website of the British Embassy in the United States is http://www.britainusa.com/embassy.

DUAL NATIONALITY: U.S. citizens who are also citizens of the United Kingdom or any other nation are reminded that U.S. law requires they enter and depart the United States documented as U.S. citizens. They are not entitled to U.S. visas or to travel to the U.S. on the visa waiver program. U.S. citizens who attempt to travel to the U.S. from the United Kingdom on foreign passports risk being denied boarding pending acquisition of a valid U.S. passport. For additional information, see the Consular Affairs home page on the Internet at http://travel.state.gov for our dual nationality flyer.

SAFETY AND SECURITY: The United Kingdom is stable and modern but shares with the rest of the world an increased threat of terrorist incidents of international origin, as well as violence related to the political situation in Northern Ireland (a part of the United Kingdom.) Americans are reminded to remain vigilant with regard to their personal security and to exercise caution. In recent months, several arrests have been made in Great Britain in connection with various possible terrorist plots. The British Home Secretary has urged its citizens to be alert and vigilant by, for example, keeping an eye out for suspect packages or people acting suspiciously at subway and train stations and airports and reporting anything suspicious to the appropriate authorities by contacting the free confidential anti-terrorist telephone hotline on 0800 789 321. Americans traveling abroad should regularly monitor the Department's Internet web site at http://travel.state.gov where any current Worldwide Cautions or Public Announcements can be found.

From time to time during periods of heightened threat of terrorism, the U.K. government deems it necessary to raise levels of security activity. Heightened activity may include the use of military personnel in support of the police and law enforcement officers. The use of troops, who remain at all times under the control of the police, is part of long-standing contingency plans. Military personnel and equipment may be deployed at airports and other transportation links, or other public locations. For more information about U.K. public safety initiatives, consult the U.K. Civil Contingencies Secretariat website at http://www.ukresilience.gov.uk

Political demonstrations are well policed and, except at times in Northern Ireland, generally orderly. Although the political situation in Northern Ireland has dramatically improved since the signing of the Good Friday Agreement in 1998, incidents of terrorist violence have, nevertheless, occurred in the past few years. Early in 2001, two explosive devices were detonated in London suburbs, injuring eight people and damaging buildings. Within Northern Ireland, flash-points for sectarian confrontations still exist, but they are generally removed from areas where tourists congregate. Sporadic incidents of street violence often erupt during the summer marching season (April to August), with tensions heightened during the month of July, especially around the July 12th public holiday. As a result, American citizens traveling in Northern Ireland have experienced delays and disruption.

CRIME: The United Kingdom and Gibraltar benefit from generally low crime rates; however crime, including violent crime, has increased over the last few years. Incidents of pickpocketing, mugging, "snatch and grab" theft of mobile phones, watches and jewelry and theft of unattended bags, especially at airports and from cars parked at restaurants, hotels and resorts. Pickpockets target tourists, especially at historic sites, restaurants, on buses, trains and the London

Underground (subway). Thieves often target unattended cars parked at tourist sites and roadside restaurants, looking for laptop computers and hand-held electronic equipment. In London, travelers should use only licensed "black taxi cabs" or car services recommended by their hotel or tour operator. Unlicensed taxis or private cars posing as taxis that may offer low fares, but are often uninsured and may have unlicensed drivers. In some instances, travelers have been robbed while using these cars.

Due to the circumstances described above, visitors should take steps to ensure the safety of their U.S. passports. Visitors in the England, Scotland, Wales and Gibraltar are not expected to produce identity documents for police authorities and thus may secure their passports in hotel safes or residences. In Northern Ireland, however, passports or other photographic I.D. should be carried at all times. The need to carry a passport to cash travelers' checks is also minimized by an abundance of ATM's able to access systems widely used in the U.S. and offering more favorable rates of exchange. Note: Common sense personal security measures utilized in the U.S when using ATMs should also be followed in the U.K.

The loss or theft abroad of a U.S. passport should be reported immediately to the local police and the nearest U.S. Embassy or Consulate. If you are the victim of a crime while overseas, in addition to reporting to local police, contact the nearest U.S. Embassy or Consulate for assistance. The Embassy/Consulate staff can, for example, assist you to find appropriate medical care, to contact family members or friends and explain how funds could be transferred. Although the investigation and prosecution of the crime is solely the responsibility of local authorities, consular officers can help you to understand the local criminal justice process and to find an attorney if needed.

U.S. citizens can refer to the Department of State's pamphlet, *A Safe Trip Abroad*, for ways to promote a more trouble-free journey. The pamphlet is available by mail from the Superintendent of Documents, U.S. Government Printing Office, Washington, D.C. 20402, via the Internet at http://www.access.gpo.gov/su_docs, or via the Bureau of Consular Affairs home page at http://travel.state.gov.

MEDICAL FACILITIES: While medical services are widely available, free care under the National Health System is allowed only to U.K. residents and certain EU nationals. Tourists and short-term visitors can expect charges roughly comparable to those assessed in the United States.

MEDICAL INSURANCE: The Department of State strongly urges Americans to consult with their medical insurance company prior to traveling abroad to confirm whether their policy applies overseas and if it will cover emergency expenses such as a medical evacuation. U.S. medical insurance plans seldom cover health costs incurred outside the United States unless supplemental coverage is purchased. Further, U.S. Medicare and Medicaid programs do not provide payment for medical services outside the United States. However, many travel agents and private companies offer insurance plans that will cover health care expenses incurred overseas including emergency services such as medical evacuations.

When making a decision regarding health insurance, Americans should consider that many foreign doctors and hospitals require payment in cash prior to providing service and that a medical evacuation to the U.S. may cost well in excess of $50,000. Uninsured travelers who require medical care overseas often face extreme difficulties. When consulting with your insurer prior to your trip, ascertain whether payment will be made to the overseas healthcare provider or if you will be reimbursed later for expenses you incur. Some insurance policies also include coverage for psychiatric treatment and for disposition of remains in the event of death. Useful information on medical emergencies abroad, including overseas insurance programs, is provided in the Department of State's Bureau of Consular Affairs brochure, *Medical Information for Americans Traveling Abroad*, available via the Bureau of Consular Affairs home page or autofax: (202) 647-3000.

OTHER HEALTH INFORMATION: Information on vaccinations and other health precautions, such as safe food and water precautions and insect bite protection, may be obtained from the Centers for Disease Control and Prevention's hotline for international travelers at 1-877-FYI-TRIP (1-877-394-8747); fax 1-888-CDC-FAXX (1-888-232-3299), or via the CDC's

Internet site at http://www.cdc.gov/travel. For information about outbreaks of infectious diseases abroad consult the World Health Organization's website at http://www.who.int/en. Further health information for travelers is available at http://www.who.int/ith.

TRAFFIC SAFETY AND ROAD CONDITIONS: While in a foreign country, U.S. citizens may encounter road conditions that differ significantly from those in the United States. The information below concerning the United Kingdom is provided for general reference only, and may not be totally accurate in a particular location or circumstance.

Safety of Public Transportation:
Excellent
Urban Road Condition/Maintenance:
Excellent
Rural Road Condition/Maintenance:
Excellent
Availability of Roadside Assistance:
Excellent

U.K. penalties for drunk driving are stiff and often result in prison sentences. In contrast to the United States and continental Europe where traffic moves on the right hand side of the road, traffic moves on the left in the U.K. Visitors uncomfortable with or intimidated by the prospect of driving on the left-hand side of the road may wish to avail themselves of extensive bus, rail and air transport networks that are comparatively inexpensive and very extensive. Roads in the United Kingdom are generally good, but are narrow and often congested in urban areas. If you plan to drive while in the U.K., you may wish to obtain a copy of the Highway Code, available in the United Kingdom. The Automobile Association (AA) of the U.K. provides information and updates on travel and traffic-related issues on its website at http://www.the-stationary-office.co.uk. If you intend to rent a car in the U.K., check that you are adequately insured. U.S. auto insurance is not always valid outside the U.S. and you may wish to purchase supplemental insurance, which is generally available from most major rental agents.

Public transport in the United Kingdom is excellent and extensive. However, poor track conditions may have contributed to train derailments resulting in some fatalities. Repairs are underway and the overall safety record is excellent.

Many U.S. citizens are injured every year in pedestrian accidents in the United Kingdom, forgetting that traffic moves in the opposite direction than in the United States. Care should be taken when crossing streets.

Driving in Gibraltar is on the right-hand side of the road, as in the U.S. and Continental Europe. Persons traveling overland between Gibraltar and Spain may experience long delays in clearing Spanish border controls.

For additional general information about road safety, including links to foreign government sites, see the Department of State, Bureau of Consular Affairs home page at http://travel.state.gov/road_safety.html. For specific information concerning United Kingdom driving permits, vehicle inspection, road tax and mandatory insurance, refer to the United Kingdom's Department of Environment and Transport web site at http://www.detr.gov.uk; the Driving Standards Agency web site at http://www.dsa.gov.uk, or consult the U.S. Embassy in London's web site at http://www.usembassy.org.uk.

The phone number for police/fire/ambulance emergency services - the equivalent of "911" in the U.S. - is 999 in the United Kingdom and 12 in Gibraltar.

AVIATION SAFETY OVERSIGHT: The U.S. Federal Aviation Administration (FAA) has assessed the Government of the United Kingdom's Civil Aviation Authority as Category 1 -- in compliance with international aviation safety standards for oversight of the United Kingdom's air carrier operations. For further information, travelers may contact the Department of Transportation within the U.S. at 1-800-322-7873, or visit the FAA's Internet website at http://www.faa.gov/avr/iasa/. The U.S. Department of Defense (DOD) separately assesses some foreign air carriers for suitability as official providers of air services. For information regarding the DOD policy on specific carriers, travelers may contact DOD at (618) 229-4801.

CUSTOMS REGULATIONS: British customs authorities may strictly enforce regulations regarding the import or export of certain items, including material deemed likely to incite racial hatred, firearms and personal defense items such as mace or knives. It is advisable to contact the British Embassy in Washington or one of the United Kingdom's consulates in the U.S. for specific information regarding customs requirements. Customs authorities encourage the use of an ATA (Admission Temporaire/Temporary Admission) Carnet for the temporary admission of professional equipment, commercial samples, and/or goods for exhibitions and fair purposes. ATA Carnet Headquarters, located at the U.S. Council for International Business, 1212 Avenue of the Americas, New York, NY 10036, issues and guarantees the ATA Carnet in the United States. For additional information call 212-354-4480, send an e-mail to atacarnet@uscib.org, or visit http://www.uscib.org for details.

CRIMINAL PENALTIES: While in a foreign country, a U.S. citizen is subject to that country's laws and regulations, which sometimes differ significantly from those in the United States and may not afford the protections available to the individual under U.S. law. Penalties for breaking the law can be more severe than in the United States for similar offenses. Persons violating British law, even unknowingly, may be expelled, arrested or imprisoned. Penalties for possession, use or trafficking in illegal drugs in the United Kingdom are strict, and convicted offenders can expect jail sentences and heavy fines. Many pocketknives and other blades, and mace or pepper spray canisters, although legal in the U.S., are illegal in the U.K. and may be confiscated. Air travelers to and from the United Kingdom should be aware that penalties against alcohol-related and other in-flight crimes ("air rage") are stiff and are being enforced with prison sentences.

CHILDREN'S ISSUES: For information on international adoption of children and international parental child abduction, please refer to our Internet site at http://travel.state.gov/children's_issues.html or telephone (202) 736-7000.

REGISTRATION/EMBASSY AND CONSULATE LOCATIONS: Americans living in or visiting the United Kingdom are encouraged to register at the Consular Section of the U.S. Embassy in London or at the U.S. Consulates General in Edinburgh or Belfast and obtain updated information on travel and security within the U.K.

The U.S. Embassy is located at 24 Grosvenor Square, London W1A 1AE; Telephone: in country 020-7499-9000, from the U.S. 011-44-20-7499-9000 (24 hours); Consular Section fax: in country 020-7495-5012; from the U.S. 011-44-20-7495-5012. The embassy web site is http://www.usembassy.org.uk.

The U.S. Consulate General in Edinburgh, Scotland is located at 3 Regent Terrace, Edinburgh EH7 5BW; Telephone: in country 0131-556-8315, from the U.S. 011-44-131-556-8315. After hours: in country 01224-857097, from the U.S. 011-44-1224-857097. Fax: in country 0131-557-6023; from the U.S. 011-44-131-557-6023. The web site is http://www.usembassy.org.uk/scotland.

The U.S. Consulate General in Belfast, Northern Ireland, is located at Queen's House, 14 Queen Street, Belfast BT1 6EQ; Telephone: in country 028-9032-8239; from the U.S. 011-44-28-9032-8239. After hours: in country 028-90-661- 629; from the U.S. 011-44-28-90-661-629. Fax: in country 028-9024-8482; from the U.S. 011-44-28-9024-8482. The web site is http://www.usembassy.org.uk.

There is no U.S. consular representation in Gibraltar. Citizen services questions should be directed to the U.S. Embassy in London. Passport questions can be directed to the U.S. Embassy in Madrid, located at Serrano 75/Madrid, Spain; telephone (34)(91) 587-2200, and fax (34)(91) 587-2303. The web site address is http://www.embusa.es.

Planning Another Trip?

See Chapter 36 for a listing of resources available to the general traveler from the U.S. Departments of State, Customs, Transportation, Health and various government and non-government organizations. Almost all of the available International travel-related pamphlets, brochures and publications issued by the U.S. Department of State and by the U.S. Customs have been reproduced in full in this book. See Table of Contents for location.

Chapter 25

Tips for Business Travelers

A Guide for Business Travelers

Officials of companies that are successful in selling overseas often tell Business America that one of the keys to their success is frequent travel to overseas markets. As in domestic business, there is nothing like a face-to-face meeting with a client or customer. Business travel abroad can locate and cultivate new customers and improve relationships and communication with current foreign representatives and associates.

The following suggestions can help officials of U.S. companies prepare for a trip. By keeping in mind that even little things (such as forgetting to check foreign holiday schedules or neglecting to arrange for translator services) can cost time, opportunity, and money, a firm can get maximum value from its time spent abroad.

Planning the Itinerary

A well-planned itinerary enables a traveler to make the best possible use of time abroad. Although travel time is expensive, care must be taken not to overload the schedule. Two or three definite appointments, confirmed well in advance and spaced comfortably throughout one day, are more productive and enjoyable than a crowded agenda that forces the business person to rush from one meeting to the next before business is really concluded. If possible, an extra rest day to deal with jet lag should be planned before scheduled business appointments. The following travel tips should be kept in mind.

The travel plans should reflect what the company hopes to accomplish. The traveler should give some thought to the trip's goals and their relative priorities. The traveler should accomplish as much as possible before the trip begins by obtaining names of possible contacts, arranging appointments, checking transportation schedules, and so on. Important meetings should be confirmed before the traveler leaves the United States.

As a general rule, the business person should keep the schedule flexible enough to allow for both unexpected problems (such as transportation delays) and unexpected opportunities. For instance, accepting an unscheduled luncheon invitation from a prospective client should not make it necessary to miss the next scheduled meeting.

The traveler should check the normal work days and business hours in the countries to be visited. In many Middle Eastern regions, for instance, the work week typically runs from Saturday to Thursday. In many countries, lunch hours of two to four hours are customary. Along the same lines, take foreign holidays into account. Business America at year-end publishes a list of commercial holidays observed in countries around the world for the following year (See Appendix 8H). The potential U.S. traveler should also contact the local Commerce Department district office(See Appendix C). to learn what travel advisories the U.S. Department of State has issued for countries to be visited. Each district office maintains a file of current travel advisory cables, which alert travelers to potentially dangerous in-country situations. The Department of State also has a telephone number for recorded travel advisories, (202) 647-5225.

The U.S. business person should be aware that travel from one country to another may be restricted. For example, a passport containing an Israeli visa may disallow the traveler from entering certain countries in the middle East.

Other Considerations

Travel agents can frequently arrange for transportation and hotel reservations quickly and efficiently. They can also help plan the itinerary, obtain the best travel rates, explain which countries require visas, advise on hotel rates and locations, and provide other valuable services.

Since travel agents' fees are paid by the hotels, airlines, and other carriers, this assistance and expertise may cost nothing.

The U.S. traveler should obtain the necessary travel documents two to three months before departure, especially if visas are needed. A travel agent can help make the arrangements. A valid U.S. passport is required for all travel outside the United States and Canada. If traveling on an old passport, the U.S. citizen should make sure that it remains valid for the entire duration of the trip.

Passports may be obtained through certain local post offices and U.S. district courts. Application may be made in person or, in some cases, by mail. A separate passport is needed for each family member who will be traveling. The applicant must provide (1) proof of citizenship, (2) proof of identify, (3) two identical passport photos, (4) a completed application form, and (5) the appropriate fees. The cost is $55 per passport ($30 for travelers under 18) plus a $10 execution fee for first-time passports or travelers applying in person. The usual processing time for a passport (including time in the mail) is three weeks, but travelers should apply as early as possible, particularly if time is needed to obtain visas, international drivers licenses, or other documents. Additional information is available from the nearest local passport office or by calling the Office of Passport Services in Washington, D.C., (202) 647-0518. (also See Appendix J).

Visas, which are required by many countries, cannot be obtained through the Office of Passport Services. They are provided for a small fee by the foreign country's embassy or consulate in the United States. To obtain a visa, the traveler must have a current U.S. passport. In addition, many countries require a recent photo. The travelers should allow several weeks to obtain visas, especially if traveling to Eastern Europe or developing nations. Some countries that do not require visas for tourist travel do require them for business travel. Visa requirements may change from time to time. (See Chapter 3).

Requirements for vaccinations differ from country to country. A travel agent or airline can advise the travelers on various requirements. In some cases, vaccinations against typhus, typhoid, and other diseases are advisable even though they are not required. (Also See Chapter 8).

Business Preparations For International Travel

Before leaving the United States, the traveler should prepare to deal with language differences by learning whether individuals to be met are comfortable speaking English. If not, plans should be made for an interpreter. Business language is generally more technical than the conversational speech with which many travelers are familiar; mistakes can be costly.

In some countries, exchanging business cards at any first meeting is considered a basic part of good business manner. As a matter of courtesy, it is best to carry business cards printed both in English and in the language of the country being visited. Some international airlines arrange this service.

The following travel checklist covers a number of considerations that apply equally to business travelers and vacations. A travel agent or various travel publications can help take these considerations into account:

- Seasonal weather conditions in the countries being visited.
- Health care (e.g., what to eat abroad, special medical problems, and prescription drugs).
- Electrical current (a transformer or plug adapter may be needed to use electrical appliances).
- Money (e.g., exchanging currency and using credit cards and travelers checks).
- Transportation and communication abroad.
- Cultural differences.
- Tipping (who is tipped and how much is appropriate).
- U.S. Customs regulations on what can be brought home.

Assistance from U.S. Embassies and Consulates

Economic and commercial officers in U.S. embassies and consulates abroad can provide assistance to U.S. exporters, both through in-depth briefings and by arranging introductions to appropriate firms, individuals, or foreign government officials. Because of the value and low cost of these services, it is recommended that the exporter visit the U.S. embassy soon after arriving in a foreign country.

When planning a trip, business travelers can discuss their needs and the services available at particular embassies with the staff of the local Commerce district office. It is also advisable to write directly to the U.S. embassy or consulate in the countries to be visited at least two weeks before leaving the United States and to address any communication to the commercial section. The U.S. business traveler should identify his or her business affiliation and complete address and indicate the objective of the trip and the type of assistance required from the post. Also a description of the firm and the extent of its international experience would be helpful to the post. Addresses of U.S. embassies and consulates are provided in Key Officers of Foreign Service Posts, a publication available from the Superintendent of Documents, U.S. Government Printing Office, Washington, D.C. 20402-9371; telephone (202) 783-3238. The cost for this publication is $5 for one year, and it is issued twice a year. (See Chapter 36).

A program of special value to U.S. business travelers is the Department of Commerce's Gold Key Service, which is custom tailored to U.S. firms visiting overseas markets. This service combines several forms of Commerce assistance, including agent and distributor location, one-on-one business counseling, prescheduled appointments with key contacts, and U.S. embassy assistance with interpreters and translators, clerical support, office services, and so on. The service is not available in all markets and may be known under a different name in some countries (e.g., RepFind in Mexico). Further information and assistance are available from any Commerce district office.

Carnets

Foreign customs regulations vary widely from place to place, and the traveler is wise to learn in advance the regulations that apply to each country to be visited. If allowances for cigarettes, liquor, currency, and certain other items are not taken into account, they can be impounded at national borders. Business travelers who plan to carry product samples with them should be alert to import duties they may be required to pay. In some countries, duties and extensive customs procedures on sample products may be avoided by obtaining an ATA (Admission Temporoire) Carnet.

The ATA Carnet is a standardized international customs document used to obtain duty-free temporary admission of certain goods into the countries that are signatories to the ATA Convention. Under the ATA Convention, commercial and professional travelers may take commercial samples; tools of the trade; advertising material; and cinematographic, audiovisual, medical, scientific, or other professional equipment into member countries temporarily without paying customs duties and taxes or posting a bond at the border of each country to be visited.

Countries are continuously added to the ATA Carnet system. The traveler should contact the U.S. Council for International Business to determine if the country to be visited is a participant. Applications for carnets should be made to the same organization. A fee is charged, depending on the value of the goods to be covered. A bond, letter of credit, or bank guaranty of 40 percent of the value of the goods is also required to cover duties and taxes that would be due if goods imported into a foreign country by carnet were not reexported and the duties were not paid by the carnet holder. The carnets generally are valid for 12 months.

To obtain a Carnet, dial Carnet headquarters at (212) 354-4480; 1-800-CARNETS (for the office nearest your calling number); or 1-800-ATA-2900 (Carnet Helpline). The Roanoke Companies, an authorized issuing agent of the U.S. Council, has Carnet issuing facilities in New York, Los Angeles, Chicago, San Francisco, Boston, Baltimore, Miami, and Houston.

Cultural Factors

Business executives who hope to profit from their travel should learn about the history, culture, and customs of the countries to be visited. Flexibility and cultural adaptation should be the guiding principles for traveling abroad on business. Business manners and methods, religious customs, dietary practices, humor, and acceptable dress vary widely from country to country. For example, consider the following:

> Never touch the head of a Thai or pass an object over it; the head is considered

458

sacred in Thailand.

Avoid using triangular shapes in Hong Kong, Korea, and Taiwan; the triangle is considered a negative shape.

The number 7 is considered bad luck in Kenya and good luck in the Czech Republic, and it has magical connotations in Benin. The number 10 is bad luck in Korea, and 4 means death in Japan.

Red is a positive color in Denmark, but it represents witchcraft and death in many African countries.

A nod of the head means no to a Bulgarian, and shaking the head from side to side means yes.

The "okay" sign commonly used in the United States (thumb and index finger forming a circle and the other fingers raised) means zero in France, is a symbol for money in Japan, and carries a vulgar connotation in Brazil.

The use of a palm-up hand and moving index finger signals "come here" in the United States and in some other countries, but it is considered vulgar in others.

In Ethiopia, repeatedly opening and closing the palm-down hand means "come here."

Understanding and heeding cultural variables such as these is critical to success in international business travel and in international business itself. Lack of familiarity with the business practices, social customs, and etiquette of a country can weaken a company's position in the market, prevent it from accomplishing its objectives, and ultimately lead to failure.

Some of the cultural distinctions that U.S. firms most often face include differences in business styles, attitudes toward development of business relationships, attitudes toward punctuality, negotiating styles, gift-giving customs, greetings, significance of gestures, meanings of colors and numbers, and customs regarding titles.

American firms must pay close attention to different styles of doing business and the degree of importance placed on developing business relationships. In some countries, business people have a very direct style, while in others they are much more subtle in style and value the personal relationship more than most Americans do in business. For example, in the Middle East, engaging in small talk before engaging in business is standard practice.

Attitudes toward punctuality vary greatly from one culture to another and, if misunderstood, can cause confusion and misunderstanding. Romanians, Japanese, and Germans are very punctual, whereas people in many of the Latin countries have a more relaxed attitude toward time. The Japanese consider it rude to be late for a business meeting, but acceptable, even fashionable, to be late for a social occasion. In Guatemala, on the other hand, one might arrive anytime from 10 minutes early to 45 minutes late for a luncheon appointment.

When cultural lines are being crossed, something as simple as a greeting can be misunderstood. Traditional greetings may be a handshake, a hug, a nose rub, a kiss, placing the hands in praying position, or various other gestures. Lack of awareness concerning the country's accepted form of greeting can lead to awkward encounters.

People around the world use body movements and gestures to convey specific messages. Sometimes the same gestures have very different meanings, however. Misunderstanding over gestures is a common occurrence in cross-cultural communication, and misinterpretation along these lines can lead to business complications and social embarrassment.

Proper use of names and titles is often a source of confusion in international business relations. In many countries (including the United Kingdom, France, and Denmark) it is appropriate to use titles until use of first names is suggested. First names are seldom used when doing business in Germany. Visiting business people should use the surname preceded by the title. Titles such as "Herr Direktor" are sometimes used to indicate prestige, status, and rank. Thais, on the other hand, address one other by first names and reserve last names for very formal occasions and written communications. In Belgium it is important to address French-speaking business contacts as "Monsieur" or "Madame," while Dutch-speaking contacts should be addressed as ``Mr.'' or "Mrs." To confuse the two is a great insult.

Customs concerning gift giving are extremely important to understand. In some cultures gifts are expected and failure to present them is considered an insult, whereas in other countries offering a gift is considered offensive. Business executives also need to know when to present gifts-on the initial visit or afterwards; where to present gifts-in public or private; what type of gift to present; what color it should be; and how many to present.

Gift giving is an important part of doing business in Japan, where gifts are usually exchanged at the first meeting. In sharp contrast, gifts are rarely exchanged in Germany and are usually not appropriate. Gift giving is not a normal custom in Belgium or the United Kingdom either, although in both countries, flowers are a suitable gift when invited to someone's home.

Customs concerning the exchange of business cards vary, too. Although this point seems of minor importance, observing a country's customs for card giving is a key part of business protocol. In Japan, for example, the Western practice of accepting a business card and pocketing it immediately is considered rude. The proper approach is to carefully look at the card after accepting it, observe the title and organization, acknowledge with a nod that the information has been digested, and perhaps make a relevant comment or ask a police question.

Negotiating-a complex process even between parties from the same nation-is even more complicated in international transactions because of the added chance of misunderstandings stemming from cultural differences. It is essential to understand the importance of rank in the other country; to know who the decision-makers are; to be familiar with the business style of the foreign company; and to understand the nature of agreements in the country, the significance of gestures, and negotiating etiquette.

It is important to acquire, through reading or training, a basic knowledge of the business culture, management attitudes, business methods, and consumer habits of the country being visited. This does not mean that the traveler must go native when conducting business abroad. It does mean that the traveler should be sensitive to the customs and business procedures of the country being visited.

460

Chapter 26

Nationality & Citizenship Issues

[The information in this chapter is reprinted verbatim from a number of bulletins issued by the U.S. State Department, Bureau of Consular Affairs. It is intended to serve as advice to Americans traveling abroad.]

Dual Nationality

The concept of dual nationality means that a person is a citizen of two countries at the same time. Each country has its own citizenship laws based on its own policy. Persons may have dual nationality by automatic operation of different laws rather than by choice. For example, a child born in a foreign country to U.S. citizen parents may be both a U.S. citizen and a citizen of the country of birth.

A U.S. citizen may acquire foreign citizenship by marriage, or a person naturalized as a U.S. citizen may not lose the citizenship of the country of birth. U.S. law does not mention dual nationality or require a person to choose one citizenship or another. Also, a person who is automatically granted another citizenship does not risk losing U.S. citizenship. However, a person who acquires a foreign citizenship by applying for it may lose U.S. citizenship. In order to lose U.S. citizenship, the law requires that the person must apply for the foreign citizenship voluntarily, by free choice, and with the intention to give up U.S. citizenship.

Intent can be shown by the person's statements or conduct. The U.S. Government recognizes that dual nationality exists but does not encourage it as a matter of policy because of the problems it may cause. Claims of other countries on dual national U.S. citizens may conflict with U.S. law, and dual nationality may limit U.S. Government efforts to assist citizens abroad. The country where a dual national is located generally has a stronger claim to that person's allegiance.

However, dual nationals owe allegiance to both the United States and the foreign country. They are required to obey the laws of both countries. Either country has the right to enforce its laws, particularly if the person later travels there. Most

U.S. citizens, including dual nationals, must use a U.S. passport to enter and leave the United States. Dual nationals may also be required by the foreign country to use its passport to enter and leave that country. Use of the foreign passport does not endanger U.S. citizenship. Most countries permit a person to renounce or otherwise lose citizenship.

Information on losing foreign citizenship can be obtained from the foreign country's embassy and consulates in the United States. Americans can renounce U.S. citizenship in the proper form at U.S. embassies and consulates abroad.

ADVICE ABOUT POSSIBLE LOSS OF U.S. CITIZENSHIP AND DUAL NATIONALITY

The Department of State is responsible for determining the citizenship status of a person located outside the United States or in connection with the application for a U.S. passport while in the United States.

POTENTIALLY EXPATRIATING STATUTES

Section 349 of the Immigration and Nationality Act, as amended, states that U.S. citizens are subject to loss of citizenship if they perform certain acts voluntarily and with the intention to relinquish U.S. citizenship. Briefly stated, these acts include:

(1) obtaining naturalization in a foreign state (Sec. 349 (a) (1) INA);

(2) taking an oath, affirmation or other formal declaration to a foreign state or its political subdivisions (Sec. 349 (a) (2) INA);

(3) entering or serving in the armed forces of a foreign state engaged in hostilities against the U.S. or serving as

a commissioned or non-commissioned officer in the armed forces of a foreign state (Sec. 349 (a) (3) INA);

(4) accepting employment with a foreign government if (a) one has the nationality of that foreign state or (b) a declaration of allegiance is required in accepting the position (Sec. 349 (a) (4) INA);

(5) formally renouncing U.S. citizenship before a U.S. consular officer outside the United States (sec. 349 (a) (5) INA);

(6) formally renouncing U.S. citizenship within the U.S. (but only "in time of war") (Sec. 349 (a) (6) INA);

(7) conviction for an act of treason (Sec. 349 (a) (7) INA).

ADMINISTRATIVE STANDARD OF EVIDENCE

As already noted, the actions listed above can cause loss of U.S. citizenship only if performed voluntarily and with the intention of relinquishing U.S. citizenship. *The Department has a uniform administrative standard of evidence based on the premise that U.S. citizens intend to retain United States citizenship when they obtain naturalization in a foreign state, subscribe to routine declarations of allegiance to a foreign state, or accept non-policy level employment with a foreign government.*

DISPOSITION OF CASES WHEN ADMINISTRATIVE PREMISE IS APPLICABLE

In light of the administrative premise discussed above, a person who:

(1) is naturalized in a foreign country;

(2) takes a routine oath of allegiance or

(3) accepts non-policy level employment with a foreign government

and in so doing wishes to retain U.S. citizenship need not submit prior to the commission of a

potentially expatriating act a statement or evidence of his or her intent to retain U.S. citizenship since such an intent will be presumed.

When, as the result of an individual's inquiry or an individual's application for registration or a passport it comes to the attention of a U.S. consular officer that a U.S. citizen has performed an act made potentially expatriating by Sections 349(a)(1), 349(a)(2), 349(a)(3) or 349(a)(4), the consular officer will simply ask the applicant if there was intent to relinquish U.S. citizenship when performing the act. If the answer is no, the consular officer will certify that it was **not** the person's intent to relinquish U.S. citizenship and, consequently, find that the person has retained U.S. citizenship.

PERSONS WHO WISH TO RELINQUISH U.S. CITIZENSHIP

If the answer to the question regarding intent to relinquish citizenship is **yes**, the person concerned will be asked to complete a questionnaire to ascertain his or her intent toward U.S. citizenship. When the questionnaire is completed and the voluntary relinquishment statement is signed by the expatriate, the consular officer will proceed to prepare a certificate of loss of nationality. The certificate will be forwarded to the Department of State for consideration and, if appropriate, approval.

An individual who has performed **any** of the acts made potentially expatriating by statute who wishes to lose U.S. citizenship may do so by affirming in writing to a U.S. consular officer that the act was performed with an intent to relinquish U.S. citizenship. Of course, a person always has the option of seeking to formally renounce U.S. citizenship in accordance with Section 349 (a) (5) INA.

DISPOSITION OF CASES WHEN ADMINISTRATIVE PREMISE IS INAPPLICABLE

The premise that a person intends to retain U.S. citizenship is **not** applicable when the individual:

(1) formally renounces U.S. citizenship before a consular officer;

(2) takes a policy level position in a foreign state;

(3) is convicted of treason; or

(4) performs an act made potentially expatriating by statute accompanied by conduct which is so inconsistent with retention of U.S. citizenship that it compels a conclusion that the individual intended to relinquish U.S. citizenship. (Such cases are very rare.)

Cases in categories 2, 3, and 4 will be developed carefully by U.S. consular officers to ascertain the individual's intent toward U.S. citizenship.

APPLICABILITY OF ADMINISTRATIVE PREMISE TO PAST CASES

The premise established by the administrative standard of evidence is applicable to cases adjudicated previously. Persons who previously lost U.S. citizenship may wish to have their cases reconsidered in light of this policy.

A person may initiate such a reconsideration by submitting a request to the nearest U.S. consular office or by writing directly to:

Director
Office of American Citizens Services
(CA/OCS/ACS)
Room 4817 NS
Department of State
2201 C Street N.W.
Washington, D.C. 20520
Each case will be reviewed on its own merits taking into consideration, for example, statements made by the person at the time of the potentially expatriating act.

LOSS OF NATIONALITY AND TAXATION

P.L. 104-191 contains changes in the taxation of U.S. citizens who renounce or otherwise lose U.S. citizenship. In general, any person who lost U.S. citizenship within 10 years immediately preceding the close of the taxable year, whose principle purpose in losing citizenship was to avoid taxation, will be subject to continued taxation. For the purposes of this statute, persons are presumed to have a principle purpose of avoiding taxation if 1) their average annual net income tax for a five year period before the date of loss of citizenship is greater than $100,000, or 2) their net worth on the date of the loss of U.S. nationality is $500,000 or more (subject to cost of living adjustments). The

effective date of the law is retroactive to February 6, 1995. Copies of approved Certificates of Loss of Nationality are provided by the Department of State to the Internal Revenue Service pursuant to P.L. 104-191. Questions regarding United States taxation consequences upon loss of U.S. nationality, should be addressed to the U.S. Internal Revenue Service.

DUAL NATIONALITY

Dual nationality can occur as the result of a variety of circumstances. The automatic acquisition or retention of a foreign nationality, acquired, for example, by birth in a foreign country or through an alien parent, does not affect U.S. citizenship. It is prudent, however, to check with authorities of the other country to see if dual nationality is permissible under local law. Dual nationality can also occur when a person is naturalized in a foreign state without intending to relinquish U.S. nationality and is thereafter found not to have lost U.S. citizenship the individual consequently may possess dual nationality. While recognizing the existence of dual nationality and permitting Americans to have other nationalities, the U.S. Government does not endorse dual nationality as a matter of policy because of the problems which it may cause. Claims of other countries upon dual-national U.S. citizens often place them in situations where their obligation to one country are in conflict with the laws of the other. In addition, their dual nationality may hamper efforts to provide U.S. diplomatic and consular protection to them when they are abroad.

ADDITIONAL INFORMATION

See also information flyers on related subject available via the Department of State, Bureau of Consular Affairs home page on the internet at http://travel.state.gov or via our automated fax service at 202-647-3000. These flyers include:

- Dual Nationality
- Advice About Possible Loss of U.S. Citizenship and Seeking Public Office in a Foreign State
- Advice About Possible Loss of U.S. Citizenship and Foreign Military Service
- Renunciation of United States Citizenship
- Renunciation of U.S. Citizenship by Persons Claiming a Right of Residence in the United States

463

QUESTIONS

For further information, please contact the appropriate geographic division of the Office of American Citizens Services:

Africa Division at (202) 647-6060;
East Asia and Pacific Division at (202) 647-6769;
Europe Division at (202) 647-6178;
Latin America and the Caribbean Division at (202) 647-5118;
Near East and South Asia Division at (202) 647-7899.

Counsel representing persons in matters related to loss of U.S. nationality may also address inquiries to Director, Office of Policy Review and Inter-Agency Liaison, Overseas Citizens Services, Room 4817 N.S., Department of State, 2201 C Street N.W., Washington, D.C. 20520, 202-647-3666.

ADVICE ABOUT POSSIBLE LOSS OF U.S. CITIZENSHIP AND SEEKING PUBLIC OFFICE IN A FOREIGN STATE

DISCLAIMER: THE INFORMATION IN THIS CIRCULAR IS PROVIDED FOR GENERAL INFORMATION ONLY. QUESTIONS INVOLVING INTERPRETATION OF SECTION 349(A)(4) INA WITH RESPECT TO A PARTICULAR CASE SHOULD BE ADDRESSED TO THE BUREAU OF CONSULAR AFFAIRS' OFFICE OF POLICY REVIEW AND INTERAGENCY LIAISON.

The Department of State is the U.S. government agency responsible for determining whether a person located outside the United States is a U.S. citizen or national. A U.S. citizen who assumes foreign public office may come within the loss of nationality statute, which is Section 349 of the Immigration and Nationality Act of 1952 (INA), as amended, or other legal provisions as discussed below.

Currently, there is no general prohibition on U.S. citizens' running for an elected office in a foreign government. Under Article 1, section 9, clause 8 of the U.S. Constitution, however, U.S. federal government officers may not accept foreign government employment without the consent of Congress. In addition, certain retired and reserve U.S. uniformed personnel may not accept foreign government positions without the express permission of the Secretary of State and the Secretary of their department. These restrictions are reflected in the Department's regulations at 22 CFR Part 3a., and are based on 37 U.S.C. 801 Note; 22 U.S.C.2658.

With respect to loss of nationality, 349(a)(4) of the Immigration and Nationality Act (INA), as amended, is the applicable section of law. Pursuant to 349(a)(4), accepting, serving in, or performing duties of in a foreign government is a potentially expatriating act. In order to come within the Act, the person must either be a national of that country or take an oath of allegiance in connection with the position. Thus, the threshold question is whether the person's actions fall within the scope of this provision. Information used to make this determination may include official confirmation from the foreign government about the person's nationality, and whether an oath of allegiance is required.

In addition, the prefatory language of section 349 requires that expatriating act be performed voluntarily and "with the intention of relinquishing U.S. nationality." Thus, if it is determined that the person's action falls within the purview of 349(a)(4) INA, an adjudication of the person's intent must be made.

The Department has a uniform administrative standard of evidence based on the premise that U.S. citizens intend to retain U.S. citizenship when they obtain naturalization in a foreign state, subscribe to routine declarations of allegiance to a foreign state, or accept non-policy level employment with a foreign government. This administrative premise is not applicable when an individual seeks public office in a foreign state, instead, the Department of State will carefully ascertain the individual's intent toward U.S. citizenship.

Because the Department's administrative practice presumes that U.S. citizens employed in non-policy level positions in a foreign government do not have the requisite intent to relinquish U.S. citizenship, there are no efforts to seek out or adjudicate the citizenship of citizens who fall into this category of employment. On the other hand, because there is no administrative presumption that

U.S. citizens who hold policy-level positions in foreign governments necessarily intend to retain their U.S. citizenship, efforts are made to fully adjudicate such cases to determine the individual's intent. (Service in a country's legislative body is considered by the Department to be a policy level position.)

An Attorney General's opinion of 1969 states that service in an important foreign political position constitutes highly persuasive evidence of intent to relinquish U.S. citizenship. In some cases, it would appear that holding a foreign office may be incompatible with maintaining U.S. citizenship (e.g. if the position necessarily entails immunity from U.S. law). The Department does not normally consider such service alone, as sufficient to sustain the burden of showing loss of U.S. citizenship by a preponderance of the evidence when the individual has explicitly expressed a contrary intent. This is particularly true when the individual continues to file U.S. tax returns, enters and leaves the U.S. on a U.S. passport, maintains close ties in the U.S. (such as maintaining a residence in the U.S.), and takes other actions consistent with an intent to retain U.S. citizenship notwithstanding the assumption of a foreign government position. Conversely, a person who publicly denied an intent to retain citizenship or who stopped paying his/her taxes, traveled to the United States on a foreign passport, and abandoned any residence in the United States might be found to have intended to relinquish U.S. citizenship notwithstanding self-serving statements to the contrary. Therefore, the Department will consider statements, as well as inferences drawn from the person's conduct, in determining one's intent to remain a U.S. citizen. Intent is determined on a case-by-case basis in light of the facts and circumstances of each individual's case. If expressed intent and conduct are consistent with a lack of intent to relinquish U.S. citizenship, the Department would generally conclude that no loss has occurred.

For further information about possible loss of U.S. citizenship and seeking public office in a foreign state, please contact:

Director
Office of Policy Review and Interagency Liaison
CA/OCS/PRI Room 4817 MS
U.S. Department of State

2201 C Street, NW
Washington, D.C. 20520-4818
(202) 647-3666

ADVICE ABOUT POSSIBLE LOSS OF U.S. CITIZENSHIP AND FOREIGN MILITARY SERVICE

A U.S. citizen who is a resident or citizen of a foreign country may be subject to compulsory military service in that country. Although the United States opposes service by U.S. citizens in foreign armed forces, there is little that we can do to prevent it since each sovereign country has the right to make its own laws on military service and apply them as it sees fit to its citizens and residents.

Such participation by citizens of our country in the internal affairs of foreign countries can cause problems in the conduct of our foreign relations and may involve U.S. citizens in hostilities against countries with which we are at peace. For this reason, U.S. citizens facing the possibility of foreign military service should do what is legally possible to avoid such service.

Federal statutes long in force prohibit certain aspects of foreign military service originating within the United States. The current laws are set forth in Section 958-960 of Title 18 of the United States Code. In *Wiborg v. U.S.*, 163 U.S. 632 (1985), the Supreme Court endorsed a lower court ruling that it was not a crime under U.S. law for an individual to go abroad for the purpose of enlisting in a foreign army; however, when someone has been recruited or hired in he United States, a violation may have occurred. The prosecution of persons who have violated 18 U.S.C. 958-960 is the responsibility of the Department of Justice.

Although a person's enlistment in the armed forces of a foreign country may not constitute a violation of U.S. law, it could subject him or her to Section 349(a)(3) of the Immigration and Nationality Act [8 U.S.C. 1481(a)(3)] which provides for loss of U.S. nationality if an American voluntarily and with the intention of relinquishing U.S. citizenship enters or serves in foreign armed forces engaged in hostilities against the United States or serves in the armed forces of any foreign country as a commissioned or non-commissioned officer.

Loss of U.S. nationality was almost immediate consequences of foreign military service and the other acts listed in Section 349(a) until 1967 when the Supreme Court handed down its decision in *Afroyim v. Rusk*, 387 U.S. 253. In that decision, the court declared unconstitutional the provisions of Section 349(a) which provided for loss of nationality by voting in a foreign election. In so doing, the Supreme Court indicated foreign election. In so doing, the Supreme Court indicated that a U.S. citizen "has a constitutional right to remain a citizen... unless he voluntarily relinquishes that citizenship."

Further confirmation of the necessity to establish the citizen's intent to relinquish nationality before expatriation will result came in the opinion in *Vance v. Terrazas*, 444 U.S. 252 (1980). The Court stated that "expatriation depends on the will of the citizen rather than on the will of Congress and its assessment of his conduct." The Court also indicated that a person's intention to relinquish U.S. citizenship may be shown by statements or actions.

Military service in foreign countries usually does not cause loss of citizenship since an intention to relinquish citizenship normally is lacking. Service as a high-ranking officer, particularly in a policy-making position, could be viewed as indicative of an intention to relinquish U.S. citizenship.

Pursuant to Section 351(b) of the Immigration and Nationality Act, a person who served in foreign armed forces while under the age of eighteen is not considered subject to the provisions of Section 349(a)(3) if, within six months of attaining the age of eighteen, he or she asserts a claim to United States citizenship in the manner prescribed by the Secretary of State.

LOSS OF NATIONALITY AND TAXATION

P.L. 104-191 contains changes in the taxation of U.S. citizens who renounce or otherwise lose U.S. citizenship. In general, any person who lost U.S. citizenship within 10 years immediately preceding the close of the taxable year, whose principle purpose in losing citizenship was to avoid taxation, will be subject to continued taxation. For the purposes of this statute, persons are presumed to have a principle purpose of avoiding taxation if 1)

their average annual net income tax for a five year period before the date of loss of citizenship is greater than $100,000, or 2) their net worth on the date of the loss of U.S. nationality is $500,000 or more (subject to cost of living adjustments). The effective date of the law is retroactive to February 6, 1995. Copies of approved Certificates of Loss of Nationality are provided by the Department of State to the Internal Revenue Service pursuant to P.L. 104-191. Questions regarding United States taxation consequences upon loss of U.S. nationality, should be addressed to the U.S. Internal Revenue Service.

ADDITIONAL INFORMATION

See also information flyers on related subject available via the Department of State, Bureau of Consular Affairs home page on the internet at http://travel.state.gov or via our automated fax service at 202-647-3000. These flyers include:

- Dual Nationality
- Advice About Possible Loss of U.S. Citizenship and Seeking Public Office in a Foreign State
- Advice About Possible Loss of U.S. Citizenship and Foreign Military Service
- Renunciation of United States Citizenship
- Renunciation of U.S. Citizenship by Persons Claiming a Right of Residence in the United States

QUESTIONS

For further information, please contact the appropriate geographic division of the Office of American Citizens Services:

Africa Division at (202) 647-6060;
East Asia and Pacific Division at (202) 647-6769;
Europe Division at (202) 647-6178;
Latin America and the Caribbean Division at (202) 647-5118;
Near East and South Asia Division at (202) 647-7899.

Counsel representing persons in matters related to loss of U.S. nationality may also address inquiries to Director, Office of Policy Review and Inter-Agency Liaison, Overseas Citizens Services, Room 4817 N.S., Department of State, 2201 C Street N.W., Washington, D.C. 20520, 202-647-

3666.

Acquisition of U.S. Citizenship By a Child Born Abroad

Birth Abroad to Two U.S. Citizen Parents in Wedlock: A child born abroad to two U.S. citizen parents acquires U.S. citizenship at birth under section 301(c) of the Immigration and Nationality Act (INA). One of the parents MUST have resided in the U.S. prior to the child's birth. No specific period of time for such prior residence is required.

Birth Abroad to One Citizen and One Alien Parent in Wedlock: A child born abroad to one U.S. citizen parent and one alien parent acquires U.S. citizenship at birth under Section 301(g) INA provided the citizen parent was physically present in the U.S. for the time period required by the law applicable at the time of the child's birth. (For birth on or after November 14, 1986, a period of five years physical presence, two after the age of fourteen is required. For birth between December 24, 1952 and November 13, 1986, a period of ten years, five after the age of fourteen are required for physical presence in the U.S. to transmit U.S. citizenship to the child.

Birth Abroad Out-of-Wedlock to a U.S. Citizen Father: A child born abroad out-of-wedlock to a U.S. citizen father may acquire U.S. citizenship under Section 301(g) INA, as made applicable by Section 309(a) INA provided:

1) a blood relationship between the applicant and the father is established by clear and convincing evidence;
2) the father had the nationality of the United States at the time of the applicant's birth;
3) the father (unless deceased) had agreed in writing to provide financial support for the person until the applicant reaches the age of 18 years, and
4) while the person is under the age of 18 years --
A) applicant is legitimated under the law of their residence or domicile,
B) father acknowledges paternity of the person in writing under oath, or
C) the paternity of the applicant is established by adjudication court.

Birth Abroad Out-of-Wedlock to a U.S. Citizen Mother: A child born abroad out-of-wedlock to a U.S. citizen mother may acquire U.S. citizenship

under Section 301(g) INA, as made applicable by Section 309(c) INA if the mother was a U.S. citizen at the time of the child's birth, and if the mother had previously been physically present in the United States or one of its outlying possessions for a continuous period of one year.
1997

Renunciation of U.S. Citizenship

A. THE IMMIGRATION & NATIONALITY ACT
Section 349(a)(5) of the Immigration and Nationality Act (INA) is the section of law that governs the ability of a United States citizen to renounce his or her U.S. citizenship. That section of law provides for the loss of nationality by voluntarily performing the following act with the intent to relinquish his or her U.S. nationality:

> "(5) making a formal renunciation of nationality before a diplomatic or consular officer of the United States *in a foreign state*, in such form as may be prescribed by the Secretary of State" (emphasis added).

B. ELEMENTS OF RENUNCIATION
A person wishing to renounce his or her U.S. citizenship must voluntarily and with intent to relinquish U.S. citizenship:
11. appear in person before a U.S. consular or diplomatic officer,
12. in a foreign country (normally at a U.S. Embassy or Consulate); and
13. sign an oath of renunciation
14.
Renunciations that do not meet the conditions described above have no legal effect. Because of the provisions of section 349(a)(5), Americans cannot effectively renounce their citizenship by mail, through an agent, or while in the United States. In fact, U.S. courts have held certain attempts to renounce U.S. citizenship to be ineffective on a variety of grounds, as discussed below.

C. REQUIREMENT - RENOUNCE ALL RIGHTS AND PRIVILEGES
In the recent case of Colon v. U.S. Department of State, 2 F.Supp.2d 43 (1998), plaintiff was a United States citizen and resident of Puerto Rico, who executed an oath of renunciation before a consular officer at the U.S. Embassy in Santo Domingo. The U.S. District Court for the District

of Columbia rejected Colon's petition for a writ of mandamus directing the Secretary of State to approve a Certificate of Loss of Nationality in the case because the plaintiff wanted to retain one of the primary benefits of U.S. citizenship while claiming he was not a U.S. citizen. The Court described the plaintiff as a person, "claiming to renounce all rights and privileges of United States citizenship, [while] Plaintiff wants to continue to exercise one of the fundamental rights of citizenship, namely to travel freely throughout the world and when he wants to, return and reside in the United States." See also Jose Fufi Santori v. United States of America, 1994 U.S. App. LEXIS 16299 (1994) for a similar case.

A person who wants to renounce U.S. citizenship cannot decide to retain some of the privileges of citizenship, as this would be logically inconsistent with the concept of citizenship. Thus, such a person can be said to lack a full understanding of renouncing citizenship and/or lack the necessary intent to renounce citizenship, and the Department of State will not approve a loss of citizenship in such instances.

D. DUAL NATIONALITY / STATELESSNESS

Persons intending to renounce U.S. citizenship should be aware that, unless they already possess a foreign nationality, they may be rendered stateless and, thus, lack the protection of any government. They may also have difficulty traveling as they may not be entitled to a passport from any country. Even if they were not stateless, they would still be required to obtain a visa to travel to the United States, or show that they are eligible for admission pursuant to the terms of the Visa Waiver Pilot Program (VWPP). If found ineligible for a visa or the VWPP to come to the U.S., a renunciant, under certain circumstances, could be permanently barred from entering the United States. Nonetheless, renunciation of U.S. citizenship may not prevent a foreign country from deporting that individual back to the United States in some non-citizen status.

E. TAX & MILITARY OBLIGATIONS /NO ESCAPE FROM PROSECUTION

Also, persons who wish to renounce U.S. citizenship should also be aware that the fact that a person has renounced U.S. citizenship may have no effect whatsoever on his or her U.S. tax or military service obligations (contact the Internal Revenue Service or U.S. Selective Service for more information). In addition, the act of renouncing U.S. citizenship will not allow persons to avoid possible prosecution for crimes which they may have committed in the United States, or escape the repayment of financial obligations previously incurred in the United States.

F. RENUNCIATION FOR MINOR CHILDREN

Parents cannot renounce U.S. citizenship on behalf of their minor children. Before an oath of renunciation will be administered under Section 349(a)(5) of the INA, a person under the age of eighteen must convince a U.S. diplomatic or consular officer that he/she fully understands the nature and consequences of the oath of renunciation and is voluntarily seeking to renounce his/her U.S. citizenship. United States common law establishes an arbitrary limit of age fourteen under which a child's understanding must be established by substantial evidence.

G. IRREVOCABILITY OF RENUNCIATION

Finally, those contemplating a renunciation of U.S. citizenship should understand that the act is irrevocable, except as provided in section 351 of the INA, and cannot be canceled or set aside absent successful administrative or judicial appeal. (Section 351(b) of the INA provides that an applicant who renounced his or her U.S. citizenship before the age of eighteen can have that citizenship reinstated if he or she makes that desire known to the Department of State within six months after attaining the age of eighteen. See also Title 22, Code of Federal Regulations, section 50.20).

Renunciation is the most unequivocal way in which a person can manifest an intention to relinquish U.S. citizenship. Please consider the effects of renouncing U.S. citizenship, described above, before taking this serious and irrevocable action. If you have any further questions regarding this matter, please contact the Director, Office of Policy Review & Interagency Liaison, Bureau of Consular Affairs, U.S. Department of State, Washington, DC 20520.

ADVICE ABOUT POSSIBLE LOSS OF U.S. CITIZENSHIP AND DUAL NATIONALITY

The Department of State is responsible for determining the citizenship status of a person located outside the United States or in connection with the application for a U.S. passport while in the United States.

POTENTIALLY EXPATRIATING STATUTES

Section 349 of the Immigration and Nationality Act, as amended, states that U.S. citizens are subject to loss of citizenship if they perform certain acts voluntarily and with the intention to relinquish U.S. citizenship. Briefly stated, these acts include:

(1) obtaining naturalization in a foreign state (Sec. 349 (a) (1) INA);

(2) taking an oath, affirmation or other formal declaration to a foreign state or its political subdivisions (Sec. 349 (a) (2) INA);

(3) entering or serving in the armed forces of a foreign state engaged in hostilities against the U.S. or serving as a commissioned or non-commissioned officer in the armed forces of a foreign state (Sec. 349 (a) (3) INA);

(4) accepting employment with a foreign government if (a) one has the nationality of that foreign state or (b) a declaration of allegiance is required in accepting the position (Sec. 349 (a) (4) INA);

(5) formally renouncing U.S. citizenship before a U.S. consular officer outside the United States (sec. 349 (a) (5) INA);

(6) formally renouncing U.S. citizenship within the U.S. (but only "in time of war") (Sec. 349 (a) (6) INA);

(7) conviction for an act of treason (Sec. 349 (a) (7) INA).

ADMINISTRATIVE STANDARD OF EVIDENCE

As already noted, the actions listed above can cause loss of U.S. citizenship only if performed voluntarily and with the intention of relinquishing U.S. citizenship. *The Department has a uniform administrative standard of evidence based on the premise that U.S. citizens intend to retain United States citizenship when they obtain naturalization in a foreign state, subscribe to routine declarations of allegiance to a foreign state, or accept non-policy level employment with a foreign government.*

DISPOSITION OF CASES WHEN ADMINISTRATIVE PREMISE IS APPLICABLE

In light of the administrative premise discussed above, a person who:

(1) is naturalized in a foreign country;

(2) takes a routine oath of allegiance or

(3) accepts non-policy level employment with a foreign government

and in so doing wishes to retain U.S. citizenship need not submit prior to the commission of a potentially expatriating act a statement or evidence of his or her intent to retain U.S. citizenship since such an intent will be presumed.

When, as the result of an individual's inquiry or an individual's application for registration or a passport it comes to the attention of a U.S. consular officer that a U.S. citizen has performed an act made potentially expatriating by Sections 349(a)(1), 349(a)(2), 349(a)(3) or 349(a)(4), the consular officer will simply ask the applicant if there was intent to relinquish U.S. citizenship when performing the act. If the answer is no, the consular officer will certify that it was **not** the person's intent to relinquish U.S. citizenship and, consequently, find that the person has retained U.S. citizenship.

PERSONS WHO WISH TO RELINQUISH U.S. CITIZENSHIP

If the answer to the question regarding intent to relinquish citizenship is **yes**, the person concerned will be asked to complete a questionnaire to ascertain his or her intent toward U.S. citizenship. When the questionnaire is completed and the voluntary relinquishment statement is signed by the expatriate, the consular officer will proceed to prepare a certificate of loss of nationality. The certificate will be forwarded to the Department of State for consideration and, if appropriate, approval.

469

An individual who has performed **any** of the acts made potentially expatriating by statute who wishes to lose U.S. citizenship may do so by affirming in writing to a U.S. consular officer that the act was performed with an intent to relinquish U.S. citizenship. Of course, a person always has the option of seeking to formally renounce U.S. citizenship in accordance with Section 349 (a) (5) INA.

DISPOSITION OF CASES WHEN ADMINISTRATIVE PREMISE IS INAPPLICABLE

The premise that a person intends to retain U.S. citizenship is **not** applicable when the individual:

(1) formally renounces U.S. citizenship before a consular officer;

(2) takes a policy level position in a foreign state;

(3) is convicted of treason; or

(4) performs an act made potentially expatriating by statute accompanied by conduct which is so inconsistent with retention of U.S. citizenship that it compels a conclusion that the individual intended to relinquish U.S. citizenship. (Such cases are very rare.)

Cases in categories 2, 3, and 4 will be developed carefully by U.S. consular officers to ascertain the individual's intent toward U.S. citizenship.

APPLICABILITY OF ADMINISTRATIVE PREMISE TO PAST CASES

The premise established by the administrative standard of evidence is applicable to cases adjudicated previously. Persons who previously lost U.S. citizenship may wish to have their cases reconsidered in light of this policy.

A person may initiate such a reconsideration by submitting a request to the nearest U.S. consular office or by writing directly to:

Director
Office of American Citizens Services
(CA/OCS/ACS)
Room 4817 NS
Department of State

2201 C Street N.W.
Washington, D.C. 20520
Each case will be reviewed on its own merits taking into consideration, for example, statements made by the person at the time of the potentially expatriating act.

LOSS OF NATIONALITY AND TAXATION

P.L. 104-191 contains changes in the taxation of U.S. citizens who renounce or otherwise lose U.S. citizenship. In general, any person who lost U.S. citizenship within 10 years immediately preceding the close of the taxable year, whose principle purpose in losing citizenship was to avoid taxation, will be subject to continued taxation. For the purposes of this statute, persons are presumed to have a principle purpose of avoiding taxation if 1) their average annual net income tax for a five year period before the date of loss of citizenship is greater than $100,000, or 2) their net worth on the date of the loss of U.S. nationality is $500,000 or more (subject to cost of living adjustments). The effective date of the law is retroactive to February 6, 1995. Copies of approved Certificates of Loss of Nationality are provided by the Department of State to the Internal Revenue Service pursuant to P.L. 104-191. Questions regarding United States taxation consequences upon loss of U.S. nationality, should be addressed to the U.S. Internal Revenue Service.

DUAL NATIONALITY

Dual nationality can occur as the result of a variety of circumstances. The automatic acquisition or retention of a foreign nationality, acquired, for example, by birth in a foreign country or through an alien parent, does not affect U.S. citizenship. It is prudent, however, to check with authorities of the other country to see if dual nationality is permissible under local law. Dual nationality can also occur when a person is naturalized in a foreign state without intending to relinquish U.S. nationality and is thereafter found not to have lost U.S. citizenship the individual consequently may possess dual nationality. While recognizing the existence of dual nationality and permitting Americans to have other nationalities, the U.S. Government does not endorse dual nationality as a matter of policy because of the problems which it may cause. Claims of other countries upon dual-national U.S. citizens often place them in situations where their obligation to one country are in conflict with the laws of the other. In addition, their dual nationality may hamper efforts to provide U.S. diplomatic and consular protection to them when they are abroad.

ADDITIONAL INFORMATION

See also information flyers on related subject available via the Department of State, Bureau of Consular Affairs home page on the internet at http://travel.state.gov or via our automated fax service at 202-647-3000. These flyers include:

- Dual Nationality
- Advice About Possible Loss of U.S. Citizenship and Seeking Public Office in a Foreign State
- Advice About Possible Loss of U.S. Citizenship and Foreign Military Service
- Renunciation of United States Citizenship
- Renunciation of U.S. Citizenship by Persons Claiming a Right of Residence in the United States

QUESTIONS

For further information, please contact the appropriate geographic division of the Office of American Citizens Services:

Africa Division at (202) 647-6060;
East Asia and Pacific Division at (202) 647-6769;
Europe Division at (202) 647-6178;
Latin America and the Caribbean Division at (202) 647-5118;
Near East and South Asia Division at (202) 647-7899.

Counsel representing persons in matters related to loss of U.S. nationality may also address inquiries to Director, Office of Policy Review and Inter-Agency Liaison, Overseas Citizens Services, Room 4817 N.S., Department of State, 2201 C Street N.W., Washington, D.C. 20520, 202-647-3666.

MARRIAGE OF UNITED STATES CITIZENS ABROAD

Who May Perform Marriages Abroad

American diplomatic and consular officers are NOT permitted to perform marriages (Title 22, Code of Federal Regulations 52.1). Marriages abroad are almost always performed by local (foreign) civil or religious officials.

As a rule, marriages are not performed on the premises of an American embassy or consulate. The validity of marriages abroad is not dependent upon the presence of an American diplomatic or consular officer, but upon adherence to the laws of the country where the marriage is performed. Consular officers may authenticate foreign marriage documents. The fee for authentication of a document is $32.00.

Validity of Marriages Abroad

In general, marriages which are legally performed and valid abroad are also legally valid in the United States. Inquiries regarding the validity of a marriage abroad should be directed to the attorney general of the state in the United States where the parties to the marriage live.

Foreign Laws and Procedures

The embassy or tourist information bureau of the country in which the marriage is to be performed is the best source of information about marriage in that country. Some general information on marriage in a limited number of countries can be obtained from Overseas Citizens Services, Room 4811, Department of State, Washington, DC 20520. In addition, American embassies and consulates abroad frequently have information about marriage in the country in which they are located.

Residence Requirements

Marriages abroad are subject to the residency requirements of the country in which the marriage is to be performed. There is almost always a lengthy waiting period.

Documentation and Authentication

Most countries require that a valid U.S. passport be presented. In addition, birth certificates, divorce decrees, and death certificates are frequently required. Some countries require that the documents presented to the marriage registrar first be authenticated in the United States by a consular official of that country. This process can be time consuming and expensive.

Parental Consent

The age of majority for marriage varies from one country to another. Persons under the age of 18 must, as a general rule, present a written statement of consent executed by their parents before a notary public. Some countries require the parental consent statement to be authenticated by a consular official of that foreign country in the United States.

Affidavit of Eligibility to Marry

All civil law countries require proof of legal capacity to enter into a marriage contract in the form of certification by competent authority that no impediment exists to the marriage. No such document exists in the United States. Unless the foreign authorities will allow such a statement to be executed before one of their consular officials in the United States, it will be necessary for the parties to a prospective marriage abroad to execute an affidavit at the American embassy or consulate in the country in which the marriage will occur stating that they are free to marry. This is called an affidavit of eligibility to marry and the fee for the American consular officer's certification of the affidavit is $55.00, subject to change. Some countries also require witnesses who will execute affidavits to the effect that the parties are free to marry.

Additional Requirements

Many countries, like the United States, require blood tests.

Some countries require that documents presented to the marriage registrar be translated into the native language of that country.

Loss of U.S. Nationality

In some countries, marriage to a national of that country will automatically make the spouse either a citizen of that country or eligible to become naturalized in that country expeditiously. The automatic acquisition of a second nationality will not affect U.S. citizenship. However, naturalization in a foreign country on one's own application or the application of a duly authorized agent may cause the loss of American citizenship. Persons planning to apply for a foreign nationality should contact an American embassy or consulate for further information.

Marriage to an Alien

Information on obtaining a visa for a foreign spouse may be obtained from any office of the Immigration and Naturalization Service, U.S. embassies and consulates abroad, or the Department of State Visa Office, Washington, DC 20520-0113. General information regarding visas

may be obtained by calling the Visa Office on 202-663-1225.

DIVORCE OVERSEAS

DISCLAIMER: THE INFORMATION IN THIS CIRCULAR IS PROVIDED FOR GENERAL INFORMATION ONLY AND MAY NOT BE TOTALLY ACCURATE IN A PARTICULAR CASE. QUESTIONS INVOLVING INTERPRETATION OF SPECIFIC U.S. STATE OR FOREIGN LAWS SHOULD BE ADDRESSED TO LEGAL COUNSEL IN THAT JURISDICTION.

STATE v. FEDERAL JURISDICTION: Marriage and divorce generally are considered matters reserved to the states rather than to the federal government. See, *Sosna v. Iowa, 419 U.S. 393, 404 (1975) and Armstrong v. Armstrong, 508 F. 2d 348 (1st Cir. 1974).* There is no treaty in force between the United States and any country on enforcement of judgments, including recognition of foreign divorces.

RECOGNITION BASED ON COMITY: A divorce decree issued in a foreign country generally is recognized in a state in the United States on the basis of comity *(Hilton v. Guyot, 159 U.S. 113, 163-64 (1895),* provided both parties to the divorce received adequate notice, i.e., service of process and, generally, provided one of the parties was a domiciliary in the foreign nation at the time of the divorce. Under the principle of comity, a divorce obtained in another country under the circumstances described above receives "full faith and credit" in all other states and countries that recognize divorce. Although full faith and credit may be given to an *ex parte* divorce decree, states usually consider the jurisdictional basis upon which the foreign decree is founded and may withhold full faith and credit if not satisfied regarding domicile in the foreign country. Many state courts which have addressed the question of a foreign divorce where both parties participate in the divorce proceedings but neither obtains domicile there have followed the view that such a divorce invalid *(Weber v. Weber, 200 Neb. 659, 265 N.W.2d 436 (1978); Everett v. Everett, 345 So. 2d 586 (La. Ct. App. 1977); Kugler v. Haitian Tours, Inc., 120 N.J. Super. 260, 293 A.2d 706 (1972); Estate of Steffke v.*

Wisconsin Department of Revenue, 65 Wis.2d 199, 222 N.W.2d 628 (1974); Commonwealth v. Doughty, 187 Pa. Super. 499, 144 A.2d 521 (1958); Bobala v. Bobala, 68 Ohio App. 63, 33 N.E.2d 845 (1940); Golden v. Golden, 41 N.M. 356, 68 P.2d 928 (1937).

AUTHORITY COMPETENT TO DETERMINE VALIDITY OF FOREIGN DIVORCE IN A U.S. STATE

Questions regarding the validity of foreign divorces in particular states in the United States should be referred to the office of the Attorney General of the state in question. It may be necessary to retain the services of a private attorney if the office of the state Attorney General does not provide such assistance to private citizens. Provide counsel with copies of foreign marriage certificates, divorce decrees and copies of foreign laws concerning divorce which may be available from the foreign attorney who handled the divorce.

MIGRATORY DIVORCES: "Foreign "migratory" divorces fall into four basic categories: (Nichols, Recognition and Enforcement: American Courts, Look at Foreign Divorces, 9 Family Advocate 9-10, 37 (1987).

-- "Ex Parte" divorces, based on the petitioner's physical presence in the foreign nation, with notice or constructive service given to the absent defendant;

-- "Bilateral" divorces, based on the physical presence of both parties in the divorcing nation, or the physical presence of the petitioner and the voluntary "appearance" by the defendant through an attorney;

-- "Void" divorces, where an *ex parte* divorce is obtained without notice, actual or constructive, to the absent defendant. Courts do not recognize or enforce this type of divorce;

-- "Practical recognition" divorces, wherein practical recognition may be afforded such decrees because of estoppel, laches, unclean hands, or similar equitable doctrines under which the party attacking the decree may be effectively barred from securing a judgment of invalidity. 13 A.L.R. 3d 1419, 1452. Many jurisdictions will prohibit the spouse who consented to the divorce from attacking it later under a principle of fairness called "estoppel". Thus, a party may be precluded from attacking a foreign divorce decree if such an attack would be inequitable under the

circumstances. *Scherer v. Scherer, 405 N.E. 2d 40, 44 (Ind. App. 1980), Rosenstiel v. Rosenstiel, 16 N.Y.2d 64, 209 N.E.2d 709, 262 N.Y.S.2d 86 (1965),* and *Yoder v. Yoder, 31 Conn.Supp. 345, 330 A.2d 825 (1974).*

REGISTERING FOREIGN DIVORCES AND THE ROLE OF U.S. EMBASSIES AND CONSULATES ABROAD

There are no provisions under U.S. law or regulation for registration of foreign divorce decrees at U.S. embassies or consulates abroad. 22 C.F.R. 52 does provide for authentication of foreign marriage and divorce records. This is not a form a registration, but simply the placing of the seal of the U.S. embassy or consulate, or other competent authority in countries party to the Hague Legalization Convention, over the seal of the foreign court. See below for a detailed discussion of the authentication process.

UNIFORM STATE LAWS AND REGISTRATION OF DIVORCES: The Uniform Act on Marriage and Divorce (1970, 1973), 9A Unif. Laws. Ann. 461 (Supp. 1965), is in force in Arizona, Colorado, Georgia, Illinois, Kentucky, Minnesota, Montana, and Washington state. Section 314(c) of the Uniform Act on Marriage and Divorce establishes a procedure for the clerk of court where the divorce decree is issued to register the decree in the place where the marriage itself was originally registered. The Uniform Divorce Recognition Act, 9 Unif. Laws Ann. 644 (1979), specifically denies recognition to a divorce decree obtaining in another jurisdiction when both spouses were domiciled in the home state. The Uniform Divorce Recognition Act is in force in California, Nebraska, New Hampshire, North Dakota, Rhode Island, South Carolina and Wisconsin. Information about uniform state laws is available from the national Conference of Comissioners on Uniform State Laws, 676 North St. Clair Street, Suite 1700, Chicago, Illinois 60611, tel: 312-915-0195 or via the Internet at http://www.law.upenn.edu/library/ulc/ulc.htm.

U.S. CONSULAR CERTIFICATES OF WITNESS TO MARRIAGE: With the repeal of the old 1860 statute on "solemnization of marriages", 22 U.S.C. 4192 on November 9, 1989, U.S. consular officers ceased issuing "Certificates of Witness to Marriage". Copies of witness to marriage issued between 1860 -1989 are available from the Office of passport Services, Vital Records Section, CA/PPT/PS/PC, Suite 510, 1111 19th Street, N.W., Washington, D.C. 20522, 202-955-0307. See also the passport Services Section of the Consular Affairs home page at http://travel.state.gov.

FOREIGN MARRIAGE CERTIFICATES: In the absence of the issuance of a "Certificate of Witness to Marriage," copies of foreign marriage certificates may be obtained directly from the civil registrar in the foreign country where the marriage occurred. Contact the embassy or consulate of the foreign country in the United States for guidance on how to obtain copies of foreign public documents. The documents may then be authenticated for use in the United States as explained below. English translations may be certified by translators in the United States before a notary public. When requesting copies of foreign public documents such as marriage or divorce records, it may be advisable to write to the foreign authorities in the language of the foreign country. Enclose copies of pertinent documents and any required fees in the form of an international money order.

PROOF OF FOREIGN DIVORCE: Obtain a certified copy of the foreign divorce decree from the court in the foreign country where the divorce decree was issued. Then have the document authenticated for use in the United States as explained below. Finally, obtain a certified English translation of the divorce decree (the translator executes a certificate before a notary public in the United States). When requesting copies of foreign public documents such as marriage or divorce records, it may be advisable to write to the foreign authorities in the language of the foreign country. Enclose copies of pertinent documents and any required fees in the form of an international money order.

AUTHENTICATION OF DIVORCE AND MARRIAGE RECORDS: It may be necessary for you to provide foreign authorities or your attorney with authenticated, translated copies of your foreign divorce decree and any other pertinent documents. Consult your foreign attorney before going to this expense

U.S. SSA, VA and IRS DETERMINATIONS REGARDING FOREIGN DIVORCES: There

have been a number of determinations by the U.S. Social Security Administration, Veterans Administration and Internal Revenue Service regarding the validity of foreign divorces based on the laws of the state of residence applicable with respect to claims for benefits. For SSA, see http://www.ssa.gov/. See also, 20 C.F.R. 404.314, SSR 66-1; 20 CFR 404.328(a), 404.1101, and 404.1104, SSR 72-61; 20 CFR 404.335(a), SSR 73-10a; 20 CFR 404.336, SSR 75-16; SSR 61-65; 20 CFR 404.340(c), SSR 88-15c, Section 202(g)(1)(A) of the Social Security Act (42 U.S.C. 402(g)(1)(A) *(Slessinger v. Secretary of Health and Human Services, 1A Unempl. Ins. Rep. (CCH),* 17,843 (1st Cir. 1987). *(Cunningham v. Harris, 658 F.2d 239, 243 (4th Cir. 1981).; Thompson v. Harris, 504 F. Supp. 653, 654 (D. Mass. 1980); Lugot v. Harris, 499 F. Supp. 1118 (D. Nev. 1980).* For Veterans Administration, see 27 FR 6281, July 3, 1962, as amended by 35 FR 16831, October 31, 1970; 40 FR 53581, November 19, 1975; 52 FR 19349, May 22, 1987. For the IRS, see *Estate of Felt v. Comm'r, 54 T.C.M. (CCH) 528 (1987).* It is our understanding that when obtained in good faith and not a sham for tax-avoidance purpose, the Internal Revenue Service recognizes foreign divorces.

OTHER CONTACTS: It may be helpful for American attorneys not familiar with enforcement and recognition of foreign divorces to consult the following resources:

ABA - the Family Law Section of the American Bar Association, 750 N. Lake Shore Drive, Chicago, IL 60611, 312-988-5000;
ABA Center on Children and the Law, 740 15th St., N.W., Washington, D.C. 20005, tel: 202-662-1740, http://www.abanet.org:80/child/home.html; State or local bar association;
American Academy of matrimonial Lawyers, 150 N. Michigan Avenue, Ste. 2040, Chicago, IL 50501, 312-263-6477, http://www.aaml.org/;
International Academy of matrimonial Lawyers, Secretariat, 13 Claybury, Bushey, Herts WD2 3ES, United Kingdom, tel: (011)(44) 0181-950-6452; fax: (011)(44) 0181.950-8895; http://www.iaml-usa.com/;
International Society of Family Law, Brigham Young University School of Law, 518 JRCB, Provo, UT 84602;
International Bar Association (IBA), 2 Harewood Place, Hanover Square, London, WIR9HB,

England, Tel: (011) (44) (171) 629-1206; Fax: (011) (44) (171) 409-0-456.

Library of Congress Law Library, Room 240, James Madison Bldg., 101 Independence Avenue, S.E., Washington, D.C. 20540, tel: 202-707-5079.

TREATIES: The United States is **not** a party to the Hague Convention on the Recognition of Divorces and Legal Separations of June 1, 1970 (978 U.N.T.S. 399 (975). See also, 5 Int'l Legal Materials 389, 393 (1966); 14 Am. J. Comp. L. 697, 700 (1966); 8 Int'l Legal Materials 31, 34 (1969); 8 Int'l Legal Materials 787, 800 (1969); 18 Int'l and Comp. L.Q. 488 (1969); 5 Family L.Q. 321 (1971); Reese, The Hague Draft Convention on Recognition of Foreign Divorces: A Comments, 14 Am. J. Comp. L. 692 (1966); Von Mehren, Draft Convention on the Recognition of Divorces and Legal Separations: Introductory Note, 16 Am. J. Comp. L. 580 (1968); Hampton, Hunning, & Wadsley, Current Legal Developments, Hague Convention on Recognition of Divorce and Legal Separation, 18 Int'l and Comp. L.Q. 483, 488 (1969). The Convention relates to such recognition but not to any ancillary matters such as findings of fault, orders for maintenance or custody of children. The Convention is in force in Australia, Cyprus, Czech Republic, Denmark, Egypt, Finland, Italy, Luxembourg, the Netherlands, Norway, Poland, Portugal, Romania, Slovenia, Sweden, Switzerland and the United Kingdom.

ENFORCEMENT OF JUDGMENTS: The Department of State, Office of Overseas Citizens Services has available a general information flyer on the subject of enforcement of judgments which is accessible via our automated fax service or our home page on the Internet as explained below.

SELECTED REFERENCES:

24 Am. Jur. 2d, Divorce and Separation, Sec. 971, 972, 27B C.J.S. Divorce Sec. 364-366.

Berke, Mexican Divorces, 7 Prac. Law. 84 (1961).

Bronstein, The Question of Haitian and Dominican Divorces, 166 N.Y.L.J., Sept. 21, 1971.

Ceschini, Divorce Proceedings in Italy: Domestic and International Procedures, 28 Family Law Quarterly, American Bar Association, 143, 150 (1994).

Comment, Mexican Bilateral Divorce -- A Catalyst

in Divorce Jurisdiction Theory?, 61 Nw. U.L. Rev. 584 (1966).

Domestic Relations - Jurisdiction, Extension of Comity to Foreign Nation Divorce, 46 Tenn. L. Rev. 238, 241 (1978).

Dyer, Recognition and Enforcement Abroad, 9 Family Advocate No. 4, ABA Family Law Section, 5, 11-14 (1987).

Forscher, Haitian, Dominican Laws of Divorce Evaluated, 166 N.Y.L.J., (October 19-20, 1971).

Foreign Divorces, A Question of Jurisdiction, 5 Southern University L. Rev. 139 (1984).

Fulton, Caribbean Divorce for Americans: Useful Alternative or Obsolescent Institution?, 10 Cornell Int'l L. J. 116, 133 (1976).

Glassman, Recognition and Enforcement at Home, 9 Family Advocate No. 4, ABA Family Law Section, 4, 6-8, (1987).

Hackworth, Digest of International Law, Office of the Legal Adviser, U.S. Department of State, Vol. II, Chapter VI, Section 168, 382-391 (1941).

Holden, Divorce in the Commonwealth, 20 Int'l and Comp. L.Q. 58, 74 (1971).

Howe, The Recognition of Foreign Divorce Decrees in New York State, 40 Colum. L. Rev. 373, 376 (1940); 23 Colum. L. Rev. 782 (1923).

Juenger, Recognition of Foreign Divorces: British and American Perspectives, 20 Am. J. Comp. L. 1 (1972).

Mendes da Costa, The Canadian Divorce Law of 1968 and its Provisions on Conflicts, 17 Am. J. Comp. L. 214 (1969).

Nichols, American Courts Look at Foreign Decrees, 9 Family Advocate No. 4, ABA Family Law Section, 9-10, 37 (1987).

Pedersen, Recent Trends in Danish Family Law and Their Historical Background, 20 Int'l and Comp. L.Q. 332, 341 (1971).

Swisher, Foreign Migratory Divorces: A Reappraisal, 21 J. Fam. L. 9, 25n, 71-72 (1982).

Stone, The New Fundamental Principles of Soviet Family Law and Their Social Background, 18 Int'l and Comp. L.Q. 392, 406 (1969).

Turner, Divorce: Australian and German "Breakdown" Provisions Compared, 18 Int'l and Comp. L.Q. 896, 937 (1969).

Whiteside, Domestic Relations - The Validity of Foreign Divorce Decrees in North Carolina (Mayer v. Mayer) 20 Wake Forrest L. Rev. 765 (1984).

ADDITIONAL INFORMATION The Office of american Citizens Srvices has available general

475

information flyers on international judicial assistance , many of which are available through our automated fax system or via our home page.

Using the Autofax System:
Dial (202) 647-3000 using the phone on your fax machine. Follow the prompts to obtain the information that you need.

Using the Internet: Many of our judicial assistance flyers are also available on the Internet via the Department of State, Bureau of Consular Affairs home page under Judicial Assistance

QUESTIONS: Additional questions may be addressed to the U.S. Department of State, Bureau of Consular Affairs, Office of American Citizens Services, Room 4817 N.S., 2201 C Street, N.W., Washington, D.C. 20520, tel: (202) 647-5225 or 202-647-5226.

Chapter 27

Getting Help Abroad from U.S. Consuls

[The information in this chapter is reprinted verbatim from a bulletin issued by the
U.S. State Department, Bureau of Consular Affairs. It is intended to serve as advice
to Americans traveling abroad.]

U.S. Consuls Help Americans Abroad

There are U.S. embassies in 160 capital cities of the world. Each embassy has a consular section. Consular officers in consular sections of embassies do two things:

they issue visas to foreigners;

they help U.S. citizens abroad.

There are also consular officers at about 60 U.S. consulates general and 20 U.S. consulates around the world. (Consulates general and consulates are regional offices of embassies.)

U.S. consuls usually are assisted by local employees who are citizens of the host country. Because of the growing number of Americans traveling abroad, and the relatively small number of consuls, the expertise of local employees is invaluable.

In this chapter, we highlight ways in which consular officers can assist you while you are traveling or residing abroad.

To help us help you while you are abroad, register with the nearest U.S. embassy or consulate. This makes it easier for consular officers to reach you in an emergency or to replace a lost passport.

Consular officers provide a range of services - some emergency, some nonemergency.

EMERGENCY SERVICES

Replace A Passport - If you lose your passport, a consul can issue you a replacement, often within 24 hours. If you believe your passport has been stolen, first report the theft to the local police and get a police declaration.

Help Find Medical Assistance - If you get sick, you can contact a consular officer for a list of local doctors, dentists, and medical specialists, along with other medical information.

If you are injured or become seriously ill, a consul will help you find medical assistance and, at your request, inform your family or friends. (Consider getting private medical insurance before you travel, to cover the high cost of getting you back to the U.S. for hospital care in the event of a medical emergency.)

Help Get Funds - Should you lose all your money and other financial resources, consular officers can help you contact your family, bank, or employer to arrange for them to send you funds. In some cases, these funds can be wired to you through the Department of State.

Help In An Emergency - Your family may need to reach you because of an emergency at home or because they are worried about your welfare. They should call the State Department's Citizens Emergency Center (202) 647-5225. The State Department will relay the message to consular officers in the country in which you are traveling. Consular officers will attempt to locate you, pass on urgent messages, and, consistent with the Privacy Act, report back to your family.

Visit In Jail - If you are arrested, you should ask the authorities to notify a U.S. consul. Consuls cannot get you out of jail (when you are in a foreign country you are subject to its laws). However, they can work to protect your legitimate interests and ensure you are not discriminated against. They can provide a list of local attorneys, visit you, inform you generally about local laws, and contact your family and friends. Consular officers can transfer money, food, and clothing to the prison authorities from your family or friends. They can try to get relief if you are held under

477

inhumane or unhealthful conditions.

Make Arrangements After The Death Of An American - When an American dies abroad, a consular officer notifies the American's family and informs them about options and costs for disposition of remains. Costs for preparing and returning a body to the U.S. may be high and must be paid by the family. Often, local laws and procedures make returning a body to the U.S. for burial a lengthy process. A consul prepares a Report of Death based on the local death certificate; this is forwarded to the next of kin for use in estate and insurance matters.

Help in a Disaster/Evacuation - If you are caught up in a natural disaster or civil disturbance, you should let your relatives know as soon as possible that you are safe, or contact a U.S. consul who will pass that message to your family through the State Department. Be resourceful. U.S. officials will do everything they can to contact you and advise you. However, they must give priority to helping Americans who have been hurt or are in immediate danger. In a disaster, consuls face the same constraints you do - lack of electricity or fuel, interrupted phone lines, closed airports.

NONEMERGENCY SERVICES

Issue a Consular Report of Birth - A child born abroad to U.S. citizen parents usually acquires U.S. citizenship at birth. The parents should contact the nearest U.S. embassy or consulate to have a "Report of Birth Abroad of a U.S. Citizen" prepared. This is proof of citizenship for all purposes.

Issue a Passport - Consuls issue approximately 200,000 passports abroad each year. Many of these are issued to persons whose current passports have expired.

Distribute Federal Benefits Payments - Over a half-million people living overseas receive monthly federal benefit payments. In many countries, the checks are mailed to the U.S. embassy or consulate and distributed through the local postal service.

Assist in Child Custody Disputes - In an international custody dispute, a consul can try to locate a child abroad, monitor the child's welfare, and provide general information to the American parent about laws and procedures which may be used to effect the child's return to the United States. Consuls may not take custody of a child, or help a parent regain custody of a child illegally or by force or deception.

Help In Other Ways - Consuls handle personal estates of deceased U.S. citizens, assist with absentee voting and Selective Service registration, notarize documents, advise on property claims, and provide U.S. tax forms. They also perform such functions as adjudicating U.S. citizenship claims and assisting U.S. courts in legal matters.

WHAT CONSULAR OFFICERS CANNOT DO

In addition to the qualifications noted above, consular officers cannot act as travel agents, banks, lawyers, investigators, or law enforcement officers. Please do not expect them to find you employment, get you residence or driving permits, act as interpreters, search for missing luggage, or settle disputes with hotel managers. They can, however, tell you how to get help on these and other matters.

If you need to pick up mail or messages while traveling, some banks and international credit card companies handle mail for customers at their overseas branches. General Delivery (Poste Restante) services at post offices in most countries will hold mail for you.

PRIVACY ACT

The provisions of the Privacy Act are designed to protect the privacy rights of Americans. Occasionally they complicate a consul's efforts to assist Americans. As a general rule, consular officers may not reveal information regarding an individual American's location, welfare, intentions, or problems to anyone, including family members and Congressional representatives, without the expressed consent of that individual. Although sympathetic to the distress this can cause concerned families, consular officers must comply with the provisions of the Privacy Act.

For more information, contact Overseas Citizens Services, Department of State, Room 4800, Washington, D.C. 20520.

Chapter 28

Crises Abroad-What the State Department Does

[The Information in this chapter is reprinted verbatim from a bulletin issued by the U.S. State Department, Bureau of Consular Affairs. It is intended to serve as advice to Americans traveling abroad.]

Crisis Abroad - What the State Department Does

What can the State Department's Bureau of Consular Affairs do for Americans caught in a disaster or a crisis abroad?

Earthquakes, hurricanes, political upheavals, acts of terrorism, and hijackings are only some of the events threatening the safety of Americans abroad. Each event is unique and poses its own special difficulties. However, for the State Department there are certain responsibilities and actions that apply in every disaster or crisis.

When a crisis occurs, the State Department sets up a task force or working group to bring together in one set of rooms all the people necessary to work on that event. Usually this Washington task force will be in touch by telephone 24 hours a day with our Ambassador and Foreign Service Officers at the embassy in the country affected.

In a task force, the immediate job of the State Department's Bureau of Consular Affairs is to respond to the thousands of concerned relatives and friends who begin to telephone the State Department immediately after the news of a disaster is broadcast.

Relatives want information on the welfare of their family members and on the disaster. The State Department relies for hard information on its embassies and consulates abroad. Often these installations are also affected by the disaster and lack electricity, phone lines, gasoline, etc. Nevertheless, foreign service officers work hard to get information back to Washington as quickly as possible. This is rarely as quickly as the press is able to relay information. Foreign Service Officers cannot speculate; their information must be accurate. Often this means getting important information from the local government, which may or may not be immediately responsive.

Welfare & Whereabouts

As concerned relatives call in, officers of the Bureau of Consular Affairs collect the names of the Americans possibly involved in the disaster and pass them to the embassy and consulates. Officers at post attempt to locate these Americans in order to report on their welfare. The officers work with local authorities and, depending on the circumstances, may personally search hotels, airports, hospitals, or even prisons. As they try to get the information, their first priority is Americans dead or injured.

Death

When an American dies abroad, the Bureau of Consular Affairs must locate and inform the next-of-kin. Sometimes discovering the next-of-kin is difficult. If the American's name is known, the Bureau's Office of Passport Services will search for his or her passport application. However, the information there may not be current.

The Bureau of Consular Affairs provides guidance to grieving family members on how to make arrangements for local burial or return of the remains to the U.S. The disposition of remains is affected by local laws, customs, and facilities which are often vastly different from those in the U.S. The Bureau of Consular Affairs relays the family's instructions and necessary private funds to cover the costs involved to the embassy or consulate. The Department of State has no funds to assist in the return of remains or ashes of American citizens who die abroad. Upon completion of all formalities, the consular officer abroad prepares an official Foreign Service Report of Death, based upon the local death certificate, and sends it to the next-of-kin or legal representative for use in U.S. courts to settle estate matters.

A U.S. consular officer overseas has statutory

479

responsibility for the personal estate of an American who dies abroad if the deceased has no legal representative in the country where the death occurred. The consular officer takes possession of personal effects, such as convertible assets, apparel, jewelry, personal documents and papers. The officer prepares an inventory and then carries out instructions from members of the deceased's family concerning the effects. A final statement of the account is then sent to the next-of-kin. The Diplomatic Pouch cannot be used to ship personal items, including valuables, but legal documents and correspondence relating to the estate can be transmitted by pouch. In Washington, the Bureau of Consular Affairs gives next-of-kin guidance on procedures to follow in preparing Letters Testamentary, Letters of Administration, and Affidavits of Next-of-Kin as acceptable evidence of legal claim of an estate.

Injury

In the case of an injured American, the embassy or consulate abroad notifies the task force which notifies family members in the U.S. The Bureau of Consular Affairs can assist in sending private funds to the injured American; frequently it collects information on the individual's prior medical history and forwards it to the embassy or consulate. When necessary, the State Department assists in arranging the return of the injured American to the U.S. commercially, with appropriate medical escort, via commercial air ambulance or, occasionally, by U.S. Air Force medical evacuation aircraft. The use of Air Force facilities for a medical evacuation is authorized only under certain stringent conditions, and when commercial evacuation is not possible. The full expense must be borne by the injured American or his family.

Evacuation

Sometimes commercial transportation entering and leaving a country is disrupted during a political upheaval or natural disaster. If this happens, and if it appears unsafe for Americans to remain, the embassy and consulates will work with the task force in Washington to charter special air flights and ground transportation to help Americans to depart. The U.S. Government cannot order Americans to leave a foreign country. It can only advise and try to assist those who wish to leave.

Privacy Act

The provisions of the Privacy Act are designed to protect the privacy and rights of Americans, but occasionally they complicate our efforts to assist citizens abroad. As a rule, consular officers may not reveal information regarding an individual Americans location, welfare, intentions, or problems to anyone, including family members and Congressional representatives, without the expressed consent of that individual. Although sympathetic to the distress this can cause concerned families, consular officers must comply with the provisions of the Privacy Act.

Chapter 29

Overseas Citizens Services/The Citizens Emergency Center

[The information in this chapter is reprinted verbatim from a bulletin issued by the U.S. State Department, Bureau of Consular Affairs. It is intended to serve as advice to Americans both at home and abroad.]

The Office of Overseas Citizens Services

When You Need Help...

Overseas Citizens Services

Overseas Citizens Services (OCS) in the State Department's Bureau of Consular Affairs is responsible for the welfare and whereabouts of U.S. citizens traveling and residing abroad. OCS has three offices: American Citizens Services and Crisis Management, the Office of Children's Issues and the Office of Policy Review and Interagency Liaison.

AMERICAN CITIZENS SERVICES AND CRISIS MANAGEMENT (ACS)

American Citizens Services and Crisis Management corresponds organizationally to American Citizens Services offices set up at U.S. embassies and consulates throughout the world. ACS has five geographical divisions with case officers who assist in all matters involving protective services for Americans abroad, including arrests, death cases, financial or medical emergencies, and welfare and whereabouts inquiries. The office also issues Travel Warnings, Public Announcements and Consular Information Sheets and provides guidance on nationality and citizenship determination, document issuance, judicial and notarial services, estates and property claims, third-country representation, and disaster assistance.

Arrests

Over 2,500 Americans are arrested abroad annually. More than 30% of these arrests are drug related. Over 70% of drug related arrests involve marijuana or cocaine.

The rights an American enjoys in this country do not travel abroad. Each country is sovereign and its laws apply to everyone who enters regardless of nationality. The U.S. government cannot get Americans released from foreign jails. However, a U.S. consul will insist on prompt access to an arrested American, provide a list of attorneys, and provide information on the host countrys legal system, offer to contact the arrested Americans family or friends, visit on a regular basis, protest mistreatment, monitor jail conditions, provide dietary supplements, if needed, and keep the State Department informed.

ACS is the point of contact in the U.S. for family members and others who are concerned about a U.S. citizen arrested abroad.

Deaths

Approximately 6,000 Americans die outside of the U.S. each year. The majority of these are long-term residents of a foreign country. ACS assists with the return of remains for approximately 2,000 Americans annually. When an American dies abroad, a consular officer notifies the next of kin about options and costs for disposition of remains. Costs for preparing and returning a body to the U.S. are high and are the responsibility of the family. Often local laws and procedures make returning a body to the U.S. for burial a lengthy process.

Financial Assistance

If destitute, Americans can turn to a U.S. consular officer abroad for help. ACS will help by contacting the destitute person's family, friends, or business associates to raise private funds. It will help transmit these funds to destitute Americans.

ACS transfers approximately 3 million dollars a year in private emergency funds. It can approve small government loans to destitute Americans abroad until private funds arrive. ACS also approves repatriation loans to pay for destitute Americans' direct return to the U.S. Each year

481

over $500,000 are loaned to destitute Americans.

Medical Assistance

ACS works with U.S. consuls abroad to assist Americans who become physically or mentally ill while traveling. ACS locates family members, guardians, and friends in the U.S., assists in transmitting private funds, and, when necessary, assists in arranging the return of ill or injured Americans to the U.S. by commercial carrier.

Welfare and Whereabouts of U.S. Citizens

ACS receives approximately 12,000 inquiries a year concerning the welfare or whereabouts of an American abroad. Many inquiries are from worried relatives who have not heard from the traveler. Others are attempts to notify the traveler about a family crisis at home. Most welfare/whereabouts inquiries are successfully resolved. However, occasionally, a person is truly missing. It is the responsibility of local authorities to investigate and U.S. consuls abroad will work to ensure their continued interest in cases involving Americans. Unfortunately, as in the U.S., sometimes missing persons are never found.

Consular Information Program

ACS issues fact sheets on every country in the world called *Consular Information Sheets* (CIS). The CIS contains information on entry requirements, crime and security conditions, areas of instability and other details relevant to travel in a particular country.

The Office also issues *Travel Warnings*. Travel Warnings are issued when the State Department recommends deferral of travel by Americans to a country because of civil unrest, dangerous conditions, terrorist activity and/or because the U.S. has no diplomatic relations with the country and cannot assist an American in distress.

Consular Information Sheets and *Travel Warnings* may be heard anytime, by dialing the Office of Overseas Citizens Services travelers' hotline at (202) 647-5225 from a touchtone phone. They are also available via Consular Affairs' automated fax system at (202) 647-3000, or at any of the 13 regional passport agencies, at U.S. embassies and consulates abroad, and through the airline computer reservation systems, or, by sending a self-addressed, stamped business size envelope to the Office of Overseas Citizens Services, Bureau

of Consular Affairs, Room 4811, U.S. Department of State, Washington, D.C. 20520-4818. If you have a personal computer and Internet access, you obtain them and other consular handouts and publications through the Consular Affairs web site at http://travel.state.gov

Disaster Assistance

ACS coordinates the Bureau's activities and efforts relating to international crises or emergency situations involving the welfare and safety of large numbers of Americans residing or traveling in a crisis area. Such crises can include plane crashes, hijackings, natural disasters, civil disorders, and political unrest.

CHILDREN'S ISSUES (CI)

The Office of Children's Issues (CI) formulates, develops and coordinates policies and programs, and provides direction to foreign service posts on international parental child abduction and international adoptions. It also fulfills U.S. treaty obligations relating to the abduction of children.

International Adoptions

CI coordinates policy and provides information on international adoption to the potential parents. In 1994, over 8,000 foreign born children where adopted by U.S. citizens. The Department of State cannot intervene on behalf of an individual in foreign courts because adoption is a private legal matter within the judicial sovereignty of the country where the child resides. This office can, however, offer general information and assistance regarding the adoption process in over 60 countries.

International Parental Child Abductions

In recent years, the Bureau of Consular Affairs has taken action in thousands of cases of international parental child abduction. The Bureau also provides information in response to thousands of additional inquiries pertaining to international child abduction, enforcement of visitation rights and abduction prevention techniques. CI works closely with parents, attorneys, other government agencies, and private organizations in the U.S. to prevent international abductions. The Hague Convention provides for the return of a child to his or her habitual place of residence if the child has been wrongfully removed or retained. CI has been designated by Congress as the Central Authority to administer the Hague Convention in the United

States.

POLICY REVIEW AND INTERAGENCY LIAISON (PRI)

The Office of Policy Review and Interagency Liaison (PRI) provides guidance concerning the administration and enforcement of laws on U.S. citizenship, and on the documentation of Americans traveling and residing abroad. The Office also provides advice on matters involving treaties and agreements, legislative matters, including implementation of new laws, conducts reconsiderations of acquisition and loss of U.S. citizenship in complex cases abroad, and administers the overseas federal benefits program.

Consular Conventions and Treaties

PRI works closely with other offices in the State Department in the negotiation of consular conventions and treaties, including prisoner transfer treaties. As a result of these prisoner transfer treaties, many U.S. citizens convicted of crimes and incarcerated abroad have returned to the U.S. to complete their sentences.

Federal Benefits

Over a half-million people receive monthly federal benefits payments outside the U.S. In many countries, the monthly benefits checks are mailed or pouched to the consular post and then distributed through the local postal service. In other countries, the checks are mailed directly into the beneficiaries foreign bank accounts. Consular officers assist in the processing of individual benefits claims and problems; investigate claims on behalf of the agency concerned; and perform other tasks requested by the agencies or needed by the beneficiaries or survivors.

Legislation

PRI is involved with legislation affecting U.S. citizens abroad. The Office participates in hearings and provides testimony to Congress on proposed legislation, particularly legislation relating to the citizenship and welfare of U.S. citizens. They also interpret laws and regulations pertaining to citizens consular services, including the administration of the Immigration and Nationality Act.

Privacy Act

PRI responds to inquires under the Privacy Act. The provisions of the Privacy Act are designed to protect the privacy and rights of Americans but occasionally complicate efforts to assist U.S. citizens abroad. As a general rule, consular officers may not reveal information regarding an individual Americans location, welfare, intentions, or problems to anyone, including family members and Congressional representatives, without the expressed consent of that individual. In all potential cases, consular officers explain Privacy Act restrictions and requirements so that all individuals involved in a case understand the Privacy Act's constraints.

Hours of Operation:

OCS is open Monday-Friday, 8:15 a.m. to 5:00 p.m. Eastern time. The OCS toll-free hotline at 1-888-407-4747 is available from 8:00 a.m. to 8:00 p.m. Eastern time, Monday-Friday, except U.S. federal holidays. Callers who are unable to use toll-free numbers, such as those calling from overseas, may obtain information and assistance during these hours by calling 317-472-2328. **For after-hours emergencies, Sundays and holidays, please call 202-647-4000 and request the OCS duty officer.**

483

Chapter 30

The State Department Travel Advisories

[The information in this chapter is reprinted verbatim from a number of bulletins issued by the U.S. State Department, Bureau of Consular Affairs. It is intended to serve as advice to Americans traveling abroad.]

TRAVEL WARNINGS AND CONSULAR INFORMATION SHEETS

What Are Travel Warnings, Consular Information Sheets & Public Announcements?

Travel Warnings are issued when the State Department decides, based on all relevant information, to recommend that Americans avoid travel to a certain country. Countries where avoidance of travel is recommended will have Travel Warnings as well as Consular Information Sheets.

Public Announcements are a means to disseminate information about terrorist threats and other relatively short-term and/or trans-national conditions posing significant risks to the security of American travelers. They are made any time there is a perceived threat and usually have Americans as a particular target group. In the past, Public Announcements have been issued to deal with short-term coups, bomb threats to airlines, violence by terrorists and anniversary dates of specific terrorist events.

Consular Information Sheets are available for every country of the world. They include such information as location of the U.S. Embassy or Consulate in the subject country, unusual immigration practices, health conditions, minor political disturbances, unusual currency and entry regulations, crime and security information, and drug penalties. If an unstable condition exists in a country that is not severe enough to warrant a Travel Warning, a description of the condition(s) may be included under an optional section entitled "Safety/Security." On limited occasions, we also restate in this section any U.S. Embassy advice given to official employees. Consular Information Sheets generally do not include advice, but present information in a factual manner so the traveler can make his or her own decisions concerning travel to a particular country.

You can access Consular Information Sheets, Travel Warnings and Public Announcements 24-hours a day in several ways.

Internet

The most convenient source of information about travel and consular services is the Consular Affairs home page. The web site address is http://travel.state.gov. If you do not have access to the Internet at home, work or school, your local library may provide access to the Internet.

Fax

From your fax machine, dial **(202) 647-3000**, using the handset as you would a regular telephone. The system will instruct you on how to proceed.

Telephone

Consular Information Sheets and Travel Warnings may be heard any time by dialing the office of American Citizens Services at **(202) 647-5225** from a touchtone phone.

In Person/By Mail

Consular Information Sheets, Travel Warnings and Public Announcements are available at any of the regional passport agencies and U.S. embassies and consulates abroad, or, by writing and sending a self-addressed, stamped envelope to the Office of American Citizens Services, Bureau of Consular Affairs, Room 4811, U.S. Department of State, Washington, D.C. 20520-4818.

Travel Warnings as of December 2, 2003

Libya - 11/20/2003
Turkey - 11/20/2003

485

Sudan - 11/14/2003
Bosnia - 11/12/2003
Iraq - 10/31/2003
Somalia - 10/31/2003
Saudi Arabia - 10/27/2003
Nepal - 10/22/2003
Israel, the West Bank and Gaza - 10/20/2003
Angola - 10/2/2003
Liberia - 9/30/2003
Kenya - 9/25/2003
Algeria - 9/5/2003
Indonesia - 8/28/2003
Yemen - 8/20/2003
Cote d'Ivoire - 8/13/2003
Burundi - 8/12/2003
Afghanistan - 7/28/2003
Nigeria - 6/26/2003
Colombia - 6/16/2003
Iran - 5/12/2003
Lebanon - 5/6/2003
Pakistan - 4/17/2003
Central African Republic - 4/7/2003
Democratic Republic of the Congo - 4/7/2003
Zimbabwe - 1/27/2003
Tajikistan - 12/20/2002

Public Announcements as December 2, 2003

Kenya - 12/2/2003, expires on 1/9/2004
Bolivia - 11/28/2003, expires on 2/21/2004
Worldwide Caution - 11/21/2003, expires on 4/21/2004
Malaysia - 11/7/2003, expires on 6/6/2004
Middle East Update - 11/6/2003, expires on 5/5/2004
Kyrgyz Republic - 10/31/2003, expires on 4/30/2004
Solomon Islands - 10/27/2003, expires on 4/9/2004
Djibouti - 10/14/2003, expires on 1/17/2004
Uzbekistan - 9/29/2003, expires on 1/1/2004
East Africa - 9/12/2003, expires on 3/13/2004
Laos - 8/28/2003, expires on 2/27/2004
Guatemala - 8/26/2003, expires on 1/15/2004
Venezuela - 8/15/2003, expires on 2/28/2004
Philippines - 7/16/2003, expires on 1/17/2004

State Department Electronic Subscriptions

You can automatically receive via email full texts of selected U.S. Department of State documents and publications that provide key official information on U.S. foreign policy; you also can receive notifications of travel warnings and Foreign Travel Per Diem updates.

To subscribe to any one of the email lists for the following information, **complete the online subscription form** or send an email to **LISTSERV@LISTS.STATE.GOV** and type in the message body "SUBSCRIBE LISTNAME YOURNAME". (Omit the quotation marks, and be sure to replace the YOURNAME portion above with your own name -- or, if preferred, ANONYMOUS -- and the LISTNAME with the name of the list below that you wish to subscribe to.)

The DOSIRAQ list. This list will distribute speeches, interviews, press briefings and other documents and releases that are pertinent to Iraq. You can expect the DOSIRAQ list to generate a substantial number of email messages per month.

The DOSINTLWMN list. This list will distribute an electronic newsletter, fact sheets, speeches, reports and other releases that are pertinent to International Women's Issues. You can expect the DOSINTLWMN list to generate 2 - 3 messages per month.

The DOSCOALITION list. This list provides official statements on the State Department's efforts to Build a Global Coalition Against Terrorism following the Attack on America September 11, 2001. You can expect the DOSCOALITION list to generate a substantial number of email messages per month.

The **DOSTRAVEL** list. This list provides notification of updates to the Travel Warnings issued when the State Department decides, based on all relevant information, to recommend that Americans avoid travel to a certain country. Countries where avoidance of travel is recommended will have Travel Warnings as well as Consular Information Sheets. You can expect the DOSTRAVEL list to generate an average of 10-15 email messages per month.

The **DOSSCHEDULE** list. The Daily Appointments Schedule of Secrtary of State Colin L. Powell and Deputy Secretary of State Richard Armitage. DOSSCHEDULE will generate a daily email.

The **DOSSEC** list. The Secretary of State regularly addresses various groups and testifies before Congress. Full texts of Secretarial addresses and remarks are disseminated by the Office of Electronic Information, Bureau of Public Affairs, for posting to the DOSSEC list as soon as they are released. You can expect the DOSSEC list to generate an average of 10-15 email messages per month.

The **DOSSDO** list. Senior State Department officials regularly address various groups and testify before Congress. These postings to the DOSSDO list are disseminated by the Office of Electronic Information, Bureau of Public Affairs, as soon as they are provided by the senior official's office. You can expect the DOSSDO list to generate about 8-12 email messages per month.

The **DOSBRIEF** list. The State Department conducts press briefings, usually Monday through Friday. The Office of the Spokesman, Bureau of Public Affairs, releases the press briefings the same day unless otherwise indicated in the Department of State State Department's daily press briefing calendar; full texts of these briefings are distributed via DOSBRIEF. You can expect the DOSBRIEF list to generate about 4-5 email messages per week.

The **DOSFACTS** list. Fact Sheets are concise (1 or 2-page) summaries of U.S. policy on current foreign affairs issues. They are updated irregularly. You can expect this listserv to generate 2-3 emails a week.

The **DOSPRESS** list. The Office of the Spokesman, Bureau of Public Affairs, releases about 2-5 press statements or notices to the press each day. You can expect the DOSPRESS list to generate about 20 email messages per month; each day's releases will be compiled into one message. Press statements are posted to our web site as they are released throughout the day.

The **DOSBACK** list. Background Notes are updated periodically and include information on U.S. bilateral relations with foreign countries and on their governments, political conditions, and foreign relations. Via DOSBACK you will receive the full-text version of newly released Background Notes. You can expect the DOSBACK list to generate about 3-4 email messages per month.

The **DOSPDIEM** list. This list provides notification of updates to the Maximum Travel Per Diem Allowance for Foreign Areas, Section 925, a supplement to the Standardized Regulations (Government Civilians, Foreign Areas). Foreign Travel Per Diem Rates are released monthly by the State Department's Office of Allowances. Via DOSPDIEM you will receive monthly notification of the availability of Travel Per Diem Rate updates.

The **DOSPPT** list. This list provides subscribers with updated passport information, including new requirements, fee changes, etc. In an effort to keep U.S. citizens informed, Passport Services will send out updated

487

information as soon as it is made available to the public. You can expect the DOSPPT list to generate 2-3 emails a year.

The DOSPPTTRV list. This list provides travel agent subscribers with updated passport information, including new requirements, fee changes, etc. In an effort to keep travel agents (and their clients) informed, Passport Services will send out updated information as soon as it is made available to the public. You can expect the DOSPPTTRV list to general 3-6 emails a year.

Chapter 31

Travel Warnings on Drugs Abroad

[The Information in this chapter is reprinted verbatim from a bulletin issued by the U.S. State Department, Bureau of Consular Affairs. It is intended to serve as advice to Americans traveling abroad.]

Things You Should Know Before You Go Abroad

HARD FACTS

Each year, 2,500 Americans are arrested overseas. One third of the arrests are on drug-related charges. Many of those arrested assumed as U.S. citizens that they could not be arrested. From Asia to Africa, Europe to South America, U.S. citizens are finding out the hard way that drug possession or trafficking equals jail in foreign countries.

There is very little that anyone can do to help you if you are caught with drugs. It is your responsibility to know what the drug laws are in a foreign country before you go, because "I didn't know it was illegal" will not get you out of jail.

In recent years, there has been an increase in the number of women arrested abroad. The rise is a result of women who serve as drug couriers or "mules" in the belief they can make quick money and have a vacation without getting caught. Instead of a short vacation, they get a lengthy stay or life sentence in a foreign jail.

A number of the Americans arrested abroad on drug charges in 1994 possessed marijuana. Many of these possessed one ounce or less of the substance. The risk of being put in jail for just one marijuana cigarette is not worth it. If you are purchasing prescription medications in quantities larger than that considered necessary for personal use, you could be arrested on suspicion of drug trafficking.

Once you're arrested, the American consular officer **CANNOT** get you out! You may say "it couldn't happen to me" but the fact is that it could happen to you if you find yourself saying one of the following:
...*"I'm an American citizen and no foreign government can put me in their jail."*

...*"If I only buy or carry a small amount, it won't be a problem."*

If you are arrested on a drug charge it is important that you know what your government **CAN** and **CANNOT** do for you.

The U.S. Consular Officer *CAN*

- visit you in jail after being notified of your arrest
- give you a list of local attorneys (The U.S. Government cannot assume responsibility for the professional ability or integrity of these individuals or recommend a particular attorney.)
- notify your family and/or friends and relay requests for money or other aid -- but only with your authorization
- intercede with local authorities to make sure that your rights *under local law* are fully observed and that you are treated humanely, according to internationally accepted standards
- protest mistreatment or abuse to the appropriate authorities

The U.S. Consular Officer *CANNOT*

- demand your immediate release or get you out of jail or the country!
- represent you at trial or give legal counsel
- pay legal fees and/or fines with U.S. Government funds

If you are caught buying, selling, carrying or using drugs -- from hashish to heroin, marijuana to mescaline, cocaine to quaaludes, to designer drugs like ecstacy....

IT COULD MEAN:

Interrogation and Delays Before Trial - including mistreatment and solitary confinement

for up to one year under very primitive conditions
Lengthy Trials - conducted in a foreign language, with delays and postponements
Weeks, Months or Life in Prison - some places include hard labor, heavy fines, and/or lashings, if found guilty
The Death Penalty - in a growing number of countries (e.g., Malaysia, Pakistan and Turkey)
Although drug laws vary from country to country, it is important to realize before you make the mistake of getting involved with drugs that foreign countries do not react lightly to drug offenders. In some countries, anyone who is caught with even a very small quantity for personal use may be tried and receive the same sentence as the large-scale trafficker.

DON'T LET YOUR TRIP ABROAD BECOME A NIGHTMARE!

This information has been provided to inform you before it is too late.

SO THINK FIRST!

- A number of countries, including the Bahamas, the Dominican Republic, Jamaica, Mexico and the Philippines, have enacted more stringent drug laws which impose mandatory jail sentences for individuals convicted of possessing even small amounts of marijuana or cocaine for personal use.
- Once you leave the United States, you are not covered by U.S. laws and constitutional rights.
- Bail is not granted in many countries when drugs are involved.
- The burden of proof in many countries is on the accused to prove his/her innocence.
- In some countries, evidence obtained illegally by local authorities may be admissible in court.
- Few countries offer drug offenders jury trials or even require the prisoner's presence at his/her trial.
- Many countries have mandatory prison sentences of seven years or life, without the possibility of parole for drug violations.

REMEMBER!

- If someone offers you a free trip and

some quick and easy money just for bringing back a suitcase.... *SAY NO!*
- Don't carry a package for anyone, no matter how small it might seem.
- The police and customs officials have a right to search your luggage for drugs. If they find drugs in **your** suitcase, **you** will suffer the consequences.
- You could go to jail for years and years with no possibility of parole, early release or transfer back to the U.S.
- Don't make a jail sentence part of your trip abroad.

The Department of State's Bureau of Consular Affairs' Office of Overseas Citizens Services provides emergency services pertaining to the protection of Americans arrested or detained abroad, the search for U.S. citizens overseas, the transmission of emergency messages to those citizens or their next of kin in the United States and other emergency and non-emergency services. Contact the Office of Overseas Citizens Services from Monday through Friday, 8:15 a.m. to 10:00 p.m. at (202) 647-5225. For an emergency after hours or on weekends and holidays, ask for the Overseas Citizens Services' duty officer at (202) 647-4000. Internet home page: http://travel.state.gov

Chapter 32

Generalized Systems of Preferences & the Traveler

[The information in this chapter is reprinted verbatim from a bulletin issued by the Department of the Treasury, U.S. Customs Service. It is intended to serve as advice to Americans traveling abroad.]

Generalized System of Preferences (GSP) & the Traveler: Bringing in Articles from Developing Countries

What is GSP?
GSP (Generalized System of Preferences) is a system used by many developed countries to help developing nations improve their financial or economic condition through exports. In effect, it provides for the duty-free importation of a wide range of products that would otherwise be subject to customs duty if imported into the U.S. from non-GSP countries.

When did GSP go into effect for the United States?
GSP went into effect on January 1, 1976. The program has expired on several occasions since that time, most recently on June 30, 1999. On December 17, 1999, President Clinton signed legislation renewing the GSP retroactively from July 1, 1999, and extending it through September 30, 2001. However, duty-free treatment for eligible products made in designated sub-Saharan African countries continues through September 30, 2008.

How is GSP administered?
GSP is administered by the United States Trade Representative in consultation with the Secretary of State. The duty suspensions are proclaimed by the President under the Trade Act of 1974 as amended. The U.S. Customs Service is responsible for determining eligibility for duty-free entry under GSP.

What products are eligible?
Approximately 4,284 items have been designated as eligible for duty-free treatment from beneficiary developing countries (BCD's). The eligible articles are identified in the Harmonized Tariff Schedule of the United States Annotated and the designated countries are also listed there.

For the traveler's convenience, an advisory list of the most popular tourist items that, in general, have been accorded GSP status is included in this chapter.

Are certain items excluded?
Under the Trade Act many items, such as most footwear, most textile articles (including clothing), watches, some electronic products, and certain glass and steel products are specifically excluded from GSP benefits.

What countries have been designated as Beneficiary Developing Countries?
Approximately 140 countries and territories have been designated. Those countries are listed elsewhere in this chapter.

Are the articles and countries subject to change?
Yes. Articles may be excluded by Executive Order if it is determined that their importation is harmful to domestic industry. Beneficiary countries may also be excluded from the GSP program at any time, due to other trade considerations. For example, beneficiary countries may graduate from GSP if they become a "high income" country as defined by the International Bank for Reconstruction and Development. The President may also withdraw a beneficiary country's GSP eligibility for other reasons, such as the country begins to give preferential treatment to imports from other developed countries, but not the United States.

In addition, some articles from specified countries may be excluded from GSP treatment, if during the preceding year:

- The level of imports of those articles exceeded a specific dollar limit indexed to the nominal growth of the U.S. gross national product, since 1984.

- That country supplied 50 percent or more of the total U.S. imports of that product.

How has the Africa Growth and Opportunity Act (AGOA) affected GSP?

The AGOA amended the GSP to provide for the duty-free treatment of many products if made in designated sub-Saharan African countries. Those countries are listed on page X. The AGOA went into effect on October 1, 2000, and expires on September 30, 2008. More detailed information may be obtained from the Customs informed compliance publication *What Every Member of the Trade Community Should Know About: The African Growth and Opportunity Act*. This publication can be found on the Customs Web site at www.customs.gov in the Importing and Exporting section

Are there any specific requirements or qualifications I must be aware of to be sure an article qualifies for duty-free treatment?

In order to take advantage of GSP, you must have acquired the eligible article in the same beneficiary country where it was grown, manufactured, or produced. Articles may accompany you or may be shipped from the developing country directly to the United States.

What forms are required?

If they are shipped, the goods should be accompanied by the merchant's invoice. No other forms are necessary unless it is a commercial importation.

What about merchandise acquired in duty-free shops?

Most items purchased in duty free shops will not be eligible for GSP treatment unless the merchandise was produced in the country in which the duty free shop is located.

What about Internal Revenue tax?

Such items as gin, liqueur, perfume, if designated as eligible articles, may be subject to Internal Revenue Service tax despite their GSP status.

What happens if I thought an article was eligible for duty-free entry and it is not?

When merchandise claimed to be free of duty under GSP is found to be dutiable, you may include it in your Customs exemption. Articles imported in excess of your exemption will be subject to duty. If you feel your article should have been passed free of duty, you may write to the director of the Customs port where you entered, giving the information concerning your entry. A determination as to whether you are due a refund will be made.

Am I still entitled to my basic Customs exemption?

Yes, as a returning U.S. resident, you may still bring in free of duty $400 worth of articles (fair retail value) acquired abroad in addition to items covered by GSP. This exemption is $1,200 if you are returning from the U.S. Virgin Islands, American Samoa, or Guam, and $600 if you are returning from certain Caribbean or Andean nations. (See pp. X-X for this list.) Remember that all articles acquired abroad, whether free of duty or not, including those entitled to GSP, must be declared to U.S. Customs on your return.

Visitors or nonresidents are entitled to bring in articles that are duty free under GSP in addition to their basic customs exemption.

Who should I contact if I have any questions about GSP?

Contact your nearest U.S. Customs office--there are 300 ports of entry throughout the United States. The address and telephone number of the nearest Customs office can be found in your local telephone directory on the U.S. Government pages under U.S. Treasury, or on the Customs website at www.customs.gov at the Office Locations button. If you are overseas, the U.S. Embassy or consulate can be of assistance.

General information on the GSP and downloadable guides are available at www.ustr.gov/gsp/general.shtml.

Please Note

Some products, although entitled to duty-free treatment under GSP, may be restricted or prohibited from entering the United States. For example, endangered species of wildlife and plants and products made from them, are protected by the Convention on International Trade in Endangered Species of Wild Fauna and Flora, and are prohibited from being exported or imported. Elephant ivory is also prohibited. Any elephant ivory brought into the United States is subject to seizure. If you are considering purchasing articles made from ivory, skin, fur, etc., please contact the U.S. Fish and Wildlife Service, or your nearest U.S. Customs port of entry, in advance of your trip.

Information in this chapter has been prepared to serve only as an advisory guide for the traveling public for entry of non-commercial importations intended for personal use only. More specific and definitive advice in this regard should be obtained from one of the Customs field offices. Please also note that details or requirements for commercial importers are not covered here.

The U.S. Customs brochure *Know Before You Go* provides information on Customs clearance, exemptions, and restricted or prohibited items.

Information for commercial importers can be found on the Customs website under the Importing and Exporting section, or in our brochure *Import Requirements*. *Import Requirements* and *Know before You Go* are available by writing to: U.S. Customs Service, P.O. Box 7407, Washington, D.C. 20004, or by telephoning 202.354.1000.

POPULAR TOURIST ITEMS

This listing is solely an advisory guide to items designated as eligible for duty-free treatment under GSP that may be of interest to travelers for their personal use. **Note that certain items, if from a particular beneficiary country, may be excluded.** Do not hesitate to check with your nearest Customs office, or the American Embassy or consulate in the country you are visiting to verify the GSP status of any article you are considering bringing into the United States.

BASKETS or bags of bamboo, willow, or rattan.
CAMERAS, motion-picture and still, lenses, and other photographic equipment.
CANDY
CHINAWARE, bone: household ware, and other articles such as vases, statues, and figurines. Non-bone: articles other than household ware (except for non-bone chinaware or subporcelain).
CIGARETTE LIGHTERS, pocket and table.
CORK, manufactures of.
EARTHENWARE or stoneware except household ware available in sets.
FLOWERS, artificial of plastic or feathers.
FURNITURE of wood, rattan, or plastic.

GAMES, played on boards: chess. Backgammon, darts, Mah-Jongg.
GOLF BALLS and EQUIPMENT
JADE, cut but not set for use in jewelry and other articles of jade.
JEWELRY of precious stones, or of precious metal set with semi-precious stones, cameos, intaglios, amber, or coral: Silver, chief value, valued not over $18 per dozen. Necklaces and neck chains, almost wholly of gold: except rope from Israel and mixed link.
JEWELRY BOXES, unlined.
MUSIC BOXES and MUSICAL INSTRUMENTS
PAPER, manufactures of.
PEARLS, cultured or imitation, loose or temporarily strung and without clasp.
PERFUME
PRINTED MATTER
RADIO RECEIVERS, solid state (not for motor vehicles) .
RECORDS, phonograph and tapes.
SHAVERS, electric.
SHELL, manufactures of.
SILVER, tableware and flatware.
SKIS and SKI EQUIPMENT, ski boots not included.
STONES cut but not set, suitable for use in jewelry. Precious and semi-precious stones including marcasites, coral and cameos.
TAPE RECORDERS
TOILET PREPARATIONS
TOYS
WIGS
WOOD, carvings.

Beneficiary Countries
The countries listed below have been designated as beneficiary developing countries in the U.S. Generalized System of Preferences.

★Antigua and Barbuda***
★Bahamas***
★Barbados***
★Belize***
★Bolivia*
★Colombia*
★Costa Rica
★Dominica ***
★Dominican Republic
★El Salvador
★Grenada***
★Guatemala
★Guyana***
★Haiti

★Honduras
★Jamaica***
★Peru*
★Saint Kitts and Nevis
★Saint Lucia***
★Saint Vincent and the Grenadines***
★Trinidad and Tobago***
Albania
Angola
Argentina
Armenia
Bahrain
Bangladesh
Belarus
Benin
Bhutan
Bosnia-Hercegovina
Bostwana
Brazil
Bulgaria
Burkina Faso
Burundi
Cameroon
Cape Verde
Central African Republic
Chad
Chile
Comoros
Congo
Cote d'Ivoire
Croatia
Cyprus
Czech Republic
Djibouti
Ecuador*
Egypt
Equatorial Guinea
Estonia
Ethiopia
Fiji
Gambia
Ghana
Guinea
Guinea Bissau
Hungary
India
Indonesia**
Israel
Jordan
Kazakhstan
Kenya
Kiribati
Kyrgyzstan
Latvia
Lebanon

Lesotho
Lithuania
Macedonia (former Republic of Yugoslavia)
Madagascar
Malawi
Malaysia**
Maldives
Mali
Malta
Maritius
Moldova
Morocco
Mozambique
Namibia
Nepal
Niger
Oman
Pakistan
Papua New Guinea
Paraguay
Philippines**
Poland
Romania
Russia
Rwanda
São Tomé and Principe
Senegal
Seychelles
Sierra Leone
Slovakia
Slovenia
Solomon Islands
Somalia
South Africa
Sri Lanka
Sudan
Surinam
Swaziland
Tanzania
Thailand**
Togo
Tonga
Tunisia
Turkey
Tuvalu
Uganda
Ukraine
Uruguay
Uzbekistan
Vanuatu
Venezuela*
Western Samoa
Yemen Arab Republic Sanaa
Zaire
Zambia

Zimbabwe

*Member countries of the Cartagena Agreement-Andean Group (treated as one country).
**Association of South East Asian Nations (ASEAN)-except Brunei Darussalam, and Singapore
(treated as one country).
***Member countries of the Caribbean Common Market (CARICOM) (treated as one country).
★ Member countries of the United States–Caribbean Basin Trade Partnership Act eligible for $600 personal duty exemption (Panama and Nicaragua are also eligible for this exemption).

Non-Independent Countries and Territories

Anguilla
★Aruba
British Indian Ocean Territory
Cayman Islands
Christmas Island (Australia)
Cocos (Keeling) Islands
Cook Islands
Falkland Islands (Islas Malvinas)
French Polynesia
Gibraltar
Greenland
Heard Island and McDonald Islands
Macau
★Monserrat ***
★Netherlands Antilles
New Caledonia
Niue
Norfolk Island
Pitcairn Islands
Saint Helena
Tokelau
Turks and Caicos Islands
★Virgin Islands, British
Wallis and Futuna
West Bank and Gaza Strip
Western Sahara

***Member countries of the Caribbean Common Market (CARICOM)
★ Member countries of the United States–Caribbean Basin Trade Partnership Act eligible for $600 personal duty exemption (Panama and Nicaragua are also eligible for this exemption).

African Growth and Opportunity Act Beneficiary Countries

Benin*
Botswana
Cape Verde*
Cameroon*
Central African Republic*
Chad*
Congo*
Djibouti*
Eritrea*
Ethiopia*
Gabonese Republic
Ghana*
Guinea*
Guinea-Bussau*
Kenya*
Lesotho*
Madagascar*
Malawi*
Mali*
Mauritania*
Mauritius
Mozambique*
Namibia
Niger*
Nigeria*
Rwanda*
São Tomé and Principe*
Senegal*
Saychelles
Sierra Leone*
South Africa
Tanzania*
Uganda*
Zambia*

*Lesser developed beneficiary sub-Saharan African countries

Report Drug Smuggling to U.S. Customs Service.
1 (800) BE-ALERT

Chapter 33

Avoiding Jet Lag

(The Traveler's Number 1 Complaint)
Jet lag has ruined more vacations, been the reason for more botched business meetings, and wreaked more general havoc on the air traveler than all the preflight or inflight irritations combined. Indeed, a term that four decades ago was an insider's expression used exclusively by an elite group of aviators, "jet lag" is now virtually a household word to 2.8 million passengers who have flown coast to coast in the United States, 2.1 million who have flown abroad from the United States, and more than 140 million people from around the globe who have flown through the world's international airports. Yet, despite the multitude of sufferers, only a handful of scientists specializing in chronobiology (the study of how time affects living organisms) and circadian regulatory biology (the study of how to control man's daily body rhythms) know its real cause, the true nature of its body-wide effect, and its simple cure.

The Phenomenon of East/West Flight

The biggest misconception that air travelers have is that jet lag is caused by being enclosed in a vehicle that is traveling at great speeds and at terrifically high altitudes. Somehow, air travelers correlate speed and altitude as key factors in jet lag. Yet the inflight velocity of the airplane and the distance traveled above the earth, per se, have absolutely nothing to do with jet lag. Nor do typical inflight symptoms of ear-popping, light-headedness, dehydration, irritability, motion sickness, and any other ailment about which air travelers might complain while en route to their destination. All these problems can be attributed to poor cabin pressure, drinking alcoholic beverages while in flight, and nerve-wracking engine noises-not jet lag. Jet lag is strictly, a phenomenon of long distance, east/west, too rapid travel to a new time frame. (caused primarily by the disruption of the sense of time, the sense of place and the sense of well being.)

The following is a list of jet lag symptoms that begin immediately upon deplaning.

Early and Late Jet Lag Symptoms

Early Symptoms	Late Symptoms
-fatigue	- constipation or diarrhea
-disorientation	-lack of sexual interest
-reduced physical ability	-limited peripheral vision -reduced mental activity
	-decreased muscle tone -contusion
	-impaired night vision upset appetite
	-reduced physical work capacity
	-off-schedule bowel and urinary movements
	-disrupted phases of body and functions onset of memory loss
	-slowed response time to visual stimulation
--	-reduced motor coordination and reflex time
	-interference with prescription drugs
	-insomnia
	-acute fatigue
	-loss of appetite
	-headache

THE ARGONNE ANTI-JET-LAG DIET

How to avoid jet lag:

1.   **DETERMINE BREAKFAST TIME** at destination on day of arrival.

2.   **FEAST-FAST-FEAST-FAST** - Start four days before breakfast time in step 1. On day one, FEAST; eat heartily with high-protein breakfast and lunch and a high-carbohydrate supper. No coffee except between 3 and 5 p.m. On day two, FAST on light meals of salads, light soups, fruits and juices. Again, no coffee except between 3 and 5 p.m. On day three, FEAST again. On day four, FAST; if you drink caffeinated beverages, take them in morning when traveling west, or between 6 and 11 p.m. when traveling east.

3.   **BREAK THE FINAL FAST** at destination breakfast time. No alcohol on the plane, if the flight is long enough, sleep until normal breakfast time at destination, but no later. Wake up and FEAST on a high-protein breakfast. Stay awake and active. Continue the day's meals according to mealtimes at the destination.

FEAST on high-protein breakfasts and lunches to stimulate the body's active cycle. Suitable meals include steak, eggs, hamburgers, high-protein cereals, green beans.

FEAST on high-carbohydrate suppers to stimulate sleep. They include spaghetti and other pastas (but no meatballs), crepes (but no meat filling), potatoes, other starchy vegetables, and sweet desserts.

FAST days help deplete the liver's store of carbohydrates and prepare the body's clock for resetting. Suitable foods include fruit, light soups, broths, skimpy salads, unbuttered toast, half pieces of bread. Keep calories and carbohydrates to a minimum.

COUNTDOWN

	1	2	3	4	
	FEAST	**FAST**	**FEAST**	**FAST**	**BREAK FINAL FAST**
BRK.FAST	feast	fast	feast	fast	
LUNCH	feast	fast	feast	fast	
SUPPER	feast	fast	feast	fast	

Westbound: If you drink caffeinated beverages, take them morning before departure.

Eastbound: take them between 6 and 11 p.m. If flight Is long enough, sleep until destination breakfast time. Wake up and FEAST, beginning with a high-protein breakfast. Lights on. Stay active.

Coffee, tea, cola, other caffeinated beverages allowed only between 3 and 5 p.m.

498

TIME ZONES AND MEDICINE--a confusing combination:[IL]

Whether you take a daily oral contraceptive, a twice-daily ulcer drug, or an every-four-hours cardiac medication, your routine is thrown off schedule when you travel out of your own time zone. Even coast-to coast travel requires an adjustment. How can you make sure you are taking pills at the proper time when the time changes? There are several strategies.

For shorter trips (less than a week), many people keep their medication schedule on home time. But since that can mean waking up in the middle of the night to take a pill, this option isn't for everyone.

In these cases, you have to adjust your schedule and perhaps even your dosage. Unfortunately there is no simple formula to follow, so your doctor's advice is crucial. You may be told to skip one dose when you travel west to east, and your day is shortened. Or, you may be told to take an extra dose on the first day of your trip if you are going east to west. The specifics depend on how many time zones you are crossing and what type of medication you are taking.

According to pharmacist, Harold Silverman, author of **Travel Healthy** (Avon Books), drugs known to be affected by shifts in biological rhythm (including jet lag and time zone changes) are antihistamines, anti-inflammatory drugs, anabolic steroids, barbiturates, benzodiazepine tranquilizers and sedatives, (including chlordiazepoxide, diazepam, and flurazepam), corticasteroids, and narcotic pain relievers, such as morphine, meperidine, and codeine.

Two other medications that are greatly affected by time changes are oral contraceptives and insulin injections. Depending on the degree of time difference and the type of oral contraceptive, many women are able to stick to their regular schedules. For instance, combination pills can still be taken at bedtime, no matter how great the time difference. But certain forms of birth control pills, such as progestin-only mini-pills, must be taken every 24 hours to be effective. If you are on this type of pill and will be for a considerable length of time, switch gradually so that you're taking a dose every 23 hours instead of every 24 until you are once again on a schedule that's convenient. The switch back should be just as gradual.(To be safe, check with your doctor.)

People with diabetes, also, should check with their physicians about altering insulin schedules when crossing two or more time zones, even if the insulin is taken in 24 hour dosages. Recommendations will be based on the severity of the disease, the type of insulin, the direction of the journey, and the number of time zones being crossed.

In many cases, the general rule is to keep your watch set to home time while you are on the plane, and follow your usual eating schedule. (You can arrange with the airline in advance for a diabetic meal, and you can request that the meal be served at a specific time.) Then, when you arrive at your destination, adjust your watch to the new time and adjust your next dose of insulin according to your doctor's instructions. Throughout your trip, frequently test your blood sugar level; the symptoms of jet lag often mimic diabetic reactions.

For more information, send a self-addressed envelope to Becton Dickinson Consumer Products, 1 Becton Drive, Franklin Lakes, NJ 07417, Attention: Diabetes Health Care, with your request for Vacations, Travel, and Diabetes. Or write to Squibb Novo, 211 Carnegie Center, Princeton, 08540, for "**Traveling with Diabetes**". The American Diabetes Association, 1660 Duke St., Alexandria, VA 22314, also provides information about how to cope while traveling with diabetes.

Chapter 34

More Information and Advice from the U.S. State Department, Customs, Transportation, Agriculture, Social Security...

[The information in this chapter is reprinted verbatim from the various U.S. government Departments It is intended to serve as advice to Americans traveling abroad.]

TRAVELING OUT OF/INTO THE U.S.; NEW GUIDELINES/PROCEDURES

(INFORMATION FROM THE U.S. TRANSPORTATION SECURITY ADMINISTRATION Post 9-11)

Prepared for Takeoff?

The following is the Transportation Security Administration's (TSA) comprehensive travel guide for you, the flying public. Here you will find everything you need to know about new airport security measures. You will discover a list of timesaving tips, information on assistance for special needs, the latest list of prohibited and permitted items, and other information that will help guide you smoothly through the security process.

Do you know what shoes you can wear that will help you move through the security line more quickly? Check "Travel Preparation" for suggestions on what to wear to the airport and how to pack for your trip.

Do you know that you can bring a paper cup of coffee through the passenger checkpoint but not a can of soda? See the section "Security Procedures" to learn about new procedures and to find timesaving tips that will help you minimize your wait time at the airport.

Do you require special assistance? Do you have religious or cultural concerns? Are you flying with family or traveling with film or sports equipment? See the " Special Considerations" section for answers and guidance.

The Prepare for Takeoff Campaign
The Prepare for Takeoff campaign reflects TSA's commitment to provide world-class security and world-class customer service. TSA's goal is to supply the traveling public with information that will not only help to ensure security, but will make air travel more efficient and less stressful for all.

Everyone needs to play an active role in contributing to air travel security. Together, airlines, airports, travel agents, government officials, and the public can contribute to making air travel safe, secure, and efficient.

Interested in Becoming a Partner?
The TSA is working in partnership with members of the travel and tourism community, and with disability groups and others, to get the word out to the traveling public. Using information provided by the TSA, partners are updating their own websites, providing links to the TSA website and distributing information to passengers through their own customer service departments.

Permitted & Prohibited Items
Can I Take It With Me? - Permitted and Prohibited Items
Prohibited items are weapons, explosives, incendiaries, and include items that are seemingly harmless but may be used as weapons-the so-called "dual use" items. You may not bring these items to security checkpoints without authorization.

What Happens to Prohibited Items?
If you bring a prohibited item to the checkpoint, you may be criminally and/or civilly prosecuted or, at the least, asked to rid yourself of the item. A screener and/or Law Enforcement Officer will make this determination, depending on what the item is and the circumstances. This is because bringing a prohibited item to a security checkpoint - even accidentally - is illegal.

Your prohibited item may be detained for use in an investigation and, if necessary, as evidence in your

501

criminal and/or civil prosecution. If permitted by the screener or Law Enforcement Officer, you may be allowed to: consult with the airlines for possible assistance in placing the prohibited item in checked baggage; withdraw with the item from the screening checkpoint at that time; make other arrangements for the item, such as taking it to your car; or, voluntarily abandon the item. Items that are voluntarily abandoned cannot be recovered and will not be returned to you.

The prohibited and permitted items list is not intended to be all-inclusive and is updated as necessary. To ensure everyone's security, the screener may determine that an item not on this chart is prohibited.

The list of items applies to flights originating within the United States. Please check with your airline or travel agent for restrictions at destinations outside of the United States.

For updates and for more information, visit our website at www.TSATravelTips.us or call our Consumer Response Center toll-free at 1-866-289-9673 or email TellTSA@tsa.dot.gov.

The following chart outlines items that are permitted and items that are prohibited in your carry-on or checked baggage. You should note that some items are allowed in your checked baggage, but not your carry-on. Also pay careful attention to the "Notes" included at the bottom of each section – they contain important information about restrictions.

The prohibited and permitted items chart is not intended to be all-inclusive and is updated as necessary. To ensure everyone's security, the screener may determine that an item not on the prohibited items chart is prohibited. In addition, the screener may also determine that an item on the permitted chart is dangerous and therefore may not be brought through the security checkpoint.

The chart applies to flights originating within the United States. Please check with your airline or travel agent for restrictions at destinations outside of the United States.

Can I take it?	Carry-on	Checked
Personal Items		
Cigar Cutters	Yes	Yes
Corkscrews	Yes	Yes
Cuticle Cutters	Yes	Yes
Eyeglass Repair Tools (including screwdrivers)	Yes	Yes
Eyelash Curlers	Yes	Yes
Knitting and Crochet Needles	Yes	Yes
Knives, round-bladed butter or plastic	Yes	Yes
Nail Clippers	Yes	Yes
Nail Files	Yes	Yes
Personal care or toiletries with		
aerosols, in limited quantities (such as hairsprays, deodorants)	Yes	Yes
Safety Razors (including disposable razors)	Yes	Yes
Scissors-plastic or metal with blunt tips	Yes	Yes
Scissors-metal with pointed tips	No	
Toy Transformer Robots	Yes	Yes
Toy Weapons (if not realistic replicas)	Yes	Yes
Tweezers	Yes	Yes
Umbrellas (allowed in carry-on baggage once they have been inspected to ensure that prohibited items are not concealed)	Yes	Yes
Walking Canes (allowed in carry-on baggage once they have been inspected to ensure that prohibited items are not concealed)	Yes	Yes

Note Some personal care items containing aerosol are regulated as hazardous materials. The FAA regulates hazardous materials. This information is summarized at http://cas.faa.gov/these.html

Medication and Special Needs Devices

Braille Note-Taker, Slate and Stylus, Augmentation Devices   Yes   Yes

Diabetes-Related Supplies/Equipment, (once inspected to ensure prohibited items are not concealed) including: insulin and insulin loaded dispensing products; vials or box of individual vials; jet injectors; pens; infusers; and preloaded syringes; and an unlimited number of unused syringes, when accompanied by insulin; lancets; blood glucose meters; blood glucose meter test strips; insulin pumps; and insulin pump supplies. Insulin in any form or dispenser must be properly marked with a professionally printed label identifying the medication or manufacturer's name or pharmaceutical label.

                                                                                         Yes   Yes

Nitroglycerine pills or spray for medical use (if properly marked with a professionally printed label identifying the medication or manufacturer's name or pharmaceutical label

                                                                                         Yes   Yes

Prosthetic Device Tools and Appliances, including drill, allen wrenches, pullsleeves used to put on or remove prosthetic devices, if carried by the individual with the prosthetic device or his or her companion

                                                                                         Yes   Yes

Electronic Devices

Camcorders   Yes   Yes

Camera Equipment

The checked baggage screening equipment will damage undeveloped film in camera equipment. We recommend that you either put undeveloped film and cameras containing undeveloped film in your carry-on baggage or take undeveloped film with you to the checkpoint and ask the screener to conduct a hand-inspection.

	Yes	Yes
Laptop Computers	Yes	Yes
Mobile Phones	Yes	Yes
Pagers	Yes	Yes
Personal Data Assistants (PDA's)	Yes	Yes

Note Check with your airline or travel agent for restrictions on the use of these and other electronic items during your flight.

Sharp Objects

Box Cutters	No	Yes
Ice Axes/Ice Picks	No	Yes
Knives (any length and type except round-bladed, butter, and plastic cutlery) No		Yes
Meat Cleavers	No	Yes
Razor-Type Blades, such as box cutters, utility knives, razor		
blades not in a cartridge, but excluding safety razors	No	Yes
Sabers	No	Yes
Scissors – metal with pointed tips		
Scissors with plastic or metal blunt tips are permitted in your carry-on. No		Yes
Swords	No	Yes

Note Any sharp objects in checked baggage should be sheathed or securely wrapped to prevent injury to baggage
handlers and inspectors.

Sporting Goods

Baseball Bats	No	Yes
Bows and Arrows	No	Yes
Cricket Bats	No	Yes
Golf Clubs	No	Yes
Hockey Sticks	No	Yes
Lacrosse Sticks	No	Yes
Pool Cues	No	Yes
Ski Poles	No	Yes
Spear Guns	No	Yes

Note Any sharp objects in checked baggage should be sheathed or securely wrapped to prevent injury to baggage handlers and security screeners.

Guns and Firearms
Ammunition
Check with your airline or travel agent to see if ammunition is permitted in checked baggage on the airline you are lying. If ammunition is permitted, it must be declared to the airline at check-in. Small arms ammunitions for personal
use must be securely packed in fiber, wood or metal boxes, or other packaging specifically designed to carry small
amounts of ammunition. Ask about imitations or fees, if any, that apply.

	No	Yes
BB guns	No	Yes
Compressed Air Guns	No	Yes
Firearms	No	Yes
Flare Guns	No	No
Gun Lighters	No	No
Gun Powder	No	No
Parts of Guns and Firearms	No	Yes

Pellet Guns	No	Yes
Realistic Replicas of Firearms	No	Yes
Starter Pistols	No	Yes

Note Check with your airline or travel agent to see if firearms are permitted in checked baggage on the airline you are flying. Ask about limitations or fees, if any, that apply. Firearms carried as checked baggage MUST be unloaded, packed in a locked hard-sided gun case, and declared to the airline at check-in. Only you, the passenger, may have the key or combination.

Tools

Axes and Hatchets	No	Yes
Cattle Prods	No	Yes
Crowbars	No	Yes
Hammers	No	Yes
Drills (including cordless portable power drills)	No	Yes
Saws (including cordless portable power saws)	No	Yes
Screwdrivers (except those in eyeglass repair kits)	No	Yes
Tools (including but not limited to wrenches and pliers)	No	Yes
Wrenches and Pliers	No	Yes

Note Any sharp objects in checked baggage should be sheathed or securely wrapped to prevent injury to baggage handlers and security screeners.

Martial Arts/Self Defense Items

Billy Clubs	**No**	**Yes**
Black Jacks	No	Yes
Brass Knuckles	No	Yes
Kubatonsq	No	Yes
Mace/Pepper Spray		
One 118 ml or 4 Fl. oz. container of mace or pepper spray is permitted in checked baggage provided it is equipped with a safety mechanism to prevent accidental discharge. For more information on these and other hazardous materials, visit http://cas.faa.gov/these.html .	No	Yes
Martial Arts Weapons	No	Yes
Night Sticks	No	Yes
Nunchakus	No	Yes

Martial Arts/Self Defense Items

Stun Guns/Shocking Devices	No	Yes
Throwing Stars	No	Yes

Note Any sharp objects in checked baggage should be sheathed or securely wrapped to prevent injury to baggage handlers and security screeners.

Explosive Materials

Blasting caps	No	No
Dynamite	No	No
Fireworks	No	No
Flares in any form	No	No
Hand Grenades	No	No
Plastic Explosives	No	No

Flammable Items

Aerosol (any except for personal care or toiletries in limited quantities)	No	No
Fuels (including cooking fuels and any flammable liquid fuel)	No	No

Gasoline	No	No
Gas Torches	No	No
Lighter Fluid	No	No
Strike-anywhere Matches	No	No
Turpentine and paint thinner	No	No

Note There are other hazardous materials that are regulated by the FAA. This information is summarized at http://cas.faa.gov/these.html

Disabling Chemicals and Other Dangerous Items		
Chlorine for pools and spas	No	No
Compressed Gas Cylinders (including fire extinguishers)	No	No
Liquid Bleach	No	No
Spillable Batteries (except those in wheelchairs)	No	No
Spray Paint	No	No
Tear Gas	No	No

Note There are other hazardous materials that are regulated by the FAA. This information is summarized at http://cas.faa.gov/these.html

Travel Preparation

There are preparations you can make before you arrive at the airport to help you move more quickly and efficiently through the new security processes. Here you will find suggestions on what to wear to the airport and how to pack for your trip. We've also included a pre-flight checklist to help you *Prepare for Takeoff.*

Dress the Part
Security does not require any particular style or type of clothing. However, certain clothing and accessories can set off an alarm on the metal detector and slow you down. Here you will find tips to help you through the checkpoint.

Pack Smart
There are restrictions on what you can pack in your carry-on and checked baggage. All of your baggage will be screened and possibly hand-searched as part of the new security measures. This inspection may include emptying most or all of the articles in your bag. Here you will find tips to help you pack.

Final Checklist
You're dressed, packed and ready to go. Or are you? Here is a pre-flight checklist to help you Prepare for Takeoff. Contact your airline or travel agent for additional information.

By familiarizing yourself with the security process and following these tips and recommendations you will be able to play an active role in ensuring your own safety and comfort.

Be Prepared - Dress the Part

Be aware that any metal detected at the checkpoint must be identified. If you set off the alarm, you will be required to undergo a secondary screening, including a hand-wanding and a pat-down inspection.

You can remove metal items at the security checkpoint and place them in the bins provided. The bins will be sent through the X-ray machine. You can save time, however, by not wearing metal items or by placing such items in your carry-on baggage before you get in line.

TIP: Avoid wearing clothing, jewelry, or other accessories that contain metal when traveling.
- Jewelry (pins, necklaces, bracelets, rings, watches, earrings, body piercings, cuff links, lanyard or bolo tie)
- Shoes with steel tips, heels, shanks, buckles or nails

- Clothing with metal buttons, snaps or studs
- Metal hair barrettes or other hair decoration
- Belt buckles
- Under-wire brassieres

Hidden items such as body piercings may result in a pat-down inspection. You may ask to remove your body piercing in private as an alternative to the pat-down search.

TIP: Avoid placing metal items in your pockets.

- Keys, loose change, lighters
- Mobile phones, pagers, and personal data assistants (PDAs)

TIP: Instead, place jewelry and other metal items in your carry-on baggage until you clear security.

TIP: Pack your outer coat or jacket in your baggage when possible.

Outer coats including trench coats, ski jackets, leather jackets, overcoats and parkas must go through the X-ray machine for inspection. If you choose to wear an outer coat to the checkpoint, you will need to either place it in your carry-on or put it in the bin that is provided for you. You will not need to remove suit jackets or blazers unless requested by the screener.

Plan Ahead - Pack Smart

Carry-on Baggage is a small piece of luggage you take onboard the airplane with you. You are allowed one carry-on in addition to one personal item such as a laptop computer, purse, small backpack, briefcase, or camera case.

Checked Baggage is luggage you check in at the ticket counter or at curbside. It will not be accessible during your flight.

Packing Tips

Below are a number of tips for packing your checked baggage that will help to speed your trip and ensure that your checked bag makes the flight with you.

- Don't put film in your checked baggage, as the screening equipment will damage it.
- Pack shoes, boots, sneakers, and other footwear on top of other contents in your luggage.
- Avoid over-packing your bag so that the screener will be able to easily reseal your bag if it is opened for inspection. If possible, spread your contents over

several bags. Check with your airline or travel agent for maximum weight limitations.
- Avoid packing food and drink items in checked baggage.
- Don't stack piles of books or documents on top of each other; spread them out within your baggage.

The following general packing tips apply to both carry-on and checked baggage and will help you to move through the screening process more quickly:

- Do NOT pack or bring prohibited items to the airport. See permitted and prohibited items.
- Put all undeveloped film and cameras with film in your carry-on baggage. If your bag will pass through the X-ray machine more than 5 times ask for a hand inspection to prevent damage.
- Check ahead of time with your airline or travel agent to determine the airline's baggage policy, including number of pieces you can bring and size and weight limitations.
- Carry-on baggage is limited to one carry-on bag plus one personal item. Personal items include laptops, purses, small backpacks, briefcases, or camera cases. Remember, 1+1.
- Don't forget to place identification tags with your name, address and phone number on all of your baggage, including your laptop computer. It is a good idea to place an identification tag inside your baggage as well.
- Avoid overpacking so that your articles don't spill out if your bag is opened for inspection.
- Think carefully about the personal items you place in your carry-on baggage. The screeners may have to open your bag and examine its contents.
- Consider putting personal belongings in clear plastic bags to reduce the chance that a TSA screener will have to handle them.
- Wait to wrap your gifts. Be aware that wrapped gifts may need to be opened for inspection. This applies to both carry-on and checked baggage.

Baggage Security Checkpoints

As of January 1, 2003, TSA began screening 100% of checked baggage at all 429 commercial airports across the United States. You will encounter one of the processes described below at the airport. Please be aware that you will not be able to access your bags after they are screened no matter which process you encounter. Therefore, you should remove everything that you want to take on the plane with you before you hand over your checked bag for screening.

Checked Bag Screening Processes
No change -- You check in at the ticket counter or with the skycaps as you have in the past. The new screening equipment will be out of your view and the screening of your checked baggage will occur behind the scenes.

Ticket counter first -- You will still check-in at the ticket counter or with the skycap as you have in the past, but you will next proceed to a new baggage screening area nearby. At most airports, you will next take your checked bag to the checked baggage screening area, where it will be screened there and afterwards delivered directly to your airline for loading. At some airports, someone will take your checked baggage from you at the ticket counter and deliver it to the screening area. In a growing number of airports, you will have the option to drop off your bags at the screening area and proceed directly to your gate without waiting for your bags to be screened.

Baggage screening first -- You will go first to the checked baggage screening area in the airport lobby. After baggage screening, the screener will direct you to the ticket counter and an authorized person will bring your bag from the screening area to the ticket counter for you to complete the check-in process.

Please watch for signs and other instructions that will direct you to the correct line. Unless you see signs directing you otherwise, go to the ticket counter to check-in with your airline.

Several methods are being used to screen 100% of checked baggage. The most common methods that you will encounter involve electronic screening, either by an Explosives Detection System (EDS) or Explosives Trace Detection (ETD) device.

The EDS machines are the large machines that can be over 20 feet long and weigh up three tons. Your baggage will be loaded on a conveyor belt of the EDS machine by a screener for screening. If your bag requires further inspection, it may be brought to an ETD machine.

The ETD machine are much smaller machines, and are the primary machine used in many airports. When your bag is screened with an ETD machine, the screener will take a swab of your bag and then place the swab into the ETD machine for analysis.

There are other methods that may be used at airports to ensure that 100% of all bags are screened. Regardless of which system is used, all checked bags will be screened before they are loaded onto the plane.

Unlocking Checked Bags
TSA suggests that you help prevent the need to break your locks by keeping your bags unlocked. In some cases, screeners will have to open your baggage as part of the screening process. If your bag is unlocked, then TSA will simply open the bag and screen the bag. However, if the bag is locked and TSA needs to open your bag, then locks may have to be broken. You may keep your bag locked if you choose, but TSA is not liable for damage caused to locked bags that must be opened for security purposes. If you are transporting a firearm, please refer to the on "Transporting Firearms and Ammunition" section at the bottom of this page for directions on locking your bag.

If TSA screeners open your bag during the screening procedure, they will close it with a tamper evident seal and place a notice in your bag alerting you to the fact that TSA screeners opened your bag for inspection.

In the near future, TSA will provide seals at the airport for you to use to secure your bags as an alternative to locks. Until that time, you may want to consider purchasing standard "cable ties," which can be found at your local hardware store. The 4 to 5 inch variety cable ties generally work best since they are the easiest to remove at your destination and can be used to close almost every bag with zippers. If TSA needs to inspect your bag, the screeners will cut off the seal and replace it with another seal.

Missing Contents
TSA screeners exercise great care during the screening process to ensure that your contents are returned to your bag every time a bag needs to be opened. TSA will assess, on an individual basis,

any loss or damage claims made to TSA. You may call the TSA Consumer Response Center toll-free at 1-866-289-9673 if you have questions.

See the section on "Travel Preparation" for a complete listing of other packing and timesaving tips.

Transporting Firearms and Ammunition

Subject to state, local, and airline restrictions, you may still transport a firearm and ammunition in your checked baggage provided it is declared to the aircraft operator (airline) at check in and that you comply with other applicable regulations. Please note that you should never unlock your bag if you are carrying a firearm and your bag serves as the locked, hard-sided case for transporting your firearm.

See the section "Travel Preparation, Frequently Asked Questions" for more details on transporting firearms and ammunition.

Travelers & Consumers

Can I still transport a firearm in checked baggage?

Subject to state and local restrictions on transporting firearms, you may still transport a firearm in your checked baggage. However, you should first check with your airline or travel agent to see if firearms are permitted in checked baggage on the airline you are flying. Ask about limitations or fees, if any, that apply. Firearms carried as checked baggage MUST be unloaded, packed in a locked hard-sided gun case, and declared to the airline at check-in. Only you, the passenger, may have the key or combination.

Ammunition may be packed in the same locked container as the firearm, so long as it is not loaded in the firearm. Small-arms ammunition must also be declared to the air carrier and placed in an appropriate container ? securely packed in fiber, wood or metal boxes or other packaging specifically designed to carry small amount of ammunition. In addition, small-arms ammunition must also be declared to the air carrier and placed in an appropriate container: "securely packed in fiber, wood, or metal boxes, or other packaging specifically designed to carry small amounts of ammunition." Ammunition may be packed in the same locked container as the firearm, so long as it is not loaded in the firearm.

What happens if my belongings are missing

from my bag when I arrive at my destination?

TSA screeners exercise great care during the screening process to ensure that your contents are returned to your bag every time a bag needs to be opened. TSA will assess any claims made to TSA on an individual basis.

Are there any tips on packing that will help me save time at the airport?

There are some tips that will help you to speed your trip through the screening process: 1. Don't put film in your checked baggage, as the screening equipment will damage it. 2. Consider putting personal belongings in clear plastic bags to reduce the chance that a TSA screener will have to handle them. 3. Pack shoes, boots, sneakers, and other footwear on top of other contents in your luggage. 4. Avoid over-packing your bag so that the screener will be able to easily reseal your bag if it is opened for inspection. If possible, spread your contents over several bags. Check with your airline or travel agent for maximum weight limitations. 5. Avoid packing food and drink items in checked baggage. 6. Don't stack piles of books or documents on top of each other; spread them out within your baggage.

Is the check-in procedure different now that TSA is screening all checked baggage?

This depends on the airport from which you are departing. If you are at an airport where the screening equipment is "behind the scenes," you will not notice any difference. In many airports you will see screening equipment in the lobby. Unless you see signs directing you otherwise, go to the ticket counter to check-in with your airline. In a limited number of airports, you will be directed to proceed to baggage screening before you check-in with your airline. Please watch for these signs and other instructions to ensure that you go the correct line.

Will TSA relock my bag if it is opened for screening?

If TSA screeners open your bag during the screening procedure, they will close it with a security seal. In addition, TSA will place a notice in your bag alerting you to the fact that TSA screeners opened your bag for inspection. Our highly trained screeners will take great care to secure your bag for the rest of your trip.

Should I lock my luggage?

In some cases, the TSA will have to open your baggage as part of the screening process. If your bag is unlocked, then TSA will simply open the bag and screen the bag. However, if the bag is locked and TSA needs to open your bag, then locks may have to be broken. Therefore, TSA suggests that you help prevent the need to break your locks by keeping your bag unlocked. In the near future, TSA will provide seals at the airport for you to use to secure your luggage as an alternative to locking your bag. Until that time, you may want to consider purchasing standard cable ties to secure your bags if it has zippers.

Will all checked baggage be screened on January 1?

The TSA will be screening all checked baggage on January 1 using several methods. Some of the screening equipment will be visible in the lobby while other equipment will be "behind the scenes." Whether you see differences or not, please be assured that all checked bags will be screened.

How early should I arrive at the airport?

Check with your airline or travel agent. Recommended check-in times differ by airline and airport.

Can I access the gate area if I am not a passenger?

1) UNACCOMPANIED CHILD, ELDERLY PERSON, OR SPECIAL NEEDS: If you are going to assist an unaccompanied child, elderly person, or person with special needs through the security checkpoint, you will need to get a gate pass/authorization at the airport ticket counter of your airline. 2) FREQUENT FLYERS CLUBS AND LOUNGES: When airline and airport clubs and lounges are located beyond the passenger security checkpoint, passengers without tickets should contact their airline representative to gain access. Access to the security checkpoints is controlled by the airlines. In regards to Frequent Fliers Clubs and Lounges, when airline and airport clubs and lounges are located beyond the passenger security checkpoint, passengers without tickets should contact their airline representative to gain access. Access to the security checkpoints is controlled by the airlines.

What are prohibited items?

Prohibited items are weapons, explosives, incendiaries, and include items that are seemingly harmless but may be used as weapons-the so-called "dual use" items. You may not bring these items to security checkpoints without authorization. A non-exclusive list of prohibited items is available at www.tsa.dot.gov.

What may happen to my prohibited item at the security checkpoint?

Your prohibited item may be detained for use in an investigation and, if necessary, as evidence in your criminal and/or civil prosecution. If permitted by the screener or law enforcement officer, you may be allowed to: consult with the airlines for possible assistance in placing the prohibited item in checked baggage, withdraw with the item from the screening checkpoint at that time, make other arrangements for the item, such as taking it to your car, or voluntarily abandon the item. Items that are voluntarily abandoned cannot be recovered and will not be returned to you.

What may happen to me if I bring a prohibited item to a security checkpoint?

You may be criminally and/or civilly prosecuted or, at the least, asked to rid yourself of the item. A screener and/or law enforcement officer will make this determination, depending on what the item is and the circumstances. This is because bringing a prohibited item to a security checkpoint-even accidentally-is illegal.

Can I transport guns or firearms?

Guns and firearms are NOT permitted in your carry-on baggage, but depending on the policy of your airline, they may be included with your checked baggage. Check with your airline or travel agent to see if firearms are permitted in checked baggage on the airline you are flying. Firearms carried as checked baggage MUST be unloaded, packed in a locked hard-sided gun case, and declared to the airline at check-in. Only you, the passenger, may have the key or combination.

What about ammunition?

Ammunition is NOT permitted in your carry-on baggage, but depending on the policy of your airline, may be included with your checked baggage. Check with your airline or travel agent to see if ammunition is permitted in checked baggage on the airline you are flying. If ammunition is permitted, it must be declared to the airline at check-in. Small arms ammunitions for personal use must be securely packed in fiber, wood or metal boxes, or other packaging specifically designed to carry small amounts of ammunition. Ask about limitations or fees, if any, that apply.

510

Final Checklist

Before You Arrive - Final Checklist

Check with your airline or travel agent
- To determine how early to arrive at the airport. Recommended check-in times differ by airline and airport.
- To determine whether you need a boarding pass and photo identification to enter the passenger checkpoint. You can also check the TSA website by looking under "Access Requirements" for a current list of airports with this requirement.

Check with your airport
- To confirm which parking lots are open if you will be parking at the airport. Some lots may be closed for security reasons. Be sure to allow extra time for parking and shuttle transportation.

Check to make sure you
- Bring a boarding pass, ticket, or ticket confirmation, such as a printed itinerary, as well as a government-issued photo ID. Children under the age of 18 do not require an ID. At some airports, only boarding passes will be accepted to enter the passenger checkpoint.
- Bring evidence verifying you have a medical implant or other device if it is likely to set off the alarm on the metal detector, bring evidence verifying this condition. Although this is not a requirement, it may help to expedite the screening process.
- Have removed prohibited items such as pocketknives, metal scissors with pointed tips (metal or plastic scissors with blunt tips are permitted), and tools from your carry-on baggage. Double check the list of prohibited and permitted items to determine what can be placed in carry-on or checked baggage if you have any questions.
- Have reviewed TSA's guidance on unlocking checked baggage.

Have a safe trip and enjoy your flight!

Travel Tips
TSA suggests that you help prevent the need to break your locks by keeping your bag unlocked

In some cases, screeners will have to open your baggage as part of the screening process. If your bag is unlocked, then TSA will simply open the bag and screen the bag. However, if the bag is locked and TSA needs to open your bag, then locks may have to be broken. You may keep your bag locked if you choose, but TSA is not liable for damage caused to locked bags that must be opened for security purposes.

Check with your airline or travel agent
- To determine how early to arrive at the airport. Recommended check-in times differ by airline and airport.
- To determine whether you need a boarding pass and photo identification to enter the passenger checkpoint. You can also check the TSA website by looking under "Access Requirements" for a current list of airports with this requirement.

Check with your airport
- To confirm which parking lots are open if you will be parking at the airport. Some lots may be closed for security reasons. Be sure to allow extra time for parking and shuttle transportation.

Check to make sure you
- Bring a boarding pass, ticket, or ticket confirmation, such as a printed itinerary, as well as a government-issued photo ID. Children under the age of 18 do not require an ID. At some airports, only boarding passes will be accepted to enter the passenger checkpoint.
- Bring evidence verifying you have a medical implant or other device if it is likely to set off the alarm on the metal detector, bring evidence verifying this condition. Although this is not a requirement, it may help to expedite the screening process.
- Have removed prohibited items such as pocketknives, metal scissors with pointed tips (metal or plastic scissors with blunt tips are permitted), and tools from your carry-on baggage. Double check the list of prohibited and permitted items to determine what can be placed in carry-on or checked baggage if you have any questions.

• Have reviewed TSA's guidance on unlocking checked baggage.

Security Procedures

TSA has Implemented New Security Procedures in U.S. Airports

The Transportation Security Administration has instituted standardized screening procedures at airports across the country. The information here describes the new enhanced procedures you will encounter. Familiarizing yourself with these procedures - particularly those that are new or different from what you may have experienced in the past - will assist you in moving quickly through your security screening.

Each passenger must go through two stages of screening:
• Baggage Checkpoints
• Passenger Checkpoints
Some passengers may go through an additional stage of screening:
• Gate Screening
For your security, only certain individuals are permitted to enter the screening area.
• Access Requirements

See Baggage checkpoints

Passenger Security Checkpoints

Passenger checkpoints are now the second checkpoints you will encounter.
You must pass through this checkpoint to access your departure gate. Security screeners will screen you and your carry-on baggage. You should find this screening process familiar, although enhanced security measures are in place.
The passenger checkpoint includes 3 primary steps you may want to become familiar with:

Step 1. X-ray machine
At the passenger security checkpoint, you will place all carry-on baggage and any items you are carrying with you on the belt of the X-ray machine. You will need to lay all items flat.

Laptop computers must be removed from their carrying cases and placed in one of the bins provided. You will also need to remove your outer coat or jacket and place it in one of the bins. These items go through the X-ray machine.
"IN - OUT - OFF"
• Place all metal items IN your carry-on baggage before you reach the front of the line.
• Take your computer OUT of its carrying case and place it in one of the bins provided.
• Take OFF your outer coat or jacket so that it can go through the X-ray machine (you do not need to remove your suit jacket, sport coat, or blazer unless you are asked to do so by one of the passenger screeners.)

Step 2. Walk-through metal detector
You will next walk through a metal detector, (or you may request a pat-down inspection instead). Objects on your clothing or person containing metal may set off the alarm on the metal detector.
You will undergo a secondary screening if you set off the alarm on the metal detector, or if you are chosen for additional screening. (See below)

TIP: Pack all metal items, including the contents of your pockets, in your carry-on baggage. Mobile phones, pagers, keys, lighters, and loose change are examples of items containing metal.
If you refuse to be screened at any point during the screening process, the screener must deny you entry beyond the screening area. You will not be able to fly.

Step 3. Secondary screening
Secondary screening occurs when an individual sets off the alarm on the metal detector, or if he or she is selected for additional screening. This screening includes a hand-wand inspection in conjunction with a pat-down inspection.

If you must go through a secondary screening, the screener will direct you from the metal detector to a screening station where he or she will brief you on the next steps.

• At this time, you should let the screener know of any personal needs you may have due to a religious or cultural consideration, disability, or other medical concern.
• Except in extraordinary circumstances, a screener of your gender will conduct your secondary screening. You may

request that your search be conducted in private.

While you will be separated from your carry-on baggage during this process, every effort will be made to help you maintain visual contact with your carry-ons.

Hand-Wand Inspection

The hand-wand inspection helps the screener to identify what may have set off the alarm on the metal detector. During the wanding procedure, you will be asked to stand with your feet apart and the screener will pass the wand over your entire body without actually touching you with the wand. Every effort will be taken to do this as discretely as possible. Please take note of the following:

- Areas of the body that have body piercings, thick hair, hats, and other items may require a pat-down inspection.
- You may ask to remove your body piercing in private as an alternative to the pat-down search.
- The screener may ask you to open your belt buckle as part of the process.
- The screener may ask you to remove your shoes, and your shoes may be X-rayed separately.

TIP: It is recommended (but not a requirement) that individuals with a pacemaker, or other device that is likely to alarm the metal detector, bring identification verifying the condition. This may help to expedite the screening process.

Your Carry-On Baggage

If your bag is selected for secondary screening, it may be opened and examined on a table in your presence. Please DO NOT attempt to assist the screener during the search, and do not attempt to retrieve the item before the screener has advised you that the search is complete and your baggage is cleared.

Your baggage might also be inspected with an Explosive Trace Detection machine (ETD), which is separate from the X-ray machine.

Pat-Down Inspection

A pat-down inspection complements the hand-wand inspection. In order to ensure security, this inspection may include sensitive areas of the body.

Screeners are rigorously trained to maintain the highest levels of professionalism.

You may request that your pat-down inspection be conducted in private.

Gate Screening
Additional Screening May Occur at the Departure Gate

Some passengers may be selected for additional screening at the departure gate. The procedures are very similar to the secondary screening process, (See STEP 3) used at the checkpoints.

Special Considerations
Do You Require Additional Assistance during the Screening Process?

The Transportation Security Administration (TSA) has developed standardized security screening procedures for all airports. Therefore, you can expect that you will encounter essentially the same procedures at each airport you visit. You can also expect to be treated with the same courtesy and respect.

While the same screening procedures are used for virtually all passengers, we recognize that some passengers may have special needs or require additional assistance during the screening process. To maintain excellent security and customer service, TSA security screeners have been trained to be sensitive to and respectful of the needs of all passengers.

The Security Process & Preparation Tips

We have identified some helpful information that explains the security screening procedures as they may apply to groups with special needs. If you fall into any one of the categories identified below, you may want to familiarize yourself with this information before arriving at the airport.

- Persons with disabilities or medical concerns
- Religious or cultural needs
- Traveling with Children
- Pets
- Film
- Sports Equipment

Your knowledge of the procedures, and observance of the tips and recommendations, will help you move through the security checkpoint quickly and efficiently.

If you have any questions while at the airport, ask

for the TSA screening supervisor. You may also contact our Consumer Response Center toll-free at 1-866-289-9673 Monday - Friday between 8am - 6pm (24 hour voicemail). You may also email us at TellTSA@tsa.dot.gov.

This information will be updated from time-to time. We recommend that you periodically check TSA's web site to obtain the latest information.

Persons with Disabilities or Medical Concerns

Do You Have a Disability?
This section provides information pertaining to specific disabilities including mobility, hearing, visual and hidden disabilities and the use of dog guides, service dogs and hearing dogs. You will also find information on medical devices for persons with diabetes, pacemakers, assistive devices and mobility aids.

Do You Have a Medical Concern?
This section provides information addressing general medical concerns, including temporary aids, injectable medication, medical implants, medical documentation, pain or sensitivity and medical, lifesaving evidentiary or scientific items and crematory containers

Before You Go
Information to be aware of and Tips for the screening process.

At the Passenger Security Checkpoint
Mobility Disability
- Don't hesitate to ask a screener for assistance with your mobility aid and carryon items as you proceed through the security checkpoint.
- Let the screener know your level of ability (e.g., whether you can walk, stand or perform an arm lift) - it will expedite the screening process.
- Inform the screener about any special equipment or devices that you are using and where this equipment is located on your body - this will help the screener be careful during a physical search if one is needed.
- Ensure that all bags and satchels hanging from, or carried on, your

equipment are put on the X-ray belt for inspection.
- Ask the screener to reunite you with your carryon items and assistive device after screening is completed.
- Let the screener know if you need assistance removing your shoes when additional screening is necessary.
- Let the screener know if your shoes cannot be removed because of your disability so that alternative security procedures can be applied to your shoes.
- Ask the screener to monitor your items during the screening process and reunite you with them and assistive devices once x-ray inspection is completed.

Hearing Disability
If the screening process is unclear to you, ask the screener to write the information down or look directly at you and repeat the information slowly.

Visual Disability
You may ask the screener to:
- Explain the security process to you.
- Verbally communicate to you throughout each step of the screening process.
- Let you know where the metal detector is located.
- Let you know when you will be going though the metal detector.
- Let you know when there are obstacles you need to avoid.
- Find someone to escort you through the security process.
- Perform a hand inspection of equipment (e.g., Braille note-takers) if the X-ray inspection will damage them.
- Reunite you with all of your carryon items and assistive devices after the X-ray or physical inspection of the items is completed, including electronic equipment which has been specially adapted for your use.
- Verbally direct you toward your gate once the screening has been completed.

Hidden Disability
Persons with a hidden disability can, if they choose, advise screeners that they have a hidden disability and may need some assistance, or need to move a bit slower than others.

- Family members or traveling companions can advise screeners when they are traveling with someone who has a hidden disability, which may cause that person to move a little slower, become agitated easily and/or need additional attention.
- Family members or traveling companions can offer suggestions to screeners on the best way to approach and deal with the person with a hidden disability, especially when it is necessary to touch the person during a pat-down inspection.
- Notify the screener if you need to sit down before and/or during the screening process.

Persons with Diabetes
- Notify the screener that you have diabetes and are carrying your supplies with you. The following diabetes related supplies and equipment are allowed through the checkpoint once they have been screened:
  - insulin and insulin loaded dispensing products (vials or box of individual vials, jet injectors, pens, infusers, and preloaded syringes),
  - unlimited number of unused syringes when accompanied by insulin, and
  - lancets, blood glucose meters, blood glucose meter test strips, insulin pumps, and insulin pump supplies.
- Insulin in any form or dispenser must be properly marked with a professionally printed label identifying the medication or manufacturer's name or pharmaceutical label.
- Notify screeners if you are wearing an insulin pump and, if necessary, advise the screener that it cannot be removed since it is surgically implanted.
- Insulin pumps and supplies must be accompanied by insulin with professionally printed labels identifying the medication or manufacturer's name or pharmacy label.
- Advise screeners if you are experiencing low blood sugar and are in need of medical assistance.
- It is recommended that used syringes be transported in your checked baggage; however, when used syringes need to

be in carry-on, ensure they are in a hard, plastic-capped container (i.e. sharps disposable container) for safety and containment.

Persons with Pacemakers
- It is recommended (but not a requirement) that individuals with a pacemaker carry a Pacemaker Identification Card (ID) when going through airport security.
- It is recommended (but not required) that you advise the screener that you have an implanted pacemaker.
- Show the screener your pacemaker ID, if you have one, and ask the screener to conduct a pat-down inspection of you rather than having you walk through the metal detector or be hand-wanded.

Persons with Assistive Devices and Mobility Aids: Canes, Walkers, Crutches, Prosthetic Devices, Body Braces, and Other Devices
- Crutches, canes and walkers will need to go through the X-ray machine.
- Notify the screener if your device requires special handling.
- Ask for assistance with your device(s) if you need it.
- The screener will perform a hand inspection of your equipment if it cannot fit through the X-ray machine.
- Collapse canes whenever possible before they are put on the X-ray belt.
- Once devices have been screened, screeners should hand back your device to you in such a manner that helps you proceed without difficulty.
- Screeners may need to see and touch your prosthetic devices and body braces as part of the inspection process.
- You can ask for a private screening for the inspection of your prosthetic device or body brace.
- Notify screeners if you need assistance during the inspection of your prosthetic devices or body braces such as a chair or someone to lean on.
- You may bring tools and appliances (e.g. wrenches, pull sleeves, etc.) used to put on or take off prosthetic devices through the security checkpoint once they have been screened.

Service Animals

- It is recommended that persons using a dog for assistance carry appropriate identification. Identification may include: cards or documentation, presence of a harness or markings on the harness, tags, or other credible assurance of the passenger using the dog for their disability.
- Advise the screener how you and your dog can go through the metal detector as a team (i.e. whether walking together or with the dog walking in front of or behind you while you continually maintain control of the dog with the leash and/or harness.
- The dog's harness will likely set off the alarm on the metal detector. In such cases, screener will perform a hand inspection of the dog and its belongings (collar, harness, leash, backpack, vest, etc.) The belongings will not be removed from your dog at any time.
- If necessary, remind the screener that you should not be separated from your dog and that removal of your dog's belongings is a sign to the dog or other service animal that it is off work.

Temporary Aids

Passengers who are temporarily using a wheelchair or assistive devices due to an injury, surgery, or medical procedure should refer to the "Mobility Disability" and/or "Persons with Assistive Devices and Mobility Aids" sections under "Persons with Disabilities." The information found there will help guide you through the screening process.

Injectable Medication

Make sure injectable medications are properly labeled (professionally printed label identifying the medication or a manufacturer's name or pharmaceutical label). Notify the screener if you are carrying a hazardous waste container, refuse container, or a sharps disposable container in your carry-on baggage used to trainsport used syringes, lancets, etc.

Medical Implants

Notify the screener if you have any implanted medical devices such as an artificial hip or knee, bone shafts, cranial plates, shrapnel, staples, pins, or metal ports that may set off the alarm on the metal detector.

Medical Documentation

If you have medical documentation regarding your medical condition, you may present this information to the screener to help inform him or her of your situation. This documentation is not required and will not exempt you from the screening process.

Pain or Sensitivity

If you are required to undergo a personal search, you can notify the screener if you are in pain due to a recent surgery or medical procedure (e.g. area where you have just undergone surgery, have staples, sutures, reconstruction areas, or newly implanted devices) that will require greater care.

Notify the screener when you have a special situation requiring sensitivity if a pat-down inspection is necessary. You may request a private area for your personal search.

Medical, Lifesaving, Evidentiary or Scientific Items and Crematory Containers

These items may be allowed through the security checkpoint and aboard an aircraft if you have made pre-arrangements with the airline. The airline and screener will confirm that you have the appropriate documents to verify the contents and establish your identity. Screeners will treat the items with the appropriate respect and dignity.

Before You Go

- Provide advance notice to your airline or travel agent if you require assistance at the airport.
- If you require a companion or assistant to accompany you through the security checkpoint to reach your gate, speak with your airline representative about obtaining a gate pass for your companion before entering the security checkpoint.
- The limit of one carry-on and one personal item (purse, briefcase or computer case) does not apply to medical supplies, equipment, mobility aids and/or assistive devices carried by a person with a disability.
- Make sure all your carry-on items, equipment, devices, etc., have an identification tag attached.
- Mobility aids and assistive devices permitted through the security

516

checkpoint include: wheelchairs, scooters, canes, walkers, crutches, prosthetic devices, body braces, augmentation and communication devices (e.g. Braille note takers, slate and stylus), dog guides, service dogs, hearing dogs, and diabetes related equipment and supplies.

- If you have a medical device (implanted on the interior or exterior of your body) check with your Doctor prior to traveling to determine if it is safe for you to go through the walk-through metal detector or be handwanded. If your Doctor indicates that you should not go through the metal detector or be handwanded or if you are concerned, ask the screener for a pat-down inspection instead.

See the Service Animals section on the Persons with Disabilities page for information on animals assisting passengers.

Tips for the Screening Process

- If a personal search is required, you may choose to remain in the wanding area or go to a private area for your screening. If you refuse either option you will not be able to fly.
- You should be offered a private screening before the beginning of a pat-down inspection if the pat-down will require the removal or lifting of clothing and/or display of a covered medical device.
- You may request a private area for your personal search at any time during the screening process.
- You may ask for a chair if you need to sit down during the screening process.
- You may request a pat-down in lieu of going through the walk-through metal detector or being hand-wanded. You do not need to disclose why you would like this option.
- If you have a disability, condition, or implant that you would like to remain private and confidential, ask the screener to please be discreet when assisting you through the screening process.

Religious or Cultural Needs

General Screening Considerations for Religious or Cultural Needs

- If you do not want to go through the metal detector, you may request a personal search (pat-down inspection) as an alternative.
- You may also ask the screener for a private area for this personal search. You will be provided a screener of the same gender, except in extraordinary situations. In the unlikely situation where a screener of the same gender is not available, you will be provided with alternatives, which may include waiting for a same-gender screener to arrive, or consenting to a search by a screener of the opposite gender.
- If you refuse appropriate screening you will not be allowed to pass the security checkpoint and you will be unable to board your plane.

Head Coverings

It may be necessary for you to remove your head covering during the screening process. If the screener asks you to remove a head covering, you may request a private area to provide privacy while the head cover is removed, inspected, and restored.

Religious, Cultural or Ceremonial Items

- There are items in this category that are not permitted through the security checkpoint (e.g., religious knives, swords). Therefore, it is advised that you place such items in your checked baggage. Check the permitted/prohibited list for more information.
- If the screener asks you to provide a religious, cultural or ceremonial item for screening, you may request a hand-inspection. If the item is prohibited from the cabin of the aircraft you will be asked to place the item in your checked baggage or speak to your airline about checking the item. If the item is delicate or fragile, or special handling is otherwise required, please let the screener know so that he or she can handle the item accordingly.

If the screener requests that you put a delicate or fragile item through the X-ray machine, you may want to ask the screener to ensure that there is no baggage immediately before or after the item so that it will not be damaged. Bins are available at the X-ray machine.

Traveling with Children

Are You Traveling with Children?

Every person, regardless of age, must undergo screening to proceed beyond the security checkpoint. Even babies must be individually screened. You will not be asked to do anything that will separate you from your child or children.

Screeners are specially trained and understand your concerns regarding children. Your children will be approached gently and treated with respect. If your child becomes uncomfortable or upset, you will be consulted about the best approach to resolving your child's concern.

The Screening Process
X-Ray

- All carry-on baggage, including children's bags and items, must go through the X-ray machine. Examples include: diaper bags, blankets, and toys.
- All child-related equipment that will fit through the X-ray machine must go through the X-ray machine. Examples include: strollers, umbrella strollers, baby carriers, car and booster seats, backpacks, and baby slings.
- When you arrive at the checkpoint, you should collapse or fold child-related equipment and secure items that are in the pockets, baskets, or attached to the equipment. You will place these items on the X-ray belt for inspection. Plastic bins are provided to deposit such items.
- When child-related equipment does not fit through the X-ray machine, the equipment must be visually and physically inspected.
- Ask screeners for assistance to help reunite you with your bags and child-related equipment, if needed.

ALERT! Babies should NEVER be left in an infant carrier while it goes through the X-ray machine.

For information regarding what is permitted or prohibited from being in carry-on luggage, please refer to our prohibited items section.

The Walk Through Metal Detector
The screener will need to resolve the alarm for both adult and child if something sets off the alarm as you are carrying a child through the metal detector.

- Babies and children must be removed from their strollers or infant carriers so they can be individually screened.
- You may not pass the child to another person behind you or in front of you during this process.
- Do not pass your child to the screener to hold.
- The screener may ask for your assistance with secondary screening of your child.
- If your child can walk unassisted, it would be best to have the child walk through the metal detector independently.

Child with a Disability
If your child has a disability, screeners may ask you what abilities your child has in order to determine the best method for screening (e.g. carry the child through the walk-through metal detector, hand-wand procedure). If your child has a disability, screeners will never attempt to remove the child from his or her equipment. This will only be done at the discretion of the accompanying adult.

Family Travel Tips

TIPS Before you reach the airport
- Please allow yourself and your family extra time to get through security - especially when traveling with younger children.
- Call your airline or travel agent for information on recommended check-in times for your departure airport.
- Talk to your children before coming to the airport and let them know that it's against the law to make threats such as, "I have a bomb in my bag." Threats made jokingly (even by a child) can result in the entire family being delayed and could result in fines.

TIPS At the airport

- Speak to your children again about the screening process so that they will not be frightened or surprised. Remind them to not joke about threats such as bombs or explosives.
- Advise your children that their bags (backpack, dolls, etc.) will be put in the X-ray machine and will come out at the other end and be returned to them.
- Let your children know that a screener may ask to see Mom or Dad's shoes, but that these too will be returned after the inspection.
- You may want to consider asking for a private screening if you are traveling with more than one child.

Pets

Traveling with a Pet?

Security procedures do not prohibit you from bringing a pet on your flight. You should contact your airline or travel agent, however, before arriving at the airport to determine your airline's policy on traveling with pets.

Security Screening

If you are planning to bring an animal on-board the plane with you, you will need to present the animal to the security checkpoint screeners for screening. You may walk your animal through the metal detector with you. If this is not possible, your animal will have to undergo a secondary screening, including a visual and physical inspection.

Your animal will NEVER be placed through an X-ray machine. You may be asked to remove your animal from its carrier so that the carrier can be placed on the X-Ray machine.

Film

WARNING: Equipment used for screening checked baggage will damage your undeveloped film.

- Never place film in your checked baggage.
- Place film in your carry-on baggage* or request a hand inspection.

*Carry-on screening equipment might also damage film if the film passes through more than 5 times. None of the screening equipment - neither the

machines used for checked baggage nor those used for carry-on baggage - will affect digital camera images or film that has already been processed, slides, videos, photo compact discs, or picture discs.

General use film*

You should remove all film from your checked baggage and place it in your carry-on baggage. The X-ray machine that screens your carry-on baggage at the passenger security checkpoint will not affect undeveloped film under ASA/ISO 800.

If the same role of film is exposed to X-ray inspections more than 5 times before it is developed, however, damage may occur. Protect your film by requesting a hand-inspection for your film if it has already passed through the carry-on baggage screening equipment (X-ray) more than 5 times.

TIP: Remember the 5x X-ray limit for your carry-on.

TIP: You may request a hand-inspection of any undeveloped film.

Specialty film*
(film with an ASA/ISO 800 or higher and typically used by professionals)

At the passenger security checkpoint, you should remove the following types of film from your carry-on baggage and ask for a hand inspection:

- Film with an ASA/ISO 800 or higher
- Highly sensitive X-ray or scientific films
- Film of any speed which is subjected to X-ray surveillance more than 5 times (the effect of X-ray screening is cumulative)
- Film that is or will be underexposed
- Film that you intend to "push process"
- Sheet film
- Large format film
- Medical film
- Scientific film
- Motion picture film
- Professional grade film

Other Tips and Precautions
- If you plan to request a hand inspection of your film, you should consider carrying your film in clear canisters, or taking the film out of solid colored canisters and putting it into clear plastic bags, to expedite the screening process.

- If you are going to be traveling through multiple X-ray examinations with the same rolls of undeveloped film, you may want to request a hand-inspection of your film. However, non-U.S. airports may not honor this request.
- If you plan to hand-carry undeveloped film on an airplane at an international airport, contact the airport security office at that airport to request a manual inspection.
- Consider having your exposed film processed locally before passing through airport security on your return trip.
- We recommend that you do not place your film in lead-lined bags since the lead bag will have to be hand-inspected. If you have concerns about the impact of the X-ray machine on your undeveloped film, you can request a hand inspection.
- You may still consider bringing a lead-lined bag if you are traveling through airports in other countries as their policies may vary. Check with your airline or travel agent for more information on foreign airports.

* This guidance was developed in cooperation with the International Imaging Industry Association (I3A).

Sports Equipment

Are You Traveling with Sports Equipment?

New screening guidelines prohibit certain sporting equipment from being brought on-board an aircraft. These items include:

- baseball bats
- bows and arrows
- cricket bats
- golf clubs
- hockey sticks
- hunting knives
- martial arts devices
- pool cues
- scuba knives
- ski poles
- spear guns
- any other equipment determined by the screener to be dangerous

While these items are prohibited from your carry-on baggage, they may be transported to your destination in your checked baggage. Any sharp opbjects in checked baggage should be sheathed or securely wrapped to prevent injury to baggage handlers and security screeners.

You may bring items such as baseballs, soccer balls, and basketballs through the passenger security checkpoint. They will need to be screened. See "Permitted and Prohibited Items" for full list.

We Welcome Your Comments and Questions

If you would like to pass on any positive feedback or concerns to TSA regarding your experience, you should contact a screener supervisor. You may also contact the TSA Consumer Response Center, toll-free, at: 1-866-289-9673 Monday - Friday between 8am - 6pm (24 hour voicemail). You may also e-mail us at TellTSA@tsa.dot.gov. The Transportation Security Administration (TSA) takes all input very seriously and will respond promptly and appropriately to all complaints or comments.

Road Safety

An estimated 1.17 million deaths occur each year worldwide due to road accidents. The majority of these deaths, about 70 percent, occur in developing countries. Sixty-five percent of deaths involve pedestrians and 35 percent of pedestrian deaths are children. Over 10 million people are crippled or injured each year. It is estimated that more than 200 U.S. citizens die each year due to road accidents abroad. The majority of road crash victims (injuries and fatalities) in developing countries are not the motor vehicle occupants, but pedestrians, motorcyclists, bicyclists and non-motor vehicles (NMV) occupants. U.S. citizens are urged to review the Road Safety segment of Department of State, Bureau of Consular Affairs Consular Information Sheets at http://travel.state.gov/travel_warnings.html and the country-specific links below for any country in which you intend to drive or travel by road as a passenger. Check with the embassy or consulate of the countries where you will visit to learn about requirements for driver's license, road permits, and auto insurance. It is important to be aware of the rules of the road in other countries, and the fact that road conditions can vary widely. It is also important to be aware of security concerns when driving abroad. Driving under the influence can have severe criminal penalties in other countries. The issue of international road safety continues to be a matter of growing concern to governments, international organizations, non-government organizations and private citizens. In 1998, the World Health Organization ranked road accidents as the 9th leading cause of mortality and disease.

Road Security

The Overseas Security Advisory Council's (OSAC) publications provide information about security and auto travel abroad. Potential victims of kidnapping and assault are probably most vulnerable when entering or leaving their homes or offices. Always carefully observe surroundings for possible surveillance upon leaving and returning. Never enter a car without checking the rear seat to ensure that it is empty. Do not develop predictable patterns. If possible, exchange company cars or swap with coworkers occasionally. Know the location of police, hospital, military, and government buildings. Avoid trips to remote areas, particularly after dark. Select well-traveled streets as much as possible. Keep vehicles well-maintained at all times. When driving, keep automobile doors and windows locked. Be constantly alert to road conditions and surroundings. Never pick up hitchhikers. Carry 3 x 5 cards printed with important assistance phrases to aid with language problems. Always carry appropriate coins for public phones. Practice using public telephones. Report all suspicious activity to the company security contact if applicable. Always lock the doors when parking a car, no matter where it is located.

Information for Students

The Department of State is engaged in outreach efforts to education-related organizations to publicize road safety risks in other countries. Students, who may chose less expensive, often less reliable methods of local travel while in foreign countries, should be aware of the potential danger. See the Center for Global Education, USC, travel and transportation web site at Travel and Transportation and the personal safety site at USC, Center for Global Education for more information. Students traveling abroad should also be aware of the dangers of potentially reckless behavior, including careless driving or driving under the influence. It should also be noted that penalties for persons judged responsible for automobile accidents resulting in injury or fatalities are treated very seriously by foreign authorities and can result in extremely stiff prison sentences. See our information for students and the Consular Information Sheet for the country you are visiting.

International Driving Permits

Although many countries do not recognize U.S. driver's licenses, most countries accept an international driving permit (IDPs). IDPs are honored in more than 150 countries outside the U.S. (See AAA's application form for the list of countries. They function as an official translation of a U.S. driver's license into 10 foreign languages. These licenses *are not intended to replace* valid U.S. state licenses and should only be used as a supplement to a valid license. *IDPs are not valid in an individual's country of residence.*

Before departure, you can obtain one from an automobile association authorized by the U.S. Department of State to issue IDPs. Article 24 of the United Nations Convention on Road Traffic (1949) authorizes the U.S. Department of State to empower certain organizations to issue IDPs to those who hold valid U.S. driver's licenses. The Department has designated the American Automobile Association (AAA) and the American Automobile Touring Alliance as the only authorized distributors of IDPs. Many foreign countries require deposit of a customs duty or an equivalent bond for each tourist automobile entering its territory, and the motoring associations are equipped with the necessary facilities for providing expeditiously a standard bond document (Article 3 of the Convention). The Convention is not applicable to United States motorists using their cars in the United States.

HOW TO APPLY FOR AN INTERNATIONAL DRIVING PERMIT: Before departure, you can obtain one at a local office of one of the two automobile associations authorized by the U.S. Department of State: the American Automobile Association (AAA) and the American Automobile Touring Alliance.

AAA (American Automobile Association), 1000 AAA Drive, Heathrow, FL 32745-5063. The application is available on-line.

American Automobile Touring Alliance (AATA), 1151 E. Hillsdale Blvd., Foster City, CA 94404, tel: 800-622-7070; fax: 650-294-7105 (www.thenac.com)

To apply for an international driving permit, you

must be at least age 18, and you will need to present two passport-size photographs and your valid U.S. license. The cost of an international driving permit from these U.S. State Department authorized organizations is under $20.00.

INTERNATIONAL DRIVING PERMITS ISSUED BY UNAUTHORIZED PERSONS: The Department of State is aware that IDPs are being sold over the Internet and in person by persons not authorized by the Department of State pursuant to the requirements of the U.N. Convention of 1949. Moreover, many of these IDPs are being sold for large sums of money, far greater than the sum charged by entities authorized by the Department of State. Consumers experiencing problems should report problems to their local office of the U.S. Postal Inspector, Federal Trade Commission (FTC), the Better Business Bureau, or their state or local Attorney General's Office.

Auto Insurance

Car rental agencies overseas usually provide auto insurance, but in some countries, the required coverage is minimal. When renting a car overseas, consider purchasing insurance coverage that is at least equivalent to that which you carry at home. In general, your U.S. auto insurance does not cover you abroad. However, your policy may apply when you drive to countries neighboring the United States. Check with your insurer to see if your policy covers you in Canada, Mexico, or countries south of Mexico. Even if your policy is valid in one of these countries, it may not meet that country's minimum requirements. For instance, in most of Canada, you must carry at least $200,000 in liability insurance, and Mexico requires that, if vehicles do not carry theft, third party liability, and comprehensive insurance, the owner must post a bond that could be as high as 50% of the value of the vehicle. If you are under-insured for a country, auto insurance can usually be purchased on either side of the border.

TIPS ON DRIVING ABROAD

Obtain an International Driving Permit (IDP). Carry both your IDP and your state driver's license with you at all times.

As many countries have different driving rules. If possible, obtain a copy of the foreign country's rules before you begin driving in that country.

Information may be available from the foreign embassy in the United States (http://www.embassy.org/embassies/index.html), foreign government tourism offices: (http://www.towd.com/), or from a car rental company in the foreign country.

Some countries have a minimum and maximum driving age.

Certain countries require road permits, instead of tolls, to use on their divided highways, and they will fine those found driving without a permit.

Always "buckle up." Some countries have penalties for people who violate this law.

Many countries require you to honk your horn before going around a sharp corner or to flash your lights before passing.

Before you start your journey, find out who has the right of way in a traffic circle.

If you rent a car, make sure you have liability insurance. If you do not, this could lead to financial disaster.

If the drivers in the country you are visiting drive on the opposite side of the road than in the U.S., it may be prudent to practice driving in a less populated area before attempting to drive during the heavy traffic part of the day.

Always know the route you will be traveling. Have a copy of a good road map, and chart your course before beginning.

Do not pick up hitchhikers or strangers.

When entering your vehicle, be aware of your surroundings.

RETAINING A FOREIGN ATTORNEY

DISCLAIMER: THE INFORMATION IN THIS CIRCULAR IS PROVIDED FOR GENERAL INFORMATION ONLY. THE DEPARTMENT OF STATE MAKES NO WARRANTY REGARDING

THE ACCURACY OF THIS INFORMATION. WHILE SOME OF THE INFORMATION IS ABOUT LEGAL ISSUES, IT IS NOT LEGAL ADVICE. QUESTIONS INVOLVING INTERPRETATION OF SPECIFIC FOREIGN LAWS SHOULD BE ADDRESSED TO FOREIGN ATTORNEYS.

PROVISO: Officers of the Department of State and U.S. Embassies and Consulates abroad are prohibited by federal regulation from acting as agents, attorneys or in a fiduciary capacity on behalf of U.S. citizens in private legal disputes abroad. (22 CFR 92.81; 10.735-206(a)(7); 72.41; 71.5.)

RECOMMENDING A FOREIGN ATTORNEY: 22 CFR 92.82 provides that Foreign Service officers shall refrain from recommending a particular foreign attorney, but may furnish names of several attorneys, or refer inquiries to foreign law directories, bar associations or other organizations.

FOREIGN ATTORNEYS REPRESENTING THE U.S. GOVERNMENT ABROAD: U.S. embassies and consulates abroad generally do not have foreign attorneys on a retainer to represent the interests of the U.S. Government. (See 22 U.S.C. 2698(a); 28 C.F.R. 0.45; Volume 2, Foreign Affairs Manual (FAM), Department of State, Sec. 283; Volume 9, Foreign Affairs Manual, Sec. 971.2.)

BACKGROUND: This information flyer was devised primarily for the lay person confronted with a private legal problem abroad. It contains general practical suggestions for dealing with a foreign attorney. General information concerning foreign legal aid is also discussed. For American lawyers facing the task of retaining foreign legal counsel, see Lewis, Selecting and Working With Foreign Counsel, The International Lawyer's Deskbook, American Bar Association, 393-410 (1996) and Epstein & Snyder, International Litigation: A Guide to Jurisdiction, Practice and Strategy, 2nd, 2.10-2.13, p. 2-17 - 2-24 (1994).

WHAT TYPE OF LAWYER WILL YOU NEED:
Barristers and Solicitors: In some foreign countries it may be necessary to retain the services of both a solicitor and a barrister. In such jurisdictions, barristers are allowed to appear in court, including trial courts and higher courts of appeal or other courts. Solicitors are allowed to advise clients and sometimes represent them in the lower courts. They may also prepare cases for barristers to try in the higher courts..**Notaries, "Notaires", "Notars", and "Huissiers":** In some countries, notaries public, "notaires", "notars" and "huissiers" can perform many of the functions performed by attorneys in the United States. A notary in a civil law country is not comparable to a notary public in the United States. Their education and training differs from that of most notaries public in the United States. They frequently draft instruments such wills and conveyances. In some countries a notary is a public official appointed by the Ministry of Justice, whose functions include not only preparing documents, but the administration and settlement of estates. Such notaries serve as repositories for wills and are empowered to serve legal documents. In some countries "huissiers" serve documents. They are not lawyers, but are very specialized members of the foreign legal profession. They may not plead cases in court. Your foreign attorney may delegate certain functions to a notary, "notaire", "notar" or "huissier".

Foreign Legal Consultants: These are U.S. law firms with offices in foreign countries. They may or may not be licensed to practice law abroad.

Selecting an Attorney: When you receive a list of attorneys, consider contacting several attorneys, briefly describing the nature of the services you desire. Find out the attorney's qualifications and experience. Find out how the attorney plans to represent you. Ask specific questions and expect the attorney to explain legal activities in language that you can comprehend. Do not turn over documents or funds until you are satisfied that the attorney understands your problem and is willing to handle your case. Find out the rules of the foreign country concerning attorney-client confidentiality.

GUIDELINES ON HOW TO DEAL WITH YOUR FOREIGN ATTORNEY:
Understanding Your Attorney: Ask your attorney to analyze your case, giving you the positive and negative aspects and probable outcome. Do not expect your attorney to give a simple answer to a complex legal question. Be sure that you understand the technical language in any contract or other legal document prepared by your attorney **before** you sign it.

Fees: Find out what fees the attorney charges and how the attorney expects to be paid. In some countries fees are fixed by local law. Establish a billing schedule that meets your requirements and is acceptable to the foreign attorney. Foreign lawyers may be unaccustomed to including a description of work performed in connection with billing. Some foreign attorneys may expect to be paid in advance; some may demand payment after each action they take on your behalf and refuse to take further action until they are paid; and some may take the case on a contingency or percentage basis, collecting a pre-arranged percentage of moneys awarded to you by the foreign court. Request an estimate of the total hours and costs of doing the work. Be clear who will be involved in the work and the fees charged by each participant. Determine costs if other attorneys or specialists need to be consulted, such as barristers. See "Payment of Attorneys and Litigation Expenses in Selected Foreign Nations", U.S. Library of Congress, Law Library, Doc. LL-95-2 (March 1995) (Includes information on Australia, Canada, China, France, Germany, Great Britain, Greece, India, Italy, Japan, Mexico, Netherlands, Poland, Sweden and Taiwan.)

Method of Payment: Find out the expected means of payment (corporate check, bank check, personal check, international money order, wire transfer), specify currency and exchange rates (when and where applicable or feasible).

Progress Reports: Ask that your attorney keep you informed of the progress of your case according to a pre-established schedule. Remember that most foreign courts work rather slowly. You may, therefore, wish the attorney to send you monthly reports, even though no real developments have ensured, simply to satisfy your doubts about the progress of the case. Ask what the fee will be for progress reports.

Language: Is the attorney fluent in English? This may or may not be important to you. If the foreign attorney does not speak or write in English, you can arrange for translation of correspondence. Attorneys on lists prepared by the U.S. embassies and consulates abroad do speak English.

Document Translations: If you need to provide complex or technical documents to your attorney, you may wish to consider having the documents translated into the attorney's native language. Remember that even a fundamental knowledge of English may not be enough to enable the attorney to understand technical documents you provide. Discuss with your attorney whether it is preferable to translate the documents in the U.S. or in the foreign country. Compare the costs.

Communication: Remember your responsibility to keep your attorney informed of any new developments in your case. Be honest and frank with your attorney. Tell the attorney every relevant fact in order to get the best representation of your interests. Establish how you be communicate with your foreign attorney (mail, phone, fax, Internet.)

Time: Find out how much time the attorney anticipates the case may take to complete. (Note: in some countries the courts recess for a period of several months. In addition, even if the case is resolved, currency control laws may delay the transfer of funds awarded to you from the foreign country for an indefinite period of time. Discuss these issues with your attorney to ensure there is no confusion.

Authentication and Translation of Documents: It may be helpful for you to provide foreign authorities or your attorney with authenticated, translated copies of pertinent documents. Consult your foreign attorney before going to this expense. An information flyer explaining the authentication process is available from the Office of American Citizens Services, either by mail or via our Internet Consular Affairs home page described below under "Additional Information". These topics include Hague Legalization Convention and General Authentication Flyer. See also the U.S. State Department's Authentications Office home page.

Records: Consider requesting copies of all letters and documents prepared on your behalf. Inquire about the costs of mailing you such documents.

Complaints Against Foreign Attorneys: If the services of your foreign attorney prove unsatisfactory, in addition to notifying the U.S. Department of State and/or the consular section of the U.S. embassy or consulate abroad, you may address your complaints to the local foreign bar association. Information about foreign bar associations may be obtained from the U.S. embassy or consulate abroad. Foreign embassies and consulates in the U.S. may also have information on this subject.

Assistance of U.S. Embassies and Consulates: Should your communication with a foreign attorney prove unsatisfactory, a U.S. consular officer may, if appropriate, communicate with the attorney on your behalf. In addition, complaints against foreign attorneys whose names appear on the consular list of attorneys can result in the removal of their names from the list.

Coordination with Attorneys in the U.S.: American attorneys may not be in a position to represent your interests abroad, particularly because generally they will not be permitted to participate in foreign court proceedings under the laws of the foreign country. American attorneys experienced in international law procedure may be helpful in explaining the complex legal issues involved in your case and some may have associates abroad to whom they can refer you.

Finding A Foreign Attorney:

U.S. Department of State, Bureau of Consular Affairs, Office of American Citizens Services and Crisis Management, (CA/OCS/ACS), Room 4811A, 2201 C Street N.W., Washington, D.C. 20520; tel: 202-647-5225 or 5226. Please send a stamped, self addressed envelope, 8 1/2 x 11, to accommodate postage for 20 sheets of paper or more. These lists of attorneys are also being added to the Internet home pages of our U.S. embassies and consulates. Lists of attorneys are prepared by U.S. embassies and consulates triennially (every three years). The lists include names, addresses, telephone numbers, etc., and information concerning the foreign attorney's educational background, areas of specialization, and language capability. When compiling the lists, U.S. consular officers send letters and questionnaires to the attorneys in their consular district in the foreign country. American attorneys licensed to practice in the foreign country or working as foreign legal consultants are also included. Local foreign bar associations are used as a resource in determining whether an attorney is in good standing. See Volume 7, Department of State Foreign Affairs Manual 990 (8/30/94) and 22 CFR 92.82.

Law Directories:

DISCLAIMER: The Department of State assumes no responsibility for the professional ability or integrity of the firms or persons whose names appear in the attached list. The order in which they appear has no significance.

Martindale-Hubbell Law Directory, 800-526-4902, on-line via Lexis. See also the Martindale-Hubbell home page.
Campbell's List - A Directory of Selected Lawyers, 407-644-8298.
Russell Law List - Legal Correspondents International, 410-820-4475.
The American Lawyer - Practice Directories, 212-973-2800.
American Bar Association, 1995 Directory of Lawyer Referral Services in the U.S. and Canada.

ABA INTERNATIONAL LIAISON SECTION: While the ABA does not provide international referrals, it can provide the names and addresses of national or local bar associations as well as the names of several reference guides. Contact the Section by e-mail at intlliaison@abanet.org or call 312-988-5107 or visit the Section's home page at American Bar Association, International Liaison Office.

LEGAL AID: There may be facilities in the foreign country for low cost or free legal services. If information is not included in the consular list of attorneys, ask the local foreign bar association or Ministry of Justice about the availability of legal aid. Contact the legal attaché or consular section of the foreign embassy in Washington for specific guidance. Legal aid information may also be available from a local branch of the International Social Service. The agencies' headquarters are in Geneva, Switzerland, but information or assistance may be available through its New York branch at 10 W. 40th Street, New York, N.Y. 10018, 212-532-6350. See also, American Bar Association, Directory of State and Local Lawyer Assistance Programs in the U.S. and Canada.

BAR ASSOCIATIONS:

DISCLAIMER: The Department of State makes no warranty or guarantee concerning the accuracy or reliability of the content of other web sites. The order in which they appear has no significance.

American Bar Association, 750 N. Lake Shore Drive, Chicago, IL 60611, 312-988-5000.
American Bar Association, Section of International Law and Practice
American Society of International Law, 2223 Massachusetts Avenue, N.W., Washington, D.C. 20008, Tel: (202) 939-6000; Fax: (202) 797-7133.
Inter-American Bar Association (IABA), 1211

Connecticut Avenue, N.W., Suite 202, Washington, D.C. 20036; tel: 202-393-1217; fax: 202-393-1241

International Bar Association (IBA), 2 Harewood Place, Hanover Square, London, WIR9HB, England, Tel: (011) (44) (171) 629-1206; Fax: (011) (44) (171) 409-0-456.

Inter-Pacific Bar Association (IPBA), Nashiazabu Sonic Building, 3-2-12 Nichiazabu, Minato-Ku, Tokyo, 106, Japan, Tel: (011) (81) (3) 34085079; Fax: (011) (81) (3) 334085505.

Law Association for Asia and the Pacific, 33 Barrack Street, 3rd Floor, Perth, W.A., 6000, Australia, Tel: (011) (61) (9) 221-5914.

National Asian Pacific Bar Association (NAPABA) Union Internationale des Avocats (UIA), 25 Rue de Jour, Paris, France, 75001, Tel: (011) (33) (1) 4508-8231; Fax: (011) (33) (1) 4508-8231.

World Jurist Association, 1000 Connecticut Avenue, N.W., Suite 202, Washington, D.C. 20036, Tel: (202) 466-5428; Fax: (202) 452-8540.

Other Resources:

Library of Congress Law Library, Room 240, James Madison Bldg., 101 Independence Avenue, S.E., Washington, D.C. 20540, tel: 202-707-5079

ADDITIONAL INFORMATION: The Office of American Citizens Services has general information flyers on international judicial assistance.

Using the Internet: Many of these flyers are also available on the Internet via the Department of State, Bureau of Consular Affairs home page under Judicial Assistance. See also, the Department of State, Office of the Legal Adviser for Private International Law home page for information regarding private international law unification. See also the home pages for many of our embassies.

Questions: Additional questions may be addressed to the U.S. Department of State, Bureau of Consular Affairs, Office of American Citizens Services at (202) 647-5225 or 202-647-5226.

TRAVEL SMART

Preparation for your trip

Start Early. Passports are required to enter and/or depart most countries around the world. Apply for a passport as soon as possible. Some countries also require U.S. citizens to obtain visas before entering. Check with the embassy of the foreign country that you are planning to visit to see if you need a visa. (Passport and visa information is available on the Internet at http://travel.state.gov. Passport information is also available by calling 1 - 900-225-5674 or, with a major credit card, 1-888-362-8668.)

Make a copy of your passport's data page. Make a copy of your passport's data page and any visas. Keep it with you, but separate from the originals, at all times while traveling.

Remember to leave an itinerary with family or friends. Leave a detailed itinerary and a copy of your passport or other citizenship documents with a friend or relative in the United States.

Find out the location of the nearest U.S. embassy or consulate. If you are traveling to a remote area or one that is experiencing civil unrest, end out the location of the nearest U.S. embassy or consulate and register with the Consular Section when you arrive. (Embassy and consulate locations can be found on the Internet at http://travel.state.gov/

Learn about the country you plan to visit. Before departing, take the time to do some research about the people and their culture, and any problems that the country is experiencing that may affect your travel plans.

Read the Consular Information Sheet. Consular Information Sheets provide up-to-date travel information on any country in the world that you plan to visit. They cover topics such as entry regulations, the crime and security situation, and the location of the U.S. embassy, consulates and consular agencies.

Check for Travel Warnings and Public Announcements. A Travel Warning advises travelers not to go to a country because of dangerous conditions. A Public Announcement provides fast-breaking information about relatively short-term conditions that pose risks to the security of travelers.

Top Ten Tips for Travelers

1. Make sure you have a signed, valid passport and visas, if required. Also, before you go, fill in

the emergency information page of your passport!

2. Read the Consular Information Sheets (and Public Announcements or Travel Warnings, if applicable) for the countries you plan to visit. (See the section "Preparation for Your Trip")

3. Leave copies of your itinerary, passport data page and visas with family or friends at home, so that you can be contacted in case of an emergency.

4. Make sure you have insurance that will cover your emergency medical needs while you are overseas.

5. Familiarize yourself with local laws and customs of the countries to which you are traveling. Remember, while in a foreign country, you are subject to its laws!

6. Do not leave your luggage unattended in public areas and never accept packages from strangers.

7. While abroad, avoid using illicit drugs or drinking excessive amounts of alcoholic beverages, and associating with people who do.

8. Do not become a target for thieves by wearing conspicuous clothing and expensive jewelry and do not carry excessive amounts of cash or unnecessary credit cards.

9. Deal only with authorized agents when you exchange money or purchase art or antiques in order to avoid violating local laws.

10. When overseas, avoid demonstrations and other situations that may become unruly or where anti-American sentiments may be expressed.

ATA Carnet

The "Admission Temporaire - Temporary Admission", or the ATA Carnet, is an international customs document which may be used for the temporary duty free importation of merchandise. This is in-lieu-of the usual customs documents required for entry. The carnet serves as a guarantee against the payment of duties which may become due if the merchandise is not re-exported.

A carnet is valid for one year, however, you may make as many trips as desired during the period the carnet is valid. It can also be used for moving goods within the United States as prescribed in the regulations under 19 C.F.R. Part 114.

Local associations issue carnets to their residents. In the United States, the U.S. Council for International Business, located at 1212 Avenue of the Americas, New York, NY, has been designated by the U.S. Customs Service as the issuing and guaranteeing organization for the United States. A fee is charged for this service.

ATA Carnet

What is an ATA carnet?

The ATA Carnet is an international Customs document that a traveler may use temporarily to import certain goods into a country without having to engage in the Customs formalities usually required for the importation of goods, and without having to pay duty or value-added taxes on the goods.

The United States allows for the temporary importation of commercial samples, professional equipment and certain advertising materials by a nonresident individual.

Carnets are a security that participating countries accept as a guarantee against the payment of Customs duties that may become due on goods temporarily imported under a carnet and not exported as required. "ATA" stands for the combined French and English words "Admission Temporaire-Temporary Admission."

Why use an ATA carnet?

The ATA carnet simplifies the Customs formalities involved in temporarily importing goods into the U.S. and other countries. Without a carnet it would be necessary to go through the Customs procedures established in each country for the temporary admission of goods. The carnet allows the business traveler to use a single document for clearing certain categories of goods through Customs in several different countries. It may be used for unlimited exits from and entries into U.S. and participating foreign countries during the one-year period of validity. They are accepted as the entry document and satisfy the importer's obligation to post a security in more than 87 countries.

Why not use Temporary Importation under Bond?

Foreign importers who choose to use a TIB to temporarily enter goods into the United States must file either Customs Form (CF) 3461, "Entry/Immediate Delivery," or 7501, "Entry Summary" to clear their shipment. This usually necessitates leaving the passenger terminal and going to the Cargo Entry Branch office, or having a Customs broker do your legwork for you. The importer will also need to secure a bond from a licensed surety. No forms, other than the carnet, need to be filed for goods entered under an ATA carnet.

What are the Importer's Obligations?

A carnet holder is obligated to present the goods and carnet to Customs to prove exportation. Failure to prove exportation on either a TIB or a carnet subjects the importer to liquidated damages equal to 110 percent of the duty and import tax. Goods imported under either a TIB or a carnet may not be offered for sale.

Who issues ATA carnets?

Domestic associations in participating countries that are members of the International Bureau of Chambers of Commerce issue carnets to residents to be used abroad. The United States Council for International Business http://www.uscib.org (USCIB) has been designated by the U.S. Customs Service as the United States issuing and guaranteeing organization. A fee is charged by the Council for its service. The guaranteeing organization is held liable for the payment of liquidated damages if the carnet holder, such as the importer, fails to comply with Customs regulations.

How long is an ATA carnet valid for?

An ATA carnet is valid for one year from the date of its issuance. Merchandise listed on an ATA carnet can be imported to and exported from any of the member countries as many times as needed during the one-year life of the carnet.

What goods may be entered under an ATA carnet?

Commercial samples, professional equipment and advertising material can be imported into the United States by a nonresident.

Other countries permit the use of a carnet to import the above materials and other categories of goods such as:

- Ordinary goods such as computers, tools, cameras and video equipment, industrial machinery, automobiles, gems and jewelry, and wearing apparel.

- Extraordinary items, for example, Van Gogh's self-portrait, circus animals, jets, band instruments, satellites, human skulls, and the New York Philharmonic's equipment.

What does a ATA carnet not cover?

Merchandise not covered by the three above listed categories of goods are not eligible for importation into the U.S. by carnet. In addition, merchandise within those three categories intended for sale or sale on approval cannot be entered on a carnet – it must be entered as a regular Customs entry.

What happens if the goods are not exported?

If the holder of an ATA carnet sells, donates or otherwise disposes of any of the goods listed on the carnet, the issuing organization will be required to pay liquidated damages equal to 100 percent of the import duties and taxes. That organization in turn will attempt to collect these moneys from the holder of the carnet who violated the terms. In some cases, the country where the violation occurred will hold both the organization that issued the carnet and the importer equally responsible. The importer is liable to his/her issuing association (and, in some cases, to the Customs authorities of the country where this transpired) for all duties and/or taxes and other sums which would normally be charged on the importation of such goods, as well as the amount charged as liquidated damages. If the U.S. Customs Service finds that there was fraud involved in the importation, additional penalties may be assessed.

What happens when goods covered by a U.S.-issued ATA carnet are reimported into the U.S.?

If goods covered by a U.S.-issued carnet are brought back into the United States within the validity period of the carnet, the carnet serves as the Customs control registration document and must be presented on re-importation. Whether the re-imported goods are subject to duty depends on exemption in the Harmonized Tariff Schedule http://www.usitc.gov/taffairs.htm and not on their status as carnet goods. See 19 CFR 141.4 for goods that are exempted from entry documentation requirements and 19 CFR 141.2 for goods exempted from duty on re-importation.

What if the ATA carnet has expired?

If the expiring ATA carnet is a U.S.-issued carnet there will be no penalties or duties assessed by the United States, however, there may be penalties assessed by a foreign government if the carnet expired before the U.S. merchandise was exported from that country.

If the carnet is foreign-issued then liquidated damages will be assessed by the U.S. Customs Service due to the carnet expiring before the merchandise could be exported out of the United States.

What is contained in an ATA carnet document?

The carnet document has a green cover page which provides the names of the carnet holder and issuing association, the carnet issue date, the carnet number, the countries in which the carnet may be used and a complete description of the goods covered. Two yellow sheets in the package are to be used upon exportation from and reimportation back into the issuing country. White sheets are used for the temporary importation into and reexportation from the second or additional countries. Blue sheets are used when transiting though countries.

Each sheet contains two parts – a counterfoil, which remains in the carnet and describes the actions taken by Customs officers each time goods enter or leave a country, and a detachable voucher, which contains a list of the goods covered by the carnet and serves as the required Customs document.

How is a U.S.-issued ATA carnet processed by Customs?

When leaving the United States, the holder of a U.S.-issued ATA carnet presents the carnet and the covered goods to a Customs officer. The carnet is reviewed for completeness and accuracy and the goods are examined to ensure that they match the carnet list. The officer then validates the carnet document and certifies the appropriate exportation counterfoil and voucher. The carnet and the U.S. Customs-certified export voucher are returned to the carnet holder who retains the voucher as the permanent record of the Customs transaction. (Note: The carnet does not affect export control requirements such as the filing of a shipper's export declaration or the requirement to obtain export licenses.) Upon return to the United States, the holder of a U.S.-issued carnet presents the carnet and covered goods to a Customs officer for examination. The officer certifies the appropriate reimportation counterfoil and voucher and returns the carnet to the holder for further use or surrender to the issuing association. (Note: On U.S.-issued carnets only, the vouchers of the yellow exportation/reimportation sheets will not be detached, but will remain with the document when departing or returning to the United States.)

It is the responsibility of the carnet holder to present the carnet to the Customs authorities when entering or leaving a country in order that the necessary verification and certification of the appropriate vouchers and counterfoils can take place. Failure to do so may result in a claim being made. A claim is a notice from a Customs authority of the country of import that a violation of the carnet system has occurred and payment of duties, taxes, and penalty are required.

How is a non-U.S.-issued ATA carnet processed?

When processing a foreign-issued carnet, Customs must create a record of the transaction in order to protect the revenue and domestic commerce. Therefore, the U.S. Customs officer responsible for clearing the temporary importation must ensure that the port of importation, dates of Customs activities, and any departure from the original list of articles, are clearly shown in the appropriate fields.

When the merchandise leaves the U.S. the Customs officer must ensure that the required exportation dates are complied with, that the original list of articles agrees with what is being exported, and that the appropriate voucher is detached and forwarded to the port of importation.

What countries use the ATA carnet?

ATA carnets can be used in the following
countries:

Algeria	Mayotte
Andorra	Melilla
Australia	Miguelon
Austria	Monaco
Balearic Isles	Morocco
Belgium	Namibia
Botswana	Netherlands
Bulgaria	New Caledonia
Canada	New Zealand
Canary Islands	Norway
Ceuta	Poland
China	Portugal
Corsica	Puerto Rico
Croatia	Reunion Island
Cyprus	Romania
Czechoslovakia	St. Barthelemy
Denmark	St. Martin,
Estonia	French part
European Union	St. Pierre
Finland	Senegal
France	Singapore
French Guiana	Slovakia
French polynesia- including Tahiti	Slovenia
Germany	South Africa
Gibraltar	Spain
Greece	Sri Lanka
Guadeloupe	Swaziland
Bailiwick of Guernsey	Sweden
Hong Kong	Switzerland
Hungary	Tahiti
Iceland	Tasmania
India	Taiwan
Ireland Isle of Man	Thailand
Israel	Tunisia
Italy	Turkey
Ivory Coast	United Kingdom
Japan	United States
Jersey	Wallis & Futuna Islands
Korea (Rep. Of)	
Lebanon	
Lesotho	
Liechtenstein	
Luxembourg	
Macedonia	
Macao	
Malaysia	
Malta	
Martinique	
Mauritius	

The listed countries are Contracting Parties to the ATA convention that established the ATA carnet system. Countries are added to the ATA system periodically. Call the Council for International Business at (212) 354-4480 to determine if the country to which you are traveling accepts carnets. The United States acceded to the ATA Convention on December 3, 1968 and began issuing ATA carnets in late 1969.

Where may I obtain additional information on the ATA carnet?

The United States Council for International Business is located at 1212 Avenue of the Americans, New York, New York 10036-1689, telephone (212) 354-4480, fax (212) 944-0012, and should be contacted for further details concerning the issuance of ATA carnets. The Internet address is http://www.uscib.org The application form for the ATA carnet can also be downloaded from that website. Other questions may be referred to the U.S. Customs Service, 1300 Pennsylvania Avenue, NW, Washington, DC 20229. Attn: Office of Trade Programs, (202) 927-0300.

Report Drug Smuggling to U.S. Customs Service

1 (800) BE ALERT

Currency Reporting

It is legal to transport any amount of currency or other monetary instruments into or out of the United States. However, if you transport, attempt to transport, or cause to be transported (including by mail or other means) currency or other monetary instruments in an aggregate amount exceeding $10,000 (or its foreign equivalent) at one time from the United States to any foreign place, or into the United States from any foreign place, you must file a report with U.S. Customs. This report is called the Report of International Transportation of Currency or Monetary Instruments, Customs Form 4790 (http://www.customs.gov/travel/forms.htm). Furthermore, if you receive in the United States, currency or other monetary instruments in an aggregate amount exceeding $10,000 (or its foreign equivalent) at one time which has been transported, mailed, or shipped to you from any foreign place, you must file a CF-4790. These forms can be obtained at all U.S. ports of entry and departure.

Monetary instruments include: 1) U.S. or foreign coins and currency; 2) traveler checks in any form; 3) negotiable instruments (including checks, promissory notes, and money orders) that are either in bearer form, endorsed without restriction, made out to a fictitious payee, or otherwise in such form that title thereto passes upon delivery; 4) incomplete instruments (including checks, promissory notes, and money orders) signed, but with they payee's name omitted; and 5) securities or stock in bearer form or otherwise in such form that title thereto passes upon delivery. However, the term "monetary instruments" does not include: 1) checks or money orders made payable to the order of a named person which have not been endorsed or which bear restrictive endorsements; 2) warehouse receipts; or 3) bills of lading.

Reporting is required under the Currency and Foreign Transaction Reporting Act (PL 97-258, 31 U.S.C. 5311, et seq.), as amended. Failure to comply can result in civil and criminal penalties and may lead to forfeiture of your monetary instrument(s).

U.S. Customs Service
1300 Pennsylvania Avenue, N.W.
Washington, D.C. 20229
Telephone (202) 927-1520

Why Are You Taking My . . .?

Plant Protection & Quarantine

If you've had food or souvenirs taken away by an inspector of the U.S. Department of Agriculture (USDA) while entering the United States at an airport, border station, or seaport, we want to be sure you understand why.

USDA restricts certain items brought into the United States from foreign countries. Prohibited items can harbor foreign animal and plant pests and diseases that could seriously damage America's crops, livestock, pets, and the environment.

Because of this threat, you are required to declare on a U.S. Customs form any meats, fruits, vegetables, plants, animals, and plant and animal products in your possession. This declaration must cover all items carried in your baggage and hand luggage. You will also be asked to indicate whether you have visited a farm or ranch outside the United States. Officers of USDA's Animal and Plant Health Inspection Service (APHIS) inspect passenger baggage for undeclared agricultural products. At some ports, APHIS personnel use beagle dogs to sniff out hidden items.

APHIS inspectors also use low-energy xray machines adapted to reveal concealed fruits and meats.
Travelers who fail to declare a prohibited item can be fined up to $1,000 or more and have their items confiscated.

Travelers are often surprised to hear that a single piece of fruit or meat can cause serious damage. In fact, one pest-infested or disease-infected item carelessly discarded can wreak havoc on American crops and livestock. The extra cost for controlling agricultural pests and diseases ripples down from farmers to consumers in the form of higher food prices. Taking prohibited agricultural items from travelers helps prevent outbreaks that could affect everyone.

Random Exams

One of Customs missions is to ensure that travelers entering the United States comply with U.S. laws.
In support of this mission, Customs conducts random compliance examinations (COMPEX).

Essentially, COMPEX examinations involve random selection of vehicles and/or air passengers that
ordinarily would not be selected for an intensive examination. By combining the results of these examinations with the results of targeted examinations, Customs is able to estimate the total number of violations being committed by the international traveling public. By comparing the results of the two types of examinations we are better able to devise enforcement techniques that prevent the entry of contraband without creating undue delay of law abiding travelers. Often trends tell us what message we need to send to ensure informed compliance by travelers who were unaware of our requirements.

It is possible that upon your entry into the United States, from a foreign country, you may be selected
for a COMPEX examination and experience a slight delay in your Customs processing. The Customs Service believes that this compliance examination is a critical component of our ability to ensure that our processing procedures are effective. We apologize for any delay or inconvenience you may experience and appreciate your cooperation.

What Gives Customs the Right To Search Me?

What Gives Customs the Right? This is certainly a normal question to ask when you have been referred to our secondary inspection area for an intensive examination.

The Congress of the United States has given the U.S. Customs Service broad authority to conduct searches of persons and their baggage, cargo, and means of transportation entering the United States. This authority is contained in Title 19 of the United States Code, Sections 482, 1467, 1496, 1581, and 1582.

The courts have also held that this search, seizure, and arrest authority is not dependent upon either probable cause or a search warrant as is required by police officers. One reason for this broad authority is the vulnerability of our borders to the illegal entry of a vast amount of dangerous and prohibited items.

We endeavor to use this authority wisely and with respect for human dignity. It is, however, the responsibility of a trained, professional Customs officer to determine the actual parameters of an examination. The officer is not permitted to release a traveler for entry into the U.S. until he or she is satisfied that no Customs or related Federal or State laws have been violated.

Why Did This Happen to Me?

Q: Why Does the Customs Service Search Passengers?
A: Customs officers must stop contraband, such as narcotics (drugs) from entering the United States. The narcotics are often found in cargo, but they are also found on passengers or in their baggage. Sometimes people swallow narcotics or insert them in their bodies to hide them.

The only way to be sure of finding narcotics

that are hidden in baggage is to open the bags and examine them thoroughly. The only way to find narcotics hidden on or inside a person is to do a personal search of the person's clothing and body.

Q: How do Officers decide which passengers to examine?
A: When a Customs officer stops a passenger, it doesn't mean the person is accused of committing a crime. The examination process is a way to confirm the passenger's U.S. Customs declaration and to allow innocent passengers to continue on their way as quickly as possible. Customs officers receive regular training in methods of identifying passengers who may be smugglers. In addition, through on the job experience, Customs officers have acquired knowledge and expertise in detecting smugglers in action. Officers are often looking for narcotics when they choose passengers for examination. This may result in innocent passengers having to undergo a personal search.

Q: Did I fit the profile of a smuggler?
A: If all smugglers shared the same characteristics, it would be easy to identify them. Smugglers, however, are continually adapting their ways of bringing contraband into the U.S. Since all cases of smuggling vary, there is no "profile" of a smuggler.

The Customs Service does not tolerate discrimination. Customs officers are not permitted to use race, gender, religion, or ethnic background to select a passenger for examination.

Q: How much authority do officers have to carry out examinations?
A: Customs officers have been given special authority by federal statutes and court decisions. The United States Congress and the courts recognize the extreme importance of protecting the United States from narcotics. Officers may examine all conveyances (car, boat, airplane), all persons and their baggage, and all cargo entering the United States. They may also conduct personal searches of passengers.

Q: Why aren't all passengers examined?
A: Our aim is to make our Customs officers highly professional at finding smugglers. Although officers have the authority to examine everyone and everything entering the U.S., there are two reasons why they don't. First, most passengers entering the U.S. are law-abiding travelers. Second, Customs resources are limited. Therefore, Customs officers concentrate on finding the few passengers who are breaking the law. So, for most people entering the U.S. there is little or no examination.

What Good Does It Do? Examinations help protect:

You and your family from narcotics and dangerous drugs,

Your job and employer from unfair foreign competition,

Our agriculture industry from devastation by harmful insects and diseases,

The health of you, your family, and community from contaminated foods and medicines,

You from very serious criminal elements bent on entering this country,

Random examinations allow us to validate compliance rates by the traveling public.

Of course, these are only a few of the many examples of what Customs accomplishes through our examination process.

The Examination: If you are ever selected for an examination upon your entry into the U.S., ask yourself, apart from the inevitable inconvenience to you, was your examination conducted politely, professionally and with tact. If not, we wish to know about it. Please discuss any problem with a Supervisor or Passenger Service Representative prior to leaving the Customs area. If that is not possible or you do not want to discuss the situation at that time, please write to us via the port where the incident took place. We will investigate your concern and respond to you as quickly as possible.

When you write, please include the date, approximate time of day, flight number (if applicable), and the badge numbers of the officers involved. If you feel that an examination deserves positive recognition, we would certainly enjoy hearing that also.

Chapter 35

Additional Information, Tips and Advice

Photocopy: Make 1-2 sets of photocopies of all of your documents including your passport, tickets, credit cards, travelers checks, drivers' license, and even prescriptions. Leave one or two sets with your family or friends at home, and carry one set with you in a separate place from the originals.

Purchases: Keep all original receipts of purchases. You may need them to satisfy U.S. Customs requirements, or in the event your luggage is lost or stolen.

Contents: Make an inventory of the contents of your check-in luggage before you leave. Such a list may become useful in the event they are lost or stolen.

Addresses: Make sure you have all the addresses and telephone numbers you may need while abroad, including those of your friends, and relatives at home and abroad, your physician, the nearest U.S. Embassy or consulate and the U.S. State Department.

Scheduling: Make sure you schedule to get your passport, visas and vaccination on time. An early start will save you a lot of heartaches. Similarly, do arrive at the airport on time, at least two hours early, and check in as early as you can. This way you will minimize the chances of being "bumped". It will, also, allow you time to make alternative plans in the event of a cancellation.

Research: No amount of information is too much for someone traveling to a foreign country, especially those dealing with the customs and laws of the foreign country, the people, the climate, transportation, food, etc. Learn as much as you can about the country from your local library, the U.S. Department of Tourism, the U.S. Department of State, the country's embassy, consulates and tourist offices, travel agencies and agents. And while you are abroad, brochures and newspapers often available in the large hotels and newsstands

may be very helpful information sources.

Itinerary: A copy of your itinerary should be left with your family or friends at home. This will be handy in the event of an emergency. Travelers very concerned about their health may also leave a copy with their physician just in case.

Getting Help: Abundant help and information are available to Americans traveling abroad. In addition to the enormous amount of information covered in this book, you could get general as well as country and region-specific travel information from the U.S. State Department, from the country's embassy, consulates and tourist offices in the U.S., and from travel agencies and travel consultants and advisors. Your local public library and bookstores should not be left out. While abroad the American Embassy and consulates will be one of your most important places to seek all forms of assistance.

Visas: Different countries have different visa requirements and may not allow you into the country without one. However, while some countries do not require visas from Americans, many others do. See Chapter 3 of this book for country by country visa and other entry requirements, including useful visa-related tips. Most countries charge a fee for their visas. Remember, visas are usually stamped in the passport, so you must have a valid passport before applying. You may, also, be denied a visa if your passport has a validity of less than six months and/or if other entry requirements have not been met.

In case you did not know, some countries do impose time restrictions on their visas, meaning that you may be required to use the visa by starting off your journey and/or entry to the country within a given time period (typically 90 days). In some cases, the visa period may also include the length of time you are allowed to stay in that country. Once the visa period has expired, you may have to re-apply.

Vaccination: Vaccination requirements vary from country to country, and some countries may deny you entry or subject you to vaccination at the airport before allowing you to enter. It will be very prudent to have your shots here in the U.S. before traveling. Make sure your shots are properly and officially documented on a yellow colored "International Vaccination Card" or the 'International Vaccination Certificate". For a list of countries and the recommended shots, visit the CDC website." You may also contact the Centers for Disease Control at (404) 329-3311 for additional diseases you should be aware of. As you go through the vaccination requirements for the various countries you plan to visit, do not overlook discussing with your physician about getting immunized for such diseases as hepatitis, polio, tetanus/diphtheria, typhoid and cholera. For those travelers who already had these shots, all that may be needed is just booster shots. A number of these shots are still controversial. Your physician however, should advise you appropriately. Whereas some of the shots you will need may be available free of charge in some places and with some health plans, in some cases you may be required to pay to get some or all of them. Contact your physician or your state or local health office on this matter. Remember, a number of these inoculations may require more than one dose of the shot and therefore, more than one visit. Some shots, may require up to several weeks apart. Furthermore, some shots have side-effects that could render you uncomfortable for several days. It is therefore, important to plan appropriately and give yourself reasonable amount of time.

Trouble: While abroad, should you find yourself in trouble (especially with local law enforcement officials) or with any other type of problem (stranded, sick, lost documents, emergency), immediately contact the nearest U.S. Embassy or consulate. When in trouble with the local law enforcement authorities, visit, or call, or request the presence of the U.S. Ambassador, consul or an official from the Embassy or consulate. While they might not help you resolve all of your problems, they are the best help available. It is recommended that you register with the nearest U.S. Embassy or consulate upon arrival. Check

Appendix A for a list of U.S. Embassies and consulates all over the world.

Physician: Your travel plans should include a discussion and consultation with your physician. Your physician may be helpful in responding to your health problems while overseas, but equally important, in counseling you regarding how to maintain good health while abroad. He or she will be in a good position to advise you on what medications to carry, what to eat and drink and what to stay away from. Do not forget a trip to your dentist.

U.S. Customs: Familiarize yourself with the U.S. Customs Services, regulations and requirements. It could save you a lot in efforts, time and money. This is especially important for those travelers contemplating returning to the U.S. with food items, animal products and other merchandise purchased abroad or originating from certain countries. The U.S. Customs publications referenced and reproduced in this book are a must read for those travelers.

Electricity: Electricity requirements vary from one country to another. In other words, appliances specifically designed for usage in the U.S. may not operate or be used in some other countries without risking disappointment, damage to the appliance, or even loss of life. For example, whereas U.S. appliances use 110 volts and 60 cycle, several countries require 220 volts and 50 cycles. Such appliances will be inappropriate and may not even function. To avoid this problem and still be able to use your 110 volt, 60 cycle American appliance, you will need a converter and an adapter plug. If your appliance is equipped with dual-voltage capability, all you may have to do in order to use it is to flip the switch accordingly. Even in the case of a dual-voltage appliance, you may still need an adapter plug with the right type of prong to fit into the wall outlet. Check your local department store or electronic shop for a converter and adapter. You may want to get a "universal adapter plug," since it has the advantage of having different size plugs which can be used when traveling to countries with different requirements. As in all cases with electrical appliances and devices, please read carefully the instructions before using them. If unsure, ask someone. Your hotel management will be of help. See appendix S for country by country electricity requirements.

Telephoning: Whereas the privilege of telephoning and telephones are taken for granted in the U.S., you must know that it is a luxury, especially in less developed countries. In other words, many countries' telephone facilities may not exist for some cities. If they do exist, they may not function properly or efficiently. In other cases, telephones may be hard to find or may be expensive. Considerable patience may be required on your part. You may have to explore alternative methods of sending messages, including telegram, cablegram, fax or telex. And while abroad you may save yourself a lot of worry by placing your overseas calls from a post office or from coin-operated phones as opposed to your hotel room. You may even benefit, through exchange rate differentials and billing procedures, if you use your credit card, calling card or call collect.

Addressing Mail: In addressing mail to or from abroad, it is important to print as clearly as possible. This will minimize the chances of your mail not getting to its destination. If you are writing to a "foreign service post," remember to use the correct format. Check the table of contents for the section on "How to communicate with a Foreign Service Post."

Writing Dates: Whereas in the U. S. the month of the year is written before the day of the month, e.g. January 10, 1992, (1/10/92), in several countries it is customary when writing dates to write the day followed by the month and the year, e.g. 10 January 1992 (10/1/92).

Visa and Other Entry Requirements: Although a U.S. passport and/or visa may not be required for Americans traveling to some countries, it is required for travel to most countries in the world. And even for those countries not requiring visas, there may be other requirements that must be met. Each country has its own set of entry and exit requirements.

The U.S. Department of State publication, <u>Foreign Entry Requirements,</u> (reprinted in Chapter 3 of this book) gives basic information on entry requirements and tells where and how to apply for visas. The best authority on a country's visa and other requirements, however, is its embassy or consulate and it is recommended that you check

with it before applying. Allow plenty of time to obtain the visas. An average of two weeks for each visa is recommended, but some countries may require at least a month. Do not forget that you may be able to get a second passport to travel on in the event your other passport is tied up with the visa application. When you make visa inquires, ask about the following:

*Entry/Exit Visas
*Visa price, length of validity, and number of entries.
*Financial data required, proof of sufficient funds, proof of onward return ticket.
*Immunizations required.
*Currency regulations.
*Import/export restrictions and limitations.
*Departure tax. Be sure to keep enough local currency to depart as planned.
*AIDS clearance certification. An increasing number of countries require certification that visitors are free from the AIDS virus.

As an international traveler, it is advisable to apply for a visa in person and at foreign consulates or embassies nearer you, especially considering that your presence may be needed for an interview. Furthermore, this will allow you to straighten things out as well as ensure that the visa has been issued properly. It is also advisable that you obtain your visa(s) before you leave home. If you decide to visit additional countries en route, it may be difficult or impossible to obtain visas. In several countries you may not be admitted into the country without a visa, and may be required to depart on the next plane if you arrive without one. This can be particularly inconvenient if the next plane does not arrive for several days, the airport hotel is full, and the airport has no other sleeping accommodations.

Should you decide to apply for your visa by mail remember to enclose the application form, the visa fee, your passport, photograph(s) and any other documents required. Should you chose to have your passport mailed to you, do enclose adequate postage money and request that it be returned to you by registered mail. Do not forget to find out what form of payments are acceptable since some embassies do not honor personal checks.

Remember, some countries require both entry and

exit visas and depending on the country, you may be better off securing a multiple or double-entry visa before departure. Travelers with only a single entry visa may find it particularly difficult to leave the country in the event of an emergency. While planning your itinerary, be aware that some countries, mostly in Africa, will refuse to admit you if you have South African visas or entry and exit stamps on your passports. Similarly, some Arab countries will refuse to admit you if your passport shows any evidence of previous or expected travel to Israel. If you have such notations in your passport or plan to visit some of these countries in conjunction with a trip to other countries, contact a U.S. passport agency for guidance.

Adoption: For those Americans traveling abroad to attempt to adopt children, be aware that several countries prohibit adoptions by foreigners or have laws governing adoption by foreigners. In some cases, the law requires formal court adoption of the child in the country before the child is permitted to immigrate to the U.S. Because of scandals over the illegal activities of some adoption agencies and attorneys both in the U.S. and abroad, you should be ready to experience some difficulties. The more knowledgeable you are about the local laws and requirements, the less burdensome the process. Americans interested in adopting a child from a particular country should contact the U.S. embassy or consulate in that country or in the U.S. the Department of State's Office of Citizen Consular Services, (202) 647-3712, to obtain information on the adoption process in that country.

Foreign Spouses: Americans traveling abroad with their foreign spouses and American children, should be aware of recent cases where the foreign spouse has prevented the children from returning to the U.S. In almost every one of those cases reported, the U.S. government, through various avenues, has continued their efforts for the safe return of the children. The results, have not always been successful, nor hopeful, due in part, to the laws and practices of those foreign countries. Remember, once overseas, you are subject to the laws and practices of the country you are in; United States laws cannot protect you. American women, in particular, should be aware that in some countries, either by law or by custom, a woman and/or her children may be required to get her husbands' permission in order to travel out of the country. If you or your children are planning to travel, be aware of the laws and customs of the places you visit. It is advisable not to visit or allow your children to visit, unless you are confident that you will be permitted to leave. Although this is not a common experience, you may want to give it some thought, as there may always be a chance of its happening. (See the Chapter on International Parental Child Abduction)

Shortages, High Prices and Other Problems: Consumer goods, gas and food are in short supply in some countries, and prices for these commodities may be high by U.S. standards. Shortages of hotel accommodations, also, exist, so confirm reservations well in advance. Some countries, especially in Africa, experience disruptions in electricity and water supply or in services, such as mail and telecommunications. Be informed, and be patient.

Tourists: Some countries, including Kuwait, Oman, Qatar and Saudi Arabia, do not permit tourism. All visitors must be sponsored either by a company in the country to be visited or by a relative or friend native to the country. Countries requiring visitors to be sponsored usually will require them to obtain exit permits from their sponsors, as well. It is advisable not to accept sponsorship to visit a country, unless you are sure you will also be able to obtain an exit permit.

Departure Tax: Some countries require all departing passengers to pay a departure tax or some type of tax or levy. You should, as part of your inquiry on entry requirements, verify if this applies and if so, keep enough local currency to ensure departure as planned.

Weather: As an international traveler, weather conditions in the countries you plan to visit should be an important consideration both as a guide to the type of clothing that you carry along and to your ability to have fun. Because weather and climatic conditions vary around the world, it is advisable to include this as part of your pre-trip plans and to verify what the conditions may be during the period of your intended travel. Remember, summer, winter, spring, and fall as commonly used to describe seasons in the U.S. are not applicable or commonly used in many parts of the world. In some parts, you may find people referring to "dry' and "rainy" (wet) seasons. You may even find many people, totally lacking in knowledge about names we are so used to in the U.S. Incidentally, there are important differences as well as similarities in characteristics between rainy and dry seasons and the seasons in the U.S.

Political/Public Gathering: Always stay away from political gathering places and avoid public demonstrations. Americans have been arrested when local authorities have thought that they were participating in civil demonstrations. Remember, public gatherings are usually surrounded by security persons.

It is also prudent to avoid engaging in political discussions or making public political statements or announcements as this may get you arrested. If you are detained or arrested for these or any other reason(s), ask to speak with a U.S. Consular Officer.

In Your Person: As a foreign visitor and for safety purposes, always carry with you your traveling papers, such as your passport with visa, tourist card and any other documentation that you may be required to carry.

Overstaying: Overstaying the validity of your visa or tourist card is often a violation. If you think, you might overstay, it is advisable to contact the local immigration office to find out whether you could be allowed to do so and what the requirements may be. In some countries, you may be granted an extension after submitting a formal application. Usually, the sooner you make such determination and/or put in your application, the better.

Contraband: (Prohibited and restricted Items): Every country has a variety of goods that are prohibited for import or export, and for which violators may be subjected to heavy fines, or imprisonment, in addition to the goods being confiscated. Often a list of such products is available with the country's foreign mission (Embassy and Consulate) and Tourist Information Office. As part of your preparation to ensure a smooth trip to a foreign country, I suggest, requesting such a list. If in doubt, verify the import/export status of whatever object, or goods you plan to carry along with you. For example, whereas firearms are generally prohibited by many countries, some countries allow hunting guns and guns used in sporting activities. There might even be restrictions or a need to get a prior permit to import or use such gadgets as computers, and radio transmitter-receivers. Products commonly found on the list of import contraband for most countries include drugs (e.g. cocaine, heroin) pornographic materials, firearms, and certain wildlife products of endangered species.

Contraband goods for export purposes will often include some of those prohibited for import, such as drugs, pornographic materials, and wildlife products of endangered species. Other forms of contraband may prohibit the export of certain products by unauthorized or unlicensed exporters; e.g., precious metals and minerals, and certain artifacts. In some cases, the contraband may be limited to certain products or to products from certain countries or regions. The United States also prohibits and restricts the importation and exportation of a variety of items. See Chapter 7.

Consumer Protection: One luxury that travelers do have in the U.S. as well as in several developed countries, is the existence of strict state and federal government rules, regulations and laws aimed at protecting them and insuring their safety and well being. These rules, regulations and laws covering such common travelers' concerns such as bumping, flight delays or cancellations, spell out your rights and privileges, thus, providing you with the legal backing for seeking redress if you feel your rights have been violated.

As an international traveler, you should be aware, however, that once you are outside the United States, you may not get the same level of protection as currently exists and is available to you in the United States. Although such protection may be provided on paper, it is not effective in many countries, particularly in less developed countries. Nevertheless, as an American traveling abroad you may still be able to take advantage of the protection provided you here at home by dealing with the U.S. offices of the airline or shipping lines, since their activities in the U.S. are, also, governed and subjected to U.S. laws.

Essentially, if you have complaints about an airline or if you feel you have not been treated fairly, you may contact the Customer Relations manager of the airline. Very often, it will make an effort to deal with your concerns. At other times, you may run into very uncooperative representatives or agents, in which case, you may consider contacting the office of Community and Consumer Affairs, U.S. Department of Transportation; 400 7th Street, S.W., Rm. 10405, Washington D.C. 20590 (202) 366-2220. Of course, your attorney is always at your disposal to take additional steps if necessary.

Before traveling, you may want to familiarize yourself with some of your rights, privileges and responsibilities as an air traveler. The U.S. Department of Transportation booklet entitled, Fly Right, is reprinted verbatim, elsewhere in this book and may be useful.

Complaints: As with many travelers, and long-haul travelers in particular, there is always a chance for cause to want to complain about one thing or the other. If such a situation should arise it is always advisable to do it immediately on the spot with the appropriate authorities or personnel. Later on, perhaps upon your return, follow up in writing. While you may at times have the urge to threaten and curse out loud, you may find a persistent, but polite approach more successful. In the event of damages, missing, or lost luggage, a verbal complaint may not be sufficient. (See Lost/Damaged Luggage).

Lost/Damaged Luggage: Losing luggage or finding your luggage damaged is a common experience among travelers, long and short haul travelers alike. Should you, upon disembarking at the airport, or seaport, train or bus station, find your luggage missing or damaged, immediately contact the appropriate personnel at the baggage area or at the lost luggage office to file your complaint. With airlines, you may have to complete a report form. Especially with missing luggage, insist on filing a written report (keep a copy) as this may become useful in the event your luggage is not found and you decide to seek legal recourse or compensation. Do not give up or release your luggage check ticket.

In addition, keep your ticket safely or any remaining portion of it. With regard to both lost or damaged luggage, you have the right to seek and receive some compensation. Rarely are you compensated fully. This right, however, does not extend to luggage misplaced elsewhere in the

airport due to your negligence. In such cases, immediately contact the airport police or security, the Lost Property office, or the Information desk for assistance.

Information Desk: For any traveler, Information Desks, readily available and visible in almost every air and sea port as well as bus and train station, are your immediate sources for a variety of assistance and information ranging from locating post offices, police offices, banks, restrooms, dining places to finding connecting flights, taxi, bus, rail and limousine services. Information desks at most large hotels are, in addition, very useful in providing you with additional information on a variety of subjects that will help make your trip more enjoyable. Use them!

Personal Appearance: While relatively few travelers ever get bothered or delayed just for their personal appearance, a tattered and weird appearance may attract an unwelcome attention and may subject you to avoidable scrutiny and or questioning by foreign immigration and security officers. A clean, smart and unsuspecting appearance and demeanor on the part of a foreigner in a foreign land, may after all, save you embarrassment and unnecessary delays.

Exchanging Your Currency: As an international traveler, knowing the host country's rules and requirements for exchanging your foreign currency is very important since the rules and requirements are different from country to country. While in some countries, the requirements are less stringent, or optional, in many other countries, especially Less Developed Countries, they may be quite strict. Obviously, if your interest is as, I will imagine, to safeguard your funds and stay out of trouble, then, follow strictly the government's requirements with regard to where to exchange foreign currency. While you might be used to using banks in the U.S., in many countries you might have the option of carrying out such transactions only at authorized banks, hotels, bureau de change and money changers. In most cases, you will be given a receipt (if not, ask for one) and/or the transaction may be endorsed in your passport. Hold on safely to your receipts and/or endorsement, since they may be requested of you, during departure.

Avoid having to exchange your money with

unauthorized dealers or in the "black market" even though their higher rates of exchange are often tempting. Remember, with high expected return is always high risk, including the risk of getting counterfeit currency, the risk of robbery, and running into problems with the law. Some of these unauthorized dealers may be undercover officers of the law.

Currency Import/Export Requirements: As an international traveler, it is important to know that many countries do have restrictions on the import and export of both foreign and local currencies. Be aware, also, of U.S. Government currency requirement. Presently, there is no limit on the amount of money or negotiable instruments which can be brought into or taken out of the United States. However, any amount over $10,000 must be reported to U.S. Customs on Customs Form 4790 when you depart from or enter into the United States.

(a)   Import of Foreign Currency: Most countries do not impose restrictions on the import of foreign currency. In several of these countries, however, there may be additional requirements, which often include declaring the amount and/or exchanging your foreign currency only at approved or authorized offices or dealers. Declaration of currency usually takes place at the airport upon arrival. In all exchange transactions, ask for a copy of your receipt and keep it safe. You may need it on departure or in reclaiming or re-converting unused currency. Although not common with most countries, some do prohibit the import of certain amounts of the country's currency. In almost every country where the import of foreign currency is allowed, the usual assumption is that it is legal to export both the currency and the given amount from your country of departure. As you may expect, very large amounts of foreign currency, especially notes, will attract additional attention and questioning.

(b)   Import of Local Currency: Most countries restrict and, in some cases, prohibit the import of local currency by both residents and non-residents, especially the latter. Where restrictions apply, they often take the form of a ceiling, above which it will be considered illegal or require that such monies be declared and even subject to visual inspection.

(c)   Export of Local Currency: Like the import of local currency, most countries restrict or prohibit the export of local currency. Where restrictions apply, they often take the form of a ceiling above which it will be considered illegal or require that such monies be declared and even subject to visual inspection. Many countries, especially Less Developing Countries, are very strict with currency movement, particularly, the import or export of local currency. Even where some amount is allowable to non-residents, it is often a very small amount usually limited to local remembrance coins. Although developed countries are generally more generous with the import and export of local currency, it is a fact that no country will allow a large or unrestricted amount of import or export of its currency.

Because the rules and requirements dealing with the import and export of currency for many countries do change constantly, I suggest you verify with the country's embassy, consulates, Tourist Information Office or with your travel agents prior to traveling for the current list of requirements.

Duty Free Import Allowances: In almost every country, foreign travelers are allowed to import, duty free, some quantity of products or products up to a specified value for personal use. Expect to pay extra, for any quantity or value over what is specified. Some of the commonest products include liquor, spirit, alcohol, beer, wine, cigars, cigarettes, perfume, and cologne. The quantity of these products allowable as duty-free varies from one country to the other and changes from time to time for some countries. In fact, in some countries, the amount allowable may be determined by your country of departure. Other familiar products that may or may not be considered duty free, depending on the quantity, the value, intended purpose and perhaps country of origin will include such gadgets as cameras, tape recorders, video machines and tapes, sports equipment, TVs, faxes and radio transmitters. It is suggested for those travelers who may be planning to carry along some of these products to contact or verify with the country's embassy, consulates or with your travel agent prior to traveling for a more current list of requirements.

For those travelers, particularly, business travelers who plan to move certain items and gadgets back and forth, consider getting an ATA CARNET. This document which is described elsewhere in this Chapter will save you money and aggravation. Returning U.S. residents and U.S importers should also familiarize themselves with the list of duty-free imports as well as the other import requirements. Your import (which ordinarily will be subject to duty) may even be duty-free under the GSP program, just because you are importing it from one of the beneficiary countries. (See Chapters 7 and 32)

What To Take With You: There is always that urge and invariably the mistake to carry along as much as we can carry and often more than we will need or use. My advice is to travel lightly and do not carry anything you would hate to lose. Unnecessary credit cards and expensive jewelry should be left at home.

Money Belt: Use a money belt or concealed pouch for your passport, cash and other valuables.

Driving Abroad: Depending on the country you are visiting, driving abroad could be both exciting and safe or could be scary and risky. Whereas the road conditions and road infrastructure in many of the Developed Countries and some urban centers of Less Developed Countries are safe, good and properly maintained, the same may not be true for most of the developing countries. Travelers to European countries should expect about the same conditions as in the U.S. However, if you are traveling to a Less Developed Country, you must anticipate such conditions as narrower roads, untarred roads, muddy or dusty roads, poorly lighted roads, loose animals and livestock, poor or nonexistent shoulders, few road signs or traffic lights, as well as a limited number of restaurants, motels, gas stations or auto-repair shops. If you plan to drive, it is advisable to familiarize yourself with the route. As always, avoid excessive speed, and, if possible, avoid driving at night. In some countries local driving signals are prevalent. Familiarizing yourself with these signals will add to the pleasure of your driving.

In addition, you may want to familiarize yourself with driving automobiles with manual (stick) shift. Unlike in the U.S. where automatic transmissions and power accessories are plentiful, you will find more cars with manual transmissions in the rest of the world. Do not be surprised therefore, if that automatic shift car you reserved with your rental agency is not available, and you are offered instead, a car with stick shift.

Further, be aware that in some countries, European countries included, you may find cars with steering wheels on the right side of the car, and you might be required to drive on the left hand side of the road. Like in the U.S., you must be properly licensed to drive, and the car must be insured. Although some countries will accept a U.S driver's license, others may require that you have an International Driver's Permit. See Appendix K for information on how to obtain an International Drivers Permit. For those planning to use their U.S. automobiles abroad, remember you may be required to obtain a vehicle import permit. Furthermore, your U.S. automobile insurance plan and coverage may or may not be acceptable. Some countries may require that you have an International Green Insurance card or obtain such coverage from a local insurance company. Needless, to say, it is important to adhere to local traffic laws. Speeding and drunk driving may land you in jail, in addition to a financial penalty.

Foreign Jails: While it is never any traveler's wish to end up in a jail or a foreign prison, it is, nevertheless, a possibility and some travelers have had this experience. For would-be visitors, do not expect anything close to the condition of U.S. penal institutions. For most countries, especially in Less Developed Countries, it is worse. Reports of jail conditions have ranged from sheer physical abuse and torture, including beatings and sexual assault to outright deprivation of any rights or privileges. There have been reports of prisoners and even those awaiting trial of not being properly fed or fed at all, of poor lighting or no lights at all in their cells, and of poor sleeping conditions and toilet facilities. In many cases, you may have to sleep on a bare, dusty or muddy floor. American traveling abroad should make every effort to avoid having to face foreign jails and jail experiences.

Minors and Traveling Restrictions: For those travelers who may be traveling with minors, be aware that the definition of minor and the age of majority vary from country to country and, importantly, that many countries do impose restrictions on minor children who travel alone with only one parent or with someone who is not their parent. In many cases, some form of documentation or written authorization for travel from the absent parent, parents or legal guardian may be required. Check with your travel agent or with the country's embassy or consulate for requirements, if any.

Criminal Assault: Any U.S. citizen who is criminally assaulted should report the incident to the local police and to the nearest U.S. embassy or consulate.

At the Pool or Beach: Do not leave your belongings on the beach while swimming. Keep your passport and other valuables in a hotel safe.

On Public Transport: Be vigilant in bus and train stations and on public transport. Do not accept beverages from other passengers. There have been reports of tourists being drugged and robbed while they slept.

Sightseeing (getting around) on Foot: Avoid dark and isolated alleys, crowds and marginal areas. These are areas where you can easily be robbed and assaulted. Be aware that women and small children as well as men can be pickpockets or purse snatchers. Do not stop if you are approached on the street by strangers, including street vendors and beggars. Whenever possible do not travel alone. Avoid traveling at night. Keep your billfold in an inner front pocket; carry your purse tucked securely under your arm; and wear the shoulder strap of your camera or bag across your chest. To guard against thieves on motorcycles, walk away from the curb and carry your purse away from the street. A money belt or concealed money pouch would be helpful to safeguard your passport and other valuables.

Foreign Laws: Foreign laws, rules and regulations may be very different from those of the United States, and violators may be subject to different penalties. For a foreigner, these penalties may be even harsher. Tourists who commit illegal acts usually have no special privileges. It is, therefore, advisable before you travel and when you are abroad to learn as much of the country's do's and don'ts as possible, in particular those aspects which often get tourists in trouble with the law. In most cases, the same type of violations that will get you in trouble in the U.S. would more than likely, get you in trouble abroad; for example, those relating to drugs, firearms, traffic, public safety, theft and robbery. Remember that while traveling in a foreign country, you are subject to that country's laws, and not U.S. laws.

Drunkenness and Drunken Driving: Public drunkenness and drunken driving is against the law in several countries and should be avoided. These social nuisances often leads to fights, traffic accidents and even death. Arrests and jail terms are common for violators. In some countries drunken driving invites mandatory jail sentences.

Hotel Bills: Many countries consider it a fraud, if you fail to pay your hotel bills or pay for other services rendered. Those accused may be subject to arrest and conviction with stiff fines and jail sentences. Keep track of your expenditures and your resources. As usual, travel with sufficient funds including a little extra for a few days subsistence in case you are stranded.

Dealing with Merchants: Always avoid disputes with merchants as this may often lead to undesirable outcomes. Although haggling over prices is common with small independently owned shops; in others, it may be insulting and unwelcome. Learning as much as you can about the modus operandi in foreign market places will be very valuable. Avoiding disputes requires you to be a careful and informed shopper. Make sure the goods you buy are in good condition, since efforts to exchange or return the goods may be unsuccessful and may lead to disputes. As always, get a receipt for your transactions.

Green Backs: The U.S. dollar notes are as popular in several countries as U.S. tourists. You will find the U.S. dollar notes are readily accepted for transactions by local merchants. While the temptation will always be there, beware of local legal requirements concerning import and use of foreign currency, as this may get you into avoidable trouble. Equally, important is to beware of how you flash your dollar notes as this may invite or attract the attention of thieves and robbers. As an American, you are always associated with the dollar, and there is the tendency to think that you are carrying some U.S. dollars.

Photography: Be cautious when taking pictures. Some countries prohibit taking photographs of some facilities, buildings, places and events; e.g., airports, police stations, military locations, oil installations, harbors, mines, and bridges. Taking a photo of demonstrations or civil disturbances is usually prohibited. Violators have often had their films and/or cameras confiscated and, at times, have been beaten or detained. A safe rule is, when in doubt whether you can take a picture, ask first. Remember, when taking pictures of or including individuals to find out if it is OK with them. Some persons detest being photographed, and or may require some form of token compensation. Be courteous. Ask first.

Restricted Areas: Travelers abroad should be aware that some countries do have strict regulations prohibiting travel in certain areas or traveling without special permission. Contact the country's embassy or consulate in the U.S., or if you are abroad, contact the U.S. Embassy or the nearest U.S. consulate for a list of such places and what may be required.

Dress Code: Some countries, especially those in the Middle East and Moslem countries, expect foreigners to adhere to their dress codes. These codes may relate to and may be restricted to certain places, such as places of worship or to women, men or children. For example, some countries require women to have their hair covered when in public or covered when in places of worship, while some prohibit wearing of shorts and miniskirts in the public or sleeveless garments.
Yet, in many other countries, such rules may not exist Check with your travel agent, the respective foreign embassy or the tourist office for the appropriate dress code in their country.

Travel Agencies/Agents: Travel Agencies and Agents can be very useful in providing answers to most of the common questions and concerns of foreign travelers and should be included as one of your important information sources. However, as in any other profession or trade, all travel agencies or agents do not possess the same degree of expertise or experience. It is important that you shop around for a reliable, reputable and competent one with experiences in foreign travels. Such agencies or agents must be committed to assisting you to have a successful and enjoyable trip by providing you with advice, answers, and other relevant information about the country or countries you plan to visit. Travel agencies and

agents that are interested only in selling you a ticket, (remember they are sales persons and/or operate on commission) should be avoided. A real helpful agency or agent ought to be willing and able to provide you not only with the "best deal" cost-wise, but also with current information on such issues as relates to hotel reservations, car rentals, visas, passports, travel conditions in the country or region you are visiting and even some cultural **do's** and **don'ts**. While no formula exists for identifying the type of travel agencies and agents mentioned here, you may want to deal primarily with those travel agencies that are members of the American Society of Travel Agents (ASTA). Members usually will have the (ASTA) sign or seal clearly affixed to a visible place in the office. The strict membership requirements give their members an edge over non-members. Yet, I must caution that membership in ASTA or the lack of it, is not a guarantee that the agency or agent you choose will deliver. Shop around. Ask your traveled colleagues, friends, and neighbors for some references. It'll be better than no reference. When you find one, seek his or her assistance. If you do not engage or ask them for assistance, all you may get from them for your money may be just a ticket, a handshake and nothing more. Interested in travel agents who are members of the Institute of Certified Travel Agents (ICTA)? These agents, upon certification, carry the title of Certified Travel Counselor (CTC). For additional information about these organizations, including members that may be in your area, write or call the American Society of Travel Agents (ASTA), 1101 King St., Alexandria, Virginia 22314. Tel: (703) 739-2782. Or the Institute of Certified Travel Agents (IGA), 148 Linden Street, Wellesley, Massachusetts 02181. Tel: (617) 237-0280.

Visa Services: (See Travel Counselors)

Travel Counselors/Travel Planners/Travel Advisors: (Also, see Travel Agencies). Travelers, in particular those planning an extensive trip, a trip for the first time or who may not have much time devoted to their travel plans, may consider using the services of a travel counselor, a travel advisor or travel planner for a fee. Although a good travel agency or agent should be able to provide you with valuable counseling and advice regarding your trip, you may find the services of a travel counselor more specialized, timely, personable and comprehensive. Remember, this is how they make their living; that is, consulting, advising and counseling you, not selling you a travel ticket or pass. A good travel counselor or travel planner, as they are sometimes referred to, should be respond and advise you on all these questions, every topic and every concern you may have regarding your trip including scheduling. How satisfied you are or how satisfactory the results are , will depend on how knowledgeable and how experienced the counselor. Some of your questions and concerns may require the counselor to do some research and, of course this means time and money. The more planning and research you do before or while using a counselor, the less costly for you and the less painful the outcome of a poor or insufficient consultation.

When looking for or researching a good travel agency or agent, you have to shop around for a reliable, reputable, knowledgeable and experienced travel counselor. Ask your colleagues, friends, and co-workers, for references. After all, levying a fee is not what makes one a good travel counselor. It is also advisable to engage the services of only those travel counselors who specialize in the country or region of the world you plan to visit or in certain aspects of travels such as ski-vacation, budget-tours, business travels, group and luxury travels. They are often more helpful than the general practitioners. You may, moreover, consider using professionally certified travel counselors, such as those certified by the Institute of Certified Travel Agents (ICTA), a U.S. based nonprofit educational organization. Upon certification, their members carry the insignia and title of "Certified Travel Counselor (CTC). Look out for the ICTA and CTC logos. Although the eligibility requirements for members of these organization give them an edge over non-certified agents, being counseled by a member may not necessarily guarantee the best results; so shop around. Be careful and be selective. For information on ICTA certified travel counselors in your area, check your local telephone directory or write or call the Institute of Certified Travel Agents, 148 Linden Street, Wellesley, Massachusetts 02181. Tel: (617) 237-0280).

Visa and Passport Services: If you plan to travel abroad and do not have the time to process your application for a visa or passport, there are businesses out there whose primary service is to assist you in obtaining them. You can find additional listing of these businesses in your local telephone directory under the heading "Visa Services."

Banking, Business and Shopping Hours: International travelers should be aware that banking, business and shopping hours vary from country to country and within a particular country. Sometimes, the hours of operation may change in response to changes between seasons. The typical differences that are likely to interest an American traveling abroad will include the fact that in some countries business is not transacted during some working days and/or during what we will generally consider as normal working hours by U.S. criteria. In some of these countries, banks, shops and offices may be closed either voluntarily or by law. In other countries you may find that government offices may be open during the weekend. Another likely observation in some countries is the "two-shift" type of operations, where banks, businesses and shops may close at mid-day for lunch, resume one to three hours later, and then close finally at night. Other than these striking differences, the others, for the most part, are merely differences in opening and closing hours. Since as an international traveler, you will inevitably be affected, I have included elsewhere in this book the banking, business and shopping hours of various countries. See Appendix X.

Weights and Measures: Most international travelers engage in some form of shopping while abroad. For these travelers, understanding the type of weights and measures used in the country will be beneficial at least in insuring that you do not end up buying something that may be cheaper in the U.S. The types and standards of weights and measures vary from country to country. Whereas, most countries use the metric system or are in the process of converting to metrication, several countries still use the imperial system or other local systems. In others, one or more of these systems of weights and measures are used. Even for those countries that have officially adopted either the metric or the imperial system, it is not uncommon to find transactions still being carried out using a different system. Understanding these differences will facilitate your shopping and may save you money. A list of countries and the type of system officially being used is provided elsewhere in this book. Provided, in addition, are conversion factor and tables of equivalent weights and measures in both metric and Imperial forms. See Appendices Z and 1A.

Clothing: If you are traveling abroad and you plan to go shopping for clothing, be aware that clothing such as shirts, pants, gowns, suits and shoes, may not carry the same size labels. Some countries employ labeling forms quite different from those used on U.S. made clothing. A table comparing the U.S. and two other labeling systems has been included elsewhere in this book. See Appendix N

Tipping: We, in America, are fond of and used to tipping in hotels, restaurants, saloons, and almost every time someone renders us some form of assistance. Well, if you are planning a trip abroad, you may want to know that, although the "rules" and expectations are the same for most countries, the amounts may be different. Importantly, in some countries, tipping may not be expected and may be officially prohibited.

Different countries have different rules and expectations regarding tipping and gratuities. In some countries, the practice is expected and clearly defined, whereas in some others, this may not be the case. For the International traveler to be confused in terms of whether to tip or not, or how much to tip, when, to whom and how is understandable. Since this could be a potential source of embarrassment, you should try to familiarize yourself with what the rules are in the country you plan to travel to. To assist you, a country by country guide to tipping has been provided in Appendix Q. It is not comprehensive, but at least acquaints you with the country's official position as well as the expectations on tipping, particularly in hotels, restaurants, taxis and saloons. You may, also, contact that country's embassy or consulate or tourist bureau for advice. Your travel agent or advisor may also be of help.

Should you decide to tip wherever such practice is allowed do restrict your gratuities to services actually rendered. Do not forget that there are really no hard and fast rules as to how much you must tip. In other words, do not expect to be thrown in jail for not tipping. Generally, a tip, and

the amount should reflect what you believe is "reasonable", and what you can afford. Sometimes, a handsome expression of appreciation (tip) may well make a difference in the quality of service you may subsequently receive, assuming you would still be around. A poor tip may be insulting and may even be worse than not giving at all. Finally, do not forget that your bill or fare may already include expected tips. The one way of knowing in most cases is to inquire.

Taboos: Travelers to foreign countries have often been embarrassed, humiliated and even isolated as a result of their inadvertently stumbling into actions and words considered as taboos. To many travelers, this could be very uncomfortable and could sour an otherwise exciting trip or relationship. Breaching a taboo in some societies could invite trouble and mean spirited treatment. It behooves the prospective foreign traveler to learn as much as possible about the cultural, and social do's and don'ts. Your local libraries and bookstores are excellent sources for general as well as country-specific books in this subject area. Also, check Chapter 36 for useful references on this subject. ** Get a copy of the book(s) "DO'S & DON'TS AROUND THE WORLD: A COUNTRY GUIDE TO CULTURAL & SOCIAL TABOOS AND ETIQUETTE", published in 9 Regional Volumes, one for every continent. Available from this publisher, major national bookstores, and on-line from Amazon.com. , or visit www.frontlinepublishers.com

Bribery and Corruption: This is a phenomenon that, admittedly, exists in every country, a phenomenon which is illegal in every country, yet, in practice, flourishes in different forms and with different degrees of impunity and tolerance. As you journey from one country to another, you may find yourself confronted with this moral dilemma. Although the effects on you for not abetting or complying may, in fact, be inconveniencing and time delaying, the consequences to you for bribing or attempting to bribe may get you into jail. For an international traveler, particularly in a foreign country or anywhere at all, your best bet is "do not attempt to give or accept a bribe." The cost for complying with the law always pays off favorably in the long run.

Clinical/Medical: For those travelers who are

particularly concerned about their health and who feel, that during their trip abroad, they may have to seek some form of medical treatment, carrying along a copy of your medical records stating any special conditions, problems and suggested treatments may be a wise idea. A similar record or log of any type of problems encountered while overseas, including treatment should also be kept. It may be needed for reference by your physician upon return. You may consider investing in a Medical Alert bracelet currently available from the Medical Alert Foundation. See Appendix 3C.

Medical Help Overseas: While no traveler wishes to be injured or ill while traveling overseas, it is a fact of life that travelers abroad do get injured and ill and may require medical attention. Americans traveling abroad may take solace in knowing that there are qualified physicians available world wide who are capable of providing them with the same level of quality treatment as is available at home. In several countries, especially in Europe and in urban centers of most developed countries, quality hospitals and medical facilities do exist. For the American traveler, the other important need may be for qualified physicians who understand and speak English. Well, for your consolation, you may want to take advantage of the services of the several international travel, medical assistance organizations listed in Appendix 3C.

While you contemplate on the topic of medical treatment abroad, you may, also, want to be aware of the fact that your medical treatment abroad, especially with private, independent physicians, may not be free of charge and you may be required to pay in advance, immediately, or initially, and/or in cash form. The cost to you may, also, be high. This is all the more reason that it is strongly recommended that before you travel abroad, that you take out some form of insurance that will cover all or most of your treatments or medical costs incurred abroad. You may, in other words, consider shopping around or delaying until you return home those routine, non-life threatening, non-essential, less urgent problems and treatments. It's really up to you.

As part of your pre-travel plans, you may want to find out the quality and status of medical facilities and treatment generally available to you in the country or countries you plan to visit, and whether

as a foreign traveler, you may have to pay or not. It is always safer to think you may have to pay and make the necessary financial or payment plans. Should there be a need to be hospitalized, University affiliated hospitals may be worth considering. Besides the quality of treatments, chances are that you may run into American or Western trained doctors who may be fluent in English.

As always, taking the proper precautions through a careful preparation in consultation with your physician will save you a bundle and will make your trip abroad a healthy, safe and enjoyable one. For example, a medical emergency kit or first aid kit (with such items as bandages, cotton wool, swabs, and disinfectants), a little extra prescription medication, and extra eyeglasses, may be worth much more than any minor inconveniences taking them along may cause. Should you decide to carry with you a substantial quantity of needed medication or a controlled or prescription drug, you may also want to secure a special note or letter from your physician stating your care and need. Failure to do so may cause your medications to be taxed or confiscated. For additional health information, see Chapter 8 Although, you may find your medical needs abroad adequate for the most part, travelers to less developed countries and to rural parts of most countries must always take extra precautions. It is safer to be overly prepared than to be under prepared. Importantly, do not always expect the same level of quality medical treatment and facilities as may exist at home.

Insurance: Obtaining adequate insurance coverage must always be paramount in the minds of every international traveler. Coverage to be considered should include automobile, life, medical, trip interruptions and cancellations, bankruptcy, luggage and personal effects insurance. The need for insurance will vary from one traveler to another. Of course, if you don't plan to drive, you obviously do not need a car insurance. If you plan to take your own car as opposed to renting one, you may find that your existing insurance policy(ies) will not cover you in case of a loss. Whatever the case, should you plan to drive abroad, first ensure that you are comprehensively insured by a reputable company and that your insurance policy is valid and will be honored in the country you are visiting. While shopping for or evaluating your health insurance needs, remember that a good medical insurance should provide you with total coverage, including full coverage for hospital stay, medications and any medically related treatment you might incur, short or long-term. Health policies must, also, include the cost of transportation to the United States, in the event of emergencies and serious conditions, including that of a traveling companion.

Because damaged and lost luggage has become a common experience for many travelers, you may consider insuring these and other accompanying possessions and valuables, especially given the limited coverage, if any, provided to travelers by their carriers. Although you may not recover in full your losses, a good insurance coverage will inevitably minimize your loss. Time-conscious travelers who are concerned about the financial loss due to unscheduled trip cancellations or interruptions, may consider purchasing a trip cancellation or a trip-interruption policy.

There is, of course, life insurance, which is even more important, while you are in transit or are abroad. Although you may already carry a life insurance policy, this may be another time to examine the adequacy of your existing policy.

All in all, your pre-travel plans, should include researching and getting the necessary insurance coverage. A good insurance broker should be able to help you, in avoiding duplication of policies and coverage. Your travel planner, advisor, travel agent and tour operators will be of assistance to you in this area. Also, check your existing automobile, medical and life insurance policies. You may already be partially or fully covered, and may or may not need additional coverage. You may, also, find that you are adequately covered by your credit card company (for those who may be charging their tickets). If you are not sure of what is covered or the extent of the coverage, contact your or credit card company. Also check with your travel agent, some of them now provide free flight insurance for their ticket clients.

Very often travelers overlook the fact that they may already be adequately covered, sometimes with double and triple indemnity clauses, for accidental death and/or dismemberment by the airline, the travel or auto clubs. Most major credit card companies for such cards as American Express, Mastercard, Visa Carte Blanche, Dinners Club and Discover automatically provide between $100,000 and $350000 for flight insurance (accident and life insurance) to cardholders who charge their trips to their cards. Cardholders desiring higher coverage can also buy them from these companies at a fairly reasonable rate. These card companies also provide insurance coverage for delayed or lost luggage; up to $500 for checked luggages and up to $1250 for carry-on baggages. It is important to also remember that in the event of an accident or death while riding as a passenger, International airlines are liable for up to $75000 if the ticket is bought in the U.S. The amount is different for tickets bought abroad.

When all is done do not forget to carry your insurance card and a photocopy of your policy with you, including the telephone numbers of your insurance company and agent, just in case a need arises. Be financially prepared as well, some insurance companies may require that you settle your expenses overseas and then apply for reimbursement. Some of the policies mentioned here can be easily purchased through your local insurance brokers. Remember, the more comprehensive the coverage (combination policies) the better. A list of some companies that provide travel-related insurance, including short-term policies is provided in Appendices 13M and 14N.

Value-Added Tax (VAT): Most foreign travelers to Western Europe are usually not knowledgeable about VAT. This is a tax, a sales tax of a sort, usually imposed on almost all goods sold in Western European countries. These taxes (ranging from 6% to 33% depending on the country) are usually included in the price of goods and services, and are levied on purchasers irrespective of the country of origin. The good news for the international traveler is that you may be able to get a refund. You must, however, ask for it, and meet the requirements.

To receive a refund, (a) you must shop at stores that are authorized to offer VAT refunds; (b) you must carry your purchases with you when you leave.

If you desire to request a refund of your VAT payments, do not forget to request the VAT form from your salesperson. The form should be signed by the salesperson. Upon departure, present the form and your receipt to the customs officers for final endorsement. Upon returning home, you may then mail the form to the store and a refund will be mailed to you.

Rail Passes: For the cost conscious international traveler, passes can be an important money saving investment. Rail passes, in particular, can be a source of a bargain for those travelers who plan to conduct a lot of their travel by train.

While some of the passes are limited to travel within the country, some do allow for travel across countries. The Eurailpass, for example, allows you to travel to all the 17 member European countries.

Rail passes and tourist cards are very popular in Europe. Similar arrangements and opportunities to travel at a discount are, also, available on other continents. Your travel agent should be able to assist you in this matter. You may, in addition, direct your inquiry to the country's tourist office in the U.S., the country's embassy, the consulate or railroad authority.

Further, children and older travelers, may take advantage of available opportunities. Several countries, especially in Europe, offer discounts of up to 50% in several areas, including rail and other travel passes. However, it is up to you to ask about the availability when making your reservation or purchasing your ticket or passes. Remember that the definition of "seniors" varies from country to country. While most countries restrict use to those 65 years and older, in some countries the definition might be different.

It is, furthermore, worth noting that despite the convenience of passes and the cost advantage, it may not be beneficial to everyone. The individual traveler should always compare the cost of a pass or tourist card with the total cost of alternative transportation, as the latter may turn out to be more convenient and/or cheaper especially, for those contemplating limited travel.

Like rail and bus passes, some airlines, also, sell limited air passes as well as other substantial discounts to older travelers. Contact your travel agent or the airlines.

Medical Emergency Kit: A good emergency medical kit should be an important carry-along

item for an international traveler. This is particularly important for those traveling to Less Developed Countries, or to rural and remote parts of foreign countries. A timely attendance to a sudden, but minor, ailment by way of a first treatment may make a difference between enjoying your vacation, terminating it or finding yourself in a hospital. A good medical kit doesn't have to be bulky or heavy. Of more importance are the contents. A sample content of a medical kit is provided in this book. Check the table of contents for location. Remember even in the possession of the best of medical kits, it is always advisable to seek immediate professional medical attention in the event of any form of illness, even more so when you are in a foreign country. Being sick away from home is not something to take lightly, and you should not depend solely on a medical kit. See Appendix 4D for a sample Emergency Medical Kit.

Airport Facilities: Airports provide a variety of facilities aimed at providing safety and comfort to the traveler, and an increasing number of international airports are taking added steps to provide for the special needs of babies, young children and the disabled.

Most international airports are now equipped with special rooms where babies can be fed and changed, and some have short-term nursery and play facilities for young children.

Disabled travelers can also take advantage of various free services available to them. A disabled traveler is entitled to ask for an escort both in the aircraft and in the airport. Deaf passengers can request written announcements from the ground staff. Blind persons are entitled to take their guide dogs, but your dog may not be exempt from both the home and country quarantine laws.

For more traveling information and tips for the disabled, see the Table of Contents. It is worth remembering, however, that to take advantage of special airport facilities, you have to request them since most of them may only be available on demand. You are always better off making your requests early, especially for those facilities with limited availability or supplies.

For travelers to Less Developed Countries, especially African countries, you may want to keep in mind that the conditions of most of their international airports are comparatively poor and inadequate; hence, some of the facilities or services noted above may not be available. It is not uncommon to find unavailable even such facilities as clean toilets or toilets that are open or accessible. Should you have access to a toilet, you may be disappointed to find that there is no toilet paper. It is based on this experience, in particular, that I have since resolved and always carried a few rolls of toilet paper with me whenever I am traveling.

Comfort Hints on Flights: It is amazing how much we value comfort and strive to achieve it on flights, especially on long flights. The act of flying, in itself, can be discomforting, especially over time zones. However, as a frequent flyer and a long-haul traveler, you may take a few steps to minimize the source of discomfort, thus, making your trip less tiring and annoying. Among other factors, discomfort often results from inadequate leg room and noise. By properly choosing your seat, you may be able to reduce the level of discomfort. Aisle seats provide more legroom than window seats; seats directly behind the emergency exit doors provide even more additional legroom. Aisle seats are more convenient for those travelers who may have to use the restrooms frequently. Having secured an aisle seat, of course, you'll hope the other passengers on your row will not move frequently move in and out.

As for the noise, because most engines are situated at the back, the further away towards the front that you are seated, the lesser the noise effect. Besides, you are more likely to find excited and rowdy holiday groups toward the rear spectrum of the plane. Sitting just behind first class, may be your best choice, unless you are a first class passenger. You may, also, minimize on noise effect by sitting away from the toilet facilities. One area you may not have much pre-planning opportunity to affect are noisy neighbors. Even with that, a little politeness and smile may do the trick.

You can furthermore, minimize some of the discomforting feelings by being selective with what you eat and drink as well as what you wear. It is advisable to minimize on the intake of alcoholic and fizzy, carbonated drinks. Instead, drink non-alcoholic liquids, such as water and fruit juices. It

is, also, advisable to wear loose-fitting clothes and shoes. Remember that feet tend to swell on long flights. Unless your shoes are sufficiently loose, you may find it difficult to put them back on.

Finally, you may consider periodically rotating your feet, ankles, and neck as an exercise or you may treat yourself to some sleep. Also, see the Chapter on Jet lag

Special Diets: One of the advantages of today's international travelers is the airlines' willingness to provide them with special diets. Whether you prefer vegetarian, fat-free, salt-free, infant, diabetic, Muslim or Jewish (Kosher and Kedassia) meals, there is a growing number of international airlines that will make an effort to get them for you. First class passengers may find their request for special meals more easily fulfilled. As with all special services, it is advisable to place your order with the airline well in advance. Remember, that not all airlines provide the wide ranges of special meals noted here. Whereas, the larger airlines are often good with providing this type of service, you may not have much luck or many choices with the smaller domestic airlines and with airlines of many Less Developed Countries. As a precaution, it is always a good idea to eat something before embarking on your flight and to take along a few of your favorite snacks.

Tickets: As a precaution, it is advisable to spend a few minutes making some sense out of your tickets, preferably right on the spot where they are being issued. You should be able to reconcile the information contained in your ticket with your travel plans. Many travelers have found, much to their disappointment and embarrassment, that the ticket they are carrying is deficient. Sometimes the tickets may contain schedules and clauses that are different, restricting and that may be expensive to rectify once you commence your trip. Double checking your ticket is, thus, essential and could save you money and time. In checking your ticket, take special note of the name of the airlines you will be traveling. The names of the airlines are usually identified by their respective two-letter codes. See the table of contents for these codes as well as the list of foreign and international airlines operating in the U.S. Your ticket check should also include reconciling the dates and times of departure and arrival, your class of ticket, the validity of your ticket and of the flight(s). Also check for the correct validation stamp or signature of the issuer. Don't forget to read all other information both in the front and on the back of the ticket. You might find additional useful information.

Air Sickness (See the Chapter on Jet Lag).

Hospitalization while Abroad: Should there be a need to be hospitalized, University affiliated teaching hospitals may be worth considering. Besides the advantage of quality treatment, the chances are that you may run into American or Western trained doctors, who may also be fluent in English.

Hold onto Your U.S. Passport[IL]**:** A U.S. passport can cause you trouble in some regions of the world. But there are ways to get around that if you meet certain requirements. Children, sometimes grandchildren, of immigrants can obtain passports from the country of their parents' birth. In many countries, once you obtain a second passport, you, also, require a dual citizenship.

This is not as easy as it sounds. You must be careful not to unintentionally renounce your U.S. citizenship. The U.S. State Department recommends the following precautions:

*Do not accept a government job from an adopted government.
*Do not serve in another country's military.
*Do not suggest, to friends or anyone else, that you intend to renounce your U.S. citizenship.
*Write a statement of intent to retain your U.S. citizenship, and send it to a U.S. Embassy or consulate.
*File U.S. income tax forms.
*Vote in U.S. elections.
*Use your U.S. passport.

Passport Scam[IL]**:** In the classifieds, you'll see advertisements for private passport companies. Some of these advertisements are legitimate; others are not. Check the advertisement carefully. Does it list a telephone number? Does it list a complete address, not just a post office box somewhere in Malaysia? Does it list some ridiculously low or exorbitantly high amount of money? Does it ask for the money right away?

If the advertisement doesn't list a telephone number and doesn't have a legitimate-looking address, chances are the company is a hoax. If you are told to hand over the money right away, forget it. You'll never see your money again, especially if the sum the company is asking for is less than the cost of obtaining a passport from a passport agency. Valid companies usually charge you twice as much as a passport agency for their services.

Call the company and ask for more information. If you are turned down, drop the entire proposition. A legitimate company would be happy to send you more information.

If you must have your passport within a week or less, some countries can help you get a passport quickly and easily. (A list of private visa and passport services is provided elsewhere in this book. Check the table of contents).

The Jet Lag Drag:[IL] Your internal clock runs on a fairly regular schedule. But every time you fly into another time zone, you disrupt your internal rhythms--and experience jet lag. (The medical term for jet lag is circadian dysynchronization.) Jet lag causes you to become overwhelmingly tired, groggy, and lightheaded. The following is a list of precautions to take:

*Before you leave, try to prepare your body for the new time zone. If you are going, for example, to London, which is five hours ahead of EST, start going to bed one hour early and getting up an hour earlier five days before your departure. By the time you depart, your body will have adjusted.

*A few days before you leave and during your flight, decrease your caffeine intake.

*Although many airline offer free alcoholic beverages, avoid them. You don't need the added impact of a hangover. If you do indulge, drink only wine. The alcohol content is lower in wine than in mixed drinks.

*Eat lightly during your flight. If you eat too heavily, you may feel nauseous.

*Try to sleep during your flight. This will reduce your exhaustion when you arrive.

*Once you land, take a few minutes to stretch. Do not go to your hotel to sleep if it is only 5 p.m. Stay awake as long as possible, try to eat a light meal, and remain active. This will allow your body to adjust more quickly to the new timetable and reduce the effects of jet lag.

How to take the Kids:[IL] Yes, you can travel with your children and still enjoy the trip. The key is planning. Following are some tips:

*Rent a car. Although public transportation is reliable and inexpensive, particularly in Europe, your children's schedules may not match those of the trains and buses. With your own car, you can come and go as you and children want, and you can carry around everything the children need.

*Take your own car seat. Some car rental agencies also rent car seats, but most won't guarantee that one will be available when you pick up the car.

*Contact the tourist bureau for the country you're planning to visit for help choosing your accommodations can tell you which hotels, pensions, and apartments welcome children, and are equipped with cribs, playrooms, and babysitting services.

*Choose an airline that welcomes children. Ask if you can bring a car seat for your child to sit in during the flight. Ask if children's meals are available, and if

training tables are provided.

*Pack a backpack carrier, a stroller, and an attachable high chair. Take along your own baby wipes (those sold in Europe are heavier, rougher, and oilier than those sold in the United States), but buy disposable diapers on the road.

Do you need a helping hand in planning and arranging travels with your children? If you do you may consider using the services of this organization: Travel With Your Children (TWYCH), 80, Eighth Ave., New York, NY. (212) 206-0688.

Traveling with Pets:[IL] Veterinarians advise against traveling with your pet. But, some dogs and cats become so miserable when their owners are away that they literally starve themselves. And, if you are moving across the ocean, you probably will want to take your pet with you. As long as your pet has had its shots, it can travel with you freely throughout Europe--with the exception of Britain, Ireland, and Norway, which have quarantine systems because their areas are rabies-free. The only restriction usually is that you possess a yellow international vaccination certificate for your pet (similar to the paper people carry to show that they have been vaccinated for smallpox).

Most airlines will make arrangements for your pet--unless it is a boa constrictor, a ferret, or a bird (birds are particularly unwelcome on airlines, because they carry diseases).

In addition to the vaccination certificate, most European countries require a health certificate for any animal taken across borders. The certificate must be filled out by a veterinarian a limited number of days before you arrive in the country. You may be required to obtain a second certificate once inside Europe if you plan to cross additional borders--check with the consulates of the country you are visiting.

Choosing Your Flight: For trans-Atlantic passages, find out if your flight is direct or nonstop. Nonstop flights have no layovers or plane changes, but direct flights may stop four or five times en route, even though you don't have to change planes. The stops can be a strain on your pet.

Most airlines allow a limited number of pets per flight, so make arrangements early. Your pet will be issued its own ticket, and you will be billed at the rate for excess baggage (which can be an insult).

Even if you have a boarding pass, you are not guaranteed a seat until you are given a seat assignment. To avoid last-minute decisions to bump you because of your pet, try to get a seat assignment as soon as possible (usually you can get a seat assignment nearly a year before the flight, even if boarding passes are not available more than 30 days before the flight). If you are unable to get your seat assignment in advance, allow extra time to board with your pet.

Storing Your Pet on Board: Some airlines will allow you to bring your pet on board with you and to store it in a compartment under your seat. However, most airlines require that you use an approved airline carrier for your pet during the flight, which is stowed in the airplanes's cargo hold. You can get one of these carriers secondhand.

Your veterinarian can help your pet endure the flight by prescribing a tranquilizer. You should arrange for it to have water during the flight (remember how dehydrated you get while flying). One trick is to freeze water in the bowl that attaches to the carrier. That way you will avoid drips while transporting the carrier.

Tips on Shipping Pets:[1]

*Ship your pet in a large, sturdy crate with a leak-proof bottom. Print on it your name, address, your pet's name and destination.

*A health certificate and a rabies inoculation and a rabies inoculation are recommended, along with distemper and hepatitis inoculations.

*Exercise pets well the day before the shipment.

*Feed the pet a light meal six hours before shipping.

*Don't give water to pets within two hours of shipping except on a very hot day. Provide a water dish for attendant's use.

*If the trip will be longer than 24 hours, provide food.

Baggage Identification: Security concerns in many countries have led to a variety of practices and procedures in several international airports. One of these practices is a Baggage identification by owner-passengers, prior to embarkation. In other words, in some countries, especially in Africa, you may be required (long after checking in) to identify your baggage. Usually, upon physical identification, your baggage is immediately loaded onto a carriage or directly into the plane. Unidentified baggage are not loaded or carried, in which case you may arrive at your destination unaccompanied by your baggage. The worst of it is that such baggage left behind may end up being misplaced, tampered with and/or lost. To avoid this, take some time (before or after checking in) and verify with the airline or airport authority if such practices or procedures are in effect, and if so, when and where.

Emergency: Telephone codes used in summoning for help during emergencies vary from country to country. Most of us are used to dialing **911** during emergencies. While this may be the code for many parts of the U.S. it may not be valid for other countries of the world. Travelers abroad should, upon arrival at their hotels, place of residence or destination, inquire and familiarize themselves with the local telephone system, particularly the correct emergency dialing code. Children accompanying parents should be included in this learning exercise. A country by country list of emergency numbers (codes) is provided in Appendix 5E.

Security Precautions: As a security protection, it is advisable for the International traveler to maintain always a low profile while in a foreign country. This is important, particularly for Americans and especially those visiting countries in the Middle East, Africa, Asia and South America. You can have a perfectly enjoyable vacation without revealing or showing off your citizenship or parading yourself as an American.

If contemporary or past events are indications to draw from, it is clear that not all countries nor all the citizens of a given country are friendly with Americans, nor with America as a country for a variety of reasons. Unfortunately, it is at times difficult to tell what country or countries, which individuals or communities as well as when and where this may be the case.

However, you can stay out of this area of controversy and uncertainty, and have yourself a safe and peaceful trip by minding what you say, when and where you say it, and what you do, how, when and where you do it and what you carry, how and where you carry it to. To improve your personal security (a) minimize stopover time you spend at airports, avoiding those airports that are known to have security problems; (b) try to book direct flights scheduling flights, preferably, on wide-body jets (two aisles) since they are more difficult for hijackers to take over and control; (c) request for window seats since passengers in aisle seats are more likely to be abused by hijackers, (d) try not to discuss your travel plans in public places, rather restrict information about your travel plans to those who need to know. For additional security-related information see Chapter 6 on security awareness overseas.

International Protocol Pointers:[RI] Whether traveling internationally for business or pleasure, here are some useful tips:

- Don't "over-gesture" with your hands; it can be offensive.

- Avoid American jargon and idioms.

- Don't refuse food; taste a little of everything.

- Don't over schedule.

- In Arab countries, don't openly admire things.

- Arrange for your own translator. Relying on someone else's translator could be a mistake.

- Gift-giving is an art and a science. Study the science and perfect the art. Giving a clock in China is a bad idea.

- You may be expected to sing after a dinner in either Japan or Korea.

- Contact the State Department for travel advisories before embarking.

- Don't photograph religious statues.

** Get a copy of the book(s) "*DO'S & DON'TS AROUND THE WORLD: A COUNTRY GUIDE TO CULTURAL & SOCIAL TABOOS AND ETIQUETTE*", published in 9 Regional Volumes, one for every continent. Available from this publisher, major national bookstores, and on-line from Amazon.com. , or visit www.frontlinepublishers.com

The Best Seat on the Plane:[RI] Of course, the best seats on a plane are in first-class. But in coach, some are better than others. In terms of safety, experts agree that the midsection of the plan, close to the wings, is safest in case of disaster. And being close to an exit door should increase your chances for survival.

Should you specify an aisle, window, or center seat? The advantages of the aisle seat are:

1. It's easier to exit the plane.

2. Your shoulders and arms have more space.

3. You can see other passengers and have a more roomy feeling.

A problem with the aisle seat is that you might repeatedly get your side brushed or toes run over by the beverage cart if you don't stay out of the way of flight attendants.

The center seat has no advantages, except when you are sitting next to someone you know (or want to know). The window seat allows a view of the sky and ground, which can help if you tend to feel claustrophobic in flight.

The closer you are to the front, the less time you will wait in line to deplane. Engine noise will also be less pronounced toward the front. The first row after the coach bulkhead gives you a ride up front plus more storage space. On smoking flights (those over six hours), a seat toward the front means you are away from smoke.

All of the major airlines, except for Southwest, offer seat selection at least 30 days in advance. The sooner you choose your seat, the better the seat you'll get - if you specify what you want. Once you get on the plane, you may request a seat reassignment.

Seats over the wing provide the smoothest ride; those in the back, the bumpiest.

Minors Traveling
Unaccompanied/Accompanied: Be aware that International Airlines may not fly children under 5 years who are unaccompanied. Some airlines, however, are willing to assist with an experienced personal hostess to take care of the child on its journey. Depending on the airline, this additional service may or may not require extra cost of a full adult fare.

For many International Airlines, children between 5 and 12 years, however, may travel unaccompanied provided certain conditions are met. The most common conditions are that (1) the unaccompanied child be brought to the airport of embarkation, and met at the airport of destination; (2) the parents or legal guardians sign a written authorization. This consent form is usually available at any of the airline offices; (3) overnight stays en route can only be included if the parents or legal guardian or representative provides an adult to accompany the child from arrival until departure the following day. Depending on the airline, and if the airlines involved allows it, two or more flights on the same day may be permitted.

For children between 5 and 12 years accompanied by a hostess, a full adult fare is often charged for the child, in addition to another full adult fare if a personal hostess is provided at a cost. Quite often no extra fare is charged if the personal hostess is an employee (hostess) of the airline.

For children over 12 years accompanied by hostess, a full adult fare is often charged, in addition to a percentage (about 50%) of the regular adult fare if the airline uses one of its own hostesses.

In all cases for children over 5 years accompanied by an independent, non-airline personal hostess a full adult fare is often charged to cover the hostess.

Because the rules and conditions vary from one airline to another, it is advisable to contact the airlines prior to departure date to find out more about their policy, cost, and conditions relating to traveling by minors. You may even be surprised to find out that the age limits differ from those discussed here.

Do remember to check visa requirements. Depending on the country or countries the child is traveling to, visas may be required for the child, the paid independent personal hostess or for the both travelers.

Babies - On Board: Many reputable international airlines do carry on board a stock of baby food, diapers and useful accessories for the care of your baby. Some do, also, provide baby baskets for babies no more than about 27 inches in length. Because of the limited number of these baskets, it is advisable to give the airline an advance notice; and, to be on the safe side, to carry along some food for your baby. It is not unusual to run into international flights that do not provide any of these services.

Liability and Insurance: As an international or air travel, remember that the luggage you carry or check into the plane is not insured by the airline against loss or damage during air transportation. Under certain conditions, the liability of the airline is limited in value, and this liability is based in principle, on weight and not on the value of the contents. This is all the more reason that it is advisable to have your luggage insured.

Transport of Animals: The transport of animal is a normal service for most international airlines. Doing it does, however, require advance notice. Usually, domestic animals are carried in the cargo hold. The holds for animals are often pressurized, well ventilated, and maintained at a comfortable temperature.

Some airlines, however, do allow small domestic animals to travel in the cabinet. Some countries or

- Infectious substances (materials that may cause human disease)
- Explosives, munitions, fireworks and flares
- Compressed gases of any kind
- Magnetized materials
- Corrosive materials
- Radioactive substances
- Oxidizing materials and peroxides (e.g. lead powder)
- Toxic materials and irritants (e.g. tear gas)
- Readily flammable solids and liquids such as gasoline or matches
- Mace, tear gas, and other irritants
  . Aerosols containing flammable material
  . Loaded firearms
  . Gunpowder
  . Loose ammunition
- Gasoline, flammables
  .Propane, butane cylinders or refills, lighter refills
  . Wet-type batteries, e.g., as used in cars
  . Any equipment containing fuel
  . Scuba tanks if pressurized
- Fireworks, flares
- Safety or "strike-anywhere" matches
  . Flammable paint and paint-related material
  . Poisonous material
  . Infectious substances

Many other hazardous materials are also prohibited. When in doubt, check with your airline.

|Violators of Federal hazardous materials regulations (49 CFR Parts 171-180) may be subject to a civil penalty of up to $25,00 for each violation and, in appropriate cases, a criminal penalty.|

Hazardous materials are prohibited in checked or carry-on luggage. However, there are certain exceptions for personal care, medical needs, sporting equipment, and items to support physically challenged travelers.

For example:

- **Toiletry and medicinal** articles containing hazardous material (e.g., flammable perfume) totaling no more than 75 ounces may be carried on board. Contents of each container may not exceed

16 fluid ounces or one pound.

Matches and lighters may only be carried on your person. However, lighters with flammable liquid reservoirs and lighter fluid are forbidden. (Smoking is prohibited on scheduled air carrier flights of six hours or less within the 48 contiguous states, and between certain other locations.)

- **Carbon dioxide gas cylinders** worn by passengers to operate mechanical limbs, and spare cylinders of a similar size for the same purpose, are permitted in both carry-on and checked luggage.

- **Carrying firearms** on board aircraft is forbidden. Unloaded firearms can be transported in checked luggage if declared to the agent at check in and packed in a suitable container. Handguns must be in a locked container. Check with your airline representative for other restrictions concerning firearms.

- **Ammunition** may not be carried on board an aircraft. However, small arms ammunition may be transported in checked luggage, but must be secure packaged in material designed for the purpose. Amounts may vary depending on the airline. Check with your airline.

- **Dry ice** for packing perishables, in quantities not to exceed 4 pounds, may be carried on board an aircraft provided the package permits the release of carbon dioxide. Further restrictions apply to dry in checked luggage. Check with air

- **Electric wheelchairs** may only be transported as checked luggage. The airline may determine that the batter must be dismounted and packed in accordance with airline requirement. Check with airline representative.

[Some items however, can be shipped or transported as air cargo. Contact your airline representative for detailed instructions regarding the shipment of hazardous material.]

Safety from Thieves:[1] Tourists are often easy and lucrative marks for thieves. Special precautions will lessen the opportunities for thieves. Here's a list of things you can do:

- Carry most of your money in traveler's checks insured for theft.

- Never leave your belongings unattended in airports, hotels or restaurants.

- Taxi drivers, also, can sometimes be thieves. If a taxi driver does not turn his meter on, ask him to turn it on or go get yourself another cab. Otherwise, he may take you to your destination, charge you a higher fee, and pocket it. If he tries to" rip you off," get his cab number and report him.

- If you agree to let someone carry your luggage and load it into a taxi watch him closely. He could run off with your bag or pretend to load your bags into the taxi while holding some back. You may not realize you've been robbed until you reach the hotel.

- When registering in hotels, do not put your brief case on the floor. That makes it a perfect target for a quick grab.

- Keep your valuables in the hotel safe.

- When you leave your hotel room, always lock your doors and windows, especially those leading to the balcony.

- When eating in the hotel restaurant or lounge never leave your hotel key on the table. A thief can note the room number, go to your room, and rob you when he knows you are out.

- If you are in town for a convention, and are required to wear a name tag remove your name tag, when you are not in a meeting. Otherwise, thieves will notice your name, find out your room number from the desk clerk, and rob your room while you are out.

- Never let a stranger into the hotel room even if he claims to be on the hotel staff. Call the desk to make sure the person is legitimate before you open the door.

- In crowds, walk against the flow of traffic, even if you do get dirty looks. That makes a pickpocket's job much harder.

- If someone jostles you in the crowd, turn around immediately while checking for your wallet. Pickpockets move fast.

- Don't keep your passport and cash in the same place.

- If you carry a purse, carry your money in a pocket. Cash should be kept in front pants pockets or skirt pockets. Pickpockets go for the purse and back pocket first. Money belts are even better. If they are well-attached, they are difficult to pick.

- to get a **shadowed baggage tag**, so that thieves cannot easily memorize your name and address.

- When shopping, do not put your package down on the ground to get your money out. Put them in front of you where you can see them or keep then in an over-the-shoulder bag. Keep your bag toward the front of your body while walking. If it's too far behind you, someone can reach in and take something out without your knowing it.

- Sleazy clubs, topless bars, and strip joints are notorious for scams. Foreigners are easy prey. For example, if you buy a bottle of champagne for a "lady," the bartender, after she's had a few drinks, may exchange the bottle for a half-empty one. By the end of the night, you are charged an exorbitant price for six bottles, while you probably only drank one full bottle of champagne.

• If you lose your checkbook and it is returned, make sure that no checks are missing.

Who Should not Fly?:[IL] A person who is undergoing severe emotional illness probably is not a good candidate for a long air trip unless absolutely necessary, and then a responsible traveling companion is essential.

In general, if good sense is used and proper consultation is made with a physician, most persons having an illness or a chronic disability, such as diabetes or epilepsy, can tolerate air travel and their disabilities will not be aggravated.

If you should have a disease that occasionally causes loss of consciousness, such as epilepsy or diabetes, carry a card in your wallet identifying the illness.

The Medic-Alert Company. has stainless-still bracelets or emblems with engraved serial numbers that, also, have key words such as **DIABETIC** written on them. The serial number enables the attending physician to call collect night or day for more specific information about the patient.

Carrying Parcels and Letters for Others: As hard as it may sometimes appear, avoid carrying parcels or letters on behalf of third persons whether or not such a person is traveling along with you in the same plane (or other means of transportation). It is highly dangerous to carry something, if you do not know its contents. Personally, if I must carry a parcel or letter for a very dear friend or relative, I insist on knowing the contents and on doing the actual packing. You can have your entire vacation or trip completely ruined by becoming a victim of a parcel or package with suspicious or illegal contents. Claiming ignorance or emphasizing your "Good Samaritan" spirit will not help you.

Credit Cards, Traveler's Checks and Personal Checks. Unless your trip abroad will entail only cash expenses, always inquire about the forms of payment widely accepted in the countries you plan to visit. If credit cards and travelers checks are acceptable, find out which ones are acceptable. This is particularly important for a variety of reasons: (a) In some countries, personal checks are not widely used and are looked upon with suspicion, especially, a check drawn on a far away foreign bank. (b) In some countries, credit cards are not widely used and in these countries, they are only gaining minimal recognition in a few select places. Even in those select places, not all types of major credit cards are readily acceptable. (c) In some countries travelers checks are not as popular as we may think. They may not be widely used and, therefore, will not be an acceptable form of payment. Like credit cards, the particular type of traveler's check may determine its acceptability. If you decide to carry travelers checks, you may consider using American Express or Thomas Cook traveler's checks. Although there are over seven brands of travelers checks world-wide, American Express and Thomas Cook traveler's checks are perhaps the most widely accepted. Their world-wide network of offices and service centers makes them easiest to replace.

It is appropriate to point out that most of the limitations noted above are more prevalent; largely in small, developing countries, in rural parts of some developed countries, and in small establishments (shops, hotels, etc.). Travelers to large metropolitan cities of most countries who plan to shop in large national boutiques or who plan to stay in large international hotels may hardly notice the limitations mentioned here. Nevertheless, it would not hurt to be quite certain and prepared. Questions regarding what forms of payments are widely acceptable in a particular country should be addressed to that country's embassy, consulate or tourist bureaus in the U.S. Your travel agent, credit card or travelers check company should assist you in this matter.

Currency Exchange: Make it a habit to find out precisely what the rules and regulations are with regard to exchanging your U.S. dollars, travelers checks and other currencies into local currency and vice versa and stick to them. In some countries, re-converting excess local currency back to U.S. dollars or other hard or convertible currency is not easy and may entail a substantial loss to you. Upon arrival, find out government authorized places for such transactions. Many travelers find themselves in trouble by failing to play by the rules either due to sheer ignorance, or taking actions on their part to short cut the regulations and procedures. The outcome for violators could spell disaster for your vacation. Do not be distracted or deceived by unauthorized entities wanting your U.S. dollars and offering you higher rates. Some of them turn out to be undercover government agents and plain clothes police. Although in many countries a large number of hotels serve as official currency exchange centers, not all of them are authorized. Personally, I restrict my currency transactions to banks; besides, they usually offer a much better rate as compared to other approved currency exchange centers. Keep in mind that coins are rarely accepted for conversion into local currency and that includes U.S. coins.

Hard Currencies Only!: In some poor, developing countries "hungry" for hard currency, non-residents and foreign visitors may be required to make virtually all of their purchases in hard or convertible currency, particularly in dollars. Beware, should your travels include some of these countries. For the most part, these are, in addition, the countries with strict rules regarding exchanging foreign currencies. They are also the countries where you might have your money confiscated with the slightest currency violations and where you might find it hard to re-convert your excess local currency to a convertible currency. Your best safeguards are (a) declare all of your currency upon arrival. This is especially important for all countries with currency restrictions. (b) Restrict your activities only to authorized currency exchange places. (c) Keep receipts of all of your currency transactions. (d) Even though the commissions may appear high, only exchange the amount you need to use in the country. To find out what the current rules and regulations are regarding currency transactions, contact that country's embassy or consulate in the U.S. or their tourist bureau in the U.S.

Customs Declaration: If in doubt, make it a habit to declare always to the customs and/or immigration anything you cannot afford to have confiscated, including all items of personal jewelry.

Records/Receipts: Make it a habit to keep all receipts of purchases and other financial transactions during your trip abroad. Arranging the receipts by country would facilitate your dealings with a host of law enforcement authorities abroad and even at home including the airlines, particularly in the case of loss or damage. The receipts you keep, in some cases, may very well prevent you from getting into trouble with the law or determine whether or not you will return home with those souvenirs you purchased abroad.

Validation on Passports: As an international traveler one observation you may not fail to see quite early is the number of times your travel documents, particularly your passport, will be requested by one authority or the other. The other observation is the number of times and accessions some form of sticker or stamp is placed or imprinted in your U.S. passport. This is not unusual. The important thing is that you should not hesitate to have any of these validations. In fact, in most cases you should ask whoever is requesting your passport if a validation by them is not required. The validations you should always look out for and ask about include: (a) visas (entry and exit) unless they are not required, in which case you will be told and (b) all currency transactions.

Do remember, however, that in some countries, some of these validations may not necessarily be made directly into your passport. They may come in the form of a sheet of paper enclosed or attached to your passport or tourist card.

Surrendering Your Passport: While the importance of safeguarding your passport must be emphasized, do not panic if your hotel or designated tour guide should request to keep it during the period you are in their service. Although not a common practice in most countries of the world, you may encounter this practice in some Communist, Middle East and developing countries.

In all cases, however, ask for an explanation, including when and under what conditions it will be returned to you. If you plan to travel to any of the regions cited above, you may want to contact the embassy, consulate, or tourist bureau of those regions here in the U.S. before leaving to find out if such practices are in effect. The U.S. Embassy in the country you plan to visit should, also, be able to advise you in this matter. You are better off getting the information here in the U.S. before departure.

Remember your passport will almost always be needed when cashing travelers checks and personal checks. You may want to carry out all necessary foreign exchange transactions before parting with your passport.

Medications/Prescription Drugs: Carry along with you any necessary medications and keep them in their original, labeled container in your hand luggage. Because of strict laws on narcotics, carry a letter from your physician explaining your need for any prescription drugs in your possession. Failure to do this may result in the confiscation of your medication and/or a fine and imprisonment.

Group Travel Versus Solo: There are advantages and disadvantages, to both group and solo traveling. These advantages and disadvantages not withstanding, an international traveler with adequate planning can always expect to have a perfectly enjoyable, exciting and successful trip abroad. Whether one plans to travel as part of a group or travel solo is really a matter of choice and personal preference, many times determined by such variables as cost (budget), age, foreign travel experience, language, privacy, flexibility, timing, health conditions and familiarity with the foreign country.

By and large, traveling as part of a group can add to the overall security of your trip, and will facilitate some of the procedural requirements that accompany traveling to a foreign country. Without a doubt, group travelers attract and get faster attention, sometimes resulting in savings of time and/or money. Because your group travel may involve a tour guide, you probably will have the advantage of sampling the best sites in town on the usual congested schedule. As a member of a tour group, you must, however, be ready to sacrifice your need for complete privacy, flexibility and independence for a schedule that may not allow them. Ultimately, it is you, and only you, who must provide the verdict as to the success of your trip abroad.

Attitude: Success with your trip abroad may depend on your attitude, particularly your degree of tolerance, as well as on how much flexibility you build into it. What will become invariably clear to you is the strangeness of the environment which, in fact, is not dramatically different from a trip to another city back home. You can break these feelings and thoughts by maintaining a positive attitude, complete with unreserved tolerance and great flexibility, and by toning down your expectations. After all, this a foreign country, not really home. The folks you see could have come from some part of the United States with their weird looks, funny accents and "wild and crazy" attire.

Essentially, I must caution that in parts of some countries you might travel to, smiles may be rare and the faces you see may not be as inviting. Do not take these looks so seriously or pre-judge them as to feel, "Oh! I have come to the wrong place," for behind these sad looking and unpolished faces are truly peaceful and loving hearts just waiting to know and understand more about you. Even if you were to run into one or two of these faces with the "wrong heart" during your very first encounters, try not to jump to a quick generalization of how hostile and unfriendly the country and its people are/or get out of town with the next available plane. You may be cutting short what could have turned out to be a wonderful and exciting learning experience.

Coming across an unfriendly host or hostess or receiving unfriendly treatment is not an unusual experience of foreign travelers. You will more than likely come across this at one time or another during your overseas trips. But, this is not very different from the same incident you might experience in your city of residence in the U.S. While overseas, it is advisable to view these isolated incidents with more smiles than something else. Unless you have done something particularly offensive, you may be sure that what you experience, and the faces you see are nothing more than expressions of momentary misunderstanding. They may, also, be, expressions of shyness, of inability to communicate appropriately, or of curiosity just waiting to be broken. And guess what will break it, **YOUR SMILES,** a product of your **ATTITUDE**, your willingness to be truly adventurous, tolerant, understanding and, above all, appreciative of cultural diversity.

CARNET:

561

What is an ATA Carnet ?

*Carnet is an international customs document, a merchandise Passport.

*Carnets facilitate **temporary** imports into foreign countries and are **valid for up to one year.**

What are the advantages of using an ATA Carnet?

***Reduces costs to the exporter.** Eliminates value-added taxes (VAT), duties, and the posting of security normally required at the time of importation.

***Simplifies Customs procedures.** Allows a temporary exporter to use a single document for all Customs transactions, make arrangements for many countries in advance, and do so at a predetermined cost.

***Facilitates reentry into the U.S.** Eliminates the need to register goods with Customs at the time of departure.

What merchandise is covered by the ATA Carnet ?

***Virtually all goods,** personal and professional, including commercial samples, professional equipment, and goods intended for use at trade shows and exhibitions.

***Ordinary goods** such as computers, tools, cameras and video equipment, industrial machinery, automobiles, gems and jewelry, and wearing apparel.

***Extraordinary items,** for example, Van Gogh Self-portrait, Ringling Brothers tigers, Cessna jets, Paul McCartney's band, World Cup-class yachts, satellites, and the New York Philharmonic.

***Carnets do not cover:** consumable goods (food and agricultural products) disposable items, or postal traffic.

Where can an ATA Carnet be used?

Currently, Carnets can be used in over 44 countries located in Europe, North America, Asia, and Africa. Additional countries are however, added periodically. To learn more about Carnets and how to apply for an ATA Carnet, contact the CARNET Headquarters at

U.S. Council for International Business:
1212 Avenue of the Americans
New York, New York 10036
(212) 354-4480 Fax: (212) 944-0012

* The U.S. Council for International Business was appointed by the Treasury Department in 1968 to manage the ATA Carnet System in the United States. Typically, the Council issues over 10,000 Carnets a year covering goods valued at over one billion dollars.

Extra Photographs: Carry with you additional passport-size photographs just in case. Six to eight will be adequate. It is not unusual to be confronted with situations requiring passport-size photographs. For example requests for certain types of permits and licenses or for extension of stay may require passport-size photographs. Having some handy will save you both time and money. Unlike in the U.S. where the requirements are less stringent, passport-size photographs you plan to use overseas should show both ears, not just one ear.

Facilities: Many of the services and gadgets that are customary in the U.S. are conspicuously missing or inadequate in many parts of the world. This is particularly true in developing countries but also occurs in rural areas and in some developed countries. Such amenities as a regular supply of heat, hot water, or air conditioning are rare in public as well as in private facilities.

In some areas even hotels lack these services. Medical services are often inadequate and transportation and telecommunications are often inefficient. Computers, color television sets and other modern gadgets remain luxury items in many parts of the world and are therefore not readily available. Even services as routine as dry cleaning may prove to be a challenge.

562

Essentially, you must be aware that many foreign countries are not as advanced, developed, rich, cultured and "blessed" as the U.S. and its citizens. Shortages abound and poverty and primitive technology are very much alive in several parts of the world. As an international traveler, you can avoid the failures, losses, disappointments and frustrations experienced by many overseas travelers through careful pre-travel research and planning. The more knowledgeable you are about the people, their culture and the level of development in the country you plan to visit, the better your chances of having an exciting and successful overseas trip.

Cash: Before you go abroad, exchange a small amount of your U.S. dollars into the local currency. This will be very handy and particularly useful in covering taxi fares, handling tips and other incidentals. It, also, assures that you have a ready supply of local currency and will save the cost of breaking larger bills into local currency that you may not need. Furthermore, it will eliminate the need to pay to re-convert currency. Furthermore, this can save you the cost of being "forced" to exchange your money with currency exchange centers whose rates, fees, and commissions may be much higher than those of banks.

Foreign (money) Exchange Centers: As an international traveler, you will have occasion to deal in foreign exchange. This will include: (a) buying travelers's checks, whether foreign currency denominated or denominated in U.S. dollars; (b) buying foreign currency (exchanging dollars for foreign currency); (c) exchanging excess foreign currency for U.S. dollars; (d) cashing foreign drafts and checks, including VAT refund checks; (e) wiring money to an account overseas. Some of these financial services can be provided directly by several large U.S. banks, however, a large number of smaller banks can only provide a limited number of these services at prices that may not be your best bargain.

Alternatively, you may consider dealing directly with specialized currency exchange firms, which provide direct currency exchange and transfer services. You are likely to get better rates from these services.

In order to save money on currency exchange transactions, you will need keep abreast of current exchange rates, fees and commissions charged by the various institutions which engage in currency transactions. Exchange rates are subject to constant fluctuations With such fluctuations your savings will depend on what is happening to the U.S. dollar vis-a-vis the foreign currency. Generally, a stronger (appreciated) dollar, will favor your position in which case you will be able to get more for the same dollar than before the appreciation. Timing, therefore, is as important, as shopping around for financial institutions that charge lower commissions and fees. Did you know, for example, as a member of the Automobile Club of America that you can get American Express Traveler's checks free of commissions; and that you can also get Thomas Cook Traveler's Checks free if purchased through any of its travel agencies? Check with your bank and credit card issuer to discover if they provide currency exchange services or other including "freebie" services. A list of dollar-foreign currency exchange rates is often published in the financial sections of some local newspapers, and in a number of national and international financial newspapers. The Wall Street Journal, and the International Herald Tribune are two excellent sources of daily rates.

Hotel Phone Calls: Placing phone calls from your hotel room may be convenient but it may also cost you considerably. Before you make that call, check with the hotel desk clerk or hotel phone operator to ascertain charges for local, long distance and overseas calls. Surcharges of up to 200% are not unusual, the quality of the connection not withstanding.

There are various options and approaches you can use to reduce the cost of hotel phone calls. If you must make your call from the hotel, (a) Find out if the hotel has low rate calling periods, and if they do, place your calls during those times. (b) Remember, that most hotels have pay phones at the lobby. If those phones are programmed to handle long distance or international calls, use them. (c) Find out if the hotel has calling card facilities. By placing your calls with a calling card, you may end up paying in U.S. dollars when you return home. (d) Alternatively, make that first time sacrifice and use a call back approach. This allows you to provide your number to your calling party while asking the other party to call you back. (e) Explore collect calls if it is available. Remember, some of these approaches may only defer payments for your calls, but most will save you money.

Another option that will help to reduce telephone costs is to place your calls at the designated central telephone stations found at most airports and in some train stations. Specially marked public telephones which allow you to use your calling cards are springing up in several large cities overseas. Because you will need a calling card to access this service, you may want to request one by signing up with one of the major long distance carriers in the U.S. before you depart.

Receiving Mail overseas: Central Post Offices in several large cities do provide facilities that allow foreign travelers to receive mail while overseas. Poste Restante as it is often referred to, is a general delivery service which allows mail to be sent to someone overseas to the care of a particular post office. The mail is then held for pick up by the owner. Proper identification, such as a passport, is often required. Important points to remember about this facility are: (1) They may not be available in every country. It is important to find and use the exact address and phone number (2) Your letter may be held only for limited time period and can only picked up during designated hours. It is very important that you inquire about these things. (3) You may be charged a nominal fee for this service. (4) It is advisable for the sender to make an appropriate note on the envelope, for example: "Hold until Dec. 31, 2004". Additionally, it is advisable to call the post office before going to pick up your mail, in this way you will be sure the post office is open and that your letter is ready for pick-up.

You could also apply this same approach with mail sent to hotels. If appropriate, have the sender place note on the envelope, for example "Mail for a guest, Hold until Dec. 31, 2004" Another available would be to use the services of the American Express Company. Customers of American Express including American Express Cardholders and those using or subscribing to any of their services may have their letters sent to American Express Office nearest their destination. This service is provided free of charge. Some restrictions may apply, therefore it is important to inquire about these services before you leave. Decide on which services you wish to use and make appropriate inquiries.

Drunks: You will probably run into them in several places. Be aware not only of their presence, but the likelihood of their nuisance turning into confrontation. Some of these drunks will try to have a chat with you, will touch and fondle you, or even spit at you. Abusive and foul language is a common trade mark of drunks and you can deal with them relatively easily by simply ignoring them. The best way to handle them is to just walk away. Any attempt on your part to deal with their harassment is at best, a waste of time.

Do not forget, many tricksters, pickpockets and baggage thieves, sometimes go about their trade, pretending to be drunks.

Auto Rental/Leasing/Purchases: Renting or leasing an automobile for use overseas may by a money-saving option, depending on your particular circumstance and travel plans. This might be an option worth considering if you are travelling with a large family or group, or plan an extended stay with travel to areas that are not accessible by public transportation. You could make your reservations upon arrival overseas or right here in the U.S. before you go. Booking your reservations in the U.S. can be done by contacting the rental agencies directly, or via several of the International Rental and Leasing Agencies .

Some travelers invest in used cars overseas and then sell them before returning to the U.S. Others buy cars in the U.S. for overseas delivery and use, or make arrangements to purchase new cars overseas which are, then, sold at the end of the stay abroad, or exported to the U.S. Several firms specialize in leasing and purchasing automobiles for overseas delivery. These firms are often knowledgeable about applicable foreign country regulations in these areas. Companies specializing in overseas delivery will also be helpful in assisting you with shipping arrangements. Those travelers who contemplate importing or exporting foreign automobiles and pleasure boats must be well aware of U.S. Government regulations and procedures.

If you plan to rent, lease or drive overseas you

should be aware of the rules and requirements. Some countries have strict age requirements, not only for renting or leasing automobiles but also for driving. Because some of these requirements may differ from the U.S. it is prudent to familiarize yourself with those of the foreign country before you go. Useful information for driving overseas can be obtained from your local automobile association or from the American Automobile Association.

Freebies: Ever wondered what free services, products, and other bargains may be available to International Travelers? You may be surprised to know that there are a number of services and products, worth hundreds of dollars, for which you may already have qualify. You may automatically qualify for some, while you will have to shop around and apply for others. In some cases its a matter of just asking for them. Those who offer these freebies obviously will be delighted if you were only to ask or pay for their services without requesting any free offer they may have. A few will give them to you, nevertheless, or use them aggressively as a promotion device. While inquiring about the freebies, we should not forget the common adage which says: "There is no such thing as a free lunch". Keep in mind that a good number of offers are, indeed, money-saving and worthwhile but there is the constant need to be cautious. It is advisable to comparative-shop and to read the fine print (if a contract or purchase is necessary) before you accept an offer for a "free" service or product.

Making Business Contacts overseas: This can be particularly, taxing for businesses seeking new overseas markets for their products and sources for their raw materials. Business contacts in some countries become even more difficult for women. U.S. businesses in need of assistance in this area or in any activity relating to international trade may contact. The U.S. International Trade Commission in the Department of Commerce. This agency will, also, provide you with advice, references and resources on a variety of issues in international business, including sources of financial assistance for U.S. exporters. Furthermore, they will provide you with information on the domestic markets, including local business customs and practices. A listing of the Department of Commerce District Offices and the International Trade Information is provided in

Appendix C and D, respectively. Other sources that should be explored are (1) the commercial section of the country's embassy or consulate in the U.S., (2) the U.S. Chamber of Commerce. A growing number of companies now have Chamber of Commerce in the U.S., (3) International Trade offices of City and State Governments, (4) Commercial attaches of American Embassies and Consulates Overseas, (5) International Business Clubs and Organization in the U.S.

Vehicle Precaution: If you plan to drive during your trip abroad, you should take safety precautions. Foreign travelers often become favored preys to local muggers and thieves. Incidentally, the same can be said of foreigners who visit the U.S. Incidents, ranging from car break-ins to car jacking, including physical assaults on the occupiers, have been reported by Americans travelers. The motives for these incidents vary, and the resultant impacts have, also, varied, and have sometimes been quite fatal. You can minimize the chances of becoming a victim by taking a few precautions, including:

- Drive the more common kinds of locally available cars; if there are not many American cars in use, don't insist on an American model.

- Make sure the car is in good repair.

- Keep car doors locked at all times.

- Wear seatbelts.

- Don't park your car on the street overnight if the hotel has a garage or secure area. If you must park it on the street, select a well-lit area.

- Don't leave valuables in the car.

- Never pick up hitchhikers.

- Don't get out of the car if there are suspicious individuals nearby. Drive away.

- If you are renting or leasing a car, request for one with a local tag as opposed to one with an international tag or clearly marked tourist tag. This way your car will not stand out.

- If you must stop to ask for directions, do so at a gas station or in a relatively populated and well lit area. In other words, avoid isolated areas when requesting services.

- If you are bumped, particularly repetitively, do not stop to check if you consider the area too isolated, or if you are suspicious of the motive. You might well be right. Instead, drive to a safe, populated, area.

- Although it may sound cruel, beware of situations that look like accidents. Some are staged just to attract your attention and sympathy. You could very well end up becoming a victim of one assault. This also include stopping to render help to, supposedly, a needy and helpless traveler or pedestrian, especially, in very isolated spots. Obviously, there are other ways besides having to stop, that you may be able to render help. If you must react to your need to help, drive to a safe area and place an emergency call on behalf of the accident or stranded victims. Remember, you are in a foreign country and environment, and may not totally understand how things work.

Need a Traveling Companion or Partner?: If you do, you are not alone. A growing number of travelers are doing just that for a variety of reasons: For some it is a way of curbing loneliness, others desire to reduce costs on accommodations by doubling up, and still others want to reduce the general risk of traveling alone. This can also create the opportunity for a new relationship.

Overseas Employment: Before considering employment overseas, you should familiarize yourself with the Internal Revenue Service rules regarding income earned abroad. Several rules and tests apply including the "foreign residence test" and the "physical presence test"; and so are exemptions and exclusions. You may avoid future confrontations with the IRS by checking the current rules and regulations. Check your local telephone directory for the IRS office nearest you.

As you embark on your search for employment

overseas, I must caution you about the growing number of unscrupulous agents and agencies with bogus claims. Many of these so called "overseas employment agencies" are not reliable, but are out to con you out of your money. It is, therefore, advisable to think really hard and long before committing any monies to them. Alternatively, you should consider applying for overseas jobs directly with the overseas employer or an overseas employment agency (assuming the latter does not require for an up-front or advance-fee). A number of international newspapers and magazines, as well as foreign magazines circulated in the U.S. carry job announcements. Other sources of information regarding overseas jobs may be obtained from the respective foreign embassies and consulates in the U.S. (See Appendix B).

Remember, an offer for a job overseas does not exempt you from the rules and regulations governing employment of foreigners in a particular foreign country, nor are you exempted from the necessary permits, including entry and exit visa, and other requirements of that country. Check with the respective embassies and consulates.

Discount Travel Opportunities: You can save a lot of money as I have, on your trips, and still enjoy the same treats as everyone else. This is true whether in the U.S. or abroad, if only, you know what it takes. And what does it take? It takes flexibility and willingness on your part to give up comfort and convenience, One must also be knowledgeable about these opportunities. The more of these you have, the greater potential for larger savings. Unfortunately, some of the opportunities for bargain fares carry risks and penalties, some of which

may end up being costly, in both time and money. Hence, it is important to shop around for the least restrictive bargain opportunities.

Generally, the longer the planning period you have for your trip and the more time you will have to explore discount opportunities. This is particularly important, because there are several carriers from which to chose and the fact that fares change continually.

As you begin exploring opportunities for discount fares, you may want to bear these generalized observations in mind. (a) Tickets for flights during peak (high) seasons cost more than those for during off (low) seasons. Incidentally, this is also true for prices charged by hotels, theaters, etc.

As you will probably guess, summers are usually considered to be peak seasons as against winters. Airlines and cruise lines have actual months (cut-off dates) signaling the start and end of the various seasons. It is important to remember that the actual dates may vary from carrier to carrier and for travel to or from some parts of the world. It is advisable to shop around and to check with the various carriers. (b) Tickets for travel during early morning or night hours tend to be cheaper. Although this may not be true for international carriers, you may find such bargains with domestic flights. (c) Tickets for weekday and holiday travel tends to be more expensive than on weekends and non-holiday periods. (d) Depending on the class of ticket you buy, you may pay more or less, and still not notice (when on board), any significant difference in services provided the different classes of passengers. In the case of travel by air, depending on the airline, you will find as many as four classes of fares. These are, (in descending order of cost, beginning with the most expensive), first class, business class, coach class (sometimes called tourist or economy) and excursion or discount fares. There is also the "super first class" as one may categorize the fare on the Concord. In the majority of the international airlines you will find the four basic fares, in some, the numbers of fare classes may be less. To complicate things for the unsuspecting and amateur traveler, you may find slight variations between airlines in their definitions of these classes. It is not unusual to find some airlines selling different types of coach or economy tickets. From time to time new packages with new terms are added to the usual economy and excursions classes of fares. In recent years, these have included the advance purchase excursion (APEX) fare, and the Youth fare. These are all potentially bargain opportunities for international travelers. Exploring some of these special fares may be worth the effort.

You will readily notice, the lower the class, the cheaper the fare will be. (e) Standby fares are considerably lower than regular fares, and are potential money-savers for those who qualify. Standby opportunities are described elsewhere in this chapter. (f) Tickets for low-fare travel, generic airlines, such as Virgin Atlantic, Icelandair and several other small carriers, are generally much cheaper than tickets for the same flight, bought for travel with any of the large, regularly scheduled carriers.

Alternatively, you could save handsomely on your overseas trip by employing the services of charter operators, ticket rebators, air couriers, and bucket shops and consolidators.

As you explore the various avenues to save on your trip expect some restrictions and learn to consider them before making any financial commitments. Read all fare permits. Some of the common conditions will include one or more of the following clauses: (a) advance reservation, (b) advance payment (purchase), (c) short notification of the traveler, (d) reconfirmation of reservation, (e) non-refundable payments, (f) no cancellations (except documented real emergency), (g) minimum and/or maximum stay (h) weekend sleep-overs (1) some stopovers/connections, (j) right to cancel on the part of the service provider.

You also have the option of booking or reserving a flight or cruise without making immediate payment. You can make reservations with more than one carrier, up to 6 or more months in advance. However, you may be required to pay and get your ticket within a few weeks before actual travel date. You could even make multiple reservations. But I must caution that carriers generally do not appreciate multiple reservations for the same traveler, since this ties up opportunities for others. Avoid booking your reservations with the airline and making a duplicate booking with a travel agency. Most airlines, once, they notice the duplication, will cancel both, and toss out your name.

Safe guarding your Camera Film: As an international traveler, you and your luggage will go through one or more airport x-Ray machines. This is a part of the security measures that are being taken worldwide. Some airline authorities have claimed that their X-ray machines will not damage camera films passing through them. This claim however, has been disputed, as some trusting passengers continue to notice the effects of X-ray exposure on their prints. Taking extra precautions to safeguard your films (including those inside the camera) will ensure that your hopes are not dashed. Imagine spending all that money, time and effort in taking the pictures just to lose them. One suggestion would be to politely ask the X-Ray operator or attending officer to pass the film through by hand, rather than through the machine. Make sure you do not open the film, as this will expose and render it useless. Let it stay in its original container (box) or wrapped in a plastic bag. Do the same with your camera, if it has film in it.

As you consider taking photographs overseas, you may also want to carry adequate film. Film is generally less expensive in the U.S. If you must buy your film overseas, expect to pay up to three times what they will cost in the U.S.

A Trip to Your Doctor: This is highly recommended for International Travelers, particularly, the elderly, the disabled and those with medical problems. To get more out of your visit, you should ask your physician to educate you on a host of health-related issues including the required vaccinations. Obviously you should be equally concerned about preventive measures. Because there are numerous diseases you may contract, and numerous related health problems that you may encounter when traveling abroad, it is fair to say, that the chances will very much depend on where you are traveling, the time of the year, and how much personal health precautions you have taken.

As you discuss these issues with your physician you may want to explore to the extent possible, what measures you can take to prevent and/or treat the following: diarrhea, blisters, stings bites (mosquitoes, dogs, and snakes, etc.), dysentery, ear aches, food poison, infections, (including fungal infections) sun burns, motion sickness, jet lag, hemorrhoids, giardia, exhaustion, tooth aches, rashes, anxiety, insomnia, and foreign objects in the eye. Discuss preventive measures for diseases such as malaria, yellow fever, hepatitis, typhoid, cholera, rabies, tetanus, AIDS, herpes syphilis, gonorrhea (STDs), measles, mumps, rubella, poliomyelities, diphtheria, pertussis, encephalitis, typhus fever, tuberculosis, schistosomiasis, trypanosomiasis (sleeping sickness) and leishmaniasis. As you will immediately notice the list can be quite extensive. The list however only includes the diseases and problems you are most likely to experience. Keep

in mind that all of them may not be relevant or applicable to your destination. You will also be encouraged to know that you may already be immunized for some of these conditions and can make arrangements to be immunized against others. You may already be adequately knowledgeable about many of these conditions, but it will not hurt to make extra inquiries to protect yourself. Some of the diseases and health concerns mentioned here are discussed in detail in chapter 8.

Vegetarians: Surely, you are not left out. Most international airlines will honor your request for a special vegetarian diet. The only requirement is that you give them advance notice. Such notice is better done when booking your reservation, and again, when re-confirming your flight. Do not be surprised, however, if you suddenly find out while already on board, that they forgot to keep to their words. You can expect apologies when this happens, although that won't be of much help. It may not be a bad idea, therefore, to carry along some food or snacks, just in case. International airlines generally do a better job in meeting your dietary needs than do local or domestic airlines. In fact, do not expect much in this area from domestic airlines. So be prepared:

Similar to international flights, you may not have difficulties getting a decent vegetarian meal in the big, well-known hotels, where salad bars are equally popular. Travelers with alternative room and board arrangements should expect to be on their own as far as feasting on a good vegetarian meal. There are obviously other ways you can make up for these deficiencies, such as a trip to the local food market. This, however, is an alternative I will not recommend for an international traveler. Do not forget that you do not have to lodge in an expensive, big-time hotel to use or eat in their restaurants. Finally, do not be surprised, depending on what part of the world you are traveling to, if your host/hostess does not understand what a vegetarian meal is, and/or perhaps find it strange. To assist you in your travel plan, you may employ the assistance of the North American Vegetarian Society at P.O. Box 72, Dolgeville, NY. 13329 (518) 568-7970.

Tricksters: Perhaps, next to pickpockets, tricksters are another group determined at fowling up your trip. They will come in all shades and colors, some well dressed, knowledgeable and well spoken, and others just the opposite. They will prey upon in your confidence and desperation with promises to do wonders for you or to render services you never requested. Essentially, Beware! What they want is your money. You will probably find more tricksters in South Asian Countries than in other parts of the world. These individuals are nothing but con men, women and children who in a flash will render you penniless, as they disappear with your money and valuables. Just be on the look out for unsolicited assistance of any form or type. Besides, always be suspicious of unsolicited samaritans. Their motives are often unpredictable and "unsamaritan". Your best approach is to avoid them, and if approached, to simply say.: "No thanks" and walk away. Do not let them distract you or get you to participate (share) in their discussion.

Security and Hotel Rooms: Do not assume that your hotel room is always safe, whether, as relates to safe guarding your valuables or for personal safety. Important valuables should be carried with you at all times or locked up in the hotel safe. To get a safe deposit box, ask the desk clerk at the hotel. And for travelers lodging in facilities without safe deposit boxes, the choice should be obvious. Carry your valuables with you. You will be amazed at how fast an item of yours can disappear. Poverty is real in several parts of the world, and hotel employees are not exceptions. An item considered so unimportant by you might just be very valuable to a poor hotel employee.

Travel Guides: The following are the more popular travel guides and their publishers and/or distributors. Several of these guides are available in most bookstores and local public libraries. You may want to check with your library first before investing in these travel guides, although it is always better to have one of your own.

Remember, these travel guides vary in coverage and depth: Some are more broad and detailed, while some others are more specialized. One feature you will find common with the publishers listed below is that they each carry a line of country-specific or region specific guides as well some special-interest guides. Depending on how already knowledgeable or sophisticated a foreign traveler you are, you will find the information in these guides useful. Before you invest in them, it is better to scan through a few of these guides, including a look at their table of contents to see if they contain what you are looking for.

Newsletters: Other than the regular travel guides and books, some of which are listed in Chapter 36, newsletters and magazines for international travelers are available. The newsletters are particularly, common with travel clubs. Whereas the newsletters, which are almost all by subscription magazines, can be bought from general bookstores, travel book stores and newsstands. Most travel newsletters, however, tend to be specialized, targeting a particular country or region, or a particular group of travelers, such as singles, women, seniors, children, disabled and gays. A good number, however, is more general with a variety of information and tips that will benefit every international traveler.

Emergencies and Restricted Reservations: We do not always expect them, but they do and can happen. I mean emergencies. And, sometimes the losses go beyond the actual emergency to include broken vacations or trips, and financial losses from restricted tickets. Certainly, airlines and other carriers and service providers are aware of such possibilities. It does not always, however, have to translate to a total loss. In other words, you can do something about it. Obviously, if you do not make the effort the loss may then become real. Remember the saying: "Nothing ventured nothing gained". Irrespective of the type of restrictions and penalties contained in your reservations and tickets, with proper and verifiable documentation and some luck, you may be able to recover. Proper documentation would include, for example, a note from your doctor in the case of illness, a copy of a newspaper release, or an obituary notice, in the case of death of a family member. Any convincing and verifiable document will help. If you are lucky you may not only be able to get some credit or refund, but you may even qualify for some discounts, such as the special bereavement fare offered by some airlines. Although these opportunities exist to minimize your loss in the event of an emergency, do not interpret this as an obligation on the part of the other party, unless specifically included in the contract. For the most part, it is a favor being rendered to you, and how you approach the other party is important. Be courteous.

Pickpockets and Baggage Thieves: These are two of the several types of menacing hosts and hostesses you will likely encounter during your trips abroad. They come in all forms and shades. They carry no name tags or special identifying features except that they are almost everywhere, but more in some places than in others, particularly at airports, train and bus stations and in crowded public gatherings. Many are well trained in the art, and operate as part of a gang, while some others may just be independent operating amateurs. Surely, you will like to be able to identify them, so as to stay away. Unfortunately, it may be difficult. It could be that 4 year old girl or boy hovering around you, that 16 year old offering to help carry one of your bags, that miserable-looking woman carrying a baby on one hand, with the other hand extended to you, or that well dressed and well spoken gentleman or woman, seemingly knowledgeable about everything around town, including your immediate need. However they are described, it should be clear that they are your worst enemies. They are capable of making you re-live all the problems faced by many travelers. Of course, pickpockets, baggage thieves and their derivatives can be found in every country, including the U.S., and their motives are the same: to take what is yours and get away with it by any means necessary. How you will deal with them in the U.S. is, therefore, no different from the approach you will use abroad? Well, not necessarily. As you journey from one country or community to another, you find that their **modus operandi** is different. Whereas, in some places, the law is there to protect you; in some countries you will find very little real help or consolation. You may even find blame for not being careful enough. Well, maybe the latter might make sense, at least to the extent that it motivates you to learn about the tricks and take necessary precautions.

Although pickpockets and baggage thieves occasionally operate overtly and with some degree of violence or force, most go about it in a subtle way. For the most part, their key strategy is DISTRACTION. Remember DISTRACTION. In other words, they will distract you by whatever means will work, and then rob you. There are numerous ways and techniques pickpockets and baggage thieves use in an effort to distract. There are stories of people using mustard or ketchup by "unintentionally" smearing it on your clothes. Some will create sudden situations and emotions such as pointing and looking to the sky for an unseen and unknown phenomenon, indirectly, encouraging, you to do the same. Some even stage events and games that will attract the unsuspecting. Some will engage you in conversations long enough for you to loose your sense of where you are. There are, furthermore, the familiar forms of distractions used by pickpockets, including crowding you up, bumping you or into you, stepping on your toes, or cornering you, so tight that you can hardly feel differently or notice any serious picking taking place. Throughout your trip you have to bear in mind that many of these individuals are very smart, and they believe you can be distracted. And, of course, you help them by giving them the opportunity, the time, and the place. What can you do to minimize your becoming a victim.

(a) Avoid crowded areas and events (2) Stay away from dark alleys and poorly lit and isolated places, including train compartments with only very few people. Remember they tend to pick more on those who appears helpless and weak. (c) Avoid conversations with groups of unknown individuals, particularly during shopping (d) Refuse unsolicited assistance, and when you must do so, be careful. If you must need help with your luggage, do the approaching, and surrender the heavier and least valuable luggage definitely, not your wallet or hand bag, (e) Stay focused and keep walking to your destination. If you have any stains or whatever, you can certainly check it out somewhere else (for example, in your hotel) not on the street. (f) Carry your valuables in a secure and hidden place, where it is apparent that somebody must totally demobilize you to get into, without you at least noticing. A number of travelers pouches, particularly money belts, are becoming very popular and many do provide better protection. (g) Do not make it a habit to tell people time when they ask. If it is so important, they can always ask some other person or invest in a cheap watch. (h) Do not make change for people. Certainly they can go to the bank. (i) Watch where you sit or stand even in trains and buses. Its better to back to the wall if you can. (j) Try to look like everyone around. Conspicuous looks and actions only expose you. You don't have to carry name tags and look like a tourist to be a tourist, or to display your valuables and money to appreciate why you must have them. (k) Do not ask strangers to watch your luggage or bags, no matter where, and no matter how short a time. (l) Be aware of your immediate environment and the people there. A careful look at faces and actions around you should be able to trigger an appropriate action on your part. A place with too many loiterers and strollers is not particularly an attractive place to be. It is often a fishing zone for pickpockets. (m) Avoid carrying your wallet or purse in a rear pocket. Carrying these items in front of you in clear view and crossed over with your arms is definitely better protection. Inside pockets are even much better, particularly, if they have zippers. Money belts (waist, leg and shoulder belts) have became popular with tourists. Every pickpocket-conscious traveler should consider getting one of these belts or making one for themselves.

And for those of you happy going travelers who, despite all the warnings and advice to the contrary, will get drunk, you are perhaps the most vulnerable.

Safety Precautions for Women Alone[1L]
Unfortunately, women need to take special precautions when traveling abroad, especially when traveling alone. Attitudes toward women vary from country to country, but here are a few general precautions that women should take when traveling:

- If you're traveling solo, use public transportation whenever possible. The incidence of rape and robbery of lone women in cabs are alarmingly high. As an American, you are an even greater temptation.

- Do most of your traveling during the day. If you must go out at night, travel with an acquaintance, especially in southern Europe, where the men tend to be sexually aggressive toward women.

- The less you carry around with you, the easier it will be to run if necessary. Do not overburden yourself with packages or luggage.

- Don't wear expensive jewelry or clothes, especially when you're alone.

- Men in Italy and Spain like to pinch. Stand with your back against the wall in elevators, and if you're traveling with a friend, ask him to walk behind you in crowds. If you figure out who's pinching you, turn around and say "Enough." That usually will put an end to it.

- Have your key ready before you reach your room so you won't be fumbling for it in the hallways.

- Don't flirt with men on the hotel staff - unless you're serious about it. They have a key to your room and may not be able to resist the invitation. If you hear anyone trying your door, call the front desk immediately. If you don't have a phone, be loud and aggressive. Yell. Threaten to notify the police.

- Ask for a hotel room near an elevator so that you won't be walking down long dim corridors alone at night.

- Try staying at a bed-and-breakfast instead of a hotel

Visa Vigilance: 14 tips to take the hassle out of traveling on a visa: Following are some useful tips to help you avoid problems when traveling to countries that require a visa:

- Don't travel on a passport that has less than six months validity. Countries that automatically extend visas for six months at a time will not give you a visa otherwise.

- Keep at least two clear pages in your passport. Many foreign consulates require both a left-and- a right-hand page for their visas. Renew your passport, whatever the expiration date, if you are running short of clear pages.

- It is sometimes possible to get a second passport to travel on while your other is tied up with visa applications.

- U.S. expatriates should avoid getting or

renewing passports in their countries of residence. Foreign consulates frequently run time-consuming checks on visa applications from people with passports issued overseas.

- Apply in good time for all the visas you'll require for a trip. Don't rely on picking up a visa at the other end, even if it is possible (as in Egypt, for example).

- Be aware that certain countries impose a time limit from the date issue (typically three months) for using the visa. This in inclusive of the length of your stay.

- Whenever possible, apply for a visa at the foreign consulate nearest your home. You are always liable to be called for an interview.

- It is best to apply in person. You can often iron ut problems on the spot and check to be sure that the visa has been issued properly before you even leave the building.

- Visa authorities are looking for evidence of financial support and your clear intention to leave their country. Always remember this.

- Know in advance whether you need a tourist or a business visa. If in doubt, ask. In some countries, there is a crucial difference in formalities.

- Ask whether an international vaccination certificate is required with your visa application.

- Be sure you get a double - or multiple-entry visa to certain countries, such as India or Saudi Arabia. If you are on a business trip, you may need to return suddenly. This is impossible with a single-entry visa.

- Check whether you need an exit visa, especially for African countries, Belize, and Brazil.

- If you're going to Israel or South Africa, use a second passport or request that your visa and entry stamp be put on a separate sheet of paper. This can help avoid problems in the future when traveling to other countries.

Limitations To Airline Compensation For Lost Luggage: Contrary to what some travelers think, airlines rarely, and are not obligated to pay you an unlimited sum in compensation for lost or damaged luggage. The limit to an airline's obligation is clearly stated at the back of your ticket. Read it carefully. Even with all of your receipts in tact, you will be entitled to usually, no more than what is stated. Generally, how much you get, depends largely in part on the weight of your luggage as indicated on your ticket when you checked in, the contents, after being subject to depreciation and any additional insurance on the luggage. The value of the contents is not the primary determining criteria. Generally, for lost or damaged items, airlines may reimburse passengers for a maximum of $12.50 per passenger on domestic flights and $9.07 per pound for each piece of checked baggage on an International flights. The maximum reimbursement for unchecked baggage on International flight is $400. If the contents of your luggage(s) are over $800 dollars in value, and you are so concerned, get additional insurance just in case. A list of Travel Insurance providers is provided in Appendices 13N and 14M.

Alternatively, consider traveling light, and importantly, leaving at home, those pieces of personal item you cannot afford to loose. Unless you have to, expensive items such as jewelry, furs cameras, should be left safely at home; otherwise, you should consider having them insured. An additional floater into your existing policy may be all that you need to cover these items.

In the event your luggage is damaged or slightly damaged, you should request a replacement baggage to carry you through the rest of your trip. Many airlines, particularly European Airlines, will often honor your request on the spot. Others may prefer to refer you elsewhere to have your luggage replaced or repaired. You may be requested to have you repaired elsewhere, of your choice, and then to send the bill for reimbursement. Because time is of essence to you, insist on immediate replacement. But, whatever your state of mind, do not forget to report immediately and document the loss or damage to the airline authorities in writing. Hold on to your copy of the report and to your ticket. Remember to not surrender your luggage tag unless you are provided with a signed letter stating that they are in possession of your luggage tag.

Road/Street Maps: Maps are very helpful tools, particularly in getting your way around town. They can save you time as well as add more thrills to your trip. Incidentally, they are one of those free items you can easily get if only you request them. Potential sources of free maps include the automobile clubs, tourist offices, travel agents, airlines, information centers and even your insurance company.

Single and Companion Travelers:. With the diversity among today's travelers, there have sprung up a number of institutions and organizations, providing services to almost every special group of traveler. One such groups include single travelers, some of them looking for companions.

Gay and Lesbian Travelers: A number of organizations and resources are available to gay and lesbian travelers. See Chapter 36 for some nice websites.

Protection Plans: As part of your overall travel insurance, do take advantage of any available services to minimize costly mistakes in planning your overseas trip. This will include ensuring that the travel planners, counselors, agents, agencies and tour operators you are dealing with are, competent, reputable and registered with their respective professional associations. In this regard, you may want to contact the Institute of Certified Travel Agents at (617)237-0280, the American Society of Travel Agents at (703) 739-2782 and the United States Tour Operators Association at (212) 944-5727. Some tour operators are part of ASTA Tour Protection Agreement, which protects clients from unscrupulous tour operators. Consider limiting your tour arrangements to these companies. To verify who is part of this plan and who is not, contact ASTA..

Hitchhiking: Avoid the temptation, unless, of course, it is your normal way of life and your preferred means of transportation, in which case you are fully aware of the thrills as well as the risks that go with it. There are many personal safety considerations and risks to worry about in a foreign land, and you do not want to complicate them or add to the risks. Should you find yourself destitute or stranded, call or request assistance from the nearest police office and the U.S. consulate. Much better, plan well and avoid those things that may necessitate hitchhiking in the first place, such as carrying adequate funds, and emergency contact telephone numbers. Remember, hitchhiking may be frowned upon and may be illegal in some countries, or prohibited in certain areas. Despite the problems and risks inherent in hitchhiking, this practice appears relatively safer and more common in Europe than in other regions of the world.

Tickets/Passes and Reservations: Get as much of what you will need for your trip in the United States. These include your tickets, visas, insurance, medications, rail passes and reservations (hotel, airlines plane seat assignment, car rental). You can always re-confirm them, if need be, when overseas. By so doing, you will save considerable time, energy, and inconveniences. You may, also, save money. You may not be able to imagine these savings and the advantages of taking care of some of these aspects of your travel before you go, until you find yourself agonizing over your lack of foresight and foreknowledge. In several countries you may find yourself literally spending hours, days and weeks, and money, to succeed in obtaining the same information and services as are in the U.S. and that would have taken just a fraction of the time and cost to obtain. In other words, many of the things we take for granted here in the U.S. constitute luxuries in several countries. From transportation, to communication to speedy and courteous services, you will be amazed at the contrasts.

Other than for the above reasons, certain discount opportunities, such as some railway passes do have stipulations requiring the passes to be purchased in the United States, to qualify.

Warranties: Do not rely on them. Carry out your

shopping on the assumption that there will be no reasons or cause for you to return the items for a refund or exchange, or to rely on the warrantee. Assume you never got one. Warranties and guarantees are not things you should take seriously when overseas. Surely, if you request a copy, you will get them, both, verbally and/or in writing, but often they are not worth much. In practice, you will have a hard time recovering on the strength of such warranties. This is not to say you should not ask for them or safeguard them, if you receive one. With every generalization, there are some exceptions. Your best approach is to examine thoroughly your agreements and purchases before you commit yourself or pay for them.

Automobile Accessories: If you plan to drive abroad, be aware that in several countries and regions, Europe included, certain accessories are standard, and are required in cars. Traffic police may stop you to check for these items. They include an emergency first-aid kit, and in some places, a jack, a spare tire, an emergency reflective triangular plate. Operating an automobile not equipped with these accessories may result in delays and/or fines. It is prudent, if you are going to drive overseas to find out the practices and requirements of that country. Your local Automobile Association should be able to assist you.

What to carry or pack: This is a subject that is not limited to international travelers. Most travelers, including seasoned travelers face the same issue. You are, therefore, not alone if you are concerned. And, to say that there is a universally accepted answer will be a joke. Obviously, you cannot carry more than what you have or can afford: While it will be up to you to decide really what is important to you, to have to carry, here are a few pointers and some things you must give careful consideration to: (a) You are only entitled to a certain number of free check-in luggages and each luggage limited to a specified weight, beyond, of which, you will be required to pay for the excess. Ask yourself, if you are within the limit and if not, if you can afford the extra cost of additional lugagges or over-weight luggages. (b) Traveling light is the ideal way to go, but in doing so, you should not sacrifice the convenience of having what you really need, or else you will have to deal with the risk and price of not taking the item(s) along with you.

Remember, you are going to a foreign country, and perhaps to a location where finding even the most essential commodities and services might not be available or may be quite expensive, or, where finding those things you need might be very time-consuming, a hassle, or even impossible? But does this mean, then stuffing you baggage with every thing imaginable? Not necessarily. Traveling light after all has a lot of advantages. Besides cost considerations, it is less aggravating, less stressful and could be time-saving. It allows you the freedom you need to react quickly, walk faster, (if need be) keep an eye on your belongings, and catch up with late commitments.

For one, thing it gives you an edge for consideration when bargaining with hotels, airlines, and taxis. Of course, if your luggage is so small to qualify as a carry-on or hand luggage, you can kiss luggage insurance good bye.

All said and done, the real questions you should ask yourself as you consider any particular item for packing are: (1) Do I really need it? Is it essential? Will I use it?, (2) If yes, to question 1, is the item cheaper and readily available where I am going. Obviously if the answer is yes and no, respectively, for the two questions, then go for it. If a lighter, but durable, form of the item is available take it, and if the item is versatile and with multiple uses, you have a must-take item for the trip. To facilitate your packing and to ensure that nothing important is left behind or left undone, a comprehensive final checklist has been provided to you elsewhere in this book. Remember, do not over do it. Research indicates many travelers do not get around to use many of the things they carry with them. And, please do not take what you cannot afford to lose.

Finally, your packing plan should include considerations for airline requirements. Some airlines restrict certain items in the cabin or in carry-on bags. There are the more familiar and perhaps obvious items generally prohibited by all airlines. These are listed elsewhere in this chapter. There are, of course, the not so familiar or obvious items such as battery-powered equipments, scissors and knives. The rules, however, from airline to airline. It is always advisable to check with the airlines.

Get The Name. As you make your plans to travel,

you will, in more than one occasion have to deal with different individuals, including travel agents, travel counselors, ticket agents, airline personnel, hotel and automobile rental reservation clerks. Because some of the information they will be providing you may determine how your trip turns out, it is prudent that you make a note or log of the person(s) you speak to including the day and time. In the event of any mix-up, this will provide you with some basis to establish your case. It makes your story credible. Whenever possible, request a written confirmation of your reservations and any important agreements made between you and the other party.

Inventory: Maintain an inventory of your luggage and have the list in a separate place. A list of what is contained in each luggage would be very useful for identification and to establish a claim in the event of a loss. Similarly, keep a log of all purchases made, including the prices paid for each item. Also, note the form of payment, whether in local or hard currency.

Jokes: Avoid stupid and careless remarks particularly, around airport premises or in the plane. They could disrupt your trip and send you to jail. Statements or conversations about or relating to bombs, grenade, terrorists and terrorism, drugs, hijacking are usually sensitive to most travelers and law enforcement authorities. Some persons, particularly law enforcement officers may take it seriously, even when you consider it to be only a joke. The consequences can be painful and could ruin your trip. Keep away from these words and lines of conversations that may employ their usage.

Checking and Boarding: Do it on time. You have spent weeks, perhaps months preparing for your trip; do not mess it up by being tardy. Tardiness could cause you, your trip and your luggage. It could even cause you your to loose money, especially, if you are traveling on a restricted ticket.

On the day of your trip whether to, or from your destination, allow yourself ample time. Try to get to the airport at least two to two and half hours before scheduled departure; and when boarding announcements are made proceed immediately to the departure gate. Arriving early will allow you time to check-in your luggage and get a seat

assignment if you have not already done so.

Upon arrival at the airport, quickly check-in your luggage and get a seat assignment and boarding pass. Then, proceed to the appropriate boarding gate, or as soon as your are allowed to. In some countries, including the United States, getting to the airport, depending on the city, the day and hour of day, could be time consuming. Worst of it, in some countries, particularly developing countries, the time required to check-in and to go through various immigrations, customs and security formalities can be enormous and so is the risk of missing your flight and other scheduled connections. You can minimize this risk, including the chances of being bumped, by giving yourself ample time. The quicker you get through the formalities and into the boarding gate, the better. There are numerous experiences of travelers who make it through to their destination just to find out that their luggage did not, because they checked in late. Similarly, there are instances where the luggage makes it through to the destination, but the owners missed the flight because they were late in boarding.

Bumped: If you are denied boarding and bumped by an airline because of overbooking, in which case they have more passengers scheduled and ticketed for the flight than these are available seats, take heart. You may have recourse. Depending upon whether you are voluntarily or involuntarily bumped, you may be entitled to compensation by the airline. But, remember, the mere fact that you are booked and have a ticket for the flight does not automatically qualify or entitle you to fly, nor does it entitle you or to a compensation if you are bumped. Failure to confirm or re-confirm your flight within the time required (usually 72 hours), or to arrive and/or check-in on time as stipulated in your ticket, may result in forfeiture of your right to fly and to a seat on the plane.

Re-Confirming Flights: The general rule with international airline tickets and reservations is that you re-confirm your flight within 72 hours. This could be done in person or over the phone. Do not take this for granted. You stand to loose your original reservation and seat in the plane, if you fail to confirm. Many airlines take it seriously, and will waste no time selling your seat. And, by the way, when you re-confirm your flight request, for confirmation number and the name of the airline personnel attending to you.

Canceled/Delayed Flights: Flight delays and cancellations are not unusual, and the effects on some travelers could be frustrating. This is all the more reason some travelers carry flight cancellation insurance coverage. The reasons for delays and cancellations vary, and may or may not entitle you to compensation, let alone, to special considerations.   It is very unlikely you can do much about it. In the instance of a protracted delay or cancellation, most airlines will often provide the travelers with alternative options and services, including meals, and lodging at no extra expense to the traveler. Sometimes, you may just have to request these services. And as upset as you may be, try not to loose your composure. In the event of flight cancellations or delays does the traveler have a legal recourse or is entitled to financial compensation? Maybe, maybe not. The rules governing flight delays and cancellations vary from country to country and, in some cases, among airlines. Unless your carrier is a U.S. based or U.S.registered airline, do not count your blessings. You may be just be wasting your time and money. In case you did not know, flight delays and cancellations are much more prevalent in developing countries. In may of these countries, do not even expect an explanation nor apologies, since none may be forthcoming. Nevertheless, do ask, and request for a substitute arrangement. If you have a suggestion on how you can be helped, make it. You may get what you ask for, especially, if your request is reasonable.

Valuables and Registration: If you plan to travel out with an item that may be subject to import duty by the U.S. Government, you may consider registering it with the U.S. Customs before you go. And if you do, retain your copy of the registration. You could have your valuables registered with the U.S. Customs at the airport, or you could check with the nearest customs office for a location. A list of U.S. Customs District Offices can be found in **Appendix E**. Remember, failure to register your valuables and other items of value may subject these items to duties when you return.   One way you can eliminate the need to register with the customs at the time of departure is to obtain an ATA Carnet. See the section on Carnet in this chapter for additional information.

Dealing with foreign law enforcement authorities: Be smart, be alert and be polite. You need these virtues when dealing with foreign law enforcement personnel, including the police, customs and immigrations. On your trip, you will very likely make contact with customs and immigration officers. How you present yourself and interact with these officials are important and may very well determine how you start-off your first few hours or day in the foreign country. In dealing with customs and immigrations and all law enforcement officers try to (1) be polite; (2) speak clearly and coherently, particularly, in stating the purpose of your trip; (3) do not fraternize or flirt with foreign law enforcement officers. They are not a breed to be trusted with your secrets or jokes, besides, you may be risking your stay. (c) Stick only to the questions asked you and avoid volunteering information. (d) If you must "declare" what you are carrying, then, do so, and do not leave out any item. Describing the contents of your luggage as "personal items" will be subject to less scrutiny than if the contents are for sale or for business. (e) Avoid carrying any goods that may be considered as contraband or subject to quantity limitations. Most non-prescription drugs are likely to be illegal, and so are pornographic materials. The quantity of liquor, cigarettes, and tobacco products you may bring or carry into a country as duty-free may also be limited. Check with your travel agent for duty-free items, and limitations, for the countries you plan to visit..

Baggage Storage Facilities: Do not leave your luggage unattended or in the care of a stranger. Most international airports are equipped with baggage storage facilities, where, for a small fee, you can store your baggages. Although many of these facilities operate seven days a week, 24 hours a day there are variations from airport to airport. In some of these facilities you can leave your baggage with them for no minimum time, and for a maximum of up to several days. Obviously you do not want to leave your luggage in these places for too long. And please, take your valuables with you, including your passport, tickets, credit cards and travelers checks. Make sure the luggage left behind have locks and your identification tag. Collect a receipt and keep it safe. If you lose your receipt you may find it difficult to re-claim your luggage. Other than storage facilities at the airports, safety lockers could be found in train stations of large cities.

Some of your excess luggages could be safely stored in these lockers for a very short period. Lockers found in Western Europe are safer than those in countries in Africa, South America and Asia.

Hotel Reservation from the Airport: For those who like to brave it by not making advance hotel reservations, you may want to know that at most international airports, there are often, specially marked or located telephones directly hooked up with the major hotels in the city. There is often, no cost to you in using these phones. All you have to do is lift up the phone and a hotel reservation clerk will be on the line to assist you. Most of these hotels also, operate free transportation to and from the airport. If you can not locate any of these phones, inquire at the information desk, located in every airport.

Finding Lodging: Finding a place to lodge is not usually difficult if you have the money to spend. However, if you are on a tight budget, you may have to do some comparison shopping, including toning down on the quality of services you expect from lodging facilities. Many large hotels in the U.S. have international subsidiaries or have reciprocal referral agreements, which makes it easier for international travelers in the U.S. to reserve accommodation overseas. All it may take is just a phone call. You could also make arrangements for lodging through your travel agents, and room-finding services provided by some international airlines tourist offices, student organizations, youth organizations, youth hostels, YMCAs, YWCAs.

Lastly, you could utilize travel guide and other publications.

Many of them list the names and addresses of a variety of foreign hotels, boarding houses or pensions, youth hostels and camps with detailed description and ranking, including price information. Do not forget, upon arrival in your destination, you can always, after the first night, find an alternative cheaper facility elsewhere, nearby. This is usually easier if you are located downtown, within the city, since you could literally do your search on foot as opposed to using a taxi. Do not get discouraged by signs saying "No Vacancy", go ahead an inquire, a room could be available right at that minute.

Besides, it is not uncommon to find such signs, even when there are vacancies. Occasionally, management forgets to take down the "no-Vacancy" signs. You can save yourself a lot of money, if you conduct your own search for lodging than to rely on your travel agent. This is important, since most travel agents/agencies operate largely on commission basis, and many not commit the time and interest to finding you a real bargain. Remember, finding overseas accommodations for travelers is not their specialty.

Lodging: A variety of lodging facilities and arrangements is available overseas. They include hotels (different sizes, types, and qualities) bread and breakfast, boarding houses, or pensions, villas, apartments, private homes, inns, youth hostels, student hotels, farm houses, camps, parks, road-side shelters, home exchange programs, and the Ys (YMCAs , YWCAs).

Addresses and telephone numbers of some of these facilities can be found in many special interest travel guides and from travel agents, foreign tourist offices and foreign embassies. You could, also, contact some of the organization specialized in one or more of the lodging types.

In planning and making reservations for your lodging, do not forget to discuss meal plans. Meal options vary, depending on the type of lodging or accommodation arrangements.

Some plans may include breakfast, while others may not. Similarly, meal plans alone, or as part of a package may include one, two or three meals a day, and may, or may not include weekends. Obviously, some comparison-shopping on your part may be a prudent thing to do, particularly, if you are looking for substantial savings. Do not forget, some packages that include room and board sometimes turn out to be cheaper, although this depends to a large extent, on the type of meal plans included. And when you make your reservation or sign the contracts, it is important not to forget to read the fine prints to ensure that what you pay or will pay for, is what you bargained.

Remember, with meal plans, there might be some restrictions which may, or may not include your favorite menu. As always the case, you do also have the choice of taking care of your food needs, outside any formal plans. In most large cities, particularly, in Europe and in other developed countries, you will have no problems, finding a wide variety of food houses, including several familiar American dishes and fast food restaurants.

Camping Carnet: If you plan to camp overseas, the international camping carnet could save you money. You can apply for a copy from the National Campers and Hikers Association at 7172 Transit Rd. Buffalo NY 14221 tel. (716) 634-5433.

U.S. Embassies Abroad and Holidays: Be aware that U.S. Embassies and consulates abroad observe a number of holidays, and are, therefore, closed during those holidays. For the most part, they observe both U.S. holidays and public holidays of the host country. See Appendix w for a country by country list of commercial holidays.

What the U.S. Embassies and Consulates Can and Cannot Do: The U.S. embassies and consulates abroad provide a number of services to Americans. A list of these services is provided in Chapter 27 & 28. While you may be tempted, in desperation, to seek their assistance remember, that embassies and consulates do not engage in travel agency functions. Approaching them for assistance, for example, to change your itinerary, re-issue your ticket may yield you very little positive results. And, certainly, embassies and consulates will not be able to assist you in such things as recovering your lost or damaged luggage or cashing your checks. Although they may direct you to assistance elsewhere, they are much more concerned with emergency and life threatening issues affecting you and other American citizens.

Catching Local (domestic) Flights and Other Transportation: Talk of orderliness and timeliness? Do not expect to find that when taking domestic flights in many countries, particularly, in developing countries. Delays are rampant, planes are often overbooked and you may have to engage in some hustling if you really want to fly or travel from one point to another. This is true, even for other means of transportation. Do not be surprised to find fellow checked-in travelers surging, and running into the waiting plane. And even after all of this, do not be surprised to find someone occupying your seat, because it has been assigned to more than one person. It seems like a tradition in some environments. You may just have to learn and join them, at least in ensuring that you make the flight. In these type of environments, I usually put on my sneakers and travel light.

Vagabonds: In your trip around the world you will, from time to time, run into vagabonds. These individuals parade and roam around, inside and outside the airports, ticketing offices, ministries, and many other places where travelers and non-travelers alike go to apply for important documents. They are neither authorized nor employed by the respective agencies and offices, nor are their activities officially condoned. These vagabonds will often offer their services to you, promising to obtain for you in record time, whatever it is you need, be it boarding passes, visas, or just forms. And, they usually promise doing this for a reasonable price. Although many do in fact succeed in providing you with the requested services in real record time, their activities are often illegal and frowned upon by the government. You will be taking a big risk dealing with them, and this could get you into trouble, including jail time. Besides, you can not be so sure, who the person you are contracting, really is. He or she may well be an undercover police officer. By supporting these vagabonds and patronizing their activities you, may end up losing, not only time and money, but also, any documents you might have advanced to them. If you plan appropriately, you will often succeed in getting legitimately, whatever it is you are applying for. Just give yourself more time.

Filing (standing) On Line: As civilized and rational as this practice may be, and as common as we find it here in the U.S., you may not always find it so in some countries. Corruption, lawlessness, favoritism and nepotism abound in may parts of the world, and you will likely find yourself a "victim". And many times, it is so blatant and overt as to make you really mad. Well, stay calm, that is all the more reason I am letting you know well in advance. It is advisable in such situations not to emulate them. Educate them instead, but do so politely and with integrity. Point out to the individual and attending official or clerk, your disapproval. Very likely, yours may be the only open incident you will witness before you are attended to. In most instances, the cost to you is time, and with proper planning, you will emerge, having your needs met.

Searches and Seizures: As your travel abroad and around the world, you will find a variety of practices which at best, could be frustrating, time wasting, and perhaps in your belief and opinion, uncalled for. Some of these practices will include road blocks, spot-checks, searches and seizures. Like many other travelers, you will hope you do not become a target. While such a feeling is OK, do anticipate them, and when confronted by these circumstances, it is in your best interest to cooperate. You will lose less time if you remain calm, and speak out politely, as opposed to acting confrontational, questioning the officer's authority, or showing signs of anger and disapproval. Law enforcement officers expect to be obeyed and respected. This is true in the U.S. and equally true of foreign law enforcement officers you will come across during your trip abroad.

Spot-checks are common in airports, but they could happen any where. A spot-check may just call for you to show or provide the officer with certain documents they normally will expect of you. Other times, they might lead to an elaborate search of your person, and your luggage. Female travelers should not expect much privacy as some foreign law enforcement officers can be especially malicious and "dirty".

Do not be surprised, if in the process the officer tells you that an item in your possession is a contraband and, therefore, will be confiscated. This is true even for such items that, in fact, are not prohibited. In other words, you may be unfortunate to come across an unscrupulous official who, in reality, would like to have your item, but figures the easiest way is to tell (scare) you that it is prohibited. When confronted with this type of situation, stay calm and polite. However, you can do one of two things. (1) Consider it a gift and let him or her have the item, particularly, if you can do without it. Besides, this may be all that the person wanted, and letting it go will likely be the end of the search or inspection. (2) Alternatively, request to speak to the boss. Chances are that the officer may, in a clever way, refuse to grant your request, but may turn around and let you keep your item. This may turn out to be the case, particularly if the original motive was suspect. On the other hand, you may have your request to see the higher in command, who may over rule the junior officer or who may reiterate the facts of the law to you.

As for road blocks, expect much more of these in developing countries of Africa, South America and in communist and police states. Routine road blocks often require checking of travel documents (passports, visas, inoculation certificate for required shots, purchase receipts); and if your are a resident or citizen, you tax receipts and voting registration. In some road blocks officers may inspect your travel luggage.

Unnecessary IDs: Before taking off on your trip, carefully go through your wallet and examine your identification cards (IDs). Remove those IDs you will not need, particularly those that could implicate and/or complicate your travels abroad. Implicating or "killer" IDs are those IDs that you do not need abroad and that may invite intense questioning by law enforcement officers. Included in this category are Federal, State and local government job IDs. IDs that indicate your title and position should also be left at home, more so, if you work in a "sensitive" industry, including weapon manufacturing nuclear laboratories, security and investigating agencies and law enforcement. Definitely, you may not need such IDs for any reason to justify the potential cost. You can, also, safely avoid using such titles as president, chairperson, director. Use instead,the common and simple titles such as Mr. Miss or Mrs., or Reverend. After all, you can have a perfectly nice time without these avoidable pieces of IDs and titles. Remember, you want to always keep a low profile when traveling abroad.

Stop-Over Flights: Unless it is necessary, always avoid stop-over flights and take direct flights instead. By so doing, you will minimize the risk of flying (including landing and take-offs), as well as save time. You also avoid such inconveniences as having, is some cases, to subject yourself to security checks. Although transit travelers rarely go through this, it is not an uncommon practice in some countries.

Acceptable Credit Cards: Not all credit cards are widely accepted overseas. The best cards, and with the most world-wide recognition and acceptance are American Express, Visa, MasterCard, Dinners Clubs, and Carte Blanche. If you have other credit cards, you may consider leaving them at home. Department stores and oil companies cards are neither popular not acceptable.

Buying Prescription and Other Drugs Unless for very quick expiring medications, fill all of your prescriptions in the U.S. before you go. Because of the lack of rigid controls on drugs and other pharmaceutical products in certain countries, particularly, in developing countries, there have been numerous case of expired and adulterated drugs being sold. This is true, even among many of the supposedly, registered and professionally staffed chemists as they are sometimes referred to overseas. The proliferation of street-side drug vendors, unlicensed and non-professional pharmacists adds even more to the risk of endangering your life when you fill your prescriptions overseas.

An additional reason for getting your prescriptions in the U.S. is that you may not be able to find your favorite brand overseas. There is, of course, the likelihood that the nearest pharmacy may be several miles away and/or with limited operating hours. Finally, do not forget that in several countries, there is acute shortage of drugs. The drugs you need may therefore, may not be available, and if you do find them, they may command exorbitant price tags, perhaps turning out more expensive than the same drugs in the U.S.

It is for these reasons that you should seriously consider carrying along extra medications. This should include both prescription and non-prescription (over-the-counter) medications. On the other hand, if you must fill all, or some part of your medications abroad, do so only, at large, professionally attended drug stores. Do not forget to request generic prescription from your physician before you go, since names of drugs abroad may differ from those in the U.S.

Authentication Services: Foreigners engaged in some official businesses and transactions are occasionally required to submit only authenticated (not notarized) documents. These documents, most of which carry or require official seals, include birth certificate, marriage license, school transcripts and divorce papers. If you must submit documents to foreign governments, agencies or institutions, find out if notarized copies are acceptable or if they must be officially authenticated. To have your documents authenticated call or write: Authentication Service Foreign Affairs Center, Bureau of Administration,

United States Department of state, 2201 C. St. NW Rm. 2815, Washington, D.C. 20520 tel: (202)647-7735.

Air Passes: This is another money-saving option, similar to rail passes. Air passes are particularly useful for those planning to engage in extensive traveling within a particular country or region. They often allow for multiple stops and unlimited mileage within the specific limitations of the particular pass. Air passes are common with European airlines. If you are interested in air passes, contact the respective airlines. Remember that air passes have their restrictions, and may not be cheaper or a money-saving alternative to every traveler. Your travel plans and the cost of alternative plans will help you determine the suitability of air passes.

Courier: If you have what it takes, you could fly for free or for a considerably cheaper cost as a courier. Good candidates for courier service are travelers who (1) are not inconvenienced traveling alone (i.e., can travel alone), (2) are flexible with their travel plans, (3) do not have baggages to check in since as a courier all you may carry is your carry-on bag. What the courier companies basically need from you is your checked baggage allowance. Of course, the courier company hopes you will deliver the baggage claim tags and the baggages to their agent on arrival. You can expect the courier company to check you in at the port of departure, and have their agent wait for you at the airport or at a designated location overseas. Courier services may be for one-way or round-trip travel. Remember as a courier you may have to subsidize part of the fare and/or be required to pay a nominal fee for the service, depending on the supply and demand for couriers. It may, also, depend on whether you are dealing with a broker or courier company. Of course you are expected to make arrangements for your visas and other entry requirements.

Traveling Standby: This type of traveling can be a source of large savings, if, indeed, you can standby . To be able to take advantage of this service, you need much flexibility with your travel schedule as well patience. Obviously, you must be willing to tolerate disappointments, especially those resulting from your not being able to make a particular flight. As a standby traveler, expect to purchase your standby ticket on a short notice.

Beyond that, it is nothing more than engaging in the waiting game at the check-in counters of the airline, and praying for seat in the plane. Remember, once on board, you will enjoy the same privileges as any regular fare passenger. The problem is only with securing a seat on board. As a standby passenger, you will have less luck on weekends, holidays and other peak traveling periods. On the contrary, you may find better luck at night, off peak seasons and during the weekdays. Various airlines, however, have their definition and rules regarding standbys. Besides, standby arrangements may not always exist with every airline. For these reasons, it is advisable to check with the airlines first, and inquire if standby fares are in existence for your intended destination . If one is available, find out what the conditions are.

Alternatively, you may employ the services of some companies that, also, specialize in standby tickets. Most of the companies require registrations or service fee.

Frequent Flyers: The frequent flyer mileage program has become a growing phenomenon in the world of travels, and it will be unimaginable not to take advantage of it. Previously offered, only by the airlines, today, even credit card companies and automobile rental agencies and big hotels are getting involved one way or the other, offering frequent flyers and frequent users, opportunities for savings towards that future trip. Besides, as a frequent flyer, you may qualify for other complementary services offered by the airline such as upgrading to first class and use of special lounges at the airport. The problem, of course, is that most travelers who can benefit, because they happen to fly more frequently, do not sign up for these free services and/or do not take the time to register or maintain a good record of amount of air miles accumulated during their trips. On the other hand, there are many travelers who have accumulated frequent flyer miles (points), but are yet to utilize them. You may loose those points. Read the fine prints. To learn more about frequent flyers and similar programs, contact the respective airlines. Many U.S. and European carriers presently have frequent flyer programs. Some newsletters and magazines, in addition, have begun to emerge, focusing on the frequent flyer and mileage programs.

Charters: Charter flights are increasing becoming very popular with budget-conscious travelers. Substantial savings can be accrued traveling on a chartered carrier. Although charter packages have been around for a long time, they are beginning to add new twists and incentives that appeal to today's sophisticated travelers. If you are considering traveling on a chartered flight either as part of a group as is often the case, or solo, you should be well aware of the characteristics and limitations of this form of travel arrangements. They include (1) advance reservation and payment, (2) sacrificing some of your comfort; (3) penalties, forfeiture of some or all of your payments in event you cancel; (4) possible postponement or cancellation of the trip by the charter operator. Generally, charters do not provide the type of flexibility as do regular flights. Some of the restrictions mentioned above may, additionally, turn out to be costly, when the time lost, and inconvenience are factored in. Of course, there are rules and regulations governing charter operators, such as those dealing with refunds, in event the operators cancel the charter. But, none of those regulations will adequately compensate you for a charter trip gone sour. It is, therefore, advisable to search around carefully for reputable and reliable specialized charter or tour operators, and compare cost. As you make your research, inquire further what services are included and what are excluded in the arrangements and the terms of the contract. The same level of prudence you apply when dealing with airlines must be applied when dealing with cruise line charters. If you are concerned about the reputation of a charter agency, check with the local Better Business Bureau. You may also check with the American Society of Travel Agents, or the National Association of Cruise only Agents listed in Appendix 6E. A trip cancellation insurance is recommended for travelers on a charted carrier.

Rebators: Rebators, and rebator services are a growing phenomena in the travel industry. Rebators operate, more or less, like travel agents except that they may charge you a fee for their service in exchange for passing on to you some portion or all of the commissions traditionally available to travel agents. Depending on the amount of travel you plan to make, the savings could be substantial. Of course, rebators are not necessarily travel agents or agencies, and are not as organized as travel agents. Find out more about

APPENDIX F

HOW TO SEND MONEY/TELEX/TELEGRAM/CABLEGRAM
(From the U.S.)

Sending Money to An American Overseas
8AM - 8PM weekdays; 9AM - 3PM Saturday; 202-647-5225

The State Department strongly encourages you to use commercial services, such as credit card advances, ATMs or Western Union. Locations of ATMs around the world can be found at www.visa.com and www.mastercard.com. Western Union services are described at www.westernunion.com and 1 800 325 6000. These services are generally much faster than the State Department transfer system.

If you cannot use a commercial service, the State Department will help you transfer money to a U.S. citizen suffering a financial emergency abroad. When you use this service, we establish a trust account in the recipient's name and send the money overseas. We charge a $30 processing fee. Remember this service is only for emergencies.

When we receive the funds, we authorize the appropriate U.S. Embassy or Consulate abroad to disburse the money. Funds are disbursed only during normal office hours, not during weekends or local holidays when the Embassy or Consulate is closed. The U.S. citizen abroad must contact the Embassy or Consulate to arrange receipt. Even if the funds are sent to the State Department in dollars, they are normally disbursed in the foreign country's currency. Whatever method you choose, be sure to provide your name, address and telephone number, as well as the recipient's name and overseas location. Otherwise, the transfer may be significantly delayed.

WESTERN UNION: Funds sent by Western Union arrive at the State Department within a few hours. Western Union charges a fee based on the amount sent and these fees can be substantial. Call Western Union at 1-800-325-6000 or 4176 or go online at www.westernunion.com and follow their instructions to transfer money using a major credit card. If you do not have a major credit card, call your local Western Union agent for instructions. Tell Western Union to send the money and message to: Overseas Citizens Services (OCS), Department of State, Washington, D.C. 20520, code (overseas emergency) and city (DC). We have a Western Union checkwriter in our office. If you send it to any other Western Union office in Washington, it will be significantly delayed.

BANKWIRE: Bankwire transfers take several days. Tell your bank that you want to wire the desired amount, plus $42, to Bank of America, Department of State Branch, 2201 C St. NW, Washington, DC 20520 at 202-624-4750 via ABA Number: 114000653; Account Number: 7476363838; Account Name: PUPID State Department; Special Instructions: OCS/Trust for benefit of (recipient's name), Embassy/Consulate (city, country). (The $42 dollar surcharge will cover processing fees assessed by the bank and the State Department.)

Other Methods: The slowest way to send money is by cashier's check or money order.
OVERNIGHT MAIL: Send a cashiers check or money order for the desired amount plus $30 (our fee), made payable to the Department of State, to: Department of State, CA/OCS, Room 4811, 2201 C St. NW, Washington, D.C. 20520.

the particular rebator its charges and much better, get references, before committing your time and money.

Bucket Shops and Discounted Tickets and Wholesalers: With careful researching you may be able to purchase air tickets at even a deeper discount from the so called "discount travel agencies" or "bucket-shops", and/or from wholesalers, often called "consolidators". Due to a number of reasons, some of these "travel agents" are able to buy and/or obtain concessions from airlines, thus, allowing them to offer many times, an unusually sizable amount of discounts. If you are a traveler interested in this type of arrangements, you should expect certain restrictions on the tickets, including penalties for any deviation from the terms of the contract. Tickets bought from bucket shops and consolidators may carry non-refundable and non-endorsable clauses, and may require cash payments. Many reputable agencies will accept alternative means of payments, including credit cards. Be aware that not all travel agencies are bucket shops and that specialize in selling at deep discount. Importantly, most bucket shops are not registered travel agencies, as we know them. The same is true with consolidators, most of whom are just wholesalers, buying from the airline and selling to travel agencies or directly to the consumers. This means that great care and providence must be applied, should you chose to use their services. Certainly, there are a number of good and reputable ones, but the same is true for a number of flight-by-night agents and agencies. You may consider restricting your dealings with registered discount travel agencies. And like every opportunity to save a buck, do some shopping around, compare costs, risks terms of the contracts before letting go your money, and certainly check out the business before you go. Additional lists can be found in the travel column of most big national and international dailies, and, further, in the advertisement sections of most travel magazines and newsletters.

Travel Clubs/Airline Clubs: Travelers interested in special treats should consider joining a travel club. Advantages accruing to club members could be wide ranged and does vary from club to club. Depending on the club, privileges often include opportunities for better services, at a bargain price. Airline clubs are becoming common with major air carriers, and the privileges members enjoy can better be appreciated when, for example, you suddenly find yourself hustling and bustling at the check-in counter or looking lost, helpless, or tired at the waiting area. During this time, club members are probably relaxing, and being provided with "free" entertainment in a private lounge, exclusive to members. Even an opportunity to take showers often exist in such lounges for club members. Its VIP treatment all the way. For the majority of travel clubs, however, benefits, in the form of savings (ticket, hotels, rentals) can be expected, including last minute reservations, some insurance coverage and regular newsletters and toll-free numbers to keep members informed of bargain opportunities. Membership in travel clubs for the most part requires an annual membership fee that could range from $30 to $200. Furthermore, some clubs charge a one time initiation fee. Lifetime membership opportunities do exist, and for a nominal fee benefits could be extended to spouses..

Time Zone Differential: Just as there is time variation, between cities in the U.S., depending on where you live, such variations, also, exist between countries. In the U.S. we have five time zones: Pacific, Mountain, Central, Eastern, and Atlantic. For example, Los Angeles, California is in the Pacific, Montana, in the Mountain, Texas and Illinois, in the Central, New York and Washington D.C., in the Eastern, and Maine in the Atlantic time zones. For example, when it is 12 noon in New York, it is 11 a.m. in Chicago because it is 1 hour behind (-1 hour) Eastern Standard Time, and it is 9 a.m. in Los Angeles because Los Angeles is 3 hours behind (-3 hours) Eastern Standard Time. Since these variations exist between countries, you should be well aware of them since they will invariably affect your flight time and schedule of appointments. The time difference between U.S. Eastern Standard Time and foreign countries is provided in Appendix R. Familiarize yourself with the time zone differential, and make appropriate adjustments.

Learning to Use Foreign Currencies: Before you go abroad, familiarize yourself with the foreign currencies you will soon be using. Check out money exchange services here in the U.S. and exchange a few of your dollars for the foreign currencies. Besides the obvious advantage of having a few foreign currency on hand, upon arrival you should make a deliberate effort to understand how they are used. This will save you time, and minimize the chances of short-changing yourself or being short-changed. Some travelers wait and only start learning how to use a foreign currency upon arrival, but only to quickly find out that it is not as simple as they had previously thought.

Cash Machines: Automatic Teller Machines, or ATMs, as they are called are becoming very popular overseas, particularly in Western Europe. With your ATM card, you may be able to access the cash machines in the same way, and with the same ease as you do in the states. As usual, a personal identification number or PIN, is required. And like in the U.S. you may only access machines at certain ATMs. Two ATM system with world-wide locations are the CIRRUS and the Plus System. Find out if your ATM is part of these systems. And if they are, find out if they are available in the country and city you plan visiting. It is, also, important to check if your card and PIN number can be used at overseas locations. If not, your credit card company may issue a new access code or PIN valid for use overseas. To reach any of the two systems mentioned here, dial 1-800-THE-PLUS or 1-800 4-CIRRUS.

Place of Worship: Finding a place to worship while overseas is as simple as just asking. Your hotel desk clerk should be able to help you locate the nearest place of worship. Alternatively, the tourist information center or local phone book will do the same. As you journey around, however, remember that you may not necessarily find a denomination of your first choice. Just as some countries may be predominantly Christian, so too are some countries and regions dominated by non-Christian faith, such as Islam. In many countries you will find a mixture of minority and majority religious denominations and places of worship scattered here and there. There are, also, non-denominational houses of worship. The more flexible you are, the greater the chance of finding a place of worship or prayer center closer to where you may be staying. Further, there is the language issue. If your preference is for an English speaking place of worship, you may or may not be able to find one, but you can certainly enjoy the activities and recite your prayers even where the local language is the used in services.

Cruise Lines and Freighters: The difference between the two may be more of quality of service and trip completion time than any other factors. These differences are, also, reflected in the cost. Cruise lines are well specialized for providing an alternative, more romantic and equally comfortable means of traveling than by air or land, but at a longer time than by air. Freighters, on the other hand, take longer time than cruises liners for the same travel, carry fewer persons and of course charge considerable less. You may, in addition, have to be much more flexible with your travel schedule with freighters than with cruise lines. Long waits and frequent schedule changes are not uncommon. For some reasons, foreign vessels, for the same quality of service, generally, tend to charge less than their U.S. counterparts. Apply the same level of prudence in dealing with cruise lines and freighters as you do in deciding what airline to fly with . Some shopping around and cost comparison are important. Ticket terms and conditions for travel with a sea vessel are different from those on your airline ticket. Read the dotted lines carefully before signing and, before letting go your money.

Your Ticket: Make it a habit to check your tickets and reservation confirmation slips once you receive them. Many of the tickets, particularly, your plane and rail tickets and passes have caveats and other details you must be clearly aware of before you go. You may ruin you entire trip, loose money and time, due in part, to information on your tickets and reservation slip you overlooked or did not know. Immediate and careful examination will give you ample time to correct mistakes, if any, as well request for clarifications, if you do not understand. Inquire about the meaning of any unfamiliar codes used, and any restrictions. Importantly, cross-check the information on the tickets with your intended itinerary.

Meal on Flight: Between international flights and domestic flights expect a wide range and variation in the quality of services provided. This is particularly true with meals. Meals on domestic flights are relatively poorer. When overseas, you may want to eat before boarding or carry some snacks with you. Do not be surprised, if no foods at all are served on journeys of reasonable distance. I have had to deal with this on more than one occasion during my trips in some African countries.

Travel Luggages: Specifications and Allowances:

As you go shopping for your luggage and carry-on cases and bags, you should be aware that airlines do have specifications. Any luggage exceeding the required dimensions for check-in and carry-on luggages may be refused. Generally, the maximum total linear dimension for a check-in-luggage ranges between 45 and 62 inches (i.e. length and width and height). Luggage with sizes no more than 21 x 16 x 48" or 23 x 13 x 9" are ideal. For carry-on, each piece cannot exceed 45 inches in total linear dimension, and must fit in the overhead luggage compartment or underneath the seat.

Equally important are the weight and amount of luggage you are entitled to. Most international airlines allow two pieces of free check-in luggage and one carry-on, per passenger, with each piece of check-in luggage not exceeding 70 lbs. Some airlines give first-class passengers allowances of up to 80 lbs, while some limit the allowances to economy class passengers to only 50 lbs. If you must carry more than two pieces of check-in luggage expect to pay extra. For heavier or larger luggage, the airline may refuse to carry them or may levy additional charges. It is better not to count on the latter.

Incidentally, specifications vary from carrier to carrier. You are, therefore, better off checking with the carrier you intend to use. Furthermore, these specifications may differ from those on domestic travels within a particular country, in which case, you may be asked have to pay extra. Again, check with your airline for guidelines on domestic flights regarding luggage requirements.

Language Barrier:

Unless English is the language of conversation in the country you plan to visit, or you are quite fluent in the language of your host country, you will, as I have, occasionally ponder, on how much you may be missing or how much exciting and easier your trip would have turned out, if only you understood and spoke the language. Well, you are not alone in this territory. Depending on the length and purpose of your trip, and how much real interest and planning time you have, you could do something about it. Some travelers enroll in language courses offered by a number of national and local organizations and schools. Others engage in home study and

self-tutoring, with the help of TVs videos, phrase books and cassette tapes. You could do any of these, or do nothing, and still have a perfectly exciting holiday. Yet, I must suggest that you familiarize yourself with a few conversational words and phrases of your host country. You will be amazed at the extra excitement and difference they will add to your trip. Check with your local colleges and libraries for basic language course offerings. Your local yellow pages and libraries would, also, have other resources, including names and addresses of foreign language institutes. There are, of course, the numerous books and other resources available in bookstores. Remember, the objective is not to be proficient in reading and writing the language, but in mastering a few important and common conversational phrases. Wouldn't you like to say "Thank you" to that cab driver, door man, waiter who just rendered you a magnificent service and in a language he or she understands?

Front Desk Service:

Not sure of something, lost, confused or forgotten? Ask the clerk at the front desk. Every hotel you will find during your trip overseas will certainly have a service desk or an information desk, with a clerk ready to assist you use them. In most cases, these clerks will have answers to most of your questions regarding your host country. If they do not know, most front desk clerks will gladly direct you to the appropriate places to get answers. They may even have stamps to sell to you. Do not, therefore, hesitate to approach them practically, on any matters of concern to you. And, while at the front desk do ask, or look around for other items of information. Hotel lobbies are often stuffed with local newspapers, maps, and other publications that you will find very useful as you explore your new environment. You may want to familiarize yourself with the language(s) spoken in the country you plan to visit. A country by country listing of official and other major languages is provided in Appendix Z

Stray Animals:

Afraid of animals, stray animals? Then, take precautions. In several parts of the world, particularly in rural communities of developing as well as some developed countries, animals, from dogs and cats, to pigs, goat, sheep and cows roam about freely. Do not be surprised also, finding yourself riding in a commercial vehicle next to these animals, or finding them in the company of local guests, or wandering around your place of residence. For the local inhabitants, these animals are, for the most part, not hostile nor a threat to them, and one will expect so for visitors. This, however, may not necessarily be true in all cases, particularly if your are not familiar with local signs and words used to communicate with these animals. Besides, some appear to be able to sense some strangeness in you in which case their reaction may be unfriendly, and unpredictable at best. My advice, is not to cuddle them, or try to play with them. Keep moving and mind your business. The last thing you want is a bite from an animal you may perceive as friendly. Remember, rabies from dogs, are alive in many developing countries. Beware!

Things Not to Buy Overseas: As you plan to go shopping overseas beware! You may buy things, but may not be able to import them into the United States. There are numerous commodities, items of seemingly, common and harmless use that are prohibited entry by the U.S. Government. These items range from certain birds, pets and wildlife, and products made from them to plants and animals. These are in addition, to many contraband items, considered dangerous and a threat to security. The latter may include unlicensed firearms, illegal drugs and pornographic materials. Beside your concern for U.S. Government requirements, and lists of prohibited items, do not forget the requirements and lists of the host country. Every country has a list of items you cannot bring in, nor take out. If you are not sure, always check with that country's customs office.

Beware of Street-Side Vendors: Like in the United States, you will find them in almost every country, particularly in the large urban centers. You will find them trading in items ranging from ornaments, jewelry, radios, stereo sets, to cameras and watches. While some of the articles they sell may be legitimately acquired, some may not. Many turn out turn out to be stolen goods. It is advisable to stay away from these street-side vendors. While their prices may be unusually attractive and tempting, their activity may be illegal, and their products fake and defective, and with no guarantees. There is, of course, the danger that you may be dealing with an undercover police officer or being set-up for a robbery. Make things easy for yourself. Avoid buying or dealing with

street vendors, whether they are registered or not.

Shopping Abroad: It is not always the case that you will find a better deal abroad. Those items you plan to buy may well turn out to be more expensive than at home. If you plan to buy any thing, it is advisable to develop a list of those items, including their U.S. prices. And while you comparison shop abroad, you should consider the taxes and duties that will be assessed on those items. You may have to pay the cost of transporting them to the U.S. Furthermore, you should consider, the exchange rate of the dollar vis-a-vis that country's currency.

If your shopping abroad, including, shopping for articles of clothing (shoes, shirts, skirt, blouses), and precious stones, you should be aware that there are significant differences between American sizes, and the sizes, as used in other parts of the world. To assist you, a guide has been provided in Appendix N. Similarly, you should be particularly careful as you shop around for precious stones. As you may already be aware of, fakes are common, and this is true, irrespective of the country of purchase. If you must shop for gems abroad, you may want to familiarize yourself with fake stones quite common in some countries. A shopper's guide is provided in Appendix 1A.

Stamps: Should you need local stamps while overseas you have a number of places to check, besides the post office. In some countries, stamps can be purchased from bookstores, department stores and stamp machines located at airports and railway stations. You may, also, be able to purchase stamps from shops located at the lobbies of hotels or from the front desk clerk. All you may need to do is ask.

Mail and Telephone Communication:
Communication in several countries is slow and, sometimes, down right inefficient when compared to the United States. And, you need to communicate this reality to your friends and relatives at home, lest they panic for fear of not hearing from you. Expect mails, including express deliveries to take between 2 to 4 weeks to reach the U.S. instead of the few days often promised or stated. The actual time will, of course, vary depending on what country you may be writing from. Communication, whether by mail or by phone is faster and much more efficient in

585

developing countries and in Western Europe than in other regions of the world. Developing countries tend to have the worst records. Not only do letters take long, telephone communication are either non-existent in most places, or do not function properly. Even reaching someone by phone from the U.S. may take you up to an hour, if you succeed. The circuits are often busy, or the connection at the other end is very poor. If you plan to write from overseas, then, keep this time frame in mind. And, if you chose to call, be prepared to spend time dialing and re-dialing, or perhaps spend time waiting on line in the central telephone office. Generally, the central telephone office or the post office provides the best chances to make calls or send telegrams. Even then, you may have to wait. Take time, therefore, to caution your loved ones here at home, before you go, not to have very high hopes of hearing from you as soon as you arrive and certainly not to panic as a result. To be sure, it is frustrating, but that is the way it is. Always send your letters by Airmail, just telling the postal officer that you would like to send your letter first class, may not be sufficient.

As an alternative, you may consider using the services of courier companies. Two well known International courier services are DHL and Federal Express. Although they are a lot more expensive than other mail services, they appear to be faster and more reliable. Before going, find out the branch offices of these companies nearest your overseas destination. Faxes are becoming popular, and you will likely find private agencies providing this and regular telephone services. Incidentally, some of these agencies have better luck getting their calls and transmission through. Of course, if you plan to use fax, do not forget to carry along the fax number (in the U.S.) you plan to forward your messages.

Public Restrooms: In many countries, public toilets or restrooms are few and poorly maintained. If all you want is to relieve your bowels, you should have little or no problems. On the contrary, if you are particular about cleanliness and other services, you may be in for a surprise. With the exceptions of urban centers of Western Europe and some developing countries, public restrooms are not generally well taken care of. Unless you have a really strong will to use one, you may find yourself totally turned off and the urge disappear in the face of a seeming "disaster zone". Expect

the following, hopefully it may not get worst than these: (1) the same facility may be used by both males and females, (2) broken toilets and sinks, (3) flooded toilets, (4) restrooms with urine and faeces on the floors, (5) restrooms with no flowing water, (6) maids cleaning the restrooms while you may be using it, and (7) restrooms without toilet papers or hand towels.

As you venture into the interiors of developing countries do not expect to find traditional toilets with water systems. Instead, you may find pits (both shallow and deep) or improvised gathering buckets, and open flat grounds for use by any one who so desires. I must add, the sight of some of these primitive toilet facilities can be frightening to use and aching to the legs. In several countries, you may also count out finding toilet tissues in their public toilets, including those at the airports and train stations. In some of these places, old newspapers and leaves substitute for toilet tissues. You can now see why I always travel with my own roll of toilet tissues.

Finally, remember that the word restroom is not universal; different names and signs are used to describe the same thing, including the equivalent of the word "toilet". If you are not sure ask. Besides, in some places the word "restroom" is used and understood literally, to represent the equivalent of a place to rest (eat, drink, or sleep). Do not be fooled or appear confused.

Water: In some parts of the world, water remains a scare resource. Potable water is scarce, and water for general purpose may not be readily available. Expect hotels without adequate water to shower, or with no hot water at all. This is true even in Europe. Of course, you may get some flimsy apologies and excuses from management, but the absence of water or hot water may be a regular occurrence rather than a sudden problem as they sometimes try to explain. Since your stay will very likely entail a hotel or similar lodging facility, find out from the reservation clerk if there is water available, and hot water, in particular, and if there are any limitations. This is important since there might be some rationing going on, in which case your room may be pre-programmed for just a few minutes of hot waters.

With regard to potable water, your best bet is to take the various precautions mentioned in Chapter

8. Not even the hotel clerks can truly guarantee the safety of the drinking water they serve you.

Beggars and Homeless Persons: As you journey round the globe, you will find beggars and homeless persons just as you will find them here in the U.S. This is common in large urban centers. It is uncertain, what to expect from these groups, as their mode of operation varies from country to country. Without a doubt, they can be a nuisance and a pest to travelers, and in some cases, a source of embarrassment. Its really up to you how you deal with them. In many countries, they will touch you, pull you, insult you, harass you and even rob you. Very often, a small token gift will satisfy them. Ironically, although they may complain of lack of food, most will not accept food, but will rather prefer money. However, you deal with this group of people, be careful, not to lose sight of your valuables, as many are in fact bona-fide professional pickpockets, luggage thieves and muggers. Many of them, including women and young children, are in fact not what they claim to be, but rather part of a robbery or extortion ring or gang in disguise. Stories of parents actually training their children in the act of begging, as well as a way of life, are common. Also, common is the reality of poverty in several parts of the world, contributing in part to these illegal practices.

Places and Gestures to Avoid: As safety concerns, without a doubt, will be paramount in your mind during your trip abroad, you ought to be careful on what you do, how and where you do it. There are places that will certainly open you up to interrogation and other actions that may invite jail term for you even though, a citizen doing the same thing may go "scott-free".

1.A partial list of places you should avoid include: (a) military facilities; (b) facilities, that manufacture military or security products; (c) places where protests/political rallies are being staged

2. A partial list of actions to avoid include:
(a) Burning or de-facing the national flag;
(b) Sitting down (in public) when the National Anthem is being played, when everyone else is standing up; or not taking off your hat or head gear in the same instance, when everybody else is doing so. (c) Making negative or derogatory remarks about the head of state, the military or the country and government as a whole; (d) Participating in rallies, riots, protests and strikes; (e) Taking photographs of military installations; (f) Taking photographs in the airport, or of the airport; (g) Taking photographs of communication facilities; (h) Defecating or urinating in public (even though you may find the latter common with local inhabitants); (i) Fraternizing or flirting with local law enforcement authorities; (j) Engaging in political discussions; (k) Engaging in discussions about, or where such words as explosives, bombs, grenades, revolt, over throw, coup and the like are used; (l) Carrying in public SPY, CIA, FBI and/or reading books that may be perceived as a source for sensitive information and for dangerous ideas; (m) Drunkenness and public nuisance; (n) drunken driving; (o) cursing. Remember, equal rights and freedom of speech and expression may be inalienable rights of U.S. citizens, in the States, and central to the constitution of the U.S. but may be hardly so in practice in many countries abroad. Being careless and not watching what you say, and do, how and where you say and do things, may just be an invitation for trouble abroad. It does not take much to stay out of these given areas, but first you must be aware of them.

The Key to a Successful Trip Abroad: A sense of humor, a positive attitude, patience, tolerance, flexibility, alertness and a careful review of the information provided in this book will assure a successful trip. With these things, you can guarantee yourself a rich, safe, exciting and successful trip abroad.

Chapter 36

References and Resources for Overseas Travelers

U.S. DEPARTMENT OF STATE
http://travel.state.gov

The following fourteen publications from the Department of State,(D.O.S.) Bureau of Consular Affairs (B.C.A) may be ordered, unless, otherwise indicated from the Superintendent of Documents, U.S. Government printing Office, Washington D.C. 20402; Tel. (202) 512-1800 (http://www.access.gpo.gov)

*Your Trip Abroad provides basic travel information - tips on passports, visas, immunizations, and more. It will help you prepare for your trip and make it as trouble - free as possible. (D.O.S. Publication # 10542, B.C.A. Revised April 1998)

*A Safe Trip Abroad gives travel security advice for any traveler, but particularly for those who plan trips to areas of high crime or terrorism. (D.O.S. Publication #10942, B.C.A. Revised March 2002)

*Tips for Americans Residing Abroad is prepared for the more than 2 million Americans who live in foreign countries. (D.O.S. Publication # 10391, B.C.A. Revised September 1996)

*Travel Tips for Older Americans provides health, safety, and travel information for older Americans (D.O.S. Publication, #10337, B.C.A. Revised August 1996)

*Tips for Travelers to Sub-Saharan Africa (D.O.S. Publication #10205, B.C.A. Revised October 1994)

*Tips for Travelers to the Caribbean (D.O.S. Publication #10439, B.C.A. Revised May 1997)

*Tips for Travelers to Central and South America (D.O.S. Publication #10407, B.C.A. Released October 1996)

*Tips for Travelers to Mexico (D.O.S. Publication #10571 B.C.A Revised August 1998)

*Tips for Travelers to the Middle East and North Africa (D.O.S. Publication #10850, B.C.A. Revised August 2001)

*Tips for Travelers to the People's Republic of China (D.O.S. Publication #10271, B.C.A. Revised October 1995)

*Tips for Travelers to South Asia (D.O.S. Publication)

*Tips for Travelers to Canada (D.O.S. Publication)

* Tips for Travelers to Russia. (D.O.S. Publication #10844, B.C.A. Revised May 2001)

Tips for Business Travelers to Nigeria (D.O.S. Publication #10786, February 2001)

Advance Business Scams (D.O.S. Publication)

*****Tips for Students** (D.O.S. Publication)

*****Tips for Women Traveling Alone** (D.O.S. Publication #10867, May 2002)

Other Department of State Publications and Resources

*****Americans Abroad** provides basic up to date information on passport, foreign laws, customs, personal safety and helpful travel tips. You may request for a free copy by writing to: Americans Abroad, Consumer Information Center, Pueblo, CO 81009. Multiple copies of 25 may be purchased from the Superintendent of Documents, U.S. Government Printing Office, Washington D.C. 20402; Tel: (202) 512-1800.

*****Foreign Entry Requirements** lists visa and other entry requirements of foreign countries and tells you how to apply for visas and tourists cards. Updated Yearly. Order this publication for 50 cents from the Consumer Information Center, Dept. 438T, Pueblo, CO 81009. (D.O.S. Publication, B.C.A. Revised May 2002)

Key Officers of Foreign Service Posts gives addresses and telephone, telex, and FAX numbers for all U.S. embassies and consulates abroad. ****(NOTE: When writing to a U.S. embassies and consulates, address the envelope to the appropriate section, such as Consular Section, rather than to a specific individual.) This publication is updated 3 times a year and may be purchased from the Superintendent of Documents, U.S. Government Printing Office, Washington, D.C. 20402; Tel. (202) 783-3238.

*****Diplomatic List** lists the addresses, and telephone and fax numbers of foreign embassies and consulates in the U.S. including the names of key offices. This publication is updated quarterly and may be purchased from the Superintendent of Documents. U.S. Government Printing Office. (D.O.S. Publication).

*****Passports the Easy Way** provides information on where to apply, how to apply and the best time to apply for a U.S. Passport, including renewals; Everything you need to know about getting a passport- cost, requirements etc. (D.O.S. Publication)

Background Notes are brief, factual pamphlets on each of 170 countries. They give current information on each country's people, culture, geography, history, government, economy, and political conditions. They also include a factual profile, brief travel notes, a country map, and a suggested reading list. To place orders or for information contact: Superintendent of Documents. U.S. Government Printing Office, Washington D.C. 20402: Tel. (202) 512-1800. Be sure to indicate the specific country or area you will be traveling to with your request.

*****Consular Information Sheets** is part of the U.S. State Department's travel advisory instruments. It covers such matters as location and telephone number of the nearest U.S. Embassy, health conditions, entry regulations, crime and security conditions that may affect travel, drug penalties and areas of instability. Consular Information Sheets are available for most countries. For a free copy of the Consular Information Sheet for the country you plan to visit write to the state Department, Bureau of Consular Affairs, Washington D.C. 20520.
 *****U.S. Consul Help Americans Abroad** explains some of the functions and services of U.S. Embassies and Consulates abroad. (D.O.S. Publication #10176 B.C.A. June 1994)

*****Crises Abroad-What the State Department Does** available free of charge from Department of State, CA/PA Rm. 5807 Washington D.C. 20520. (D.O.S. Publication #10176, B.C.A. June 1994)

International Parental Child Abduction available free of charge. Write to Office of Citizens Consular Services, Bureau of Consular Affairs, Department of State, Rm.4817 Washington D.C. 20520. (D.O.S. Publication #10862 B.C.A. Revised July 2001)

*International Adoptions discusses the issue of International Adoptions including valuable tips, guidelines and procedures. This circular (publication) is available free of charge from the Department of State, Overseas Citizens Services or call (202) 647-2688.

*Travel Warnings on Drugs Abroad available free of charge from the Department of State, CA/PA Rm. 5807 Washington D.C. 20520. (D.O.S. Publication B.C.A. Revised February 2000)

***Travel advisories, issued by the State Department, caution U.S. citizens about travel to specific countries or areas. If you are concerned about existing conditions in a given area, contact your travel agent or airline, the nearest passport agency or the Department of State's Citizens Emergency Center at (202) 647-5225.

* Security Awareness Overseas: An Overview provides guidelines and tips on a variety of topics relating to personal safety and security while overseas.(D.O.S. Overseas Security Advisory Council, Bureau of Diplomatic Security).

U.S. DEPARTMENT OF COMMERCE

* Climates of the World provides data on climatic conditions around the world, including temperatures and precipitations. This publication may be ordered from the Superintendent of Documents, U.S. Government Printing Office. (Department of Commerce, Environmental Science Services Administration, Environmental Data Service Publication).

DEPARTMENT OF TREASURY/CUSTOMS

http://www.customs.treas.gov   or
http//www.customs.gov

*Know Before You Go, Customs Hints for Returning U.S. Residents gives detailed information on U.S. Customs regulations, including duty rates. Single copies are available free from any local customs or by writing to the Department of the Treasury, U.S. Customs Service, P.O. Box 7407, Washington D.C. 20044. (U.S. Customs Publication #0000-0512

*U.S. Customs: International Mail Imports provides information on procedures and requirements pertaining to parcels mailed from abroad to the U.S. (U.S. Customs Publication No. 0000-0514, Revised September 2002).

*U.S. Customs: Importing or Eporting a Car provides essential information for persons importing a vehicle into the U.S. It also includes U.S. Custom requirements and those of other government agencies whose regulations are enforced by the U.S. Customs. (U.S. Customs Publication)

*Pleasure Boats provides essential information for persons importing pleasure boats into the U.S. It includes requirements and charges. This publication is available free of charge from the Public Information Office, U.S. Customs Service, P.O. Box 7407, Washington D.C. 20044. (U.S. Customs Publication #: 0000-0544.)

*Pets, Wildlife: U.S. Customs (U.S. Customs Publication #509. Revised September 1992)

*G.S.P. and the Traveler provides basic information regarding the Generalized System of Preference which allows some products from certain countries to be brought into the U.S. duty-free. The leaflet only treats those non-commercial importation intended for personal use only. (U.S. Customs Publication #0000-0515. Revised July 2000)

*Personal Search: What to Expect (U.S. Customs Publication)

*Why U.S. Customs Conduct Examinations (U.S. Customs Publication #0000-0119)

*Internet Purchases (U.S. Customs Publication)

*Moving Household Goods to the U.S. (U.S. Customs Publication #0000-0518. Revised April 2000)

*Pets & Wildlife (U.S. Customs Publication #0000-0509)

*Importing or Exporting A Car (U.S. Customs Publication #0000-0520)

*ATA Carnet (U.S. Customs Publication #0000-0127)

*Currency Reporting (U.S. Customs Publication #0000-0503. October 2001)

*International Mail Imports (U.S. Customs Publication #0000-0514. Revised September 2003)

U.S. DEPARTMENT OF AGRICULTURE
http://www.usda.gov

*Travelers Tips on Bringing Food, Plant, And Animal Products Into the United States lists the regulations on bringing these items into the United States from most parts of the world. Fresh fruits and vegetables, meat, potted plants, pet birds, and other items are prohibited or restricted. Obtain the publication free from the Animal and Plant Health Inspection Service, U.S. Department of Agriculture, 732 Federal Bldg., 6505 Belcrest Road, Hyattsville, Maryland 20782. Tel. (301) 734-7885. (Program Aid No. 1083. Revised December 1993).

*Shipping Foreign plants Home. Provides tips and guidelines. Obtain the publication free from the Animal and Plant Health Inspection Service, U.S. Department of Agriculture, 732 Federal Bldg., 6505 Belcrest Road, Hyattsville, Maryland 20782. Tel. (301) 734-7885. (Program Aid No. 1162. Revised September 1988)

*Travelers Tips on Prohibited Agriculture Products Free copies may be obtained from the address above.

*Traveling By Air with Your Pet (USDA: Animal & Plant Health Inspection Service, (Miscellaneous Publication # 1536 revised October 998)

U.S. DEPARTMENT OF HEALTH

Centers For Disease Conrols-CDC (http://www.cdc.gov/travel/index.htm)

*+Health Information for International Travel is a comprehensive listing of immunization requirements of foreign governments. In addition, it gives the U.S. Public Health Service's recommendations on immunizations and other health precautions for the international traveler. Copies are available from the Superintendent of Documents, U.S. Government Printing Office, Washington, D.C. 20402; Tel. (202) 512-1800 or go to http://www.cdc.gov/travel/index.htm

DEPARTMENT OF INTERIOR

*Buyer Beware! tells about restrictions on importing wildlife and wildlife products. For a free copy, write to the Publications Unit, US Fish and Wildlife Service, Department of the interior, Washington D.C. 20240; (202) 343-5634.

ENVIRONMENTAL PROTECTION AGENCY

*Buying a Car Overseas? Beware! Free copies may be ordered from Publication Information Center PM-211B, 401 M Street S.W. Washington DC 20460 (202) 260-7751. (U.S. Environmental Protection Agency, February 1988)

DEPARTMENT OF TRANSPORTATION

*Fly Rights explains your rights and responsibilities as an air traveler (U.S. Department of Transportation, Tenth Revised Edition, September 1994)

Although essential requirements are provided in the leaflets listed above and, all regulations cannot be covered in detail. If you have any questions, or are in doubt , write or call the specific agency or organization mentioned. Their addresses including the type of subject matter they might provide some assistance are noted below.

SOCIAL SECURITY ADMINISTRATION
*Your Payments While You are Outside the United States (SSA #: 05-10137, ICN 480085, October 2002

AMERICAN SOCIETY FOR THE PREVENTION OF CRUELTY TO ANIMALS
American Society for the Prevention of Cruelty to Animals. Write to A.S.P.C.A. Education Department, 424 E. 49th Street, NY, N.Y. 10128

*Air Travel Tips (free)

*Airline Travel with Your Bird (free)

Agency/Source and Type of Inquiry/Assistance
Center For Disease Control: Travel Information
International Travelers Hotline 404-323-4559

[Telephone or fax back information about required and recommended vaccinations for foreign destinations]

U.S. Public Health Services
Centers for Disease Control
Division of Quarantine
Atlanta, Georgia 30333
Tel. (404) 539-2574

[On bringing food, plant and animal products into the U.S.]

Animal and Plant Health Inspection Service (APHIS)
U.S. Department of Agriculture
613 Federal Building
6505 Belcrest Road
Tel. (301) 734-7885,
http//www.aphis.usda.gov/travel/travel.htm

[On Importing meat and mea products]

USDA-APHIS
Verterinary Services
National Center for Import/Export (NCIE)

4700 River Rd. Unit 401
Riverdale MD 20737-1231
301-74-7830

[On bringing food, plant, and animal products into the U.S.]

U.S. Fish and Wildlife Service
Department of the Interior
Washington, D.C. 20240
Tel. (202) 343-9242,
(202) 343-5634
http://www.fws.gov

[Fish and Wildlife]

Department of the Treasury
U.S. Customs Service
P.O. Box 7407
Washington D.C. 20044
(202) 927-2095

[Imports and Exports, duties (tariffs) restricted and prohibited products]

Food and Drug Administration
Import Operations Unit
Room 12-8(HFC-131)
5600 Fishers Lane
Rockville, MD 20857

[Import of food and drugs into the U.S]

Office of Community and   Consumer Affairs
U.S. Department of Transportation
400 7th Street, S.W., Rm. 10405
Washington, D.C. 20590 . Tel: (202) 366-2220

[To complain about an airline or cruise line or to check out the records of an airline or cruise line.]

Executive Director
Passenger Programs
U.S. Customs Service
1300 Pennsylvania Ave. N.W.; Rm 5.4D
Washington , DC 20229

[For information about Customs procedures, requirements or policies regarding travelers; or if you have complaints about treatment you have received from customs inspectors or about your Customs processing]

Community and Consumer
Liaison Division
APA - 400
Federal Aviation Administration
800 Independence Avenue, S.W.
Washington, D.C. 20591. Tel: (202) 267-3481

593

[To complain about safety hazards.]

U.S. Environmental Protection Agency
Public Information Center
PM-211B, 401 M Street
S.W. Washington, D.C. 20460. Tel: (202) 382-2504

[Environmental issues dealing with imports of certain products or goods, including cars.]

TRAFFIC U.S.A.
World Wildlife Fund - U.S.
1250 24th Street
N.W. Washington, D.C. 20520

[On import of wildlife.]

U.S. Department of State
CA/PA Rm. 5807 Washington ,D.C. 20402
(202) 647 4000 or (202) 647 1488 *[Citizen safety, whereabouts, and welfare abroad, passports, visas, U.S. embassies and consulates abroad, foreign embassies and consulates in the U.S.*

Department of Justice
800-375-5283

[For questions concerning resident Alien & Non resident visa, passport information]

Superintendent Of Documents
U.S. Government Printing Office
Washington, D.C. 20402. Tel: (202) 512-1800
[U.S. government publications, including publications of various agencies and departments of the Federal Government.]

Office Of Foreign Assets Control
Department Of The Treasury
Washington, D.C. 20220. Tel: (202) 566-2761

[Import of merchandise from foreign countries.]

Quarantines, USDA-APHIS-PPQ 6505 Belcrest Rd. (301) 436-7472

[For permits and information on import of plants, meat products, livestock and poultry.]

Office Of Munitions Control
Department Of State
Washington, D.C. 20520

[Export/ import of weapons, ammunition and firearms.]

Bureau Of Alcohol, Tobacco and
Firearms
Department Of The Treasury
Washington, D.C. 20226. Tel: 202-927-8320

[Import of alcohol, tobacco and firearms.]

**Office Of Vehicle Safety Compliance
(NEF 32)
Department Of Transportation**
Washington, D.C. 20590
[Import of vehicles (standards).]

U.S. Information Agency
Washington, D.C.
(202) 619-4700

[Import/export of Cultural property.]

Consumer Information Center
*Pueblo, Colorado 81009   or P.O. Box 100
Pueblo Colorado 81002
[Publications of interest to the general public.]*

RECOMMENDED GOVERNMENT WEBSITES

Department of Homeland Security [http://dhs.gov]

U.S. State Department [http://travel.state.gov]

U.S. Customs [http://www.customs.gov]

Transportation Security Administration [http://www.tsa.gov]

Federal Aviation Administration [http://www1.faa.gov]

Office of Aviation Enforcement & Proceedings (Aviation Consumer Protection Division)
[http://airconsumer.ost.dot.gov]

Federal Consumer Information Center [http://www.pueblo.gsa.gov]

Centers For Disease Control [http://www.cdc.gov]

OTHER TRAVEL WEBSITES

SENIORS:
http://www.seniors.gov
SeniorNet [http://www.seniornet.org]
Elderhostel [http://www.elderhostel.org]
American Association of Retired Persons [http://www.aarp.org/travel)

DISABLED TRAVELERS:
Assess-Able Travel Source [http://www.access-able.com]
GlobalAccess [http://www.geocites.com]

HEALTH ADVICE:
Your Health Abroad [http://armchair.com/info/health.html]
Healthy Flying [http://www.flyana.com]
U.S. Centers for Disease Control [http://www.cdc.gov/travel/travel.html]

Travel Health Online [http://www.tripprep.com]
International Society of Travel Medicine [http://www.istm.org/clinidir.html]

GAY/LESIAN TRAVELERS

PlanetOut Travel [http://www.planetout.com]
Travelook [http://www.tavelook.com]
Out & About [http://www.outandabout.com]
-[http://www.gaytravelig.com]

FAMILY TRAVEL:

Family Travel Forum [http://www.familytravelforum.com]
-[http://www.familytravelguides.com

SECURITY/TRAVEL ADVISORIES
U.S. State Department Travel Warnings [http://travel.state.gov/travel_warnings.htm]
Kroll Travel Watch [http://www.krollassociates.com/kts]
CIA World Factbook [http://www.pdci.gov/cia/pulications/factbook]

OTHER TRAVEL SERVICES:

WEATHER [http://weather.com; http://www.accuweather.com]

CURRENCY CONVERTER [http://www.xe.net/currency] [http://www.oanda.com]

FOREIGN LANGUAGES HELP [http://www.travlang.com/languages]

PASSPORT SERVICES [http://travel.state.gov/passport_services.html]

CREDIT CARD ATM LOCATORS
[http://visa.com/pd/atm]   [http://wwmastercard.com/atm]

ROAD SAFETY:

Association For Safe International Road Travel
[http://www.asirt.org]

A FINAL CHECKLIST
FORGET-ME-NOTs

**Please see chapter 9 for new U.S. Government airport, packing, and other security requirements and procedures for travelers!!!

Addresses book.
Addresses.
Adhesive tape.
Alarm clock.
Alcohol pads
Alcohol.
Antacid.
Anti-acid tablets
Anti-diarrhea medication.
Antibiotics.
Aspirin.
Athletes Foot medication.
Auto repair kit
Band Aids
Bandage.
Battery charger
Belt.
Binoculars/telescope
Birth Certificate (copy)
Birth Control Pills.
Blank Personal Checks.
Blood pressure kit
Blouses
Bra.
Buttons (assorted).
Calculator (pocket).
Calling Card, telephone.
Camera.
Card (playing).
Cash.
Chapstick.
Clothes line
Coat (trench).
Coat (overcoat).
Coats.
Cold tablets.
Cologne.
Comb.
Compass.
Condoms.
Cone remover.
Contact lenses.
Contact lens cleaning solution.
Converter
Cotton swab.
Credit Cards.

Cufflinks.
Curling Iron.
Currency (Foreign)
Currency (U.S).
Customs registration Certificate
Decongestant.
Dental Floss.
Dentures.
Deodorant.
Diary.
Dress.
Driver's License.
Ear plugs.
Ear drops
Electric adapters and plugs.
Emergency Kit.
Envelopes.
Extra batteries.
Extra bag (collapsible).
Extra Prescriptions.
Eye drops.
Films (camera).
Flashlight.
Flask.
Foreign Language dictionary.
Fur.
Gifts (presents).
Gloves.
Glue
Golf clubs.
Guide books.
Hair Conditioner.
Hair Dryers.
Hair Remover.
Hair blower
Hair Spray.
Hair shaving blades
Hairbrush.
Hand luggage.
Hangers.
Hat.
Head gear.
Hearing aid.
Hemorrhoidal cream.
Hostel Card.
Hydrocortisone cream.

Immunizations.
Insect Repellant.
Insulin needles
Insurance ID cards.
Insurance claim forms.
International Driver's Permit.
International Vaccination certificate
Iron.
Jewelry.
Language dictionary.
Lint remover.
Lipsticks.
log book (diary).
Lotion (suntan).
Lotion (facial).
Lotion (body).
luggage keys (and extra set, put elsewhere).
Luggage carts.
Luggage (to be checked in).
Magnifying glasses.
Makeup Kit.
Maps.
Medic Alert bracelet.
Medical/clinical records.
Medication (prescription and non-prescription).
Mirror (pocket-size).
Money belt.
Nail Polish.
Neck Ties.
Needle.
Night Gown.
Pajamas.
Panties.
Pants.
Passport.
Pen.
Perfume.
Personal checks.
Photos:(passport-size).
Phrase Book..
Plastic bags.
Plastic utensils
Polish Remover.
Prescription glasses(reading).
Q-tips.
Rain Coat.
Raincoat
Razor.
Reading glasses carrying cases.
Reservation slips.
Rollers (hair).
Safety pins.

Sandals.
Sanitary pads.
Sanitary napkins.
Scarves.
Scissors (small).
Sewing Kit
Shampoo.
Shaving cream/powder.
Shaving blades.
Shirts (dress).
Shoe Polish.
Shoe brush
Shoe laces.
Shoes.
Shower cap.
Ski-equipments.
Ski-jacket.
Skirt.
Skis.
Slacks.
Sleeping bag.
Sleeping pills.
Slip (waist).
Snacks, favorite.
Sneakers.
Soap (bathing).
Soap (laundry).
Socks.
Souvenirs
Spare glasses.
Stain remover.
Stockings
Suit (bathing).
Suit.
Sun Glasses.
T-shirts.
Tape recorder
Tape recorder
Tape measure
Tape (fiberglass).
Thermal wear.
Thermometer.
Thread (assorted).
Timetables
Toilet tissue
Toothbrush.
Toothpaste.
Toothpicks
Tourist card.
Towel.
Tranquilizers
Transformer
Traveler's checks.
Tweezers.

Umbrella
Underwear.
Vaccination Card.
Visas.
Vitamins
Walkman radio/cassette.
Wallet.
Washcloth.
Watch.
Water pills.
Water heater
Whistle
Windbreaker.
Writing pads.
Zip lock plastic bags

HAVE YOU

A copy of your medical report?

Checked your credit card and bank account balances?

Checked medications for clear labelling?

Checked the dress code for the countries you are visiting?

Checked currency requirements of host country?

Checked medication for clear labelling?

Checked your insurance coverage?

Consulted with your physician?

Consulted with your dentist?

Discussed with your loved ones, key code words to use in case of an emergency?

Familiarized yourself with a few conversational phrases of your host country?

Had your shots?

Jotted down addresses and phone number of the nearest U.S. embassy or consulate?

Jotted down addresses and telephone numbers of overseas offices of

traveler's checks issuing companies, in case of a refund or lost or stolen checks?

Left a copy of your itinerary with relatives, friends?

Made arrangements for money to be transferred to you in case of an emergency?

Made a final telephone call to your host/hostess?

Obtained a Carnet?

Obtained a copy of your medical report?

Obtained your ATM Card?

Obtained your telephone dialing card?

Picked up your prescriptions?

Picked up letters of authorization/explanation from your doctor regarding drugs you are be carrying?

Picked up a dialing card from your long distance telephone carrier?

Picked up your travelers checks?

Picked up your passport?

Picked up your tickets?

Placed tags on all of your luggage?

Re-confirmed your flight/ reservations?

Registered your valuables with the U.S. Customs?

Requested your special diet with the airline/cruise line?

Updated your insurance?

Written down important, addresses, telephone and fax numbers?

599

APPENDIX A

U.S. EMBASSIES AND CONSULATES ABROAD

Note: APO/FPO addresses may only be used for mail originating in the United States. When you use an APO/FPO address, do not include the local street address. For more information

Albania - Tirana (E), Tirana Rruga Elbasanit 103 -- AmEmbassy Tirana, Department of State, Washington, D.C. 20521-9510, Tel [355] (42) 47285 thru 89, Fax 32222

Algeria - Algiers (E), 4 Chemin Cheikh Bachir El-Ibrahimi -- B.P. Box 408 (Alger-Gare) 16000, Tel [213] (2) 69-12-55, 69-32-22, 69-11-86, 69-14-25, Fax 69-39-79; GSO Fax 69-17-82; COM Tel 69-23-17, Fax 69-18-63; PAO Fax 69-14-88. Internet address: - us-embassy.eldjazair.net.dz -

Angola - Luanda (E), Rua Houari Boumedienne No. 32, Miramar, Luanda -- International Mail: Caixa Postal 6484, Luanda, Angola, or Pouch: American Embassy Luanda, Dept. of State, Washington, D.C., 20521-2550; INMARSAT: Int'l Operator 873-151-7430, Tel [244] (2) 347-028/345-481, Fax 346-924; DAO Fax 347-217; Admin/Consular Annex: Casa Inglesa, Rua Major Kanhangula No. 132/135, Angola, or use above pouch address; ADMIN Tel 392-498; CON Tel 396-927, Fax 390-515

Argentina - Buenos Aires (E), International Mail: 4300 Colombia, 1425 Buenos Aires -- APO Address: Unit 4334, APO AA 34034, Tel [54] (1) 777-4533 and 777-4534, Fax 777-0197; COM Fax 777-0673, Telex 18156 AMEMBAR

Armenia - Yerevan (E), 18 Gen Bagramian (local address) --

American Embassy Yerevan, Dept. of State, Washington, D.C. 20521-7020 (pouch address), Tel 3742-151-551, Fax 3742-151-550, Telex 243137 AMEMY. Internet address: - www.embgso@arminco.com -

Australia - Canberra (E), Moonah Pl., Canberra, A.C.T. 2600 -- APO AP 96549, Tel [61] (2) 6214-5600, afterhours Tel 6214-5900, Fax 6214-5970. Internet website: www.usis-australia.gov

Austria - Vienna (E), Boltzmanngasse 16, A-1091, Vienna, Tel [43] (1) 313-39, Fax [43] (1) 310-0682; CON: Gartenbaupromenade 2, 4th Floor, A-1010 Vienna, Tel [43] (1) 313-39, Fax 513-4351; COM Fax [43] (1) 310-6917 or 31339-2911; EXEC Fax [43] (1) 317-7826; ADM Fax [43] (1) 31339-2510; ECON/POL Fax [43] (1) 313-2916

Azerbaijan - Baku (E), Azadliq Prospekt 83, Baku 370007, Azerbaijan -- AmEmbassy Baku, Dept. of State, Washington, D.C. 20521-7050 (pouch address), Tel [9] (9412) 98-03-35, 36, 37, Fax 90-66-71; Tie Line 841-0289; EXEC Fax 98-91-79; CON Fax 98-37-55; COM Fax 98-61-17; PAO Tel & Fax 98-93-12. Internet address: http://www.usia.gov/posts/baku.html

Bahamas, The - Nassau (E), Queen St. (local/express mail address) P.O. Box N-8197; Amembassy Nassau, P.O. Box 599009, Miami, Fl. 33159-9009 (stateside address); -- Nassau, Dept. of State, Wash., D.C. 20521-3370 (pouch address), Tel (242) 322-1181, afterhours Tel 328-2206, EXEC Fax (242) 356-0222; ECO/COM Fax 328-3495; ADM Fax 328-7838; NAS Fax 356-0918; PAO Fax 326-5579; Visas Fax 356-7174

Bahrain - Manama (E), Building No. 979, Road 3119, Block 331, Zinj District -- AmEmbassy Manama, PSC 451, FPO AE 09834-5100; International Mail: American Embassy, Box 26431, Manama, Bahrain, Tel [973] 273-300, afterhours Tel 275-126, Fax 272-594; ADM Fax 275-418; ECON/COM Fax 256-717; PAO Tel 276-180, Fax 270-547; OMC Tel 276-962, Fax 276-046. Web site address: http://www.usembassy.com.bh

Bangladesh - Dhaka (E), Diplomatic Enclave, Madani Ave., Baridhara, Dhaka 1212 or -- G.P.O. Box 323, Dhaka 1000, Tel [880] (2) 882-4700-22, Fax 882-3744; USAID Fax 882-3648; PAO address: House No. 110, Road No. 27, Banani, Dhaka 1213, Tel [880] (2) 881-3440-44, Fax 9881677; workweek: Sunday thru Thursday. E-mail address: Dhaka@usia.gov.

Barbados - Bridgetown (E), Canadian Imperial Bank of Commerce Bldg., Broad Street -- P.O. Box 302 or FPO AA 34055, Tel (246) 436-4950, Fax 429-5246, Telex 2259 USEMB BGI WB, Marine Sec. Guard, Tel 436-8995; CON Fax 431-0179; AID Fax 429-4438; PAO Fax 429-5316; MLO Fax 427-1668; LEGATT Fax 437-7772

Belarus - Minsk (E), 46 Starovilenskaya Str., 220002 Minsk · PSC 78, Box B Minsk, APO 09723, Tel [375] (17) 210-12-83 and 234-77-61, afterhours Tel 226-1601, Fax 234-78-53, CON Fax 217-7160; Fax 577-4650; PAO Tel [375] (17) 217-04-81, Fax 217-88-28

Belgium - Brussels (E), 27 Boulevard du Regent, B-1000 Brussels -- PSC 82, Box 002, APO AE 09710, Tel [32] (2) 508-2111,

Fax [32] (2) 511-2725; COM Fax 512-6653; direct-in-dial: Amb [32] (2) 508-2444; Amb sec 508-2444; DCM 508-2446; POL 508-2475; ECO 508-2448; COM 508-2425; CON 508-2382; ADM 508-2350; RSO 508-2370; PAO 508-2412; IRM 508-2200; DAO 508-2505; ODC 508-2664; FAS 508-2437; FAA 508-2703

Belize - Belize City (E), Gabourel Lane -- P.O. Box 286, Unit 7401, APO AA 34025, Tel [501] (2) 77161 thru 63, Fax 30802; ADM Fax 35321; DAO Fax 32795; DEA Fax 33856; PC Fax 30345; IBB Tel [501] (7) 22091/22063, Fax 22147; MLO Tel 25-2009/2019, Fax 25-2553. Internet address: embbelize@belizwpoa.us-state.gov. Web site address: http://www.usemb-belize.gov

Benin - Cotonou (E), rue Caporal Bernard Anani, B.P. 2012, Tel [229] 30-06-50, 30-05-13, 30-17-92, Fax 30-14-39 and 30-19-74, workweek: Monday through Friday. Internet address: amemb.coo@intnet.bj

Bermuda - Hamilton (CG), Crown Hill, 16 Middle Road, Devonshire -- P.O. Box HM325, Hamilton HMBX, Bermuda, or AmConGen Hamilton, Department of State, Wash., D.C. 20520-5300, Tel [441] 295-1342, Fax 295-1592or 296-9233

Bolivia - La Paz (E), Ave. Arce No. 2780 -- P.O. Box 425, La Paz, Bolivia, APO AA 34032, Tel [591] (2) 430251, Fax 433900; USAID Tel 786544, Fax 786654; Direct lines: AMB [591] (2) 432524; DCM 431340; POST 1 432540; DEA 431481; CON 433758, Fax 433854; PAO Tel 432621; USAID DIR Tel 786179, USAID EXEC OFF Tel 786399

Bosnia and Herzegovina - Sarajevo (E), Alipasina 43, 71000 Sarajevo, Tel [387] (71) 445-700, Fax [387] (71) 659-722

Botswana - Gaborone (E), P.O. Box 90, Tel [267] 353-982,

afterhours Tel 357-111 or 374-498, Fax 356-947; AID Tel 324-449, Fax 324-404; CDC Tel 301-696; VOA Tel 810-932. E-mail address: usembgab@global.co.za

Brazil - Brasilia (E), Avenida das Nacoes, Quadra 801, Lote 3, Brasilia, D.F. Cep 70403-900 Brazil -- American Embassy Brasilia, Unit 3500, APO AA 34030, Tel [55] (61) 321-7272, Fax 225-9136 (Stateside address); ADM Fax 225-5857; COM Fax 225-3981; PAO Fax 321-2833, 322-0554; AID Fax 323-6875; FCS Fax 225-3981; NAS Fax 226-0171; SCI Fax 321-3615; POL Fax 223-0497; ECO Fax 224-9477. Internet address: http://www.embaixada-americana.org.br/

Brunei - Bandar Seri Begawan (E), Third Floor - Teck Guan Plaza, Jalan Sultan, Bandar Seri Begawan, Brunei Darussalam -- PSC 470 (BSB), FPO AP 96507, Emb Tel [673] (2) 220-384, 229-670, Fax [673] (2) 225-293; Amb direct line 240-763; DCM direct line 241-645; COM Fax 226-523; STU III Fax 240-761. E-mail: amembbsb@brunet.bn. Embassy website: http://members.xoom.com/amembr unei

Bulgaria - Sofia (E), 1 Saborna St. -- AMEmbassy Sofia, Dept. of State, Washington, D.C. 20521-5740, Tel [359] (2) 980-5241 thru 48, Fax 981-8977; CON Fax 963-2859; ADM/GSO/PER Fax 963-0086; COM Fax 980-6850; AGR Fax 981-6568; AID Fax 951-5070; PAO Fax 980-3646; PC Tel 980-0217, Fax 981-7525. CON Internet address: bgcons@hotmail.com

Burkina Faso - Ouagadougou (E), 602 Avenue Raoul Follerau, 01 B.P. 35, Tel (226) 30-67-23, afterhours Tel 31-26-60 and 31-27-07, Fax (226) 30-38-90. Internet address: amembouaga@ouagadougb.us-state.gov

Burma - Rangoon (E), 581 Merchant St. (GPO 521) -- Box B,

APO AP 96546, Tel [95] (1) 282055, 282182, Fax [95] (1) 280409, Telex (083) 21230 AMBYGN BM; direct-in-dial: EXEC Tel [95] (1) 283668; DAO Tel 277507; GSO Tel 543354, 542608, Fax 543353; Health Unit Tel 511072, Fax 511069; PAO Tel 221585, 223106, 223140, Fax 221262. Internet address: Embassy.info-rangoon@dos.us-state.gov

Burundi - Bujumbura (E), B.P. 1720, Avenue Des Etas-Unis, Tel [257] 22-34-54, afterhours Tel 21-48-53, Fax 22-29-26; AID/OFDA Tel 22-59-51, Fax 22-29-86. E-mail: (user last name plus initials) @bujumburab.us-state.gov

Cambodia - Phnom Penh (E), 27 EO Street 240 -- Box P, APO AP 96546, Tel [855] 23-216-436/438, Fax 23-216-811; ADM Fax 23-216437

Cameroon - Yaounde (E), rue Nachtigal, B.P. 817, Tel (237) 23-40-14, and (237) 23-05-12 -- Pouch address: American Embassy, Dept. of State, Washington, D.C. 20521-2520, Tel [237] 23-45-52, Fax 23-07-53; ADM Tel 23-13-87; IRM Tel [237] 23-43-72; DAO Tel 22-03-17. Internet address: yaounde@youndeb.us-state.gov

Canada - Ottawa, Ontario (E), 100 Wellington St., K1P 5T1 -- P.O. Box 5000, Ogdensburg, NY 13669-0430, Tel (613) 238-5335 or 238-4470, Fax 238-5720; COM Fax 238-5999

Cape Verde - Praia (E), Rua Abilio Macedo 81, C.P. 201, Tel [238] 61-56-16, Fax 61-13-55

Central African Republic - Bangui (E), Avenue David Dacko, B.P. 924, Tel [236] 61-02-00, 61-02-10, 65-25-78, Fax 61-44-94, duty phone (236) 50-12-08

Chad - N'Djamena (E), Ave. Felix Eboue, B.P. 413, Tel [235] (51) 70-09, 51-90-52, 51-92-33, Telex 5203 KD, Fax 51-56-54, or 56-54; Direct system dialing via system 85

in Dept: AMB 924-2002, DCM 924-2112; POL 924-2372; RSO 924-2342; IRM 924-2122, Fax 924-2302. Internet Admin address: paschallrc@ndjamenab.us-state.gov

Chile - Santiago (E), Av. Andres Bello 2800, APO AA 34033, Tel [56] (2) 232-2600, Fax 330-3710; COM Fax 330-3172; AID Fax 638-0931; AGR Fax 56-2-330-3203; FBO Fax 233-4108; CON 56-2-330-3710; GSO Fax 330-3020

China - Beijing (E), Xiu Shui Bei Jie 3, 100600 -- PSC 461, Box 50, FPO AP 96521-0002, Tel [86] (10) 6532-3831, Telex AMEMB CN 22701; EXEC/ECO Fax 6532-6422; POL/ES&T/RSO Fax 6532-6423; ESO/MSG Fax 6532-6421; GSO Travel Fax 6532-2483; Health Unit Fax 6532-6424; AGR Fax 6532-2962; CUS Fax 6500-3032; INS Fax 6561-4507; PAO Fax 6532-2039; CON Fax 6532-3178; COM Tel 6532-6924 thru 27, Fax 6532-3297; ADM/Personnel Fax 6532-5141; APHIS address: 12-21 China World Trade Ctr., No. 1 Jianguomenwai Ave., Beijing, FAX [86] (10) 6505-4574; American Center for Education Exchange (ACEE) address: Jing Guang Center, Tel 6510-5242, Fax 6501-5247; Federal Aviation Administration (FAA) address: No. 15 Guang Hua Li, Jian Guo Men Wai, Chao Yang District, Tel 6504-2571, Fax 6504-5154

Colombia - Bogota (E), Calle 22D-BIS, No. 47-51, Apartado Aereo 3831, -- APO AA 34038, Tel [57] (1) 315-0811, Fax 315-2197; CON Tel. 315-1566; COM Fax [571] (315) 2171/2190; GSO Fax [571] (315) 2207

Congo, Democratic Republic of - Bogota (E), Calle 22D-BIS, No. 47-51, Apartado Aereo 3831, -- APO AA 34038, Tel [57] (1) 315-0811, Fax 315-2197; CON Tel. 315-1566; COM Fax [571] (315) 2171/2190; GSO Fax [571] (315) 2207

Congo, Republic of - Brazzaville (E), The Brazzaville Embassy

Office is co-located with Embassy Kinshasa at 310 Avenue Des Aviateurs, Kinshasa, DRC, Tel [243] (88) 43608, Fax (88) 41036. Address/phone of temporary office in Brazzaville: 70 rue Bayardelle, Tel [242] 81-14-72; additional information: [243] (88) 40520 or (88) 40252

Costa Rica - San Jose (E), Pavas, San Jose -- APO AA 34020, Tel (506) 220-3939, afterhours Tel 220-3127, Fax 220-2305; COM Fax 231-4783

Cote d'Ivoire - Abidjan (E), 5 rue Jesse Owens, 01 B.P. 1712, Tel [225] 20-21-09-79 or 20-21-46-72, Fax 20-22-32-59

Croatia - Zagreb (E), Andrije Hebranga 2, 1000 Zagreb, Croatia, Tel [385] (1) 455-5500, afterhours Tel 455-5281, Fax 455-8585; EXEC Fax 455-0394; ADM Fax 455-0892; GSO Fax 481-7711. Website address: www.usembassy.hr

Cuba - -3975; ADM Fax 66-2095, INS switchbHavana (USINT), Swiss Embassy, Calzada between L and M Sts., Vedado, Havana, USINT Tel [53] (7) 33-3551/9, 33-3543/5, Fax 33-3700; Refugee inquiries telephone numbers 33-3546/7, afterhours Marine Post 1 33-3026; PAO direct line 33-3967, Fax 33-3869; T+T Fax 33-3975, FBO direct line: 33-4096/97, Fax 33oard 33-4511/33-3586, Fax 33-4512

Cyprus - Nicosia (E), Metochiou and Ploutarchou Streets, Engomi, Nicosia, Cyprus -- P.O. Box 24536, PSC 815 FPO AE 09836, Tel [357] (2) 776400, afterhours Tel 776934, Fax 780944; CON Fax 781146; PAO Tel 677143, Fax 668003; Internet address: amembsys@spidernet.com.cy

Czech Republic - Prague (E), Trziste 15, 11801 Prague 1, Tel [420] (2) 5753-0663, Fax 5753-0920; GSO Fax 5753-0584; DAO Fax 5753-2718; ODC Fax 5753-1175; CON Fax 5753-4028;

POL/ECO Fax 5753-2717; COM Fax 5753-1165 or 5753-1168; AGR Fax 5753-1173; Pub. Diplomacy and IRC: Hybernska 7A 11716 Prague 1, PAO Tel Fax 2422-0983

Denmark - Copenhagen (E), Dag Hammarskjolds Alle 24, 2100 Copenhagen -- PSC 73, APO AE 09716, Tel [45] 3555-3144, afterhours Tel 3555-9270, Fax 3543-0223; POL/ECO/EST Fax 3542-8075; ADM Fax 3526-9611; CON Fax 3538-9616; PAO Fax 3542-7273; AGR Fax 3543-0278; USAF Fax 3526-5108; COM Fax 3542-0175; DAO Fax 3542-2516. Embassy home page: www.usembassy.dk

Djibouti - Djibouti (E), Plateau du Serpent, Blvd. Marechal Joffre, B.P. 185, Tel [253] 35-39-95, Fax 35-39-40, afterhours 35-13-43

Dominican Republic - Santo Domingo (E), corner of Calle Cesar Nicolas Penson and Calle Leopoldo Navarro -- Unit 5500, APO AA 34041-5500, Tel [809] 221-2171, afterhours Tel 221-8100 or 562-3560, Fax 686-7437; CON Tel 221-5511, Fax 685-6959; AID Tel 221-1100, Fax 221-0444; INS Tel 221-0113, Fax 221-0110; PC Tel 685-4102, Fax 686-3241. Fax 686-4326; ADM ext. 255, Fax 686-7166; FCS ext. 400, Fax 688-4838; PAO ext. 486, Fax 541-1828; DEA ext. 381, Fax 685-7507; DAO ext. 220, Fax 687-5222; MAAG ext. 487, Fax 682-3991; APHIS ext. 357, Fax 686-0979; AGR ext. 344, Fax 685-4743; ECO/POL x 335 Fax 686-4038; website: www.usia.gov/posts/santodomingo. E-mail: Last name first, initial, middle initial@state.gov

Copenhagen, Denmark - Dag Hammarskjölds Allé 24, 2100 København Ø. Tl: +45 35 55 31 44 Fax: +45 35 43 02 23

Ecuador - Av. Patria y Av. 12 de Octubre Tel:(593) 2 256 2890 Fax:(593) 2 250 2052 Tel: de emergencia: (593) 2 223 4126

Egypt - 5, Latin America St.,

Garden City, Cairo, Egypt Tel: [20] [2] 797-3300 Fax: [20] [2] 79 7 - 32 00

El Salvador - Boulevard Santa Elena,Urbanización Santa Elena, Antiguo Cuscatlán La Libertad, El Salvador General info: [503] 278 4444

Equatorial Guinea - Yaounde, Cameroun - Rue Nachtigal P.O. Box 817, Yaounde Tel: (237) 223-05-12 (237) 222-25-89 (237) 222-17-94 (237) 223-40-1

Eritrea - Asmara (E), Franklin D. Roosevelt St. P.O. Box 211, Asmara, Eritrea Tel: [291] (1) 120004 Fax: 127584 USAID Tel: 121895; Fax: 123093 Peace Corps Tel: 12 63 54 Fax: 122870 DAO/SAO Tel: 126381 DOD/SAO Fax: 126339

Estonia - Kentmanni 20, 15099 Tallinn, Estonia Tel: (372) 668 8100 Fax (372) 668 8134 Public E-mail:tallinn@usemb.ee **U.S. Consular Section in Tallin, Estonia** - Kentmanni 20, 15099 Tallinn, Estonia Tel: (372)-668 8100 Consular Section Fax: (372)-668 8267 Visa information: E-mail:VisaTallinn@state.gov American Citizen Services:ACSTallinn@state.gov

Addis Ababa, Ethiopia - P.O.Box 1014, Addis Ababa , Ethiopia E-mail:usemaddis@state.gov Tel. 251-1-550666, Fax 251-1-551328

U.S. Consular Section in Addis Ababa, Ethiopia - Entoto Street, P.O.Box 1014 Addis Ababa,Ethiopia Tel: 251-1-55 06 66, Fax: 251-1-55 10 94 E-mail:consaddis@state.gov

Fiji - 31 Loftus Street P.O. Box 218 Suva, Fiji Tel: (679) 3314-466 Fax: (679) 3300-081 ; **U.S. Consular Section in Suva, Fiji** - 31 Loftus Street P.O. Box 218 Suva, Fiji Tel: (679) 3314-466 Fax: (679) 3300-081 E-mail: consularsuva@state.gov.

Finland - Itäinen Puistotie 14 B,

FIN-00140 Helsinki, Finland Tel: +358-9-171 931 E-mail:webmaster@usembassy.fi ;**U.S. Consular Section in Helsinki, Finland** - Itäinen Puistotie 14 B, FIN-00140 Helsinki, Finland Tel: +358-9-171 931 E-mail:consular@usembassy.fi

France - 2 avenue Gabriel 75008 Paris, France Switchboard (33) 1 43 12 22 22 Fax: (33) 1 42 66 97 83 ; **U.S. Consular Section in Paris, France** - 2, rue St. Florentin 75382 Paris, Cedex 08; **Visa Services :** Tel: 08-99-70-37-00 (fee charged) Fax: 01-42-86-82-91 (From outside France 33-1-42-86-82-91) ; **U.S. General Consulate in Marseille, France** - **Office address:** Place Varian Fr 13006 Marseille Tel: (33) 4-91-54-92-00 Fax: (33) 4-91-55-09-47 - ; Mailing address: Consulat Général des Etats-Unis d'Amérique Place Varian Fry 13286 Marseille Cedex 6 - Mailing address within the U.S.: U.S. Consulate General PSC 116 (MAR) APO AE 09777 ; **U.S. General Consulate in Strasbourg, France** - 15, Avenue d'Alsace 67082 Strasbourg Cedex Tel: (33) 3 88 35 31 04 Fax: (33) 3 88 24 06 95

Gabon - Blvd. De la Mer B.P. 4000 Libreville Gabon Tel:(241) 76.20.03 or (2004/1241) Fax: (241) 74.55.07

Georgia - 25 Atoneli Street, Tbilisi 380005, Georgia. Tel:(995-32) 98-99-67 or 98-99-68 Fax:(995-32) 92-29-53 E-mail:consulate-tbilisi@state.gov

Germany - Neustädtische Kirchstr. 4-5 10117 Berlin Federal Republic of Germany Tel: (030) 8305-0 ; **U.S. General Consulate in Düsseldorf, Germany** - Willi- Becker- Allee 10 40227 Düsseldorf ;Tel: (0211) 788 - 8927 ;**U.S. General Consulate in Frankfurt, Germany** - Siesmayerstraße 21 60323 Frankfurt Federal Republic of Germany Tel: (49) (69) 7535-0 ;**U.S. General Consulate in Hamburg, Germany** - Alsterufer

27/28 20354 Hamburg Federal Republic of Germany Tel: (040) 411 71 100 Fax: (040) 411 71 222 ;**U.S. General Consulate in Leipzig, Germany** - Wilhelm-Seyfferth- Straße 4 04107 Leipzig Federal Republic of Germany

U.S. General Consulate in Munich, Germany - Königinstraße 5 80539 Munich, Federal Republic of Germany

Ghana - Ring Road East P.O. Box 194 Accra, Ghana Tel: (233) 21 - 775-348. After Hours Emergency Number: (233) 21-775-297 Fax: (233) 21-776-008

Greece - E-mail:usembassy@usembassy.gr ; **U.S. General Consulate in Thessaloniki, Greece** - 43 Tsimiski , 7th Floor GR-54623 Thessaloniki Tel : 003 2310 242 905,6,7 Fax : 003 2310 242 927 Public Affairs Fax : 003 2310 242 910 E-mail : amcongen@compulink.gr

Grenada - St. George's (E), P.O. Box 54, St. George's, Grenada, W.I., Tel [473] 444-1173/6, Fax 444-4820. E-mail address: usemb-gd@caribsurf.com

Guatemala - Avenida Reforma 7-01, Zona 10 Ciudad de Guatemala, Guatemala.

Guinea - Rue KA 038, Conakry, Republic of Guinea Tel: (224) 41-15-20/21/23 Fax: (224) 41-15-22

Haiti - Consular Section 104, rue Oswald Durand Port au Prince, Haiti.

Holy see (Vatican City) - Via delle Terme Deciane, 26 00162 - Rome, Italy Tel: (+39) 06-4674-3428 Fax: (+39) 06-575-8346

Hong Kong and Macau -26 Garden Road, Hong Kong Tel: (852) 2523-9011 Fax: (852) 2845-1598

Honduras - La Paz, Apartado Postal No. 3453 Tegucigalpa, Honduras.

Hungary - Szabadság tér 12., H-1054 Budapest Tel: (36-1) 475-4400 After-Hours: (36-1) 475-4703/4924.

Iceland - - Laufasvegur 21, 101 Reykjavik, Iceland Tel: +354 5629100 Fax: +354 5629123

India - Shantipath, Chanakyapuri New Delhi - 110021. Tel: 011-2419-8000 E-mail:newdelhi@pd.state.gov ; **U.S. General Consulate in Calcutta, India** - 5/1, Ho Chi Minh Sarani Calcutta- 700071 Tel: 033-2282-3611 E- mail:pascal@pd.state.gov ;**U.S. General Consulate in Mumbai, India** - Lincoln House 78, Bhulabhai Desai Road Mumbai - 400026 Tel: 022-2363-3611 E-mail:webmastermumbai@state.gov ;**U.S. Information Service in**

Chennai, India - No. 220, Anna Salai Chennai - 600006 Tel: 044-2811-2000 E-mail:chennaic@state.gov

Indonesia - Jl. Medan Merdeka Selatan 4-5, Jakarta 10110, Indonesia Tel: (62-21) 3435-9000 Fax: (62-21) 385-7189; **U.S. Consular Agency in Bali, Indonesia** - Jl. Hayam Wuruk 188, Denpasar 80235, Bali, ;; Indonesia Tel: (62-361) 233-605, Fax: (62-361) 222-426 E-mail:amcobali@indosat.net.id ; **U.S. General Consulate in Surabaya, Indonesia** - alan Raya Dr. Soetomo 33 Surabaya 60264, Indonesia Tel: 62-31-568-2287 Facsimile: 62-31-567-4492

Ireland - 42 Elgin Road, Dublin 4, Ireland Tel: +353 1 6688777 / 687122 Fax: +353 1 6689946

Israel - 1 Ben Yehuda Street Tel Aviv POB 26180 Israel Tel: 972 3822 Fax: 972-3-5103828 E-mail: webmaster@usembassy-israel.org.il

Italy - Via Vittorio Veneto 119/A 00187 Roma, Italia Telephone: (+39) 06.4674.1 (switchboard) Fax: (+39) 06.4882.672 or 06.4674.2356;

U.S. General Consulate in Florence, Italy - Lungarno Vespucci, 38 - 50123 FIRENZE, Italy Tel: +39 055-266-951 Fax:+39 055-284-088 ; **U.S. General Consulate in Milan, Italy** - Via Principe Amedeo, 2/10 - 20121 MILANO (Italy) Tel:+39 02-290-351 Fax: +39 02-2900-1165 ; **U.S. General Consulate in Naples, Italy** - Piazza della Repubblica - 80122 NAPOLI, Italy Tel:+39 081-5838-111 Fax: +39 081-7611-869

Jamaica - 2 Oxford Road, Kingston 5, Jamaica, W.I.Tel: 1 (876) 935-6053/4. Fax: 1(876) 929-3637 E-mail:opakgn@pd.state.gov

Japan - - 1-10-5 Akasaka, Minato-ku, Tokyo Japan 107-8420 Tel: 03-3224-5000 ; **U.S. Consulate in Fukuoka, Japan** - Fukuoka American Center Solaria Parkside Building 8th floor 2-2-67 Tenjin Chuo-ku, Fukuoka 810-0001 Phone: 092-733-0246 Fax: 092-716-6152; E-Mail:facres@gol.com ; **U.S. General Consulate in Osaka, Japan** - 11-5 Nishitenma 2-chome, Kita-ku, Osaka 530-8543 Tel: 06-6315-5900 Fax:06-6315-5914

Jordan - P.O. Box 354, Amman 11118 Jordan Tel: 962-6-592-0101, Fax: 962-6-592-0121.

Kazakhstan - Seyfullin Ave., 531 Almaty, Kazakstan Tel: 7 3272 633094 Fax: 7 3272 633045 E-mail:usembassy@freenet.kz

Kenya - Consular Section APO AP 96205-5550 USA

Kuwait - Bayan, Area 14, Al-Masjed Al-Aqsa Street, P. O. Box 77, Safat 13001, Tel: (965)539-5307/8; Fax: (965) 538-0282.

Laos- 19 Rue Bartholonie Vientiane, Lao P.D.R. Tel: (856-21) 212581 Fax: (856-21) 213045

Latvia - Raina Blvd.7 Riga LV-1510 Tel: +371 7036-200 Fax: +371 7820-047 E-mail:pas@usembassy.lvConsular E-

mail:AskConsular@USRiga.lv

Lebanon - Beirut (E), Antelias -- P.O. Box 70-840, or PSC 815, Box 2, FPO AE 09836-0002, Tel: [961] (4) 543-600, 542-600, 544-130/131/133, Fax 544-136; ADM Fax: 544-604

Lesotho - Tel:+ 266- 312666 Fax:+ 266-310116 E-mail:info@embassy.org.ls

Liberia - 111 United Nations Drive, Mamba Point P.O. Box 10-0098 1000 Monrovia, 10 Liberia Telephone: (231)226-370/-380 Fax:(231)226-148

Lithuania - -2600 Akmenu 6 Vilnius, Lithuania Tel:(370-5)2665500 Fax:(370-5)2665510 E-mail:mail@usembassy.lt

Luxembourg - 22 Boulevard Emmanuel Servais L-2535 Luxembourg Tel: +352-460123 Fax: +352-461401

Macedonia - bul. Ilinden bb 1000 Skopje, Macedonia. Tel +389 2 116 180; Fax:+ 389 2 117 103 E-mail:irc@usembassy.mpt.com.mk

Madagascar - 14 - 16, rue Rainitovo - Antsahavola-Antananarivo 101 Tel.: 261 20 22 212 57/ 212 73 / 209 56 Fax: 261 20 22 345 39

Malaysia - 376 Jalaln Tun Razak, 50400 Kuala Lumpur. Tel: 603-2168-5000 Fax: 603-2142-2207.

Malta - Development House, 3rd Floor St. Anne Street, Floriana, Malta VLT 01 - P.O. Box 535, Valletta, Malta, CMR 01 Tel: (356) 2561 4000 Fax: (356) 21 243229

Marshall Islands - P.O. Box 1379 Majuro, MH 96960 Tel: (692) 247-4011 Fax: (692) 247-4012

Mauritius - 4th floor, Rogers House, John Kennedy Avenue, Port Louis, Mauritius.Tel : (230) 202 4400 Fax: (230) 208 9534 E-mail:usembass@intnet.mu

605

Mexico - Av. Lopez Mateos 924 Nte.Ciudad Juarez, Mexico ; **Mexico City, Mexico** -From Mexico: Paseo de la Reforma 305 Col. Cuauhtémoc 06500 México, D.F. Tel: (01- 55) 5080 - 2000 Fax: (01- 55) 5511- 9980 From USA: American Embassy Mexico P.O. Box 9000 Brownsville, TX 78520-9000 Tel:(011- 52 - 55) 5080 - 2000 Fax: (011- 52 - 55) 5511- 9980; **U.S. General Consulate Guadalajara, Mexico** - Progreso 175, Col. Americana Guadalajara, Jalisco ZP C. 44100 Tel: (01-33) 3825-2700 Fax: (01-33) 3826-6549 Emergency phone (01-33) 3826-5553; **U.S. General Consulate in Monterrey, Mexico** - Ave. Constitución 411 Pte. Monterrey, Nuevo León. México 64000 Phone from the U.S. 011 (52 81) 8345-2120; **U.S. General Consulate in Tijuana, Mexico** - Tapachula 96, Colonia Hipódromo, Tijuana, Baja California, México 22420 Tel.: (664) 622-7400 Fax: (664) 681-8016 From USA: P.O. Box 439039, San Diego, CA 92176-9039

Micronesia - P.O. Box 1286 Kolonia, Pohnpei FSM 96941 Phone: (691) 320-2187 Fax: (691) 320-2186 E-mail:USEmbassy@mail.fmfm

Moldova - 103 Mateevivi Street, Chisinau MD-2009, Tel:373 -2 - 23 3772 Fax:373-2-233044

Mongolia - P.O. Box 21Ulaanbaatar-13 ; MONGOLIA Tel: 976-11-329095 Fax: 976-11-320776

Morocco - The international mailing address:2 Avenue de Mohamed El Fassi Rabat, Morocco Mail from the U.S. to the Embassy can be sent via APO. The address is: Embassy PSC 74 Box 021 APO AE 09718 Tel: (212)(37)-76-22-65 Fax: (212)(37)-76-56-61 After-hours telephone: (212)(37)-76-96-39

Mozambique - Avenida Kenneth Kaunda, 193 Maputo, Mozambique

Telephone: 258-1-492797 Fax: 258-1-490448 E-mail:consularmaputo@state.gov

Namibia - Mail Address Private Bag 12029 Windhoek, Namibia Street Address 14 Lossen Street Windhoek, Namibia Local Phone 221601 International Phone 264-61-221601 E-mail:kopfgb@state.gov

Nepal - U.S. Embassy, Panipokhari, Kathmandu, Nepal Tel: +977 1 4411179 Fax: +977 1 4419963

Netherlands - - Lange Voorhout 102 2514 EJ The Hague the Netherlands Tel: +31 70 310-9209 Fax: +31 70 361-4688

New Zealand - Km 4 1/2 Carretera Sur P.O. Box #: 327 TeL: 011-(505)-268-0123 Fax: 011 - (505) - 2669943

Nigeria - 7, Mambilla Street Off Aso Drive Maitama District, Abuja, Nigeria Telephone: (234)-9-523-0916/0960/5857/2235/2205 Fax: (234)-9-523-0353 E-Mail:usabuja@pd.state.gov

Norway - Drammensveien 18 0244 Oslo, Norway Tel:(+47)22 44 85 50

Samoa - Apia (E) -- P.O. Box 3430, Apia, Tel [685] 21-631, afterhours Tel 23-617, Fax 22-030.Mobile Tel [685] 7-1776. Internet address: usembassy@samoa.net

Saudi Arabia - Riyadh (E), Collector Road M, Riyadh Diplomatic Quarter or American Embassy, Unit 61307, APO AE 09803-1307, international mail: P.O. Box 94309, Riyadh 11693, Tel 966 (1) 488-3800, Fax 488-7360; PAO address: P.O. Box 94310, Riyadh 11693, Fax 488-3989; COM Fax 488-3237; POL/ECO Fax 488-3278; RSO Fax 488-7867; FMC Fax 482-2765; GSO Fax 488-7939; ATO Tel 488-4364, ext. 1560, Fax 482-4364; ISC Fax 488-7867; ADM Fax 488-7765; workweek: Saturday–

Wednesday /// Dhahran (CG), Between Aramco Hdqtrs and Dhahran Int'l Airport, P.O. Box 81, Dhahran Airport 31932 -- Unit 66803, APO AE 09858-6803, Tel [966] (3) 891-3200; ADM Fax 891-7416; COM Fax 891-8332; CON Fax 891-6816; EXEC Fax 891-0464; GSO Fax 891-3296, afterhours 891-2203 /// Jeddah (CG), Palestine Rd., Ruwais -- P.O. Box 149, Jeddah 21411, or Unit 62112, APO AE 09811, Tel [966] (2) 667-0080, Fax 669-2991; ADM Fax 669-3074; CON Fax 669-3078; COM Tel 667-0040, Fax 665-8106; ATO Tel 661-2408, Fax 667-6196; PAO Tel 660-6355, Fax 660-6367; workweek: Saturday through Wednesday /// U.S. Representative to the Saudi Arabian U.S. Joint Commission on Economic Cooperation (USREP/-JECOR), P.O. Box 5927, Riyadh, Tel [966] (1) 248-3471, ext.] 263, Fax 248-3471, ext. 857

Senegal - Dakar (E), B.P. 49, Avenue Jean XXIII, Tel [221] 823-4296 or 823-7384, Fax 822-2991; PAO Tel 823-1185 or 823-8124; AID Tel 823-5880, 823-1602, 823-6680, Fax 823-2965, Telex 21793 AMEMB SG, Fax 822-2991; E-mail user last name and initials, i.e.: doejt@state.gov

Serbia and Montenegro - Belgrade (E), American Embassy Belgrade -- U.S. Department of State, Washington, D.C. 20521-5070, Tel [381] (11) 645-655, afterhours Tel 646-481, tie line (8) 754-0000, Fax [381] (11) 645-221; E ec Fax 645-332; POL/ECO Fax 646-054; PAO Fax 646-924; CON Fax 644-053; GSO Fax 645-221. Internet address: amembassybelgrade@dos.us-state.gov./ (Operations temporarily suspended)./ Pristina (USOP), Dragodan – Nazim Hikmet 30, 38000 Pristina, Kosovo Province -- Pouch address: Embassy Skopje, Department of State, Washington, DC 20521-7120, Satellite phone 873 762 029 525, Fax 873 762 029 526; USAID: Dragodan – Nazim Hikmet, 38000 Pristina, Kosovo Province Tel [381] (38) 590 174,

Fax [381] (38) 590438, Saturday Tel 873 761 393 321

Seychelles - Port Louis (E), Rogers House (4th Fl.), John Kennedy St., Tel [230] 208-2347, 208-2354, 208-9763 thru 9767, Fax 208-9534;Int'l. mail: P.O. Box 544, Port Louis, Mauritius; U.S. mail: Am. Emb., Port Louis, Dept. of State, Wash., D.C. 20521-2450. Internet address: usembass@intnet.mu [*Note: Port Louis is now responsible for Comoros and assumed responsibility for Seychelles on October 1, 1996.]

Sierra Leone - Freetown (E), corner of Walpole and Siaka Stevens Sts., Tel [232] (22) 226-481 through 226-485, AMB Tel 226-155, DCM Tel 227-192, Fax 225-471

Singapore - Singapore (E), 27 Napier Rd., Singapore 258508 -- PSC Box 470, FPO AP 96534-0001, Tel [65] 476-9100, Fax 476-9340. Internet home page address: http://www.homepacificnet.sg/˜am emb

Slovakia - Bratislava (E), Hviezdoslavovo Namestie 4, 81102 Bratislava (int'l address), Tel [421] (7) 5443-3338, ADM Fax 5441-5148; CON Tel 5443-0809, GSO/CON Fax 5441-8861, POL Tel 5443-5990, POL/ECO Fax 5443-0096. Internet address: www.usis.sk

Slovenia - Ljubljana (E), Presernova 31, 1000 Ljubljana or -- AmEmbassy Ljubljana, Dept. of State, Washington, D.C. 20521-7140, Tel [386] (61) 200-5000, Fax 200-5555; PAO address: Cankarjeva 11 1000 Ljubljana, Tel 200-21-80, Fax 126-4284. Internet address: us-embassy@usis.si

South Africa - Pretoria (E), 877 Pretorius St., Arcadia 0083 -- P.O. Box 9536, Pretoria 0001, Tel [27] (12) 342-1048, Fax 342-2244; PAO Tel 342-3006, Fax 342-2090; AID Tel 323-8869, Fax 323-6443 /// Cape Town (CG), Broadway Centre

Hertzog Boulevard, Heerengracht, Foreshore, Cape Town, P.O. Box 6773, Roggebaai, Cape Town 8012, Tel [27] (21) 421-4280, ADM Fax 418-1989. Internet address: socapetown@pixie.co.za /// Durban (CG), 2901 Durban Bay House, 333 Smith St., Durban 4000, Tel [27] (31); 304-4737, Fax 301-0265; PAO Tel 305-5060, Fax 304-2847; COM Tel 304-4737, Fax 3301-0577 /// Johannesburg (CG), 1 River Street -- corner of Riviera, Killarney -- P.O. Box 1762, Houghton, 2041, Tel [27] (11) 646-6900, Fax 646-6913; COM Tel 442-3571, Fax 442-3770; PAO Tel 838-2231, Fax 838-3920; SCO Tel 442-3571, Fax 442-3770. E-mail address: amcongen.jhb@pixie.co.za

Spain - Madrid (E), Serrano 75, 28006 Madrid -- PSC 61, APO AE 09642, Tel [34] (1) 91587-2200, Fax 91587-2303. Inward dial (DID) numbers: AMB [34] 91587-2201; DCM 91587-2205; POL 91587-2387; ECO 91587-2286; ADM 91587-2208; IRM 91587-2308; DAO 91587-2278; PAO 91587-2502; DEA 91587-2280; FAA 91587-2300; ODC 91549-1339; CON 91587-2236; B&F 91587-2211; PER 91587-2226; RSO 91587-2230; IRM duty phone 91587-2355; EMB duty phone 619-276-782. Internet address: http://www.embusa.es /// Barcelona (CG), Paseo Reina Elisenda De Montcada 23, 08034 Barcelona -- PSC 61, Box 0005, APO AE 09642, Tel [34] (93) 280-2227, Fax (93) 205-5206; ADM Fax (93) 205-7764; PAO Fax (93) 205-5857; COM Fax (93) 205-770 /// La Coruna (CA), Canton Grande, 16-17, 8E, 15003; Tel. [34] 981213-233; Fax [34] 981228 808 /// Las Palmas (CA), Los Martinez De Escobar, 3 Oficina 7- 35007, Tel 34-928-271 259, Fax 34-928-22-58-63 /// Fuengirola (Malaga) (CA), Centro Comercial "Las Rampas" Fase 2, Planta 1, Locales 12-G-7 y 12-G-8, Fuengirola, 29640 Malaga, Tel. 34-952-47-48-91, Fax 34-952-46-51-89 /// Palma de Mallorca (CA), Avenida Jamime 111, No. 26,

Entresuelo (97) 07012; Tel. 34-971-725051, Fax 34-971-71-87-55 /// Seville (CA), Paseo de las Delicias, 7 Seville, 41012, Tel. 34-95-42 31885, Fax 34-95-42 32040 /// Valencia (CA), CL de la Paz, 6-5 Local 5, 46003 Valencia; Tel. 34-96-351-6973, Fax 34-96-352-9565

Sri Lanka - Colombo (E), 210 Galle Road, Colombo 3, Tel [94] (1) 448007, Fax 437345, 4446013; USAID: 44 Galle Road, Colombo 3, Tel [94] (1) 472855, Fax 472850; PAO: 44 Galle Road, Colombo 3, Tel [94] (1) 421121, Fax 449070; IBB: 228/1 Galle Road, Colombo 4, Tel 589245, Fax 502675; Peace Corps: 751/1 Kynsey Road, Colombo 8, Tel 687617. Internet address: http://www.usia.gov/posts/sri lanka. COM E-mail address: com@eureka.lk. Information Resource Center E-mail address: amcenter@sri.lanka.net.USAID. E-mail address: lisachiles@usaid.gov

Sudan - Khartoum (E), Sharia Ali Abdul Latif -- P.O. Box 699, APO AE 09829, Tel [249] (11) 774611 or 77-47-00, Fax [249] (11) 774137, Telex 22619 AMEM SD, Fax (873) (151) 6770

Suriname - Paramaribo (E), Dr. Sophie Redmondstraat 129 -- P.O. Box 1821, AmEmbassy Paramaribo, Dept. of State, Washington, D.C., 20521-3390, Tel [597] 472900, 477881, 476459; AMB 78300; DCM 476507; IRM 476793; GSO Fax 479829; AMB Fax 420800; ADM Fax 410972. Internet address: embuscen@sr.net

Sweden - Stockholm (E), Dag Hammarskjšlds VŠg 31, S-115 89 Stockholm, Sweden -- pouch address: AmEmb Stockholm, Dept. of State, Wash, D.C. 20521-5750, Tel [46] (8) 783-5300, Fax (46) (8) 661-1964; AMB SEC Tel 783-5314; afterhours Tel 783-5310; CON Fax 660-5879; COM: Fax 660-9181; AGR: Fax 662-8495; PAO Fax 665-3303; DAO Fax 662-8046

Switzerland - Bern (E), Jubilaumsstrasse 93, 3005 Bern, Tel [41] (31) 357-7011, Fax 357-7344; Telex (845) 912603, AMB Tel 357-7259; DCM Tel 357-7258; POL/ECO Tel 357-7424; ADM Tel 357-7295; PAO Tel 357-7238, Fax 357-7379; IRM Tel 357–7201; RSO Tel 357-7296; DEA Tel 357-7367, Fax 357-7253; DAO Tel 357-7244, Fax 357-7381; AGR Tel 357-7279, Fax 357-7363; LEGATT Tel 357-7340, Fax 357-7268; CON Fax 357-7398; FCS Fax 357-7336; COM Fax 357-7336. Embassy website: www.usembassy.ch /// US Mission to the European Office of the UN and Other International Organizations (Geneva), Mission Permanente Des Etats-Unis, Route de Pregny 11, 1292 Chambesy-Geneva, Switzerland, Tel [41] (22) 749-4111, Fax 749-4880, Amb. Tel 749-4300, Fax 749-4892; DCM Tel 749-4302; PSA (POL) Tel 749-4621; IAEA (ECON) Tel 749-4629, Fax 749-4883; RMA Tel 749-4617, Fax 4671; LEGATT: 749-4460; ADM Tel 749-4391, Fax 749-4491; PAO Tel 749-4360, Fax 749-4314; RSO Tel 749-4397; LAB Tel 749-4624; IRM Tel 749-4306 /// US Trade Representative (USTR), Botanic Bldg., 1-3 Avenue de la Paix, 1202 Geneva, Switzerland, Tel [41] (22) 749-4111, Fax 749-5308 /// US Delegation to the Conference on Disarmament (CD), U.S. Mission Bldg., Route de Pregny 11, 1292 Chambesy-Geneva, Tel [41] (22) 749-4407, Fax 749-4833 /// Geneva (CA), 11 route de Pregny, 1292 Chambesy/Geneva, Tel [41] (22) 798-1605, Fax 798-1630 /// Zurich (CA), Dufourstrasse 101, 8008 Zurich, Tel [41] (01) 422-2566, Fax 383-9814

Syria - Damascus (E), Abou Roumaneh, Al-Mansur St., No. 2 -- P.O. Box 29, Damascus, Syria, Tel [963] (11) 333-1342, Fax 224-7938; 24 hours: 333-3232; PAO Tel 333-1878, 333-8413, Fax 332-1456; CON Fax 331-9678

Taiwan - American Institute in Taiwan, No. 7 Lane 134, Hsin Yi Road, Section 3, Taipei, Taiwan, Tel [886] (2) 2709-2000, afterhours Tel 2709-2013, Fax 2702-7675. For further information, contact the Washington, D.C., office of the American Institute in Taiwan, 1700 N. Moore St. Suite 1700, Arlington, VA 22209-1996, Tel (703) 525-8474, Fax 841-1385. /// American Trade Center, Room 3207, International Trade Building, Taipei World Trade Center, 333 Keelung Road, Section 1, Taipei 10548, Taiwan, Tel [886] (2) 2720-1550; COM Fax 2757-7162 American Institute in Taiwan, 5th Fl., #2 Chung Cheng 3rd Rd. Kaohsiung, Taiwan, Tel [886] (7) 224-0154/7, Fax 223-8237

Tajikistan - Dushanbe (E), Octyabrskaya Hotel, 105A Prospect Rudaki, Dushanbe, Tajikistan 734001, Tel [7] (3772) 21-03-56, Fax [7] (3772) 21-03-62. Internet address: amemb@usis.td.silk.org

Tanzania - Dar Es Salaam (E), 140 Msese Road, Kinondoni District -- P.O. Box 9123, Tel [255] (51) 666010-5, Fax 666701. Internet address: usembassy-dar2@cats-net.com

Thailand - Bangkok (E), 120 Wireless Rd. -- APO AP 96546, Tel [66] (2) 205-4000, Fax 205-4131;COM 3rd Fl., Diethelm Towers Bldg., Tower A, 93/1 Wireless Rd., 10330, Tel 255-4365 thru 7, Fax 255-2915 /// Chiang Mai (CG), 387 Vidhayanond Rd., Chaing Mai 50300 -- U.S. Embassy, Box C, APO AP 96546, Tel [66] (53) 252-629, Fax 252-633

Togo - Lome (E), rue Pelletier Caventou and rue Vauban, B.P. 852, Tel [228] 21-29-91 thru 94, ADM Fax 21-79-52. Internet address: ustogo1#caf.tg

Trinidad and Tobago - Port-of-Spain (E), 15 Queen's Park West -- P.O. Box 752, Tel (809) 622-6372/6, 6176, Fax 628-5462; EXEC OFF Fax 628-8134; ECO/COM Fax 622-2444

Tunisia - Tunis (E), 144 Ave. de la Liberte, 1002 Tunis-Belvedere, Tel [216] (1) 782-566, Fax 789-719; USATO Fax 785-345; CON Fax 788-923; FSI Tel 741-672 or 746-991, Fax 741-062; GSO Tel 707-166 or 715-785, Fax 715-735; PAO Tel 799-895, 789-800, 798-833, Fax 789-313; DAO Fax 794-677; ODC Fax 788-609; AGR Fax 785-345

Turkey - Ankara (E), 110 Ataturk Blvd. -- PSC 93, Box 5000, APO AE 09823, Tel [90] (312) 468-6110, Fax 467-0019; ADM/ECO Fax 468-6138; GSO Fax 467-0057; PER Fax 467-8847; POL Fax 468-4775; CON Fax 468-6131; PAO Tel 468-6102 thru 6106; PAO EXEX OFF Fax 467-3624 and 468-6145; AGR Fax 467-0056; COM Fax 467-1366. Internet address: http://www.usis-ankara.orgt.tr. /// Istanbul (CG), 104-108 Mesrutiyet Caddesi, Tepebasi, 80050 Istanbul, Turkey -- PSC 97, Box 0002, APO AE 0927-0002, Tel [90] (212) 251-3602, Fax 251-3218; ADM Fax 251-3632; CON Fax 252-7851; DEA Fax 251-5213; FAS Fax 243-5262; FCS/COM Fax 252-2417; GSO Fax 251-2554; PAO Fax 252-7986. Web site address: http://www.usisist.org.tr /// Adana (C), Ataturk Caddesi -- PSC 94, APO AE 09824, Tel [90] (322) 459-1551, Fax 457-6591. Website address: http://www.usconadana.org.tr /// Izmir (CA), PSC 88, Box 5000, APO AE 09821, Tel [90] (232) 441-0072 and 441-2203; Fax 441-2373; COM: c/o Izmir Chamber of Commerce, Ataturk Caddesi 126, Kat 5, 35210 Pasaport, Izmir, PSC 88 Box 5000, APO AE 09821, Tel 441-2446; Fax 489-0267

Turkmenistan - Ashgabat (E), 9 Puskin Street, Tel [9] (9312) 35-00-37, 35-0 0-42, 51-13-06, tie line 962-0000, Fax 51-13-05, tie line 962-2159

Uganda - Kampala (E), Parliament Ave. -- P.O. Box 7007, Tel [256] (41) 259792/3/5, Fax 259794; ADM Tel 234142, Fax 341863; PAO Tel 233231, Fax 250314;

608

AID Tel 235879, Fax 233417

Ukraine - Kiev (E), 10 Yuria Kotsubynskoho, 2..54053 Kiev 53, Tel [380] (44) 246-9750, afterhours Tel 216-3805, Fax 244-7350; PAO Tel 213-2532, Fax 213-3386; USAID Tel 462-5678, Fax 462-5834; COM Tel 417-2669, Fax 417-1419; PC Tel 220-1183; AGR Tel 417-1268

United Arab Emirates - Abu Dhabi (E), [post does not have access to APO/FPO] Al-Sudan St. -- P.O. Box 4009, Pouch: AmEmbassy Abu Dhabi, Dept. of State, Washington, D.C. 20521-6010, Tel [971] (2) 436-691 or 436-692, afterhours Tel 434-457, Fax 434-771; ADM Fax 435-441; CON Fax 435-786; PAO Fax 434-802; USLO Fax 434-604; COM: Blue Tower Bldg., 8th Fl., Sheikh Khalifa Bin Zayed St., Tel 273-666, Fax (2) 271-377, workweek: Saturday–Wednesday. Internet address: uscmbabu@emirates.net.ae /// Dubai (CG), [post does not have access to APO/FPO] Dubai World Trade Center, 21st Fl. -- P.O. Box 9343, Pouch AMCONGEN Dubai, Dept. of State, Washington, D.C., 20521-6020, Tel [971] (4) 3313-115, Fax 3314-043; COM Tel 3313-584, Fax 3313-121; PAO Tel 3314-882, Fax 3314-254; ATO Tel 3313-612/3314-063, Fax 3314-998; NRCC Tel 3311-888, Fax 3315-764, workweek: Saturday–Wednesday. Internet E-mail address: max@emirates.net.ae

United Kingdom - London, England (E), 24/31 Grosvenor Sq., W1A 1AE -- PSC 801, Box 40; FPO AE 09498-4040, Tel [44] (0207) 499-9000; ECO Fax [44] (0207) 409-1637; COM/FCS Fax [44] (0207) 408-8020; CON Fax [44] (0207) 495-5012; ADM Fax [44] (171) 629-9124. Website: www.usembassy.org.uk /// Belfast, Northern Ireland (CG), Queen's House, 14 Queen St., BT1 6EQ -- PSC 801, Box 40, APO AE 09498-4040, Tel [44] (028) 9032-8239, Fax [44] (028) 9024-8482 ///

Edinburgh, Scotland (CG), 3 Regent Ter. EH7 5BW -- PSC 801, Box 40, FPO AE 009498-4040, Tel [44] (131) 556-8315, Fax [44] (131) 557-6023. Website: www.usembassy.org.uk/scotland/ /// European Bank for Reconstruction and Development, One Exchange Square, London EC2A 2EH, Tel [44] (171) 338-6502, Fax [44] (171) 338-6487 /// Cayman Islands (CA), Office of Adventure Travel, Seven Mile Beach, Georgetown, Grand Cayman, Tel 345-945-1511, Fax 345-945-1811

United States - US Mission to the United Nations (USUN), 799 United Nations Plaza, New York, NY 10017-3505, Tel (212) 415-4000, afterhours Tel 415-4444, Fax 415-4443 /// US Mission to the Organization of American States (USOAS), Department of State, Washington, D.C. 20520, Tel (202) 647-9376, Fax 647-0911

Uruguay - Montevideo (E), Lauro Muller 1776 • APO AA 34035, Tel [598] (2) 203-6061 or 408-7777, Fax 408-7777. Internet address: www.embeeuu.gub.uy

Uzbekistan - Tashkent (E), 82 Chilanzarskaya, Tel [998] 71 120-5450, Fax 120-6335, tie-line Tel 793-0000, tie-line Fax 793-0131; PAO Fax [998] (71) 120-6224; USAID Fax 120-6309; COM Fax 120-6692; duty officer cellular Tel [998] (71) 180-4060

Venezuela - Caracas (E), Calle F con Calle Suapure, Colinas de Valle Arriba -- P.O. Box 62291, Caracas 1080-A or APO AA 34037, Tel [58] (2) 975-6411/975-7811 or 975-9821 (afterhours); IVG 643 plus ext. or 643-0000 (operator); MILGP [58] (2) 682-7749/2877, Emb Fax 975-6710; ADM Fax 975-9429; AGR Fax 975-7615; CON Fax 753-4534; CON ACS FAX 975-8991; COM and FCS Fax 975-9643; CUS Fax 975-6556; DAO Fax 975-6542; DEA Fax 975-8519; POL and ECO FAX 975-9778; FAS Fax 975-7615; FMC Fax 975-7903; GSO Fax 975-8406;

RSO Fax 975-8972; LEGATT Fax 975-9629; MILGP Fax 682-5844; NAS Fax 975-9685; PAO Fax 975-6998; PER Fax 975-6292. Website address: www.usia.gov/posts/caracas /// Maracaibo (CA), CEVAZ -- Centro Venezolano-Americano del Zulia, Calle 63 Numero 3E60, Apartado 419, Maracaibo, Estado Zulia, Venezuela, Tel 58-61-982-164 or 58-61-925-953, Fax 58-61-921-098

Vietnam - Hanoi (E), 7 Lang Ha Road, Ba Dinh District, Hanoi, Vietnam (Int'l mail), U.S. Embassy-Hanoi, PSC 461, Box 400, FPO AP 96521-0002 (U.S. mail), U.S. Embassy-Hanoi, Dept. of State, Washington, D.C. 20521-4500 (pouch address), Tel [84] (4) 843-1500, ADM Fax 843-1510; CON Fax 831-3017; USDAO Fax 831-3239; AGR Fax 843-8932; POL/ECO Fax 733-2614; PAO Tel 822-5439, Fax 822-5435; USCS Tel 824-2422, Fax 824-2421 /// Ho Chi Minh City (CG), 51 Nguyen Dinh Chieu, District 3 -- PSC 461, P.O. Box 400, FPO AP 96521-0002, Tel [84] (8) 822-9433, Fax 822-9434

Yemen - Sanaa (E), Dhahr Himyar Zone, Sheraton Hotel District -- P.O. Box 22347, Sanaa, Republic of Yemen, Tel [967] (1) 238-843/52, Fax 251-563; CON Fax 238-870; PAO Tel 238-819, Fax 226-649; post one/afterhours: 238-855; RMO Fax 238-874; workweek: Saturday–Wednesday, 8:00 a.m. to 4:30 p.m. Internet address: usembassyol@y.net.ye

Zambia - Lusaka (E), corner of Independence and United Nations Aves. -- P.O. Box 31617, Tel [260] (1) 250-955 or 252-230, front office Tel 254-301, afterhours Tel 252-234, Telex AMEMB ZA 41970, Fax 252-225; AID Tel 254-303 thru 6, ext. 212, Fax 254-532; PAO Tel 227-993 thru 4, ext. 211, Fax 226-523

Zimbabwe - Harare (E), 172 Herbert Chitepo Ave. -- P.O. Box 3340, Tel [263] (4) 250-593, 250-594, 250-595, Fax 796-488;

Executive Office direct line 704679, Fax 796487; Embassy Fax 797488; IPU direct tel line 708941; DAO Fax 705752; PAO Tel 758800/1, Fax 758802; USAID Tel 720630, Fax 722418, 720722; PC Tel 752273. Internet address: amembzim@africaonline.co.zw

---

Note:

ACM	Assistant Chief of Mission
ADM	Administrative Section
ADV	Adviser
AGR	Agricultural Section (USDA/FAS)
AID	Agency for International Development
ALT	Alternate
AMB	Ambassador
AMB SEC	Ambassador's Secretary
APHIS	Animal and Plant Health Inspection Service Officer
APO	Army Post Office
ATO	Agricultural Trade Office (USDA/FAS)
BCAO	Branch Cultural Affairs Officer (USIS)
Bg	Brigadier General
BIB	Board for International Broadcasting
BO	Branch Office (of Embassy)
BOB/EUR	Board of Broadcasting, European Office
BPAO	Branch Public Affairs Officer (USIS)
B.P.	Boite Postale
C	Consulate
CA	Consular Agency/Agent
CAO	Cultural Affairs Officer (USISO
Capt	Captain (USN)
CDC	Centers for Disease Control
Cdr	Commander
CEO	Cultural Exchange Officer (USIS)
CG SEC	Consul General's Secretary
CHG	Charge d' Affaires
CINCAFSOUTH	Commander-in Chief Allied Forces Southern Europe
CINCEUR	Commander-in Chief U.S. European Command
CINCUSAFE	Commander-in Chief U.S. AirForces Europe
CINCUSAREUR	Commander-in Chief U.S. Army Europe
Col	Colonel
COM (FCS)	Commercial Section
CON	Consul, Consular Section
COUNS	Counselor
C.P.	Caixa Postal
CPO	Communications Program Officer
CUS	Customs Service (Treasury)
DAC	Development Assistance Committee
DCM	Deputy Chief of Mission
DEA	Drug Enforcement Agency
DEP	Deputy
DEP DIR	Deputy Director
DIR	Director
DOE	Department of Energy
DPAO	Deputy Public Affairs Officer (USIS)
DPO	Deputy Principal Officer
DSA	Defense Supply Adviser
E	Embassy
ECO	Economic Section
ECO/COM	Economic/Commercial Section
EDO	Export Development Officer
ERDA	Energy Research and Development Administration
EX-IM	Export-Import
FAA	Federal Aviation Administration
FIC/JSC	Finance Committee and Joint Support Committee
FIN	Financial Attache (Treasury)
FODAG	Food and Agriculture Organizations
FPO	Fleet Post Office
IAEA	International Atomic Energy Agency
IAGS	Inter-american Geodetic Survey
ICAO	International Civil Aviation Organization
IMO	Information Management Officer
IO (USIS)	Information Officer
IRM	International Resources Management
IRS	Internal Revenue Service
ISM	Information Systems Manager
JUS/CIV	Department of Justice, Civil Division
JUSMAG	Joint US Military Advisory Group
LAB	Labor Officer
LO	Liaison Officer
Ltc	Lieutenant Colonel
LEGAT	Legal Attache
M	Mission
Mg	Major General
MAAG	Military Assistance Advisory Group
MILGP	Military Group
MSG	Marine Security Guard
MIN	Minister
MLO	Military Liaison Office
MNL	Minerals Officer
NARC	Narcotics
NATO	North Atlantic Treaty Organization
NAU	Narcotics Assistance Unit
OAS	Organization of American States
ODA	Office of the Defense Attache
ODC	Office of Defense Cooperation
OIC	Office in Charge
OMC	Office of Military Cooperation
PAO (USIS)	Public Affairs Officer
PO	Principal Officer
PO SEC	Principal Officer's Secretary
POL	Political Section
POL/LAB	Political and Labor Section
POLAD	Political Adviser
POL/ECO	Political/Economic Section
Radm	Rear Admiral
REDSO	Regional Economic Development Services Office
REF	Refugee Coordinator
REP	Representative

RES   Resources
RHUDO   Regional Housing and
Urban Development Office
ROCAP   Regional Officer for
Central American Programs
RPSO   Regional Procurement
             and Support Office
RSO   Regional Security
Officer
SAO   Security Assistance
Office
SCI   Scientific Attache
SEC DEL Secretary of Delegation
SHAPE   Supreme Headquarters
             Allied Powers Europe
SLG   State and Local
             Government
SR   Senior
STC   Security Trade Control
UNEP   United Nations
Environment Program

APPENDIX B

FOREIGN EMBASSIES IN THE UNITED STATES

The Republic of Afghanistan
2341 Wyoming Ave., NW,
Washington DC 20008
Telephone: (202) 234-3770
Fax: (202) 328-3516

The Republic of Albania
2100 S Street, NW, Washington
DC 20008
Telephone: (202) 223-4942
Fax: (202) 628-7342

**The Democratic and Popular
Republic of Algeria**
2118 Kalorama Road NW,
Washington DC 20008
Telephone: (202) 265-2800
Fax: (202) 667-2174
E-mail: embalgus@cais.com
http://www.algeria-us.org/

Andorra
Two United Nations Plaza, 25th
Floor, New York NY 10017

Angola
1615 M Street, NW Suite 900,
Washington DC 20036
Telephone: (202) 785-1156
Fax: (202) 785-1258
E-mail: angola@angola.org
http://www.angola.org/

Antigua and Barbuda
3216 New Mexico Avenue, NW,
Washington DC 20016
Telephone: (202) 362-5122
Fax: (202) 362-5225

The Argentine Republic
1600 New Hampshire Avenue,
NW, Washington DC 20009
Telephone: (202) 238-6400
Fax: (202) 332-3171
E-mail: argentina@veriomail.com
http://www.embassyofargentina-usa.org/

The Republic of Armenia
2225 R Street, Washington DC
20008

Telephone: (202) 319-1976
Fax: (202) 319-2982
E-mail: amembusadm@msn.com
http://www.armeniaemb.org/

Australia
1601 Massachusetts Avenue, NW,
Washington DC 20036
Telephone: (202) 797-3000
Fax: (202) 797-3168
http://www.austemb.org/

Austria
3524 International Court, NW,
Washington DC 20008-3035
Telephone: (202) 895-6700
Fax: (202) 895-6750

The Republic of Azerbaijan
927 15th Street, NW, Suite 700,
Washington DC 20035
Telephone: (202) 842-0001
Fax: (202) 842-0004
E-mail: azerbaijan@tidalwave.net
http://www.azembassy.com/

**The Commonwealth of the
Bahamas**
2220 Massachusetts Avenue, NW,
Washington DC 20008
Telephone: (202) 319-2660
Fax: (202) 319-2668

The State of Bahrain
3502 International Drive, NW,
Washington DC 20008
Telephone: (202) 342-0741
Fax: (202) 362-2192
E-mail: info@bahrainembassy.org
http://www.bahrainembassy.org/

**The People's Republic of
Bangladesh**
3510 International Drive, NW,
Washington DC 20007
Telephone: (202) 244-2745
Fax: (202) 244-5366
E-mail: bdenq@bangladoot.org
http://www.bangladoot.org/

Barbados
2144 Wyoming Avenue, NW,

Washington DC 20008
Telephone: (202) 939-9200
Fax: (202) 332-7467

The Republic of Belarus
1619 New Hampshire Avenue,
NW, Washington DC 20009
Telephone: (202) 986-1606
Fax: (202) 986-1805
E-mail: embassy@capu.net
http://www.belarusembassy.org

Belgium
3330 Garfield Street, NW,
Washington DC 20008
Telephone: (202) 333-6900
Fax: (202) 333-3079
E-mail: washington@diplobel.org

http://www.diplobel.org/usa/default.htm

Belize
2535 Massachusetts Avenue, NW,
Washington DC 20008
Telephone: (202) 332-9636
Fax: (202) 332-6888
E-mail: belize@oas.org
http://www.embassyofbelize.org/

The Republic of Benin
2124 Kalorama Road, NW,
Washington DC 20008
Telephone: (202) 232-6656
Fax: (202) 265-1996

Bhutan
(Consulate-General) 2 UN Plaza,
27th Floor, New York NY 10017
Telephone: (212) 826-1919
Fax: (212) 826-2998

Bolivia
3014 Massachusetts Avenue, NW,
Washington DC 20008
Telephone: (202) 483-4410
Fax: (202) 328-3712
http://www.bolivia-usa.org/

Bosnia and Herzegovina
2109 E Street NW, Washington DC

20037
Telephone: (202) 337-1500
Fax: (202) 337-1502
E-mail: info@bosnianembassy.org
http://www.bosnianembassy.org/

Botswana
1531-3 New Hampshire Avenue,
NW, Washington DC 20036
Telephone: (202) 244-4990
Fax: (202) 244-4164

Brazil
3006 Massachusetts Avenue, NW,
Washington DC 20008
Telephone: (202) 238-2700
Fax: (202) 238-2827
E-mail: webmaster@brasilemb.org
http://www.brasilemb.org/

Embassy of Brunei Darussalam
3520 International Court, NW,
Washington DC 20008
Telephone: (202) 237-1838
Fax: (202) 885-0560
E-mail: info@bruneiembassy.org
http://www.bruneiembassy.org/

The Republic of Bulgaria
1621 22nd Street, NW, Washington
DC 20008
Telephone: (202) 387-0174
Fax: (202) 234-7973
E-mail: office@bulgaria-
embassy.org
http://www.bulgaria-embassy.org

Burkina Faso
2340 Massachusetts Avenue, NW,
Washington DC 20008
Telephone: (202) 332-5577
Fax: (202) 667-1882
E-mail: bf@burkinaembassy-
usa.org
http://www.burkinaembassy-
usa.org/

The Republic of Burundi
2233 Wisconsin Avenue, NW, Suite
212, Washington DC 20007
Telephone: (202) 342-2574
Fax: (202) 342-2578

The Republic of Cameroon
2349 Massachusetts Avenue, NW,
Washington DC 20008
Telephone: (202) 265-8790
Fax: (202) 387-3826

Canada

501 Pennsylvania Avenue, NW,
Washington DC 20001
Telephone: (202) 682-1740
Fax: (202) 682-7726
E-mail:
webmaster@canadianembassy.org
http://www.canadianembassy.org

The Republic of Cape Verde
3415 Massachusetts Avenue, NW,
Washington DC 20007
Telephone: (202) 965-6820
Fax: (202) 965-1207

http://www.capeverdeusaembassy.o
rg/

The Central African Republic
1618 22nd Street, NW, Washington
DC 20008
Telephone: (202) 483-7800
Fax: (202) 332-9893
The Republic of Chad
2002 R Street, NW, Washington
DC 20009
Telephone: (202) 462-4009
Fax: (202) 265-1937
E-mail: info@chadembassy.org
http://www.chadembassy.org

Chile
1732 Massachusetts Avenue, NW,
Washington DC 20036
Telephone: (202) 785-1746
Fax: (202) 887-5579
http://www.chile-usa.org/

The People's Republic of China
2300 Connecticut Ave., NW,
Washington DC 20008
Telephone: (202) 328-2500
Fax: (202) 588-0032
E-mail:
chinaembassy_us@fmprc.gov.cn
http://www.china-embassy.org/

Colombia
2118 Leroy Place, NW,
Washington DC 20008
Telephone: (202) 387-8338
Fax: (202) 232-8643
E-mail: emwas@colombiaemb.org
http://www.colombiaemb.org/

**The Federal and Islamic Republic
of the Comoros**
420 E. 50th St., New York NY
10022
Telephone: (212) 972-8010
Fax: (212) 983-4712

The Republic of Congo
4891 Colorado Avenue, NW,
Washington DC 20011
Telephone: (202) 726-5500
Fax: (202) 726-1860
E-mail: info@embassyofcongo.org
http://www.embassyofcongo.org/

**The Democratic Republic of
Congo**
1800 New Hampshire Avenue,
NW, Washington DC 20009
Telephone: (202) 234-7690
Fax: (202) 234-2609

Costa Rica
2114 S Street, NW, Washington
DC 20008
Telephone: (202) 234-2945 or 46
Fax: (202) 265-4795
E-mail: embassy@costarica-
embassy.org
http://costarica-embassy.org/

**The Republic of Cote d'Ivoire
(Ivory Coast)**
2424 Massachusetts Avenue, NW,
Washington DC 20008
Telephone: (202) 797-0300

The Republic of Croatia
2343 Massachusetts Avenue, NW,
Washington DC 20008
Telephone: (202) 588-5899
Fax: (202) 588-8936
E-mail: webmaster@croatiaemb.org
http://www.croatiaemb.org/

Cuba Interests Section
2630 and 2639 16th Street, NW,
Washington DC 20009
Telephone: (202) 797-8518
Fax: (202) 986-7283
E-mail: cubaseccion@igc.apc.org

The Republic of Cyprus
2211 R Street, NW, Washington
DC 20008
Telephone: (202) 462-5772
Fax: (202) 483-6710
E-mail: cypembwash@earthlink.net
http://www.cyprusembassy.net

The Czech Republic
3900 Spring of Freedom Street,
NW, Washington DC 20008
Telephone: (202) 274-9100
Fax: (202) 966-8540
E-mail:

613

washington@embassy.mzv.cz
http://www.mzv.cz/washington/

Royal Danish Embassy
3200 Whitehaven Street, NW,
Washington DC 20008
Telephone: (202) 234-4300
Fax: (202) 328-1470
E-mail: wasamb@wasamb.um.dk
http://www.denmarkemb.org/

The Republic of Djibouti
1156 15th Street, NW, Suite 515,
Washington DC 20005
Telephone: (202) 331-0270
Fax: (202) 331-0302

The Commonwealth of Dominica
3216 New Mexico Avenue, NW,
Washington DC 20016
Telephone: (202) 364-6781/2
Fax: (202) 364-6791
E-mail: Embdomdc@aol.com

The Dominican Republic
1715 22nd Street, NW, Washington
DC 20008
Telephone: (202) 332-6280
Fax: (202) 265-8057
E-mail: embdomrepusa@msn.com
http://www.domrep.org/

Ecuador
2535 15th Street, NW, Washington
DC 20009
Telephone: (202) 234-7200
Fax: (202) 667-3482
E-mail: mecuawaa@erols.com
http://www.ecuador.org/

The Arab Republic of Egypt
3521 International Court, NW,
Washington DC 20008
Telephone: (202) 895 5400
Fax: (202) 244-4319
E-mail: embassy@egyptembdc.org
h
ttp://www.embassyofegyptwashingtondc.or
g/

El Salvador
2308 California Street, NW,
Washington DC 20008
Telephone: (202) 265-9671
E-mail: cbartoli@elsalvador.org
http://www.elsalvador.org
Equatorial Guinea
2020 16th Street, NW, Washington
DC 20009
Telephone: (202) 518-5700

Fax: (202) 518-5252

Eritrea
1708 New Hampshire Ave, NW,
Washington DC 20009
Telephone: (202) 319-1991
Fax: (202) 319-1304
E-mail:
veronica@embassyeritrea.org

Estonia
1730 M Street, Suite 503, NW,
Washington DC 20036
Telephone: (202) 588-0101
Fax: (202) 588-0108
E-mail: info@estemb.org
http://www.estemb.org/

Ethiopia
3506 International Drive, NW,
Washington DC 20008
Telephone: (202) 364-1200
Fax: (202) 686-9551
E-mail: info@ethiopianembassy.org
http://www.ethiopianembassy.org/

Fiji
2233 Wisconsin Avenue, NW, Suite
240, Washington DC 20007
Telephone: (202) 337-8320
Fax: (202) 337-1996
E-mail: fijiemb@earthlink.net

Finland
3301 Massachusetts Avenue, NW,
Washington DC 20008
Telephone: (202) 298-5800
Fax: (202) 298-6030
E-mail: info@finland.org
http://www.finland.org/

France
4101 Reservoir Road, NW,
Washington DC 20007
Telephone: (202) 944-6000
Fax: (202) 944-6072
E-mail: info@amb-wash.fr
http://www.ambafrance-us.org/

The Gabonese Republic
2034 20th Street, NW, Suite 200,
Washington DC 20009
Telephone: (202) 797-1000
Fax: (202) 332-0668

The Gambia
1155 15th Street, NW, Suite 1000,
Washington DC 20005
Telephone: (202) 785-1399
Fax: (202) 785-1430

E-mail: gamembdc@gambia.com

http://www.gambia.com/index.html

The Republic of Georgia
1615 New Hampshire Ave. NW,
Suite 300, Washington DC 20009
Telephone: (202) 387-2390
Fax: (202) 393-4537
http://www.georgiaemb.org/

Germany
4645 Reservoir Road, NW,
Washington DC 20007-1998
Telephone: (202) 298-4000
Fax: (202) 298-4249 or 333-2653
http://www.germany-info.org/

Ghana
3512 International Drive NW,
Washington DC 20008
Telephone: (202) 686-4520
Fax: (202) 686-4527
E-mail: ghtrade@cais.com

Greece
2221 Massachusetts Avenue, NW,
Washington DC 20008
Telephone: (202) 939-5800
Fax: (202) 939-5824
http://www.greekembassy.org/

Grenada
1701 New Hampshire Ave., NW,
Washington DC 20009
Telephone: (202) 265-2561

Guatemala
2220 R Street, NW, Washington
DC 20008
Telephone: (202) 745-4952
Fax: (202) 745-1908
E-mail: info@guatemala-
embassy.org
http://www.guatemala-
embassy.org

The Republic of Guinea
2112 Leroy Place, NW,
Washington DC 20008
Telephone: (202) 483-9420
Fax: (202) 483-8688

The Republic of Guinea-Bissau
15929 Yukon Lane, Rockville MD
20855
Telephone: (301) 947-3958

Guyana
2490 Tracy Place, NW,

614

Washington DC 20008
Telephone: (202) 265-6900
Fax: (202) 232-1297
E-mail:
Guyanaembassy@hotmail.com

http://www.guyana.org/govt/embas
sy.html

The Republic of Haiti
2311 Massachusetts Avenue, NW,
Washington DC 20008
Telephone: (202) 332-4090
Fax: (202) 745-7215
E-mail: embassy@haiti.org
http://www.haiti.org/

**Apostolic Nunciature, the Holy
See**
3339 Massachusetts Avenue, NW,
Washington DC 20008
Telephone: (202) 333-7121

Honduras
3007 Tilden Street, NW, Suite 4M,
Washington DC 20008
Telephone: (202) 966-7702
Fax: (202) 966-9751
E-mail: embhondu@aol.com
http://www.hondurasemb.org/

The Republic of Hungary
3910 Shoemaker Street, NW,
Washington DC 20008
Telephone: (202) 362-6730
Fax: (202) 966-8135
E-mail: office@huembwas.org
http://www.huembwas.org/

Iceland
1156 15th Street, NW, Suite 1200,
Washington DC 20005-1704
Telephone: (202) 265-6653
Fax: (202) 265-6656
E-mail: icemb.wash@utn.stjr.is
http://www.iceland.org/

India
2107 Massachusetts Avenue, NW,
Washington DC 20008
Telephone: (202) 939-7000
Fax: (202) 265-4351
http://www.indianembassy.org/

The Republic of Indonesia
2020 Massachusetts Avenue, NW,
Washington DC 20036
Telephone: (202) 775-5200
Fax: (202) 775-5365

Iranian Interests Section
2209 Wisconsin Avenue NW,
Washington DC 20007
Telephone: (202) 965-4990
Fax: (202) 965-1073

http://www.daftar.org/default_eng.
htm

Iraqi Interests Section
1801 P Street, NW, Washington
DC 20036
Telephone: (202) 483-7500
Fax: (202) 462-5066

Ireland
2234 Massachusetts Avenue, NW,
Washington DC 20008
Telephone: (202) 462-3939
Fax: (202) 232 5993
E-mail: ireland@irelandemb.org
http://www.irelandemb.org/

Israel
3514 International Drive, NW,
Washington DC 20008
Telephone: (202) 364-5500
Fax: (202) 364-5423
E-mail: ask@israelemb.org
http://www.israelemb.org/

Italy
3000 Whitehaven Street, NW,
Washington DC 20008
Telephone: (202) 612-4400
Fax: (202) 518-2154
http://www.italyemb.org/

Jamaica
1520 New Hampshire Avenue,
NW, Washington DC 20036
Telephone: (202) 452-0660
Fax: (202) 452-0081
E-mail: info@emjamusa.org
http://www.emjamusa.org/

Japan
2520 Massachusetts Avenue NW,
Washington DC 20008
Telephone: (202) 238-6700
Fax: (202) 328-2187
http://www.embjapan.org/

**The Hashemite Kingdom of
Jordan**
3504 International Drive, NW,
Washington DC 20008
Telephone: (202) 966-2664
Fax: (202) 966-3110
E-mail: HKJEmbassyDC@aol.com

http://www.jordanembassyus.org/

The Republic of Kazakhstan
1401 16th Street, NW, Washington
DC 20036
Telephone: (202) 232-5488
Fax: (202) 232-5845
E-mail: kazak@intr.net
http://www.kazakhstan-embassy-
us.org

Kenya
2249 R. Street, NW, Washington
DC 20008
Telephone: (202) 387-6101
Fax: (202) 462-3829
E-mail: info@kenyaembassy.com
http://www.kenyaembassy.com/

The Kyrgyz Republic
1732 Wisconsin Avenue, NW,
Washington DC 20007
Telephone: (202) 338-5141
Fax: (202) 338-5139
E-mail: Embassy@kyrgyzstan.org
http://www.kyrgyzstan.org/

The Republic of Korea
2450 Massachusetts Avenue, NW,
Washington DC 20008
Telephone: (202) 939-5600
Fax: (202) 797-0595
http://www.koreaembassy.org/

The State of Kuwait
2940 Tilden Street, NW,
Washington DC 20008
Telephone: (202) 966-0702
Fax: (202) 364-2868

**The Lao People's Democratic
Republic**
2222 S Street, NW, Washington
DC 20008
Telephone: (202) 332-6416
Fax: (202) 332-4923
http://www.laoembassy.com/

Latvia
4325 17th Street, NW, Washington
DC 20011
Telephone: (202) 726-8213
Fax: (202) 726-6785
E-mail: Embassy@Latvia-USA.org
http://www.latvia-usa.org/

Lebanon
2560 28th Street, NW, Washington
DC 20008
Telephone: (202) 939-6300

615

Fax: (202) 939-6324
E-mail:
info@lebanonembassyus.org
http://www.lebanonembassyus.org/

The Kingdom of Lesotho
2511 Massachusetts Avenue, NW,
Washington DC 20008
Telephone: (202) 797-5533
Fax: (202) 234-6815

The Republic of Liberia
5201 16th Street, NW, Washington
DC 20011
Telephone: (202) 723-0437
Fax: (202) 723-0436
E-mail: info@liberiaemb.org
http://www.liberiaemb.org/

Lithuania
2622 Sixteenth Street, NW,
Washington DC 20009-4202
Telephone: (202) 234-5860
Fax: (202) 328-0466
E-mail: admin@ltembassyus.org
http://www.ltembassyus.org/

Luxembourg
2200 Massachusetts Avenue, NW,
Washington DC 20008
Telephone: (202) 265-4171
Fax: (202) 328-8270
E-mail: infos@luxembourg-usa.org
http://www.luxembourg-usa.org/

The Republic of Macedonia
3050 K Street, NW, Suite 210,
Washington DC 20007
Telephone: (202) 337-3063
Fax: (202) 337-3093
E-mail: rmacedonia@aol.com

Malawi
2408 Massachusetts Avenue, NW,
Washington DC 20008
Telephone: (202) 797-1007

Malaysia
3516 International Court, NW,
Washington DC 20008
Telephone: (202) 572-9700
Fax: (202) 483-7661

The Republic of Mali
2130 R Street, NW, Washington
DC 20008
Telephone: (202) 332-2249
Fax: (202) 332-6603
E-mail: info@maliembassy-usa.org
http://www.maliembassy-usa.org

Malta
2017 Connecticut Avenue NW,
Washington DC 20008
Telephone: (202) 462-3611
Fax: (202) 387-5470
E-mail:
Malta_Embassy@compuserve.com

http://www.foreign.gov.mt/ORG/m
inistry/missions/washington2.htm

**The Republic of the Marshall
Islands**
2433 Massachusetts Avenue, NW,
Washington DC 20008
Telephone: (202) 234-5414
Fax: (202) 232-3236
E-mail: info@rmiembassyus.org

http://www.rmiembassyus.org/use
mb.html

**The Islamic Republic of
Mauritania**
2129 Leroy Place, NW,
Washington DC 20008
Telephone: (202) 232-5700
Fax: (202) 319-2623
E-mail: info@mauritaniembassy-
usa.org
http://www.mauritaniembassy-
usa.org/

Mauritius
4301 Connecticut Avenue, NW,
Suite 441, Washington DC 20008
Telephone: (202) 244-1491
Fax: (202) 966-0983
E-mail:
MAURITIUS.EMBASSY@prodigy.
net

http://www.idsonline.com/usa/embasydc.ht
ml

Mexico
1911 Pennsylvania Avenue, NW,
Washington DC 20006
Telephone: (202) 728-1600
Fax: (202) 728-1698
E-mail: mexembusa@sre.gob.mx
http://www.embassyofmexico.org

**The Federated States of
Micronesia**
1725 N Street, NW, Washington
DC 20036
Telephone: (202) 223-4383
Fax: (202) 223-4391
E-mail: fsm@fsmembassy.org

http://www.fsmembassy.org/

The Republic of Moldova
2101 S Street, NW, Washington
DC 20008
Telephone: (202) 667-1130/31/37
Fax: (202) 667-1204
E-mail: moldova@dgs.dgsys.com
http://www.moldova.org/

Mongolia
2833 M Street NW, Washington
DC 20007
Telephone: (202) 333-7117
Fax: (202) 298 9227
E-mail: monemb@aol.com
http://members.aol.com/monemb/

The Kingdom of Morocco
1601 21st Street, NW, Washington
DC 20009
Telephone: (202) 462-7979
Fax: (202) 265-0161

The Republic of Mozambique
1990 M Street, NW, Suite 570,
Washington DC 20036
Telephone: (202) 293-7146
Fax: (202) 835-0245
E-mail: embamoc@aol.com
http://www.embamoc-usa.org/

The Union of Myanmar
2300 S Street, NW, Washington
DC 20008
Telephone: (202) 332-9044
Fax: (202) 332-9046
E-mail: MEWashDC@aol.com

http://members.aol.com/mewashdc/

The Republic of Namibia
1605 New Hampshire Avenue,
NW, Washington DC 20009
Telephone: (202) 986-0540
Fax: (202) 986-0443

Royal Nepalese Embassy
2131 Leroy Place, NW,
Washington DC 20008
Telephone: (202) 667-4550
Fax: (202) 667-5534
E-mail: nepali@erols.com

Royal Netherlands Embassy
4200 Linnean Avenue, NW,
Washington DC 20008
Telephone: (202) 244-5300
Fax: (202) 362-3430
http://www.netherlands-

616

embassy.org/

New Zealand
37 Observatory Circle, Washington
DC 20008
Telephone: (202) 328-4800
Fax: (202) 667-5227
E-mail: nz@nzemb.org
http://www.nzemb.org/

The Republic of Nicaragua
1627 New Hampshire Avenue,
NW, Washington DC 20009
Telephone: (202) 939-6570
Fax: (202) 939-6542

The Republic of Niger
2204 R Street, NW, Washington
DC 20008
Telephone: (202) 483-4224
Fax: (202) 483-3169
E-mail: embassyofniger@ioip.com
http://www.nigerembassyusa.org/

The Federal Republic of Nigeria
1333 16th Street, NW, Washington
DC 20036
Telephone: (202) 986-8400
Fax: (202) 462-7124
http://www.nigeriaembassyusa.org

Royal Norwegian Embassy
2720 34th Street, NW, Washington
DC 20008
Telephone: (202) 333-6000
Fax: (202) 337-0870
http://www.norway.org/

The Sultanate of Oman
2535 Belmont Road, NW,
Washington DC 20008
Telephone: (202) 387-1980
Fax: (202) 745-4933

The Islamic Republic of Pakistan
2315 Massachusetts Avenue, NW,
Washington DC 20008
Telephone: (202) 939-6200
Fax: (202) 387-0484
E-mail: info@pakistan-
embassy.com
http://www.pakistan-embassy.com/

The Republic of Panama
2862 McGill Terrace, NW,
Washington DC 20008
Telephone: (202) 483-1407

Papua New Guinea
1779 Massachusetts Ave. NW,

Suite 805, Washington DC 20036
Telephone: (202) 745-3680
Fax: (202) 745-3679
E-mail: Kunduwash@aol.com
http://www.pngembassy.org

Paraguay
2400 Massachusetts Avenue, NW,
Washington DC 20008
Telephone: (202) 483-6960
Fax: (202) 234-4508

Peru
1700 Massachusetts Avenue, NW,
Washington DC 20036
Telephone: (202) 833-9860
Fax: (202) 659-8124
E-mail: peru@peruemb.org
http://www.peruemb.org

The Philippines
1600 Massachusetts Avenue, NW,
Washington DC 20036
Telephone: (202) 467-9300
Fax: (202) 467-9417
http://www.philippineembassy-
usa.org/

Poland
2640 16th Street, NW, Washington
DC 20009
Telephone: (202) 234 3800
Fax: (202) 328-6271
E-mail: information@ioip.com
http://www.polandembassy.org/

Portugal
2125 Kalorama Road, NW,
Washington DC 20008
Telephone: (202) 328-8610
Fax: (202) 462-3726
E-mail: portugal@portugalemb.org
http://www.portugalemb.org/

The State of Qatar
4200 Wisconsin Ave, NW, Suite
200, Washington DC 20016
Telephone: (202) 274-1600
Fax: (202) 237-0061

Romania
1607 23rd Street, NW, Washington
DC 20008
Telephone: (202) 332-4848
Fax: (202) 232-4748
E-mail: romania1@roembus.org
http://www.roembus.org/

The Russian Federation
2650 Wisconsin Avenue, NW,

Washington DC 20007
Telephone: (202) 298-5700
Fax: (202) 298-5735
http://www.russianembassy.org

The Republic of Rwanda
1714 New Hampshire Avenue,
NW, Washington DC 20009
Telephone: (202) 232-2882
Fax: (202) 232-4544
E-mail: rwandemb@rwandemb.org
http://www.rwandemb.org/

Saint Kitts and Nevis
3216 New Mexico Avenue, NW,
Washington DC 20016
Telephone: (202) 686-2636
Fax: (202) 686-5740
E-mail: info@stkittsnevis.org
http://www.stkittsnevis.org/

Saint Lucia
3216 New Mexico Avenue, NW,
Washington DC 20016
Telephone: (202) 364-
6792/93/94/95
Fax: (202) 364-6723

Saint Vincent and the Grenadines
3216 New Mexico Avenue, NW,
Washington DC 20016
Telephone: (202) 364-6730
Fax: (202) 364-6736

Royal Embassy of Saudi Arabia
601 New Hampshire Avenue, NW,
Washington DC 20037
Telephone: (202) 337-4076
E-mail: info@saudiembassy.net
http://www.saudiembassy.net/

The Republic of Senegal
2112 Wyoming Avenue, NW,
Washington DC 20008
Telephone: (202) 234-0540

The Republic of Seychelles
800 Second Avenue, Suite 400,
New York NY 10017
Telephone: (212) 687-9766
Fax: (212) 972-1786

Sierra Leone
1701 19th Street, NW, Washington
DC 20009
Telephone: (202) 939-9261
Fax: (202) 483-1793

The Republic of Singapore
3501 International Place, NW,

Washington DC 20008
Telephone: (202) 537-3100
Fax: (202) 537-0876
E-mail: singemb@bellatlantic.net

http://www.gov.sg/mfa/washington
/

The Slovak Republic
3523 International Court, NW,
Washington DC 20008
Telephone: (202) 237-1054
Fax: (202) 237-6438
E-mail: info@slovakembassy-us.org
http://www.slovakembassy-us.org/

The Republic of Slovenia
1525 New Hampshire Avenue,
NW, Washington DC 20036
Telephone: (202) 667-5363
Fax: (202) 667-4563
E-mail: slovenia@embassy.org
http://www.embassy.org/slovenia/

Somalia
The Embassy of the Somali
Democratic Republic ceased
operations May 8, 1991

South Africa
3051 Massachusetts Avenue, NW,
Washington DC 20008
Telephone: (202) 232-4400
Fax: (202) 265-1607
E-mail: info@saembassy.org
http://www.saembassy.org

Spain
2375 Pennsylvania Avenue, NW,
Washington DC 20037
Telephone: (202) 452-0100
Fax: (202) 833-5670
E-mail: spain@spainemb.org

http://www.spainemb.org/ingles/indexing.h
tm

Sri Lanka
2148 Wyoming Avenue, NW,
Washington DC 20008
Telephone: (202) 483-4025 to 28
Fax: (202) 232-7181
E-mail: slembassy@starpower.net
http://www.slembassyusa.org/

The Republic of the Sudan
2210 Massachusetts Avenue, NW,
Washington DC 20008
Telephone: (202) 338-8565
Fax: (202) 667-2406

E-mail: info@sudanembassyus.org
http://www.sudanembassyus.org/

The Republic of Suriname
4301 Connecticut Avenue, NW,
Suite 460, Washington DC 20008
Telephone: (202) 244-7488
Fax: (202) 244-5878

The Kingdom of Swaziland
3400 International Drive, NW,
Washington DC 20008

Sweden
1501 M Street, NW, Washington
DC 20005
Telephone: (202) 467-2600
Fax: (202) 467-2656
E-mail:
ambassaden.washington@foreign.m
inistry.se
http://www.swedish-embassy.org/

Switzerland
2900 Cathedral Avenue, NW,
Washington DC 20008
Telephone: (202) 745-7900
Fax: 202-387-2564
E-mail:
vertretung@was.rep.admin.ch
http://www.eda.admin.ch/

The Syrian Arab Republic
2215 Wyoming Avenue, NW,
Washington DC 20008
Telephone: (202) 232-6313
Fax: (202) 234-9548

The Republic of China on Taiwan
4201 Wisconsin Avenue, NW,
Washington DC 20016
Telephone: (202) 895-1800
Fax: (202) 966-0825

The United Republic of Tanzania
2139 R Street, NW, Washington
DC 20008
Telephone: (202) 939-6125
Fax: (202) 797-7408
E-mail: balozi@tanzaniaembassy-
us.org
http://www.tanzaniaembassy-
us.org/

Royal Thai Embassy
1024 Wisconsin Avenue, NW, Suite
401, Washington DC 20007
Telephone: (202) 944-3600
Fax: (202) 944-3611
E-mail: thai.wsn@thaiembdc.org

http://www.thaiembdc.org/

The Republic of Togo
2208 Massachusetts Avenue, NW,
Washington DC 20008
Telephone: (202) 234-4212
Fax: (202) 232-3190

The Kingdom of Tonga
800 Second Avenue, Suite 400B,
New York NY 10017

**The Republic of Trinidad and
Tobago**
1708 Massachusetts Avenue, NW,
Washington DC 20036
Telephone: (202) 467-6490
Fax: (202) 785-3130
E-mail: embttgo@erols.com
http://ttembassy.cjb.net/

Tunisia
1515 Massachusetts Avenue, NW,
Washington DC 20005
Telephone: (202) 862-1850
Fax: (202) 862-1858

The Republic of Turkey
2525 Massachusetts Avenue, NW,
Washington DC 20008
Telephone: (202) 612-6700
Fax: (202) 612-6744
E-mail: info@turkey.org
http://www.turkey.org/

Turkmenistan
2207 Massachusetts Avenue, NW,
Washington DC 20008
Telephone: (202) 588-1500
Fax: (202) 588-0697
E-mail: turkmen@earthlink.net

http://www.turkmenistanembassy.o
rg

The Republic of Uganda
5911 16th Street, NW, Washington
DC 20011
Telephone: (202) 726-7100
Fax: (202) 726-1727
E-mail: ugembassy@aol.com

http://www.ugandaweb.com/ugaem
bassy/

Ukraine
3350 M Street, NW, Washington
DC 20007
Telephone: (202) 333-0606
Fax: (202) 333-0817

618

E-mail: infolook@aol.com
http://www.ukremb.com/

The United Arab Emirates
1255 22nd Street, NW, Suite 700,
Washington DC 20037
Telephone: (202) 243-2400
Fax: (202) 243-2432

**The United Kingdom of Great
Britain and Northern Ireland**
3100 Massachusetts Ave, NW,
Washington DC 20008
Telephone: (202) 588-6500
Fax: (202) 588-7870

http://www.britainusa.com/consular
/embassy/embassy.asp

Uruguay
2715 M Street, NW, 3rd Floor,
Washington DC 20007
Telephone: (202) 331-1313
Fax: (202) 331-8142
E-mail: uruguay@erols.com
http://www.embassy.org/uruguay/

The Republic of Uzbekistan
1746 Massachusetts Avenue, NW,
Washington DC 20036
Telephone: (202) 887-5300
Fax: (202) 293-6804
E-mail: emb@uzbekistan.org
http://www.uzbekistan.org/

The Republic of Venezuela
1099 30th Street NW, Washington
DC 20007
Telephone: (202) 342-2214
Fax: (202) 342-6820
E-mail: prensa@embavenez-us.org
http://www.embavenez-us.org/

The Socialist Republic of Vietnam
1233 20th Street NW, Suite 400,
Washington DC 20037
Telephone: (202) 861-0737
Fax: (202) 861-0917
E-mail: info@vietnamembassy-
usa.org
http://www.vietnamembassy-
usa.org/

Independent State of Samoa
800 Second Avenue, Suite 400D,
New York NY 10017
Telephone: (212) 599-6196
Fax: (212) 599-0797

The Republic of Yemen

2600 Virginia Avenue, NW, Suite
705, Washington DC 20037
Telephone: (202) 965-4760
Fax: (202) 337-2017
E-mail: info@yemenembassy.org
http://www.yemenembassy.org

**The Former S. F. Republic of
Yugoslavia**
2410 California Street, NW,
Washington DC 20008
Telephone: (202) 332-0333
Fax: (202) 332-3933
E-mail: yuembusa@aol.com
http://www.yuembusa.org/

The Republic of Zambia
2419 Massachusetts Avenue, NW,
Washington DC 20008
Telephone: (202) 265-9717
Fax: (202) 332-0826

The Republic of Zimbabwe
1608 New Hampshire Avenue,
NW, Washington DC 20009
Telephone: (202) 332-7100
Fax: (202) 483-9326
E-mail: zimemb@erols.com
http://www.zimembassy-usa.org/

APPENDIX C

U.S. GOVERNMENT PASSPORT AGENCIES

APPLY EARLY FOR YOUR PASSPORT!

Passport Agencies
Please Remember to Apply Early For Your Passport!
All public inquiries should be referred to the National Passport Information Center at telephone number 1-900-225-5674* (or 1-888-362-8668 with a credit card).

* (Please see information about these telephone numbers.)
** Twenty-four hour recording.

Boston Passport Agency
Thomas P. O'Neill Fed. Bldg., Room 247
10 Causeway Street
Boston, Massachusetts 02222-1094
**Recording: 617-565-6990

Chicago Passport Agency
Suite 380, Kluczynski Federal Bldg.
230 South Dearborn Street
Chicago, Illinois 60604-1564
**Recording: 312-341-6020

Honolulu Passport Agency
First Hawaiian Tower
1132 Bishop Street, Suite 500
Honolulu, Hawaii 96813-2809
**Recording: 808-522-8283

Houston Passport Agency
Mickey Leland Fed. Bldg.
1919 Smith Street, Suite 1100
Houston, Texas 77002-8049
**Recording: 713-209-3153

Los Angeles Passport Agency
1st Floor, Federal Building
11000 Wilshire Boulevard, Suite 1000
Los Angeles, California 90024-3615
**Recording: 310-575-5700

Miami Passport Agency
3rd Floor, Federal Office Bldg.
51 Southwest First Avenue
Miami, Florida 33130-1680
**Recording: 305-539-3600

New Orleans Passport Agency
Postal Services Building
701 Loyola Avenue, Rm. T-12005
New Orleans, Louisiana 70113-1931
**Recording: 504-589-6161

New York Passport Agency
Greater New York Federal Building
376 Hudson Street
10th Floor
New York, New York 10014
**Recording: 212-206-3500

Philadelphia Passport Agency
U.S. Customs House
200 Chestnut Street, Room 103
Philadelphia, Pennsylvania 19106-2970
**Recording: 215-597-7480

San Francisco Passport Agency
95 Hawthorne Street
5th Floor
San Francisco, California 94105-3901
**Recording: 415-538-2700

Seattle Passport Agency
Room 992, Federal Office Bldg.
915 Second Avenue
Seattle, Washington 98174-1091
**Recording: 206-808-5700

Stamford Passport Agency
One Landmark Square

620

Broad and Atlantic Streets
Stamford, Connecticut 06901-2667
**Recording: 203-325-4401

Washington Passport Agency
1111 19th Street, N.W.
Washington, D.C. 20522-1705
**Recording: 202-647-0518

* The cost per minute for 1-900 calls is $.35 for
the automated system and $1.05 for operator
assistance. This service also includes an optional
number: 1-888-362-8668 (TDD 1-888-498-3648)
for those calling with blocked 1-900 service. These
calls require a credit card payment of a flat rate of
$4.95 per call.

** The twenty-four hour recording includes
general passport information, passport agency
location, hours of operation, and information
regarding emergency passport services during non-
working hours. Some passport agencies require
appointments for applicants with proof of
departure within 14 days. When necessary, the
recording will provide instructions on making an
appointment

APPENDIX *D*

HOW TO OBTAIN AN INTERNATIONAL DRIVER'S PERMIT

Although most countries no longer require an International Drivers Permit (IDP), it is advisable to verify in advance if such a permit is required or recommended for the country you plan to visit. Your travel agent, travel advisor, or the country's tourist bureau or Embassy should be able to provide you with that information. You may also contact your local automobile association or the American Automobile Association. One of the important advantages of the IDP is that it is written in nine different, major languages.

Here are the requirements to apply for an International Drivers Permit from the American Automobile Association (AAA).

Requirements:	(1)	A completed application form;
......	(2)	two recent signed passport size photograph not larger than 2 1/2" by 2 1/2";
......	(3)	A $10 permit fee;
......	(4)	Applicant must be 15 years or older;
......	*(5)	Applicant must hold a valid U.S. or Territorial Driver's License.

You may request for an IDP by mail or in person. You are not required to be an AAA member to get and IDP from them. Check your telephone directories for an AAA office in your area you, or you may contact their headquarters at AAA Drive, Heathrow, Florida 32746-5063. Telephone: (407) 444-4000.

---

*Applicants with driving violations may be refused permit.

APPENDIX E

TO REPORT LOST OR STOLEN CREDIT/CHARGE CARD*
OR TO ARRANGE FOR CARD REPLACEMENT

CARD	IN U.S./CARIBBEAN	OUTSIDE U.S./OVERSEAS
VISA	800-336-8472	CALL COLLECT:(314) 275-6690
VISA GOLD	800-847-2911	CALL COLLECT:(314) 275-6690
MASTERCARD	800-826-2181	CALL COLLECT:(314) 275-6690
DINNERS CLUB	800-525-9135	CALL COLLECT:(303) 790-2433
AMERICAN EXPRESS*		
Personal Card (Green)	800-528-4800	CALL COLLECT:(919) 668-6668
Corporate Card	800-528-2122	CALL COLLECT:(602) 492-5450
Gold Card	800-528-2121	CALL COLLECT:(305) 476-2166
Platinum Card	800-525-3355	CALL COLLECT:(602) 492-5450
Optima Card	800-635-5955	CALL COLLECT:(602) 492-5450
Travelers Checks	800-221-7282	CALL COLLECT:(801) 964-6665
THOMAS COOK		
Travelers Checks	800-223-7373	CALL COLLECT:(609) 987-7300

*In the event of a stolen or lost Credit/Charge Card, it is advisable to quickly file a report with the local Police. Request a copy of the report for your file. American Express Cardholders are advised to call or visit the nearest American Express Travel Service Office immediately and/or call collect. Apply the same procedure as with cards, in the event your travelers checks are stolen or lost.

OFFICES OF CORPORATE CHARGE CARD ISSUERS

Air Travel Card
1301 Pennsylvania Ave., NW
Washington, DC 20004
(800) 222-4688, (202)
 624-4224
Fax: (202) 626-4242

American Express Travel Management Services
World Financial Center
200 Vesey St.
New York, NY 10285
(800) 528-2122; (212) 640-2000
Fax: (312) 380-5483

Citicorp Diners Club
8430 W. Bryn Mawr Ave.
Chicago, IL 60631
(800) 2-DINERS; (312) 380-5467
Fax: (3112) 380-5483

Mastercard International
Seventh Ave.
New York, NY 10106
(800) 727-8825; (212) 649-5535
Fax: (212) 649-4772

VISA USA
P.O. Box 8999
San Francisco, CA 94128
(800) 847-2221; (415) 432-2076
Fax: (415) 432-8153

Delivery of overnight mail takes 2 to 3 days to reach our office. REGULAR MAIL: Regular mail can take 3 to 4 weeks to reach the State Department due to on-going irradiation procedures. We strongly discourage this method for emergency use.

......

WIRING MONEY

WESTERN UNION	800-325-6000 or 800-257-4900
AMERICAN EXPRESS (MONEYGRAM)	800-543-4080.
......	From Abroad CALL COLLECT: (303) 980-3340
BANK OF AMERICA **(GLOBAL SELLERS NETWORK)**	800-227-3460
CITIBANK	(212) 657-5161
BARCLAYS⁺	(212) 233-4200

TELEX/TELEGRAM/CABLEGRAM

WESTERN UNION	800-325-6000 or 800-257-4900
AT&T (EASYLINK)*	800-242-6005

---

* May be available only to subscribers.

+ Must have a Barclays account.

APPENDIX G

COMPARATIVE CLOTHING SIZES

Suits and Overcoats (men)

American	32	34	36	38	40	42	44	46
Continental	42	44	46	48	50	52	54	56
British	32	34	36	38	40	42	44	46

Dresses and Suits (women)

American		6	8	10	12	14	16	18
Continental		36	38	40	42	44	46	48
British		8	10	12	14	16	18	20

Shirts (men)

American	14	14.5	15	15.5	16	16.5	17	17.5
Continental	36	37	38	39	41	42	43	44
British	14	14.5	15	15.5	16	16.5	17	17.5

Women's Hosiery

American	8	8.5	9	9.5	10	10.5
Continental	0	1	2	3	4	5
British	8	8.5	9	9.5	10	10.5

Socks

American	8.5	9	9.5	10	10.5	11	11.5

Continental	36/37	37/38	38/39	39/40	40/41	41/42	42/43
British	8.5	9	9.5	10	10.5	11	11.5

Shoes(Men)

American 7	8	8.5	9.5	10.5	11	11.5	12 13
Contl.39.5	41	42	43	44	44.5	45	46	47
British 6	7	7.5	8.5	9.5	10	10.5	11 12

Shoes (women)

American	6	6.5	7	7.5	8	8.5 9
Continental	38	38	39	30	40	41 42
British	4.5	5	5.5	6	6.5	7 7.5

Children's Clothes

American	2	4	6	8	10	12	14

Continental

Height (cm)	115	125	135	150	155	160	165
Age	5	7	9	12	13	14	15

British

Height (in)	38	43	48	55	58	60	62
Age	2-3	4-5	6-7	9-10	11	12	13

Shoes (children)

American 1	2	3	4.5	5.5	6.5	8	9 10 11 12 13
Continental 32	33	34	36	37	38.5	24	25 27 28 29 30
British 13	1	2	3	4	5.5	7	8 9 10 11 12

APPENDIX H

INTERNATIONAL WEIGHTS AND MEASURES

CONVERSION TABLES

DISTANCE

1 mile (Mi) = 1.609 Kilometers (Km)
1 kilometer (Km) = .6214 miles (Mi)

VOLUME (capacity)

IMPERIAL WEIGHT MEASURE

1 Imperial gallon = 4.5 liters (L)
1 liter (L) = .222 Imperial gallon (IGal)

Imperial gallons are larger than U.S. gallons
1mperial gallon = 1.2 U.S. gallons

TEMPERATURE

Degrees Fahrenheit (F^0) = 9/5 x Degrees
Centigrade + 32
Degrees Centigrade/Celsuis (C^0) = (5/9
Degrees Fahrenheit - 32)

SPEED

1 Mile per hour (MPH) = 1.6 (KMH)
1 kilometer per hour (KMH) = .625
(MPH)
1 inch = 2.54 centimeter (cm)
1 centimeter = .3937 inches (in)   1 foot
= .3048 meters (m)
1 meter = 3.281 feet (ft)

WEIGHTS

1 ounce (oz) = 28.349 grams (gm)
1 gram (gm) = .0353 ounces (oz)
1 pound (lb) = .4536 Kilograms
1Kg Kilogram (Kg) = 2.205 pounds (lb)

In = Cm	
1	= 2.54
2	= 5.08
3	= 7.63
4	= 10.16
5	= 12.70
6	= 15.24
7	= 17.78
8	= 20.32
9	= 22.86
10	= 25.40
11	= 27.94
12	= 30.48

Cm = In	
1	= 0.40
2	= 0.80
3	= 1.20
4	= 1.60
5	= 2.00
6	= 2.40
7	= 2.80
8	= 3.20
9	= 3.50
10	= 3.90
11	= 4.30
12	= 4.70

Lb = Kg	
1	= 0.45
2	= 0.91
3	= 1.36
4	= 1.81
5	= 2.27
6	= 2.72
7	= 3.18
8	= 3.63
9	= 4.08
10	= 4.54
50	= 22.68
100	= 45.36

Kg = Lb
1 = 2.21
2 = 4.41
3 = 6.61
4 = 8.82
5 = 11.02
6 = 13.23
7 = 15.43
8 = 17.64
9 = 19.84
10 = 22.05
50 = 110.23
100 = 220.46

Mi = Km
1 = 1.61
2 = 3.22
3 = 4.83
4 = 6.44
5 = 8.05
6 = 9.66
7 = 11.27
8 = 12.88
9 = 14.48
10 = 16.09
50 = 80.47
100 = 160.90

Km = Mi
1 = 0.62
2 = 1.24
3 = 1.86
4 = 2.49
5 = 3.11
6 = 3.73
7 = 4.35
8 = 4.97
9 = 5.59
10 = 6.21
50 = 31.07
100 = 62.14

Gal = L
1 = 3.79
2 = 7.57
3 = 11.35
4 = 15.14
5 = 18.93
6 = 22.71
7 = 26.50
8 = 30.28
9 = 34.16
10 = 37.94
50 = 189.70
100 = 379.40

L = Gal
1 = 0.26
2 = 0.53
3 = 0.79
4 = 1.06
5 = 1.32
6 = 1.58
7 = 1.85
8 = 2.11
9 = 2.38
10 = 2.64
50 = 13.20
100 = 26.40

TEMPERATURE
F = C
32 = 0
40 = 5
50 = 10
60 = 15
70 = 20
75 = 25
85 = 30
105 = 40
140 = 60
175 = 80

SPEED
MPH = KMH
20 = 32
30 = 48
40 = 64
50 = 80
60 = 96
70 = 112
80 = 128
90 = 144
100 = 160

APPENDIX I

INTERNATIONAL SYSTEMS OF WEIGHTS & MEASURES

AFGHANISTAN	M	CZECH REP.	M	LAOS	M
ALBANIA	M	DENMARK	M	LATVIA	M
ANGOLA	M	DOMINICA	I*	LEBANON	M
ANGUILLA	M,I	DOMINICAN REP.	I*	LESOTHO	M
ANTIGUA &		ECUADOR	M	LIBERIA	I
BARBUDA	I*	EGYPT	M*	LIBYA	M
ARGENTINA	M	EL SALVADOR	M*	LIECHTENSTEIN	M
ARMENIA	M	EQUAT. GUINEA	M	LITUANIA	M
AUSTRALIA	M	ESTONIA M		LUXEMBOURG	M
AUSTRIA	M	ETHIOPIA	M*	MADAGASCAR	M
AZERBAIJAN	M	FIJI	M	MALAWI	M
BAHAMAS	I	FINLAND	M	MALAYSIA	M*
BAHRAIN	M	FRANCE	M	MALI	M
BANGLADESH	I*	FRENCH GUIANA	M	MALTA	M
BARBADOS	M	FR. ANTILLES	M	MARTINIQUE	M
BELGIUM	M	FR. POLYNESIA	M	MAURITANIA	M
BELIZE	I	GABON	M	MAURITIUS	M
BERMUDA	M,I	GEORGIA	M	MEXICO	M
BHUTAN	M	GERMANY	M	MOLDOVA	M
BOLIVIA	M	GHANA	M	MONACO	M
BOTSWANA	M	GREECE	M	MONGOLIA	M
BRAZIL	M	GRENADA	M	MONTSERRAT	I*
BRITISH V.I.	I	GUADELOUPE	M	MOROCCO	M
BRUNEI	I**	GUATEMALA	M	MOZAMBIQUE	
BULGARIA	M	GUINEA	M	NAMIBIA	M
BURKINA FASO	M	GUINEA-BISSAU	M	NAURU	M
BURUNDI	M	GUYANA	M	NETHERLANDS	M
BYELARUS	M	HAITI	M	NETH. ANTILLES	M
CAMBODIA	M	HONDURAS	M*	NEW ZEALAND	M
CAMEROON	M	HONG KONG	M	NICARAGUA	M*
CANADA	M	HUNGARY	M	NIGER	M
CAYMAN IS	I	ICELAND	M	NIGERIA	M
CENTRAL		INDIA	M,I*	NORWAY	M
AFRICAN REP.	M	INDONESIA	M	OMAN	M,I*
CHAD	M	IRAN	M*	PAKISTAN	M,I*
CHILE	M	IRAQ	M*	PANAMA	M,I
CHINA,		IRELAND	I*	PAPUA	
PEOPLES REP.	M*	ISRAEL	M	NEW GUINEA	M
CHINA, TAIWAN	M	ITALY	M	PARAGUAY	M
COLOMBIA	M	JAMAICA	M,I	PERU	M
COMOROS	M	JAPAN	M	PHILIPPINES	M
CONGO,		JORDAN	M	PORTUGAL	M
PEOPLE'S REP.	M	KAZAKHSTAN	M	QATAR	M*
COSTA RICA	M	KENYA	M	REP. OF	
COTE D'IVOIRE	M	KOREA, NORTH	M	CAPE VERDE	M
CUBA	M	KOREA, SOUTH	M*	ROMANIA	M
CYPRUS	M*,I*	KUWAIT	M	RUSSIA	M
CZECHOSLO-		KYRGYZSTAN	M	RWANDA	M
				SAN MARINO	M

SAO TOME &			--------------------	
PRINCIPE	M			
SAUDI ARABIA	M	I =	Imperial system of	
SENEGAL	M		Weights and	
SEYCHELLES	I*		Measures is in use.	
SIERRA LEONE	M			
SINGAPORE	M*	I* =	Imperial system of	
SOMALIA	M,I		Weights and	
SOUTH AFRICA	M		Measures is in use,	
SPAIN	M		however	
SRI LANKA	M*		metrication	
ST. VINCENT	I		program is being	
ST. KITTS			introduced.	
	I	I** =	Imperial and /or	
ST. LUCIA	I		local systems of	
ST.PIERRE &			Weights and	
MIQUELON	M		Measures are	
SUDAN	I*		being used.	
SURINAME	M	M =	Metric system of	
SWEDEN	M		Weights and	
SWITZERLAND	M		Measures is in use.	
SYRIA	M	M* =	Traditional	
TAJIKISTAN	M		systems of Weights	
TANZANIA	M		and Measures is	
THAILAND	M*		still in use.	
THE GAMBIA	I*	M,I =	Metric and	
TOGO	M		Imperial systems	
TONGA	M		of Weights and	
TRINIDAD &			Measures are in	
TOBAGO	I*		use.	
TUNISIA	M			
TURKEY	M			
TURKMENISTAN	M			
TURKS & CAICOS	I			
UGANDA	M			
UKRAINE	M			
UN. ARAB				
EMIRATES	I,M			
U.K	I*			
URUGUAY	M			
UZBEKISTAN	M			
VENEZUELA	M			
VIETNAM	M			
YEMEN, P.D.M.	I*			
YUGOSLAVIA	M			
ZAIRE	M			
ZAMBIA	M			
ZIMBABWE	M			

APPENDIX J

INTERNATIONAL GUIDE TO TIPPING[*]

	HOTELS	TAXIS	OTHERS
ANDORRA	10-20%	10%	YES
ANGUILLA	D	D	YES
ANTIGUA & BARBUDA	10%	D	YES
ARGENTINA	10-22%	10%	YES
ARMENIA	YES	OD	OD
AUSTRALIA	10%	D	YES
AUSTRIA	10-15%	10%	YES
AZERBAIJAN	YES	OD	OD
BAHAMAS	15%	15%	YES
BANGLADESH	5-10%	5-10%	YES
BARBADOS	10%	10%	YES
BELARUS	YES	OD	OD
BELGIUM	15%	D	YES
BELIZE	D 10%	D	YES
BENIN	D	D	D
BOLIVIA	10-23%	D	YES
BRAZIL	D	YES	
BURMA	10%	10%	YES
CAMEROON	10%	D	YES
CANADA	15-20%	15-20%	YES
CAYMAN IS	NC 10-15%	NC	YES
CHILE	10%	NC	YES
CHINA, PEOPLES REP.	F	F	F
CHINA, TAIWAN	D 10%	D 10%	YES
COLUMBIA	10%	NC	YES
COSTA RICA	10%	NC	YES
COTE D'IVOIRE	5-10%	5-10%	YES
CYPRUS	10%	NT	YES
CZECHOSLOVAKIA	OD 5-10%	5-10%	YES
DENMARK	15%	upto 15%	YES
DOMINICA	10%	D	YES
DOMINICAN REP.	10%		
ECUADOR	10%	NC	YES
EGYPT	10-12%	10%	YES
ETHIOPIA	5-10%	NC	YES
FIJI	D	D	YES
FINLAND	14-15%	NT	YES
FRANCE	upto 25%	15%	YES
FRENCH GUIANA	12 1/2%	NC	YES
GERMANY	10%	5%	YES
GHANA	YES	YES	YES
GIBRALTAR	10-12%	10%	YES

GREECE	10-15%	10%	YES
GRENADA	D	D	YES
GUADELOUPE	10-15%	YES	
GUATEMALA	10%	10%	YES
GUINEA	D	D	YES
GUYANA	10%	10%	YES
HAITI	NC 10%	D	YES
HONDURAS	10%	10%	YES
HONG KONG	10-15%	10%	YES
HUNGARY	OD 10-15%	YES	YES
ICELAND	NC	NC	NC
INDIA	10%	NC	YES
INDONESIA	NC 10%	NC 10%	YES
IRELAND	10-15%	YES	YES
ISRAEL	10%	NC	YES
ITALY	12-15%	15%	YES
JAMAICA	15%	10-20%	YES
JAPAN	NC 10-20%	NC	YES
JORDAN	10%	10%	YES
KAZAKHSTAN	OD	OD	OD
KENYA	10-15%	10%	YES
KOREA, SOUTH	NC 10%	NC 10-15%	YES
KUWAIT	10%	D	YES
KYRGYZSTAN	OD	OD	OD
LATVIA	NT	10-20%	YES
LIBERIA	10-15%	NC	YES
LIECHTENSTEIN	10-15%		
LITHUANIA	NC	NC	NC
LUXEMBOURG	NC 10-20%	15-20%	YES
MALAYSIA	NC 10%	NC 10%	YES
MALTA	10%	10%	YES
MARTINIQUE	10-15%	D	YES
MEXICO	7-15%	D	YES
MOLDOVA	OD	OD	OD
MONTSERRAT	10%	10%	YES
MOROCCO	10-15%	10-15%	YES
NEPAL			YES
NETHERLANDS	15%	10-15%	YES
NEW CALEDONIA		F	F
NEW ZEALAND	NC 10%	NC	
NICARAGUA	10%	NC	YES
NIGERIA	10%	D	YES
NORWAY	15%	D	YES
PAKISTAN	5-10%	D	YES
PANAMA	10-15%	NC	YES
PAPUA NEW GUINEA	NC	NC	NC
PARAGUAY	10%	5-12%	YES
PERU	5-10%	NC	YES
PHILIPPINES	10%	D 10%	YES
POLAND	10%	10%	YES
PORTUGAL	10-15%	15%	YES
ROMANIA	NC	NC	
RUSSIA	10-15%	10-15%	YES
SAUDI ARABIA	10-15%	NC	YES
SENEGAL	10%	D	YES
SEYCHELLES	10%	D	YES

634

SINGAPORE	OD	10%	OD
SOUTH AFRICA	10%	10%	YES
SPAIN	5-10%	10-15%	YES
SRI LANKA	10%	D	YES
ST. KITTS	D	D	YES
ST. LUCIA	10%	10%	YES
ST. VINCENT	10-15%	10-15%	YES
ST. MAARTEN	10%	10%	YES
SURINAME	10%	NC	YES
SWEDEN	12-15%	10-15%	YES
SWITZERLAND	12-15%	12-15%	YES
TAJIKISTAN	OD	OD	OD
TANZANIA	5%	(OD) D	YES
THAILAND	D 10%	NC	YES
TOGO	OD	OD	
TRINIDAD & TOBAGO	10%	10-15%	YES
TUNISIA	10%	10%	YES
TURKEY	10-15%	D	YES
TURKMENISTAN	OD	OD	OD
UKRAINE	OD	OD	OD
UNITED KINGDOM	12-15%	10-15%	YES
URUGUAY	10%	10%	YES
UZBEKISTAN	OD	OD	OD
VENEZUELA	10%	NC	YES
YUGOSLAVIA	10%	10%	YES
ZAIRE	10%	D	YES
ZAMBIA	10%	OD	YES

xxx		YES, persons who perform other services such as porters, luggage handlers, door persons, etc. may be tipped or may expect to be tipped. Tipping and amount of tip is at your discretion.
D	=	Tipping is expected. Amount of tip is at your discretion.
OF	=	Tipping is Officially Discouraged although privately welcome.
NC	=	Tipping is not customary, nevertheless welcome.
NT	=	Not usually tipped
F	=	Tipping is prohibited

APPENDIX K

INTERNATIONAL TIME ZONES

(TIME DIFFERENCE, IN
HOURS, BETWEEN
U.S.EASTERN STANDARD
TIME AND FOREIGN
CAPITAL CITIES)

COUNTRIES	HOURS
AFGHANISTAN	9.5
ALBANIA	6
ALGERIA**	6
AMERICAN SAMOA	6
ANDORRA	6
ANGUILLA	1
ANTIGUA &	
BARBUDA	1
ARGENTINA	2
ARMENIA	8
AUSTRALIA*	15
AUSTRIA	6
AZERBAIJAN	8
BAHAMAS	0
BAHRAIN	8
BANGLADESH	11
BARBADOS	1
BELGIUM	6
BELIZE	-1
BENIN	6
BERMUDA	1
BHUTAN	11
BOLIVIA	1
BOTSWANA	7
BRAZIL*	2
BRITISH VIRGIN IS	1
BRUNEI	13
BULGARIA	7
BURKINA FASO	5
BURMA	11.5
BURUNDI	7
BYELARUS	8
CAMBODIA	12
CAMEROON	6
CANADA*	0
CAYMAN IS	0
CENT. AFRICAN REP.	6
CHAD	6
CHILE**	1
CHINA, PEOPLES	

REPUBLIC.	13
CHINA, TAIWAN	3
COLUMBIA	0
COMOROS	8
CONGO,	
PEOPLE'S REP	6
COSTA RICA	-1
COTE D'IVOIRE	5
CUBA**	0
CYPRUS	7
CZECH REP.	6
DENMARK	6
DOMINICA	1
DOMINICAN REP.	0
ECUADOR	0
EGYPT	7
EL SALVADOR	-1
ESTONIA	8
EQUAT. GUINEA	6
ETHIOPIA	8
FAEROW IS	5
FIJI	17
FINLAND	7
FRANCE	6
FR. POLYNESIA	-5
FR. ANTILLES	1
FRENCH GUIANA	2
GABON	6
GEORGIA	6
GHANA	5
GIBRALTAR	6
GREECE	7
GREENLAND	2
GRENADA	1
GUADELOUPE	1
GUAM	15
GUANTANAMO BAY	0
GUATEMALA	-1
GUINEA	5
GUINEA-BISSAU	5
GUYANA	2
HAITI	0
HONDURAS	-1
HONG KONG	13
HUNGARY	6
ICELAND	5
INDIA	10.5

INDONESIA*	12
IRAN	8.5
IRAQ	8
IRELAND	5
ISRAEL	7
ITALY	6
JAMAICA**	0
JAPAN	14
JORDAN	7
KAZAKHSTAN	11
KENYA	8
KIRIBATI	-5
KOREA, SOUTH	14
KOREA, NORTH	14
KUWAIT	8
KYRGYZSTAN	11
LAOS	12
LATVIA	8
LEBANON	7
LESOTHO	7
LIBERIA	5
LIBYA	6
LIECHTENSTEIN	6
LITUANIA	8
LUXEMBOURG	6
MADAGASCAR	8
MALAWI	7
MALAYSIA*	13
MALDIVES	10
MALI	5
MALTA	6
MARSHALL IS	17
MAURITANIA	5
MAURITIUS	9
MAYOTTE IS	8
MEXICO*	1
MICRONESIA*	16
MOLDOVA	8
MONACO	6
MONGOLIA	13
MONTSERRAT	1
MOROCCO	5
MOZAMBIQUE	7
MUSTIQUE	1
NAMIBIA	7
NAURU	17
NEPAL	10.5

NETHERLANDS	6		TONGA	18
NETHERLANDS			TRANSKEI	7
ANTILLES	1		TRINIDAD &	
NEW CALEDONIA	16		TOBAGO	1
NEW ZEALAND**	17		TUNISIA	6
NICARAGUA	-1		TURKEY	7
NIGER	6		TURKMENISTAN	10
NIGERIA	6		TURKS &	
NORWAY	6		CAICOS	**0
OMAN	9		U.S.A.	0
PAKISTAN	10		UGANDA	8
PANAMA	0		UKRAINE	8
PAPUA N. GUINEA	15		UNION IS	1
PARAGUAY	2		U.K**	5
PERU	0		UNITED ARAB	
PHILIPPINES	13		EMIRATES	9
POLAND	6		URUGUAY	2
PORTUGAL	5		UZBEKISTAN	11
PUERTO RICO	1		VATICAN CITY	6
QATAR	8		VENEZUELA	1
REP. OF DJIBOUTI	8		WESTERN SAMOA	-6
REP. OF CAPE VERDE	4		YEMEN, .P.D.R.	8
REUNION IS	9		YEMEN,	
ROMANIA	7		ARAB REP.	8
RUSSIA	8		YUGOSLAVIA	6
RWANDA	7		ZAIRE*	6
SAIPAN	15		ZAMBIA	7
SAN MARINO	6		ZIMBABWE	7
SAO TOME &				
PRINCIPE	5		*	Countries with
SAUDI ARABIA	8			multiple Time
SENEGAL	5			Zones. Hours
SEYCHELLES	9			indicated may be
SIERRA LEONE	5			different
SINGAPORE	13			depending on your
SOLOMON IS	16			location in these
SOMALIA	8			countries.
SOUTH AFRICA	7			
SPAIN	6			
SRI LANKA	10.5			
ST. MARTIN	1		**	Countries with
ST. LUCIA	1			varying time,
ST. KITTS-NEVIS	1			depending on the
ST. PIERRE & MIQUELON	2			month.
ST. VINCENT	1			
SUDAN	7			
SURINAME	2			
SWAZILAND	7			
SWEDEN	6			
SWITZERLAND	6			
SYRIA	7			
TAJIKISTAN	11			
TANZANIA	8			
THAILAND	12			
THE GAMBIA	5			
TOGO	5			

APPENDIX L

INTERNATIONAL ELECTRICITY REQUIREMENTS

COUNTRIES	Volts/AC	COUNTRIES	Volts/AC
AFGHANISTAN	20/50 AC	DENMARK	220/50
ALGERIA	110-115/50, 220/50 AC*	DOMINICA	220-240/50 AC
ANDORRA	125/50 AC	DOMINICAN REP.	110/60 AC
ANGUILLA	220	ECUADOR	110/60 AC
ANTIGUA	110/60 AC	EGYPT	220/50, 110-120/50*
ARGENTINA	220/60 AC	EL SALVADOR	110/60
ARMENIA	220/50	ESTONIA	220/50
AUSTRALIA	240 AC	EQUAT. GUINEA	220/50
AUSTRIA	220/50	ETHIOPIA	220/60 AC
AZERBAIJAN	220/50	FIJI	240/50 AC
BAHAMAS	120/60 AC	FINLAND	220/60 AC
BAHRAIN	220/50 AC	FRANCE	220/50
BANGLADESH	220 AC	FRENCH GUIANA	220 & 110/50 AC
BARBADOS	110/50 AC	GABON	220/240/50
BELGIUM	220/50 AC	GEORGIA	220/50
BELIZE	110/220/60 AC	GERMANY	220/50 AC
BENIN	220/50	GHANA	220-240/50 AC
BERMUDA	110/60 AC	GIBRALTAR	240-250/50 AC
BHUTAN	110-220/50 AC*	GREECE+	220/50 AC
BOTSWANA	220	GRENADA	220-240/50 Ac
BRAZIL+ 110/60; 220/60, 127/60 AC*		GUADELOUPE	220/50 AC
BRITISH V.I	115-210/60 AC	GUAM	120/60 AC
BULGARIA	220/50 AC	GUATEMALA	110/60 AC
BURKINA FASO	220/50	GUINEA	220/50
BURMA	220/50 AC	GUYANA	110-120/60 AC
BURUNDI	220/50	HAITI	110/60 AC
BYELARUS	220/50	HONDURAS	110 or 220/60 AC*
CAMEROON	110-220	HONG KONG+ +	200-220/60 AC
CANADA	110/60 AC	HUNGARY	220/50 AC
CAYMAN ISLANDS	110/60 AC	ICELAND	220/50 AC
CENTRAL AF. REP.	220	INDIA+	220/50 AC
CHAD	220	INDONESIA	220/50 AC
CHILE+	220/50 AC	IRAN	220/50
CHINA	110/50	IRAQ	220 DC
CHINA, TAIWAN	110/60 AC	IRELAND	220/50 AC
COLOMBIA	150/60 AC, 110/60**	ISRAEL	220/50 AC
COMOROS	220/50	ITALY	220/50, 110-127/50 AC*
CONGO, REP.	220/50	JAMAICA	110/50 AC
COSTA RICA	110/60 AC	JAPAN	110/50, 100/60 AC*
COTE D'IVOIRE	220/50 AC	JORDAN	220/50 AC
CUBA	110/60	KAZAKHSTAN	220/50
CYPRUS+ +	240/50 AC	KENYA	220/50 AC
ZECH REP.	220/50 AC	KOREA, SOUTH	110/60 AC

638

KUWAIT	240/50 AC	SOMALIA	220/50
KYRGYZSTAN	220/50	SOUTH AFRICA	220-230/50 AC
LATVIA	220/50	SPAIN	110-220/50 AC
LEBANON	110-220/50	SRI LANKA	230-240/50 AC
LESOTHO	220 AC	ST. KITTS	230/60 AC
LIBERIA	120/60 AC	ST. LUCIA	220/50 AC
LIBYA	220/50	ST. MARTIN	220/60 AC
LIECHTENSTEIN	220/50 AC	ST. VINCENT	220-230/50 AC
LITHUANIA	220/50	SUDAN	240 AC
LUXEMBOURG	220/110	SURINAME	110-115/60 AC
MADAGASCAR	220/50	SWAZILAND	240/50
MALAWI	220	SWEDEN+	220/50 AC
MALAYSIA	220/50 AC	SWITZERLAND	220/50 AC
MALI	220	TAJIKISTAN	220/50
MALTA	240/50 AC	TANZANIA	240/50/60 AC
MARTINIQUE	220/50AC	THAILAND	220/50 AC
MAURITANIA	220/50	TOGO	220/50 AC
MAURITIUS	220/230	TONGA	220 AC
MEXICO	110/60 AC	TRINIDAD & TOB.	110/60 AC
MICRONESIA	110/60 AC	TUNISIA	110-115/50, 220/50 AC*
MOLDOVA	220/50	TURKEY	220/50
MONTSERRAT	230/60 AC	TURKMENISTAN	220/50
MOROCCO	110-120/50 AC	TURKS & CAICOS	110/60
MOZAMBIQUE	220/50	U.S.A	110-115/60 AC
NAMIBIA	220/240/60	UKRAINE	220/50
NEPAL	220/50 AC	UNITED ARAB EM.	240/415 AC
NETHERLANDS		UNITED KINGDOM	220/50 AC
ANTILLES.	110-130/50,120/60 AC*	URUGUAY	220/50 AC
NETHERLANDS	220/50 AC	UZBEKISTAN	220/50
NEW CALEDONIA	220/50 AC	VENEZUELA	110/60 AC
NICARAGUA	110/60 AC	YEMEN, ARAB REP.	220/50 AC
NIGER	220-240/50	YEMEN, P.D.R	220/240/50
NIGERIA++	220/50 AC	YUGOSLAVIA	220/50 AC
NORWAY	220/50 AC	ZAIRE	220/50
OMAN	220/240/50	ZAMBIA	220/50 AC
PAKISTAN	220/240/50 AC	ZIMBABWE++	220/240/50
PANAMA	110/60 AC		
PAPUA NEW GUINEA	240 AC		
PARAGUAY+	220/50 AC	------------------	
PERU	220/60 AC	*	Electricity requirements vary in some
PHILIPPINES	220/60 AC		parts of the country.
POLAND	220/50 AC		
PORTUGAL	210-220/50 AC	+	Some parts of the country still use DC.
PUERTO RICO	110-115/60 AC		
QATAR	220/50	++	In some or most parts of the country,
REP. OF DJIBOUTI	220/50		you may need three square pin plugs.
CAPE VERDE	220/50		
ROMANIA	220/50		
RUSSIA	220/50		
RWANDA	220/50		
SAUDI ARABIA	110 & 120/60 AC		
SENEGAL	110 & 220/50 AC		
SEYCHELLES	240/50 AC		
SIERRA LEONE	220/50		
SINGAPORE++	230-250 AC		
SAO TOME & PRIN.	220/50		

639

APPENDIX M

INTERNATIONAL TELEPHONE DIALING CODES

COUNTRY/COUNTRY CODE

City & Codes

Albania   355
Durres 52 plus 4 digits, Elbassan 545 plus 4 digits,
Korce 824 plus 4 digits, Shkoder 224 plus 4 digits,
Tirana 42 plus 5 digits

Algeria   213

City code not required.

American Samoa   684

City code not required.

Andorra   376

Use 628 for all cities.

Anguilla   809

Dial 1 + 809 + Local Number.

Antigua   809
Dial 1 + 809 + Local Number.

Argentina   54

Bahia Blanca 91. Buenos Aires 1, Cordoba 51,
Corrientes 783, La Plata 21, Mar Del Plata 23,
Mendoza 61, Merlo 220, Posadas 752, Resistencia
772, Rio Cuarto 586, Rosario 41, San Juan 64, San
Rafael 627, Santa Fe 42, Tandil 293

Armenia   374
City codes not required

Aruba   297
Use 8 for all cities.

Ascension Island   247
City code not required.

Australia   61
Adelaide 8, Ballarat 53, Brisbane 7, Canberra 62,
Darwin 89, Geelong 52, Gold Coast 75, Hobart

02, Launceston 03, Melbourne 3, Newcastle 49,
Perth 9, Sydne 2, Toowoomba 76, Townsville 77,
Wollongong 42

Austria   43

Bludenz 5552, Graz 316, Innsbruck 5222,
Kitzbuhel 5356, Klagenfut 4222, Krems An Der
Donau 2732, Linz Donau 732, Neunkirchen
Niederosterreich 2635, Salzburg 662, St. Polten
2742, Vienna 1, Villach 4242, Wels 7242, Wiener
Neustadt 2622

Bahamas   809

Dial 1 + 809 + Local Number.

Bahrain   973
City code not required.

Bangladesh   880
Barisal 431, Bogra 51, Chittagong 31, Comilla 81,
Dhaka 2, Khulna 41, Maulabi Bazar 861,
Mymensingh 91, Rajshaki 721, Sylhet 821

Barbados   809

Dial 1 + 809 + Local Number.

Blarus   375
Loev 2347, Minsk 172, Mogilev 222

Belgium   32
Antwerp 3, Bruges 50, Brussels 2, Charleroi 71,
Courtrai 56, Ghent 91, Hasselt 11, La Louviere 64,
Leuven 16, Libramont 61, Liege 41, Malines 15,
Mons 65, Namur 81, Ostend 59, Verviers 87

Belize   501
Belize City (City code not required), Belmopan 08,
Benque Viejo Del Carmen 093, Corozal Town 04,
Dangviga 05, Independence 06, Orange Walk 03,
Punta Gorda 07, San Ignacio 092

Benin   229
City code not required.

Bermuda   809

Dial 1 + 809 + Local Number.

Bolivia   591
Cochabamba 42, Cotoga 388, Guayafamerin 47, La Belgica 923, La Paz 2, Mineros 984, Montero 92, Oruro 52, Portachuelo 924, Saavedra 924, Santa Cruz 33, Trinidad 46, Warnes 923

Bosnia-Herzegovina   387
Mostar 88, Sarajevo 71, Zenica 72

Botswana   267
Francistown 21, Gaborone 31, Jwaneng 38, Kanye 34, Lobatse 33, Mahalapye 41, Maun 26, Mochudi 37, Molepoloe 32, Orapa 27, Palapye 42, Ramotswana 39, Selibe (Phikwe) 8, Serowe 43

Brazil   55
Belem 91, Belo Horizonte 31, Brasilia 61, Curitiba 41, Fortaleza 85, Goiania 62, Niteroi 21, Pelotas 532, Porto Alegre 512, Recife 81, Rio de Janeiro 21, Salvador 71, Santo Andre 11, Santos 132, Sao Paulo 11, Vitoria 27

British Virgin Islands 809
Dial 1 + 809 + Local Number in the following cities: Anegada, Camanoe Island, Guana Island, Josh Vah Dyke, Little Thatch, Marina Cay, Mosquito Island, North Sound, Peter Island, Salt Island, Tortola, Virgin Gorda.

Brunei   673
Bandar Seri Begawan 2, Kuala Belait 3, Mumong 3, Tutong 4

Bulgaria   359
Kardjali 361, Pazardjik 34, Plovdiv 32, Sofia 2, Varna 52

Burkina Faso   226
Bobo Dioulasso 9, Fada N'Gorma 7, Koudougou 4, Ouagadougou 3

Burma   95
Akyab 43, Bassein 42, Magwe 63, Mandalay 2, Meikila 64, Moulmein 32, Pegu 52, Prom 53, Rangoon 1

Cameroon 237
City code not required.

Canada   NPA's

Dial 1 + Area Code + Local Number.
Cape Verde Islands   238

City code not required.

Caymen Islands   809
Dial 1 + 809 + Local Number.

Chile   56
Chiquayante 41, Concepcion 41, Penco 41, Recreo 31, San Bernardo 2, Santiago 2, Talcahuano 41, Valparaiso 32, Vina del Mar 32

China   86
Beijing (Peking) 1, Fuzhou 591, Ghuangzhou (Canton) 20, Shanghai 21

Colombia   57
Armenia 60, Barranquilla 5, Bogota 1, Bucaramanga 73, Cali 3, Cartagena 59, Cartago 66, Cucuta 70, Giradot 832, Ibague 82, Manizales 69, Merdellin 42, Neiva 80, Palmira 31, Pereira 61, Santa Marta 56

Costa Rica 506
City code not required.

Croatia   387
Dubrovnik 20, Rijeka 51, Split 21, Zagreb 41.

Cyprus   357
Kythrea 2313, Lapithos 8218, Lamaca 41, Lefkonico 3313, Limassol 51, Moni 5615, Morphou 71, Nicosia 2, Paphos 61, Platres 54, Polis 63, Rizokarpaso 3613, Yialousa 3513. The following cities are handled by the Turkish Telephone Network. Use country code 90 for Turkey: Famagusta 536, Kyrenia 581, and Lefka 57817.

Czech Rep.   42
Brno 5, Havirov 6994, Ostrava 69, Prague (Praha) 2,

Denmark   45
City code not required.

Djibouti   253
City code not required.

Dominica   809
Dial 1 + 809 + Local Number.

Dominican Republic   809
Dial 1 + 809 + Local Number.

Ecuador   593
Ambato 2, Cayambe 2, Cuenca 7, Esmeraldas 2, Guayaquil 4, Ibarra 2; Loja 4, Machachi 2,

641

Machala 4, Manta 4, Portoviejo 4, Quevedo 4, Quito 2, Salinas 4, Santa Domingo 2, Tulcan 2

Egypt   20
Alexandria 3, Answan 97, Asyut 88, Benha 13, Cairo 2, Damanhour 45, El Mahallah (El Kubra) 43, El Mansoura 50, Luxor 95, Port Said 66, Shebin El Kom 48, Sohag 93, Tanta 40

El Salvador   503
City code not required.

Estonia   372
Tallinn 2, Tartu 7.

Ethiopia   251
Addis Ababa 1, Akaki 1, Asmara 4, Assab 3, Awassa 6, Debre Zeit 1, Dessie 3, Dire Dawa 5, Harrar 5, Jimma 7, Makale 4, Massawa 4, Nazareth 2, Shashemene 6

Faeroe Islands   298
City code not required.

Fiji Islands   679
City code not required.

Finland   358
Epoo-Ebbo 15, Helsinki 0, Joensuu 73, Jyvaskyla 41, Kuopio 71, Lahti 18, Lappeenranta 53, Oulu 81, Port 39, Tammefors-Tampere 31, Turku 21, Uleaborg 81, Vaasa 61, Vanda-Vantaa 0

France   33
Aix-en-Provence 42, Bordeaux 56, Cannes 93, Chauvigny 49, Cherbourge 33, Grenoble 76, Le Havre 35, Lourdes 62, Lyon 7, Marseille 91, Nancy 8, Nice 93, Paris 1, Rouen 35, Toulouse 61, Tours 47

French Antilles   596
City code not required.

French Guiana   594
City code not required.

French Polynesia   689
City code not required.

Gabon Republic   241
City code not required.

Gambia   220
City code not required.

Georgia   7

Sukhumi 881, Tblisi 88

Germany, Fed. Rep. 49
Bad Homburg 6172, Berlin 30, Bonn 228, Bremen 421, Cologne (Koln) 221, Cottbus 355, Dresden 351, Dusseldorf 211, Erfurt 361, Essen 201, Frankfurt am Main (west) 69, Frankfurt an der Oder (east) 335, Gera 365, Halle 345, Hamburg 40, Heidellberg 6221, Karl-Stadt 9353, Koblenz 261, Leipzig 341, Magdeburg 391, Mannheim 621, Munich 89, Numberg 911, Postdam 331, Rostock 381, Saal 38223, Schwerin 385, Stuttgart 711, Wiesbaden 6121

Ghana   233
City code not required.

Gibraltar   350
City code not required.

Greece   30
Argos 751, Athens (Athinai) 1, Corinth 741, Iraklion (Kristis) 81, Kavala 51, Larissa 41, Patrai 61, Piraeus Pireefs 1, Rodos 241, Salonica (Thessaloniki) 31, Sparti 731, Thessaloniki 31, Tripolis 71, Volos 421, Zagora 426

Greenland 299
Goatham 2, Sondre Stromfjord 11, Thule 50

Grenada   809
Dial 1 + 809 + Local Number.

Guadeloupe   590
City code not required.
Guam   671
City code not required.

Guantanemo Bay   5399
City code not required.

Guatemala502
Guatemala City 2. All other cities 9.

Guinea   224
City code not required.

Guyana   592
Anna Regina 71, Bartica 5, Beteryerwaging 20, Cove & John 29, Georgetown 2, Ituni 41, Linden 4, Mabaruma 77, Mahaica 28, Mahalcony 21, New Amsterdam 3, New Hope 66, Rosignol 30, Timehri 61, Vreed-En-Hoop 64, Whim 37

Haiti   509
Cap-Haitien 3, Cayes 5, Gonalve 2, Port au Prince

I

51, Wexford 53

Honduras   504
City code not required.

Hong Kong   852
Castle Peak 0, Cheung Chau 5, Fan Ling 0, Hong Kong 5, Kowloon 3, Kwai Chung 0, Lamma 5, Lantau 5, Ma Wan 5, Peng Chau 5, Sek Kong 0, Sha Tin 0, Tai Po 0, Ting Kau 0, Tsun Wan 0

Hungary   36
Abasar 37, Balatonaliga 84, Budapest 1, Dorgicse 80, Fertoboz 99, Gyongyos 37, Kaposvar 82, Kazincbarcika 48, Komlo 72, Miskolc 46, Nagykaniza 93, Szekesfehervar 22, Szolnok 56, Varpalota 80, Veszprem 80, Zalaegerzeg 92

Iceland   354

Akureyi 6, Hafnafijorour 1, Husavik 6, Keflavik Naval Base 2, Rein 6, Reykjavik 1, Reyorarjorour 7, Sandgerol 2, Selfoss 9. Siglufijorour 6, Stokkseyri 9, Suoavik 4, Talknafijorour 4, Varma 1, Vik 9

India   91

Ahmedabad 272, Amritsar 183, Bangalore 812, Baroda 265, Bhopal 755, Bombay 22 Calcutta 33, Chandigarh 172, Hyderabad 842, Jaipur 141, Jullundur 181, Kanpur 512, Madras 44, New Dehli 11, Poona 212, Surat 261

Indonesia   62
Bandung 22, Cirebon 231, Denpasar (Bali) 361, Jakarta 21, Madiun 351, Malang 341, Medan 61, Padang 751, Palembang 711, Sekurang 778, Semarang 24, Solo 271, Surabaya 31, Tanjungkarang 721, Yogykarta 274

Iran   98

Abadan 631, Ahwaz 61, Arak 2621, Esfahan 31, Ghazvin 281, Ghome 251, Hamadan 261, Karadj 2221, Kerman 341, Mashad 51, Rasht 231, Rezaiyeh 441, Shiraz 71, Tabriz 41, Tehran 21

Iraq   964
Baghdad 1, Basiah 40, Diwanyia 36, Karbala 32, Kirkuk 50, Mosul 60, Nasryia 42

Ireland   353
Arklow 402, Cork 21, Dingle 66, Donegal 73, Drogheda 41, Dublin 1, Dundalk 42, Ennis 65, Galway 91, Kildare 45, Killamey 64, Sligo 71, Tipperary 62, Tralee 66, Tullamore 506, Waterford

Israel   972
Afula 65, Ako 4, Ashkelon 51, Bat Iam 3, Beer Sheva 57, Dimona 57, Hadera 63, Haifa 4, Holon 3, Jerusalem 2, Nazareth 65, Netania 53, Rehovot 8, Tel Aviv 3, Tiberias 67, Tsefat 67

Italy   39
Bari 80, Bologna 51, Brindisi 831, Capri 81, Como 31, Florence 55, Genoa 10, Milan 2, Naples 81, Padova 49, Palermo 91, Pisa 50, Rome 6, Torino 11, Trieste 40, Venice 41, Verona 45

Ivory Coast   225
City code not required.

Jamaica   809
Dial 1 + 809 + Local Number.

Japan   81
Chiba 472, Fuchu (Tokyo) 423, Hiroshima 82, Kawasaki (Kanagawa) 44, Kobe 78, Kyoto 75, Nagasaki 958, Nagoya 52, Nahat (Okinawa) 988, Osaka 6, Sapporo 11, Sasebo 956, Tachikawa (Tokyo) 425, Tokyo 3, Yokohama 45, Yokosuka (Kanagawa) 468

Jordan   962
Amman 6, Aqaba 3, Irbid 2, Jerash 4, Karak 3, Maam 3, Mafruq 4, Ramtha 2, Sueeleh 6, Sult 5, Zerqa 9

Kazakhstan   7
Alma-Ata 3272, Chimkent 325, Guryev 312, Petropavlovsk 315.

Kenya   254
Anmer 154, Bamburi 11, Embakasi 2, Girgiri 2, Kabete 2, Karen 2882, Kiambu 154, Kikuyu 283, Kisumu 35, Langata 2, Mombasa 11, Nairobi 2, Nakuru 37, Shanzu 11, Thika 151, Uthiru 2

Kiribati   686
City code not required.

Korea   82
Chung Ju 431, Chuncheon 361, Icheon 336, Incheon 32, Kwangju (Gwangju) 62, Masan 551, Osan 339, Osan Military (333+414), Pohang 562, Pusan (Busan) 51, Seoul 2, Suwon (Suweon) 331, Taegu (Daegu) 53, Ulsan 552, Wonju (Weonju) 371

Kuwait   965
City code not required.

643

Kyrgyzstan   7
Osh 33222 plus 5 digits, Pishpek 3312

Latvia   371
Riga 0132

Lebanon   961
Beirut 1, Juniyah 9, Tripoli 6, Zahlah 8

Lesotho   266
City code not required.

Liberia   231

City code not required.

Libya   218

Agelat 282, Benghazi 61, Benina 63, Derma 81, Misuratha 51, Sabratha 24, Sebha 71, Taigura 26, Tripoli 21, Tripoli International Airport 22, Zawai 23, Zuara 25

Liechtenstein   41
Use 75 for all cities.

Lithuania   370
Kaunas 7, Klaipeda 6, Panevezys 54, Siauliai 1, Vilnius 2.

Luxembourg   352
City code not required.

Macao   853
City code not required.

Macedonia   389
Asamati 96, Bitola 97, Gostivar 94, Kicevo 95, Krusevo 98, Lozovo 92, Skopje 91.

Malawi   265
Domasi 531, Likuni 766, Luchenza 477, Makwasa 474, Mulanje 465, Namadzi 534, Njuli 664, Thondwe 533, Thornwood 486, Thyolo 467, Zomba 50, City code not required for other cities.

Malaysia   60
Alor Star 4, Baranang 3, Broga 3, Cheras 3, Dengil 3, Ipoh 5, Johor Bahru 7, Kajang 3, Kepala Batas 4, Kuala Lampur 3, Machang 97, Maran 95, Port Dickson 6, Semenyih 3, Seremban 6, Sungei Besi 3, Sungei Renggam 3

Maldives   960

City code not required.

Mali   223
City code not required.
Malta   356
City code not required.
Marshall Islands   692
Ebeye 871, Majuro 9

Mauritius   230
City code not required.

Mayotte Islands   269
City code not required.

Mexico   52
Acapulco 748, Cancun 988, Celaya 461, Chihuahua 14, Ciudad Juarez 16, Conzumel 987, Culiacan 671, Ensenda 667, Guadalajara 36, Hermosillo 621, La Paz 682, Mazatlan 678, Merida 99, Mexicali 65, Mexico City 5, Monterrey 83, Puebla 22, Puerto Vallarta 322, Rasarito 661, San Luis Potosi 481, Tampico 121, Tecate 665, Tijuana 66, Torreon 17, Veracruz 29

Micronesia   691
Kosrae 851, Ponape 9, Truk 8319, Yap 841

Moldova   373
Benderi 32, Kishinev 2

Monaco   33
Use 93 for all cities.

Mongolian People's Rep. 976
Ulan Bator 1

Montserrat   809
Dial 1 + 809 + Local Number.

Morocco   212
Agardir 8, Beni-Mellal 48, Berrechid 33, Casablanca (City code not required). El Jadida 34, Fes 6, Kenitra 16, Marrakech 4, Meknes 5, Mohammedia 32, Nador 60, Oujda 68, Rabat 7, Tanger (Tangiers) 9, Tetouan 96

Mustique   809
Dial 1 + 809 + Local Number.

Namibia   264
Gobabis 681, Grootfontein 673, Industria 61, Keetmanshoop 631, Luderitz 6331, Mariental 661, Okahandja 622, Olympia 61, Otjiwarongo 651, Pioneerspark 61, Swakopmund 641, Tsumeb 671, Windhoek 61, Windhoek Airport 626

Nauru Island   **674**
City code not required.

Nepal   **977**
City code not required.

Netherlands   **31**
Amsterdam 20, Arnhem 85, Eindhoven 40, Groningen 50, Haarlem 23, Heemstede 23, Hillegersberg 10, Hoensbraoek 45, Hoogkerk 50, Hoogvliet 10, Loosduinen 70, Nijmegen 80, Oud Zuilen 30, Rotterdam 10, The Hague 70, Utrecht 30

Netherlands Antilles **599**
Bonaire 7, Curacao 9, Saba 4, Eustatius 3, St. Maarten 5

Nevis   **809**
Dial 1 + 809 + Local Number.

New Caledonia   **687**
City code not required.

New Zeland   **64**
Auckland 9, Christchurch 3, Dunedin 24, Hamilton 71, Hastings 70, Invercargill 21, Napier 70, Nelson 54, New Plymouth 67, Palmerston North 63, Rotorua 73, Tauranga 75, Timaru 56, Wanganui 64, Wellington 4, Whangarei 89

Nicaragua   **505**
Boaco 54, Chinandega 341, Diriamba 42, Esteli 71, Granada 55, Jinotepe 41, Leon 311, Managua 2, Masatepe 44, Masaya 52, Nandaime 45, Rivas 461, San Juan Del Sur 466, San Marcos 43, Tipitapa 53

Niger Republic   **227**
City code not required.

Nigeria   **234**
Lagos 1 (Only city direct dial)

Niue   **683**

Norfolk Island   **672**

Norway   **47**
Arendal 41, Bergen 5, Drammen 3, Fredrikstad 32, Haugesund 47, Kongsvinger 66, Kristiansund N. 73, Larvik 34, Moss 32, Narvik 82, Oslo 2, Sarpsborg 31, Skien 35, Stavanger 4, Svalbard 80, Tonsberg 33, Trondheim 7

Oman   **968**
City code not required.

Pakistan   **92**
Abbotabad 5921, Bahawalpur 621, Faisalabad 411, Gujtanwala 431, Hyderabad 221, Islamabad 51, Karachi 21, Lahore 42, Multan 61, Okara 442, Peshawar 521, Quetta 81, Sahiwal 441, Sargodha 451, Sialkot 432, Sukkur 71

Palm Island   **809**
Dial 1 + 809 + Local Number.

Panama   **507**
City code not required.

Papau New Guinea   **675**
City code not required.

Paragua   **595**
Asuncion 21, Ayolas 72, Capiata 28, Concepcion 31, Coronel Bogado 74, Coronel Oviedo 521, Encarnacion 71, Hermandarias 63, Ita 24, Pedro J. Caballero 36, Pilar 86, San Antonio 27, San Ignacio 82, Stroessner: Ciudad Pte. 61, Villarica 541, Villeta 25

Peru   **51**
Arequipa 54, Ayacucho 6491, Callao 14, Chiclayo 74, Chimbote 44, Cuzco 84, Huancavelica 6495, Huancayo 64, Ica 34, Iquitos 94, Lima 14, Piura 74, Tacna 54, Trujillo 44

Phillippines   **63**
Angeles 55, Bacolod 34, Baguio City 442, Cebu City 32, Clark Field (military) 52, Dagupan 48, Davao 35, Lloilo City 33, Lucena 42, Manila 2, San Fernando: La Union 46, San Fernando: Pampanga 45, San Pablo 43, Subic Bay Military Base 89, Subic Bay Residential Housing 89, Tarlac City 47

Poland   **48**
Bialystok 85, Bydgoszcz 52, Crakow (Krakow) 12, Gdansk 58, Gdynia 58, Katowice 32, Lodz 42, Lubin 81, Olsztyn 89, Poznan 48, Radom 48, Sopot 58, Torun 56, Warsaw 22

Portugal   **351**
Alamada 1, Angra Do Heroismo 95, Barreiro 1, Beja 84, Braga 53, Caldas Da Rainha 62, Coimbra 39, Estoril 1, Evora 66, Faro 89, Horta 92, Lajes AFB 95, Lisbon 1, Madalena 92, Madeira Islands 91, Montijo 1, Ponta Del Gada 96, Porto 2, Santa Cruz (Flores) 92, Santarem 43, Setubal 65, Velas 95, Vila Do Porto 96, Viseu 32

Qatar   **974**

City code not required.

Reunion Island   262
City code not required.

Romania   40
Arad 66, Bacau 31, Brasov 21, Bucharest 0,
Cluj-Napoca 51, Constanta 16, Crajova 41, Galati
34, Lasi 81, Oradea 91, Pitesti 76, Ploiesti 71,
Satu-Mare 97, Sibiu 24, Timisoara 61, Tirgu Mures
54

Russia   7
Magadan 413, Moscow 095, St. Petersburg 812

Rwanda   250
City code not required.

St. Kitts   809
Dial 1 + 809 + Local Number.

St. Lucia   809
Dial 1 + 809 + Local Number.

St. Pierre & Miquelon   508
City code not required.

St. Vincent   809
Dial 1 + 809 + Local Number.

Saipan   670
Capitol Hill 322, Rota Island 532, Susupe City 234,
Tinian Island 433

San Marino   39
Use 541 for all cities.

Saudi Arabia   966
Abha 7, Abqaiq 3, Al Khobar 3, Al Markazi 2, Al
Ulaya 1, Damman 3, Dhahran (Aramco) 3, Jeddah
2, Khamis Mushait 7, Makkah (Mecca) 2, Medina
4, Najran 7, Qatif 3, Riyadh 1, Taif 2, Yenbu 4

Senegal   221
City code not required.

Seychelles Islands   248
City code not required.

Sierra Leone   232
Freetown 22, Juba 24, Lungi 25, Wellington 23

Singapore   65
City code not required.

Solomon Island   677

City code not required.

Slovakia   42
Bratislava 7, Presov 91.

Slovenia   386
Ljubljana 61, Maribor 62

South Africa   27
Bloemfontein 51, Cape Town 21, De Aar 571,
Durban 31, East London 431, Gordons Bay 24,
Johannesburg 11, La Lucia 31, Pietermaritzburg
331, Port Elizabeth 41, Pretoria 12, Sasolburg 16,
Somerset West 24, Uitenhage 422, Welkom 171

Spain   34
Barcelona 3, Bibao 4, Cadiz 56, Ceuta 56, Granada
58, Igualada 3, Las Palmas de Gran Canaria 28,
Leon 87, Madrid 1, Malaga 52, Melilla 52, Palma
De Mallorca 71, Pamplona 48, Santa Cruz de
Tenerife 22, Santander 42, Seville 54,
Torremolinos 52, Valencia 6

Sri Lanka   94
Ambalangoda 97, Colombo Central 1, Galle 9,
Havelock Town 1, Kandy 8, Katugastota 8, Kotte
1, Maradana 1, Matara 41, Negomgo 31, Panadura
46, Trincomalee 26

Suriname   597
City code not required.

Swaziland   268
City code not required.

Sweden   46
Alingsas 322, Boras 33, Eskilstuna 16, Gamleby
493, Goteborg 31, Helsinborg 42, Karlstad 54,
Linkoping 13, Lund 46, Malmo 40, Norrkoping
11, Stockholm 8, Sundsvall 60, Trelleborg 410,
Uppsala 18, Vasteras 21

Switzerland   41
Baden 56, Basel 61, Berne 31, Davos 83, Fribourg
37, Geneva 22, Interlaken 36, Lausanne 21,
Lucerne 41, Lugano 91, Montreux 21, Neuchatel
38, St. Gallen 71, St. Moritz 82, Winterthur 52,
Zurich 1

Taiwan   886
Changhua 47, Chunan 36, Chunghsing-Hsintsun
49, Chungli 34, Fengyuan 4, Hsiaying 6, Hualien
38, Kaohsiung 7, Keelung 2, Lotung 39, Pingtung
8, Taichung 4, Tainan 6, Taipei 2, Taitung 89,
Taoyuan 33

Tajikistan   7
Dushanbe 3772

Tanzania   255
Dar Es Salaam 51, Dodoma 61, Mwanza 68, Tanga 53

Thailand   66
Bangkok 2, Burirum 44, Chanthaburi 39, Chien Mai 53, Cheingrai 54, Kamphaengphet 55, Lampang 54, Nakhon Sawan 56, Nong Khai 42, Pattani 73, Pattaya 38, Ratchaburi 32, Saraburi 36, Tak 55, Ubon Ratchathani 45

Togo   228
City code not required.

Tonga Islands   676
City code not required.

Trinidad & Tabago   809
Dial 1 + 809 + Local Number.

Tunisia   216
Agareb 4, Beja 8, Bizerte 2, Carthage 1, Chebba 4, Gabes 5, Gafsa 6, Haffouz 7, Hamman-Souse 3, Kairouan 7, Kef 8, Khenis 3, Medenine 5, Tabarka 8, Tozeur 6, Tunis 1

Turkey   90
Adana 711, Ankara 41, Antalya 311, Bursa 241, Eskischir 221, Gazianter 851, Istanbul 1, Izmir 51, Izmit 211, Kayseri 351, Konya 331, Malatya 821, Mersin 741, Samsun 361

Turka & Caicos   809
Dial 1 + 809 + Local Number.

Turkmenistan   7
Ashkkhabad 3632, Chardzhou 378

Tuvalu   688

Ukraine   380
Kharkiv 572, Kiev 44, Lviv 322
Uganda   256
Entebbe 42, Jinja 43, Kampala 41, Kyambogo 41

Union Island   809
Dial 1 + 809 + Local Number.

United Arab Emirates 971
Abu Dhabi 2, Ajman 6, Al Ain 3, Aweer 58, Dhayd 6, Dibba 70, Dubai 4, Falaj-al-Moalla 6, Fujairah 70, Jebel Ali 84, Jebel Dhana 52, Khawanij 58, Ras-al-Khaimah 77, Sharjan 6, Tarif 53,

Umm-al-Quwain 6

United Kingdom   44
Belfast 232, Birmingham 21, Bournemouth 202, Cardiff 222, Durham 385, Edinburgh 31, Glasgow 41, Gloucester 452, Ipswich 473, Liverpool 51, London (Inner) 71, London (Outer) 81, Manchester 61, Nottingham 602, Prestwick 292, Sheffield 742, Southampton 703

Uruguay   598
Atlantida 372, Colonia 522, Florida 352, La Paz 322, Las Piedras 322, Los Toscas 372, Maldonado 42, Mercedes 532, Minas 442, Montevideo 2, Parque De Plata 372, Paysandu 722, Punta Del Este 42, Salinas 372, San Jose 342, San Jose De Carrasco 382

Uzbekistan   7
Karish 375, Samarkand 3662, Tashkent 3712

Vanuatu, Rep. of   678

Vatican City   39
Use 6 for all cities.

Venezuela   58
Barcelona 81, Barquisimeto 51, Cabimas 64, Caracas 2, Ciudad Bolivar 85, Coro 68, Cumana 93, Los Teques 32, Maiquetia 31, Maracaibo 61, Maracay 43, Maturin 91, Merida 74, Puerto Cabello 42, San Cristobal 76, Valencia 41

Vietnam   84
Hanoi 4, Ho Chi Minh City 8

Wallis & Futuna Islands 681

Western Samoa   685
City code not required.

Yeman (North)   967
Al Marawyah 3, Al Qaidah 4, Amran 2, Bayt Al Faquih 3, Dhamar 2, Hodeidah 3, Ibb 4, Mabar 2, Rada 2, Rawda 2, Sanaa 2, Taiz 4, Yarim 4, Zabid 3

Yugoslavia   38
Belgrade (Beograd) 11, Dubrovnik 50, Leskovac 16, Ljubljana 61, Maribor 62, Mostar 88, Novi Sad 21, Pirot 10, Rijeka 51, Sarajevo 71, Skopje 91, Split 58, Titograd 81, Titovo-Uzice 31, Zagreb 41

Zaire   243
Kinshasa 12, Lubumbashi 222

Zambia   **260**

Chingola 2, Kitwe 2, Luanshya 2, Lusaka 1, Ndola 26

Zimbabwe 263

Bulawayo 9, Harare 0, Mutare 20

APPENDIX N

INTERNATIONAL TELEX CODES

AFGHANISTAN	930	COMOROS	942
ALGERIA	936	CONGO, PEOPLE'S REP.	971
AME. SAMOA	782	COOK IS	717
ANDOA	833	COSTA RICA	303
ANGOLA	998	COTE D'IVOIRE	969
ANGUILLA	317	CUBA	307
ANTIGUA & BARBUDA	306	CYPRUS	826
ARGENTINA	390	CZECH REPUBLIC	849
ARMENIA	871	DENMARK	855
ARUBA	364, 384	DIEGO GARCIA IS	919
ASCENSION IS.	920	DOMINICA	304
AUSTRALIA	790	DOMINICAN	
AUSTRIA	847	REP.	326, 346, 366
AZERBAIJAN	871	ECUADOR	393
AZORES	835	EGYPT	927
BAHRAIN	955	EL SALVADOR	301
BALERIC IS	831	ELLICE IS	726
BANGLADESH	950	EQUAT GUINEA	939
BARBADOS	386	ESTONIA	871
BELARUS	871	ETHIOPIA	976
BELGIUM	846	FAEROE IS	853
BELIZE	310	FIJI	792
BENIN	979	FINLAND	857
BERMUDA	380	FRANCE	842
BHUTAN	733	FR. POLYNESIA	711
BOLIVIA	336, 355, 356, 376	FRENCH GUIANA	313
BOTSWANA	991	FR. ANTILLES	340
BRAZIL	391	GABON	981
BRITISH V.I.	318	GEORGIA	871
BRUNEI	799	GERMANY	841
BULGARIA	865	GHANA	974
BURKINA FASO	985	GIBRALTAR	837
BURMA	713	GREECE	863
BURUNDI	977	GREENLAND	859
CAMBODIA	720	GRENADA	320
CAMEROON	978	GUADELOUPE	340
CANADA	389	GUAM	721
CANARY IS	966	GUANTANAMO BAY	606
CAYENNE	313	GUATEMALA	305
CAYMAN IS	309	GUINEA	995
CENT. AFR.REP.	980	GUINEA-BISSAU	931
CHAD	984	GUYANA	312
CHANNEL IS	851	HAITI	349
CHILE	332, 352, 359, 392	HONDURAS	311
CHINA, PEOPLES REP.	716	HONG KONG	780
CHINA, TAIWAN	785	HUNGARY	861
COLOMBIA	396	ICELAND	858

INDIA	953	NIGERIA	961
INDONESIA	796	NIUE	772
IRAN	951	NORFOLK IS	756
IRAQ	943	NORWAY	856
IRELAND	852	OKINAWA	781, 789
ISRAEL	922	OMAN	926
ITALY	843	PAKISTAN	952
JAMAICA	381	PANAMA	328, 348, 368
JAPAN	781	PAPUA NEW GUINEA	798, 795
JORDAN	925	PARAGUAY	399
KAZAKHSTAN	871	PERU	334, 394
KENYA	963	PHILIPPINES	712, 722,
KIRIBATI	727		732, 742, 762, 778
KOREA, SOUTH	787	PITCAIRN IS	604
KOREA, NORTH	779	POLAND	867
KUWAIT	959	PORTUGAL	832
KYRGYZSTAN	871	PUERTO RICO	324, 325,
LAOS	715		345, 365, 385
LATVIA	871	QATAR	957
LEBANON	923	REP. OF	
LESOTHO	990	CAPE VERDE	938
LIBERIA	937	REP. OF DJIBOUTI	994
LIBYA	929	REUNION ISLAND	941
LIECHTENSTEIN	845	RODRIGUEZ IS	996
LITHUANIA	871	ROMANIA	864
LUXEMBOURG	848	RUSSIA	871
MADAGASCAR	983	RWANDA	967
MALAWI	988	SAIPAN	724, 783
MALAYSIA	784	SAN MARINO	868
MALDIVES	940	SAO TOME & PRINCIPE	916
MALI	972	SAUDI ARABIA	928
MALTA	838	SENEGAL	962
MARSHALL IS	730	SEYCHELLES	997
MARTINIQUE	300	SIERRA LEONE	989
MAURITANIA	935	SINGAPORE	786
MAURITIUS	996	SOLOMON IS	769
MAYOTTE IS	942	SOMALIA	999
MEXICO	383	SOUTH AFRICA	960
MICRONESIA	729	SPAIN	831
MIDWAY IS	603	SPANISH SAHARA	933
MOLDOVA	871	SRI LANKA	954
MONACO	842	ST. THOMA IS	916
MONGOLIA	719	ST. THOMAS	327, 347, 367
MONTSERRAT	360	ST. MARTEEN	384
MOROCCO	933	ST. MARTIN	340
MOZAMBIQUE	946	ST. PIERRE & MIQUELON	316
NAMIBIA	964	ST. VINCENT	321
NAURU	739	ST. KITTS-NEVIS	361
NEPAL	947	ST. LUCIA	341
NETHERLANDS ANTILLES	384	SUDAN	970
NETHERLANDS	844	SURINAME	397
NEVIS	361	SWAZILAND	993
NEW CALEDONIA	714	SWEDEN	854
NEW ZEALAND	791	SWITZERLAND	845
NICARAGUA	388	SYRIA	924
NIGER	982	TAHITI	711

TAJIKISTAN	871
TANZANIA	975
THAILAND	788
THE GAMBIA	992
TIBET	716
TOGO	986
TOKELAU IS	731
TONGA	765
TRINIDAD & TOBAGO	387
TUNISIA	934
TURKEY	821
TURKMENISTAN	871
TURKS & CAICOS	315
UGANDA	973
UKRAINE	871
U.K	851
UNITED ARAB EMIRATES	949, 958
URUGUAY	398
US. V.I.	327, 347,367
UZBEKISTAN	871
VANUATU	718
VATICAN CITY	803
VENEZUELA	395
VIETNAM	798
WESTERN SAMOA	793
YEMEN, PEOPLE'S DEM REP.	956
YEMEN, ARAB REP.	948
YUGOSLAVIA	862
ZAIRE	968
ZAMBIA	965
ZIMBABWE	987

APPENDIX O

CURRENCIES OF THE WORLD

COUNTRY UNIT Unit = 100 Unless otherwise stated

AFGHANISTAN	Afghani	Puls
ALBANIA	Lek	quindarka
ALGERIA	Dinar	Quintars
ANGOLA	Kwanza	Lweis
ANGUILLA	E.C. Dollar	Cents
ARGENTINA	Peso	Centavos
ARMENIA	Luma	Dram
AUSTRALIA	Aust. Dollar	Cents
AUSTRIA	Euro	Euro Cents
AZERBAIJAN	Manat/Rubles	Kopek
BAHAMAS	Bahamian Dollar	Cents
BAHRAIN	Bahrain Dinar	1000 Fils
BANGLADESH	Taka	Poisha
BARBADOS	Dollar	Cents
BELGIUM	Euro	Euro Cents
BELIZE	Dollar	Cents
BENIN	Franc (CFA)	---
BERMUDA	Dollar	Cents
BHUTAN	Ngultrum	
BOLIVIA	Boliviano	Centavos
BOTSWANA	Pula	Thebe
BOSNIA-HERZEGOVINA		Bosnian Dinar
BRAZIL	Cruzeiro	Centavos
BRITISH V.I.	Dollar USC	Cents
BRUNEI	Brunei Dollar	Cents
BULGARIA	Lev	Stotinki
BURKINA FASO	Franc (CFA)	---
BURMA	Kyat	Pyas
BURUNDI	Burundi Franc	Centimes
BYELARUS	Rubles	Kopeks
CAMBODIA	Riel	
CAMEROON	Franc (CFA)	---
CANADA	Canadian Dollar	Cents
CAYMAN IS	Cayman Is.Dollar	Cents
CENTRAL A. REP.	Franc (CFA)	Centimes
CHAD	Franc (CFA)	Cents
CHILE	Chilean Peso	Centesimos
CHINA, P. REP.	Ren Min Bi	Fen
CHINA, TAIWAN	New Taiwan Dollar	
COLOMBIA	Colombian Peso	Centavos
COMOROS	Franc (CFA)	---
COSTA RICA	Colon	Cenavos
COTE D'IVOIRE	Franc (CFA)	---
CROATIA	Croatian Kuna	
CUBA	Peso	Centavos
CYPRUS	Cyprus Pound	1000 Mills

COUNTRY UNIT Unit = 100 Unless otherwise stated

CZECH REPUBLIC	Koruna	Halers
DENMARK	Krone	Ore
DOMINICA	E.C. Dollar	Cents
DOMINICAN REP.	Peso	Centavos
ECUADOR	Sucre	Centavos
EGYPT	Egyptian Pound	Piastres
CONGO, P. REP.	Franc (CFA)	---
EL SALVADOR	Colon	Centavos
EQUAT. GUINEA	Ekuele	Centimos
ESTONIA	Kroon	
ETHIOPIA	Birr	Cents
FAEROE IS	Faeroese Krona	
FIJI	Fiji Dollar	Cents
FINLAND	Euro	Euro Cents
FRANCE	Euro	Euro Cents
FR. POLYNESIA	Franc	Centimes
FRENCH GUIANA	Franc	Centimes
GABON	Franc (CFA)	---
GEORGIA	Lari	Kopek
GERMANY	Euro	Euro Cents
GHANA	Cedi	Pesawas
GIBRALTAR	Pound	Pence
GREECE	Euro	Euro Cents
GRENAD	E.C. Dollar	Cents
GUATEMALA	Quetzal	Centavos
GUINEA	Franc	Couris
GUINEA-BISSAU	Peso	Centavos
GUYANA	Guyana Dollar	Cents
HAITI	Gourde	Centimes
HONDURAS	Lempira	Centavos
HONG KONG	Hong Kong Dollar	Cents
HUNGARY	Forint	Fillers
ICELAND	Icelandic Krona	Aur
INDIA	Indian Rupee	Naya Paise
INDONESIA	Rupiah	Sen
IRAN	Iranian Rial	Dinars
IRAQ	Iraqi Dinar	1000 Fils
IRELAND	Euro	Euro Cents
ISRAEL	New Shekel	10 Agorot
ITALY	Euro	Euro Cents
JAMAICA	Jamaican Dollar	Cents
JAPAN	Yen	---
JORDAN	Jordanian Dinar	1000 Fils
KAMPUCHEA	Riel	Centimes
KAZAKHSTAN	Tenge	
KENYA	Kenya Shilling	Cents
KIRIBATI	Australian Dollar	Cents

KOREA, NORTH	Won	Jun		**SAO TOME**	Dobra	---
KOREA, SOUTH	Won	Chon		**SAUDI ARABIA**	Saudi Riyal	Hallalah
KUWAIT	Kuwaiti Dinar	1000 Fils		**SENEGAL**	Franc (CFA)	---
KYRGYZSTAN	Som	Kopeks		**SEYCHELLES**	Seychelles Rupee	Cents
LAOS	Kip Pot Po	Centimes		**SIERRA LEONE**	Leone	Cents
LATVIA	Latvian Lats	Santimis		**SINGAPORE**	Singapore Dollar	Cents
LEBANON	Lebanese Pound	Piastres		**SLOVAKIA**	Slovak Crown	Hellers
LESOTHO	Loti	Licente		**SLOVENIA**	Slovene Tolar	
LIBERIA	Liberian Dollar	Cents		**SOLOMON IS**	Dollar	Cents
LIBYA	Libyan Dinar	1000 Dirham		**SOMALIA**	Somali Schilling	Cents
LIECHTENSTEIN	Franc			**SOUTH AFRICA**	Rand	Cents
LITHUANIA	Litas	Cents		**SPAIN**	Euro	Euro Cents
LUXEMBOURG	Euro	Euro Cents		**SRI LANKA**	Sri Lanka Rupee	Cents
MACEDONIA	Macedonia Deni	Denars		**ST. KITTS-NEVIS**	E.C. Dollar	Cents
MADAGASCAR	Franc	Centimes		**ST. VINCENT**	E.C. Dollar	Cents
MALAWI	Kwacha	Tambala		**ST. LUCIA**	E.C. Dollar	Cents
MALAYSIA	Ringgit	Sen		**SUDAN**	Sudanese Pound	Piastres
MALDIVES	Rufiyaas	Laree		**SURINAME**	Surinam Guilder	Cents
MALI	Mali Franc	Centimes		**SWAZILAND**	Lilangeni	Cents
MALTA	Maltese Lira	Cents		**SWEDEN**	Swedish Kronor	Ore
MAURITANIA	Ouguiya	5 Khoums		**SWITZERLAND**	Franc	Centimes
MAURITIUS	Mauritian Rupee	Cents		**SYRIA**	Syrian Pound	Piastre
MEXICO	Mexican Peso	Centavos		**TAJIKISTAN**	Ruble	Kopeks
MICRONESIA	U.S. Dollar	Cents		**TANZANIA**	Tanzanian Shilling	Cents
MOLDOVA	Leu	Bani		**THAILAND**	Baht	Satang
MONACO	Franc			**THE GAMBIA**	Dalasi	Batut
MONGOLIA	Tugrik			**TOGO**	Franc (CFA)	---
MONTSERRATE.	Caribbean Dollar	Cents		**TONGA**	Pa'anga	Seniti
MOROCCO	Dirham	Centimes		**TRINIDAD/TOBAGO**	Dollar	Cents
MOZAMBIQUE	Metical	Centavos		**TUNISIA**	Tunisian Dinar	1000 Millimes
NAMIBIA	Rand			**TURKEY**	Turkish LiraKurus	
NAURU	Australian Dollar			**TURKMENISTAN**	Ruble	Kopeks
NEPAL	Nepalese Rupee	Pice		**TURKS & CAICOS**	U.S. Dollar	Cents
NETH. ANTILLES	Guilder	Cents		**U.S.A**	Dollar	Cents
NETHERLANDS	Euro	Euro Cents		**UGANDA**	Uganda Shilling	Cents
NEW ZEALAND	N.Zealand Dollar	Cents		**UKRAINE**	Karbovanets	
NEW CALEDONIA	Franc	Centimes		**UN.ARAB EMIRATE.**	UAE Dirham	Fils
NICARAGUA	Cordoba	Centavos		**UNITED KINGDOM**	Pound Sterling	Pence
NIGER	Franc (CFA)	---		**URUGUAY**	New Uruguayan Peso	Centimos
NIGERIA	Naira	Kobos		**UZBEKISTAN**	Ruble/Coupons	Kopeks
NORWAY	Norwegian Krone	Ore		**VANUATU REP.**	Vatu	Centimes
OMAN	Rial	1000 Baizas		**VENEZUELA**	Bolivar	Centimos
PAKISTAN	Pakistani Rupee	Paisa		**VIETNAM**	Dong	10 Hao
PANAMA	Balboa	Cents		**YEMEN, ARAB REP.**	Yemeni Rial	Fils
PAPUA N. GUINEA	Kina	Toea		**YEMEN, P.D.R.**	Yemeni Dinar	1000 Fils
PARAGUAY	Guaranie	Centimos		**ZAIRE**	Zaire	Makutas
PERU	Sol	Centavos		**ZAMBIA**	Zambian Kwacha	Ngwee
PHILIPPINES	Philippine Peso	Centavos		**ZIMBABWE**	Zimbabwe Dollar	Cents
POLAND	Zloty	Groszy				
PORTUGAL	Euro	Euro Cents		**CFA =**	Communaute Financiere Africaine	
PUERTO RICO	U.S. Dollar	Cents				
QATAR	Qatar Riyal	Dirhams		**E.C. =**	East Caribbean	
REP. OF CAPE VERDE	Escudo	Centavos				
REP. OF DJIBOUTI	Franc	Centimes		* =	Several of the countries of the former Soviet	
REUNION ISLAND	Franc	Centimes			Union are in the process of introducing their	
ROMANIA	Lei	Bani			own currency. For now most are still using	
RUSSIA	Ruble	Kopeks			and accepting the Soviet Ruble.	
RWANDA	Rwandese Franc	Centimes				
SAN MARINO	Lira					

APPENDIX P

WORLD COMMERCIAL HOLIDAYS

Virtually every day this year will be a holiday somewhere in the world with business and government offices closed while employees watch parades, pray, or perhaps enjoy a quiet holiday at home with their family. Seasoned business travelers build their schedules around these holidays, because the alternative can be a frustrating day wasted in a hotel room while the local people, from the top executives on down observe their traditional holiday rituals.

The following pages list alphabetically by country, the hundreds of commercial holidays around the world each year that will close business and government offices for a day or more. Major regional holidays that are observed in many countries are included, plus any other pertinent information.

In cases where holidays fall on Saturday or Sunday commercial establishments may be closed the preceding Friday or following Monday. For many countries, such as those in the Moslem world, holiday dates can be only approximated because the holidays are based on actual lunar observation and exact dates are announced only shortly before they occur. Note that references to the Moslem holidays often vary in spelling and dates, and that businesses in many Moslem countries are closed on Fridays.

Although U.S. holidays are not listed in this schedule, they should also be considered when appointments are made with U.S. and Foreign Commercial Service officers abroad. This calendar is intended as a working guide only. For some countries that have not yet announced holidays for 2003, the schedule was projected based on 2002 holidays. Corroboration of dates is suggested in final travel planning.

Algeria
March 13 Aid El Fitr; May 1 Labor Day; May 21 Aid El Adha; June 11 Awal Mouharem; June 19 Revolutionary Recovery Day; June 20 Achoura; July 5 Independence Day; August 20 El Moulid Ennaboui; November 1 Revolution Day.

Argentina
January 1 New Year's; April 1 Good Friday; May 1 Labor Day; May 25 Revolution (1810) Day; June 10 Sovereignty Day; June 20 Flag Day; July 9 Independence (1816) Day; August 17 Death of General J. de San Martin; October 12 Discovery of America; December 25 Christmas.

Australia
January 1 New Year's; January 26 Australia Day; April 14 Good Friday; April 17 Easter Monday; April 25 ANZAC Day; June 13 Queen's Birthday; December 26 Christmas; December 27 Boxing Day. [The preceding list is based on Australia's 2002 holiday schedule.]

Austria
January 1 New Year's; January 6 Epiphany; April 17 Easter Monday; May 1 Labor Day; May 25 Ascension; June 5 Whit Monday; June 6 Corpus Christi; August 15 Assumption; October 26 National Day; November 1 All Saint's; December 8 Immaculate Conception; December 25 Christmas; December 26 St. Stephen's Day.

Bahrain
January 1 New Year's; March 2-4 Eid Al Fitr; May 9-11 Eid Al Adha; May 29 Islamic New Year; June 8-9 Ashoora; August 7 Prophet's Birthday; December 16 National Day.

Bangladesh
February 21 Martyrs' Day; March 11 Shab-i-Qadr; March 13-14 Eid-ul-Fitr; March 26 Independence Day; April 14 Bangla New Year's Day; May 1 May Day; May 21-24 Eid-ul-Azha; June 20 Muharram (Ashura); August 29 Janmaausthami; November 7 Solidarity Day. (The Bangladesh Government announces holidays for the next year in late December. Muslim religious holidays vary with appearance of the moon. Religious holidays may move one or two days in either direction.)

Barbados
January 1 New Year's; January 21 Errol Barrow's Birthday; April 14 Good Friday; April 17 Easter

Monday; May 1 May Day; June 5 Whit Monday; First Monday in August Kadooment Day; First Monday in October United Nation's Day; Last weekday of November Independence Day; December 25 Christmas; December 26 Boxing Day.

Belgium

January 1 New Year's; April 17 Easter Monday; May 1 Belgian Labor Day; May 25 Ascension; June 5 Whit Monday; July 21 Belgian Independence Day; August 15 Assumption; November 1 All Saints' Day; November 10-11 Veterans' Day; December 25 Christmas.

Brazil

January 1 New Year's; February 14-15 Carnival; April 14 Good Friday; April 21 Tiradentes' Day; June 2 Corpus Christi; September 7 Independence Day; October 12 N. Sra. Aparecida; November 2 All Souls; November 15 Proclamation of the Republic; December 25 Christmas; (The preceding list is based on Brazil's 1994 holiday schedule.)

Bulgaria

January 1 New Year's; March 3 Liberation from the Ottoman Yoke Day; May 1 Labor Day; First Monday after the Orthodox Easter Easter Monday; May 24 Cyril and Methodius Day; December 25-26 Christmas.

Canada

January 1-2 New Year's; January 3 New Year's (Quebec only); February 20 Family Day (Alberta only); April 14 Good Friday; April 17 Easter Monday; May 22 Victoria Day; June 26 St. Jean Baptiste Day (Quebec only); July 3 Canada Day; August 7 Civic Holiday (most provinces); September 4 Labor Day; October 9 Thanksgiving; November 13 Remembrance Day; December 25 Christmas; December 26 Boxing Day.

Chile

January 1 New Year's; April 1 Good Friday; April 3 Easter Sunday; May 1 Labor Day; May 21 Commemoration of the Battle of Iquique; June 2 Corpus Christi; June 29 Saint Peter and Saint Paul; August 15 Assumption; September 11 Official Holiday; September 18 Independence Day; September 19 Day of the Army; October 12 Columbus Day; November 1 All Saints' Day; December 8 Immaculate Conception; December 25 Christmas.

China

February 10-12 Spring Festival; May 1 International Labor Day; October 1-2 Chinese

National Day.

Colombia

January 1 New Year's; January 6 Epiphany*; March 19 St. Joseph's Day*; April 13 Holy Thursday; April 14 Good Friday; May 1 Labor Day; May 29 Ascension; June 19 Feast of the Sacred Heart; June 26 Corpus Christi; June 29 Saints Peter and Paul* (When holidays marked with an asterisk do not fall on Monday, they are transferred to the following Monday.)

Costa Rica

March 31 Holy Thursday; April 1 Good Friday; April 11 Juan Santamaria; June 2 Corpus Christi; June 29 Saint Peter and Saint Paul; July 25 Annexation of Guanacaste; August 2 Our Lady of Los Angeles; August 15 Assumption; September 15 Independence Day; October 12 Columbus Day; December 8 Immaculate Conception; December 26 Christmas.

Cote d'Ivoire

January 1 New Year's; March End of Ramadan; April 17 Easter Monday; May 1 Labor Day; May 25 Ascension; May Tabaski; June 5 Pentecost Monday; August 15 Assumption; August Prophet Mohammed's Birthday; October Houphouet Boigny's Birthday; November 1 All Saint's; November 15 National Peace Day; December 7 Independence Day; December 25 Christmas.

Czech Republic

January 1 New Year's; May 8 Liberation Day; July 5 Cyril & Methodius Day; July 6 Jan Hus Day; October 28 National Day; December 25 Christmas; December 26 St. Stephen's Day.

Denmark

January 1 New Year's; April 13 Maundy Thursday; April 14 Good Friday; April 17 Easter Monday; May 12 Prayer Day; May 23 Ascension; June 5 Whit Monday and Constitution Day; December 25 Christmas; December 26 Second Christmas Day.

Dominican Republic

January 1 New Year's; January 6 Epiphany; January 21 Our Lady of Grace; January 26 Duarte's Birthday; February 27 Dominican Independence; April 1 Good Friday; May 1 Dominican Labor Day; May 16 Dominican Election Day; June 2 Corpus Christi; August 16 Dominican Restoration Day; September 25 Our Lady of the Mercedes; December 25 Christmas.

Ecuador

April 1 Good Friday; May 24 Battle of Pichincha; July 25 Founding of Guayaquil (Guayaquil only); August 10 Independence Day; November 2 All Souls' Day; November 3 Independence of Cuenca; December 6 Founding of Quito (Quito only).

Egypt

January 1 New Year's; *March 13-15 Ramadan Bairam (End of Ramadan Fasting Month); April 25 Sinai Liberation Day; May 1 Labor Day; May 2 Sham El Nessim (Spring Day); *May 20-23 Kurban Bairam (Pilgrimage); *June 10 Islamic New Year; July 23 National Day; *August 19 Moulid El Nabi (Prophet's Birthday); [*Depends on Lunar Calendar; a difference of one day may occur.]

El Salvador

January 1 New Year's; January 16 Salvadoran Peace Day; April 14 Holy Thursday; April 15 Good Friday; May 1 Labor Day; June 30 Bank Holiday; August 3-6 San Salvador Feasts; September 15 Independence Day; October 12 Columbus Day; November 2 All Souls' Day; November 5 Day of First Cry of Independence; December 25 Christmas.

Finland

January 1 New Year's; January 6 Epiphany; April 14 Good Friday; April 16 Easter; April 17 Easter Monday; May 1 May Day; May 25 Ascension; June 25 Mid-Summer Day; December 6 Independence Day; December 25-26 Christmas.

France

January 1 New Year's; April 17 Easter Monday; May 1 Labor Day; May 8 Veterans' Day (WWII); May 25 Ascension; June 5 Whit Monday; July 14 French National Day; August 15 AssumptionGabon; January 1 New Year's; April 17 Easter Monday; May 1 Labor Day; June 5 Pentecost Monday; August 15-17 Independence Day; November 1 All Saint's; December 25 Christmas; [Two muslim holidays Id el Fitr and the Last Day of Ramadan are; celebrated in Gabon, but their dates are known only at the last moment.]

Georgia

January 1 New Year's; January 7 Christmas; January 19 Baptism Day; March 3 Mother's Day; April 9 Memorial Day; May 2 Recollection of the Deceased; May 26 Independence Day; August 28 August Day of the Virgin; October 14 Svetitskhovloba; November 23 St. George's Day.

Germany

January 1 New Year's; April 14 Good Friday; April 17 Easter Monday; May 25 Ascension; June 5 Whit Monday; October 3 Day of German Unity; November 16 Repentance Day; December 25-26 Christmas; [The preceding list is based on Germany's 1994 holiday schedule.]

Greece

January 1 New Year; January 6 Epiphany; 49 days prior to Greek Easter Sunday Kathara Deftera; March 25 Independence Day; Movable Holiday Good Friday; Movable Holiday Holy Saturday; Movable Holiday Easter Sunday; Movable Holiday Easter Monday; May 1 May Day; 50 days after Greek Easter Sunday Whit Monday; August 15 Assumption; October 20 OXI Day; December 24 Christmas Eve; (half-day holiday, only shops open all day); December 25 Christmas Day; December 26 Boxing Day; December 31 New Year's Eve; (half-day holiday, only shops open all day); [Regional holidays: Liberation of Ioannina, February 20 (observed; in Ioannina only); Dodecanese Accession Day, March 7 (observed in; Dodecanese Islands only); Liberation of Xanthi, October 4 (observed; in Xanthi only); St. Demetrios Day, October 26 (observed in; Thessaloniki only); St. Andreas Day, November 30 (observed in; Patras only).]

Guatemala

January 1 New Year's; April 12 p.m.-April 15 Holy Week; May 1 Labor Day; June 30 Army Day; August 15 Feast of the Assumption; September 15 Independence Day; October 20 Revolution Day; November 1 All Saints'; December 24 (p.m. only) Christmas Eve; December 25 Christmas; December 31 (p.m. only) New Year's Eve; [In addition, the banking sector celebrates the following holidays: July 1 Bank Workers's Day, and October 12, Columbus Day. Business; travelers should avoid arriving in Guatemala on a holiday, if possible,; because of the unpredictability of transportation and other services,; especially during the Holy Week, when almost everything is shut down.]

Guinea

January 1 New Year's; Variable Holiday end of Ramadan; (in 1994, it was celebrated March 19); April 3 Anniversary of the Second Republic; May 1 Labor Day; May 25 Anniversary of Organization of African Unity (OAU); Variable Holiday Tabaski; (in 1994, it was celebrated June 8); August 25 Assumption; Variable Holiday Prophet Mohammed's Birthday; (in 1993, it was observed

September 23); October 2 Independence Day; December 25 Christmas.

Honduras

January 2 New Year's Day; April 13 Holy Thursday; April 14 Good Friday and Americas' Day; May 1 Labor Day; September 15 Honduran Independence Day; October 3 Francisco Morazan's Birthday; October 12 Discovery of America Day; October 21 Armed Forces' Day; December 25 Christmas.

Hong Kong

January 2 First Weekday after New Year's Day; January 31 Lunar New Year's Day; February 1 Second Day of Lunar New Year; February 2 Third Day of Lunar New Year; April 5 Ching Ming Festival; April 14 Good Friday; April 15 The day following Good Friday; April 17 Easter Monday; June 2 Dragon Boat Festival; August 26 The Saturday preceding the last Monday in August; August 28 Liberation Day; November 1 Chung Yeung Festival; December 25 Christmas; December 26 First Weekday after Christmas Day.

Hungary

January 1-2 New Year's; March 15 Revolution Day; April 17 Easter Monday; May 1 Labor Day; June 5 Whit Monday; August 20 National Day; October 23 Republic Day; December 25 Christmas; December 26 Boxing Day.

India

January 26 Republic Day; March 10 Mahashhivratri; March 14 Id'ul Fitr; April 14 Good Friday; April 20 Ramnavami; May 22 Bakrid; May 25 Buddha Purnima; June 20 Muharram; August 15 Independence Day; August 29 Janmashtami; October 13 Dussehra; November 3 Diwali; November 18 Guru Nanak's Birthday; [The preceding list is based on India's 1994 holiday schedule.]

Indonesia

January 1-2 New Year's; January 10 Ascension of Mohammad; March 14-15 Idulfitri 1414H; April 14 Good Friday; May 1 Ascension of Christ; May 21 Idul Adha 1414H (Haj New Year); June 11 Moslem New Year 1415H; August 17 Independence Day; August 20 Mohammad's Birthday; December 25 Christmas; December 30 Ascension Day; [The preceding list is based on Indonesia's 1994 holiday schedule.]

Ireland

January 1 New Year's Day; March 17 Saint Patrick's Day; April 16 Easter Monday; First Monday in May May Holiday; First Monday in June June Holiday; First Monday in August August Holiday; First Monday in October October Holiday; December 25 Christmas; December 26 Saint Stephen's Day; [If New Year's Day, Saint Patrick's Day, Christmas Day, or; Saint Stephen's Day fall on a weekend, the following Monday is; a public holiday.; Most businesses close from December 24 through January 2 during; the Christmas festive period.; Certain other days are celebrated as holidays within local; jurisdictions.]

Israel

April 15 Passover (first day); April 21 Passover (last day); May 4 Independence Day; June 4 Shavuot (Pentecost); September 25 Rosh Hashana (New Year-first day); September 26 Rosh Hashana (New Year-second day); October 4 Yom Kippur (Day of Atonement); October 9 Succot (Feast of Tabernacles); October 16 Simhat Torah (Rejoicing of the Law); [Jewish holidays are determined according to lunar calendars, so their dates change from year to year.]

Italy

January 6 Epiphany; April 17 Easter Monday; April 25 Anniversary of the Liberation; May 1 Labor Day; August 15 Assumption; Patron Saint's Days are observed by the following cities: Florence, June 24, St. John's Day; Rome, June 29, St. Peter's and St. Paul's Day; Palermo, July 15, St. Rosalia's Day; Naples, September 19, St. Gennaro's Day; July and [August are poor months for conducting business in Italy; since most business firms are closed for vacation during this period. The same is true during the Christmas and New Year period. Certain; other days are celebrated as holidays within local jurisdictions. When; an Italian holiday falls on a Saturday, offices and stores are closed.]

Jamaica

January 1 New Year's; Variable Ash Wednesday; Variable Good Friday; Variable Easter Monday; May 23 National Labor Day; August 5 Independence Day; October 21 National Heroes' Day; December 25 Christmas Day; December 26 Boxing Day.

Japan

January 1 New Year's; January 15 Adult's Day; February 11 National Foundation Day; March 21 Vernal Equinox Day; April 29 Greenery Day; May 3 Constitution Memorial Day; May 4 Declared Official Holiday; May 5 Children's Day; September

15 Respect-for-the-Aged; September 23 Autumnal Equinox Day; October 10 Health/Sports Day; November 3 Culture Day; November 23 Labor Thanksgiving Day; December 23 Emperor's Birthday; [If a national holiday falls on a Sunday, the following Monday is a compensatory day off. May 4 is also a national holiday, although; it has no specific title. In addition to the above public holidays, many Japanese companies and government offices traditionally close; for several days during the New Year's holiday season (December 28- January 3). Many also close during ``Golden Week'' (April 29-May 5); and the traditional ``O-Bon'' (Festival of Souls') period for several; days in mid-August (usually August 12-15).]

Korea

January 1-2 New Year's; January 30-; February 1 Lunar New Year Days; March 1 Independence Movement Day; April 5 Arbor Day; May 5 Children's Day; May 7 Buddha's Birthday; June 6 Memorial Day; July 17 Constitution Day; August 15 Independence Day; September 8-10 Korean Thanksgiving Days; October 3 National Foundation Day; December 25 Christmas.

Kuwait

January 1 New Year's; February 25 Kuwait National Day; February 26 Kuwait Liberation Day. [A number of variable Islamic holidays are also observed in Kuwait. Government offices operate with very limited business hours during the Holy Month of Ramadan (the dates of which vary from one year to the next). Appointments should not be scheduled on Thursdays and Fridays.]

Latvia

January 1 New Year's; April 14 Good Friday; May 1 Constitution Day; June 23-24 Midsummer Holiday; November 18 Proclamation Day; December 25-26 Christmas; December 31 New Year's Eve.

Lebanon

January 1 New Year's; February 9 St. Maron's Day; Variable Feast of Ramadan; Variable Good Friday Western Rite; May 1 Labor Day; Variable Eastern Orthodox Good Friday; May 6 Martyr's Day; Variable Feast of Al-Adha; Variable Ashura; Variable Moslem New Year; August 15 Assumption; Variable Prophet's Birthday; November 1 All Saint's Day; November 22 Independence Day; December 25 Christmas.

Lesotho

March 12 Moshoeshoe Day; March 21 National Tree Planting Day; April 14 Good Friday; April 17 Easter Monday; July 4 Ascension and Family Day; July 17 King's Birthday; October 4 Independence Day; December 26 Boxing Day.

Madagascar

January 1 New Year's; March 29 Day Commemorating Martyrs; April 14 Easter; April 17 Easter Monday; May 1 Labor Day; 6th Thursday after Easter Ascension; 7th Sunday after Easter Pentecost,; followed by Pentecost Monday; May 25 OAU Day; June 26 Independence Day; August 15 Assumption; November 1 All Saint's Day; December 25 Christmas.

Malawi

January 3 New Year's; March 3 Martyrs' Day; April 14 Good Friday; April 17 Easter Monday; May 16 Kamuzu Day; July 6 Republic Day; October 17 Mothers' Day; December 21 National Tree Planting Day; December 26 Boxing Day; December 27 Christmas observed.

Malaysia

January 1 New Year's; January 31-; February 1 Chinese New Year; February 1 Kuala Lumpur City Day; March 4 and 5 (variable, and subject to change); Hari Raya Puasa May 1 Labor Day; May 12 (variable, and subject to change) Hari Raya Haji; May 14 Wesak Day; May 31 Awal Muharam; June 3 Agong's Birthday; August 9 Prophet Mohammed's Birthday; August 31 National Day; October or November (variable) Deepavali; December 25 Christmas.

Mali

January 1 New Year; January 20 Army Day; March 14 (approximate) Ramadan; March 26 Day of Democracy; April 17 (approximate) Easter Monday; May 1 International Labor Day; May 21 (approximate) Tabaski; May 25 Day of Africa; August 21 (approximate) Mawloud; August 28 (approximate) Prophet's Baptism; September 22 Independence Day; December 25 Christmas; [Dates listed as approximate, other than Easter, are Muslim holidays; based on the lunar calendar and therefore subject to one or two days'; variation from the date given.]

Mexico

January 1 New Year's; February 5 Anniversary of Mexican Constitution; March 21 Benito Juarez' Birthday; April 14 Good Friday; May 1 Mexican Labor Day; May 5 Anniversary of Independence;

September 16 Mexican Independence Day; November 2 All Soul's Day; November 20 Anniversary of the Mexican Revolution; December 25 Christmas; [The preceding list is a projection based on Mexican holidays in 2002.]

Morocco

March 3 Throne Day; March 30* Aid El Fitr; May 1 Labor Day; May 23 National Holiday; June 5* Aid El Adha; June 25* Moslem New Year; July 9 King's Birthday; August 14 Saharan Province Day; September 5* Prophet's Birthday; November 6 Green March Day; November 18 Independence Day. [Holidays marked with an asterisk are based on the lunar calendar; and change every year.]

Mozambique

January 1 New Year's; February 3 Mozambican Heroes' Day; April 7 Women's Day; May 1 Labor Day; June 25 Independence Day; September 7 Lusaka Agreement Day; September 25 Revolution Day; November 10 Maputo City day, a holiday only for Maputo; December 25 Christmas.

Netherlands

January 1 New Year's; April 14 Good Friday; April 17 Easter Monday; April 30 Queen's Birthday; May 5 Liberation Day; May 28 Ascension; December 25 Christmas; December 26 Second Christmas Day; [Certain other days are celebrated as holidays within; local jurisdictions.]

New Zealand

January 1-3 New Year's; January 23 Wellington Anniversary Day (Wellington only); January 30 Auckland Anniversary Day (Auckland only); February 6 Waitangi Day; April 14 Good Friday; April 17 Easter Monday; April 25 ANZAC Day; June 5 Queen's Birthday; October 23 Labor Day; November 6 Marlborough Anniversary (Blenheim only); November 10 Canterbury Anniversary (Christchurch only); December 25 Christmas; December 26 Boxing Day.

Nicaragua

January 1 New Year's Day; April 13 Holy Thursday; April 14 Good Friday; May 1 Labor Day; July 19 Sandinista Revolution Day; August 1 Festival of Santo Domingo; September 14 Battle of San Jacinto; September 15 Independence Day; December 8 Immaculate Conception; December 25 Christmas.

Nigeria

January 1 New Year's; April 1 Good Friday; April

4 Easter Monday; May 1 Labor Day; October 1 National Day; December 25 Christmas; December 26 Boxing Day.

Holidays falling on Saturdays are likely to be observed on the preceding Friday, while those falling on Sunday are likely to be observed on the following Monday.

[The Muslim holidays of Eid-El-Fitri and Eid-El-Kabir are usually celebrated for two consecutive work days. Their dates, as well as the date of Eid-El-Maulud, vary and are announced by the Ministry of Internal Affairs shortly before they occur.]

Norway

April 13 Holy Thursday; April 14 Good Friday; April 17 Easter Monday; May 1 Labor Day; May 17 Independence Day; May 25 Ascension; December 25 Christmas. [Some Norwegian manufacturing plants and major businesses are closed for three to four weeks for summer holidays from mid-July to mid-August. Easter (a 10-day holiday season for many Norwegians) also is a period of low business activity.]

Oman

March 1-2 Eid Al Fitr; May 9-10 Eid Al Adha; May 30 Islamic New Year; August 18 Birth of the Prophet; November 18-19 National Day; December 29 Ascension Day. [Most of these dates are approximations. The religious holidays are determined by locally observed phases of the moon. The actual date and duration of the National Day holiday is announced shortly before the holiday is to take place].

Pakistan

March 3-5* Eid-ul-Fitr; March 23 Pakistan Day; May 1 May Day; May 12-13 Eid-ul-Azha; June 10-11* 9th and 10th of Muharram; August 10 Milad-An-Nabi; August 14 Independence Day; September 6 Defense of Pakistan Day; September 11 Death Anniversary of Quaid-i-Azam; November 9 Iqbal Day; December 25 Birthday of Quaid-i-Azam. [*Based on the Islamic lunar calendar and may differ by one or two days from the expected dates. In addition, there is often a one or two day discrepancy in timing among different parts of the country).

Panama

January 1 New Year's; January 9 Mourning Day; February 28 Carnival; April 14 Good Friday; May 1 Labor Day; November 3 Independence Day from

Colombia; November 4 Flag Day; November 10 The Uprising of Los Santos; November 28 Independence Day from Spain; December 8 Mother's Day; December 25 Christmas.

Paraguay

January 1 New Year's; February 3 San Blas; March 1 Heroes' Day; April 14 Holy Thursday; April 15 Good Friday; May 1 Labor day; May 15 Independence Day; June 12 Chaco Armistice; August 15 Founding of Asuncion; December 8 Virgin of Caacupe Day; December 25 Christmas.

Philippines

January 1 New Year's; April 9 Bataan & Corregidor Day and Heroism Day; April 13 Maundy Thursday; April 14 Good Friday; May 1 Labor Day; June 12 Independence Day; August 28 National Heroes Day; November 1 All Saints' Day; November 30 Bonifacio Day; December 25 Christmas; December 30 Rizal Day. [June 24, Manila Day, is observed only in the City of Manila, and August 19, Quezon Day, is observed only in Quezon City. In addition, special public holidays such as Election Day and EDSA Revolution Day, may be declared by the President and are observed nationwide.]

Poland

January 1 New Year's; April 17 Easter Monday; May 1 Labor Day; May 3 Constitution DayLate; May or early; June Corpus Christi; August 15 Assumption; November 1 All Saints' Day; November 11 Independence Day; December 25-26 Christmas. [One Saturday per month is by custom considered a working Saturday, but there is no consistency among institutions or exact observance as such.]

Qatar

February 22 Anniversary of the Accession of the Amir; September 3 Independence Day [Officially, Qatar uses the Gregorian calendar year for all purposes. The Hijra (Islamic) calendar is also widely used. Religious holidays vary from year to year. Eid Al-Fitr (four days) marks the end of the fasting month of Ramadan and Eid Al-Adha marks the conclusion of the pilgrimage (Haj) to Mecca.]

Romania

January 1-2 New Year's; April 23-24 Orthodox Easter; May 1-2 Labor Day; December 1 National Day; December 25 Christmas.

Russia

January 1-2 New Year's; January 7 Orthodox Christmas; March 8 International Women's Day; May 1 International Labor Day; May 2 Spring Day; May 9 Victory Day; June 12 Independence Day; November 7 Revolution Day. [When holidays occur on weekends, Russian authorities announce during the week prior to the holiday, if the day will be celebrated on the following Monday. It is likely that January 2 and 3 will be holidays in 1995 since January 1 is a Sunday.]

Saudi Arabia

Beginning about March 1 Eid al-Fitr; Beginning about May 9 Eid al-Adha; September 22 National Day. [There are two Islamic religious holidays around which most businesses in Saudi Arabia close for at least three working days. Eid al-Fitr occurs at the end of the holy month of Ramadan. Eid al-Adha celebrates the time of year when pilgrims arrive from around the world to perform the Haj. Their timing is governed by the Islamic lunar calendar and they fall approximately 11 days earlier in each successive year. In 1995, the Eid al-Fitr holiday will begin on or about March 1 and the Eid al-Adha holiday on or about May 9.]

Senegal

January 1 New Year's; April 4 Independence Day; 1st Monday in April Easter Monday; May 1 International Labor Day; August 15 Assumption; November 1 All Saints' Day; December 25 Christmas. [The following holidays are moveable according to the religious calendar: Korite, Tabaski, Tamxarit, Mawlud, Ascension, and Pentecost (in May).]

South Africa

January 1-2 New Year's; April 6 Founders' Day; April 14 Good Friday; April 17 Family Day; May 1 Workers' Day; May 25 Ascension; May 31 Republic Day; October 10 Kruger Day; December 16 Day of the Vow; December 25 Christmas; December 26 Day of Goodwill.

Spain

January 1 New Year's; January 6 Epiphany; April 14 Good Friday; August 15 Assumption; October 12 National Day; November 1 All Saints' Day; December 6 Constitution Day; December 8 Immaculate Conception. [Regional holidays: April 13 (Holy Thursday), Bilbao/Madrid; April 17 (Easter Monday), Barcelona/Bilbao; May 2 (Labor Day), Madrid; May 16 (St. Isidro), Madrid; June 5 (Whit Monday), Barcelona; June 24 (St. John), Barcelona; July 25 (St. James), Bilbao/Madrid; September 24 (La Merced), Barcelona; November 9 (Our Lady of Almudena), Madrid; December 26,

Barcelona/Madrid. The list of Spain's commercial holidays for 1995 is not available yet. It will not differ much from the preceding list for 1994.]

Sri Lanka

January 15 Thai Pongal; January 16 Duruthu Poya; February 4 National Day; February 14 Navam Poya; February 27 Maha Sivarathri; March 3 Ramazan Festival; March 16 Medin Poya; April 13 Day Prior to Sinhala and Tamil New Year; April 14 Sinhala and Tamil New Year Good Friday; April 15 Bak Poya; May 1 May Day; May 10 Hadji Festival; May 14 Vesak Poya; May 15 Day Following Vesak Poya; May 22 National Heroes' Day; June 12 Poson Poya; July 12 Esala Poya; August 10 Nikini Poya and Holy Prophet's Birthday; September 8 Binara Poya; October 8 Vap Poya; October 23 Deepavali Festival; November 6 Il Poya; December 6 Unduvap Poya; December 25 Christmas; December 31 Special Bank Holiday. [Sri Lankan holidays are connected with the country's four religions: Buddhism, Hinduism, Islam, and Christianity. Dates change from year to year. Holidays with fixed dates include National Day (February 4), National Heroes' Day (May 22), and Christmas (December 25). Each full moon is marked by a Poya Day holiday.]

Suriname

January 1 New Year's; About March 13 Holi Phagwa; About March 27 Ied Ul Fitr; April 14 Good Friday; April 17 Easter Monday; May 1 Labor Day; July 1 Emancipation Day; November 25 Independence Day; December 25 Christmas.

Swaziland

January 1 New Year's; April 14 Good Friday; April 17 Easter Monday; April 19 King Mswati III's Birthday; April 25 National Flag Day; May 12 Ascension; July 22 Public Holiday; August or September Umhlanga (Reed Dance); September 6 Independence Day; December 25 Christmas; December 26 Boxing Day; December or January Incwala. [The preceding list is a projection based on Swaziland holidays in 1994. Swaziland holidays falling on a Sunday are observed on the following Monday. Swaziland holidays falling on a Saturday are observed on that day unless an announcement to the contrary is made by the Government.]

Sweden

January 1 New Year's; January 6 Epiphany; April 14 Good Friday; April 17 Easter Monday; May 1 Swedish Labor Day; May 25 Ascension; June 5 Whit Monday; June 24 Midsummer Day; November 4 All Saints' Day; December 25-26 Christmas. [Offices are also closed on Mid-Summer Eve, Christmas Eve, and New Year's Eve. Government and many business offices generally close 1:00 p.m. on the day before major holidays.]

Switzerland

January 1 New Year's; January 2 Baerzelistag; April 14 Good Friday; April 17 Easter Monday; May 25 Ascension; June 5 Whit Monday; August 1 Swiss National Day; December 25 Christmas; December 26 St. Stephan's Day.

Syria

Jauary 1 New Year's; March 8 Revolution Day; March 13-15 Al-Fitr Holiday; March 21 Mothers' Day; April 3 Western Easter; April 10 Eastern Easter; April 17 In dependence Day; May 1 Labor Day; May 6 Martyrs' Day; May 22-25 Al-Adha Holiday; June 9 Muslim New Year; August 18 Prophet's Birthday; October 6 Tishree War; December 25 Christmas. [The Muslim religious holidays listed above are based on the lunar calendar; the exact dates are to be confirmed.]

Taiwan

January 1 Founding Day; Late January Mid-February Spring Festival; (Chinese New Year) March 29 Youth Day; April 4 Women and Children's Day; April 5 Tomb Sweeping Day and President Chiang Kai-Shek Day; Late May Mid-June Dragon Boat Festival; September Mid-Autumn Festival; September 28 Confucius' Birthday; October 10 Double Ten National Day; October 25 Taiwan Retrocession Day; October 31 President Chiang Kai-Shek's Birthday; November 12 Dr. Sun Yat-Sen's Birthday; December 25 Constitution Day. [There are 10 holidays and three festivals in Taiwan. Dates for the three festivals which include Chinese Lunar New Year Day, Dragon Boat Festival, and Mid-Autumn (Moon) Festival change with the lunar calendar.]

Tanzania

January 1 New Year; January 12 Zanzibar Revolutionary Day; March 3-4* Idd-El-Fitr; April 14 Good Friday; April 17 Easter Monday; April 26 Union Day; May 1 International Workers' Day; May 11* Idd-El-Hajj; August 8 Peasants' Day; August 11 Maulid Day; December 9 Independence Day; December 25 Christmas; December 26 Boxing Day. [Holidays marked with an asterisk are subject to the sighting of the moon and may vary from the dates shown.]

Thailand

January 3 New Year's; February 9-10 Chinese New Year; February 25 Magha Puja Day; April 6 King Rama I Memorial and Chakri Day; April 12-14 Songkran Days; May 2 Labor Day; May 5 Coronation Day; May 24 Visakha Puja Day; July 25 Buddhist Lent Day; August 12 Her Majesty the Queen's Birthday; October 24 Chulalongkorn Day; December 5 His Majesty the King's Birthday; December 12 Constitution Day. [The preceding list is based on the list of Thailand holidays in 1994.]

Trinidad and Tobago

January 1 New Year's; April 14 Good Friday; April 17 Easter Monday; June 2 Corpus Christi; June 5 Whit Monday; June 19 Labor Day; August 1 Emancipation Day; August 31 Independence Day; September 24 Republic DayDate to be determined Divali; December 25 Christmas; December 26 Boxing Day. [The dates for Carnival Monday and Tuesday (the Monday and Tuesday preceding Ash Wednesday) change from year to year. Carnival Monday and Tuesday are not official public holidays but most businesses are closed.]

Turkey

January 1 New Year's; March 2-5 Sugar Holiday; April 23 National Sovereignty and Children's Day; May 9-13 Sacrifice Holiday; May 19 Ataturk Memorial, Youth, and Sports Day; August 30 Zafer Bayrami (Victory Day); October 28-29 Turkish Independence Day.

Uganda

January 1 New Year's; January 26 Liberation Day; April 14 Good Friday; April 17 Easter Monday; March 8 International Women's Day; May 1 Labor Day; Date to be determined Idd-el-Fitr; Date to be determined Iddi Aduha; June 3 Uganda Martyrs' Day; June 9 National Heroes' Day; October 9 Independence Day; December 25 Christmas; December 26 Boxing Day.

United Arab Emirates

January 1 New Year's; January 19* Ascension; March 2-4 Eid Al Fitr; May 9* Waqfa; May 10-12* Eid Al-Adha; May 31* Islamic New Year; August 6 Shaykh Zayed Accession Day; August 8* Prophet's Birthday; December 2-3 UAE National Day. [UAE religious holidays are marked with an asterisk and are dependent upon the sighting of the moon.]

United Kingdom

England and Wales: January 1 New Year's; April 14 Good Friday; April 17 Easter Monday; May 1 May Day; May 29 Spring Holiday-May; August 28 Summer Bank Holiday; December 25 Christmas; December 26 Boxing Day.

Scotland

Scotland observes the above except Easter Monday, Spring Holiday, and Summer Bank Holiday, and also observes the following: January 2 Bank Holiday; April 3 Spring Holiday; May 15 Victoria Day; August 7 Bank Holiday; September 18 Autumn Holiday.

Northern Ireland:

In addition to the U.K.-listed holidays, the following are observed: March 17 St. Patrick's Day; April 18 Easter Tuesday; July 12-13 Orangeman's Day.

Venezuela

February 27-28 Carnival; April 13 Good Thursday; April 14 Good Friday; April 19 Signing of Independence; May 1 Labor Day; July 5 Independence Day; July 24 Bolivar's Birthday.

Zambia

January 1 New Year's; March 12 Youth Day; April 14 Good Friday; April 17 Easter Monday; May 1 Labor Day; May 25 African Freedom Day; July 4 Heroes' Day; July 5 Unity Day; August 1 Farmers' Day; October 24 Independence Day; December 25 Christmas.

APPENDIX Q

COUNTRIES: BANKING, BUSINESS AND SHOPPING HOURS

AFGHANISTAN
Business/Shopping Hours: 8:AM - 6:AM (Sun-Thur)Businesses are closed Thursday and Friday afternoons

ALGERIA
Banking Hours: 9:AM - 4:PM (Sun-Thur) Business Hours: 8:AM - 12:Noon, 1:PM - 5:PM (Sat-Wed) Businesses are closed Thursday and Friday

AMERICAN SAMOA
Banking Hours: 9:AM - 2:PM (Mon-Thur) 9:AM - 5:PM (Fri)

ANDORRA
Banking Hours: 9:AM - 1:PM; 3:PM - 7:PM Business Hours: 9:AM - 1:PM; 3:PM - 7:PM, Shopping Hours: 10:AM - 1:PM; 3:PM - 8:PM

ANGUILLA
Banking Hours: 8:AM - 12:00 Noon (Mon-Fri); 3:PM (Fri)Business Hours: 8:AM - 4:PM, Shopping Hours: 8:AM - 5:PM (Mon-Sat)

ANTIGUA AND BARBUDA
Banking Hours: 8:AM - 1:PM (Mon,Tue,Wed,Thur) 8:AM - 1:PM & 3:PM - 5:PM (Fri); Business Hours: 8:AM - 12:Noon & 1:PM - 4:PM (Mon-Fri) Shopping Hours: 8:AM - 12:Noon & 1:PM - 5:PM (Mon-Sat)

ARMENIA
Banking Hours: 9:AM - 6:PM
Business Hours: 9:AM - 6:PM
Shopping Hours: 8:AM - 9:PM

ARGENTINA
Banking Hours: 10:AM - 4:PM (Mon-Fri); Business Hours: 9:AM - 6:PM (Mon-Fri); Shopping Hours: 9:AM - 8:PM (Mon-Sat)

AUSTRALIA
Banking Hours: 10:AM - 3:PM (Mon-Thur); 10:AM - 5:PM (Fri)Banks are closed on Saturdays; Business/Shopping Hours: 9:AM - 5:30PM (Mon-Thur); 8:30AM - 12:Noon (Sat)

AUSTRIA
Banking Hours: 8:AM - 12:30 PM, 1:30 - 3:30 PM (Mon, Tue, Wed, Fri); 1:30 -5:30PM(Thur) Business Hours: 8:30 AM - 4:30 PM Shopping Hours: 8:AM - 6:PM (Mon - Fri); 8:AM -12:Noon (Sat)

AZERBAIJAN
Banking Hours: 9:AM - 6:PM; Business Hours: 9:AM - 6:PM; Shopping Hours: 8:AM - 9:PM

BAHAMAS
Banking Hours: 9:30AM - 3:PM (Mon-Thur); 9:30AM - 5:PM (Fri)

BAHRAIN
Banking Hours: 7:30AM - 12:Noon (Sat-Wed); 7:30AM - 11:AM Thur)

BARBADOS
Banking Hours: 8:AM - 3:PM (Mon-Thur); 8:AM - 1:PM & 3:PM - 5:PM (Fri); Business Hours: 8:30AM - 4:PM (Mon-Fri); Shopping Hours: 8:AM - 4:PM (Mon-Fri); 8:AM - 12:Noon (Sat)

BANGLADESH
Banking Hours: 9:30AM - 1:30PM (Mon-Thur); 9:AM - 11:AM (Fri- Sat); Business/Shopping Hours: 9:AM - 9:PM (Mon-Fri); 9:AM - 2:PM (Sat)

BELARUS
Banking Hours: 9:AM - 6:PM
Business Hours: 9:AM - 6:PM
Shopping Hours: 9:AM - 9:PM

BELGIUM
Banking Hours: 9:AM - 3:PM (Mon-Fri); Business Hours: 9:AM - 12:Noon & 2:PM - 5:30PM; Shopping Hours: 9:AM - 6:PM (Mon-Sat)

BELIZE
Banking Hours: 8:AM - 1:PM (Mon-Fri); 3:PM - 6:PM (Fri)Business Hours: 8:AM - 12:Noon; 1:PM - 5:PM (Mon-Fri)Shopping Hours: 8:AM - 4:PM (Mon-Sat)

BENIN
Banking Hours: 8:AM - 11:AM; 3:PM - 4:PM (Mon-Fri); Business Hours: 8:AM - 12:30PM; 3:PM - 6:30PM (Mon-Fri) Shopping Hours: 9:AM - 1:PM, 4:PM -7:PM (Mon-Sun)

BERMUDA
Business/Shopping: 9:AM - 5:PM (Mon-Sat)

BOLIVIA
Banking Hours: 9:AM - 12:Noon & 2:PM - 4:PM (Mon-Fri) Business Hours: 9:AM - 12:Noon & 2:30PM - 6:PM (Mon-Fri) Shopping Hours: 9:AM - 6:PM; 9:AM - 12:Noon (Sat)

BOSNIA HERZEGOVINA
Banking Hours: 7:AM - Noon or &:AM - 7:PM; Business Hours: 8:AM - 3:30 PM; Shopping Hours: 8:AM - 8:PM (Mon-Fri)

BOTSWANA
Banking Hours: 8:15 - 12:45PM (Mon-Fri), 8:15AM - 10:45 AM (Sat) Shopping Hours: 8:AM - 6:PM (Mon-Sat)

BRITISH VIRGIN ISLANDS
Banking Hours: 9:AM - 2:PM (Mon-Fri); Business Hours: 8:30AM - 2:00PM & 4:PM - 5:PM (Mon-Fri); Shopping Hours: 8:AM - 5:PM (Mon-Sat)

BRAZIL
Banking Hours 10:AM - 4:30PM (Mon-Fri) Shopping Hours: 9:AM - 6:30PM (Mon-Fri) & 9:AM - 1:PM (Sat)

BURKINA FASO
Business Hours: 7:AM - 12:Noon, 3:PM - 5:PM (Mon-Fri) Shopping Hours: 7:AM - 12:Noon, 2:PM - 7:PM (Mon-Sat)

BURMA
Banking Hours: 10:AM - 2:PM (Mon-Fri); 10:AM - 12:Noon (Sat) Bussiness/Shopping Hours: 9:30Am - 4:PM (Mon-Sat)

BURUNDI
Business Hours: 8:AM - 12:Noon (Mon-Fri); Shopping Hours: 8:AM - 6:PM (Mon-Sat)

CAMEROON
Banking Hours: French Speaking Part: 8:AM - 11:AM, 2:30PM - 4:PM (Mon-Fri)English Speaking Part: 8:AM - 2:PM (Mon-Fri) Business Hours: French Speaking Part: 7:30AM - 12: Noon, 2:30PM - 6:PM (Mon-Fri) English Speaking Part: 7:30AM - 2:30PM - (Mon-Fri), 7:30AM - 1:PM

Shopping Hours: 8:AM - 12:30PM, 4:PM - 7:PM (Mon-Sat)

REPUBLIC OF CAPE VERDE
Banking Hours: 8:AM - 12: Noon (Mon-Fri); Business Hours: 8:AM - 12: Noon (Mon-Fri)

CAYMAN ISLANDS
Banking Hours: 9:AM - 2:30PM (Mon-Thur) & 9:AM -PM, :30PM -4:30PM (Fri) Business Hours: 8:30AM - 5:PM Shopping Hours: 8:30AM - 5:PM

CENTRAL AFRICAN REPUBLIC
Banking Hours: 8:AM - 11:30AM (Mon-Fri); Shopping Hours: 7:30AM - 9:PM (Mon-Sun)

CHAD
Banking Hours: 7:AM - 11:AM (Mon-Thur, Sat), 7:AM -10:AM (Fri) Business Hours: 7:AM - 2:PM (Mon-Thur, Sat), 7:AM -12: Noon (Fri)Shopping Hours: 8:AM - 1:PM, 4:PM - 6:PM (Mon-Sat)

CHILE
Banking Hours: 9:AM - 1:PM & 2:30PM - 6:PM (Mon-Fri); 9:AM -2:PM (Sat) Shopping Hours: 9:AM - 1:PM & 2:30PM - 6:PM (Mon-Fri)

CHINA, PEOPLES REPUBLIC
Banking Hours: varies (Mon-Sat)

CHINA, TAIWAN
Banking Hours: 9:AM - 3:30PM (Mon-Fri); 9:AM - 12:Noon (Sat)

COLUMBIA
Banking Hours: 9:AM - 3:PM (Mon-Thur); 9:AM - 3:30 (Fri); Business Hours: 8:30AM - 5:PM (Mon-Fri); Shopping Hours: 10:AM - 7:PM (Mon-Sat)

COMOROS ISLAND
Banking Hours: 9:AM - 12:30PM, 3:PM - 5:PM (Mon-Fri), 9:AM - 12:30PM (Sat); Shopping Hours: 8:AM - 8:PM (Mon-Sat)

CONGO, PEOPLE'S REPUBLIC
Banking Hours: 7:AM - 2:PM (Mon-Fri); Shopping Hours: 7:AM - 7:PM (Mon-Sat)

COSTA RICA
Banking Hours: 9:AM - 3:PM (Mon-Fri); Shopping Hours: 8:30AM - 11:30AM & 2:PM - 6:PM (Mon-Fri) 8:30AM - 11:30AM (Sat)

COTE D'IVOIRE
Banking Hours: 8:AM - 11:30AM, 2:30PM - 4:PM (Mon-Fri) Business Hours: 8:AM - 12:Noon, 2:30PM - 5:30PM (Mon-Fri) Shopping Hours: 8:30AM - 12:Noon, 2:30PM - 7:PM (Mon-Sat)

CUBA
Banking Hours: 9:AM - 3:PM (Mon-Fri); Business Hours: 8:30AM - 12:30PM & 1:30PM - 5:30PM (Mon - Fri) Shopping Hours: 9:AM - 5:PM (Mon-Fri); 9:AM - 12:Noon (Sat)

CYPRUS
Banking Hours: 8:30AM - 12: Noon (Mon-Sat); Business Hours: 8:AM - 1:PM, 2:30PM - 6:PM (Mon-Fri)8:AM -1:PM (Sat)Shopping Hours: 8:AM - 1:PM; 4:PM - 7:PM (Mon-Fri) Closed Wednesday and Saturday afternoons.

CZECH REPUBLIC
Banking Hours: 8:AM - 4:PM (Mon-Fri); Business Hours: 8:30AM - 5:PM Shopping Hours: 9:AM - 6:PM (Mon-Fri), 9:AM - 1:PM (Sat)

DENMARK
Banking Hours: 9:30AM - 4:PM; (Mon,Tue,Wed, & Fri), 9:30AM -6:PM (Thur) Business Hours: 8:AM - 4:PM (Mon-Fri) Shopping Hours: 9/10:AM - 5:30/7:PM (Mon-Thur) 9/10:AM - 7/8:PM (Fri) 9/10:AM - 1/2:PM (Sat)

REPUBLIC OF DJIBOUTI
Banking Hours: 7:15AM - 11:45AM (Sun-Thur); Shopping Hours: 7:30AM - 12:Noon, 3:30PM - 7:30PM (Sat-Thur)

DOMINICA
Banking Hours: 8:AM - 1:PM (Mon-Fri); 3:PM - 5:PM (Fri) Business Hours: 8:AM - 1:PM & 2:PM - 4:PM (Mon-Fri); 8:AM - 1:PM (Sat) Shopping Hours: 8:AM - 1:PM & 2:PM - 4:PM (Mon-Fri); 8:AM- 1:PM (Sat)

DOMINICAN REPUBLIC
Banking Hours: 8:AM - 12:Noon (Mon-Fri); Business Hours: 9:AM - 6:PM (Mon-Fri) & 9:AM -12:Noon (Sat); Shopping Hours: 8:30AM - 12:Noon & 2:30PM - 6:PM (Mon-Fri); 8:30AM - 1:PM (Sat)

ECUADOR
Banking Hours: 9:AM - 1:30PM (Mon-Fri); Shopping Hours: 8:30AM - 12:30PM (Mon-Sat) & 3:30PM - 7:PM (Mon-Sat)

EGYPT
Banking Hours: 8:30AM - 1:PM (Mon-Thur, Sat), 10:AM - 12:Noon (Sat) Shopping Hours: 10:AM - 7:PM (Tue-Sat), 10:AM - 8:PM (Mon - Thur)

EL SALVADOR
Banking Hours: 8:AM - 12:Noon & 2:PM - 4:PM (Mon-Fri); Shopping Hours: 8:AM - 12:Noon & 2:30PM - 6:PM (Mon-Sat)

EQUATORIAL GUINEA
Banking Hours: 8:AM - 3:PM (Mon-Fri), 8:AM - 1:PM(Sat) Business Hours; 8:AM - 3:PM (Mon-Fri), 8:AM - 1:PM (Sat) Shopping Hours: 8:AM - 3:PM, 5:PM - 7:PM (Mon-Sat)

ESTONIA
Banking Hours: 9:AM - 3:PM
Business Hours: 9:AM - 6PM
Shopping Hours: 9:am - 9:PM (Mon-Sat)

ETHIOPIA
Banking Hours: 9:AM - 5:PM (Mon-Fri); Business Hour: 8:AM - 12:Noon, 1:PM - 4:PM (Mon-Fri);Banks close for 3 hours for lunch

FIJI
Banking Hours: 10:AM - 3:PM (Mon-Thur); 10:AM - 4:PM (Fri); Business/Shopping Hours: 8:AM - 5:PM

FINLAND
Banking Hours: 9:15AM - 4:15PM (Mon-Fri); Business Hours: 8:30AM - 4:PM (Mon-Fri);Shopping Hours: 9:AM - 5/6:PM (Mon-Fri), 9:AM - 2/3:PM (Sat)

FRANCE
Banking Hours: 9:AM - 4:30PM (Mon-Fri); Business Hours: 9:AM - 12:Noon; 2:PM - 6:PM (Mon-Fri), 9:AM - 12:Noon (Sat); Shopping Hours: 9:AM -6:30PM (Tue-Sat)

FRENCH GUIANA
Banking Hours: 7:15AM - 11:45AM (Mon,Tue,Thur, Fri); 7:AM -12:Noon (Wed)

GABON
Banking Hours: 7:AM - 12:Noon (Mon-Fri); Business Hours: 8:AM - 12:Noon, 3:PM - 6:PM (Mon-Fri); Shopping Hours: 8:AM - 12:Noon, 4:PM - 7:PM (Mon-Sat)

GEORGIA
Shopping Hours: 9:AM - 7:PM

THE GAMBIA
Banking Hours: 8:AM - 1:PM (Mon-Fri); 8:AM - 11:AM (Sat); Business/Shopping Hours: 8:AM - 5:PM (Mon-Fri); 8:AM -12:Noon (Sat)

FEDERAL REPUBLIC OF GERMANY
Banking Hours: 8:30AM - 12:30PM; 1:45PM - 3:45PM (Mon-Fri), Thur- 5:45PM Business Hours: 8:AM - 5:PM Shopping Hours: 8:AM - 6:30PM (Mon-Fri), 8:AM - 2:PM (Sat)

GHANA
Banking Hours: 8:30AM - 2:PM (Mon-Fri); Business Hours: 8:30AM - 5:PM (Mon-Fri); Shopping Hours: 8:30AM - 5:PM (Mon-Sat)

GIBRALTAR
Banking Hours: 9:AM - 3:30PM (Mon-Fri), 4:30PM - 6:PM (Fri) Business Hours: 9:AM - 6:PM; Shopping Hours: 9:AM - 1:PM & 3:30PM - 7:PM (Mon-Fri), 9:-1:PM (Sat)

GREECE
Banking Hours: 8:AM - 2:PM (Mon-Fri); Business Hours: 8:30AM - 1:30PM, 4:PM - 7:30PM; Shopping Hours: 8:AM - 2:30PM (Mon, Wed, Sat), 8:AM - 1:30PM, 5:PM- 8:PM (Tue, Thur, Fri)

GRENADA
Banking Hours: 8:AM - 12:Noon (Mon-Fri) & 2:30 PM - 5:PM (Fri) Business Hours: 8:AM -4:PM (Mon-Fri) 8:AM - 11:45 AM (Sat) Shopping Hours: 8:AM -4:PM (Mon-Fri); 8:AM - 11:45 AM (Sat)

GUADELOUPE
Banking Hours: 8:AM - 12:Noon & 2:PM - 4:PM; Shopping Hours: 9:AM - 1:PM & 3:PM - 6:PM (Mon-Fri); Sat mornings

GUATEMALA
Banking Hours: 9:AM - 3:PM (Mon-Fri); Shopping Hours: 9:AM - 7:PM (Mon-Sat)

GUINEA, REPUBLIC
Banking Hours: 7:30AM - 3:PM (Mon-Sat); Business Hours: 7:30 - 3:PM (Mon-Sat); Shopping Hours: 8:AM - 6:PM (Mon-Sun)

GUYANA
Banking Hours: 8:AM - 12:30PM (Mon-Fri); Business Hours: 8:AM - 4:PM (Mon-Fri); Shopping Hours: 8:AM - 12:Noon; 2:PM - 4:PM

HAITI
Banking Hours: 9:AM - 1:PM (Mon-Fri); Business Hours: 8:AM - 5:PM (Mon-Fri); 8:AM - 12:Noon (Sat) Shopping Hours: 8:AM - 5:PM (Mon-Fri); 8:AM - 12:Noon (Sat)

HONDURAS
Banking Hours: 9:AM - 3:30PM (Mon-Fri); Shopping Hours: 8:AM - 6:30PM (Mon-Sat)

HONG KONG
Banking Hours: 10:AM - 3:PM (Mon-Fri); 9:AM - 12:Noon (Sat) Business/Shopping Hours: 9:AM - 5:PM; 9:AM - 1:Pm (Sat)

HUNGARY
Banking Hours: 8:30AM - 3:PM (Mon-Sat); Business Hours: 8:30AM - 5:PM Shopping Hours: 10:AM - 6:PM (Mon-Fri); 10:AM - 2:PM (Sat)

ICELAND
Banking Hours: 9:15AM - 4:PM (Mon-Fri); Business Hours: 9:AM - 5:PM (Mon-Fri); Shopping Hours: 9:AM - 6:PM (Mon-Fri); 9:AM - 12:Noon (Sat)

INDIA
Banking Hours: 10:30AM - 2:30PM (Mon-Fri); 10:30AM - 12:30PM (Sat); Business/Shopping Hours:Government Offices: 10:AM - 1:PM; 2:PM - 5:PM (Mon-Sat); Non-Gov't Offices: 9:30AM - 1:PM; 2:PM - 5:PM (Mon-Sat)

INDONESIA
Banking Hours: 10:AM - 3:PM (Mon-Fri); 9:AM - 12:Noon (Sat)

IRAN
Banking Hours: 8:AM - 1:PM; 4:PM - 6:PM (Sat-Thur); Business/Shopping Hours:Gov't Office: 8:AM - 4:30PM (Sat-Wed) Non-Gov't. Offices: 8:AM - 4:30PM (Sat-Thur) Offices closed on Friday

IRELAND
Banking Hours: 10:AM - 12:30PM; 1:30PM - 3:PM (Mon-Fri); Business Hours: 9:AM - 1:PM, 2:PM - 5:PM; Shopping Hours: 9:AM - 5:30PM (Mon-Sat)

ISRAEL
Banking Hours: 8:30AM - 12:30PM; 4:PM - 5:30PM (Sun-Tue,Thur) 8:30AM -12:30PM (Wed); 8:30AM -12:Noon (Fri)Business Hours: Non-Gov't Office: 8:AM - 4:PM (Mon-Fri) Offices close early on Friday

ITALY

Banking Hours: 8:35AM - 1:35PM; 3:PM - 4:PM (Mon-Fri) Business Hours: 8:30AM - 12:30PM, 3:30PM- 7:30PM Shopping Hours: 9:AM - 1:PM, 3:30/4:PM - 7:30/8:PM

JAMAICA

Banking Hours: 9:AM - 2:PM (Mon - Thur); 9:AM - 12:Noon & 2:PM- 5:PM (Fri) Business Hours: 8:AM - 4:PM Shopping Hours: 8:30AM - 4:30PM

JAPAN

Banking Hours: 9:AM - 3:PM (Mon-Fri); 9:AM - 12:Noon (Sat) Business/Shopping: 9:AM - 5:PM (Mon-Fri); 9:AM - 12:Noon (Sat)

JORDAN

Banking Hours: 8:AM - 12:30PM (Sat-Thur) Business/Shopping Hours: 8:AM - 6:PM (Sat-Thur)

KENYA

Banking Hours: 9:AM - 2:PM (Mon - Fri); 9:AM - 11;AM (1st & last saturday of month) Business Hours: 8:30AM - 4:30PM (Mon -Fri), 8:30 - 12:Noon (Sat) Shopping Hours: 8:30AM - 12:30PM, 2:PM - 5:PM (Mon - Sat)

KOREA, SOUTH

Banking Hours: 9:30AM - 4:30PM (Mon-Fri); 9:30AM - 11:PM (Sat) Business/Shopping Hours: 9:AM - 5:PM (Mon-Fri): 9:AM - 1:PM (Sat)

KUWAIT

Banking Hours: Mostly in the morning ;Business/Shopping Hours: Gov't Offices: 7:30AM - 1:30PM Non-Gov't Offices: 7:30AM - 2:30PM (Sat-Wed);7:AM - 1:PM; 5:PM - 8:PM

KYRGYZSTAN

Banking Hours: 9:AM - 6:PM
Business Hours: 9:AM - 6:PM
Shopping Hours: 8:AM - 9:PM

LATVIA

Banking Hours: 9:AM - 12:Noon
Business Hours: 9:AM - 6:PM
Shopping Hours: 8:Am - 10:PM

LEBANON

Banking Hours: 8:30AM - 12:30PM (Mon-Fri); 8:30AM -12:Noon (Sat)

LESOTHO

Banking Hours: 8:30AM - 1:PM (Mon-Fri); 9:AM - 11:AM (Sat) Business Hours: 8:AM - 4:30PM (Mon-Fri) Shopping Hours: 8:AM - 4:30PM (Mon-

Fri); 8:AM - 1:PM (Sat)

LIBERIA

Banking Hours: 9:AM - 5:PM (Mon-Sat); Business Hours: 9:AM - 6:PM (Mon-Sat)

LIBYA

Banking Hours: 8:AM - 4:PM (Sat-Thur); Business Hours: 8:AM - 4:PM (Sat-Thur)

LIECHTENSTEIN

Banking Hours: 8:30AM - 12:Noon, 1:30 - 4:30PM (Mon-Fri) Business Hours: 8:AM - 12:Noon, 2:30PM - 6:PM; Shopping Hours: 8:AM - 12:15PM, 2:PM - 6:30PM (Mon-Fri), 8:AM - 4:PM (Sat)

LITHUANIA

Banking Hours: 9:AM - 12:Noon; Business Hours: 9:AM - 1:PM, 2:PM - 6:PM (Mon-Sat)

LUXEMBOURG

Banking Hours: 9:AM - 12:Noon; 2:PM - 5:PM (Mon-Sat); Business Hours: 9:AM - 12:Noon, 2:PM - 5:30PM; Shopping Hours: 8:AM - 12:Noon, 2:PM - 6:PM (Mon-Sat)

MADAGASCAR

Banking Hours: 8:AM - 11:AM, 2:PM -4:PM (Mon-Fri); Shopping Hours: 9:AM - 6:PM (Mon-Sat); Business Hours: 8:AM - 12:Noon, 2:PM - 6:PM (Mon-Fri)

MALAWI

Banking Hours: 8:AM - 1:PM (Mon-Fri); Business Hours: 7:30AM - 5:PM (Mon-Fri); Shopping Hours: 8:AM - 6:PM

MALAYSIA

Business/Shopping Hours: 8:30/9:AM - 1:PM, 2:30PM - 4:30PM (Mon-Fri); 9:AM - 1:PM (Sat) Gov't Offices: 9:AM - 4:30Pm (Mon-Fri); 9:AM - 1:PM (Sat)

MALI

Banking Hours: 8:AM - 12:Noon, 2:PM - 4:PM (Mon-Fri); Business Hours: 7:30AM - 2:30PM (Mon-Sat), 7:30AM -12:30PM (Fri)Shopping Hours: 9:AM - 8:PM (Mon-Sat)

MALTA

Banking Hours: 8:30AM - 12:30PM (Mon-Fri), 8:30AM - 11:30AM (Sat) Business Hours: 8:30AM - 5:30PM (Mon-Fri), 8:30AM - 1:PM (Sat) Shopping Hours: 9:AM - 1:PM, 4:PM - 7:PM (Mon-Fri), 9:AM -1:PM, 4:PM - 8:PM (Sat)

MARTINIQUE
Banking Hours: 7:30AM - 4:PM (Mon-Fri); Shopping Hours: 8:30AM - 6:PM (Mon-Fri); 8:30AM - 1:PM (Sat)

MAURITANIA
Banking Hours: 8:AM - 3:PM (Sun-Thur);Business Hours: 8:AM - 3:PM (Sun-Thur); Shopping Hours: 8:AM - 1:PM, 3:PM - 6:PM (Sun-Thur)

MAURITIUS
Banking Hours: 10:AM - 2:PM (Mon - Fri), 9:30AM - 11:30AM (Sat) Shopping Hours: (Varies) 9:AM - 5:PM (Mon-Fri), 9:AM -12:Noon (Sat, Sun)

MEXICO
Banking Hours: 9:AM - 1:30PM (Mon-Fri); Business Hours: 9:AM - 6:PM (Mon-Fri) Shopping Hours: 10:AM - 5:PM (Mon-Fri); 10:AM 8:/9:PM

MICRONESIA
Banking Hours: 9:30Am - 2:30PM (Mon-Fri)

MONACO
Banking Hours: 9:AM - 12:Noon, 2:PM - 4:PM (Mon-Fri); Business Hours: 8:30AM - 6:PM Shopping Hours: 9:AM - 12:Noon, 2:PM - 7:PM (Mon-Sat)

MONTSERRAT
Banking Hours: 8:AM - 1:PM (Mon-Thur); Business Hours: 8:AM - 4:PM; Shopping Hours: 8:AM - 4:PM

MOROCCO
Banking Hours: 8:30AM - 11:30AM, 3:PM - 5:30PM (Mon-Fri) Business Hours: 8:30AM - 12:Noon, 2:30PM - 6:30PM (Mon-Fri), 8:30AM - 12:Noon (Sat) Shopping Hours: 8:30AM - 12:Noon, 2:PM - 6:30PM (Mon-Sat)

MOZAMBIQUE
Banking Hours: 7:30 -12:Noon, 2:PM - 5:PM (Mon-Fri), 7:30AM - 12:Noon (Sat) Business Hours: 7:30AM - 12:Noon, 2:PM - 5:PM (Mon-Fri), 7:30AM - 12:Noon (Sat)

NAMIBIA
Banking Hours: 9:AM - 3:30PM (Mon-Fri), 8:30AM - 11:AM (Sat) Business Hours: 8:30AM - 5:PM (Mon-Fri) Shopping Hours: 8:30AM - 5:30PM (Mon-Fri) 9:AM - 1:PM (Sat)

NEPAL
Banking Hours: 10:AM - 3:PM (Sat-Thur);10:AM - 12:Noon (Sat)

NETHERLANDS
Banking Hours: 9:AM - 4/5:PM (Mon-Fri); Business Hours: 8:30 - 5:30PM; Shopping Hours: 8:30/9:AM - 5:30/6:PM (Mon-Fri)

NETHERLANDS ANTILLES
Banking Hours: 8:30AM - 11:AM; 2:PM - 4:PM (Mon-Fri) Business/Shopping Hours: 8:AM - 12:Noon; 2:PM - 6:PM (Mon-Sat)

NEW CALEDONIA
Banking Hours: 7:AM - 10:30AM; 1:30PM - 3:30PM (Mon-Fri); 7:30 - 11:AM (Sat)

NEW ZEALAND
Banking Hours: 10:AM - 4:PM (Mon-Fri); Business/Shopping Hours: 9:AM - 5:PM (Mon-Fri)

NIGARAGUA
Banking Hours: 8:30AM - 12:Noon; 2:PM - 4:PM (Mon-Fri); 8:30AM - 11:30AM (Sat); Business/Shopping Hours: 8:AM - 5:30PM (Mon-Sat)

NIGER
Banking Hours: 7:30AM - 12:30PM, 3:30PM - 5:PM; Business Hours: 7:30AM - 12:30:PM, 3:30PM - 6:30PM; Shopping Hours: 7:30AM - 12:30PM, 3:30PM - 6:30PM

NIGERIA
Banking Hours: 8:AM - 3:PM (Mon), 8:AM - 1:30PM (Tues-Fri):Business Hours: Gov't Offices: 7:30AM - 3:30PM (Mon-Fri) Private Firms: 8:AM - 5:PM (Mon-Fri)

NORWAY
Banking Hours: 8:15AM - 3:30PM (Mon, Tue, Wed, Fri); 8:15AM - 5:PM (Thur); Business Hours: 9:AM - 4:PM; Shopping Hours: 9:AM - 5:PM (Mon-Fri); 9:AM - 6/7:PM (Thur); 9:AM- 1/2:PM (Sat)

PAKISTAN
Banking Hours: 9:AM - 1:PM (Mon-Thur); 9:AM - 11:30AM (Sat) Business/Shopping Hours: 9:30AM - 1:PM (Mon-Thur); 9:AM -10:30AM (Sat)

PANAMA
Banking Hours: 8:30AM - 1:PM (Mon-Fri); Business Hours: 8:30AM - 12:30PM & 1:30PM - 4:PM (Mon-Fri); Shopping Hours: 8:30AM - 6:PM (Mon-Sat)

PARAGUAY

Banking Hours: 7:AM - 12:Noon (Mon-Fri); Shopping Hours: 7:AM - 12:Noon & 3:PM - 7:PM

PERU

Banking Hours: 9:AM - 1:PM (Mon-Fri); Business Hours: 9:AM - 5:PM (Mon-Fri);Shopping Hours: 9:AM - 7:PM (Mon-Sat)

PHILIPPINES

Banking Hours: 9:AM - 6:PM (Mon-Fri); 9:AM - 12:30 (Sat)

POLAND

Banking Hours: 8:AM - 1:PM; Business Hours: 8:30AM - 3:30PM; Shopping Hours: 9:AM - 8:PM

PORTUGAL

Banking Hours: 8:AM - 3:PM (Mon-Fri) Business Hours: 10:AM - 6:PM Shopping Hours: 9:AM - 1:PM, 3:PM - 7:PM (Mon-Fri), 9:AM -12:Noon (Some Shops)

PUERTO RICO

Banking Hours: 9:AM - 5:PM (Mon-Fri); Business Hours: 8:AM - 5:PM (Mon-Fri); Shopping Hours: 9:AM - 6:PM (Mon-Sat)

QATAR

Banking Hours: 7:30AM - 11:30AM (Sat-Thur)

REUNION ISLAND

Business/Shopping Hours: 8:AM - 12:Noon; 2:PM - 6:PM

ROMANIA

Banking Hours: 8:30 - 11:30AM Business Hours: 8:AM - 4:PM (Mon-Fri), 8:AM - 12:30PM (Sat); Shopping Hours: 9:AM - 1:PM, 4:PM-6/8:PM

RUSSIA

Banking Hours: 9:AM - 6:PM; Business Hours: 9:AM - 6:PM; Shopping Hours: 9:AM - 9:PM (Mon-Sat)

RWANDA

Banking Hours: 8:AM - 11:AM, 2:PM - 5:PM (Mon-Fri), 8:AM -1:PM (Sat) Business Hours: 7:AM - 12:Noon, 2:PM - 6:PM (Mon-Fri) Shopping Hours: 8:AM - 6:PM (Mon-Fri), 11:AM - 6:PM (Sat)

SRI LANKA

Banking Hours: 9:AM - 1:PM (Mon-Fri); 9:am - 11:AM (Sat)

ST. KITTS & NEVIS

Banking Hours: 8:AM - 1:PM (Mon-Fri); 8:AM - 1:PM; 3:PM -5:PM (Fri) Business Hours: 8:AM - 12:Noon, 1:PM - 4:30PM (Mon, Tues); 8:AM - 12:Noon; 1:PM - 4:PM (Wed Thur, Fri) Shopping Hours: 8:AM - 12:Noon, 1:PM -4:PM Shops closed on Thursday afterNoons

ST. LUCIA

Banking Hours: 8:AM - 12:30PM (Mon-Thur); 8:AM - 12:Noon & 3:PM - 5:PM (Fri) ; Shopping Hours: 8:AM - 4:30PM (Mon-Fri); 8:AM - 1:PM (Sat)

SAN MARINO

Banking Hours: 8:30AM - 12:Noon, 2:30PM - 3:15PM; Business Hours: 8:AM - 12:Noon, 2:PM - 6:PM; Shopping Hours: 8:AM - 12:Noon 3:PM - 7:PM

ST. MAARTEN

Banking Hours: 8:30AM - 1:PM (Mon-Thur); 8:30AM - 1:PM & 4:PM - 5:PM (Fri); Business Hours: 8:AM -12:Noon & 2:PM - 6:PM; Shopping Hours: 8:AM - 12:Noon & 2:PM - 6:PM

ST. MARTIN

Banking Hours: 9:AM - 12:Noon & 2:PM - 3:PM (Mon-Fri); Shopping Hours: 9:AM - 12/12:30 & 2:PM - 6:PM (Mon-Sat)

SAO TOME AND PRINCIPE

Banking Hours: 7:30AM - 12:30PM, 2:30PM - 4:30PM (Mon-Fri); Businss Hours: 7:30AM - 12:30PM, 2:30PM - 4:30PM (Mon-Fri); Shopping Hours: 9:AM - 12:30PM, 2:30PM - 6:PM (Mon-Sat)

ST. VINCENT & THE GRENADINES

Banking Hours: 8:AM - 12/1:PM (Mon - Thur); 8:AM - 12:/1:PM & 2:/3:PM -5:PM (Fri) Business Hours: 8:AM - 12:Noon & 1:PM - 4:PM (Mon - Fri); 8:AM- 12:Noon (Sat)

SAUDI ARABIA

Banking Hours: 7/8:AM - 2:30PM (Sat-Thur); Business Hours: Gov't Offices: In Winter 8:AM - 4:PM (Sat- Wed); In Summer 7:AM - 3:PM; During Ramadan 8:AM - 2:PM Others: 8:30AM-1:30PM; 4:30AM -8PM (Sat-Thur) closed Friday

SENEGAL

Banking Hours: 8:AM - 11:AM, 2:30PM - 4:30PM (Mon-Fri) Business Hours: 8:AM - 12:Noon, 3:PM - 6:PM (Mon-Fri), 8:AM - 12:Noon (Sat) Shopping Hours: 8:AM - 7:PM (Mon-Sat)

SEYCHELLES
Banking Hours: 8:30AM - 1:30PM (Mon-Sat)
Business Hours: 8:AM - 12:Noon, 1:PM - 4:PM
(Mon-Fri) Shopping Hours: 8:AM - 5:PM (Mon-Fri), 8:AM - 1:PM (Sat)

SIERRA LEONE
Banking Hours: 9:AM - 2:PM (Mon-Fri); Business Hours: 9:AM - 2:PM (Mon-Fri); Shopping Hours: 9:AM - 6:PM (Mon-Sat)

SINGAPORE
Banking Hours: 10:AM - 3:PM (Mon-Fri); 9:30AM - 11:30AM (Sat) Business Hours: Gov't: 9:AM - 4:30PM (Mon-Fri); 9:AM - 1:PM (Sat) Shopping Hours: 9:AM - 6:PM (Mon-Sat)

SOUTH AFRICA
Banking Hours: 9:AM - 3:PM (Mon,Tue,Thur,Fri); 9:AM - 1:PM (Wed); 9:AM - 11:AM (Sat) Business/Shopping Hours: 8:30AM - 5:PM (Mon-Fri); 8:30AM - 12:Noon (Sat) Some stores'

SPAIN
Banking Hours: 9:AM - 2:PM (Mon-Fri), 9:AM - 1: PM (Sat)Business Hours: 9:AM - 2:PM, 4:PM - 7:PM Shopping Hours: 9:AM - 1:PM, 4:PM - 8:PM

SUDAN
Banking Hours: 8:30AM - 12:Noon (Sat-Thur); Business/Shopping Hours: 8:AM - 1:PM; 5:PM - 8:PM (Sat-Thur)

SURINAME
Banking Hours: 8:AM - 3:PM (Mon-Fri); Business Hours: 7:AM - 3:PM (Mon-Fri); Shopping Hours: 7:30AM - 4:PM (Mon-Fri)

SWEDEN
Banking Hours: 9:30AM - 3:PM (Mon,Tue,Wed,Fri), 9:30AM -3:PM, 4:PM - 5:30PM (Thur) Business Hours: 8:AM - 5:PM Shopping Hours: 9:30AM - 6:PM (Mon-Fri), 9:30AM - 1:PM (Sat), Noon - 4:PM (Sun)

SWITZERLAND
Banking Hours: 8:30AM - 4:30PM (Mon-Fri); Business Hours: 8:AM - 12:Noon; 2:PM - 6:PM; Shopping Hours: 8:AM - 12:15PM, 1:30PM - 6:30AM (Mon-Fri); 8:AM - 4:PM (Sat)

SYRIA
Banking Hours: 8:AM - 12:30PM (Sat-Thur);

Business Hours: 8:AM - 1:30PM; 4:30PM - 9:PM (Sat-Thur)

TANZANIA
Business/Shopping Hours: 8:AM - 5/6:PM (Mon-Sat)

TAJIKISTAN
Bankng Hours: 9:AM - 6:PM; Business Hours: 9:AM - 6:PM; Shopping Hours: 8:AM - 9:PM

THAILAND
Business/Shopping Hours: 8:30AM - 7/8:PM

TOGO
Banking Hours: 7:30AM - 11:30AM; 1:30 - 3:30PM (Mon-Fri); Business/Shopping Hours: 8:AM - 6:PM (Mon-Fri); Sat morning

TONGA
Banking Hours: 9:30AM - 4:30PM (Mon-Fri)

TRINIDAD AND TOBAGO
Banking Hours: 9:AM - 2:PM (Mon-Thur) & 9:AM - 12:Noon; 3:PM -5:PM (Fri); Shopping Hours: 8:AM - 4:PM (Mon-Fri); 8:AM - 12:Noon (Sat)

TUNISIA
Banking Hours: 8:AM - 11:AM; 2:PM - 4:PM (Mon-Fri)

TURKEY
Banking Hours: 8:30AM - 12:Noon, 1:30 - 5:PM (Mon- Fri) Business Hours: 8:30AM - 12:30PM, 1:30PM - 5:30PM Shopping Hours: 9:AM - 1:PM, 2:PM - 7:PM (Mon-Sat)

TURKMENISTAN
Banking Hours: 9:AM - 6:PM
Business Hours: 9:AM - 6:PM
Shopping Hours: 8:AM - 9:PM

TURKS AND CAICOS
Banking Hours: 8:30AM - 3:30PM
Business Hours: 8:30AM - 5:PM
Shopping Hours: 9:AM - 7:PM

UKRAINE
Banking Hours: 9:AM - 6:PM
Business Hours: 9:AM - 6:PM
Shopping Hours: 8:AM - 9:PM

UNITED KINGDOM
Banking Hours: (Varies) England & Wales: 9:AM - 3:PM (Mon-Fri) Scotland: 9:30 - 12:30PM, 1:30 - 3:30PM (Mon - Wed), 9:30AM -12:30PM, 1:30 -

3:30PM, 3:30PM -4:30PM-6PM (Thur) 9:30AM - 3:30PM (Fri), North Ireland: 10:AM - 3:30PM (Mon - Fri) Business Hours: 9:AM - 5:PM Shopping Hours: 9:AM - 5:30PM

UZBEKISTAN
Banking Hours: 9:AM - 6:PM
Business Hours: 9:AM - 6:PM
Shopping Hours: 8:AM - 9:PM

URUGUAY
Banking Hours: 1:PM - 5:PM (Mon-Fri)
Business Hours: 7:AM - 1:30PM (Mon-Fri) Summer & 12:30 - 7:PM (Mon-Fri) Winter Shopping Hours: 10:AM - 7:PM (Mon-Sat)

VENEZUELA
Banking Hours: 9:AM - 12:Noon & 3:PM - 5:PM (Mon-Fri) Business Hours: 8:AM - 12:Noon & 2:PM - 5:PM (Mon-Fri) Shopping Hours: 9:AM - 12:Noon & 2:PM - 5:PM (Mon-Sat)

VIETNAM
Banking Hours: 8:AM - 11:30AM; 2:PM - 4:PM (Mon-Fri); 8:AM - 11:AM (Sat)

WESTERN SAMOA
Banking Hours: 9:30AM - 3:PM (Mon-Fri); 9:30AM - 11:30AM (Sat)

YUGOSLAVIA
Banking Hours: 7:AM - 12:Noon or 7:AM - 7:PM; Business Hours: 8:AM - 12:30PM Shopping Hours: 8:AM - 12:Noon, 4:PM - 8:PM or 8:AM - 8:PM (Mon-Fri) 8:AM - 3:PM (Sat)

ZAIRE
Banking Hours: 8:AM - 11:30 (Mon-Fri); Business/Shopping Hours: 8:AM - 12:Noon; 3:PM - 6:PM (Mon- Sat)

ZAMBIA
Banking Hours: 8:AM - 1:PM (Mon-Fri); 8:AM - 11:AM (Sat) Business/Shopping Hours: 8:AM - 5:PM (Mon-Fri); 8:AM - 3:PM (Sat)

ZIMBABWE
Banking Hours: 8:30AM - 2:PM (Mon,Tue, Thur, Fri); 8:30AM -12:Noon (Wed); 8:30AM - 11:AM (Sat)Business/Shopping Hours: 8:AM - 5:PM

APPENDIX R

DIRECT FLIGHT TIME FROM THE U.S.++
(Time is expressed in Hours)

ALGERIA	9	JORDAN	11.5	YUGOSLAVIA	9
ANTIGUA & BARBUDA	3.5	KENYA	16.5	ZAIRE	18
ARGENTINA	10.25	KOREA, SOUTH	11.75**	ZAMBIA	18.5
AUSTRIA	8.5	KUWAIT	13		
BAHAMAS	2.5	LIBERIA	8.75		
BARBADOS	4.25	LUXEMBOURG	9	------------	
BELGIUM	7.5	MALAYSIA	18**		
BELIZE	4.75	MALTA	9	++These are approximate
BERMUDA	2	MARTINIQUE	5.5	flight time from New York to
BOLIVIA	9.25	MEXICO	5.75	the country's Capital City or
BRITISH VIRGIN IS	3.75	MONTSERRAT	5	the nearest airport to the
BULGARIA	10	MOROCCO	8	Capital City, usually not more
CAYMAN IS	3.5	NEPAL	18	than 25 miles away. Countries
CHINA, TAIWAN	13**	NETHERLANDS	7	omitted are those without
COLOMBIA	5.5	NEW CALEDONIA	14.75*	direct flights from New York
COSTA RICA	6.25	NICARAGUA	7	and /or may require 1-2
COTE D'IVOIRE	10.75	NIGERIA	11.25	connecting flights. They also
CZECH REPUBLIC	10	NORWAY	7.75	include countries with
DENMARK	8	PANAMA	5.5	International Airports located
DOMINICAN REP.	3.75	PARAGUAY	9.5	in cities other than the capital
ECUADOR	6	PERU	7.5	and over 25 miles away.
EGYPT	11.25	PHILIPPINES	14.5**	
ETHIOPIA	16	POLAND	9	
FINLAND	8	PORTUGAL	6.5	* From Los Angeles,
FRANCE	7	PUERTO RICO	4	California
FRENCH GUIANA	7	ROMANIA	10	
FED. REP. OF GERMANY	7.5	RUSSIA	11	** From San Francisco,
GHANA	10.5	ST. KITTS	4	California
GIBRALTAR	7.5	ST. LUCIA	5.5	
GREECE	10	ST. VINCENT	4.75	
GRENADA	4.5	SAUDI ARABIA	12	
GUATEMALA	4.75	SENEGAL	7	
GUINEA	8.75	SEYCHELLES	19.5	
GUYANA	5.25	SINGAPORE	17.25**	
HAITI	3.75	SPAIN	6	
HONDURAS	6	SURINAME	4.5	
HONG KONG	14**	SWEDEN	9	
HUNGARY	8.25	TANZANIA	18	
ICELAND	6	THAILAND	22*	
INDIA	16.75	TONGA	18.75	
INDONESIA	18.25**	TRINIDAD AND TOBAGO	4.75	
IRELAND	6	TUNISIA	9	
ISRAEL	10.5	UNITED KINGDOM	6.75	
ITALY	8.25	URUGUAY	11.25	
JAMAICA	3.5	VENEZUELA	4.5	

APPENDIX S

COUNTRIES AND OFFICIAL LANGUAGES

COUNTRY	OFFICIAL LANGUAGE	OTHER LANGUAGES
AFGHANISTAN	Dari, pashto	Uzbek, Turkmen
ALBANIA	Albanian	Greek
ALGERIA	Arabic	Berber, French
ANDORRA	Catalan	Spanish, French
ANGOLA	Portuguese	
ANTIGUA & BARBUDA	English	
ARGENTINA	Spanish	English, Italian, German
ARMENIA	Armenian	Azerbaijani, Russian
AUSTRALIA	English	
AUSTRIA	German	
AZERBAIJAN	Azeerbaijani	Russian , Armenian
BAHAMAS	English	Creole
BAHRAIN	Arabic	English, Farsi, Urdu
BANGLADESH	Bangla (Bengali)	English
BARBADOS	English	
BELARUS	Byelorussian	Russian
BELGIUM	Dutch (Flemish)	French, German
BELIZE	English	Spanish, Garifuna, Mayart
BENIN	French	Fon, Adja,
BERMUDA	English	
BHUTAN	Dzongkha	Tibeatan & Nepalese
BOLIVIA	Spanish	Quechua, Aymara
BOSNIA-HERCEGORVINA	Serb, Croat, Albanian	
BOTSWANA	English	Tswana
BRAZIL	Portuguese	Spanish, English
BRITISH VIRGIN IS.	English	
BRUNEI	Malay	English, Chinese
BULGARIA	Bulgarian	
BURKINA FASO	French	
BURMA	Burmese	
BURUNDI	French, Kirundi	Swahili
CAMBODIA	Cambodian (Khmer)	French
CAMEROON	English, French	
CANADA	English, French	
CENTRAL AFRICAN REP.	French	Sango, Arabic,
CHAD	French	Arabic
CHILE	Spanish	
CHINA, PEOPLES REP.	Chinese	
CHINA, TAIWAN	Chinese	
COLUMBIA	Spanish	
COMOROS	French	Abrabic, Shaafi Islam
CONGO, PEOPLE'S REP.	French	
COSTA RICA	Spanish	
COTE D'IVOIRE	French	
CROATIA	Croat	Serb

CUBA	Spanish	
CYPRUS	Greek, Turkish, English	
CZECH REP.	Czech & Slovak	Hungarian
DENMARK	Danish	
DOMINICA	English	
DOMINICAN REP.	Spanish	
ECUADOR	Spanish	Quechua
EGYPT	Arabic	
EL SALVADOR	Spanish	Nahua
EQUATORIAL GUINEA	Spanish	
ESTONIA	Estonian	Russian
ETHIOPIA	Amharic	Tigrinya, Orominga, Arabic
FAEROW ISLANDS	Danish, Faroese	
FIJI	English	Fiji
FINLAND	Finnish	Swedish
FRANCE	French	
FRENCH POLYNESIA	French	Tahitian, Chinese
FRENCH GUIANA	French	
FRENCH ANTILLES	French	
GABON	French	Fang
GEORGIA	Georgian	Russian, Armenian
GERMANY	German	
GHANA	English	Akan
GIBRALTAR	English	Spanish
GREECE	Greek	
GREENLAND	Danish	Greenlandic, Inuit
GRENADA	English	
GUADELOUPE	French	Creole
GUAM	English	Chamorro, Tagalog
GUATEMALA	Spanish	
GUINEA	French	
GUINEA-BISSAU	Portuguese	Crioulo
GUYANA	English	
HAITI	French	Creole
HONDURAS	Spanish	
HONG KONG	Chinese (Cantonese)	English
HUNGARY	Magyar	
ICELAND	Icelandic	
INDIA	Hindi	English
INDONESIA	Indonesian	Javanese, Sundanese
IRAN	Farsi	Turkish, Kurdish, Arabic
IRAQ	Arabic	Kurdish, Assyrian, Armenian
IRELAND	English, Gaelic	Irish
ISRAEL	Hebrew, Arabic	Yiddish, English
ITALY	Italian	
JAMAICA	English	Creole
JAPAN	Japanese	
JORDAN	Arabic	
KAZAKHSTAN	Kazakh	Russian, German, Ukraine
KENYA	English	Swahili
KIRIBATI	English	Gilbertese
KOREA, SOUTH	Korean	
KOREA, NORTH	Korean	
KUWAIT	Arabic	English
KYRGYZSTAN	Kirghiz	Russian, Uzbek
LAOS	Lao	French, Tai

LATVIA	Latvian	Russian
LEBANON	Arabic	French, Armenian, English
LESOTHO	English	Sesotho, Zulu, Xhosa
LIBERIA	English	
LIBYA	Arabic	
LIECHTENSTEIN	German	
LITHUANIA	Lithuanian	Russian, Polish
LUXEMBOURG	French, German	Luxembourgish
MADAGASCAR	Malagasy, French	
MALAWI	Chichewa, English	Tombuka
MALAYSIA	Malay	Chinese, English, tamil
MALDIVES	Divehi	
MALI	French	Bambara
MALTA	English, Maltese	
MARSHALL ISLANDS	English	Malay-Polynesian, Japanese
MARTINIQUE	French	Creole
MAURITANIA	Arabic, French	
MAURITIUS	English	Creole, Bhohpuri, Hindi
MAYOTTE ISLANDS	French	Swahili
MEXICO	Spanish	
MICRONESIA	English	Malay-Polynesian
MOLDOVA	Moldavian	Russian, Ukrainian
MONACO	French	English, Italian, Monegasque
MONGOLIA	Khalkha Mongol	Kazakh, Russian, Chinese
MONTSERRAT	English	
MOROCCO	Arabic	Berber, FRench
MOZAMBIQUE	Portuguese	
NAURU	Nauruan	English
NEPAL	Nepali	Maithali, Bhojpuri
NETH. ANTILLES	Dutch	Papiamento, English
NETHERLANDS	Dutch	
NEW CALEDONIA	French	
NEW ZEALAND	English	Maori
NICARAGUA	Spanish	English
NIGER	French	Hausa, Ndjerma
NIGERIA	English	Hausa, Yoruba, Ibo
NORWAY	Norwegian	Lapp
OMAN	Arabic	English, Baluchi, Urdu
PAKISTAN	Urdu	English, Punjab, Pashto, Sindhi, Saraiki
PANAMA	Spanish	English
PAPUA NEW GUINEA	English	Motu, Pidgin
PARAGUAY	Spanish	Guarani
PERU	Spanish, Quechua	Aymara
PHILIPPINES	English, Philipino	Tagalog
POLAND	Polish	
PORTUGAL	Portuguese	
QATAR	Arabic	English
REP. OF DJIBOUTI	Arabic	French, Somali, Afar
REP. OF CAPE VERDE	Portuguese, Crioulo	
REP. OF PALAU	Paluan, English	
REUNION ISLAND	French	Creole
ROMANIA	Romanian	Hungarian, German
RUSSIA	Russian	Tatar, Ukrainian
RWANDA	French, Kinyarwanda	
SAN MARINO	Italian	
SAU TOME & PRINCIPE	Portuguese	Fang

SAUDI ARABIA	Arabic	
SENEGAL	French	
SEYCHELLES	English, French	Creole
SIERRA LEONE	English	Krio
SINGAPORE	Chinese, English,	Malay, Tamil
SLOVAK REP.	Slovak, Czech	Hungarian
SLOVANIA	Slovene	
SOLOMON ISLANDS	English	
SOMALIA	Somali	Arabic, English, Italian
SOUTH AFRICA	Afrikaans, English	Zulu, Xhosa
SPAIN	Spanish (Castilian)	Catalan, Galician, Basque
SRI LANKA	Sinhala, Tamil	English
ST. KITTS & NEVIS	English	
ST. LUCIA	English	French
ST. PIERRE & MIQUELON	French	
ST. VINCENT	English	French
SUDAN	Sudan	English
SURINAME	Dutch	Sranan, Tongo, English, Hindustani, Javanese
SWAZILAND	English, Siswati	
SWEDEN	Swedish	
SWITZERLAND	German, French, Italian	Romansch
SYRIA	Arabic	Kurdish, Armenian, Aramaic, Circassian
TAJIKISTAN	Tajik	Uzbek, Russian
TANZANIA	English, Swahili	
THAILAND	Thai	
THE GAMBIA	English	Malinke, Wolof, Fula
TOGO	French	
TONGA	Tongan	English
TRINIDAD & TOBAGO	English	Hindi, French, Spanish
TUNISIA	Arabic	French
TURKEY	Turkish	Kurdish, Arabic
TURKMENISTAN	Turkmen	Russian, Uzbek, Kazakh
TURKS & CAICOS	English	
UGANDA	English	Luganda, Swahili
UKRAINE	Ukrainian	Russian
UNITED KINGDOM	English	Welsh, Gaelic
UNITED ARAB EMIRATES	Arabic	English, Fashi, Hindi, Urdu
URUGUAY	Spanish	
UZBEKISTAN	Uzbek	Russian, Kazakh, Tajik
VATICAN CITY	none	Italian, Latin
VENEZUELA	Spanish	
VIETNAM	Vietnamese	French, Chinese, Khmer
WESTERN SAMOA	Samoan, English	
YEMEN, ARAB REP.	Arabic	
YEMEN, P.D. REP.	Arabic	
YUGOSLAVIA	Macedonian, Serbo-Croatian	Slovene, Albanian, Hungarian
ZAIRE	French	Kikongo, Lingala, Swahili, Tshiluba
ZAMBIA	English	Tonga, Lozi
ZIMBABWE		English
		ChiShona

676

APPENDIX T

WHERE TO FIND THOSE GEMS (PRECIOUS STONES)[IL]

Country:	Gems Indigenous to the area	Practices to beware:
Australia & New Zealand	opal, emerald, sapphire, & jade	dyed jades, synthetic emeralds and sap-phires, and doublet opals
Brazil	amethyst, aquamarine, emerald, garnet, topaz, tourmaline, citrine, and diamond (uncut)	misleading names, synthetic emeralds and amethysts, color alteration, and stone substitutes
Colombia	emerald	look-alikes and synthetics
Egypt	turquoise and camelian	plastic or imitation turquoise and dyed stones
Hong Kong	jade and pearl	Simulated pearls, misleading names, dyed opaque stones,synthetics, and high prices
India	fine Kashmit sapphire, ruby	poor quality, star ruby, and garnet synthetic rubies and sapphires, color alteration, and look-alike substitutes
Israel	diamond	poor quality, flaw concealment, color alterations, and look-alike substitutes
Japan	pearl, coral, & jade	simulated pearls, premature pearls that chip easily, and dyed jades and corals
Mexico	jelly, water, fire & cherry opal; moss, fire, & plume agate; and turquoise	plastic and simulated turquoise, color alterations, synthetics, and doublets
South Africa	diamond, emerald, green substitutions, garnet, & semi-precious colored is a vorite stone	misleading names, synthetics, and color alteration

677

Sri Lanka	fine and star sapphire, precious cats-eye (chrysobery), alexandrite and moonstone	synthetics, doublets, and pink rubies; sapphires and rubies said to be flawless should be looked upon with suspicion
Tahiti	fine and black pearl	simulated and dyed and coral pearls and corals
Thailand	ruby, sapphire, and zircon stone	synthetics, substitutions, mis-misleading names, and dark sapphires

APPENDIX U

TRAVEL INSURANCE PROVIDERS

Some companies and organizations specialize in providing a variety of insurance coverage and travel related services to domestic as well as international travelers including coverage for medical expenses, accidental injury and sickness, medical assistance, baggage loss, trip cancellation or trip interruption.   Check with your travel agent/agency, broker, or travel advisor for reputable insurers in your area. Members of travel clubs and automobile clubs may also check with their associations for availability of such policies.

Here are a few companies widely known in the country to provide travel-related insurance coverage.   These companies also sell short-term policies.

TRAVEL INSURANCE COMPANIES

ACCESS AMERICA, INC.
Richmond, VA
866-807-3982

AIGAssist
American International Group, Inc.
New York, NY
800-382-6986

ASA, INC.
International Health Insurance
Phoenix, AZ
888-ASA-8288

AXA ASSISTANCE
Bethesda, MD
301-214-8200

CLEMENTS INTERNATIONAL
Washington, DC
800-872-0067 / 202-872-0060
http://www.clements.com
e-mail: info@clements.com

GATEWAY
Seabury & Smith
Washington, DC
800-282-4495 / 202-457-7707
e-mail: gateway.dc@seabury.com

HEALTH CARE GLOBAL
(also known as MEDHELP or WALLACH & COMPANY or HEALTHCARE ABROAD)
Middleburg, VA
800-237-6615 / 540-687-3166

HIGHWAY TO HEALTH
Fairfax, VA
703-322-1515
(Also provides destination-based travel health information for cities worldwide.)

InsureMyTrip.com
Commack, NY
800-487-4722
e-mail: info@insuremytrip.com

INTERNATIONAL MEDICAL GROUP (IMG)
Indianapolis, IN
800-628-4664 / 317-655-4500

MultiNational Underwriters, Inc.
Indianapolis, IN
800-605-2282
e-mail: insurance@mnui.com

MUTUAL OF OMAHA
Tele-Trip Company
Omaha, NE
800-228-9792

PETERSEN INTERNATIONAL UNDERWRITERS, INC.
Valencia, CA
800-345-8816
e-mail: piu@piu.org

TRAVELEX
Omaha, NE
800-228-9792

TRAVEL GUARD
Stevens Point, WI
800-826-4919

TRAVEL INSURED INTERNATIONAL
E. Hartford, CT
800-243-3174

TRAVEL INSURANCE SERVICES
InterMedical Division
Walnut Creek, CA
800-937-1387/925-932-1387

TRIPGUARD PLUS
Northridge, CA
800-423-3632

UNICARD TRAVEL ASSOCIATION
Overland Park, KS
800-501-0352

UNIVERSAL SERVICE AND ASSISTANCE
Alexandria, VA
800-770-9111 / 703-370-7800

WORLDWIDE ASSISTANCE
Washington, DC
800-777-8710 ext. 417

EXECUTIVE MEDICAL SERVICES
AMERICAN MEDICAL CENTERS
Moscow, Russia
Offices in Moscow, St. Petersburg, Kiev,
Prague, Warsaw, Istanbul
(7-095) 933-77-00 (Moscow)

GlobaLifeline
Phoenix, AZ
800-890-8209

HEALTH QUEST TRAVEL INC.
Wexford, PA
888-899-3633
e-mail: HQT@HealthQuestTravel.com

WORLD CLINIC
Burlington, MA
800-636-9186

APPENDIX V

MEDICAL ASSISTANCE ORGANIZATIONS/AIR AMBULANCE SERVICE

Several private organizations will provide medical information and insurance for overseas travelers. Most charge a fee for this service. The following is provided FOR INFORMATIONAL PURPOSES ONLY and in no way constitutes an endorsement, expressed or implied, by the Department of State.

AIR AMBULANCE / MED-EVAC

U.S.-based Companies

ABLE JET
Fort Pierce, FL
800-225-3538

ACADIAN AMBULANCE & AIR MED
SERVICE, INC.
Lafayette, LA
800-259-3333

ADVANCED AIR AMBULANCE
Miami, FL
800-633-3590 / 305-232-7700

AAA - AIR AMBULANCE AMERICA
Austin, TX
800-222-3564 / 512-479-8000

AIR AMBULANCE CARE FLIGHT
INTERNATIONAL, INC.
Clearwater, FL
800-282-6878 / 1-727-530-7972 (international)

AIR AMBULANCE NETWORK
Sarasota, FL
800-327-1966

AIR AMBULANCE PROFESSIONALS
Fort Lauderdale, FL
800-752-4195 / 954-491-0555

AirEvac
Phoenix, AZ

800-421-6111
AIR MEDIC - AIR AMBULANCE OF
AMERICA
Washington, PA
800-245-9987

AIRescue INTERNATIONAL
Van Nuys, CA
800-922-4911 / 818-994-0911

AIR RESPONSE
Orlando, FL
800-631-6565 / 303-858-9967

AIR STAR INTERNATIONAL
Thermal, CA
877-570-0911 / 800-991-2869
e-mail: AirStar1@aol.com

AMERICAN CARE, INC.
San Diego, CA
800-941-2582 / 619-486-8844

AMERICAN JET AIR MEDICAL
Houston, TX
888-I-FLY-AJI / 713-641-9700

CRITICAL AIR MEDICINE
San Diego, CA
800-247-8326 / 619-571-0482

CRITICAL CARE MEDFLIGHT
Lawrenceville, GA
800-426-6557

GLOBAL CARE / MEDPASS
Alpharetta, GA
800-860-1111

INFLIGHT MEDICAL SERVICES
INTERNATIONAL INC.
Naples, FL
800-432-4177 / 941-594-0800

INTERNATIONAL SOS ASSISTANCE
Philadelphia, PA
800-523-8930 / 215-244-1500
Also provides travel insurance services.

MedAire
Phoenix, AZ
602-452-4300

MED ESCORT INTERNATIONAL INC.
Allentown, PA
800-255-7182 / 610-791-3111

MEDEX ASSISTANCE CORPORATION
Timonium, MD
888-MEDEX-00 / 410-453-6300 (call collect)
(Also provides travel insurance services.)

MEDJET ASSISTANCE
Birmingham, AL
1-800-963-3538

MEDJET INTERNATIONAL, INC.
Birmingham, AL
800-356-2161 / 205-592-4460

MEDWAY AIR AMBULANCE
Lawrenceville, GA
800-233-0655

MERCY MEDICAL AIRLIFT
Manassas, VA
800-296-1217
(Service area: Caribbean and part of Canada
only. If necessary, will meet commercial
incoming patients at JFK, Miami and other
airports.)

NATIONAL AIR AMBULANCE
Ft. Lauderdale, FL
800-327-3710 / 305-525-5538

SMARTRAVEL
Alexandria, VA
800-730-3170 / 703-379-8645
Provides a range of travel medicine services.

TRAVEL CARE INTERNATIONAL, INC.
Eagle River, WI
800-524-7633 / 715-479-8881

TRAVELERS EMERGENCY NETWORK
Tierra Verde, FL

800-ASK-4-TEN
e-mail: ten@intrex.net
Foreign-based Companies

AEA INTERNATIONAL
Singapore
U.S. Phone: 800-468-5232
Service worldwide, also provides travel
insurance services

AUSTRIAN AIR AMBULANCE
Vienna, Austria
43-1-40-144

EURO-FLITE LTD.
Helsinki International Airport
Vantaa, Finland
358-9-870-2544

EUROPASSISTANCE
Johannesburg, South Africa
27-11-315-3999

GERMAN AIR RESCUE (DRF)
Filderstadt, Germany
49-0711-7007-0
e-mail: alarmzentrale@drf.de

MEDIC'AIR
Paris, France
331-41-72-14-14

TYROL AIR AMBULANCE
Innsbruck, Austria
43-512-22422

APPENDIX **W**

MEDICAL EMERGENCY KIT

Listed below are some items you may wish to include in your medical emergency kit. These items are readily available (in various brands) in your local pharmacy. Consult your physician for advice on other useful items and health matters.

Aspirin, 5 gr., or Tylenol, 325 mg.
Aluminum Hydroxide with Magnesium Trisilicate Tablets
Milk of Magnesia Tablets
Chlorpheniramine Tablets
Antihistamine Nasal Spray
Antimicrobial Skin Ointment
Calamine Lotion
Liquid Surgical Soap
Tweezers
Antifungal Skin Ointment
Zinc Undecylenate Foot Powder
Vitamin Mineral Tablets
Oil of Clove and Benzocaine Mixture
Opthalmic Ointment
Throat Lozenges
Kaolin Pectin Mixture, Tablets or Liquid
Paregoric or Lomotil
Adhesive Bandages
3-inch Wide Elastic Bandage
2-foot-by-19-Yard Gauze Bandage
4-inch by 4-inch Gauze Pad
Adhesive Medical Tape
Medium-Size Safety Pins
Thermometer
Insect Repellent
Sleeping Pills
Small Pack of Cotton Wool
Tampons
Tissues
A Pair of Scissors

APPENDIX X

INTERNATIONAL EMERGENCY CODES

Country	Emergency #	Ambulance #	Police #
Algeria			17
Andorra		182-0020	21222
Andorra	11/15	20020	
Anguilla	999		
Antigua	999		20045/20125
Argentina			101
Austria		144	133
Bahamas		3222221	3224444
Barbados			112/60800
Belgium	900/901	906	101
Belize			2222
Bermuda			22222
Bolivia	118		110
Brazil	2321234		2436716
Columbia			12
Costa Rica	2158888		117
Cyprus	999		
Czech Republic	155		
Denmark	000		
Dominican Republic			6823000
Egypt			912644
Ethiopia			91
Fiji Islands	000		
Finland	000	002/003	
France	17	12/17	
French Guiana			18
Germany	110		
Gibraltar	199		
Great Britain	999		
Greece	100		171
Guyana	999		
Haiti	0		
Hong Kong	999		
Hungary	04		
Iceland			
(Reykavik)	11100	11166	
(elsewhere dial 02 for the operator who will then place the call)			
India		102	100
Ireland	999		
Israel			100
Italy		113	112
Jamaica		110	119
Japan		119	100
Jordan	19		
Kenya	999		

684

Liechtenstein		144	117
Luxembourg	012		
Malaysia	0		
Malta	99		
Maltese Island		196	191
Monaco		933-01945	17
Morocco			19
Nepal	11999		
Netherlands			
Amsterdam	559-9111	5555555	222222
(elsewhere dial 008 for the operator who will then place the call)			
New Zealand	111		
Norway		003	110011
Pakistan	222222		
Papua New Guinea			255555
Paraguay			49116
Peru	05		
Phillipines			599011
Poland		999	997
Portugal	115		
San Marino	113		
Singapore	999		
Spain	091		
Sri Lanka			26941/21111
St. Vincent			71121
St. Kitts & Nevis	999		
St. Lucia	95		99
Suriname	99933		711111/77777
Sweden	90000		
Switzerland		144	117
Tanzania	999		
Thailand			2810372/2815051
Tunisia			243000
U.S. Virgin Is.		922	915
Uruguay	401111		890
Venezuela			169/160
Yugoslavia	94		92

685

APPENDIX Y

ORGANIZATIONS THAT PROVIDE SERVICES TO INTERNATIONAL TRAVELERS

Academic Travel Abroad, 3210 Grace St., N.W. 1st flr. Washington, D.C. 20007, Tel. (202) 333-3355

Airline passenger of America, 4212 King St., Alexandria, VA 22302, Tel. (703) 824-0505

Airport Operators Council International, Inc., 1220 19th St. NW, Suite 200, Washington DC, 20036, Fax. (202) 331-1362.

American Council for International Studies, 19 Bay State, Road, Boston, MA. 02215, Tel. (617) 236-2051

American Automobile Association (AAA), AAA Drive, Heathrow, Florida 32746 (404) 444-4000

American Youth Hostels, P.O. Box 37613 Washington DC 20013, Tel. (202) 783-4943.

American Association of Retired Persons (AARP), 1909 K-Street, NW Washington DC 20049 Tel. (800) 441-7575 or (800) 927-0111.

American Society of Travel Agents (ASTA), 1101 King St., Alexandria, VA 22314, Tel. (703) 739-2782

Association of Group Travel Executives, c/o Arnold H. Light A.H. Light Co., Inc. 424 Madison Ave., Suite 705, New York, NY. 10017 Tel. (212) 486-4300

Association of Corporate Travel Executives, P.O. Box 5394, Parsippany, N.J. 07054, Tel. (201) 537-4614

Citizens Emergency Center, Bureau of Consular Affairs, Rm 4811, N.S. U.S. Department of State, Washington DC 20520, Tel. (202) 647-5225.

Council on International Education Exchange (CIEE), 205 E. 42nd St., New York, NY 10017 (212) 661-1414.

Cruise Lines International Association, 500 Fifth Ave, Suite 407, New York, NY. 10110, Tel. (212) 921-0066

Fly Without Fear (FWF), 310 Madison Ave., New York, NY 10017, Tel. (212) 697-7666

Freighter Travel Club of America (FTC), P.O. Box 12693, Salem OR, 97309, Tel. (503) 399-8567

Hideaways International, 15 Goldsmith St., P.O. Box 1270, Littleton, MA 01460, Tel. (508) 486-8955, (800) 843-4433

Institute of Certified Travel Agents (ICTA), P.O. Box, 8256, 148 Linden St., Wellesley, MA. 02181 Tel. (617) 237-0280

Interexchange, 356 W. 34th St., 2nd flr. New York, NY., 10001 Tel. (212) 947-9533

International Gay Travel Association, P.O. Box 18247, Denver, CO. 80218, Tel. (303) 467-7117

International Federations of Women's Travel Organizations, 4545 N. 36th St., Suite 126, Phoenix, AZ, 85018 Tel. (602) 956-7175

International Association for Medical Assistance to Travellers (IAMAT), 417 Center St. Lewiston, NY. 14092 Tel. (716) 754-4883

International Airline Passengers Association (IAPA), 4341 Lindburg Dr., Dallas, TX, 75244, Tel. (214) 404-9980

International Association of Tour Managers, 1646 Chapel St., New Haven, CT. 06511, Tel. (203) 777-5994

International Cruise Passengers Association (ICPA), Box 886 F.D. R. Station, New York, NY 10150, Tel. (212) 486-8482

International Visitors Information Service, 733 15th Street, NW Suite 300, Washington DC 20005, Tel. (202) 783-6540.

International Bicycle Tours, Champlin Square, Box 754 Essex, CT 06426 Tel. (203) 767-7005

National Association of Cruise Only Agents, (NACOA) P.O. Box 7209, Freeport, NY. 11520

National Campers and Hikers Association, 4804 Transit Rd., Building 2, Depend, NY 1404, Tel. (716) 668-6242.

North American Vegetarian Society, P.O. Box 72, Dolgeville, NY 1339, Tel. (518) 568-7970.

SCI International Voluntary Service, Innisfree Village, Rt.2, BOX 506 Crozet, VA 22932, Tel. (804) 823-1826.

Share-A-Ride International (SARI), 100 Park Ave. Rockville, Maryland, Tel. (301) 217-0871

Society of Incentive Travel Executives, 347 Fifth Ave., Suite 610, New York, NY. 10016, Tel. (212) 725-8253

Society for the Advancement of Travel for the Handicapped (SATH), 347 Fifth Ave., Suite 610, New York, NY 10016 Tel. (212) 447-7284. 858-5483

Travel Information Service (TIS), Moss Rehabilitation Hospital , 12th St., and Tabor Rd, Philadelphia, PA. 19141, Tel. (215) 456-9600

U.S. Department of Commerce, International Trade Information Center, Tel (800) 872-8723.

U.S. Department of Transportation, Office of General Counsel, 400 7th St. SW, Rm. 10422, Washington DC 20590, Tel. (202) 366-9306 (voice), (202) 755-7687 (TDD)

U.S. Public Health Services, Centers for Disease Control, Atlanta Georgia, Tel. (404) 539-2574.

Volunteers for Peace International Work Camps, 43 Tiffany Rd., Belmont VTY 05730, Tel. (802) 259-2759.

World Ocean and Cruise Liner Society, P.O. Box 92, Stamford, CT. 06904, Tel. (203) 329-2787

Institute of Certified Travel Agents (ICTA), 148 Linden St., P.O. Box, 812059, (800) 542, 4282.

International Air Passenger Association (IAPA), P.O. Box 870188, Dallas TX. 75287, (800) 821-4274.

International Air Transport Association (IATA), 2000 Peel St., Montreal, QC Canada, H3A 2R4, (514) 844-6311.

International Airlines Travel Agent Network (IATAN), 300 Garden City Plaza, Ste. 342, Garden City, NY. 11530, (7516) 747-4716.

International Association for Medical Assistance to Travelers (IAMAT), 417 Center St., Lewiston, NY. 14092, (716) 754-4883

International Association of Convention and Visitor Bureaus (IACVB), 2000 L. St., NW., Ste. 702, Washington, D.C. 20036, (202) 296-7888.

International Civil Aviation Organization (ICAO), 1000 Sherbrooke West, Montreal, QC Canada H3A 2R2, (514) 285-8219.

National Business travel Association (NBTA), 1650 King St., STe. 301, Alexandria, VA. 22314, (703) 684-0836.

Society of Incentive Travel Executives (SITE), 21 W. 38th St., 10th Fl., New York, 10018, (212) 575-0910.

Society of Travel Agents in Government (STAG), 6935 Wisconsin Ave, Bethesda, MD. 20815, (301) 654-8595.

Travel and Tourism Government Affairs Council, 1100 New York Ave., NW., Ste. 450, Washington, DC. 20005, (202) 408-9600.

Travel and Tourism Research Association, 10200 W. 44th Ave., Ste. 304, Wheat ridge, CO. 80033, (303) 940-6557.

Travel Industry Association of America (TIA), 1100 New York AVe. NW. Ste. 450, Washington, D.C. 20005, (202) 408-8422.

U.S. Travel Data Center, 1100 New York Ave, NW., Ste. 450, Washington, D.C. 20005, (202) 408-1832.

World Travel & Tourism Council, Chaussee de La Hulpe 181, Box 10, 1170 Brussels, Belgium, (32-2) 660 20 67.

OTHER BOOKS BY THE SAME AUTHOR

Americans Traveling Abroad: What You Should Know Before You Go (3rd Ed.) Bestseller! paperback, 720 pages, ISBN: 1-890605-10-7, $39.99

Americans Living Abroad: What You Should Know While You are There. paperback, 375 pages, ISBN: 1-890605-11-5, $34.99

Traveling Abroad Post "9-11" and in the Wake of Terrorism: A Practical Guide for Americans & Other International Travelers, paperback, 265 pages, ISBN: 1-890605-13-1, $24.99

American Businesses Abroad: How to Protect Your Assets and Personnel, paperback, 320 pages, ISBN: 1-890605-12-3, $39.99; (Hard Cover, ISBN: 1-890605-26-3, $49.99)

Weapons of Mass Destruction, What You Should Know: A Citizen's Guide To Biological, Chemical and Nuclear Agents & Weapons paperback, 300 pages, ISBN: 1-890605-14-X, $39.99 (Hard Cover, ISBN: 1-890605-25-5, $49.99)

Natural Disasters and Other Emergencies, What You Should Know: A Family Planning & Survival Guide. paperback, 250 pages, ISBN: 1-890605-15-8, $29.99 (Hard Cover, ISBN: 1-890605-27-1, $39.99)

Do's and Don'ts Around the World: A Country Guide to Cultural and Social Taboos and Etiquette. paperback, available in 9 different volumes/editions: Europe, Asia, Africa, South America, The Caribbean, The Middle East, Russia and the Independent States, Oceania, USA-Canada-Australia. These books contain hundreds of country-specific do's and don'ts and much more!.

Series Title: *DO'S AND DON'TS AROUND THE WORLD: A COUNTRY GUIDE TO CULTURAL AND SOCIAL TABOOS AND ETIQUETTE*

EUROPE 1-890605-00-X; (*1-890605-17-4) 400 pages; $39.99; **SOUTH AMERICA** 1-890605-03-4; (*1-890605-20-4) 230 pages; $24.99; **AFRICA** 1-890605- 04-2 (*1-890605-16-6); 450 pages; $39.99; **THE CARIBBEAN** 1-890605-02-6; (*1-890605-19-0) 230 pages; $24.99; **ASIA** 1-890605-01-8; (*1-890605-18-2) 260 pages; $24.99; **RUSSIA & THE INDEPENDENT STATES** 1-890605-06-9; (*1-890605-22-0) 120 pages; $15.99; **USA, CANADA & AUSTRALIA** 1-890605-08-5; (*1-890605-24-7) 75 pages; $15.99; **OCEANIA & JAPAN** 1-890605-07-7; (*1-890605-23-9) 200 pages; $19.99; **THE MIDDLE EAST** 1-890605-05-0; (*1-890605-21-2) 120 pages; $15.99

Note: Books marked with * refer to a new ISBN planned for the same book under a different title called " *Ethics and Etiquette Around the World: A Country Guide To Cultural and Social Do's, Don'ts, & Taboos* "

Individual Country Reports are *of the Do's & Don'ts Books currently* online and may be ordered for $7 per country per report (www.frontlinepublishers.com)

LIBRARY RECOMMENDATION FORM

(This form should be hand delivered to your local Head Librarian or Reference Librarian)

Sir/Madam:

I regularly use the following book(s) published by **Frontline Publishers** **(www.frontlinepublishers.com)**:

(1)_____ISBN #:_____Price $_____

(2)_____ISBN #:_____Price $_____

(3)_____ISBN #:_____Price $_____

(4)_____ISBN #:_____Price $_____

(5)_____ISBN #:_____Price $_____

(6)_____ISBN #:_____Price $_____

(7)_____ISBN #:_____Price $_____

(8)_____ISBN #:_____Price $_____

(9)_____ISBN #:_____Price $_____

(10)_____ISBN #:_____Price $_____

(11)_____ISBN #:_____Price $_____

(12)_____ISBN #:_____Price $_____

Your records indicate that the library does not carry these valuable and comprehensive travel reference books. Could you please order them for our library?

Name of Recommender: _____

Address:_____

_____

Phone:_____

ORDERING INFORMATION

Mail or Fax your orders to:

Frontline Publishers
P.O. Box 32674-1A,
Baltimore, MD 21282-2674 U.S.A.
Fax: (410) 922-8009.
Make check or money order payable to **Frontline Publishers**
We also accept, International Money Orders.

Shipping/Postage Cost for books:
U.S. Residents add $4.50 U.S. dollars per book for postage.
Canadian Residents add $6 U.S. dollars per book for postage.
Mexican Residents add $7 U.S. dollars per book for postage.
Other Countries: add $15 U.S. dollars for airmail delivery; $7 for surface mail delivery.

Books may also be ordered on-line at *amazon.com* or *frontlinepublishers.com*, and other major online bookstores, or from major bookstores throughout the country.

Remember, individual **Country Reports** of the *Do's and Don'ts* books are now available on-line through several sites including:
frontlinepublishers.com

ORDER FORM

Telephone Orders: Directly from the publisher- FRONTLINE PUBLISHERS at 1-410-922-4903

Fax Orders: 1-410-922-8009 (Send this form)

Postal Orders: Frontline Publishers, P.O. Box 32674-1A, Baltimore, Maryland 21282-2674-8674 U.S.A.{Tel: (410) 922-4903}. Make Check or Money Order payable to **FRONTLINE PUBLISHERS**

Online Orders: Visit *amazon.com* or *frontlinepublishers.com*. Also available through several online bookstores

☐ Please enter my order for the following books:
- **Do's and Don'ts:**

Europe	$39.99 + $____	postage: Total $____
South America	$24.99 + $____	postage: Total $____
Africa	$39.99 + $____	postage: Total $____
The Caribbean	$24.99 + $____	postage: Total $____
Asia	$24.99 + $____	postage: Total $____
Russia/The Independent States	$15.99 +$____	postage: Total $____
USA, Canada & Australia	$15.99 + $____	postage: Total $____
The Middle East	$15.99 + $____	postage: Total $____
Oceania & Japan	$19.99 + $____	postage: Total $____

(Please refer to the section containing shipping/postage information for applicable postage rates.)

- **Americans Traveling Abroad.**	$39.99 + $____	postage Total $____
- **Americans Living Abroad**	$34.99 + $____	postage Total $____
- **American. Businesses Abroad (paper)**	$39.99 + $____	postage Total $____
- **American. Businesses Abroad (Hard)**	$49.99 + $____	postage Total $____
-**Traveling Abroad Post 9-11**	$24.99 + $____	postage Total $____
- **Weapons of Mass Destruction (paper)**	$39.99 + $____	postage Total $____
- **Weapons of Mass Destruction (Hard)**	$49.99 + $____	postage Total $____
- **Natural Disasters (paper)**	$29.99 + $____	postage Total $____
- **Natural Disasters (Hard)**	$39.99 + $____	postage Total $____

- **Do's and Don'ts - COUNTRY REPORTS:** Available online for $7 at www.frontlinepublishers.com

Sales Tax: (Maryland Residents Only) Add 5%
$____

Enclosed is my Total Payment of $____ by

☐ Check ☐ Money Order ☐ This is a gift from:____

Ship To:____ **Firm Name:**____
Your Name:____ **Address:**____
City:____ **State:**____ **Zip:**____ **Country**:____

COMMENT FORM FOR OUR BOOKS

YOUR OPINION MEANS A LOT TO US
Please use this post card to tell us how you feel about any of our books. Remember, we may quote you and/or use your comments, testimonials or suggestions in our promotions and future editions.

Title of Book:_____

Name:_____

Organization:_____Position:_____

Address:_____

City, State, Zip & Country:_____

_____

_____

( ) Check here if we may quote you.

Signature:_____Date:_____

[Mail your comments to Frontline Publishers, P.O. Box 32674 Baltimore, MD 21282-2674, USA.]

COUNTRY REPORTS FOR "*DO'S & DON'TS*" BOOKS

[Note: Individual Country reports are currently available for $7 per country, per report at www. frontlinepublishers.com]

AFGHANISTAN	DOMINICA	LIBYA	SINGAPORE
ALBANIA	DOMINICAN REP.	LIECHESTEIN	SLOVAK REP.
ALGERIA	ECUADOR	LITHUANIA	SLOVENIA
AMERICAN SAMOA	EGYPT	LUXEMBOURG	SOLOMON ISLAND
ANDORRA	EL SALVADOR	MACAU	SOMALIA
ANGUILLA	EQUATORIAL GUINEA	MACEDONIA	SOUTH AFRICA
ANTIGUA & BARBUDA	ERITREA	MADAGASCAR	SPAIN
ARGENTINA	ESTONIA	MALAWI	SRI LANKA
ARMENIA	ETHIOPIA	MALAYSIA	ST. PIERRE &
ARUBA	FALKLAND ISLANDS	MALDIVES	MIQUELON
AUSTRALIA	FAROE ISLAND	MALI	ST. MARTIN
AUSTRIA	FIJI	MALTA	ST. KITTS & NEVIS
AZERBAIJAN	FINLAND	MARSHALL ISLANDS	ST. LUCIA
BAHAMAS	FRANCE	MAURITIUS	ST. VINCENT
BAHRAIN	FRENCH GUIANA	MAYOTTE	SUDAN
BANGLADESH	FRENCH POLYNESIA	MEXICO	SURINAME
BARBADOS	GABON	MOLDOVA	SWAZILAND
BELGIUM	GAMBIA, THE	MONACO	SWEDEN
BELIZE	GEORGIA	MONGOLIA	SWITZERLAND
BENIN	GERMANY	MONTESERRAT	SYRIA
BERMUDA	GHANA	MOROCCO	TAJIKISTAN
BHUTAN	GIBRALTA	MOZAMBIQUE	TANZANIA
BOLIVIA	GREECE	MUSTIQUE	THAILAND
BOTSWANA	GREENLAND	MYANMAR (BURMA)	TOGO
BRAZIL	GRENADA	NAMIBIA	TONGA
BRITISH VIRGIN	GUADELOUPE	NAURU	TRINIDAD & TOBAGO
ISLANDS	GUAM	NEPAL	TUNISIA
BRUNEI-DARUSSALEM	GUANTANAMO BAY	NETHERLANDS	TURKEY
BULGARIA	GUATEMALA	NEW ZEALAND	TURKMENISTAN
BURKINA FASO	GUINEA	NEW CALEDONIA	TURKS & CAICOS
BURMA (SEE	GUINEA BISSAU	NICARAGUA	TUVALU
MYANMAR)	GUYANA	NIEU	UGANDA
BURUNDI	HAITI	NIGER	UKRAINE
BYLERUS	HONDURAS	NIGERIA	UNION ISLAND
CAMBODIA	HONG KONG	NORWAY	UNITED KINGDOM
CAMEROON	HUNGARY	OMAN	UNITED ARAB
CANADA	ICELAND	PAKISTAN	EMIRATES
CAPE VERDE, REP. OF	INDIA	PANAMA	UNITED STATES
CAYMAN	INDONESIA	PAPUA NEW GUINEA	URUGUAY
CENTRAL AFRICAN	IRAN	PARAGUAY	UZBEKISTAN
REP.	IRAQ	PERU	VENEZUELA
CHAD	IRELAND	PHILIPPINES	VIETNAM
CHILE	ISRAEL	POLAND	WESTERN SAMOA
CHINA, PEOPLE'S REP.	ITALY	PORTUGAL	YEMEN, ARAB REP.
COLOMBIA	JAMAICA	PUERTO RICO	YEMEN, P.D.R.
COMOROS	JAPAN	QUATAR	YUGOSLAVIA
CONGO, PEOPLE'S	JORDAN	REUNION ISLAND	ZAIRE
REP.	KAZAKHSTAN	ROMANIA	ZAMBIA
COOK ISLANDS	KENYA	RUSSIA	ZIMBABWE
COSTA RICA	KIRIBATI	RWANDA	
COTE'IVOIRE	KOREA, NORTH	SAIPAN	
CROATIA	KOREA, SOUTH	SAN MARINO	
CUBA	KUWAIT	SAO TOME &	
CURACAO	LAOS	PRINCIPE	
CYPRUS	LATVIA	SAUDI ARABIA	
CZECH REP.	LEBANON	SENEGAL	
DENMARK	LESOTHO	SEYCHELLES	
DJIBOUTI, REP.	LIBERIA	SIERRA LEONE	

INDEX

NOTES

ABOUT THE AUTHOR

Dr. Gladson I. Nwanna (Ph.D.) is a university professor, a former consultant to the World Bank, and a veteran traveler. He has over the past 20 years traveled to several countries of the world, logging thousands of miles in the process. Dr. Nwanna is the author of several books.

OTHER BOOKS BY THE SAME AUTHOR

Americans Traveling Abroad: What You Should Know Before You Go (3rd Ed.) Bestseller! paperback, 720 pages, ISBN: 1-890605-10-7, $39.99

Americans Living Abroad: What You Should Know While You are There. paperback, 375 pages, ISBN: 1-890605-11-5, $34.99

Traveling Abroad Post "9-11" and in the Wake of Terrorism: A Practical Guide for Americans & Other International Travelers, paperback, 265 pages, ISBN: 1-890605-13-1, $24.99

American Businesses Abroad: How to Protect Your Assets and Personnel, paperback, 320 pages, ISBN: 1-890605-12-3, $39.99; (Hard Cover, ISBN: 1-890605-26-3, $49.99)

Weapons of Mass Destruction, What You Should Know: A Citizen's Guide To Biological, Chemical and Nuclear Agents & Weapons paperback, 300 pages, ISBN: 1-890605-14-X, $39.99 (Hard Cover, ISBN: 1-890605-25-5, $49.99)

Natural Disasters and Other Emergencies, What You Should Know: A Family Planning & Survival Guide. paperback, 250 pages, ISBN: 1-890605-15-8, $29.99 (Hard Cover, ISBN: 1-890605-27-1, $39.99)

Do's and Don'ts Around the World: A Country Guide to Cultural and Social Taboos and Etiquette. paperback, available in 9 different volumes/editions: Europe, Asia, Africa, South America, The Caribbean, The Middle East, Russia and the Independent States, Oceania, USA-Canada-Australia. These books contain hundreds of country-specific do's and don'ts and much more!.

Series Title: *DO'S AND DON'TS AROUND THE WORLD: A COUNTRY GUIDE TO CULTURAL AND SOCIAL TABOOS AND ETIQUETTE*

EUROPE 1-890605-00-X; (*1-890605-17-4) 400 pages; $39.99; **SOUTH AMERICA** 1-890605-03-4; (*1-890605-20-4) 230 pages; $24.99; **AFRICA** 1-890605- 04-2 (*1-890605-16-6); 450 pages; $39.99; **THE CARIBBEAN** 1-890605-02-6; (*1-890605-19-0) 230 pages; $24.99; **ASIA** 1-890605-01-8; (*1-890605-18-2) 260 pages; $24.99; **RUSSIA & THE INDEPENDENT STATES** 1-890605-06-9; (*1-890605-22-0) 120 pages; $15.99; **USA, CANADA & AUSTRALIA** 1-890605-08-5; (*1-890605-24-7) 75 pages; $15.99; **OCEANIA & JAPAN** 1-890605-07-7; (*1-890605-23-9) 200 pages; $19.99; **THE MIDDLE EAST** 1-890605-05-0; (*1-890605-21-2) 120 pages; $15.99

Note: Books marked with * refer to a new ISBN planned for the same book under a different title called " *Ethics and Etiquette Around the World: A Country Guide To Cultural and Social Do's, Don'ts, & Taboos"*

Individual Country Reports are *of the Do's & Don'ts Books currently* online and may be ordered for $7 per country per report (www.frontlinepublishers.com)

[See inside pages 691-692 for ordering information & ORDER FORM]

WHAT OTHERS ARE SAYING ABOUT
AMERICANS TRAVELING ABROAD

This is one publication that truly lives up to its description. It should be read at least in part, if not in its entirety, by anyone embarking on foreign travel for the first time. Even seasoned travelers would benefit from it...this book will be a most welcome addition to any travel reference collection. *ALA BOOKLIST, December 15, 1993.*

"Nwanna provides an extremely comprehensive and well-researched resource guide for the American traveler abroad....A traveler would be hard pressed to find information not included in this volume. Its excellent table of contents and index make it easy to use. Well recommended." *Library Journal, September 1993.*

"This all-in-one guide packs in details on everything from health and safety to money tips, terrorism, funds replacement, driving and visa requirements, making it the most comprehensive handbook in print on international travel. A "must" for any who frequently go overseas." *The Midwest Book Review (BOOKWATCH), January 1994.*

"'Americans Traveling Abroad: What You Should Know Before You Go' is a nice big book filled with helpful information. It is excellent for the first timer or the experienced business traveler or tourist. Travel agents should invest in a copy of this and keep it handy." *The press Tribune, Dec. 1993.*

"The Americans Traveling Abroad Resource Guide is without a doubt the most complete compilation of information I believe I have ever seen in one publication. There isn't anything that I am aware of that has been left out. An excellent resource guide." *Robert W. Whitley, President United States Tour Operators Association.*

"...a very thorough compilation of travel information which should be helpful to Americans traveling abroad." *H. Wayne Berens, Chairman, Institute of Certified Travel Agents.*

"Every American traveling abroad should buy a copy of this ultimate guide. It's a definitive international traveler's resource covering everything from abduction to vaccinations. This remarkable tome sets a new standard for world travel and tourism. No inexperienced traveler should leave home without it." *Andrew S. Linick, Ph.D, Chairman/CEO, Travel, Tourism, Transportation and Hospitality Adviceline. Bestselling Author of Guide to Trouble-Free Travel.*

"Terrific! It's great to have all the necessary international travel information at your finger tips rather than trying to find the one single publication. A great asset for Human Resource departments that are responsible for relocating employees and their families overseas." *John H. Hintz, President National Business Travel Association.*

"This is an extremely useful compilation of information, much of which would not be available in small libraries, and useful in large libraries with U.S. Documents because it compiles the wealth of information in one easy source." *Harriet C. Jenkins, Librarian, Enoch Pratt Free Library, Baltimore, MD.*

"Americans Traveling Abroad is very detailed, it contains everything from what to do if you are held hostage to how to obtain visas. This book would be an excellent addition as a reference work for libraries, travel agents and companies doing business abroad." *Christopher J.J. Thiry, Map Librarian, New York Public Library.*

"A very unique complete book. Contains much useful information... The nitty gritty of traveling that looks deeper than the usual tourist attractions. A must for the frequent traveler or public library collection." *Jean Alexander, Regional Administrator, County of Los Angeles, Public Library.*

"Anything that promotes the goal of traveler safety and security must be applauded. Your effort to compile and organize a comprehensive anthology of information on the subject is a positive and useful step toward this goal." *Edward R. Book, President, Travel Industry Association of America.*

"Information is relevant, reliable, and easy to use. This resource delivers on all it promises. It is a great book! Very highly recommended." *American Reference Book Annual, 1995.*

[See inside pages 691-692 for ordering information &
ORDER FORM]

Printed in the United States
21935LVS00002B/310-312